CONTEMPORARY SOCIETY

Contemporary Society

SOCIAL PROCESS AND SOCIAL STRUCTURE
IN URBAN INDUSTRIAL SOCIETIES

JACKSON TOBY

Professor of Sociology and Chairman
Department of Sociology
College of Arts & Sciences
Rutgers University

JOHN WILEY & SONS, INC.
New York London Sydney

Second Printing, June, 1966

To the memory of Anna Toby, my first teacher, and of Samuel Andrew Stouffer, who taught his students how exciting sociology can be.

Preface

When Socrates was condemned to death for raising too many philosophical questions, he remarked to his accusers, "An unexamined life is not worth living." The world has become safer for philosophical and religious speculation. Yet even in an intellectually freer world, many doubt the wisdom of questioning established institutions. In seeking to understand how societies function, sociologists are professionally committed to questioning the benefit of respected institutions like the family and the harm of condemned activities like theft or sexual license. Such a commitment is bound to appear subversive to those who are still unconvinced that Socrates was right and his accusers wrong. I like to think that Socrates, if he were alive today, might be a sociologist. He would justify his research to suspicious critics by remarking that an unexamined society is not worth living in. In this connection, I note with some pride that a majority of the world's sociologists live and work in the United States. Unlike the Athenians two thousand years ago or the Russians today, Americans are willing to expose the minds of the young to searching questions.

This book seeks to examine contemporary society. Understanding one's society, no less than understanding oneself, is the obligation of an educated man. In the first chapter, the concept of human interaction is introduced; interaction is the substance out of which more complicated social structures are patterned. In Chapter 2, the scientific inclinations of present-day sociologists are discussed—although some sociologists still regard sociology as a humanistic discipline akin to history and philosophy; such a conception was more common a generation ago. Chapter 2 emphasizes the *scientific* conception of sociology—including techniques of empirical research—because an empirical emphasis seems to predominate among living sociologists, particularly in the United States, and to be the direction in which sociology is moving. In Chapter 3, the concept of *culture* is introduced. This idea, borrowed from anthropology, is essential to an understanding of the meaning of interaction.

In the remainder of the book, an attempt is made to describe contemporary society with scientific detachment. Each chapter relies implicitly or explicitly on the assumption that complex systems of interaction cannot be maintained without shared meanings contributed by the culture. Chapters 4 through 7 are concerned with the economic, ecological, and status aspects of urban industrial societies as the necessary context for later discussions of social processes in these societies. Chapter 4 shows that industrial societies have a relatively autonomous "economy"; in preindustrial societies the economic aspect of life is not differentiated from other functions. Chapter 5 describes the urban way of life made possible by technological advances in transportation, communication, and productivity generally, a way of life radically different from that supported by subsistence agriculture. Chapter 6 considers the cultural characteristics of industrial populations and points out the existence of unassimilated elements within industrial societies. Chapter 7 analyzes inequalities of status. ("Social stratification" is the term sociologists use to describe these inequalities within a society regardless of whether the ranks are formally acknowledged as in feudal society or overlaid with an ideology of social equality as in Western industrial countries. It calls attention to the relatively stable structure of evaluations within the system.)

Chapters 8, 9, 10, and 11 deal with the processes of socialization and social control. These processes are not treated in abstract terms, general enough to apply to preliterate as well as to urban societies. They are concerned with harnessing individual motivation to the social requirements of *contemporary* industrial societies. Chapter 8 deals with child socialization, Chapters 9 and 10 with nonconformity and its control, and Chapter 11 with socialization in stages of the life cycle beyond early childhood.

Chapters 12 to 15 describe formal organizations that lend stability to urban industrial societies: schools, governments, and churches. Chapter 12 shows how mass education makes possible the transmission of a complex cultural tradition despite rapid changes in technology. In Chapter 13, political institutions are viewed as resolving conflicts of interest, arriving at decisions, and choosing leaders. Chapter 14 examines religious institutions in the light of the universal problem of the meaning of human existence and the special problem of reconciling traditional religious values with the doubts engendered by science. Chapter 15 deals with a phenomenon that cuts across economic, political, educational, and religious institutions: bureaucracy.

The concluding two chapters tackle the most difficult intellectual problem of contemporary sociology: dynamics. Chapter 16 discusses the processes whereby individuals and groups rise and fall in status within urban industrial societies. Chapter 17 attempts to provide some understanding of the rapid rate of sociocultural change in such societies—and illustrates this rapid rate with an examination of the changing position of Negroes in the United States.

Note that the book contains an expository framework and a variety of illustrative articles, most of them from professional journals, a few from popular magazines. I included journalistic articles calculatingly. Some students keep academic sociology in one compartment of their minds and stereotypes about "criminals" or "Negroes" in another. Perhaps they do not see the relevance of academic sociology for the world in which they live. I hope that the inclusion of journalistic articles will help to emphasize that truth is indivisible; common-sense sociology and academic sociology cannot be contradictory and equally correct. Sociologists have no monopoly on sociological insights; novelists and journalists are often able to illuminate a social situation superlatively well. On the other hand, many popular notions are misleading—as are some interpretations of personal experience. The task of a scholarly discipline is to base its conclusions on evidence, not on plausibility or popularity. In some cases I have edited articles slightly because parts of the original source were irrelevant to the point I meant it to make; I have renumbered tables, figures, and footnotes.

Practical necessity compels an introductory textbook to discuss one topic at a time—even though the author might like to use concepts early in the book that he will not present systematically until later. For example, in the analysis of social stratification in Chapter 7, I was tempted to refer briefly to social mobility although social mobility was not scheduled for discussion until Chapter 16. In a few places, I yielded to such temptation and introduced concepts out of their planned sequence in order to present a topic more adequately. In other places, I refrained from using a sociological concept because the student was unfamiliar with it. This dilemma is a special case of a broader presentation problem: striking a balance between an oversimplified sketch and a scholarly description that qualifies all generalizations in order to take account of complexities.

A word about the bibliography. Bibliographies have been waggishly defined as lists of books an author intends to read after the writing chore is over. This facetious definition calls attention to the dispensability of most bibliographies; the student is usually not given enough information about the listed books and articles to be useful to him—not even enough to decide whether he wishes to read them. In this book, the bibliography at the end of each chapter has been constructed with an explicit educational purpose in mind. Even the professional sociologist cannot read thoroughly the hundreds of new books and scholarly articles published each year. In the *American Sociological Review* alone, 76 articles were published during 1962, and 279 books were reviewed. The professional keeps up with the field by *selective* attention to the current literature. He reads reviews of new books to help him decide which deserve further attention; he scans the major journals for articles in his specialties; he may read a journal of abstracts such as *Excerpta Criminologica*. The undergraduate taking a first course in sociology cannot be expected to pick a judicious path through this voluminous literature. To help the student obtain a reasonable sample of the sociological literature, I have summarized some significant books and articles in the bibliographies of Chapters 2 through 17. In many cases I prepared the summary with the help of book reviews published in the *American Sociological Review* and indexed in a volume distributed to members of the American Sociological Association. I leaned on published reviews either because I had read the book long ago and could not rely on memory or because I had read reviews rather than the book itself. The references to the original reviews are in every case appended to my summary.

A textbook is, by definition, made up of ideas on loan from other people. I have tried to acknowledge my debts explicitly by appropriate footnotes. Some I cannot acknowledge because ideas developed in the course of discussions with colleagues are not attributable to particular persons. The following colleagues enlightened me on one or more occasions about sociology or how it should be taught: Wendell D. Baker, Harry C. Bredemeier, Richard M. Cohn, John Gerald Condran, Joseph M. Conforti, Roger E. Craig, Frank F. Fasick, Myron Glazer, Nathan H. Gould, Robert Gutman, Larry J. Jakubsen, Richard N. Juliani, Larry Karacki, Michael Lewis, Arthur Liebman, Simon Marcson, Charles F. Marden, Paul W. Massing, Joseph Neyer, Solomon Poll, John W. Riley, Jr., Matilda White Riley, Earl Rubington, Brian F. Sherry, Charles H. Stember, Richard M. Stephenson, Marcia L. Toby, and Robert L. York.

I am grateful to Marvin Bressler, Richard F. Curtis, Joseph R. Gusfield, Philip M. Hauser, Wilbert E. Moore, Leonard Reissman, Peter I. Rose, Peter Rossi, Richard L. Simpson, David P. Street, and Stanton Wheeler for reading and criticizing drafts of the manuscript and for causing me sufficient anguish to make extensive revisions. Richard Simpson made detailed comments on each chapter; I relied heavily on his editorial judgment. I cannot resist mentioning what every author knows: the time for writing a book has to be stolen from one's family. I hope that my wife, Marcia, and my children, Gail and Stevie, feel that the sacrifice was justified.

Jackson Toby

February 1964
Highland Park, New Jersey

Contents

PART I

Goals, Methods, Concepts

CHAPTER 1

Understanding Systems of Interaction

"What exactly is sociology?"

There is no pat answer to this question. One sociologist tries looking his questioner in the eye and saying in a firm voice, "The study of human groups." This will not do. Neither will such capsule definitions as "The study of interaction" or "The study of social institutions."

The field of psychology has a clearer public image. Laymen think they know the subject matter of psychology: the "mind." On the other hand, the words associated with sociology —"interaction," "group," "society," "institutions," "norms"—sound vague. What do sociologists *do*? If one replies that they study the character of human interaction this recalls the gibe that sociology tells you what you already know in words that you can't understand.

It is only a half truth to say that sociology is concerned with the group and psychology with the individual. The group is composed of individuals. Groups cannot think or feel or act except in a metaphorical sense. Since mental and physical behavior are produced only by individuals, sociologists cannot surrender their curiosity about "the individual" without also surrendering any serious interest in "the group."

This does not mean that sociology and psychology are different terms for the same discipline —although there is some overlap between the two. (An entire field, social psychology, lies in the border region between them.) Sociology abstracts and analyzes a different aspect of behavior from psychology. Psychology is interested in the individual's needs and abilities and in their organization within the personality; sociology is concerned with the way individuals relate to one another. Both deal with human motivation, but they search for the *source* of the motivation in different places. For the psychologist, it lies within the organism and includes such variables as intelligence and aggressiveness. For the sociologist, it lies within the group and includes the ideas and sentiments the individual learns from society.

THE SOCIAL PATTERNING OF BIOLOGICAL DRIVES

Sociologists are deeply impressed with the effect of societal values on the expression of individual motivation. Even physiological drives like hunger are channeled by social and cultural rules. While there are certain nutritional requirements that no society can ignore, a tremendous range of substances are nutritionally adequate: whale blubber, beefsteak, horsemeat, human flesh, grubs and worms, mice, fruit, nuts, vegetables, berries, roots. Nutrition cannot explain why Eskimos like whale blubber and Navahos like rattlesnake meat. Every society makes a selection from the edible things available and defines some of these as "food." Thus, Americans think of beefsteak as succulent and horsemeat as fit only for pets. The explanation of America's discrimination against horses is not nutritional. The faculty club at a leading university had horsemeat steak on the menu for years. What it comes down to is this: Americans have sentimental attachments to horses, not to cattle. We remember weeping over the story of Black Beauty as children; we watch horses race and we bet on them; we look at television programs in which horses are given near-human qualities. As a result, horsemeat is not given a fair chance to qualify as food on nutritional or taste grounds. Not recognizing how deeply our own food habits are affected by American values, we may consider Hindus unreasonable to regard cows as inedible and to become upset when someone kills one. Yet the Hindu religion, affirming as it does the doctrine of reincarnation, provides a very good reason for the devout to dote on a cow. According to the ideas of Hindu society, the cow might be a reincarnation of a close relative.

Reactions to pain are similarly responsive to societal values. Although male infants cry just as much as female infants when they are hurt, American society teaches older boys to respond to pain differently from girls. The same level of physical suffering that causes American women to cry produces curses from American men or silent heroism. Other societies have even more extreme ideals of male fortitude. In the puberty rites of some American Indian tribes, the boy was required to undergo physical torture without flinching. Naive observers of these ceremonies were misled by the boy's pretense that the pain did not exist and came to the erroneous conclusion that the threshold of pain was higher for Indians than for whites.

THE CENTER OF SOCIOLOGICAL INTEREST: INTERACTION

In short, sociology looks for the *sources* of human motivation in the tradition of the society whereas psychology looks for sources of motivation within the personality. Sociologists differ from psychologists also in the behavioral *outcomes* that interest them. Psychologists are largely concerned with *individual* behavior, sociologists with the *interactions* of more than one person. It may not be immediately apparent that "interaction" involves anything more than the simultaneous behavior of two or more individuals. A fist fight or a conversation are certainly interaction, but they are also individual behavior. *Interaction* is not, however, merely the action of A and the subsequent action of B. Interaction implies the taking account on the part of each participant of the potential reactions of the other. For example, suppose you are a weekend guest at the home of a classmate. Your classmate's mother has just served you a plate of scrambled eggs for breakfast and is chatting with you as you eat. Suddenly you start chewing on a hard, crackly substance: eggshell. Your first impulse is to spit it out, but you do not wish to offend your hostess. You swallow the eggshell with your egg. No one watching you would know that you are reacting to the presence of your hostess. This is interaction, nevertheless. The fact that you did *not* spit out the eggshell is just as much a response as spitting it out would have been. Interaction depends on sensitivity to the approval and disapproval of others and to the *anticipation* of their approval or disapproval. This sensitivity makes a social order possible. Without it, society would be a jungle—a "war of all against all."

Professor Solomon Asch, a social psychologist, devised an ingenious laboratory experiment to test the coercive power of group pressure. In the experiment, the evidence of the individual's eyes suggested one judgment and the expectations of the other members of the group suggested another.

Sensitivity of the Individual to Group Pressures

Reprinted by permission. From Solomon E. Asch, "Opinions and Social Pressure," *Scientific American*, Vol. 193, November 1955, pp. 4–8.

A group of seven to nine young men, all college students, are assembled in a classroom for a "psychological experiment" in visual judgment. The experimenter informs them that they will be comparing the lengths of lines. He shows two large white cards. On one is a single vertical black line—the standard whose length is to be matched. On the other card are three vertical lines of various lengths. The subjects are to choose the one that is of the same length as the line on the other card. One of the three actually is of the same length; the other two are substantially different, the difference ranging from three quarters of an inch to an inch and three quarters.

The experiment opens uneventfully. The subjects announce their answers in the order in which they have been seated in the room, and on the first round every person chooses the same matching line. Then a second set of cards is exposed; again the group is unanimous. The members appear ready to endure politely another boring experiment. On the third trial there is an unexpected disturbance. One person near the end of the group disagrees with all the others in his selection of the matching line. He looks surprised, indeed incredulous, about the disagreement. On the following trial he disagrees again, while the others remain unanimous in their choice. The dissenter becomes more and more worried and hesitant as the disagreement continues in succeeding trials; he may pause before announcing his answer and speak in a low voice, or he may smile in an embarrassed way.

What the dissenter does not know is that all the other members of the group were instructed

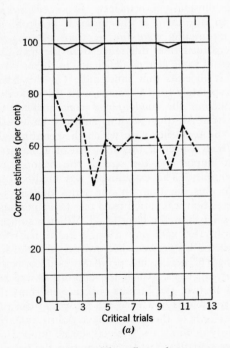 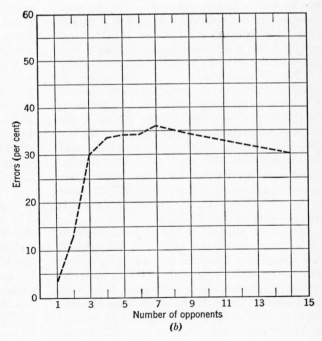

FIGURE 1. The effect of group pressure on individual errors in judgment. (*a*) Error of 123 subjects, each of whom compared lines in the presence of six to eight opponents, is plotted in the broken curve. The accuracy of judgments not under pressure is indicated in the solid curve. (*b*) Size of majority which opposed them had an effect on the subjects. With a single opponent the subject erred only 3.6 per cent of the time; with two opponents he erred 13.6 per cent; three, 31.8 per cent; four, 35.1 per cent; six, 35.2 per cent; seven, 37.1 per cent; nine, 35.1 per cent; 15, 31.2 per cent.

by the experimenter beforehand to give incorrect answers in unanimity at certain points. The single individual who is not a party to this prearrangement is the focal subject of our experiment. He is placed in a position in which, while he is actually giving the correct answers, he finds himself unexpectedly in a minority of one, opposed by a unanimous and arbitrary majority with respect to a clear and simple fact. Upon him we have brought to bear two opposed forces: the evidence of his senses and the unanimous opinion of a group of his peers. Also, he must declare his judgments in public, before a majority which has also stated its position publicly.

The instructed majority occasionally reports correctly in order to reduce the possibility that the naive subject will suspect collusion against him. (In only a few cases did the subject actually show suspicion; when this happened, the experiment was stopped and the results were not counted.) There are 18 trials in each series, and on 12 of these the majority responds erroneously.

How do people respond to group pressure in this situation? I shall report first the statistical results of a series in which a total of 123 subjects from three institutions of higher learning (not including my own, Swarthmore College) were placed in the minority situation described above.

Two alternatives were open to the subject: he could act independently, repudiating the majority, or he could go along with the majority, repudiating the evidence of his senses. Of the 123 put to the test, a considerable percentage yielded to the majority. Whereas in ordinary circumstances individuals matching the lines will make mistakes less than 1 per cent of the time, under group pressure the minority subjects swung to acceptance of the misleading majority's wrong judgments in 36.8 per cent of the selections.

Of course individuals differed in response. At one extreme, about one quarter of the subjects were completely independent and never agreed with the erroneous judgments of the majority. At the other extreme, some individuals went with the majority nearly all the time. The performances of individuals in this experiment tend to be highly consistent. Those who strike out on the path of independence do not, as a rule, succumb to the majority even over an extended series of trials, while those who choose the path of compliance are unable to free themselves as the ordeal is prolonged.

The reasons for the startling individual differences have not yet been investigated in detail. At this point we can only report some tentative generalizations from talks with the subjects, each of whom was interviewed at the end of the experiment. Among the independent individuals were many who held fast because of staunch confidence in their own judgment. The most significant fact about them was not absence of responsiveness to the majority but a capacity to recover from doubt and to reestablish their equilibrium. Others who acted independently came to believe that the majority was correct in its answers, but they continued their dissent on the simple ground that it was their obligation to call the play as they saw it.

Among the extremely yielding persons we found a group who quickly reached the conclusion: "I am wrong, they are right." Others yielded in order "not to spoil your results." Many of the individuals who went along suspected that the majority were "sheep" following the first responder, or that the majority were victims of an optical illusion; nevertheless, these suspicions failed to free them at the moment of decision. More disquieting were the reactions of subjects who construed their difference from the majority as a sign of some general deficiency in themselves, which at all costs they must hide. On this basis they desperately tried to merge with the majority, not realizing the longer-range consequences to themselves. All the yielding subjects underestimated the frequency with which they conformed.

Which aspect of the influence of a majority is more important—the size of the majority or its unanimity? The experiment was modified to examine this question. In one series the size of the opposition was varied from one to 15 persons. The results showed a clear trend. When a subject was confronted with only a single individual who contradicted his answers, he was swayed little: he continued to answer independently and correctly in nearly all trials. When the opposition was increased to two, the pressure became substantial: minority subjects now accepted the wrong answer 13.6 per cent of the time. Under the pressure of a majority of three, the subjects' errors jumped to 31.8 per cent. But further increases in the size of the majority apparently did not increase the weight of the pressure substantially. Clearly the size of the opposition is important only up to a point.

Disturbance of the majority's unanimity had a striking effect. In this experiment the subject was given the support of a truthful partner—either another individual who did not know of the prearranged agreement among the rest of the group, or a person who was instructed to give correct answers throughout.

The presence of a supporting partner depleted the majority of much of its power. Its pressure on the dissenting individual was reduced to one fourth: that is, subjects answered incorrectly only one fourth as often as under the pressure of a unanimous majority (*see* Figure 1 *c*). The weakest persons did not yield as readily. Most interesting were the reactions to the partner. Generally the feeling toward him was one of warmth and closeness; he was credited with inspiring confidence. However, the subjects repudiated the suggestion that the partner decided them to be independent.

Was the partner's effect a consequence of his dissent, or was it related to his accuracy? We now introduced into the experimental group a person who was instructed to dissent from the majority but also to disagree with the subject. In some experiments the majority was always to choose the worst of the comparison lines and the instructed dissenter to pick the line that was closer to the length of the standard one; in others the majority was consistently intermediate and the dissenter most in error. In this manner we were able to study the relative influence of "compromising" and "extremist" dissenters.

Again the results are clear. When a moderate dissenter is present, the effect of the majority on the subject decreases by approximately one third, and extremes of yielding disappear. Moreover, most of the errors the subjects do make are moderate, rather than flagrant. In short, the dissenter largely controls the choice of errors. To this extent the subjects broke away from the majority even while bending to it.

On the other hand, when the dissenter always chose the line that was more flagrantly

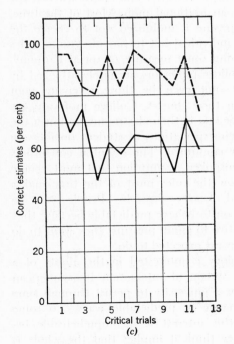

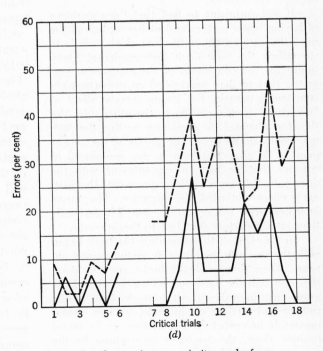

FIGURE 1 (*continued*). (*c*) Two subjects supporting each other against a majority made fewer errors (broken curve) than one subject did against a majority (solid curve). (*d*) Partner left subject after six trials in a single experiment. The broken curve shows the error of the subject when the partner "deserted" to the majority. The solid curve shows error when partner merely left the room.

different from the standard, the results were of quite a different kind. The extremist dissenter produced a remarkable freeing of the subjects; their errors dropped to only 9 per cent. Furthermore, all the errors were of the moderate variety. We were able to conclude that dissent *per se* increased independence and moderated the errors that occurred, and that the direction of dissent exerted consistent effects.

In all the foregoing experiments each subject was observed only in a single setting. We now turned to studying the effects upon a given individual of a change in the situation to which he was exposed. The first experiment examined the consequences of losing or gaining a partner. The instructed partner began by answering correctly on the first six trials. With his support the subject usually resisted pressure from the majority: 18 of 27 subjects were completely independent. But after six trials the partner joined the majority. As soon as he did so, there was an abrupt rise in the subjects' errors. Their submission to the majority was just about as frequent as when the minority subject was opposed by a unanimous majority throughout.

It was surprising to find that the experience of having had a partner and of having braved the majority opposition with him had failed to strengthen the individuals' independence. Questioning at the conclusion of the experiment suggested that we had overlooked an important circumstance; namely, the strong specific effect of "desertion" by the partner to the other side. We therefore changed the conditions so that the partner would simply leave the group at the proper point. (To allay suspicion it was announced in advance that he had an appointment with the dean.) In this form of the experiment, the partner's effect outlasted his presence. The errors increased after his departure, but less markedly than after a partner switched to the majority.

In a variant of this procedure the trials began with the majority unanimously giving correct answers. Then they gradually broke away until on the sixth trial the naive subject was alone and the group unanimously against him. As long as the subject had anyone on his side, he was almost invariably independent, but as soon as he found himself alone, the tendency to conform to the majority rose abruptly.

As might be expected, an individual's resistance to group pressure in these experiments depends to a considerable degree on how wrong the majority is. We varied the discrepancy between the standard line and the other lines systematically, with the hope of reaching a point where the error of the majority would be so glaring that every subject would repudiate it and choose independently. In this we regretfully did not succeed. Even when the difference between the lines was seven inches, there were still some who yielded to the error of the majority.

The foregoing experiment revealed the power of the group over the individual even when the group made a scientifically incorrect judgment. This same phenomenon, individual suggestibility, is demonstrated in race riots and panty raids.[1] Socially undesirable behavior can and does result from the desire of the individual to conform to the expectations of the people with whom he is interacting. On the other hand, it should not be assumed that the individual is always creative and kindly whereas the group is an irrational mob. Most of the time, social pressure is mobilized not to coerce the creative individual but to provide ground rules establishing some measure of social harmony. Thus, college professors are rarely attacked by students—not even by those receiving poor grades in their courses. College professors expect to be safe in their classrooms, and over the years their expectations of student docility are routinely confirmed. The essential correctness of the unspoken assumption that most people will follow the rules most of the time makes organized society possible. People can be counted on to behave predictably because they are sensitive to group pressure; they *want* to do what they are expected to do.

Sociology is interested in the ability of a complex system of interaction like American society or a university to persist through time or to change in predictable ways. To some people, this interest is incomprehensible because they think it implies that the whole is

[1] Ralph H. Turner and Lewis M. Killian, *Collective Behavior*, Englewood Cliffs, N.J.: Prentice-Hall, 1957.

more than the sum of its parts. In the following passage, a distinguished psychologist pokes fun at the notion that a university constitutes an entity with needs of its own.

The Concept of Society: Reality or Illusion?

Reprinted by permission. From Floyd Allport, *Institutional Behavior*, Chapel Hill: University of North Carolina Press, 1933, p. 3.

At a meeting of the faculty of a certain large university a proposal for a new administrative policy was being discussed. The debate was long and intense before a final vote of adoption was taken. As the professors filed out of the room an instructor continued the discussion with one of the older deans.

"Well," observed the latter official, "it may be a little hard on some people; but I feel sure that, in the long run, the new plan will be for the best interests of the institution."

"Do you mean that it will be for the good of the students?" inquired the younger man.

"No," the dean replied, "I mean it will be for the good of the whole institution."

"Oh, you mean that it will benefit the faculty as well as the students."

"No," said the dean, a little annoyed, "I don't mean *that*; I mean it will be a good thing for the institution itself."

"Perhaps you mean the trustees then—or the Chancellor?"

"No, I mean the institution, the *institution*! Young man, don't you know what an institution is?"

ROLES: THE INTERNAL STRUCTURE OF INTERACTIVE SYSTEMS

Sociology is dedicated to the proposition that it makes sense to talk about "the best interests of the institution." Take the complex system of interaction called a university. It has organizational requirements apart from the needs and wants of students, faculty, and trustees. This point of view has implications for the basic unit of analysis. For the sociol-ogist, a university, or any social system, is composed of an organized system of meshing *roles*, not an aggregation of concrete *individuals*. The role concept is a way of looking at human behavior that emphasizes the requirements of a social structure.

To be specific, a professor participates in the interactive system known as Rutgers University. But this is not the only role he plays in American society. He is also a husband, a father, a son, a neighbor, a member of the Parent-Teachers Association of his community, a consultant to a private foundation, and a member of the American Civil Liberties Union. His students know only a small part of him because most of their knowledge of him is confined to interactions in which he participates as a professor and in which they participate as students. He is similarly ignorant about them; he does not know them as a parent, a neighbor, a chum, or a girlfriend might know them. Sociology assumes that it makes sense to ignore all the other roles that the professor and his students play outside of Rutgers, while concentrating on the problem of fitting together his activities as professor, the activities of students, the activities of deans and department heads, and so on, such that the interactive system, the University, continues to function. From the sociological point of view, the problems of Rutgers are *not* the problems of the individuals making up the University all added together. Thus, the difficulty the professor has in meeting the mortgage payments on his house is not a problem of Rutgers University—except indirectly if it makes him an inadequate teacher. The problems of Rutgers University are problems of organizing a role structure capable of getting teaching and research accomplished.

1. *Recruiting students, faculty, and nonteaching staff*. This function is discharged by the Admissions Office, the various deans and department chairmen, and the Personnel Office.

2. *Teaching new members of the Rutgers community how to play their roles*. For faculty members, this function is handled rather in-

formally. The new instructor learns his role by observing and conversing with his older colleagues and by attending faculty meetings and serving on committees.[2] For students, formal orientation sessions, for example, Freshman Week, supplement the informal tutelage of upperclassmen, teachers, fraternity brothers, and dormitory preceptors.

3. *Dismissing from the Rutgers community those who cannot learn to play their roles adequately and advancing those who perform well.* Some members of the staff have to be fired; some students have to be expelled or, more politely, "requested to withdraw." Faculty members are promoted and eventually retired; students are graduated. This movement of people through the role structure of the University requires elaborate evaluative procedures.

4. *Accommodating to the larger society so as to obtain the financial support and social approval necessary for continued operation.* The Treasurer must collect fees from students, research grants from government agencies and private foundations, gifts from alumni, and appropriations from the state legislature (since Rutgers is a state university) to pay staff, maintain the physical plant, and provide essential services. The ability to do this depends on the attitude of people outside the University toward it, and this is affected to some extent by the activities of the Office of Public Relations.

5. *Setting goals for future development and resolving conflicts between subgroups within the Rutgers community.* This decision making and coordinating function goes on at many levels. If it did not, department chairmen would come to blows with one another over the most favorable schedule for their courses and the largest share of the budget. But there must be an ultimate source of authority in a complex organization—a court of last resort. At a university it is the President and the Board of Trustees.

This list does not exhaust the problems of

2 Logan Wilson, *The Academic Man*, New York: Oxford University Press, 1942.

a university. It serves, however, to indicate the sociological level of analysis. Note that the problems of the university are not reduced to the more microscopic level of the human beings who participate in its community. The university is regarded as having problems, not in a mystical sense, but as a result of the fact that coordination is necessary to get roles to mesh in a complex system of interaction. The more important centers of coordination may be labeled "institutions"; this is a shorthand way of expressing the idea that certain activities going on in and around a university are more important than others to the continuation of the university. By calling these more crucial activities "institutions," a sociologist is able to concentrate on variables which, taken together, help him to understand the functioning of the university. He cannot, of course, hope to understand everything that is going on in the university. From his point of view, the courses being taught and the discoveries being made in the various laboratories of the university are of no interest in themselves. They become relevant to his interests only when they have significance for the maintenance or the change of the complicated system of interaction called a university. That is, the sociologist ignores a great deal of the concrete activities, not to mention thought processes, within the university. He abstracts only a small part of human behavior—the actions and reactions that link individual to group—and he tries to understand how some interactive systems persist and why others disintegrate.

One might argue that it makes no sense to study an interactive system as though it were self-contained, that is, to abstract the roles that people play in the university while disregarding the much larger number of roles they play in other social structures. Sociologists do not accept this argument. Sociologists believe that the first place to look if you want to understand the *academic* behavior of the teachers, students, deans, and administrative personnel of a university is at its role structure. Thus, sociologists assume that the policy set by the director of admissions is primarily determined by the classroom and dormitory space available and only secondarily by the quarrels he might be having with his wife or by a possible sadistic streak in his character. True, there are occasions when commitments to social structures other than the university—for example, to his family—may interfere with the adequate discharging of obligations to the university. This situation, called "role conflict," has received considerable attention in the sociological literature.

Role Conflict: Competing Commitments of the Individual to Several Systems of Interaction

Reprinted by permission. From Jackson Toby, "Some Variables in Role Conflict Analysis," *Social Forces*, Vol. 30, March 1952, pp. 323–327.

Social roles are the institutionally proper ways for an individual to participate in his society and thus satisfy his needs and wants. But roles are also *demands* upon the individual, norms which prescribe certain acts and forbid others. These demands come from the various groups in which the individual holds membership: his family, peer group, social class, occupational group, and so on. Usually the individual's role in one group is quite distinct from his role in another group. A man can be both a *father* and a *factory worker* at the same time. But sometimes role obligations are difficult to reconcile. Thus, the non-com is subject to one set of pressures from commissioned officers in authority over him and to another from his fellow enlisted men. Such competing obligations have been labeled "role conflicts," and several studies exist of verbal responses to hypothetical role conflict situations.

It is obvious that an individual in a role conflict situation is uncomfortable. For him, the crossfire of competing claims is an obnoxious problem to be solved as quickly as possible. From society's point of view, however, role conflicts may be useful; they often give a social system flexibility by providing an entering wedge for social change. For example, Gunnar Myrdal points out that white Americans face a role conflict over the status of Negroes. The subordinate status of Negroes has a certain traditional legitimacy. But this inferiority of status, ascribed on a racial basis, is not compatible with the American creed, with the norms by which we define the role of a human being in a democratic state. Hence white Americans are inhibited in their tendency to "keep the Negro in his place" because of their conflicting role of democrat. Therefore, Myrdal predicts the gradual deinstitutionalization of the ascribed inferior status for Negroes.

Valuable as role conflict may be as an initiator of necessary change, it is not entirely desirable from the viewpoint of the social system either. For, after all, a social system must make provisions for stability as well as for progress. Some control over incompatible claims must exist in every society—lest available motivation be channeled into internal tensions instead of into the maintenance of the social structure. If a social system is too flexible, stable expectations cannot exist, and anomie results. Hence, even in a society as dynamic as ours, mechanisms must exist to provide minimum control over role conflicts. These mechanisms are institutionalized. They serve to prevent inevitable strains from developing into disruptive intra-society conflicts. The following are a few of the more obvious integrative mechanisms of American society:

HIERARCHIES OF ROLE OBLIGATIONS

Role conflicts resemble a jurisdictional dispute between two unions in that both the groups defining the roles of the individual insist that their claim is the legitimate one. Further, just as jurisdictional disputes are exceptional enough in union activity to be newsworthy, so role conflicts are unusual in that they represent situations where the institutionalized system of priorities have proved insufficient to avert friction. To illustrate the ordinary operation of this system of priorities, consider the following question we posed to Harvard undergraduates:

"Imagine that your mother is en route to Cambridge and has sent a wire asking you to meet her train at South Station at 9 P.M. Suppose you have a seminar meeting from 8 to 10 that evening, and you have been scheduled to deliver a paper. You have no way of leaving a message for your mother at the station and no friend who can meet her for you. What would you probably do?"

The students questioned were unanimous in saying that they would attend the seminar and explain to their mother later why they were unable to meet her. When pressed further, they usually added that they were sure that their mother would consider the presentation of a seminar paper more important than meeting her train. One respondent went so far as to say that his mother would have expected him to attend the seminar and would have been angry if he had cut the seminar to meet her train.

Similarly, a death in the immediate family is recognized as compelling reason for not appearing at one's place of business; kinship obligations have so clear a priority under such circumstances that a person who fulfilled his occupational obligations instead of staying home with his family would probably be regarded as peculiar by his fellow workers. In other words, institutionalization is more specific than the mere cataloguing of an individual's rights and obligations vis-a-vis other individuals and groups. Rights and obligations are defined *relative* to one another. The applicability of a claim depends in part upon the absence of other legitimate claims. Thus, the "excuse" is a highly important sociological category. *It is an approved technique for avoiding sanctions by asserting that an equally high or higher claim prevented the individual from fulfilling his obligations.* Excuses are most prevalent in informal interpersonal relations, but even the law recognizes their validity. For example, the obligation to respect human life is violated whenever one person kills another. But, under circumstances where the "excuse" of self-defense can be established, penalties are waived.

THE ACCIDENT

Another kind of legitimate non-compliance, a cousin of the "excuse," is the claim of the actor that his failure to fulfill his obligations is involuntary. No higher claims are invoked, but the actor escapes sanctions by demonstrating that circumstances beyond his control prevented him from carrying out his good intentions. For example, a bomber crew may not complete its combat mission because of engine trouble. Of course, only if the individual's failure to fulfill his obligations is regarded as involuntary will he remain in good standing with the group. Quite obviously, some claims of "accident" are fabricated for the purpose of avoiding penalties. Hence group skepticism is necessary to check abuses. (In the case of motorcycle policemen, skepticism verges on utter disbelief.) Even though the group is not in a position to investigate whether the accident really happened, a rough calculation of probabilities can usually be made. An individual

can blame his tardiness on the public transportation system occasionally, but not daily.

RITUALS FOR REDUCING SOCIAL FRICTION: ETIQUETTE

Emily Post is sometimes ridiculed by people who pride themselves on being rational. They naively suppose that etiquette consists of meaningless ceremonials, for they do not realize the importance of prescribed rituals in solving the dilemmas of daily life. Consider the chaos of competing demands for social recognition which would ensue if etiquette did not exist. Etiquette formalizes the rank order of claims for deference, thus avoiding in most cases the problem of deciding between one individual's right to attention and another's. The very arbitrariness of the ritual takes the problem out of the realm of idiosyncratic judgment; precedence is automatically evaluated according to the institutionalized criteria. Less specific than etiquette but analogous in function are rules of social intercourse like "first come, first served."

In the play of small children we see what happens before etiquette is institutionalized. Tom steps on Dick's foot. Dick pushes him off with a vigorous shove. "You don't need to push that hard," says Tom, pushing him back. And the fight is on. After they have beaten one another up and gone home in tears, a parent may feel called upon to heal the breach. Observe what he does. Instead of insisting that Tom was wrong and should be ashamed of himself (or that Dick should not have started the pushing), the peacemaker ignores the question of fault and seeks to induce the boys to apologize *mutually and to shake hands.*

With adults there is less likelihood for essentially trivial issues to produce conflict. The automatic apology of two strangers who accidentally collide on a busy street illustrates the integrative function of etiquette. In effect, each of the parties to the collision says, "I don't know whether I am responsible for this situation, but *if* I am, you have a right to be angry with me, a right that I pray you will not exercise." By defining the situation as one in which both parties must abase themselves, society enables each to keep his self-respect. Each may feel in his heart of hearts, "Why can't that stupid ass watch where he's going?" But overtly each *plays the role of the guilty party* whether he feels he has been miscast or not.

LEGITIMATE DECEPTION: TACT

Lies are generally regarded as reprehensible, and truth is held to be a virtue. But there are certain circumstances—held to be exceptional—where it is considered "tactless" to tell the truth, where the "white lie" is regarded as the proper response. Consider an example of such circumstances: Tom invites Mary to go to dinner with him on a certain evening. Mary does not like Tom, so she refuses the invitation, fabricating a previous appointment as the reason for not accepting his invitation. She may or may not deceive him. If she has on another occasion rejected a proposed "date," he may recognize that the "previous appointment" may have been her way of indicating that she does not care for his company. But Tom has no right to become indignant, for Mary has been *tactful*. True, she refused the invitation, which was an injury, especially if he suspects the motive for her refusal. But she does not add insult to injury by explaining it.

This solicitude for the feelings of others is the circumstance that makes the white lie socially "right." The ordinary lie is unreservedly disapproved because it lacks precisely this quality. It is a selfish attempt to manipulate other people by controlling their access to information. Tact, on the other hand, is institutionalized deception for the primary purpose of sparing the feelings of others. Mary did not lie to Tom because she feared losing a friend if she did not consider his feelings. Tactful behavior is a social obligation of adults. We are trained to avoid hurting one another because otherwise it would be too difficult to control the aggressions and hostilities at large in the system.

SEGREGATION OF ROLES

Another important device for preventing role conflicts is the definition of roles so that attendant circumstances have to be appropriate in order to activate the role behavior in question. For example, the personnel director of a corporation has a role obligation to hire the best qualified people; he also has obligations to his family. But if his daughter were looking for a job and did not have the qualifications for any that were open, no one would accuse him of failing in his father role because he did not hire her. In our society the occupational and the familial roles are *defined* as segregated. Nepotism, though it occurs, is regarded as a fault rather than a virtue.

The fact that the same person is properly treated differently when he occupies different roles is of incalculable importance in clarifying the limits of obligations. An Air Force major who is in command of a fighter squadron is entitled to one kind of treatment from a pilot in his squadron because he is a major and quite different treatment because he is the Commanding Officer. And it may be important to understand when the major is occupying one role, when the other, and when he occupies neither. At the Officers Club, for instance, it may be appropriate to regard him in the role of friend. Interestingly enough, officers frequently dress in civilian clothes at their clubs, perhaps because this has functional significance for the segregation of military roles from the roles appropriate to convivial interaction.

In spite of these various mechanisms to prevent incipient conflicts from developing, individuals do find themselves in situations where two or more groups make incompatible demands upon them. This is due in part to the imperfect integration of all social systems; if the integrative mechanism functioned perfectly, *true* role conflicts would be impossible. By true role conflicts, we refer to situations where the claims of the two groups are institutionally defined as legitimate, but where there exists no institutionalized formula for making the demands compatible. However, pseudo-role conflicts arise even where true role conflicts are impossible, and these appear very much like the genuine article to the individuals involved. By pseudo-role conflicts, we refer to situations where the claims of the two groups are institutionally defined as legitimate but where a skillful individual might have prevented the conflict from arising. For example, the anguish resulting from appointments at two widely removed places at the same time is potentially avoidable. Nevertheless, whether an individual is caught in a true or a pseudo-role conflict, there are only a limited number of alternatives open to him:

REPUDIATION OF HIS ROLE IN ONE GROUP. The individual gets out of the dilemma but in a manner analogous to Alexander's cutting of the Gordian knot. Complete repudiation of role obligations is a drastic solution, inviting sanctions from the group which is defied. Depending on the group's importance to him—his identification with it and the severity of the sanctions it is likely to impose—he may be unable to face the consequences of defiance. A sergeant whose commanding officer instructs him to enforce an unpopular regulation may not be willing either to disobey his superior or to outrage the sentiments of his men. Other sergeants might be willing to enforce the regulation, no matter how their men griped. Still others might refuse to carry out the order.

PLAYING OFF ONE GROUP AGAINST THE OTHER. The individual achieves a precarious equilibrium by indicating to each group the incompatible demands simultaneously being made upon him by the other. In this way he induces each group to mitigate its demands sufficiently so that his role obligations are compatible. A union official might be under pressure from union members to press for a substantial wage increase and under pressure from the Federal Government to hold the line against inflation. If he could convince the rank and file that the national welfare permitted only a small wage increase and the appropriate federal agency that a token wage boost was necessary to avert a wild-cat strike, the problem would be solved. There is a certain similarity between this technique of resolving a role conflict and the invoking of institutionalized priorities to prevent the conflict from arising. But an important difference should be noted. The individual who plays off one group against another does not have institutionalized backing for his compromise. It is by dint of his personal skill in negotiation and his ability to communicate his plight and invoke sympathy that he solves the problem.

STALLING UNTIL THE PRESSURES SUBSIDE. If the cross-pressure are of a *temporary* nature, it may be possible for the individual to postpone making a decision until one or both of the groups relax their demands. Stalling is, however, not passive waiting; it is an art. It involves placating and promising while the competing obligations are not being fulfilled. A role conflict amenable to such a tactic occurs when a woman comes to visit her son and daughter-in-law, and the two women resent one another. The son might stall until his mother's visit is over, thus avoiding a fight with either his wife or his mother.

REDEFINITION OF THE ROLE (OR ROLES). The individual reacts upon the situation and changes it so that the role expectations are no longer incompatible. For example, the daughter of immigrant parents may be able to redefine her role in the family according to American patterns, thus resolving the conflicting claims of her parents and her girl friends. Of course the opportunities for reeducating a group are comparatively infrequent. More often, a different type of redefinition of role is possible. The individual does not change the role requirements of the group, but he finds a formula whereby his behavior can, by Procrustean efforts, be defined as fulfilling the requirements. For example, suppose that the parents of an adolescent boy forbid him to drink intoxicating beverages, whereas his friends drink a good deal and bring pressure upon him to join them. He might solve this role conflict by drinking beer —if he could convince his parents that "beer isn't liquor" and his friends that beer is a manly and highly satisfactory "drink."

THE DOUBLE LIFE. The individual takes advantage of the fact that he is not simultaneously in contact with both groups. He plays the approved role in each group, ignoring its expectations when in contact with the other. Deception is a vital element in this solution, and thus it is limited to circumstances where deception is possible. Moreover, this sort of deception, unlike the white lie, is entirely self-oriented and would be recognized as such by others—if they found out about it. It is not always necessary to practice *double* deception. That is to say, one of the groups might have no objection to the individual's playing a different role when not in contact with it. A nudist colony would, for example, probably approve of its members wearing clothes "on the outside." But nudists might still have to keep their membership in the colony secret.

ESCAPE FROM THE FIELD. The individual may find his position in the cross-fire so unpleasant that he moves to a different social system. Of course this does not necessarily imply geographic mobility, although that is the most common device. A foreman under pressure both from his superiors in the company and from the shop steward of the union may resign his job. Escape from the field, though similar to role repudiation, involves retirement from *both* groups and withdrawal from the effective range of their sanctions. Suicide would be the limiting case.

ILLNESS. If the pressures become unbearable and the individual does not perceive as appropriate to his problem any of the above mentioned devices, he may become prey to mental or physical illness. Illness is an excuse for failing to conform to role expectations, an excuse which has general acceptability. Thus, we might call this a solution to the conflict. On the other hand, it may simply signify the breakdown of the coping mechanisms of the organism under the pressure of the problem.

To sum up: Institutionalized techniques exist for preventing role conflicts from arising. These are not perfect, however, and role conflicts arise. But there are only a limited number of possible solutions to these dilemmas. The problem for research is the conditions under which one solution is chosen over another.

If role conflict were nothing more than a dilemma for the individual, a choice between two incompatible courses of action, it would be of interest to the psychologist alone. The sociologist is interested in role conflicts because they place individuals under strain, and strain is often the starting point of social change. Furthermore, in urban industrial societies role conflicts are chronic because the social structure is so highly differentiated that the individual is simultaneously a member of a number of independent interactions systems. He is a member of the family into which he was born (the family of orientation), the family he creates by marriage (the family of procreation), the corporation that he works for, his neighborhood, the educational institution in which he is taking courses, his circle of friends, and so on. Therefore, the probability of role conflict is much greater than in preliterate societies like that of the Australian Murngin where one social structure—kinship—predominates.

INTEGRATION: THE PROBLEM OF COORDINATING INTERACTIVE SYSTEMS

Another way of looking at role conflict is to see it as an effort of the individual to integrate his motivational commitments among multiple social structures. This is not the same thing as *societal* integration or, on a less inclusive level, *group* integration. When the sociologist talks about *societal* integration, he is concerned with conflicts among groups and between individuals, not with intrapsychic conflicts. Consider for a moment New York City as an illustration of a social system with integrative problems. The Police Department and the Traffic Commissioner of New York City spend much time, effort, and money to keep motor vehicles moving on the hundreds of miles of streets and highways within the city limits. The Port of New York Authority, which owns and operates the bridges and tunnels leading into New York City (as well as the airports and bus terminals), charges motor vehicles tolls for using the bridges or tunnels. The more passenger cars, buses, and trucks using the bridge and tunnel facilities of the Authority, the more money the Authority takes in and the more additional bridges and tunnels it can build. The officials of the Authority are not responsible for traffic congestion on the streets of New York City, and the Traffic Commissioner of New York City cannot stop the Port of New York Authority from building an additional tunnel or from double-decking the George Washington Bridge. There may be conflict here between officials of the City of New York and officials of the Port of New York Authority; but this is not role conflict. No person is torn apart by incompatible loyalties to different social structures. The trouble is rather that the social structures have not been coordinated adequately.

It is obvious why societies have integrative problems. Groups, organizations, and institutions develop to deal with particular functions. Roles are established to mobilize individual effort in the discharge of these functions. Often, however, there are unanticipated consequences for other social structures dealing with other functions.[3] As an example of this phenomenon, consider the rapid introduction of automated processes in American industry. Corporation officials decide on self-regulating machines to reduce costs or to improve quality, or both. They are conscientiously playing their roles. But the cumulative impact of large numbers of companies simultaneously introducing such equipment is to create massive retraining

[3] Robert K. Merton, "The Unanticipated Consequences of Purposive Social Action," *American Sociological Review*, Vol. 1, December 1936, pp. 894–904.

and relocation problems for workers. And, since workers are usually members of families, the ultimate impact of automation may be far indeed from the economic area in which it originates. The following article traces the impact of a seemingly trivial technological innovation on a small community.

Societal Malintegration: The Failure to Consider the Effect of One Interactive System on Other Interactive Systems

Reprinted by permission. From W. F. Cottrell, "Death by Dieselization: A Case Study in the Reaction to Technological Change," *American Sociological Review*, Vol. 16, June 1951, pp. 358–365.

In the following instance it is proposed that we examine a community confronted with radical change in its basic economic institution and to trace the effects of this change throughout the social structure. From these facts it may be possible in some degree to anticipate the resultant changing attitudes and values of the people in the community, particularly as they reveal whether or not there is a demand for modification of the social structure or a shift in function from one institution to another. Some of the implications of the facts discovered may be valuable in anticipating future social change.

The community chosen for examination has been disrupted by the dieselization of the railroads. Since the railroad is among the oldest of those industries organized around steam, and since therefore the social structure of railroad communities is a product of long-continued processes of adaptation to the technology of steam, the sharp contrast between the technological requirements of the steam engine and those of the diesel should clearly reveal the changes in social structure required. Any one of a great many railroad towns might have been chosen for examination. However, many railroad towns are only partly dependent upon the railroad for their existence. In them many of the effects which take place are blurred and not easily distinguishable by the observer. Thus, the "normal" railroad town may not be the best place to see the consequences of dieselization. For this reason a one-industry town was chosen for examination.

In a sense it is an "ideal type" railroad town, and hence not complicated by other extraneous economic factors. It lies in the desert and is here given the name "Caliente" which is the Spanish adjective for "hot." Caliente was built in a break in an eighty-mile canyon traversing the desert. Its reason for existence was to service the steam locomotive. There are few resources in the area to support it on any other basis, and such as they are they would contribute more to the growth and maintenance of other little settlements in the vicinity than to that of Caliente. So long as the steam locomotive was in use, Caliente was a necessity. With the adoption of the diesel it became obsolescent.

This stark fact was not, however, part of the expectations of the residents of Caliente. Based upon the "certainty" of the railroad's need for Caliente, men built their homes there, frequently of concrete and brick, at the cost, in many cases, of their life savings. The water system was laid in cast iron which will last for centuries. Business men erected substantial buildings which could be paid for only by profits gained through many years of business. Four churches evidence the faith of Caliente people in the future of their community. A twenty-seven bed hospital serves the town. Those who built it thought that their investment was as well warranted as the fact of birth, sickness, accident and death. They believed in education. Their school buildings represent the investment of savings guaranteed by bonds and future taxes. There is a combined park and play field which, together with a recently modernized theatre, has been serving recreational needs. All these physical structures are material evidence of the expectations, morally and legally sanctioned and financially funded, of the people of Caliente. This is a normal and rational aspect of the culture of all "solid" and "sound" communities.

Similarly normal are the social organizations. These include Rotary, Chamber of Commerce, Masons, Odd Fellows, American Legion and the Veterans of Foreign Wars. There are the usual unions, churches, and myriad little clubs to which the women belong. In short, here is the average American community with normal social life, subscribing to normal American codes. Nothing its members had been taught would indicate that the whole pattern of this normal existence depended completely upon a few elements of technology which were themselves in flux. For them the continued use of the steam engine was as "natural" a phenomenon as any other element in their physical environment. Yet suddenly their life pattern was destroyed by the announcement that the railroad was moving its division point, and with it destroying the economic basis of Caliente's existence.

Turning from this specific community for a moment, let us examine the technical changes which took place and the reasons for the change. Division points on a railroad are established by the frequency with which the rolling stock must be serviced and the operating crews changed. At the turn of the century when this particular road was built, the engines produced wet steam at low temperatures. The steel in the boilers was of comparatively low tensile strength and could not withstand the high temperatures and pressures required for the efficient use of coal and water. At intervals of roughly a hundred miles the engine had to be disconnected from the train for service. At these points the cars also were inspected and if they were found to be defective they were either removed from the train or repaired while it was standing and the new engine being coupled on. Thus the location of Caliente, as far as the railroad was concerned, was a function of boiler temperature and pressure and the resultant service requirements of the locomotive.

Following World War II, the high tensile steels developed to create superior artillery and armor were used for locomotives. As a consequence it was possible to utilize steam at higher temperatures and pressure. Speed, power, and efficiency were increased and the distance between service intervals was increased.

The "ideal distance" between freight divisions became approximately 150 to 200 miles whereas it had formerly been 100 to 150. Wherever possible, freight divisions were increased in length to that formerly used by passenger trains, and passenger divisions were lengthened from two old freight divisions to three. Thus towns located at 100 miles from a terminal became obsolescent, those at 200 became freight points only, and those at three hundred miles became passenger division points.

The increase in speed permitted the train crews to make the greater distance in the time previously required for the lesser trip, and roughly a third of the train and engine crews, car inspectors, boilermakers and machinists and other service men were dropped. The towns thus abandoned were crossed off the social record of the nation in the adjustment to these technological changes in the use of the steam locomotive. Caliente, located midway between terminals about six hundred miles apart, survived. In fact it gained, since the less frequent stops caused an increase in the service required of the maintenance crews at those points where it took place. However, the introduction of the change to diesel engines projected a very different future.

In its demands for service the diesel engine differs almost completely from a steam locomotive. It requires infrequent, highly skilled service, carried on within very close limits, in contrast to the frequent, crude adjustments required by the steam locomotive. Diesels operate at about 35 per cent efficiency, in contrast to the approximately 4 per cent efficiency of the steam locomotives in use after World War II in the United States. Hence diesels require much less frequent stops for fuel and water. These facts reduce their operating costs sufficiently to compensate for their much higher initial cost.

In spite of these reductions in operating costs the introduction of diesels ordinarily would have taken a good deal of time. The change-over would have been slowed by the high capital costs of retooling the locomotive works, the long period required to recapture the cost of existing steam locomotives, and the effective resistance of the workers. World War II altered each of these factors. The locomotive works were required to make the change in order to provide marine engines, and the costs of the change were assumed by the government. Steam engines were used up by the tremendous demand placed upon the railroads by war traffic. The costs were recaptured by shipping charges. Labor shortages were such that labor resistance was less formidable and much less acceptable to the public than it would have been in peace time. Hence the shift to diesels was greatly facilitated by the war. In consequence, every third and sometimes every second division point suddenly became technologically obsolescent.

Caliente, like all other towns in similar plight, is supposed to accept its fate in the name of "progress." The general public, as shippers and consumers of shipped goods, reaps the harvest in better, faster service and eventually perhaps in lower charges. A few of the workers in Caliente will also share the gains, as they move to other division points, through higher wages. They will share in the higher pay, though whether this will be adequate to compensate for the costs of moving no one can say. Certain it is that their pay will not be adjusted to compensate for their specific losses. They will gain only as their seniority gives them the opportunity to work. These are those who gain. What are the losses, and who bears them?

The railroad company can figure its losses at Caliente fairly accurately. It owns 39 private dwellings, a modern clubhouse with 116 single rooms, and a twelve-room hotel with dining-room and lunch-counter facilities. These now become useless, as does much of the fixed physical equipment used for servicing trains. Some of the machinery can be used elsewhere. Some part of the roundhouse can be used to store unused locomotives and standby equipment. The rest will be torn down to save taxes. All of these costs can be entered as capital losses on the statement which the company draws up for its stockholders and for the government. Presumably they will be recovered by the use of the more efficient engines.

What are the losses that may not be entered on the company books? The total tax assessment in Caliente was $9,946.80 for the year 1948, of which $6,103.39 represented taxes assessed on the railroad. Thus the railroad valuation was about three-fifths that of the town. This does not take into account tax-free property belonging to the churches, the schools, the hospital, or the municipality itself which included all the public utilities. Some ideas of the losses sustained by the railroad in comparison with the losses of others can be surmised by reflecting on these figures for real estate alone. The story is an old one and often repeated in the economic history of America. It represents the "loss" side of a profit and loss system of adjusting to technological change. Perhaps for sociological purposes we need an answer to the question "just who pays?"

Probably the greatest losses are suffered by the older "non-operating" employees. Seniority among these men extends only within the local shop and craft. A man with twenty-five years' seniority at Caliente has no claim on the job of a similar craftsman at another point who has only twenty-five days' seniority. Moreover, some of the skills formerly valuable are no longer needed. The boilermaker, for example, knows that jobs for his kind are disappearing and he must enter the ranks of the unskilled. The protection and status offered by the union while he was employed have become meaningless now that he

is no longer needed. The cost of this is high both in loss of income and in personal demoralization.

Operating employees also pay. Their seniority extends over a division, which in this case includes three division points. The older members can move from Caliente and claim another job at another point, but in many cases they move leaving a good portion of their life savings behind. The younger men must abandon their stake in railroad employment. The loss may mean a new apprenticeship in another occupation, at a time in life when apprenticeship wages are not adequate to meet the obligations of mature men with families. A steam engine hauled 2,000 tons up the hill out of Caliente with the aid of two helpers. The four-unit diesel in command of one crew handles a train of 5,000 tons alone. Thus, to handle the same amount of tonnage required only about a fourth the man-power it formerly took. Three out of four men must start out anew at something else.

The local merchants pay. The boarded windows, half-empty shelves, and abandoned store buildings bear mute evidence of these costs. The older merchants stay, and pay; the younger ones, and those with no stake in the community will move; but the value of their property will in both cases largely be gone.

The bondholders will pay. They can't foreclose on a dead town. If the town were wiped out altogether, that which would remain for salvage would be too little to satisfy their claims. Should the town continue there is little hope that taxes adequate to carry the overhead of bonds and day-to-day expenses could be secured by taxing the diminished number of property owners or employed persons.

The church will pay. The smaller congregations cannot support services as in the past. As the church men leave, the buildings will be abandoned.

Homeowners will pay. A hundred and thirty-five men owned homes in Caliente. They must accept the available means of support or rent to those who do. In either case the income available will be far less than that on which the houses were built. The least desirable homes will stand unoccupied, their value completely lost. The others must be revalued at a figure far below that at which they were formerly held.

In a word, those pay who are, by traditional American standards, *most moral*. Those who have raised children see friendships broken and neighborhoods disintegrated. The childless more freely shake the dust of Caliente from their feet. Those who built their personalities into the structure of the community watch their work destroyed. Those too wise or too selfish to have entangled themselves in community affairs suffer no such qualms. The chain store can pull down its sign, move its equipment and charge the costs off against more profitable and better located units, and against taxes. The local owner has no such alternatives. In short, "good citizens" who assumed family and community responsibility are the greatest losers. Nomads suffer least.

The people of Caliente are asked to accept as "normal" this strange inversion of their expectations. It is assumed that they will, without protest or change in sentiment, accept the dictum of the "law of supply and demand." Certainly they must comply in part with this dictum. While their behavior in part reflects this compliance, there are also other changes perhaps equally important in their attitudes and values.

The first reaction took the form of an effort at community self-preservation. Caliente became visible to its inhabitants as a real entity, as meaningful as the individual personalities which they had hitherto been taught to see as atomistic or nomadic elements. Community survival was seen as prerequisite to many of the individual values that had been given precedence in the past. The organized community made a search for new industry, citing elements of community organization themselves as reasons why industry should move to Caliente. But the conditions that led the railroad to abandon the point made the place even less attractive to new industry than it had hitherto been. Yet the effort to keep the community a going concern persisted.

There was also a change in sentiment. In the past the glib assertion that progress spelled sacrifice could be offered when some distant group was a victim of technological change. There was no such reaction when the event struck home. The change can probably be as well revealed as in any other way by quoting from the Caliente *Herald*:

". . . (over the) years . . . (this) . . . railroad and its affiliates . . . became to this writer his ideal of a railroad empire. The (company) . . . appeared to take much more than the ordinary interest of big railroads in the development of areas adjacent to its lines, all the while doing a great deal for the communities large and small through which the lines passed.

"Those were the days creative of (its) enviable reputation as one of the finest, most progressive—and most human—of American railroads, enjoying the confidence and respect of employees, investors, and communities alike!

"One of the factors bringing about this confidence and respect was the consideration shown communities which otherwise would have suffered serious blows when division and other changes were effected. A notable example was . . . (a town) . . . where the shock of division change was made almost unnoticed by installation of a rolling stock reclamation point, which gave (that town) an opportunity to hold its community intact until tourist traffic and other industries could get better established—with the result that . . . (it) . . . is now on a firm foundation. And through this display of consideration for a community, the railroad gained friends—not only among the people of . . . (that town) . . . who were perhaps more vocal than others, but also among thousands of others throughout the country on whom this action made an indelible impression.

"But things seem to have changed materially during the last few years, the . . . (company) . . . seems to this writer to have gone all out for glamor and the dollars which glamorous people have to spend, sadly neglecting one of the principal factors which helped to make . . . (it) . . . great: that fine consideration of communities and individuals, as well as employees, who have been happy in cooperating steadfastly with the railroad in times of stress as well as prosperity. The loyalty of these people and communities seems to count for little with the . . . (company) . . . of this day, though other 'Big Business' corporations do not hesitate to expend huge sums to encourage the loyalty of community and people which old friends of . . . (the company) . . . have been happy to give voluntarily.

"Ever since the . . . railroad was constructed . . . Caliente has been a key town on the railroad. It is true, the town owed its inception to the railroad, but it has paid this back in becoming one of the most attractive communities on the system. With nice homes, streets and parks, good school . . . good city government . . . Caliente offers advantages that most big corporations would be gratified to have for their employees—a homey spot where they could live their lives of contentment, happiness, and security.

"Caliente's strategic location, midway of some of the toughest road on the entire system, has been a lifesaver for the road several times when floods have wreaked havoc on the roadbed in the canyon above and below Caliente. This has been possible through storage in Caliente of large stocks of repair material and equipment—and not overlooking manpower—which has thus become available on short notice.

". . . But (the railroad) or at least one of its big officials, appearing to be almost completely divorced from policies which made this railroad great, has ordered changes which are about as inconsiderate as anything of which 'Big Business' has ever been accused! Employees who have given the best years of their lives to this railroad are cut off without anything to which they can turn, many of them with homes in which they have taken much pride; while others, similarly with nice homes, are told to move elsewhere and are given runs that only a few will be able to endure from a physical standpoint, according to common opinion.

"Smart big corporations the country over encourage their employees to own their own homes —and loud are their boasts when the percentage of such employees is favorable! But in contrast, a high (company) official is reported to have said only recently that 'a railroad man has no business owning a home!' Quite a departure from what has appeared to be (company) tradition.

"It is difficult for the Herald to believe that this official, however 'big' he is, speaks for the . . . (company) . . . when he enunciates a policy that, carried to the letter, would make tramps of (company) employees and their families!

"No thinking person wants to stand in the way of progress, but true progress is not made when it is overshadowed by cold-blooded disregard for the loyalty of employees, their families, and the communities which have developed in the good American way through the decades of loyal service and good citizenship."

This editorial, written by a member of all the service clubs, approved by Caliente business men, and quoted with approbation by the most conservative members of the community, is significant of changing sentiment.

The people of Caliente continually profess their belief in "The American Way," but like the editor of the *Herald* they criticize decisions made solely in pursuit of profit, even though these decisions grow out of a clear-cut case of technological "progress." They feel that the company should have based its decision upon consideration for loyalty, citizenship, and community morale. They assume that the company should regard the seniority rights of workers as important considerations, and that it should consider significant the effect of permanent unemployment upon old and faithful employees. They look upon community integrity as an important community asset. Caught between the support of a "rational" system of "economic" forces and laws, and sentiments which they accept as significant values, they seek a solution to their dilemma which will at once permit them to retain their expected rewards for continued adherence to past norms and to defend the social system which they have been taught to revere but which now offers them a stone instead of bread.

IMPLICATIONS

We have shown that those in Caliente whose behavior most nearly approached the ideal taught are hardest hit by change. On the other hand, those seemingly farthest removed in conduct from that ideal are either rewarded or pay less of the costs of change than do those who follow the ideal more closely. Absentee owners, completely anonymous, and consumers who are not expected to cooperate to make the gains possible are rewarded most highly, while the local people who must cooperate to raise productivity pay dearly for having contributed.

In a society run through sacred mysteries whose rationale it is not man's privilege to criticize, such incongruities may be explained away. Such a society may even provide some "explanation" which makes them seem rational. In a secular society, supposedly defended rationally upon scientific facts, in which the pragmatic test "Does it work?" is continually applied, such discrepancy between expectation and realization is difficult to reconcile.

Defense of our traditional system of assessing the costs of technological change is made on the theory that the costs of such change are more than offset by the benefits to "society as a whole." However, it is difficult to show the people of Caliente just why *they* should pay for advances made to benefit others whom they have never known and who, in their judgment, have done nothing to justify such rewards. Any action that will permit the people of Caliente to levy the costs of change upon those who will benefit from them will be morally justifiable to the people of Caliente. Appeals to the general welfare leave them cold and the compulsions of the price system are not felt to be self-justifying "natural laws" but are regarded as being the specific consequence of specific bookkeeping decisions as to what should be included in the costs of change. They seek to change these decisions through social action. They do not consider that the "American Way" consists primarily of acceptance of the market as the final arbiter of their destiny. Rather they conceive that the system as a whole exists to render "justice," and if the consequences of the price system are such as to produce what they consider to be "injustice" they proceed to use some other institution as a means to reverse or offset the effects of the price system. Like other groups faced with the same situation, those in Caliente seize upon the means available to them. The operating employees had in their unions a device to secure what they consider to be their rights. Union practices developed over the years make it possible for the organized workers to avoid some of the costs of change which they would otherwise have had to bear. Feather-bed rules, make-work practices, restricted work weeks, train length legislation and other similar devices were designed to permit union members to continue work even when "efficiency" dictated that they be disemployed. Members of the "Big Four" in Caliente joined with their fellows in demanding not only the retention of previously existing rules, but the imposition of new ones such as that requiring the presence of a third man in the diesel cab. For other groups there was available only the appeal to the company that it establish some other facility at Caliente, or alternatively a demand that "government" do something. One such demand took the form of a request to the Interstate Commerce Commission that it require inspection of rolling stock at Caliente. This request was denied.

It rapidly became apparent to the people of Caliente that they could not gain their objectives by organized community action nor individual endeavor but there was hope that by adding their voices to those of others similarly injured there might be hope of solution. They began to look to the activities of the whole labor movement for succor. Union strategy which forced the transfer of control from the market to government mediation or to legislation and operation was widely approved on all sides. This was not confined to those only who were currently seeking rule changes but was equally approved by the great bulk of those in the community who had been hit by the change. Cries of public outrage at their demands for make-work rules were looked upon as coming from those at best ignorant, ill-informed or stupid, and at worst as being the hypocritical efforts of others to gain at the workers' expense. When the union threat of a national strike for rule changes was met by government seizure, Caliente workers like most of their compatriots across the country welcomed this shift in control, secure in their belief that if "justice" were done they could only be gainers by government intervention. These attitudes are not "class" phenomena purely nor are they merely occupational sentiments. They result from the fact that modern life, with the interdependence that it creates, particularly in one-industry communities, imposes penalties far beyond the membership of the groups presumably involved in industry. When make-work rules contributed to the livelihood of the community, the support of the churches, and the taxes which maintain the schools; when feather-bed practices determine the standard of living, the profits of the business man and the circulation of the press; when they contribute to the salary of the teacher and the preacher; they can no longer be treated as accidental, immoral, deviant or temporary. Rather they are elevated into the position of emergent morality and law. Such practices generate a morality which serves them just as the practices in turn nourish those who participate in and preserve them. They are as firmly a part of what one "has a right to expect" from industry as are parity payments to the farmer bonuses and pensions to the veterans, assistance to the aged, tariffs to the industrialist, or the sanctity of property to those who inherit. On the other hand, all these practices conceivably help create a structure that is particularly vulnerable to changes such as that described here.

Practices which force the company to spend in Caliente part of what has been saved through technological change, or failing that, to reward those who are forced to move by increased income for the same service, are not, by the people of Caliente, considered to be unjustifiable. Confronted by a choice between the old means and resultant "injustice" which their use entails, and the acceptance of new means which they believe will secure them the "justice" they hold to be their right, they are willing to abandon (in so far as this particular area is concerned) the liberal state and the omnicompetent market in favor of something that works to provide "justice."

The study of the politics of pressure groups will show how widely the reactions of Caliente people are paralleled by those of other groups. Amongst them it is in politics that the decisions as to who will pay and who will profit are made. Through organized political force railroaders maintain the continuance of rules which operate to their benefit rather than for "the public good" or "the general welfare." Their defense of these practices is found in the argument that only so can their rights be protected against the power of other groups who hope to gain at their expense by functioning through the corporation and the market.

We should expect that where there are other groups similarly affected by technological change, there will be similar efforts to change the operation of our institutions. The case cited is not unique. Not only is it duplicated in hundreds of railroad division points but also in other towns abandoned by management for similar reasons. Changes in the location of markets or in the method of calculating transportation costs, changes in technology making necessary the use of new materials, changes due to the exhaustion of old sources of materials, changes to avoid labor costs such as the shift of the textile industry from New England to the South, changes to expedite decentralization to avoid the consequences of bombing, or those of congested living, all give rise to the question, "Who benefits, and at whose expense?"

The accounting practices of the corporation permit the entry only of those costs which have become "legitimate" claims upon the company. But the tremendous risks borne by the workers and frequently all the members of the community in an era of technological change are real phenomena. Rapid shifts in technology which destroy the "legitimate" expectations derived from past experience force the recognition of new obligations. Such recognition may be made voluntarily as management foresees the necessity, or it may be thrust upon it by political or other action. Rigidity of property concepts, the legal structure controlling directors in what they may admit to be costs, and the stereotyped nature of the "economics" used by management make rapid change within the corporation itself difficult even in a

"free democratic society." Hence while management is likely to be permitted or required to initiate technological change in the interest of profits, it may and probably will be barred from compensating for the social consequences certain to arise from those changes. Management thus shuts out the rising flood of demands in its cost-accounting only to have them reappear in its tax accounts, in legal regulations or in new insistent union demands. If economics fails to provide an answer to social demands then politics will be tried.

The author of the foregoing article contrasts the economic balance sheet of a particular organization (the railroad) with the broader balance sheet of American society. Railroad officials were not considering all of the social costs of switching to diesels.[4] Even if they were aware of the hardships to the residents of Caliente, their occupational roles required them to consider only costs appearing in the balance sheet of the railroad. Professor Cottrell goes on to point out that the cost to society must be paid by someone: either by the residents of Caliente themselves or by government (meaning taxpayers generally). In society's balance sheet, the economic advantage to the railroad might have been offset by the economic and personal losses of the families and other social systems of Caliente.

A society must achieve some minimum level of integration if it is to continue functioning, just as an individual must achieve some unity of purpose. But there is no over-all responsibility for societal unity as there is for the integration of the personality. If John's right hand decided, for its own good reasons, to drop heavy weights on John's right foot, this would be analogous to the social phenomenon of groups and institutions working at crosspurposes in contemporary societies. Nevertheless, societies persist, and within societies smaller interactive systems manage to function. A major problem for sociology is to understand how a minimum level of integration within

[4] Karl William Kapp, *The Social Costs of Private Enterprise*, Cambridge, Mass.: Harvard University Press, 1950.

interactive systems is achieved. Many sociologists hope that a checklist of functions can be identified which are crucial for describing any interactive system from the small family to the self-contained society. In his book, *The Social System*, the eminent sociological theorist, Talcott Parsons, tried to do precisely this.[5] Many sociologists do not believe that Parsons succeeded, and some are doubtful that anyone will ever be able to describe all interactive systems, varying as they do in size, complexity, and focus, with the same checklist of basic variables.

If it is not possible to develop such a checklist, sociology will have to be subdivided into several distinct disciplines, perhaps along the following lines: one discipline studying interaction in small groups like families, cliques of friends, mobs (and other ephemeral groups); another studying interaction and role differentiation in formal organizations like schools, prisons, and government agencies; and a third studying the integration of entire societies. Such a division of the field, however, would violate the scientific ideal of parsimony: to use as few variables as possible to explain adequately the phenomenon under study. One may be skeptical about the feasibility of a single set of variables adequate for explaining interaction in small groups and in complex societies. Many professional sociologists would agree. The issue is unsettled, and it probably will not be possible to resolve it for many decades. Sociology is a relatively young discipline. Consider its founding fathers: Émile Durkheim and Auguste Comte in France, Max Weber in Germany, Herbert Spencer and Leonard Hobhouse in England, William I. Thomas, William Graham Sumner, and Charles Horton Cooley in the United States.[6]

[5] Talcott Parsons, *The Social System*, Glencoe, Ill.: Free Press, 1951.
[6] Harry Elmer Barnes, Ed., *An Introduction to the History of Sociology*, Chicago: University of Chicago Press, 1948.

Most of these men were alive and productive at the turn of the twentieth century.

CONCLUSION

Sociologists are fascinated by the extraordinary dependence of the human individual on the human group. It is not too much to say that the human individual is partially created by his society. The very language that he speaks is a group legacy, enabling him to communicate with others, to express his emotions, to think, to remember, to anticipate. Advantageous though it is to walk erect and to have a thumb opposed to the other fingers, these do not account for the dominance of the human species on this planet. It is the social rather than the biological potentialities of human beings that make them distinctive.

Sociologists are also fascinated by the idea that interaction tends to be organized in *systems*. Just as the physicist sees parallels between the solar system and the atom, so the sociologist sees similarities between the small family as a unity of interacting personalities and giant industrial societies differentiated into complex institutions. The rest of this book consists of an effort to break down enormously complicated societies into comprehensible subsystems. Everyone does not interact with everyone else in a large society, but interaction nevertheless proceeds in an orderly manner. Sociologists yearn to understand the underlying laws of social organization which can explain the absence of chaos.

As noted at the outset, there is no capsule answer to the question of what exactly is sociology. Like other disciplines in the modern university, sociology is part of man's desire to understand the world around him. The formulations in this book will certainly be different from those in a sociology textbook published in the year 2000.

SOME SIGNIFICANT PERIODICALS

Dozens of sociological journals exist including those published in France, England, Denmark, India, and Japan. The following list is a selection of journals in the English language where articles of sociological interest may be found. All of them are readily available in American universities.

American Journal of Sociology. Founded in 1894, this journal is published bimonthly at the University of Chicago, which long has been a major center of sociological teaching and research.

American Sociological Review. Founded in 1936, this is the official journal of the American Sociological Association, largest organization of professional sociologists in the world. The prestige of the *Review* is such that, although six issues appear each year, about 85 per cent of the manuscripts submitted for publication are rejected. As in other professional journals, authors of articles receive no payment except for a small number of free reprints. In 1962, 11,000 copies of each issue of the *Review* were published, about 7000 of which went to members of the Association. The editor of the *Review* is elected by the Council of the American Sociological Association, from among distinguished members of the Association, for a three-year term and the editorial office moves to the University (or other institution) with which the editor is associated.

British Journal of Sociology. Founded in 1949, this quarterly journal is closely associated with the London School of Economics where sociology has developed more strongly than at Oxford or Cambridge. An interesting feature of this journal is long review articles of important books—in addition to shorter reviews such as are published in most professional journals.

Current Sociology. Founded in 1952 and sponsored by UNESCO, the United Nations Educational, Scientific, and Cultural Organization, this journal is published three times a year. It specializes in compiling exhaustive bibliographies on specific topics. Thus, three issues covering 1961–1962 were devoted to trend reports and bibliographies in the fields of (1) the sociology of law, (2) the sociology of human fertility, and (3) the sociology of medicine.

Human Organization. Founded in 1941, this quarterly journal is the official organ of the Society for Applied Anthropology. Since it is concerned with the application of social science to practical problems, a wide range of topics are covered from mental illness to technical assistance to underdeveloped countries. However, industrial sociology is a special emphasis, perhaps because the journal is published by the New York School of Industrial and Labor Relations of Cornell University.

Journal of Abnormal and Social Psychology. Founded in 1906, and appearing monthly, this is a psychological rather than a sociological journal. Nevertheless, articles of sociological interest often appear. For example, the October 1963 issue contained the following articles:

"Influence and Reward in Structured Two-Person Interactions," "Effect of Expecting to be Liked on Choice of Associates."

Psychiatry. Founded in 1938, this quarterly journal is published by the William Alanson White Psychiatric Foundation in Washington, D.C. Until his death Harry Stack Sullivan was an influential figure in this psychoanalytic group and his theories of the interpersonal basis of mental illness make the journal receptive to sociological contributions. Several sociologists are currently on the Board of Editors: William Caudill, Leonard S. Cottrell, Jr., Erving Goffman, and Talcott Parsons.

Public Opinion Quarterly. Founded in 1936, this quarterly journal is devoted to survey research concerned with the mass media and with political behavior. It is the official organ of the American Association for Public Opinion Research, an organization made up of academic sociologists, psychologists, and political scientists, on the one hand, and market research professionals, on the other. The *POQ* is edited at Princeton University by the distinguished social statistician, Professor Frederick F. Stephan.

Rural Sociology. Founded in 1935, this quarterly journal is the official organ of the Rural Sociological Society, which is entirely independent of the American Sociological Association. Although the journal is an excellent one, explanation of its separate existence apart from the rest of sociology is historical rather than intellectual. The field of urban sociology is not similarly represented by a society and a journal.

Sociological Abstracts. Founded in 1952, this bimonthly publication makes available summaries of sociological articles published in hundreds of periodicals from many countries. Thus, it is an invaluable help to the sociologist who wishes to learn about recent developments on a particular topic and cannot himself consult all of the original sources. The articles are indexed under such headings as the following: methodology, research technology, statistical methods, history and present state of sociology, sociological theories and ideas, interaction within (small) group structure, interaction between (large) groups, culture, social change and economic development, rural sociology (village), urban sociology (metropolis), social stratification, sociology of occupations and professions, industrial sociology, leadership studies, military sociology, bureaucratic structures, political sociology, social movements (and revolutions), communication (mass and otherwise), collective behavior, sociology of language and literature, sociology of education, sociology of knowledge (and ideology), sociology of religion, sociology of law, demography and ecology, sociology of the child (and socialization), sociology of the family, sociology of leisure, sociology of medicine, social psychiatry (mental health), social disorganization (criminology, alcoholism, etc.).

CHAPTER 2

The Scientific Aspirations of Contemporary Sociology

"Is sociology objective?"

Most contemporary sociologists believe that it is. This was not always so. One hundred years ago, when sociology was just beginning, sociologists were more likely to be social reformers, eager to change the society in which they lived, than detached scientific observers trying only to describe how their society worked. Even a generation or two ago sociologists tended to be ministers or ex-ministers. Most contemporary sociologists find this historical association burdensome. They explain that they are *not* social workers or social reformers but *scientists*. They point out the aim of sociology is to increase knowledge about human societies just as the aim of chemistry is to increase knowledge about elements and compounds. Although sociologists as individuals may be kindly and generous, they are not professionally dedicated to helping people with problems, as social workers are. Partly for historical reasons, sociologists teach courses on "social problems," but these courses are intended to be descriptive and not preparatory for a crusade.

Thus, some sociologists try to understand why people violate the criminal laws. This does not necessarily mean that they wish to *prevent* crime. Conceivably, they might wish to devote their knowledge to *increasing* delinquency and crime. Such bad citizenship would risk the disapproval of officials at the universities in which they are employed, but, as scientists, their behavior could not be criticized. Sociologists are usually respectable citizens, and, indeed, they frequently are consultants to or employees of government agencies or private foundations concerned with the alleviation of social problems. But the question of how knowledge is applied is not, strictly speaking, a scientific one. Atomic physicists may not be happy that their discoveries are being used for the construction of bombs, but their scientific task was finding out whether atomic energy *could* be released, not deciding the use to which atomic energy *should* be put.

Contemporary sociologists try to be as objective as contemporary physicists. They do not always succeed, but in principle objectivity is possible in sociology just as it is in any descriptive discipline. Objectivity means simply that an observation does not depend on the peculiarities of the observer. When a physicist says that water freezes at 32° Fahrenheit, he

25

means that a dozen trained observers will read the thermometer at about 32° when water starts to freeze. If one observer read the thermometer at 27° and another at 36°, the physicist could no longer talk about the freezing point of water as an objective fact. *Objectivity means that trained observers agree.* Consider the implications of this statement not only for sociology but for any field with scientific aspirations. *The greater the precision of the measuring instruments, the greater the likelihood of consensus among trained observers.* The measurement of temperature is objective because the contemporary physicist has available standardized, precisely calibrated thermometers. If the contemporary physicist had the technical equipment of the ancient Greeks, temperature would move toward the realm of the subjective.

There are many technical difficulties that sociologists must overcome if they are to be rigorously objective. They must develop better tools for interviewing, for questionnaire construction, for observing interaction in groups. The technical difficulties of social research, however, are less responsible than the subject matter for the popular conception of sociology as inherently "subjective." For example, laymen may think that prejudice against minorities cannot be studied scientifically because prejudice is itself subjective. This kind of reasoning can be proved fallacious. Suppose a sociologist interviews an individual in connection with a survey of attitudes toward ethnic minorities. During the course of the interview, the respondent makes the statement, "I hate Negroes. I'd be happy if all of them were lined up against a wall and shot." (However much the sociologist disagrees with the statement, he is careful to record it because that statement is his datum about the respondent's feelings toward Negroes, just as the thermometer reading is the physicist's datum about temperature.) Later, when the researcher analyzes interviews from various respondents, he categorizes the one who wanted to see Negroes shot as the most prejudiced in the survey. The test of whether his research has been objective

is: Would other sociologists having access to the transcript of the interview agree that this respondent were the most prejudiced? If rather good consensus occurs among trained observers on ratings of various degrees of prejudice, the ratings are objective *in precisely the same sense that temperature measurements are objective in physics.*[1]

Though it is *possible* to study with scientific detachment even controversial phenomena like prejudice and juvenile delinquency, such detachment is not always easily attained. If a sociologist believes that prejudice is morally wrong, can he faithfully interview an individual who tells him that Negroes should be lined up against the wall and shot? If a certain type of sex offense shocks his sensibilities, can he avoid communicating this repugnance to the prison inmate whose life history he wishes to record? Either is possible, but it requires training and self-discipline. Social scientists are fully aware of the tendency for the observer to be more than an observer—for example, to give the respondent subtle (or not so subtle) cues as to what answers the interviewer will approve.[2] A tremendous literature exists on interviewer bias and how to avoid it—including the report of a tendency in voting surveys for Republican pollsters to get more Republican political preferences than Democratic pollsters.[3]

Training and self-discipline on the part of the social scientist, however, would not suffice to make sociology scientific if social life were capricious and unpredictable. Science assumes that there are regularities in nature which become laws of the particular subject under study, and that these can be discovered by controlled observation. If there were no reg-

[1] Scientists describe a measure as "reliable" when trained observers can agree as to how it should be applied. Reliability can be measured quantitatively—and often is. For all practical purposes, "objective" and "reliable" are synonymous.
[2] Curiously enough, this principle is equally applicable to physics. Heisenberg pointed out that some subatomic particles defy accurate measurement because the light beam necessary for observation affects their velocity.
[3] Herbert H. Hyman, et al., *Interviewing in Social Research*, Chicago: University of Chicago Press, 1954.

ularities in social life, if human behavior were completely unpredictable, scientific sociology would be impossible—just as physics would be impossible if the freezing point of water and the acceleration of gravity varied chaotically from day to day. Human behavior is unpredictable only in the sense that perfect predictions about an *individual* are impossible. In a statistical sense—that is, predictions about categories of people—human behavior is highly predictable.

Thus, when he comes to the assigned room at the beginning of the semester to give his first lecture, the professor is not surprised to find that students are waiting for him. He *predicted* that they would be there by consulting the schedule of classes. The students also made predictions: not only that the professor would come but how he would be dressed and what he would do when he got there. Students are so accustomed to making *correct* predictions about human behavior, for example, that men will wear trousers, that cars will drive on the right side of the road and try to avoid hitting pedestrians, and that professors will talk about the subject promised in the course catalog, that most of them are not aware of being prophets. They are bewildered and outraged when someone violates one of these predictions, for human beings not only make predictions about behavior but also have great confidence in the confirmation of these predictions by experience.

A student might say, "It is true that we make correct predictions in a statistical sense —such as that a professor will come to class dressed in a business suit. But this isn't a very interesting prediction. What we mean when we say that human behavior is unpredictable is that we cannot tell in advance what *color* suit he will wear." This goes to the heart of the issue. Sociology, like all sciences, is concerned with generalizations about classes of phenomena, not about unique cases. The sociologist gloats over his ability to describe a uniformity of dress among American men and regards the differences in color and texture of fabrics as unimportant. To the suggestion that

the difference is more important than the uniformity the sociologist has two answers. First, he can reply that science is concerned only with generalizations, not with idiosyncratic exceptions. Second, he can point out that far more is asked of the sociologist than one expects of the zoologist. Thus, if a zoologist described to his class the feeding and swimming habits of whales, the student would not insist that he explain why Moby Dick drowned Captain Ahab. Students are not as interested in individual whales or in individual electrons as they are in individual human beings, and therefore they are more satisfied with statistical statements in the physical sciences than in the social sciences.

EMPIRICAL RESEARCH IN SOCIOLOGY

Because contemporary sociology is interested in describing what *is* rather than in suggesting what *should be*, a great deal of our professional literature consists of the patient collection of data about interaction (or about factors related to interaction) in face-to-face groups, in formal organizations, in communities of varying size and complexity, and in complex societies. The topics covered by these studies are virtually limitless—from a content analysis of a popular comic strip to an investigation of trends in mental disease, from the autobiographical account of a delinquent career to studies of differential voting behavior of various population segments.[4] The techniques of data collection vary almost as widely —from elaborate questionnaire surveys analyzed by means of computers to qualitative accounts by participant-observers, such as the description of a lynching in a small Southern town.[5]

[4] Donald Auster, "A Content Analysis of 'Little Orphan Annie,'" *Social Problems*, Vol. 2, July 1954, pp. 26–33; Herbert Goldhamer and Andrew Marshall, *Psychosis and Civilization*, Glencoe, Ill.: Free Press, 1953; Clifford R. Shaw, *The Natural History of a Delinquent Career*, Chicago: University of Chicago Press, 1931; Paul F. Lazarsfeld, Bernard Berelson, and Hazel Gaudet, *The People's Choice*, 2nd ed., New York: Columbia University Press, 1948.
[5] Leon Festinger and Daniel Katz, Eds., *Research Methods in the Behavioral Sciences*, New York: Dryden, 1953.

In the course of reading the rest of this book, you will encounter many examples of sociological research. However, these examples will be incidental to developing basic sociological concepts or to stating substantive conclusions about the functioning of human societies. Therefore, it seems worthwhile to spend much of this chapter in reviewing the more common types of investigations undertaken by sociologists.

THE COMMUNITY STUDY. In 1892 Charles Booth published the first volume of his nine-volume survey of living conditions in the slums of London, *The Life and Labor of the People of London*. Perhaps inspired by this monumental work, sociologists on both sides of the Atlantic have attempted to describe the social life of communities of varying sizes. In 1929 Robert S. Lynd and Helen Merrill Lynd published *Middletown*, a study of Muncie, Indiana, and in 1937 brought their account up to date by reporting the changes that the Great Depression helped to effect since their first visit.[6] In 1934 a three-volume study of the city of Liverpool was published.[7] In 1941 W. Lloyd Warner, already well-known for his study of the preliterate people of the Australian desert, published the first volume of what was destined to be a six-volume report on the way of life in Newburyport, Massachusetts.[8] Within the next decade the patterns of interaction in several other American communities came to be described.[9]

Most of these community surveys were carried out by research teams rather than by lone scholars. The number of man-hours involved in preparing questionnaires, interviewing hundreds of respondents, coding their responses to facilitate mechanical tabulation, analyzing quantitative as well as qualitative data, and pulling the entire operation together in a final report became too great an enterprise for the lone scholar working without research assistance. That is to say, community surveys are costly. Without financial support from governments, private foundations, or university research funds, sociologists are not ordinarily able to undertake such studies. Even organized research teams, however, cannot describe *all* the patterns of interaction in Newburyport, Massachusetts, much less in London. This means that every community study is highly selective. Within the limits of a particular interpretive framework, a community study may be a model of objectivity. But the reader must bear in mind that an interpretive framework exists: Booth was interested in the effects of poverty, Hollingshead in "the impact of social classes on adolescents."

If so much interpretive discretion is permitted the sociological researcher, is his report more scientific than the observations of an intelligent resident of the community? It is—provided that the research is competently done. One difference between living in a community and conducting a community survey is that a survey will involve many *more* observations than would be made in the course of mere residence. Even more important than the *number* of observations, however, is the *perspective* from which the observations are made. The ordinary resident observes the community from the vantage point of his roles in it. A 27-year-old garage attendant who left high school at the age of 16 and is not yet married sees a different community from that seen by the middle-aged wife of the town's leading industrialist. The researcher, aware that the community

[6] Robert S. Lynd and Helen M. Lynd, *Middletown*, New York: Harcourt, Brace, 1929; Robert S. Lynd and Helen M. Lynd, *Middletown in Transition*, New York: Harcourt, Brace, 1937.

[7] D. Caradog Jones, *The Social Survey of Merseyside*, 3 vols., Liverpool, England: University Press of Liverpool, 1934.

[8] W. Lloyd Warner, *A Black Civilization: A Social Study of an Australian Tribe*, rev. ed., New York: Harper, 1958; W. Lloyd Warner and Paul S. Lunt, *The Social Life of a Modern Community*, New Haven, Conn.: Yale University Press, 1941.

[9] Allison Davis, Burleigh B. Gardner, and Mary R. Gardner, *Deep South*, Chicago: University of Chicago Press, 1941; John Useem, Pierre Tangent, and Ruth Useem, "Stratification in a Prairie Town," *American Sociological Review*, Vol. 7, June 1942, pp. 331–342; James West, *Plainville, U.S.A.*, New York: Columbia University Press, 1945; August B. Hollingshead, *Elmtown's Youth*, New York: Wiley, 1949.

presents a different face to persons differently situated in the social structure, attempts to collect observations from many perspectives. To the extent that he succeeds, his description of the community is more objective than that of *any* of his informants. The same principle applies to other types of sociological research. The criminologist who studies a few dozen adolescent delinquents in their neighborhood milieu may learn more about delinquency than the policeman who has known thousands of delinquents. The policeman has extensive experience with delinquents, but it is obtained in the course of trying to arrest them. Thus, he is not aware of the perspectives of their mothers, of their girlfriends, and of their street-corner associates. The criminologist, although his experience may be more limited numerically, is likely to achieve objectivity. Personal experience is not always trustworthy.[10]

In recent years sociologists have become less interested in studying total geographic communities and more concerned with specialized segments of them. Thus, hospitals, prisons, and factories have been studied as though they were self-contained.[11] And even when a geographic community is studied, it tends to be more circumscribed than the older studies; it is limited to a residential suburb or a slum neighborhood being redeveloped.[12] This change is not merely a vagary of sociological fashion. More likely, the interest in specialized segments of modern communities is due to increasing

recognition that the differentiated parts of complex societies are relatively independent of each other. That is, a university or a factory or a prison is a distinct interactive system—even though the individual member also has roles in other systems. This is one big difference between urban industrial societies and the small, isolated, homogeneous preliterate societies studied by cultural anthropologists.[13]

THE STUDY OF ROLES. Since "role" is the fundamental unit of social structure, it is not surprising that sociologists have described the ways of life involved in a wide variety of roles: medical students, prize fighters, union organizers, jazz musicians, clerks, business executives.[14] Many of these are species of *occupational* roles and, as such, are found only in industrial societies. But nonoccupational roles have been studied also: the male role, the female role, the criminal, the role of the adolescent, and the roles of military commander, political leader, and religious specialist.[15] In

---

[10] Jackson Toby, "Undermining the Student's Faith in the Validity of Personal Experience," *American Sociological Review*, Vol. 20, December 1955, pp. 717–718.
[11] William A. Caudill, *The Psychiatric Hospital as a Small Society*, Cambridge, Mass.: Harvard University Press, 1958; Gresham M. Sykes, *Society of Captives*, Princeton, N.J.: Princeton University Press, 1958; Fritz R. Roethlisberger and William J. Dickson, *Management and the Worker*, Cambridge, Mass.: Harvard University Press, 1939.
[12] Bennett M. Berger, *Working-Class Suburb: A Study of Auto Workers in Suburbia*, Berkeley: University of California Press, 1960; Herbert J. Gans, *The Urban Villagers: Group and Class in the Life of Italian-Americans*, New York: The Free Press of Glencoe, 1962.

[13] Robert Redfield, "The Folk Society," *American Journal of Sociology*, Vol. 52, January 1947, pp. 293–308.
[14] Robert K. Merton, George G. Reader, and Patricia Kendall, *The Student-Physician*, Cambridge, Mass.: Harvard University Press, 1957; S. Kirson Weinberg and Henry Arond, "The Occupational Culture of the Boxer," *American Journal of Sociology*, Vol. 57, March 1952, pp. 460–469; Bernard Karsh, Joel Seidman, and Daisy M. Lilienthal, "The Union Organizer and His Tactics: A Case Study," *American Journal of Sociology*, Vol. 59, September 1953, pp. 113–122; Howard S. Becker, "The Professional Dance Musician and His Audience," *American Journal of Sociology*, Vol. 57, September 1951, pp. 136–144; Peter M. Blau, *The Dynamics of Bureaucracy*, Chicago: University of Chicago Press, 1955; William H. Whyte, Jr., *The Organization Man*, New York: Simon and Schuster, 1956.
[15] Talcott Parsons, "Age and Sex in the Social Structure of the United States," *American Sociological Review*, Vol. 7, October 1942, pp. 604–616; Mirra Komarofsky, "Functional Analysis of Sex Roles," *American Sociological Review*, Vol. 15, August 1950, pp. 508–516; Clifford R. Shaw, *The Natural History of a Delinquent Career*, Chicago: University of Chicago Press, 1931; Kingsley Davis, "Adolescence and Social Structure," *Annals of the American Academy of Political and Social Science*, Vol. 236, November 1944; Robert L. Hall, "Social Influence on the Aircraft Commander's Role," *American Sociological Review*, Vol. 20, June 1955, pp. 292–299; David E. Apter, *The Gold Coast in Transition*, Princeton, N.J.:

addition to learning the requirements of the role under scrutiny, often by systematic interviews with persons playing that role and sometimes by observing the role players directly, the sociologist tries to understand the process of recruitment into the role, the stresses on incumbents of the role, and the various ways in which incumbents of the role leave it. Role studies, it should be noted, are not studies of people in their full concreteness. Thus, in the following investigation of the role of the teacher in a big-city school system, the researcher ignored all aspects of the lives of the 60 teachers he interviewed, except those directly relevant to their careers in the Chicago school system.

The Career of the Chicago Public Schoolteacher

Reprinted by permission. From Howard S. Becker, "The Career of the Chicago Public Schoolteacher," *American Journal of Sociology*, Vol. 57, March 1952, pp. 470–477.

The positions open to a particular teacher in the system at a given time appear, in general, quite similar, all having about the same prestige, income, and power attached to them. This is not to deny the existence of variations in income created by the operation of seniority rules or of differences in informal power and prestige based on length of service and length of stay in a given school. The fact remains that, for an individual with a given amount of seniority who is about to begin in a school new to her, all teaching positions in the Chicago system are the same with regard to prestige, influence, and income.

Though the available teaching positions in the city schools are similar in formal characteristics, they differ widely in terms of the configuration of the occupation's basic work problems which they present. The teacher's career consists of movement among these various schools in

Princeton University Press, 1955; Robert K. Merton, *Social Theory and Social Structure*, rev. ed., Glencoe, Ill.: Free Press, 1957, Chap. 10, "Patterns of Influence: Local and Cosmopolitan Influentials," pp. 387–420; Waldo W. Burchard, "Role Conflicts of Military Chaplains," *American Sociological Review*, Vol. 19, October 1954, pp. 528–535.

search of the most satisfactory position in which to work, that being the position in which these problems are least aggravated and most susceptible of solution. Work problems arise in the teacher's relations with the important categories of people in the structure of the school: children, parents, principal, and other teachers. Her most difficult problems arise in her interaction with her pupils. Teachers feel that the form and degree of the latter problems vary considerably with the social-class background of the students.

Without going into any detailed analysis of these problems, I will simply summarize the teacher's view of them and of their relation to the various social-class groups which might furnish her with students. The interviewees typically distinguished three class groups: (1) a bottom stratum, probably equivalent to the lower-lower and parts of the upper-lower class, and including, for the teacher, all Negroes; (2) an upper stratum, probably equivalent to the upper-middle class; and (3) a middle stratum, probably equivalent to the lower-middle and parts of the upper-lower class. Three major kinds of problems were described as arising in dealings with pupils: (1) the problem of *teaching*, producing some change in the child's skills and knowledge which can be attributed to one's own efforts; (2) the problem of *discipline*, maintaining order and control over the children's activity; and (3) the problem of what may be termed *moral acceptability*, bringing one's self to bear some traits of the children which one considers immoral and revolting. The teacher feels that the lowest group, "slum" children, is difficult to teach, uncontrollable and violent in the sphere of discipline, and morally unacceptable on all scores, from physical cleanliness to the spheres of sex and "ambition to get ahead." Children of the upper group, from the "better neighborhoods," were felt to be quick learners and easy to teach but somewhat "spoiled" and difficult to control and lacking in the important moral traits of politeness and respect for elders. The middle group was considered to be hard-working but slow to learn, extremely easy to control, and most acceptable on the moral level.

Other important problems arise in interaction with parents, principal, and colleagues and revolve primarily around the issue of authority. Parents of the highest status groups and certain kinds of principals are extremely threatening to the authority the teacher feels basic to the maintenance of her role; in certain situations colleagues, too, may act in such a way as to diminish her authority.

Thus, positions at the teaching level may be very satisfactory or highly undesirable, depending on the presence or absence of the "right" kind of pupils, parents, principal, and colleagues. Where any of these positions are filled by the "wrong" kind of person, the teacher feels that she is in an unfavorable situation in which to deal with the important problems of her work. Teachers in schools of this kind are dissatisfied and wish to move to schools where "working conditions" will be more satisfactory.

Career movement for the Chicago teacher is, in essence, movement from one school to another, some schools being more and others less satisfactory places in which to work. Such movement is accomplished under the Board of Education's rules governing transfer, which allow a teacher, after serving in a position for more than a year, to request transfer to one of as many as ten other positions. Movement to one of these positions is possible when an opening occurs for which there is no applicant whose request is of longer standing, and transfer takes place upon approval by the principal of the new school.

The career patterns which are to be found in this social matrix are not expected to be typical of all career movements of this horizontal type. It is likely that their presence will be limited to occupational organizations which, like the Chicago school system, are impersonal and bureaucratic and in which mobility is accomplished primarily through the manipulation of formal procedures.

The greatest problems of work are found in lower-class schools and, consequently most movement in the system is a result of dissatisfaction with the social-class composition of these school populations. Movement in the system, then, tends to be out from the "slums" to the "better" neighborhoods, primarily in terms of the characteristics of the pupils. Since there are few or no requests for transfer to "slum" schools, the need for teachers is filled by the assignment to such schools of teachers beginning careers in the Chicago system. Thus, the new teacher typically begins her career in the least desirable kind of school. From this beginning two major types of careers were found to develop.

The first variety of career is characterized by an immediate attempt to move to a "better" school in a "better" neighborhood. The majority of interviewees reporting first assignment to a "slum" school had already made or were in the process of making such a transfer. The attitude is well put in this quotation:

"When you first get assigned you almost naturally get assigned to one of those poorer schools, because those naturally are among the first to have openings because people are always transferring out of them to other schools. Then you go and request to be transferred to other schools nearer your home or in some nicer neighborhood. Naturally the vacancies don't come as quickly in those schools because people want to stay there once they get there. I think that every teacher strives to get into a nicer neighborhood."

Making a successful move of this kind is contingent on several factors. First, one must have fairly precise knowledge as to which schools are "good" and which are not, so that one may make requests wisely. Without such a knowledge, which is acquired through access to the "grapevine," what appears to be a desirable move may prove to be nothing more than a jump from the frying pan into the fire, as the following teacher's experience indicates:

"When I put my name down for the ten schools I put my name down for one school out around ———— ['nice' neighborhood]. I didn't know anything about it, what the principal was like or anything, but it had a short list. Well, I heard later from several people that I had really made a mistake. They had a principal there that was really a terror. She just made it miserable for everyone. . . .

"But I was telling you about what happened to me. Or almost did. After I had heard about this principal, I heard that she was down one day to observe me. Well, I was really frightened. If she had taken me I would have been out of luck, I would have had to stay there a year. But she never showed up in my room. . . . But, whatever it was, I was certainly happy that I didn't have to go there. It just shows that you have to be careful about what school you pick."

Second, one must not be of an ethnic type or have a personal reputation which will cause the principal to use his power of informal rejection. Though a transferee may be rejected through formal bureaucratic procedure, the principal finds it easier and less embarrassing to get the same result through this method, described by a Negro teacher:

"All he's got to do is say, 'I don't think you'll be very happy at our school.' You take the hint. Because if the principal decides you're going to be unhappy, you will be, don't worry. No question about that. He can fix it so that you have every discipline problem in the grade you're teaching right in your room. That's enough to do it right there. So it really doesn't pay to go if you're not wanted. You can fight it if you want, but I'm too old for that kind of thing now."

This has the effect of destroying the attractive qualities of the school to which transfer was desired and of turning choice in a new direction.

Finally, one must be patient enough to wait for the transfer to the "right" school to be consummated, not succumbing to the temptation to transfer to a less desirable but more accessible school:

"When I got assigned to ——— [Negro school], for instance, I went right downtown and signed on ten lists in this vicinity. I've lived out here for twenty-five years and I expect to stay here, so I signed for those schools and decided I'd wait ten years if necessary, till I found a vacancy in the vicinity."

The majority of teachers have careers of this type, in which an initial stay in an undesirable "slum" schools is followed by manipulation of the transfer system in such a way as to achieve assignment to a more desirable kind of school.

Thirteen of the interviewees, however, had careers of a different type, characterized by a permanent adjustment to the "slum" school situation. These careers were the product of a process of adjustment to the particular work situation, which, while operating in all schools, is seen most clearly where it has such a radical effect on the further development of the career, tying the teacher to a school which would otherwise be considered undesirable. The process begins when the teacher, for any of a number of possible reasons, remains in the undesirable school for a number of years. During this stay changes take place in the teacher and in the character of her relations with other members of the school's social structure which make this unsatisfactory school an easier place in which to work and which change the teacher's view of the benefits to be gained by transferring elsewhere. Under the appropriate circumstances, a person's entire career

may be spent in one such school.

During this initial stay changes take place in the teacher's skills and attitudes which ease the discomfort of teaching at the "slum" school. First, she learns new teaching and disciplinary techniques which enable her to deal adequately with "slum" children, although they are not suited for use with other social-class groups:

"Technically, you're not supposed to lay a hand on a kid. Well, they don't, technically. But there are a lot of ways of handling a kid so that it doesn't show—and then it's the teacher's word against the kid's, so the kid hasn't got a chance. Like dear Mrs. G———. She gets mad at a kid, she takes him out in the hall. She gets him stood up against the wall. Then she's got a way of chucking the kid under the chin, only hard, so that it knocks his head back against the wall. It doesn't leave a mark on him. But when he comes back in that room he can hardly see straight, he's so knocked out."

Further, the teacher learns to revise her expectations with regard to the amount of material she can teach and learns to be satisfied with a smaller accomplishment; a principal of a "slum" school described such an adjustment on the part of her teachers:

"Our teachers are pretty well satisfied if the children can read and do simple number work when they leave here. . . . They're just trying to get these basic things over. So that if the children go to high school they'll be able to make some kind of showing and keep their heads above water."

She thus acquires a routine of work which is customary, congenial, and predictable to the point that any change would require a drastic change in deep-seated habits.

Finally, she finds for herself explanations for actions of the children which she has previously found revolting and immoral, and these explanations allow her to "understand" the behavior of the children as human, rather than as the activity of lunatics or animals:

"I finally received my permanent assignment at E———. That's that big colored school. Frankly, I wasn't ready for anything like that. I thought I'd go crazy those first few months I was there. I wasn't used to that kind of restlessness and noise. The room was never really quiet at all. There was always a low undertone, a humming, of conversation, whispering, and shoving. . . . I didn't think I would ever be able to stand it. But as I came to understand them, then it seemed different. When I could understand the conditions they were brought up in, the kind of family life and home background that they had, it seemed more natural that they should act that way. And I really kind of got used to it after awhile."

At the same time that these changes are taking place in the teacher's perspectives, she is also gradually being integrated into the network of social relations that make up the school in such a way as to ease the problems associated with the "slum" school. In the first place, the teacher, during a long stay in a school, comes to be accepted by the other teachers as a trustworthy equal and acquires positions of influence and prestige in the informal colleague structure. These changes make it easier for her to maintain her position of authority vis-à-vis children and principal. Any move from the school would mean a loss of such position and its advantages and the need to win colleague acceptance elsewhere.

Second, the problem of discipline is eased when the teacher's reputation for firmness begins to do the work of maintaining order for her: "I have no trouble with the children. Once you establish a reputation and they know what to expect, they respect you and you have no trouble. Of course, that's different for a new teacher, but when you're established that's no problem at all."

Finally, problems of maintaining one's authority in relation to parents lessen as one comes to be a "fixture" in the community and builds up stable and enduring relationships with its families: "But, as I say, when you've been in that neighborhood as long as I have everyone knows you, and you've been into half their homes, and there's never any trouble at all."

The "slum" school is thus, if not ideal, at least bearable and predictable for the teacher who has adjusted to it. She has taken the worst the situation has to offer and has learned to get along with it. She is tied to the school by the routine she has developed to suit its requirements and by the relationships she has built up with others in the school organization. These very adjustments cause her, at the same time, to fear a move to any new school, which would necessitate a rebuilding of these relationships and a complete reorganization of her work techniques and routine. The move to a school in a "better" neigh-

borhood is particularly feared, desirable as it seems in the abstract, because the teacher used to the relative freedom of the "slum" school is not sure whether the advantages to be gained in such a move would not be outweighed by the constraint imposed by "interfering" parents and "spoiled" children and by the difficulties to be encountered in integrating into a new school structure. This complete adjustment to a particular work situation thus acts as a brake on further mobility through the system.

Either of these career patterns results, finally, in the teacher's achieving a position in which she is more or less settled in a work environment which she regards as predictable and satisfactory. Once this occurs, her position and career are subject to dangers occasioned by ecological and administrative events which cause radical changes in the incumbents of important positions in the school structure.

Ecological invasion of a neighborhood produces changes in the social-class group from which pupils and parents of a given school are recruited. This, in turn, changes the nature and intensity of the teacher's work problems and upsets the teacher who has been accustomed to working with a higher status group than the one to which she thus falls heir. The total effect is the destruction of what was once a satisfying place in which to work, a position from which no move was intended:

"I've been at this school for about twenty years. It was a lovely school when I first went there. . . . Of course, the neighborhood has changed quite a bit since I've been there. It's not what it used to be.

"The neighborhood used to be ninety, ninety-five per cent Jewish. Now I don't think there are over forty per cent Jews. The rest are Greek, Italian, a few Irish, it's pretty mixed now. And the children aren't as nice as they used to be."

Ecological and demographic processes may likewise create a change in the age structure of a population which causes a decrease in the number of teachers needed in a particular school and a consequent loss of the position in that school for the person last added to the staff. The effect of neighborhood invasion may be to turn the career in the direction of adjustment to the new group, while the change in local age structure may turn the career back to the earlier phase, in which transfer to a "nicer" school was sought.

A satisfactory position may also be changed for the worse by a change in principal through transfer or retirement. The departure of a principal may produce changes of such dimension in the school atmosphere as to force teachers to transfer elsewhere. Where the principal has been a major force upholding the teachers' authority in the face of attacks by children and parents, a change can produce a disastrous increase in the problems of discipline and parental interference:

"I'm tempted to blame most of it on our new principal. . . . [The old principal] kept excellent order. Now the children don't seem to have the same feeling about this man. They're not afraid of him, they don't respect him. And the discipline in the school has suffered tremendously. The whole school is less orderly now."

This problem is considered most serious when the change takes place in a "slum" school in which the discipline problem has been kept under control primarily through the efforts of a strict principal. Reactions to such an event, and consequent career development, vary in schools in different social-class areas. Such a change in a "slum" school usually produces an immediate and tremendous increase in teacher turnover. A teacher who had been through such an experience estimated that faculty turnover through transfer rose from almost nothing to 60 per cent or more during the year following the change. Where the change takes place in a "nicer," upper-middle-class school, teachers are reluctant to move and give up their hard-won positions, preferring to take a chance on the qualities of the new incumbent. Only if he is particularly unsatisfying are they likely to transfer.

Another fear is that a change in principals will destroy the existing allocation of privilege and influence among the teachers, the new principal failing to act in terms of the informal understandings of the teachers with regard to these matters. The following quotations describe two new principals who acted in this fashion:

"He knows what he wants and he does it. Several of the older teachers have tried to explain a few things to him, but he won't have any part of it. Not that they did it in a domineering way or anything, but he just doesn't like that."

"He's a goodhearted man, he really means well, but he simply doesn't know anything about running a school. He gets things all mixed up, listens to people he shouldn't pay any attention to. . . . Some people assert themselves and tell him what to do, and he listens to them when he shouldn't."

These statements are the reaction of more strongly intrenched, "older" teachers who depend greatly for their power on their influence with the principal. Their dissatisfaction with a new principal seldom affects their careers to the point of causing them to move to another school. On the other hand, the coming of a new principal may be to the great advantage of and ardently desired by younger, less influential teachers. The effect of such an event on the career of a younger teacher is illustrated in this quotation:

I was ready to transfer because of the old principal. I just couldn't stand it. But when this new man came in and turned out to be so good, I went downtown and took my name off the transfer list. I want to stay there now. . . . Some of those teachers have been there as long as thirty years, you see, and they feel like they really own the place. They want everything done their way. They always had things their way and they were pretty mad when this new principal didn't take to all their ideas."

Any of these events may affect the career, then, in any of several ways, depending on the state of the career development at the time the event occurs. The effect of any event must be seen in the context of the type of adjustment made by the individual to the institutional organization in which she works.

SURVEYS OF POPULATION CHARACTERISTICS. In order to understand how a society works, the sociologist needs to know a great deal about the characteristics of the population and about recurring events that affect the population. Fortunately for him, births, deaths, marriages, accidents, immigration, emigration, and other such events are subject to official registration. Hence the sociologist can discover, relatively easily and cheaply, the level of birth and death rates in a particular society, the trends in marriage and divorce, and so forth. Fortunately also, every industrial nation, in the course of enumerating the population, collects statistical data of great interest to the sociologist. Thus, the United States Bureau of the Census makes a decennial count of the American people as required by the Constitution for determining the representation of each state in the House of Representatives. But the information gathered in the 1960 census, for example, went far beyond the simple enumeration contemplated in the Constitution. The age, sex, and marital composition of the population, its relative distribution between rural and urban areas, its educational attainment and occupational characteristics, its income, its household arrangements, its national and racial origins, all these data and more were carefully collected in April 1960 by thousands of specially trained enumerators. The following tables are a small sample of the wealth of information tabulated from the 1960 census by means of high-speed computers and published by the Bureau of the Census:

Table 1 shows the age distribution of the American population in 1960 (for each sex separately). Taken by itself, Table 1 is not too enlightening—although it does reflect the higher mortality rates of males as compared with females. The ratio of males under 15 to females under 15 is 103.4, whereas the ratio of males 65 and over to females of the same age is 82.8. But Table 1 can be compared with other data. Thus, a backward look at statistics from previous censuses shows that the median age of the American population has almost doubled in a century and a half.

Table 2, like Table 1, is of most interest when viewed in comparative perspective. That nearly 70 per cent of the American population lived in urban places in 1960 becomes more

TABLE 1

Male and Female Population of the United States, by Age, 1960

| Ages | Males | | Females | |
	Number	Per Cent	Number	Per Cent
Under 5 years	10,339,475	11.7	9,982,389	11.0
5 to 9 years	9,448,557	10.7	9,170,588	10.1
10 to 14 years	8,562,507	9.7	8,253,463	9.1
15 to 19 years	6,698,833	7.6	6,588,606	7.2
20 to 24 years	5,283,228	6.0	5,519,941	6.1
25 to 29 years	5,333,271	6.0	5,537,115	6.1
30 to 34 years	5,840,287	6.6	6,111,422	6.7
35 to 39 years	6,089,776	6.9	6,418,540	7.1
40 to 44 years	5,649,404	6.4	5,917,812	6.5
45 to 49 years	5,374,935	6.1	5,553,943	6.1
50 to 54 years	4,764,728	5.4	4,931,770	5.4
55 to 59 years	4,184,653	4.7	4,411,294	4.8
60 to 64 years	3,384,493	3.8	3,727,404	4.1
65 to 69 years	2,883,429	3.3	3,303,334	3.6
70 to 74 years	2,138,977	2.4	2,522,159	2.8
75 years and over	2,286,560	2.6	3,072,778	3.4
Total, all ages	88,303,113	100.0	91,022,558	100.0
Median age [a]	28.5		30.4	

[a] The median is the value that divides the distribution into two equal parts—one-half of the cases falling below this value and one-half exceeding this value.

Source: Bureau of the Census, *U.S. Census of Population: 1960, United States Summary, General Social and Economic Characteristics*, Final Report PC

TABLE 2

Urban and Rural Population of the United States, by Size of Place, 1960

| Size of Urban and Rural Places | Population | |
	Number (in thousands)	Per Cent
Urban total	125,269	69.9
Places of 1,000,000 or more	17,484	9.8
Places of 500,000 to 1,000,000	11,111	6.2
Places of 250,000 to 500,000	10,766	6.0
Places of 100,000 to 250,000	11,652	6.5
Places of 50,000 to 100,000	13,836	7.7
Places of 25,000 to 50,000	14,951	8.3
Places of 10,000 to 25,000	17,568	9.8
Places of 5,000 to 10,000	9,780	5.5
Places of 2,500 to 5,000	7,580	4.2
Places under 2,500	690	0.4
Unincorporated parts of urbanized places	9,851	5.5
Rural total	54,054	30.1
Places of 1,000 to 2,500	6,497	3.6
Places under 1,000	3,894	2.6
Other rural	43,664	24.3
United States total	179,323	100.0

Source: U.S. Bureau of the Census, *Statistical Abstract of the United States: 1962*, Washington: Government Printing Office, 1962, p. 21.

(1)-1C, Washington: Government Printing Office, 1962, pp. 199–200.

significant when one recalls that only 5.1 per cent of the population was classified as urban in the census of 1790. Or, to make a contemporary comparison, only 17 per cent of the population of India was classified as urban in the census of 1951.[16]

TABLE 3

Years of School Completed by Persons Age 25 and Over, by Color, 1960

Years of School Completed	Whites		Nonwhites	
	Number (in thousands)	Per Cent	Number (in thousands)	Per Cent
Less than 5 years	5,989	6.7	2,314	23.4
5 to 7 years	11,451	12.8	2,303	23.4
8 years	16,179	18.1	1,264	12.8
9 to 11 years	17,274	19.3	1,842	18.7
12 years	23,100	25.7	1,356	13.8
13 to 15 years	8,311	9.3	431	4.4
16 years or more	7,278	8.1	347	3.5
Total, all educational levels	89,581	100.0	9,857	100.0
Median school years completed	10.9		8.2	

Source: U.S. Bureau of the Census, *Statistical Abstract of the United States: 1962*, Washington: Government Printing Office, 1962, p. 117.

Table 3 is more complicated than either Table 1 or Table 2. Table 3 does not refer to the entire American population, only to those persons 25 years old or older. The explanation for this lies in the type of data being presented. The data in Table 3 are being used to show the comparative educational attainment of whites and nonwhites.[17] It would confuse the issue to include persons whose educations are not yet completed (children). The selection of 25 years was made in order to separate those persons whose educations are presum-

16 *Demographic Yearbook of the United Nations, 1952*, New York: Statistical Office of the United Nations, 1952, p. 11.
17 In 1960 the decennial census counted 18,871,831 Negroes and 1,619, 612 nonwhites other than Negroes. (See U.S. Bureau of the Census, *Statistical Abstract of the United States: 1962*, Washington: Government Printing Office, 1962, p. 29.) Thus, the comparison between whites and nonwhites in Table 3 is, for all practical purposes, a Negro-white comparison.

ably complete from those whose educations are still in process. Why 25 years? Some people continue their educations beyond the age of 25. If data are to be presented bearing on the educational attainment of Americans, however, *some definite* age must be chosen or else the issue will be hopelessly confused. The object is to select an age by which most people have completed their educations but that is still young enough to catch those whose educations have been completed quite recently. No doubt Census Bureau experts spent many hundreds of hours on this decision when questions on educational attainment were added to the census schedule in 1940.

Table 3 clearly demonstrates that *white* Americans receive, on the average, more years of formal education than *colored* Americans. The median years of school completed by whites were 10.9 years in 1960 as compared with 8.2 years completed by nonwhites. Or, to express the same point another way, a majority of the nonwhites (59.6 per cent) got no further than grade school as contrasted with a minority of whites (37.6 per cent). This does not mean, of course, that *all* whites were better educated in 1960 than nonwhites. The two distributions of educational attainment overlapped considerably. Thus, the 7.9 per cent of the nonwhites with some college had *more* education than all but 17.4 per cent of the whites. Table 3 gives no hint as to the reasons for the differences between the races in educational attainment.

Important as the decennial census is as a source of basic population data, the ten-year intervals between censuses is a serious disadvantage not only to sociologists but also to government agencies and private businesses needing up-to-date population information. For instance, the President's Council of Economic Advisers and the Department of Labor require *monthly* estimates of unemployment. But it is impractical to conduct a complete population census every month. Not only is a census expensive; equally important, it takes many months to tabulate the results of millions of separate schedules. In 1940 the Bureau of the Census solved this problem by establishing the Current Population Survey.

The Current Population Survey is a monthly survey of about 35,000 American households (containing about 80,000 persons 14 years old and over).[18] The strategy of the Survey is to use this tiny sample to give accurate estimates of hours worked during a given calendar week by the American labor force, the length of time the unemployed have been looking for work, and other aspects of American occupational activity. How can such a small sample represent the entire American labor force? The sample is so shrewdly drawn from the universe of American households that the discrepancy between its values and the values of the larger universe (the sample error) is negligible. Statisticians explain that a *random* sample has a known probability of error—just as an evenly balanced coin has a known probability of coming up "heads." Since we assume that extremely improbable events do not happen, some question would be raised about the balance of the coins (or the honesty of the tosser) if 50 coins in sequence turned up "heads." In the same way, it is extremely unlikely for the estimate of unemployment based on the Current Population Survey to differ more than 1 per cent from the true percentage of unemployment in the United States.

The mathematical basis of random sampling is well established. Agricultural research, quality control in industry, and various branches of the physical and biological sciences use statistical theory for the design of experiments. But the application of random sampling to survey research on human populations presents special problems. A sample of people has the option of refusing to cooperate. Yet the basic requirement of random sampling is that each member of the population under investigation *has an equal chance of appearing in the sample*.

If suspicious, uncooperative individuals have

less chance of appearing in the sample than friendly members of the population, it is no longer a random sample. Similarly, if people who are not at home when the field researcher calls are eliminated from the sample, the sample is biased in favor of those who spend more time at home. These considerations make clear that a random sample, far from being a *casual* collection of representatives of a larger universe, must be drawn from the universe in a rigorous fashion. It is not easy to obtain a random sample. A *quota control* sample—in which interviewers stand on street corners or knock on convenient doors until they get so many men and so many women of certain ages, educational levels, and incomes—is not a random sample. If the quotas are filled in Newark, New Jersey, at 3 P.M., persons who happen to live in rural Kentucky at the time do not have much opportunity to be included in the sample. Quotas guarantee that the sample contains persons representative of the parent universe with respect to characteristics controlled by quotas, such as age, sex, educational attainment, income. Whether the sample is representative of the parent universe with respect to characteristics *not* controlled by quotas is another matter. The laws of probability are no help unless the sample is a random one.

In short, researchers face a dilemma in sampling from human populations. A random sample of people is extremely difficult to obtain. Only a random sample, however, permits characteristics of the parent universe to be estimated with a known probability of error. In recent years, organizations concerned with the accuracy of results, including the Bureau of the Census, have elected to approximate random samples as best they can. The basis for these approximations is the assumption that a random sample of dwelling units approximates a random sample of Americans. This assumption is not exactly correct, but it is correct enough for practical purposes. It is the basis for *area sampling*, the approximation of random sampling used not only by the Current Population Survey but also by such respected organizations as the National Opinion Research

18 Daniel B. Levine and Charles B. Nam, "The Current Population Survey: Methods, Content, and Sociological Uses," *American Sociological Review*, Vol. 27, August 1962, pp. 585–590. For a discussion of the comparative merits of a complete census and a survey, see Appendix A at the end of this chapter.

Center of the University of Chicago and the Survey Research Center of the University of Michigan. The following description of area sampling is based on research conducted by the latter organization.

An Illustration of Area Sampling in Survey Research

Reprinted by permission. From Rensis Likert, "The Sample Interview Survey as a Tool of Research and Policy Formation," in Daniel Lerner and Harold D. Lasswell, *The Policy Sciences*, Stanford, Calif.: Stanford University Press, 1951, pp. 239–246.[19]

The Survey Research Center has been conducting for several years an annual nationwide Survey of Consumer Finances for the Board of Governors of the Federal Reserve System. The general objective of these studies is to obtain data to show: (*a*) distribution of liquid holdings at the beginning of each year; (*b*) past and expected disposition of accumulated assets, and factors affecting the disposition of assets; (*c*) past and expected rate of saving, and factors affecting rate of saving; (*d*) plans for the purchase of consumer durable goods for the coming year and actual purchases during the past year; (*e*) expectations with regard to personal well-being and with regard to the economy in general.

To obtain these data a total of three to four thousand interviews has been conducted on a nationwide sample. To increase the accuracy of the results, more persons were interviewed in the upper income groups than would normally occur in a cross-section sample. This was done primarily by increasing the sampling ratio in those areas having high rental values. The probability sampling method employed always involves strictly random procedures and as a rule utilizes area methods.

The dwellings in which interviews were conducted were selected by the Center's sampling staff. The interviewers had no freedom or latitude in selecting respondents; they were instructed to interview the heads of all spending units in the designated dwellings.

[19] For a discussion of the specific type of sampling used in the survey reported in this article, see Appendix B at the end of this chapter.

The designing of the sample involved two major steps: first, the selection of localities in which interviewing would be done, and second, the selection of the specific dwelling units within those designated localities. Both of these steps were conducted so that each dwelling unit (and spending unit) in the country had an equal—or, where oversampling occurred, a known—probability of appearing in the sample. The sample was designed to be truly random and without biases.

In the selection of the localities in which interviews would be conducted, all the metropolitan areas having over one million population were necessarily included. These cities include too many people and too much of the income and savings of the nation to omit any one of them. All the rest of the nation was then grouped by counties. There were fifty-four of these groups of counties, each group containing approximately the same proportion of total population. Technically speaking, samplers call these groups of counties "strata." From each stratum one county was selected by using random numbers to represent it.

The purpose in arranging the counties into strata was to have the counties in each stratum as homogeneous as possible and to use variables for the grouping which were known or suspected to be related to factors being studied in the sample survey.

After the metropolitan areas and counties which were to be sampled had been selected, the task was to designate specific dwelling units. In cities, census block statistics were used to group homogeneous blocks and a sample of blocks was picked by means of random numbers. Then by means of up-to-date, detailed maps or a list of all dwellings on the block, specified dwellings were selected at random and used in the sample. In rural areas the county was broken into small geographical units containing about three to five farms. These were numbered in such a way that when one of the units between 1 and n was selected at random and every nth unit thereafter, the selected units would be widely scattered over the county. Aerial photographs on an enlarged scale, showing each farmhouse, were then obtained for the units that had been selected and the interviewers were instructed to interview the heads of all spending units in each dwelling located within the designated area.

The interviewers were instructed to complete

interviews with the heads of all the spending units selected in the sample even though they had to make two or three calls. In case the person could not be found or the interview completed, a full report was sent to the Center but no substitution was made. In designing the sample, a somewhat larger sample was included than was finally needed. This allowed leeway in case a small proportion of respondents could not be located or interviewed. But people who were easy to find were not substituted for people who were hard to find, because these two groups of peoples differed in many important respects.

The method of sampling employed by the Center enabled the expansion of the data obtained from the interviews to estimates for the entire population. Each year, for example, the results from the three thousand to four thousand interviews were expanded to national estimates for income, ownership of government bonds, deposits in savings accounts, amounts held in checking acccounts for personal use, number of new and used cars to be purchased, number of new and used cars purchased the preceding year, total number of cars owned, and so on. All these national estimates were, of course, for the universe covered by the sample, namely, consumers living in the United States in private households but not including members of the armed forces, persons living in institutions, or persons living in hotels. The quota method of sampling, which is ordinarily used by consumer market research agencies, yields results which are difficult and often impossible to expand to estimates for the entire population. Results obtained from quota samples often have biases in them which introduce substantial errors into any total estimates. At times these errors can be reduced by weighting the data from the sample so as to make them correspond with certain known facts. However, to use this procedure to remove biases on known factors offers no assurance that all of the biases are removed from the variables being studied. In fact, some of this weighting may even increase the biases in the variables that are being measured.

In designing the interview for the Federal Reserve study, the first step was to list the specific tables that would be needed to meet the objectives of the study. From this list of tables, the questions required to obtain the desired data were prepared. After this preliminary draft of the interview form was completed, those in charge of the study spent over two weeks in the field testing and improving it. They were assisted in this by a few of the Center's best interviewers.

Each interview form is tested in the field before it is used and changes are always necessary. There are several reasons for this pretest. Some of the more important are:

1. To test the wording of questions. Each question must be so clearly worded that it is readily and correctly understood by all respondents. In fact, it should be so clear that it cannot be misunderstood. In addition, the question wording should be in an easy, conversational style. It is more important to have the wording easy in style than to have it phrased in the best English.

2. To test whether the questions secure all the data required for the tables that have been specified. An important part of the pretest of each interview form is to discover whether the questions, as finally worded and arranged, obtain answers which when coded and analyzed will yield data meeting the objectives of the study. The study director consequently codes the pretest questionnaires. Often it is necessary to add a question here or there so as to obtain clear and complete information from each respondent on each variable that is to be analyzed.

3. To test question order. It is important to check the influence of order to be sure that certain questions are not influenced in an undesirable manner by preceding questions. Moreover, it is essential that the questions flow easily from one to another, forming a natural, conversational pattern. Too many sudden shifts confuse the respondent and have an adverse effect upon his cooperation.

4. To test whether any important variables have been overlooked in the design of the study. At times, interviewing on the pretest will reveal through the thinking or experience of respondents that there is an important dimension that has not been recognized previously. The study usually will be materially improved by incorporating this variable into the design and securing adequate data on it.

5. To test whether the interview form is constructed so as to obtain a high level of respondent co-operation. In addition to having the questions worded in a vocabulary familiar to respondents and flowing from one to an-

other in an easy conversational manner, it is essential that the respondents feel that the questions asked call for information that they should supply. It is possible, of course, to start an interview by bluntly asking, "What is your income?" "How much money do you have in your checking account?" "How much in your savings account?" But to do so produces an antagonistic attitude in respondents and yields results of little value.

Over the past several years the Survey Research Center has done a great deal of experimentation and has learned that to secure cooperation it must make clear to respondents why the information covered by the questions is needed and why it is to their interest to give it. A step that helps to do this is to phrase the questions so that they are stated in terms of problems of concern and interest to the respondent. Thus, for example, the interview form on the Federal Reserve study starts with the following questions:

1. Would you say you people are better off or worse off financially now than you were a year ago? (1a) Why do you say so?
2. Are you making as much money now as you were a year ago, more or less? (2a) Why is that?
3. How about a year from now—do you think that you will be making more money or less money than you are now, or will you be making about the same? (3a) Why will that be?
4. Now considering the country as a whole, do you think we will have good times or bad times or what during the next twelve months or so? (4a) Can you tell me a little more about what you see for 1949? Or: Just how do you think the good (bad) times will show up? (4b) Do you consider that we are having good times or bad times now?
5. What do you think will happen to the prices of things you buy during 1949—do you think they will go up, or down, or stay about where they are now? (5a) Why will they do that? (5b) (If any change at all is mentioned) Do you think that prices in general will be a lot lower (higher) or only a little lower (higher) by the end of 1949?

In addition to an interview form designed to facilitate a high level of respondent co-operation, it is essential that the interviewers have a good understanding of each study and its purpose. They need this information so that they can make clear to respondents the purpose of the study when they introduce themselves. They need it also in order to answer readily any questions that respondents ask.

One of the interviewers who works on the survey for the Federal Reserve Board has stated: "With a $12,000-a-year broker I use something like: 'You are of course familiar with the functions of the Federal Reserve Board in regulating inflationary and deflationary tendencies, both in the securities market and in the general economy. . . .' With a small commercial photographer I say: 'I don't know whether you know just how the Federal Reserve Board works and how much it can do to prevent inflation. For example, by regulating the banks, it can increase or decrease the amount of money in circulation, and you know that has a great deal to do with general business conditions. . . .' And with an elderly widow in poor circumstances: 'Nobody can tell whether we are going to have good times or poor times during the next year or so, and the Government would like to get ready to do what it can to make sure we don't have another depression. . . .'"

The interviewers are instructed to ask all questions exactly as they appear on the interview form and to record fully the respondent's answers. When a respondent fails to understand a question, the interviewer rephrases it to make it clear to the respondent and reports the rewording used as well as the respondent's answer.

After the final draft of the interview form has been turned over to the field staff to secure the necessary interviews, the study director and his staff start putting the codes into final form. The codes show for each question, or group of questions, how each of the different answers obtained from respondents is to be categorized for purposes of tabulation and analysis. As fast as the completed interviews are returned from the field they are coded and a random sub-sampling of them is check-coded. By the time the interviewing is completed, the answers are ready to be punched on cards for machine tabulation.

As a rule, the coding is done in the office rather than using fixed alternative questions or having the interviewers code the answers in the field. There are several reasons for this preference. As previously mentioned, the fixed-question, free-answer method is superior to other methods in building rapport and providing the data to assure a correct understanding of what each respondent means by his answer. The full answers of respondents also provide material to help appraise the quality of work done by each interviewer. In addition, coding in the field by the interviewer proves in tests to be appreciably less reliable than office coding. Different interviewers, even when working under close supervision, will vary more in their coding than will a group of coders working together in an office.

Moreover, it is essential to check-code a sample of all data and this is possible only with office coding. This check-coding is necessary because the reliability of coding varies for each category under each question. The analysis and interpretation of the tabulations prepared from the coded material must be done in relation to the reliability of the coding as well as the sampling errors. Results from questions which have low coding reliability for one reason or another should not be used or should be used only if the differences in results are large relative to the coding errors. Often the reliability of coding certain categories can be increased if some categories of answers are combined. Attempts to make discriminations in coding that are too fine often result in unreliable coding.

Great emphasis is placed in survey research on the design of the study and the process of analysis. The Survey Research Center, it is believed, consistently has spent relatively more money on this phase of research than any similar research organization. This is surely a wise and necessary expenditure. Good research and useful results depend on good design. The direct answers to direct questions cannot be taken at face value. Consequently, several related questions are asked and often an indirect approach is used. In the Federal Reserve study, people are asked what their plans are for the use of their government bonds, and elsewhere in the interview they are asked how they are going to finance the consumer durable goods they propose to purchase. The answers to one question help to act as a check on the answers to the other.

EXPERIMENTS. The research ideal of science is experimentation. An experiment enables the researcher to investigate the effect of Factor A on Factor B while excluding the effects of all other potentially confounding factors. Inso-

far as sociologists have scientific aspirations, they yearn to use controlled experiments in their investigations.[20] Often, however, sociological experiments are not feasible. For example, consider the hypothesis that broken homes are more likely to produce juvenile delinquents than intact homes. In order to test this hypothesis in the classical experimental manner, it would be necessary to select (by some random procedure) two populations of infants, to break up the homes of infants in the experimental group, to let alone the homes of infants in the control group, and, after some years pass, to observe carefully the comparative incidence of delinquency in the two groups. From a technical point of view, this would be a rigorous experiment, but neither the sociologist nor the general public wants to pay the price (in human suffering) of experimenting with broken homes.

Does this mean that the relationship between broken homes and delinquency cannot be investigated? Instead of *contriving* an experiment which relates broken homes to delinquency, the sociologist can let the experiment conduct itself. Some homes break up naturally; others do not. Some children become delinquent; others do not. The researcher can observe how many delinquents come from broken homes and how many from intact homes even though he had nothing to do with producing the broken homes. This is called a *natural* experiment. Natural experiments are often used to test hypotheses relating one social variable to another. Sociologists are not alone in using natural experiments. Astronomers cannot manipulate the orbits of planets or stars; hence, they also depend on natural experiments. There is no use pretending that the natural experiment is fully equivalent to the contrived experiment; it is not. But the natural experiment is often the sociologist's best approximation to controlled observation.

Table 4 illustrates the strengths and weaknesses of natural experiments. It presents a tab-

[20] Samuel A. Stouffer, "Some Observations on Study Design," *American Journal of Sociology*, Vol. 55, January 1950, pp. 355–361.

ulation of responses from undergraduates from 11 universities to a question about cheating on examinations. This tabulation was made to ex-

TABLE 4

The Percentage of Fraternity and of Independent Students Who Admit Having Cheated on Examinations, by Year in College

Year in College	(Percentage [a] who admit having cheated more than once)	
	Fraternity Members	Independent Students
First	15 (178)	12 (498)
Second	24 (255)	16 (375)
Third	30 (320)	22 (437)
Fourth	32 (306)	23 (440)
Fifth	42 (49)	31 (48)

[a] The figures in parentheses are the bases on which each per cent was computed. Excluded from these bases are six fraternity members and eleven independent students who could not be classified as to year in college, as well as 52 students who could not be classified according to fraternity membership.

Source: Rose K. Goldsen et al., *What College Students Think*, Princeton, N.J.: Van Nostrand, 1960, p. 79. The data were derived from questionnaires administered anonymously to students at eleven universities.

plore the possibility that fraternity membership may be conducive to cheating. The percentage of admitted cheaters among *fraternity* members is greater than the percentage of admitted cheaters among *independent* students in all five years. Does this mean that fraternities somehow encourage cheating? Perhaps boys more likely to cheat are also more likely to join fraternities. Or perhaps boys more likely to tell the truth on anonymous questionnaires are more likely to join fraternities. In either case, it is a weakness of the study that the experimental group (fraternity members) and the control group (independents) *selected themselves*. The researcher cannot say with assurance that these groups were precisely the same before joining fraternities. Moreover, if the groups were different with respect to financial resources, religious affiliations, or values,

perhaps these differences account for the greater tendency of fraternity members to confess to cheating. A *contrived* experiment would not be open to such questions. If, for the purposes of the experiment, entering freshmen at these 11 universities had been randomly allocated to fraternities or to the independent group, probability theory would guarantee that initial differences were minimal.

Actually, statistical techniques exist for coping with the self-selection problem in natural experiments. If it turns out that fraternity members come from higher socioeconomic levels, on the average, than independents, the researcher can separate both fraternity members and independents by socioeconomic level and make the fraternity-independent comparison separately for two (or more) socioeconomic levels. Thus, it is possible to accomplish by statistical manipulation what has not been done in the real world: to make the experimental and control groups initially comparable.

Helpful though statistical procedures are, they do not solve the problem completely. Statistical control is only possible if the researcher is aware of a potentially confounding characteristic and sets out to control it. If a confounding characteristic exists and he does not happen to consider it, its uncontrolled variation is free to mislead him. When individuals have been randomly allocated to experimental and control groups, probability theory guarantees that the two groups are initially alike with respect to all characteristics, whether the researcher is aware of them or not. This problem does not exist for the contrived experiment.

Table 4 does not directly address this problem of the initial comparability of fraternity members and independent students. Instead it tabulates the data by class in college. The small difference in the percentages of freshman fraternity members and of freshman independent students who admit to having cheated suggests that whatever *initial* differences existed between the two groups have little effect on the propensity to cheat. The fact that the differences between fraternity men and independents are *greater* in the sophomore and later years suggests that fraternity membership somehow makes for cheating. The data could, however, have supported the hypothesis much more strongly. There could have been *no* difference between fraternity men and independents in the freshman year and a progressive increase in the difference from the second to the fifth year.

This discussion of natural experiments should not be taken to mean that contrived experiments are unknown in sociology. Efforts are frequently made to reduce prejudice, to prevent delinquency, to improve morale, and so on. On the rare occasions that these efforts are systematically evaluated, a contrived experiment is added to the sociological literature. Needless to say, the value of such experiments does not depend on a demonstration that the goal of the action program was fulfilled. Sometimes the failure of the experimental group to differ from the control group has important implications. For instance, between 1924 and 1927 researchers from the Harvard University and the Western Electric Company conducted at the Hawthorne works of the Company a variety of controlled experiments in order to discover whether higher levels of illumination would result in higher productivity.[21] At first the researchers were jubilant because productivity rose in the experimental groups. But it rose in the control groups also. Furthermore, *decreases* in illumination to a point considerably below ordinary levels in the main shop did not bring productivity down. The experiments had failed to show that level of illumination was an important variable in productivity. But the by-product of this failure was the discovery that *human relations* within the work group could enormously affect morale and, indirectly, productivity. The following report describes some of the further experiments in a field which became known as "industrial sociology."

[21]   Roethlisberger and Dickson, *op. cit.*, pp. 14–18.

When Experiments Fail:
The Importance of Interpretation

Reprinted by permission. From George C. Homans, "The Western Electric Researches," in *Fatigue of Workers: Its Relation to Industrial Production*, New York: Reinhold, 1941, Chap. 4.

In April, 1927, six girls were selected from a large shop department of the Hawthorne works. They were chosen as average workers, neither inexperienced nor expert, and their work consisted of the assembling of telephone relays. A coil, armature, contact springs, and insulators were put together on a fixture and secured in position by means of four machine screws. The operation at that time was being completed at the rate of about five relays in six minutes. This particular operation was chosen for the experiment because the relays were being assembled often enough so that even slight changes in output rate would show themselves at once on the output record. Five of the girls were to do the actual assembly work; the duty of the sixth was to keep the others supplied with parts.

The test room itself was an area divided from the main department by a wooden partition eight feet high. The girls sat in a row on one side of a long workbench. The bench and assembly equipment were identical with those used in the regular department, except in one respect. At the right of each girl's place was a hole in the bench, and into this hole she dropped completed relays. It was the entrance to a chute, in which there was a flapper gate opened by the relay in its passage downward. The opening of the gate closed an electrical circuit which controlled a perforating device, and this in turn recorded the completion of the relay by punching a hole in a tape. The tape moved at the rate of one-quarter of an inch a minute and had space for a separate row of holes for each operator. When punched, it thus constituted a complete output record for each girl for each instant of the day. Such records were kept for five years.

In this experiment, then, as in the earlier illumination experiments, great emphasis was laid on the rate of output. A word of caution is needed here. The Western Electric Company was not immediately interested in increasing output. The experiments were not designed for that purpose.

On the other hand, output is easily measured, i.e., it yields precise quantitative data, and experience suggested that it was sensitive to at least some of the conditions under which the employees worked. Output was treated as an index. In short, the nature of the experimental conditions made the emphasis on output inevitable.

From their experience in the illumination experiments, the investigators were well aware that factors other than those experimentally varied might affect the output rate. Therefore arrangements were made that a number of other records should be kept. Unsuitable parts supplied by the firm were noted down, as were assemblies rejected for any reason upon inspection. In this way the type of defect could be known and related to the time of day at which it occurred. Records were kept of weather conditions in general and of temperature and humidity in the test room. Every six weeks each operator was given a medical examination by the company doctor. Every day she was asked to tell how many hours she had spent in bed the night before and, during a part of the experiment, what food she had eaten. Besides all these records, which concerned the physical condition of the operators, a log was kept in which were recorded the principal events in the test room hour by hour, including among the entries snatches of conversation between the workers. At first these entries related largely to the physical condition of the operators: how they felt as they worked. Later the ground they covered somewhat widened, and the log ultimately became one of the most important of the test room records. Finally, when the so-called Interviewing Program was instituted at Hawthorne, each of the operators was interviewed several times by an experienced interviewer.

The girls had no supervisor in the ordinary sense, such as they would have had in a regular shop department, but a "test room observer" was placed in the room, whose duty it was to maintain the records, arrange the work, and secure a cooperative spirit on the part of the girls. Later, when the complexity of his work increased, several assistants were assigned to help him.

When the arrangements had been made for the test room, the operators who had been chosen to take part were called in for an interview in the office of the superintendent of the Inspection Branch, who was in general charge of the experiment and of the researches which grew out of it.

The superintendent described this interview as follows: "The nature of the test was carefully explained to these girls and they readily consented to take part in it, although they were very shy at the first conference. An invitation to six shop girls to come up to a superintendent's office was naturally rather startling. They were assured that the object of the test was to determine the effect of certain changes in working conditions, such as rest periods, midmorning lunches, and shorter working hours. They were expressly cautioned to work at a comfortable pace, and under no circumstances to try and make a race out of the test." This conference was only the first of many. Whenever any experimental change was planned, the girls were called in, the purpose of the change was explained to them, and their comments were requested. Certain suggested changes which did not meet with their approval were abandoned. They were repeatedly asked, as they were asked in the first interview, not to strain but to work "as they felt."

The experiment was now ready to begin. Put in its simplest terms, the idea of those directing the experiment was that if an output curve was studied for a long enough time under various changes in working conditions, it would be possible to determine which conditions were the most satisfactory. Accordingly, a number of so-called "experimental periods" were arranged. For two weeks before the operators were placed in the test room, a record was kept of the production of each one without her knowledge. In this way the investigators secured a measure of her productive ability while working in the regular department under the usual conditions. This constituted the first experimental period. And for five weeks after the girls entered the test room no change was made in working conditions. Hours remained what they had been before. The investigators felt that this period would be long enough to reveal any changes in output incidental merely to the transfer. This constituted the second experimental period.

The third period involved a change in the method of payment. In the regular department, the girls had been paid according to a scheme of group piecework, the group consisting of a hundred or more employees. Under these circumstances, variations in an individual's total output would not be immediately reflected in her pay, since such variations tended to cancel one another in such a large group. In the test room, the six operators were made a group by themselves. In this way each girl received an amount more nearly in proportion to her individual effort, and her interests became more closely centered on the experiment. Eight weeks later, the directly experimental changes began. An outline will reveal their general character: Period IV: two rest pauses, each five minutes in length, were established, one occurring in midmorning and the other in the early afternoon. Period V: these rest pauses were lengthened to ten minutes each. Period VI: six five-minute rests were established. Period VII: the company provided each member of the group with a light lunch in the midmorning and another in the midafternoon, accompanied by rest pauses. This arrangement became standard for subsequent Periods VIII through XI. Period VIII: work stopped a half-hour earlier every day—at 4:30 P.M. Period IX: work stopped at 4 P.M. Period X: conditions returned to what they were in Period VII. Period XI: a five-day work week was established. Each of these experimental periods lasted several weeks.

Period XI ran through the summer of 1928, a year after the beginning of the experiment. Already the results were not what had been expected. The output curve, which had risen on the whole slowly and steadily throughout the year, was obviously reflecting something other than the responses of the group to the imposed experimental conditions. Even when the total weekly output had fallen off, as it could hardly fail to do in such a period as Period XI, when the group was working only five days a week, daily output continued to rise. Therefore, in accordance with a sound experimental procedure, as a control on what had been done, it was agreed with the consent of the operators that in experimental Period XII a return should be made to the original conditions of work, with no rest pauses, no special lunches, and a full-length working week. This period lasted for twelve weeks. Both daily and weekly output rose to a higher point than ever before: the working day and the working week were both longer. The hourly output rate declined somewhat but it did not approach the level of Period III, when similar conditions were in effect.

The conclusions reached after Period XII may be expressed in terms of another observation. Identical conditions of work were repeated in three different experimental periods: Periods VII, X, and XIII. If the assumptions on which the study was based had been correct, that is to say, if the output rate were directly related to the physical conditions of work, the expectation would be that in these three experimental periods there would be some similarity in output. Such was not the case. The only apparent uniformity was that in each experimental period output was higher than in the preceding one. In the Relay Assembly Test Room, as in the previous illumination experiments, something was happening which could not be explained by the experimentally controlled conditions of work.

The question remains:

With what facts, if any, can the changes in the output rate of the operators in the test room be correlated? Here the statements of the girls themselves are of the first importance. Each girl knew that she was producing more in the test room than she ever had in the regular department, and each said that the increase had come about without any conscious effort on her part. It seemed easier to produce at the faster rate in the test room than at the slower rate in the regular department. When questioned further, each girl stated her reasons in slightly different words, but there was uniformity in the answers in two respects. First, the girls liked to work in the test room; "it was fun." Secondly, the new supervisory relation or, as they put it, the absence of the old supervisory control, made it possible for them to work freely without anxiety.

For instance, there was the matter of conversation. In the regular department, conversation was in principle not allowed. In practice it was tolerated if it was carried on in a low tone and did not interfere with work. In the test room an effort was made in the beginning to discourage conversation, though it was soon abandoned. The observer in charge of the experiment was afraid of losing the cooperation of the girls if he insisted too strongly on this point. Talk became common and was often loud and general. Indeed, the conversation of the operators came to occupy an important place in the log. T. N. Whitehead has pointed out that the girls in the test room were far more thoroughly supervised than they ever had been in the regular department. They were watched by an observer of their own, an interested management, and outside experts. The point is that the character and purpose of the supervision were different and were felt to be so.

The operators knew that they were taking part in what was considered an important and interesting experiment. They knew that their work was expected to produce results—they were not sure what results—which would lead to the improvement of the working conditions of their fellow employees. They knew that the eyes of the company were upon them. Whitehead has further pointed out that although the experimental changes might turn out to have no physical significance, their social significance was always favorable. They showed that the management of the company was still interested, that the girls were still part of a valuable piece of research. In the regular department, the girls, like the other employees, were in the position of responding to changes the source and purpose of which were beyond their knowledge. In the test room, they had frequent interviews with the superintendent, a high officer of the company. The reasons for the contemplated experimental changes were explained to them. Their views were consulted and in some instances they were allowed to veto what had been proposed. Professor Mayo has argued that it is idle to speak of an experimental period like Period XII as being in any sense what it purported to be—a return to the original conditions of work. In the meantime, the entire industrial situation of the girls had been reconstructed.

Another factor in what occurred can only be spoken of as the social development of the group itself. When the girls went for the first time to be given a physical examination by the company doctor, someone suggested as a joke that ice cream and cake ought to be served. The company provided them at the next examination, and the custom was kept up for the duration of the experiment. When one of the girls had a birthday, each of the others would bring her a present, and she would respond by offering the group a box of chocolates. Often one of the girls would have some good reason for feeling tired. Then the others would "carry" her. That is, they would agree to work especially fast to make up for the low output expected from her. It is doubtful whether this "carrying" did have any effect, but the important point is the existence of the practice, not its effectiveness. The girls made friends in the test room and went together socially after hours. One of the interesting facts which has appeared from Whitehead's analysis of the output records is that there were times when variations in the output rates of two friends were correlated to a high degree. Their rates varied simultaneously and in the same direction—something, of course, which the girls were not aware of and could not have planned. Also, these correlations were destroyed by such apparently trivial events as a change in the order in which the girls sat at the workbench.

Finally, the group developed leadership and a common purpose. The leader, self-appointed, was an ambitious young Italian girl who entered the test room as a replacement after two of the original members had left. She saw in the experiment a chance for personal distinction and advancement. The common purpose was an increase in the output rate. The girls had been told in the beginning and repeatedly thereafter that they were to work without straining, without trying to make a race of the test, and all the evidence shows that they kept this rule. In fact, they felt that they were working under less pressure than in the regular department. Nevertheless, they knew that the output record was considered the most important of the records of the experiment and was always closely scrutinized. Before long they had committed themselves to a continuous increase in production. In the long run, of course, this ideal was an impossible one, and when the girls found out that it was, the realization was an important element of the change of tone which was noticeable in the second half of the experiment. But for a time they felt that they could achieve the impossible. In brief, the increase in the output rate of the girls in the Relay Assembly Test Room could not be related to any changes in their physical conditions of work, whether experimentally induced or not. It could, however, be related to what can only be spoken of as the development of an organized social group in a peculiar and effective relation with its supervisors.

The failure of physiologically oriented experiments on worker productivity opened the eyes of the Harvard Business School researchers to social factors. This new turn which their investigations took proved rewarding. As a result, descriptions of the Western Electric researches are usually eulogies, and it is not always remembered how the later achievements were built on initial failures. An awkward word, "serendipity,' describes "the fairly common experience of observing an unanticipated, anomalous and strategic datum which becomes the occasion for developing a new theory or for extending an existing theory." [22] Serendipity deserves credit for important discoveries, including that of the drug penicillin. Unfortunately, not every researcher has the flexibility to recognize the importance of unanticipated results, to distinguish between an experimental failure that is a dead-end and one that opens new vistas.

Sometimes an experiment fails, and it is not clear, even to creative minds in that field, what the failure means. For example, the Cambridge-Somerville Youth Study was a rigorous evaluation of an attempt to arrest delinquent tendencies in predelinquents. As you will see, this experiment produced rather baffling results.

A Contrived Experiment in Delinquency Prevention

Reprinted by permission. From Joan and William McCord, "A Follow-up Report on the Cambridge-Somerville Youth Study," *Annals of the American Academy of Political and Social Science*, Vol. 322, March 1959, pp. 89–96.

One of the most extensive attempts to prevent delinquency and crime was the famous Cambridge-Somerville Youth Study. Founded in 1935 by Richard Clark Cabot, a physician and social philosopher on the faculty of Harvard University, the project aimed at decreasing delinquency in two densely populated, factory dominated cities, Cambridge and Somerville, Massachusetts.

With the aid of a $500,000 grant, Dr. Cabot established a center for the project. After careful interviews, the staff selected subjects from among hundreds of boys referred by schools, welfare agencies, police, and churches as difficult children or as ones who were average in behavior and personality. Each boy was given medical and

[22] Robert K. Merton, *Social Theory and Social Structure*, rev. ed., Glencoe, Ill.: Free Press, 1957, p. 104.

psychological examinations. Social workers consulted the families and reported on their homes. On the basis of this information, each boy was matched to another as closely similar in background and in personality as was possible. One in each pair was then selected, by toss of a coin, to receive the services of the Youth Study. Thus 325 boys were to be given friendly, regular attention from counselors, as well as whatever medical and educational service seemed needed. A matched set of 325 boys, a control group, was to be left to the usual services of the community.

Beginning in 1939, for an average of five years, the "treatment boys" were given assistance ranging from academic tutoring to psychological counseling. The intensity and calibre of treatment varied from counselor to counselor and boy to boy. In some cases, as Dr. Cabot had hoped, treatment involved an intimate friendship between boy and counselor. In most cases, however, the treatment relationship was less close. Treatment had many aspects: talks between the boys and counselors, trips and other recreation for the children, and medical aid whenever it was required. In addition, many counselors, focusing on school problems, tutored their boys in reading and arithmetic. Others acted primarily as co-ordinators for welfare and family agencies, the YMCA, and summer camps. Large numbers of boys were encouraged to participate in shop classes or informal games at the project's center. Religion formed an important part of the treatment: Boys and their families were encouraged to attend church, and ministers and priests were alerted to their problems. Police departments, particularly the juvenile bureaus, kept in close touch with the project. Counselors often visited the boys' families to offer advice and general support.

The Cambridge-Somerville Youth Study differed from most social agencies in three ways: Its subjects were selected by the staff and were therefore, in a sense, "drafted" into the project. It tried to maintain contact with the boys and their families until the boys were about seventeen instead of "closing" cases after shorter treatment. Most importantly, it incorporated a control group of boys who could later be examined in an objective assessment of the effectiveness of the treatment program.

The first attempt to measure effectiveness was carried out while the program was in progress.

Psychological tests, checks on school adjustment, and a review of court records failed to uncover significant differences between the treatment and the control groups.

In 1948, almost three years after the project had ended treatment, a second assessment was made by Edwin Powers, the project's Director, and Helen Witmer, a social scientist. At that time it was found that, according to juvenile court and criminal records, the treatment group had committed as many and approximately as serious offenses as had the control group. Dr. Witmer's ratings of the terminal adjustment of the boys also indicated few differences between the treatment and control groups. Since the conclusions of Powers and Witmer are fully presented in *An Experiment in the Prevention of Delinquency*, we will not attempt to duplicate their report.

In 1956 the authors of this article received a grant from the Cabot Foundation to trace the lives of these boys now that they had reached manhood. We dropped from our study those who had died or who had received very little treatment; also, of course, we dropped their matched mates from the control group. We then secured criminal records for the remaining boys who had passed through Massachusetts or Federal courts. By 1948, 90 per cent of a random sample of 200 boys from the study were still living in the Boston area.

We had decided that the presence or absence of criminal behavior would be our criterion of success in treatment and that criminality would be determined through official court convictions. Objections can be made both to the criterion of success and to the method by which we measured it. We might, for example, have attempted to gauge the general mental health, adjustment, or character of the men. Yet since the major avowed aim of the project was the prevention of crime—and since other standards of success seemed relatively difficult to define or measure—we concluded that criminality should be the yardstick of success.

We recognize, of course, the many defects of official criminal records as a standard of criminality. An earlier study made by the Cambridge-Somerville staff revealed that many delinquent acts known to the counselors had gone undetected by the police. Admittedly, official records are incomplete and, in some cases, may reflect a variety of community biases. Nevertheless, no satisfactory substitute has yet been developed. Moreover, we believe that a confirmed criminal is unlikely to pass through the first thirty years of his life without being apprehended at least once. Furthermore, most of our subjects emerged from deteriorated neighborhoods; therefore the usual middle-class biases in court convictions would be equally applicable to all the boys. Thus, for a variety of reasons, court convictions appeared to be the most practical, objective standard of crime.

The final group used for this assessment of treatment was made up of 506 men predominantly from lower-class and lower-middle-class backgrounds. Approximately half of these men, divided equally between the treatment and the control group, had been considered predelinquent. Their median I.Q. in childhood was 98; their median age, when treatment began, was 11.

COMPARISON OF TREATMENT GROUP AND CONTROL GROUP

When we compared the court records of the boys who had received treatment with those of the control group, we found that a slightly greater number of treatment boys had been convicted for at least one crime, although their number of convictions was slightly lower. Neither of these differences, however, is statistically significant.[23]

	Number of Boys Convicted	Number of Convictions
Treatment group	107	315
Control group	95	344

Both Professor Gordon Allport, in his foreword, and Edwin Powers had expressed the hope that the treatment boys would evidence better adjustment as they matured. To check this possibility, we grouped the boys according to the age at which they committed crimes. We found that a slightly larger number of treatment boys had criminal records in each of three groups: those convicted only as juveniles, those convicted only after "maturation," and those convicted as both juvenile and as adult criminals. These differences, too, were not statistically significant.

[23] For a discussion of the chi-square test of significance used in most of the tables of this article, see Appendix C at the end of this chapter.

Age of Criminality	Number of Boys Convicted	
	Treatment Group	Control Group
Under 18 only	34	29
18 or older only	35	32
Under and over 18	35	34

Nor was there a significant difference in the number of crimes committed during either the juvenile or the adult period.

Age of Boy	Number of Convictions	
	Treatment Group	Control Group
Under 18	152	157
18 and over	163	186

Thus again we had failed to uncover evidence that the treatment had successfully deterred criminality. We looked in another direction for such evidence. Although the treatment and control groups had been carefully matched before treatment began, we knew that much had been discovered since the 1930's about the causes of crime. To control against erroneous matching, we held constant the affectional attitudes of the parents, their techniques of discipline, and the neighborhoods in which the subjects had been reared. Nevertheless, we found no statistically significant differences in favor of the treatment group. Nor did we find differences in favor of the treatment group when we held constant the intelligence and the personalities of the boys.

As a result of these various analyses, we were forced to conclude that the treatment program, considered in its totality, had been ineffectual as a preventative of crime.

COMPARISON OF VARIATIONS
IN TREATMENT

A comparison of treatment and control groups failed to indicate that the treatment, in general, had been beneficial. One possibility suggested itself as perhaps being responsible for the failure: During World War II, many counselors had joined the armed forces, and the turnover in counselors had been marked. We thought these changes might account for the over-all failure of treatment. Yet when we compared criminal rates

—per cent convicted of crimes—we found that they did not significantly reflect this factor.

Number of Counselors		Per Cent Convicted of Crimes
One	(N: 72)	43
Two	(N: 88)	30
Three	(N: 47)	53
More than three	(N: 46)	48

Despite changes in counselors, the first counselor could be expected to have a degree of influence unmatched by his successors. One of the results of the turnover in counselors was that few boys maintained their relationships with their first counselors for an extended period of time. We anticipated that the duration of treatment by the first counselor would influence criminal rates. Again, we found no confirmation for this view.

Length of Treatment by First Counselor		Per Cent Convicted of Crimes
Less than two years	(N: 38)	47
2–3 years	(N: 134)	39
More than 3 years	(N: 81)	42

Since neither the number of counselors nor the length of treatment by the first counselor seemed to be responsible for the apparent failure of treatment in preventing criminality, we next considered the total duration of treatment. One could argue that programs utilizing the tactics of the Cambridge-Somerville Youth Study must operate over extended periods of time. Length of treatment, to a considerable extent, reflected the staff's estimate of the seriousness of a case. Yet we found no support for the belief that lengthy treatment decreased criminality.

Total Length of Treatment		Per Cent Convicted of Crimes
Less than 4 years	(N: 82)	35
4–6 years	(N: 65)	29
More than 6 years	(N: 106)	53

In addition to variations in the duration of treatment, there was, of course, wide variation in the intensity of treatment. In almost every case, counselors devoted close attention to family problems. Nevertheless, there were considerable differences in the amount of interaction they had with the boys themselves. Using six months as the minimum time span, we divided the boys according to the greatest intensity of contact they had with any counselor.

Greatest Intensity of Contact		Per Cent Convicted of Crimes
Once a week	(N: 32)	25
Once in two weeks	(N: 84)	51
Once a month	(N: 47)	43
Less than once a month	(N: 82)	33

If we assume that cases considered most serious were seen at least once in two weeks, then the comparison between the group seen every two weeks and those seen every week (for a minimum of six months) gives a measure of the efficacy of intensive treatment. When the criminal rates for these two groups are compared, we find that those seen every week had a significantly smaller incidence of criminality (X^2 6.4; $P < .02$). This finding suggests that frequent contact between a boy and an adult counselor may deter criminality and that sporadic contact has little effect.

Besides reflecting the intensity of treatment, the effectiveness of treatment was found to be related to the age of the boys when they first became participants in the program (X^2 18.9; d.f. 4; $P < .001$).

Age on Nearest Birthday		Per Cent Convicted of Crimes
5–8	(N: 39)	26
9	(N: 35)	29
10	(N: 47)	66
11	(N: 56)	45
12–13	(N: 76)	37

Clearly, early treatment appeared to have been most beneficial; possibly, the drop in crime rate for older boys—over 10 years old—was due to the fact that a higher proportion continued to have guidance through the difficult adolescent period.

We hypothesized that the sex of the counse-

lors, too, might make a difference in the effectiveness of treatment. One might assume, on the one hand, that female counselors would best satisfy a rejected child's desire for maternal care —or, on the other hand, that male counselors would be most effective for they would furnish a masculine model for the boy. To check the relationship between the sex of the first counselor and treatment, we held the boy's age constant.

	Sex of First Counselor			
	Female		Male	
Age of Boy	Per Cent Convicted		Per Cent Convicted	
5–9	(N: 42)	29	(N: 32)	25
10	(N: 6)	67	(N: 41)	66
11–13	(N: 48)	29	(N: 84)	46

The group of boys in the 11- to 13-year age group who had female counselors had a significantly lower crime rate than did those guided by male first counselors (X^2 3.9; $P < .05$). This may be a reflection of independent variables which we were unable to measure, but it appears that female guidance may be more valuable than male guidance for adolescent boys. On the other hand, the very young boy seems to respond equally to male and female counseling. These findings would seem to recommend a reversal in programs which leave adolescent guidance to men and frequently discourage the treatment of very young children by males.

In summary, these comparisons point again to the general ineffectiveness of those forms of counseling which consisted in family assistance plus infrequent interaction with the boy. The analyses suggest, however, that frequent contact with the child—particularly if begun when the child is under 10 or by a female after the boy has reached adolescence—may effectively prevent criminality. . . .

SUMMARY

Three forms of analyses were used to check the efficacy of the Cambridge-Somerville Youth Study in preventing crime. In the first form, we compared 253 boys who had received treatment with 253 boys, carefully matched in personality and family background, who had received no special treatment. In this comparison, we found that the general program—consisting in guidance for the family, medical and academic assistance for the boys, co-ordination of community agencies, and supplementary entertainment of the boys— had been no more effective in crime prevention than other community services: Approximately equal numbers of treated boys and control boys had committed approximately equal numbers of crimes in childhood and adulthood.

In the second form of analysis, we concentrated upon variations within the treatment group. Negatively, we found that neither the change in counselors nor the length of treatment—which, for many boys, was shorter than had been planned —could be held responsible for the failure. On the other hand, we found evidence that the program might have been more successful had a greater number of boys been seen at least once a week by their counselors and had treatment been started during the first decade of the boys' lives. In addition, we found that male counselors were apparently as effective as female counselors with very young boys, although they were less effective with adolescents. . . .

Thus, using the standard of "official" criminal behavior, we must conclude that the Cambridge-Somerville Youth Study was largely a failure. Some individuals undoubtedly benefited from the program; but the group, as a whole, did not. Yet even in its failure, the program must be regarded as a magnificent experiment, for its provision of a control group and its careful attention to research have produced a fund of information invaluable to future studies of the causation and prevention of crime.

Magnificent failure? If the Cambridge-Somerville Youth Study corrected *wrong* notions held about the causes of, or cures for, delinquency, or if it suggested *new* approaches to delinquency control, it was worth $500,000. At issue was the *interpretation* of the finding that protracted guidance from understanding adults had no measurable effect. Does this mean that family influences in the first few years of life are irreversible? Or that the influence of neighborhood playmates is stronger than the influence of kindly counselors who visit occasionally? One trouble with the Cambridge-Somerville Youth Study was that its negative finding

was susceptible to a multiplicity of interpretations.[24] The Study was well designed to discover whether counselors could arrest the delinquent tendencies of a specific group of predelinquents, but not to assess the *implications* of their success or failure. Yet the half-million-dollar expenditure could best be justified in terms of some larger theoretical significance of the project, some insight into the general process of making or unmaking criminals.

THE IMPORTANCE OF SOCIOLOGICAL THEORY

Some people think of science as preoccupied with the collection of facts. If this conception were correct, the Manhattan telephone directory would be the greatest scientific achievement of the twentieth century—1800 pages of names, addresses, and telephone numbers, alphabetically organized, four columns to the page. Despite the fabulous amount of time and painstaking effort that goes into the Manhattan telephone directory, it is *not* regarded as monumental research. It has no relevance for a body of theory.

Scientifically important research is research that helps to define the fundamental units of the subject or the relationships among them. In other words, it contributes to the development of improved theories of what is going on. Therefore, sociology, for the very reason that it has scientific aspirations, cannot allow facts about interaction to pile up without attempting to set them in a theoretical framework. Human interaction is such an inclusive subject that almost any inquiry about human relations could be called sociological research. But sociological *theory* provides criteria for judging the value of sociological *research*. Do the facts discovered by the research suggest a *new* way of conceptualizing the processes of interaction that will be more fruitful? Although much research falls short of this ideal, a theoretical

[24] For one interpretation, see Jackson Toby, "Early Identification and Intensive Treatment of Predelinquents: A Negative View," *Social Work*, Vol. 6, July 1961, pp. 3–13.

implication is, nevertheless, the criterion of important research.

Sometimes all of the theoretical implications of a piece of research are not grasped by the person who carries it out. More often, the theoretical implication can be grasped only when the results of two or more researchers are juxtaposed. Since researchers are customarily reported in the professional journals and in monographs, other members of the profession are in as good a position to perceive the theoretical implication of several independent research projects as are the researchers themselves. That is to say, it is possible to make significant theoretical contributions, which is the ultimate goal of research, without engaging in direct research at all. Talcott Parsons, for example, is regarded as an outstanding sociological theorist, but he has had negligible research experience.

The rest of this book, like most introductory textbooks in sociology, is mainly concerned with theory. The research reported will be incidental to explicating the concepts and the substantive propositions held by contemporary sociologists. In this respect, an introductory textbook has quite a different flavor from *The American Sociological Review, The British Journal of Sociology,* or *Acta Sociologica* (the journal published by Scandinavian sociologists); the professional journals assume that readers are acquainted with sociological theory and emphasize research reports.

CONCLUSION

The origins of sociology are diverse; intellectual debts are owed to history, philosophy, political theory, and economics as well as to religiously inspired humanitarianism and secular reform movements. Nevertheless, the direction of contemporary sociology is away from the traditions out of which the field emerged. Theorists like Talcott Parsons and organizers of huge research projects like Samuel A. Stouffer share a scientific approach to sociology. Such an approach is anathema to many intellectuals who vacillate between denying that science is applicable to human behavior and protesting

that social science leads directly to the evil society depicted by George Orwell in his novel *1984*.[25] Sociological studies are increasingly concerned both with methodological sophistication and implications for systematic theory. The objective is ambitious indeed: to work back and forth between empirical data and descriptive concepts until a system of variables is developed capable of analyzing the complexities of even the most intricate human society.

APPENDIX A

The accuracy of the Current Population Survey may be *greater* than the accuracy of the decennial census because the errors in the decennial census are probably larger than the sampling error of the Survey. Consider the errors attributable to overlooked persons and to faulty communication between the enumerator and the respondent.

(*a*) *Underenumeration.* In the hectic couple of weeks in April of a census year, every man, woman, and child is supposed to be enumerated. However, the population of an industrial society moves about; it does not stand still waiting for the census taker. As a result, some people are enumerated twice and others are not counted at all. The Census Bureau estimated that 1,309,000 people were *over*enumerated in 1950 and 3,400,000 people were *under*enumerated out of a total population of 152,788,000—a net underenumeration of 2,091,000 people. Underenumeration does not occur uniformly throughout the population. Certain categories of persons are more likely to be missed than others. For example, newborn infants sometimes are missed, apparently because they are not yet thought of as residents of the household. Thus, the 1950 census reported 3,146,948 children under one year; ten years later the 1960 census reported 3,481,131 children between 10 and 11. Since these were essentially the same children enumerated

[25] Bennett M. Berger, "Sociology and the Intellectuals: An Analysis of a Stereotype," *Antioch Review,* Vol. 17, September 1957, pp. 275–290.

at different ages, underenumeration of infants had occurred.

(b) *Response error.* Communication between the enumerator and the respondent may be faulty. The respondent may misunderstand the enumerator's question or the enumerator may misunderstand the respondent's answer. The enumerator may forget to ask a question he was supposed to ask. Or he may record an answer incorrectly. Although it is difficult to estimate the magnitude of these various response errors on the decennial census, it is certain that they are far greater than response errors on the Current Population Survey. The research workers conducting field work for the Current Population Survey are full-time, permanent employees of the Census Bureau with extensive training and experience, whereas the census enumerators are temporary workers, sometimes recruited through political connections. The short training course the enumerators receive prevents the most serious blunders, but it is no substitute for professional commitment to the Survey task.

APPENDIX B

Stratified sampling is a modification of random sampling. Instead of drawing *one* random sample from a large and heterogeneous population, the researcher divides the population into relatively homogeneous subpopulations and selects random samples from *each* of the subpopulations. Ultimately, the estimates for each subpopulation must be pooled to get an estimate for the entire population. Stratified sampling may not sound economical, but it is. *Stratified sampling enables a researcher to attain the same level of accuracy with a smaller total sample.*

An illustration will show the advantages of stratified over simple random sampling. Suppose the Health Department of a university needed to know the average height of its students. There are 4000 students attending the university. If an alphabetical list of all the students were available, a researcher could select every *twentieth* name, find out the heights of

each of these students from health records, and compute the average height of students in the 5 per cent sample. Since the sample is a random one, the sample average would be a good estimate of the average for the total university population, which is 20 times as large. The sampling procedure, however, disregards at least two known facts: (1) the university contains female students as well as males, and (2) the average height of females is several inches less than the average height of males. Consider how these facts might be utilized to reduce the size of the sample *without sacrificing the accuracy of the sample estimate.* The researcher selects every *fiftieth* name and obtains the heights from health records as before. This time, however, the girls are separated from the boys and the average height is computed for each sex separately.

Even though a 2.5 per cent sample is smaller than a 5 per cent sample, it may be just as good. The smaller sample attempts two relatively easy tasks, estimating the average heights of boys and estimating the average heights of girls, whereas the larger sample attempts a more difficult task, estimating the heights of all students taken together. The latter task is more difficult, as Figure 2 shows, because the

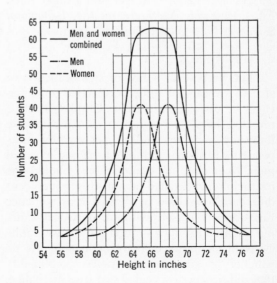

FIGURE 2. Distribution of heights of a sample of college-age men and women.

variation of heights around the average height for all students is far greater than the variation around the average height for boys or the variation around the average height for girls. From the estimates of the average height for boys and the average height for girls, it is a simple matter to compute the average height for all students at the university. The girls' average is multiplied by the female enrollment at the university, the boys' average by the male enrollment at the university. Both are added and the sum is divided by the total enrollment.

This explanation of stratified sampling illustrates the underlying principle—even though the content is unrealistic. It simplifies the exposition to discuss the heights of males and females rather than the financial behavior of persons in rural and urban counties. In his discussion of surveys conducted by the Survey Research Center for the Federal Reserve Board, Likert referred to strata of counties, probably based on socioeconomic criteria or the extent of urbanization. A second inadequacy of this explanation is its avoidance of precise statistical concepts (like variance). Students with sufficient mathematical or statistical training will find a more rigorous treatment of stratified sampling in Leslie Kish, "Selection of the Sample," in Leon Festinger and Daniel Katz, Eds., *Research Methods in the Behavioral Sciences*, New York: Dryden, 1953.

APPENDIX C

The purpose of a test of significance is to give the researcher some perspective on differences he discovers in various samples. Table 4 revealed that 15 per cent of freshmen who were fraternity members and 12 per cent of independent freshmen admitted having cheated more than once on examinations. Should the researcher get excited about this 3 per cent difference, or should he dismiss it as a chance variation? A person without statistical training might think such a question unanswerable. Tests of significance, however, enable the researcher to compute the precise probability that differences of specified size arise by chance. In Table 4, for instance, the question at issue

is: Are fraternity members and independent students essentially similar in their disposition to cheat or are they essentially different? That is to say, are they from the same universe or from different universes? For the freshman year, there are two samples, one of 178 fraternity members, one of 498 independents.

A test of significance can tell the researcher whether, with samples of those sizes, the 3 per cent difference could have arisen by chance from a population in which fraternity members and independents were indistinguishable regarding cheating behavior. If the test of significance reveals a probability of less than five chances in a hundred that random samples from a single population would have differed by as much as 3 per cent, the researcher may reject the hypothesis of no difference between fraternity men and independents. Or he may insist on a one in a hundred probability before he is willing to reject what statisticians call "the null hypothesis." It is, of course, an arbitrary decision as to how small the probability must be before the researcher assumes that the difference could not have arisen by chance. Most commonly, statisticians use the 5 per cent and the 1 per cent levels. Differences labeled "significant at the .01 level" are a shorthand way of saying, "The chances are only one in a hundred that such a difference could have arisen as a result of random sampling from a single population."

Even if the 3 per cent difference were significant (at the .05 level or less), the researcher could not yet say that freshmen with fraternity affiliations differed from independent freshmen in cheating tendencies. Bear in mind that the statistical basis for tests of significance is random sampling. Suppose that the chances of fraternity members filling out a questionnaire were not the same as the chances of an independent filling out a questionnaire. This would violate the conditions of random sampling and would therefore invalidate the inference from the test of significance.

There are many tests of significance. The selection of the appropriate test of significance requires knowledge of its underlying assumptions. In the article based on the Cambridge-Somerville Youth Study, the chi-square test is used. Thus, on page 50 you see that for an X^2 value of 6.4, the probability is less than two chances in a hundred.

SOME SIGNIFICANT LITERATURE ON SOCIOLOGICAL RESEARCH

Kurt W. Back and J. Mayone Stycos, *The Survey Under Unusual Conditions: The Jamaica Human Fertility Investigation*, Ithaca, N.Y.: Society for Applied Anthropology, 1959. This is a methodological report on an interview survey of the knowledge of underprivileged Jamaican women about contraception and their attitudes toward it. Very few women refused to answer questions although this delicate subject was raised among a poorly educated population unfamiliar with polling and other types of scientific social research. One reason for the cooperative attitude of respondents was the careful program of interviewer selection and training. This summary is based on a review by Hyman Rodman, *American Sociological Review*, Vol. 25, October 1960, p. 768.

Bernard Berelson, *Content Analysis in Communication Research*, Glencoe, Ill.: Free Press, 1952. The analysis of the symbolic content of newspapers, magazines, radio broadcasts, and motion pictures has been used for a number of purposes: (1) to trace trends, (2) to compare one medium of mass communication with another, (3) to audit the quality of the communication, (4) to measure readability, (5) to obtain military intelligence, and more. Professor Berelson describes the technical problems involved in content analysis. What units of analysis should be used—small units like the word or larger units like the sentence or the theme? How should material be sampled so as to increase the reliability and validity of the quantitative analysis? He also addresses the criticisms of content analysis and especially the complaint of humanists that it is unrealistic to hope to reduce the subtlety of linguistic communication to rows of percentages. This summary is based on a review by Ithiel De Sola Pool, *American Sociological Review*, Vol. 17, August 1952, pp. 515–516.

James S. Davie and A. Paul Hare, "Button-down Collar Culture: A Study of Undergraduate Life at a Men's College," *Human Organization*, Vol. 14, Winter 1956, pp. 13–20. The description in this article of undergraduate life in an eastern Ivy League university is based on interviews with eight juniors and seniors attending its undergraduate college. The eight informants were selected to be representative of the student body in five respects: (1) type of secondary school attended, (2) section of the country in which home is located, (3) source of financial support at college, (4) field of study, and (5) grades in college. Each informant participated in two group interviews, lasting two hours each, and one individual interview. It was assumed that this small but purposively selected sample could provide a valid composite description of undergraduate life.

Herbert Hyman, *Survey Design and Analysis: Principles, Cases and Procedures*, Glencoe, Ill.: Free Press, 1955. This volume is a product of the Columbia University Planning Project for Advanced Training in Social Research. Since Columbia is a major center of graduate instruction in sociology that includes a quasicommercial social research organization, the Bureau of Applied Social Research, the book offers a bird's-eye view of what the professional sociologist ought to know about survey research. One axis on which the book turns is the distinction between descriptive and explanatory surveys. Whereas the objective of descriptive surveys is to categorize a population as precisely as possible, the objective of explanatory surveys is to relate one variable to another and, in particular, to find out whether factor A is a cause of factor B. This summary is based on a review by Edward A. Suchman, *American Sociological Review*, Vol. 21, April 1956, pp. 232–233.

Herbert H. Hyman, William J. Cobb, Jacob J. Feldman, Clyde W. Hart, and Charles H. Stember, *Interviewing in Social Research*, Chicago: University of Chicago Press, 1954. This book is concerned with an important source of error in survey research: communication failure between the interviewer and the respondent. A leading survey organization, the National Opinion Research Center, brought data from its own files to bear on this problem as well as examining the survey research literature. Communication failure results from a variety of sources: (1) The interviewer expects certain responses because he assumes consistency within a particular frame of reference. (2) The interviewer expects certain responses because he assumes people in a certain category will give them. (3) The interviewer interacts with the respondent in the interview situation in such a way as to influence the response. (4) Lack of structure in the interviewing situation permits responses irrelevant to the purposes of the study. These and other sources of interviewer bias may be offset partially, although probably not completely, by better methods of selection, training, and supervision of interviewers. This summary is based on a review by Charles E. Bowerman, *American Sociological Review*, Vol. 20, June 1955, pp. 356–357.

Robert L. Kahn and Charles F. Cannell, *The Dynamics of Interviewing: Theory, Techniques, and Cases*, New York: Wiley, 1957. This book is described by the director of the Survey Research Center at the University of California at Berkeley as ". . . without question the most thorough and painstaking examination of the interviewing process in print." It discusses the practical questions of how to motivate the respondent, how to design questionnaires, and how to probe to obtain answers required by the research project. But it is also concerned with the psychology of the interview and in particular with the theory of nondirective interviewing (Carl Rogers) and field theory (Kurt Lewin). This summary is based on a review by Charles Y. Glock, *American Sociological Review*, Vol. 22, December 1957, pp. 761–762.

Allen H. Barton and Paul F. Lazarsfeld, "Some Functions of Qualitative Analysis in Social Research," *Frankfurter Beiträge zur Soziologie*," Vol. 1, 1955, pp. 321–361, reprinted in Seymour Martin Lipset and Neil J. Smelser, *Sociology: The Progress of a Decade*, Englewood Cliffs, N.J.: Prentice-Hall, 1961, pp. 95–122. These two distinguished social researchers examined 100 studies in which investigators analyzed *qualitative* rather than *quantitative* data. They sought to contribute, on the basis of current research practice, a tentative answer to the following question: "What can a researcher do when confronted by a body of qualitative data—detailed, concrete, nonmetric descriptions of people and events, drawn from direct observation, interviews, case studies, historical writings, the writings of participants?" They found that qualitative data can, in the early stages of the investigation of a problem, contribute to the formulation of the problem, to classification of variables, and to hypotheses relating one variable to another. Qualitative observation can also provide support for large-scale, wide-ranging theories not amenable to quantitative testing, for example, theories of social change. Here qualitative data are ". . . more than simply illustration, but less than definitive proof."

Samuel A. Stouffer et al., *The American Soldier*, 2 vols., Princeton, N.J.: Princeton University Press, 1949. These volumes represent a reanalysis of data collected during the Second World War by the Research Branch of the Information and Education Division of the United States Army. "The Research Branch existed to do a practical engineering job, not a scientific one. Its purpose was to provide the Army Command quickly and accurately with facts about the attitudes of soldiers which . . . might be helpful in policy formation." For instance, it found out through anonymous questionnaire surveys how enlisted men felt about officers and reported the findings to those responsible for officer training and soldier morale. Thus, the Research Branch functioned for the Army much the way a market research firm functions for

a manufacturer. The reanalysis was undertaken to utilize the Army data to answer questions raised by sociological and social psychological theories. This summary is based on a review by John W. Riley, Jr., *American Sociological Review*, Vol. 14, August 1949, pp. 557–559.

William Foote Whyte, *Street Corner Society: The Social Structure of an Italian Slum*, 2nd ed., Chicago: University of Chicago Press, 1955. First published in 1943, this account on an Italian slum community in the North End of Boston in the years from 1936 to 1940 is a classic illustration of the participant-observer method of social research. The author was then a Junior Fellow at Harvard University. He lived in the North End for three and a half years, hung around street corners with a group of unemployed young men in their twenties, and learned Italian so as to communicate better with the older generation. In short, he became a member of the community in order to describe it firsthand. The result is a marvelously perceptive account of corner boys and, to a lesser extent, college boys, as well as racketeers and politicians, all observed at close range over a period of several years. Since Whyte was a one-man research staff, what is missing from the book is whatever a 23-year-old graduate student was not in a good position to observe, such as family life. Participant-observation at its best provides deep insights, but it cannot deal as systematically with all aspects of community life as can an organized research project. Whyte, now a professor in the School of Industrial and Labor Relations of Cornell University, has turned his hand to directing large-scale investigations of the social organization of factories, restaurants, and other occupational communities.

Theodore D. Woolsey, "Sampling Methods for a Small Household Survey," Public Health Monograph No. 40, Washington: Government Printing Office, 1956. The survey reported in this monograph furnished estimates of the amount of illness and the number of persons available for work in the age group 45 years and over in Hagerstown, Maryland, in the summer of 1953. It is included in this bibliography because it serves as a model of a household survey based on a probability sample. The city directory provided a list of street addresses. Every seventh residential listing was marked for inclusion in the sample. (In the case of addresses of apartment houses or other multiple dwellings, the ratio of one in seven was preserved by listing the separate dwelling units and by designating households in a random way from the list.) Interviewers were then instructed to go to the designated households and ask whether a person in them had passed the forty-fifth birthday. If not, the interview was concluded. If so, the interviewer was instructed to list *all* of the persons in the household. This listing was necessary so that, if there were several persons past 45 in the household, the interviewer would know, in accordance with previously prepared instructions, which one to interview. For example, in households containing *two* persons over 45, *half* the interviewers were instructed to interview the older and *half* the younger. Households in which no one was available on repeated calls (including calls on Saturdays and Sundays and sometimes calls at the place of work) were dropped from the study. A table was compiled at the end of the survey showing how far the sample had departed from the ideal design. Thus, there were 19 refusals to be interviewed, 11 households in which no one could ever be found at home, and 600 completed interviews.

CHAPTER 3

Culture: The Symbolic
Prerequisite of a Way of Life

Interaction can occur on subhuman levels. When two dogs fight, growls, lunges, bites, and strategic retreats fit a pattern of action and reaction. One dog interprets the other's growl as a sign of hostility, and the battle is on. The dogs understand one another because there is an inherent connection between growling and hostility in the animal world; wherever they are, animals express themselves in much the same way.

THE MEANING DIMENSION IN HUMAN INTERACTION

Human interaction is more complicated. Take as an example a policeman who arrested a drunk on the streets of New Brunswick, New Jersey. The drunk, resentful, muttered a curse in Hungarian, his native tongue. The policeman happened to be of Hungarian extraction himself, understood the curse, and filed an additional charge against his prisoner: abusing an officer. Note that the drunk expressed his hostility not by growling but by using a linguistic code. In order to decode the message contained in the curse, the policeman had to know Hungarian. There are two differences between a curse and a growl. In the first place,

58

the drunk had to *learn* to curse. He did not invent for the occasion the sound he uttered. Nor was the curse linked directly to his feeling of hostility, as is a dog's growl. He drew it from the Hungarian cultural tradition—in much the same way as cooks draw upon the Hungarian cultural tradition for goulash. Second, the policeman had to *share* knowledge of the cultural tradition with the drunk for communication to occur. The policeman could not have inferred from the sound the drunk made or the expression on his face that he was "abusing an officer."

Learning of meanings is crucial to human communication—and therefore to human interaction—because the messages are usually in a cultural code. Language is the most obvious example of a cultural code, but virtually all human behavior has a *cultural dimension*, including behavior usually thought of as physiological. An American adult, for example, does not belch in public, no matter how acute his gastric distress, because American culture disapproves. In Japan, on the other hand, belching is considered an appropriate way to indicate to one's host that the meal was good. As a result, Japanese adults *produce* belches for the same reason that American adults *suppress* them: to be polite.

Similarly, cultures define the meaning of masculinity and femininity.[1] All cultures begin with an initial biological difference between males and females, but each culture elaborates this initial difference in a distinctive way. In the United States, different haircuts are given to boys and girls; they receive different toys to play with, different clothing to wear, and, to some extent, different words to use when expressing themselves. Girls may or may not know the meanings of "bad words"; they are tempted to pretend not to know them whether they do or not, as an indication of their femininity. Boys, however, are expected to know the horrifying words and, on occasion, to use them as an expression of virility. Consider the situation in which two boys fight and one gets considerably the worse of it. If the loser cries because of his frustration at defeat and injury, he identifies himself as a "sissy" (according to American culture). On the other hand, if he lets loose with a stream of four-letter Anglo-Saxon profanity, he reassures himself and everyone around him that he is "tough" and will not resort to the female pattern of crying.[2] Careful study of the occasions when profanity is used shows that, far from being an irrational phenomenon, profanity is skillfully selected by males to express hostility, virility, or both simultaneously.[3]

Not only do conceptions of masculinity and femininity vary from one culture to another. So do conceptions of the ease or difficulty of *becoming* men and women, that is, of the adolescent role. Ruth Benedict, the anthropologist, comments as follows about cultural variability in expectations for the adolescent boy and girl.

1 Margaret Mead, *Male and Female: A Study of the Sexes in a Changing World*, New York: William Morrow, 1949.
2 Ashley Montagu, "Should Strong Men Cry?" *New York Times Magazine*, May 26, 1957, pp. 17–18.
3 Henry Elkin, "Aggressive and Erotic Tendencies in Army Life," *American Journal of Sociology*, Vol. 51, March 1946, pp. 408–413.

Becoming an Adult in Various Preliterate Societies

Reprinted by permission. From Ruth Benedict, *Patterns of Culture*, Boston: Houghton Mifflin, 1934, pp. 25–29.

The most casual survey of the ways in which different societies have handled adolescence makes one fact inescapable: even in those cultures which have made most of the trait, the age upon which they focus their attention varies over a great range of years. At the outset, therefore, it is clear that the so-called puberty institutions are a misnomer if we continue to think of biological puberty. The puberty they recognize is social, and the ceremonies are a recognition in some fashion or other of the child's new status of adulthood. This investiture with new occupations and obligations is in consequence as various and as culturally conditioned as the occupations and obligations themselves. If the sole honourable duty of manhood is conceived to be deeds of war, the investiture of the warrior is later and of a different sort from that in a society where adulthood gives chiefly the privilege of dancing in a representation of masked gods. In order to understand puberty institutions, we do not most need analyses of the necessary nature of *rites de passage*; we need rather to know what is identified in different cultures with the beginning of adulthood and their methods of admitting to the new status. Not biological puberty, but what adulthood means in that culture conditions the puberty ceremony.

Adulthood in central North America means warfare. Honour in it is the great goal of all men. The constantly recurring theme of the youth's coming-of-age, as also of preparation for the war-path at any age, is a magic ritual for success in war. They torture not one another, but themselves: they cut strips of skin from their arms and legs, they strike off their fingers, they drag heavy weights pinned to their chest or leg muscles. Their reward is enhanced prowess in deeds of warfare.

In Australia, on the other hand, adulthood means participation in an exclusively male cult whose fundamental trait is the exclusion of women. Any woman is put to death if she so much as hears the sound of the bull-roarer at the ceremonies, and she must never know of the rites. Puberty ceremonies are elaborate and symbolic repudiations of the bonds with the female sex; the men are symbolically made self-sufficient and the wholly responsible element of the community. To attain this end they use drastic sexual rites and bestow supernatural guaranties.

The clear physiological facts of adolescence, therefore, are first socially interpreted even where they are stressed. But a survey of puberty institutions makes clear a further fact: puberty is physiologically a different matter in the life-cycle of the male and the female. If cultural emphasis followed the physiological emphasis, girls' ceremonies would be more marked than boys'; but it is not so. The ceremonies emphasize a social fact: the adult prerogatives of men are more far-reaching in every culture than women's, and consequently, as in the above instances, it is more common for societies to take note of this period in boys than in girls.

Girls' and boys' puberty, however, may be socially celebrated in the same tribe in identical ways. Where, as in the interior of British Columbia, adolescent rites are a magical training for all occupations, girls are included on the same terms as boys. Boys roll stones down mountains and beat them to the bottom to be swift of foot, or throw gambling-sticks to be lucky in gambling; girls carry water from distant springs, or drop stones down inside their dresses that their children may be born as easily as the pebble drops to the ground.

In such a tribe as the Nandi of the lake region of East Africa, also, girls and boys share an even-handed puberty rite, though, because of the man's dominant rôle in the culture, his boyhood training period is more stressed than the woman's. Here adolescent rites are an ordeal inflicted by those already admitted to adult status upon those they are now forced to admit. They require of them the most complete stoicism in the face of ingenious tortures associated with circumcision. The rites for the two sexes are separate, but they follow the same pattern. In both the novices wear for the ceremony the clothing of their sweethearts. During the operation their faces are watched for any twinge of pain, and the reward of bravery is given with great rejoicing by the lover, who runs forward to receive back some of his adornments. For both the girl and the boy the rites mark their *entrée* into a new sex status: the boy is now a warrior and may take a sweetheart, the girl is marriageable. The adolescent tests are for both a pre-marital ordeal in which the palm is awarded by their lovers.

Puberty rites may also be built upon the facts of girls' puberty and admit of no extension to boys. One of the most naïve of these is the institution of the fatting-house for girls in central Africa. In the region where feminine beauty is all but identified with obesity, the girl at puberty is segregated, sometimes for years, fed with sweet and fatty foods, allowed no activity, and her body rubbed assiduously with oils. She is taught during this time her future duties, and her seclusion ends with a parade of her corpulence that is followed by her marriage to her proud bridegroom. It is not regarded as necessary for the man to achieve pulchritude before marriage in a similar fashion.

The usual ideas around which girls' puberty institutions are centred, and which are not readily extended to boys', are those concerned with menstruation. The uncleanness of the menstruating woman is a very widespread idea, and in a few regions first menstruation has been made the focus of all the associated attitudes. Puberty rites in these cases are of a thoroughly different character from any of which we have spoken. Among the Carrier Indians of British Columbia, the fear and horror of a girl's puberty was at its height. Her three or four years of seclusion was called "the burying alive," and she lived for all that time alone in the wilderness, in a hut of branches far from all beaten trails. She was a threat to any person who might so much as catch a glimpse of her, and her mere footstep defiled a path or a river. She was covered with a great headdress of tanned skin that shrouded her face and breasts and fell to the ground behind. Her arms and legs were loaded with sinew bands to protect her from the evil spirit with which she was filled. She was herself in danger and she was a source of danger to everybody else.

Girls' puberty ceremonies built upon ideas associated with the menses are readily convertible into what is, from the point of view of the individual concerned, exactly opposite behaviour. There are always two possible aspects to the sacred: it may be a source of peril or it may be a source of blessing. In some tribes the first menses of girls are a potent supernatural blessing. Among the Apaches I have seen the priests themselves pass on their knees before the row of solemn little girls to receive from them the blessing of their touch. All the babies and the old people come also of necessity to have illness removed from them. The adolescent girls are not segregated as sources of danger, but court is paid to them as to direct sources of supernatural blessing. Since the ideas that underlie puberty rites for girls, both among the Carrier and among the Apache, are founded on beliefs concerning menstruation, they are not extended to boys, and boys' puberty is marked instead, and lightly, with simple tests and proofs of manhood.

The meaning of masculinity and femininity, the meaning of sexual intimacy, and the meaning of adolescence differs from one culture to another. These differences of meaning have implications for interaction. In a society that regards sexual intercourse as expressing the emotional intimacy of a *married* couple, courtship behavior may exclude coitus. In a society in which sexual intercourse is the tangible evidence of male success in a game of seduction, promiscuity may be a feature of adolescent life. Thus, cultural definitions of the situation do not merely add a dimension of interpretation to factual events. Culture helps to complete a world that nature has left indeterminate. Sexual intimacy *can* symbolize love, but it can also symbolize conquest. For animals, sex is uninterpreted; it simply *is*. For human beings, the meaning dimension is always part of the situation. *Some* meaning is supplied by the cultural tradition and is shared, to varying degrees, by all members of the society. (The degree of sharing varies because these meanings are not inborn but must be learned—and it is too much to expect that everyone will learn precisely the same interpretation of the cultural definition.) *Some* meaning is contributed by the idiosyncratic values of the individual. (When and if the idiosyncratic values of a particular individual spread to the rest of his society, they stop being idiosyncratic and become part of the culture; to this extent the culture has changed.) But in either case the meaning dimension is part of the situation confronting human beings just as the time dimension is part of the situation.

Culture not only defines *physiological processes* like belching and *biological facts* like masculinity and femininity. Culture also defines the *physical environment*. Snow does not not mean the same thing to Americans as it does to Eskimos. Nor is space understood in the same way by contemporary man as it was before the invention of airplanes, rockets, and missiles. Human beings do not perceive the world as events in space and time except in infancy. Adults see clearly what their culture calls attention to and disregard what their culture ignores. As linguists have pointed out, these cultural emphases are imbedded in the language we speak and thus, indirectly, in the thoughts we think.

Language, the Definition of Reality

Reprinted by permission. From Benjamin Lee Whorf, "Science and Linguistics," in John B. Carroll, Ed., *Language, Thought, and Reality: Selected Writings of Benjamin Lee Whorf*, Cambridge, Mass.: M.I.T. Press, 1956, Chap. 15.

Natural logic says that talking is merely an incidental process concerned strictly with communication, not with formulation of ideas. Talking, or the use of language, is supposed only to "express" what is essentially already formulated nonlinguistically. Formulation is an independent process, called thought or thinking, and is supposed to be largely indifferent to the nature of particular languages. Languages have grammars, which are assumed to be merely norms of conventional and social correctness, but the use of language is supposed to be guided not so much by them as by correct, rational, or intelligent *thinking*.

Thought, in this view, does not depend on grammar but on laws of logic or reason which are supposed to be the same for all observers of the universe—to represent a rationale in the universe that can be "found" independently by all intelligent observers, whether they speak Chinese or Choctaw. In our own culture, the formulations of mathematics and of formal logic have acquired the reputation of dealing with this order of things, i.e., with the realm and laws of pure thought.

Natural logic holds that different languages are essentially parallel methods for expressing this one-and-the-same rationale of thought and, hence, differ really in but minor ways which may seem important only because they are seen at close range. It holds that mathematics, symbolic logic, philosophy, and so on, are systems contrasted with language which deal directly with this realm of thought, not that they are themselves specialized extensions of language. . . .

When linguists became able to examine critically and scientifically a large number of languages of widely different patterns, their base of reference was expanded; they experienced an interruption of phenomena hitherto held universal, and a whole new order of significances came into their ken. It was found that the background linguistic system (in other words, the grammar) of each language is not merely a reproducing instrument for voicing ideas but rather is itself the shaper of ideas, the program and guide for the individual's mental activity, for his analysis of impressions, for his synthesis of his mental stock in trade. Formulation of ideas is not an independent process, strictly rational in the old sense, but is part of a particular grammar and differs, from slightly to greatly, as between different grammars. We dissect nature along lines laid down by our native languages. The categories and types that we isolate from the world of phenomena we do not find there because they stare every observer in the face; on the contrary, the world is presented in a kaleidoscopic flux of impressions which has to be organized by our minds—and this means largely by the linguistic systems in our minds. We cut nature up, organize it into concepts, and ascribe significances as we do, largely because we are parties to an agreement to organize it in this way—an agreement that holds throughout our speech community and is codified in the patterns of our language. The agreement is, of course, an implicit and unstated one, *but its terms are absolutely obligatory*; we cannot talk at all except by subscribing to the organization and classification of data which the agreement decrees.

The fact is very significant for modern science, for it means that no individual is free to describe nature with absolute impartiality but is constrained to certain modes of interpretation even while he thinks himself most free. The person most nearly free in such respects would be a linguist familiar with very many widely different linguistic systems. As yet even no linguist is in any such position. We are thus introduced to a new principle of relativity, which holds that all observers are not led by the same physical evidence to the same picture of the universe, unless their linguistic backgrounds are similar, or can in some way be calibrated.

This rather startling conclusion is not so apparent if we compare only our modern European languages, with perhaps Latin and Greek thrown in for good measure. Among these tongues there is a unanimity of major pattern which at first seems to bear out natural logic. But this unanimity exists only because these tongues are all Indo-European dialects cut to the same basic plan, being historically transmitted from what was long ago one speech community; because the modern dialects have long shared in building up a common culture; and because much of this culture, on the more intellectual side, is derived from the linguistic backgrounds of Latin and Greek. Thus this group of languages satisfies the special case of the clause beginning "unless" in the statement of the linguistic relativity principle at the end of the preceding paragraph. From this condition follows the unanimity of description of the world in the community of modern scientists. But it must be emphasized that "all modern Indo-European-speaking observers" is not the same thing as "all observers." That modern Chinese or Turkish scientists describe the world in the same terms as Western scientists means, of course, only that they have taken over bodily the entire Western system of rationalizations, not that they have corroborated that system from their native posts of observation.

When Semitic, Chinese, Tibetan, or African languages are contrasted with our own, the divergence in analysis of the world becomes more apparent; and when we bring in the native languages of the Americas, where speech communities for many millenniums have gone their ways independently of each other and of the Old World, the fact that languages dissect nature in many different ways becomes patent. The relativity of all conceptual systems, ours included, and their dependence upon language stand revealed. That American Indians speaking only their native tongues are never called upon to act as scientific observers is in no wise to the point. To exclude the evidence which their languages offer as to what the human mind can do is like expecting botanists to study nothing but food plants and hothouse roses and then tell us what the plant world is like!

Let us consider a few examples. In English we divide most of our words into two classes, which have different grammatical and logical properties. Class 1 we call nouns, e.g., "house," "man"; Class 2, verbs, e.g., "hit," "run." Many words of one class can act secondarily as of the other class, e.g., "a hit," "a run," or "to man" the boat, but on the primary level the division between the classes is absolute. Our language thus gives us a bipolar division of nature. But nature herself is not thus polarized. If it be said that strike, turn, run, are verbs because they denote temporary or short-lasting events, i.e., actions, why then is fist a noun? It also is a temporary event. Why are lightning, spark, wave, eddy, pulsation, flame, storm, phase, cycle, spasm, noise, emotion, nouns? They are temporary events. If man and house are nouns because they are long-lasting and stable events, i.e., things, what then are keep, adhere, extend, project, continue, persist, grow, dwell, and so on, doing among the verbs? If it be objected that possess, adhere, are verbs because they are stable relationships rather than stable percepts, why then should equilibrium, pressure, current, peace, group, nation, society, tribe, sister, or any kinship term, be among the nouns? It will be found that an "event" to *us* means "what our language classes as a verb" or something analogized therefrom. And it will be found that it is not possible to define event, thing, object, relationship, and so on, from nature, but that to define them always involves a circuitous return to the grammatical categories of the definer's language.

In the Hopi language, lightning, wave, flame, meteor, puff of smoke, pulsation, are verbs—events of necessarily brief duration cannot be anything but verbs. Cloud and storm are at about the lower limit of duration for nouns. Hopi, you see, actually has a classification of events (or linguistic isolates) by duration type, something strange to our modes of thought. On the other hand, in Nootka, a language of Vancouver Island, all words seem to us to be verbs, but really there are no Classes 1 and 2; we have, as it were, a monistic view of nature that gives us only one class of word for all kinds of events. "A house occurs" or "it houses" is the way of saying "house," exactly like "a flame occurs" or "it burns." These terms seem to us like verbs because they are inflected for durational and temporal nuances, so that the suffixes of the word for house event make it mean long-lasting house, temporary house, future house, house that used to be, what started out to be a house, and so on.

Hopi has a noun that covers every thing or being that flies, with the exception of birds, which class is denoted by another noun. The former noun may be said to denote the class FC—B, i.e., flying class minus bird. The Hopi actually call insect, airplane, and aviator all by the same word, and feel no difficulty about it. The situation, of course, decides any possible confusion among very disparate members of a broad linguistic class, such as this class FC—B. This class seems to us too large and inclusive, but so would our class "snow" to an Eskimo. We have the same word for falling snow, snow on the ground, snow packed hard like ice, slushy snow, wind-driven flying snow —whatever the situation may be. To an Eskimo, this all-inclusive word would be almost unthinkable; he would say that falling snow, slushy snow, and so on, are sensuously and operationally different, different things to contend with; he uses different words for them and for other kinds of snow. The Aztecs go even farther than we in the opposite direction, with cold, ice, and snow all represented by the same basic word with different terminations; ice is the noun form; cold, the adjectival form; and for snow, "ice mist."

What surprises most is to find that various grand generalizations of the Western world, such as time, velocity, and matter, are not essential to the construction of a consistent picture of the universe. The psychic experiences that we class under these headings are, of course, not destroyed; rather, categories derived from other kinds of experiences take over the rulership of the cosmology and seem to function just as well. Hopi may be called a timeless language. It recognizes psychological time, which is much like Bergson's "duration," but this "time" is quite unlike the mathematical time, T, used by our physicists. Among the peculiar properties of Hopi time are that it varies with each observer, does not permit of simultaneity, and has zero dimensions; i.e., it cannot be given a number greater than one. The Hopi do not say, "I stayed five days," but "I left on the fifth day." A word referring to this kind of time, like the word day, can have no plural. The puzzle picture (Figure 3), will give mental exercise to anyone who would like to figure out how the Hopi verb gets along without tenses. Actually, the only practical use of our tenses, in one-verb sentences, is to distinguish among five typical situations, which are symbolized in the picture. The timeless Hopi verb does not distinguish between the present, past, and future of the event itself but must always indicate what type of validity the *speaker* intends the statement to have: (*a*) report of an event (situations 1, 2, 3 in the picture); (*b*) expectation of an event (situation 4); (*c*) generalization or law about events (situation 5). Situation 1, where the speaker and listener are in contact with the same objective field, is divided by our language into the two conditions, 1*a* and 1*b*, which it calls present and past, respectively. This division is unnecessary for a language which assures one that the statement is a report.

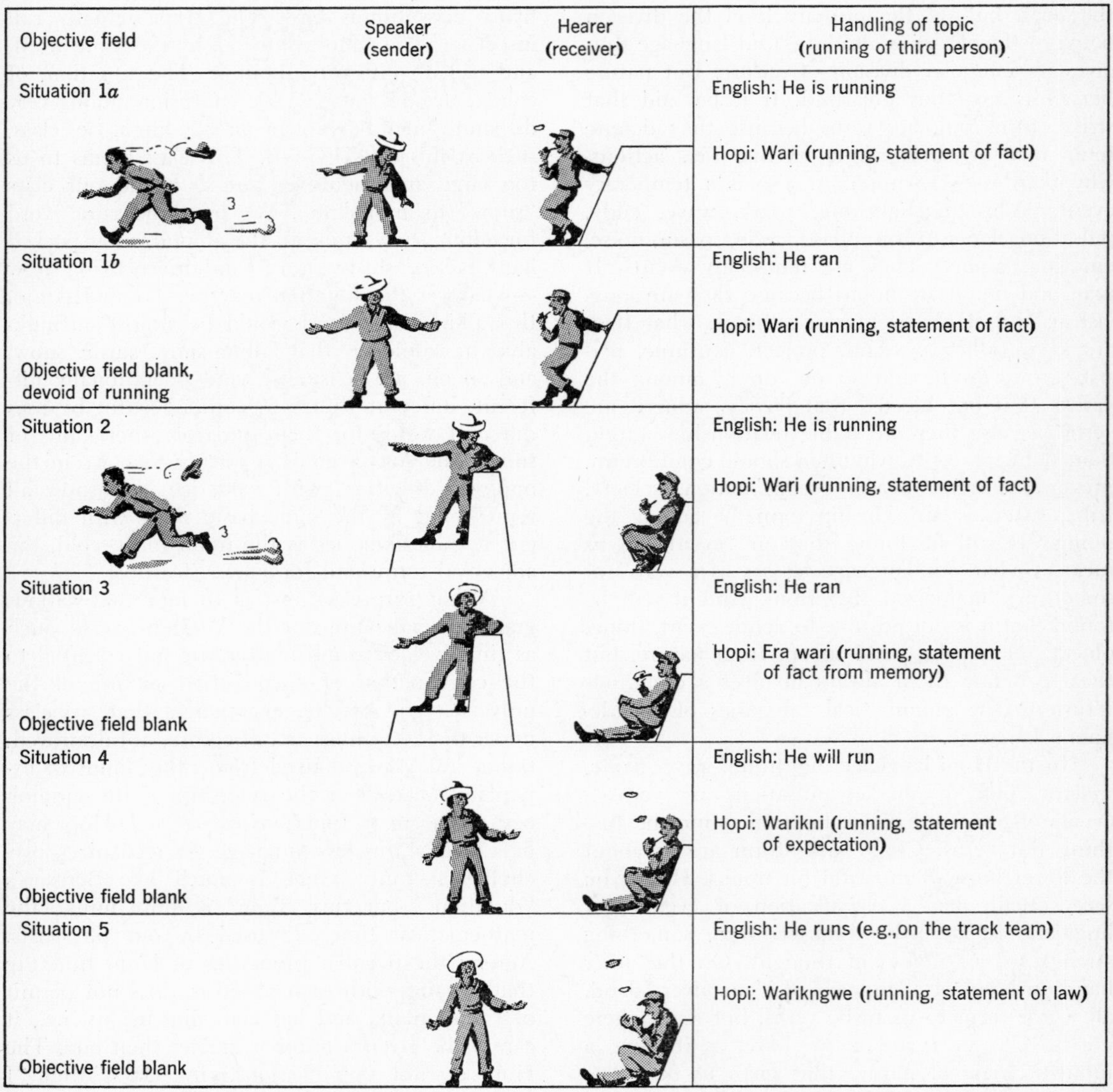

Objective field	Speaker (sender)	Hearer (receiver)	Handling of topic (running of third person)
Situation 1*a*			English: He is running Hopi: Wari (running, statement of fact)
Situation 1*b* Objective field blank, devoid of running			English: He ran Hopi: Wari (running, statement of fact)
Situation 2			English: He is running Hopi: Wari (running, statement of fact)
Situation 3 Objective field blank			English: He ran Hopi: Era wari (running, statement of fact from memory)
Situation 4 Objective field blank			English: He will run Hopi: Warikni (running, statement of expectation)
Situation 5 Objective field blank			English: He runs (e.g., on the track team) Hopi: Warikngwe (running, statement of law)

FIGURE 3. Contrast between a "temporal" language (English) and a "timeless" language (Hopi). What are to English differences of time are to Hopi differences in the kind of validity.

Hopi grammar, by means of its forms called aspects and modes, also makes it easy to distinguish between momentary, continued, and repeated occurrences, and to indicate the actual sequence of reported events. Thus the universe can be described without recourse to a concept of dimensional time. How would a physics constructed along these lines work, with no T (time) in its equations? Perfectly, as far as I can see, though of course it would require different ideology and perhaps different mathematics. Of course V (velocity) would have to go too. The Hopi language has no word really equivalent to our "speed" or "rapid." What translates these terms is usually a word meaning intense or very, accompanying any verb of motion. Here is a clew to the nature of our new physics. We may have to introduce a new term I, intensity. Every thing and event will have an I, whether we regard the thing or event as moving or as just enduring or being. Perhaps the I of an electric charge will turn out to be its voltage, or potential. We shall use clocks to measure some intensities, or, rather, some *relative* intensities, for the absolute intensity of anything will be meaningless. Our old friend acceleration will still be there but doubtless under a new name. We shall perhaps call it V, meaning not velocity but variation. Perhaps all growths and accumulations will be regarded as V's. We should not have the concept of rate in the temporal sense, since, like velocity, rate introduces a mathematical and linguistic time. Of course we know that all measurements are ratios, but the measurements of intensities made by comparison with the standard intensity of a clock or a planet we do not treat as ratios, any more than we so treat a distance made by comparison with a yardstick.

A scientist from another culture that used time and velocity would have great difficulty in getting us to understand these concepts. We should talk about the intensity of a chemical reaction; he would speak of its velocity or its rate, which words we should at first think were simply words for intensity in his language. Likewise, he at first would think that intensity was simply our own word for velocity. At first we should agree, later we should begin to disagree, and it might dawn upon both sides that different systems of rationalization were being used. He would find it very hard to make us understand what he really meant by velocity of a chemical reaction.

We should have no words that would fit. He would try to explain it by likening it to a running horse, to the difference between a good horse and a lazy horse. We should try to show him, with a superior laugh, that his analogy also was a matter of different intensities, aside from which there was little similarity between a horse and a chemical reaction in a beaker. We should point out that a running horse is moving relative to the ground, whereas the material in the beaker is at rest.

One significant contribution to science from the linguistic point of view may be the greater development of our sense of perspective. We shall no longer be able to see a few recent dialects of the Indo-European family, and the rationalizing techniques elaborated from their patterns, as the apex of the evolution of the human mind; nor their present wide spread as due to any survival from fitness or to anything but a few events of history—events that could be called fortunate only from the parochial point of view of the favored parties. They, and our own thought processes with them, can no longer be envisioned as spanning the gamut of reason and knowledge but only as one constellation in a galactic expanse. A fair realization of the incredible degree of diversity of linguistic system that ranges over the globe leaves one with an inescapable feeling that the human spirit is inconceivably old; that the few thousand years of history covered by our written records are no more than the thickness of a pencil mark on the scale that measures our past experience on this planet; that the events of these recent millenniums spell nothing in any evolutionary wise, that the race has taken no sudden spurt, achieved no commanding synthesis during recent millenniums, but has only played a little with a few of the linguistic formulations and views of nature bequeathed from an inexpressibly longer past. Yet neither this feeling nor the sense of precarious dependence of all we know upon linguistic tools which themselves are largely unknown need be discouraging to science but should, rather, foster that humility which accompanies the true scientific spirit, and thus forbid that arrogance of the mind which hinders real scientific curiosity and detachment.

In short, human beings live in a world one constituent of which is their cultural tradition.

Language is perhaps the clearest illustration of this point, but nonverbal behavior and cultural artifacts also communicate shared meanings. If New York City were destroyed in a nuclear war, archeologists five centuries hence might learn a little about American life from the material objects found in the ruins: houses, clothes, toothbrushes, typewriters, boxes of cigars, diamond rings, automobiles, and fluorescent lights. They would infer from typewriters, for example, that written communications were common. If the streets were sufficiently intact for the distribution of mailboxes to be observed, further inferences could be made about the communications habits of New Yorkers. Thus, cultural meanings are to some extent encapsulated in physical objects—but never completely.

A SPECIAL CASE OF SYMBOLIC COMMUNICATION: EXPRESSIVE SYMBOLS

Knowing that New Yorkers clean their teeth with toothbrushes would not make clear the full meaning of the morning and evening ritual. Brushing teeth is more than dental hygiene just as eating caviar is more than reducing hunger pangs; both are rituals of different kinds. The physical artifact is a good clue to one level of meaning, especially when the main significance is utilitarian, as is the case with a chair or a pot. But there is at least a second level of meaning: the significance of the physical object for defining the person using it. Thus, a red Cadillac convertible is not only a means of transport; it is also a way for its driver to communicate to others his youthful, adventurous image of himself. Some material objects are better understood on this second level of meaning than on the first. Consider the cigarette from this point of view. What is the 13-year-old boy communicating to the world by puffing on a cigarette? That he is an adult? That he is rough and tough? That he is sophisticated? True, each 13-year-old boy communicates a somewhat different message, but the range of meanings is limited by the significance of the cigarette in American culture.

Advertising agencies are well aware that cigarettes, liquor, automobiles, soft drinks, perfume, and virtually every other commodity have characteristic meanings to potential buyers. Thus, Coca-Cola evokes one "product image" and Ford Thunderbirds another.[4] That is to say, one of the main objectives of the advertising industry is to develop favorable "product images" for its clients. If an unfavorable image develops inadvertently, the advertising agency handling the account seeks to change it. For example, when scientific studies demonstrated a relationship between cigarette smoking and lung cancer, new brands of cigarettes were developed with filter tips. Sales were poor, however, because a filter-tipped cigarette had a *female* product image, and men would not buy them. Whereupon one tobacco company launched a massive advertising campaign featuring a tattooed Marlboro Man smoking filter-tipped cigarettes. Apparently the meaning of smoking filter-tipped cigarettes changed. A virile image of the Marlboro smoker developed in American culture. At any rate, sales boomed. The cigar industry has an equally dramatic history of cultural ups and downs.

The Changing Meaning of Cigars

Reprinted by permission. From Keith Monroe, "They Made the Cigar Respectable," *Harper's Magazine*, Vol. 210, February 1955, pp. 37–41.

There were cigar stores in America before the Revolution. One in Lancaster, Pennsylvania, was opened in 1770 and is still owned by the same family. The earliest cigar-makers in this country were Colonial dames, who rolled them by hand and sold them to itinerant peddlers for pin money. These good wives sampled their own wares as a matter of course. In colonial days cigar-smoking was no less ladylike than cigarette-smoking is today.

The first world war came closer to killing the cigar than any other event had. During that war, men switched to cigarettes. Until then the cigarette had seemed vaguely degenerate. Almost no-

[4] Martin Mayer, *Madison Avenue, U.S.A.*, New York: Harper, 1958.

body smoked it except mysterious Orientals, absinthe drinkers, Tenderloin girls, and other slinky characters. But the doughboys, burdened with bulkier equipment than any warriors since the Crusades, discovered the advantages of the handy little pack in an outside pocket. They learned to enjoy a quick puff at odd moments in the trenches. Suddenly a cigarette was a he-man's pleasure.

This trend started by default, because cigars weren't in the field. Service men had yearned for cigars in the early months of the war, so Washington had ordered millions for distribution to the armed forces. Unfortunately its policy was to buy from the lowest bidders.

"Many bidders for cigar contracts," the Cigar Institute of America records bitterly, "were neither experienced nor reputable. It was their practice to produce something that had the appearance of a cigar, deliver it to government depots, then disappear with their profit. Much of this product was in no condition for anything but the incinerator. It was moldy or dried or wormy, or the most sordid combination of assorted vegetables and wrapping paper."

So the AEF tried cigarettes. Soon all the armies of the Allied and the Central Powers were smoking them too. Cigarette manufacturers shrewdly reinvested their profits in massive advertising and distribution drives which led to complete saturation of their markets.

By 1920 they were strong enough to suggest that women might smoke too. They began cautiously, with advertisements which showed winsome and fashionable girls imploring men to "Blow Some My Way." Finally they risked a picture of a girl actually smoking. Another barrier between the sexes fell, and millions of women bought cigarettes.

Meanwhile, trainloads of war-surplus cigars were being dumped on civilians. Retailers put baskets of cigars in their stores with signs like "Take a handful for 5 cents" and "Free cigars with every purchase." Only the most hardened roughnecks could smoke them at any price. A cigar in the mouth became the mark of a tough mug.

The infant movie industry noticed this. Thrifty casting directors realized they didn't need a good actor to play a house detective, gangster, or ward heeler. All they needed was a $5-a-day extra with plug hat and cigar.

Movie audiences learned to identify the cigar-smoker as the villain. The impact of Hollywood on our folkways has been felt many times. This time it knocked cigars out the mouths of almost everyone except Grandpa. Without malice aforethought, the movie-makers nearly finished off the cigar-makers.

Dealers buried cigars on bottom counters, and stopped bothering to humidify them. Four of every five cigar factories closed. In 1933 most of the remaining manufacturers sat down in one room to form the Cigar Manufacturers Association.

THE INDIRECT APPROACH

They were a jealous and suspicious crowd: Cubans, Puerto Ricans, New Yorkers and Southerners and New Englanders. Each considered his product a work of art, and was as egoistic as a chef or a novelist. No one would agree to anything smacking of standardization. No system of classifying cigar shapes or sizes would suit them —nor has, to this day. "Perfecto" or "Panatela" can mean almost anything in length and thickness, depending on which company is doing the labeling.

However, the manufacturers did agree to hire a market-research man. But when he recommended spending $150,000 on publicity to make cigar-smoking fashionable, the CMA shuddered and voted him down.

Another two years passed. Cigars were becoming as old-fashioned as chin whiskers. Then the sales curve took a feeble turn upward. Why? Some tobacco men said cigar sales had followed the prosperity graph downward, and now would follow it up again. Others noted that Cremo, Dutch Masters, and Bayuk Phillies had lashed out on their own with vigorous advertising; perhaps they were pulling the whole industry upward.

Not until 1940, when the "national defense" boom had failed to bring prosperity to them, did the cigar-makers pull out their checkbooks and agree on joint, bold action. They would finance a subtle but widespread promotion to stop Americans' drift away from cigars.

The manufacturers rented offices in Rockefeller Center, established the Cigar Institute of America, and hired a manager: Berthold Nussbaum, an adman who had wrestled for years with cigar-company accounts.

Mr. Nussbaum remembered the blunder of the movie men, who wasted vast sums bellowing

"Movies Are Your Best Entertainment." (Their billboards, banners, radio commercials, and newspaper pages were hastily canceled when someone pointed out that the initials of the slogan spelled MAYBE. But even when reborn as "Motion Pictures Are Your Best Entertainment" the campaign flopped.) He knew that a blatant smoke-more-cigars theme would merely remind people that few cigars were being smoked.

When the meat packers had wanted to sell more bacon, he remembered, they had sought the advice of the legendary Ivy Lee, a public-relations counsel who believed in persuasion by indirection. Mr. Lee had sprinkled the newspapers with statements from doctors urging people to eat bigger breakfasts. The doctors never mentioned bacon. But millions of people bought bacon, because a big breakfast usually includes bacon and eggs.

Mr. Nussbaum devised an even more oblique approach. His campaign did not urge anybody to do anything. Instead he sent emissaries to newspaper offices, empty-handed. They bore no mimeographed press releases, no invitations to press conferences. They had nothing in writing—but they discreetly passed the word to news photographers that there would be cash prizes each month for the best published photos of people smoking cigars.

Cameramen, who had previously suggested to a cigar-smoking subject that he hide his cigar before posing, now decided that he looked better with cigar. They sometimes went so far as to offer him one if he didn't have it. News pictures began to show cigars in the mouths of the Duke of Windsor, Lauritz Melchior, Darryl Zanuck, Benny Goodman. When American wire-service men photographed Winston Churchill, they waited patiently for chances to catch him with cigar in teeth.

By text as well as by photo, cigars eased into newspapers and magazines. Cigar Institute agents had begun feeding copy to editors. The nation heard cigars mentioned casually amid the thunder of big games. There were reminders of Churchill's fifteen cigars a day; of the five-dollar Havanas Coolidge had cherished, and the humidor Roosevelt kept for distinguished visitors; of Babe Ruth's passion for expensive Perfectos, and Douglas MacArthur's habit of sitting down with a cigar to mull a military problem.

Cigar sales showed a walloping increase of one

billion in 1941. Mr. Nussbaum died of a heart attack the week before Pearl Harbor, but the manufacturers kept their campaign rolling. As their new manager they picked Harry W. McHose, fresh from Lexington, Kentucky, where he had been a publicity man for American Tobacco Company during the government's monopoly suit against cigarette manufacturers.

CIGARS ARE FOR HEROES

Mr. McHose saw that the new war threatened final ruin of the cigar business if the government repeated its 1917 policy. He persuaded Washington to buy only from established cigar-makers. Cigars for the armed forces were as good as those for civilians, and service men asked for more and more. The first Allied soldier to land in France was reported to be a young American paratrooper who arrived bolt upright with a lighted cigar in his mouth. The Cigar Institute, naturally, prevented this incident from being overlooked.

By 1944 there was a world-wide cigar shortage. Manufacturers could not keep up with demand. They had only 36,000 factory workers, with no hope of hiring more while the war lasted. But they knew that even if they made enough cigars for everyone who wanted them, sales would be far below the eight-billion peak of 1910. Mr. McHose kept hatching ideas.

He had plenty of problems. Younger men by no means overwhelmed cigar counters. Women still complained about the "vile smell." Hollywood still used cigars incessantly as a prop for heavies.

Mr. McHose begged Hollywood to stop putting stogies in the mouths of Edward G. Robinson and his ilk. Hollywood paid no attention. Finally he loaded a briefcase and stormed the studios in person.

He showed movie magnates a tabulation which revealed that 27,500,000 people a week passed cigar counters near theaters. "Whenever you make a movie with a good cigar scene," he offered, "I'll put posters advertising it on 25,000 cigar counters across the nation. Free of charge."

Free advertising is meat and drink to showmen. Hollywood heavies stopped smoking, and heroes started. Tyrone Power puffed cigar smoke all over the screen in "Blood and Sand." So did Gary Cooper as Sergeant York. When the Cigar Institute heard that Hollywood was filming

George Gershwin's life story, it hastened to concoct twenty-five pages of alleged historical data about Gershwin's cigar-smoking. The subsequent movies showed Gershwin wreathed in smoke at each high point of triumph or delight. In "Saratoga Trunk," Gary Cooper flourished Havanas intermittently, and Ingrid Bergman cooed, "A house isn't really a house unless it has about it the scent of a good cigar after breakfast."

If they thought about it at all, men may have been puzzled that cigar counters were all flaunting movie posters. But movie patronage picked up. By the end of 1947 the Cigar Institute was able to boast that forty major movies of that year contained "good cigar scenes" and that "Seldom, if ever, is a cigar misused today in action or dialogue."

Mr. McHose combed literature for endorsements of cigars. Robert Louis Stevenson, he found, had advised women never to marry a non-smoker. Bert Leston Taylor had suggested that when things go wrong it is a good idea to "meditate on interstellar spaces,/ And smoke a mild seegar." Bulwer-Lytton called the cigar "as great a comfort to a man as a good cry to a woman." Thackeray called it "a kind companion, a gentle stimulant, an amiable anodyne, a cementer of friendship." Kipling wrote "A woman is only a woman, but a good cigar is a smoke!"

People softened up toward cigars. Without analyzing why, men began smoking them and women did not protest. Cigar missionaries kept the vogue growing. Boxes of cigars became prizes on radio shows. Store-window displays urged cigars for Father's Day and Christmas. Service clubs and American Legion posts presented cigars to boys entering the armed forces. Elks gave them away to new fathers.

The extent to which advertising agencies are successful in changing the meaning of commodities for consumers is not clear. Maybe cigars would have come back into popular favor without the efforts of the Cigar Institute of America. Maybe filter-tipped cigarettes would have been adopted by American men without the Marlboro Man. That such efforts are made at all is an indication that meanings *do* change with the passage of time; the advertising industry simply tries to guide cultural change in the interests of its clients.

A more significant cultural change than that which increased the acceptability of the cigar is occurring in relation to skin color. Whereas a century ago the meaning to white Americans of a darkly pigmented skin was "slave" or "biologically inferior person," now pigmentation is less likely to be regarded as an index of social worth. There are many reasons for this cultural change, including the increased contact of Americans with colored persons from the nations of Asia and Africa. However, most students of race relations agree that a factor in the changed meaning of pigmentation is scientific research. Anthropologists have demonstrated the impurity of all so-called pure races.[5] Psychologists have demonstrated the effect of the sociocultural milieu in changing supposedly unchangeable characteristics like the Intelligence Quotient.[6] And sociologists have explained how it was possible for unprejudiced whites to observe "evidence" of Negro inferiority without realizing that white prejudices indirectly produced it.[7]

THE SELF-FULFILLING PROPHECY: A FACTOR IN THE STABILITY OF CULTURAL PREJUDICES

The sociological contribution to the re-evaluation of pigmentation is an instance of the effect of scientific knowledge on the American concept of "race," but it has more general significance. The principle of the *self-fulfilling prophecy* accounts for the stability of cultural meanings in other aspects of social life. A self-fulfilling prophecy is a cultural definition, initially untrue, which affects interactions in such a way as to become valid. Take the belief in the inherent inferiority of darkly pigmented people. When Americans believed this to be true, Negroes could be enslaved, denied op-

[5] Franz Boas, *The Mind of Primitive Man*, rev. ed., New York: Macmillan, 1938; Ruth Benedict, *Race: Science and Politics*, New York: Modern Age Books, 1940.
[6] Otto Klineberg, *Negro Intelligence and Selective Migration*, New York: Columbia University Press, 1935.
[7] Robert K. Merton, "The Self-Fulfilling Prophecy," *Antioch Review*, Vol. 8, June 1948, pp. 193–210.

portunities for education, and relegated to service and menial occupations. Even after emancipation, these cultural definitions lingered on and disturbed the balance of the Negro family.[8] Negro women had a better chance of getting jobs as domestic servants than Negro men had of being employed in factories and offices. As a result, women were more often the breadwinners in Negro families —and more often the authority figures. A Negro man not crucial to the economic stability of his family was more likely to desert, and his wife was more likely to ask him to leave the household. Thus, the broken family has been more characteristic of Negro than of white Americans.

For related reasons, Negroes have higher venereal disease rates than whites, higher delinquency rates, higher rates of illegitimacy, and higher rates of mental illness.[9] But it would be improper to infer from this greater incidence of social pathology among Negroes that the initial belief in their inferiority was valid. What happened rather was that belief in their inferiority led to their being given fewer opportunities than whites of no greater ability. The pathologies resulted from lack of opportunities, not from the correctness of the initial belief in Negro inferiority. In short, cultural definitions can create self-fulfilling prophecies.

Fulfillment of the prophecy reinforces the original definition of the situation, not only with regard to *racial* stereotypes but also under any circumstances where a widely shared belief generates its own supporting evidence. A folk notion maintains, for example, that redheaded persons have fiery tempers. If this interpretation of red hair results in a general expectation that redheaded persons cannot control themselves as well as other people, redheads may be encouraged to live up to their reputations. It then becomes difficult to persuade the public that there is no biological connection between the gene controlling hair color and the complex emotional reactions involved in a temper tantrum. Experience appears to confirm the folk belief. In the case of American racial stereotypes, the cumulative impact of anthropological, psychological, and sociological opinions has denied intellectual respectability to the old meaning of pigmentation.[10] Certainly it *cannot* be said that skin color is regarded as casually as eye color—even in the North and West. Yet the position of Negroes is improving, partly because of a greater willingness of whites to make available educational, occupational, and voting opportunities and partly because of new militancy on the part of Negro protest organizations.[11]

This discussion of the meaning of pigmentation points up another dimension of culture —morality. Culture not only defines the world *intellectually*. It also determines what members of the society appreciate as *pleasurable* and evaluate as *moral*. Thus, American culture teaches that ice cream sodas, romantic songs, and rides on roller coasters are pleasant and that cruelty to dogs, sexual promiscuity, and murder are immoral. Racial attitudes belong to this moral dimension. That is to say, members of White Citizens' Councils do not simply *think* that Negroes are inferior to whites; they *feel* morally outraged when the "inferiority of Negroes" is doubted. White supremacy is a sacred principle to some Southerners. It is fanatical commitment to this principle that

8 E. Franklin Frazier, *The Negro Family in the United States*, Chicago: University of Chicago Press, 1939.
9 For venereal disease statistics, see U. S. Department of Health, Education, and Welfare, Communicable Disease Center, *V.D. Fact Sheet, 1961: Basic Statistics on the Venereal Disease Problem in the United States*, Public Health Service Publication No. 341, 1961; for statistics on arrests, see U. S. Department of Justice, *Uniform Crime Reports for the United States, 1960*, Washington: Government Printing Office, 1961, pp. 95, 101; for statistics on illegitimacy, see U. S. Bureau of the Census, *Statistical Abstract of the United States: 1962*, Washington: Government Printing Office, 1962, p. 57; for statistics on mental hospital patients, see U. S. Bureau of the Census, *Special Report on Institutional Population*, Vol. IV, Part 2, Chap. C, Washington: Government Printing Office, 1953, p. 16.

10 Gunnar Myrdal, *An American Dilemma: The Negro Problem and Modern Democracy*, New York: Harper, 1944.
11 Chapter 17 returns to this example of sociocultural change.

explains Southern lynchings, as exemplified in the Texas incident studied by Durward Pruden.

What Rape Means to White Supremacists in the South

Reprinted by permission. From Durward Pruden, "A Sociological Study of a Texas Lynching," *Studies in Sociology*, Vol. 1, Summer 1935, pp. 3–9.

One Saturday morning in the spring of the early 1930's the Negro laborer on a white man's farm, near Leeville, Texas, came to his employer's house to collect his wages. On being told by the farmer's wife that her husband had gone to town and had not left the wages, the Negro, disappointed, left the house, but returned shortly with a shotgun, forced the woman into her bedroom, and assaulted her several times. Fearing that the woman's five-year-old son in the back yard might give an alarm, the Negro went to look for him, but first tied his victim to the bed, telling her he would return soon. She broke loose and fled across a field to a neighbor's house where the sheriff was telephoned. Meanwhile, some men came walking along the road, and the Negro fled toward a creek bottom.

Although the above is the commonly accepted story of the crime, there are other versions, as is frequently the case in charges of this nature. Most of the Leeville Negroes and some whites believe that no assault occurred. Medical records show that the illicit relationship did occur.

THE ARREST AND BEGINNINGS OF MOB ACTION

One deputy sheriff came to the scene and arrested the Negro, who, it is claimed, fired at him. The Negro confessed, agreed to plead guilty, waived all rights, and was secreted in a jail in a town some miles distant from Leeville. The next Monday night a small group of men and boys loitered near the Leeville jail. By Tuesday many exaggerated versions of the details of the assault were being repeated on the street. Tuesday night a large group of boys and men appeared at the jail and demanded the Negro. They refused to leave until the sheriff allowed some of their leaders to go through the jail and see that the Negro was not there. There were no more attempts at mob action until the next Friday, the date set for the trial.

THE ATTEMPT AT TRIAL

On the morning of the trial many people came to the Leeville business center, both local residents and others from farms and small communities of the adjacent trading area. The judge refused to change venue, but had four Texas Rangers present to guard the court. The Rangers took the Negro into the courthouse early in the morning before the crowd gathered. All morning, as the jury was being selected, the crowd around the courtyard and in the courthouse halls grew larger and more belligerent. Just as the situation was hanging in the balance between an orderly trial and a riot, a rumor was circulated that the governor of the state had telegraphed the Rangers not to shoot anyone in trying to protect the Negro. Although the rumor was untrue, yet it was accepted by the mob and so encouraged its members as to make the Rangers practically helpless without extensive bloodshed. The precipitating event which changed the huge, curious crowd into a vicious and active mob, was the bringing of the woman from the hospital to the courthouse in an ambulance, and carrying her on a stretcher through the crowd into the courtroom. This was about 1 o'clock. After that the mob went wild. It broke in the courtroom, and was repeatedly driven back by the Rangers, with drawn guns and tear gas. Several shots were fired. The judge at last decided to change venue, and the Negro was hurried into the second-floor, fireproof vault room of the district clerk's office.

BURNING THE COURTHOUSE

When the mob saw that the Rangers were determined to hold the courthouse, they determined to burn it. A group of teen-age boys, led by an excited and vociferous woman dressed in red, broke out the courthouse windows with rocks, threw gasoline in, and fired the building about 2:30 in the afternoon. The fire department used its ladders to carry the people from the second-floor courtroom. There was some objection to the rescuing of the judge, county attorney, sheriffs, and Rangers; but, finally, all were removed except the Negro in the district clerk's vault. As the firemen tried to fight the blaze during the afternoon, the mob cut the fire hose and sometimes attacked the firemen.

THE BATTLE WITH THE SOLDIERS

The Rangers, who had left the courthouse, telephoned the governor for assistance, and about 4 P.M. a small detachment of National Guards arrived from a neighboring town. They marched around the falling ruins of the courthouse, saw that they were too far outnumbered to restore order, and returned home. About 6 P.M. a larger unit of 52 soldiers from a large city to the south arrived. Leaving a detachment to garrison their headquarters at the county jail three blocks west of the courthouse, the remainder deployed around the smoldering courthouse ruins to push the crowd back from the hanging walls. As darkness fell, the spirit of the mob became uglier. They reasoned that if the governor would not let the Rangers shoot at them, he surely would not let soldiers shoot either. They began to abuse the soldiers, and soon a pitched battle ensued in which the troops were forced to retreat the three blocks back to the jail, followed by the angry mob throwing bricks, rocks, pieces of timber, chunks of concrete, broken bottles, sticks of dynamite, etc. Several soldiers were badly cut and beaten, others had their rifles taken from them, and some of the mobsters received minor bullet wounds. Reinforced by their comrades at the jail the troops made a determined stand there and started shooting into the air. The mob then withdrew and returned to the courthouse square to open the vault and get the Negro, about whose condition there was much speculation.

From around 8 P.M. to midnight various efforts were made to open the upper room of the great two story steel and cement vault. A gigantic crowd packed the entire square and side streets. Finally, the mob leaders confiscated an acetylene torch; and, working from the top of a ladder, were able to open a hole large enough to insert dynamite and blow out a hole which the mob leader entered and threw out the dead body of the Negro.

The corpse was dragged behind a Ford roadster containing two young men and two girls to the Negro business section, a distance of seven blocks. Thousands of people followed in a frenzied midnight parade, yelling, singing, tooting horns of automobiles. At an important corner in the Negro section the body was drawn up to the limb of a cottonwood tree in front of a Negro drug store. The store was forcibly entered and ran-

sacked, the money and valuables pocketed, confections passed out to the crowd, and the furniture and furnishing piled under the Negro's body for fuel. Some versions have it that the leader unsexed the Negro in the presence of the crowd of men, women, and children before lighting the fire. The crowd gave a mighty cheer as flames enveloped the Negro's body. After the burning of the body some of the crowd—the onlookers—went home, but the more vicious elements continued ransacking and burning with gasoline the Negro business places including a hotel, drug store, two cafes, two barber shops, two dentists' offices, a doctor's office, two undertaking establishments, an Odd Fellows' Hall, a Knights of Pythias building, a theater, a lawyer's office, a life insurance office, a cleaning and pressing shop, and several residences. They swore that they would "run all the damn niggers out of Leeville." Many of the remaining mob were very drunk. The fire department was not permitted to put any water on the fires except on nearby property owned by whites.

EXODUS OF THE NEGROES

Meanwhile all of Leeville's 2,000 Negro inhabitants were under cover. Some were given refuge by white friends and employers in Leeville; the others, with their old people, their sick, their babies and children, hurried away in old automobiles, wagons, buggies, on mules, and by foot. Some reached Negro friends in adjacent cities; less fortunate individuals spent a harrowing night in ditches, ravines, clumps of bushes, under houses or bridges, etc.

MARTIAL LAW

About 1 o'clock Saturday morning 150 more National Guards arrived with machine guns, rifles, side arms, and tear gas. They, together with the previously mentioned soldiers at the jail, were at last able to break the mob and disperse it. At 3 A.M. more troops arrived. At dawn the soldiers had the town under control with machine guns mounted at strategic points. Martial law was declared and arrests began. During the next few days there were continual rumors that the mob would reassemble on the outskirts of town at dark, make a new march against the soldiers, and complete their avowed job of burning all Negro dwellings and driving their occupants out of town permanently. The armed force was increased to 419 men and more arms were brought in, but nothing more of importance occurred. A notice was found tacked on a white employer's office door warning him to fire his Negro workers and engage whites. Warnings to leave town were discovered on some Negro dwellings. A military court of investigation turned over 29 persons and 600 typewritten pages of confidential evidence to the civil authorities, who indicted 14 men and boys. They were removed to jail in the large metropolitan city to the south; a citizens' committee to maintain order was organized, and the troops left Leeville after being there nine days.

LEGAL DISPOSITIONS

After many seemingly unnecessary delays on the part of the Leeville county attorney, the rioters were brought to trial in the aforementioned metropolitan city, where, to the surprise and chagrin of the judge, a jury of urban men could not be found who would agree to convict even if the defendants were proved guilty. On another change of venue to the state capital city, one young man was finally given a two-year term for arson. This was more than a year after the lynching. The defendant was already at odds with the law on other charges. Before ending his sentence he was released by the governor on petition of Leeville citizens on account of the illness of his mother. The other 13 men were never tried.

Why did the lynching occur? Clearly, the lynch mob felt outraged over what the Negro laborer was alleged to have done. But why? Because they considered rape a horrifying act? This could not be the explanation because *Negro* men who rape *Negro* women do not arouse comparable hostility. Nor do *white* men who rape *white* women (or Negro women) get lynched. As a matter of fact, Pruden mentioned in a part of his account which is not reprinted that one of the leaders of the mob "later had trouble with a farmer because he raped the farmer's wife." Why is it that the rape of a *white* woman by a *Negro* man taps a special reservoir of indignation? In order to answer this question satisfactorily, one must understand how white supremacy is traditionally symbolized in the South. The following

rules of etiquette are observed by those who subscribe to the implicit assumption of Negro inferiority.

Whites should never shake hands with Negroes on being introduced. No matter how well educated the Negro, no matter what his professional attainments, white persons should always address him by his first name. Negroes, on the other hand, must address whites as "Mr.," "Mrs.," or "Miss."

Whites should never eat a meal with Negroes.

Negroes should sit in the *back* of a bus, train, or street car, whites in the *front*.

A white person must not marry a Negro.

These rules of etiquette used to be strictly enforced. Negroes who violated them were suspected of getting "uppity," that is, of resenting the inferior place assigned to them by whites. The penalties for not knowing "their place" was often harassment and sometimes violence. In the context of these rules for symbolizing social inferiority, the rape of a white woman by a Negro man is not so much a sexual act as an attack on the system of white supremacy. For a white supremacist, it is presumptuous for a Negro man to stare at a white woman; it is impertinent for him to speak to her on a first-name basis; it is unthinkable to ask her for a date, much less to aspire to sexual relations with her. But to force sexual relations upon her is simply inconceivable. The degree of coercion exerted on the alleged victim was not examined too closely in Leeville, as it would have been in a Northern court, because the mere existence of a sexual act between a Negro man and a white woman was defined as an attack on white supremacy. The *men* felt violated; the woman became almost a secondary issue.

ETIQUETTE: THE SYMBOLIC
EXPRESSION OF MORAL JUDGMENTS

It may seem paradoxical to conclude that a lynching resulted from a breach of etiquette but only if etiquette is construed as trivial. If etiquette is thought of as the symbolic expression of important moral judgments, of what is good and bad, of who is important and who unimportant, then a breach of etiquette can be a very serious matter. Professor Erving Goffman devised an ingenious natural experiment to gauge the importance of social ceremonies. In the following article he reports the violations of conventional social rituals on two wards of a mental hospital.

The Mental Hospital: Where Rules of Etiquette Are Not Followed

Reprinted by permission. From Erving Goffman, "The Nature of Deference and Demeanor," *American Anthropologist*, Vol. 58, June 1956, pp. 474–502.

Data for the paper are drawn chiefly from a brief observational study of mental patients in a modern research hospital. I use these data on the assumption that a logical place to learn about personal proprieties is among persons who have been locked up for spectacularly failing to maintain them. Their infractions of propriety occur in the confines of a ward, but the rules broken are quite general ones, leading us outward from the ward to a general study of our Anglo-American society. . . .

An act that is subject to a rule of conduct is, then, a communication, for it represents a way in which selves are confirmed—both the self for which the rule is an obligation and the self for which it is an expectation. An act that is subject to rules of conduct but does not conform to them is also a communication—often even more so— for infractions make news and often in such a way as to disconfirm the selves of the participants. Thus rules of conduct transform both action and inaction into expression, and whether the individual abides by the rules or breaks them, something significant is likely to be communicated. For example, in the wards under study, each research psychiatrist tended to expect his patients to come regularly for their therapeutic hours. When patients fulfilled this obligation, they showed that they appreciated their need for treatment and that their psychiatrist was the sort of person who could establish a "good relation" with patients. When a patient declined to attend

his therapeutic hour, others on the ward tended to feel that he was "too sick" to know what was good for him, and that perhaps his psychiatrist was not the sort of person who was good at establishing relationships. Whether patients did or did not attend their hours, something of importance about them and their psychiatrist tended to be communicated to the staff and to other patients on the ward. . . .

Students of society have distinguished in several ways among types of rules, as for example, between formal and informal rules; for this paper, however, the important distinction is that between substance and ceremony. A substantive rule is one which guides conduct in regard to matters felt to have significance in their own right, apart from what the infraction or maintenance of the rule expresses about the selves of the persons involved. Thus, when an individual refrains from stealing from others, he upholds a substantive rule which primarily serves to protect the property of these others and only incidentally functions to protect the image they have of themselves as persons with proprietary rights. The expressive implications of substantive rules are officially considered to be secondary; this appearance must be maintained, even though in some special situations everyone may sense that the participants were primarily concerned with expression.

A ceremonial rule is one which guides conduct in matters felt to have secondary or even no significance in their own right, having their primary importance—officially anyway—as a conventionalized means of communication by which the individual expresses his character or conveys his appreciation of the other participants in the situation. This usage departs from the everyday one, where "ceremony" tends to imply a highly specified, extended sequence of symbolic action performed by august actors on solemn occasions when religious sentiments are likely to be invoked.

In all societies rules of conduct tend to be organized into codes which guarantee that everyone acts appropriately and receives his due. In our society the code which governs substantive rules and substantive expressions comprises our law, morality, and ethics, while the code which governs ceremonial rules and ceremonial expressions is incorporated in what we call etiquette. All of our institutions have both kinds of codes, but in this paper attention will be restricted to the ceremonial one.

The acts or events, that is, the sign-vehicles or tokens which carry ceremonial messages, are remarkably various in character. They may be linguistic, as when an individual makes a statement of praise or depreciation regarding self or other, and does so in a particular language and intonation; gestural, as when the physical bearing of an individual conveys insolence or obsequiousness; spatial, as when an individual precedes another through the door, or sits on his right instead of his left; task-embedded, as when an individual accepts a task graciously and performs it in the presence of others with aplomb and dexterity; part of the communication structure, as when an individual speaks more frequently than the others, or receives more attentiveness than they do. The important point is that ceremonial activity, like substantive activity, is an analytical element referring to a component or function of action, not to concrete empirical action itself. While some activity that has a ceremonial component does not seem to have an appreciable substantive one, we find that all activity that is primarily substantive in significance will nevertheless carry some ceremonial meaning, provided that its performance is perceived in some way by others. The manner in which the activity is performed, or the momentary interruptions that are allowed so as to exchange minor niceties, will infuse the instrumentally oriented situation with ceremonial significance. . . .

Ceremonial activity seems to contain certain basic components. As suggested, a main object of this paper will be to delineate two of these components, deference and demeanor, and to clarify the distinction between them.

DEFERENCE

By deference I shall refer to that component of activity which functions as a symbolic means by which appreciation is regularly conveyed *to* a recipient *of* this recipient, or of something of which this recipient is taken as a symbol, extension, or agent. These marks of devotion represent ways in which an actor celebrates and confirms his relation to a recipient. In some cases, both actor and recipient may not really be individuals at all, as when two ships greet each other with four short whistle blasts when passing. In some cases, the actor is an individual but the recipient is some object or idol, as when a sailor salutes the quarterdeck upon boarding ship, or

when a Catholic genuflects to the altar. I shall only be concerned, however, with the kind of deference that occurs when both actor and recipient are individuals, whether or not they are acting on behalf of something other than themselves. Such ceremonial activity is perhaps seen most clearly in the little salutations, compliments, and apologies which punctuate social intercourse, and may be referred to as "status rituals" or "interpersonal rituals." I use the term "ritual" because this activity, however informal and secular, represents a way in which the individual must guard and design the symbolic implications of his acts while in the immediate presence of an object that has a special value for him. . . .

The individual may desire, earn, and deserve deference, but by and large he is not allowed to give it to himself, being forced to seek it from others. In seeking it from others, he finds he has added reason for seeking them out, and in turn society is given added assurance that its members will enter into interaction and relationships with one another. If the individual could give himself the deference he desired there might be a tendency for society to disintegrate into islands inhabited by solitary cultish men, each in continuous worship at his own shrine. . . .

Those who render deference to an individual may feel, of course, that they are doing this merely because he is an instance of a category, or a representative of something, and that they are giving him his due not because of what they think of him "personally" but in spite of it. Some organizations, such as the military, explicitly stress this sort of rationale for according deference, leading to an impersonal bestowal of something that is specifically directed toward the person. . . .

Where an actor need show no concern about penetrating the recipient's usual personal reserve, and need have no fear of contaminating him by any penetration into his privacy, we say that the actor is on terms of familiarity with the recipient. (The mother who feels at liberty to pick her child's nose is an extreme example.) Where the actor must show circumspection in his approach to the recipient, we speak of nonfamiliarity or respect. Rules governing conduct between two individuals may, but need not, be symmetrical in regard to to either familiarity or respect.

There appear to be some typical relations between ceremonial distance and other kinds of sociological distance. Between status equals we may expect to find interaction guided by symmetrical familiarity. Between superordinate and subordinate we may expect to find asymmetrical relations, the superordinate having the right to exercise certain familiarities which the subordinate is not allowed to reciprocate. Thus, in the research hospital, doctors tended to call nurses by their first names, while nurses responded with "polite" or "formal" address. Similarly, in American business organizations the boss may thoughtfully ask the elevator man how his children are, but this entrance into another's life may be blocked to the elevator man, who can appreciate the concern but not return it. Perhaps the clearest form of this is found in the psychiatrist-patient relation, where the psychiatrist has a right to touch on aspects of the patient's life that the patient might not even allow himself to touch upon, while of course this privilege is not reciprocated. (There are some psychoanalysts who believe it desirable to "analyze the countertransference with the patient" but this or any other familiarity on the part of the patient is strongly condemned by official psychoanalytical bodies.) Patients, especially mental ones, may not even have the right to question their doctor about his opinion of their own case; for one thing, this would bring them into too intimate a contact with an area of knowledge in which doctors invest their special apartness from the lay public which they serve.

While these correlations between ceremonial distance and other kinds of distance are typical, we must be quite clear about the fact that other relationships are often found. Thus, status equals who are not well acquainted may be on terms of reciprocal respect, not familiarity. Further, there are many organizations in America where differences in rank are seen as so great a threat to the equilibrium of the system that the ceremonial aspect of behavior functions not as a way of iconically expressing these differences but as a way of carefully counterbalancing them. In the research hospital under study, psychiatrists, psychologists, and sociologists were part of a single ceremonial group as regards first-naming, and this symmetrical familiarity apparently served to allay some feeling on the part of psychologists and sociologists that they were not equal members of the team, as indeed they were not. Similarly, in a study of small business managers, the writer (1952) found that filling-station attendants had

the right to interrupt their boss, slap him on the back, rib him, use his phone, and take other liberties, and that this ritual license seemed to provide a way in which the manager could maintain morale and keep his employees honest. We must realize that organizations that are quite similar structurally may have quite different deference styles, and that deference patterns are partly a matter of changing fashion. . . .

Violation of rules regarding privacy and separateness is a phenomenon that can be closely studied on mental wards because ordinarily there is so much of it done by patients and staff. Sometimes this results because of what are felt to be the substantive or instrumental requirements of the situation. When a mental patient checks into a hospital, an itemized account is usually made of every one of his belongings; this requires his giving himself up to others in a way that he may have learned to define as a humiliation. Periodically his effects may have to be searched in a general effort to clear the ward of "sharps," liquor, narcotics, and other contraband. The presence of a microphone known to be concealed in each patient's room and connected with a speaker in the nurses' station is an additional invasion (but one provided only in the newest hospitals); the censoring of outgoing mail is another. Psychotherapy, especially when the patient appreciates that other staff members will learn about his progress and even receive a detailed report of the case, is another such invasion; so too is the practice of having nurses and attendants "chart" the course of the patient's daily feelings and activity. Efforts of staff to "form relations" with patients, to break down periods of withdrawal in the interest of therapy, is another example. Classic forms of "nonperson treatment" are found, with staff members so little observing referential avoidance that they discuss intimacies about a patient in his presence as if he were not there at all. There will be no door to the toilet, or one that the patient cannot lock; dormitory sleeping, especially in the case of middle-class patients, is a similar encroachment on privacy. The care that is given to "very disturbed" patients in many large public hospitals leads in a similar direction, as with forced medication, cold packs applied to the naked body, or confinement while naked in an empty strongroom into which staff and patients may look. Another instance is forced feeding, whereby a frightened mute patient who may want to keep certain food out of his mouth is matched against an attendant who must see that patients are fed.

Invasions of privacy which have an instrumental technical rationale can be paralleled with others of a more purely ceremonial nature. Thus "acting out" and "psychopathic" patients are ones who can be counted on to overreach polite bounds and ask embarrassing questions of fellow-patients and staff, or proffer compliments which would not ordinarily be in their province to give, or proffer physical gestures of appreciation such as hugging or kissing, which are felt to be inappropriate. Thus, on Ward B, male staff members were plagued by such statements as "Why did you cut yourself shaving like that," "Why do you always wear the same pants, I'm getting sick of them," "Look at all the dandruff you've got." If seated by one of the patients, a male staff member might have to edge continuously away so as to keep a seemly safe distance between himself and the patient.

Some of the ways in which individuals on Ward A kept their distance were made clear in contrast to the failure of Ward B's patients to do so. On Ward A the rule that patients were to remain outside the nurses' station was observed. Patients would wait for an invitation or, as was commonly the case, stay in the doorway so that they could talk with those in the station and yet not presume upon them. It was therefore not necessary for the staff to lock the station door when a nurse was in the station. On Ward B it was not possible to keep three of the patients out of the station by request alone, and so the door had to be kept locked if privacy was to be maintained. Even then, the walls of the station were effectively battered down by continuous banging and shouting. In other words, on Ward A the protective ring that nurses and attendants drew around themselves by retreating into the station was respected by the patients, whereas on Ward B it was not. . . .

In suggesting that there are things that must be said and done to a recipient, and things that must not be said and done, it should be plain that there is an inherent opposition and conflict between these two forms of deference. To ask after an individual's health, his family's well-being, or the state of his affairs, is to present him with a sign of sympathetic concern; but in a certain way to make this presentation is to invade the individual's personal reserve, as will be made clear if an actor of wrong status asks him these questions, or if a recent event has made such a question painful to answer. As Durkheim suggested, "The human personality is a sacred thing; one dare not violate it nor infringe its bounds, while at the same time the greatest good is in communion with others." I would like to cite two ward illustrations of this inherent opposition between the two forms of deference.

On Ward A, as in other wards in the hospital, there was a "touch system." Certain categories of personnel had the privilege of expressing their affection and closeness to others by the ritual of bodily contact with them. The actor places his arms around the waist of the recipient, rubs a hand down the back of the recipient's neck, strokes the recipient's hair and forehead, or holds the recipient's hand. Sexual connotation is of course officially excluded. The most frequent form that the ritual took was for a nurse to extend such a touch-confirmation to a patient. Nonetheless, attendants, patients, and nurses formed one group in regard to touch rights, the rights being symmetrical. Any one of these individuals had a right to touch any member of his own category or any member of the other categories. (In fact some forms of touch, as in playful fighting or elbow-strength games, were intrinsically symmetrical.) Of course some members of the ward disliked the system, but this did not alter the rights of others to incorporate them into it. The familiarity implicit in such exchanges was affirmed in other ways, such as symmetrical first-naming. It may be added that in many mental hospitals, patients, attendants, and nurses do not form one group for ceremonial purposes, and the obligation of patients to accept friendly physical contact from staff is not reciprocated.

In addition to these symmetrical touch relations on the ward, there were also asymmetrical ones. The doctors touched other ranks as a means of conveying friendly support and comfort, but other ranks tended to feel that it would be presumptuous for them to reciprocate a doctor's touch, let alone initiate such a contact with a doctor.

Now it should be plain that if a touch system is to be maintained, as it is in many hospitals in America, and if members of the ward are to receive the confirmation and support this ritual system provides, then persons other than doctors coming to live or work on the ward must make themselves intimately available to the others present. Rights of apartness and inviolability which are demanded and accorded in many other establishments in our society must here be forgone, in this particular. The touch system, in short, is only possible to the degree that individuals forego the right to keep others at a physical distance.

A second illustration of the sense in which the two forms of deference act in opposition to each other turns upon the point of social participation. On Ward A there was a strong feeling of in-group solidarity among all nonmedical ranks —nurses, attendants, and patients. One way in which this was expressed was through joint participation in meals, card-games, room-visits, TV parties, occupational therapy, and outings. Ordinarily individuals were ready not only to participate in these activities but also to do so with visible pleasure and enthusiasm. One gave oneself to these occasions and through this giving the group flourished. . . .

DEMEANOR

It was suggested that the ceremonial component of concrete behavior has at least two basic elements, deference and demeanor. Deference, defined as the appreciation an individual shows of another to that other, whether through avoidance rituals or presentational rituals, has been discussed and demeanor may now be considered.

By demeanor I shall refer to that element of the individual's ceremonial behavior typically conveyed through deportment, dress, and bearing, which serves to express to those in his immediate presence that he is a person of certain desirable or undesirable qualities. In our society, the "well" or "properly" demeaned individual displays such attributes as: discretion and sincerity; modesty in claims regarding self; sportsmanship; command of speech and physical movements; self-control over his emotions, his appetites, and his desires; poise under pressure; and so forth.

When we attempt to analyze the qualities conveyed through demeanor, certain themes become apparent. The well-demeaned individual possesses the attributes popularly associated with "character training" or "socialization," these being implanted when a neophyte of any kind is housebroken. Rightly or wrongly, others tend to use such qualities diagnostically, as evidence of

what the actor is generally like at other times and as a performer of other activities. In addition, the properly demeaned individual is someone who has closed off many avenues of perception and penetration that others might take to him, and is therefore unlikely to be contaminated by them. Most importantly, perhaps, good demeanor is what is required of an actor if he is to be transformed into someone who can be relied upon to maintain himself as an interactant, poised for communication, and to act so that others do not endanger themselves by presenting themselves as interactants to him.

It should be noted once again that demeanor involves attributes derived from interpretations others make of the way in which the individual handles himself during social intercourse. The individual cannot establish these attributes for his own by verbally avowing that he possesses them, though sometimes he may rashly try to do this. (He can, however, contrive to conduct himself in such a way that others, through their interpretations of his conduct, will impute the kinds of attributes to him he would like others to see in him.) In general, then, through demeanor the individual creates an image of himself, but properly speaking this is not an image that is meant for his own eyes. Of course this should not prevent us from seeing that the individual who acts with good demeanor may do so because he places an appreciable value upon himself, and that he who fails to demean himself properly may be accused of having "no self-respect" or of holding himself too cheaply in his own eyes.

As in the case of deference, an object in the study of demeanor is to collect all the ceremonially relevant acts that a particular individual performs in the presence of each of the several persons with whom he comes in contact, to interpret these acts for the demeanor that is symbolically expressed through them, and then to piece these meanings together into an image of the individual, an image of him in others' eyes.

Rules of demeanor, like rules of deference, can be symmetrical or asymmetrical. Between social equals, symmetrical rules of demeanor seem often to be prescribed. Between unequals many variations can be found. For example, at staff meetings on the psychiatric units of the hospital, medical doctors had the privilege of swearing, changing the topic of conversation, and sitting in undignified positions; attendants, on the other hand, had the right to attend staff meetings and to ask questions during them (in line with the milieu-therapy orientation of these research units) but were implicitly expected to conduct themselves with greater circumspection than was required of doctors. (This was pointed out by a perceptive occupational therapist who claimed she was always reminded that a mild young female psychiatrist was really an M.D. by the fact that this psychiatrist exercised these prerogatives of informal demeanor.) The extreme here perhaps is the master-servant relation as seen in cases where valets and maids are required to perform in a dignified manner services of an undignified kind. Similarly, doctors had the right to saunter into the nurses' station, lounge on the station's dispensing counter, and engage in joking with the nurses; other ranks participated in this informal interaction with doctors, but only after doctors had initiated it.

On Ward A, standards of demeanor were maintained that seem to be typical in American middle-class society. The eating pace maintained at table suggested that no one present was so over-eager to eat, so little in control of impulses, so jealous of his rights, as to wolf down his food or take more than his share. At pinochle, the favorite card game, each player would coax spectators to take his hand and spectators would considerately decline the offer, expressing in this way that a passion for play had in no way overwhelmed them. Occasionally a patient appeared in the dayroom or at meals with bathrobe (a practice permitted of patients throughout the hospital) but ordinarily neat street wear was maintained, illustrating that the individual was not making his appearance before others in a lax manner or presenting too much of himself too freely. Little profanity was employed and no open sexual remarks.

On Ward B, bad demeanor (by middle-class standards) was quite common. This may be illustrated from meal-time behavior. A patient would often lunge at an extra piece of food or at least eye an extra piece covetously. Even when each individual at table was allowed to receive an equal share, over-eagerness was shown by the practice of taking all of one's share at once instead of waiting until one serving had been eaten. Occasionally a patient would come to table half-dressed. One patient frequently belched loudly at meals and was occasionally flatulent. Messy manipulation of food sometimes occurred. Swearing and cursing were common. Patients would occasionally push their chairs back from the table precipitously and bolt for another room, coming back to the table in the same violent manner. Loud sounds were sometimes made by sucking on straws in empty pop bottles. Through these activities, patients expressed to the staff and to one another that their selves were not properly demeaned ones.

These forms of misconduct are worth study because they make us aware of some aspects of good demeanor we usually take for granted; for aspects even more usually taken for granted, we must study "back" wards in typical mental hospitals. There patients are denudative, incontinent, and they openly masturbate; they scratch themselves violently; drooling occurs and a nose may run unchecked; sudden hostilities may flare up and "paranoid" immodesties be projected; speech or motor activity may occur at a manic or depressed pace, either too fast or too slow for propriety; males and females may comport themselves as if they were of the other sex or hardly old enough to have any. Such wards are of course the classic settings of bad demeanor.

A final point about demeanor may be mentioned. Whatever his motives for making a well demeaned appearance before others, it is assumed that the individual will exert his own will to do so, or that he will pliantly co-operate should it fall to someone else's lot to help him in this matter. In our society, a man combs his own hair until it gets too long, then he goes to a barber and follows instructions while it is being cut. This voluntary submission is crucial, for personal services of such a kind are done close to the very center of the individual's inviolability and can easily result in transgressions; server and served must co-operate closely if these are not to occur. If, however, an individual fails to maintain what others see as proper personal appearance, and if he refuses to co-operate with those who are charged with maintaining it for him, then the task of making him presentable against his will is likely to cost him at the moment a great deal of dignity and deference, and this in turn may create complex feelings in those who find they must cause him to pay this price. This is one of the occupational dilemmas of those employed to make children and mental patients presentable. It is easy to order attendants to "dress up" and shave male patients on visitors' day, and no doubt when this is done patients make a more favorable appearance, but while this appearance is in the process of being achieved—in the showers or the barbershop, for example—the patients may be subjected to extreme indignities.

DEFERENCE AND DEMEANOR

Deference and demeanor are analytical terms; empirically there is much overlapping of the activities to which they refer. An act through which the individual gives or withholds deference to others typically provides means by which he expresses the fact that he is a well or badly demeaned individual. Some aspects of this overlapping may be cited. First, in performing a given act of presentational deference, as in offering a guest a chair, the actor finds himself doing something that can be done with smoothness and aplomb, expressing self-control and poise, or with clumsiness and uncertainty, expressing an irresolute character. This is, as it were, an incidental and adventitious connection between deference and demeanor. It may be illustrated from recent material on doctor-patient relationships, where it is suggested that one complaint a doctor may have against some of his patients is that they do not bathe before coming for an examination; while bathing is a way of paying deference to the doctor it is at the same time a way for the patient to present himself as a clean, well demeaned person. A further illustration is found in acts such as loud talking, shouting, or singing, for these acts encroach upon the right of others to be let alone, while at the same time they illustrate a badly demeaned lack of control over one's feelings. . . .

We are to see, then, that there are many occasions when it would be improper for an individual to convey about himself what others are ready to convey about him to him, since each of these two images is a warrant and justification for the other, and not a mirror image of it. The . . . notion that the individual takes toward himself the attitude others take to him seems very much an oversimplification. Rather the individual must rely on others to complete the picture of him of which he himself is allowed to paint only certain parts. Each individual is responsible for the demeanor image of himself and the deference image of others, so that for a complete man to be expressed, individuals must hold hands in a chain of ceremony, each giving deferentially with proper demeanor to the one on the right what will be received deferentially from the one on the left. While it may be true that the individual has a unique self all his own, evidence of this possession is thoroughly a product of joint ceremonial labor, the part expressed through the individual's demeanor being no more significant than the part conveyed by others through their deferential behavior toward him.

CEREMONIAL PROFANATIONS

There are many situations and many ways in which the justice of ceremony can fail to be maintained. There are occasions when the individual finds that he is accorded deference of a misidentifying kind, whether the misidentification places him in a higher or lower position than he thinks right. There are other occasions when he finds that he is being treated more impersonally and unceremonially than he thinks proper and feels that his treatment ought to be more punctuated with acts of deference, even though these may draw attention to his subordinate status. . . .

In some psychiatric wards, face-to-face ritual profanation is a constant phenomenon. Patients may profane a staff member or a fellow-patient by spitting at him, slapping his face, throwing feces at him, tearing off his clothes, pushing him off the chair, taking food from his grasp, screaming into his face, sexually molesting him, etc. On Ward B, on occasion, Betty would slap and punch her mother's face and tramp on her mother's bare feet with heavy shoes; and abuse her, at table, with those four-letter words that middle-class children ordinarily avoid in the presence of their parents, let alone in reference to them. It should be repeated that while from the point of view of the actor these profanations may be a product of blind impulse, or have a special symbolic meaning, from the point of view of the society at large and its ceremonial idiom these are not random impulsive infractions. Rather, these acts are exactly those calculated to convey complete disrespect and contempt through symbolic means. Whatever is in the patient's mind, the throwing of feces at an attendant is a use of our ceremonial idiom that is as exquisite in its way as is a bow from the waist done with grace and a flourish. Whether he knows it or not, the patient speaks the same ritual language as his captors; he merely says what they do not wish to hear, for patient behavior which does not carry ritual meaning in terms of the daily ceremonial discourse of the staff will not be perceived by the staff at all.

In addition to profanation of others, individuals for varieties of reasons and in varieties of situations give the appearance of profaning themselves, acting in a way that seems purposely designed to destroy the image others have of them as persons worthy of deference. Ceremonial mortification of the flesh has been a theme in many social movements. What seems to be involved is not merely bad demeanor but rather the concerted efforts of an individual sensitive to high standards of demeanor to act against his own interests and exploit ceremonial arrangements by presenting himself in the worst possible light.

In many psychiatric wards, what appears to staff and other patients as self-profanation is a common occurrence. For example, female patients can be found who have systematically pulled out all the hair from their head, presenting themselves thereafter with a countenance that is guaranteed to be grotesque.

Professor Goffman's study demonstrates that the failure to use certain ceremonies on occasions when they are expected is itself a communication. The failure to respect the privacy of mental patients reflects a staff view that, by their bizarre conduct, patients have lost their status as full members of the human community. Ward B patients, who did not follow the rules of etiquette while eating, communicated their acceptance of this degraded position; they did not try to keep up appearances. Finally, the willingness of patients to use ceremonial profanations not allowed to American adults, such as spitting in the faces of staff members, was an equally clear communication. These communications were, of course, implicit; we must not exaggerate the extent to which the patients and the staff of a mental hospital understand one another intellectually. An important aspect of mental illness is communication failure. Whatever else is wrong with a patient, the most obvious symptom of his illness is the breakdown of communication with other members of his society. When a patient is described as "withdrawn" or "out of touch with reality," what

is meant is that he no longer interprets cultural symbols as other members of his society do; he has a catalog of private meanings that no one else understands.

THE CAUSES OF COMMUNICATION FAILURE IN A COMPLEX SOCIETY

Dramatic as is the communication failure of a schizophrenic or paranoid patient, communication failure is a frequent occurrence in *normal* social intercourse. Human communication is a precarious venture. It relies so heavily on symbols, and symbols are, by definition, arbitrary means of conveying meanings. The man who removes his hat on entering a church performs what is for him an act of respect in a sacred place. However, if he were an Orthodox Jew and were entering a synagogue, he would keep his hat *on* for precisely the same reason. A Christian, unaware that Jewish men cover their heads out of deference, might be shocked to see men with their hats on in a synagogue. This communication failure would result from the circumstance that the *same* symbol (uncovering the head) has *opposite* meanings in the Christian and the Jewish cultural traditions.

This is a general problem. Modern societies are so large that many subcultures coexist within them. Persons reared in the South interpret skin pigmentation differently from persons reared in the North and West. Beethoven symphonies are considered masterpieces of artistic achievement by intellectuals and regarded contemptuously as "long-hair" music by devotees of "rock and roll." Difficulties in communications can even occur within the same family when the same symbol is interpreted differently by males and females or by adolescents and adults. A 14-year-old girl arrives home from school wearing lipstick; all her friends do, so wearing lipstick is a symbol of her membership in her clique. Her parents, coming as they do from a fundamentalist Lutheran background, are horrified. To them, lipstick means sex and sin. Such a failure of communication can have tragic consequences. Studies of the early lives of prostitutes have shown that some started to define themselves as "bad" because of this type of experience with excessively strict parents.[12]

Thus, communication failures can occur accidentally, despite the best efforts of human beings to understand one another, because different subcultures attach different meanings to the same symbol. On the other hand, communication failures can be engineered for self-seeking reasons, as when one person lies to another. A boy tells a girl that he loves her, brings her flowers and candy, and in other ways implies that he is interested in marriage; in reality he is interested only in sexual intimacies.[13] The advertiser or the salesman tries to communicate messages that will induce people to buy a product; oftentimes these messages are misleading if not outright fabrications. In short, symbolic communication is a tremendous achievement of the human species, but the looseness of the connection between the cultural symbol and its meaning makes possible not only accidental communication failures but also deliberate deception.

CONCLUSION

Reality has for human beings a cultural dimension. Words, acts, and even the physical environment are examined for *meaning* before they are reacted to. Culture, in providing a shared vocabulary of meanings for the members of a society, makes possible common interpretations of the world and of human behavior in it. Thus, culture is a prerequisite for sustained systems of interaction.

In common speech "culture" is used to refer to the creditable traditions of a society,

[12] Edwin M. Lemert, *Social Pathology*, New York: McGraw-Hill, 1951, pp. 236–280.
[13] Willard Waller, "The Rating and Dating Complex," *American Sociological Review*, Vol. 2, December 1937, pp. 727–734.

such as painting, poetry, music, and literature. As this chapter has made clear, sociologists and anthropologists do not use the term in this way. For the social scientist, the cultural tradition of a society includes safe cracking, profanity, cooking, and furniture making as well as artistic achievements. Every society, from the most advanced industrial countries to technologically primitive tribes, has a stock of intellectual and evaluative ideas shared by the bulk of its population. *This is its culture.* Culture is the cement that holds systems of interaction together. Without culture human communication would necessarily remain at the level of the snarls and barks by means of which dogs express themselves.

The advantages of symbolic communication are obvious. The disadvantages should be noted also. The doctrine of white supremacy is a cultural phenomenon. A Southern lynching, far from being a reversion to subhuman brutality, is comprehensible only when the cultural definition of pigmentation is understood, when the rape of a white woman by a Negro male is interpreted in the context of the etiquette of race relations defined by white supremacy. Tigers kill, but only human beings hate. In short, some of the least attractive features of human society—cruelty, greed, lust, envy—depend on culture. The second disadvantage of symbolic communication is a consequence of the fact that the meanings of symbols are arbitrary. Since meanings must be *learned* from other people, the possibility always exists that misunderstandings will arise because different persons learn different meanings for the same symbol. And even when the meaning of a symbol is shared, there is no guarantee that communication failure will not occur. Symbols facilitate deception as well as honest communications.

SOME SIGNIFICANT LITERATURE ON CULTURE

Bernard Barber, *Science and the Social Order*, Glencoe, Ill.: Free Press, 1952. The possession of a method for adding systematically to knowledge is one of the distinguishing features of the cultures of urban industrial societies. In his book Professor Barber analyzes the place of science in democratic and despotic societies, the social control of science, and the social organization of science. Concentrating particularly on American society, he discusses the scientist in the university, in industry, and in government. The book concludes with a chapter on the social sciences. This summary is based on a review by Robert Bierstedt, *American Sociological Review*, Vol. 18, December 1953, pp. 721–722.

James H. Barnett, *The American Christmas: A Study in National Culture*, New York: Macmillan, 1954. If a sociologist from Mars came to the United States, he would be interested in national festivals and their significance in American life. Professor Barnett subjects Christmas to this kind of analysis. This summary is based on a review by Frederick Elkin, *American Sociological Review*, Vol. 20, June 1955, p. 366.

Ruth Benedict, *Patterns of Culture*, Boston: Houghton Mifflin, 1934. What Ruth Benedict attempts in this book is to show that it is possible to describe three preliterate cultures as *wholes* rather than to catalog hundreds of unrelated customs and practices. The Zuni of New Mexico are a ceremonious people who pursue moderation in all things; the Dobu of Melanesia are violently suspicious; and the Kwakiutl of the Pacific Northwest are fiercely competitive. When the dominant theme of each culture is recognized (the *pattern* of its culture), the detached observer from a totally different society can understand how the culture organizes its social life meaningfully around this theme. Of course, the well-integrated preliterate society is more amenable to such configurational analysis than urban industrial societies, but Professor Benedict also tries (in another book) to apply the configurational approach to contemporary Japan. See her book, *The Chrysanthemum and the Sword*, Boston: Houghton Mifflin, 1946.

Henry Elkin, "Aggressive and Erotic Tendencies in Army Life," *American Journal of Sociology*, Vol. 51, March 1946, pp. 408–413. The author of this article drew upon his observations of Army life while he served in the Armed Forces during the Second World War. Specifically, he was struck by the exaggerated emphasis on certain symbols of masculine virility among American troops: excessive drinking, preoccupation with sex, brawling, and constant use of profane language. "Apart from expressing a general rebelliousness, profanity most perfectly suggests that the user is capable of asserting his will, using his fists, drinking inordinate quantities of alcohol, taking women in contemptuous, domineering stride, and engaging in such other pursuits as are becoming to the virile American male."

Raymond Firth, *We, the Tikopia: A Sociological Study of Kinship in Primitive Polynesia*, New York: American Book Co., 1936. This account of the kinship system of a Polynesian community is typical of the anthropological method. The author immersed himself in the culture, living in a primitive village of 1200 individuals for one year. He learned to speak with the natives in their own language. The result is a work rich in detail. Professor Firth showed that informal behavior toward relatives—much more than formal behavior—depended on the closeness of the kinship tie, the number of persons involved, and how far away they lived. This summary is based on a review by A. Irving Hallowell, *American Sociological Review*, Vol. 2, October 1938, pp. 558–560.

Richard Hoggart, *The Uses of Literacy: Changing Patterns in English Mass Culture*, Fair Lawn, N.J.: Essential Books, 1957. This book is concerned with the effect of widespread literacy and the mass media on the culture of the English working class. The author analyzes the content of the popular press and compares the values it offers with the values of the folk culture. Mass communications ". . . tend towards a view of the world in which progress is conceived as a seeking of material possessions, equality as a moral leveling, and freedom as the ground for endless irresponsible pleasure." Hoggart is not a sociologist, and his book is more polemical than descriptive. His hypothesis about the effect of the mass media on English working-class culture is worth the attention of sociologists, however, because it shows the usefulness of the culture concept in an analysis of a contemporary industrial society. This summary is based on a review by Asher Tropp, *American Sociological Review*, Vol. 23, April 1958, p. 221.

John Irwin and Donald R. Cressey, "Thieves, Convicts and the Inmate Culture," *Social Problems*, Vol. 10, Fall 1962, pp. 142–155. Criminologists have observed that the culture in prisons differs from the culture of the larger society. This article is a sophisticated attempt to analyze the components of the "inmate culture." One component of inmate culture is the *thief* subculture of the larger society: the traditions of those who steal for a living and who regard incarceration as one of the hazards of their profession. Another component is the system of utilitarian and manipulative values of those who compete for status and power within the prison—"convicts". Not all inmates of a prison are oriented to either of these components of inmate culture. Some inmates bring to the prison both antithief and anticonvict values. "They are people such as a man who, on a drunken Saturday night, ran over a pedestrian and was sent to the prison for manslaughter, a middle-class clerk who was caught embezzling his firm's money, and a young soldier who stole a car in order to get back from a leave."

Edward Sapir, *Language: An Introduction to the Study of Speech*, New York: Harcourt, Brace, 1921. Professor Sapir defines language as follows: "Language is a purely human and non-instinctive method of communicating ideas, emotions, and desires by means of a system of voluntarily produced symbols." He contrasts locomotion, which depends on biological maturation, with speech, which depends on learning the culture of one's society. He argues that speech makes thought possible and that in the evolution of man prerational speech antedated the intellectual uses of language. However, speech and thought are mutually stimulating; ". . . thought processes set in, as a kind of psychic overflow, almost at the beginning of linguistic expression . . . the concept, once defined, necessarily reacted on the life of its linguistic symbol, encouraging further linguistic growth." Some experts in the field of linguistics have criticized the Sapir-Whorf theory of language in recent years; other experts maintain that Professors Sapir and Whorf are correct in their emphasis on the patterning of thought by language.

W. Lloyd Warner, *A Black Civilization: A Social Study of an Australian Tribe*, rev. ed., New York: Harper, 1957. The Murngin tribes are aboriginal inhabitants of Northern Australia. They live in a tropical area marked by sharp seasonal cycles of rainy and dry periods and possess a Stone Age culture. The men spear kangaroos, wallabies, and emus, and harpoon turtles and porpoises. "The fundamental basis of the society is an elaborate kinship system in which everyone is related to everyone else." Seven lines of descent are recognized with five generations in each line. The 35 different relatives are distinguished by sex, thus creating 70 categories of relationship; to this is added the distinction between an older and a younger brother, making 71 relationships possible for each member of the society. Asymmetrical cross-cousin marriage is institutionalized. This means that a man marries his maternal uncle's daughter but not his father's sister's daughter. Vertical lines rather than horizontal lines are stressed in the kinship structure; a man's relations with his children are stronger than the relationships created by marriage. There is much feuding, which results in a scarcity of men. Perhaps because of chronic warfare, Murngin society permits polygamy; the average number of wives for middle-aged men is three and a half.

J. Milton Yinger, "Contraculture and Subculture," *American Sociological Review*, Vol. 25, October 1960, pp. 625–635. In societies as complicated as the contemporary United States, sociologists have felt a need to develop a concept capable of distinguishing *internal* variations in culture. The word "subculture" has been used for this purpose. Professor Yinger argues, on the basis of his review of 100 uses of the concept of subculture in the sociological literature, that it is an overworked concept. He suggests that some of the meanings attached to "subculture" should be allocated to "*contra*culture," a word he coined to express these meanings. Subculture and contraculture are defined as follows: Subcultures are normative systems of groups smaller than a society, which, because of isolation or other inadequacies of communication, have a different tradition from the larger society of which they are a part—for example, the subculture of American Indians. Contracultures are the normative systems of groups caught in frustrating situations; they are understandable in terms of social and psychological reactions hostile to the larger society—for example, delinquent gangs.

PART II

The Development
of Urban Industrial Societies

CHAPTER 4

The Industrial Way of Life

Although goods and services are exchanged in all known societies, institutions regulating exchange and the meaning of transactions to participants vary from society to society. In preliterate societies, for example, barter is not a purely economic transaction but a social ritual. Raymond Firth, the anthropologist, illustrates this point with a story of his purchase of a fish in a Malayan village.[1] He went to the beach where fishermen gather with their catch, found a fish he wanted, asked its price from a fisherman, paid it without a word, and started off with his purchase. The flabbergasted fisherman pursued Firth, screaming his tale of frustrated expectations to all who would listen, "He didn't bargain! He took my first price!" The fisherman had quoted an initial price three times what he ultimately planned to receive for the fish; he expected Firth to respond with a lower offer than he intended to pay. A violent argument should have followed in the course of which the fisherman would have reduced his price and Firth would have raised his offer. After much dickering and sharp words,

[1] The story comes from an unpublished lecture delivered at Harvard University. For background, see Raymond Firth, *Malay Fishermen: Their Peasant Economy*, London: Kegan Paul, Trench, Trubner, 1946, Chap. 7.

a price should have been agreed upon, and each party to the transaction should have stamped off, protesting loudly that he had been cheated while secretly believing that he had had the better of the bargain. When Firth paid the initial price, the fisherman was disappointed to the point of shock. True, he received three times what he expected to *get* for the fish, but he was deprived of participating in a haggling ritual. On balance, he felt cheated.

INSTITUTIONALIZED EXCHANGE IN INDUSTRIAL SOCIETIES

In contemporary industrial societies, exchange relationships are depersonalized and separated from the rest of social life. On the New York Stock Exchange, for example, buyers and sellers never meet; they execute orders through brokers—solely on the basis of price. If a customer instructed his broker to purchase 100 shares of American Can "provided that the seller had good morals," the broker would suspect the customer of having lost his mind. In a large department store in New York, London, Paris, Stockholm, or in any large city of an industrialized society, the buyer and the seller meet face to face, but the relationship is al-

THE INDUSTRIAL WAY OF LIFE 87

most as impersonal and devoid of ritual. Customers of R. H. Macy & Company do not expect to haggle with the sales clerk, and the sales clerk is not trained (or permitted) to do so. The price is written on a tag; the customer decides to buy or not, and the transaction ends. Not only goods but *services* are impersonally bought and sold in contemporary industrial societies. In a hotel, for example, complete strangers can obtain food, drink, and a bed in which to stay one or more nights merely by paying money. Such an arrangement would shock a Murngin because he lives in a society where sleeping accommodations are determined by kinship and are therefore far too personal to sell. A Murngin would be equally horrified to learn that Americans pay nurses to take care of them when they are sick and buy blood from blood donors.

In contemporary industrial societies, most valuable goods and services are transferred impersonally in what is called a "market." A market is not, of course, a physical location but a form of relationship between buyer and seller. In the pure market situation, the buyer and seller are connected only by their economic interests; their other human qualities are irrelevant. Even in contemporary industrial societies, not all goods and services are for sale in the market place. For instance, the unpaid volunteer performs crucial services in hospitals and social agencies. Because she does not sell her services, she is not regarded as part of "the labor force" for purposes of economic calculation. What is remarkable about industrial societies, however, as contrasted with preindustrial societies, is *the extent to which exchange occurs in an impersonal market place where transactions are stripped of all except economic meaning.* Robert Heilbroner, the economic historian, describes industrial society as a "market society" and explains how it emerged out of feudalism.

The Development of a Market Society

Reprinted by permission. From Robert L. Heilbroner, *The Making of Economic Society*, Englewood Cliffs, N.J.: Prentice-Hall, 1962, pp. 42, 56–65, 67.

One prerequisite of a market society should by now be clear: a market society must involve the process of exchange, of buying and selling, at every level of society. But for this to take place men must have the wherewithal to enter a market; that is, they must have cash. And, in turn, if society is to be permeated with cash, men must earn money for their labors. In other words, *for a market society to exist, nearly every task must have a monetary reward.*

Even in our highly monetized society we do not pay for *every* service: most conspicuously not for the housekeeping services of a wife. But all through the pre-market era, the number of unpaid services—the amount of work performed by law without monetary compensation—was vastly larger than in our society. Slave labor was, of course, unpaid. So was most serf labor. Even the labor of apprentices was remunerated more in kind, in food and lodging, than in cash. Thus at least 60 or 70 per cent of the actual working population of an ancient or medieval economy labored without anything resembling full payment in money.

Clearly, in such a society the possibilities for a highly involved exchange economy were limited. But a still more important consequence must be noted. The absence of a widespread monetization of tasks meant the absence of a widespread *market for producers.* Nothing like the flow of "purchasing power" which dominates and directs our own productive efforts could be forthcoming in a society in which money incomes were the exception rather than the rule. . . .

THE BREAKDOWN OF THE MANORIAL SYSTEM

. . . Yet, with all due caution we can now begin to comprehend the immense coalition of events—some as specific as the Crusades, some as diffuse as a change in religious ideals—which jointly cooperated to destroy the medieval framework of economic life and to prepare the way for a new dynamic framework of market transactions.

One important aspect of this profound alteration was the gradual *monetization of feudal obligations*. In locality after locality we can trace the conversion of the old feudal payments in *kind* —the days of labor or chickens or eggs which a lord received from his tenants—into payments of *money* dues and money rents with which they now discharged their obligations to him.

A number of causes lay behind this commutation of feudal payments. One was the growing urban demand for food, as city populations began to swell. In concentric circles around the cities, money filtered out into the countryside, at one and the same time raising the capacity of the rural sector to buy urban goods and whetting its desire to do so. At the same time, in a search for larger cash incomes to buy a widening variety of goods, the nobility looked with increasing favor on receiving its rents and dues in money rather than in kind. In so doing, however, it unwittingly set into motion a cause for the further serious deterioration of the manorial system. Often the old feudal services were converted into *fixed* sums of money payments. This temporarily eased the cash position of the lord, but soon placed him in the squeeze which always hurts the creditor in times of inflation. And even when dues were not fixed, rents and money dues lagged sufficiently behind the growing monetary needs of the nobility, so that still further feudal obligations were monetized to keep the lord in cash. But as prices rose and the monetized style of life expanded still further, these too failed to keep him solvent. . . .

THE EMERGENCE OF THE ECONOMIC ASPECT OF LIFE

We can discern an immense process of change which literally revolutionized the economic organization of Europe. Whereas in the tenth century, cash and transactions were only peripheral to the solution of the economic problem, by the sixteenth and seventeenth centuries cash and transactions were already beginning to provide the very molecular force of social cohesion.

But over and above this general monetization of life, another and perhaps even more profound change was taking place. This was the emergence of a separate *economic* sphere of activity visible within, and separable from, the surrounding matrix of social life. It was the creation of a whole aspect of society which had never previously existed, but which was thenceforth to constitute a commanding facet of human existence.

In antiquity and feudal times, . . . one could not easily separate the economic motivations or even the economic actions of the great mass of men from the normal round of existence itself. The peasant following his immemorial ways was hardly conscious of acting according to "economic" motives; indeed, he did not: he heeded the orders of his lord or the dictates of custom. Nor was the lord himself economically oriented. His interests were military or political or religious, and not basically oriented toward the idea of gain or increase. Even in the towns, as we have seen, the conduct of ordinary business was inextricably mixed with noneconomic concerns. The undeniable fact that men were acquisitive, not to say avaricious, did not yet impart its flavor to life in general; the making of money, as we have been at some pains to indicate, was a peripheral rather than a central concern of ancient or medieval existence.

With the monetization of daily activity, however, a genuinely new element of life came slowly to the fore. Labor, for example, emerged as an activity quite different from the past. No longer was "labor" part of an explicit social relationship in which one man (serf or apprentice) worked for another (lord or guildmaster) in return for at least an assurance of subsistence. Labor was now a mere quantum of effort, a "commodity" to be disposed of on the market place for the best price it could bring, quite devoid of any reciprocal responsibilities on the part of the buyer, beyond the payment of wages. If those wages were not enough to provide subsistence—well, that was not the buyer's responsibility. He had bought his "labor," and that was that.

This emergence of "pure" labor—labor as a quantity of effort detached from a man's life and bought on the market in fixed quantities—was followed also in respect to two other main elements of economic life. One of these was land. Formerly conceived as the territory of a great lord, as inviolable as the territory of a modern nation-state, land was now also seen in its economic aspect as something to be bought or leased for the economic return it yielded. An estate which was once the core of political and administrative power became a "property" with a market price, available for any number of uses, even as a site for a factory. The dues, the payments in kind, the intangibles of prestige and power which once flowed from the ownership of land gave way to the single return of *rent*; that is, to a money return derived from putting land to *profitable* use.

• The same transformation became true of property. As it was conceived in antiquity and throughout most of the Middle Ages, property was a sum of tangible wealth, a hoard, a treasury of plate, bullion, or jewels. Very logically, it was realized in the form of luxurious homes, in castles and armaments, in courtly robes and trappings. But with the monetization and commercialization of society, property, too, became expressible in a monetary equivalent: a man was now "worth" so many *livres*, or *écus*, or pounds, or whatever. Property became *capital*, manifesting itself no longer in specific goods, but as an abstract sum of infinite flexibility whose value was its capacity to earn *interest* or *profits*.

None of these changes, it should be emphasized, was planned, clearly foreseen, or for that matter, welcomed. It was not with equanimity that the feudal hierarchies saw their prerogatives nibbled away by the mercantile classes. Neither did the tradition-preserving guildmaster desire his own enforced metamorphosis into a "capitalist," a man of affairs guided by market signals and beset by competition. But perhaps for no social class was the transition more painful than for the peasant, caught up in a process of history which dispossessed him from his livelihood and made him a landless laborer.

THE ENCLOSURES

This process, which was particularly important in England, was the *enclosure movement*, a by-product of the monetization of feudal life. Starting as early as the thirteenth century, the landed aristocracy, increasingly squeezed for cash, began to view their estates not merely as the ancestral fiefs, but as sources of cash revenue. In order to raise larger cash crops, they began to "enclose" the pasture which had previously been deemed "common land." Communal grazing fields which had in fact always belonged to the lord, despite their communal use, were now claimed for the exclusive benefit of the lord and turned into sheepwalks. Why sheepwalks? Because a rising demand for woolen cloth was making sheep-raising a highly profitable occupation. The medieval historian Eileen Power writes:

"The visitor to the House of Lords, looking respectfully upon that august assembly, cannot fail to be struck by a stout and ungainly object facing the throne—an ungainly object upon which in full session of Parliament, he will observe seated the Lord Chancellor of England. The object is a woolsack, and it is stuffed as full of pure history as the office of the Lord Chancellor itself. . . . The Lord Chancellor of England is seated upon a woolsack because it was upon a woolsack that this fair land rose to prosperity."

The enclosure process in England proceeded at an irregular pace which reached twin climaxes in the sixteenth and again in the late eighteenth and early nineteenth centuries: By its end, some ten million acres, nearly *half* the arable land of England, had been "enclosed"—in its early Tudor days by the more or less high-handed conversion of the "commons" to sheep-raising; in the final period, by the forced consolidation of tenants' strips and plots into tracts suitable for large-scale commercial farming. Presumably there was fair compensation.

From a strictly economic point of view, the enclosure movement was unquestionably salutary in that it brought into productive employment land which had hitherto yielded only a pittance. Indeed, particularly in the eighteenth and nineteenth centuries, enclosure was the means by which England "rationalized" its agriculture and finally escaped from the inefficiency of the traditional manorial strip system. But there was another, crueler side to enclosure. As the common fields were enclosed, it became ever more difficult for the tenant to support himself. At first slowly, then with increasing rapidity, he was pressed off the land, until in the fifteenth and sixteenth centuries, when the initial enclosure of the commons reached its peak, as many as three-fourths to nine-tenths of the tenants of some estates were simply turned off the farm. Whole hamlets were thus wiped out. Sir Thomas More described it savagely in Book I of his *Utopia*:

"Your sheep that were wont to be so meek and tame, and so small eaters, now, as I hear say, be become so great devourers and so wild, that they eat up and swallow down the very men themselves. They consume, destroy and devour whole fields, houses and cities. For look in what parts of the realm doth grow the finest, and therefore dearest wool, there noblemen and gentlemen, yea and certain abbots, holy men God wot, not contenting themselves with the yearly revenues and profits that were wont to grow to their forefathers and predecessors of their land . . . leave no ground for tillage, they enclose all into pastures, they throw down houses, they pluck down towns and leave nothing standing, but only the church to make of it a sheep house. . . ."

The enclosure process provided a powerful force for the dissolution of feudal ties and the formation of the new relationships of a market society. By dispossessing the peasant, it "created" a new kind of labor force—landless, without traditional sources of income, however meagre, impelled to find work for wages wherever it might be available.

From the agricultural proletariat came in turn the urban proletariat, although there was, in addition, a process of proletarianization *within* the cities as guild structures gave way to more "business-like" firms. But many of the landless peasantry who had been evicted from the great estates wended their way cityward in search of work. Population increases further augmented their numbers. As a result, we find England, from Elizabethan times on, plagued with the problem of the "wandering poor." One not untypical proposal of the eighteenth century was that they be confined in what a reformer candidly termed "Houses of Terror."

Thus did the emergence of a market-oriented system grind into being a "labor force," and though the process of adjustment for other classes of society was not so brutal, it, too, exacted its social price. Tenaciously the guildmasters fought against the invasion of their protected trades by manufacturers who trespassed on traditional preserves or who upset established modes of production with new machinery. Doggedly the landed nobility sought to protect their ancient privileges against the encroachment of the moneyed *nouveaux riches*.

Yet the process of economization, breaking down the established routines of the past, rearranging the power and prestige of all social classes, could not be stopped. Ruthlessly it pursued its historic course and impartially it distributed its historic rewards and sacrifices. Although stretched out over a long period, it was not an evolution but a slow revolution which overtook European economic society. Only when that society had run its long gauntlet, suffering one of the most wrenching dislocations of history, would the

world of transactions appear "natural" and "normal" and the categories of "land," "labor," and "capital" became so matter-of-fact that it would be difficult to believe they had not always existed. . . .

Along with the new relationships of man to man in the market place, there arose a new form of *social control* to take over the guidance of the economy from the former aegis of tradition and command.

THE PRECONDITIONS OF MARKET OPERATION

What was this new form of control? Essentially, it was a pattern of social behavior, of normal, everyday action which the new market environment imposed on society. And what was this pattern of behavior? In the language of the economist, it was the drive to maximize one's income (or to minimize one's expenditures) by concluding the best possible bargains on the market place. In ordinary language, it was the drive to buy cheap and sell dear.

The market society had not, of course, invented this drive. Perhaps it did not even intensify it. But it did make it a *ubiquitous* and *necessitous* aspect of social behavior. Although men may have *felt* acquisitive during the Middle Ages or antiquity, they did not, in fact, enter into market transactions for the basic economic activities of their livelihoods. And even if they did (when a peasant sold his few eggs at the town market), rarely was the transaction a matter of overriding importance for his continued existence. Market transactions in a fundamentally nonmarket society were thus a subsidiary activity, a means of supplementing a livelihood which, however sparse, was largely independent of buying or selling.

With the monetization of labor, land, and capital, however, transactions became *universal* and *critical* activities. Now everything was for sale, and the terms of transactions were anything but subsidiary to existence itself. To a man who sold his labor on a market, in a society which assumed no responsibility for his upkeep, the price at which he concluded his bargain was all-important. So it was with the landlord and the budding capitalist. For each of these a good bargain could spell riches—and a bad one, ruin. Thus the pattern of economic maximization was generalized throughout society and given an inherent urgency which made it a powerful force for shaping human behavior.

The new market society did more than merely bring about an environment in which men were forced to follow their economic self-interest. It brought into being at the same time a social environment in which men could be *controlled* in their economic activities. With the generalized drive to maximize income, it was now possible to direct the application of men's energies in various directions by raising or lowering the rewards offered for different tasks. If more effort was needed in the making of shoes, the market mechanism raised the rewards for land, labor, and capital employed in shoe manufacture. Or if society, operating through that market mechanism, wished to diminish the amount of social energy employed in making hats, it had but to lower the rewards—wages, rents, profits—of hat manufacture, and there would ensue an exodus of the factors of the production from hat-making toward other, more profitable fields. In the universalized presence of a drive toward income maximization, society possessed a powerful tool for *allocating its resources.*

Note, however, that this regulatory device required more than just the drive of self-interest. Equally necessary was a mobility of the factors of production. To the extent that labor was tied to its manorial estates or to its guild establishments, or that guildmasters were forbidden to expand their scales of operation or to venture into new endeavors, the control mechanism would not work. In that case, raising rewards for shoes or lowering rewards for hats could not bring about any substantial increase or decrease in the distribution of social effort.

An essential part of the evolution of the market society was thus not only the monetization of life but the mobilization of life—that is, the dissolution of those ties of place and station which were the very cement of feudal existence. And this essential requirement of mobility leads to a further point. Mobility meant that any job or activity was now open to all comers. Competition appeared. The traditional compartmented division of feudal labor had to give way to a universal rivalry among employments. No longer was each employment a protected haven for apprentice and guildmaster alike. Now any worker and any employer could be displaced from his task by a competitor who would do the job more cheaply. . . .

Only one final point remains to be noted. We have seen how a competitive market economy operated to fulfill the wants of society. But who was to say what its wants were?

In pre-market economies such a question does not pose subtle problems. The "wants" of such societies are either codified by ageless tradition or specifically formulated by its rulers. But in a market society, the specification of wants takes on a new dimension. It now consists of the demands of everyone who has the wherewithal to enter the market. The "wants" of society are thus expressed by millions of daily orders placed on the market by an entire community. As these orders enter the market place they affect the prices at which goods sell. Thus shifts in prices become, in effect, signals to producers, rising prices betokening an increase in demand and an actual or prospective increase in rewards; falling prices signaling the opposite.

In this way the market society catapults the consumer into a position of extraordinary importance. On his ability and willingness to buy hinges the schedule of demands which confront society's producers. If consumers do not want a good or service, or if they do not wish to buy it at its offered price, that good or service will go unsold. In that case, the production effort needed to supply it will not pay for itself and will soon terminate. *In a market society, the consumer is the ultimate formulator of the pattern of economic activity.* He is now the sovereign of the economic process—sovereign not as an individual, but as a member of an entire society which collectively guides and controls the on-going productive effort of society.

A *pure* market society as described by Robert Heilbroner perhaps existed in nineteenth-century England. It does not exist today, certainly not in the Soviet Union where centralized planning of production limits the sovereignty of consumers, nor in the United States where tariffs, strikes, and the rigid price policies of great corporations interfere with the free market.[2] Nevertheless, all contemporary

[2] National Resources Committee, *The Structure of the American Economy*, Washington: Government Printing Office, 1939, pp. 153–170, reprinted in Bendix and Lipset, Eds., *Class, Status and Power*, Glencoe, Ill.: Free Press, 1953.

industrial societies involve a great deal of market behavior. This is because the industrial societies, both communist and capitalist, have pushed the division of labor to the point where *everyone* must enter the market in order to consume, even farmers. In the United States, for example, subsistence farming is rare. Even small farmers produce one or more cash crops to be sold in the market. The income so obtained is used to buy much the same goods and services as city people: packaged foods, ready-made clothing, automobiles, television sets, magazines, admission to the latest Hollywood movie.

Because money is the means—and usually the only means—of consuming part of the production of an industrial society, Americans and Russians and Swedes worry about money. In preliterate societies, where very little consumption is organized through markets, lack of interest in money is understandable. Malinowski reported that the Trobriand islanders,

TABLE 5

Relationship between Per Capita Income and Per Capita Consumption of Energy, 60 Countries, 1957

Country	Per Capita Income (in U.S. dollars)	Per Capita Energy Consumption (in kilograms of coal or equivalent)	Country	Per Capita Income (in U.S. dollars)	Per Capita Energy Consumption (in kilograms of coal or equivalent)
United States	$2101	7771	Lebanon	304	531
Canada	1458	5543	Colombia	153	464
United Kingdom	954	4775	Jamaica	257	436
Belgium	920	4225	Panama	254	392
Luxembourg	1066	4225	Greece	291	360
West Germany	741	3631	Iraq	135	351
Australia	1074	3522	Portugal	197	335
Iceland	1218	3458	Brazil	251	303
Sweden	1276	2974	Peru	123	297
Venezuela	806	2593	Turkey	365	257
Netherlands	690	2538	Egypt	112	248
France	847	2508	Costa Rica	274	240
Norway	914	2359	Malaya	355	237
Denmark	869	2346	Syria	153	223
South Africa	336	2311	South Korea	135	173
Austria	543	2044	Dominican Republic	239	163
New Zealand	1166	2028	Honduras	181	158
Switzerland	1223	1752	Bolivia	69	156
Ireland	451	1750	Ecuador	151	150
Finland	648	1463	Guatemala	162	131
Puerto Rico	473	1088	Philippines	194	129
Argentina	475	1085	India	62	127
Israel	722	1079	Ceylon	116	122
Japan	252	926	Ghana	161	99
Italy	403	915	Belgian Congo	74	86
Chile	360	840	Paraguay	115	62
Spain	310	829	Pakistan	52	53
Mexico	234	820	Thailand	85	53
Cuba	362	735	Burma	48	41
Southern Rhodesia	122	565	Nigeria	69	38

Sources: Suphon Andic and Alan T. Peacock, "The International Distribution of Income, 1949 and 1957," *Journal of the Royal Statistical Society*, Series A (General), Vol. 124 (Part 2, 1961), pp. 214–215; United Nations, *Statistical Yearbook: 1961*, New York: United Nations, 1961, pp. 278–280.

though excellent divers, could not be induced to dive for pearls because the monetary rewards offered to them by traders had little meaning in their society.[3] A similar situation prevails in underdeveloped countries starting to industrialize. High factory wages are not as effective an incentive as in fully industrialized societies because the population does not depend much on money to satisfy its wants.[4] The good things of life are not for sale in the market place. This circumstance helps to explain the difference in the per capita incomes of in-industrialized and underdeveloped countries (Table 5). Part of the reason the average Pakistani can survive with an average income of $52, less than one-fiftieth the average American's income, is that some of his consumption is not reflected in his money income; he is less dependent than an American on market consumption.[5]

Thus, the United States and the Soviet Union are alike in a respect that all industrial societies are alike; both have highly developed market economies; Americans and Russians are equally dependent on money incomes for an opportunity to consume. One important *difference* between the Soviet Union and the United States is in the extent to which *wealth* is marketable. In the United States, virtually every possession is transferable through the market place: buildings and real estate; automobiles and other consumer durables; home furnishings, clothing, jewelry; and, most important of all, fractional shares of ownership in huge corporations. That is, American society is unusual not only for its per capita wealth, but also for the latitude given the individual to hold his wealth in whatever form he wishes: bank balances, stocks and bonds, real estate, small business enterprises, precious stones and metals.[6] This freedom to liquidate one's hold-

ings whenever one wants to receive their "market value" in cash encourages savings and investment. The high rate of capital formation in free-enterprise industrial societies reflects confidence in the continued liquidity of investments.[7] Of course, capital losses occur.[8] Money functions not only as a medium of exchange and a storehouse of value, but also as a unit of account in terms of which wealth is constantly reevaluated. Especially in time of crisis, the monetary value of investments may rise sharply or fall precipitously. The prospect of capital gains or losses adds a speculative flavor to investment. The chance of loss is not sufficient, however, to dim the long-run confidence that one can invest wealth today with a good prospect of liquidating the investment tomorrow.

In communist countries, severe restrictions are placed on the transfer of wealth through the market place. Factories, mines, farms, utilities, and other productive organizations are owned by the government instead of privately as in the Western countries.[9] No stock exchanges exist where shares of ownership in such enterprises may be transferred. However, Soviet citizens do have bank accounts and own clothing, jewelry, and home furnishings much as Americans do. Although the market is a more important exchange institution in the United States than in the Soviet Union, it

[3] Dorothy Lee, *Freedom and Culture*, Englewood Cliffs, N.J.: Prentice-Hall, 1959, pp. 98–99.
[4] Wilbert E. Moore, "Primitives and Peasants in Industry," *Social Research*, Vol. 15, March 1948, pp. 44–81.
[5] Needless to add, the differential scope of the market economy is only *part* of the explanation; the rest of it is sheer poverty.
[6] What is true for the individual is not true of American society as a whole. If everyone wanted to liquidate

his real-estate holdings simultaneously, the market price of real estate would drop precipitously, but title would continue to be held by somebody. See John Maynard Keynes, *The General Theory of Employment, Interest and Money*, New York: Harcourt, Brace, 1936, Chaps. 13 and 15.
[7] In totalitarian industrial societies like the Soviet Union, the rate of capital formation is as high or higher than free-enterprise industrial societies, but it does not depend on confidence in the continued liquidity of investments because it is largely involuntary.
[8] The late economist, Joseph Schumpeter, felt that the destruction of capital values as a result of technological innovations is a creative (and inescapable) feature of capitalism. See his *Capitalism, Socialism and Democracy*, 2nd ed., New York: Harper, 1947.
[9] The corporate form of organization spreads *ownership* of large business enterprises while retaining centralized control. See Adolph A. Berle, *The Twentieth Century Capitalist Revolution*, New York: Harcourt, Brace, 1954; Edward S. Mason, Ed., *The Corporation in Modern Society*, Cambridge, Mass.: Harvard University Press, 1959.

plays a much greater role in both these industrial societies than in preliterate economies.

THE COMMERCIALIZATION OF LABOR IN INDUSTRIAL SOCIETIES

People work in all societies. But the *organization* of work differs fundamentally in pre-industrial and industrial societies. A Murngin hunter hunts because all Murngin men hunt—just as all Murngin women cook; hunting is not his "occupation." He would find it difficult to understand what an "occupation" is because he has no experience with a work role unrelated to his kinship and tribal roles. Nor could he comprehend the buying and selling of a specified number of hours of a worker's services for a given price, the main mechanism by which industrial societies place workers in jobs.

In industrial societies persons playing occupational roles do the bulk of the productive work. Since one of the features of occupational roles is that they yield money income, or perquisites of monetary value, occupations constitute the link between production and distribution. By virtue of his work, the worker receives title to a portion of what his society has available for consumption. Of course, some persons in industrial societies do not play occupational roles and still receive money incomes. This refers not to the dependents of workers or even to recipients of welfare allowances but rather to privileged persons who *need* not work. In the United States the "idle rich" constitute only a tiny fraction of the adult male population. In Western European countries with a titled aristocracy, especially those with constitutional monarchies (Great Britain, The Netherlands, Denmark, Sweden, and Norway), the landed gentry tradition of the Middle Ages persists and makes for a larger leisure class than in the United States.[10] However, the expectation that adult males will follow an occupation is

strong in industrial societies; many possessors of inherited wealth or social position are "gainfully employed" even though their incomes do not depend mainly upon working.

The phrase "gainfully employed" refers to persons having an occupation in which they earn money or a money equivalent. Some gainfully employed persons are self-employed—a physician in private practice, the owner of a restaurant, a farmer. Such persons are directly dependent on the market for income; they sell goods or services to the public. Most Americans are only *indirectly* dependent on the sale of the goods and services they help to produce. They work for an employer or, more usually, an employing organization, such as General Motors, the Pennsylvania Railroad, the Post Office Department of the Federal government. Table 6 documents the extent to which American workers are employees rather than self-employed entrepreneurs.[11] Only in agriculture are a ma-

TABLE 6
Self-employed Male Workers Age 14 and over in the Five Largest American Industries, 1960

Industry	Total Employed Workers	Self-employed Workers	
		Number	Per Cent
Manufacturing	13,111,965	331,579	2.5
Wholesale and retail trade	7,398,070	1,563,104	21.1
Agriculture	3,932,225	2,462,351	62.6
Transportation, communication, and other public utilities	3,687,448	177,553	4.8
Construction	3,662,393	722,136	19.7
All industries (including those not among the the largest 5)	43,466,955	6,834,327	15.7

Source: Bureau of the Census, *United States Census of Population: 1960, United States Summary, Detailed Characteristics,* Washington: Government Printing Office, 1963, p. 571.

---

[10]   Soviet society is less than 50 years old. It has no leisure class at present, and Soviet ideology strongly condemns "parasites." Time works changes, however. Possibly high communist officials will form the nucleus for a hereditary aristocracy.

[11]   Peter F. Drucker, "The Employee Society," *American Journal of Sociology,* Vol. 58, January 1953, pp. 358–363.

jority of male workers self-employed. In manu-facturing, the largest industry, less than 4 per cent of the male workers are self-employed. Table 6 shows that nearly 85 per cent of American male workers were employees in 1960. More than 90 per cent of *female* workers were employees in 1960.[12]

The extent to which industrial societies are employee societies points up the fact that the market for *services* is at least as important as the market for *goods* in the contemporary world. Economists need not concern themselves about this development. To the economist, labor is a factor of production precisely as natural resources and capital are factors of production; labor markets, commodity markets, and capital markets fit the same framework of supply and demand. To the sociologist, the difference between services and commodities is more important than the similarity. Commodities lie wholly within the economy—until they reach the consumer and disappear. The worker,

on the other hand, plays other roles besides his occupational role. He interacts in the economy, but *not only* in the economy. To go back to some of the issues discussed in Chapter 1, workers have *role conflicts;* commodities do not.[13] These role conflicts explain why labor markets are, in the words of the economist, "imperfect," why workers are reluctant to move from an economically stagnant community to a growing community paying higher wages. A worker may have relatives and friends whom he does not wish to leave behind; he may want his children to continue in the same school; he may enjoy his home and garden. Unlike the economist, the sociologist must consider the consequences for the worker's *other* roles of his participation in the occupational system.

The United States Bureau of the Census measures with precision the occupational involvement of various population segments. So do the statistical offices of other industrial countries. Table 7 shows the differential partic-

TABLE 7
Labor-Force Participation in the United States, by Age and Sex, 1960

| | Male Population, Age 14 and over | | | Female Population, Age 14 and over | | |
| | Total of | In Labor Force | | Total of | In Labor Force | |
Age	Specified Age	Number	Per Cent	Specified Age	Number	Per Cent
14–15	2,823,032	452,943	16.0	2,697,727	186,902	6.9
16–17	2,891,892	1,064,523	36.8	2,791,152	581,791	20.8
18–19	2,337,550	1,548,520	66.2	2,406,632	1,114,666	46.3
20–24	5,236,986	4,510,798	86.1	5,492,006	2,462,697	44.8
25–29	5,298,596	4,975,113	93.9	5,506,465	1,933,693	35.1
30–34	5,805,617	5,562,577	95.8	6,078,049	2,156,467	35.5
35–39	6,055,047	5,802,969	95.8	6,386,767	2,569,986	40.2
40–44	5,619,690	5,360,030	95.4	5,893,104	2,667,149	45.3
45–49	5,349,759	5,052,877	94.5	5,535,365	2,624,207	47.4
50–54	4,744,298	4,372,149	92.2	4,917,741	2,253,086	45.8
55–59	4,167,829	3,656,323	87.7	4,399,358	1,744,365	39.7
60–64	3,374,074	2,618,958	77.6	3,719,035	1,096,055	29.5
65–69	2,876,754	1,261,842	43.9	2,297,013	546,732	16.6
70–74	2,133,158	611,429	28.7	2,517,769	241,122	9.6
75 and over	2,280,630	352,939	15.5	3,068,168	129,411	4.2
Total, all ages	60,994,912	47,203,990	77.4	64,706,351	22,308,329	34.5

Source: Bureau of the Census, *United States Census of Population: 1960, United States Summary, Detailed Characteristics,* Washington Government Printing Office, 1963, p. 499.

[12] Bureau of the Census, *United States Census of Population: 1960, United States Summary,* Washington: Government Printing Office, 1963, p. 549.

[13] Karl Polanyi speaks of "the commodity fiction." See his *The Great Transformation,* New York: Farrar and Rinehart, 1944.

ipation in the labor force of men and women and of adolescents, adults, and the elderly. A much higher percentage of males than of females was in the labor force in 1960 at every age. The explanation of the difference is, of course, that many women, especially married women with young children, devote their full-time efforts to homemaking. Nine-tenths of American *males* between the ages of 25 and 55 were in the labor force. The remaining tenth included the mentally ill and deficient, the permanently disabled, and inmates of prisons and other institutions. For practical purposes, therefore, all American men between 25 and 55 who *could* pursue an occupation in 1960 did so. Going to school kept many younger males out of the labor force. As for men over 55, retirement and the increasing incidence of disabilities pushed large numbers out of the labor force, especially after 65, when they became eligible for Social Security payments.

As with all statistical tabulations, Table 7 becomes more meaningful when the definitions used in classifying the population are thoroughly understood. For example, the Census Bureau classified a person as a member of the labor force even though he happened to be unemployed during the calendar week in April 1960 preceding the enumerator's visit (the "census week"). The enumerator could tell whether the person was an unemployed member of the labor force or was uninterested in working or unable to work and therefore *not* a member of the labor force. This was because the Census Bureau had a clear conception of what it meant by "employed," "unemployed," "in the labor force," and "not in the labor force"—and included a series of questions on the census schedule designed to define these concepts operationally.

The Census Bureau *concepts* were as follows:

"Employed.—Employed persons comprise all civilians 14 years old and over who were either (*a*) 'at work'—those who did any work for pay or profit, or worked without pay for 15 hours or more on a family farm or in a family business; or (*b*) were 'with a job but not at work'—those who did not work and were not looking for work but had a job or business from which they were temporarily absent because of bad weather, industrial dispute, vacation, illness, or other personal reasons.

"Unemployed.—Persons are classified as unemployed if they were 14 years old and over and not 'at work' but looking for work. A person is considered as looking for work not only if he actually tried to find work during the reference week but also if he had made such efforts recently (i.e., within the past 60 days) and was awaiting the results of these efforts. Examples of looking for work are:

1. Registration at a public or private employment office.
2. Meeting with or telephoning prospective employers.
3. Being on call at a personnel office, at a union hall, or from a nurses' register or other similar professional register.
4. Placing or answering advertisements.
5. Writing letters of application.

Persons waiting to be called back to a job from which they had been laid off or furloughed were also counted as unemployed. . . .

"Labor force.—The labor force includes all persons classified as employed or unemployed, as described above, and also members of the Armed Forces (persons on active duty with the United States Army, Air Force, Navy, Marine Corps, or Coast Guard). The 'civilian labor force' comprises only the employed and unemployed components of the labor force. The experienced civilian labor force comprises the employed and the unemployed who have had previous work experience.

"Not in labor force.—This category consists of all persons 14 years old and over who are not classified as members of the labor force and includes persons doing only incidental unpaid family work (less than 15 hours during the week). Most of the persons in this category are students, housewives, retired workers, seasonal workers enumerated in an 'off' season who were not looking for work, inmates of institutions, or persons who cannot work because of long-term physical or mental illness or disability." [14]

The 1960 *data* on employment characteristics were derived from the following questions on the Household Questionnaire: [15]

P22. Did this person work at any time last week?

Include part-time work such as a Saturday job, delivering papers, or helping without pay in a family business or firm. Do not count own housework.

Yes_____☐   No_____☐

P23. How many hours did he work last week (at all jobs)? (if exact figure not known, give best estimate)

1 to 14 hours____☐   40 hours_____☐
15 to 29 hours___☐   41 to 48 hours_____☐
30 to 34 hours___☐   49 to 59 hours_____☐
35 to 39 hours___☐   60 hours or more___☐

P24. Was this person looking for work, or on layoff from a job?

Yes_____☐   No_____☐

P25. Does he have a job or business from which he was temporarily absent all last week because of illness, vacation, or other reasons?

Yes_____☐   No_____☐

THE SEPARATION OF OCCUPATIONAL AND FAMILY ROLES

As Wilbert Moore has pointed out, the "labor force" concept is useful for describing the economically active segment of the population only in industrial societies.[16] In preliterate societies where food gathering, agriculture, or hunting are not specialized activities but aspects of kinship or communal roles, the concept is irrelevant. The market test of labor force participation—remuneration for services —does not apply. As an approximate measure of the development of a labor market in a society moving toward industrialization, Professor Moore suggested computing the proportion of all males 15 to 64 years of age who were wage and salary earners. He showed, for example, that the Philippines had 35.7 per cent of its eligible males working for wages or salaries in 1939 as compared with 65.5 per cent in the United States in 1940. He concluded that "the goal of economic growth in undeveloped areas may be expressed as the attempt to create a 'labor force' in the technical sense." [17]

In industrial societies, occupational roles are relatively autonomous of kinship roles. There are family businesses and family farms where one's work role is a consequence of family membership, but most jobs are not obtained on this basis. Indeed, giving a relative a job rather than filling it on the basis of impersonal qualifications may be considered reprehensible. Congressmen charged with nepotism in filling positions on their staff find themselves at a disadvantage at election time. And President Kennedy was accused of attempting to establish a dynasty because of the political offices held by his brothers and his brothers-in-law. Not every industrial society separates the occupational realm from family life as completely as does the United States. Japan, for example, has a strong familistic tradition which seems to be compatible with industrial development. Thomas Wilkinson has shown that the proportion of unpaid family workers in the Japanese labor force is far larger than in the United States or Great Britain.[18] Apparently the family is more frequently the unit of economic activity in Japan than in Western industrial countries. Nevertheless, even in this familistic society, the forces of industrialization tend to separate the occupational from the kinship roles. Professor Wilkinson pointed out that the larger the city, the smaller was the proportion of unpaid family workers.[19]

There tends also to be a *physical* separation of occupational and family roles in industrial societies. True, on family farms the place of residence of the farm family and the place of work of the farmer are *not* separated. But this is an exceptional situation. More typically, the

---

[14] Bureau of the Census, *United States Census of Population: 1960, United States Summary*, Washington: Government Printing Office, 1962, pp. xxvii–xxviii.
[15] *Ibid.*, p. xxvii.
[16] Wilbert E. Moore, "The Exportability of the 'Labor Force' Concept," *American Sociological Review*, Vol. 18, February 1953, pp. 68–72.

[17] *Ibid.*
[18] Thomas O. Wilkinson, "Family Structure and Industrialization in Japan," *American Sociological Review*, Vol. 27, October 1962, p. 681.
[19] *Ibid.*

worker's *home*, the place of his kinship roles, is distinct from his *job* location. The "rush hour" traffic jams in the cities of industrial societies —Tokyo is just as jammed as Los Angeles— attest to the separation of work and residence. This physical separation of work and residence is the essence of what economic historians call "the factory system." A factory is commonly thought to be a building containing specialized machinery for manufacturing products. But the history of the factory shows that the emphasis should not be placed on equipment but on social organization. Professor Usher's scholarly account of the development of the British woolen industry shows that the great innovation was the removal of production from the cottage (home) of the craftsman to premises owned and supervised by the capitalist employer.

The Factory System: Separation of Work and Residence

Reprinted by permission. From Abbott Payson Usher, *The Industrial History of England*, Boston: Houghton Mifflin, 1920, pp. 11–15, 346–351.

There are two distinct stages in the development of the crafts which are of primary importance. In the earlier stages of industrial specialization, the crafts emerge as occupations which produce a finished product, or at least a salable product. Cloth, for instance, can be used without being bleached or dyed, and it is fairly certain that "grey" cloth was used extensively in the ancient and medieval periods. It may be that a weaver would sell the grey cloth to a prospective consumer, and thus he would not strictly speaking deal in a finished product. We cannot be sure whether weavers preceded dyers or dyers preceded weavers as persons exercising distinct crafts. It would seem likely, however, that some persons would find a regular and distinct occupation in bleaching and dyeing crude homespuns appreciably before weaving became a specialized occupation. The dyers took the product of undiversified household industry and gave the cloth a finish that made it substantially a new product. Such a craft would represent more or less exactly the

notions commonly held of craft industry. A single craft, represented always by a particular workman, stands between the "raw product" and the consumer. There is no middleman, no intermediate processes of production and sale.

Such a simple situation cannot long persist; the development of craft differentiation tends to disintegrate the process of production into its essential stages, and finally each phase of the transformation of the primary raw material becomes the basis of a separate craft. Thus in the textile trades, we ultimately find distinct crafts of woolcombers, weavers, fullers, dyers, and drapers. Spinning never became a craft operation in the legitimate sense of the word; it was a subsidiary employment of women and children that required no specialized skill. The production of textiles thus came to be the work of a group of crafts, so that some of the workers never came in contact with the consumer. The direct contact with the consumer that is so strongly emphasized in descriptions of craft industry does not apply to the later stages of craft development. The disintegration of the process of production required at least successive sales of partly finished goods. Combers might sell combed wool to weavers, weavers would sell grey cloth to fullers or dyers, fullers and dyers would sell finished cloth to the drapers who undertook to sell the cloth in the distant market that was usually contemplated. A considerable division of labor might thus develop without breaking down the independence of the craftsmen. In this second period of craft diversification each craft was a link in a chain of correlated crafts. Sufficient differentiation to give rise to many of these phenomena undoubtedly existed at a relatively early period in the development of craft industry. The notion of direct contact between producer and consumer cannot be regarded as characteristic of the chief period of craft industry. The simplicity of industrial life during the craft period, too, has been seriously exaggerated. The multiplicity of special crafts gave rise at an early date to all these loose coordinations of groups of crafts that are so hard for us to appreciate.

The recognition of this second stage of craft development is particularly important because it furnishes the basis for the beginnings of capitalistic control of industry. The formation of a considerable group of crafts in a single industry brought with it certain technical advantages from specialization of skill, but there were certain economic disadvantages as long as the crafts remained entirely independent. The successive buying and selling of partly finished products were sheer waste of energy. There was also no possibility of exercising any supervision over the process of production. These disadvantages could be overcome if some one bought the primary raw material at the outset and then hired the various craftsmen to perform their craft work for wages. A capitalist employer of this type was necessary to prevent specialization from degenerating into disorder. The tendency toward disintegration was thus offset by a tendency towards integration: there was disintegration in the technique of production followed speedily by integration of control.

The general industrial system by which this control was exercised passes under a great variety of names. It has been called the "domestic system," because the workmen are generally able to pursue their craft in their homes. This term presents an antithesis to the factory system, but it fails to suggest any distinction between this form and the craft system. Until the factory appeared the household was the scene of nearly all industrial labor; the fact that the work was done at home is thus of no distinctive significance. The phrase "commission system" has also been used, but such a term suggests a relation between principal and agent that is meaningless in this particular phase of industrial history. The term "putting-out system" is neither euphonious nor elegant, but it has the merit of describing the salient characteristics of this type of industrial organization, and it suggests the features that distinguish this type both from the craft forms that precede it and from the factory system that follows. The employer owns the materials and gives them out to various craft workers who carry the goods through a process or group of processes. The goods are then returned to the employer, and, if they are not yet finished, they are passed on to other workmen. The employer must needs be a capitalist: he owns the materials during the process of production and advances wages to the craftsmen. At times the employer may own tools or other equipment used in production. Instances occurred in the nineteenth century in which the employer owned the cottages used by the workmen; the cottages were prepared for the weavers or other craftsmen and rented completely equipped. Not infrequently part of the work was done in workshops belonging to the capitalist employer and under immediate supervision. This was most commonly the case with reference to some of the finishing processes of the woolen manufacture.

The putting-out system is by nature highly elastic, admitting of many gradations of capitalistic control of the process of production, and corresponding variety in the degree to which the disintegration of industry into separate crafts is remedied by centralized direction. The scale of production, too, might vary within wide limits. Many establishments in the woolen industry organized on this system employed a thousand hands, and though the number of employees was of course somewhat increased by the absence of power machinery the scale of the undertaking was considerable. The variety of detail possible in this system enables us to appreciate clearly all the phases of the long transition from craftwork to the factory, and the minuteness of the changes affords interesting illustrations of the continuity of industrial development. At no point is there an abrupt transition from the old to the new.

In the main, the putting-out system merely brought a number of workmen under a moderate degree of supervision and direction. The establishment was the loosest possible aggregation of workers. The development of this form does not ordinarily bring with it any increase in the division of labor. It was primarily an antidote for excessive disintegration. . . .

Description of the genesis of the modern factory is difficult because all historical accounts are so profoundly influenced by the definition of the factory. Accounts that may seem to differ in important details represent merely different conceptions of the thing described. It would seem desirable that the matter be approached from a purely historical point of view, without the prejudices created by elaborately formulated notions of the factory. It is of course impossible to avoid definition even in a purely historical account, but if the ideal of historical investigation is achieved these definitions will be an interpretation of events that occurred rather than an artificial form or mould into which events have been crowded with Procrustean indifference to the adaptability of the events to the mould.

The preconceived notions that are most likely to cause confusion appear both in popular conceptions of the factory and in some special writing. These views are therefore peculiarly dangerous. The presence of machinery in the factory and the relatively large scale of production both seem to be highly characteristic features, so that it is not strange to find these elements emphasized as the fundamental features of the factory. The early English factory acts; Dr. Ure, a sympathetic observer; and Marx, a most bitter critic were united in the opinion that machinery made the factory. It became necessary to distinguish the tool from the machine, but though there were difficulties they did not seem insuperable. This was largely in accord with the opinions of the average citizen. In the words of Marx, the instruments of labor employed the workman; instead of being the foundation of the industrial process the workman became an incidental feature of the productive system, his numbers determined by the needs of the machines, his skill subordinated to the ingenuity of the new contrivance. Ure describes the factory in less forceful language, "a vast automaton, composed of various mechanical and intellectual organs, acting in uninterrupted concert for the production of a common object, all of them being subordinate to a self-regulated moving force." Legislative definitions and census enumerations generally define the factory in terms of numbers; it is of course freely recognized that such definitions are somewhat artificial, but it is none the less easy to assume that the essential feature of the factory consists in the number of hands employed.

The other aspect of the factory has also been the basis of distinctions from the outset: the factory workers are gathered together in buildings or rooms wholly devoted to their work; the establishment does not serve as a home for either employer or employee. The aggregation of workers created new problems of discipline. When work was done in the household no regularity of hours was necessary. The craft worker enjoyed considerable freedom as to the manner and time of doing such work as was necessary for his support. Even when the putting-out system had become elaborately organized it was not possible to exert much pressure on the workers as to the time of finishing the work allotted to them. The aggregation of the workers in factories made it possible to improve the timing of the productive process; the work could be made to flow along without interruptions; no group of workers need be obliged to wait for the group engaged on the earlier stages of the work. The division of labor

that existed under the putting-out system could thus be more effectively carried out, but on one condition—the subjection of the whole body of workmen to a systematic schedule.

The organization of factories thus gave a different meaning to the relation between the capitalist employer and the workman. The dependence of the worker on the capitalist was not increased; under the putting-out system every possible degree of dependence existed: at an early date it became common for the capitalist to own the machines or tools, and in the later phases of this system the capitalists owned the entire establishment. The Hand-Loom Weavers' Commissioners reported that a firm at Newark, Notts, employed about one hundred weavers in cottages; "the system is for the manufacturer to build cottages adapted for weavers, and filled up with looms, and to let these cottages at a moderate weekly rental: every weaver taking a house and not having a family sublet portions of the cottage." The gathering together of such cottage workers into a factory involved only one change: the introduction of discipline. The capitalist employer became a supervisor of every detail of the work; without any change in the general character of the wage contract, the employer acquired new powers which were of great social significance. He acquired authority which was irksome to the men and almost certain to become the source of much friction.

It is doubtless possible to exaggerate the extent of the increased authority of the employer under the factory system; the small master of the earlier periods undoubtedly exercised some supervision over his journeymen and apprentices, but in theory his authority was that of a parent or fellow-workman, and it seems likely that in actual practice supervision amounted to nothing that would imply a different relation between master and journeyman. The capitalist employer of the putting-out system certainly exercised no powers of supervision. It was therefore an essentially new thing for the capitalist to be a disciplinarian.

The irksomeness of discipline to the workmen would seem to explain the slow development of the factory system. Experimentation with the factory system begins in England as early as the sixteenth century and in France in the seventeenth century, if the presence of power machinery is not made the essential test of the factory. The relative failure of these early attempts is curiously puzzling. In England actual legislation in the interest of the older system must have played some part in preventing a significant development of factories, but the usual futility of legislation to check a powerful social tendency makes one hesitate to account for the late development of factories solely, or even primarily, by reason of antagonistic legislation. Toward the close of the seventeenth century the restrictive legislation was still in force, but there were developments toward the factory even in those trades and areas that were included within the restrictive laws. Furthermore, there was little legislative restriction in France, and yet the sporadic experiments with the factory system led to no large change in industrial organization. Factories became permanently established only when there were special features which overcame the social and economic drawbacks.

Although we cannot be certain, there is reason to believe that the factory system did not afford a significant margin of profit as compared with the putting-out system until machinery became relatively elaborate. The factory thus held out little hope of special profits to the capitalist in the early period, and, as it was bitterly opposed by the men, there was no general tendency to substitute the factory for the organization of cottage industry under the putting-out system. Unfortunately, we cannot determine the relative importance of these two factors in the postponement of the factory development; but the late evidence makes it clear that factories developed slowly even after they had become profitable to the capitalist. This was notably the case with weaving factories; the handloom weavers could not be induced to forsake the freedom of the old system under which they had enjoyed more independence even than farm laborers.

Speaking of the conditions in Coventry, the special commissioner writes:

"With all its usual distress and degradation, the trade of single hand weaving (requiring a minimum of strength and skill) offers half the liberty of savage life, for which the uninstructed man is almost tempted to sacrifice half the enjoyments of the civilized. Thus, there is a well known feeling among the farm laborers, the brick-layers, and other ordinary artizans in this district, that it is very hard on them to be turned out at early hours every day instead of being able to take

what hours they please, like the ribbon weaver, and like him, take saint Monday, and saint Tuesday too if they choose. Precisely the counterpart of these feelings is also found in the other sex. Notwithstanding the wretched state in which, until recently, the trade had long been, it was impossible for respectable families to procure domestic servants. There is the greatest difficulty in prevailing upon parents to let their children come to service. The young women look down with scorn upon it, and prefer the liberty of the Monday and Saturday, the exemption from confinement, and the little finery, with the liberty to wear it, which the loom furnishes them."

From all sections of England there came similar testimony. The great attraction of hand-loom weaving was the degree of freedom enjoyed, the weavers refusing to leave their cottages for the factory even when the factory offered higher wages. It would seem that the discipline of the factory was not merely a distinguishing feature, but an obstacle to the introduction of the system. Machinery became important in the development of the system because its introduction ultimately forced the workman to accept the discipline of the factory. As long as there were some measure of freedom of choice between cottage and factory the workman preferred the cottage. The general development of the factory thus required the existence of commanding economic advantages, advantages so great as to destroy any real freedom of choice on the part of the worker. The development of the factory is thus closely associated with the introduction of machinery, but it would inevitably distort one's conception of the rise of the system if the use of machinery were made the characteristic test of the existence of a factory. Machinery made the factory a successful and general form of organization, but there can be a factory "without machinery."

Professor Usher places his main emphasis on changes in social organization in discussing the origins of the factory. His argument can be extended. If the factory consists of premises controlled by the employer to which employees come to work for pay, a hospital, a school, a post office, and a jet airplane are factories no less than a manufacturing establishment.

Clearly, the factory method of organizing production had to be invented to make possible a modern economy. The extensive division of labor in automobile production, for example, presupposes rigid adherence to specifications in manufacturing each of thousands of parts. Quality control is feasible in *factory* production, but not under the *domestic* system. Imagine the frequency of breakdowns in automobile assembly lines if the home production of parts were attempted. Not only would parts fail to arrive on time; they would also vary so much from specifications that unlikely coincidences would be required in order to assemble a complete automobile. Another feature of contemporary industrial economies, large investments in plant and equipment, depends on factory production. True, *some* investment in machinery occurred even during the cottage-industry phase of British economic history. But elaborate, bulky, expensive, and easily damaged machines can prove profitable only if the employer can supervise their operation and maintenance, and can keep them busy. Beyond a relatively primitive stage of industrial development, this requires factory production. A steel mill, for instance, or an oil refinery requires such tremendous investment in plant and equipment that less than full-scale production tends to be unprofitable.

Before the development of the factory system, human and animal brawn were the main sources of energy for production. (The term "horsepower" was bequeathed to us from that era.) The factory system was conducive to the development of *inanimate* sources of energy: coal, oil, natural gas, electricity, and, most recently, atomic energy. Utilization of these inanimate sources of energy enormously increased productivity per worker. Table 8 shows how rapidly the per capita consumption of inanimate energy increased in the United States over the past century. The high American standard of living is made possible by this harnessing of inanimate energy. Of course, other industrial societies are also high-energy societies.[20] And they likewise enjoy high standards of living.[21] Table 5 provides statistical documentation of the proposition that high-energy societies tend to be high-income societies and, conversely, that societies with primitive technologies are low-income societies.

Thus, the invention of the factory method of production ultimately helped to raise the standard of living in Western industrial countries beyond the expectations of all but utopians. In the early stages of the factory system, however, the transformation of the *social* aspects of the work situation was more obvious. Workers did not like the long hours and the harsh discipline. They reacted to factory discipline, first, by preferring lower wages in the cottages to higher wages in the factories; then, after factories became the wave of the future, they expressed their frustration by sporadic riots and sabotage. (The derivation of "sabotage" is the French word, *sabot*, meaning wooden shoe; apparently considerable damage resulted when *sabots* were thrown into machinery.) Karl Marx and his followers put this resentment into words. Communist ideology developed in direct opposition to what Marxists called the "exploitation" of the working class, and Marx drew most of his illustrations from official reports of working conditions in British factories and mines during the first half of the nineteenth century.[22]

Marxist predictions proved incorrect. Instead of the increasing misery of the working class that Marx believed inevitable, the standard of living of workers in capitalist countries rose steadily.[23] Equally important, instead of the polarization of society into a mass of downtrodden proletariat and a tiny stratum of oppressors, an increasing proportion of the population in industrial societies consists of neither *manual workers* nor *capitalists* but *white-col-*

20   Fred Cottrell, *Energy and Society: the Relationship between Energy, Social Change, and Economic Development*, New York: McGraw-Hill, 1955.

21   William F. Ogburn and Francis R. Allen, "Technological Development and Per Capita Income," *American Journal of Sociology*, Vol. 65, September 1959, pp. 127–131.

22   Karl Marx, *Capital: a Critique of Political Economy*, New York: Modern Library, no date, Chaps. 10 and 15.

23   Simon Kuznets, "Economic Growth and Income Inequality," *American Economic Review*, Vol. 45, March 1955, pp. 1–28.

lar administrative, professional, technical, clerical, or sales persons.[24] Marx did not foresee the tremendous need for engineers, teachers, secretaries, clerks, technicians, and supervisory employees in industrial societies. In the early stages of industrialism, it was almost impossible to exaggerate the importance of the factory or the wretchedness of factory workers, but Marx managed to do it.

Nevertheless, Marxist diatribes against capitalism had important intellectual as well as practical consequences. Much scholarly work in economics and sociology during the past century was undertaken in order to reformulate Marxist exaggerations or errors.[25] And the sense of mission of many pioneering trade unionists derived, directly or indirectly, from Marxism. Marx was influential despite his misplaced

TABLE 8

Growth in the Horsepower of Prime Movers in the United States, 1850 to 1960

Year	Factories	Mines	Railroads	Merchant Ships, Powered	Sailing Vessels	Farms	Windmills	Electric Central Stations
1850	1,150	60	586	325	400	—	14	—
1860	1,675	170	2,156	515	597	—	20	—
1870	2,453	380	4,462	632	314	—	30	—
1880	3,664	715	8,592	741	314	668	40	—
1890	6,308	1,445	16,980	1,124	280	1,452	80	447
1900	10,309	2,919	24,501	1,663	251	4,009	120	2,443
1910	16,697	4,473	51,308	3,098	220	10,460	180	6,228
1920	19,422	5,146	80,182	6,508	169	21,443	200	17,050
1930	19,519	5,620	109,743	9,115	100	28,610	200	43,427
1940	21,768	7,332	92,361	10,094	26	42,488	130	53,542
1950	32,921	9,167	110,969	11,032	11	63,090	59	87,965
1960	37,360	34,000	46,856	23,890	2	201,756	44	217,173

Year	Aircraft	Work Animals	Automobiles, Trucks, Buses, Motorcycles	Total Horsepower	Population	Total Horsepower per 100,000 Population
1850		5,960	—	8,495	23,191,876	37
1860	—	8,630	—	13,763	31,443,321	44
1870	—	8,660	—	16,931	39,818,449	43
1880	—	11,580	—	26,314	50,155,783	52
1890	—	15,970	—	44,086	62,947,714	70
1900	—	18,730	100	65,045	75,994,575	86
1910	—	21,460	24,686	138,810	91,972,266	151
1920	—	22,430	280,900	453,450	105,710,620	429
1930	3,382	17,660	1,426,568	1,663,944	122,775,046	1353
1940	7,455	12,510	2,511,312	2,759,018	131,669,275	2095
1950	22,000	7,040	4,403,617	4,747,871	150,697,361	3151
1960	36,534	2,790	10,366,880	10,967,285	178,464,236	6145

Sources: Bureau of the Census, *Historical Statistics of the United States, Colonial Times to 1957*, Washington: Government Printing Office, 1960, p. 506; Bureau of the Census, *Statistical Abstract of the United States: 1962*, Washington: Government Printing Office, 1962, pp. 5, 528.

[24] Lewis Corey, "The Middle Class," *Antioch Review*, Vol. 5, Spring 1945, pp. 1–20.

[25] See, for example, Max Weber, *General Economic History*, New York: Collier, 1961.

emphasis, perhaps because he recognized the changing character of industrial societies. Once work shifted from the home to the factory, its meaning changed. Regardless of the level of remuneration paid to the worker, which was the central question for Marx, the factory worker interacts for a considerable portion of his waking life with other workers instead of with his family. Since the work role is relatively autonomous of kinship roles, meaningful questions about *work* satisfaction can now be raised. Before the separation of work and residence, *work* satisfaction was entangled with *marital* and *family* adjustment and with the more general problem of *life* satisfaction. Marx was right to call attention to work satisfaction as a new problem. But he committed the error of supposing that an empirical question could be settled by philosophical analysis. He *assumed* that the meaning of work had to be dehumanization and frustration ("alienation") as it was during the early stages of industrialization. American data accumulated within the past generation show that work satisfaction varies among occupational roles, but also that work satisfaction in at least one industrial society is considerably more prevalent than Marx would have predicted.

The Meaning of Work in an Industrial Society

Reprinted by permission. From Robert Blauner, "Work Satisfaction and Industrial Trends in Modern Society," in Walter Galenson and Seymour M. Lipset, Eds., *Labor and Trade Unionism: An Interdisciplinary Reader*, New York: Wiley, 1960, pp. 339–369.

The present paper surveys research on attitudes of workers toward their work, especially those investigations commonly called job satisfaction studies. To assess the absolute level of job satisfaction in the working population is not my aim, for this is an impossible task, but rather, my purposes are, (1) to locate differences in the incidence and intensity of work satisfaction among those in diverse occupations and work settings, and (2) to discern the factors that, in accounting

for these differences, seem to indicate the important preconditions of satisfaction in work. Further, the paper considers the implications of these findings for theories of work and workers in modern society, in the light of industrial and social trends.

EXTENT OF SATISFACTION: A REVIEW OF GENERAL RESEARCH

Before considering occupational differences and the factors that account for them, I shall briefly consider evidence on the general extent of job satisfaction by looking at the results of six representative sample studies. In Table 9 the figure in the extreme right-hand column indicates the percentage of workers who gave the dissatisfied response to such a question as "Taking into consideration all the things about your job (work), how satisfied or dissatisfied are you with it?"

In the 1946 issue of the *Personnel and Guidance Journal*, Robert Hoppock began summarizing the results of all published studies of job satisfaction, most of which were non-representative samples of individual companies or occupations. When, by 1958, 406 percentages of the proportion of persons dissatisfied with their jobs in these several hundred studies had been averaged out, they yielded a median percentage of 13 per cent dissatisfied. This figure is quite similar to the summary percentages of dissatisfaction resulting from more representative labor force samples.

Thus the most recent American research on satisfaction attitudes seems to support the generalization that: "Even under the existing conditions, which are far from satisfactory, most workers like their jobs. Every survey of workers' attitudes which has been carried out, no matter in what industry, indicates that this is so."

But a caveat should be inserted at this point. Many of these studies, which seek to determine the proportion of workers who are satisfied or dissatisfied with their jobs, fail to specify sufficiently an inherently vague concept and ignore the cultural pressures on workers to exaggerate the degree of actual satisfaction. Despite this, the evidence shows that in the numerous samples of the labor force which have been interviewed, more than 80 per cent indicate general job satisfaction. Even though the methodological limitations make it hard to accept the findings of any one of these studies by itself, it is much harder to reject the weight of their cumulative evidence.

Although it is difficult, therefore, not to accept the proposition that at least the majority (and possibly a very large majority) of American workers are moderately satisfied in their work, such a finding is neither particularly surprising nor sociologically interesting. Under "normal" conditions there is a natural tendency for people to identify with, or at least to be somewhat positively oriented toward, those social arrangements in which they are implicated. Attitude surveys show that the majority of employees like their company, that the majority of members are satisfied with their unions, and undoubtedly research would show a preponderance of positive over negative attitudes toward one's own marriage, family, religion, and nation-state. It is the presence of marked occupational *differences* in work attitudes to which I turn in the next section that is of more theoretical interest.

OCCUPATIONAL DIFFERENCES IN
WORK SATISFACTION

Work satisfaction varies greatly by occupation. Highest percentages of satisfied workers are usually found among professionals and businessmen. In a given plant, the proportion satisfied is higher among clerical workers than among factory workers, just as in general labor force samples it is higher among middle-class than among manual working class occupations. Within the manual working class, job satisfaction is highest among skilled workers, lowest among unskilled laborers and workers on assembly lines.

When a scale of relative job satisfaction is formed, based on general occupational categories, the resulting rank order is almost identical with the most commonly used occupational status classification—the Edwards scale of the Bureau of the Census. For example, the mean indexes of satisfaction in Table 10 resulted from a survey of all New Hope, Pa., jobholders in 1935.

A similar rank order resulted in a national survey when the proportions of workers in each occupational group who would continue the same kind of work in the event they inherited enough money to live comfortably were computed (Table 11).

The generally higher level of job satisfaction

TABLE 9
Proportion of Dissatisfied Workers in Major Job Satisfaction Studies

Researchers	Scope of Sample	Composition of Study	Date	Per Cent Dissatisfied
Morse and Weiss [a]	Random national	401 employed men	1955	20
Centers [b]	Representative national	811 men	1949	17
Palmer [c]	Norristown, Pa.	517 labor force members	1957	10
Shister and Reynolds [d]	New England city	800 manual workers	1949	12
				21 [g]
Hoppock [e]	New Hope, Pa.	309 labor force members	1935	15
Kornhauser [f]	Detroit area	324 employed persons	1952	11

[a] Nancy C. Morse and Robert S. Weiss, "The Function and Meaning of Work and the Job," *American Sociological Review*, 20, 1955, pp. 191–198.

[b] Richard Centers, *The Psychology of Social Classes*, Princeton, N.J.: Princeton University Press, 1949, p. 172.

[c] Gladys L. Palmer, "Attitudes toward Work in an Industrial Community," *American Journal of Sociology*, 63, 1957, pp. 17–26.

[d] Joseph Shister and L. G. Reynolds, *Job Horizons: A Study of Job Satisfaction and Labor Mobility*, New York: Harper, 1949, p. 33.

[e] Robert Hoppock, *Job Satisfaction*, New York: Harper, 1935, p. 246.

[f] Arthur Kornhauser, *Detroit as the People See It*, Detroit: Wayne University Press, 1952, p. 54.

[g] Two separate samples.

of white-collar over blue-collar workers is confirmed by a study of twelve different factories in 1934, in which the scores of clerical workers on job satisfaction were considerably higher than those of factory workers; by the Centers national sample, which found that only 14 per cent of workers in middle-class occupations were dissatisfied with their jobs, compared to 21 per cent of those in working class occupations; and by a 1947 *Fortune* poll, which revealed that the proportion of employees who said their jobs were interesting was 92 per cent among professionals and executives, 72 per cent among salaried employees and 54 per cent among factory workers. However, a study of the Detroit area population found that only among such upper white-collar employees as secretaries, draftsmen, and bookkeepers was the incidence of job satisfaction greater than among manual workers; such lower white-collar employees as clerks, typists, and retail salespeople were somewhat less satisfied than blue-collar workers.

Further evidence of the relation of job satisfaction to occupational status is provided by studies of retirement plans. Although there are a number of factors which affect the retirement decision, it is plausible to argue that the more satisfying a job is to the worker, the more likely he will choose not to retire. In a study of work and retirement in six occupations it was found that the proportion of men who wanted to continue working or had actually continued working after age sixty-five was more than 67 per cent for physicians, 65 per cent for department store salesmen, 49 per cent for skilled printers, 42 per cent for coal miners, and 32 per cent for unskilled and semiskilled steelworkers.

As has been shown in the preceding section of this paper, the majority of workers in all occupations respond positively when asked whether or not they are satisfied with their jobs. But that does not mean they would not prefer other kinds of work. The average worker in a lower-status occupation says that he would choose another line of work if he had the chance to start his working life anew. This question then, is perhaps a more sensitive indicator of latent dissatisfactions and frustrations; the occupational differences it points to, though forming the same pattern as the other, are considerably greater. For example, when a survey of 13,000 Maryland youths was made during the depression it was found that 91 per cent of professional-technical workers preferred their own occupation to any other, compared to 45 per cent of managerial personnel and farm owners, 41 per cent of skilled manual workers, 37 per cent of domestic workers, 36 per cent of office and sales personnel, 14 per cent of unskilled, and 11 per cent of semiskilled manual workers.

More detailed data for a number of professional and manual working class occupations strongly confirm these general findings. Note how for six different professions, the proportion of satisfied persons ranges from 82 per cent to 91 per cent, whereas for seven manual occupations it varies from 16 per cent for unskilled automobile workers to 52 per cent for skilled printers. (See Table 12.)

To some extent, these findings on occupational differences in job satisfaction reflect not only differences in the objective conditions of work for people in various jobs, *but also occupational differences in the norms with respect to work attitudes.* The professional is expected to be dedicated to his profession and have an intense intrinsic interest in his area of specialized com-

TABLE 10

Occupational Group	Mean Index	Number in Sample
Professional and managerial	560	23
Semiprofessional, business, and supervisory	548	32
Skilled manual and white collar	510	84
Semiskilled manual workers	483	74
Unskilled manual workers	401	55

TABLE 11

Occupational Group	Per Cent Who Would Continue Same Kind of Work	Number in Sample
Professionals	68	28
Sales	59	22
Managers	55	22
Skilled manual	40	86
Service	33	18
Semiskilled operatives	32	80
Unskilled	16	27

petence; the white-collar employee is expected to be "company" oriented and like his work; but the loyalty of the manual worker is never taken for granted and, more than any other occupational type, cultural norms permit him the privilege of griping. In fact, it has been asserted that "the natural state of the industrial worker . . . is one of discontent." The same point has been clearly made in an analysis of the latent function of the time clock:

"The office staff does not 'clock-in'—ostensibly because they are not paid by the hour, but it seems likely that at least part of the reason for this is the supposition that, unlike labourers, they do not necessarily dislike work and can be placed on their honour to be punctual. The working classes, as we have seen, are supposed to dislike work and therefore need 'discipline' to keep them

in order. Since 'clocking-in' has been abolished in many firms, it cannot be accepted as absolutely necessary."

FACTORS THAT ACCOUNT FOR OCCUPATIONAL DIFFERENCES IN SATISFACTION

The literature on work is filled with numerous attempts to list and often to estimate the relative importance of the various components, elements, or factors involved in job satisfaction. These lists do not correspond neatly with one another; they bear a large number of labels, but they all are likely to include, in one way or another, such variables as the income attached to a job, supervision, working conditions, social relations, and the variety and skill intrinsic in the work itself. The classification of these terms is quite arbitrary and the number of factors considered relevant can be broken down almost indefinitely.

Whereas most studies attempt to explain variations in job satisfaction among individual employees in the same company or occupation, the interest of the present paper is to explain the gross differences in work attitudes that exist among those in *different* occupations and industries. Four factors that seem useful in accounting for these differences are discussed: occupational prestige, control, integrated work groups, and occupational communities.

OCCUPATIONAL PRESTIGE. Occupational prestige is the one best explanatory factor in the sense that if all occupations (for which sufficient data are available) were ranked in order of extent of typical job satisfaction, and these ranks were compared with the rank order in which they partake of public esteem, the rank-order correlations would be higher than those resulting from any other factor. This is because the prestige of any occupation depends on the level of skill the job entails, the degree of education or training necessary, the amount of control and responsibility involved in the performance of the work, the income which is typically received—to mention the most readily apparent factors. Since occupational prestige as a kind of composite index partly subsumes within itself a number of factors which contribute heavily to differences in satisfaction, it is not surprisng that it should be itself the best individual measure of satisfaction.

In addition, jobs that have high prestige will

TABLE 12
Proportion in Various Occupations Who Would Choose Same Kind of Work if Beginning Career Again

Professional Occupations, Per Cent		Working Class Occupations,[d] Per Cent	
Mathematicians [a]	91	Skilled printers	52
Physicists [a]	89	Paper workers	52
Biologists [a]	89	Skilled automobile workers	41
Chemists [a]	86	Skilled steelworkers	41
Lawyers [b]	83	Textile workers	31
Journalists [c]	82	Unskilled steelworkers	21
		Unskilled automobile workers	16

Sources:
[a] "The Scientists: A Group Portrait," *Fortune*, October 1948, pp. 106–112.
[b] "The U.S. Bar," *Fortune*, May 1939, p. 176.
[c] Leo Rosten, *The Washington Correspondents*, New York: Harcourt, Brace, 1938, p. 347.
[d] These are unpublished data which have been computed from the IBM cards of a survey of 3,000 factory workers in 16 industries, conducted by Elmo Roper for *Fortune* magazine in 1947. A secondary analysis of this survey is being carried out by the Fund for the Republic's Trade Union Project. The general findings of the original study appeared in "The Fortune Survey," *Fortune*, May 1947, pp. 5–12, and June 1947, pp. 5–10.

tend to be valued for their status rewards even when "objective" aspects of the work are undesirable; similarly, low-status jobs will tend to be undervalued and disliked.

". . . the lowliness or nastiness of a job are subjective estimates. . . . A doctor or a nurse, for example, or a sanitary inspector, have to do some things which would disgust the most unskilled casual laborer who did not see these actions in their social context. Yet the status and prestige of such people is generally high. . . . Above all, it is the prestige of his working group and his position in it which will influence the worker's attitude to such jobs."

That the actual findings on differences in job satisfactions correspond quite closely to the scale of occupational prestige has been shown in the previous section. Professionals and business executives have the highest prestige in our society; they also consistently report the highest degree of work satisfaction. According to the most thorough occupational prestige study, doctors are the most esteemed major occupational group in the United States. It is not surprising therefore that this public esteem is an important source of their satisfaction with their work:

"[For] physicians . . . work is a source of prestige. Some doctors stated that to be a physician meant that one belonged to an elite class. It meant that one associated with important people and was in a position of leadership in the community."

Among non-professional or managerial employees, white-collar workers are generally more satisfied with their jobs than manual workers. Again status considerations play an important role. Even when white-collar work does not outrank manual jobs in income or skill, office workers are accorded higher social prestige than blue-collar personnel.

Although this is so, manual work seems to be viewed with greater respect in America, with its democratic frontier traditions, than in many other nations. The historic "social inferiority complex," the "sense of social subordination" of the European industrial worker, to use the words of Henri DeMan, has never been well developed in the United States. We might expect, therefore, that the level of work satisfaction among manual workers would be higher in this country than in Europe. With the rapidly increasing number of attitude surveys of European workers since the war, such a comparison would be of considerable interest.

Within the world of manual work, occupational differences in satisfaction are also related to the differences in prestige that exist among various working class jobs. The higher incidence of positive work attitudes consistently found among skilled workers is not only caused by the skill factor per se; the craftsman takes pride in the fact that he is looked on with more respect in the community than the factory operative or the unskilled laborer. Moreover, those manual workers in occupations which are particularly looked down on will find difficulty in deriving overall positive satisfactions in their work. Interviewers of coal miners have remarked on the great pride with which they are shown various home improvements made possible by the higher wages of a period of prosperity, and on the sensitivity with which some miners react to the public image of the occupation, which has been, in part, created by the hostility of the mass media to the militancy of the union.

"I don't like to strike, because people all get mad at the miners then. I wish the people would realize that the miner has to live too, and not hate him when he tries to better conditions for himself. It bothers me the way people say bad things about the miners, and makes me ashamed of my job."

An attempt has been made to illustrate the manner in which variations in work satisfaction among different occupations tend to follow variations in occupational prestige. Although this generalization is, to an impressive extent, supported by the evidence, it does not hold unfailingly. We can note occupations with relatively high prestige whose general level of satisfaction is lower than would be expected, whereas some low-status jobs seem to be highly satisfying. This suggests that in certain cases other factors play a role even more important than status. A good test of the approach applied here is to see whether the other factors which have been advanced as critical ones can indeed account for discrepancies in the generally marked association between occupational prestige and job satisfaction.

CONTROL. In a perceptive passage, the Belgian socialist Henri DeMan remarks that "all work is felt to be coercive." The fact that work inherently involves a surrender of control, a "subordination of the worker to remoter aims," is probably what makes the relative degree of control in work so important an aspect of job attitudes. As Max Weber, the German sociologist, suggested long ago, "no man easily yields to another full control over the effort, and especially over the amount of physical effort he must daily exert."

There seem to be significant cultural as well as individual differences in the need for control and independence in work. In America, where individual initiative has long been a cultural ideal, we would expect strong pressures in this direction. And we do find that surprising proportions of manual workers in this country have attempted to succeed in small business, and that for many others the idea of running a gas station or a number of tourist cabins is a compelling dream.

Lack of control over the conditions of work is most pronounced for industrial workers.

"The very evidence of his daily work life brings home to the manual worker the degree to which he is directed in his behavior with only limited free choices available. From the moment of starting work by punching a time clock, through work routines that are established at fixed times, until the day ends at the same mechanical time recorder, there is impressed upon the industrial worker his narrow niche in a complex and ordered system of interdependency . . . a system over which he, as an individual, exercises little direct control."

The factory worker is at the bottom of the bureaucratic hierarchy; he is a person for whom action is constantly being originated, but who himself originates little activity for others.

At the same time, diverse factory jobs and working class occupations vary greatly in the degree of control they permit over the conditions of work: it is these variations, of which workers are keenly aware, that are most interesting for the purpose of accounting for differences in satisfaction.

The notion of control in work, as I am using it, is, of course, a vague, *sensitizing* concept which covers a wide range of phenomena rather than a concept which is precisely delimited and identifiable by precise indicators. Among its most important dimensions are control over the use of one's *time* and physical *movement*, which is fundamentally control over the *pace* of the work process, control over the *environment*, both technical and social, and control as the *freedom* from *hierarchal authority*. Naturally, these dimensions are highly interrelated; a business executive high on the occupational ladder will tend to be high in each, whereas an unskilled laborer will have little control from any of these viewpoints. *It is possible to generalize on the basis of the evidence that the greater the degree of control that a worker has (either in a single dimension or as a total composite) the greater his job satisfaction.*

Control over Time, Physical Movement and Pace of Work. Assembly line work in the automobile industry is a good example of the almost complete absence of this aspect of control.

"Its coerced rhythms, the inability to pause at will for a moment's rest, and the need for undeviating attention to simple routines made it work to be avoided if possible and to escape from if necessary. So demanding is the line that one worker, echoing others, complained: 'You get the feeling, everybody gets the feeling, whenever the line jerks everybody is wishing, "break down, baby!" ' "

The consensus of the work literature is that assembly line work, especially in the automobile industry, is more disliked than any other major occupation, and the prime factor in dissatisfaction with the assembly line is the lack of control over the pace of production. Workers in assembly line plants have strong preferences for jobs off the line. A study of the job aspirations of 180 men on the line found that the "workers' motivations were not what might normally be expected. It was not promotion or transfer in order to improve one's economic status. Rather, it was primarily a desire 'to get away from the line.' " *Only 8 per cent* were satisfied, in the sense of not preferring to get an off-line job. The difference between line and off-line jobs has been clearly stated by the sociologist Ely Chinoy who worked in an automobile plant and studied automobile workers:

"Work at a machine may be just as repetitive, require as few motions and as little thought as line assembly, but men prefer it because it does not keep them tied as tightly to their tasks. 'I can stop occasionally when I want to,' said a machine-operator. 'I couldn't do that when I was on the line.' Production standards for a particular machine may be disliked and felt to be excessive, but the machine operator need only approximate his production quota each day. The line-tender must do all the work that the endless belt brings before him. . . ."

The greater dissatisfaction with mass production assembly line jobs is confirmed by the findings in an automobile plant that "men with highly repetitive jobs, conveyor paced, and so forth, were far more likely to take time off from work than those whose jobs did not contain such job characteristics," and that quit rates were almost twice as high among men on the assembly line as among men off the line. In a study of Maryland youth during the depression, it was found that the occupation most disliked by female workers was that of operator on cannery conveyor belts. Every one of the fifty-three cannery operatives in the sample expressed a preference for different work! The control of these workers over the pace of production is at least as minimal as that of automobile workers, and in addition they lack even the protection of a strong union.

A machine operator may go all out in the morning to produce 100 pieces, take it easy in the afternoon, only putting out 50; at any rate, it is his own decision. In similar fashion a few assembly line workers may be able to build up a "bank" of automobile seats which they assemble to the oncoming bodies; a few try to get ahead and gain time for rest by working up the line, but for the great majority it is hopeless. Assembly line workers are "alienated," according to the researchers who have studied them. In their work they "can secure little significant experience of themselves as productive human beings." As one automobile worker put it a little wistfully:

"You understand, if you get a job that you're interested in, when you work you don't pay attention to the time, you don't wait for the whistle to blow to go home, you're all wrapped up in it and don't pay attention to other things. *I don't know one single job like that.*"

According to David Riesman, what these wage earners are deprived of is "any chance to extend themselves, to go all-out." A stark example is the worker on the packinghouse assembly line who goes home after his day's work in order to "try to accomplish something for that day." How do these workers stand it? Here is the deadly answer of a Hormel meat worker: "The time passes."

"Most workers are so busily engaged in pushing the flow of work that they do not *consciously* suffer from the inherent monotony of their work. They are well adjusted, because they have reduced their level of aspirations to the rather low level of the job. They coast along, keeping busy, visiting, talking, making time go by, and getting the work done in order to get 'out of there' in order to get home!'"

The great dissatisfaction with automobile assembly work is an example of a discrepancy between occupational status and job satisfaction. The status of the automobile worker is not lower than that of other semiskilled American factory workers; in fact, the level of wages would suggest that it is higher than manual workers in many other industrial occupations, especially those in nondurable goods manufacturing. But the control of the automobile assembly line worker over the work process is considerably less than in other major industrial occupations, and this is a big factor in accounting for the prevalence of job discontent.

It is interesting to contrast automobile manufacturing with mining, an occupation which, though considered lower in prestige, seems to provide marked work satisfaction. Alvin Gouldner, in his study of a gypsum plant, found that although the miners had considerably less status in the community than surface workers, they showed much greater work motivation. He attributed this high job satisfaction to the fact that miners "were not 'alienated' from their machines: that is, they had an unusually high degree of control over their machine's operation. The pace at which the machines worked, the corners into which they were poked, what happened to them when they broke down, was determined mainly by the miners themselves. On the surface, though, the speed at which the machines worked and the procedures followed were prescribed by superiors."

Finally, the higher job satisfaction of skilled workers (documented in the preceding sections of this paper) is related to the fact that they have a large measure of control over the pace of their work. The fact that craftsmen themselves largely determine the speed at which they work gives them a marked advantage over most factory workers.

Control over the Technical and Social Environment. In those occupations in which the physical environment or the technological work process is particularly challenging, control over it seems to be an important aspect of job satisfaction. Coal-miners have "a very personal sense of being pitted against their environment" and express "feelings of accomplishment and pride at having conquered it." That steel production is found fascinating is suggested by a mill worker: "It's sort of interesting. Sometimes you have a battle on your hands. You have to use your imagination and ability to figure out what move to make." Similarly, it has been noted that railroad workers derive a sense of power in "the manipulation of many tons of railroad equipment." Engineers derive more pleasure in running large engines rather than small ones; switchmen and brakemen "give the signals that move fifty or so freight cars back and forth like so many toys."

A further source of the dissatisfaction with automobile assembly, then, is the fact that these jobs provide so little scope for control over the technical environment; there is little that is challenging in the actual work operation. As a man on the line puts it:

"There is nothing more discouraging than having a barrel beside you with 10,000 bolts in it and using them all up. Then you get a barrel with another 10,000 bolts, and you know that every one of those 10,000 bolts has to be picked up and put in exactly the same place as the last 10,000 bolts."

Paralleling the control of industrial workers over the technical environment is the satisfaction derived by professional and white-collar employees from control over a social environment, namely, clients and customers. A study of salespeople concluded that "the completion of the sale, the conquering of the customer, represents the challenge or the 'meaningful life-experience' of selling." As one salesclerk, contemplating the import of his retirement, said: "I think to be perfectly truthful about it, the thing I miss most is being able to project myself into a sphere, conquer it, and retire with a pleased feeling because I have conquered it."

Control as the Freedom from Direct Supervision. On a slightly different level of analysis is this third dimension, which refers not to the aspects of the work process under control, but rather to the locus of control. One of the most consistent findings of work research is that industrial workers consider light, infrequent supervision, "foremen who aren't drivers," a crucial element in their high regard for particular jobs and companies.

The absence of close supervision in the mines has been considered an important determinant of the miners' high level of satisfaction. And truck drivers and railroad workers, in explaining their preference for their own trades, stress the independence they experience in these jobs where the contact between employees and supervisor is so much less frequent than in factory work. As two railroad engineers put it:

"I'd work anywhere except at a shop or in the factory. Just don't like a place where someone is watching you do your work all the time. That's why I like my job on the railroad now.

"I wouldn't last three days working in a shop with a foreman breathing down my neck. Here I'm my own boss when I run the trains, nobody tells me what to do. . . ."

Such impressionistic evidence is confirmed by the more systematic comparisons of Hoppock, who found that the mean job satisfaction index of railroad employees ranked only below professional men and artists; it was higher than managers, clerical workers, small business proprietors, salesmen, and storeclerks! Although railroading is a high-status industrial occupation—railroaders have historically been part of the labor aristocracy—its occupational prestige is below most white-collar occupations. On the other hand, truck driving is a lower-status manual occupation (truck drivers are classified as semi-skilled operatives by the census, and the popular stereotypes of this occupation are somewhat derogatory), and yet in the Hoppock survey the satisfaction of truck drivers outranked all industrial occupations except railroading and was approximately the same level as that of salesmen.

It is plausible that the marked discrepancy between job satisfaction and occupational status in these industries can be explained by the high degree of control, especially as reflected in freedom from supervision, which the workers enjoy.

If control in the work process is a crucial determinant of a worker's subjective feelings of well-being on the job, as I am trying to demonstrate, the question whether industrial trends are increasing or decreasing these areas of control becomes quite significant. It is interesting that Faunce's recent study of an *automated* engine plant shows that various dimensions of control may not change in the same direction. Compared to work in a non-automated, non-assembly line engine plant, automation greatly decreased the worker's direct control over his machine and pace of work, and this was felt to be a source of serious dissatisfaction. On the other hand, the increased responsibility and control over a complex technical environment of automated equipment was seen as a source of greater satisfaction and heightened status. Thus, while Faunce was able to locate the elements which made for satisfaction and those which made for dissatisfaction in these jobs (his analysis seems very congruent with the present discussion), it was rather difficult to assess the overall effect of the change on work satisfaction.

INTEGRATED WORK GROUPS. A third factor that is important in explaining occupational differences in work satisfaction is the nature of on-the-job social relations. The technological structure of certain industries such as steel production and mining requires that the work be carried out by *teams* of men working closely together, whereas in industries such as automobile assembly the formation of regular work groups is virtually prohibited by the organization of production. There is much evidence to support the proposition that the greater the extent to which workers are members of integrated work teams on the job, the higher the level of job satisfaction.

In a steel mill in which 85 per cent of sixty-two workers interviewed were satisfied with their jobs, Charles Walker found that "the source of satisfaction most often articulated or implied was that of being part of, or having membership in, the hot mill crew." As three steel workers express it:

"(A heater helper) We work for a while, it's like playing baseball. First one fellow is up and then you have your turn at bat. We can knock off every so often and take a smoke and talk. I like working with men I know and working like a team.

"(A piercer plugger) The crew I am in is very good. Our foreman likes to see his men on top and he does everything to help us . . . this attitude makes a lot of people put out more steel. . . . Over here it's teamwork. . . . You can have a lot of Hank Greenbergs on the team but if you don't work together, it isn't a team at all. And we like our work because we carry on a lot of conversation with signs and the men laugh and joke and the time passes very quick.

"(A piercer dragout worker) There's nothing like working here in this mill. Everybody cooperates. Every man works as a member of a team and every man tries to turn out as much steel as they possibly can. We work hard and get satisfaction out of working hard."

While recognizing that close kinship ties and a small town atmosphere encouraged such cooperative spirit, Walker attributed the principal cause of the integrated work teams to the basic technological process of making steel, which requires small group operations. He compared this technology and its results with that of the automobile assembly plants in which the technological structure is such that the majority of workers perform their operations individually. There, the pattern of social interaction produced by the moving line is such that although workers will talk to the man in front of them, behind them, and across from them, no worker will interact with exactly the same group of men as any other worker will; therefore, no stable work groups are formed. Walker considered this a major element in the greater dissatisfaction he found among automobile workers compared to steel workers.

Mining is another occupation where technological conditions seem to favor the development of closely knit work groups. Since, as one miner expressed it, "the mines are kind of a family affair," where "the quality of the sentiment is of a depth and complexity produced only by long years of intimate association," it is not surprising that many miners feel that the loss of social contacts at work is a major disadvantage of retirement. The dangerous nature of the work is another factor that knits miners together:

"To be an old-timer in the mines means something more than merely knowing the technique of a particular job; it also means awareness and acceptance of the responsibility which each man has for his fellow-workers. The sense of interdependence in relation to common dangers is undoubtedly an important factor in the spirit of solidarity which has characterized miners in all countries for many generations."

Within the same factory, departments and jobs vary considerably in the extent to which the work is carried out by individuals working alone or by groups; the consequences of these differences have been a major interest of the "human relations in industry" movement. A recent study of one department in a factory manufacturing rotating equipment found that the employees who were integrated members of informal work groups were, by and large, satisfied with both the intrinsic characteristics of their jobs, and such "extended characteristics" as pay, working conditions, and benefits, whereas the non-group members tended to be dissatisfied. Sixty-five per cent of "regular" group members were satisfied, compared to 43 per cent of members of groups which were deviant in accepting less fully the values of the factory community, and compared to only 28 per cent of isolated workers.

The classic investigations of the functions of informal work groups in industry have been produced by the "human relations in industry" school, associated most directly with the Harvard Business School and the writings of Elton Mayo, and represented by the pioneering experiments at the Hawthorne plant of the Western Electric Company. These studies have demonstrated that informal work groups establish and enforce norms which guide the productive and other behavior of workers on the job, and that such management problems as absenteeism, turnover, and morale can often be dealt with through the manipulation of work groups and supervisorial behavior. But it is striking that the human relations school has concerned itself so little with the job itself, with the relation between the worker and his work, rather than the relation between the worker and his mates. A typical human relations discussion of the conditions of employee morale is likely to give all its emphasis to matters of communication, supervision, and the personality of workers and ignore almost completely intrinsic job tasks. In a recent study by the Harvard Business School entitled *Worker Satisfaction and Development*, the only sources of work satisfaction discussed are those which directly concern workers' integration in work groups and cliques. Although creativity is a major concern of the author, it is the creativity of the *work group* to adapt to new circumstances, rather than the creative expression of an individual in his work, that he is interested in.

In its emphasis on the importance of integrated work groups the human relations approach has made an important contribution. But "a way of seeing is a way of not seeing," and its neglect of the other factors imposes serious limitations on the usefulness of this approach, at least in providing an adequate theory of the conditions of work satisfaction.

OCCUPATIONAL COMMUNITIES. The nature of the association among workers *off-the-job* is also a factor in work satisfaction. The evidence of the work literature supports the notion that levels of work satisfaction are higher in those industries and in those kinds of jobs in which workers make up an "occupational community." One such industry is mining. Not only is the actual work carried out by solidary work groups, but, in addition, miners live in a community made up largely of fellow workers. This kind of "inbreeding" produces a devotion to the occupation which is not characteristic of many other working class jobs:

"Somehow when you get into mining and you like the men you work with, you just get to the place after a while that you don't want to leave. *Once that fever gets hold of a man, he'll never be good for anything else.*

"A fellow may quit the mines, but when they whistle, he goes back. I've had a lot better jobs, but I've always liked to work in the mines. I can't explain it, except I like being with the gang; I never could just sit around much."

Such occupational communities are likely to develop in occupations that are isolated, either spatially or on the basis of peculiar hours of work. Coal mining and textile industries characteristically have grown up in *isolated small communities*; sailors, cowboys, and long-distance truck drivers are also isolated from contact with persons in other jobs. Similarly, *off-hours shifts* favor the development of occupational communities; this is the case with printers, a large proportion of whom work nights, steelworkers, who often rotate between day, swing, and graveyard shifts, firemen, and, of course, railroad men.

The essential feature of an occupational community is that workers in their off-hours socialize more with persons in their own line of work than with a cross section of occupational types. Printers generally go to bars, movies, and baseball games with other printers. In a small town steel mill, 87 per cent of the workers had spent "in the last week," at least some time off the job with other workers in their department; almost half said they had seen many or almost all of their fellow workers. However, in a large tractor plant of 20,000 people only 41 per cent of the employees said that they got together socially outside the plant with employees from their own work groups. *Occupational communities rarely exist among urban factory workers.*

A second characteristic of an occupational community is that its participants "talk shop" in their off-hours. That this is true of farmers, fishermen, miners, and railroaders has been described far more by novelists than by social scientists. The significance of talking about work off the job has been well expressed by Fred Blum, who notes that the assembly line workers in the meat packing plant he studied rarely do so.

"Whether they are with their family or their friends, rare are the occasions when workers feel like talking about their work. In response to the question: 'Do you talk with your friends about the work you are doing?' only a very small number indicated that they do talk with their friends —or their wife—about their work. Quite a few said that they 'only' talk with their friends 'if they ask me' or that they talk 'sometimes' or 'seldom.' Some workers are outspoken in saying that they do not like to talk about their work. 'If we get out of there, we are through with that to the next day.' Another worker said, 'When I leave down there, I am through down there. I like to talk about something else.' *He adds to this with some astonishment: 'Railroadmen always want to talk about their work.'* "

Third, occupational communities are little worlds in themselves. For its members the occupation itself is the reference group; its standards of behavior, its system of status and rank, guide conduct.

"Railroading is something more than occupation. Like thieving and music, it is a world by itself, with its own literature and mythology, with an irrational system of status which is unintelligible to the outsider, and a complicated rule book for distributing responsibility and rewards."

We can suggest a number of mechanisms by means of which occupational communities increase job satisfaction. First, when workers know their co-workers off the job, they will derive deeper social satisfactions on the job. In the second place, an effect of the isolation of the occupation is that workers are able to develop and maintain a pride in and devotion to their line of work; at the same time, isolation insulates them from having to come to grips with the general public's image of their status, which is likely to be considerably lower than their own. Participation in an occupational community means not only the reinforcement of the group's sense of general prestige; in such worlds one's skill and expertise in doing the actual work becomes an important basis of individual status and prestige. Finally, unlike the "alienated" assembly line worker, who is characterized by a separation of his work sphere from his non-work sphere—a separation of work

from life as Mills and Blum put it—the work and leisure interests of those in occupational communities are highly integrated. If the integration of work and non-work is an important element in general psychic adjustment, as some assert, then these workers should exhibit higher job satisfaction, since satisfaction with life in general seems to be highly related to satisfaction in work.

CONCLUSIONS

When we read modern accounts of what work and workers were like before the industrial revolution, we continually find that the dominant image of the worker of that period is the craftsman. Viewed as an independent producer in his home or small shop with complete control over the pace and scheduling of his work, making the whole product rather than a part of it, and taking pride in the creativity of his skilled tasks, his traits are typically contrasted with those of the alienated factory worker—the allegedly characteristic producer of modern society. . . .

But, *work has significant positive meanings to persons who do not find overall satisfaction in their immediate job.* A still viable consequence of the Protestant ethic in our society is that its work ethic (the notion of work as a calling, an obligation to one's family, society, and self-respect, if no longer to God), retains a powerful hold. This is most dramatically seen in the reactions of the retired and unemployed. The idea is quite common to American workers at all occupational levels that soon after a worker retires, he is likely to either "drop dead" or "go crazy" from sheer inactivity. An English industrial psychiatrist states that this is actually a common calamity in British industry. Similarly, the studies made in the 1930's of unemployed people show that the disruption of the work relationship often leads to the disruption of normal family relations, to political apathy, and to a lack of interest in social organizations and leisure-time activities.

The studies of job satisfaction reviewed in this paper further question the prevailing thesis that most workers in modern society are alienated and estranged. There is a remarkable consistency in the findings that the vast majority of workers, in virtually all occupations and industries, are moderately or highly satisfied, rather than dissatisfied, with their jobs.

However, the marked occupational differences in work attitudes and the great significance which workers impute to being, at least to some extent, masters of their destiny in the work process, along with the fact that surrender of such control seems to be the most important condition of strong dissatisfaction are findings at least as important as the overall one of general satisfaction. Perhaps the need for autonomy and independence may be a more deep-seated human motive than is recognized by those who characterize our society in terms of crowdlike conformity and the decline of individualism. . . .

Finally, the findings of this paper indicate a need for considerable further research on industrial statistics and industrial trends. If the evidence shows that extreme dissatisfaction is concentrated among assembly line workers, it becomes terribly important, for a total assessment of the conditions of work in modern America, to know what proportion of the labor force works on assembly lines or in other job contexts involving little control over their work activities. It is startling, considering the importance of such data, that such figures do not exist. This situation helps maintain the conventional belief that the mechanized assembly line worker is today's typical industrial worker in contrast to the craftsman of the past.

An indication that the actual proportion of assembly line workers is quite small is suggested by figures of the automobile industry, the conveyor belt industry par excellence. If we consider total employment in the industrial groupings involved in the manufacture, sales, repair, and servicing of automobiles, we find that assembly line workers make up less than 5 per cent of all workers in this complex. There are approximately 120,-000 automobile workers who are line assemblers, yet the number of skilled repair mechanics in all branches of the industry, a job which in many ways resembles the craft ideal, exceeds 500,000. In addition, the 120,000 assemblers are outnumbered by 400,000 managers who own or operate gas stations, garages, new and used car lots, and wrecking yards, and by 200,000 *skilled* workers in automobile plants. Recent developments, especially automation, have served further to decrease the proportion of assembly line operatives in the industry.

If the situation in the automobile industry is at all typical, research might well show that those kinds of job contexts which are associated with high work satisfaction and control over one's time

and destiny, such as skilled repair work and self-employment, are more representative than is commonly believed, and are even increasing over the long run. Such a prospect should bring considerable satisfaction to all those in the diverse intellectual traditions who have been concerned with what happens to human beings in the course of their major life activity, their work. And yet, this would not necessarily mean that the problem of the lack of fulfillment in work had become less serious. For as one industrial sociologist has suggested, this problem *may become more acute*, not because work itself has become more tedious, fractionated, and meaningless, but because the ideal of pride in creative effort is shared by an increasingly large proportion of the labor force as a result of the rise of democratic education and its emphasis on individualism and occupational mobility.

In the closing sentences of the foregoing article, Professor Blauner calls attention to what has been called the "revolution of rising expectations." The phrase, in its more usual application, refers to the rising economic and political aspirations of people in underdeveloped countries. Curiously enough, although the twentieth century has witnessed progress in the standard of living in backward countries and great increases in their political autonomy, aspirations have arisen *faster* than changes. A similar phenomenon has been noted in affluent, democratic, industrial societies. At a time when *objective* deprivation is on the wane, resentment of *relative* deprivation continues.[26] The *feeling* of poverty does not necessarily correspond to the extent of *objective deprivations.*[27] Professor Blauner's suggestion that rising expectations applies to the work situation is intriguing. Rising expectations for the work situation could account for increases of dissatisfaction despite objective improvements in some or all of the four factors that, according to Blauner,

[26] Samuel A. Stouffer et al., *The American Soldier*, Vol. 1, Princeton, N.J.: Princeton University Press, 1949, pp. 124–130, 172–173, 178–182, 208–211, 250–251, 219–280, 369, 525–527, 542–543, 562–564.
[27] Harry C. Bredemeier and Jackson Toby, *Social Problems in America: Costs and Casualties in an Acquisitive Society*, New York: Wiley, 1960, p. 60.

bear a relationship to work satisfaction.

Take control over the work situation, for instance. Blauner argues persuasively that the closer the supervision over the worker and the less the choice he can exercise over the timing of his operations, his physical movements, and the pace of his work, the less is his work satisfaction. Is worker control over the work situation *decreasing?* Not clearly so; this is a complicated problem. Some technological developments in machine-line operations seem to reduce worker autonomy; other technological developments seem to increase it. Apart from technology, two industrial developments *favor* worker control over the work situation. One is a change in managerial ideology.

Partly as a result of studies conducted by Elton Mayo of the Harvard Business School and his colleagues, business executives are aware of "human relations in industry." [28] They recognize that the character of supervision is an important factor in worker morale and therefore, indirectly, in productivity. For instance, take the oft-cited study of absenteeism and labor turnover in a California aircraft factory during the Second World War.[29] In a new factory, some inexperienced foremen had natural talent for leadership; others thought that a foreman was supposed to bark orders at underlings. The researchers discovered that variation in supervisory skill accounted for the tremendous rate of absenteeism and labor turnover in certain departments and the negligible rate in others. Government and industry learned from such wartime experiences that supervisory skill can be developed through training. More than a million foremen were taught methods of handling workers in the Training Within Industry Program of the War Manpower Commission.[30] And since the end of the war,

industry has continued the stress on human relations in its training programs for supervisory personnel. The human-relations climate in many large corporations means that management tries to exercise supervision *tactfully*. An industrial corporation can never be as democratic as the ideal New England town meeting, but the feelings of subordinates can be considered or ignored in the communication of decisions from the top. Insofar as the new human-relations ideology has permeated the company, workers experience a *less* coercive atmosphere.

The second change, the power of giant unions to limit managerial authority, tends to increase worker influence in the work situation. In 1960 more than 18 million American workers were enrolled in 184 unions, three of which contained more than a million members each [31] (See Table 13). In the steel, coal, automobile, and electrical industries, giant corporations bargain with giant unions.[32] In the garment and coal industries, the unions are more powerful than individual corporate employers and have on occasion loaned money to employers to save tottering businesses. This strength of unions has resulted in contracts with employers which customarily provide protection for the worker against arbitrary actions on the part of management. Two officials of the Steelworkers Union went so far as to explain the appeal of unions largely in terms of worker desire for a Bill of Rights. "Labor unions have their origin in the desire of workers for self-protection against arbitrary acts of management in layoff, promotions, wage distributions, speed-ups, and other matters that vitally affect them." [33] The main thrust of this statement is *not* on wage benefits but on what is known in constitutional law as "due process." "Due process" is what a leading labor economist was emphasizing when he called collective bargaining a system of "industrial jurisprudence." [34]

28   Reinhard Bendix, *Work and Authority in Industry: Ideologies of Management in the Course of Industrialization*, New York: Wiley, 1956, pp. 308–340.
29   Elton Mayo and George F. Lombard, *Teamwork and Labor Turnover in the Aircraft Industry of Southern California*, Boston: Harvard Graduate School of Business Administration, Business Research Studies, No. 32, 1944.
30   Stuart Chase, *The Proper Study of Mankind*, rev. ed., New York: Harper, 1956, p. 166.

31   Bureau of the Census, *Statistical Abstract of the United States: 1962*, Washington: Government Printing Office, 1962, pp. 241–242.
32   John Kenneth Galbraith, *American Capitalism: The Theory of Countervailing Power*, Boston: Houghton Mifflin, 1952.
33   Clinton S. Golden and Harold J. Ruttenberg, *The*
(continued on next page)

TABLE 13
National and International Labor Unions Reporting 100,000 Or More Members in 1960

Name of Union	Number of Members
1. International Brotherhood of Teamsters, Chauffeurs, Warehousemen, and Helpers of America (Independent)	1,484,433
2. United Steelworkers of America	1,152,000
3. United International Union of Automobile, Aircraft, and Agricultural Implement Workers of America	1,136,140
4. International Association of Machinists	898,139
5. United Brotherhood of Carpenters and Joiners of America	800,000
6. International Brotherhood of Electrical Workers	771,000
7. United Mine Workers of America (Independent)	600,000
8. International Ladies' Garment Workers' Union	446,554
9. Hotel and Restaurant Employees and Bartenders International Union	443,000
10. International Hod Carriers', Building, and Common Laborers' Union of America	442,473
11. Amalgamated Clothing Workers of America	377,000
12. Retail Clerks International Association	342,000
13. Amalgamated Meat Cutters and Butcher Workmen of North America	333,482
14. Brotherhood of Railway and Steamship Clerks, Freight Handlers, Express and Station Employees	300,000
15. International Union of Operating Engineers	291,000
16. International Union of Electrical, Radio, and Machine Workers	287,937
17. Building Service Employees' International Union	272,000
18. American Federation of Musicians	266,618
19. Communications Workers of America	259,917
20. United Association of Journeymen and Apprentices of the Plumbing and Pipe Fitting Industry of the United States and Canada	251,273

Name of Union	Number of Members
21. American Federation of State, County, and Municipal Employees	210,000
22. Brotherhood of Painters, Decorators, and Paperhangers of America	192,568
23. Textile Workers Union of America	192,000
24. Oil, Chemical, and Atomic Workers International Union	174,000
25. International Brotherhood of Pulp, Sulphite, and Paper Mill Workers	170,554
26. United Rubber, Cork, Linoleum, and Plastic Workers of America	170,000
27. Brotherhood of Maintenance of Way Employees	164,447
28. United Electrical, Radio, and Machine Workers of America (Independent)	160,000
29. Brotherhood of Railroad Trainmen	159,384
30. Bricklayers, Masons, and Plasterers' International Union of America	155,000
31. International Association of Bridge, Structural, and Ornamental Iron Workers	147,982
32. Retail, Wholesale, and Department Store Union	143,300
33. International Brotherhood of Boilermakers, Iron Shipbuilders, Blacksmiths, Forgers, and Helpers	140,000
34. United Papermakers and Paperworkers	140,000
35. National Association of Letter Carriers of the United States of America	138,000
36. Transport Workers Union of America	135,000
37. Amalgamated Association of Street, Electric Railway, and Motor Coach Employees of America	132,100
38. Brotherhood of Railway Carmen of America	125,000
39. International Printing Pressmen and Assistants' Union of North America	113,903
40. International Typographical Union	105,033
41. United Packinghouse, Food, and Allied Workers	102,598
42. Sheet Metal Workers' International Association	100,000
43. International Union of Mine, Mill, and Smelter Workers (Independent)	100,000

Dynamics of Industrial Democracy, New York: Harper, 1942, p. 255.
[34] Sumner H. Slichter, James J. Healy, and E. Robert Livernash, *The Impact of Collective Bargaining on Management*, Washington: Brookings Institution, 1960.

Source: *Directory of National and International Labor Unions in the United States, 1961*, United States Department of Labor, Bureau of Labor Statistics, Bulletin No. 1320, March, 1962, pp. 49, 16–32.

Union contracts place limitations on the authority of the employer to hire, fire, promote, and make work rules. Some employers resent this. They feel that promotions based on seniority, for example, prevent them from rewarding the best workers and thereby reduce overall efficiency. On the other hands, seniority provisions in the contract give workers a feeling of job security; they are less likely to suspect that favoritism or discrimination underlies management decisions. In Professor Blauner's terms, seniority gives workers more *control* over the work situation. If morale of the work force thereby improves, seniority might *increase* productivity even though it is a demonstrable violation of the logic of efficiency.

Giant unions do not guarantee the individual worker greater control over his immediate work situation. If the union is undemocratic, the worker may feel subjected to two tyrannies, that of union bureaucrats and that of his supervisors, instead of one.[35] The likelihood is, however, that even in undemocratic unions, shop stewards and other union officials cannot ignore their members' concern over the work situation.

To sum up: both a human-relations ideology on the part of management and the power of big unions may have increased worker independence over the past generation. As Professor Blauner points out, however, worker satisfaction depends not only on the *objective* work situation, but also on the aspirations of the worker. Thus, improvements in the work situation and *in*creases in worker dissatisfaction could be compatible.

SOME SOCIAL CONSEQUENCES OF THE DIFFERENTIATION OF ECONOMIC INSTITUTIONS

The separation of work and residence in industrial societies does more than create traffic jams for commuters. The relative independence of the world of work and of the neighborhood where the worker resides makes for jurisdictional problems. Talcott Parsons notes

that the English language implicitly assumes that the residential community is the paramount commitment of the worker; ". . . the place of residence, the 'home,' is said to be the place where the person 'lives,' as though, when away from home, he were not alive."[36] This assumption was approximately correct in the preindustrial era. Today it sounds quaint. Contemporary man not only *lives* when away from home; he may feel that his life away from home, his *career*, is as important to him as his family. The term "career" is usually applied to prestige occupational roles in government, business, or the professions; manual workers have "jobs," not "careers." This explains why a conflict in allegiance between work and family is most acute on the *upper* levels of the occupational structure. Newspaper accounts of divorce actions among film stars, for instance, hint that career problems underlie many of the legal charges. Husbands are away from home for months at a time to make movies in foreign countries; wives are more interested in nightclubbing with other film celebrities than in homemaking. Commitments to careers are especially disruptive when *both* spouses have strong career commitments, as in the entertainment world. For business executives, on the other hand, the husband's commitment to his career need not disrupt the marriage because the wife is often willing to subordinate family life to the demands of her husband's workload. In the colorful words of a *Fortune* editor, William H. Whyte, Jr., home is not a sanctuary but a "branch office."

The Major Allegiance of the Executive: To His Career

Reprinted by permission. From William H. Whyte, Jr., *The Organization Man*, New York: Simon and Schuster, 1956, pp. 142–150.

There is a widespread assumption that executives don't work as hard as they used to, for which apparent fact many people voice thanks. We are

---

[35] Chapter 15 takes up the problem of union bureaucracy at greater length.

[36] Talcott Parsons, *Structure and Process in Modern Society*, Glencoe, Ill.: Free Press, 1960, pp. 252.

hearing more and more now about the trend to more hobbies and outside interests, a more rational appreciation of the therapy of leisure, the desirability of being fully involved in community life, and it has now become virtually a cliché that today's effective executive is not the single-minded hard driver of old, but the man who is so well organized himself as to strike a sane balance between work and the rest of his life.

My colleagues and I, half persuaded that executives were in fact working more moderately, tried to test the proposition. We checked such things as country club attendance, commuter peak hours and travel schedules, and, more to the point, talked at length to several hundred organization men. We came to the conclusion that: (1) executives are working as hard as they ever did—possibly even harder; (2) grumbling notwithstanding, high income taxes have had little effect on executive drive; (3) executives are prey to more tension and conflict than ever before, for while the swing to committee management has eliminated many old work pressures it has substituted new ones just as frustrating.

By "executive" I do not mean management men in general; in many respects the two are rather different. I am abitrarily defining "executive" as corporation men who are presidents or vice-presidents plus those men in middle management who have so demonstrably gone ahead of their contemporaries as to indicate that they are likely to keep on going.

Common to these men is an average work week that runs between fifty and sixty hours. Typically it would break down something like this: each weekday the executive will put in about 9½ hours in the office. Four out of five weekdays he will work nights. One night he will be booked for business entertaining, another night he will probably spend at the office or in a protracted conference somewhere else.

On two of the other nights he goes home. But it's no sanctuary he retreats to; it's a branch office. While only a few go so far as to have a room equipped with dictating machines, calculators, and other appurtenances of their real life, most executives make a regular practice of doing the bulk of their business reading at home and some find it the best time to do their most serious business phone work. ("I do a lot of spot-checking by phone from home," one executive explained. "I have more time then, and besides most people

have their guard down when you phone them at home.") . . .

Why do they work so hard? No voice has been louder than the businessman's in damning the income tax as encouraging slothfulness, and they have repeatedly complained that its worst effect has been to rob management of the incentive to hard work. With this plaint in mind, we asked each of the executives we interviewed this question: "Would you, personally, be working harder now if your taxes were less?" Well, said the executives, now don't get them wrong, they don't take back anything about taxes, but as far as their own particular case went—no, they wouldn't be working harder now. . . .

When the executive talks of himself and why he works—a subject of quite compelling interest to him—he speaks about many things. He speaks often of service to others. It is a genuine feeling on his part, for he does not himself belabor the point. Convention rhetoric notwithstanding, he has so little self-doubt on the matter that he is rather bored with the kind of soul-searching questions ("Is management a profession?" "Is public relations at the crossroads?") that worry the staff. He takes it for granted that management work is one of the most vital functions in the United States—sometimes he talks as if it were the only one.

Labor leaders talk like any other executive. Here, in excerpt, is a vice-president of a big CIO union on the subject of work load:

"I'm working harder than I ever have in my life, and I once was a cushion builder. The incentive isn't monetary gain. There is much more than that. There is never a dull moment in the labor movement. I feel I'm part of a crusade, making the world a better place in which to live. I like everything about my job.

"My usual work week is seventy to eighty hours, I would say. I get to the office at 8:30 A.M. and usually am at my desk until 6:00 P.M. There's usually a luncheon conference daily, and three nights a week I take home a brief case with reading material and reports. I spend about two hours those nights on the reports.

"Two nights a week is about the average for attending local union meetings that require my attention. Every Saturday and Sunday there is a membership conference, an executives' conference, a convention, or a union picnic.

"Forty per cent of the time I'm on the road

in top-level negotiations, trouble-shooting, speaking or attending a CIO board meeting. Here is an example of out-of-town work: Last week end a workshop conference was ending at Purdue University. I left Detroit at 3:05 P.M., flying to Indianapolis and taking a car from there to Lafayette, Indiana. I spoke at 7:30 P.M., finished at 9:30, and then was in a conference until 11:15 P.M. I drove back to Indianapolis, left at 1:10 by plane and got home at 3 A.M.

"Do I work too hard? My doctor and my wife think so, but I don't. If I am, it's my own fault because I don't delegate enough work."

Service is not the basic motivation. In talking about why he works, the executive does not speak first of service, or of pressures from the organization; very rarely does he mention his family as a reason. He speaks of himself—and the demon within him. He works because his ego demands it. "People are like springs," explains one company president. "The energy you have within you has to come out one way or another. I would really get in bad shape if I didn't work." "It's like baseball," another president puts it. "A good player doesn't think of the contract when he is up to bat. He drives for the fences." Whatever the analogy—two presidents compare themselves to concert pianists—the theme is self-expression.

Work, then, is dominant. Everything else is subordinate and the executive is unable to compartmentalize his life. Whatever the segment of it—leisure, home, friends—he instinctively measures it in terms of how well it meshes with his work. Is it *overwork*? The executive's ability to describe a crushing work load and in the next breath deny that it's overwork is prodigious. Here, for example, is the way a utility company president answered the overwork question:

"In the old days, I used to work eighteen and twenty hours a day, but when it was all finished, I didn't give a damn until work rolled around again the next day. Now, hell, I go home thinking about decisions I have to make. I just don't like to sit and think, so I pick up a detective story—something light—and sit there wondering what I'll tell Mike Quill when he says such-and-such or what I'll say at the next fare-increasing hearing.

"In the middle of a rate or a wage fight, I lie awake nights wondering what the hell I'll say next. Sometimes I get up from one wage-bargaining session, go home, lie awake thinking until it gets light, and then go back to the bargaining

table with maybe only an hour's sleep. I've got an ulcer that acts up on me in times like that. It goes to sleep again when the bargaining is all over and I can start eating decent meals again. I turn in at the hospital every once in a long while just to get some time off to think quietly. Is it overwork? Well . . . I grew up in this business. I like it. There's always something happening. I like it for itself and the fact that I've got some share in helping millions of people get where they want to go. That gives me some feeling of accomplishment."

Most executives are not as sheepish. For some reason the question of whether they overwork touches a very sensitive nerve; equably as they discuss other aspects of their life, on this one they fairly jump. Ninety per cent of the executives we queried said they didn't work too hard, and when they said it they answered with "Absolutely not!" "Of course not!" and similar expostulation. (The few executives who did say they worked too hard were described by colleagues as lazy.)

Why do they protest so much? Executives' reactions to a follow-up question give a clue. Did other people—their wives, their doctors, their friends—think they worked too hard? A little sadly the executive would answer, Yes, others did think that he worked too hard. *They just didn't understand.*

To the executive there is between work and the rest of his life a unity he can never fully explain, and least of all to his wife. One of the few secrets many an executive manages to keep from his wife is how much more deeply he is involved in his job than in anything else under the sun. Thus he can never really explain to his wife that what he is doing is not overwork, for the explanation would be tactless. "Overwork as I see it," says one company president, "is simply work that you don't like. But I dearly love this work. You love only one time and you might as well do something you like." He was not talking about his wife.

Unlike the Catholic Church, the corporation cannot require celibacy, and because its members are subject to the diversions of family ties, the corporation does fall short of complete effectiveness. But not so very far short, and if it officially praises the hearth and family, it is because it can afford the mild hypocrisy. It is true that wives often try to have their men violate their contract, and it is also true that many men have a much stronger attachment to after-hours with their families than to their work, but such cases are the minority; the men on whom The Organization depends most are generally the ones able to resolve successfully any dual allegiance.

Executives try to be dutiful husbands and parents, and they are well aware that their absorption in work means less time with their family even when they are physically with them. Younger executives in particular accuse themselves. They are not, they say, the fathers they should be and they often mention some long-term project they plan to do with their boy, like building a boat with him in the garage. But, they add ruefully, they probably never will. "I sort of look forward to the day my kids are grown up," one sales manager said. "Then I won't have to have such a guilty conscience about neglecting them."

What of leisure? When they talk about it, executives betray a curiously split feeling. They envy the worker his forty-hour week and they deplore the impulse that bedevils them into thinking about work after hours. Yet . . . "Instead of relaxing at night with a mystery story," one executive said of himself, "I keep at it until eleven o'clock and finally I say to myself, The devil with it, I'm going to have a highball or two and go to bed. But I sit there stewing until 12:30 or 1:00. As a result, I am very uncompanionable at breakfast. My wife says I just sit there and dream and maybe she's right. But I do get a kick out of being well informed in business." . . .

We have, in sum, a man who is so completely involved in his work that he cannot distinguish between work and the rest of his life—and is happy that he cannot. Surrounded as he is by a society ever more preoccupied with leisure, he remains an anomaly. Not only does he work harder, his life is in a few respects more ascetic than the businessman of half a century ago. His existence is hardly uncomfortable, yet, save for the Cadillac, the better address, the quarter acre more of lawn, his style of living is not signally different from that of the men in middle management.

The tone of Whyte's description of the home life of the "organization man" is critical. Whyte implies that the executive invests too much of himself in his career and not enough in his family. But Whyte is honest enough to admit that the executive is happy in his work, so happy "that he cannot distinguish between work and the rest of his life. . . ." For the organization man, work is *fun*. To eliminate the value judgment from Whyte's argument and yet retain his data, one might say that certain interesting and prestigious occupational roles attract major commitments of time and energy. A corresponding *decrease* is likely in the *family* commitments of persons in such executive roles.

At the opposite end of the socioeconomic scale the disruptive effects of occupational demands on family life are easier to demonstrate (Table 14). American men with less than $4000 income per year were *ten* times more likely to be divorced or separated from their wives in 1950 than men with $4000 or more.[37] Part of the explanation of this pattern is that financial problems are a factor in marital conflict. The lower the level of skill and hence of earnings, the greater is the pressure of family obligations on the worker. Monetary transactions have implications for all phases of social life in industrial societies, including family stability.

Thus, the differentiation of economic institutions has created a world of work that may compete with or fail to support family life. At the same time the tremendous efficiency of the industrial economy has steadily driven down the average work week. The increase in leisure may contribute to family solidarity. To put this point another way, the Industrial Revolution took the worker out of the home and put him in the factory; the high levels of productivity made possible by industrialism is sending him back. There is, however, an important difference between the preindustrial and the contemporary industrial family situation. In the preindustrial era the worker shared his *work* with his family; in industrial society he shares his *leisure*. In preindustrial societies a small leisure class was common. But not until the industrial era did *mass* leisure appear—

[37] Note that the relationship between low income and marital breakup is about as strong for whites and nonwhites.

and with it the commercialization of recreation.[38]

Mass Recreation in the United States

Reprinted by permission. From Robert Coughlan, "A $40 Billion Bill Just for Fun," *Life*, Vol. 47, Dec. 28, 1959, pp. 69–70, 73–74.[39]

With mounting productive efficiency (and militant unionism) wages have gone up and hours

[38] Eric Larrabee and Rolf Meyersohn, Eds., *Mass Leisure*, Glencoe, Ill.: Free Press, 1958; Nels Anderson, *Work and Leisure*, New York: Free Press of Glencoe, 1961.
[39] The statistics in the article generally refer to 1958, so they probably understate current expenditures for commercial recreation.

of work down—so much so that the average wage earner now has about 3,700 free hours, the equivalent of 230 full 16-hour days off a year, besides time for sleep. And, almost as much as anything else that has happened, it is this growth of leisure time that has kept the American economy strong and growing.

Even rats in a maze, if given alternative routes to food, will mix them up apparently just for the hell of it. People too get bored doing nothing or doing the same old thing. Americans have a low threshold of boredom, and they have fought it with every device from anagrams to parachute jumping. In so doing, they have created a vast *new* economic force, the Leisure Business, which could not exist if everyone worked at "useful things" and which, by the buying power it releases

TABLE 14
Rate of Separation and Divorce among Ever-Married American Men in 1950, Crosstabulated by 1949 Income

White Men, 14 Years and Over

Income	Ever Married	Separated	Divorced	Separated per 1000 of Ever Married	Divorced per 1000 of Ever Married	Both Divorced and Separated per 1000 of Ever Married
No income	1,794,750	46,950	64,800	26.16	36.10	62.26
$1–$999	4,242,940	119,940	188,580	28.27	44.44	72.71
$1000–$1999	5,211,410	98,130	167,190	18.82	32.08	50.90
$2000–$2999	8,334,000	131,220	255,150	15.74	30.62	46.36
$3000–$3999	7,320,240	70,740	167,610	9.66	22.90	32.56
$4000 and over	7,261,920	5,100	18,090	.70	2.49	3.19
Total	34,165,260	472,080	861,420	13.82	25.21	39.03

Nonwhite Men, 14 Years and Over

Income	Ever Married	Separated	Divorced	Separated per 1000 of Ever Married	Divorced per 1000 of Ever Married	Both Divorced and Separated per 1000 of Ever Married
No income	254,660	28,590	7,770	112.27	30.51	142.78
$1–$999	1,096,740	98,130	25,440	89.47	23.20	112.67
$1000–$1999	1,022,010	86,190	23,700	84.33	23.19	107.52
$2000–$2999	802,860	57,120	19,650	71.14	24.48	95.62
$3000–$3999	239,670	12,870	6,840	53.70	28.54	82.24
$4000 and over	63,390	210	210	3.31	3.31	6.62
Total	3,479,330	283,110	83,610	81.37	24.03	105.40

Source: Compiled from the 1950 census by Karen G. Hillman and published in Winch, McGinnis, and Barringer, Eds., *Selected Studies in Marriage and the Family*, rev. ed., New York: Holt, Rinehart and Winston, 1962, pp. 604–605.

and by the dreams it satisfies, has filled the whole economy with energy and ambition.

The size of this leisure business is almost anybody's guess, because it is made up of a great many kinds of business and is embedded in many industries that are considered utilitarian. Clothing, for instance: the big shift in that multi-billion-dollar industry has been toward "casual" clothes, and this reflects the growth of leisure activities. No one can say closely how many items are sold because of the change in living habits. Yet obviously the amount of money spent is enormous. Has anyone stopped to count the tassels that have to be replaced each year on the fezzes of the Shriners? How many paper clips are consumed in filing the applications for country club memberships? How many salted nuts are consumed at bridge parties? Where does the liquor business fit in? Despite the rise of alcoholism and the prevalence in some centers of the lubricating cocktail at business lunches, most drinking is of the "social," off-the-job type. Since the liquor industry grosses almost $10 billion a year, it could be maintained that drinking is America's favorite sport.

The economics of leisure not only are inexact: they defy logic and sometimes almost defy belief. Who would suppose that Florida's deep-sea fishing, supported mainly by sportsmen, is nearly as big as its citrus fruit and cattle industries combined? That six times as many people attend ballroom dancing classes today as attend colleges and universities? That the amount spent on dogs is equal to all the salaries and fees paid for legal services?

In short, in the leisure business you take your choice of the moneys paid. A reasonable guess as to the total would be at least $40 billion a year, which is more than 8% of the gross national product. It is almost as big as this year's national defense budget, more than all U.S. personal income tax receipts, more than the amount spent on new housing and new automobiles combined. The most important thing about this market, however, is not its size in dollars but its size in people, for the leisure market is supported mainly by people who make from $4,000 up a year after taxes. There are 34 million families in that category now, a majority of all the U.S. families, and among them they control most of the $84 billion "discretionary income" (money left after necessary expenditures) in the country.

These new "leisure masses" have acquired not only the money and the time to spend it in, but also—and most significantly—an appetite for the good life. And their enjoyment expresses itself more and more in active terms. The Oxford Dictionary, that scholarly work, makes an inadvertent summary of the situation in one of the several definitions of leisure it gives: "Leisure . . . a period or spell of unoccupied time. Now *rare*." Truly, idleness has little to do with the average American's use of his leisure; *rare* is his unoccupied time. In filling it he has created a host of businesses, some brand new, some of them surprising, and many of them important by any financial standard.

The biggest and most diverse leisure business consists of going someplace to see someone or something. The span covers a Sunday drive to grandmother's and a flight to Las Vegas, uncounted roadside gas stations and hot dog stands, a trip to the nearest midget golf course and a trip to Monument Valley. A few items: Georgia's tourist business is bigger than the cash value of its cotton crop. Mrs. Wickham Ames of Cape Cod, who in her spare time puts up and sells beach plum jelly to the summer vacationers, earns enough to take herself on a winter vacation to Florida, where she sometimes buys guava jelly from ladies who go north for summer vacations. Wallace Johnson and Kemmons Wilson of Memphis, originators of the luxury motel chain idea, have in the last seven years built 116 elaborately equipped Holiday Inns with an investment of $115 million. All told, Mrs. Ames, Messrs. Johnson and Wilson and their hundreds of thousands of colleagues take in $10.5 billion a year. The national restlessness also sent 1.4 million Americans abroad last year on $2 billion worth of vacations, not even counting the amount spent on postcards and remedies for tourist-stomach.

In the huge variety of domestic leisure-time travel there is one most-common denominator: sooner or later, when the average American gets in the car and begins moving, he heads for water. *Life* queried its correspondents all over the country to find out what people were doing with their spare time and money, and with extraordinary unanimity the answers emphasized boating, fishing, swimming, skin diving, water skiing, and the numerous variations of what appears to be a national aquamania. This is so important a part of the leisure business that it needs to be looked at in some individual categories. . . .

Today there are close to 8 million recreational boats in the U.S. . . .

There are several reasons for this boating boom, but perhaps the most important is simply that there has been a big increase in the indispensable facility—water. Whereas modern highways were built because cars became popular, boats have become popular partly because so many artificial lakes are being built. The TVA, for instance, converted the Tennessee River valley into a watering pleasure area with 10,000 miles of shoreline. The Army Engineers, with their flood control projects, have created hundreds of large artificial lakes, and the Department of Agriculture has encouraged farmers to build hundreds of thousands of ponds, most of them big enough at least to float a rowboat. (North Carolina alone now has 33,605 ponds.) There are around 5.5 million outboards in use now; $300 million worth of them were sold last year, and the industry estimates that nearly half were bought by people in the skilled or semiskilled worker category. Thirty-seven million people went boating—a fifth of the whole population of the U.S. . . .

Anyone who owns a boat is bound eventually, by the laws of chance and the incurable optimism of man's nature, to put a hook and line over the side. Hence boating has boomed fishing. And while the expenditures on the two sports are inextricably entangled, imaginative statisticians have produced a figure of $2.6 billion a year for fishermen, covering car expenses to the shore, boat hire, licenses, equipment ($200 million), lodging, food, sun lotion, seasick pills and, not least, drink. Be that as it may, at least 30 million people went fishing last year. . . .

The most surprising development in the leisure economy has been the growth of the swimming pool business. It seems hardly yesterday that the accepted formula for acquiring a pool was to become a Hollywood star. In 1950 there were only 3,600 residential pools in the whole country, and even counting municipal, club and hotel pools there were only 12,000 in all. Now suddenly there are more than 250,000 of them. The swimming pool—counting maintenance and equipment— has become a $1 billion a year business.

The biggest reason for the pool boom has been improved construction techniques which have made mass production possible. Around 1955–56 people began really to catch on to the fact that a family-size pool could be had for not much more than the price of a good car (average pool price last year: $4,170), and banks began to understand that whereas a car can be driven away and is soon obsolete, pools are nondetachable and add permanent value to a property. The result: a coast-to-coast plunge featured by builders' innovations like the "house-pool-package," the two items rolled up in one price. A new housing development in California's San Fernando Valley has 37 houses and 37 pools, making this the wettest small place per capita in the country.

Beyond the confines of swimming pools, six million Americans are water skiers. In California alone there are around 225 companies making water skis. About $15 million was spent this year on such aquatic items as swim fins, goggles, masks, diving suits and scuba tanks. Another $40 million went for inflatable water toys and mattresses. Spending more and more for less and less, women bought $225 million worth of bathing suits, a 100% increase in a dozen years.

Hunting, a good share of which also takes place in watery terrain, is still a major sport practically everywhere, with 20 million participants laying out close to $1 billion a year. In fact, the only major active adult sport that has nothing to do with water is bowling.

Not many years ago sociologists would go to bowling alleys to study the ways of the shiftless classes, but bowling today has much of the ruddy good-fellowship and aggressive virtue of the reformed sinner. Efforts by the American Bowling Congress and equipment manufacturers started the change 15 years or so ago, but the most important factor was a technological revolution in the form of the automatic pin-setting machine, which did away with the undependable, usually surly pin boy and almost overnight improved the whole atmosphere of the sport. . . .

Along with becoming better, bowling alleys have become very much bigger and have added all sorts of diversions, personal services and esthetic touches. The 112-lane Edison Lanes of Edison, N.J., the world's largest, is so long (twice the length of a football field) that an electric trolley has been installed to carry mechanics to the scene of equipment failure. Many alleys provide baby-sitting for bowling mothers. One has an aviary and an art gallery. Bowling has suddenly become a $1 billion yearly business.

Two other big consumers of time and money

deserve special notice, although both are marked by ambiguity as to whether they really are "leisure" pursuits. The first is the hodgepodge known generically as do-it-yourself; the other is gardening. If one were to believe all the advertisements, everyone in the U.S. has fun painting it, papering it, tiling it, lathing, gouging, reaming, soldering, grinding, gluing and sanding it, not to speak of cutting and sewing it. Somewhere in this vast market—estimated at $12 billion—many people doubtless really are having a ball. Others, it may reasonably be supposed, are simply sweating away at tasks they wish they could afford to have performed by professionals; protracted brooding on this theme can lead to divorce. As for gardening, the famous exodus from the cities to the suburbs has given that earthy pastime a lift such as has not been seen since Jack's beanstalk. The woods are full of people stealing violets for the front border. Gardening can be fun but, gratifying as some of it may be, hedge trimming, bug spraying, leaf raking, lawn watering, and, most emphatically, lawn mowing, are pure work for most people. Call it what you will, the home gardening business—seeds, nursery items, implements, insecticides, birdbaths, three-tier waterfall fountains (the hottest gardening item in California; sales last year amounted to almost $2 million), canvas gloves, mowers with and without mulchers, soil analyzers and conditioners, rain-making machines, dousing rods and good-luck charms—came to a good $2 billion last year, enough to establish a new Garden of Eden.

It may exasperate five million golfers to hear that theirs is still a minor sport but such is the case, 40 million lost or ruinously gashed golf balls a year notwithstanding. The National Golf Association has put forward a figure of $750 million a year for golf expenses, but this surely must represent a clerical error (maybe the figure represents interest on clubhouse mortgages). Half that would be more like it for transportation, equipment and fees, 19th hole drinks being extra. The only time a regulation golf course turns a profit worth mentioning is when it expires and becomes a housing development, as in fact so many have done that today—in spite of many new courses being opened—there are no more of them than there were 30 years ago.

Softball (eight million enthusiasts) is bigger than golf and still growing fast. Seven million people in this country still pitch horseshoes, although there are now only two million horses left (are horses dying out for want of shoes?) There are more skiers in the U.S. than in Switzerland—three million of them, and almost as many archers—five million—as inhabitants of the land of William Tell. Americans cooked two billion meals in the open last year and spent $100 million for grills and accessories. They also spent $700 million on photography. A man in Iowa named Nissen has made a fortune selling Trampolines—springy platforms for bouncing—to amateur tumblers.

Disneyland took in $13.5 million last year; a Disneylike amusement park planned for the New York area will cost $65 million just to build. The United States Playing Card Company, the Krupp of its industry, has never felt better: a house of cards constructed of their annual product would be unimaginably high. Movies are doing fine, for last year the box office showed 2.2 billion admissions and receipts of $1.2 billion.

Where does all this swirling activity leave the pursuit of knowledge, the enjoyment of man's cultural heritage, the search for a meaning in the past and a guide to the future? These things are certainly not measurable in dollars. The libraries, museums and many of the great music programs are free, and the adult education courses are almost all heavily subsidized. Even so, some of the items tell a story consequential alike to the economic and intellectual environment of the country. A key figure is the endowment for higher educational institutions: $4.5 billion. Financially this sum helps supply an underpinning for the real estate and security markets. Culturally it is paid-up insurance guaranteeing the support of dedicated institutions and of the people who staff them. In the ordinary, out-of-pocket spending habits of Americans there also is evidence of a national appreciation of values beyond "fun." The lines are inexact, but here are some approximate totals for what might be called serious or worthwhile leisure enjoyments: $1.2 billion for books, $2 billion for magazines, $83 million for classical phonograph records, $500 million for musical instruments, $313 million for theater, opera and concerts, $30 million merely for amateur art supplies. There are more than 1,000 symphony orchestras, mostly in smaller cities and towns.

If, as some observers maintain . . . , Americans are not realizing the potentialities their new leisure opens up to them, they are swindling themselves in the most literal sense. But if so, the fault certainly is not lack of effort. Never have so many been so determined to get so much out of *everything*.

Industrialization made possible mass leisure. With mass leisure has come mass restlessness. The growth of commercial recreation indicates that many people like outside stimulation to help them deal with leisure. Not everyone is happy about the new leisure. Some social critics are pessimistic about the capacity of the average man to spend his leisure wisely. At best he litters the countryside and the public beaches. At worst he drinks himself numb in taverns and looks for kicks driving cars at high speeds or smoking marijuana. These critics do not rejoice at the mass market for the novel, the motion picture, the television play. They are concerned with debasement of taste, with the impact of Mass Culture on High Culture.[40] Others are more hopeful that the talent for consuming leisure can be developed.

*The Consumption of Leisure:
A New Problem*

Reprinted by permission. From Russell Lynes, "Time on Our Hands," Harper's Magazine, Vol. 217, July 1958, pp. 34–39.

There are, of course, a great many professional and business men who wonder what all this talk about leisure is; somehow it is no problem to them—or so they think. There are also a good many women, especially young married women, who would give their heirlooms for a few minutes to themselves. They have only to wait.

But leisure is making some thoughtful people uneasy. In January the American Council of Churches met in Columbus to discuss the spare time of our increasingly urbanized populace. The Twentieth Century Fund is deep in an in-

40 Dwight Macdonald, "A Theory of Mass Culture," *Diogenes*, No. 3, 1953, pp. 1–17; Bernard Rosenberg and David M. White, Eds., *Mass Culture: The Popular Arts in America*, Glencoe, Ill.: Free Press, 1956.

vestigation of leisure and the University of Chicago is (with the help of Ford Foundation funds) making a study of the nature of leisure and how people use it. Corporations not only worry about the leisure of their employees; they do something about it. Schoolteachers and social workers and local politicians worry about it, about footloose youngsters, about long summer vacations for teenagers, and about juvenile delinquency. City planners, safety experts, highway engineers watch the growing number of hours when families are not at work and feel they have to go somewhere. Where? To what extent is the boredom of leisure responsible for young drug addicts, for the common cold, for muggings on city streets?

Every new scientific development, whether it is aimed at saving our skins or washing our dishes, leads in one way or another to reducing still further the sweat of the public brow. The four-day week which looms on the immediate horizon (and which causes such consternation in the corporate breast) is, of course, less the product of labor's demands than of manufacturing genius. Machines not men have created the three-day weekend, and men are worried about what to do with it. Not long ago the Oil, Chemical, and Atomic Workers Union made a survey of its membership. It asked them: ". . . if and when the Union enters a bargaining program for shorter hours" how would they like this additional leisure to be distributed? Would a housewife, for example, "want her husband at home three consecutive days?" Good question.

The attitude of many large corporations has been somewhat different. They have attacked the problem of employee leisure head on. They have provided all sorts of sports facilities, music clubs, theater groups, and bowling leagues. IBM has its own golf courses for its employees. Bell and Howell has baseball fields lighted for night games. Ford's River Rouge plant has an indoor shooting range, tennis courts, baseball diamonds (nine of them), and horseshoe pits. Corning Glass has its own museum, visiting repertory theater, and changing exhibitions, in addition to automatic bowling alleys, basketball courts, and dancing classes.

Business is not sentimental about the new leisure. "Many of these off-the-job or after-hours activities," the head of employee relations for General Motors has said, "have not only a therapeutic value, but can actually sharpen or increase employees' skills." And the President of Bell and Howell has said, "Everyone in the organization gains from a well-planned recreational program." . . .

Leisure is not a new problem born of automation, but it is a new problem for a great many kinds of people who were never much concerned with it when Bridget was working her seventy- or eighty-hour week in the one-maid house. America has had a leisure class since the industrialization of our country began, and in the 1850s the art critic James Jackson Jarves complained in shocked tones of the number of scions of wealthy families who threw themselves into rivers because they were so bored that life seemed not worth living. (Mr. Jarves wanted to interest such young men in the arts as a suitable outlet for their energies and money.) These young men, whom we would call the idle rich, had on a large scale the same problem that nearly everybody in America has today on a small scale. In its simplest terms, the primary problem of leisure is how to avoid boredom.

We used to be more accomplished at being bored than we are today, or at least we seem to have taken boredom with better grace in the days of party calls and decorous parlor games. We assumed a high moral tone toward leisure, and in some respects this tone persists. "The devil finds work for idle hands," our parents said and shook their heads; and when they said, "All work and no play makes Jack a dull boy," they meant, of course, that Jack should work most of the time but not quite all of it. Primarily leisure was thought of as a way to get a man back on his feet so that after Sunday he could put in sixty or so productive hours from Monday through Saturday. Leisure for women (few women in those days had jobs) was something quite else—it was the custody of culture and good works. Women in their spare time were expected to cultivate the arts, foster the education of their children, and play the role of Lady Bountiful in the community.

It was a neat division of family functions and a tidy way of life. Father's leisure was restorative; mother's was extremely productive. But more has changed than just the roles of men and women; the whole complex machinery of leisure has changed.

Briefly the changes are these:

In the last few decades what had started about a century ago as a trickle of people from the country and small towns to the cities became a torrent. Cities filled like cisterns and overflowed into suburbs, and as we shifted from a predominantly agricultural economy to a predominantly industrial one, we changed the nature of much of our leisure from what might be called a natural one to an artificial one, from pleasures provided by nature to pleasures concocted by man. Ways of using leisure began to come in packages—in cars, in movies, in radios, and most recently in television sets, and what was once the sauce only for the city goose became the sauce for the country gander as well. City culture is now within easy reach of everyone everywhere and everyone has the same access to talent that only a few decades ago used to be reserved for the rich and the urbane.

During the time when we were changing from a rural to an urban culture, the length of the work-week fell from sixty hours or more to forty or thirty-five. Gradually the five-day week became an almost universal reality, and the four-day week is on the immediate horizon. With more leisure time, men have, quite naturally, taken on some of the household chores that only a short while ago they wouldn't have been caught dead at, and have assumed some of the cultural responsibilities which were once the domain of their wives. They have also, with time on their hands and cars at their disposal, turned again to many kinds of rural recreation . . . to fishing and hunting, especially, but also to sailing and skiing. The most solitary of all sports, fishing, is also the most popular of all sports with American men.

But the greatest assault on old patterns of leisure and on the shibboleths about devil's work for idle hands, has been industry's discovery that it needs the consuming time of workers as much as it needs their producing time. In an economy, geared as ours is to making life comfortable for everyone, it is essential to business that people have time to enjoy their comfort and to use up the things that make life comfortable. . . .

Urbanization, the shorter working day and week, and the changing roles of the sexes have, heaven knows, produced tremendous changes in the ways Americans live. But the premium put on the consuming time of the worker by our economic system presents us with a tidily packaged moral dilemma. When idleness is a public virtue, what becomes of the moral value of work?

What are we going to substitute for the old adages on which we were brought up? What are we going to tell our children? What will happen to the economy if we go on saying that virtue is its own reward, that work is good for the soul, and that leisure is only a reward for toil? What happens to the Calvinist ethic?

This is a problem I would rather refer to a dilettante than to an economist or a clergyman or certainly to an engineer. The economist would consider it from the point of view of wealth, the clergyman of the after life, and the engineer of production. The dilettante can be counted on to look at it from the point of view of life, liberty, and especially the pursuit of happiness. . . .

Originally *dilettante* meant a lover of the fine arts (it comes from the Latin word for delight) and it was used to distinguish the consumer from the producer. Its application spread beyond the arts in England, and in the eighteenth century the Society of the Dilettanti was a club of influential men interested not only in the arts but in the sciences and in archaeology. It meant the man of intellectual curiosity who devoted part of his time to the intelligent cultivation of the arts and sciences, to the resources of leisure and the satisfactions of the mind.

If you transplant the idea of the eighteenth-century dilettante from England to America, you discover that he was Thomas Jefferson and Benjamin Franklin—one a farmer who dabbled in architecture and introduced a new style to America, the other a printer who dabbled in natural science and flew a kite into a thunderstorm. You discover several others who got together and started a talkfest that became the Philosophical Society of Philadelphia, and others who, dabbling in the arts, somehow founded a string of distinguished museums across the nation and filled them with masterpieces, and, of course, a good many bad guesses. These men were dilettantes. There is no other word that fits them. . . .

The dilettante is just a consumer. He is a man who takes the pursuit of happiness seriously, not frivolously, and he works at it. He is part sensualist, part intellectual, and part enthusiast. He is also likely to be a proselytizer for those causes in which his interests are involved, and to be rather scornful of those people who do not take their pleasures seriously and who are passive instead of active in the cultivation of them. But whatever else he may be he is not lazy. He may

or may not have a job that he finds interesting, but he does not use his leisure in a miscellaneous and undirected fashion. He knows what he wants out of life and will go to a lot of trouble to get it. Primarily, in Voltaire's sense, he wants to cultivate his own garden.

You will find dilettantes everywhere and in every aspect of our culture. I found one a few weeks ago driving a taxi in New York. He was a man in his early sixties.

"I only drive this hack three days a week," he said. "The other four days I go fishing. I like to fish and I'm pretty good at it."

By the time he had delivered me home I knew what he fished for at what times of year, what bait he used and where and in what weather, and which were the best fishing boats and captains going out of New York harbor. I asked him what he did with all the fish he caught.

"I got a son-in-law runs a saloon," he said. "I give them to his customers."

Probably the most common and in some ways the most accomplished of American dilettantes is the baseball fan, though the national pastime is being crowded out of its position as top banana of entertainment these days by serious music. The baseball fan knows his subject with something very close to genuine scholarship. He is an expert in the minutiae of its history and understands the nuances and subtleties of its performance. He takes as much pleasure from the refinements of its details as from the outcome of any single game, and he enjoys the company of others with whom he can argue the relative virtues of performance and make comparisons with other similar situations. He demands skill on the field of a truly professional caliber, and he lets his displeasure with anything less be known in the most direct and uncompromising manner. He is, by and large, a less tolerant dilettante than the one whose interest is devoted to art, for his expert eye is less subject to changes in fashion. Unquestionably without him the standards of baseball would long since have gone to pot.

The simple fact is that the dilettante is the ideal consumer, not ideal, perhaps, from the point of view of those producers who would like their customers to accept their products with blind confidence, but ideal from the point of view of maintaining standards of quality . . . whether material or cultural. He takes his functions as a consumer seriously. He takes the trouble to know what he likes and to sort out the shoddy and the meretricious from the sound and reasonable. If he is a dilettante of music, for example, he demands the best performance from his record-player. He is unimpressed by an imitation mahogany cabinet in the Chippendale manner, but he knows that the components of his hi-fi equipment are the very best that he can afford. (He can, in fact, be credited with the very great improvement in mass-produced sound equipment; it was his interest in high-fidelity that spread the word to the general public and raised the level of public acceptance.) . . .

Several months ago I found myself in an argument, or the beginnings of one, in a radio interview with a well-known broadcaster. "Our colleges need to produce more and better trained men," he said, and I countered with the suggestion that they needed to produce better educated men. "We need experts," he said.

"We need dilettantes," I replied, and the word so surprised him that he gingerly changed the subject to safer ground.

I would like to change my position, but only slightly. What we need are trained men with the capacity for being dilettantes. There can be no argument with the fact that an industrialized society must have a great many highly trained men and women with specialized knowledge and skills. But in this country the consumers and the producers are the same people; all of us work both sides of the economic street. We are, the great majority of us, the part-time idle rich, and no nation, so far as I know, has ever found itself in such a position before. Ours is a society in which no man's nose need be permanently to the grindstone, and where every man is a potential dilettante.

We have thought of our know-how as our most exportable commodity, and when somebody else demonstrated, moon-fashion, a superior know-how, we took it as a blow to our "national prestige." In fact our most exportable commodity has been a cultural one, a way of life that balances work and leisure for almost everyone and distributes the fruits of labor with astonishing, if not complete, evenness. Our most effective know-how has been in the production of leisure, a commodity filled with promise and booby traps. It is the engineer with his slide rule who knows how to produce leisure, but it is the dilettante who knows how to use it and make it productive.

The increase in leisure is made possible by the productivity of industrial societies. It is *made possible* by industrialization but is not an inevitable consequence of it. In 1798 Thomas Robert Malthus published *An Essay on the Principle of Population* in which he warned that population growth might wipe out the gains of productivity and keep the standard of living low.[41] Malthus assumed that people would have as many children as they could afford to support. This did *not* happen during the nineteenth century in industrializing countries. Birth rates *fell* in such countries as Sweden, France, Switzerland, and the United States.[42] Even though industrialization made possible more children per family, what actually happened was conscious family limitation, apparently motivated by a desire to enjoy a higher standard of living. Furthermore, *within* industrial societies, the better-educated, higher-income, white-collar, and urbanized segments of the population tended to have fewer children than elements less committed to the urban industrial way of life. Demographers concluded that Malthus' pessimism was unjustified; population explosions are temporary phases. Whereas a preindustrial society achieves a stable population through the cruel balancing of a high birth with a high death rate, industrial societies achieve balance because high standards of living depress both birth and death rates.

41 Thomas R. Malthus, *An Essay on the Principle of Population as It Affects Future Improvement of Society*, 1st ed., London: Macmillan, 1926. See the bibliography at the end of this chapter for a more precise statement of Malthus' argument.
42 Dennis H. Wrong, *Population*, New York: Random House, 1956, p. 53.

The Demographic Transition

Reprinted by permission. From Kingsley Davis, "The Demographic Consequences of Changes in Productive Technology: An Essay on the Problem of Measurement," in Georges Baladier et al., *Social, Economic and Technological Change: a Theoretical Approach*, Paris: Conseil International des Sciences Sociales, 1958, pp. 195–227.

The theory of modern population change revolves around the idea of a "demographic transition"—a cycle in which there are three phases: First, a regime of *slow* population growth characterized by *high* birth and death rates; second, a period of *rapid* population growth characterized by *high* fertility but *low* death rates, due to the lag of fertility decline behind mortality decline (the "demographic gap"); and, third, a regime of *slow* population growth characterized by *low* birth and death rates. These three phases can be put in tabular form as follows:

	First	Second	Third
Birth rate	high	high	low
Death rate	high	low	low
Growth rate	low	high	low

The cycle can be represented diagrammatically as in Figure 4. This notion of a demographic cycle associated with industrialization has such wide applicability that it has become a fruitful principle

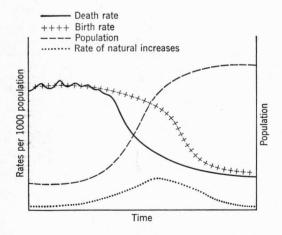

FIGURE 4. Vital rates and population growth during the demographic transition.

in population theory and research. Yet it is obviously only a rough generalization, more perfect as an abstraction than as a description of fact. Empirically, the precise length of the transition cannot be specified in any given case. Our statistics hardly go back to the beginning of the cycle in any country and there is no certainty that the end of it has been reached even in the most advanced nations. In Western Europe the cycle seems to have begun sometime *before* 1750 and to have lasted until the great depression—a period of more than 200 years. But in view of the subsequent rise in fertility in the West, the depression can hardly be viewed as the end of the cycle. In Sweden, for example, the net reproduction rate fell typically to .73 in 1933–34, but rose again to 1.21 in 1945–49 and 1.09 in 1950–51. Between 1945 and 1954 Sweden's population (in the absence of emigration) grew faster than at any time since 1860. The advanced countries of the New World, furthermore, have not really experienced the full cycle, for their modern history began *after* the transition had started in Europe. Thus Australia, which as late as 1811 had only 12,000 Europeans, got started long after the homeland of its people, Britain, had entered the demographic transition. This recency of European settlement was even truer of New Zealand, which as late as 1951 had less than 30,000 Europeans in its population.

Not only the duration of the cycle, but also the magnitude and contour of the various elements in it, have varied from one country to another. The rate of population growth in France remained rather stable at a low figure from 1800 to 1930. During the nineteenth century, on the other hand, the rate of increase in Britain and Germany doubled and tripled, despite a greater emigration from these countries. There is no certainty that those countries which are only now beginning to enter the demographic transition will go through the cycle in the same way or at the same rate as did the countries that have already passed through it. Numerous changes have occurred which make a sheer repetition unlikely.

Industrialization offers hope of a better standard of living to the underdeveloped countries of the world. But industrialization cannot guarantee that these countries will succeed in passing through "the demographic transition."

The developing countries must reduce their fertility *quickly*—or else the growth in population will consume the increase in productivity made possible by industrialization, and the standard of living will remain the same or fall. Japan is virtually alone in having done this.[43] In the rest of the world the specter of Thomas Malthus is haunting the leaders of underdeveloped countries. Mexico's population increased between 1953 and 1960 at the rate of 3.1 per cent per year, fast enough to double Mexico's population every 23 years.[44] Extrapolation of the current rate of growth of *world* population yields a prediction of 50 billion people in less than 200 years.[45] Only the most optimistic scholars believe that the earth can feed such a large population.

If underdeveloped countries succeed in passing through the demographic transition, fantastic improvements in their standards of living are possible. If these countries fail to control the population explosion, Malthus' gloomy predictions of war, famines, and pestilence may prove to be correct.

CONCLUSION

While economic activities are performed in every society, only an industrial society has an "economy" differentiated from other institutions. A necessary condition for this differentiation is the commercialization of exchange. A further condition is the separation of work and residence. Once separation occurs, the organization of production becomes fundamentally different. Occupational roles emerge. The ratio of capital to labor grows along with the increased utilization of inanimate sources of energy. Provided that population growth is not too rapid, the standard of living of the average family rises, and the disparity of income between the rich and the poor decreases. Recreational industries develop. Finally, as Chapter 5 will demonstrate, the urban way of life becomes dominant throughout the society.

SOME SIGNIFICANT LITERATURE ON THE INDUSTRIAL WAY OF LIFE

Gertrude Bancroft, *The American Labor Force: Its Growth and Changing Composition*, New York: Wiley, 1958. This volume is one of a series of studies of the 1950 census sponsored by the Social Science Research Council. The author tries to account for the increasing propensity of both men and women to enter the labor market in the United States. To some extent, the increase can be explained in terms of age, marital status, and farm or nonfarm residence of the American population, but changes in *attitudes* toward labor-force participation must have also occurred. The increasing employment of married women can only be explained in this way. This summary is based on a review by Charles D. Stewart, *American Sociological Review*, Vol. 24, October 1959, pp. 743–744.

Theodore Caplow and Reece J. McGee, *The Academic Marketplace*, New York: Basic Books, 1958. The authors studied 237 professorial vacancies that occurred

in the liberal-arts departments of ten major American universities between June 30, 1954, and July 1, 1956. Professors Caplow and McGee are concerned with professors as *employees* in a competitive labor market rather than with their academic duties or achievements. Hence, the book concentrates on the motivations of the professor for leaving his position and the motives of department chairmen and other recruiters in searching for replacements. Prestige considerations are perceived as of major importance to both the professor and the recruiters, especially at leading universities. Thus, a department is often more interested in hiring a well-known scholar, who adds to the reputation of the university, than a good teacher. Although professors are paid to teach, they are evaluated mainly on the basis of research contributions (publications); hence, professors preoccupied with career advancement are tempted to put more of their energies into research than into teaching. At secondary universities, teaching ability, service to the university, and acceptability to the local community are weighed more heavily in the evaluation of professors both for initial recruitment and for promotion.

William J. Goode, "Community within a Community: The Professions," *American Sociological Review*, Vol.

[43] William Peterson, *Population*, New York: Macmillan, 1961, pp. 486–490.
[44] Bureau of the Census, *Statistical Abstract of the United States: 1962*, Washington: Government Printing Office, 1962, p. 911.
[45] Philip M. Hauser, *Population Perspectives*, New Brunswick, N.J.: Rutgers University Press, 1960, p. 7.

22, April 1957, pp. 194–200. Occupational roles are a feature of industrial societies. Professions are high-prestige occupations having some of the characteristics of communities, although not a physical center: (1) Members of a profession have a sense of identity and share common values. (2) Within the scope of professional action, members communicate by means of a common language only partially comprehensible to outsiders. (3) The profession has power over its members. (4) "Though it does not produce the next generation biologically, it does so socially through its control over the selection of professional trainees, and through its training processes it sends these recruits through an adult socialization process." Furthermore, like a community a profession exists within and depends on a larger society, and this circumstance gives rise to interesting sociological problems of the relationship between the contained community and the society.

Clark Kerr, "Changing Social Structures," in Wilbert E. Moore and Arnold S. Feldman, Eds., *Labor Commitment and Social Change in Developing Areas*, New York: Social Science Research Council, 1960. This article interprets industrialism as a new way of life toward which all underdeveloped societies are moving. Four stages of commitment of workers to industrial life may be distinguished: In Stage 1 the *uncommitted* worker takes a job in order to earn money for a specific purpose; when he accumulates enough, he quits. In Stage 2 the *semicommitted* worker has a regular job, but he also maintains connections with a nonindustrial way of life, usually in rural areas. In Stage 3 the *committed* worker has severed his connections with his rural or tribal roots; he is permanently resident in a city, and it is not unusual for his wife to enter the labor market. In Stage 4 the *overcommitted* worker has tied himself so closely to a particular occupation or to a particular employer that he cannot easily move to another job. Kerr concludes that differences in cultural backgrounds are less important to an understanding of the process of industrial commitment than might be supposed. ". . . the future into which workers are going is much more determinative of what happens to them than the past from which they are drawn."

Thomas Robert Malthus, *An Essay on the Principle of Population as It Affects Future Improvement of Society*, 1st ed., London: Macmillan, 1926. Malthus wrote the first edition of his *Essay* in response to the radical ideas generated by the French Revolution. Condorcet in France and William Godwin in England argued that the corrupting influence of social institutions led to human misery; hence, they advocated anarchy. Condorcet and Godwin believed that men were basically reasonable and good and that therefore anarchy would produce social harmony, prosperity, and happiness. Malthus was horrified. He sought to justify social institutions, and he used the danger of overpopulation as an argument in support of the status quo. Marriage is necessary so that a man cannot escape the responsibility to provide for the children he brings into the world. Private property gives him the resources to discharge this responsibility. Without familial and economic institutions, men would have no incentive for procreative restraint and would multiply like fruit flies. Since the food supply of the world is limited, eventually population growth would be checked by war, disease, and famine. The *Essay* was of course the special pleading of a conservative. But it was also an early statement of the regulatory function of social institutions. This summary is based on the discussion of Malthus in Talcott Parsons, *The Structure of Social Action*, New York: McGraw-Hill, 1937, pp. 102–107.

C. Wright Mills, *White Collar: The American Middle Classes*, New York: Oxford University Press, 1951. The United States has experienced a decline in the relative proportion of the labor force composed of small manufacturers, retailers, farmers, and self-employed professionals and an increase in the relative proportion of executives, salaried professionals, salespeople, and office workers. This new middle class is distinguished from other strata not only by a generally middle position with reference to income, prestige, and power but also by the fact that it works with symbols and with other people. Mills interprets the situation of white-collar people as being rather bleak, but this interpretation rests on certain value judgments of the author; other reputable sociologists disagree with him. This summary is based on a review by Paul K. Hatt, *American Sociological Review*, Vol. 16, October 1951, pp. 727–728.

Edward A. Shils, "Daydreams and Nightmares: Reflections on the Criticism of Mass Culture," *Sewanee Review*, Vol. 65, Autumn 1957, pp. 597–608. This article is concerned with the charge that popular culture has vulgarized the taste of the average man by exposing him to comic books, sensational newspapers, and magazines that concentrate on illicit sexual activity and crimes of violence. Professor Shils replies that preindustrial societies have at least as impoverished an esthetic life as contemporary societies. "Hunger and the imminence of death, work such as we in the West would now regard as too burdensome even for beasts, over very long hours, [prevent] the development of individuality, of sensitivity or refinement in any except those very few in the lower classes who [are] either extremely strong personalities or extremely talented or extremely fortunate in forming a connection with the aristocratic or mercantile classes, or all three together." In short, Professor Shils does not defend the level of mass culture in industrial societies, but he deplores the romantization of preindustrial societies.

Max Weber, *General Economic History*, New York: Collier, 1961. When Max Weber died in 1920, he had just finished giving a course of lectures on economic history. His colleagues decided that his insights should not be lost, and they put together this volume from his fragmentary notes and from the lecture notes of his students. The last section of the book, "The Origin of Modern Capitalism," is particularly interesting to sociologists. It discusses not only the economic and political conditions necessary for the development of capitalism, but also "the capitalist spirit." Weber denies that capitalists are as rapacious as, say, oriental traders. He argues that the acquisitive impulse is disciplined under capitalism so as to produce "a regulated economic life with the economic impulse functioning within bounds." The early entrepreneurs possessed some of the ascetic inclinations and the religious anxieties of monks, but unlike monks they labored in the world. The concept of a "calling"—an occupation to which one felt called by God—reflected these motivations.

Harold L. Wilensky, "Orderly Careers and Social Participation: The Impact of Work History on Social Integration in the Middle Class," *American Sociological Review*, Vol. 26, August 1961, pp. 521–539. The work role in urban industrial societies usually takes the adult male out of his neighborhood of residence. Professor Wilensky hypothesizes nonetheless that the vitality of social participation and the strength of attachment to the local community *increases* with involvement in the economic system. He tested this hypothesis by classifying 648 interviews with Detroit males from 21 to 55 years of age on the basis of the orderliness of their work histories, that is, the extent to which their work histories constituted a career rather than a succession of unrelated jobs. ("A career is a succession of related jobs, arranged in a hierarchy of prestige, through which persons move in an ordered . . . sequence.") Wilensky shows that men with more orderly work histories have on the average stronger attachments (1) to community organizations and (2) to relatives, friends, and neighbors. "Participation in community life is a natural extension of participation in the labor market: orderly and pleasant experiences in the latter provide motive and opportunity for the former. . . . chaotic experiences in the economic order foster a retreat from both work and the larger communal life."

Harold L. Wilensky and Charles N. LeBeaux, *Industrial Society and Social Welfare: The Impact of Industrialization on the Supply and Organization of Social Welfare Services in the United States*, New York: Russell Sage Foundation, 1958. Industrial development has led to changes in the character of the welfare problems in advanced societies. In addition to an over-all discussion of American conceptions of social welfare and the scope of existing welfare programs, the authors consider in detail two fields, family services and agencies designed to cope with juvenile delinquency. They also deal with social work as a profession and with the social agency as a bureaucratic organization. This summary is based on a review by Zena Smith Blau, *American Sociological Review*, Vol. 23, August 1958, pp. 461–462.

CHAPTER 5

The Urban Way of Life

Descriptions of industrial societies cannot fail to include a discussion of urbanization. The tendency for a *majority* of the population to live and work in cities—that is, to *urbanize* —is a characteristic of industrial societies. On the other hand, cities existed long before the Industrial Revolution. Preindustrial cities have been trade centers, centers of handicrafts, centers of administration, educational centers, fortresses, and religious communities.[1] In industrial societies, too, some cities are organized around functions unrelated to industrial activities, for example, resort cities.[2] Furthermore, the underdeveloped countries of the contemporary world contain 463 cities with more than 100,000 population.[3] To put it the other way around, of the 897 cities of that size in the world, only 434 are in industrial societies.

THE URBANISM STIMULATED BY INDUSTRIALIZATION

Until the Industrial Revolution, cities constituted an occasional clustering of population in essentially rural societies. With industrialization came the *urbanized society* in which clustered population is the dominant pattern. Figure 5 documents this development in the United States. Of course, many parts of the contemporary world are still preindustrial ("underdeveloped"). This circumstance provides an opportunity to examine the relationship between *degree* of industrialization and *degree* of urbanization. Table 15 shows that the *lower* the percentage of the gainfully employed males in agriculture, the *larger* the percentage of the population in cities of over 100,000 population. This not a tautology. Industrialization makes an impact in rural areas, too. The tremendous increase in productivity per farm worker results from the application of power-driven machinery, from scientific methods of fertilizing the soil, rotating crops, and checking erosion, and from more efficient

[1] Gideon Sjoberg, "The Preindustrial City," *American Journal of Sociology*, Vol. 60, March 1955, pp. 438–445.
[2] Albert J. Reiss, Jr., "Functional Specialization of Cities," in Hatt and Reiss, *Cities and Society: The Revised Reader in Urban Sociology*, Glencoe, Ill.: Free Press, 1957.
[3] Three-quarters of the world's population lives in underdeveloped countries, but these countries have slightly more people living in cities of 100,000 or more than do the industrialized nations. See Kingsley Davis and Hilda Hertz Golden, "Urbanization and the Development of Pre-Industrial Areas," *Economic Development and Cultural Change*, Vol. 3, October 1954, p. 9.

farm management. Conceivably, industrialization could occur without much clumping of population. Workers not needed for industrialized farming might remain in rural areas in manufacturing or other nonfarming occupations. This has not happened. Of the 17,513,086 manufacturing workers enumerated in the 1960 census in the United States, 13,348,151 lived in cities.[4] And a considerable proportion of the remaining manufacturing workers, though technically "rural nonfarm," probably lived in the suburban fringes of metropolitan areas.[5] Modern industrialism, accompanied as it is by technological advances in transportation and communication as well as great increases in productivity, created the urbanized society.

TABLE 15

Degree of Urbanization in World's Countries and Territories Classified by Degree of Agriculturalism

Per Cent of Gainfully Occupied Males in Agriculture	Number of Counties	Per Cent of Population in Cities 100,000-plus
0–19	11	32.3
20–29	11	23.6
30–39	7	23.2
40–49	7	21.9
50–59	16	17.7
60–69	17	8.9
70–plus	86	6.3

Source: Kingsley Davis and Hilda Hertz Golden, "Urbanization and the Development of Pre-Industrial Areas," *Economic Development and Cultural Change*, Vol. 3, October 1954, p. 8.

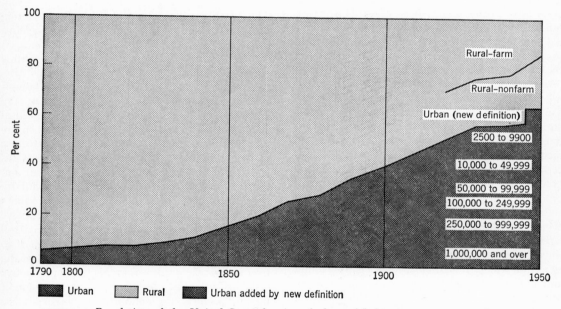

FIGURE 5. Population of the United States by size of place of habitation, 1790–1950. Source: Donald J. Bogue, "Urbanism in the United States, 1950," *American Journal of Sociology*, Vol. 60, March 1955, p. 472.

Bureau of the Census, *United States Census of Population: 1960, United States Summary*, Washington: Government Printing Office, 1962, p. 221. The Census Bureau definition of the urban population is complicated. Essentially it includes persons living in incorporated places of 2500 population or more and also persons living in the densely settled fringe of large cities.

[5] Vincent H. Whitney, "Changes in the Rural-Nonfarm Population, 1930–1950," *American Sociological Review*, Vol. 25, June 1960, pp. 363–368.

From Cities to Urban Societies

Reprinted by permission. Fom Kingsley Davis, "The Origin and Growth of Urbanization in the World," *American Journal of Sociology*, Vol. 60, March 1955, pp. 429–437.

Urban phenomena attract sociological attention primarily for four reasons. First, such phenomena are relatively recent in human history. Compared to most other aspects of society—e.g., language, religion, stratification, or the family—cities appeared only yesterday, and urbanization, meaning that a sizable proportion of the population lives in cities, has developed only in the last few moments of man's existence. Second, urbanism represents a revolutionary change in the whole pattern of social life. Itself a product of basic economic and technological developments, it tends in turn, once it comes into being, to affect every aspect of existence. It exercises its pervasive influence not only within the urban milieu strictly defined but also in the rural hinterland. The third source of sociological interest in cities is the fact that, once established, they tend to be centers of power and influence throughout the whole society, no matter how agricultural and rural it may be. Finally, the process of urbanization is still occurring; many of the problems associated with it are unsolved; and, consequently, its future direction and potentialities are still a matter of uncertainty. This paper examines the first and last points: the origin, growth, and present rate of progress of urbanization in the world. Since good statistics on urban concentration do not exist even today for substantial parts of the world, and hardly exist for any part during most of the time since cities have been in existence, we are forced to rely on whatever credible evidence can be found and so can reach only broad conclusions concerning early periods and only approximations for recent times. . . .

THE RISE OF EARLY URBAN CENTERS

Because the archeological evidence is fragmentary, the role of cities in antiquity has often been exaggerated. Archeologists in particular are inclined to call any settlement a "city" which had a few streets and a public building or two. Yet there is surely some point in not mistaking a town

for a city. Moreover, what is important is not only the appearance of a few towns or cities but also their place in the total society of which they were a part. Thus, even though in particular regions around the Mediterranean and in southern and western Asia many towns and a few cities arose prior to the Christian Era, there were severe limitations both on the size that such cities could reach and on the proportion of the total population that could live in them.

Speaking generally, one can agree with the dominant view that the diverse technological innovations constituting Neolithic culture were necessary for the existence of settled communities. Yet one should not infer that these innovations, which began some 8,000–10,000 years ago, were sufficient to give rise to towns as distinct from villages. Even though the Neolithic population was more densely settled than the purely hunting or food-gathering peoples, it was nevertheless chiefly engaged in an occupation—agriculture—which requires a large amount of land per person. The Neolithic population density was therefore not a matter of town concentration but rather a matter of tiny villages scattered over the land.

What had to be added to the Neolithic complex to make possible the first towns? Between 6000 and 4000 B.C. certain inventions—such as the ox-drawn plow and wheeled cart, the sailboat, metallurgy, irrigation, and the domestication of new plants—facilitated, when taken together, a more intensive and more productive use of the Neolithic elements themselves. When this enriched technology was utilized in certain unusual regions where climate, soil, water, and topography were most favorable (broad river valleys with alluvial soil not exhausted by successive cropping, with a dry climate that minimized soil leaching, with plenty of sunshine, and with sediment-containing water for irrigation from the river itself), the result was a sufficiently productive economy to make possible the *sine qua non* of urban existence, the concentration in one place of people who do not grow their own food.

But a productive economy, though necessary, was not sufficient: high productivity per acre does not necessarily mean high per capita productivity. Instead of producing a surplus for town dwellers, the cultivators can, theoretically at least, multiply on the land until they end up producing just enough to sustain themselves. The rise of towns and cities therefore required, in addition to highly favorable agricultural conditions, a form of social organization in which certain strata could appropriate for themselves part of the produce grown by the cultivators. Such strata—religious and governing officials, traders, and artisans—could live in towns, because their power over goods did not depend on their presence on the land as such. They could thus realize the advantages of town living, which gave them additional power over the cultivators.

The first cities, doubtless small and hard to distinguish from towns, seem to have appeared in the most favorable places sometime between 6000 and 5000 B.C. From that time on, it can be assumed that some of the inventions which made larger settlements possible were due to towns and cities themselves—viz., writing and accountancy, bronze, the beginnings of science, a solar calendar, bureaucracy. By 3000 B.C., when these innovations were all exercising an influence in Egypt, Mesopotamia, and India, there were in existence what may be called "true" cities. After that there appears to have been, for some 2,000 years, a lull during which the most important innovations, toward the end of the period, were alphabetic writing and the smelting of iron. Curiously, the cities in the regions where city life had originated eventually went into eclipse, and it was not until Greco-Roman times that new principles made possible, in new regions, a marked gain in city existence. The fact that the greatest subsequent cultural developments did not occur primarily in the regions where the first cities arose suggests that cities are not always and everywhere a stimulant of economic and social advance. . . . [I]f anything, the first cities had a stultifying effect on cultural progress, due perhaps to the unproductive insulation and excessive power of the urban elite. There is no doubt that the religio-magical traditionalism of the early cities was profound.

Why was there so little urbanization in ancient times, and why did it proceed so slowly from that point? The sites of the earliest "cities" themselves show that they were small affairs. The walls of ancient Babylon, for example, embraced an area of very roughly 3.2 square miles, and "Ur, with its canals, harbors, and temples, occupied some 220 acres; the walls of Erech encompass an area of just on two square miles." This suggests that the famous Ur could hardly have boasted more than 5,000 inhabitants and Erech hardly

more than 25,000. The mounds of Mohenjo-daro in Sind cover a square mile, and Harappa in the Punjab had a walled area visible in 1853 with a perimeter of 2½ miles. These were evidently "cities" of 5,000–15,000 inhabitants, yet they were the chief centers for the entire Indus region, an area nearly two-thirds the size of Texas. Less is known about the earliest Egyptian cities, for they were built with mudbricks and have long since disappeared beneath the alluvial soil. Tell el 'Amarna, the temporary capital built much later, about 1400 B.C., perhaps held something like 40,000 people. The wall of Hotep-Sanusert, an earlier capital built about 1900 B.C. on the Fayum, measured 350 by 400 meters and inclosed an area of approximately one-twentieth of a square mile. Thebes, at the height of its splendor as the capital of Egypt about 1600, was described by Greek writers as having a circumference of 14 miles. By a liberal estimate it may have contained 225,000 inhabitants.

To the questions why even the largest cities prior to 1000 B.C. were small by modern standards, why even the small ones were relatively few, and why the degree of urbanization even in the most advanced regions was very slight, the answer seems as follows: Agriculture was so cumbersome, static, and labor-intensive that it took many cultivators to support one man in the city. The ox-drawn plow, the wooden plowshare, inundation irrigation, stone hoes, sickles, and axes were instruments of production, to be sure, but clumsy ones. Not until iron came into use in Asia Minor about 1300 B.C. could general improvement in agriculture be achieved. The static character of agriculture and of the economy generally was fostered perhaps by the insulation of the religio-political officials from the practical arts and the reduction of the peasant to virtually the status of a beast of burden. The technology of transport was as labor-intensive as that of agriculture. The only means of conveying bulky goods for mass consumption was by boat, and, though sails had been invented, the sailboat was so inefficient that rowing was still necessary. The oxcart, with its solid wheels and rigidly attached axle, the pack animal, and the human burden-bearer were all short-distance means of transport, the only exception being the camel caravan. Long-distance transport was reserved largely for goods which had high value and small bulk—i.e., goods for the elite—which could not maintain a large urban population. The size of the early cities was therefore limited by the amount of food, fibers, and other bulky materials that could be obtained from the immediate hinterland by labor-intensive methods, a severe limitation which the Greek cities of a later period, small as they remained, nevertheless had to escape before they could attain their full size.

There were political limitations as well. The difficulty of communication and transport and the existence of multifarious local tribal cultures made the formation of large national units virtually impossible. The first urban-centered units were city-states, and when so-called "empires" were formed, as in Egypt, in the Sumerian region, and later in Assyria, much local autonomy was left to the subordinated areas, and the constant danger of revolt prevented the extension of the hinterlands of the cities very far or very effectively. It is symptomatic of the weakness of the early cities that they were constantly threatened and frequently conquered not only by neighboring towns but also by nonurban barbarians. Each wave of barbarians tended to rebuild the urban centers and to become agricultural and sedentary, only to be eventually overwhelmed in turn by new invaders. Other limiting factors were the lack of scientific medicine (which made urban living deadly), the fixity of the peasant on the land (which minimized rural-urban migration), the absence of large-scale manufacturing (which would have derived more advantage from urban concentration than did handicraft), the bureaucratic control of the peasantry (which stifled free trade in the hinterland), and the traditionalism and religiosity of all classes (which hampered technological and economic advance).

The limitations explain why we find, when the sites furnish adequate evidence, that the earliest cities were small affairs, usually no more than towns. Whether in the new or in the old world, even the biggest places could scarcely have exceeded 200,000 inhabitants, and the proportion of the total population living in them must have been not more than 1 or 2 per cent. From 50 to 90 farmers must have been required to support one man in a city.

SUBSEQUENT CITY DEVELOPMENT

If urbanization was to escape its early limitations, it had to do so in a new region, a region more open to innovation and new conceptions.

As it turned out, the region that saw a later and greater urban development was farther north, the Greco-Roman world of Europe, flourishing approximately during the period from 600 B.C. to 400 A.D. Iron tools and weapons, alphabetic writing, improved sailboats, cheap coinage, more democratic institutions, systematic colonization— all tended to increase production, stimulate trade, and expand the effective political unit. Towns and cities became more numerous, the degree of urbanization greater. A few cities reached a substantial size. Athens, at its peak in the fifth century B.C., achieved a population of between 120,-000 and 180,000. Syracuse and Carthage were perhaps larger.

The full potentialities of the ancient world to support a large city were realized only with the Romans. Through their ability to conquer, organize, and govern an empire, to put the immediate Italian hinterland to fruitful cultivation, to use both force and trade to bring slaves, goods, food, and culture to the imperial capital, they were able to create in Rome (with the possible exception of Constantinople some centuries later) the largest city that was to be known in the world until the rise of London in the nineteenth century. Yet, despite the fact that Rome and Constantinople came to hold populations of several hundred thousand, they were not able to resist conquest by far less urbanized outsiders. The eclipse of cities in Europe was striking. Commerce declined to the barest minimum; each locale became isolated and virtually self-sufficient; the social system congealed into a hereditary system. When finally towns and cities began to revive, they were small, as the following estimates suggest: Florence (1338), 90,000; Venice (1422), 190,000; Antwerp (sixteenth century), 200,000; London (1377), 30,000; Nuremberg (1450), 20,165; Frankfort (1440), 8,719.

Yet it was precisely in western Europe, where cities and urbanization had reached a nadir during the Dark Ages, that the limitations that had characterized the ancient world were finally to be overcome. The cities of Mesopotamia, India, and Egypt, of Persia, Greece, and Rome, had all been tied to an economy that was primarily agricultural, where handicraft played at best a secondary role and where the city was still attempting to supplement its economic weakness with military strength, to command its sustenance rather than to buy it honestly. In western Europe, starting at the zero point, the development of cities not only reached the stage that the ancient world had achieved but kept going after that. It kept going on the basis of improvements in agriculture and transport, the opening of new lands and new trade routes, and, above all, the rise in productive activity, first in highly organized handicraft and eventually in a revolutionary new form of production—the factory run by machinery and fossil fuel. The transformation thus achieved in the nineteenth century was the true urban revolution, for it meant not only the rise of a few scattered towns and cities but the appearance of genuine urbanization, in the sense that a substantial portion of the population lived in towns and cities.

THE WORLD TREND FROM 1800 TO 1950

Urbanization has, in fact, gone ahead much faster and reached proportions far greater during the last century and a half than at any previous time in world history. The tremendous growth in world trade during this period has enabled the urban population to draw its sustenance from an ever wider area. Indeed, it can truly be said that the hinterland of today's cities is the entire world. Contemporary Britain, Holland, and Japan, for example, could not maintain their urban population solely from their own territory. The number of rural inhabitants required to maintain one urban inhabitant is still great—greater than one would imagine from the rural-urban ratio *within* each of the highly urbanized countries. The reason is that much of agriculture around the world is still technologically and economically backward. Yet there can be no doubt that, whether for particular countries or for the entire globe, the ratio of urban dwellers to those who grow their food has risen remarkably. This is shown by the fact that the proportion of people living in cities in 1950 is higher than that found in any particular country prior to modern times and many times higher than that formerly characterizing the earth as a whole.

The rapidity of urbanization in recent times can be seen by looking at the most urbanized country, England. In 1801, although London had already reached nearly the million mark (865,-000), England and Wales had less than 10 per cent of their population in cities of 100,000 or more. By 1901 no less than 35 per cent of the population of England and Wales was living in cities of 100,000 or more, and 58 per cent was

living in cities of 20,000 or more. By 1951 these two proportions had risen to 38.4 and 69.3 per cent, respectively.

Britain was in the van of urban development. A degree of urbanization equal to that she had attained in 1801 was not achieved by any other country until after 1850. Thereafter the British rate of urbanization began slowly to decline, whereas that of most other countries continued at a high level. By assembling available data and preparing estimates where data were lacking, we have arrived at figures on urbanization in the world as a whole, beginning with 1800, the earliest date for which anything like a reasonable estimate can be obtained. The percentage of the world's population found living in cities is as shown in Table 16. It can be seen that the proportion has tended to do a bit better than double itself each half-century and that by 1950 the world as a whole was considerably more urbanized than Britain was in 1800. As everyone knows, the earth's total population has grown at an extremely rapid rate since 1800, reaching 2.4 billion by 1950. But the urban population has grown much faster. In 1800 there were about 15.6 million people living in cities of 100,000 or more. By 1950 it was 313.7 million, more than twenty times the earlier figure. Much of this increase has obviously come from rural-urban migration, clearly the most massive migration in modern times.

In 1800 there were apparently less than 50 cities with 100,000 or more inhabitants. This was less than the number in the million class today and less than the number of 100,000-plus cities currently found in many single countries. By 1950 there were close to 900 cities of 100,000 or more people, which is more than the number of towns and cities of 5,000 or more in 1800.

TABLE 16

Percentage of World's Population Living in Cities

	Cities of 20,000 or More	Cities of 100,000 or More
1800	2.4	1.7
1850	4.3	2.3
1900	9.2	5.5
1950	20.9	13.1

As yet there is no indication of a slackening of the rate of urbanization in the world as a whole. If the present rate should continue, more than a fourth of the earth's people will be living in cities of 100,000 or more in the year 2000, and more than half in the year 2050. For places of 20,000 or more, the proportions at the two dates would be something like 45 per cent and 90 per cent. Whether such figures prove too low or too high, they nevertheless suggest that the human species is moving rapidly in the direction of an almost exclusively urban existence. We have used the proportion of the population in cities of 20,-000 and 100,000 or more as a convenient index of differences and changes in degree of urbanization. Places of less than 20,000 also fit a demographic definition of "urban." When, therefore, more than a third of the population of a country lives in cities of the 100,000 class (38.4 per cent in England and Wales in 1951), the country can be described as almost completely urbanized (81 per cent being designated as "urban" in the English case in 1951). We thus have today what can be called "urbanized societies," nations in which the great majority of inhabitants live in cities. The prospect is that, as time goes on, a greater and greater proportion of humanity will be members of such societies.

The question may be raised as to how such an extreme degree of world urbanization will prove possible. Who will grow the food and fibers necessary for the enormous urban population? The answer is that agriculture may prove to be an archaic mode of production. Already, one of the great factors giving rise to urbanization is the rather late and as yet very incomplete industrialization of agriculture. As farming becomes increasingly mechanized and rationalized, fewer people are needed on the land. On the average, the more urbanized a country, the lower is its rural density.[6] If, in addition to industrialized agriculture, food and fiber come to be increasingly produced by manufacturing processes using materials that utilize the sun's energy more efficiently than plants do, there is no technological reason why nearly all of mankind could not live in conurbations of large size.

[6] Rural density *decreases* because agriculture has to become more efficient in order to supply the increasing proportion of the population living in cities. This means not only a relative decline in the farm population, but also, as happened in the United States, an absolute decline. See Davis and Golden, *op. cit.,* p. 10.

THE REGIONAL PATTERN OF URBANIZATION

The highest levels of urbanization are found today in northwestern Europe and in those new regions where northwest Europeans have settled and extended their industrial civilization. The figures are as shown in Table 17. Oceania is the most urbanized of the world's major regions, because Australia and New Zealand are its principal components. North America is next, if it is defined as including only Canada and the United States. The regions least urbanized are those least affected by northwest European culture, namely, Asia and Africa.

The figures for world regions are less valuable for purposes of analysis than are those for individual countries. The latter show clearly that urbanization has tended to reach its highest point wherever economic productivity has been greatest —that is, where the economy is industrialized and rationalized. This explains why urbanization is so closely associated with northwest Europeans and their culture, since they were mainly responsible for the industrial revolution. Of the fifteen most urbanized countries in the world, all but one, Japan, are European in culture, and all but four derive that culture from the northwest or central part of Europe.

The rate of urbanization in the older industrial countries, however, is slowing down. During the twenty years from 1870 to 1890 Germany's proportion in large cities more than doubled; it

TABLE 17

Percentage of World's Population Living in Cities, by Regions

	In Cities of 20,000 Plus	In Cities of 100,000 Plus
World	21	13
Oceania	47	41
North America (Canada and U.S.A.)	42	29
Europe (except U.S.S.R.)	35	21
U.S.S.R.	31	18
South America	26	18
Middle America and Caribbean	21	12
Asia (except U.S.S.R.)	13	8
Africa	9	5

nearly doubled again from 1890 to 1910; but from 1910 to 1940 the increase was only 36 per cent. In Sweden the gain slowed down noticeably after 1920. In England and Wales the most rapid urbanization occurred between 1811 and 1851. Contrary to popular belief, the fastest rate in the United States occurred between 1861 and 1891. Since, as we noted earlier, there has been no slowing-down of urbanization in the world as a whole, it must be that, as the more established industrial countries have slackened, the less-developed countries have exhibited a faster rate. In fact, such historical evidence as we have for underdeveloped areas seems to show that their rates of urbanization have been rising in recent decades. This has been the case in Egypt, where the rate is higher after 1920 than before; in India, where the fastest urbanization has occurred since 1941; in Mexico, where the speed-up began in 1921; and in Greece, where the fastest period ran from 1900 to 1930. Asia, for example, had only 22 per cent of the world's city population in 1900 but 34 per cent of it in 1950, and Africa had 1.5 per cent in 1900 but 3.2 per cent at the later date.

With respect to urbanization, then, the gap between the industrial and the preindustrial nations is beginning to diminish. The less-developed parts of the world will eventually, it seems, begin in their turn to move gradually toward a saturation point. As the degree of urbanization rises, it of course becomes impossible for the rate of gain to continue. The growth in the urban proportion is made possible by the movement of people from rural areas to the cities. As the rural population becomes a progressively smaller percentage of the total, the cities no longer can draw on a noncity population of any size. Yet in no country can it be said that the process of urbanization is yet finished. Although there have been short periods in recent times in England, the United States, and Japan when the city population increased at a slightly slower rate than the rural, these were mere interludes in the ongoing but ever slower progress of urban concentration.

THE TENDENCY TOWARD METROPOLITAN EXPANSION

The continuance of urbanization in the world does not mean the persistence of something that remains the same in detail. A city of a million inhabitants today is not the sort of place that a city of the same number was in 1900 or in 1850. Moreover, with the emergence of giant cities of five to fifteen million, something new has been added. Such cities are creatures of the twentieth century. Their sheer quantitative difference means a qualitative change as well.

One of the most noticeable developments is the ever stronger tendency of cities to expand outward—a development already observed in the nineteenth century. Since 1861, the first date when the comparison can be made, the Outer Ring of Greater London has been growing more rapidly than London itself. French writers prior to 1900 pointed out the dispersive tendency, as did Adna Weber in 1899. There is no doubt, however, that the process of metropolitan dispersion has increased with time. This fact is shown for the United States by comparing the percentage gains in population made by the central cities with those made by their satellite areas in forty-four metropolitan districts for which Thompson could get comparable data going back to 1900. The gains are as shown in Table 18.[7] The difference increases, until in 1930–40 the population outside the central city is growing more than three times as fast as that inside the central city. Furthermore, Thompson has shown that *within the metropolitan area outside the central cities* it was the "rural" parts which gained faster than the urban parts, as the percentage increases per decade shown in Table 19 indicate.

TABLE 18
Percentage Increase in Population in 44 Metropolitan Districts in the United States, 1900–1940

	Central Cities	Rest of Districts
1900–1910	33.6	38.2
1910–20	23.4	31.3
1920–30	20.5	48.7
1930–40	4.2	13.0

[7] Warren S. Thompson, *The Growth of Metropolitan Districts in the United States, 1900–1940*, Washington: Government Printing Office, 1948, p. 5. The picture is much the same for the rest of the metropolitan districts for decades in which comparability could be established.

Clearly, the metropolitan districts were increasingly dependent on the areas outside the central cities, and especially upon the sparsely settled parts at the periphery of these areas, for their continued growth. Thompson showed that, the greater the distance from the center of the city, the faster the rate of growth.

The same forces which have made extreme urbanization possible have also made metropolitan dispersion possible, and the dispersion itself has contributed to further urbanization by making large conurbations more efficient and more endurable. The outward movement of urban residences, of urban services and commercial establishments, and of light industry—all facilitated by improvements in motor transport and communications—has made it possible for huge agglomerations to keep on growing without the inconveniences of proportionate increases in density. In many ways the metropolis of three million today is an easier place to live and work in than the city of five hundred thousand yesterday. Granted that the economic advantages of urban concentration still continue and still push populations in the direction of urbanization, the effect of metropolitan dispersion is thus to minimize the disadvantages of this continued urban growth.

The new type of metropolitan expansion occurring in the highly industrial countries is not without its repercussions in less-developed lands as well. Most of the rapid urbanization now occurring in Africa and Asia, for example, is affected by direct contact with industrial nations and by a concomitant rise in consumption standards. Although private automobiles may not be available to the urban masses, bicycles and busses generally are. Hence Brazzaville and Abidjan, Takoradi and Nairobi, Jamshedpur and New Delhi, Ankara and Colombo, are not evolving in the same manner as did the cities of the eighteenth and nineteenth centuries. Their ecological pattern, their technological base, their economic activity, all reflect the twentieth century, no matter how primitive or backward their hinterlands may be. Thus the fact that their main growth is occurring in the present century is not without significance for the kind of cities they are turning out to be.

FUTURE TRENDS IN WORLD URBANIZATION

Speculation concerning the future of urbanization is as hazardous as that concerning any other aspect of human society. Following the direction of modern trends, however, one may conclude that, with the industrial revolution, for the first time in history urbanization began to reach a stage from which there was no return. The cities of antiquity were vulnerable, and the degree of urbanization reached was so thin in many societies as to be transitory. Today virtually every part of the world is more urbanized than any region was in antiquity. Urbanization is so widespread, so much a part of industrial civilization, and gaining so rapidly, that any return to rurality, even with major catastrophes, appears unlikely. On the contrary, since every city is obsolescent to some degree—more obsolescent the older it is—the massive destruction of many would probably add eventually to the impetus of urban growth.

The fact that the rate of world urbanization has shown no slackening since 1800 suggests that we are far from the end of this process, perhaps not yet at the peak. Although the industrial countries have shown a decline in their rates, these countries, because they embrace only about a fourth of the world's population, have not dampened the world trend. The three-fourths of humanity who live in underdeveloped countries are still in the early stages of an urbanization that promises to be more rapid than that which occurred earlier in the areas of northwest European culture.

How urbanized the world will eventually become is an unanswerable question. As stated earlier, there is no apparent reason why it should not become as urbanized as the most urban countries today—with perhaps 85–90 per cent of the population living in cities and towns of 5,000 or more and practicing urban occupations. Our present degree of urbanization in advanced countries is still so new that we have no clear idea of

TABLE 19
Percentage Population Increase outside Central Cities in 44 Metropolitan Districts

	Urban Parts	Rural Parts
1900–1910	35.9	43.2
1910–20	30.2	34.5
1920–30	40.6	68.1
1930–40	7.3	28.1

how such complete world urbanization would affect human society; but the chances are that the effects would be profound.

In visualizing the nature and effects of complete urbanization in the future, however, one must guard against assuming that cities will retain their present form. The tendency to form huge metropolitan aggregates which are increasingly decentralized will undoubtedly continue but probably will not go so far as to eliminate the central business district altogether, though it may greatly weaken it. At the periphery, it may well be that the metropolis and the countryside, as the one expands and the other shrinks, will merge together, until the boundaries of one sprawling conurbation will touch those of another, with no intervening pure countryside at all. The world's population doubles itself twice in a century, becoming at the same time highly urbanized, and as new sources of energy are tapped, the possibility of centrifugal metropolitan growth is enormously enhanced. If commuting to work could be done with the speed of sound and cheaply, one would not mind living two hundred miles from work. Almost any technological advance from now on is likely to contribute more to the centrifugal than to the centripetal tendency. It may turn out that urbanization in the sense of emptying the countryside and concentrating huge numbers in little space will reverse itself—not, however, in the direction of returning people to the farm but rather in that of spreading them more evenly over the land for purposes of residence and industrial work. "Rurality" would have disappeared, leaving only a new kind of urban existence.

The blurring of the line between rural and urban has already taken place in urban industrial societies. Industrialization ties together the rural and urban economies more closely than in preindustrial societies. Commercial farming is a business, and it resembles urban businesses in its consciousness of costs, its orientation to the market, its investment in capital equipment, and even in its use of modern accounting. One author has called commercial farms "factories in the field," and others talk about "agribusiness" instead of "agriculture." [8] The average size of commercial farms in the United States is growing. In 1940 the average

size was 220 acres; in 1959, 404 acres.[9] Small farms cannot use power machinery efficiently; economic pressure forces the small farmer to sell out or expand. From 1930 to 1961 the number of farms *decreased* from 6,546,000 to 3,811,000; and the proportion of the American population living on farms decreased from 24.9 per cent to 8.1 per cent.[10] In the same period the average value of farmland and buildings (not including equipment) *increased* from $7,313 to $35,578.[11] To cite the United States or Canada as examples of the industrialization of agriculture may be misleading; these countries contained vast open spaces during much of their recent history. None of the urban industrial societies of Western Europe have been able to utilize agricultural power machinery on the same scale.[12] And the problem of fractionated, inefficient farms is even more acute in the underdeveloped countries. In 1960, 4,256,734 American agricultural workers were able to feed a total population of nearly 180 million people—as well as to produce a politically embarrassing food surplus. The swift urbanization of the United States cannot be fully understood without an awareness of the special circumstances facilitating the industrialization of agriculture.

The industrialization of agriculture in the United States helps to explain the narrowing of the difference between the style of life of city and farm families. Rural populations in all of the urban industrial societies are deeply involved in the money economy, but the integration of rural and urban economies is closer

8   Carey McWilliams, *Factories in the Field: The Story of Migratory Farm Labor in California*, Boston: Little, Brown, 1939; John H. Davis and Roy A. Goldberg, *A Concept of Agribusiness*, Boston: Division of Research, Graduate School of Business Administration, Harvard University, 1957.
9   Bureau of the Census, *Statistical Abstract of the United States: 1962*, Washington: Government Printing Office, 1962, p. 610.
10   *Ibid.*, p. 608.
11   *Ibid.*
12   Fred Cottrell, *Energy and Society: The Relationship between Energy, Social Change, and Economic Development*, New York: McGraw-Hill, 1955, pp. 110–165, especially 128.

in the United States, thus accounting for some of the increased homogeneity. For instance, not only has rural electrification eliminated such laborious tasks as pumping water and milking cows by hand; it has also enabled farm families to listen to the same radio programs and see the same television programs as urban families.[13] Good roads not only enable farmers to transport their crops speedily to distant markets; they also make urban recreational and educational facilities accessible. Farm families dispose of their incomes much as city people do. Like city people, they talk on telephones and ride in airplanes. They live in the same culture.

The line between rural and urban has been blurred in yet another way in urban industrial societies: by the emergence of suburbs. From one point of view, suburbs are the inevitable consequence of urbanization. An urbanized society cannot develop without booming city growth. Such growth usually means spilling over beyond original political boundaries. Even with high-rise apartment houses, there are limits to population density. From this point of view then, suburbs are political accidents. They represent urban growth occurring outside the boundaries of the city. Had the annexation of outlying areas kept pace with the functional growth of cities, there would be less need to talk about "suburbs." However, suburbs emerge for another reason: improved transportation and communication makes a larger area accessible to the central business district. This accessibility of the hinterland necessitates greater transportation costs, but industrial societies are affluent societies. Many people are willing to pay the cost in time and money which commutation involves in order to escape high population density. Suburbia is a compromise between urban work and rural residence. In the United States, for example, large cities are not merely increasing the scope of their influence over larger and larger areas; the population density at their centers is de-

creasing.[14] Cities are not as concentrated as they once were; they sprawl. For instance, Boston's population decreased from 801,444 in 1950 to 697,197 in 1960, a loss of 13 per cent.[15] Most of these people fled to communities in the Boston commuting zone: to Cambridge, Chelsea, Everett, Lynn, Malden, Medford, Melrose, Quincy, Revere, Waltham, or Woburn.

In 1950, the Census Bureau defined 168 population clusters called "standard metropolitan areas" to measure the new kind of sprawling urbanism emanating from large cities. A standard metropolitan area consists of one or more central cities containing at least 50,000 population and surrounding built-up areas in close economic and social communication with the central city (or cities). By 1960, the Census Bureau identified 212 metropolitan areas containing nearly 113 million persons, out of a total American population of 180 million.[16] While the American population as a whole rose 18.5 per cent between 1950 and 1960, metropolitan population increased 26.4 per cent, whereas the suburban segments of metropolitan areas alone increased 48.6 per cent.[17]

The Rise of the Metropolis

Reprinted by permission. From Donald J. Bogue, "Urbanism in the United States, 1950," American Journal of Sociology, Vol. 60, March 1955, pp. 471–486.

The phenomenon of growth of cities to large size and the fact that large cities acquire unique attributes have given rise to a theory that major cities are focal points in the economic and social organization of modern industrial-commercial nations. From piecemeal evidence it appears that, as a nation becomes highly industrialized and

[13] U. S. Department of Agriculture, "Farming in the United States," Agricultural Information Bulletin No. 246, Washington: Government Printing Office, 1961.

[14] Amos H. Hawley, *The Changing Shape of Metropolitan America: Deconcentration since 1920*, Glencoe, Ill.: Free Press, 1956.
[15] Bureau of the Census, *Statistical Abstract of the United States: 1962*, Washington: Government Printing Office, 1962, p. 13.
[16] *Ibid.*
[17] *Ibid.*, pp. 12–13.

committed to a system of interregional commerce and industry, its economic activities tend to be located with reference to large urban centers, or metropolises, as well as to natural resources and available raw materials. The specific forces and factors that produce a concentration of population and economic activities in metropolitan centers and distribute the remainder in a metropolitan hinterland have not been measured or studied in detail. Among its advantages are, one may say tentatively, low transportation costs, a concentrated market, a joint location for several industries, a large and varied labor supply, a large and varied supply of employment opportunities, and the opportunity for wholesalers and manufacturers to assemble a wide range of items. Also, business management tends to locate sales offices and its home office in large centers to have ready access to other business management, financial institutions, and good transportation and communication facilities. The term "dominance" has been used as a class name to refer to the combined force of these factors in determining location. New economic units seeking to establish themselves, or old ones seeking to expand their activities, find that these forces are integral parts of the environment over which they have no control and to which they must adjust. Since they emanate from the metropolis and tend to locate activities with respect to the latter, large metropolitan centers are said to be dominant in determining the distribution of population and economic activities. Not an insignificant aspect of the dominant role of the metropolitan centers is the fact that medium-size and small cities, as well as dispersed rural populations, appear to perform their functions with reference to the metropolitan centers, while they themselves exert a more limited and integrative influence upon the territory about them. Thus metropolitan centers are dominant conditioners of the physical environment in the modern industrial-commercial society, while the smaller urban places are subdominant environmental conditioners.

A most familiar aspect of metropolitan dominance is the fact that a large territory outside the metropolis is directly under the influence of the metropolitan center. This territory corresponds approximately to what one would regard as the combined labor market and retail trade area of the metropolis. Since transportation facilities now make it possible to live several miles distant from the place of work, a broad ring outside the urban fringe but adjacent to it is growing rapidly. A high proportion of the population in this ring is rural-nonfarm. Many new factories and other business establishments are locating themselves there. Even the rural-farm population in this zone differs from the farm population elsewhere, for there are numerous residential farms, part-time farms, and specialized farms. After all these aspects are considered, it is evident that the economic and social entity that may be termed "the metropolis and its immediate environs" or "metropolitan area" is much greater in scope than either the central city or even the urbanized area.

Despite the blurring of differences between rural and urban areas as a result of common participation in industrial development, some distinctive characteristics remain, even in the United States where metropolitan dominance is far advanced because cities lead and rural areas follow. Table 20 demonstrates the concentration of college-educated males in urban areas. Whereas 22.7 per cent of urban white males, 25 years old or older, had completed at least one year of college in 1960, only 7.4 per cent of white males living on farms had done so. Nonwhite males were much less likely to have completed one or more years of college than white males, and nonwhite males were

TABLE 20
Per Cent of Urban, Rural Nonfarm, and Rural Farm Males, Age 25 and Over, Who Completed One or More Years of College, United States, 1960

Residence	White Males	Nonwhite Males
Urban	22.7%	9.5%
Rural Nonfarm	13.4%	3.7%
Rural Farm	7.4%	1.7%

Source: Bureau of the Census, *United States Census of Population: 1960, United States Summary, General Social and Economic Characteristics*, Final Report PC(1)–1C, Washington: Government Printing Office, 1962, p. 208.

even more concentrated in urban areas than white males in 1960. The chances were better than one in 11 in cities that a nonwhite male had completed some college, but only about one in 59 on farms. Other differences between urban and rural communities persist. Women are less likely to seek gainful employment outside of the home and birth rates are higher in rural areas.[18] Cities have a preponderance of females and rural areas a preponderance of males.[19] Rural farm people are much more likely to have lived in the same house for five years or more than rural nonfarm or urban people.[20] Nonetheless, these are differences of degree; in the urban society, rural communities are *not* isolated; they respond to the influences arising in urban areas.

THE RELATIVE PACE OF URBANIZATION AND ECONOMIC DEVELOPMENT

When sociologists examine the history of urbanization in Western Europe and the United States, they relate it to economic development. They do not mean, of course, that all urbanites are engaged in manufacturing or that all manufacturing is done in cities. Nor do they mean that the fabrication of goods is more crucial to an industrial society than the wide variety of activities that develop concomitantly: transportation, communication, public utilities, wholesale and retail trade, banking, insurance, real estate, public administration, health, education, and other professional services. As a matter of fact, while a predominantly manufacturing city like Manchester, England, could grow fairly large, the real giants (New York, London, Paris) were also commercial, financial, and administrative centers. Nevertheless, the major impetus for urban growth in the Western world for the past three centuries has been industrial development. Urban populations grew because rural people

were attracted to urban areas by genuine occupational opportunities. When sociologists concern themselves with urbanization in the underdeveloped countries of Asia, Africa, and South America, however, they face a new situation: a larger flow of population into cities than is necessary to keep up with economic growth or increased administrative functions.

This new situation arose largely because the underdeveloped countries have been strongly influenced by Western industrial countries. For instance, during the nineteenth century, when Burma was politically as well as economically dominated by Great Britain, the city of Rangoon grew because it served as an economic link between Burma and the world market.[21] Imported European manufactured products and Burmese raw materials exported in exchange passed through Rangoon. Shanghai, Hong Kong, Karachi, and Djakarta also flourished because they served as centers of Western influence.[22] For similar reasons, swift urbanization is now taking place in Central and West Africa. By 1950 Nairobi had grown to 119,000 population, Leopoldville to 211,000, Lagos to 230,000, Dakar to 209,000, and Accra to 136,000.[23] "This sudden juxtaposition of 20th-century cities and extremely primitive cultures (virtually stone-age in their organization and technology) gives rise in some respects to a sharper rural-urban contrast than can be found anywhere in the world."[24]

In short, some underdeveloped countries are undergoing more rapid urbanization than is necessary for the level of economic differentiation. This is partly because of the pull of Western consumption standards that are visible, if not easily attainable, in the cities, and partly because of the impoverishment of the rural population.[25] Demographers have pointed out, for example, that 19.3 per cent of the Egyptian population lived in cities of 100,000 population or more in 1947—about the same

---

[18] Bureau of the Census, *United States Census of Population: 1960, United States Summary*, Washington: Government Printing Office, 1962, pp. 212, 214.
[19] *Ibid.*, p. 200.
[20] *Ibid.*, p. 204.

[21] Bert F. Hoselitz, *Sociological Aspects of Economic Growth*, Glencoe, Ill.: Free Press, 1960, pp. 204–205.
[22] *Ibid.*, p. 223.
[23] Davis and Golden, *op. cit.*, p. 21.
[24] *Ibid.*, p. 20.
[25] Hoselitz, *op. cit.*, p. 202.

proportion of the population as in France, Switzerland, and Sweden, which are far more industrialized.[26] The Egyptian system of absentee landlords living in the cities heightens the contrast between rural and urban standards of living and thereby leads to overurbanization.[27] A similar explanation accounts for overurbanization in Latin America generally and Argentina in particular.

Overurbanization of Latin America

Reprinted by permission. From Kingsley Davis and Ana Casis, "Urbanization in Latin America," *Milbank Memorial Fund Quarterly*, Vol. 24, April 1946, pp. 186–207.

Progress in Latin America did not begn spontaneously or indigenously. Instead, coming as a foreign, ocean-borne intrusion, it began on the coastal borders, where the Europeans first settled and where water transport was available. This might have been a prelude for gradual penetration and settlement of the interior, and so it was in a sense. But the Central and South American land masses were tropical or semi-tropical, mountainous or jungly, excessively wet or dry, and peopled by hostile or at least alien peoples. The conditions offered formidable barriers to settlement, and the Spaniards hardly had hard work in mind. As a consequence, the interior was not developed along the lines of homestead farming, but was given to large landowners (*encomenderos*) who used native or slave labor and aimed at getting out from forest, field, or mine as quickly as possible a commercial product for foreign shipment. The market lay across the ocean. The city, usually a port, was the necessary nexus, without which the interior would be worthless.

The interior, inaccessible and undeveloped, had little of culture or convenience to offer. It was remote from the center of civilization (Europe), and from the cities through which European influence filtered. Nobody wanted to stay there any longer than necessary. To live in the city was every man's dream. Persons who owned enough land in the interior lived in the city, where they formed a class of absentee landowners, educating their children abroad, doting on Eu-

rope, and in general neglecting the interior from which their wealth came. The existence of this class also drew to the cities a numerous body of retainers giving service to the rich.

As time went by the interior improved very little. Absentee ownership, the use of slave or peon labor, the lack of local industry and local demand all impeded agricultural progress, despite the effort to raise commercial crops. In the absence of mechanization, human labor had to bear the burden of agricultural production. The competition with more mechanized and accessible agriculture in other continents, plus the peon system, drove rural "wages" down to virtual subsistence. To the agricultural worker almost any city wage looked attractive, and he filled the need of the aristocracy in the towns for "unspoiled" menial labor. There was thus a stimulus to cityward migration for both the laboring and landowning classes.

The emphasis upon urban dwelling among the wealthy meant that living conditions in cities were improved greatly, whereas little improvement was made in the country. Sanitation, education, utilities, and amusements were fostered in the city, but not elsewhere. The resulting gulf between city and country, still noticed by travelers and amply documented in rural-urban statistics, served to reinforce the initial preference for the city as a place to live. The idea of a quiet home in the country, far from the urban crowd, was not prominent in the Latin-American mind.

The growth of cities was also fostered by political factors. Despite an expressed preference in the leading republics for federalism and decentralization, the Latin American countries have usually had centralized governments. Since everything, including economic advantage, political patronage, and cultural support revolved about politics, the capitals became the national nerve-centers. It is therefore no accident that in every Latin American country the largest city is also the capital.

In short, the rural-urban migration that has given rise to unusual urbanization has not been due to heavy industrialization, but rather to the peculiar institutions of the Spaniards and Portuguese and the environmental conditions in their part of the new world. Today there is the prospect that industrialization will play a greater role, and that some of the Latin American nations will carry urban concentration still further.

[26] Davis and Golden, *op. cit.*, p. 16.
[27] *Ibid.*, pp. 17–18.

THE CASE OF ARGENTINA

The most urbanized of the larger republics, Argentina is experiencing a "de-peopling of the pampas." In 1930 the rural population (persons in places of less than 1,000) was estimated to be 3.58 million; by 1938, 3.32 million. In percentage terms, the rural population dropped during this time from 32 to 26 per cent of the total population. Since 1938 the rural population has probably declined still further, both in absolute and in percentage figures.

This rural decline bespeaks a huge rural-urban migration. Between 1930 and 1939, for example, an estimated 260,000 rural dwellers, or 7.3 per cent of all such dwellers, migrated to the towns. The rural exodus, plus foreign immigration, explains the phenomenal expansion of the urban population—an expansion that has exceeded the rate of rural growth since 1895.

It is primarily the larger cities that have gained. The census of 1914 showed 24 per cent of the total population living in cities of 100,000-plus, while estimates for 1943 place the figure at 34 per cent. "Between 1914 and 1943 the population of Argentina increased by 74.6 per cent, while the population of the cities that in 1914 had 100,000 or more inhabitants increased by 106 per cent." Greater Buenos Aires contains today close to 3.4 million persons, or above one-fourth of the Argentine population. It is, as Preston James points out, the largest city in the Southern Hemisphere and is second only to Paris among the world's Latin cities. Truly, for a predominantly agricultural country, Argentina is extremely urbanized. Its closest parallel is Australia, which is even more urban.

It is the organization of agriculture on the one hand, and the birth of industry on the other, that explains the Argentine phenomenon. Argentina resembles many another Latin American country in the concentration of land ownership. It has been estimated that almost half of Buenos Aires Province, by far the richest and most populous province, is controlled by not more than 3,500 people, or one-tenth of one per cent of the provincial population; and most other parts of the country are similarly controlled. Large *estancias* and *latifundios* dominate the agricultural scene. The holdings are organized along two different lines. Some of them (about 38 per cent) are run by their owners or by salaried managers; others (about 62 per cent) are cultivated by tenants, sharecroppers, etc. The class of persons who own their own farm and work it with their own hands is extremely small. Most of the big landholders are absentee owners—many of them being simply stock-holders in agricultural corporations.

Though resembling her neighbors in the concentration of landownership, Argentina differs from them in the degree to which her estates are mechanized and the need for manpower thus reduced. The equipment, even in the case of large estates, is often not owned by the cultivators; rather it is leased by the day from machine-renting enterprises. Moreover, livestock raising, which requires a relatively small amount of labor, has recently regained its historical dominance over other agricultural activities. The net effect of mechanization and livestock raising has been to reduce the amount of labor needed. Bunge points out that the per capita product of the agricultural population is in Argentina approximately four times what it is in France. Carl C. Taylor has given a graphic account of the labor force of a cattle *estancia*. This *estancia*, covering 50,000 acres, grazing about 32,000 head of livestock, and grossing approximately $300,000 per year, had a permanent working population of 72 persons.

One might think that agricultural mechanization would make rural wages high. But such is not the case in Argentina, because the agricultural proletariat, as against the politically dominant landowning class, has little bargaining power on the *estancia*. It seems generally agreed that rural labor in Argentina is poorly paid and poorly housed, insecure and extremely mobile. If we add that the system of rural credit favors larger holders, and that the tendency toward concentration of ownership is increasing rather than decreasing, it becomes clear why Argentine agriculturalists should desire to leave the land.

At the same time, Argentine industry, concentrated in the cities, has been growing at a fast pace for several decades. It has drawn hard-pressed laborers and tenants from the pampas like a magnet. Thus there have been two forces—agriculture pushing and industry pulling—which have carried huge numbers to the cities.

THE GROWTH PATTERN OF INDUSTRIAL CITIES

Industrialization is urbanizing the entire world. Nevertheless, advanced industrial countries like Great Britain and the United States offer better opportunities to study the growth processes of modern cities. Cities like Manchester and Chicago developed gradually—as contrasted with the explosive growth of Buenos Aires or Johannesburg. In the decade following the First World War, sociologists from the University of Chicago devoted thousands of man-hours to mapping the distribution of various kinds of activities and events throughout the metropolis. They did this, not because of an intrinsic interest in stores, rooming houses, mental illness, or juvenile delinquency, but rather because they believed that study of such phenomena would lead to a theory of differential land use in the city and ultimately to an explanation of the changing character of neighborhoods as the city grew. They identified *competition for scarce space* as a natural tendency in the crowded city, and they demonstrated how the economic expression of this competition resulted in concentric rings with characteristic land uses.[28]

The inner ring, being most accessible to people from all parts of the city, is a favorable location for department stores and office buildings. Therefore, such business enterprises are willing to outbid all other potential users of land in the central business district. If one did not mind the noise and congestion, one might still reside in a one-family house in Chicago's Loop. However, most people are not willing to pay ten times the taxes the same land use would cost on the fringe of the city. Rational economic calculation induces a flow of business enterprises *into* the central business district as it becomes accessible to a larger and larger population. Simultaneously, it produces a flow of residential users *out* of the area. Thus,

as the metropolis expands, so too does the central business district. To draw upon one of the ecological concepts which the Chicago sociologists borrow from biology, business *invades* a residential area and, because business firms are willing to pay more for the use of available space than residential users, one land use succeeds another.

Invasion and succession take time, however. Between the anticipation of the expansion of the central business district and the actual razing of residential structures to make way for stores and offices is a period of uncertainty for the neighborhood in question. The land is beginning to appreciate in value, but the structures on it have no future; the owners hardly see the practicality of making repairs. This "zone in transition," as the University of Chicago ecologists called it, is the second concentric ring; it is a slum. Into its deteriorating structures crowd those who can pay least for living space: first-generation immigrants and their families, ethnic minorities, alcoholics and petty criminals, elderly persons on small pensions.

The third concentric ring is the "zone of workingmen's homes." Unlike the zone in transition, it is *not* a slum; often it is the next step for those who have escaped from the slum and are on the way "up." Cheap rents and proximity to work are important considerations for the factory workers who live in this zone, but this is an area of thrift rather than of deprivation and public welfare. The fourth concentric ring is a middle-class residential zone, and the fifth concentric ring contains the spacious homes of affluent commuters.

The zonal theory developed by Ernest Burgess and his colleagues fitted large American cities fairly well. It was predicated on realistic assumptions for an urban industrial society: (1) Cities will continue to grow. (2) The centers of cities will continue to be accessible for these larger populations. (3) The real-estate market will continue to be the main mechanism determining land use. (4) Business uses will continue to outbid residential uses in the central neighborhoods of maximum

[28] Robert E. Park, Ernest W. Burgess, and Roderick D. McKenzie, *The City*, Chicago: University of Chicago Press, 1925.

accessibility. (5) The demand for spacious residential uses and the costs of commutation will continue to push the "best" residential neighborhoods into remote suburbs.

Although obviously irrelevant to preindustrial cities, these assumptions are reasonably descriptive of American society. On the other hand, the zonal theory was never fulfilled *in its entirety* even in American cities. For example, Beacon Hill remains a high-rent, high-prestige area in the heart of Boston instead of turning into a slum.[29] Furthermore, some of the assumptions of the theory are less true today than when the theory was developed. Zoning laws and other planning efforts of local governments are interfering with the free play of the real-estate market. Second, as the metropolis spreads, centers develop in outlying areas, thus reducing the dominance of the main business district. Finally, as suburbia recedes further into the countryside and as commuting traffic becomes a more and more serious problem, élite residential neighborhoods have returned to the heart of the city. These changes may explain why recent survey of the New York metropolitan area described the evolution of neighborhoods in terms only faintly reminiscent of the University of Chicago ecologists.

The Evolution of Neighborhoods in New York

Reprinted by permission. From Edgar M. Hoover and Raymond Vernon, *Anatomy of a Metropolis: The Changing Distribution of People and Jobs within the New York Metropolitan Region*, Cambridge, Mass.: Harvard University Press, 1959, pp. 191–204.

The shifting pattern of metropolitan residence areas has often been schematically described in terms of gradually widening concentric zones pushing out in all directions from a growing central business core like ripples from a splash. Nonresidential "downtown" land uses, pre-empting the very center of the metropolitan area almost exclusively, expand into the immediately surrounding old residential areas, and also extend an aura of blight far beyond the range of their actual landtaking. Housing nearest the center is mainly slum —because it is the oldest, because it is cramped, because the street traffic and other aspects of downtown development make it undesirable for residence, and because it comes to house a concentration of disadvantaged people who are shunned as neighbors by those more fortunate or longer in residence. These slum characteristics are persistent, even cumulative, since the economics of slum property deters extensive replacement, modernization, or even maintenance of the antiquated housing.

The near-central slum area, eroded from the inside and along its main streets by competing land uses, and having to accommodate an influx of bottom-income people, expands outward into the next nearest and next oldest zone, mainly by the down-grading and conversion of old apartments and houses to higher densities. This pressure, as well as over-all population growth, forces the population of the next zone to push outward in turn, and so it goes till we reach the out-crawling fringe of urban development where new houses replace farms, woodland, or golf courses.

This highly simplified picture is not unrelated to reality in the New York Metropolitan Region, but it needs a good deal of modification to take account of observed facts. In the first place, there is not just one high-density commercial center but many, of different orders of magnitude; there is not only Manhattan but Newark, Jersey City, Paterson, Passaic, Elizabeth, New Brunswick, and many other old cities. The widening ripples come, then, not from a single pebble dropped into a puddle, but from a scattered handful of large, middling, and small pebbles, each a focus of expansion. Secondly, the pattern does not really shape up into neat concentric circular zones, because of manifold variation in transport facilities, topography, zoning, and so on which "distort" the picture. Thirdly, people do not just "shove over" from one block to the next, like a row of dominoes falling, but often move to a quite different part of the metropolitan area once they decide to move at all. New residential developments too, as we have already seen, do not simply extend the built-up area into the countryside in solid sequence, but "leap-frog" across intervening vacant land in order to use sites better matched to the current demand for new housing. Finally,

[29] Walter Firey, *Land Use in Central Boston*, Cambridge, Mass.: Harvard University Press, 1947.

the housing supply responds to changing demand in several alternative ways.

We can get a realistic view of what has been happening in the New York Metropolitan Region by identifying areas in sequential stages of development. Some of the oldest communities in the Region have evolved through the whole succession while other less "mature" parts of the Region are still in earlier stages. Our hypothesis is that the historical pattern of sequence, as exhibited in cross-section in the present structure of the Region, does have enough predictive value to be useful, if we can allow for certain evident changes in the impact of such basic determinants as means of transport.

What then are the stages of evolution we can identify, and where in the Region are they found?

Stage 1 is residential development in single-family houses. This stage, the earliest of all, is just beginning to appear in some outlying parts of the Region, is currently in full swing in the outer parts of the Inner Ring, and was passed long ago in most of the Core and in the central parts of the large Inner Ring cities, notably Newark. Table 21 shows that new residential construction in the outer counties of the Region is primarily single-family. In every Outer Ring county, more than 72 per cent of the new housing covered by permits issued in the first half of 1958 was in one-family structures, and all of the counties with more than half of their new housing in multifamily structures in that period were Core counties except Essex. . . .

Stage 2 is a transition stage in which there is substantial new construction and population growth in the area, but in which a high and increasing proportion of the new housing is in apartments, so that average density is increasing. Much of the apartment construction replaces older single-family houses. . . .

Stage 3 is a down-grading stage, in which old housing (both multifamily and single) is being adapted to greater-density use than it was originally designed for. In this stage there is usually little actual new construction, but there is some population and density growth through conversion and crowding of existing structures. This stage appears most clearly in areas of recent "slum invasion" located on Manhattan's upper West Side, in sections of the Bronx and Brooklyn, and in certain old urban areas in and around Newark, Paterson, Passaic, Elizabeth, and the Hudson County cities.

Of course, the sequence to this stage from the preceding one is not always clean-cut. Thus in the down-grading stage there may be a certain amount of new housing construction too, involving the replacement of single-family homes by apartment houses at the same time that other structures are being subdivided. Moreover, Stage 2 does not inevitably lead to Stage 3: an area converted to apartments may not undergo any down-grading then or later. The Riverdale area of the Bronx, for instance, promises to hold its present quality for some time to come. The stretch of Fifth Avenue facing Central Park was almost entirely transformed from one-family residences to towering apartment buildings after about 1910 and has maintained its character. On the other hand, Riverside Drive, similarly redeveloped at about the same time, has been subject to down-grading.

The down-grading stage is often associated with the spread of districts occupied by more or less segregated ethnic and minority groups. In the spread of such districts, conversion of structures to accommodate more families plays a significant part, but not always a decisive one. Thus, the number of dwelling units in the 17-county

TABLE 21

Percentage of New Dwelling Units in Single-Family Structures, New York Metropolitan Region, First Half of 1958

Entire Region	54.1	Union	70.9
		Richmond	75.5
Core	9.3	Nassau	81.3
Manhattan	None	Outer Ring	87.9
Brooklyn	1.7	Fairfield	72.0
Bronx	12.0	Middlesex	72.2
Queens	20.6	Dutchess	78.9
Hudson	59.1	Rockland	94.9
		Somerset	95.4
Inner Ring	65.9	Suffolk	96.2
Essex	35.2	Morris	98.1
Passaic	55.1	Orange	98.3
Westchester	56.0	Monmouth	98.4
Bergen	69.5	Putnam	100.0

Source: Regional Plan Association, *New Homes in the New Jersey–New York–Connecticut Metropolitan Region*, RPA Bulletin 90, No. 3, December 1958.

Standard Metropolitan Area with nonwhite household heads showed a net increase of about 100,-000 between 1950 and 1956. Of this increase, at least 85 per cent appears to have been accounted for by net shift from white to nonwhite occupancy in dwelling units that were occupied in both 1950 and 1956 and were not converted. The remainder of the increase was split fairly evenly between conversions and post-1950 construction. In particular areas of the Region, of course, the relative importance of conversions in the shifting character of neighborhoods was much greater than these over-all figures might suggest. . . .

All of which brings us to *Stage 4*, the thinning-out stage. This is the phase in which density and dwelling occupancy are gradually reduced. Most of the shrinkage comes about through a decline in household size in these neighborhoods. But the shrinkage may also reflect merging of dwelling units, vacancy, abandonment, and demolition. This stage is characterized by little or no residential construction and by a decline in population.

To find the reasons for this thinning-out process, we shall have to retrace our steps and have another look at the families which characteristically participate in the preceding stage of slum invasion. Those families are, on the whole, recently arrived in-migrants to the Region, with low incomes and a limited housing choice. The limitations are imposed not only by their income levels but also by restrictions and prejudices against many of them in various parts of the Region, by an inadequate knowledge of the housing market, and by uncertain employment alternatives. At the same time, these in-migrants tend to be predominantly young married couples or marriageable individuals in their twenties, that being the time of life when mobility is much the greatest for all classes of people.

Households with these characteristics expand rapidly in size through the arrival of children and also, commonly, by taking in relatives or other lodgers even more recently arrived in the City and seeking a foothold. As a result, at the stage when a down-grading neighborhood is having an increase in the number of dwelling units (that is, households) per structure, it is likely also to have —either at the same time or very shortly after— an increase in the number of persons per dwelling unit.

But once settled, the main couple of the household does not characteristically move soon again. The tendency to stay put strengthens fast after people pass their early twenties. Also . . . dwellers in central-city areas are distinctly less mobile than residents of other types of areas in the Region.

Once the in-migrant couples have settled down and raised families, the continued aging of them and their neighborhoods leads to the "thinning-out" stage characteristic of slum areas after they reach peak density—a thinning-out provided in considerable part by the shrinkage of household size.

The thinning-out stage began several decades ago in some of the Region's oldest slums, and those areas are now far less crowded than they were, both in absolute terms and in comparison with more recently created slums. In Manhattan's lower East Side the population, after having risen from 339,000 to 532,000 between 1890 and 1910, declined in the next twenty years by more than half, reaching 250,000 in 1930.

The importance of reduced household size in the thinning-out process in the highest density areas is reflected in a comparison of population and housing trends. Although population declined between 1950 and 1957 in Manhattan, Brooklyn, and the Bronx, according to federal Census reports, the number of dwelling units apparently went on increasing in each borough.

We come at last to *Stage 5*. This is the renewal stage, in which obsolete areas of housing, after arriving at Stage 4, are being replaced by new multifamily housing. Quality and the effective use of space are improved, but the over-all population density of the area affected may not change much. By and large, such redevelopment in recent years has tended to increase over-all densities somewhat in Manhattan projects and to reduce them a little in projects elsewhere in the City.

This stage has assumed importance only quite recently, but it is safe to assume that the renewal effort will grow in magnitude. It is most conspicuous in Manhattan, particularly in the oldest slum areas, though appearing also in parts of Brooklyn, the Bronx, and Newark. It takes mainly two contrasting forms: first, subsidized medium-income and the low-income housing, and second, luxury apartments. So far, the unsubsidized luxury structures which have been built in the Region on the razed sites of decayed slums have appeared almost exclusively in the middle East Side of Manhattan.

Still another slum-renewal process, less important to date but with significant further potentialities in a few parts of the Region, is exemplified in Greenwich Village. Old areas of felicitous design and conveniently central location, originally high-income but deteriorated, are restored piecemeal to high-grade occupancy by extensive repair and remodeling, merger of dwelling units, and a little new construction.

To a large extent, however, Stage 5 has depended on public intervention: on the use of condemnation powers to assemble the site, on the use of public grants to bring down the site costs to levels at which medium-income rentals could be charged, and in some cases on the use of continuing operating subsidies to bring the rentals within reach of low-income families. About 500,-000 people in the Region are now housed in structures falling in one or another of these categories, most of them in New York City. Though the effect of such programs on some neighborhoods has been of major importance, their impact on land use in the Region as a whole has been small. In Manhattan, Brooklyn, and the Bronx, where renewal programs of all sorts have made the greatest relative progress in the Region, the land area affected by the subsidized renewal programs adds up to about two square miles, or 1.4 per cent of the total.

THE MEANING OF URBANISM

Even though it is difficult to describe the difference precisely, the character of interaction in an urban society differs from interaction in rural societies. Rural societies are more traditional, slower to change their patterns of interaction.[30] In addition, they tend to be oriented to the *local* community in contrast to the more *cosmopolitan* orientation of urban societies. A city is interdependent with the rural area supplying it with food; a rural community, on the other hand, can be self-sufficient. Even in predominantly rural societies, then, cities are dramatic evidence of the economic and social division of labor. Urban societies push interdependence further; they represent an increase in the *scale* of social organization beyond the local community. The individual still interacts extensively within a limited space, a neighborhood, but he also has commitments to economic, political, educational, and religious organizations that transcend the local community. Unlike the peasant in a preindustrial rural society, who has no alternative but to immerse himself psychologically in the world of the village, the individual in an urban society can orient himself toward the diffuse solidarities of family and neighborhood (primary groups) or toward narrower, more specialized relationships in more inclusive social structures (secondary groups).[31] Members of an urban society who orient themselves consistently toward primary groups may for comparative purposes be described as *local* types.[32] Those who orient themselves consistently toward secondary groups may be described as cosmopolitans. But the logic of urban societies is to induce most people to adopt both orientations at different times depending on social context.

Of course, within urban societies some communities contain more local types and others more cosmopolitans. Generally speaking, the smaller, rural communities are more likely to contain locals than cosmopolitans. Conversely, cosmopolitan types are more likely to be represented in the metropolis. These are differences

---

30 Robert Redfield, "The Folk Society," *American Journal of Sociology*, Vol. 52, January 1947, pp. 293–308; Fredrik Barth, "Subsistence and Institutional System in a Norwegian Mountain Valley," *Rural Sociology*, Vol. 17, March 1952, pp. 28–38.

31 Charles Horton Cooley defined a primary group as follows: "By primary groups I mean those characterized by intimate face-to-face association and cooperation. They are primary in several senses, but chiefly in that they are fundamental in forming the social nature and ideals of the individual." See his discussion in *Social Organization*, New York: Scribner's, 1929. Another sense in which they are primary is that they are the *first* groups of which the child is a member: his family, his play group, his neighborhood. This does not mean, however, that the normal *adult* in an urban industrial society lacks primary group affiliations. His membership in purposive, specialized associations (secondary groups) does not reduce his need for diffuse solidarities, and he finds them in his family, his friendship group, his clique at work.

32 See Robert K. Merton, "Patterns of Influence: Local and Cosmopolitan Influentials," in Merton, *Social Theory and Social Structure*, rev. ed., Glencoe, Ill.: Free Press, 1957.

in degree, not in kind. Research has demonstrated that some neighborhoods within the supposedly impersonal metropolis are in actuality a mosaic of local communities. Herbert Gans coined the apt phrase "urban villagers" to describe the dominant orientations of the people in such communities.[33] And, as the following case study of urbanization in Turkey shows, a cosmopolitan type can appear even in a peasant village.

An Urban Prophet in a Rural Village

Reprinted by permission. From Daniel Lerner, "The Grocer and the Chief," *Harper's Magazine*, Vol. 211, September 1955, pp. 47–56.

The Turkish village of Balgat lies about five miles out of Ankara, in the southerly direction. It does not show on the standard maps and it does not figure in the standard histories. I first heard of it in the autumn of 1950 and most Turks have not heard of it today. Yet the story of the modern Middle East is summed up in the recent career of Balgat. Indeed the personal meaning of modernization in underdeveloped lands everywhere is traced in miniature in the lives of two Balgati —the Grocer and the Chief.

My first exposure to Balgat came while leafing through several hundred interviews that had been recorded in Turkey during the spring of 1950. One caught my eye because of the underlying tone of bitterness in the interviewer's summary of his impressions, his earnest sense of the hopelessness of place and people. I was moved by his five interviews in this village; even so, something in the perspective seemed awry. For one thing, the interviewer was clearly more sensitized to what he saw than what he heard. The import of what had been said to him, and duly recorded in his reports, had somehow escaped his attention. For another, in the interval between the interviews and my reading of them, there had been a national election in which, as a stunning surprise to everybody, practically all Turks over twenty had voted and the government had been turned out of office.

Nothing like this ever happened before in

[33] Herbert Gans, *The Urban Villagers*, New York: Free Press of Glencoe, 1962.

Turkey, possibly because universal suffrage with an opposition party in a fair election had never been tried before. The dazed experts who explain Middle Eastern events could only say of this epochal deed, while sparring for time, that the Anatolian villagers had done it. Since it would be hard to imagine Anatolian villagers of more standard pattern than the Balgati whose collected opinions were spread before me, I had it on top authority that during the summer of 1950 they had entered History. But it was not immediately obvious by what route.

Four years later, the Balgat interviews had become part of an oversized draft manuscript on the modernizing of the Middle East. To provide at least the internal satisfaction of having been "there," I went out to Turkey myself in the spring of 1954—an odyssey which terminated where my ideas began: in Balgat, on the eve of a second national election.

The interviewer who recorded Balgat on the verge—his name was Tosun B.—had detected no gleam of the future during his sojourn there. "The village is a barren one," he wrote. "The main color is gray, so is the dust on the divan on which I am writing now." Tosun was a serious young scholar from Ankara and he loved the poor in his own fashion. He had sought out Balgat to find the deadening past rather than the brave new world. He found it: "I have seen quite a lot of villages in the barren mountainous East, but never such a colorless, shapeless dump. This was the reason I chose the village. It could have been half an hour to Ankara by car if it had a road, yet it is about two hours to the capital by car without almost any road and is just forgotten, forsaken, right under our noses."

Tosun also sought and found persons to match the place. Of the five villagers he interviewed, his heart went straight out to the village shepherd. "The respondent was literally in rags and in this cold wheather [sic] he had no shoe," wrote Tosun, in his own spelling, "but the mud and dirt on his feet were as thick as any boot. He was small, but looked rugged and sad, very sad. He was proud of being chosen by me and though limited tried his best to answer the questions. Was so bashfull [sic] that his blush was often evident under the thick layer of dirt on his face. He at times threw loud screams of laughter when there was nothing to laugh about. These he expected to be accepted as answers, for when I said

'Well?' he was shocked, as if he had already answered the question."

Tosun attributed to the Chief of Balgat his frustration in not getting more interviews. He reported that the chief "imposed himself on me all the time I was in the village, even tried to dictate to me, which I refused in a polite way. I couldn't have followed his directions, as I would have ended up only interviewing his family." Tosun did succeed in talking privately with two Balgat farmers, but it is clear that throughout these interviews he was still haunted by the shepherd and bedeviled by the Chief. Not until he came to interview the village grocer did Tosun find another Balgati who aroused in him a comparable emotional response. Tosun's equal hostility to these very different men made me curious, and eventually convinced me of the notion that the parable of modern Turkey was the story of the Grocer and the Chief.

Aside from resenting the containment strategy which the Chief was operating against him, Tosun gave few details about the man. He reported only the impression that "the *Muhtar* is an unpleasant old man. Looks mean and clever. He is the absolute dictator of this little village." Nor did Tosun elaborate his disapproval of the *Muhtar's* opinions beyond the comment that "years have left him some sort of useless, mystic wisdom." But the main source of Tosun's hostility, it appeared, was that the Chief made him nervous. His notes concluded: "He found what I do curious, even probably suspected it. I am sure he will report it to the first official who comes to the village."

Against the Grocer, however, Tosun reversed his neural field. He quickly perceived that he made the Grocer nervous; and for this Tosun disliked *him*. His notes read:

"The respondent is comparatively the most city-like dressed man in the village. He even wore some sort of a necktie. He is the village's only grocer, but he is not really a grocer, but so he is called, originally the food-stuffs in his shop are much less than the things to be worn, like the cheapest of materials and shoes and slippers, etc. His greatest stock is drinks and cigarettes which he sells most. He is a very unimpressive type, although physically he covers quite a space. He gives the impression of a fat shadow. Although he is on the same level with the other villagers, when there are a few of the villagers around, he seems

to want to distinguish himself by keeping quiet, and as soon as they depart he starts to talk too much. This happened when we were about to start the interview. He most evidently wished to feel that he is closer to me than he is to them and was curiously careful with his accent all during the interview. In spite of his unique position, for he is the only unfarming person and the only merchant in the village, he does not seem to possess an important part of the village community. In spite of all his efforts, he is considered by the villagers even less than the least farmer. Although he pretended to take the interview naturally, he was nervous and also was proud to be interviewed although he tried to hide it."

All of this posed a weighty question: Why did the Chief make Tosun nervous and why did Tosun make the Grocer nervous? Looking for answers, I turned to the responses each had made to the fifty-seven varieties of opinion called for by the standard questionnaire used in Tosun's interviews.

The Chief, it became clear immediately, was a man of few words on many subjects. He dismissed most of the items on Tosun's schedule with a shrug or its audible equivalent. What interested him were questions having to do with the primary modes of human deportment. Only when the issues involved first principles of conduct did he consider the occasion appropriate for pronouncing judgment. Of the Chief it might be said, as Henry James said of George Eliot's salon style, *"Elle n'aborde que les grandes thèmes."*

The Chief has so little trouble with first principles because he desires to be, and usually is, a vibrant sound box through which the traditional Turkish virtues may resonantly echo. His themes are obedience, courage, loyalty—the classic values of the Ottoman Imperium reincarnate in the Ataturk Republic. For the daily round of village life these are adequate doctrine; and as the Chief had been outside of his village only to fight in two wars he has never found his austere code wanting. When asked what he wished for his two grown sons, for example, the Chief replied promptly: "I hope they will fight as bravely as we fought and know how to die as my generation did."

With his life in Balgat, as with the Orphic wisdom that supplies its rationale, the Chief is contented. At sixty-three his desires have been quieted and his ambitions achieved. To Tosun's question on contentment he replied with another question. "What could be asked more? God has brought me to this mature age without much pain, has given me sons and daughters, has put me at the head of my village, and has given me strength of brain and body at this age. Thanks be to Him."

The Grocer is a very different style of man and, though born and bred in Balgat, lives in a different world—an expansive world, populated more actively with imaginings and fantasies, hungering for whatever is different and unfamiliar. To Tosun's probe, the Grocer replied staccato: "I have told you I want better things. I would have liked to have a bigger grocery shop in the city, have a nice house there, dress nice civilian clothes." He perceives his story as a drama of Self *versus* Village. "I am not like the others here. They don't know any better. And when I tell them, they are angry and they say that I am ungrateful for what Allah has given me."

Clearly, from the readiness and consistency of his responses to most questions, the Grocer had in fact brooded much over his role. At one point in the interviews, after asking each respondent to state the greatest problem facing the Turkish people, Tosun was obliged by the questionnaire to ask what the person would do about this problem if he were the president of Turkey. Some were shocked by the impropriety of the very question. "My God! How can you say such a thing?" gasped the shepherd. "How can I . . . I cannot . . . a poor villager . . . master of the whole world."

The Chief, Balgat's virtuoso of the traditional style, summarized prevailing sentiment by his laconic reply to this question with another question: "I am hardly able to manage a village, how shall I manage Turkey?" When Tosun prodded him (by rephrasing the question to ask "What would you suggest for *your village* that you can not handle yourself?"), the Chief said he would ask for "help of money and seed for some of our farmers." When the turn of the Grocer came, he told what he would and would *not* do, if he were president of Turkey, without embarrassment or hesitation: "I would make roads for the villagers to come to towns to see the world and would not let them stay in their holes all their life."

To get out of his hole the Grocer even declared himself ready—and in this he was quite alone in Balgat—to live outside of Turkey. This came out when Tosun asked: "If you could not live in Turkey, where would you want to live?" The standard reply of the villagers was simply that they *would not* live anywhere else. When Tosun persisted by asking, "Suppose you *had* to leave Turkey?" the shepherd replied finally that he would rather kill himself.

The Chief again responded on this issue with the clear and confident voice of traditional man. "Nowhere," said the Chief, and then added, with a calm assurance that this was all the reason required, "I was born here, grew old here, and hope God will permit me to die here." To Tosun's further probe, the Chief responded firmly: "I wouldn't move a foot from here." Only the Grocer found no trouble in imagining himself outside of Turkey, living in a strange land. Indeed he seemed fully prepared, as a man does when he has already posed a question to himself many times. "America," said the Grocer, and, without waiting for Tosun to ask him why, stated his reason, "because I have heard that it is a nice country, and with possibilities to be rich even for the simplest persons."

The vivid sense of cash displayed by the Grocer was perhaps his most grievous offense against Balgat ideas of taboo talk. In the code regulating the flow of symbols among Anatolian villagers, cravings for blood and sex are permissible but not for money. To talk of money at all—possibly because so little of it exists—is an impropriety. To reveal a *desire* for money is—Allah defend us! —an impiety. The Grocer, with his "city-dressed" ways and his "eye at the higher places" and his visits to Ankara, provoked the Balgati to wrathful and indignant expressions of this code. But occasional, and apparently trivial, items in the survey suggested that some Balgati were talking loud about the Grocer to keep their own inner voices from being overheard by the Chief—or even by themselves.

As we were interested in knowing who says what to whom in such a village as Balgat, Tosun had been instructed to ask each person whether others ever came to him for advice, and if so what they wanted advice about. Naturally, the Balgati whose advice was most sought was the Chief, who reported: "Yes, that is my main duty, to give advice. [Tosun: *What about?*] About all that I or you could imagine, even about their wives and how to handle them, and how to cure their sick cow." But this conjunction of wives and cows, to illustrate all the Chief could imagine, runs the gamut only from A to B. Tosun discovered that some Balgati went for advice also to the disreputable Grocer. What did they ask his advice about? "What to do when they go to Ankara, where to go and what to buy, how much to sell their things. . . ."

The cash nexus, this suggested, was somehow coming to Balgat and with it a new role for the Grocer as cosmopolitan specialist in how to avoid wooden nickels in the big city. Also, how to spend the nickels one got, for the Grocer was a man of clear convictions on which coffee houses played the best radio programs for their customers and which were the best movies to see in Ankara. While his opinions on these matters were heterodox as compared, say, to the Chief's, they had an open field to work in, since most Balgati had never heard a radio or seen a movie and were not aware of what constituted orthodoxy with respect to them.

At the time of Tosun's visit, there was only one radio in Balgat, owned by no less a personage than the Chief. In the absence of a standard doctrine on radio inherited from the great tradition, the Chief—who was also of course the large landowner of Balgat—had bought a radio to please his sons. He had also devised an appropriate ceremonial for its use. Each evening a select group of Balgati forgathered in the Chief's guest room as he turned on the newscast from Ankara. They heard the newscast through in silence and, at its conclusion, the Chief turned the radio off and made his commentary. "We all listen very carefully," he told Tosun, "and I talk about it afterwards."

Tosun inquired of the Grocer, a frequent attendant at the Chief's salon, how he liked this style of radio session. Without complaining directly about the Chief's exclusive preoccupation with Radio Ankara news of "wars and the danger of wars"—which turned out in fact to be a rather single-minded interest in the Korean War to which a Turkish brigade had just been committed—the Grocer indicated that after all *he* had opportunities to listen in the coffee houses of Ankara where the audiences exhibited a more cosmopolitan range of interests. "It is nice to know what is happening in the other capitals of the world," said the Grocer. "We are stuck in this hole, we have to know what is going on outside our village."

The Grocer had his own aesthetic of the movies as well. Though the Chief had been to the movies several times, he viewed them mainly as a moral prophylactic: "There are fights, shooting. The people are brave. My sons are always impressed. Each time they see such a film they wish more and more their time for military service would come so that they would become soldiers too." For the Grocer, movies were more than a homily on familiar themes; they were his avenue to the wider world of his dreams. It was in a movie, he told Tosun, that he had first glimpsed what a *real* grocery store could be like—"with walls made of iron sheets, top to floor and side to side, and on them standing myriads of round boxes, clean and all the same dressed, like soldiers in a great parade."

This fleeting glimpse of what sounds like the Campbell Soup section of a supermarket had provided the Grocer with an abiding image of how his fantasy world might look. No petty pedantries obstructed his full sensory relationship to the movies; he delivered clear net judgments in unabashedly hedonist categories. "The Turkish ones," he said, "are gloomy, ordinary. I can guess at the start of the film how it will end. . . . The American ones are exciting. You know it makes people ask what will happen next?"

Here, precisely, arose the question that speculation could only rephrase but not answer. In Balgat, the Chief carried the sword, but did the Grocer steer the pen? When the Balgati sought his advice on how to get around Ankara, would they then go to see the movies that taught virtue or those that taught excitement? True, few Balgati had ever been to Ankara. But things were changing in Turkey and many more Balgati were sure to have a turn or two around the big city before they died. What would happen next in Balgat if more people discovered the tingle of wondering what will happen next?

I reached Ankara last April via a circuitous route through the Middle East. The glories of Greece, Egypt, Lebanon, Syria, Persia touched me only lightly, for some part of me was already in Balgat. Even the Blue Mosque and Santa Sophia seemed pallid and I left Istanbul, three days ahead of schedule, for Ankara. I had saved this for last, and now here I was. I was half afraid to look.

I called a limousine service recommended by the hotel clerk and explained that I wanted to go out the following day, a Sunday, to a village some five miles south that might be hard to reach. As I wanted to spend the day, would the driver meet me at 8:00 A.M. and bring along his lunch?

While I waited for the car, next morning, my reverie wandered back through the several years since my first reading of the Balgat interviews. Was I chasing a phantom? Tahir S. appeared. With solitude vanished anxiety; confidently we began to plan the day. Tahir had been a member of the original interview team, working in the Izmir area. As Tosun had joined the Turkish foreign service and was stationed in North Africa, where he was conducting an inquiry among the Berbers, I had arranged in advance for Tahir to revisit Balgat with me in his place. Over a cup of sirupy coffee, we reviewed the questions that had been asked in 1950, noted the various responses and silences, decided the order in which we would repeat the old questions and interpolate the new ones.

As our plan took shape, Zilla K. arrived. She had had no connection with the original survey, but I had decided to take along a female interviewer who could add some Balgat women to our gallery while Tahir and I were working over the men. I had not seen Zilla before, but had "ordered" her, through a colleague at Ankara University, "by the numbers": thirtyish, semitrained, alert, compliant with instructions, not sexy enough to impede our relations with the men of Balgat but chic enough to provoke the women. A glance and a word were enough to demonstrate that Zilla filled the requisition. The hall porter came in to say our car was waiting. We settled back for a rough haul, debating niceties of procedure. Twenty minutes later, the driver said briskly: "There's Balgat."

We looked puzzled at each other until Tosun's words of 1950 recurred to us: "It could have been half an hour to Ankara if it had a road." Now it did have a road. What was more, a *bus* was coming down the road, heading toward us from the place our driver had called Balgat. As it passed, jammed full, none of the passengers inside waved or even so much as stuck out a tongue at us. Without these unfailing signs of villagers out on a rare chartered bus to celebrate a great occasion of some sort, we could only make the wild guess that Balgat had acquired a regular bus service. And indeed, as we entered the village, there it was—a "bus station," freshly painted benches under a handsome new canopy. We got out and looked at the printed schedule of trips. "The bus leaves every hour, on the hour, to *Ulus* Station. Fare: 20 Kurus." For about 6 cents Balgati could now go, whenever they felt the whim, to the heart of Ankara.

The villagers were getting out of their holes at last.

Overhead wires were stretched along the road, with branch lines extending over the houses of Balgat. The village had been electrified. Alongside the road deep ditches had been dug, in which the graceful curve of new water pipe was visible. Feeling strange, we made our way along the erratic path through the old village, led and followed by a small horde of children, to the house of the Chief. Tahir knocked, an old woman with her head covered by a dark shawl appeared; the children scattered. We were led into the guest room.

The Chief looked as I had imagined. His cheeks a bit more sunken, perhaps, but the whole *présence* quite familiar. Tall, lean, hard, he walked erect and looked me straight in the eye. His own eyes were Anatolian black and did not waver as he stretched out a handful of long, bony fingers. "*Gün aydin, Bey Efendim,*" he said, "good day, sir, you are welcome to my house." I noted in turn the kindness which opens a door to strangers and the Chief responded that we honored his house by our presence. This completed the preliminary round of *formules de la politesse* and steaming little cups of Turkish coffee were brought in by the Chief's older son. The son was rather a surprise—short, pudgy, gentle-eyed, and soft spoken. He bowed his head, reddening slightly as he stammered, "*Lütfen*" (Please!) and offered the tray of demitasses to me. I wondered whether he had learned to fight bravely and die properly.

As the Chief set down his second cup of coffee, signifying that we could now turn to the business of our visit, I explained that I had come from America, where I taught in a university, with the hope of meeting him. There, in my own country, I had read about Balgat in some writing by a young man from Ankara who, four years ago, had talked at length with the Chief and other persons in his village. This writing had interested me very much and I had often wondered, as the years passed by, how things were going in the village of Balgat and among its people. When I had the opportunity to come to Turkey, I immediately decided that I would visit Balgat and see the Chief if I could.

The Chief heard me through gravely, and when he spoke I knew I was in. He by-passed the set of formulas available to him—for either rejecting or evading my implied request—and responded directly to the point. I was right to have come to see Balgat for myself. He remembered well the young man from Ankara. Much had changed in Balgat since that time. Indeed, Balgat was no longer a village. It had, only last month, been incorporated as a district of Greater Ankara. This was why they now had bus service and electricity and a supply of pure water that would soon be in operation. Where there had been fifty houses there were now over five hundred, and even he, the *Muhtar*, did not know any more all the people living here.

Yes, he had lived in Balgat all his life and never in all that time seen so much happen as had come to pass in these four years. "It all began with the election that year. The *Demokrat* men came to Balgat and asked us what was needed here and told us they would do it when they were elected. They were brave to go against the government party. We all voted for them, as the *Halk* men knew no more what to do about the prices then, and the new men did what they said. They brought us this road and moved out the *gendarmerie*. Times have been good with us here. We are all *Demokrat* party in Balgat now."

The Chief spoke in a high, strong, calm voice, and the manner of his utterance was matter-of-fact. His black eyes remained clear and his features retained their shape. Only his hands were animated, though he invoked only the thumbs and the index fingers for punctuation. When he had completed his statement, he picked his nose thoughtfully for a moment and then laid the finger alongside the bridge. The tip of the long, bony finger reached into his eye socket.

I explained then that the young lady had come with us to learn how such changes as the Chief mentioned were altering the daily round of life for the village women. Might she talk with some of them while Tahir Bay and I were meeting the men? The Chief promptly suggested that Zilla could speak with the females of his household. (We recalled Tosun's resentful remark that, had he followed the Chief's suggestions, "I would have ended up only interviewing his family," when Zilla reported on her interviews later that day. All had identified the biggest problem of

Balgat as the new fashion of young men to approach girls shamelessly on the village outskirts—precisely what the Chief had told me, in answer to the same question.)

But if the Chief still used his containment tactics with the women, in other directions he had taken a decidedly permissive turn. Tahir and I, he said, could walk about Balgat entirely as we wished and speak with whomsoever it pleased us to honor—even, he added with a smile in response to my jest, some non-*Demokrat* party men, if we could find any. We chatted a bit longer and then, having agreed to return to the Chief's house, we set out for a stroll around Balgat. Our next goal was to find the Grocer.

After a couple of bends and turns, we came to a coffee house. Here was something new and worth a detour. We stopped at the door and bade the proprietor *"Gün aydin!"* He promptly rushed forward with two chairs, suggested that we sit outdoors to get the benefit of the pleasant sunshine, and asked us how we would like our coffee. (There are five ways of specifying the degree of sweetening in Turkish coffee.) Obviously, this was to be on the house, following the paradoxical Turkish custom of giving gratis to those who can best afford to pay. In a matter of minutes, the male population of Balgat was assembled around our two chairs, squatting, sitting on the ground, looking us over with open and friendly curiosity.

Top man among the group was one of the two farmers Tosun had interviewed in 1950. He too was tall, lean, hard. He wore store clothes with no patches and a sturdy pair of store shoes. His eyes were Anatolian black and his facial set was much like the Chief's. He sat with his chair tilted back and kept his hands calmly dangling alongside, as he ambled along in conversation, with no apparent terminus in view. Interrupting him, even long enough to steer his flow of words in another direction, was not easy. His voice was deep and harsh, with the curious suggestion of strangling in the throat that Anatolian talk has, and the content was elusive. He spoke from such a height to such a height, located somewhere in the space above my head into which he gazed steadily, that little of his discourse made concrete contact with my notebook.

As I review my notes on that hour of monologue-with-choral murmurs, he appears to have certified the general impression that great changes had occurred in Balgat during the four years past.

But in his recital, these great events lost some of their luster. The tough old farmer did not look shining at new styles of architecture, nor did he look scowling, but simply looked. Under his gaze the new roofs in Balgat were simply new roofs; the wonder of there being new roofs in *Balgat* brightened other eyes and cadenced other voices.

These other voices were finally raised—either because he had exhausted the prerogative of his position (he had certainly exhausted Tahir S., whose eyes were glazed and vacant) or because the issue was grave enough to sanction discourtesy toward a village elder—when the quondam farmer undertook to explain why he was no longer a farmer. He had retired, over a year ago, because there was none left in Balgat to do an honest day's work for an honest day's lira. Or rather two lira (about 36 cents)—the absurd rate, he said, to which the daily wage of farm laborers had been driven by the competition of the voracious Ankara labor market. Now, all the so-called able-bodied men of Balgat had forsaken the natural work which Allah had intended men to do and swarmed off to the factories of Ankara where, for eight hours of so-called work, they could get five lira a day.

The protests that rose did not aim to deny these facts, but simply to justify them. Surprised, we asked whether it was indeed true that there were no farm laborers left in Balgat. "How many of you," we quickly rephrased the question, "work on farms now?" Four hands were raised among the twenty-nine present, and all of these turned out to be small holders working their own land. (These four were sitting together and, it later developed, were the only four members of the *Halk* party among the group.)

Galvanized by the intelligence now suddenly put before us (even Tahir S. had reawakened promptly upon discovering that there were hardly any farmers left in Balgat), we started to fire a battery of questions of our own. As this created a din of responding voices, Tahir S.—once again the American-trained interviewer—restored order by asking whether each man around the circle would tell us, in turn, what he was now working at and how long he had been at it. This impromptu occupational census was never quite completed. As it became clear that most of the male population of Balgat was now in fact working in the factories and construction gangs of Ankara—*for cash*—our own impatience to move

on got the better of us.

How did they spend the cash they earned? Well, there were now over a hundred radio receivers in Balgat as compared to the lone receiver Tosun had found four years earlier. There were also seven refrigerators, four tractors, three trucks, and one Dodge sedan. Also, since there was so little farming in Balgat now, much of the food came from the outside (even milk) and had to be bought in the grocery stores (of which there were now seven in Balgat). Why milk? Well, most of the animals had been sold off during the last few years. What about the shepherd? Well, he had moved to a village in the east a year or so ago, as there were no longer any flocks for him to tend. How was the Grocer doing? *"Which one?"* The original one, the great fat one that was here four years ago? *"Oh that one, he's dead!"*

Tahir S. later told me that my expression did not change when the news came (always the American-trained interviewer). I asked a few more questions in a normal way—"What did he die of?" "How long ago?"—and then let the questioning pass to Tahir. I don't recall what answers came to my questions or to his. I do recall suddenly feeling very weary and, as the talk went on, slightly sick. The feeling got over to Tahir S. and soon we were saying good-by to the group of Balgati, relieved that the ritual for leave-taking is less elaborate than for arriving. We promised to return and said our thanks. *"Güle, güle,"* answered those who remained ("Smile, smile" signifying farewell).

"What a lousy break," growled Tahir in a tone of reasonable indignation as we started back toward the house of the Chief. He was speaking of the Grocer. I didn't know what to say by way of assent. I felt only a sense of large and diffuse regret, of which indignation was not a distinct component. "Tough," I agreed. As we came up to the Chief's house, I told Tahir we might as well return to Ankara. We had gathered quite a lot of information already and might better spend the afternoon putting it together. We could come back again the next day to interview the Chief. The Chief was agreeable to this plan and invited me to be his guest for lunch next day. We collected Zilla K. and our driver, and drove back to the city.

I slept late the next morning and was tired when I awoke. While dressing slowly and ingesting a full-scale breakfast, I decided that the

Grocer was—and, to face right up to it, had been right from the start—*my* man.

I recalled Tosun's unflattering sketch of him as a pretentious phony, as "the only unfarming person in the village . . . who is even less than the least farmer." But I had never minded this about the Grocer, nor Tosun's disgust that "he even wore some sort of a necktie." What had located all these details in a context I could understand, what had made the Grocer a man I recognized, was Tosun's acid remark: "He most evidently wished to feel that he is closer to me than he is to the other villagers and was curiously careful with his accent all during the interview."

There was something in this sentence that had sounded to me like History. Maybe it was the eighteenth-century field hands of England who had left the manor to find a better life in London or Manchester or Liverpool. Maybe it was the nineteenth-century French farm lad, who, wearied by his father's burdens of the *taille* and the *tithe* and the *gabelle*, had gone off to San Francisco to hunt gold and finding none, tried his hand as a mason, mechanic, printer's devil; though none of these brought him fortune, as he cheerfully wrote home (in a letter noted by the perspicacious Karl Marx), he was going to stay in this exciting new city where the chance to try his hand at anything made him feel "less of a mollusk and more of a man."

The Grocer of Balgat stood for some part of all these figures as he nervously edged his psyche toward Tosun, the young man from the big city. I'm like you, the Grocer might have been feeling, or I'd like to be like you and wish I could get the chance. It was harsh of Tosun, or perhaps only the antibourgeois impatience of a consecrated young scholar looking for the suffering poor in a dreary village, to cold-shoulder this fat and middle-aged man yearning to be comfortably rich in an interesting city. But the Grocer had his own sort of toughness. He had, after all, stood up to the other villagers and had insisted, even when they labeled him infidel, that they ought to get out of their holes.

This time I was going out to Balgat by bus instead of taxi, to see how the villagers traveled. The way the villagers traveled, it turned out, was in a shiny new bus from Germany that held three times as many passengers as there were seats. The bus was so new that the signs warning the passengers not to smoke or spit or talk to the driver (while the bus is moving) in German, French, and English had not yet been converted into Turkish. There was, in fact, a great deal of smoking (some Turkish tobacco is used *in* Turkey) and several animated conversations between the driver and various passengers occurred, in the intervals between which the driver chatted with a crony whom he had brought along for just this purpose.

In Balgat I reported directly to the Chief. He was out on his land but appeared after a few minutes, steaming and mopping his large forehead. He had been pruning some trees and, in this warm weather, such work brought the sweat to his brow. This was about the only work he did any more, he explained, as he had sold or rented most of his land in the last few years, keeping for himself only the ground in which he had planted a small grove of trees that would be his memorial on earth. The Chief agreed to show me his trees and as we strolled away from the house he resumed his discourse of yesterday.

Things had changed, he repeated, and a sign of the gravity of these changes was that he—of a lineage that had always been *Muhtars* and landowners—was no longer a farmer. Nor was he long to be *Muhtar*. After the coming election, next month, the incorporation of Balgat into Greater Ankara was to be completed and thereafter it would be administered under the general municipal system.

"I am the last *Muhtar* of Balgat, and I am happy that I have seen Balgat end its history in this way that we are going."

The new ways, then, were not bringing evil with them? "No, people will have to get used to different ways and then some of the excesses, particularly among the young, will disappear. The young people are in some ways a serious disappointment; they think more of clothes and good times than they do of duty and family and country. But it is to be hoped that as the *Demokrat* men complete the work they have begun, the good Turkish ways will again come forward to steady the people. Meanwhile, it is well that people can have to eat and to buy shoes they always needed but could not have."

And as his two sons were no longer to be farmers, what of them? The Chief's voice did not change, nor did his eyes cloud over, as he replied: "They are as the others. They think first to serve themselves and not the nation. They had no wish to go to the battle in Korea, where Turkey fights before the eyes of all the world. They are my sons and I speak no ill of them, but I say only that they are as all the others."

I felt at this moment a warmth toward the Chief which I had not supposed he could evoke. His sons had not, after all, learned to fight bravely and die properly. These two sons through whom he had hoped to relive his own bright dreams of glory had instead become *shopkeepers*. The elder son owned a grocery store and the younger one owned Balgat's first clothing store. As we turned back to the house, the Chief said we would visit the shops after lunch and his sons would answer all my questions.

That afternoon we went first to the elder son's grocery store, just across the road from the Chief's house and alongside the village fountain. The central floor space was set out with merchandise in the immemorial manner—heavy, rough, anonymous hemp sacks each laden with a commodity requiring no identity card, groats in one and barley in another, here lentils and there chicory. But beyond the sacks was a distinct innovation, a counter. What is more, the counter turned a corner and ran parallel to two sides of the square hut. Built into it was a cash drawer and above each surface a hygienic white porcelain fixture for fluorescent lighting. Along the walls was the crowning glory—a case of shelves running from "top to floor and side to side, and on them standing myriads of round boxes, clean and all the same dressed, like soldiers in a great parade." The Grocer's words of aspiration came leaping back to mind as I looked admiringly around the store. His dream house had been built in Balgat—in less time than even he might have forecast—and by none other than the Chief!

The irony of the route by which Balgat had entered History stayed with me as we walked in quartet, the Chief and I ahead, the sons behind, to the clothing store of the younger son. This was in the newer part of the village, just across the new road from the bus station. The stock inside consisted mainly of dungarees, levis, coveralls—all looking rather like U. S. Army surplus stocks. There was a continuous and growing demand for these goods, the Chief stated solemnly, as more and more men of Balgat went into the labor market of Ankara, first discarding their *shalvars* (the billowing bloomers of traditional garb in which Western cartoons always still portray the "sultan" in a harem scene). In a corner of the store there was also a small stock of "gentleman's haberdashery"—ready-made suits, shirts, even a rack of neckties.

The younger son, who maintained a steady silence in the presence of the Chief, replied to a direct question from me that he had as yet sold very few items from this department of the store. The Balgat males by and large were still reticent about wearing store-bought clothes. A few, however, had purchased in a *sub rosa* sort of way neckties which remained to be exhibited in public. But wearing them would come, now that several owned them, as soon as an older man was bold enough to wear his first. The owners of the neckties had only to get used to them in private, looking at them now and then, showing them to their wives and elder sons, and some one of them had to show the way. I remembered Tosun's rather nasty comment, as though this was his most telling evidence against the Grocer's preposterous pretences, "*He even wore some sort of a necktie.*" As one saw it now, the Grocer *had* shown the way, and it was now only a hop, skip, and jump through history to the point where most men of Balgat would be wearing neckties.

The Grocer's memory stayed with me all afternoon, after I had expressed intense satisfaction with the shops, wished the sons good fortune, thanked the Chief again and, with his permission, started out to walk among the alleys and houses of Balgat. On the way, I absently counted sixty-nine radio antennas on the roofs and decided that yesterday's estimate of "over a hundred" was probably reliable. And only four years ago, I reminded myself, there was but a single radio in this village. The same theme ran through my recollection of the numbers of tractors, refrigerators, and "unfarming persons." That was what Tosun had called the Grocer—"the only unfarming person in the village." Several of these newly unfarming persons, recognizing their interlocutor of yesterday's coffee-house session, greeted me as I strolled along. One stopped me long enough to deliver his opinion of the Turkish-Pakistani pact (strong affirmation) and to solicit mine of the proposed law to give Americans prospecting rights on Turkish oil (qualified affirmative).

Weary of walking, I turned back to the coffee house. The ceremony of welcome was warm and the coffee was again on the house, but the conversational group was smaller. Only eleven Balgati appeared to praise the weather and hear my questions. The group got off on politics, with some attention to the general theory of power but more intense interest in hearing each other's predictions of the margin by which the *Demokrat* party would win the elections next month. There was also general agreement, at least among the wiser heads, that it would be better to have a small margin between the major parties. "The villagers have learned the basic lesson of democratic politics," I wrote in my notebook.

The afternoon was about over before I got an appropriate occasion to ask about the Grocer. It came when the talk returned to the villagers' favorite topic of how much better life had become during the past four years of *Demokrat* rule. Again they illustrated the matter by enumerating the new shops in Balgat and the things they had to sell that many people could buy. "How are these new grocery shops better than the old grocery shop of years ago owned by the fat grocer who is now dead?" I asked. The line of response and the examples cited were obvious in advance, but the question served to lead to another. What sort of man had the Grocer been? The answers were perfunctory, consisting mainly of *pro forma* expressions of good will toward the departed. I tried to get back of these ritual references to the Grocer by indirection. How had he dressed? Why had he been so interested in the life of Ankara? The light finally shone in one of the wiser heads and he spoke the words I was seeking: "Ah, he was the cleverest of us all. We did not know it then, but he saw better than all what lay in the path ahead. We have none like him among us now. He was a prophet."

As I look back on it now, my revisit to Balgat ended then. I went back to the village several times of course, once to bring some gifts for the grandchildren of the Chief, another time with a camera (as he had coyly suggested) to take his picture. On these visits, I felt less tense, asked fewer questions, than during the earlier visits. The last time I went out with Ahmet Emin Yalman, publisher of a prominent Istanbul newspaper and then a devoted *Demokrat* man, who was eager to see the transformed village I had described to him over an endless series of "Screwdrivers" (Turkish vodka with orange juice) in the bar of the Ankara Palas Hotel.

He was enchanted with the Chief, the stores, the bus service and electricity, and other symbols of the History into which his party had ushered Balgat. He decided to write a feature story about it and asked permission to call it "Professor Lerner's Village." I declined, less from modesty than a sense of irrelevance. The Balgat his party needed was the suburb inhabited by the sons of the Chief. The Village I had known for what now seemed only four short years was passing, had already passed. The Grocer was dead. The Chief—"the last *Muhtar* of Balgat"—had reincarnated the Grocer in the flesh of his sons. Tosun was in North Africa studying the Berbers.

To the Grocer, urbanization was not a threat but an opportunity. The Chief was not so sure. This difference in the interpretation of the meaning of urbanization can be duplicated in the industrial cities of the West. Many persons regard the city as the place for the development of cultural potentialities: art museums, universities, symphony orchestras, theater, ballet, libraries, book stores. Because transportation of persons requires time and money, a considerable concentration of persons is required in order to develop a following for an activity with limited appeal, such as concert going.[34] The infinite variety of New York, London, or Tokyo results from the size and heterogeneity of their populations. In a city of 7,000,000 persons, probability favors the emergence of constituencies for the most esoteric and bizarre interests.[35]

FREEDOM TO CHOOSE. The freedom of choice which urban life offers is obtained at a price. The more choices people have as to what roles they will play and what goals they will pursue, the less certain it is that everyone will be included in the web of community. Take the matter of dating among young adults. Boys are free to seek out girls who are pretty, well poised, and good conversationalists and to ignore those who are not. This means competition. And in the competition for dates, attractive girls are

34 Hans L. Zetterberg, *Social Theory and Social Practice*, New York: Bedminster Press, 1962, Chap. 4.
35 Karl W. Deutsch, "On Social Communication and the Metropolis," in Lloyd Rodwin, Ed., *The Future Metropolis*, New York: Braziller, 1961, pp. 129–143.

popular, whereas other girls are lonely. Freedom to choose is freedom to ignore. The probability is that the more ignored one is, the less adequate will one feel. A person cannot easily maintain a good opinion of himself if nobody wants him as a friend or if he finds it much more difficult than the average person to obtain a job. And when he begins to agree that he is worthless, he becomes a problem not only to himself but also to the community. He may withdraw into a world of his own where he does not get pushed around; and even a skilled psychiatrist may not be able to induce him to leave it. Or he may turn for consolation to liquor or drugs.[36]

To emphasize freedom of choice is to look at social life from the viewpoint of the individual. From the group standpoint, however, freedom of choice is simply a competitive method of allocating people to roles. Thus, occupational roles are filled by a competitive struggle among individuals who prefer one particular kind of work to another. A role filled by competition among potential candidates for it on the basis of their supposed capacities to play it is called an *achieved* role. Even in urban societies, however, many roles are filled by assigning the individual to a role on the basis of qualities he possesses without considering how well he can play that role or whether he wishes to play it. Age and sex roles are examples of *non*competitive assignment to roles; the technical term for this is *ascription*. As soon as an infant arrives in the world, he is assigned to the "boy" or the "girl" role on the basis of a genital examination. The assignment determines how he will be defined and what people will expect from him. Sometimes a male child prefers to play with dolls and sew rather than wrestle, but he cannot compete with female children for feminine roles.

Achieved roles are certainly more prominent in urban industrial socieites than in preliterate societies. Modern societies carry role differentiation too far for a mechanical transmission of roles from father to son. The peculiar combination of talent and training entering into a brain surgeon must be mobilized afresh in each generation. An advantage of a competitive system of role allocation is obvious: it increases the chances of finding adequate candidates, particularly for roles requiring special abilities. The disadvantage is that the preferences of the population and the role structure of the society may not match. More people aspire to be business tycoons than there are openings in top management. On the other hand, dirty, dangerous, or menial jobs have to be filled, but are intrinsically unattractive.

Urban industrial societies face a dilemma: the more attractive they make roles at the top of the occupational hierarchy, the more eager will people be to play *them* and the less eager to play roles at the bottom. The labor market provides a partial solution to the problem. Since the average person has to find employment to support himself and his family, he is driven by economic considerations to take less attractive jobs if he cannot compete for better jobs. The economist can demonstrate by supply and demand analysis how impersonal market mechanisms induce people to take jobs. Persons from underdeveloped countries, of course, are skeptical.

The Invisible Planning in Competitive Role Allocation

Reprinted by permission. From Robert L. Heilbroner, *The Making of Economic Society*, Englewood Cliffs, N.J.: Prentice-Hall, 1962, pp. 15–16.

Because we live in a market-run society, we are apt to take for granted the puzzling—indeed, almost paradoxical—nature of the market solution to the economic problem. But assume for a moment that we could act as economic advisers to a society which had not yet decided on its mode of economic organization. Suppose, for instance, that we were called on to act as consultants to one of the new nations emerging from the continent of Africa.

We could imagine the leaders of such a nation saying, "We have always experienced a highly

---

[36] Harry C. Bredemeier and Jackson Toby, *Social Problems in America: Costs and Casualties in an Acquisitive Society*, New York: Wiley, 1960.

tradition-bound way of life. Our men hunt and cultivate the fields and perform their tasks as they are brought up to do by the force of example and the instruction of their elders. We know, too, something of what can be done by economic command. We are prepared, if necessary, to sign an edict making it compulsory for many of our men to work on community projects for our national development. Tell us, is there any other way we can organize our society so that it will function successfully—or better yet, more successfully?"

Suppose we answered, "Yes, there is another way. Organize your society along the lines of a market economy."

"Very well," say the leaders. "What do we then tell people to do? How do we assign them to their various tasks?"

"That's the very point," we would answer. "In a market economy no one is assigned to any task. The very idea of a market society is that each person is allowed to decide for himself what to do."

There is consternation among the leaders. "You mean there is *no* assignment of some men to mining and others to cattle raising? No manner of selecting some for transportation and others for cloth weaving? You leave this to people to decide for themselves? But what happens if they do not decide correctly? What happens if no one volunteers to go into the mines, or if no one offers himself as a railway engineer?"

"You may rest assured," we tell the leaders, "none of that will happen. In a market society, all the jobs will be filled because it will be to people's advantage to fill them."

Our respondents accept this with uncertain expressions. "Now look," one of them finally says, "let us suppose that we take your advice and let our people do as they please. Now let's talk about something important, like cloth production. Just how do we fix the right level of cloth output in this 'market society' of yours?"

"But you don't," we reply.

"We don't! Then how do we know there will be enough cloth produced?"

"There will be," we tell him. "The market will see to that."

"Then how do we know there won't be *too much* cloth produced?" he asks triumphantly.

"Ah, but the market will see to that too!"

"But what *is* this market that will do all these wonderful things? Who runs it?"

"Oh, nobody runs the market," we answer. "It runs itself. In fact there really isn't any such *thing* as 'the market.' It's just a word we use to describe the way people behave."

"But I thought people behaved the way they wanted to!"

"And so they do," we say. "But never fear. They will want to behave the way you want them to behave."

"I am afraid," says the chief of the delegation, "that we are wasting our time. We thought you had in mind a serious proposal. But what you suggest is madness. It is inconceivable. Good day, sir." And with great dignity the delegation takes its leave.

Candidates for attractive roles vie with one another in the labor market until the supply is brought into balance with available vacancies. The price of unattractive roles, on the other hand, is bid up until sufficient applicants appear to satisfy the demand. Logical though this process may be, it creates additional tensions in the society. The losers may deal with their disappointments by accepting their own inadequacy. As long as it is believed that the varsity football team contains the best football players in the college, unsuccessful candidates for the team cannot protest too loudly. Yet the competitive system does not always choose the best man. Sometimes the boss promotes a "yes-man" instead of the most competent worker. The ideal in competitive role allocation remains the filling of roles with those most capable of performing them. However, it is sometimes easier for failures to suspect that the ideals of the system are violated than to concede their own incompetence. If the unsuccessful competitor is forced to admit that the competition was fair, the tensions are likely to be even greater.

The complex, rapidly changing role structure of an urban industrial society necessitates a competitive method of role allocation not only in the occupational system, but also in such personal contexts as friendship and marriage. The individual competes for a wife as well as for a job. The *pervasiveness* of competition in industrial societies makes for widespread feelings of inadequacy because everyone is an unsuccessful competitor in one context or another. Ruth Benedict suggested that race prejudice, the belief that persons of different racial or ethnic stock were *inferior*, served to quell doubts about competitive adequacy. She pointed out that racism was a modern ideology invented in the West following urban industrial development and well suited to allay the anxieties of a competitive society.[37]

Competition, although not necessarily market competition, is characteristic of urban industrial societies because competition is the most feasible mechanism for filling the roles in a dynamic, fluid society. That same dynamism is responsible for the anonymity of urban life, which stems partly from the sheer numbers of people but partly from the specialized kind of interaction required by an industrial society. In the preliterate society, where role differentiation is at a minimum, interaction is personal, diffuse. As Robert Redfield put it, ". . . the personal and intimate life of the child in the family is extended, in the folk society, into the social world of the adult and even into inanimate objects." [38] In contemporary urban societies, social participation is often organized around specific functions and therefore is less personal than in preliterate societies. The supermarket customer interacts with the checker over such limited segments of their respective personalities that calling their relationship "personal" would distort reality. In the same way, in a subway train during the morning rush-hour, the other riders are *bodies* rather than *people*; they are physically close but psychologically remote. The interactions that take place in these specialized contexts are efficient, but they tend to be emotionally unsatisfying. Gordon Allport, the social psychologist, has suggested that *participation* (in the sense of psychic commitment) is a crucial problem of urban life.[39]

Urban anonymity does not mean that personal, emotionally significant relationships are disappearing, even for cosmopolitan types. Primary groups persist in the metropolis, most notably in the family, but also in the neighborhood, the work situation, and in voluntary associations. In recent years, sociologists have rediscovered the primary group, imbedded though it often is in formal organizations.[40] The enormous number of secondary groups, an organizational necessity given the scale of urban societies, make it possible for an adult to *survive* without much primary group involvement. He can live in a hotel, eat in restaurants, and work as a solitary street cleaner. In short, urban society permits one to lead the life of a hermit without residing in a wilderness. For the overwhelming majority of urban people, however, this opportunity is not attractive. Hence, they live in two worlds, "the world of physically close but socially distant strangers" and the world of primary groups.[41] The existence of the two worlds means that the individual can escape primary group controls if he wishes. He can escape them to join the American Civil Liberties Union, to wear a beret, to eat with chopsticks at an oriental restaurant, or to paint abstract pictures. He can also escape them to rob a bank. The following account of a small-town bank robbery reveals, by implication, the advantages of urban anonymity to the thief.

Small-Town Cohesiveness: A Contrast with Metropolitan Anonymity

Reprinted by permission. From Ted Hall, "The Great But Very, Very Late Bank Robbery," *Life*, Vol. 52, Jan. 5, 1962, pp. 10–11.

When the Great Bank Robbery was finally over, everyone in Mendham, N.J. breathed a deep

37 Ruth Benedict, *Race: Science and Politics*, rev. ed., New York: Viking, 1945.
38 Redfield, *loc. cit.*
39 Gordon W. Allport, "The Psychology of Partici-

pation," *Psychological Review*, Vol. 53, May 1945, pp. 117–132.
40 William F. Whyte, "Social Organization in the Slums," *American Sociological Review*, Vol. 8, February 1943, pp. 34–39.
41 Kingsley Davis, *Human Society*, New York: Macmillan, 1948, p. 331.

sigh of relief. Mendham (pop. 2,700) is not used to much excitement, and getting ready for the robbery had kept things stirred up for a year and a half. Everybody was pretty sick of it. The butcher store across the street from the bank had been thrown into confusion by false alarms. Eddie Fagan, the school custodian who lives within sight of the bank, had got good and tired of sitting in the window every Friday night with his carbine in his lap (the bank stays open late Fridays). One of the robbers kept dropping in on the grocery store and the grocer began to worry that maybe *he* was going to be held up. Police Chief Earl Moore had been so busy following the two robbers while they were casing the bank that he had little time for anything else. It really was too much, and everyone was glad when it was over.

Mendham is a pleasant country town, well removed from any main road. It is the kind of place where everybody knows everybody else— and newcomers are noticed the first time they appear and studied closely the second time. So when a pair of strangers showed up one day in March of 1960, parked in front of the Morris County Savings Bank and studied it with obvious appetite, Chief Moore, who was shoveling snow a little way down the street, could not help paying attention.

It happens that in Mendham the bank is not far from the police station, which is located —along with the borough tax office, the local civil defense organization, and the room where the Borough Council and the ladies' garden club meet—in an old white brick colonial hostelry on Main Street called Phoenix House. So it is not an ideal bank for stick-ups. When Chief Moore wanted a better look at the two strangers all he had to do was shovel in their direction. As he approached they hastily drove away.

He finished shoveling the walk, then went indoors and recorded the incident on a card which he dropped into an unmarked manila folder.

The next day was full of developments. To begin with, Chief Moore got a telephone tip that someone was planning to rob the Mendham bank. The chief typed out this information on a new card and dropped it into the folder. Then he labeled it, "Planned Robbery of Mendham Bank."

Later that day he was standing on Main Street when a car drew up right in front of him and the two visitors of the previous day asked him for directions to an auto body repair shop. The chief, startled, told them he had never heard of the place. As they drove off, Moore stepped back into the station and dropped a new card into the folder.

Half an hour later the chief strolled past the Mendham Soda Shop, a few stores down from the bank, and saw one of the men there. He noted that the man had a mustache and a moon-shaped scar above his right eye.

"After that I kept seeing that car, or some other one with the same men in it," says the chief. "It was always where they could see the bank."

Fascinated, Moore sent out tracers on the license numbers and made inquiries among other police departments. In nearby Madison he hit pay dirt. A man there had boasted within earshot of a police officer that the bank at Mendham would be easy to knock off if you first lured the cops away from the center of town.

Moore dropped more cards into his folder. By now information was starting to pour in. These were surely the world's gabbiest bank robbers. It seemed that they planned to use a red 1950 Ford sedan for the job. They were going to switch to an old Nash for the getaway; the Nash would be parked on Ironia Road, west of town. The number of men involved appeared to fluctuate, but the ringleaders were two Madisonians named William Redic, an odd-jobs man with a moon-shaped scar over his eye, and Robert Grogan, a Madison candy-store proprietor.

After Moore had amassed all this data there was a lull. For a while the would-be bank robbers stopped showing up in Mendham. The chief was a little unnerved by this—what had gone wrong? Had they found a better bank? But he made good use of the lull. For the first time he passed word around Mendham that a bank robbery seemed to be in the offing. "I kind of confided in the bank manager, the postmaster, storekeepers along Main Street and other interested parties," the chief says. Naturally, there were no *un*interested parties; soon most of Mendham knew.

And then in December of 1960, after a hiatus of nine months, a car pulled up in front of the bank and, much to Chief Moore's satisfaction, William Redic stepped out and entered the bank for the first time.

The Mendham branch of the Morris County Savings Bank is enough to throw any orthodox bank robber off his stride. Instead of being located in the kind of severe brick or stone building that a bank robber feels most at home in, the Mendham bank is in a pleasant 140-year-old shuttered frame house furnished with antique pine and cherry tables. The walls are hung with oil paintings.

This decor seems to have thrown Redic into confusion. At any rate, he acted extremely nervous. That made Bank Manager Herbert Miller nervous too. Miller is a six-foot, 28-year-old former Morristown High School football and basketball star who does not ordinarily get upset easily. But he recognized Redic immediately, and saw that he was jittery—and if there is one thing bankers do not like it is nervous bank robbers.

Yet their meeting went well. Redic said he had come to discuss getting a mortgage and they talked about this for a while. Toward the end of the visit Miller was called away to the phone and Redic wandered around the bank's homelike lobby getting a good look at things.

Miller's call was from Murph Rae, who works in the butcher shop across the street. Murph reported that he had just seen one of the bank robbers enter the bank but that the other one was sitting in a car outside. "It doesn't look so good," Murph said. But just as he was hanging up he saw Redic walk sedately out of the bank and get into the car, which quickly drove off.

During his visit to the bank Redic had asked Miller about night banking hours. Miller told Redic that the bank stayed open until 8 P.M. on Fridays. As soon as Redic left, Miller did two things. He arranged to have the main office of the bank in Morristown phone in periodically during banking hours, just to make sure everything was all right. And he suggested to Chief Moore that perhaps some special precaution was indicated for Friday nights.

Accordingly, the following Friday found Chief Moore staked out in the darkened butcher shop along with Mendham's other cop, Officer James Cillo. School Custodian Eddie Fagan, a special officer on the force, took up his window watch with a loaded carbine. Five minutes before closing time, the two bank robbers drove up in front of the bank and the watchers tensed. Then, inexplicably, the robbers drove off, and the police officers went home, disgruntled.

From that night on, the bank robbers stepped up the frequency of their visits to Mendham.

Soon they were coming into town almost every day, usually heralded by helpful citizens. "The bank robbers are here again," the callers would say. There was some discussion about whether the police shouldn't intervene right then and there but Moore decided against it. "After all," he said reasonably, "you can't just walk up and say, 'Hey, you waiting to rob the bank?' You just can't do that."

Six months passed.

Then one day last September William Redic swung his car through the municipal parking lot and pulled up by the bank's drive-in window, in plain sight of Phoenix House. He made it that far, then got so excited he became almost incoherent. "I want 10 cents' worth of dimes," he blurted.

Miller, at the window, stared in astonishment.

"I mean a dollar's worth," said Redic hastily.

Redic got his dimes and drove off with half the people in town watching him. He parked in front of a grocery store owned by Bill Fagan, Eddie's brother, and went in. Chief Moore watched from a discreet distance.

Bill Fagan, loading groceries into a customer's car, dropped them and hastened into the store after Redic. But Redic had merely bought cigarets and was on his way out. "Hiyah," Redic said. "Hiyah," said Fagan.

A week later Redic showed up at Fagan's grocery again and asked Mrs. Fagan for a job repairing disabled shopping carts. The Fagans didn't give Redic the job, but they began to worry. Had the bank robbers decided to switch to grocery robbing? Chief Moore said he doubted it.

It was apparent from the stepped-up pace that the big moment was approaching. Mendham got ready. Murph Rae in the butcher shop was set to pass the word the minute the robbers showed up. Mrs. Ann Neill, the lone woman employee of the bank, had instructions to head for the ladies' room and lock herself in the minute the robbery started. The bank in Morristown was making regular telephone checks, ready to flash the alarm. Officer Cillo, attired in white coveralls, began painting the rectory of St. Joseph's Roman Catholic Church, next door to the bank, with his gun hidden in the rain gutter. Officer Frank Geraghty of the Mendham Township police (the township is the governmental unit of which the Borough of Mendham is a part, and it has its own police force) was brought in to help keep watch. Chief Moore planted himself in a basement window of the Phoenix House, where he could see without being seen.

One day last fall a girl from the tax collector's office upstairs hurried down to the chief in the basement and reported that he was wanted on the phone urgently. The caller was Captain Benjamin Waer of the Morris County Police Radio. Mrs. Neal Uptegrove of Mendham had just been warned by an anonymous phone caller to get her children out of school because a bomb was to go off in 50 minutes. Was this the diversion everyone had been expecting?

Diversion or not, both of the town's schools —Mendham Township school and St. John Baptist, an Episcopal school for girls—were warned to start evacuating their students. Officer Geraghty ostentatiously drove off to oversee the procedure and Chief Moore slipped over to the bank. Meanwhile everyone else swung into action. Murph Rae took up his sentry post in front of the butcher shop; Mrs. Neill edged toward the bank's ladies' room; the main office in Morris-

town stepped up the frequency of its calls and Officer Cillo began painting his way closer to the rain gutter.

Nothing happened. Chief Moore watched the bank robbers heading out of town. He questioned Mrs. Uptegrove later and learned that the caller had been a man apparently in a pay booth, and that she had heard voices and the tinkle of glassware in the background. There are only a half-dozen pay telephones in Mendham. One of them is in the Mendham Soda Shop, and there a waitress told Chief Moore that just about the time Mrs. Uptegrove had been getting the phone call a man with a moon-shaped scar over his eye was using the phone booth.

Chief Moore went back to the police station and wrote out a new card for his "Planned Robbery of Mendham Bank" folder. But what did it mean? Was it a rehearsal? He ordered the state of readiness maintained.

The next day it happened.

Officer Cillo had got in several hours of painting on St. Joseph's rectory when the bank robbers' car drove up and parked in front of the

When the thieves approached, the townspeople were all at their battle stations.

church. Across the street in the butcher shop Murph Rae recognized the car and tried to telephone Chief Moore, but the line was busy—two visiting cops were using the phone to check out a local resident they were investigating. The butcher handed a bag of bones to customer Mary Cacchio as a cover, and asked her to deliver it to headquarters and tell the chief that the bank robbers were back.

Meanwhile bank manager Miller, who had brought his lunch to work that day because his wife needed the car, went out to throw his sandwich wrappings into the incinerator behind the bank and saw the robbers cruising slowly around the block. They passed the bank three times and then stopped at the end of the walk, 30 feet from the front door of the bank. The bank manager hurried inside, checked the phone arrangement with Morristown, warned Ann Neill to head for the ladies' room, and turned to greet the bank robbers, Redic and Grogan.

"I want to open an account," Redic said. He took the application card Miller handed him and went to one of the tables near the front door. Grogan engaged Miller in conversation. He said he had a headache and Miller advised him to go to Robinson's Drug Shop and get some aspirin. Then the only honest customer in the bank departed. Grogan produced a .38 caliber revolver, pointed it at the bank manager and told him it was a stick-up.

"I'm desperate, I'm desperate," said Grogan, who appears to have been a close student of television crime shows. "I have cancer and don't care what happens. Make no false moves and nobody'll get hurt!"

"Yeah! Yeah!" Redic yelled anxiously. He asked for a bag for the money Miller was piling on the counter. The bank manager then produced a nice new bag marked "Federal Reserve," which seemed to please Redic. He began to stuff the money into it.

The telephone rang. Grogan motioned for the bank manager to answer it but Redic didn't see his partner's motion. When Miller answered, Redic punched him in the face. It was the main bank in Morristown calling, and they got the idea right away.

The bank robbers, with $10,679 stuffed in that new Federal Reserve bag, proceeded to herd the manager and Jerre Budd, a substitute teller, into a small supply room. Redic set about tying

them up, but the rope kept slipping. Seeing that Redic's temper was getting worse, Miller and Budd finally obliged by holding the rope in place so it would look as if they were bound.

Outside the bank the police—who knew the robbery was on—were frantic. In front of Phoenix House a crowd of women had arrived for a meeting of the Mendham Garden Club and completely blocked the view and path of the police. At last Chief Moore and Officer Geraghty, who had been staked out in Phoenix House, squirmed their way through the ladies and took up positions on the sidewalk covering the front door of the bank. The two visiting policemen, drafted for the occasion, likewise took battle stations and Officer Cillo grabbed his gun out of the rain gutter and moved in quickly from his side of the bank.

The bank robbers stepped out onto the sidewalk. Chief Moore met them, pointing his carbine, and said, "Git 'em up!"

Neither robber complied. Instead Redic hurried frantically toward the getaway car, explaining loudly that he didn't have anything to do with all this—he had just stopped in to cash a check. Grogan ducked back into the bank. Moore called for him to come out, and Grogan did. "Git 'em up!" the chief repeated. When the bank robber hesitated, Moore fired a blast over his head. Grogan put up his hands and dropped the $10,679.

The bank robbers were handcuffed and marched across the street, up the front steps of Phoenix House, through the room where the Mendham Garden Club was assembling, and into police headquarters. Mrs. James L. McFadden, in charge of refreshments for the garden club meeting, arrived with bottles of cider to find the Phoenix House swarming with police and other people. The 35 ladies fretfully switched their meeting to Mrs. McFadden's home.

The Great Bank Robbery at Mendham was over. The butcher went back to his butchering; Redic and Grogan went to jail; the police chief went back to helping schoolchildren across the street and enforcing Main Street's 25-mph speed limit; Officer Cillo thankfully removed the ladder from St. Joseph's rectory and Herbert Miller, the bank manager, explained to interested citizens that it wasn't so bad getting punched in the face, but he never again wanted to go through another wait like that as long as he lived.

Amusing as the story of the Mendham bank robbery is, it illustrates a social fact: the tighter control over nonconformity in less urbanized communities. This is not an argument for the general superiority of less urbanized communities over the metropolis. The looser control of the big city makes it easier for vice and crime to escape detection, but it also makes more likely creditable adventures of the human spirit. The balance sheet is a complicated one. Urban industrial societies combine diminished social control over the individual with increased freedom for him to choose his own role commitments. These circumstances foster an ideology of individual fulfillment, a pursuit of happiness and good times, which is quite alien to the stress on primary group obligations in most preindustrial societies.[42] True, some urban industrial societies are more individualistic than others. (Contrast the United States, for example, with Japan.) And large cities are generally more individualistic than the rural hinterland. But an individualistic ideology tends to permeate every part of all the urban industrial societies because the individual is the unit of social organization in these societies, and ideologies cannot be too remote from social reality. The achievement of individual "success"—meaning accomplishments, material possessions, power over others, and prestige—is as important to many people in urban industrial societies as marriage, children, and friendship, which are more prominent values in preindustrial societies.

Television, radio, and movies, themselves products of industrial technology, reinforce an individualistc ideology. The glimpses provided in the mass media of impeccably groomed men and women dining in expensive restaurants, living in luxurious homes, and riding in sleek new automobiles arouse aspirations for individual "success." These aspirations are reinforced by the explicit temptations of advertising. The appetite for fame is also whetted by the mass media—for example, by their implicit

[42] Martha Wolfenstein, "The Emergence of Fun Morality," *Journal of Social Issues*, Vol. 7, No. 4, 1951, pp. 15–24.

suggestion that individuals whose activities are chronicled in newspapers and magazines are more valuable than "ordinary" people. Envy was certainly not invented by urban industrial societies, but envy is stimulated more systematically in them. This is partly an unintended consequence of the existence of mass media which make visible the rewards of success. It is also the result of relying on envy as the motivational basis for a competitive system of role allocation.

The scientific secularism of contemporary societies also contributes to the concern with individual achievement and individual welfare. The ability of science and technology to harness the forces of nature cannot be forgotten when human problems arise. Whatever the explicit religious commitments of industrial societies, to Christianity, to Judaism, to Buddhism, to Islam, or to Marxism, an implicit value is the importance of the here and now, and an implicit faith is activism. Frustrations need not be borne with resignation in a scientific age. Rational thinking and hard work may lead to a solution. Thus, the individual dissatisfied with his lot is prone to *do* something about it. This helps to explain the hunger for fame of a musician or painter—and also the lure of "easy money" for the professional criminal.

CONCLUSION

Modern industrialism, accompanied as it is by technological advances in transportation and communication as well as by scientific methods of farming, makes possible the urban society. In the urban society, cities are the rule rather than the exception. A majority of the population lives in metropolitan areas and depends on the labor market for income, on the real-estate market for housing, on the retail store for food and clothing, and on commercial entertainment for recreation. Even in rural areas, the style of life is radically different from that of subsistence agriculture; rural areas in the urban society are more closely integrated with cities than are rural areas in preindustrial societies.

The pattern of growth of industrial cities reflects the salience of economic activities. Competition for scarce space is reflected in sales prices, rental costs, and property taxes. Through the market mechanism, commercial uses typically preempt accessible locations in the center of the city—even though the expansion of the central business district spreads blight in surrounding residential areas.

An urban industrial society is a fluid society. Although age and sex roles continue to be *ascribed*, a wide range of occupational and other roles are *achieved*, that is, filled through competitive processes, which necessarily involve some freedom of choice—and also some disappointed aspirations. The individual continues to find meaningful relationships in primary groups (particularly in the family). But he also interacts in more specialized relationships in political organizations, professional societies, churches, and schools. The distinction between *cosmopolitan* and *local* types hinges on the extent to which the individual utilizes specialized secondary groups as the basis for his values, opinions, and goals.

An urban industrial society is an individualistic society. The individual (rather than the kinship unit) is the unit of social participation. The individual enrolls in school, votes at election time, looks for a job, and gets married. An individualistic ideology reflects this social fact. No one should be startled by the materialism or by the humanitarianism of urban industrial societies. Both preoccupations have a common source: the belief in individual fulfillment. And the belief in individual fulfillment, though not an inevitable consequence of industrialism, is promoted by the characteristic form of social organization.

SOME SIGNIFICANT LITERATURE ON URBANISM

Otis Dudley Duncan and Albert J. Reiss, Jr., *Social Characteristics of Urban and Rural Communities*, 1950, New York: Wiley, 1956. This volume is part of the Census Monograph Series which was sponsored by the Social Science Research Council to take advantage of new data made available by the 1950 census. The authors use detailed tabulations of census data by size of place to find out whether there is a sharp discontinuity between rural and urban communities or a continuous variation suggested by the concept of a rural-urban continuum. The findings of the authors are relevant to the interpretive problem of users of census statistics in dealing with the "rural" and "urban" categories. This summary is based on a review by Robert G. Burnight, *American Sociological Review*, Vol. 22, April 1957, pp. 247-248.

Philip M. Hauser, *Population Perspectives*, New Brunswick, N.J.: Rutgers University Press, 1960, Chap. 4 and 5. These chapters present data on the explosive growth of metropolitan areas in the world generally and in the United States in particular. Professor Hauser considers the consequences and implications of this explosion. For example, metropolitan growth has reduced to an absurdity many existing political boundaries; in 1950 the 162 Standard Metropolitan Areas of the United States included over 16,000 governmental units with powers to tax and spend (including school districts). Professor Hauser discusses briefly the physical problems of metropolitan housing and transportation and the human-relations problems resulting from a new ethnic mix in the central cities.

Philip M. Hauser, *Urbanization in Asia and the Far East*, Calcutta: UNESCO, 1957. This volume consists of papers contributed to a conference on urbanization in Asia and the Far East at Bangkok in August 1956. These papers reviewed the changing rates of urbanization in various countries with an eye to their social and economic consequences. This summary is based on a review by Britton Harris, *American Sociological Review*, Vol. 24, December 1959, pp. 924-925.

Sheridan T. Maitland and Reed E. Friend, *Rural Industrialization: A Summary of Five Studies*, Agricultural Information Bulletin No. 252, Washington: Government Printing Office, November 1961. This report summarizes the results of five surveys on the effects of industrial plants in economically depressed rural areas—two in Utah, one in Mississippi, one in Louisiana; and one in Iowa. The survey method included two random samples in each community: (1) of the employees of the industrial plant recently established in the community and (2) of all rural households in the community. A major finding was that older rural workers and workers with little industrial experience were least likely to seek and find jobs in the new plant. Nevertheless, the new plant provided rural workers an opportunity to shift from farm to factory work without migrating to distant industrial centers. Even if it only postpones the migration, it gives the worker some industrial experience which may facilitate his later adjustment to urban life.

Walter T. Martin, *The Rural-Urban Fringe: A Study of Adjustment to Residence Location*, Eugene, Ore.: University of Oregon Press, 1953. A random sample of residents of the unincorporated countryside contiguous to the cities of Eugene and Springfield, Oregon, was interviewed concerning satisfaction with the locations of its homes. It was hypotheszied that ". . . the extent of satisfaction of family members varies directly with the degree of accessibility of the center (of the city) to that location," but this hypothesis was not borne out by the data. Other factors did distinguish the more satisfied from the less satisfied. Males were more satisfied with the location of their homes than females, high-income persons than low-income persons, persons with a large number of memberships in formal associations than persons with few such memberships. This summary is based on a review by Richard Dewey, *American Sociological Review*, Vol. 19, December 1954, pp. 799–800.

Horace Miner, *The Primitive City of Timbuctoo*, Princeton, N.J.: Princeton University Press, 1953. Sociological study of cities suffer from a sampling bias. Most of the cities studied have been deeply influenced by the culture of Western Europe; hence, it is difficult to know whether the urban characteristics that have been identified are the inevitable result of population concentration or the result of population concentration under special cultural conditions. Professor Miner's study of the African city of Timbuctoo was undertaken ". . . to see whether such phenomena as crime, secularization, and group conflict are products of city life per se or whether they are the products of our particular type of urban civilization." Timbuctoo dates back to the eleventh century, and it was not until the twentieth century that appreciable European influence appeared. Thus, it proved a crucial case in which to examine the hypothesis that certain phenomena of city life are independent of culture. This summary is based on a review by D. B. Stout, *American Sociological Review*, Vol. 19, June 1954, pp. 367–368.

Peter H. Rossi, *Why Families Move: A Study in the Social Psychology of Urban Residential Mobility*, Glencoe, Ill.: Free Press, 1955. This study is based on depth interviews in high-income and low-income neighborhoods and in neighborhoods of high and low rates of residential mobility. Change of residence has long been thought about by sociologists as due to a double motivation: rejection of the old neighborhood and attraction for the new one (a push and a pull). This study shows the relationship of pushes and pulls to the family's stage in the life cycle. Specifically, the tendency to move is greatest during the period when the family is increasing in size. Lack of adequate space overshad-

ows objectionable qualities of the neighborhood as a "push." The relationship between mobility and stage of the family cycle explains an otherwise puzzling finding: Families are more mobile than unattached persons even in areas of high mobility containing large numbers of single, divorced, or widowed persons. This summary is based on a review by Donald O. Cowgill, *American Sociological Review*, Vol. 21, June 1956, pp. 395–396.

Gresham M. Sykes, "The Differential Distribution of Community Knowledge," *Social Forces*, Vol. 29, May 1951, pp. 376–382. In the summer of 1949, Professor Sykes conducted a questionnaire survey of white male wage earners in Plainfield, New Jersey. The questionnaire consisted of three parts: a test of knowledge of the community, a set of questions dealing with political participation, and background information (income, occupation, education, length of residence in the community, home ownership, and so forth). On the basis of the background information some respondents could be categorized as being oriented to the local community by virtue of long residence, location of work in the community, children in the schools, and other characteristics. Others worked outside of the community, rented their homes, lived only a short time in Plainfield, and did not have children in the schools; these were presumably less oriented to the local community. Sykes found that *locals* had much greater community knowledge than *nonlocals* (cosmopolitans).

Max Weber, *The City*, Glencoe, Ill.: Free Press, 1958. In these essays, the famous German sociologist considered the historical evolution of cities and city life. Weber attempted to formulate an inductive definition of the city based on his historical research. "To constitute a full urban community a settlement must display a relative predominance of trade-commercial relations, with the settlement as a whole displaying the following features: (1) a fortification; (2) a market; (3) a court of its own and at least partially autonomous law; (4) a related form of association; and (5) . . . an administration by authorities in the election of whom the burghers participated." Obviously a rather restrictive definition, in terms of which only the Occident produced urban communities, it is not useful for contemporary urban research. This summary is based on a review by Albert J. Reiss, Jr., *American Sociological Review*, Vol. 24, April 1959, pp. 267–268.

Louis Wirth, "Urbanism as a Way of Life," *American Journal of Sociology*, Vol. 44, July 1938, pp. 1–24. This classic article deduces the anonymity and impersonality of urban life from population density and heterogeneity. "The multiplication of persons in a state of interaction under conditions which make their contact as full personalities impossible produces that segmentalization of human relationships which has sometimes been seized upon by students of the mental life of the cities as an explanation for the 'schizoid' character of urban personality." Although this view is almost traditional in sociology, counting among its exponents Max Weber, Georg Simmel, and Robert E. Park, contemporary urban sociologists have criticized it on both theoretical and empirical grounds. Herbert J. Gans, for example, has pointed out that Wirth failed to distinguish conceptually between *urban* characteristics and characteristics of the type of *mass* society produced by industrialism. Furthermore, Wirth assumed that bulk of the urban population consisted of unattached individuals such as are found in rooming-house districts, whereas, in fact, the majority of urban populations have social and cultural moorings. See Herbert J. Gans, "Urbanism and Suburbanism as Ways of Life: a Reevaluation of Definitions," in Arnold M. Rose, Ed., *Human Behavior and Social Processes: An Interactionist Approach*, Boston: Houghton Mifflin, 1962.

CHAPTER 6

In-group and Out-group Cultures
of an Industrial Society

To speak of the division of the world into industrialized and underdeveloped societies—the haves and the have nots—is to repeat a cliché.[1] This division pertains not only to the distribution of automobiles and television sets but also to the opportunities for health and for life itself. The American people had in 1959 a crude death rate (deaths, exclusive of still-births, per thousand population) one-half the rate of the Burmese people.[2] The American infant mortality rate (deaths of children under one year per 1000 live births) was in 1959 one-fifth the Burmese rate—26.4 per thousand compared to 130.3 per thousand.[3] Such striking differences in life expectancies are, however, decreasing with the introduction of insecticides and other techniques of disease control.

In Ceylon the control of malaria resulting from DDT spraying raised the life expectancy from 43 years in 1946 to 52 years in 1947, as big an increase as most Western countries accomplished in half a century.[4] In Mexico the crude death rate dropped from 26.6 per thousand in 1930 to 11.7 per thousand in 1960.[5] The differences between the standards of living of industrialized and underdeveloped countries have *not* narrowed. In fact, they have widened in recent years; the rich nations have gotten richer and the poor poorer.[6] One important factor in this division of the world into have and have-not countries is that the underdeveloped countries have not succeeded in reducing fertility rates. For example, Mexico had in 1960 a crude birth rate (live births per thousand persons in the population) of 45.9 compared with the American rate for that year of 23.6.[7]

1 Robert Theobald, *The Rich and the Poor: A Study of the Economics of Rising Expectations*, New York: New American Library, 1961; Robert L. Heilbroner, *The Great Ascent: The Struggle for Economic Development in Our Time*, New York: Harper & Row, 1963.
2 Bureau of the Census, *Statistical Abstract of the United States: 1962*, Washington: Government Printing Office, 1962, p. 913.
3 *Ibid.*

4 William Peterson, *Population*, New York: Macmillan, 1961, pp. 467–474.
5 *Ibid.*, p. 37, gives the Mexican death rate in 1930. For the 1960 Mexican death rate, see Bureau of the Census, *Statistical Abstract of the United States: 1962*, Washington: Government Printing Office, 1962, p. 913.
6 Suphon Andic and Alan T. Peacock, "The International Distribution of Income, 1949 and 1957," *Journal of the Royal Statistical Society*, Series A (General), Vol. 124, Part 2, 1961, pp. 214–215.
7 Bureau of the Census, *Statistical Abstract of the United States: 1962*, Washington: Government Printing Office, 1962, p. 913.

Within industrial countries there is also a division into haves and have nots: between persons adjusted to the industrial way of life, who function adequately in the complex role structure of a highly differentiated society, and persons who do not understand the cultural values of industrialism and are excluded from its material rewards. The latter group constitutes a welfare and dependency problem for the former group. However, unlike the division between industrial and underdeveloped countries, the internal cleavage seems to be growing *less* sharp. The proportion of the population adjusted to the industrial way of life is increasing as larger numbers of people are upgraded educationally and economically. One indication of better adjustment to industrial culture is the tendency for consumer goods to be distributed more equitably in rich industrial societies. "It is, indeed, a regular occurrence endowed almost with the dignity of an economic law that the poorer the country, the greater the difference between poor and rich." [8]

In short, the division of industrial societies into *in*-group (haves) and *out*-group (have nots) cultures may well be transitional. Welfare-minded Sweden has moved far enough toward a homogeneous culture that slums are nonexistent in Swedish cities. For the time being, however, an advanced industrial country like the United States should be thought of as having two cultures: that of the industrially oriented in-group and that of the demoralized out-group.

THE CULTURE OF THE IN-GROUP

What is an "in-group"? *An in-group consists of persons linked to one another by feelings of solidarity.*[9] An in-group can be small in size: a family or a squad of soldiers. It can

also include an entire nation, as when Americans emphasize their common allegiance, which excludes all "foreigners." Thus, the in-group concept is relevant to many levels in a complex society: wherever a feeling of solidarity unites some people and excludes others. The *out*-group is defined residually, by subtracting the in-group from a larger category. Sometimes members of an out-group are drawn together by the bond of their common exclusion; sometimes they feel rejected in isolation. Racial discrimination in the United States creates a Negro out-group, but Negro protest organizations like the National Association for the Advancement of Colored People, the Urban League, and the Congress of Racial Equality help to create *esprit de corps* among victims of racial discrimination, thus transforming an out-group into a kind of in-group. On the other hand, discrimination against the blind, the deaf, the crippled, and those with speech impediments creates an out-group of *individual* unfortunates.

This chapter will attempt to distinguish industrially oriented segments of the population in an advanced society from the rest of the population. In what sense do these segments constitute an in-group? They are not linked by such obvious characteristics as skin color or the absence of physical handicaps. Their unity depends on sharing certain values and skills. For example, they utilize the media of mass communication for information and for entertainment; they regard formal education as an important asset in adjusting to their society; they are prepared to relocate in other communities to provide a better environment for children or better occupational opportunities for the breadwinner. If acceptance of the institutions of their society is inferred from active participation in them, they are conformists. Obviously, some members of the in-group exemplify its values more strongly than others. Since many values and skills are involved, it might be argued that no sharp separation occurs between the in-group and the out-group, that instead there is continuous variation from those most at home in the society to the totally inadequate. The evidence is not sufficient to

[8] Gunnar Myrdal, *An International Economy*, New York: Harper, 1956, p. 133. Quoted in Seymour Martin Lipset and Reinhard Bendix, *Social Mobility in Industrial Society*, Berkeley: University of California Press, 1959, p. 108, along with supporting United Nations data.

[9] For an excellent discussion of the in-group concept, see Robert Bierstedt, *The Social Order: An Introduction to Sociology*, New York: McGraw-Hill, 1957, pp. 263–268.

resolve the issue with confidence. Nevertheless, this chapter will assume that the white Protestant business executive living with his wife and two children in a $40,000-ranch house in Westfield, New Jersey, has more in common with the Catholic carpenter who lives with his larger family in a smaller, less expensive house on Staten Island than the carpenter has with a migrant laborer or a prostitute. In short, this chapter will assume that the real differences among the industrially oriented segments of the population are less important than the similarities. The ultimate test of the validity of this assumption is actual behavior.

In the following section of the chapter, three aspects of the in-group culture will be described in an effort to make more vivid the basis for the solidarity we are assuming.

SENSITIVITY TO MASS COMMUNICATIONS. In all societies, including urban industrial ones, face-to-face communication is the most important type of communication. Electronic devices and the printing press have not supplanted face-to-face exchange. They have added a new technique for transmitting information through the intervention of nonhuman media. Although a human agency is the ultimate source of mass media messages, the relationship between sender and receiver is no longer symmetrical as in ordinary face-to-face communication. The recipient of information from newspapers or television is necessarily more passive than the participant in a conversation. Interaction still occurs between the initiator of the communication and its recipients, but response requires more initiative and more training than in the face-to-face situation. Thus, readers of a newspaper can interact with the editorial staff through letters to the editor if they have enough education and patience to compose a coherent one. Similarly, television viewers can exert considerable influence on sponsors and network officials by expressing reactions in letters or by telephone. Yet it takes a certain level of self-confidence (or indignation) to attempt to interact with something as impersonal as a television station.

Members of the industrially oriented in-group have incorporated the mass media into their lives. They depend on the newspaper not only for current events but also for the radio and television logs, information about the movies at neighborhood theaters, sales in retail stores, stock-market prices, and other activities and events. The following article reports a piece of research which took advantage of a newspaper strike to gauge the place of the newspaper in the lives of New Yorkers.

Dependence on the Newspaper in a Literate Society

Reprinted by permission. From Bernard Berelson, "What 'Missing the Newspaper' Means," in Paul F. Lazarsfeld and Frank N. Stanton, Eds., *Communications Research, 1948–1949*, New York: Harper, 1949, pp. 111–129.

In the late afternoon of Saturday, June 30, 1945, the deliverymen of eight major New York City newspapers went on strike. They remained on strike for over two weeks, and during that period most New Yorkers were effectively deprived of their regular newspaper reading. They were able to buy the newspaper *PM* and a few minor and specialized papers at newsstands, and they could buy copies over the counter at central offices of some newspapers. But the favorite papers of most readers were simply inaccessible to them for seventeen days.

These unusual circumstances presented a good opportunity for various interested parties—advertisers, newspaper publishers, radio executives, social scientists—to gauge public attitudes toward the newspaper, and at least three general polls of opinion were independently conducted during the strike. Some if not all findings of two polls have been made public, one by the Elmo Roper agency and the other by Fact Finders Associates, Inc. This article is a report on the third, an exploratory survey conducted for the Bureau of Applied Social Research, Columbia University.

According to the published findings, the Roper and Fact Finder organizations directed their efforts to determining what people had done in order to keep up with the news, what parts of the newspaper they particularly missed, and how much they missed the newspapers as the strike went on. On no specific question are their results strictly comparable, but in three ways they aimed at the same general attitudes or behavior, although in quite different ways. Both agencies attempted to get at the nature of the substitute for the newspaper, and in both cases respondents stressed that they listened to news broadcasts over the radio. Both attempted, in quite different ways, to discover what parts of the newspaper were particularly missed, and in both cases respondents stressed news (national, local, and war news) and advertising. Finally, both attempted to get at the degree to which the newspapers were actually missed, and in both cases respondents indicated that they missed the papers intensely.

Because the questions used by the two polling agencies differed greatly, the results are not strictly comparable. Furthermore, neither poll is able to interpret its data, which consist altogether of "surface facts," relevant only to the specific question at hand. Saying that one "misses the newspaper," or a part of it, can cover a variety of psychological reactions. What does "missing the newspaper" mean? Why do people miss it? Do they really miss the parts they claim, to the extent they claim? Why do they miss one part as against another? The Roper and Fact Finders polls bring little or nothing to bear on such questions, which are at the core of the basic problem, namely, to understand the function of the modern newspaper for its readers. Neither poll succeeds in getting at the more complex attitudinal matters operating in the situation.

It was to attack this problem that the present study was conducted. At the end of the first week of the strike, the Bureau of Applied Social Research of Columbia University sponsored a quite different kind of study of people's reactions to the loss of their newspapers. Where the Roper and Fact Finders surveys were extensive, the Bureau's was intensive, designed to secure psychological insight in order to determine just what not having the newspaper meant to people. It is an axiom in social research, of course, that such studies can most readily be done during a crisis period like that represented by the newspaper strike. People are not only more conscious of what the newspaper means to them during such a "shock" period than they are under normal conditions, but they also find it easier to be articulate about such matters.

Accordingly, the Bureau conducted a small number (60) of intensive interviews. The sample, stratified by rental areas in Manhattan, provided a good distribution by economic status although it was high in education. No attempt was made to secure statistically reliable data on poll questions of the Roper or Fact Finders sort (although for a few similar questions, such as what was missed in the papers, the results are the same as those from the Roper survey). Instead, the Bureau's interviews were designed to supply so-called qualitative data on the role of the newspaper for its readers, as that became evident at such a time. The results are not offered as scientific proof, but rather as a set of useful hypotheses.

In brief, then, the two polls on the subject present certain "surface facts," without knowing just what they mean. This study tries to suggest what "missing the newspaper" really means. Let us start with people's stereotyped responses to questions about missing the newspaper.

Because of people's inclination to produce accepted slogans in answer to certain poll questions, there is always the danger that verbal response and actual behavior may not correspond. This danger was confirmed here. Intensive follow-up interviewing of the respondents demonstrated that practically everyone *pays tribute* to the value of the newspaper as a source of "serious" information about and interpretation of the world of public affairs, although not everyone uses it in that way. During the interview our respondents were asked whether they thought "it is very important that people read the newspapers or not." Almost everyone answered with a strong "Yes," and went on to specify that the importance of the newspaper lay in its informational and educational aspects. For most of the respondents, this specification referred to the newspaper as a source of news, narrowly defined, on public affairs.

However, not nearly so many people use the newspaper for this approved purpose, as several previous reading and information studies have shown. The general tribute without supporting behavior was evident in this study as well. When the respondents were given the opportunity to say spontaneously why they missed reading their regular newspapers, only a very few named a specific "serious" news event of the period (such as the Far Eastern war or the British elections) whereas many more answered with some variant of the "to-keep-informed" cliché or named another characteristic of the newspaper (e.g., its departmental features).

At another point in the interview, respondents were asked directly, "What news stories or events which happened last week (i.e., before the strike) did you particularly miss not being able to follow up?" Almost half the respondents were unable to name any such story or event whereas others named such non-"serious" news stories as the then-current Stevens murder case. About a third of the respondents did cite a "serious" news event, most of them the Far Eastern war. Furthermore, directly following this question, the respondents were asked which of a list of six front-page stories of the week before they had missed "not being able to follow up in your regular paper." Here, too, only a little more than a third of the respondents said that they had missed reading about the average serious event in this list. Thus, although almost all the respondents speak highly of the newspaper's value as a channel of "serious" information, only about a third of them seemed to miss it for that purpose.

In brief, there seems to be an important difference between the respondents' *general* protestations of interest in the newspaper's "serious" purposes and their *specific* desires and practices in newspaper reading. The respondents' feeling that the newspaper "keeps me informed about the world" seems to be rather diffuse and amorphous, and not often attached to concrete news events of a "serious" nature. Again, for example, take the answer to our question, "Now that you don't read your regular newspaper, do you feel you know what's going on in the world?" Fully two-thirds of the respondents felt that they did not know what was going on although, as we have seen, only about half that many had any notion of what in the world they wanted more information about. To miss the newspaper for its "serious" news value seems to be the accepted if not the automatic thing to say.

But this does not mean that the newspapers were not genuinely missed by their readers. There were many spontaneous mentions of the intensity with which the respondents missed their papers, and several of those who missed them a good deal at the beginning of the strike felt even more strongly about it as the week wore on. The question is, *why* did people miss the newspaper so keenly. However, let us first review the several uses to which readers typically put the newspaper. This is the next step in our effort to put content into a check mark on a poll questionnaire by suggesting what "missing the newspaper" really means.

The modern newspaper plays several roles for its readers. From the analysis of our intensive interviews, we have attempted to construct a typology of such roles, or functions, of the newspaper. Obviously the types enumerated here, while discrete, are not necessarily mutually exclusive for any one newspaper reader. Undoubtedly, different people read different parts of the newspaper for different reasons at different times. The major problem is to determine the conditions under which the newspaper fulfills such functions as those developed here—and perhaps others—for different kinds of people. In this connection, the special value of a small group of detailed interviews lies in the identification of hypotheses which can then be tested, one way or the other, by less intensive methods. In other words, such "qualitative" interviews suggest the proper questions which can then be asked, in lesser detail, for "quantitative" verification.

In this section we shall mention briefly several immediate uses of the newspaper which we found in the interviews. The illustrative quotations are typical of those appearing in the interviews. Some of these uses correspond to acknowledged purposes of the newspaper, others do not.

FOR INFORMATION ABOUT AND INTERPRETATION OF PUBLIC AFFAIRS

There is a core of readers who find the newspaper indispensable as a source of information about and interpretation of the "serious" world of public affairs. It is important to stress, in this connection, that this interest is not limited simply to the provision of full information about news events. Many people are also concerned with commentaries on current events from both editorials and columnists, which they use as a touchstone for their own opinions. For example:

"I don't have the details now, I just have the result. It's almost like reading the headlines of the newspaper without following up the story. I miss the detail and the explanation of events leading up to the news. I like to get the story behind and the development leading up to—it's more penetrating . . . I like to analyze for myself why things do happen and after getting the writers' opinions of it from the various newspapers, in which each one portrays the story in a different manner, I have a broader view and a more detailed view when I formulate my own opinion."

AS A TOOL FOR DAILY LIVING

For some people the newspaper was missed because it was used as direct aid in everyday life. The respondents were asked, "Since you haven't been able to get your regular newspaper, have you found some things that you can't do as well without it?" Fully half of them indicated that they had been handicapped in some way. Many people found it difficult if not impossible to follow radio programs without the radio log published in the newspaper. Others who might have gone to a motion picture did not like the bother of phoning or walking around to find out what was on. A few business people missed such merchandising comments as the arrival of buyers; others were concerned about financial and stock exchange information. Several women interested in shopping were handicapped by the lack of advertisements. A few close relatives of returning soldiers were afraid they would miss details of embarkation news. A couple of women who regularly followed the obituary notices were afraid that acquaintances might die without their knowing it. Finally, there were scattered mentions of recipes and fashion notes and even the daily weather forecast in this connection. In short, there are many ways in which many people use the newspaper as a daily instrument or guide and it was missed accordingly.

FOR RESPITE

Reading has respite value whenever it provides a vacation from personal care by transporting the reader outside his own immediate world. There is no question but that many newspaper stories with which people readily identify supply this "escape" function satisfactorily for large numbers of people. Exhibit A in this connection is the comics, which people report liking for their story and suspense value. Beyond this, however, the newspaper is able to refresh readers in other ways, by supplying them with appropriate psychological relaxation. The newspaper is particularly effective in fulfilling this need for relief from the boredom and dullness of everyday life not only because of the variety and richness of its "human interest" content or because of its inexpensive accessibility. In addition, the newspaper is a good vehicle for this purpose because it satisfies this need without much cost to the reader's conscience; the prestige value of the newspaper as an institution for "enlightening the citizenry" carries over to buttress this and other uses of the newspapers.

"When you read it takes your mind off other things."

"It [the strike] gave me nothing to do in between my work except to crochet, which does not take my mind off myself as much as reading."

"I didn't know what to do with myself. I was depressed. There was nothing to read and pass the time. I got a paper on Wednesday and felt a whole lot better."

FOR SOCIAL PRESTIGE

Another group of readers seem to use the newspaper because it enables them to appear informed in social gatherings. Thus the newspaper has conversational value. Readers not only can learn what has happened and then report it to their associates but can also find opinions and interpretations for use in discussions on public affairs. It is obvious how this use of the newspaper serves to increase the reader's prestige among his fellows. It is not that the newspapers' content is good in itself but rather that it is good *for* something—and that something is putting up an impressive front to one's associates.

"You have to read in order to keep up a conversation with other people. It is embarrassing not to know if you are in company who discuss the news."

"Not that I am uneasy about what's happening but I like to know about the country so when people ask you questions you don't feel dumb and silly."

"It makes me furious, absolutely furious, because I don't know what's going on and all my friends who are getting the papers do know."

FOR SOCIAL CONTACT

The newspaper's human interest stories, personal advice column, gossip columns, and the like provide some readers with more than relief from their own cares and routine. They also supply guides to the prevailing morality, insight into private lives as well as opportunity for vicarious participation in them, and indirect "personal" contact with distinguished people.

One explanation of the role of the human interest story is that it provides a basis of common experience against which urban readers can check their own moral judgments and behavior (the "ethicizing" effect). The requirements for such stories are that they shall be understandable in terms of the reader's own experience and that they shall be "interesting." (One respondent who read the tabloids although he disliked them remarked that "the *Times* isn't written interestingly enough" and that "*PM* is the most honest paper but should have more interesting stuff like the *Journal-American*.") From the comments of a few respondents, it appears that the human interest stories and the gossip columnists do serve something of this purpose. In fact, a few respondents indicated that they missed the newspaper because, so to speak, some of their friends resided in its pages. A few women who read the gossip columnists and the society pages intensively seemed to take an intimate personal interest in their favorite newspaper characters and to think of them in congenial terms.

"I miss Doris Blake's column [advice to the lovelorn]. You get the opinions in Doris Blake of the girls and boys and I find that exciting. It's like true life—a girl expressing her life. It's like everyday happenings."

"I always used to condemn the mud-slinging in the *News* and *Mirror*, and many times I swore I'd never buy them if it weren't for the features I like. But just the other day I said to a friend of mine that I'd never, never talk like that about the papers again, because now I know what it is to be without them."

"I missed them [favorite columnists] for their information, their news, their interviews with various people, their interaction with people. It is interesting to know people's reactions. If you read the background of individuals, you can analyze them a little better."

"I like the *Daily News*. It's called the 'scandal sheet' but I like it. It was the first paper that I bought when I came to New York. When you live in a small town and read the papers you know everybody who's mentioned in the papers. The *News* is the closest thing to them. The pictures are interesting and it makes up for the lack of knowing people . . . You get used to certain people; they become part of your family, like Dorothy Kilgallen. That lost feeling of being without papers increases as the days go on. You see, I don't socialize much. There's no place that you can get Dorothy Kilgallen—chit-chat and gossip and Louella Parsons with Hollywood news."

The foregoing article reported a natural experiment. Researchers inferred the dependence of urban industrial man on his newspapers from observing him when they were temporarily unavailable. But the newspaper is not the only instrument of mass communications in industrial societies. Glossy magazines are sold in kiosks and newsstands all over the world. In 1960 the United States had 54 million television sets in use, Great Britain had 11 million sets, Japan six million sets, the Soviet Union and West Germany five million each, Canada four million, France and Italy two million each, and Australia, Brazil, and Sweden one million each.[10] Radio receivers are even more common than television receivers. The motion picture industry has a world market. Mass communications carry so much information that a British or American family without a radio, television set, newspapers, or magazines would be almost as isolated as the shipwrecked household in *Swiss Family Robinson*.

Living in an urban industrial society without responding to some extent to mass communications is impossible. Poorly educated segments of the population respond minimally: to comic strips, soap operas, news of sports.[11] Better educated persons use the mass media more extensively: to keep abreast of public affairs, new books, comparative values in consumer goods.

FAMILY STABILITY. Much research has been done on desertion, divorce, marital conflict, and other forms of family disorganization in urban industrial societies. Chapter 8 will consider these matters at some length. For the purposes of the present chapter, it is necessary to challenge the notion that the individualistic culture of industrial societies produces *general*

10 Bureau of the Census, *Statistical Abstract of the United States: 1962*, Washington: Government Printing Office, 1962, pp. 933–934.
11 For a classic study of the psychology of the listener to radio soap operas, see Herta Herzog, "What Do We Really Know about Daytime Serial Listeners?," in Paul F. Lazarsfeld and Frank N. Stanton, Eds., *Radio Research, 1942–1943*. New York: Duell, Sloan, and Pearce, 1944, pp. 3–33.

family breakdown.[12] Family breakdown occurs, but it is the exception rather than the rule. Of the 99 million Americans recorded in the 1960 census as having *ever* been married, 81 million were living with their spouses at the time of census; ten million were widows or widowers; five million persons were living apart from their spouses due to marital discord, institutionalization, or other reasons; and only three million were divorced (and not remarried).[13] These statistics do not fully reflect family breakup in the United States because some of the 81 million persons living with their spouses in 1960 had been *previously* married. Fourteen per cent of the 99 million Americans reported as "ever married" had been married more than once.[14] Usually though, divorces occurred after a relatively brief period of marriage and did not discourage the individuals involved from establishing more stable marriages.[15]

The increase in the birth rate is another indication that family life is not deteriorating. The American birth rate rose from 77.2 live births per thousand females aged 15–44 in 1935 to 119.0 in 1960.[16] The rise in the birth rate after the Second World War is not restricted to the United States. All industrial countries have enjoyed a baby boom along with the prosperity that encouraged married couples to undertake larger families. In the United States the baby boom has been accompanied by an expansion of home ownership. In 1940 only 41.1 per cent of nonfarm homes were occupied by their owners; in 1960 61.0 per cent of nonfarm homes were owner occupied.[17] If a higher birth rate and increased home ownership are indices of family stability, family stability has increased in recent decades.

The difficulty with such data as these is that they combine statistics on Negroes and whites, on city slums and wealthy suburbs, on Americans who share the culture of the industrially oriented in-group and Americans who do not. Even these combined data challenge the notion of general family breakdown. Yet family disorganization is much more concentrated among population elements poorly integrated into urban industrial society. For instance, more of the Negro population belong to the nonindustrial out-group, which creates greater family instability among Negroes. While 73 per cent of the "ever married" white women 45 to 49 years old were living with their *first* spouse at the time of the 1960 census, only 48 per cent of nonwhite women in the same age bracket were doing so.[18]

A clearer instance of the family pattern of the in-group can be found in homogeneous suburban communities such as Westfield, New Jersey. Westfield, a city of 31,447 people in 1960, is situated within commuting distance of New York City. The 1960 census reported that 88 per cent of its population were native whites, 7 per cent were foreign-born whites, and only 5 per cent were nonwhites.[19] A majority of the families in this affluent community had incomes in 1959 of $10,000 or more. A majority of Westfield men were employed in high-level white-collar occupations: professional or technical workers, managers, officials, proprietors. Two-fifths of them had graduated

12   The argument in this paragraph and the one following leans on Talcott Parsons, "The American Family: Its Relations to Personality and to Social Structure," in Talcott Parsons and Robert F. Bales, *Family, Socialization and Interaction Process*, Glencoe, Ill.: Free Press, 1955, Chap. 1.
13   Bureau of the Census, *United States Census of Population: 1960, United States Summary, Detailed Characteristics*, Washington: Government Printing Office, 1963, pp. xxi–xxii.
14   *Ibid.*, p. xxii.
15   William M. Kephart, "The Duration of Marriage," *American Sociological Review*, Vol. 19, June 1954, pp. 287–295.
16   Department of Health, Education and Welfare, *Health, Education, and Welfare Trends: 1961*, Washington: Government Printing Office, 1961, p. 6.

17   Bureau of the Census, *Statistical Abstract of the United States: 1962*, Washington: Government Printing Office, 1962, p. 758.
18   Bureau of the Census, *United States Census of Population: 1960, United States Summary, Detailed Characteristics*, Washington: Government Printing Office, 1963, p. xxii.
19   The data in the paragraphs to follow come from the 1960 Census of population. See Bureau of the Census, *United States Census of Population: 1960, General Social and Economic Characteristics, New Jersey*, Washington: Government Printing Office, 1962, various tables.

from college. Unemployment was insignificant. Eight times as many families had incomes over $10,000 in 1959 as had incomes under $3000. Westfield had proportionally more husband-wife families than the United States as a whole and proportionally fewer divorced persons.

Why do people live in suburbs like West-field? Some sociologists regard suburbanization as partly explainable by the desire to promote better family living. In the following article Wendell Bell reports on his research into motives for moving into suburban communities.

The Desire to Promote Family Stability as a Factor in Suburbanization

Reprinted by permission. From Wendell Bell, "Familism and Suburbanization: One Test of the Social Choice Hypothesis," *Rural Sociology*, Vol. 21, September–December 1956, pp. 276–283.

INTRODUCTION

SOCIAL CHOICE AND POPULATION TYPES. Within certain population types, the relationship between the food economy and population growth fairly well resembles the conditions described by Malthus.[20] These societies, described by Notestein as having high growth potential [21] and described by Schultz as having endogenous relationships between the agricultural economy and population changes,[22] contain populations which tend to expand to the limits of the food supply. In these societies, the "positive checks" of Malthus operate to control population size; birth rates remain high and relatively stable, variations in population growth being tied to variations in the death rate. Although a large proportion of the world's people still live under such conditions, it has been demonstrated that in other societies, especially large-scale industrial societies, population changes cannot be explained by changes in the agricultural sector of the economy. These societies are freed from the Malthusian limits, and population variations within them will be an expression of a

wide range of alternatives for individuals, death rates being characteristically low and stable and variations in population growth being tied to variations in the birth rate rather than to variations in the death rate. Thus the pressure of the population on the food supply no longer explains population growth in such societies as the United States, and other explanatory concepts are needed. A range of available choices which may affect the birth rate has been postulated. These include *familism, upward vertical mobility,* and *consumership,* among others.

THE THREE ALTERNATIVE CHOICE PATTERNS DEFINED. By familism is meant investment in the familial system of the society; marriage at young ages, a short childless time-span after marriage, large families, and other such characteristics are indicators of familism. By upward mobility is meant movement into social positions of greater prestige, property, and power.

These are fairly common notions and many writers have discussed the relationship between the family and economic systems, usually positing an inverse relationship between familism and upward vertical mobility. Recent writers have pointed out, for example, that the investment of time and money in family life may have deleterious consequences for upward mobility; and, conversely, that the investment of time and money in one's career may limit one's family life by delaying marriage or postponing children.

Those persons who eschew investment in either career or family and prefer having as high a standard of living as possible in the present represent the consumership choice pattern. These persons expend their efforts on "having a good time," "living it up," or "enjoying life as much as possible," and they do this in ways which are unconnected with family or career goals.

THE HYPOTHESIS

There is some evidence that these alternative choice patterns and the recent shift of population to the suburbs may be linked together, although there does not seem to be complete agreement concerning which choice patterns are most reflected in the suburban shift. Demographic comparisons between central cities and their suburbs have shown that there is generally a higher socio-economic status group in the suburbs, suggesting that vertical mobility was involved in the

[20] See Chapter 4, pp. 129–131.
[21] Frank W. Notestein, "Population—The Long View," in Theodore W. Schultz, *Food for the World,* Chicago: University of Chicago Press, 1945.
[22] Theodore W. Schultz, *The Economic Organization of Agriculture,* New York: McGraw-Hill, 1953.

suburban move.[23] On the other hand, these comparisons also have shown for the suburbs a larger family size, more married males, more intact families, and more women not in the labor force, suggesting that a preference for familism was reflected in the outward move. Statistically analyzed surveys as well as impressionistic articles by popular writers have reflected one or another aspect of these two themes, and in some cases both themes are present.

The hypothesis of this study is *that the move to the suburbs expresses an attempt to find a location in which to conduct family life which is more suitable than that offered by central cities*, i.e., *that persons moving to the suburbs are principally those who have chosen familism as an important element of their life styles*. This is not offered as a complete explanation of the move to the suburbs. The sheer growth of our cities has brought about an expansion into the areas around them. This hypothesis concerns the selective or differentiating factors involved in the movement.

THE SAMPLE

One hundred interviews were obtained in two adjacent suburbs in the Chicago metropolitan area. These were Park Ridge and Des Plaines, both of which have had relatively large increases since the end of World War II. Park Ridge increased 37.6 per cent between 1940 and 1950 and about 44.6 per cent between 1950 and 1955. Des Plaines has had a somewhat larger relative growth, increasing its population 57.5 per cent between 1940 and 1950 and about 80 per cent between 1950 and 1955. Both have increased every decade since 1880; the largest relative increase over the years in each case occurred during the 1920's. Both suburbs are primarily residential in character, and are located along a Chicago and Northwestern Railway commuter line. Park Ridge has a somewhat higher average income, oc-

cupation, and education than does Des Plaines; and the sample, having been drawn from both places, contains a relatively wide range with respect to economic status characteristics. Thirty-two per cent of the sample are classified as blue-collar; 24 per cent, lower white-collar; and 44 per cent, upper white-collar.[24]

A sample of dwelling units was randomly drawn from those areas where about 30 per cent or more of the housing consisted of post-World War II building. Substitution of next-door neighbors was allowed in case the selected respondent refused or was not at home. Half of the field work was done on the weekends in order to obtain about an equal split between men and women respondents. The interviewing was done during the early summer of 1955. Most of the interview schedule was memorized by the interviewers, and the average interview was about 30 minutes long.

THE FINDINGS

Sixty-eight per cent of the respondents had been living in Chicago just prior to their present move to the suburbs; 24 per cent came from nearby areas, mostly other suburbs, outside of Chicago; and only 8 per cent came from other places. Persons of lower socio-economic status were more likely to have moved from Chicago than were those of higher socio-economic status —88 per cent of the blue-collar, 62 per cent of the lower white-collar, and 57 per cent of the upper white-collar persons reported their last residence within the city limits of Chicago.

Characteristically, the suburbanites interviewed had been apartment dwellers before moving to their present residence, 65 per cent so reporting. Thus the shift to these two suburbs typically involves not only a move from the central city, but also entails a move from an apartment to a house.

The bulk of each interview was devoted to probing the reasons the respondent gave for moving to the suburbs. The reasons given for the move were classified into five broad categories

---

23 For example, see J. Allan Beegle, "Characteristics of Michigan's Fringe Population," *Rural Sociology*, September 1947, pp. 254–263; Donald J. Bogue, "A Few Facts about Chicago's Suburbs," Chicago Community Inventory (1954); Beverly Duncan, "Demographic and Socio-Economic Characteristics of the Population of the City of Chicago and the Suburbs and Urban Fringe: 1950," Chicago Community Inventory (1954); U. S. Bureau of the Census, *Census of Population: 1950*, Vol. IV, *Special Reports*, Part V, Chap. A, "Characteristics by Size of Place."

24 Professionals, managers, officials, and proprietors were classified upper white collar; clerical and sales workers were classified lower white collar; and craftsmen, foremen, operatives, private household workers, service workers, and laborers were classified blue collar. None of the sample dwelling units contained persons reporting the occupation of farm laborer, farm manager, or farm proprietor.

(Table 22). Four-fifths of the respondents gave reasons which had to do with bettering conditions for their children. Three-fourths of these responses concerned physical features of the suburbs in contrast to those of the city (Table 23). More space outside the house with less traffic and cleaner areas were cited as allowing the children to play out of doors "like children should," with

TABLE 22

Broad Classes of Reasons Given for Moving to the Suburbs, and Percentage of Respondents Mentioning Each Type

Type of Reason	Per Cent [a]
Better for children	81
Enjoy life more	77
Husband's job	21
Near relatives	14
Other	3

[a] Since many respondents gave more than one reason, the sum of the percentages does not equal 100.

TABLE 23

Percentage Distribution of Specific Reasons in the "Better for Children" Category

Specific Reasons for Moving to the Suburbs	Per Cent
Physical reasons (N = 172):	72.3
More space outside house	19.7
More space inside house	14.3
"The outdoors" (fresh air, sunshine, etc.)	12.6
Less traffic	11.8
Cleaner	6.3
No neighbors in same building	3.8
Quiet	2.1
No stairs	1.7
Social reasons (N = 66):	27.7
Better schools	10.2
"Nice" children to play with	9.2
Other children to play with	2.5
More organized activities	2.5
Home of own (security)	1.7
Adults "nice" to children	0.8
Better churches	0.8
Total reasons in this category (N = 238)	100.0

much less worry and supervision on the part of the parents. Also, the fresh air, sunshine, and other features of "the outdoors" were mentioned as providing a "more healthy" life for the children. Living in a single-family detached house—instead of next to, above, or below other persons as in an apartment—was cited as giving the children more freedom to run and play in the house without the constant repressive demands of the parents. Also, the additional space inside the house, according to the respondents, allows the children to have a place of their own within the house, and permits them to "be children" without constantly "being on top" of their parents. Naps are less interfered with in the quiet of the suburbs.

Only a quarter of the responses having to do with moving for the children's sake referred to social factors. The most frequent reason was the belief that the schools would be better in that classes would be smaller, more individual attention would be given by the teachers, and the teachers in the suburbs would be more interested in the children as well as generally more competent than those in Chicago. Other features concerning the social aspect of suburban living thought to be better for children were the following: other children of about the same age to serve as playmates for the respondent's children; more organized activities available for children; owning one's own home, which gives the children a sense of security they could never get in an apartment; other adults in the suburbs have children and, therefore, the adults treat all children with understanding; and better churches in the suburbs to which the children can go.

In 9 per cent of these responses (a third of those classed as "social") there were words to the effect that there were "nicer" children in the suburbs to serve as playmates for one's children. When this reason was given, extensive probing was employed to determine whether or not an upward mobility motif was involved. In one case this seemed to be so. The mother said, "We moved here mainly because of my daughter. The environment and schools are better, and her companions are of high caliber." (Interviewer probed "high caliber.") "I mean more highly educated families." (Interviewer asked what difference that made.) "If it's a girl I suppose you're thinking of who she's going to marry and grow up with." (Pause.) "When it comes down to it, it's a matter of income isn't it? We want to give our child the best possible chance." (Interviewer asked what she meant by "chance.") "So she can enjoy life to the fullest and live graciously, I suppose."

This case was an exception, however, for probing indicated that other respondents giving this response seemed to be referring to their belief that there are fewer "juvenile delinquents" and "bad" influences among their children's playmates in the suburbs. Thus, the response generally seems to indicate a maintenance of present social status rather than upward mobility aspirations for children.

Three-fourths of the respondents (Table 22) gave reasons for their move to the suburbs which have been classified as "enjoying life more." These are shown in detail in Table 24. In these reasons, social features were mentioned more often than the physical features of the suburbs as being important influences in the decision to move. The respondents expected more friendly neighbors,

TABLE 24
Percentage Distribution of Specific Reasons in the "Enjoy Life More" Category

Specific Reasons for Moving to the Suburbs	Per Cent
Physical reasons (N = 141):	44.1
"The outdoors" (fresh air, sunshine, etc.)	13.1
Gardening and "puttering around the house"	10.9
Quiet	7.2
Less crowded	6.6
Cleaner	4.1
More modern conveniences in house	2.2
Social reasons (N = 179):	55.9
Friendly neighbors	14.1
Feeling of belonging	8.8
Easier living, slower pace	8.1
Home of own (investment)	7.2
Privacy	4.1
Age, marital, and family status the same	4.1
Financial status the same	3.1
"Higher class" of people	2.8
Education the same	1.2
Racial stock the same	1.2
Friends moved here	0.9
Occupational level the same	0.3
Total reasons in this category (N = 320)	100.0

greater participation in the community, and easier living at a slower pace than they had had in the city.

Another theme was the "people-like-ourselves" idea. Some respondents said they wanted to live in a neighborhood where people had the same age, marital, family, financial, educational, occupational, or ethnic status as themselves. Ten per cent of the responses fell into this category, and extensive probing seemed to indicate that the mobility motif was not involved. Instead, it appeared that it was more a matter of feeling more comfortable and having more in common with persons of similar interests. For example, a white-collar man living in a predominantly blue-collar block indicated that he would move elsewhere in the suburbs because he didn't have much of a common interest with his neighbors. He went on to say that his chief concern, although by no means his only one, was the fact that none of his neighbors played bridge.

Only 9 per cent of the respondents indicated that one of their reasons for moving to the suburbs was that they expected a "higher class" of person to be living there as compared with the central city. When probed on this point, the respondents referred to higher education and income, better occupations—especially engineering and sales occupations—good manners, quiet rather than loud and boisterous habits, a gracious manner of living, and intelligence. Certainly, a mobility motif must be admitted in most of these cases, but even here some persons seemed to be trying to find a group of persons "like themselves" with which to live, rather than trying to "better themselves" socially.

The physical features which attracted these suburbanites were the fresh air, sunshine, growing trees and other characteristics of the "open country" in contrast to the central city; also, the opportunity to garden and to "putter" around their "own home" was important. The quiet, lack of congestion, and cleanliness of the suburbs were also mentioned, as was the fact that a new house with modern conveniences was to be had in the suburbs for a lower price than its equivalent in the city.

As is also shown in Table 22, a fifth of the respondents said that the husband's job was a factor in their move to the suburbs. Of these, more than half were transferred without a promotion or increase in salary or were just moving closer to a job which they had held for some time. The others, 9 per cent of the respondents, indicated that their move was a consequence of upward mobility, although none felt that their move was consequential for future increases on the job.

SOCIAL CHOICE TYPES

The following interpretation should be accepted with caution since these findings may not hold for the movement into suburbs of different types from those studied here. Even though a fairly wide range with respect to value of homes and occupations of the respondents was included in the sample, different reasons for moving may be found in other types of suburbs, such as industrial suburbs or suburbs in which only families of the very top socio-economic stratum reside. For the two suburbs studied, however, the findings are quite convincing.

The respondents were classified with respect to the dominant theme underlying their reasons for moving to the suburbs. Upward vertical mobility does not seem to be greatly associated with choosing to live in the suburbs, despite the contention of some recent writers. In fact, only 10 per cent of the respondents could be classified as having upward mobility aspirations involved in their move to the suburbs, and even here most of these persons also had other reasons for moving.

On the other hand, 31 per cent of the respondents can be classified as exemplifying pure familism, and a familistic orientation entered into the decision to move to the suburbs in a total of 83 per cent of the cases. That familism as it enters into the suburban move is largely "conjugal familism" is indicated by the fact that only a relatively small percentage of the respondents moved in order to be closer to relatives not living with them while a much larger percentage indicated that they moved "because of the children." In fact, several who moved because of the children also noted that it was a little farther away from their relatives—a condition which they considered desirable.

In many of the responses which were categorized as familistic, it was evident that the respondents tended to think of the move to the suburbs in terms of the move from an apartment to a house. Thus, some respondents pointed out that if they could have found the same house in the city they would have preferred to live in the city. Although they realized such sections did exist within the city, they also noted that homes in them cost more than in the suburbs. Also in these responses there was the definite notion that the move from apartment to house was mutually beneficial for parent and child. In fact, several of the wives, according to their own testimony, had been on the verge of nervous collapse living with small children in an apartment. Since moving to a house in the suburbs, they reported they were no longer "nervous."

In general, the respondents reported moving because of the children, but they also reported that since they had lived in the suburbs they had learned to enjoy "suburban living" so much that they would never move back to the city. Seven per cent of the respondents, however, said that they would move back to an apartment in the city as soon as their children were married.

Ten per cent of the respondents were classified as pure examples of the consumership pattern, and an additional 43 per cent gave consumership reasons along with other reasons.

The three original life styles did not seem adequate to account for all of the responses given. A fourth theme, labeled the "quest-for-community," was apparent. This was the idea of moving to the suburbs to get more friendly neighbors, greater community participation, and a sense of belonging to the community. About 73 per cent of the respondents included such reasons as important factors in their decision to move to the suburbs, and usually this was in conjunction with the familistic orientation.

Thus the data support the hypothesis that the new suburbanites are largely persons who have chosen familism as an important element in their life styles, and in addition suggest a relationship between the desire for community participation or sense of belonging and the move to the suburbs.

When suburbs mushroomed in the United States following the Second World War, their homogeneity was exaggerated. Very few suburbs are Westfields. Some have a working-class flavor. For example, a suburban tract in Milpitas, California, is inhabited by Ford auto workers who relocated along with their plant.[25]

[25] Bennett M. Berger, *Working Class Suburb: A Study of Auto Workers in Suburbia*, Berkeley: University of California Press, 1960.

Most suburbs, however, have an intermediate socioeconomic character. The *culture* of the suburbs, as Professor Bell points out, is family oriented. Educators remark on the preoccupation with education.[26] Readership of newspapers and magazines is high. Thus, in one sense suburbia *is* homogeneous. Its cultural climate supports urban industrial society because a large proportion of its people function adequately within the institutions of that society.

A HIGH RATE OF GEOGRAPHIC MOBILITY. An apparent exception to the image of suburban stability is the high rate of population turnover. In Westfield, for instance, 23.5 per cent of the population five years old and over came from some other county than the one in which Westfield is located within the five-year period preceding the 1960 census.[27] This high rate of residential mobility is not, however, incompatible with family stability. As William H. Whyte, Jr., observes in his book, *The Organization Man*, business and professional men accept "transfers" as a matter of course; transiency is a way of life.

The Mobile American

Reprinted by permission. From William H. Whyte, Jr., *The Organization Man*, New York: Simon & Schuster, 1956, pp. 269–271, 275.

The man who leaves home is not the exception in American society but the key to it. Almost by definition, the organization man is a man who left home and, as it was said of the man who went from the Midwest to Harvard, kept on going. There have always been people who left home, and the number of them is not decreasing but increasing—and so greatly that those who stay put in the home town are often as affected by the emigration as those who leave.

When a man moves from one place to an-

26 James B. Conant, *Slums and Suburbs: A Commentary on Schools in Metropolitan Areas*, New York: McGraw-Hill, 1961.
27 Bureau of the Census, *United States Census of Population: 1960, United States Summary, Detailed Characteristics*, Washington: Government Printing Office, 1963, p. xxii.

other he is not necessarily moving socially. If we look at the figures for geographic mobility, however, we find that there is a rough connection between the two kinds of movement. Consider the relationship between the physical movement and age, education, and occupation. Men in the twenty-five-to-thirty-four age group are only 7.5 per cent of the total population, but they account for 12.4 per cent of the migration. The second characteristic is education: the more of it, the more mobility. If a man goes to college now, the chances are almost even that he won't end up in his home state. Recent census figures and *Time*'s study, *They Went to College*, indicate that the educational level is higher among migrants than nonmigrants, and the higher the educational level, the more intensive the migration. Only 27.3 per cent of high-school grads aged twenty-five to thirty-four, for example, were interstate migrants, versus 45.5 per cent of those who had had at least one year of college. Of those who worked their way through in a college outside their home state, 69 per cent don't come back. And for all college men, incidentally, the higher the grades, the more likely they are to move. Next, income. As the correlation with education would suggest, the more the mobility, the more one is likely to be in the higher income brackets. Census figures do not break down migration by income groups, but the experience of direct-mail people indicates that address changes are most frequent in the $5,000 and over bracket. There are also indications that address changes are becoming more frequent in this group. In 1953, 14.8 per cent of *Fortune*'s subscribers changed addresses during the year. In 1954, 16.6 per cent, and in 1955, 17.4 per cent.

Records of long-distance movers show the same concentration of organization people. The greatest single group of their clients—between 40 and 50 per cent—is composed of corporation people being transferred from one post to another (with the corporation directly paying the bill). If to this group are added government, Army and Navy people, and corporation people leaving one company for another, roughly three quarters of all moves are accounted for by members of large organizations. . . .

The export movement that brings them together has become thoroughly basic to our society. It is no longer a case of the special boy who had to get out of town to cross the tracks to find an outlet for his energies; now as many as three quarters of the town's young college men may be in the same position. Where are they to go after college? Back home? Lawyers and doctors can, and the majority do; they are in the happy position of being able to go home, to keep professionally alert, and to make a good bit of money at the same time. But for the others, opportunity seems to be elsewhere—not just for the delivery boy who became an Air Force lieutenant, but for the young man on the Hill who's gone off to join Du Pont. . . .

Let me turn for a moment to corporation transfer policy, for it helps illuminate the self-perpetuating nature of the mobility. When the recruit joins up he does not do so because he *wants* to move a lot, and it is often in spite of it. But moving, he knows, has become part of the bargain, and unsettling as transfer might be, even more unsettling are the implications of not being asked to transfer. "We never plan to transfer," as one company president explains a bit dryly, "and we never make a man move. Of course, he kills his career if he doesn't. But we never *make* him do it." The fact is well understood; it is with a smile that the recruit moves—and keeps on moving—year after year, until, perhaps, that distant day when he is summoned back to Rome.

It is not just more moves per man. Even companies reporting no increase in the number of times each individual moves report an increase in the sheer number of men being moved. G.E. has compared a cross section of its forty-five-year-old executives with one of its thirty-five-year-olds. In the ten years after they were twenty-five, 42 per cent of the older group had moved at least once; during the same age period, 58 per cent of the younger had moved.

Corporations never planned it quite that way. Decentralization and expansion, rather than deliberate personnel policy, have determined the pattern. Companies have systematized it, to be sure. Moves are settling into more of a rhythm, and almost invariably they are sweetened by special departments that handle all the housekeeping fuss of the trip. By and large, however, the question of the man's personal development—however emphasized when the boss breaks the news to him—has been secondary to the day-to-day necessity of filling vacancies out in the empire.

Business and professional families move from one part of the United States to another. Homes are sold and new ones bought. New friendships are developed; children are enrolled in different schools; charge accounts are opened in other stores. Yet the impact on family life and community organization does not seem appreciable. The moving about takes place with so little disruption partly because of the homogeneity of American communities. Westfield, New Jersey may be three thousand miles from Palo Alto, California, but each is an affluent suburb on the periphery of a metropolis; this socioeconomic similarity means that a Westfielder understands the way of life in Palo Alto even before he moves there. The organization man moves from one urban community to another very much like it; hence he feels "transferred," but not uprooted. Second, in a society in which moving around is so common, geographic mobility is the normal expectation. Only 6.3 per cent of the Americans enumerated in the 1960 census (including infants!) were living in the houses they occupied at birth.[28] People who feel justified in moving to a new community out of boredom or a desire for adventure are psychologically prepared for the adjustments that moves entail.

These considerations are most relevant for the *interurban* moves of white-collar persons. For poorly educated, rural Negroes, migration to urban areas *is* a threatening experience. This is the exception that proves the rule. Migration has an entirely different meaning to a Mississippi farm laborer who moves to Chicago and an electronics engineer who is transferred from New York to San Francisco. An industrial society is never wholly industrialized. Preindustrial population elements persist, often in rural areas. In the United States, the preindustrial minority consists mostly of visible ethnic groups: Negroes, Puerto Ricans, Mexicans. Thus, problems of prejudice and intergroup relations make economic and educational up-

28 Bureau of the Census, *United States Census of Population: 1960, United States Summary*, Washington: Government Printing Office, 1962, p. 205.

grading and the move into the in-group more difficult.

DEMORALIZATION OF THE OUT-GROUP: THE CULTURE OF POVERTY

Poverty in industrial societies is quantitatively if not qualitatively different from poverty in many underdeveloped countries of Asia, Africa, and Latin America. It is concentrated in the backwaters; it is not mass poverty. Even in agriculture, where poverty is a legacy of the preindustrial era,[29] it is dwindling as scientific production techniques spread. In the United States, for example, the misery of migrant laborers and their families will become an historical curiosity as mechanical crop pickers take over more and more of the toil of harvesting. Meanwhile, however, the migrant labor problem has been called a national disgrace.

A Pocket of Poverty in the Rural United States: Migrant Labor

Reprinted by permission. From Paul Jacobs, "The Forgotten People," *The Reporter*, Vol. 20, Jan. 22, 1959, pp. 13–30.

The hired farm work force in the United States is composed of three main groups: regular workers, seasonally employed workers, and the foreign farmhands, mostly Mexicans brought in under a special program approved by Congress. The seven hundred thousand regular hired workers, those employed for more than 150 days a year by one employer, are almost all male; they take care of livestock, repair buildings, maintain equipment, drive tractors, and generally work without supervision. Frequently they live on or near the farm where they are employed. About half of this group are hired by the largest farms; forty-eight per cent of them are working for farms of more than 1,900 acres.

The million seasonal farm workers normally work less than 150 days in a year, and they work for more than one employer. They do work that

[29] Conference on Economic Progress, *Poverty and Deprivation in the U.S.: the Plight of Two-Fifths of a Nation*, Washington: Conference on Economic Progress, April 1962, p. 48.

can be completed in a short time and are usually paid by the day, hour, or piece. They clear land, lay fertilizer, chop, weed, and do the harvest work —cutting, picking, packing, and toting. Forty-eight per cent of all hired seasonal workers were employed on the two largest groups of cotton and fruit-and-nut farms in Texas, California, Arkansas, Mississippi, Louisiana, Tennessee, and North Carolina.

The seasonal farm workers split into two main groups: the larger group of local day-haul employees who may go out with a different farmer each day and are picked up by truck from a central employment point; and the much smaller number of migrants, mostly employed by labor contractors in the South and West and by crew leaders in the East. The contractors or crew leaders take the migrants from farm to farm along the migrant stream. They set a flat price with the farmer for the harvesting work, then paying the workers from their own pockets, or else they get a commission from the farmer for each worker supplied. The lush financial rewards open to an unscrupulous labor contractor are obviously tempting, and there has been a sharp increase in the number of people with criminal records who have applied for contractors' licenses in California.

There are six major streams of migratory workers:

(1) The one on the Atlantic Coast is made up of about 60,000 workers, most of whom are Negro, supplemented by workers from Puerto Rico and Mexican-Americans.

(2) The sugar-beet stream starts in Texas and goes up into the North Central and Mountain States. This group, too, consists of about 60,000 workers, almost all Mexican-Americans.

(3) The wheat and small-grain harvest migrants also come up from Texas, generally as combine teams, and work north to Montana and North Dakota. About 30,000 men, also of Mexican descent, do this work.

(4) About 80,000 workers of Mexican descent plus Negroes harvest cotton, starting out from Texas with one group moving off into the Mississippi Delta and a bigger one going westward into New Mexico, Arizona, and southern California.

(5) From Oklahoma, Arkansas, and western Tennessee, about 30,000 people of early American stock move north and west during the

harvest season, picking fruit and tomatoes.
(6) Finally, there are about 120,000 workers, of all backgrounds, working in the Western States, up and down the Pacific Coast.

In addition to the 380,000 American migrant workers, about half a million foreign farm laborers are brought into the United States each year. Most of these are the "braceros" from Mexico, who more and more are replacing the seasonal American workers, both local and migrant.

Seventy-five per cent of the regular year-round farm workers and nearly fifty per cent of all the seasonal workers were employed by only little more than one-tenth of all the farmers. Thus one-tenth of farmers cultivate nearly half the land, producing three-fifths of all the vegetables, nearly half of all the fruits and nuts, and two-fifths of all the cotton. Since 1940, the number of the nation's farms has declined from 6,350,-000 to less than 5,000,000 in 1957. At the same time, the average farm increased from 174 acres in 1940 to more than 242 acres in 1954.

The average yearly income for all farm workers is only $1,250, including all nonfarm cash income and roughly $200 for perquisites. Farm workers, in fact, only receive twice as much pay now as they did in 1933, even though farm productivity has gone up nearly threefold since then. In some farm work, like the picking of cotton, the real value of the wages paid to the farm workers has actually declined since 1943.

It is because farm workers have such a low income level that so many of their children work alongside them in the fields. The money earned by the children is essential to keep the family on even a bare below-subsistence level. And so the children grow up badly educated because local schools are reluctant to take them as pupils, sickly because medical facilities are not easily available to them.

Why does this large group of people continue in farm work? Primarily because no other work is open to them. The minority groups among them find that much industrial employment is closed to them, while the white workers are generally unskilled and are ill adapted to urban life. The kind of lives they lead incapacitates them— and their children—for leading any other. And so they go on living as regular farmhands in shabby houses on the fringes of agricultural communities or on the farms, the migrants in tents, barracks, and occasionally decent camps.

ALL NIGHT IN A TRUCK

These men, women, and children are utterly exhausted after working long hours in the field. Many of the children suffer from chronic diarrhea. They get horribly cramped, traveling long distances without sleep in broken-down trucks. And if some growers had their way, the trucks would never stop for rest. When the Interstate Commerce Commission held a hearing in May, 1957, to consider setting up safety regulations to govern interstate transportation of farm workers, it was informed by S. H. Butler of the Green Giant Company, Dayton, Wisconsin: "We feel that the requirement banning travel from 8:00 P.M. to 6:00 A.M. would work a hardship on the laborers being transported as well as upon employers. It has been our experience that these trucks can complete the trip from Texas to Washington in from fifty to sixty hours, with stops only for meals, gasoline, and general 'stretching.' The men seem to arrive in good physical condition and with a good mental attitude."

At the same 1957 ICC hearing, the Tri-State Packers Association, Inc., of Easton, Maryland, protested a proposal that trucks carrying farm workers be required to have seats. "The floors of the truck in which the persons are transported are normally covered with bedding or sacks of clothing which provide a more suitable resting place than would seats of the type suggested by the Commission—the requirement that seats be provided appears to be extremely undesirable. It is unsatisfactory as a safety measure for the reason that if seats are not provided, the transients will sit or lie on bedding or clothing and they would be in far less danger in the event of a sudden stop than would be true if they were sitting on wooden benches. In addition, these trucks are used to haul produce to the processor—it would be practically impossible to attach the seats securely and still use the vehicle to haul produce."

But a lack of seats did not act "as a safety measure" for the forty-one American men, women, and child farm workers jammed into the eight-by-fifteen-foot back of a dilapidated one-and-a-half-ton truck that pulled out from the side of a North Carolina highway on June 6, 1957, directly into the path of a ten-ton tractor-trailer. Seconds later, after a grinding crash, twenty broken and mutilated bodies were strewn over the highway. Of the forty-one who had been crammed together in that tiny space without seats, only five were unhurt. The North Carolina crash broke the record for this kind of accident—a record set previously in August, 1947, in Texas, when nineteen farm workers were killed.

Just as on the national level some powerful farm organizations bitterly—and usually successfully—resist any Federal regulation that affects them (except increased subsidies, of course), so too on the state level is the farm worker left unprotected. The prospects for including farm workers under the compensation acts are "bleak," writes Harold Katz, an authority on workmen's compensation law, "since farm organizations, which have traditionally opposed such coverage, exert considerable influence in our state legislatures."

The extent of the influence of farm organizations on state legislatures can easily be seen even in a state like California, where farm workers are somewhat better off than in many other states. A California state law provides that an illegally employed minor who suffers an accident while working shall receive an additional fifty per cent increased payment in workmen's compensation, paid by the employer—unless the employer is a farmer. In that case, the penalty payment is not made.

Why this exception? State officials shrug. "It's the farm lobby in Sacramento," they say. "That lobby has lots of power."

Efforts have been made to arouse public concern over the conditions under which migrant laborers work and live. The Columbia Broadcasting System documented their situation in an hour-long television program entitled "Harvest of Shame" and narrated by Edward R. Murrow. One reason the problem persists is that the American Farm Bureau Federation and other farm lobbies have managed to prevent effective regulatory legislation from being passed. In only a handful of states are farm workers covered by workmen's compensation laws—even though agriculture has more accidents than any other industry, except mining and construction.[30] Similarly, the federal minimum wage law specifically exempts agriculture.

[30] Paul Jacobs, "The Forgotten People," *The Reporter*, Vol. 20, Jan. 22, 1959, p. 13.

Exceptions such as these, by keeping labor costs down, reduce the incentive for introducing labor-saving harvesting equipment. The exceptions have been permitted because population shifts from rural to urban areas have not yet resulted in proportional shifts in political power. These exceptions are concessions to the political power of rural legislators, especially from the South—concessions made partly because farm laborers are predominantly Negroes and other low-status minorities. Despite the democratic ideal of equal protection under law for all citizens, discrimination against certain ethnic groups is traditional in the United States. This discrimination contributes to the migrant labor problem as well as to the more persistent problem of *urban* poverty.

To identify ethnic minorities with the "culture of poverty" would be an oversimplification. Large numbers of Negroes, Puerto Ricans, Mexican-Americans, Indians, and Orientals have completed high school; they work at white-collar jobs, and own their homes. On the other hand, white Protestants can be found in the worst slums, living on welfare allowances. Still, there can be no doubt that the underdogs of American society come disproportionately from visible ethnic minorities. In 1960 more than 60 per cent of nonwhite families had less than $4000 a year income as compared with less than 30 per cent of the white families.[31] Furthermore, income does not tell the complete story; discrimination in rental housing, hotel and restaurant accommodations, recreational facilities, and educational opportunities compound the cultural poverty of many nonwhites. The incredible congestion and dilapidation of the Negro neighborhoods of New York, Chicago, Cleveland, and other large American cities reflects not only Negro poverty but also the resistance to Negro "invasion" of white neighborhoods.

The logic of urban industrial societies denies ethnic considerations. Gypsy or Slav, white or Negro, Jew or Hindu, all racial and ethnic groups can participate in an industrial

[31] Conference on Economic Progress, *op. cit.*, p. 59.

society because all are potentially literate; all can adapt to the factory system; all are willing to live in cities. If one considers only the requirements of industrialism, one might conclude that urban industrial societies are gigantic melting pots in which ethnic origin is becoming less and less important. However, a society is a prisoner of its ethnic history. Although slavery has not existed in the United States for more than a century, the place of Negroes in contemporary American cities is affected by the circumstance that their ancestors were slaves brought here to work as farm laborers. To varying degrees, the Lapps in Sweden, the Eta in Japan, the Irish in England, the Moslem North Africans in France, and the Indonesians in Holland are also disadvantaged in their respective societies. Cultural pluralism sounds workable, and ethnic cleavages lead to demonstrable inefficiencies and problems. Nevertheless, prejudice and discrimination do not automatically disappear, as the following analysis of American metropolitan areas demonstrates.

Racial Cleavages within American Metropolitan Areas

Reprinted by permission. From Morton Grodzins, *The Metropolitan Area as a Racial Problem*, Pittsburgh: University of Pittsburgh Press, 1958, pp. 1–13.

Some 95 million people, more than half the population of the United States, now live in what the Bureau of the Census defines as a standard metropolitan area: a central city of at least 50 thousand population with its ring of satellite communities "essentially metropolitan in character and socially and economically integrated with the central city." Fewer than one-third of the nation's population lived within these areas in 1900; slightly more than half resided there in 1950; and it is estimated that 70 per cent of the nation's total population will be metropolitan area dwellers by 1975.

The fourteen largest metropolitan areas, those with populations of over one million, contain more than half of the total metropolitan population and almost one-third of the nation's. These areas attract the largest number of Negro in-migrants from the South, and in them, generally, Negroes constitute a larger proportion of the total population. The consequences of the urban-suburban racial and class bifurcation, therefore, are most acute in these largest metropolitan areas. Some smaller metropolitan areas face the same problems in less acute form while others, because of their small number of Negroes, do not face them at all.

For several decades the Negro population of the great cities has been increasing more rapidly than the white population. The great changes come in time of full employment, and the explosive growth, as measured by the decennial censuses, took place between 1940 and 1950. In that decade, the total population of the fourteen largest metropolitan areas increased by 19 per cent, the total Negro percentage gain (65.1 per cent) being more than four times greater than the white increase (15.6 per cent). Negroes increased proportionately more rapidly in both central cities and suburbs, but the significant growth differential was inside the great cities. Whites increased by 3.7 per cent, Negroes 67.8 per cent. (For individual cities, see Figure 6.) The Negro population at least doubled in four central cities while whites in five cities decreased in number.

As late as 1950 non-whites constituted only a minor fraction of the total population in most of the central cities of the fourteen largest metropolitan areas. Washington, D.C., with non-whites totalling 35.4 per cent of total population, and Baltimore (23.8 per cent) had the largest group of non-whites in proportion to total population. In addition to these, only three other cities had 1950 Negro populations in excess of 15 per cent; three had less than 10 per cent.

Continued Negro migration, the comparatively greater rate of natural increase among non-whites, and the exodus of whites to the suburbs will dramatically raise the proportion of non-whites in central cities. The few special censuses that have been made since 1950 indicate this trend. In Los Angeles non-whites moved up from 6.5 per cent of the population in 1940, to 11 per cent in 1950, to 14 per cent in 1956. In Chicago, according to a careful unofficial estimate by Otis Dudley Duncan and Beverly Duncan of the University of Chicago, Negroes now comprise 19 per cent of the total, compared with 8 per cent in 1940. The city is expected to be one-third Negro by 1970. An official census in New York City showed that non-whites in the nation's largest city increased by 41 per cent from 1950 to 1957, while the white population decreased by 6 per cent. Non-whites made up 13 per cent of New York's population in 1957, as compared with 6 per cent in 1940 and 10 per cent in 1950. (Only a tiny fraction of New York's Puerto Rican population is enumerated as being "non-white.") New York City officials have forecast that in 1970 Negroes and Puerto Ricans together will constitute 45 per cent of the population of Manhattan and nearly one-third of the entire city. Washington, D.C. may already have an actual Negro majority.

Estimates of future population trends must take into account some reurbanization of white suburbanites as the proportion of older people increases and the suburbs become less attractive to those whose children have grown up and left home. Even making allowances for shifts of this

sort, all evidence makes it highly probable that within 30 years Negroes will constitute from 25 to 50 per cent of the total population in at least 10 of the 14 largest central cities.

The suburbs of the metropolitan areas exhibit very different population trends. Negroes made up only 4 per cent of their population in 1940 and less than 5 per cent in 1950. (Central city non-whites were 9 per cent of total population in 1940, 13.2 per cent in 1950.)

Some suburban areas experienced non-white percentage gains between 1940 and 1950, and even the fourteen-area totals show Negro increases greater than white ones. But the actual number of Negroes was small. A suburban non-white gain of 130 per cent in Minneapolis-St. Paul, for example, represented an actual increase of exactly 337 persons. Moreover, even the non-white "suburban" increases noted are rarely to the suburbs themselves. Rather they largely represent Negro migration to the smaller industrial towns within the metropolitan rings of the central cities. Spe-

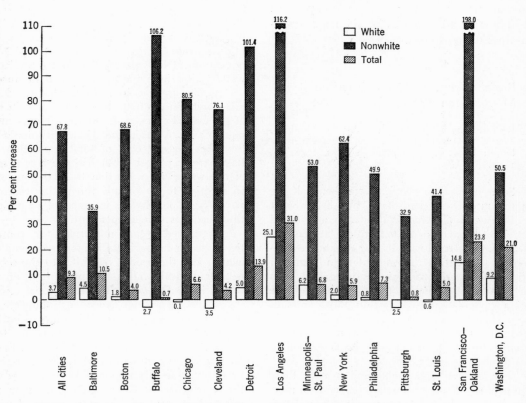

FIGURE 6. Center cities: largest metropolitan areas population growth, by race, 1940–1950.

cial censuses made of suburban places since 1950 strengthen the impression of Negro exclusion. There is evidence of absolute decreases in the numbers of Negroes in some suburban areas; in other areas there has been a movement of one or two non-white families into all-white communities. The only statistically significant suburban growth of Negro population, however, has taken place in industrial fringe cities—Gary, Indiana, for example—or in segregated Negro dormitory communities—Robbins, Illinois, for example.

The growing racial schism of population between central cities and suburbs is revealed sharply in the megaphone-like lines of Figure 7. There is no exception in the 14 cities to the pattern of a widening gap between Negro city percentages and Negro suburban percentages. Where Negroes in 1940 were proportionally most numerous in both central cities and suburbs (as in Baltimore and Washington, D.C.), the subsequent decade saw non-whites decrease markedly as a percentage of suburban populations and increase markedly as a percentage of central city populations. This record very likely traces the future for other cities whose urban-suburban population distribution by race in 1950 approximated the 1940 distribution of Baltimore and Washington.

The general picture of the future is clear enough: large non-white concentrates (in a few cases, majorities) in the principal central cities; large white majorities, with segregated Negro enclaves, in the areas outside.

GROWTH PATTERNS WITHIN CITIES

The pattern of Negro population growth within the central cities follows established and well-understood patterns. It is based upon in-migration from the South, and it is accelerated by a larger rate of natural increase of the non-white in-migrants in comparison with the older white residents. Migration has been the source of the largest increase in most non-southern cities, and continued industrial expansion may actually increase this movement in the years immediately ahead. The "push" from the South may grow stronger as the consequence of growing white antagonisms following attempts to enforce the Supreme Court's nonsegregation decisions. And

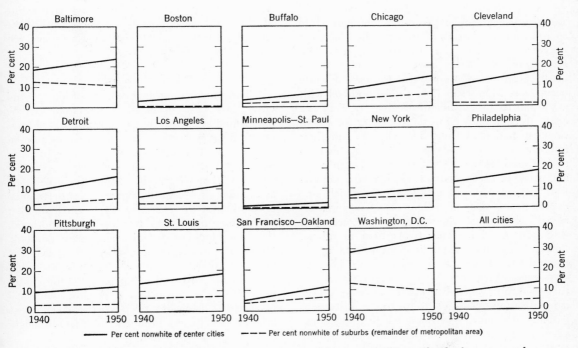

FIGURE 7. Largest metropolitan areas, per cent non-whites, center cities and suburbs, 1940 and 1950.

the "pull" of the northern cities may become more forceful as the Negro communities there become larger and more firmly established and as information concerning job and other opportunities correspondingly flows back to relatives and friends. On the other hand, the relatively more rapid natural increase of Negroes, in comparison with white residents, will almost certainly become less striking with the passage of years.

The spatial expansion of Negro population in the larger cities follows roughly similar patterns. One universal rule is that residential concentrations are segregated. In every major city with a considerable number of Negroes there exists a "black belt" or a series of "black areas." In Chicago, 79 per cent of all Negroes in 1950 lived in census tracts in which at least 75 per cent of the residents were Negroes. At the opposite extreme, 84 per cent of the non-Negroes resided in census tracts in which less than 1 per cent of the residents were Negro, and the disparity would be even higher if Negro servants "living in" were not counted. Chicago's segregation pattern is somewhat extreme, but all cities follow this pattern. Negroes live preponderantly or exclusively with Negroes, whites with whites.

A second rule is equally general: once an urban area begins to swing from predominant white to predominant Negro occupancy, the change is rarely reversed. Between 1920 and 1950 in Chicago there are no cases in which areas of predominantly Negro residents reverted to areas of white occupancy. More than this, a neighborhood with a substantial proportion of Negroes (say 25 per cent) rarely retains its mixed character for a considerable period of time. The Duncans, in their intensive study of neighborhood changes in Chicago, found not a single instance between 1940 and 1950 of a census tract "with mixed population (25–75 per cent non-white) in which succession from white to Negro occupancy was arrested" though, as they remark, the succession was more rapid in some tracts than in others. Postwar programs of public housing and urban renewal have somewhat altered this rule, in some cases establishing new Negro concentrates where they had not previously existed and in others demonstrating that relatively stable interracial patterns of living can be achieved. But new housing programs in predominantly Negro areas have for the most part meant the simple exchange of one Negro population group for another; and

urban renewal programs, by displacing Negro families in one area, have frequently had the effect of hastening the succession of adjacent areas to all-Negro occupancy.

A third generalization is that the pattern of Negro residential expansion is from the core of the city outward. The original concentration is almost everywhere near the center of the city. It subsequently expands radially or in concentric circles. A map by zones for virtually every city with a sizeable Negro population shows higher percentages of Negro residence in areas closest to the city center with decreasing proportions as the distance from the city center increases.

A fourth generalization is also possible. The Negro population moves generally into areas already characterized by high residential mobility. Furthermore, there is a rough comparability between the social characteristics of the in-migrant Negro population and the out-migrant white population with respect to such factors as educational attainment, rate of unemployment, room crowding, home ownership, and white collar employment. Lower-class Negroes, in other words, tend to move into lower-class neighborhoods; middle-class Negroes into middle-class neighborhoods. The "piling up" process—the gross overcrowding of dwellings and areas—occurs only after the transition from white to Negro dominance has taken place.

THE "TIPPING" MECHANISM

The process by which whites of the central cities leave areas of Negro in-migration can be understood as one in the social-psychology of "tipping a neighborhood." The variations are numerous, but the theme is universal. Some white residents will not accept Negroes as neighbors under any conditions. But others, sometimes willingly as a badge of liberality, sometimes with trepidation, will not move if a relatively small number of Negroes move into the same neighborhood, the same block, or the same apartment building. Once the proportion of non-whites exceeds the limits of the neighborhood's tolerance for interracial living (this is the "tip point"), the whites move out. The proportion of Negroes who will be accepted before the tip point is reached varies from city to city and from neighborhood to neighborhood.

The process is not the simple one of "flight" that is a part of the real estate mythology of changing neighborhoods. It may take a number of years before the "invaded" neighborhood becomes an all-Negro one. Nor is the phenomenon uniformly one in which Negroes "push" whites out. As already noted, areas of heavy Negro inmigration are most often areas already characterized by high mobility; and the process of Negroes taking up vacancies as they occur cannot be conceived as one in which the old residents have been "pushed." This is to say that tipping may come slowly and does not necessarily indicate any immediate downgrading of the given neighborhood. What it signifies is the unwillingness of white groups to live in proximity to large numbers of Negroes.

Many people in many ways for many purposes have explored how the tip point operates. Real estate operators, seeking the higher revenues that come with Negro overcrowding, talk freely among themselves about "tipping a building" or "tipping a neighborhood." (Sometimes this can be done by selling a single house to a "block busting" family.) Quakers in the Philadelphia suburbs of Concord Park and Greenbelt Knoll have utilized the tip point for the opposite purpose: to build interracial communities. They have concluded that this goal can be achieved only if the proportion of Negroes is rigidly controlled and does not exceed the point at which whites (even Quakers) will refuse to participate. An official of these developments has written: "Early in our sales program we found that white buyers would not buy without assurance that Negroes would be in a minority."

Public housing officials have faced the tip-point phenomenon from another angle. In some Eastern cities it is possible to maintain low cost housing projects on an interracial basis as long as non-whites do not exceed roughly 20 per cent of the total residents. Once this point is reached, whites will not remain in, or move into, the project. One method used to combat the process of tipping public housing has been to raise rents. This has the effect of decreasing the number of Negroes who can afford to live in the projects. So the tip point leads to a shifting of public housing goals, subordinating the first principle of low rentals to that of maintaining interracial occupancy.

In a few areas around the country Negroes and whites live side by side without fuss or fanfare. This is true even in Chicago, where segregation patterns are extreme, and examples of "open occupancy" can be found from New York to San Francisco. Furthermore, in recent years, there has been a tendency for a single Negro family— usually of considerable income and of the professions—to find a dwelling in an all-white neighborhood. In every such case of "interracial living," however, some factor—economic or other— limits the ingress of Negro residents.

Education and community organization can extend tolerance and thus increase the proportion of Negroes in a given area before the tip point is reached. But the limits have not proved to be infinitely elastic. Even where goodwill, community effort, and financing have been maximized, the psychology of tipping has operated. The only interracial communities in the United States, with the exception of some abject slums, are those where limits exist upon the influx of non-whites.

PATTERNS OF SUBURBAN EXCLUSION

The sheer cost of suburban housing excludes Negroes from many suburban areas. Furthermore, the social satisfactions of slum or near-slum existence for a homogeneous population have been insufficiently studied, and it is undoubtedly true that many Negro urban dwellers would not easily exchange life in all-Negro big-city neighborhoods for interracial suburban homes, even if moderately priced. The crucial fact, however, is that Negroes do not have any free choice in the matter. They are excluded from suburbia by a wide variety of devices.

Social antagonisms of suburban communities are themselves effective. Where it is plainly understood that Negroes are not wanted, Negro suburbanization is for all practical purposes impossible. In addition, suburban communities use their control of zoning, subdivision, and building regulations to achieve exclusion. Minimum lot sizes are increased to two or more acres; requirements for expensive street improvements are made —and then waived only in favor of "desirable" developments; large-scale building operations are defined as "business" for zoning purposes, thus excluding the possibility of low or moderate income suburban building; the suburb itself purchases all vacant land parcels that are large enough for subdivision and resells only to favored purchasers; builders are required to obtain certificates from the school board that educational accommodation will be adequate for the new residences;

ordinances regulating "look alike" features or requiring certain building materials make home building expensive.

Where legal barriers of this sort are not sufficient to maintain a "white only" policy, land use controls are used informally—and of course illegally—to exclude Negroes. A Philadelphia builder recently told an interviewer that he would very much like to sell suburban houses to Negroes, but that it was impossible because it would ruin him economically. "If I sold just one suburban home to a Negro, the local building inspectors would have me moving pipes three-eighths of an inch every afternoon in every one of the places I was building; and moving a pipe three-eighths of an inch is mighty expensive if you have to do it in concrete."

These practices are combined with social and economic pressures upon white owners of older homes and upon real estate brokers. Mortgage bankers habitually discriminate against the Negro buyer in the white neighborhood, and not always for purely economic reasons. Where all else fails, suburban residents have often turned to violence to prevent Negro occupancy. The total suburban façade is relatively impenetrable.

Suburban restrictions are everywhere aimed at Negroes as a racial group and not simply against people of low or moderate income. When such restrictions are applied uniformly, they of course also affect whites. But even this has an indirect effect upon the Negro concentrates within the cities. If middle- and lower-class whites who live next door to the slums were able to move to the suburbs, their places would quickly be taken by the slum-dwellers, especially those Negroes whose presence in the slums is due less to income than to the prejudice which excludes them from more desirable places. By raising the price of housing in the suburbs, land use regulations reduce the movement of the white middle and lower classes out of the city. And this in turn holds the slum-dweller in the slums and, accordingly, the Negro in the ghetto.

CONSEQUENCES OF POPULATION DISTRIBUTION

Some of the consequences of the urban-suburban racial and class schism are already apparent, and others can be reasonably predicted. SOCIAL CONSEQUENCES. Within the cities the first result is a spreading of slums. There is no free market for Negro housing. The Negro population always increases faster than the living space available to it. New areas that open up to Negro residence become grossly overcrowded by conversion of one-family houses to multiple dwellings and by squeezing two or more Negro families into apartments previously occupied by a single white one. Though complete statistical evidence is lacking, it is likely that Negroes pay substantially more rent for such accommodations than do whites, and the higher rent itself produces higher densities. Housing occupied by Negroes is more crowded, more dilapidated, and more lacking in amenities such as private baths than housing occupied by whites with equivalent incomes.

Income factors account in part for the condition of life of the Negro community. Negroes are heavily over-represented in low income jobs; in the menial services, in unskilled and semi-skilled factory labor, and in "dirty work" generally. In this respect they are not unlike some earlier immigrants to the city; the Irish and the Poles, for example, also settled mainly in the slums.

Like previous newcomers to the city tasting the freedom of urban life for the first time, a significant portion of the Negro group does not possess the stable patterns of thought and action that characterize the "better" older inhabitants. And, as with all immigrant groups, old community patterns of control do not operate well in the new environment. Family disorganization among urban Negroes is high as measured by such indices as broken marriages, families headed by females, and unrelated individuals living in the same household. The development of social stabilization pivoted on family and community ties takes place against great odds. How does a mother keep her teen-age son off the streets if an entire family must eat, sleep, and live in a single room? What utility can be found in sobriety among a society of drinkers and in a block of taverns? What opportunity for quiet amidst the din of a tightly packed, restless neighborhood?

The conditions of urban life, rather than socializing new Negro residents to "desirable" life patterns, frequently have the opposite effect. They encourage rowdiness, casual and competitive sexuality, and a readiness for combat. The result is that the neighborhoods acquired by Negro residents eventually spiral downward. Disease and crime rates are high. Family stability is further prejudiced. Filth accumulates. The slum spreads outward.

These very conditions of life in the predominantly Negro neighborhoods lead the larger population to resist the expansion of Negro residential areas. The racial attribute—skin color—is added to the social attributes of lower class behavior. And while Negroes, like other urban immigrants, can readily lose undesirable social attributes, they cannot lose their color. They therefore do not have the mobility of other immigrant groups. They are racially blocked, whatever their social *bona fides*.

The Negro "black belts" of the great American cities as a consequence are by no means homogeneous. The very concentration of population within them plus the visible badge of color give them a spurious air of likeness. They contain, in fact, wide ranges of every social attribute: from illiteracy to high learning, from filth to hospital-like hygienic standards, from poverty to riches, from political backwardness to sophistication. Though the casual observer of the "black belt" neighborhoods sees only slums, the fact is that in every such area there are sub-areas, frequently on the periphery of the high-density mass, that are anything but slums. These are usually neighborhoods of newest acquisition, inhabited by the well-to-do of the Negro community. Density is low, lawns and gardens are well-tended, church attendance is high, neatness and cleanliness are apparent, parental standards of propriety for children higher than for comparable white groups.

Negro neighborhoods in the shadows of white luxury apartments are not unknown; but the more usual pattern is for low-income non-Negroes to occupy a buffer zone between all-Negro and the better white neighborhoods. Some of these are themselves new migrants to the city: Southerners and Japanese-Americans in Chicago, Puerto Ricans in New York, for example. Others are old residents on the lower ends of the income scale, people who, like the Negroes themselves, do not find success in life, or life itself, easy.

With the exodus of middle and upper classes to the suburbs, lower-income groups constitute a larger and larger fraction of the population of the central cities. Members of these groups generally exhibit a greater degree of intolerance and racial prejudice than do other whites. And the increasing juxtaposing of the Negro and the low-income non-Negro populations produces increased interracial tensions. Shirley Star of the National Opinion Research Center has shown that the greatest white animosity towards Negroes is found on the edge of the expanding Negro residential areas where whites fear their block or neighborhood will soon be "invaded." In these lower class and lower-middle class transitional areas, violence is incipient. Individual differences within the minority group are ignored. A young white resident of such an area in Chicago recently beat a Negro to death with a hammer. "I just wanted to get one of them," he explained, "which one didn't matter."

The total situation produces Negro communities in which people live their whole lives without, or with minimum, contact with the other race. With a Negro population numbering in the hundreds of thousands, and with this population densely concentrated, one can live, eat, shop, work, play, and die in a completely Negro community. The social isolation of the northern urban Negro is, for very large numbers, more complete than it ever was for the Negro rural resident in the South.

Even in education, the urban residential segregation of the non-southern cities has produced consequences that are not dissimilar to what the South is trying to maintain by the use of violence and unconstitutional law. If segregation is defined not in legal terms but in the numbers of students who attend all-Negro schools, then it is undoubtedly true that more Negro students are segregated in the schools of New York and Chicago than in any other cities or some states.

This general picture of segregation needs some qualification. A small number of church groups have succeeded in building interracial congregations. Qualified Negro workers are finding employment in places previously barred to them, not only in manufacturing, but also in the professions and in retail establishments. On a few blocks in urban America, Negroes and whites have demonstrated that they can live together as neighbors. Labor unions, though traditionally anti-Negro, have in some places accepted Negroes as full partners in leadership as well as membership.

These are evidences of advances toward social integration. Other advances have been made within the Negro community itself. As this community in a given city grows larger, satisfactory career lines, economic security, and the home and community life that accompany such developments become possible. Here, however, Negroes and whites meet each other across separate societies rather than within a single group. The Negro shares with whites the better things of life, but he does so in isolation with other Negroes. The disadvantaged segregated community even produces advantages for some individuals within it, providing protected markets for Negro professionals and businessmen and protected constituencies for Negro political and church leaders. Yet even those who profit from segregation suffer from it. They feel the pin-pricks as well as the sledges of discrimination, and they must suppress their dissatisfaction in accordance with standards of conduct expected of all "better" people, whatever their race.

The larger evidence is neither that of social integration nor of intra-community social gains. Rather it is evidence pointing to the expansion of Negro slums within the largest cities and the separation of whites and Negroes by intra-city neighborhoods and especially on central city-suburban lines.

ECONOMIC CONSEQUENCES. Population shifts bring with them major economic consequences. Of first importance is the further decline of a large segment of business activity and associated property values, in the central cities. For reasons only remotely related—or unrelated—to the Negro-white population distribution, the economic feasibility of decentralized retail shopping has already been demonstrated. Suburban shopping centers have captured a large segment of the market in clothing, furniture, and other consumption goods; almost everywhere the "downtown" shops of the central cities have lost ground, absolutely and proportionally, to the peripheral developments. Retail sales in the central business district of Chicago decreased by 5 per cent between 1948 and 1954, while sales in the metropolitan area outside the city increased by 53 per cent. The relative sales loss of downtown areas has been even greater in other central cities.

Further developments can be foreseen. The downtown stores, with non-white and low-income customers more and more predominant in their clientele, will tend to concentrate on cheaper merchandise. " 'Borax' for downtown, Herman Miller for the suburb," is already a slogan of the furniture business. The decline of the central-city department store will be accompanied by a general deterioration of the downtown area. There are some striking exceptions, most notably in mid-town Manhattan. But in most cities—Chicago, Boston, Los Angeles are good examples—the main streets are becoming infested with sucker joints for tourists: all night jewelry auctions, bargain linens and cheap neckties, hamburger stands and jazz dives. The slums, in other words, are spreading to the central business districts.

A further, though more problematic, development is that the offices of the large corporations will join the flight from the city, taking along with them their servicing businesses: banks, law offices, advertising agencies, and others. The rapid development of closed circuit television, facsimile reproduction, and other technical aids relieves these businesses of the necessity of clustering at a central point. Their exodus from the city is already underway. New highways will make it easier in many places to get from one suburb to another than from suburb to downtown; and the losses of giving up central headquarters can be amortized over a number of years, frequently at considerable tax savings. Even the downtown hotel is likely to give way to the suburban motel except for convention purposes, an incidental further boost to the honkey-tonk development within the downtown business areas.

The rule seems to be a simple one: retail trade, the white collar shops, and the service industries will follow population. (Once their exodus is well underway, they also lead population.) The same general rule at least partially applies for manufacturing: the greatest suburbanization of manufacturing has taken place in those metropolitan areas where there has also been the most marked suburbanization of population, and some evidence indicates that manufacturing precedes population, rather than vice versa. Though the central cities have lost some manufacturing to both suburban and non-metropolitan areas, they have nevertheless maintained the preponderant share of the nation's total manufacturing enterprise. As Kitagawa and Bogue have shown, "the over-all spatial distribution [of manufacturing] in the United States has changed comparatively little in the past 50 years." The relative immobility of heavy industry has the result of fixing the laboring and semi-skilled groups, including large numbers of Negroes, within the central cities.

Even a conservative view must anticipate the exodus of a large segment of retail and other non-manufacturing businesses from downtown centers. Abandonment of these centers will lead to a host of municipal problems, not least of which is the loss of a substantial tax base. These economic developments are at once a step towards, and a consequence of, the city-suburban bifurcation of races that promises to transform many central cities into lower class ethnic islands. Successful attempts by central cities to encourage the establishment of new manufacturing plants as a means of rebuilding their tax base will of course hasten this process.

Minority problems are more serious in the United States than in other industrial societies. The task of integrating into American society a Negro minority composing 10 per cent of the population is vastly more difficult than the problem Sweden faces with Lapp reindeer herders in the Arctic region. Nevertheless, all industrial countries and most developing societies contain minorities; it would be unrealistic to discuss them as ephemeral remnants of the preindustrial past. The tendency is for these minorities to live in a different cultural world from the majority—a meaner, smaller world. When the anthropologist Oscar Lewis talks about "the culture of poverty," he means more than the absence of money.[32] A family that has become impoverished does not necessarily share the culture of poverty; the members may continue to hold the same values and aspirations as before. The culture of poverty refers to a climate of hopelessness arising either from generations of deprivation or from personal defeats so crushing that the future holds no further promise, such as long-time unemployment.[33] Professor Lewis suggests that poverty produces essentially the same attitudes and values whether it appears among the Untouchables in

[32] Oscar Lewis, *Five Families: Mexican Case Studies in the Culture of Poverty*, New York: Basic Books, 1959, p. 2.
[33] Mirra Komarovsky, *The Unemployed Man and His Family*, New York: Dryden, 1940; E. Wight Bakke, *Citizens without Work*, New Haven: Yale University Press, 1940.

India, among detribalized natives in the slums of Johannesburg, among dwellers in the *vecindades* of Mexico City, or among migrant laborers in the United States. People react with the same quiet desperation regardless of geography. If the concept of the culture of poverty is valid, the following account of a visit to a New York slum tenement would be fully understood by social workers in Hong Kong.

Life in an Urban Slum

Reprinted by permission. From Richard Harris, "The Slum," *The Nation*, Vol. 194, Feb. 17, 1962, pp. 143–147.

I recently took advantage of a chance to visit a classical slum house. . . . On that occasion, I was in the company of Mrs. Juliet F. Brudney, a vigorous middle-aged woman with curly brown hair and a determined manner who is associated with the Neighborhood Conservation Program, which is an official attempt, on a city-wide basis, to stop the deterioration of buildings that are on their way to becoming slums. Our destination was a place called the Armstrong, an apartment house situated on 103rd Street and Amsterdam Avenue, a once-hale neighborhood that has been sinking fast since the end of the war. As we walked from her nearby office to the Armstrong, which Mrs. Brudney was visiting for the first time to see if its state was as bad as reported, she gave me a quick rundown on it.

"First of all," she said, "the Armstrong is said to be one of the worst places on the entire upper West Side. In fact, it's bad enough so that the city is talking about condemning and demolishing it. My job is to see what can be done for the tenants until that happens. For the past several days, an inspector from the Department of Buildings and one from the Department of Health have been going through there, at our request. That's the first step in taking legal action against the landlord." I asked how many people lived in the Armstrong. "At the last count," she answered, "there were 440 tenants, more than half of whom are under twelve years old. They live in forty-nine apartments and 108 single rooms. Five of the families are white, and the rest are Negro. From what I hear, the place scarcely qualifies as housing at all. Last summer, they had an average of one fire a week. There's been a constant run of robberies and rapes and assaults. The building has no protection—no locks on the apartment doors, no watchman, so people just wander in and out. It's not a building any more—just an extension of the street."

The Armstrong turned out to be a seven-story, brownish-brick structure festooned with fire escapes. Since brick and stone easily survive—and conceal—the most flagrant internal disorder and display only the wear of the elements and an accretion of urban grime, from the outside the building was more drab than ramshackle. A couple of dozen children were playing around the stoop, while half as many adults were either sitting there or standing idly on the sidewalk in groups of two and three. Mrs. Brudney asked a woman in one of the latter where she could find the superintendent, and was directed to a heavy-set colored man in faded overalls and a brown hat who was lounging against the fender of a parked car. Going up to him, she identified herself and asked if it were all right for her to go into the Armstrong, whereupon he shrugged indifferently, and said, "Make yourself to home, lady."

"I suppose you realize there have been a great many complaints about this building," Mrs. Brudney said.

"There's nothing wrong with this building," he replied. "It's a good building, a good solid building. Sure, it's old, but it's still good. There is any complaints, they're about the people living in it. They're the ones to complain about."

"That's the usual excuse," Mrs. Brudney said to me as we started up the steps to the entrance. "People are kept in an inhuman state all their lives, and then criticized for not having the sensibilities of an Emily Post." In the lobby, a dimly lighted, narrow room, we made our way through another crowd of playing children to the elevator. When she pushed the button, a girl of about ten with long pigtails came running over and said, "The elevator don't work, misses. You've got to be pretty fast to catch it when it's working." Thanking her, we started up a littered stairway with old-fashioned, fancy, iron balustrades that, from the looks of the accumulation of dust and soot on them, hadn't been cleaned for years.

At the second-floor landing, Mrs. Brudney opened a door onto the hall, and at once we were enveloped in a stench of rotting garbage and urine. "I never get used to that smell in places like this—never," she said, quickening her pace. As we turned a corner of the corridor, we came upon one cause of the odor—an enormous burlap bag nailed to the wall at shoulder level; it was overflowing with refuse, which covered the floor for several feet around it. "My God!" Mrs. Brudney gasped. "Just look at that filth!" Hurrying on, she chose a door at random and knocked. I could hear the sound of voices inside, but no one answered—possibly because it was not the custom of the house to knock before entering. In any event, the next knock brought to the door a young and very pregnant colored woman who was wearing a soiled gingham housedress and bedroom slippers. Once Mrs. Brudney had identified herself, the woman let us in—less, I gathered from her rather sullen expression, because of any desire to be hospitable than from a way of life that made it out of the question for her to doubt our right to be there.

Inside, we found five children—three boys and two girls, the oldest of whom was around seven—in a room about ten by twelve feet, with two small windows that let out on an airshaft. Connected to this room by an archway was another, which was slightly smaller and windowless, and at one end of it was a tiny bathroom. At one time, the walls had been painted a glossy dark green, but they had been turned almost black by age and the fumes from a gas stove, an ancient piece of equipment on top of which a large kettle of beans were simmering. Elsewhere in the front room were a refrigerator of the same vintage, a small sink, a single bed and two wooden armchairs, whose stuffing was coming out of their imitation leather seats; the other room contained a double bed and a large chest of drawers. Here and there, throughout the place, great patches of plaster were missing from the walls and ceilings, leaving bare lath showing.

"Excuse me for bothering you like this," Mrs. Brudney said. "I'm trying to get some idea of the conditions here so we can do something about them." The woman looked at her listlessly, and after a moment, Mrs. Brudney went on, "How many of you live here?"

"Seven all told," the woman answered. "There are the kids here," she added, waving a hand at the children, who had stopped whatever they had been doing when we entered and were watching in awe. "Then there's me and my mother."

"How much rent do you pay?"

"Up 'til they cut the rent, we paid $32 a week."

"$140 a month?"

"That's right. Some bargain, huh? Then they cut it, and now it's $26 a week."

"Have you seen any rats?"

"Seen any!" the woman cried. "Why, they about knock you down. There's one big one that just devils us 'till we like to go crazy. He runs through here daytime, nighttime, any time he feels like it. He does everything but cook here. I got a cat once—Skippy. But that rat run Skippy right on out of the house."

"Have you tried to find another place to live?" Mrs. Brudney asked.

"Sure, plenty of times," she answered. "But they won't take you with so many kids. And, besides, you got to give them two, three months' rent. Where's the money to come from?" Pausing, she shrugged heavily and then went on, "This is no good for kids, a place like this. There are winos and hopheads lying around in the halls and cursing and carrying on like they was already in hell. My kids are hearing all that kind of stuff. They need a fit place to live. It's wrong for them to be living in the same room and all. Another thing I'll tell you about is those policemen. Every time something happens here and the police come, they treat you just like them that stirred up the trouble. They figure if there's some bad people here, they're all bad. Somebody give me another place to live, I'd show I wasn't bad. Just 'cause we're here doesn't mean we *like* it."

With that, the woman lapsed into a glum silence, and Mrs. Brudney then thanked her and we left. As we started upstairs, I asked her about the rent reduction the woman had mentioned, and she explained that the State Rent Commission had investigated the building a year ago and, on the basis of the woeful state of the place, had cut the rent roll from a total of $140,000 annually to half that amount; apparently, she added, the decreases had varied, since the apartment we had visited had been reduced by less than a quarter. "Even at that rent you can imagine what the returns are in a place like this," she said. "The answer is for the Rent Commission to cut the rents to a dollar a month. For some people, the only thing that talks louder than money is the lack of it."

Graphic as is the foregoing account of slum conditions, it does not *explain* the psychology of the poor. While it is true that some people, white and nonwhite, are trapped in the slum because of circumstances beyond their control —such as illness or old age—others do not take advantage of opportunities to make a better life for themselves. Even Jacob Riis, whose muckraking accounts of New York slums won the friendship of Theodore Roosevelt, had to admit that poverty leaves marks on the psyche which cannot be erased by a better environment. The following paragraph is from his famous book, published in 1890, *How the Other Half Lives.*

The Perversity of the Poor

Reprinted by permission. From Jacob A. Riis, *How the Other Half Lives: Studies among the Tenements of New York*, New York: Sagamore Press, 1957, pp. 207–208.

The causes that operate to obstruct efforts to better the lot of the tenement population are, in our day, largely found among the tenants themselves. This is true particularly of the poorest. They are shiftless, destructive, and stupid; in a word, they are what the tenements have made them. It is a dreary old truth that those who would fight for the poor must fight the poor to do it. It must be confessed that there is little enough in their past experience to inspire confidence in the sincerity of the effort to help them. I recall the discomfiture of a certain well-known philanthropist, since deceased, whose heart beat responsive to other suffering than that of human kind. He was a large owner of tenement property, and once undertook to fit out his houses with stationary tubs, sanitary plumbing, wood-closets, and all the latest improvements. He introduced his rough tenants to all this magnificence without taking the precaution of providing a competent housekeeper, to see that the new acquaintances got on together. He felt that his tenants ought to be grateful for the interest he took in them.

They were. They found the boards in the wood-closets fine kindling wood, while the pipes and faucets were as good as cash at the junk shop. In three months the owner had to remove what was left of his improvements. The pipes were cut and the houses running full of water, the stationary tubs were put to all sorts of uses except washing, and of the wood-closets not a trace was left. The philanthropist was ever after a firm believer in the total depravity of tenement-house people. Others have been led to like reasoning by as plausible arguments, without discovering that the shiftlessness and ignorance that offended them were the consistent crop of the tenement they were trying to reform, and had to be included in the effort. The owners of a block of model tenements uptown had got their tenants comfortably settled, and were indulging in high hopes of their redemption under proper management, when a contractor ran up a row of "skin" tenements, shaky but fair to look at, with brown-stone trimmings and gewgaws. The result was to tempt a lot of the well-housed tenants away. It was a very astonishing instance of perversity to the planners of the benevolent scheme; but, after all, there was nothing strange in it. It is all a matter of education, as I said about the landlord.

More recently, a social psychologist surveyed the public-opinion literature in an effort to specify the apathy of the American underdog. The composite portrait that emerges from Genevieve Knupfer's survey is not only internally consistent; it also fits in with Professor Lewis' observations on the "culture of poverty."

The Poverty-Stricken State of Mind

Reprinted by permission. From Genevieve Knupfer, "Portrait of the Underdog," *Public Opinion Quarterly*, Vol. 11, Spring 1947, pp. 103–114.

This paper considers the disadvantages of low status, the restriction of "life chances" which low status carries with it. From this point of view, the tendency of different aspects of status to "cluster" together takes on the aspect of a vicious circle which recalls the Biblical dictum: "to him that hath shall be given." Thus, the lack of financial reserves prevents people from taking advantage of the few opportunities for making more money which do present themselves; the people who need it least have friends who can lend them money in an emergency. Moreover, the economic restrictions, because of the accompanying lack of education and perhaps a certain adaptation to submission and failure, result in psychological restrictions which reinforce the economic. For example, those who need it least are under the most social pressure to keep themselves informed and to participate in community activities; not being able to go to college not only prevents a person from acquiring a college education but also makes it much less likely that he will use those educational opportunities which *are* available to him. . . .

More specifically stated, the purpose of the present paper is to present some evidence in support of the following hypothesis: that the economic and educational limitations accompanying low status produce a lack of interest in and a lack of self-confidence in dealing with certain important areas of our culture; as a result, there is reduced participation—a *withdrawal from* participation in these areas. It is interesting to recall that C. C. North made a very similar statement, many years ago, when he said that low status produces a kind of mental isolation which operates to "limit the sources of information, to retard the development of efficiency in judgment and reasoning abilities, and to confine the attention to the more trivial interests of life."

The constant interaction of the different factors involved makes it difficult to distinguish between cause and effect. Lack of education and information, of facility in reading and writing, of interest in relatively abstract things; habits of submission, feelings of inferiority, low income, absorption with the problem of mere survival—all these factors continually influence one another, so that we cannot attempt to show where one begins and the other ends.

Another difficulty for interpretation is that the data on this subject are generally crude. The pattern of limited psychological horizons among the lower as compared with the higher socio-economic groups is certainly not unambiguous. Statistical comparisons show differences between groups, but the differences are not all large, and the groups are heterogeneous. We do not know from such data, for example, what are the different effects of different *types* of low status. In rough classifications of status there may be manual workers, farmers, and small businessmen in the lower group. The over-all figures do not reveal whether or not these different groups react differentially.

Before presenting the following data, our terms need to be clarified. By status we refer to rank position with respect chiefly to income, prestige and power—one or all of these. "Low" is used in a purely relative sense. The definition varies: sometimes it may be the lower half, sometimes it may be measured by income, sometimes by occupation, sometimes by impressionistic ratings. In the case of individual studies cited, a more exact description of the status index used will usually be given.

In order to simplify our language we will use the initials LS and HS for "low status" and "high status." Short cuts in stating statistical comparisons will also be used. Thus, a statement that "the LS person is more inclined to . . ." should be understood to mean "a larger proportion of persons in the lower socio-economic status group . . ."

The data will be presented in three sections, dealing respectively with (*a*) the differential participation of status groups in social contacts or interaction, both organized and informal, (*b*) with their differential participation in the thought-life of society, and (*c*) with their differential efforts and aspirations to control and to enjoy life.

There is ample evidence to show that LS groups participate in fewer organized activities and know fewer people. As far as membership in clubs and organizations goes, one illustration among many is provided by a study made in Franklin, Indiana (pop. 6,000). The percentage of men in the income class earning less than $100 per month who had no group affiliations at all was eight times as great as that of the men in the higher income class: "In every type of group without exception—church, fraternal, service, recreational, patriotic, political, cultural—membership on the part of the lower income class was markedly lower."

In part the lesser membership is, of course, caused by economic considerations—the cost of membership and of going to meetings, and the many other incidental expenses. There is also the factor of lack of time and energy, due to longer and more strenuous working hours. The explanation most likely to be given by individuals themselves is probably "lack of interest." Of the implications of this lack of interest we shall have more to say later. In some cases there may be a reluctance to mix with persons of higher status. This would operate in the case of organizations which are predominantly middle class. The lower class mother may hesitate to go to Parent Teachers Association meetings, being unwilling to meet with women who have more money and education, because of her cheap clothes and her poor grammar. It may be that the relatively high degree of social mobility in this country, and its even greater *ideological* "classlessness," makes the participation of LS persons particularly difficult, because separate organizations are not usually provided for different classes. The great majority of Americans consider themselves middle class and so they are all ostensibly on an equal basis. If they feel themselves too severely handicapped in the competition, they simply withdraw. More investigation is needed to determine which of the factors suggested above actually are most important in different situations.

Studies of participation in civilian defense activities showed that almost all the members were white-collar people. It was the experience of the writer that attempts to bring in manual workers often uncovered an exaggerated fear on the part of the latter of even trying to take the required examination in air raid protection procedures, which was, as a matter of fact, probably well within their capacities to pass.

We might expect to find that LS people compensate for their relative lack of more demanding types of participation by a greater development of informal relationships, just as we find more radio listening among the poor than among the well-to-do, because the latter have so many other opportunities for entertainment and information. But evidence indicates that even in face-to-face contacts LS people are more limited. Informal social activities, such as visiting friends, are more infrequent among them. In Middletown, for example, it was found that 3% of the "business class" women (who gave the information) said they had no friends whatever, 13% said they had no intimate friends, while for the working class women the proportions were 13% and 34% respectively. A study of a rural New York community made in 1940–41 brings additional evidence. People were asked "What persons not members of your household do you visit most when away from your business or work?" If two persons in answer to this question mentioned each other, this was a mutual choice. Mutual choices were regarded as indicating an intimate interpersonal relationship. The community was further divided into 11 prestige groups. The mean number of mutual choices for the highest group was 6, for the lowest 2.

Comments made by working class women on this question in Middletown bring out a corollary of social isolation: suspicion and dread of the foreign, the definition of the foreign being more or less inclusive:

"It doesn't pay to be too friendly."

"I never chum with anyone; it's dangerous."

Whether such reactions are characteristic of LS persons generally is a question which needs further study. Friendliness, solidarity and mutual aid have sometimes been cited as characteristic of the ethic of the underprivileged as opposed to bourgeois competitiveness and self-reliance. Many factors would have to be more precisely determined in order to clarify the issue. There are different types of community, different definitions of "stranger" and "friendliness" and different types of low status groups. The results may well depend on the particular combination of these elements which is involved. Whatever the true interpretation, it seems well established that in many American communities there is a correlation between income and the number of friends or acquaintances an individual associates with.

Moreover, what friendship contacts there are among LS people are apt to be confined to a narrower area. In Middletown, more than half the best friends of the working-class wives, less than a tenth of the friends of the business group, were reported to have been met in the "neighborhood." In a South Dakota town, comparison of the top group with the lowest showed that over 90% of the "Tops" and only 27% of the "Bottoms" exchanged visits with friends outside the immediate neighborhood. It has also been shown that propinquity is more important to the selection of a spouse in the LS group than in the other.

The geographical circumscription apparently attendant upon relatively low socio-economic status is shown in the extent of travel outside the community. In Prairieton, "the average lower class person in the course of a lifetime . . . (had) traveled within a radius of but 145 [miles] from Prairieton; in contrast the average for upper class individuals was 1,100 miles."

It is clear that a major factor in the geographical restrictions cited above is the economic one: travel costs money, even within a city. But there may also be a psychological factor: the richer classes have had more chance to cultivate the habit of ignoring obstacles, of conceiving their potentialities generously. They have perhaps acquired the idea that it is worth while to make an effort to choose one's associates freely instead of allowing them to be dictated by circumstances.

Other restrictions in informal social contacts among LS groups appear to be the larger proportion of them which consist of associations with "own kin." In the study of a New York rural community mentioned above, the lowest prestige classes had the highest proportion of mutual choices with their own relatives. A study comparing the political opinions of parents with those of their (grown-up) children in Cleveland, Ohio, showed less divergence between parents and children in the lower occupational groups than in the higher groups. The reason for this, according to the authors, is that the less privileged individual has less variety of "institutional pulls" outside the family.

The lack of reading and writing *facility* as distinct from mere technical literacy is a very important handicap in keeping people isolated from the "thought life of the group." Although only 6% of the lowest socio-economic group in the U.S. (the D group according to the ABCD rating system) do not read newspapers, reading of magazines and books shows sharp socio-economic differentials. In a study of Sandusky, Ohio, based on about 1,600 interviews, respondents were classified into three economic groups. In the lowest socio-economic group, about 35% said they did not read magazines, whereas in the highest group only 7% said they did not. Another group in the same study were asked how many books they had read. 82% of the LS group (C and D levels) read less than one book a month, while only 59% of the HS groups read no more than that.

More significant than the amount of reading are the kinds of material the LS person reads, which, together with data from some public opinion surveys, give us a picture of the differences in interests between socio-economic groups.

A large body of data on magazine reading and radio listening exists as a result of many years of research in this area, undertaken chiefly for commercial purposes. This data shows a consistent tendency for LS people to be less interested in "serious" reading and listening. The term "serious," though somewhat vague, is used here for want of a better term. One might try to define it as indicating an interest in subjects whose applicability to one's personal life is not immediately perceptible but which helps one to become a richer person and to see the world more fully.

To take one example among many, a nation-wide survey of women magazine readers showed that more of the "prosperous" read *Time* Magazine than read *True Confessions*. Among the "poor" more read *True Confessions* than read *Time*. Direct questions about reading preferences asked of women readers also showed relatively more interest in fiction, less in public affairs, among the poorer women.

Surveys on radio listening showed similar regularities. Asked "Do you listen to classical music on the radio, such as the Ford Hour or the Metropolitan Opera?", 73% of the HS group, 57% of the LS group, said "yes." Educational programs, serious dramatizations, and programs on public affairs were less listened to by LS groups, according to a Buffalo survey. The most popular programs among a group of people in a Midwestern town were studied. It was found that the programs heard more by LS persons than by HS persons were: comedy and variety, sports, serial stories, religious programs, and service programs.

On the other hand, the HS person heard the following programs more frequently: news, popular music, quiz programs, other than serial dramatizations, serious music, and talks, forums and discussions.

Public opinion surveys give a good deal of evidence showing that the LS group has on the whole less interest in international affairs, and in news of any kind, than the HS group. In a survey of attitudes toward Russia, it was found that in the "top 12%" of the population 63% were interested in getting more information about Russia, whereas in the "bottom 12%" only 24% were interested, in spite of the fact that more of the lower group were favorably disposed towards that country. In a study of reactions in one county to the 1940 presidential election, an index of "interest in the election" was devised. Great interest in the election was shown by 33% of the top socio-economic half of the population while only 24% of the lower half displayed a great interest. It is noteworthy that the differences between socio-economic groups in this case are not very great. A presidential election, during the campaign when there is much excitement and publicity about it everywhere, is, of course, less remote than other political issues.

Naturally enough, LS persons are consistently less well informed on a wide variety of subjects. To cite just a few examples: Asked to name the Senators of their own state, 69% of the lowest (of three) income groups could name neither, while only 28% of the highest income group were ignorant of both. In another survey, people were asked to pair the names of a list of public figures with their functions. 84% of those who had gone to college knew that Elmer Davis was head of the Office of War Information, while 29% of those with only a grade school education knew this.

Paralleling lack of interest and information, differences in opinion between socio-economic groups show a certain amount of naivete and credulity among LS persons. Data on this point are more scanty and the differences less pronounced than they were for the points made earlier. In a study of reactions to Boake Carter, the question was asked: "Do you think Carter interpreted the news, or gave you straight news?" More of the LS people thought that Carter gave them straight news. A study of reactions to testimonials in advertisement showed that the LS people less often than the HS believe that the testimonials are paid for. Asked in 1939 whether they thought the war had increased President Roosevelt's chances for reelection, the LS persons were less inclined to believe that it had.

A study of the panic created by Orson Welles' radio drama, "The Invasion from Mars," showed that a relatively larger proportion of the LS group believed the "invasions" to be a reality. "One of the outstanding indices of suggestibility," the authors say, "is the complete absence of awareness that things might be otherwise than they are made out to be." Those who have no relevant standard of judgment into which they can fit an unfamiliar stimulus are inadequately equipped to withstand suggestion. And the narrowed outlook of the LS person, the lack of range in his thought and experience, fails to give him relevant standards of judgment in many areas of life. Some people during the "Invasion from Mars" incident tried to check the truth of what they had heard over the radio. Many, however, did not know how to evaluate evidence, so they ended by accepting what was ostensibly offered them as an interpretation, namely, that the broadcast was news, not fiction. Here we see the effect of the lack of training which is one of the serious forms of underprivilege in LS groups.

In view of the naivete and lack of information we have been describing, one might say it is only to be expected that the LS person has so much timidity about voicing an opinion. One of the most consistent results of public opinion polls is the higher proportion of "don't know" and "no opinion" in the LS group. What should the government do to avoid postwar unemployment? Can Russia be trusted? Are there any prominent individuals in this country who might be harmful to our future unless curbed? Could the Germans get rid of the Nazis if they wanted to? (asked in 1944) Should automobile owners be forced to take out insurance against the damage they might do to others? If extra taxes have to be levied should they be sales or income taxes?

On all these questions the LS person is less likely to venture an opinion than the HS person. Of course, he is less well informed about all the issues. But amount of information is probably not the only factor involved. It is not only, we suggest, that the LS person does not know the answer, for most of those who give an opinion probably do not know enough for a rational defense of their views. Very possibly there is another factor: the LS person feels less competent to judge. This implies that he will leave decisions to wiser men. The "wiser" men are those who have been taught that it is more shameful to have no opinion than to have the wrong opinion, who take it for granted that their views are at least as good as the next man's.

One might object that perhaps all this apparent lack of interest in and understanding of things not directly related to personal life is merely lack of interest in a certain area, whereas an opposite picture would emerge if we selected different areas for investigation. We might find, for example, that awareness of minute differences in the standings of big league baseball players, or understanding of the workings of political machines in wards, would be much greater among LS persons than among others. However, the areas in modern American life which appear to be relatively closed to the person of low status are certainly sufficiently important to affect his well being in a material way.

True, there are large segments of so-called "general information" of upper class culture which do not seem to serve any purpose other than marking one as a member of a sub-group in the society. For example, the person who has heard of Aeschylus, but knows only that he wrote a play called "Agamemnon," knows nothing which has any bearing on the enrichment of his personal life. But it so happens that the LS persons are also apt to be ignorant of things which do concern them and which might increase their control and enjoyment of life—such as the existence of price ceilings. As we have mentioned, only 6% of even the lowest income group do not read newspapers. Price control legislation was front-page news for a period of time. Moreover, prices are, if anything, of more direct concern to LS persons than to others. Yet a survey made in 1942 showed that fewer of the LS than of the HS knew that price ceilings had been established. The knowledge differential grew with more detailed and exact questions about the workings of the price control system.

The importance of the mental attitude, aside from the mere accessibility of the information, is suggested by the fact that when asked, "Have you seen any ceiling prices displayed in stores or marked on goods?" more of the prosperous than of the poor said "yes." Since most stores have a list of ceiling prices posted, this difference appears to be largely a matter of alertness. The LS person, it would seem, does not see as much of what goes on around him.

Another example of ignorance in a matter which could be detrimental to the LS person is the question of income taxes. Asked how much income tax they thought people should pay at various levels of income, the LS group consistently selected a sum very much smaller than the amount actually paid by people with incomes over $10,000.

Other cases in point include the history of consumer cooperatives, both for information and retail services. By and large, they do not reach the groups who need them most. Birth control practices show the same discrepancy: the poor use less effective contraceptives and use them less frequently. They do not avail themselves readily of the services of birth control clinics even when these are accessible, and even women who express dread of having any more children show an apparent inability to exercise the necessary care and patience in practicing contraception.

These manifestations of a lack of effort to control the environment may spring from deeply ingrained habits of doing what one is told. There is some indication from personality tests that LS persons are more submissive than others, but the evidence is far from definitive.

We do know that there is much more indifference to voting among LS groups. A nationwide survey included a question on voting in the 1944 presidential elections. The sample was divided into three economic groups: the upper fourth, the middle half, and the lower fourth. The proportion of voters in these three groups were, respectively, 84%, 68% and 53%.

The reasons for non-voting have been described by Lazarsfeld, Berelson and Gaudet as follows: ". . . three-quarters of the non-voters stayed away from the polls deliberately because they were thoroughly unconcerned with the election. . . . Only a small number of people were kept from the polls by a last minute emergency. . . . A long range program of civic education would be needed to draw such people into the orbit of political life, and further studies are needed to unearth the specific nature of their lack of interest."

Is this lack of interest in elections due to a more or less conscious cynicism about their value —a lack of interest in deciding "once every few years which member of the ruling class is to repress and oppress the people through Parliament"? This appears from the facts to be unlikely. In an earlier study of non-voting, Merriam and Gosnell state that general indifference was the chief reason for non-voting, and that "the most common partners of general indifference were ignorance and timidity." Recent research has borne this statement out remarkably well. A series of questions in nationwide polls showed that non-voters are not only less informed about political issues but are less willing to criticize the status quo or even to believe that newspapers should be allowed to criticize "our form of government."

This is not to say that LS persons have fewer complaints about their life than others. A survey on political opinions in Chicago included questions on whether or not respondents were satisfied with the following: their children's opportunities, the kind of work they did, their pay, their treatment at work, their opportunity to enjoy life, and the chance to get ahead. In every case, LS people were more dissatisfied than other groups.

The same study also demonstrated, as have many others, that LS groups tend to be more "radical" than HS groups. That is, they tend more to favor social security measures, labor unions, government regulation of business, and to regard it as the rightful function of government to redistribute the wealth more equally. It would seem from this that LS groups do take a rational view of their plight and support measures which would improve their lot. Our picture of mental isolation and withdrawal hardly fits in with these facts. Possibly one might explain the difference as follows: a larger proportion of LS people do not vote but those who do are alive to their own interests and vote for them. For we cannot be sure when we bring together evidence from various studies showing differences between socioeconomic groups, that it is always the same portion of the LS group which displays the given characteristic.

An interesting parallel to the limited efforts of the LS person to control his environment is the apparent fact that he is also limited in what he permits himself to wish for.

When a large sample of people were asked how much income they wanted, it was found that those who had less wished for less. A group of children were given an opportunity to choose Christmas gifts. LS children had fewer desires than the others. High school girls were asked what occupation they would like to enter, as distinct from the occupation they expected to enter. Those from LS groups are less likely than the others to choose such relatively lucrative and interesting professions as medicine and commercial art, and more likely to limit their wishes to such things as stenography and beautician's work.

The low level of aspiration just described cannot, of course, be regarded entirely as a handicap. It performs a useful service in making life tolerable for the LS person. Too wide a discrepancy between what one has and what one aspires to would create frustration and discourage effort. Nevertheless, the low level of aspiration may well be, in some cases, a sign of apathy and ingrained acceptance of defeat rather than of adjustment to reality, and may be just as unrealistic as excessive ambition. Studies of unemployed youth showed a tendency for "frightened" youth to go into blind alley jobs, "to crowd into overfilled, unproductive lines of work where they could produce nothing, out of anxiety over unemployment."

In this paper an attempt has been made to present evidence to show that closely linked with economic underprivilege is psychological underprivilege: habits of submission, little access to sources of information, lack of verbal facility. These things appear to produce a lack of self-confidence which increases the unwillingness of the low status person to participate in many phases of our predominantly middle-class culture even beyond what would be a realistic withdrawal adapted to his reduced chances of being effective.

Our theme is summed up by P. F. Lazarsfeld in his conclusion from a study of youth in Austria: "The underprivileged youth has seen less, read less, heard about less, has in his whole environment experienced fewer changes than the socially privileged, and he simply knows of fewer possibilities."

CONCLUSION

Industrialism is a way of life. The economic aspects of the industrial way of life were discussed in Chapter 4: the expansion of the market, the differentiation of occupational roles, the growth in affluence. The ecological aspect of the industrial way of life was discussed in Chapter 5: the concentration of population in urban areas and the opportunities for individual fulfillment which urbanism makes possible. This chapter has been concerned with the cultural differentiation of industrial societies.

The population of an industrial society can be roughly divided into a majority that shares its cultural values and material rewards, and a minority that does not understand the urban industrial way of life and is excluded from its benefits. In the United States, the industrially oriented majority consists largely of urbanized whites. Majority Americans usually have stable families, a low death rate, and high educational aspirations. They live in pleasant homes, often in the suburbs of large cities, but many are willing to move at short notice to distant parts of the country in order to advance the career of the male breadwinner. These moves are not disorganizing, partly because neighborhood roots are shallow in industrial societies and partly because American communities have remarkably similar social organization and cultural characteristics.

The nonindustrial minority of the American population includes both rural and urban segments. The rural poor, including migrant laborers, may ultimately disappear as the demand for unskilled farm workers declines. Rural Negroes and Mexicans move to cities where they join the slum-dwelling remnants of previous migrations, including the failures left behind by the trans-Atlantic migration of European peasants. This nonindustrial population of American cities has a higher incidence of broken families and illegitimacy, a higher death rate, more welfare problems, and lower educational attainment, on the average, than the industrially oriented majority. Whether these malintegrated elements of American cities will maintain a permanent culture of poverty or be assimilated into the mainstream of urban industrial life is not clear; massive rural-to-urban population shifts are still going on. The test will come when rural areas are industrialized and no longer export surplus unskilled labor, and when city slums begin to be dominated by second-generation and third-generation natives of the cities.

Meanwhile, however, they exist within American society but are not of it. When in the next chapter social stratification is discussed, they will pose a problem of classification. Should they be considered the lowest stratum of the society or should they be thought of as not belonging to industrial society at all?

SOME SIGNIFICANT LITERATURE ON IN-GROUP AND OUT-GROUP CULTURES

Kurt W. Back, *Slums, Projects, and People: Social Psychological Problems of Relocation in Puerto Rico*, Durham, N.C.: Duke University Press, 1962. Some of the families from a Puerto Rico slum in process of demolition moved to a modern apartment in a housing project; others preferred the shacks of another slum neighborhood. Professor Back explains the reasons for these choices. Those who chose public housing were either families at the bottom of the socioeconomic hierarchy who welcomed the services available to a tenant in a project or were young, mobile families in which the husband was employed in a white-collar job. Other low-income families did not want to be tenants complying with bureaucratic regulations and chose instead to be homeowners—although the home was a shack. This summary is based on a review by Herbert J. Gans, *American Sociological Review*, Vol. 28, February, 1963, p. 156.

St. Clair Drake and Horace R. Cayton, *Black Metropolis*, New York: Harcourt Brace, 1945. This 800-page book about the Negro community of Chicago traces the social, economic, and political history of that community as well as its contemporary way of life. In particular, the authors discuss the forces which created a "black ghetto" on the South Side of Chicago and the forces making for increased political influence of Negroes. The styles of life of upper-class and middle-class Negroes are described as well as detailed descriptions of the Negro culture of poverty. This summary is based on a review by Samuel M. Strong, *American Sociological Review*, Vol. 11, April 1946, pp. 240–241.

Herbert J. Gans, *The Urban Villagers: Group and Class in the Life of Italian-Americans*, New York: Free Press of Glencoe, 1962. Professor Gans lived in the West End section of Boston between October 1957 and May 1958 in connection with a study of the relocation of people displaced by urban redevelopment. According to standards of physical dilapidation, the West End was a slum, but this was not the evaluation of the local residents. Gans thinks of the West End—torn down between 1958 and 1960 to make way for a luxury apartment-house complex—as possessing a different way of life from middle-class Americans but an equally viable one. Gans considers his book a contribution to ". . . the continuing conversation between the upper and the lower levels of our culture. Actually, most of the talking has usually been done by the upper level; the people of the lower one sit by quietly, and even sullenly, often without listening. . . . I have tried to describe the way of life of lower level people as they might describe it themselves if they were so-

ciologists. In a sense, then, I am reporting to the upper level for them and urging that they be given more consideration when policy decisions are made."

Nathan Glazer and Davis McEntire, Eds., *Studies in Housing and Minority Groups*, Berkeley: University of California Press, 1960. This book includes seven studies of housing for ethnic minorities in nine American cities: Atlanta, Birmingham, San Antonio, Houston, New Orleans, Miami, New York City, San Francisco, and Detroit. Considerable variation of housing opportunities exists, and one important task is to explain this variation. Nathan Glazer, in his introduction, suggests that the organization and the values of the banking, real estate, and construction interests of the local community in conjunction with local government influence financing and site selection for ethnic housing. Hence, the weaker the ethnic minority politically and the more hostile banking, real estate, and construction interests are toward that minority, the smaller its housing opportunities. This generalization is based on American data and would have to be qualified in industrial societies with different approaches to housing. This summary is based on a review by Scott Greer, *American Sociological Review*, Vol. 25, December 1960, p. 991.

Robert Gutman, "Population Mobility in the American Middle Class," in Leonard J. Duhl, *The Urban Condition*, New York: Basic Books, 1963, pp. 172–183. Suburban developments do not integrate all newcomers smoothly and quickly. "Working-class wives, or wives with only high school or less than high school education had more distant relationships with neighbors . . . than did wives of middle-class husbands and wives with some college experience." And if residents of the developments studied are divided into those who regard the community as their permanent home and those who regard it as a temporary stopping place on the way to better things, the transients are more likely than the permanents to report extensive social contact with their neighbors. In established suburbs—as contrasted with developments—newcomers sink roots into the community by joining established organizations rather than by informal neighboring. Again it is the middle-class newcomer who is more likely to accomplish this, partly because the voluntary associations in the suburb is likely to be oriented to middle-class interests, partly because middle-class newcomers are more likely than working-class newcomers to assume initiative for meeting other people and to devote time and energy to community activities.

Hilde T. Himmelweit, A. N. Oppenheim, and Pamela Vince, *Television and the Child: An Empirical Study of the Effect of Television on the Young*, New York: Oxford University Press, 1958. This book reports on two studies of the effects of television on British children. One study compares a thousand children (half aged 10–11, half 13–14) who have television at home with an equally large group of children who do not have television at home. Since the researchers were aware of the possibility that the families who purchased television sets might have been different from apparently similar families who did not, the second study took advantage of the introduction of television into a community. Prior to the advent of television, a large group of children filled out questionnaires, and these same children were retested a year later. Although many specific conclusions are drawn from the two studies, the most striking finding is a negative one. Television does not seem to damage the children exposed to it. This summary is based on a review by Eleanor E. Maccoby, *American Sociological Review*, Vol. 24, August 1959, pp. 595–597.

Robert K. Merton, Marjorie Fiske, and Alberta Curtis, *Mass Persuasion: The Social Psychology of a War Bond Drive*, New York: Harper, 1946. In 1943 Kate Smith staged an 18-hour radio broadcast for the purpose of selling war bonds. Listeners were subjected to a variety of patriotic and personal appeals and asked to telephone their pledges of bond purchases to local stations on the national hookup. Thousands of people responded, and millions of dollars worth of bonds were sold. Within two weeks of the broadcast, a sample of 100 listeners were interviewed at length; each interview took three to four hours, and in a majority of cases there were follow-up interviews. These interviews enabled researchers to determine which themes stressed by Kate Smith triggered the decision to buy bonds and which were ineffective. The title of the book, *Mass Persuasion*, emphasizes the responsiveness of an urban industrial population to mass-media messages. This summary is based on a review by Walter B. Bodenhafer, *American Sociological Review*, Vol. 12, April 1947, p. 234.

James N. Morgan et al., *Income and Welfare in the United States*, New York: McGraw-Hill, 1962. This book is a report of an interview survey of 2800 families conducted by the Survey Research Center of the University of Michigan. The determinants of family income are reported in a 14-chapter section ranging from "Hourly Earnings of Working Wives" to "The Economics of Living with Relatives." A special subsample of 300 low-income families provides data on poverty in the United States and in particular on the contribution of physical disabilities, educational deficiencies, and ethnic discrimination to the perpetuation of poverty. The redistribution of income through welfare programs, both public and private, is analyzed.

William Peterson, *Population*, New York: Macmillan, 1961. The in-group and out-group cultures referred to in Chapter 6 have qualitative aspects not reflected in birth rates, death rates, migration statistics, marriage and divorce rates, sex and age composition, and so forth. Nevertheless, demographic data are the quantitative expression of sociological, social psychological, and cultural factors; hence, one should seize the opportunity to use such relatively precise indices of the culture of poverty or of the culture of the industrial in-group wherever possible. To take advantage of opportunities to use demographic data for index purposes one must understand demographic *concepts* and the *sources* of population data—as well as some substantive facts about preindustrial, industrializing, and fully industrialized populations. Professor Peterson's textbook is an excellent treatment of these topics.

Conference on Economic Progress, *Poverty and Deprivation in the United States: The Plight of Two-fifths of a Nation*, Washington: Conference on Economic Progress, 1962. Certain groups within the American population are more likely than others to have inadequate incomes: nonwhites, the disabled, the aged, the unemployed, the farm population, the poorly educated, the unskilled, families headed by women (broken homes), and families with teen-age heads. This monograph estimates that in 1960 38 million Americans lived in poverty and 39 million in some deprivation out of a total population of 180 million people. Persons in social categories vulnerable to poverty are likely to live in blighted areas; low income usually forces families and even unattached individuals to accept substandard housing in the less desirable neighborhoods. In 1960 out of 58 million dwelling units in the United States, about nine and a half million were seriously deficient according to Census Bureau standards—five million inside large metropolitan areas and four and a half million outside. These social and ecological concentrations of low-income people provide a favorable climate for the development and maintenance of the culture of poverty.

CHAPTER 7

Social Stratification

Social rules apply to *people* indirectly. Their direct application is to *roles*, whoever happens to perform them. Thus, a college student is expected to register for courses at certain times, attend class meetings, borrow books from the library, live in a dormitory, and so forth. Although each student is unique, the college disregards his uniqueness for the sake of organizational efficiency. The application of rules to *roles* rather than to *people* means that one rule is relevant to the situations of hundreds or even thousands of individuals. The expectations for students apply not only to students currently enrolled but also, with some modification, to future generations of students.

The *content* of expected behavior—what the individual does or is supposed to do in a role—is the *instrumental* side of social organization. There is also an *expressive* side: how the person feels about what he is doing in the role and how other people feel about him. Erving Goffman has analyzed with great sensitivity the expression of these feelings.[1] Professor Goffman calls the individual's expression of *his* feelings about his role "demeanor"; he calls the expression of reactions to him (on the part

of those with whom he interacts) "etiquette"; and he distinguishes deferential from contemptuous reactions. This sounds rather complicated—especially in industrial societies with thousands of different roles. But a further complication has yet to be mentioned: a person normally occupies dozens of roles, some of them sequentially, some of them simultaneously. This multiplicity of roles sometimes places the individual under cross-pressures; sociologists say that he is in a "role conflict."[2] Multiplicity of roles also poses a choice for the community. How is an adult male regarded in a particular situation: as a college professor, as a parent, as a taxpayer in the local community? Or does he receive a composite evaluation based on all of his roles simultaneously? Which roles of the individual are the basis for his social evaluation? For many sociologists, this issue is central to the system of social stratification prevailing in a society.

STATUS AND STRATIFICATION

Social stratification, by definition, refers to inequality within a society. Inequality with respect to what? Here sociologists differ. Some

[1] See pp. 74–81.

[2] See pp. 10–14.

believe that stratification can most fruitfully be thought of in multidimensional terms: variations in economic power, variations in political authority, and variations in community prestige.[3] Other sociologists prefer a unidimensional conception of stratification even though they are aware that a high position in one dimension is correlated with a high position in another. In this book, social stratification is defined unidimensionally: as *the organization of deference*. An individual's *status* is his level of community prestige, the approximate consensus prevailing in his society as to how much deference he is entitled to receive and from whom. Such a conception of stratification is deliberately contentless; it treats the religious, educational, economic, or political characteristics associated with certain positions in the hierarchy as an open question, to be settled by empirical research.

Implicit in such a conception of social stratification is the assumption that a hierarchy of social honor is an inescapable feature of human life, however variable its basis in different societies. Most sociologists would agree that social inequality *is* inevitable. Certainly it is ubiquitous, arising even in societies dedicated to the ideal of classlessness. The emergence of social inequality despite egalitarian ideals is a tribute to the strength of the forces tending to produce *in*equality.[4] What are these forces? First must be mentioned the tendency for members of a social system to evaluate one another's behavior in the course of interaction. "Social stratification" is the end-product of an *evaluative process:* the giving and receiving of deference. Although "stratification" may suggest rigidity instead of dynamism, the evaluation of interaction creates the stratification system anew every day. One reason social stratification seems to be universal is that human

beings make value judgments, for example, whether role A is being played well and whether role A is more valuable to the society than role B.[5]

There is a second reason. As long as value judgments are confined to *roles* and not extended to *people*, stratification does not emerge. For example, suppose Mr. Jones, a banker, is evaluated by his neighbors exactly as they evaluate Mr. Smith, a factory worker living on the same street. They ignore differences between Mr. Jones and Mr. Smith in education, income, wealth, and occupational achievement and respond to Jones and Smith as "neighbors." If such specific reactions were the rule in a society, Mr. Jones would have no consistent worth; he would be judged quite differently depending on the role he occupied at the moment. The concept of social stratification assumes a tendency for all of the people who interact with Mr. Jones to evaluate him in approximately the same way, to judge him as a composite which transcends momentary roles. What makes for stratification is the *generalization* of many specific role evaluations to a rating of the person as a whole and, by extension, of other persons closely related to him. Thus, Talcott Parsons defines a *social class* as "an aggregate of kinship units of approximately equal status in the system of stratification." [6] Not only does Mr. Jones enjoy the same deference (or contempt) from a variety of persons who interact with him; his *children* also share his status and thereby possess opportunities in American society different from those of the children of other parents. This transmission of status from one generation to the next violates the American ideal of equality of opportunity.[7]

[3] Reinhard Bendix and Seymour Martin Lipset, *Class, Status and Power: A Reader in Social Stratification*, Glencoe, Ill.: Free Press, 1953.
[4] Eva Rosenfeld, "Social Stratification in a 'Classless' Society," *American Sociological Review*, Vol. 16, December 1951, pp. 766–774; Alex Inkeles, "Social Stratification and Social Mobility in the Soviet Union: 1940–1950," Vol. 15, August 1950), pp. 465–479.

[5] Talcott Parsons, *Essays in Sociological Theory: Pure and Applied*, Glencoe, Ill.: Free Press, 1949, Chap. 7, pp. 166–184; Kingsley Davis and Wilbert E. Moore, "Some Principles of Stratification," *American Sociological Review*, Vol. 10, April 1945, pp. 242–249; Melvin Tumin, "On Inequality," *American Sociological Review*, Vol. 28, February 1963, pp. 19–26.
[6] Talcott Parsons, *The Social System*, Glencoe, Ill.: Free Press, 1951, p. 172.
[7] Seymour Martin Lipset and Reinhard Bendix, *Social Mobility in Industrial Society*, Berkeley: University of California Press, 1960, Chap. 3, pp. 76–113.

Yet social inequality is compatible with American ideology as long as the inequalities result from individual qualities and achievements; *inherited* inequality seems unjust.

American sociologists, sharing as they do the values of their countrymen, may dislike the inequitable life-chances inherent in social stratification. There have been in fact, lengthy discussions of this issue in the sociological literature.[8] From the scientific point of view, however, the personal feelings of sociologists about equality of opportunity do not matter; their task is to describe how the stratification system operates in a given society. More than 20 years ago, August Hollingshead described the five classes he found in a small city in Illinois (about 6200 inhabitants in 1941). The following is a long excerpt from his classic study.

Styles of Life on the Different Prestige Levels of a Small City

Reprinted by permission. From August B. Hollingshead, *Elmtown's Youth: the Impact of Social Classes on Adolescents*, New York: Wiley, 1949, Chap. 5, pp. 83–120.

Elmtowners in general are inconsistent in the way they talk and act with reference to the idea of classes. If they are asked bluntly, "Do you believe there are 'classes' in the community?" they are very likely to say, "No." Yet, they will tell you the Binghams are "a leading family here," or the "Sweitzers are like the Binghams, Woodsons, McDermotts, and Jennings'. These families are different from the rest of us; they are very exclusive. I guess you'd call them our aristocracy." During the course of the conversation, the same speaker will say that there are several different "types of families" in the community and, justifying his judgment by describing the "way they live," place them in different categories. The democratic tradition that there are no classes in American society is the reason for this type of

8 Walter Buckley, "Social Stratification and the Functional Theory of Social Differentiation," *American Sociological Review*, Vol. 23, August 1958, pp. 369–375; Kingsley Davis, "The Abominable Heresy: A Reply to Dr. Buckley," *American Sociological Review*, Vol. 24, February 1959, pp. 82–83.

behavior. Therefore, Elmtowners deny the existence of class directly but act as if classes exist. However, many Elmtowners openly say that there are three classes in the community, "upper," "middle," and "lower," but when they are requested to name persons in, let us say, the "lower class" they generally divide the class into the "good" lower class people and the "worthless, ne'er-do-wells." The same kind of break appears in the "middle class." Separation of the "middle class" into "upper middle" and "lower middle" is quite conventional.

Even though Elmtowners are inconsistent in their designations of a particular class, the systematic analysis of selected cultural traits associated with each of the five classes, based upon data collected from the 535 families of the adolescents, supplemented by interviews and observations, reveal that the possession of a constellation of differentially evaluated social symbols—functional, pecuniary, religious, educational, reputational, power, lineage, proper associates, memberships in associations—are relied upon by Elmtowners to "hang people on the peg they belong on," to determine "their place in the community" or "their standing in life."

CLASS I

Wealth and lineage are combined through the economic, legal, and family systems in such a manner that membership in class I is more or less stabilized from one generation to another. Consequently the members of class I tend to have their position ascribed through inheritance. In view of this, very few of its members have achieved their positions in the prestige structure through their own efforts. Because the station of the family is transferred to the children and because few persons achieve class I positions through their own efforts, only a very few persons are able to enter its ranks in any one generation. Although wealth is the prime requisite for achieving positions associated with class I, once such positions have been attained, they do not need to be reinforced by further pecuniary accumulation. . . .

Marriage between social equals is desired but achieved only in about four cases out of five. Marriage with a family from a lower stratum is strongly disapproved—even the threat of one brings the force of gossip and personal pressures into play to "break the affair off" before "something happens." On the other hand, a potential marriage between equals is approved, and subtle pressures are brought to bear by relatives and friends to see it consummated, for a "successful" marriage will bring two estates together and assure the family of its station for another generation. . . .

When children are born, they are delivered in a large city hospital, usually in Chicago, by a specialist recommended to the family by a local doctor to take the case during the lying-in period. Children are carefully attended and given every consideration due future scions of a proud "old family" whose reputation in future years will rest on their shoulders after the present generation has been borne to rest beneath the green sod of "Everest" in the shadow of majestic tombstones that signify prestige of a bygone era, or rolled into the marble crypts of the mausoleum to face eternity by the side of relatives and friends of this "exclusive 2 per cent" of the community's families to which Elmtowners refer as "the society class."

Accumulated wealth provided these families with the highest incomes in the community. The two banks, the large industries, practically all the business buildings in town, as well as extensive farm lands, were owned by class I families. . . . The men were almost exclusively engaged in large business or farming enterprises, but there were a few independent professionals who had either been born into this stratum or married into it; in two or three cases they had moved into it by personal effort.

Large tax bills accompany extensive ownership; consequently these families have a direct interest in keeping assessments and tax rates low. They accomplish this effectively, within the community and the county, through the control of the two major political party organizations on the township and county levels. The candidates for public office, except the district attorney and the judge, are generally not members of class I, but this does not mean they are free from controls exerted by class I interests. Money, legal talent, and political office are instruments used to translate interests into effective power. They are relied upon to implement decisions in contests which involve raising tax bills through public improvements, such as new public buildings, schools, roads, or welfare programs. This behind-the-scenes control results in the formulation of conservative policies and the election of officials who act in the capacity of agents for class I interests.

Although class I families have the highest standard of living, their level of consumption does not exhaust their incomes; so a sizable proportion is saved. All homes are owned; many have been inherited. They are located in two residential areas, but concentrated mostly in one. . . . Practically every family owns two or three cars. The "family car" is generally a Packard, Cadillac, or Buick, less than two years old. The "business car" may range from a Cadillac to a Ford; in age, it may be the latest model or an old "jalopy." Some of the older men have been running these "business cars" for twenty years without undue cost or trouble; their sentimental attachments to the car have replaced their earlier feelings about their saddle horses. The "young folks" usually have a late model light-weight coupé or roadster as a personal car.

Leisure, not labor, is dignified; consequently as little time as possible is devoted to making a living. Wealth invested in lands, securities, and businesses assures the family a secure income with a minimum of effort. The wealthier families have managers who supervise their holdings, and only nominal supervision of these agents is necessary. The men may spend a few hours a day in the office, but most of the work is done by "the office girl." The remainder of the day may be spent in going out to the farm or farms, "to see how things are going." A walk over the farms is always in order in good weather. There are fine, blooded cattle, either Angus or Herefords, to be admired, hogs to be inspected, and instructions to be given to the tenant or farm manager. Almost all families keep one full-time maid who does the daily chores of cooking, cleaning, washing, ironing, and keeping the house in order, and a considerable minority hires an additional woman part-time to do the heavy cleaning. Yard men do the gardening in the summer months and fire the furnace in the winter. This hired help frees both the men and the women several hours each day from the confining requirements of making a living and keeping the household in order. The leisure time thus gained is consumed in many ways by different persons. In fall and early winter, the men spend several mornings each week in the duck blinds at the Hunt Club, owned and maintained by a select group of upper class families. In spring and summer there is the thrill of fishing in local lakes or in the "game fish" lakes a hundred miles to the north. Practically all families belong to the Country Club, where they while away many pleasant hours during the summer months either on the golf course or lounging and visiting on the veranda over a coke, a beer, or a long highball. The women belong to the "Friday Morning Club"; they meet and listen to speakers or just visit and gossip.

Travel is an avidly followed leisure time pursuit. Most families own or rent cottages near the northern lakes, and the women and children move to "the lake" for the summer. The head of the family makes trips there over a week end that lasts from Friday afternoon to Monday evening. A trip to Florida, the Gulf Coast, or California during January or February is the order of the season. . . .

CLASS II

Class II's prestige appears to depend as much upon civic leadership as upon economic success. A considerable proportion of the working day of many business and professional men is donated to community affairs, and the donor neither receives nor expects any compensation for his efforts other than the pleasure derived from the manipulation of human relationships in a controversial situation. A sense of personal assurance, self-mastery, and keen awareness of the way in which power is exercised is found among these men and women. As the outwardly prominent prestige bearers of community leadership, they are generally respected by the bulk of the population who look to them for "community betterment." Few people realize that these leaders may be controlled from behind the scenes, and often are, by powerful class I families who desire to have a particular person in a given office to act as their agent. Extreme personal rivalry for coveted offices often leads to personal feuds between near and would-be titans who form with other leaders alliances and power blocks pledged to back their efforts to gain control of a given office or community situation.

Approximately four out of five families in class II trace their ancestry to pioneer "American" stock, the remainder tracing their origins directly to Norwegian, German, and Irish elements who have lived in the area for two or three generations; no Poles are represented here. One-half of the class II town families live in the "best residential" section. Ninety per cent own their own nicely furnished, well-kept homes which they have either built themselves or bought. Greater prestige is attached to a house with a genealogy than to a recently built one, even though the new home is more comfortable, more convenient, and better built. Elmtown reveres the homes of its "old families," and the halo of past glory is somehow transferred from the old to the new owner.

The family's income is earned largely by the male head through active daily participation in the practice of a large independent profession (law, medicine, engineering, dentistry); in the operation of a family-owned business; as a salaried executive in an enterprise owned by class I families (the president of the Home County Bank); or as a salaried professional in a public office (the Superintendent of Schools). It may be supplemented by income from a farm or two that the family has inherited or bought; some securities; perhaps a small rental house or two. Insurance is considered a protection against the hazards of disaster and old age. . . . Most, but seldom all, of the family income is spent on daily living; however, the fraction left over for investment is not so large as it is in class I. Prudence in spending is exercised widely, for the family saves to educate its children; to buy durable quality goods, such as nice homes, furniture, automobiles; and for investment in insurance policies, a few stocks and bonds, a farm, a rental house, possibly a small business building. Security rather than wealth appears to be the economic goal. This is not to imply these people would not like to become wealthy—they would; but since they realize that they cannot achieve wealth in the normal course of events, they content themselves with striving for security. They were successful enough in the depression years to avoid all types of direct public assistance. There may have been some indirect forms, such as mortgage relief, but data were not collected on this point. All families have commercial accounts in the local banks, and all but three have savings accounts. In a crisis, bank credit is available and used when necessary. Another important point is that lawyers are used extensively as agents and for counsel in normal business activities rather than in a crisis only.

Wives as homemakers, mothers, and social secretaries run the home with the help of one general servant, usually part-time, or the hourly services of a scrub woman. The laundry is done at home, generally by the "help." Their homes, well-managed and run with a minimum of menial labor by the housewife, are a source of feminine pride, but an ambitious wife should not allow her home to outweigh "community interests," for both husband and wife must work as a team in the promotion of "community interests" if the family is to enjoy maximum prestige. Women's "community activities" generally are arranged to take place in the afternoons; the wife is seldom expected to be "out in the evening." Community demands on the husband's evenings, however, are so numerous that he is home only a few nights a week. Almost every Saturday night there are "get-togethers" in private homes; cliques of husbands and wives eat, drink, play cards, talk, and relax from the strains of daily life with obvious enjoyment.

A family car is a necessity. Prestige factors decree that it shall be a new one, under four years old, preferably large but not necessarily so, and well kept. Only a half-dozen families own two cars; in each case one car is used by the father in his business. Typically, the car is shared by the family. . . .

Parents jointly accept the duty of rearing children correctly so the family will not be "disgraced" by their "misbehavior." Parents sacrifice time, energy, and their own desires "to rear the children properly" and "to give them advantages" they may not have had themselves. Education is believed to be the prime requisite to success. Thus, an education is indispensable in the family's plan for the children's future. In passing it may be well to point out that class II adults are the most highly educated group in Elmtown. Four out of five parents have completed high school and one-half have attended a college or university from one to four years. All have graduated from the eighth grade. The college-educated fathers are concentrated in the large professions; a few are in business. The non-college fathers are in business enterprises of one kind or another. Those who have achieved success without a college education admit the lack of it, often in an indirect way, and indicate, none too subtly, their belief that they could have gone much further in business if they had had better educations. Both college and non-college fathers and mothers emphasize the need for a college education to their children. The children expect their parents to assist them materially in reaching and consolidating a desirable future. The boys are headed for

business or a profession. The girls are steered toward a desirable marriage after an education has been secured; for they must be trained for the kind of life that is expected of them. Girls are respected, well treated, and are not married off for the purpose of getting rid of them.

Almost every family is affiliated with and active in one way or another in church work. Ministers rely upon them for lay leadership in money-raising drives, Sunday School work, dinners, and other forms of the church program. Class II is predominantly Protestant (91 per cent) with a very heavy concentration in the Federated Church (60 per cent); the Methodists are a poor second (20 per cent). The remainder are split equally between the Catholic and all other Protestant churches. Approximately one-half of the adults attend church regularly and as a couple, if married. The men who do not come give as an excuse that Sunday is the only morning in the week they can sleep or that they need to work or to go out of town. They seldom admit that they have no interest in religious services, at least not enough to make the effort to go. They have, however, no objection to their wives going to or supporting the church in a financial way.

Since class II families have neither the time nor the money to travel extensively they usually make a few trips each year to a neighboring city to attend the theater or an intercollegiate football game. Their vacations are spent most often in automobile trips to various parts of the country or in a rented cabin at one of the northern lakes. Only limited use is made of public recreational facilities such as parks and playgrounds, as they have access to the Country Club. Eighty-five per cent of the class II families belong to the Country Club. Golf and gossip are the chief activities in this "social" center, but each member normally has two or three large private parties each year to pay "social debts."

CLASS III

The pivotal position of class III, lying as it does between the two extremes of the prestige structure, was demonstrated by the attitudes its members revealed toward themselves, as well as toward the other classes. As a rule, class III's exhibited strong class feelings. Above them they saw the class I's, who, they realized, were superior to themselves because of their wealth, leisure, lineage, and way of life. They also knew that the class II's occupied a position superior to their own, but a position that rested on different bases: dignified occupations, income, higher education, leadership and social activity—traits that they too possess, but not in such generous amounts. . . .

Forty-two per cent of the 129 families in class III own small businesses, farms, or are independent professionals. The other 58 per cent derive their livelihood from wages and salaries. This employed group is scattered in the mines, mills, offices, banks, and in the public service. Owners of businesses and farms and the professional workers enjoy some independence of action and leisure in the daily work routine. The employee group has little freedom of choice as to how they spend their time on the job.

One-sixth of the mothers are gainfully employed outside the home, largely as school teachers, nurses, music teachers, stenographers, bookkeepers, secretaries, seamstresses, and beauticians. These women received their training prior to marriage, were working usually when they were married, and three-fourths continued intermittently to supplement the family income rather than to support the family. A few operate small businesses, such as corner groceries, tobacco and dress shops. About one-fourth of these working mothers have had to make the family living after their husband's death.

Class III families have sufficient income for the conveniences and comforts of life, but they have little surplus to invest in productive, wealth-producing enterprises. The family income is spent on consumer goods—automobiles, clothes, electric appliances, radios, telephones, furniture, club dues, commercial amusements, popular magazine subscriptions, some domestic help, and a two-week vacation. They live under more or less standard conditions in their homes where quantity of furniture and convenience are stressed rather than quality. Home furnishings tend to be standard in design, similar in price, and uniform in the kind of article in a room; one can almost predict the arrangement of furniture. These families most nearly fit the typical American stereotype represented in popular magazines. . . .

Class III's strive to live in the better residential areas, and they have succeeded to a large extent. Twenty-five per cent have managed to locate in the best residential area, not on the best streets, but within the district. . . . Some 53 per cent live in the second best or "old residential" area.

Thus, almost eight out of ten families live in desirable areas. The remainder are scattered throughout the other districts, except that none live below the canal. Their homes are largely bungalows of five, six, or seven rooms. A few families live in commodious apartments in remodeled upper class mansions of an earlier era in the older residential area. Two-thirds of the homes are owned by the occupants. Home ownership is general among the families who own small businesses and the professional people. However, less than one-half of the foremen at the mill, salesmen, and service workers own their homes. . . .

Church guilds, study groups, missionary societies, and welfare organizations are kept alive, in large measure, by class III women. The women are twice as likely to be avid church workers as the men, but there is a significantly higher average attendance at church services among both men and women than in any other class. Regular church attendance appears to confer a kind of moral respectability peculiar to this stratum. To resign from church membership is widely condemned; to do so flaunts a class value and possibly implies the personal rejection of religious and ethical values, or so it is interpreted. The Sunday Schools are staffed almost completely by men and women from class III. Church committees are made up in four cases out of five from it. These people, along with the class II's, run the high-prestige churches. . . .

Class III is not so well educated as the higher classes; moreover, there is a distinct difference in the amount of education received by the men and women. Eighty-six per cent of the fathers have completed the eight grammar grades, 23 per cent have completed high school, and 7 per cent have taken some type of advanced training, but only one has graduated from college, and none holds an advanced collegiate degree. Ninety-nine per cent of the mothers have completed eight grades; 63 per cent have completed high school; and 46 per cent have received some type of specialized training beyond high school. Twenty-six per cent have completed a course in technical training, and 10 per cent have graduated from a recognized college or university. It is interesting to note that approximately one-half of the fathers have no formal school training beyond the eighth grade, but 97 per cent of the mothers have at least one or more years of high school.

Leisure tends to be utilized in some type of

organized group activity segregated on a sex basis and, to a considerable extent, an age basis. Both men and women are ardent joiners of lodges with auxiliaries, social clubs, church groups, patriotic societies, civic betterment groups, political party organizations, and the ubiquitous clique. It has often been observed that Americans are joiners; this is particularly true in class III, where membership in many associations, implemented by active participation, confers high prestige within the class. To be elected to office or to be on a committee adds a few additional cubits to one's stature. The most coveted memberships are in the Country Club and Rotary. An estimated 15 per cent of the Country Club's membership and 10 per cent of Rotary's comes from class III, the rest from classes I and II. However, an estimated 85 per cent of the Lion's Club membership is drawn from this stratum. The picture is similar for the exclusive women's organizations. Although class III's cannot "make the grade" to these relatively exclusive organizations in appreciable numbers, a few do, thus preserving the traditional belief that "one can go anywhere if he only has the stuff in him." The majority belongs to clubs with lesser prestige, but clubs dominated by class III; clubs where they will not be snubbed by people who consider themselves better than these above-average people who aspire "to climb the social ladder" but do not quite have the symbols which would lift them into more selective organizations with higher prestige. These people, like the typical member of each class, want to associate with people similar to themselves. Here they feel comfortable, for they are "among my kind of people." This appeared to be an important principle in the organization of the leisure time activities of each class.

Although class III persons are more actively engaged in politics than the other classes, evidence gained from interviews and direct experience in Elmtown politics did not lead to the conclusion that class III is politically powerful. On the contrary, it looks to classes I and II for leadership, direction, and policy making. As a consequence, many politically active class III's resent their impotence in the light of the work they do, but their control is limited because all policy-making offices are in the hands of the higher classes. Then, too, a very potent factor in this situation is the local paper. *The Elmtown Bugle* is owned and published by a class I family whose chief con-

cern outside the paper is the political control of the county. By common consent, this family has been singularly successful since the early 1890's; even during the depression of the 1930's, it held the county solidly Republican and on the side of "*The Bugle*'s candidates." . . .

The public record of criminal charges and convictions contains a few names of persons in class III, but none from classes I and II. This indicates either that class III persons are more likely than the higher classes to commit criminal offenses, or they lack the power to avoid charges after an offense has been committed.

CLASS IV

. . . Class IV works for a living day after day on the farms, in the mines, the mills, and the shops of Elmtown; its members are wage earners. The economic folkways prescribe that the father should support his family, but 30 per cent of the mothers are gainfully employed outside the home either as supplementary or chief breadwinner in occupations that carry little prestige, and low hourly or weekly wages. . . . Their income is large enough to provide the necessities of life and a few comforts, but few if any luxuries. Family income is spent as it is earned; little is left over for a "rainy day." As a rule, the family buys wherever it can get the most for its money. Its groceries come from the local chain outlets when the family has cash; when it is short of money, purchases are often made at a locally owned grocery that will extend credit. . . .

The meager savings of a lifetime are generally invested in a small home, bought on contract or mortgaged to a local bank, lumber yard, or a national insurance company; furniture for the house; and a family car. However, 25 per cent of the families do not own an automobile, and only 35 per cent either own or are buying a home. . . .

Cash reserves at best are not more than a few hundred dollars. Thirty-five per cent have small commercial bank accounts, and 17 per cent have savings accounts. The commercial bank accounts are limited largely to the farmers, little businessmen, and the craft and skilled workers; only 11 per cent of the laborers and service workers have commercial accounts. Bank credit is available to approximately two families out of five. Farmers, very small businessmen, and craftsmen may procure loans if they have security for a chattel mortgage. For families who do not have bank credit the local small loans broker acts as the credit agency. He does an extensive and lucrative business in class IV; 28 per cent of the families maintain an account with him (19 per cent had loans they were paying on in the spring of 1942). These families are considered to be excellent risks by the broker, for they have borrowed sums ranging from $50 to $300 repeatedly and his losses have been less than 1 per cent. . . .

The family pattern is sharply different from class III. Family stability so characteristic of the higher classes begins to give way to instability; exactly one-third of the families have been broken by separation, divorce, or death. This is a strong contrast to class III, where only 18 per cent have been broken by these same factors. Males marry when they are in their early twenties, females in their late teens. Children normally are born from 10 to 18 months later. In our families, 55 per cent of the class IV mothers gave birth to their first child before they were 20 years of age, whereas only 19 per cent of the class III mothers gave birth to their first child before their twentieth birthday. Class IV women also have more children. The mean number per family is 4.3.

The roles of the wife and mother are encompassed by her domestic duties—cleaning, washing, ironing, mending, preparation of the family's meals, cutting out and making the children's clothes, particularly little girls'. There is no part-time help except in an emergency such as childbirth or illness; even then, it is dispensed with as soon as possible. Class IV housewives are discriminated against if they have ambitions to join the Women's Club or other "social" organizations. "Their place" is "in the home" or "on the job." They are judged by the way they keep their houses, dress their children, and manage the family budget. Emphasis is placed on wifely virtues —good housekeeper, good cook, good mother, good sewer, careful of her children's welfare. The husbands are judged as providers and by their moral actions. Neither the men nor the women are expected to do more than work hard, pay their bills, raise their family in the manner expected of this class, vote "right" in elections, and, above all, eschew any radical or "bolshevik" ideas.

Formal educational experience is limited almost exclusively to the public elementary and high schools. One-third of the fathers and a fifth of the mothers have not graduated from the eighth grade; one-sixth of the fathers and one-fourth of the mothers have attended high school, but only slightly more than one father out of twenty and one mother out of eleven have graduated from high school. The present generation is receiving more education than its parents did, but the average is not more than two years of high school. Most class IV children aspire to a high school diploma, but the parents often are not convinced of its value, and they have few, if any, scruples about letting a child quit school or actually taking him out to work without a good reason. . . .

Class IV persons more or less active in religious affairs are concentrated in the Lutheran, Catholic, and low-ranking Protestant churches. The Catholic and Lutheran churches are attended very well each Sunday, but the class IV's stay away in significantly larger proportions than the higher classes. The low-ranking Protestant churches are all small except the Baptist, which is sometimes referred to as "the society church of the mill workers."

Proportionately, class IV's are not so active in the churches as the higher classes. Only 5 per cent of the fathers are reported by the ministers to be "church workers," whereas 40 per cent of the class II fathers are in this category. The mothers are more active than the fathers, but even here only 18 per cent are church workers. Among the class II mothers, the figure is 67 per cent. Obviously this class does not manifest its spirituality by work on church boards, committees, and societies. In the Methodist Church the chances are 20 to 1 that an active class IV woman will be found in the kitchen at a church dinner rather than on the planning committee for the affair. Several active class IV Methodist women are known as "kitchen Methodists."

Civic and community organizations are largely outside the experience of these people. Exclusive organizations, such as the Country Club, the Friday Morning Club, Rotary, and Lions, are closed to them, and only a few women belong to the supposedly "community-wide" Women's Club. Even the Farm Bureau and rural women's clubs are not joined in appreciable numbers. A few men belong to the Masonic Lodge, the Knights of Columbus, the Knights of Pythias, and the Odd Fellows. Their wives join the appropriate feminine complements to these organizations, but the preponderant majority of the members in these organizations come from the three higher classes. On the other hand, the Eagles, Redmen, Woodmen, and their auxiliaries are composed in large part of class IV persons who not only belong but take an active part in fraternal affairs. The local labor organizations are run almost exclusively by class IV men. . . .

There appears to be a definite attempt on the part of the factory workers to "get away from the wife" for a few hours at least once or twice a week. While the men are away, the women may call on a neighbor, putter about the house, or just relax from the labor, noise, and excitement of the daily grind of preparing meals, putting up lunches, cleaning the house, washing and ironing clothes, going to market, and caring for the children. The man's escape from home may be an adjustment to a tired, irritable, and frustrated wife who has a task that is too difficult for her to do "with what she has to do it with." The higher classes know little about the leisure activities of the class IV's, and they care less. This class is taken for granted, and the existence of its members is largely ignored except in so far as they perform economic and political functions.

Periodically, the attention of the community is focused very briefly on some person who has committed a crime. This occurs more frequently in class IV than in class III, for 14 per cent of class IV fathers were convicted in local courts of offense between 1934 and 1941, but only 4 per cent of class III fathers.

CLASS V

Class V occupies the lowest-ranking stations in the prestige structure. It is looked upon as the scum of the city by the higher classes. It is believed generally that nothing beyond charity can be done for these people, and only a minimum of that is justified since they show little or no inclination to help themselves. It is the opinion of the upper classes that:

"They have no respect for the law, or themselves.

"They enjoy their shacks and huts along the river or across the tracks and love their dirty, smoky, low-class dives and taverns.

"Whole families—children, in-laws, mistresses, and all—live in one shack.

"This is the crime class that produces the delinquency and sexual promiscuity that fills the paper.

"Their interests lie in sex and its perversion. The girls are always pregnant; the families are huge; incestual relations occur frequently.

"They are not inspired by education, and only a few are able to make any attainments along this line.

"They are loud in their speech, vulgar in their actions, sloppy in their dress, and indifferent toward their plight. Their vocabulary develops as profanity is learned.

"If they work, they work at very menial jobs.

"Their life experiences are purely physical, and even these are on a low plane.

"They have no interest in health and medical care.

"The men are too lazy to work or do odd jobs around town.

"They support the Democratic party because of the relief obtained during the depression.

"This group lives for a Saturday of drinking or fighting. They are of low character and breed and have a criminal record for a pedigree." . . .

Family support comes from many sources. The father is the chief breadwinner in three families out of five, but his earnings are meager. Ninety-two per cent are unskilled and semi-skilled laborers or machine operators. Not one is a farm owner, and only 8 are farm tenants; 2 are notions salesmen; and 8 operate very small businesses, such as hauling coal from local mines, ash and trash hauling, repair and sales of old cars. Fifty-five per cent of the mothers "work out" part or full time as waitresses, dishwashers, cooks, washwomen, janitresses, cleaning women, and unskilled domestic workers. Many younger women and girls work on the production line of a local manufacturer who is reputed to give them preference in his shops because they can be hired for lower wages than class IV workers. . . .

The uncertain nature of their employment results in long periods of idleness; also illness, real or imagined, may result in a voluntary layoff for a few days that, to persons in the higher classes, appears to be laziness. Whatever the conditioning factors, these people are far more irregular in their employment than the class IV's. They will leave a job casually, often without notice, and for flimsy reasons. Employers do not like to hire them unless labor is scarce or they can be induced to work for low wages. Even then they are placed in the simplest and most menial jobs. The work history of a father or mother is generally known to employers, and he acts in the light of it when a son or daughter of one of these families asks him for employment.

All population elements are represented, but three families out of five (58 per cent) trace their ancestry to "American stock" that came to Elmtown before the Civil War. In spite of popular belief, "the Irish element" has contributed less than 9 per cent to the ranks of class V. The Poles are found here twice as frequently, and the Germans and Norwegians only one-third as frequently as we may expect if chance factors alone are operating. The concentration of "American stock" is overlooked by Elmtowners who commonly use a European ancestral background as a symbolic label. This is understandable in the case of the Poles; they were imported as strikebreakers, and they have not outlived this experience or their ethnic background. Many of these "American" families have lived in Elmtown as long as its "leading families"; however, length of residence is their only similarity to leading families, for through the generations they have achieved notorious histories. Unfortunately, the unsavory reputation of an ancestor is remembered and often used as an explanation for present delinquency. It is interesting to note that the doctrine of "blood" which explains the rise to eminence of class I is used in the same way to justify the derogation of class V. And, significantly, present behavior of class V gives the people who hold such beliefs a basis for their conviction. Sociologically, such an explanation is unwarranted, but Elmtowners are not sociologists! Often such remarks as the following are made about these families or some member of them, "Blood will out"; "You can't expect anything else from such people"; "His great-grandfather was hanged for killing a neighbor in cold blood!" . . .

The dilapidated, box-like homes contain crude pieces of badly abused furniture, usually acquired secondhand. A combination wood and coal stove, or kerosene burner, is used for both cooking and heating. An unpainted table and a few chairs held together with baling wire, together with an ancient sideboard—with shelves above to hold the assorted dishes and drawers below for pots, pans, and groceries—furnish the combined kitchen and dining room. There may be some well-worn linoleum or strips of roofing on the floor. The "front room" generally serves a dual purpose, living room by day and bedroom by night. Here too the floor is often covered with linoleum or roofing strips, seldom with a woven rug. Two or three overly used chairs in various stages of disrepair share the room with a sagging sofa that leads a double life as the routine of day alternates with that of night. If an additional bed is needed, an iron one may stand in a corner or along one wall. A simple mirror that shows signs of age, perhaps abuse, shares the wall with a few cheap prints or pictures cut from magazines that show how undressed a woman may be without being nude. Now and again a colored print of a saint and a motion picture star will be pasted or nailed beside a siren. An improvised wardrobe made by driving a row of nails in the wall generally occupies one corner. A table, radio, and some means of lighting the room complete its furnishings. Old iron beds that sag in the middle, made with blankets and comforts in the absence of sheets, a chest of drawers, a chair or two, and a mirror that looks out on the stringy curtains and the bare floor complete the furnishings of the tiny bedrooms. Musical instruments, magazines, and newspapers other than *The Bugle* seldom find their way into these homes. Less than 1 per cent have telephones.

Privacy in the home is almost non-existent; parents, children, "in-laws" and their children, and parts of a broken family may live in two or three rooms. There is little differentiation in the use of rooms—kitchen, dining room, living room, and bedroom functions may be combined from necessity into a single use area. Bath and toilet facilities are found in approximately one home in seven. City water is piped near or into 77 per cent of the homes within the city limits, except those below the canal. Water for these homes is either carried from the town pump, also located in this area, or from the river. Outside the town, wells, springs, and creeks are used for a water supply. Some 4 per cent of the homes were equipped with furnace heat; the rest were heated with wood- or coal-burning stoves. . . .

The family pattern is unique. The husband-wife relationship is more or less an unstable one, even though the marriage is sanctioned either by law or understandings between the partners. Disagreements leading to quarrels and vicious fights, followed by desertion by either the man or the woman, possibly divorce, is not unusual. The evidence indicates that few compulsive factors, such as neighborhood solidarity, religious teachings, or ethical considerations, operate to maintain a stable marital relationship. On the contrary, the class culture has established a family pattern where serial monogamy is the rule. Legal marriages are restricted within narrow limits to class equals. However, exploitive sex liaisons between males from the higher classes frequently occur with teen-age girls, but they rarely result in marriage. Marriage occurs in the middle teens for the girls and the late teens or early twenties for the boys. Doctors, nurses, and public officials who know these families best estimate that from one-fifth to one-fourth of all births are illegitimate. Irrespective of the degree of error in this estimate, 78 per cent of the mothers gave birth to their first child before they were 20 years of age. Another trait that marks the family complex is the large number of children. The mean is 5.6 per mother, the range, 1 to 13. There is little pre-natal or post-natal care of either mother or child. . . . Death, desertion, separation, or divorce has broken more than half the families (56 per cent). The burden of child care, as well as support, falls on the mother more often than on the father when the family is broken. The mother-child relation is the strongest and most enduring family tie.

Formal educational experience is limited in large part to the elementary school. Two parents out of three (67 per cent) quit school before the eighth grade was reached; the third completed it. Seven fathers and six mothers out of 230 have completed a year or more of high school; only one father and four mothers have graduated. None has attended any type of school after leaving the public school system. . . .

Class V persons are almost totally isolated from organized community activities. A few men claim membership in veterans' organizations, but they neither pay dues nor attend meetings. Workers in the Mill belong to the union, since this is a closed shop; the others follow lines of work not organized by the unions. Time has little value in the daily routine. Even getting to work on time and staying on the job are not too highly regarded. Employers complained bitterly about their loose work habits. They claim that these people come to work at irregular times, leave when they feel like it, and lay off on the least excuse. Since they do not participate in organized community affairs, hours off the job and during the periods of unemployment or layoff are spent the way the person chooses without too much interference from neighbors. Leisure is expended in loafing around the neighborhood, in the downtown district, along the river, and at home. Their social

life consists of informal visits between neighbors, gossip, petty gambling, visits to the cheaper theaters, going to town, drinking in the home or public taverns, with now and again a fist fight. The family is so loosely organized that the members usually go their own way in search of amusement or pleasure. The cliques are severely age- and sex-graded; men associate with men and women with women, except in their ubiquitous sex play.

Organized dinners and parties where guests are invited to the home on a Saturday night are unknown. Festive gatherings take place on Sunday when many branches of the family unite for a brief spell of merrymaking. The low-ranking taverns are filled on Saturday nights with class V's of all ages who gather there for their big social night. Small children are kept up until after midnight in the hot, smoke-filled, poorly lighted, noisy "poor man's night club." Young couples wander in and out; often preliminary "passes" are made in preparation for a later seduction. Almost every Saturday night the police are called to some low-ranking tavern to break up a fight between half-drunk customers.

The police, sheriff, prosecuting attorney, and judge know these families from frequent contact through the years, whereas the ministers and school officials may be only slightly acquainted with them. Between 1934 and 1941, 8 per cent of the mothers and 46 per cent of the fathers had been convicted once or more in the local courts. Public drinking, disorderly conduct, family neglect, and sex offenses were the charges against the women; they averaged 1.5 convictions each. The men were more or less chronic offenders who were convicted of habitual public drunkenness, 49 per cent; miscellaneous offenses, 30 per cent; offenses against property, 12 per cent; sex and family neglect, 9 per cent. They averaged 4.1 convictions each in the eight years covered by reliable court records. Their misdeeds are prominently written up in *The Bugle*. If they do not reach the paper, they are known by some persons in the higher classes who delight in telling about them to their acquaintances.

The foregoing description of social classes in Elmtown has a ring of authenticity about it. Remember, however, that Elmtown contained only about 6200 people when Professor Hollingshead was studying its system of social stratification. Neat ranking of community prestige may be feasible in a small community but not in an anonymous metropolis. Sociologists at the University of Michigan investigated this problem by surveying a random sample of residents of the Detroit metropolitan area.[9] Professors Lenski and Landecker examined the positions of 749 respondents on four dimensions: income level, educational attainment, occupational prestige, and racial or ethnic origins. Although three-quarters of their respondents had consistent ratings on all four dimensions, one-quarter had markedly inconsistent standings in two or more of them; for example, some well-educated Negroes had low-paid jobs. Lenski and Landecker hypothesized that these persons whose status had not *crystallized* would have distinctive political attitudes, and they found evidence supporting their hypothesis. Even if we ignore what Lenski and Landecker were most interested in studying, the *effect* of lack of class crystallization, the *existence* of inconsistent evaluations in the stratification system of a large city challenges the assumption of a clear-cut status hierarchy. Class lines are not as simple to draw in Detroit as they were in Elmtown.

First, the standards of evaluation may not be fully shared by all members of the society. And the larger the society, the more probable is lack of consensus; Detroiters are more likely than Elmtowners to disagree as to who belongs where. Second, status ratings necessarily refer to a particular moment. This would not constitute a serious problem in feudal or caste societies where the standing of the individual does not change much during his lifetime. But industrial societies permit considerable upward and downward movement on the prestige scale. Hence, an assessment of the status of an individual in an industrial society is like taking a

photograph of a moving object with a slow lens. The faster it moves, the worse the picture. And there is evidence that upward and downward movement is faster (more common) in large cities than in small ones.[10] Finally, in a highly differentiated society, the individual's multiplicity of roles cannot be fully known to all of the persons with whom he interacts. Yet global status evaluations depend on such knowledge.

TECHNIQUES FOR MEASURING STATUS IN SMALL AND LARGE COMMUNITIES

Despite the difficulties of status measurement in fluid industrial societies, sociologists have plunged in zestfully. Hundreds of studies have been carried out in which individuals are allocated to social classes and their differential behaviors compared. Table 25, an example of such studies, reports data collected in 1947 on the value placed on higher education by different social classes in a national sample of approximately 3000 persons. Several different techniques for breaking the sample into social classes lead to the same result: persons in the lower echelons of the American stratification system are less likely than persons in higher echelons to consider college education essential for young people.[11]

REPUTATIONAL RATINGS. Sociologists have used a variety of techniques for allocating people to social classes. Studies in the field of social stratification show, however, that, by and large, *different* techniques are used in small communities and in the "mass society" of big cities. *Reputational* measures, for instance, are common in community studies like Elmtown.[12]

---

[9] Gerhard E. Lenski, "Status Crystallization: a Nonvertical Dimension of Social Status," *American Sociological Review*, Vol. 19, August 1954, pp. 405–413; Werner S. Landecker, "Class Crystallization and Its Urban Pattern," *Social Research*, Vol. 27, August 1960, pp. 308–320; Werner S. Landecker, "Class Crystallization and Class Consciousness," *American Sociological Review*, Vol. 28, April 1963, pp. 219–229.

[10] Seymour Martin Lipset and Reinhard Bendix, *Social Mobility in Industrial Societies*, Berkeley: University of California Press, 1960, pp. 204–213.
[11] Herbert H. Hyman, "The Value Systems of Different Classes: A Social Psychological Contribution to the Analysis of Stratification," in Bendix and Lipset, Eds., *Class, Status and Power*, Glencoe, Ill.: Free Press, 1953, pp. 426–442.
[12] W. Lloyd Warner and Paul S. Lunt, *The Social Life of a Modern Community*, New Haven: Yale University Press, 1941; Harold F. Kaufman, "Prestige (continued on next page)

In such a study, the status rating for an individual hinges on the votes he receives from other members of his community in a poll conducted by the researcher. In the Elmtown study, Hollingshead adopted the following procedure:

1. He asked 12 Elmtowners to assign a control list of 20 well-known families to different status levels.

TABLE 25
The Differential Emphasis Among Economic Classes upon College Education as an Essential to Advancement

Interviewer's Rating of Economic Level	Per Cent Recommending College Education	N
Wealthy and prosperous	68	512
Middle class	52	1531
Lower class	39	856
Occupation		
Professional	74	301
Businessmen and proprietors	62	421
White collar workers	65	457
Skilled labor	53	392
Semiskilled	49	416
Domestic and personal service workers	42	194
Farmers	47	417
Nonfarm laborers	35	132
Highest Education Achieved		
Attended college	72	564
Attended high school	55	1411
Attended grammar school	36	926
Among renters, Monthly rental		
Above $60	70	327
$40–60	64	666
$20–40	54	990
Below $20	37	403

Source: Herbert H. Hyman, "The Value Systems of Different Classes: A Social Psychological Contribution to the Analysis of Stratification," in Bendix and Lipset, Eds., *Class, Status and Power*, Glencoe, Ill.: Free Press, 1953, p. 430.

Classes in a New York Rural Community," Ithaca, N.Y.: Cornell University Agricultural Experiment Station, Memoir 260, 1944, pp. 3–46; John Useem, Pierre Tangent, and Ruth Useem, "Stratification in a Prairie Town," *American Sociological Review*, Vol. 7, June 1942, pp. 331–342.

2. Since most of the 12 judges distributed the 20 well-known families among five levels, Hollingshead assigned his 20 control families to these five levels.

3. He then used 31 Elmtowners (other than the 12 original raters) to assign each of the 535 families in the study to one of the five prestige levels established by the 20 control families.

Since the 31 raters were carefully chosen on the basis of long residence in Elmtown (and other criteria) and since at least two well-known families from the control list exemplified each status level, the raters did not have difficulty assigning the families to status levels. Some families were identified by as many as 22 raters; ten families were identified by only seven of them. In general, the status level assigned the family by Hollingshead was the average assignment given to it by those who rated it. Complicated though Hollingshead's procedure was, it amounted to having 31 residents of Elmtown serve as *representatives* of the community for the purpose of assigning ratings. Hollingshead might equally well have asked *all* Elmtowners instead of 31 to rate the 535 families; he devised an ingenious short-cut to avoid asking every member of the community about everyone else. The 20 control-list families functioned as a single pretested question. Essentially then, Hollingshead delineated the deference hierarchy in a small city in Illinois by asking representatives of the community to answer the following question about every family that they recognized: "Is the community standing of this family more like that of families A and B, of families C, D, and E, of families F, G, H, and I, of families J, K, L, M, N, and O, or of families P, Q, R, S, and T?"

SELF-PLACEMENT IN THE CLASS STRUCTURE. The reputational method of measuring status has obvious limitations. If the community is large, no rater can evaluate more than a tiny fraction of the total population. Furthermore, ratings from *different* communities within the same society are incomparable. These drawbacks of reputational methods do not apply to techniques that permit the respondent to assess his *own* standing (self-placement). One of the best self-placement measures of status was developed by a social psychologist, Richard Centers, for inclusion in surveys conducted by polling organizations.[13] Respondents are assigned to socioeconomic classes on the basis of their replies to the following question: "If you were asked to use one of these four names for your social class, which would you say you belonged in: the middle class, lower class, working class, or upper class?" Table 26 shows how a national sample of white American men answered this question in 1945. Very few respondents defined themselves as "upper class" or "lower class"; "working class" and "middle class" were the attractive choices.

The self-placement method of measuring status has limitations of its own. For example, the class with which the respondent identifies himself may represent his aspirations rather than his current interactions. The self-placement technique relies on the honesty as well as on the class awareness of the respondent. Neither of these limitations destroys the validity of the self-placement method. The problem of obtaining truthful answers to potentially embarrassing questions is not unique to studies of stratification; some respondents lie in order to increase their sense of self-importance, but

not many. And most people are aware of the existence of a hierarchy of prestige and power in their community. Interestingly enough, self-placement did not look like a promising technique before Centers added "working class" to the "upper class, middle class, lower class" choices. Faced with "upper class, middle class, lower class," 88 per cent of American respondents said they were "middle class." [14] This was interpreted to mean that Americans were not class conscious. A better interpretation would have been that Americans did not like the ideological implications of calling themselves

TABLE 26
Class Identifications of a National Cross Section of White Males (July 1945)

Response	Per Cent
Upper class	3
Middle class	43
Working class	51
Lower class	1
Don't know	1
"Don't believe in classes"	1
Total	100

Source: Richard Centers, *The Psychology of Social Classes: A Study of Class Consciousness*, Princeton, N.J.: Princeton University Press, 1949, p. 77.

TABLE 27
Differential Identification with the Middle and Upper Classes on the Part of Respondents from Various Occupational, Educational, and Income Levels

	Number	Per Cent Identifying with Middle and Upper Classes
Occupational and Educational Levels		
Business, professional, and white collar		
Graduate school	49	92
College graduate	68	90
Some college	81	83
High school graduate	96	71
Some high school	69	64
All grade school levels	53	58
Manual workers		
All college levels	18	—
High school graduate	75	28
Some high school	97	22
Seventh and eighth grades	134	22
Sixth grade or less	84	7
Interviewer Rating of Economic Status		
Wealthy	49	86
Average plus	135	84
Average	345	60
Poor plus	275	30
Poor	292	19

Source: Richard Centers, *op. cit.*, pp. 164, 110.

---

13 Richard Centers, *The Psychology of Social Classes: A Study of Class Consciousness*, Princeton, N.J.: Princeton University Press, 1949.

14 George Gallup and S. F. Rae, *The Pulse of Democracy*, New York: Simon & Schuster, 1940, p. 169.

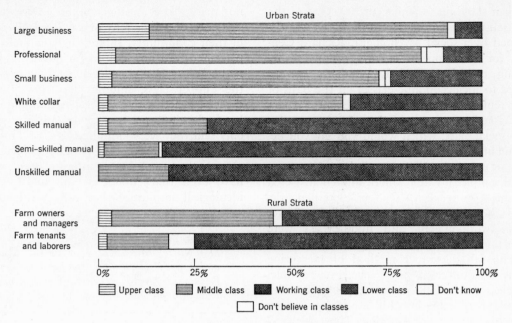

FIGURE 8. Class identifications of occupational strata.

"lower class." The fact is that subjectively determined class identifications correlate strongly with more objective indices: educational attainment, occupation, and income—and also with economic and political attitudes. Table 27 and Figure 8 present data tabulated by Centers which illustrate this point.

THE EVALUATION OF CULTURAL ARTIFACTS. In some research projects, people are classified in one social rank or another, not on the basis of what they say about themselves or of what others say about them, but because of cultural symbols associated with them. Public-opinion polls often use interviewer ratings of the socioeconomic status of respondents. On the basis of their style of dress, the furnishings of their homes, their manner of speech, and other symbols known to be associated with socioeconomic status, respondents are rated A, B, C+, C, or D.[15] Figure 9 shows that such ratings of socioeconomic status bear a consistent relationship to voting behavior.

Despite the training that interviewers receive from the polling organization to achieve consistency in their ratings, much discretion is necessarily left to the interviewers. A generation ago F. Stuart Chapin constructed a less intuitive scale of socioemonomic status, which also used interviewer assessment of cultural symbols. Professor Chapin's Living Room Scale of status depended on notations made by an interviewer of the furnishings and appearance of a family's living quarters.[16] A schedule of questions was supplied the interviewer; his task was to check on various items, such as whether there was a rug on the living room floor. Once the interviewer handed in his filled-out schedule, previously determined weights were applied, and a status score for the family emerged. Although none of the items on the schedule dealt with the interaction of one family with another (or the prestige of one family vis-à-vis another), Chapin meant the status scores gen-

15   Paul F. Lazarsfeld, Bernard Berelson, and Hazel Gaudet, *The People's Choice: How the Voter Makes Up His Mind in a Presidential Campaign*, New York: Duell, Sloan and Pearce, 1944, pp. 17–18.

16   F. Stuart Chapin, *Contemporary American Institutions*, New York: Harper, 1935, pp. 373–398; Louis Guttman, "A Revision of Chapin's Social Status Scale," *American Sociological Review*, Vol. 7, June 1942, pp. 362–369.

TABLE 28

Differential Readership of LIFE Magazine by Education and Annual Household Income

Repeat Audiences of LIFE by Education (People Age 20 and Older)

Number of issues read out of six issues	LAST GRADE OF SCHOOL COMPLETED						
	0–4th grade	5–7th grade	Finished grade school	1–3rd year high school	Finished high school	1st year college or beyond	All people 20 years old and older
Audience coverage							
One or two	18.2%	21.1%	27.3%	33.8%	30.6%	25.1%	27.3%
Three or four	2.3	9.6	7.6	11.9	14.6	21.6	12.1
Fixe or six	2.2	3.0	4.7	6.8	11.0	22.7	9.0
Total: Read one or more	22.7%	33.7%	39.6%	52.5%	56.2%	69.4%	48.4%

Repeat Audiences of LIFE by Annual Household Income

Number of issues read out of six issues	ANNUAL HOUSEHOLD INCOME					
	Under $2,000	$2,000–$2,999	$3,000–$4,999	$5,000–$6,999	$7,000 or more	All people
Audience coverage						
One or two	18.8%	34.2%	30.4%	29.1%	27.9%	29.1%
Three or four	4.9	11.7	12.9	17.9	20.0	12.7
Five or six	4.5	4.3	8.5	13.0	22.0	8.8
Total: Read one or more	28.2%	50.2%	51.8%	60.0%	69.9%	50.6%

Source: Alfred Politz Research, Inc., *A Study of Four Media: Their Accumulative and Repeat Audiences*, New York: Time, Incorporated, 1953, pp. 21, 23.

erated by his Scale to be compared with one another. He developed the Living Room Scale because interactive evaluations struck him as more difficult to measure than the possession of certain cultural objects and because he assumed that such possessions reflected the social standing of their owners.

STATUS RATINGS BASED ON OCCUPATION, EDUCATION, OR INCOME. The most common measures of social class used by contemporary sociologists are, as might be expected, the simplest and the cheapest. Research has demonstrated that status ratings based on occupation, education, or income correlate with reputational and self-placement ratings as well as with certain cultural symbols. For example, Table 28 shows that higher-status people are more likely to read *Life* magazine whether status is measured

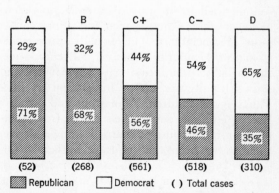

Those high in socioeconomic status (SES level) are more likely to vote Republican than Democratic.

FIGURE 9. Voting behavior by socioeconomic status. Source: Paul F. Lazarsfeld, Bernard Berelson, and Hazel Gaudet, *The People's Choice: How the Voter Makes Up His Mind in a Presidential Campaign*, New York: Duell, Sloan and Pearce, 1944, p. 19.

by educational achievement or by annual household income.

Implicit in the use of occupation, education, or income to rank a population into strata is some *theory* of social stratification. In this book, stratification is defined unidimensionally: as a gradient of prestige. A theory is required to account for the emergence of this gradient and to explain why status ratings (of prestige) correlate with ratings based on occupation, education, and income. The theory of stratification in American society to be presented in the next section attempts to satisfy these requirements. Like all theories it tries to fit known facts and succeeds in fitting some better than others.

STRATIFICATION IN AMERICAN SOCIETY [17]

The key to social stratification in industrial societies is the occupational structure and specifically the place of adult males in it. The first question to ask in seeking to understand the status of an American family is, "What is the occupation of the husband-father?" Gainful employment of women, including married women, is a continuing trend, but the married woman derives her status more from her husband's job than from her own. That is why women tend to be wary about marrying men of lower status whereas men can afford to be more democratic.[18] The socially prominent woman who marries a laborer falls in status; the socially prominent man who marries a showgirl pulls her up to his station in life. What about children? Adolescent and preadolescent children derive their status from that of their fathers just as married women derive their status from that of their husbands. Of course, once they become adults, marry, and establish their own households, their status no

longer depends on that of their parents. Occupation becomes the crucial status determinant for sons; for daughters, the main criterion is the men they marry.

The occupational role is the key to social stratification in industrial societies for two reasons, one direct, the other indirect. What a man *does* occupationally tends to define him to himself as well as to others—and therefore to provide a *direct* basis for social assessment. In addition, the occupational role of the adult male is the main source of money income for most families. Since money income influences the neighborhood in which the family lives, the type of car it can afford, and the clothing its members wear (as well as its expenditures for food and recreation), the occupational role of the breadwinner is an indirect determinant of the *style of life* of the family. In short, the occupational role has two aspects: (1) what the worker *produces* for society and (2) the remuneration he receives for his productive contribution, and thus what he and his dependents *consume*.

The rank order of prestige of 90 occupations was measured in a study conducted by the National Opinion Research Center (N.O.R.C.) in 1947. The N.O.R.C. field staff interviewed a United States sample containing 2920 respondents. Each respondent was asked to select the number on a card (handed to him by the interviewer) corresponding to his evaluation of each occupation.[19] The card looked like this:

For each job mentioned, please pick out the statement that best gives *your own personal opinion* of the *general standing* that such a job has.
1. *Excellent* standing
2. *Good* standing
3. *Average* standing
4. *Somewhat below average* standing
5. *Poor* standing
X. I don't know where to place that one

---

17 The analysis that follows leans heavily on Talcott Parsons, "A Revised Analytical Approach to the Theory of Social Stratification," in Bendix and Lipset, Eds., *Class, Status and Power*, Glencoe, Ill.: Free Press, 1953, pp. 92–128.

18 August B. Hollingshead, "Cultural Factors in the Selection of Marriage Mates," *American Sociological Review*, Vol. 15, October 1950, pp. 625–626.

19 Albert J. Reiss, Jr., *Occupations and Social Status*, New York: Free Press of Glencoe, 1961, pp. 18–19.

Table 29 compares the prestige ratings of 45 of these occupations with the levels of remuneration they afford. Note that high-prestige occupations like architects and bankers usually had high incomes; and low-prestige occupations like bootblacks and counter and fountain workers usually had low incomes. On the other hand, clergymen had high prestige and low in-

TABLE 29

Comparison of the N.O.R.C. Prestige Ratings and the 1949 Incomes of 45 Occupations

Census Occupational Title (NORC title in parenthesis)	NORC Prestige Rating [a]	1949 Income [b]
Accountants and auditors (accountant for a large business)	82	62
Airline pilots and navigators (airline pilot)	83	72
Architects (architect)	90	75
Authors (author of novels)	76	55
Chemists (chemist)	90	64
Clergymen (minister)	87	21
College presidents, professors, and instructors (college professor)	93	64
Dentists (dentist)	90	80
Editors and reporters (reporter on a daily newspaper)	52	67
Engineers, civil (civil engineer)	88	72
Funeral directors and embalmers (undertaker)	57	42
Lawyers and judges (lawyer)	89	76
Physicians and surgeons (physician)	97	76
Social and welfare workers, except group (welfare worker for a city government)	59	41
Teachers (instructor in the public schools)	73	48
Conductors, railroad (railroad conductor)	38	76
Managers, officials, and proprietors: Construction (building contractor)	76	53
Manufacturing (owner of a factory that employs about 100 people)	81	60
Retail trade (manager of a small store in a city)	45	42
Banking and other finance (banker)	92	78
Bookkeepers (bookkeeper)	39	29
Mail carriers (mail carrier)	34	48
Insurance agents and brokers (insurance agent)	41	55
Salesmen and sales clerks, retail trade (clerk in a store)	16	29
Carpenters (carpenter)	33	21
Electricians (electrician)	53	47
Locomotive engineers (railroad engineer)	67	81
Machinists (trained machinist)	57	36
Mechanics and repairmen, automobile (automobile repairmen)	26	22
Plumbers and pipe fitters (plumber)	29	44
Attendants, auto service and parking (filling-station attendant)	10	15
Mine operatives and laborers, coal mining (coal miner)	15	7
Motormen, street, subway, and elevated railway (streetcar motorman)	19	42
Taxicab drivers and chauffeurs (taxi driver)	10	9
Truck and tractor drivers (truck driver)	13	21
Operatives and kindred workers, manufacturing (machine operator in a factory)	24	21
Barbers, beauticians, and manicurists (barber)	20	16
Bartenders (bartender)	7	16
Bootblacks (shoe shiner)	3	9
Cooks, except private household (restaurant cook)	16	14
Counter and fountain workers (soda fountain clerk)	6	12
Guards, watchmen, and doorkeepers (night watchmen)	11	17
Janitors and sextons (janitor)	8	7
Policemen and detectives, government (policemen)	41	34
Waiters and waitresses (restaurant waiter)	10	8

[a] Per cent of respondents rating occupation "excellent" or "good"; base of per cent excludes "don't know" responses.

[b] Per cent of males in the 1950 experienced civilian labor force with incomes of $3500 or more in 1949, adjusted by age of respondents.

Source: Albert J. Reiss, Jr., *Occupation and Social Status*, New York: Free Press of Glencoe, 1961, pp. 122–123, in a chapter prepared by Otis Dudley Duncan.

comes; and railroad conductors had low prestige and high incomes. Which is more relevant to social status: occupational prestige or money income?

Money income is certainly a *convenient* index of social status; it generates an unequivocal rank order without elaborate attitude surveys. Furthermore, prestigeful consumption patterns are correlated with money income. Although ostentatious displays of wealth by *nouveaux riches* prove that purchasing power is not sufficient to maintain a prestigeful style of life, most of the symbols of high-prestige consumption are expensive. The difficulty with money income as an index of status is that industrial societies contain parallel rank systems within the occupational realm with comparable prestige and different levels of remuneration.[20] Within business and professional occupations, for example, the self-employed restaurateur or dentist may earn more than a middle-level executive or a research scientist in a large corporation, yet the standing of the executive and the scientist in the community would be at least as high. Second, there exists a class of occupations dependent on philanthropy or taxation rather than on the sale of products or services in the market place. The low level of remuneration in government service (including the Armed Forces), in churches, in hospitals, and in social-work agencies reflects the subsidized character of these occupations, but their prestige is high. That a Metropolitan opera star earns less than Elvis Presley and a Supreme Court justice less than a corporation lawyer is ironic; but it does not prove who outranks whom in social status.

Perhaps the question of the relative importance of occupational prestige and style of life in the American class system is unanswerable —given the fluidity of industrial societies generally and of big cities in particular. Such a wide range of goods and services are for sale in

the market place—cigarettes, automobiles, hotel accommodations, theater tickets—that lack of clarity in the ranking system is a tolerable form of ambiguity. In an affluent industrial society, consumers have an enormous range of discretionary expenditures. Even a laborer can buy a Cadillac if he can scrape up enough cash for a down-payment. In feudal Europe, on the other hand, only a noble could participate in knightly tournaments. This difference is important; it means that Americans frequently find themselves in situations where status comparisons do not have to be made or status credentials scrutinized too closely.

This fluidity of the class structure in industrial societies helps to explain why the precise *number* of social classes is a matter of dispute among sociologists. W. Lloyd Warner counts six, Hollingshead five, and so on.[21] In most contexts, especially for males, occupational prestige is the crucial factor in social ranking. In some contexts, especially for females, style of life is more important. An element of arbitrariness necessarily enters into any classification of social classes because the scientific observer must settle questions that interaction leaves unsettled. Furthermore, a complex society is a mosaic of separate worlds. The university professor lives in a world of university professors, a business man in a world of business men. These worlds may be physically close, as when a professor and a business man are neighbors, but they have independent standards of evaluation. Thus, a university professor can drive a ten-year-old car without the slightest loss of status in *his* reference group whereas his entrepreneurial neighbor *must* drive a later-model car to maintain *his* standing in the business community. In sum, the many rank systems of an industrial society do not fully coalesce—except in sociological analyses of stratification. People tend to care more about the judgments of their immediate neighbors or work associates than they do about their overall standing in the larger society. This reference-group aspect of stratification further blurs an already fluid class system. John Kenneth Gal-

[20]   Paul K. Hatt, "Occupation and Social Stratification," *American Journal of Sociology*, Vol. 55, May 1950, pp. 533–543; Richard T. Morris and Raymond J. Murphy, "The Situs Dimension in Occupational Structure," *American Sociological Review*, Vol. 24, April 1959, pp. 231–239.

[21]   Warner and Lunt, *op. cit.*; Hollingshead, *op. cit.*

braith, a Harvard economist and former ambassador to India, commented on the subjective restriction of the world by members of his own profession.

A Reference Group Phenomenon: Hierarchy in a Closed World

Reprinted by permission. From John Kenneth Galbraith, "The Language of Economics," *Fortune*, Vol. 56, December 1962, pp. 128–130, 169, 171.

Professional economists, like members of city gangs, religious congregations, public schools, aboriginal tribes, fashionable regiments, craft unions, clubs, learned disciplines, holders of diplomatic passports, and, one is told, the intellectually more demanding criminal pursuits, have the natural desire of all such groups to delineate and safeguard the boundary between those who belong and those who do not. This has variously been called the tribal, gang, club, guild, union, or aristocratic instinct.

The differentiation of those who belong from those who do not is invariably complemented by a well-graded prestige system within the tribal group. And—a vital point—the two are closely interdependent. If the members of the tribal group are sufficiently conscious of the boundary that separates them from the rest of the world, the tribe becomes *the* world to its members. Its limits and the mental horizons of the members are coterminous. This means, in turn, that the prestige system of the tribe is the only one that has meaning to a member and it is all-important. The most honorific position in the tribal group then becomes the most honorific position in the universe. If the school is all that counts, then the head boy is a person of the greatest possible grandeur. In the Barchester Close the eminence of the Bishop was absolute because no one was aware of the world beyond. Everything within, in each case, depends on the exclusion of what is without.

The prestige system of economics is wholly in accord with these principles. It assigns, and for good reason, the very lowest position to the man who deals with everyday policy. For this individual, in concerning himself with the wisdom of a round of wage increases or the need for an addition to the deficit, is immediately caught up in a variety of political and moral judgments.

As such he is a threat to the sharp delineation that separates the tribal group from the rest of society and thus to the prestige system of the profession. Moreover, his achievements are rated not by his professional peers but by outsiders. This causes difficulty in fitting him into the professional hierarchy and argues strongly for leaving him at the bottom.

A very low position is also assigned to economists who, even though forswearing any interest in practical affairs, occupy themselves with related disciplines—urban sociology, political theory, cultural anthropology, juvenile delinquency. The reason is the same. These men are also inimical to the tribal delineation and their achievements depend on the judgment of non-economists and thus cannot be integrated into the established scale. An economist who concerns himself with sociology is assumed by his colleagues to be escaping the rigors of his own subject and by sociologists to be showing slightly broadened tendencies of mind.

If Professor Galbraith is correct, economists disregard the evaluations of everybody but other economists; and so it is with each occupational community. Such parochialism would be incompatible with social stratification. Stratification implies *consensus* on who stands high and who stands low. If bankers looked down on garbage collectors, and garbage collectors reciprocated by looking down on bankers, no clear-cut hierarchy of prestige could exist. A slight tendency was observed in the 1947 N.O.R.C. survey for members of an occupational category to evaluate their own category more favorably than other respondents did; but this tendency was dwarfed by a much more powerful tendency for respondents to *agree* on the relative prestige of particular occupations regardless of the region of the country they came from, the size of the place they lived in, their own occupational group, their age, sex, educational attainment, or economic position.[22] Furthermore, this consensus on occupational ratings prevails not only in the United States but also in several other industrial societies.

22   Reiss, *op. cit.*, Chap. 8, pp. 162–237.

Comparative Occupational Prestige in Six Industrial Societies

Reprinted by permission. From Alex Inkeles and Peter H. Rossi, "National Comparisons of Occupational Prestige," *American Journal of Sociology*, Vol. 61, January 1956, pp. 329–339.

During the latter part of the nineteenth and the first half of the twentieth centuries the factory system of production was introduced, at least on a small scale, to most areas of the world. The factory has generally been accompanied by a relatively standard set of occupations, including the factory manager (sometimes also owner) and his administrative and clerical staff, engineering and lesser technical personnel, foremen, skilled, semi-skilled, and unskilled workers. In the factory, authority and responsibility are allocated largely according to the degree of technical or administrative competence required for the job. In addition, the allocation of material and social rewards, the latter generally in the form of deference, is closely adjusted to levels of competence and degrees of authority and responsibility. The pattern of differentiation of authority is undoubtedly functionally necessary to the productive activity of the factory, and it may be that the associated pattern of reward differentiation is also functionally necessary.

There is, however, no clear-cut imperative arising from the structure of the factory as such which dictates how the incumbents of its typical statuses should be *evaluated* by the population at large. One possibility is that in popular esteem the typical occupations will stand relative to one another in a rank order strictly comparable to their standing in the formal hierarchy of competence, authority, and reward in the factory. It is also possible, however, that the popular evaluation of these occupations will be quite different. Indeed, where the factory system has been introduced into societies like those of Spain or Japan, with well-established values based on tradition and expressive of the culture, one might expect significant differences between an occupation's standing in the formal hierarchy of the industrial system and its position in the popular ranking scheme.

Thus the interaction of the two systems—the standardized modern occupational system and the individual national value pattern for rating occupations—presents an interesting and important problem in comparative sociology.

We may posit two extreme positions in this interaction, while granting that it might be difficult to find live exponents of either. The extreme "structuralist" would presumably insist that the modern industrial occupational system is a highly coherent system, relatively impervious to influence by traditional culture patterns. Indeed, he might go so far as to insist that the traditional ranking system would in time have to be subsumed under, or integrated into, the industrial system. Consequently, his argument would run, even such occupations as priest, judge, provincial governor, not part of the modern occupational system and often given unusual deference, would come in time to have roughly the same standing relative to one another and to other occupations, no matter what their national cultural setting.

By contrast, an extreme "culturalist" might insist that within each country or culture the distinctive local value system would result in substantial—and, indeed, sometimes extreme—differences in the evaluation of particular jobs in the standardized modern occupational system. For example, he might assume that in the United States the company director would be rated unusually high because of our awe of the independent businessman and large corporations or that in the Soviet Union the standing of industrial workers would be much higher relative to managerial personnel than in Germany, with its emphasis on sharply differentiated status hierarchies. Furthermore, he might argue that the more traditional occupational roles assigned special importance in particular cultures would continue to maintain their distinctive positions in the different national hierarchies. Indeed, he might hold that the characteristic roles of the modern industrial system would come to be subsumed within the traditional rating system, each factory occupation being equated with some traditional occupation and then assigned a comparable rank.

A systematic test of these contrasting positions is not beyond the capacity of contemporary social research. A standard list of occupations—say thirty or forty in number—might be presented for evaluation to comparable samples from countries presenting a range of culture types and degrees of industrialization. The list should contain both standard industrial occupations and the common, but differentially valued, traditional roles (e.g., priest, legislator, etc.).

Data are available which, though far from completely adequate, will carry us a long way beyond mere speculation on these matters. In the postwar years studies of occupational ratings have been conducted in and reported on five relatively industrialized countries: the United States, Great Britain, New Zealand, Japan, and Germany. In addition, the authors have available previously unpublished data for a sixth country, the Soviet Union.

Since these six studies were, on the whole, undertaken quite independently, our ideal research design is clearly far from being fulfilled. Nevertheless, the data do permit tentative and exploratory cross-national comparisons.

I. THE COMPARABILITY OF RESEARCH DESIGNS

The elements of similarity and difference in the six studies may be quickly assessed from the following summary of their essential features:

A. POPULATION STUDIED. *United States:* National sample of adults fourteen years and over; 2,920 respondents. *Japan:* Sample of males twenty to sixty-eight years of age in the six large cities of Japan; 899 respondents. *Great Britain:* Written questionnaires distributed through adult-education centers and other organizations; 1,056 returns (percentage returned unspecified). *U.S.S.R.:* Sample of displaced persons, mostly in DP camps near Munich, Germany, and some former DP's now residing on eastern seaboard of U.S.; 2,100 written questionnaires. *New Zealand:* Sample collected mainly by interviews with inhabitants of town of 2,000, partly by mailed questionnaires (12 per cent returns) sent out to town of 4,000; 1,033 questionnaires and interviews used. *Germany:* 1,500 Schleswig-Holsteiners: vocational-school students, university students, and male adults (not otherwise specified); adult sample only used here.

B. OVERLAP AMONG OCCUPATIONS STUDIED. Each study involved a different number of occupations, ranging from 88 in the case of the National Opinion Research Center American study to 13 in the Soviet research. Only the New Zealand and the British groups studied exactly the same occupations. Each of the remaining four studies used a different, but partially overlapping, set of occupations. In order to make comparisons between pairs of countries, each occupation studied in each research was matched, when possible, with an occupation in the data gathered in the other country. In many cases it was necessary to disregard the information about an occupation in one of the paired countries because no comparable occupation was studied in the other. In other instances, in order to increase the number of occupations which could be compared for any given pair of countries, occupations were matched which were only very roughly comparable, e.g., Buddhist priest and minister, or collective farm chairman and farm owner and operator. In most cases, however, a direct correspondence characterizes the pairs of occupations which are being equated. The reader is invited to turn to Table 34 (below), where the lists of occupations used from each of the researches are printed. The occupations listed on any row or line were matched. The number of pairs of similar or identical occupations for each cross-national comparison is shown in Table 30.

C. NATURE OF RATING TASK. *United States:* Respondents were asked: ". . . Please pick out the statement that best gives your own *personal opinion* of the *general standing* that such a job has. Excellent standing, good standing, average standing, somewhat below average, poor standing." *Japan:* Respondents were given a set of thirty cards and asked: ". . . Think of the general reputations they have with people, and sort them into five or more groups, from those which people think highly of to those which are not thought so well of." *Great Britain:* Respondents were told: "We should like to know in what order, *as to their social standing*, you would grade the occupations in the list given to you. [Rate them] . . . in terms of five main social classes . . . ABCDE." *U.S.S.R.:* Respondents were asked: "Taking everything into consideration, how desirable was it to have the job of (———) in the Soviet Union? Very desirable? Desirable? So-so? Undesirable? Very undesirable?" *New Zealand:* Same as in Great Britain. *Germany:* The source is unfortunately not very specific about the rating task assigned. The respondents were apparently asked to rank-order a list of 38 occupations presented as one slate.

D. COMPUTING PRESTIGE POSITION. With the exception of the German study, each research presents a "prestige score" for each of the occupations studied. These scores, computed variously, represent in each case the "average" rating given to each of the occupations by the entire sample of raters used. The German study presented only the rank-order positions of the occupations.

One is not sure whether differences between nations are generated by the differences in the questionnaires or the differences in the nations themselves. However, similarities in the prestige hierarchies, particularly when they are striking, are somewhat strengthened by the same lack of comparability in research designs and in the occupations matched to one another. Similarities may be interpreted as showing the extent to which design and other differences are overcome by the comparability among the prestige hierarchies themselves.

II. COMPARABILITY OF OCCUPATIONAL PRESTIGE HIERARCHIES

Since each study included some occupations used in another study, it is possible to compare the prestige hierarchies of occupations in pairs of countries by computing correlation coefficients for the scores (or ranks) of occupations. The fifteen correlation coefficients which result are presented in Table 31. It will be seen immediately that the levels of correlation are considerably higher than the magnitude to be expected if there were only rough agreement on placement in the top and bottom halves of the prestige hierarchy. Indeed, twelve of the fifteen coefficients are above

.9, and only one is below .8. The three coefficients below .9 all concern the Soviet ratings, which, it will be recalled, involve only a very small number of occupations, maximizing the chances for lower correlations arising from merely one or two "mismatches."

For most of the comparisons, furthermore, the findings go beyond establishing mere comparability of rank orders. With the exception of the correlations involving Germany, each coefficient represents the relationships between prestige *scores* given to the same occupations in two different nations. Hence there is a high relationship between the relative "distance" between occupations, as expressed in score differences, as well. In other words, if, of two occupations, one is given a much lower score than the other by the raters in one country, this difference in prestige scores and not merely crude rank order also obtains in another country.

It should also be noted that these high correlations were obtained by using samples of occupations which were not strictly identical from country to country, including such very crude comparisons already mentioned as that of collective farm chairman and farm owner and operator. One may anticipate that if the occupations studied were more uniform, the similarities of prestige hierarchies from country to country would be even higher.

In other words, *despite the heterogeneity in research design, there exists among the six nations a marked degree of agreement on the relative prestige of matched occupations.* To this extent, therefore, it appears that the "structuralist" expectation is more nearly met than is the expectation based on the culturalist position.

TABLE 30

Number of Identical or Similar Occupations Rated between Six Industrial Countries

	U.S.	Great Britain	U.S.S.R.	Japan	New Zealand	Germany
United States	..	24	10	25	24	20
Great Britain	..	..	7	14	30	12
U.S.S.R.	..	..	..	7	7	8
Japan	..	..	..	..	14	19
New Zealand	..	..	..	..	..	12
Total occupations studied	88	30	13	30	30	38

Each of the six nations differs in the extent to which its prestige hierarchy resembles those of other nations. The average of the correlations for each nation, contained in the bottom row of Table 32, expresses these differences among na-tions quantitatively. Thus we may see that the American and German occupational prestige hi-erarchies are most similar to those of other na-tions, while the Soviet and Japanese hierarchies are most dissimilar. When we consider that the

TABLE 31 [a]

Correlations between Prestige Scores (or Ranks) Given to Comparable Occupations in Six National Studies

	U.S.S.R.	Japan	Great Britain	New Zealand	U.S.	Germany [b]
U.S.S.R.	...	.74	.83	.83	.90	.90
Japan	...	...	.92	.91	.93	.93
Great Britain	...	...	...	.97	.94	.97
New Zealand	...	...	...	...	.97	.96
United States	...	...	...	...	...	.96
Av. correlation	.84	.89	.93	.93	.94	.94

[a] See Table 30 for numbers of occupations involved in each comparison.

[b] All coefficients are product-moment correlations, with the exception of those involving Germany, which are rank-order coefficients.

TABLE 32

Discrepancies [a] in the Rating of Matched Occupations by Pairs of Nations

	Rated Higher in Japan	Rated Higher in U.S.	Rated Higher in Great Britain	Rated Higher in New Zealand	Rated Higher in U.S.S.R.
Rated lower in Japan		Minister, farmer, insurance agent, car-penter	Minister, farmer, insurance agent	Minister, farmer, insurance agent	Accountant
Rated lower in U.S.	Company director, labor leader, re-porter (news), street sweeper, shoe shiner		Accountant, chef, street sweeper	Accountant, farmer, truck driver, street sweeper	Engineer, worker
Rated lower in Great Britain	Reporter (news), street sweeper	Civil servant truck driver, minister, build-ing contractor, electrician		Truck driver	Worker
Rated lower in New Zealand	Reporter (news), street sweeper	Civil servant, building con-tractor, book-keeper, electri-cian, dock worker	Chef, bartender		Worker
Rated lower in U.S.S.R.	Factory manager, farmer	Scientist, farmer	Farmer	Farmer	

[a] We consistently designate any cited occupation by the title closest and most familiar to Americans. For example, we used minister in preference to Buddhist priest, electrician rather than fitter (electrical). For the exact titles see Table 34.

Soviet Union and Japan are, of the six, the more recently industrialized cultures, we may see there some small degree of evidence for the culturalist position.

Furthermore, if we examine the correlations among the three nations which have the closest cultural ties and which share a common historical background and language—Great Britain, the United States, and New Zealand—we find these coefficients to be among the highest in Table 31. Again, the evidence to some extent supports the interpretation of a small "cultural" effect. However, the coefficients in question are not sufficiently distinguished in size from those involving Germany and the three Anglo-Saxon nations to allow much weight to be given to the influence of the common Anglo-Saxon culture. In other words, whatever the national differences between the six, they do not greatly affect the general pattern of the prestige hierarchy.

III. NATIONAL PATTERNS OF OCCUPATIONAL PRESTIGE

Although the relationships among the six occupational hierarchies are very high, they do not indicate one-to-one correspondences among the national ranks of occupations. Each nation shows some variation from every other, and the international discrepancies may perhaps throw further light on the relationships between social structure, culture, and occupational prestige.

One possibility is that unique aspects of the culture or social structure of a particular country determine distinctive appraisals of a certain type or types of occupation. National differences are thus to be interpreted in a unique fashion for each country.

A second possible explanation is that it is the type of occupation which engenders disagreement, some occupations being similarly rated everywhere and others yielding no consistent rating. To some extent these contrasting explanations are similar, respectively, to the culturalist and structuralist positions discussed earlier.

Here again the available data place marked limits on the possibility of a definitive answer, but it is nevertheless feasible for us to go some distance in exploring the problem. In order to obtain some means by which to assess the presence or absence of disagreement among nations, regression equations were computed to predict the prestige positions of the occupations in one

country as against the prestige positions of the comparable occupations in each other country. Ten such equations were computed, interrelating the prestige hierarchies in the United States, Japan, Great Britain, New Zealand, and the Soviet Union but excluding Germany, since the published data on that country indicated only the rank order of occupations. Those occupations which lay more than one standard deviation of the estimate off the regression lines were arbitrarily characterized as occupations over which there was a disagreement between the two nations involved.

Applying this criterion, we have, in Table 32, presented the discrepancies in ratings between all the relevant pairs of nations. The columns show the occupations rated higher by a given country in relation to each of the other countries represented in the rows. Reading the table by rows, we find the occupations rated lower by one country than by other nations, not forgetting that each comparison of a pair of countries involves a somewhat different set of occupations from the comparison of ratings for any other two countries. Only a few occupations, such as farmer, teacher, doctor, factory manager, and some form of industrial worker, were rated in all five countries and therefore appear in all the pairs of comparisons. Some occupations, such as judge, were rated in only two countries and therefore appear in only one paired comparison.

Table 32 serves to highlight the special positions held by certain occupations in particular countries. For example, the Japanese Buddhist priest rates lower than a minister in each of the three available comparisons, and this undoubtedly reflects the cultural differences in structure and role between the Buddhist religion in Japan and the Judeo-Christian religion in the three Anglo-Saxon countries. Equally notable is the consistently lower position of farm manager as rated by displaced persons from the Soviet Union. While the occupation collective farm chairman is not strictly comparable to those with which it is matched, there can be no doubt that the displaced persons regard that occupation with a special ambivalence arising out of the position of agriculture in the Soviet economy during the last three decades.

Despite the clarity with which a particular occupation may stand out, it is difficult to find any definite *pattern* characterizing the disagreements expressed by any one country. Of course, such a pattern, if it does exist, may be obscured in our data by the modest number of occupations rated by each country. There are seldom more than one or two occupations of a given type in each of the comparisons, and it is hazardous to assume from the fact, for example, that since the Japanese rate the occupation newspaper reporter higher than Americans, Britishers, or New Zealanders, they would rate occupations *of this type* higher than the other two countries. Nevertheless, it will be noticed that in the country with the largest number of comparisons, the instances of disagreement involve a wide variety of quite disparate occupations. Those rated higher in the United States, for example, range from building contractor to farmer and from scientist to dock worker and appear to have little in common. The same range and absence of a common denominator are shown by the occupations rated lower in the United States. Furthermore, the discrepancies do not consistently appear in all the relevant comparisons: farm owner is out of line in only two out of four comparisons; as to truck driver, the two recorded disagreements go in opposite directions, that occupation being rated higher in comparison with Britain and lower in comparison with New Zealand.

IV. INTERNATIONAL COMPARABILITY OF TYPES OF OCCUPATION

If there is no clear-cut pattern of deviance by country, is there perhaps a tendency for certain types of occupation to be foci of disagreement? Perhaps if we classify occupations according to the features of social structure or culture to which they are most closely related, we may gain further insight into the interaction between culture, social structure, and occupational prestige hierarchies. To explore this question, we grouped all the occupations into seven basic types: industrial, clerical and commercial, professional, political, traditional crafts, agricultural and service occupations. In Table 33 we have indicated the number of international comparisons between pairs among the five countries, again excluding Germany, which could be made involving the occupations in each class of occupations. We have also indicated the proportions of those comparisons which yielded disagreements. Disagreements were recorded on the same basis as in the preceding table,

that is, on the basis of predictions from regression equations.

Because our findings so far have so strongly supported the structuralist expectation concerning the influence of industrialization in producing uniformity, our initial expectation may well be that occupations closely allied to the industrial system will enjoy highly comparable standings from country to country, while occupations more remotely connected would be the focus of international discrepancies. Table 33 indicates that industrial occupations do enjoy comparable standing in all five countries. Nevertheless, the *lowest* proportion of disagreements is shown by the professions. In addition, other occupational types, such as the political occupations and the traditional crafts, which are not necessarily closely allied to the industrial system, manifested levels of disagreement as low as that enjoyed by the industrial occupations. Only the agricultural and service occupations yield a degree of disagreement which sets them apart from the other occupational groups.

Accounting for these discrepancies appears to require a combination of arguments. In the first place, some types of non-industrial occupations

TABLE 33

Discrepancies in Prestige Position according to Type of Occupation

Occupation Types [a]	Proportion of Discrepancies (Per Cent)	No. of Comparisons
Professional	16	31
Industrial	24	29
Political	25	16
Traditional crafts	27	11
Clerical and commercial	32	37
Agricultural	50	16
Service	63	20

[a] Examples of occupations included in each type are as follows: *Professional*: doctor, minister, teacher, etc.; *industrial*: industrial worker, company director, factory manager, engineer; *political*: judge, civil servant, etc.; *traditional crafts*: bricklayer, carpenter, fisherman; *clerical and commercial*: accountant, bookkeeper, salesman, small entrepreneur, etc.; *agricultural*: farm owner and operator, farm hand; *service*: shoe shiner, barber, porter, streetcar conductor, etc.

TABLE 34

The Comparative Prestige of Occupations in Six Industrial Societies

Occupation	Score	Occupation	Rank	Occupation	Score	Occupation	Score	Occupation	Score	Occupation	Score
United States:		*Germany:*		*Great Britain:*		*New Zealand:*		*Japan:*		*U.S.S.R.*	
Physician	93	Doctor	2	Medical officer	1.3	Medical officer	1.4	Doctor	7.0	Doctor	75
State governor	93							Prefectural gov.	3.8		
College professor	89	Univ. professor	1					Univ. professor	4.6		
Scientist	89									Scientific worker	73
County judge	87							Local court judge	4.7		
Head of dept. in state government	87	High civil servant (Regierungsrat—höherer Beamter)	4	Civil servant	6.0	Civil servant	7.0	Section head of a government office	7.2		
Minister	87	Minister (Pfarrer)	6	Non-conformist minister	6.4	Non-conformist minister	5.9	Priest of a Buddhist temple	12.5		
Architect	86	(Elec. engineer)	10					(Architect)	9.5		
Lawyer	86			Country solicitor	2.6	Country solicitor	3.8				
Member of board of directors of large corporation	86	Factory director (Fabrikdirektor)	5	Company director	1.6	Company director	3.6	Officer of large company	5.5	Factory manager	65
Civil engineer	84	Elec. engineer	10					(Architect)	9.5	Engineer	73
Owner of factory that employs about 100 people	82							Owner of a small or medium-sized factory	10.2		
Accountant for a large business	81			Chartered accountant	3.2	Chartered accountant	5.7	(Company office clerk)	16.1	Bookkeeper	62
Captain in regular army	80	Major (in armed forces)	8							Officer in the armed services	58
Building contractor	79			Jobbing master builder	11.4	Jobbing master builder	10.7				
Instructor in public schools (teacher)	78	Elem.-school teacher (Volksschullehrer)	11	Elem.-school teacher	10.8	Elem.-school teacher	10.3			Teacher	55
Farm owner and operator	76	Farmer (Bauer—mittelgrosser Betrieb)	13	Farmer	7.3	Farmer	8.1	Small independent farmer	16.4	Chairman of collective farm	38
Official of international labor union	75							Chairman of national labor federation	10.8		
Electrician	73			Fitter (elec.)	17.6	Fitter (elec.)	15.8				
Trained machinist	73	Skilled industrial worker (Industriefacharbeiter)	24								
Reporter on daily newspaper	71			News reporter	11.8	News reporter	13.8	Newspaper reporter	11.2		
Bookkeeper	68	Bank teller (bookkeeper in bank)	19	Routine clerk	16.1	Routine clerk	16.4	Company office clerk	16.1	(Bookkeeper)	62

United States		Germany		Great Britain		Japan		U.S.S.R.	
Insurance agent	68	Insurance agent	20	Insurance agent	14.6	Insurance agent	16.1	Insurance agent	20.2
Traveling salesman for wholesale concern	68			Commercial traveler	12.0	Commercial traveler	14.1		
Policeman	67	Postman	23	Policeman	16.1	Policeman	15.5	Policeman	16.4
Mail carrier	66								
Carpenter	65	Carpenter	18	Carpenter	18.6	Carpenter	17.0	Carpenter	20.2
Corporal in regular army	60	Non-commissioned officer	31						
Machine operator in factory	60	Machine operator (Maschinenschlosser-Geselle)	26	(Composite of fitter, carpenter, bricklayer, tractor driver, coal hewer)	20.5	Composite of fitter, carpenter, bricklayer, tractor driver, coal hewer)	20.9	Latheman	21.1
								Rank-and-file worker	48
Barber	59	Barber	16					Barber	20.5
Clerk in a store	58	Store clerk (Verkäufer im Lebensmittelgeschäft)	28	Shop assistant	20.2	Shop assistant	20.2	Department-store clerk	19.8
Fisherman who owns own boat	58							Fisherman	22.0
Streetcar motorman	58	Conductor	33					Bus driver	20.9
Restaurant cook	54			Chef	13.8	Chef	21.8		
Truck driver	54			Carter	25.8	Carrier	20.2		
Farm hand	50	Farm laborer (worker)	36	Agricultural laborer	25.5	Agricultural laborer	24.4		
Coal miner	49			Coal hewer	23.2	Coal hewer	24.7	Coal miner	23.7
Restaurant waiter	48	Waiter (Kellner)	30						
Dock worker	47			Dock laborer	27.0	Dock laborer	28.3		
Bartender	44			Barman	26.4	Barman	28.3		
		(Unskilled laborer) **	38	Road sweeper	28.9	Road sweeper	28.9	Road worker	24.8
Street sweeper	34								
Shoe shiner	33							Shoe shiner	26.9
		Bricklayer	27	Bricklayer	20.2	Bricklayer	19.3		
				Business manager	6.0	Business manager	5.3		
				Works manager	6.4	Works manager	7.9		
		Clothing-store owner	12					Owner of a retail store	15.3
				News agent and tobacconist	15.0	News agent and tobacconist	15.4		
		Tailor	14					Tailor	17.7
				Tractor driver	23.0	Tractor driver	22.8		
		Street peddler	35					Street-stall keeper	24.9
				Railway porter	25.3	Railway porter	25.3		
								Rank-and-file collective farmer	18

Sources: (1) A. A. Congalton, "The Social Grading of Occupations in New Zealand," *British Journal of Sociology*, Vol. 4, March 1953 (New Zealand data); (2) John Hall and D. Caradog Jones, "The Social Grading of Occupations," *British Journal of Sociology*, Vol. 1, January 1950 (British data); (3) National Opinion Research Center, "Jobs and Occupations: A Popular Evaluation," in Reinhard Bendix and Seymour Martin Lipset, Ed., *Class, Status and Power*, Glencoe, Ill.: Free Press, 1953 (United States data); (4) *Der Spiegel*, June 30, 1954 (German data); (5) Research Committee, Japan Sociological Society, "Report of a Sample Survey of Social Stratification and Mobility in Six Large Cities of Japan," December 1952 (Japanese data); and (6) Unpublished materials from the Project on the Soviet Social System of the Russian Research Center at Harvard University (U.S.S.R. data).

are easily assimilated to the industrial system. The traditional crafts serve as the prime example here, since the skills involved in such occupations as bricklayer, carpenter, and plumber have a close resemblance to the skills of industrial workers. Indeed, some crafts have been partly incorporated into the industrial system, and, it may be argued, such occupations are easily placed within the hierarchy of industrial occupations and may tend to assume roughly the same position vis-à-vis industrial occupations. Likewise, some professions, such as engineering and applied scientific research, have a most immediate connection with the industrial system, and others, such as architecture, are easily equated with it.

However, closeness or assimilability to the industrial system will not suffice to explain the relatively stable position of other professions, such as doctor. Nor will it serve to explain the low proportion of disagreement concerning the political occupations. We must recognize that the nations being compared have certain structural and cultural features in common, in addition to the presence of industry. For example, they share certain needs, as for socialization, and values, such as health and systematic knowledge, which insure relatively comparable standing to doctors, teachers, and scientists. Furthermore, all the countries compared have in common the national state, with which is associated a relatively standardized occupational structure ranging from ministers of state to local bureaucrats. In addition, both the professions and the political occupations are highly "visible," and agreement as to their standing is probably facilitated by the relatively objective and easily perceived indexes of power, knowledge, and skill manifested by their incumbents.

The types of occupation which generate the greatest amount of disagreement are highly variant and unstandardized or difficult to assimilate to the industrial structure. Agriculture may be conducted, as in Japan, on relatively small holdings, on collective farms as in the U.S.S.R., or, as in the western plains of the United States, in "agricultural factories." Being a farmer means very different things in each of the five countries, quite unlike the standardized image of the machinist or the factory manager. It can be anticipated, however, that as agriculture tends to be similarly organized in different countries, agricultural occupations will achieve more uniform standing.

The "service" occupations—barber, shoe shiner, chef, street sweeper—show the greatest amount of variation. Many of them antedate the industrial system and are in agrarian as well as industrial societies. They have no fixed position relative to the industrial order, nor are they similar to typical industrial occupations, as are many of the traditional crafts. They therefore appear to be most easily evaluated according to the traditional culture. Personal service in countries like Japan and Great Britain, in which a servant class was historically well developed and benefited from intimate association with an aristocratic upper class, may still be regarded as not so degrading as in the more democratic societies, such as the United States and New Zealand. In fact, the greatest discrepancy to be found among all the comparisons involves the differences in prestige position accorded to chef in Great Britain as compared with either the United States or New Zealand, although in the case of the former the match was poor, since the comparable occupation was "restaurant cook." As these services come to be organized and mechanized—as in modern laundries or restaurants—they will become more thoroughly integrated into the larger economic order and may in time achieve more strictly comparable status from country to country.

All told, it would appear from this examination of international discrepancies that a great deal of weight must be given to the cross-national similarities in social structure which arise from the industrial system and from other common structural features, such as the national state. The greatest incidence of discrepancies occurs for occupations which are hardest to fit into either the one or the other structure. To this extent the structuralist position which we outlined earlier seems to be more heavily borne out in these data.

V. SUMMARY AND CONCLUSIONS

To sum up, our examination of occupational ratings in six modern industrialized countries reveals an extremely high level of agreement, going far beyond chance expectancy, as to the relative prestige of a wide range of specific occupations, despite the variety of sociocultural settings in which they are found. This strongly suggests that there is a relatively invariable hierarchy of prestige associated with the industrial system, even when it is placed in the context of larger social systems which are otherwise differentiated in important respects. In addition, the fact that the countries compared also have in common the national state and certain needs or values, such as interest in health, apparently also contributes to the observed regularity of the ratings, since both professional and political occupations are foci of agreement. Perhaps the most striking finding is the extent to which the different classes of occupation have been woven together into a single relatively unified occupational structure, more or less common to the six countries. At the same time, there is strong evidence that this relatively standardized occupational hierarchy does not apply without major exception to all occupations in all large-scale industrialized societies. In some instances, important disagreement may arise from the distinctive role of a single occupation in a particular country. In the majority of cases, however, the disagreement appears to involve certain classes of occupation, notably agricultural and service, about which there is only modest agreement. Disagreement probably reflects differences in the length and "maturity" of industrialization in various countries but also clearly results from differentiations in sociocultural systems which may well be relatively enduring.

The similarity in the prestige ratings of occupations in six industrial countries not only supports the hypothesis of the ubiquity of stratification; such similarity for societies with different histories and cultures also suggests that occupational structure is the key to status in industrialized countries. Even the exceptions tend to reinforce this conclusion. Note the low prestige of "small independent farmer" in Japan (in Table 34) as compared to the relative standing of this occupation in the United States, Great Britain, and New Zealand. (Similarly, farm laborers rank relatively lower in Germany and in the Soviet Union than in the United States, Great Britain, and New Zealand.) The people of Japan, Germany, and the Soviet Union have not yet forgotten the *peasant* status with which farming was traditionally associated in these countries. In the United States and New Zealand, on the other hand, a feudal past cannot be remembered because it did not exist, and in Great Britain it is not as recent as in Japan, Germany, and the Soviet Union.

No society completely escapes its history. Just as agricultural work has a *lower* status in an industrial society with a feudal past, so some occupations have *higher* status due to historical associations which may be irrelevant to the current functioning of the society. The samurai tradition in Japan probably inflates the prestige of military officers; this occupation was unfortunately not rated in the Japanese survey, so this guess cannot be put to the test with the data at hand. The United States does not have a feudal past, but the distribution of prestige in contemporary American society is also affected by historical circumstances. The low status of Negroes is partly the result of Negro enslavement during the eighteenth and nineteenth centuries and the low status of Spanish-speaking Americans of the struggle with Mexico over Texas and other parts of the Southwest.

Historical and cultural circumstances, then, distort the hierarchy of prestige in an industrial society from what it would be if occupational structure were the only factor in social stratification. Moreover, the history of individuals as well as the history of the society affects the distribution of prestige. The son of class I parents in Elmtown would retain some prestige directly by virtue of his origins even if he became an unskilled laborer. Although family connections also count in more dynamic urban areas, the son of middle-class parents in New York City who became an unskilled laborer would probably be upgraded *indirectly* by his family background—because of his taste in clothing and home furnishings, his hobbies, his childhood friends, and the educational history reflected in his speech. The *direct* assessment of family background is less likely in the more anonymous city.

Although it is probably true that an unskilled laborer with a college education enjoys greater prestige in the American system of stratification than a laborer with less education, the *independent* contribution of education to social status is small. What confuses the issue is that educational achievement is highly correlated with position in the occupational structure. Hence, using educational achievement as an index of social status is almost as good as evaluating occupations directly. (In view of the difficulty of avoiding classificatory errors in assessing thousands of occupational categories, an index of social status based on education may be more valid than one based on occupation.[23]) This is not to minimize the relationship between education and social stratification. Education is the single most important factor in the class position of American adult males, as Chapter 12 will show. But the significance of education lies in its preparatory value for middle-class occupational roles, not in its direct contribution to status.

CONCLUSION

Members of a society evaluate one another's role behavior, partly because judgment is inherent in human interaction, partly because performance in one role is a basis for admission to, or exclusion from, another role. Industrial societies are especially prone to base role allocations on the evaluation of past performances.

Some sociologists believe that mutual evaluations can occur without generating a system of social stratification, but the majority of sociologists assume that a hierarchy of deference emerges in all societies. The religious, educational, economic, or political characteristics associated with particular positions in the hierarchy in particular societies is an empirical matter. Several factors account for the crystallization of status in the form of social strata.

1. Judgments tend to be generalized to the *person* instead of remaining confined to specific *roles*. Thus, the individual receives a composite prestige rating based on his social participation in all of his roles.

2. Judgments tend to be generalized to the kinship unit instead of remaining confined to the individual. Thus, infants automatically occupy the status possessed by their parents.

[23] For a study of the relationship between the educational requirements of various American occupations and their prestige ratings, see Otis Dudley Duncan, "A Socioeconomic Index for All Occupations," in Reiss, *op. cit.*, pp. 109–138.

3. The advantages inherent in a hierarchy of prestige and rewards are often transmitted from one generation to the next because high-status parents can provide better opportunities for their children than lower-status parents.

Social classes can be distinguished in industrial societies despite the fluidity resulting from heterogeneous populations, geographic mobility, and opportunities to rise or fall in status during one's lifetime. Sociologists have developed several techniques for measuring class membership: (1) reputational ratings, (2) self-placement, (3) evaluation of cultural artifacts, and (4) indirect ratings based on the correlation between social honor and occupation, education, and income. Implicit in these various techniques are assumptions about the process of status determination in industrial societies. Reputational ratings assume that members of a community are sufficiently aware of the prestige hierarchy that they are able to place their friends and acquaintances in it. The self-placement technique assumes that a respondent's *identification* with a social class is a good indication of his objective position in the stratification system. Evaluation of cultural artifacts is based on the premise that different symbols are used at different levels of the deference hierarchy. Status ratings based on occupation rest on the theory that the occupational role is the main determinant of status in industrial societies, directly for adult males, indirectly for women and children. Status ratings based on educational achievement rest on the correlation observed between occupational and educational attainments. Finally, status ratings based on income rest on the assumption that the more luxurious style of life made possible by a large income is positively valued in industrial societies and must therefore be at least roughly related to judgments of social worth.

Some evidence exists that classes are generated by the occupational system in essentially the same way in all industrial societies despite differences in historical and cultural circumstances. This increases the confidence of sociologists in the generality of the conclusions reached on the basis of stratification studies done in a few countries. If, however, social stratification in industrial societies depended on occupational achievement, population elements not integrated into the occupational system could not be rank ordered. W. Lloyd Warner dealt with this classificatory problem by attaching the label "lower-lower" to low-status people which Chapter 6 identified with the culture of poverty and the label "upper-upper" to élites whose high status transcended occupational considerations. An alternative approach would be to recognize that some people live in an industrial society but have no clear position in its institutions or its system of social stratification.

SOME SIGNIFICANT LITERATURE ON SOCIAL STRATIFICATION

E. Digby Balzell, *Philadelphia Gentlemen: The Making of a National Upper Class*, Glencoe, Ill.: Free Press, 1958. Professor Balzell is concerned with the inheritance of élite status in the United States. To explore this problem he identified the 770 Philadelphians whose names were listed in the 1940 edition of *Who's Who in America* by virtue of their occupational and other achievements. He found that 226 of these 770 (29 per cent) were also listed in the Philadelphia *Social Register* for 1940 on the basis of their upper-class family background. Professor Balzell infers from this correlation that upper-class birth, while not a guarantee of élite status, gives the individual an excellent chance to attain it. Taking these 226 individuals for intensive scrutiny, he examines their family backgrounds, neighborhoods of residence, religious affiliations, prep schools and colleges commonly attended, and club memberships. This summary is based on a review by William Miller, *American Sociological Review*, Vol. 23, August 1958, pp. 451–452.

Norval D. Glenn, "Negro Prestige Criteria: A Case Study in the Bases of Prestige," *American Journal of Sociology*, Vol. 68, May 1963, pp. 645–657. Many studies have shown that educational achievement is the most important single factor in prestige rankings among American Negroes. In the general American community, on the other hand, occupational attainment and educational achievement are correlated with prestige to about the same extent. Why should Negroes give education greater weight as a determinant of prestige than whites? Dr. Glenn offers three possible explanations: (1) Negroes may value education more than whites do, perhaps because higher education is rarer among Negroes than among whites. Higher education is rarer among Negroes: in 1950 nonwhites constituted 10.5 per cent of the American population and had about 7.6 per cent of the total years of school completed by persons 25 years old and older. (2) Education is more unequally distributed among Negroes than among whites, and relative scarcity may make for prestige. In 1950 the best-educated tenth of the white population had completed 16.8 per cent of the years of school completed by whites, whereas the best-educated tenth of the nonwhite population had completed 21.4 per cent of the schooling completed by nonwhites. (3) Perhaps because higher education is rarer among Negroes, higher education may make a greater difference for Negroes than for whites in opening up high-level jobs. This is true only for male college graduates. Nonwhite college graduates get far better jobs than nonwhites who have had some college but have not graduated; graduation is less crucial to whites.

Neal Gross, "Social Class Identification in the Urban Community," *American Sociological Review*, Vol. 18, August 1953, pp. 398–404. Professor Gross conducted an interview survey of household heads (935) in four types of neighborhoods in Minneapolis: high-rental to low-rental. He used unstructured and highly structured questions with the same respondents to assess class identification. The results differed depending on the form of the questions, thus raising doubts that a forced-choice question about class identification—such as the one used by Richard Centers—results in a valid picture of the class consciousness of Americans.

August B. Hollingshead and Frederick G. Redlich, *Social Class and Mental Illness: A Community Study*, New York: Wiley, 1958. The authors investigated psychiatric cases active in New Haven, Connecticut, between June 1, 1950, and December 1, 1950, in order to find out whether the differing life circumstances of various social classes generate differing amounts and types of mental illness. They reported much higher prevalence of mental illness in lower strata than in higher strata. The concept of *prevalence* refers, however, to all cases known during the period of observation, not to new cases alone (*incidence*). The prevalence of mental illness during this five-month period was much greater than the incidence because mental illness typically requires lengthy treatment. In fact, the prevalence of psychosis was 21 times the incidence of psychosis in the lowest class but only seven times the incidence in the highest. One explanation of this class difference in the ratio of prevalence to incidence is that psychiatric treatment was less successful among lower-class persons, probably because of communication difficulties with middle-class psychiatrists. Variation in incidence by class level was by no means as sharp, but the data supported the hypothesis that lower-class persons were more likely than persons at higher social levels to break down psychologically. This summary is based on a review by Herbert Goldhamer, *American Sociological Review*, Vol. 24, August 1959, pp. 579–581.

Alex Inkeles, "Social Stratification and Social Mobility in the Soviet Union: 1940–1950," *American Sociological Review*, Vol. 15, August 1950, pp. 465–479. Soviet leaders originally hoped for a one-class society with approximate equality of economic rewards. In 1931, however, Stalin launched an attack against "equality mongering" and instituted a system of wage incentives based on differential economic rewards. By 1940 these economic differentials had reinforced social distinctions, thus giving rise to nine distinct social groups: (1) the ruling élite consisting of high Communist Party and government officials as well as prominent scientists, artists, and writers; (2) intermediate ranks of officialdom and important technical specialists; (3) professionals, managers of small enterprises, junior military officers, technicians; (4) petty bureaucrats, clerks, office workers; (5) highly skilled and productive manual workers; (6) rank-and-file manual workers; (7) unskilled, unproductive workers (at minimum wage levels); (8) well-to-do peasants; and (9) peasants on less productive farms.

Ruth R. Kornhauser, "The Warner Approach to Stratification," in Bendix and Lipset, Eds., *Class, Status and Power: A Reader in Social Stratification*, Glencoe, Ill.: Free Press, 1953, pp. 224–255. This analysis of W. Lloyd Warner's approach to social stratification is a careful, yet readable, summary of what Warner himself reports about his research methods in half a dozen books. In addition, the article contains a searching discussion of the methodological problems in Warner's researches, most of them gleaned from critical discussions in the sociological literature. For example:

1. Warner's definition of social class is based mainly on community prestige, but it takes too seriously what the members of the community *say* are the reasons for differential prestige. This tempts him to lump together (in his concept of class) prestige, economic power, political influence, and style of life instead of exploring empirically the relationships among these factors.
2. Since the places studied by Warner and his collaborators were small, well-integrated communities, findings based on them are not applicable to highly urbanized, more anonymous communities. In the metropolis, stratification may be thought of more fruitfully in terms of power hierarchies and interest groups than in terms of a prestige hierarchy.
3. Warner's analysis is essentially static, ignoring the immigration of the foreign-born and the emigration of ambitious youngsters to large cities.
4. Warner's portrayal of the prestige structure of the communities he studied gives heavier weight to the *social* values of upper- and middle-class residents than to the *economic* values of lower-class residents. Class differences in the criteria of allocating persons to strata forced Warner to construct a composite prestige hierarchy built from the varied perspectives of local residents. But he paid disproportional attention to the values of high-prestige respondents.

John C. Leggett, "Uprootedness and Working-Class Consciousness," *American Journal of Sociology*, Vol. 68, May 1963, pp. 682–692. Three hundred and seventy-five blue-collar male workers were interviewed in Detroit in 1960 concerning four aspects of class consciousness. The purpose of the study was to ascertain how workers born in rural areas (migrants) compare in class consciousness with workers reared in industrial settings. The four aspects of class consciousness explored in the study are as follows: (1) The tendency to discuss politics in class terms, which was measured by the worker's response to questions about his favorite president and about the candidate he voted for in the 1956 presidential election. (2) The tendency to perceive ordinary people as exploited by the rich, which was measured by the worker's response to the question, "When business booms in Detroit, who gets the profits?" (3) The tendency to take *action* on behalf of other workers, which was measured by the worker's expressed willingness to join with other workers in action (including picketing) against a landlord. (4) The belief in equality of wealth and opportunity, which was measured by asking the worker whether he agreed with the notion that the wealth of the country should be divided up equally so that people would have an equal chance to get ahead. Dr. Leggett found that the "uprooted" migrants from rural areas expressed a higher level of class consciousness than did workers reared in and adjusted to the industrial way of life.

Albert J. Reiss, Jr., *Occupations and Social Status*, New York: Free Press of Glencoe, 1961. This book consists of a searching analysis of poll data concerned with the prestige of occupations. These data, collected by the National Opinion Research Center in 1947, show remarkable consensus among Americans about the relative prestige of occupations. The part of the country in which the respondent lives does not influence his perspective on the prestige of occupations; neither does the size of the community, his educational attainment, occupation, sex, or age. To be sure, low-status raters give greater weight than higher-status raters to income as the basis for their ratings, but the rank order of prestige is not appreciably affected by this difference in criteria. Despite the general consensus, some variation occurs. Respondents upgrade the prestige of their own occupations and downgrade the occupations immediately below them. Poorly educated respondents tend to bestow higher ratings on manual occupations than well-educated respondents. The major difficulty with occupational prestige ratings stems from the fact that little-known occupations are, by definition, difficult to rate. This being so, the occupational titles presented to respondents for rating cover *groups* of specialized occupations; hence their prestige ratings tend to overlap. This summary is based on a review by Richard L. Simpson, *American Sociological Review*, Vol. 27, October 1962, pp. 713–714.

Eva Rosenfeld, "Social Stratification in a 'Classless' Society," *American Sociological Review*, Vol. 16, December 1951, pp. 766–844. Ideologically committed to social equality, collective farms in Israel (*kibbutz*) are deliberately organized so that economic rewards are minimized. Food is eaten in a communal dining room. Children are brought up from birth in communal child-care arrangements. Room allocations have nothing to do with the importance of the individual's job. Nevertheless, in these small agricultural settlements—averaging 200 members—a managerial stratum and a rank-and-file stratum occupy distinct prestige levels. Eva Rosenfeld explains the emergence of prestige ranks as due to a scarcity of administrative talent in the pioneering days of the settlements. The survival of the settlements required continuity of management, and successful managers tended to be reelected. It is not clear what happened to the earlier glorification of manual labor. The pioneers insisted on turnover in managerial positions, which they considered unproductive, but this attitude must have changed subsequently to one of deference, which is apparently the present sentiment toward managers.

William H. Sewell, "Social Class and Childhood Personality," *Sociometry*, Vol. 24, December 1961, pp. 340–356. On the assumption that the position of the child's family in the stratification system selects to some extent the learning experiences to which the child will be exposed, theorists have anticipated personality differences between middle-class and lower-class children. Professor Sewell carefully reviews relevant research on child development, considering the respects in which lower-class child-rearing practices differ from middle-class ones and also the respects in which the resulting personalities differ. He concludes that the relationship between social class and personality is small, possibly because differences in child-rearing practices are not as great as was at first anticipated. Insofar as personality tests reveal differences between middle-class and lower-class children, they show that middle-class children are somewhat *better* adjusted.

PART III

Role Commitment
in Urban Industrial Societies

CHAPTER 8

Initial Socialization

From the point of view of every society, industrial or preliterate, infants constitute a barbarian invasion. They want what they want when they want it. Such amorality is intolerable. Hence all societies try to civilize the barbarians: to teach children to play roles that adults define for them. Sociologists call this process whereby the individual is taught to fill existing roles "socialization." This may seem a pretentious way of saying that the infant learns from his parents. Its virtue is that it emphasizes the contribution of society to the humanization of the infant, a contribution which is easy to overlook.

BARBARIAN BY BIRTH

Since nearly everybody is routinely exposed to parental guidance, one might conclude that the infant is *born* human just as the squirrel is born a squirrel. However, a squirrel taken from its mother at birth and raised in total isolation from other squirrels grows up to be a recognizable member of the species: climbing trees, eating nuts, and so on. The essence of being a squirrel is to have squirrel heredity. Parental guidance is not crucial.[1] For the infant, on the

other hand, heredity is only a beginning, a potentiality for human development. A normal infant can develop into a subhuman monster if he does not have sufficient contact with human beings to learn not only the culture of his society but also its role structure. Cases of children raised with minimal parental care provide an opportunity to see the effect of social impoverishment on child development. They are unintended experiments, illustrations of the sociological assertion that human beings are made and not born.

The Human Infant: Barbarian by Nature

Reprinted by permission. From Kingsley Davis, "Final Note on a Case of Extreme Isolation," *American Journal of Sociology*, Vol. 52, March 1947, pp. 432–437.

Early in 1940 there appeared . . . an account of a girl called Anna. She had been deprived

[1] Recent research has demonstrated that certain types of monkeys, like human beings, require training by other monkeys for normal development. See Leonard Engel, "The Troubled Monkeys of Madison," New York *Times Magazine*, Jan. 29, 1961, pp. 62–64. As far as we know, however, members of most species of animals do not require group guidance—except to facilitate physical survival.

of normal contact and had received a minimum of human care for almost the whole of her first six years of life. At that time observations were not complete and the report had a tentative character. Now, however, the girl is dead, and, with more information available, it is possible to give a fuller and more definitive description of the case from a sociological point of view.

Anna's death, caused by hemorrhagic jaundice, occurred on August 6, 1942. Having been born on March 1 or 6, 1932, she was approximately ten and a half years of age when she died. The previous report covered her development up to the age of almost eight years; the present one recapitulates the earlier period on the basis of new evidence and then covers the last two and a half years of her life.

EARLY HISTORY

The first few days and weeks of Anna's life were complicated by frequent changes of domicile. It will be recalled that she was an illegitimate child, the second such child born to her mother, and that her grandfather, a widowed farmer in whose house her mother lived, strongly disapproved of this new evidence of the mother's indiscretion. This fact led to the baby's being shifted about.

Two weeks after being born in a nurse's private home, Anna was brought to the family farm, but the grandfather's antagonism was so great that she was shortly taken to the house of one of her mother's friends. At this time a local minister became interested in her and took her to his house with an idea of possible adoption. He decided against adoption, however, when he discovered that she had vaginitis. The infant was then taken to a children's home in the nearest large city. This agency found that at the age of only three weeks she was already in a miserable condition, being "terribly galled and otherwise in very bad shape." It did not regard her as a likely subject for adoption but took her in for a while anyway, hoping to benefit her. After Anna had spent nearly eight weeks in this place, the agency notified her mother to come to get her. The mother responded by sending a man and his wife to the children's home with a view to their adopting Anna, but they made such a poor impression on the agency that permission was refused. Later the mother came herself and took the child out of the home and then gave her to this couple.

It was in the home of this pair that a social worker found the girl a short time thereafter. The social worker went to the mother's home and pleaded with Anna's grandfather to allow the mother to bring the child home. In spite of threats, he refused. The child, by then more than four months old, was next taken to another children's home in a near-by town. A medical examination at this time revealed that she had impetigo, vaginitis, umbilical hernia, and a skin rash.

Anna remained in this second children's home for nearly three weeks, at the end of which time she was transferred to a private foster-home. Since, however, the grandfather would not, and the mother could not, pay for the child's care, she was finally taken back as a last resort to the grandfather's house (at the age of five and a half months). There she remained, kept on the second floor in an attic-like room because her mother hesitated to incur the grandfather's wrath by bringing her downstairs.

The mother, a sturdy woman weighing about 180 pounds, did a man's work on the farm. She engaged in heavy work such as milking cows and tending hogs and had little time for her children. Sometimes she went out at night, in which case Anna was left entirely without attention. Ordinarily, it seems, Anna received only enough care to keep her barely alive. She appears to have been seldom moved from one position to another. Her clothing and bedding were filthy. She apparently had no instruction, no friendly attention.

It is little wonder that, when finally found and removed from the room in the grandfather's house at the age of nearly six years, the child could not talk, walk, or do anything that showed intelligence. She was in an extremely emaciated and undernourished condition, with skeleton-like legs and a bloated abdomen. She had been fed on virtually nothing except cow's milk during the years under her mother's care.

Anna's condition when found, and her subsequent improvement, have been described in the previous report. It now remains to say what happened to her after that.

LATER HISTORY

In 1939, nearly two years after being discovered, Anna had progressed, as previously reported, to the point where she could walk, understand simple commands, feed herself, achieve some neatness, remember people, etc. But she still did not speak, and, though she was much more like a normal infant of something over one year of age in mentality, she was far from normal for her age.

On August 30, 1939, she was taken to a private home for retarded children, leaving the county home where she had been for more than a year and a half. In her new setting she made some further progress, but not a great deal. In a report of an examination made November 6 of the same year, the head of the institution pictured the child as follows:

"Anna walks about aimlessly, makes periodic rhythmic motions of her hands, and, at intervals, makes guttural and sucking noises. She regards her hands as if she had seen them for the first time. It was impossible to hold her attention for more than a few seconds at a time—not because of distraction due to external stimuli but because of her inability to concentrate. She ignored the task in hand to gaze vacantly about the room. Speech is entirely lacking. Numerous unsuccessful attempts have been made with her in the hope of developing initial sounds. I do not believe that this failure is due to negativism or deafness but that she is not sufficiently developed to accept speech at this time. . . . The prognosis is not favorable." . . .

More than five months later, on April 25, 1940, a clinical psychologist, the late Professor Francis N. Maxfield, examined Anna and reported the following: large for her age; hearing "entirely normal"; vision apparently normal; able to climb stairs; speech in the "babbling stage" and "promise for developing intelligible speech later seems to be good." He said further that "on the Merrill-Palmer scale she made a mental score of 19 months. On the Vineland social maturity scale she made a score of 23 months."

Professor Maxfield very sensibly pointed out that prognosis is difficult in such cases of isolation. "It is very difficult to take scores on tests standardized under average conditions of environment and experience," he wrote, "and interpret them in a case where environment and experience have been so unusual." With this warning he gave it as his opinion at that time that Anna would eventually "attain an adult mental level of six or seven years."

The school for retarded children, on July 1, 1941, reported that Anna had reached 46 inches in height and weighed 60 pounds. She could bounce and catch a ball and was said to conform to group socialization, though as a follower rather than a leader. Toilet habits were firmly established. Food habits were normal, except that she still used a spoon as her sole implement. She could dress herself except for fastening her clothes. Most remarkable of all, she had finally begun to develop speech. She was characterized as being at about the two-year level in this regard. She could call attendants by name and bring in one when she was asked to. She had a few complete sentences to express her wants. The report concluded that there was nothing peculiar about her, except that she was feebleminded—"probably congenital in type."

A final report from the school, made on June 22, 1942, and evidently the last report before the girl's death, pictured only a slight advance over that given above. It said that Anna could follow directions, string beads, identify a few colors, build with blocks, and differentiate between attractive and unattractive pictures. She had a good sense of rhythm and loved a doll. She talked mainly in phrases but would repeat words and try to carry on a conversation. She was clean about clothing. She habitually washed her hands and brushed her teeth. She would try to help other children. She walked well and could run fairly well, though clumsily. Although easily excited, she had a pleasant disposition.

INTERPRETATION

Such was Anna's condition just before her death. It may seem as if she had not made much progress, but one must remember the condition in which she had been found. One must recall that she had no glimmering of speech, absolutely no ability to walk, no sense of gesture, not the least capacity to feed herself even when the food was put in front of her, and no comprehension of cleanliness. She was so apathetic that it was hard to tell whether or not she could hear. And all this at the age of nearly six years. Compared with this condition, her capacities at the time of her death seem striking indeed, though they do not amount to much more than a two-and-a-half-year mental level. One conclusion therefore seems safe, namely, that her isolation prevented a considerable amount of mental development that was undoubtedly part of her capacity. Just what her original capacity was, of course, is hard to say; but her development after her period of confinement (including the ability to walk and run, to play, dress, fit into a social situation, and, above all, to speak) shows that she had at least this much capacity—capacity that never could have been realized in her original condition of isolation.

A further question is this: What would she have been like if she had received a normal upbringing from the moment of birth? A definitive answer would have been impossible in any case, but even an approximate answer is made difficult by her early death. If one assumes, as was tentatively surmised in the previous report, that it is "almost impossible for any child to learn to speak, think, and act like a normal person after a long period of early isolation," it seems likely that Anna might have had a normal or near-normal capacity, genetically speaking. On the other hand, it was pointed out that Anna represented "a marginal case, [because] she was discovered before she had reached six years of age," an age "young enough to allow for some plasticity." While admitting, then, that Anna's isolation *may* have been the major cause (and was certainly a minor cause) of her lack of rapid mental progress during the four and a half years following her rescue from neglect, it is necessary to entertain the hypothesis that she was congenitally deficient.

In connection with this hypothesis, one suggestive though by no means conclusive circumstance needs consideration, namely, the mentality of Anna's forebears. Information on this subject is easier to obtain, as one might guess, on the mother's than on the father's side. Anna's maternal grandmother, for example, is said to have been college educated and wished to have her children receive a good education, but her husband, Anna's stern grandfather, apparently a shrewd, hard-driving, calculating farmowner, was so penurious that her ambitions in this direction were thwarted. Under the circumstances her daughter (Anna's mother) managed, despite having to do hard work on the farm, to complete the eighth grade in a country school. Even so, however, the daughter was evidently not very smart. "A schoolmate of [Anna's mother] stated that she was retarded in school work; was very gullible at this age; and that her morals even at this time were discussed by other students." Two tests administered to her on March 4, 1938, when she was thirty-two years of age, showed that she was mentally deficient. On the Stanford Revision of the Binet-Simon Scale her performance was equivalent to that of a child of eight years, giving her an I.Q. of 50 and indicating mental deficiency of "middle-grade moron type."

As to the identity of Anna's father, the most persistent theory holds that he was an old man about seventy-four years of age at the time of the girl's birth. If he was the one, there is no indication of mental or other biological deficiency, whatever one may think of his morals. However, someone else may actually have been the father.

To sum up: Anna's heredity is the kind that *might* have given rise to innate mental deficiency, though not necessarily.

COMPARISON WITH ANOTHER CASE

Perhaps more to the point than speculations about Anna's ancestry would be a case for comparison. If a child could be discovered who had been isolated about the same length of time as Anna but had achieved a much quicker recovery and a greater mental development, it would be a stronger indication that Anna was deficient to start with.

Such a case does exist. It is the case of a girl found at about the same time as Anna and under strikingly similar circumstances. A full description of the details of this case has not been published, but, in addition to newspaper reports, an excellent preliminary account by a speech specialist, Dr. Marie K. Mason, who played an important role in the handling of the child, has appeared. Also the late Dr. Francis N. Maxfield, clinical psychologist at Ohio State University, as was Dr. Mason, has written an as yet unpublished but penetrating analysis of the case. Some of his observations have been included in Professor Zingg's book on feral man. The following discussion is drawn mainly from these enlightening materials. The writer, through the kindness of Professors Mason and Maxfield, did have a chance to observe the girl in April, 1940, and to discuss the features of her case with them.

Born apparently one month later than Anna, the girl in question, who has been give the pseudonym Isabelle, was discovered in November, 1938, nine months after the discovery of Anna. At the time she was found she was approximately six and a half years of age. Like Anna, she was an illegitimate child and had been kept in seclusion for that reason. Her mother was a deaf-mute, having become so at the age of two, and it appears that she and Isabelle had spent most of their time together in a dark room shut off from the rest of the mother's family. As a result Isabelle had no chance to develop speech; when she communicated with her mother, it was by means of gestures. Lack of sunshine and inadequacy of diet had caused Isabelle to become rachitic. Her legs in particular were affected; they "were so bowed that as she stood erect the soles of her shoes came nearly flat together, and she got about with a skittering gait." Her behavior toward strangers, especially men, was almost that of a wild animal, manifesting much fear and hostility. In lieu of speech she made only a strange croaking sound. In many ways she acted like an infant. "She was apparently utterly unaware of relationships of any kind. When presented with a ball for the first time, she held it in the palm of her hand, then reached out and stroked my face with it. Such behavior is comparable to that of a child of six months." At first it was even hard to tell whether or not she could hear, so unused were her senses. Many of her actions resembled those of deaf children.

It is small wonder that, once it was established that she could hear, specialists working with her believed her to be feebleminded. Even on nonverbal tests her performance was so low as to promise little for the future. Her first score on the Stanford-Binet was 19 months, practically at the zero point of the scale. On the Vineland social maturity scale her first score was 39, representing an age level of two and a half years. "The general impression was that she was wholly uneducable and that any attempt to teach her to speak, after so long a period of silence, would meet with failure."

In spite of this interpretation, the individuals in charge of Isabelle launched a systematic and skilful program of training. It seemed hopeless at first. The approach had to be through pantomime and dramatization, suitable to an infant. It required one week of intensive effort before she even made her first attempt at vocalization. Gradually she began to respond, however, and, after the first hurdles had at last been overcome, a curious thing happened. She went through the usual stages of learning characteristic of the years from one to six not only in proper succession but far more rapidly than normal. In a little over two months after her first vocalization she was putting sentences together. Nine months after that she could identify words and sentences on the printed page, could write well, could add to ten, and could retell a story after hearing it. Seven months beyond this point she had a vocabulary of 1,500–2,000 words and was asking complicated questions. Starting from an educational level of between one and three years (depending on what aspect one considers), she had reached a normal level by the time she was eight and a half years old. In short, she covered in two years the stages of learning that ordinarily require six. Or, to put it another way, her I.Q. trebled in a year and a half. The speed with which she reached the normal level of mental development seems analogous to the recovery of body weight in a growing child after an illness, the recovery being achieved by an extra fast rate of growth for a period after the illness until normal weight for the given age is again attained.

When the writer saw Isabelle a year and a half after her discovery, she gave him the impression of being a very bright, cheerful, energetic little girl. She spoke well, walked and ran without trouble, and sang with gusto and accuracy. Today she is over fourteen years old and has passed the sixth grade in a public school. Her teachers say that she participates in all school activities as normally as other children. Though older than her classmates, she has fortunately not physically matured too far beyond their level.

Clearly the history of Isabelle's development is different from that of Anna's. In both cases there was an exceedingly low, or rather blank, intellectual level to begin with. In both cases it seemed that the girl might be congenitally feebleminded. In both a considerably higher level was reached later on. But the Ohio girl achieved a normal mentality within two years, whereas Anna was still marked inadequate at the end of four and a half years. This difference in achievement may suggest that Anna had less initial capacity. But an alternative hypothesis is possible.

One should remember that Anna never received the prolonged and expert attention that Isabelle received. The result of such attention, in the case of the Ohio girl, was to give her speech at an early stage, and her subsequent rapid development seems to have been a consequence of that. "Until Isabelle's speech and language development, she had all the characteristics of a feeble-minded child." Had Anna, who, from the standpoint of psychometric tests and early history, closely resembled this girl at the start, been given a mastery of speech at an earlier point by intensive training, her subsequent development might have been much more rapid.

The hypothesis that Anna began with a sharply inferior mental capacity is therefore not established. Even if she were deficient to start with, we have no way of knowing how much so. Under ordinary conditions she might have been a dull normal or, like her mother, a moron. Even after the blight of her isolation, if she had lived to maturity, she might have finally reached virtually the full level of her capacity, whatever it may have been. That her isolation did have a profound effect upon her mentality, there can be no doubt. This is proved by the substantial degree of change during the four and a half years following her rescue.

Consideration of Isabelle's case serves to show, as Anna's case does not clearly show, that isolation up to the age of six, with failure to acquire any form of speech and hence failure to grasp nearly the whole world of cultural meaning, does not preclude the subsequent acquisition of these. Indeed, there seems to be a process of accelerated recovery in which the child goes through the mental stages at a more rapid rate than would be the case in normal development. Just what would be the maximum age at which a person could remain isolated and still retain the capacity for full cultural acquisition is hard to say. Almost certainly it would not be as high as age fifteen; it might possibly be as low as age ten. Undoubtedly various individuals would differ considerably as to the exact age.

Anna's is not an ideal case for showing the effects of extreme isolation, partly because she was possibly deficient to begin with, partly because she did not receive the best training available, and partly because she did not live long enough. Nevertheless, her case is instructive when placed in the record with numerous other cases of extreme isolation. This and the previous article about her are meant to place her in the record. It is to be hoped that other cases will be described in the scientific literature as they are discovered (as unfortunately they will be), for only in these rare cases of extreme isolation is it possible "to observe *concretely separated* two factors in the development of human personality which are always otherwise only analytically separated, the biogenic and the sociogenic factors."

Anna and Isabelle, when they were discovered, were unable to participate in American society. They were unresponsive, partly because they did not know how to communicate symbolically and partly because they had not learned to care about other people's reactions to them. As a result, they failed to conform to expectations made of those in the role of "child." Beyond behavioral nonconformity, their *attitudes* were barbaric. Socialization is not mere conformity. Socialization is learning to *like* doing what one has to do anyway.[2] Perhaps an example will point up the importance of attitude in socialization. In American society, as in most societies, toilet training is part of early socialization. Americans teach children about toilets and toilet paper, about closing the bathroom door, and about washing their hands afterwards. Once Americans learn these lessons though, they greatly *prefer* using bathrooms to a return to the free and easy ways of the infant.

Not all socialization is as successful as toilet training. Taught as children that they must not steal, some American adults are incapable of theft. They think of themselves as honest, and this self-conception prevents them from even considering opportunities to steal. However, in 1960 more than eight hundred thousand burglaries, three hundred thousand auto thefts, and four hundred thousand cases of larceny of property valued at $50 or more were known to the American police.[3] And it is likely that more stealing would have occurred had it not been for police forces. Apparently Americans are less deeply committed to honesty than they are to the use of modern plumbing.

The difference arises because American society is so organized that honesty does not *always* seem to be the best policy. The next chapter will show how the temptation to commit crimes frequently overcomes the individ-

2   My discussion draws upon the unpublished lectures of Talcott Parsons. See also his treatment of socialization in Chapter 6 of *The Social System*, Glencoe, Ill.: Free Press, 1951.
3   Federal Bureau of Investigation, Department of Justice, *Uniform Crime Reports*, 1960, Washington: Government Printing Office, 1961, p. 2.

ual's moral scruples. Since crimes occur with some regularity—crime is a "normal phenomenon," as the French sociologist, Émile Durkheim, put it—the thought of stealing may cross one's mind even though most people ultimately abandon the idea. On the other hand, no one defecates in the street; such an idea is *unthinkable*. Socialization is thus a matter of degree. Some norms are *internalized* so completely that the individual does not perceive any conflict between social rules and his own inclinations. In other instances, the norms are imbedded deeply enough to prevent the individual from violating them, but he experiences some temptation. With regard to still other norms, the individual is socialized only to the extent that he is aware of the social disapproval which would result from public violations. He treats the rule pragmatically, violating it if the chances for his escaping social sanctions are good and conforming if he believes that he cannot get away with it.

Differences among individuals exist in the extent to which norms of society are internalized. These internal variations are small and unimportant compared with the enormous differences in self-conceptions from one society to another. If one chooses to focus on the *content* of socialization, human beings seem very different depending on their society of origin— virtually a different species. If one focuses instead on the *process* of socialization, the similarities seem more remarkable than the differences. In all societies the individual joins the human community in the same way: by identifying with previously socialized members of the society and by adopting *their* values.

THE SOCIALIZATION PROCESS

Socialization might well be described as miraculous. It is not miraculous in the sense of unusual; most people are socialized. It is miraculous in the sense that the end-product, a moral being, is so far removed from an amoral barbarian that the transitional process is difficult to describe credibly. How is the egocentric infant transformed?

Consider the starting point: the prolonged helplessness of the infant. Most animals are helpless at birth and must be cared for by the mother for a while. But human infancy lasts longer than the infancy of any other species. What for other species is an episode, for the human infant is a career. This prolonged dependence on the mother is fortunate. Without it, the infant would not be so receptive to parental guidance. An infant perceives the world as a frightening and potentially frustrating place. Strange noises startle him because he does not yet share the cultural interpretation of the ringing of a doorbell or the honking of an automobile horn. There is a hard object called a "floor" that comes up and hits him every once in a while. And a shiny object that looks and sounds interesting turns out to be dangerously hot. Or course, there are pleasant things in the world, too: that warm white stuff that comes in bottles and those marbles and rattles that he can touch and take into his mouth. Best of all, there is a benevolent monster who brings good things to eat and is generally helpful at critical times, for example, when a diaper pin is sticking him. A loud cry brings her on the run. In short, his first interest in his mother is thoroughly egocentric. She is not a *person*, only a source of important gratifications. He does not care about *her*; he cares about what she does for him.

Gradually the infant learns that his mother is not merely "the monster" who feeds him and changes his diapers. She possesses a unique feature: reactions. He smiles; she smiles back. He cries; she cuddles. They begin to participate in an interactive relationship. He has developed an interest in her *attitudes* and moods because he dimly recognizes that they underlie the services she renders. Furthermore, he learns that what *he* does can please her or make her angry. For reasons beyond his comprehension, the monster is delighted when he performs the dangerous feat of getting about on two limbs the way she does. So, although crawling is a perfectly satisfactory way of getting about, he humors her and tries to walk. On the other hand, she gives him a sour look when he sends a pile of dishes crashing to the floor. Since her attitude is important to him, he tries to control the impulse to destroy the crockery. Note that he does not consider breaking dishes *wrong*; he considers it *dangerous* because, for inexplicable reasons, it antagonizes "the monster." This is pragmatism, not morality.

A further stage of socialization is reached when the child identifies with his mother and looks at *his* behavior from the perspective of *her* values. Charles Horton Cooley compared the process by which the child internalizes parental values with the observation of one's reflection in a looking glass.

How the Self-concept Develops

Reprinted by permission. From Charles Horton Cooley, *Human Nature and the Social Order*, New York: Scribner's, 1922, pp. 184–185.

As we see our face, figure, and dress in the glass, and are interested in them because they are ours, and pleased or otherwise with them according as they do or do not answer to what we should like them to be; so in imagination we perceive in another's mind some thought of our appearance, manners, aims, deeds, character, friends, and so on, and are variously affected by it.

A self-idea of this sort seems to have three principal elements: the imagination of our appearance to the other person; the imagination of his judgment of that appearance and some sort of self-feeling, such as pride or mortification. The comparison with a looking-glass hardly suggests the second element, the imagined judgment, which is quite essential. The thing that moves us to pride or shame is not the mere mechanical reflection of ourselves, but an imputed sentiment, the imagined effect of this reflection upon another's mind. This is evident from the fact that the character and weight of that other, in whose mind we see ourselves, makes all the difference with our feeling. We are ashamed to seem evasive in the presence of a straightforward man, cowardly in the presence of a brave one, gross in the eyes of a refined one, and so on. We always imagine, and in imagining share, the judgments of the other mind. A man will boast to one person of an action—say some sharp transaction in trade—which he would be ashamed to own to another.

In the context of the relationship with his mother, the child learns to transcend egocentricity. He not only cares about her judgments of his behavior; he also adopts the values implicit in them as his own. Furthermore, the lesson he learns is applied beyond the family. His sensitivity to disapproval is gradually extended to human beings generally. As George Herbert Mead put it, the individual develops the capacity *to treat himself as an object*.[4] And the perspective that he takes toward himself, although initially that of his parents, ultimately becomes that of society—or, as Mead put it, that of the "generalized other." This adoption of societal standards makes it possible to civilize the barbarians. Once this internalization occurs, society has an ally within the psyche of the child. Parental vigilance can be reduced because, from then on, the child helps to police himself.

Many gaps exist in this explanation of socialization. Especially puzzling is the child's step from conforming pragmatically to the demands of an external authority to identifying with his mother and adopting her standards of right and wrong. Most students of socialization agree that the mother is crucial to moral development, not necessarily the biological mother, but some adult (1) who gives the child love and (2) who judges the child's behavior in terms of adult standards. These two conditions are to some extent contradictory. If maternal affection were unconditional, gushing forth regardless of the child's behavior, the child would have no incentive to judge his behavior from his mother's perspective. If, on the other hand, he were judged but not loved, his mother's disapproval would not be so threatening, and therefore he would once again lack the incentive to identify with her and, concomitantly, to internalize her moral standards.

Successful socialization steers a middle course between overindulgence and rejection. Maternal love convinces the child of a qualitative distinction between a frustration imposed by the physical environment (touching a hot

[4] George Herbert Mead, *Mind, Self, and Society*, Chicago: University of Chicago Press, 1934.

radiator) and a frustration imposed by his mother in the name of discipline (a spanking). The two experiences may be equally painful. One has moral significance, however, and the other does not. The child has no reason to empathize with the radiator. It burned him because that is its nature. If he touches it again, it will burn him again, regardless of whether he has been "good" or "bad." His action in touching it was foolish, careless, ill-advised, *but not wrong.* On the other hand, when his mother spanks him, a relationship is at stake. His mother punishes him, not because it is her nature to do so, but because she evaluated his behavior unfavorably. The spanking symbolizes her righteous indignation: "You have done something so wrong that I don't feel like loving you at this moment. You had better mend your ways." In these traumatic moments when maternal affection is in jeopardy, the child exerts the prodigious effort necessary to transcend infantile egocentricity: "What did I do to make her angry?" In order to win back his mother's approval, he must look at his behavior through her eyes. Conscience is built upon experiences in which the child transcends his egocentric perspective in order to forestall or cut short parental disapproval.

SOCIALIZATION FAILURE

To say that successful socialization steers a middle course between overindulgence and rejection evades the crucial difficulty. *How* unconditional must parental love be before it can properly be described as "overindulgence"? *How* judgmental and cold must a parent's attitude be before it can properly be described as "rejecting"? Unfortunately, "overindulgence" and "rejection" are subtle concepts. They refer to the meaning of parental behavior to the child, not to objective acts. In some families, spankings communicate rejection, in others they do not. The difficulties involved in rigorous operational definitions of "overindulgence" and "rejection" have been an obstacle to research on the conditions making for *successful* socialization. It has proved easier to investigate *unsuccessful* socialization. Pathological indul-

gence and extreme rejection are more readily identified. The following excerpt from a classic study of overprotected children shows how excessive mothering can interfere with socialization.

Excessively Indulged Children: A Failure of Maternal Control

Reprinted by permission. From David M. Levy, "Maternal Overprotection," *Psychiatry,* Vol. 2, November 1939, pp. 563–567.

Of the four criteria of maternal overprotection, the first three have to do with facts relating to activity of mothers—excessive contact, infantilization and prevention of development of independent behavior. They are based on observations of maternal behavior operating on the child. The fourth criterion, lack or excess of maternal control, contains data derived primarily from the behavior of the child, data indicating a defect in maternal discipline. As a criterion of maternal overprotection, the inclusion of such findings may be questioned since they do not show evidence directly of maternal activity and appear to be a resultant of the forms of maternal overprotection previously described. Nevertheless, they show those aspects of maternal care that involve discipline of the child and are most readily observed directly through the child's activity rather than the mother's. Instead of describing acts, for example, in terms of "the mother allows this or that," or "dominates the child in this way or that," we may collect objective data on maternal control in terms of the child's activity. Furthermore, it is difficult to learn in any given act how much the mother has "allowed," or actively indulged the child, and how much the child has appropriated as a privilege fought for against parental opposition.

Overindulgence is a weakness in maternal control. It consists in yielding to the wishes or actions of a child or submitting to demands ordinarily not tolerated by most parents. It is the commonest evidence of "spoiling." A demarcation line between the mother's inability to deny the infant's wish and her later apparently unwilling submission to his tyranny is difficult to draw. The former situation, one of willing active catering to the child, is overindulgence in a true sense. Submitting unwillingly to his excessive demands is a passive form of indulgence. Allowing the child to eat whatever he wishes, to sleep regardless of hours, because one "doesn't wish to deny him anything" is typical of the former; surrender to the child's insistence in these matters, of the latter. In either situation, whether of willing or unwilling submission to the child's demands, the child appears to be active, the mother passive. Yet in the overindulgent act, the mother may be as actively overprotective as in the other forms.

The extreme example of overindulgence is that of complete maternal surrender to the child, to the point that the child's merest wish becomes the mother's absolute command. In such a hypothetical case, the child represents a deity on whose altar the mother willingly sacrifices her life. Maternal obeisance of that type would then be transformed into a psychosis in which every sense of proportion is perverted by the maternal attitude. All the social orientations of the mother, as wife, housekeeper, worker, member of various social groups, would completely deteriorate. She would live on only for the purpose of fulfilling the wishes of her offspring.

This quality of maternal overprotection, of submission to the child's demands for certain kinds of food, and later, toys, clothes or money; or of surrender to his refusal to conform to requirements of eating, time of sleeping, bowel and bladder control, later of home work, elementary politeness or deportment, differs sufficiently in its expression from the other forms to require special formulation.

Overindulgence as an overprotective phenomenon shows a distinct resemblance to the other forms. Theoretically, one may argue that excessive contact, infantilization and refusal to take risks for the child likewise represent evidence of overindulgent behavior. However, in sorting out the data there is little difficulty in differentiating items for the fourth criterion. . . . Items that show closest similarity to lack of maternal control have to do with infantilization when they concern especially prolonged breast or bottle feeding or helping the child with bathing or dressing long past infancy. In Case 2, for example, the mother continued bottle feeding until her boy was 3½ years old because "he didn't want to give it up." She helped to bathe and dress him until age 14, at the time when he was referred for treat-

ment. Such activities may be regarded as evidence of overindulgence on the part of the mother. Presumably, she refuses to give up the pleasure of handling her son as an infant, and prefers to continue bottle feeding long past the weaning period. On the other hand, one may assume as readily, on the basis of the facts given, that the mother did not yield to her wish to prolong the child's infancy but to a stubborn refusal on the part of the infant to give up the bottle. Furthermore, excessive bottle feeding, as an easy way of avoiding the more troublesome diet, may occur in maternal rejection of infants. The facts recorded under infantilization can be interpreted per se as evidence only of a prolongation of infantile care. . . .

Complete maternal submission, as described in the fictitious example given, is not found in any of our cases of maternal overprotection. Various forms and degrees of overindulgence are present though not as extreme as in the hypothetical case. Nevertheless, in eleven of the twenty Group I cases, there are numerous instances showing remarkable submission to the tyranny of infantile demands. Two questions present themselves: first, why are these parents willing to take as much punishment as they do from their children; and second, why does the submissive maternal attitude to the infant's undisciplined behavior fall short of the extreme instance?

An answer to the second question is found in the development of a situation impossible for family life at a certain stage in the growth of the unmodified, aggressive infant. Even should the father remain submissive to a life in which the whims of the child dominate the family activity, the mother at some point or other can no longer hold out. As a matter of self-defense, she is compelled to turn against the "monster." The numerous and incessant complaints of the mother against all she "has had to endure," in spite of all the sacrifices she has made, attest to this situation. A review of the data indicates how difficult the situation becomes. Besides disrespectful behavior, insulting refusals to comply with the parents' requests, the mother is also spit at and slapped (Case 1); not allowed to go out in the evening because the child refuses to let her go (Case 2); compelled to prepare meals whenever the child wishes to eat regardless of meal times, to have food that is disliked thrown to the floor (Case 4); compelled to sleep in the bed the son chooses (Case 11); hit, teased and bullied, muddy shoes tramped on newly scrubbed floors, etc. (Case 12); kicked, pinched and sworn at (Case 14).

Rebellious, defiant, tyrannizing behavior toward mothers occurred in eleven cases of the twenty. In each case, difficulties began in infancy and increased with the growing aggression of the child. Yet only three of the eleven mothers sought help directly because the child made life intolerable for them. Of the remaining eight, three were referred for reasons other than rebellious behavior (Case 4 by mother through a settlement worker because the child, age 4, could not be persuaded to stay in kindergarten without the mother; Case 9, age 4, by mother through advice of the family physician because the child was afraid of the dark; Case 13, age 14, by a visiting teacher because of school retardation.) Five were referred for rebellious behavior primarily by agents other than the mother, with or without her cooperation (Case 2 by a visiting teacher, Case 3 by a settlement house psychiatrist, Case 10 and Case 14 by fathers, Case 17 by a public school vocational counselor).

After referral of the aggressive children, regardless of the reason originally given or the agency that made examination possible, complaints by mothers of the suffering they endured followed regularly. The mothers of this group appeared to relish the opportunity to give expression to the "punishment" they had to undergo. Nevertheless, they regularly interfered with treatment, tried to spoil the growing relationship of child and psychiatrist, and, presumably, to control the interviews, especially in the early stages. To borrow material from the forthcoming section on treatment, several mothers, after expressing great satisfaction at release from the tyranny of a child, exerted every effort to restore the status that preceded the treatment period. Indeed, in reviewing the therapeutic history one discerns clearly that the entire group of overprotecting mothers were caught hard and fast in the relationship even when some of them put forth strenuous efforts at release. The situation is revealed in high light in Case 12, in which the mother, driven to desperation by the tyrannical role of her son, moved the entire household during the night, while the son was visiting at the home of a relative. She hoped in this way to prevent his return since he did not know the new address. Yet in a few days the mother brought him back. . . .

Theoretically, a sharp contrast may be drawn between overprotecting mothers who dominate and those who indulge. The former express to the fullest degree that phase of maternal love that corresponds to possession of the love object. The latter represent in exaggerated degree the phase of surrender to the love object. The former attempt with great concentration of energy to mould the child according to the maternal conception, thwarting any expression that is not in the determined direction. The latter abandon themselves to the child's emotional development however it proceeds, making feeble attempts to modify insistent behavior. The former act as though saying, "This is my child. He must do whatever I wish"; the latter as though saying, "I am his mother. I will do whatever he wishes."

Both exceed the usual parental overvaluation of the child. The former, however, attempt to constrict its personality, to trim it to the desired shape; the latter allow the child's personality to expand, giving luxuriant growth to infantile tendencies.

The behavior problems of the children are consistently rebellious and aggressive in indulgent overprotection; submissive and dependent in dominating overprotection. However, the child's share in the direction of maternal manoeuvers is more clearly observed in relation to the fourth criterion than to the others. Granting that all overprotecting mothers start with strong infantilizing behavior, it is easy to understand how the child's response may swing the overprotection into the dominating or indulgent form. If the child responds with sweet submission to infantilizing behavior, the dominating tendencies of the parent are unhindered and strengthened. If the child rebels against discipline, the submissive tendencies of the parent are brought into evidence. We need start only with the premise of excessive maternal love. In a milder degree, if the child yields readily, the control exerted by the mother in the first year of life continues in the form "dominating mother—obedient child." If he rebels, he is given his way and the maternal domination in the early months gives way to overindulgence. In a milder form such variation in parental response is typical of family life in general.

The overprotective mother gives her children too much love, which is no favor to them.

A rejecting mother, in contrast, gives too little love, sometimes because of her own personality problems, sometimes because her situation poses obstacles to her playing the role of mother. The unwed mother, for example, faces an extremely hostile social reception in all of the industrial societies, except Sweden, if she elects to keep her baby. If she chooses to give up the child, that youngster must face a complicated world without the parental support most children need. How such consequences can be transformed into societal rejection may be seen from the following case history of an illegitimate child.

Case Study of an Illegitimate Child in America

Reprinted by permission. From Croswell Bowen, *They Went Wrong*, New York: McGraw-Hill, 1954, pp. 33–44.

The story of Robert Brown begins in the social-service records of New York City before he was born. On May 16, 1928, a woman who gave her name as Madge Clark and her age as twenty-seven called at the charity clinic of the Lying-In Hospital, then at 307 Second Avenue. She said she had no money and was pregnant. The father of her unborn child, she claimed—apparently falsely—was William Clark, a thirty-year-old chauffeur, whose whereabouts she said she did not know. She was given a physical examination, found to be in good condition, and told to report back to the hospital at the first indication that labor had commenced.

Early in the morning of June 13, Madge Clark returned to the clinic and said she was having labor pains. She was examined and put to bed. After she had undergone three hours and forty minutes of labor, according to the hospital records, "a male, white child weighing 3,265 grams" was born to her. "Delivery was normal." She named the child Robert Handel Clark, and the circumstances of his birth were recorded at the Department of Health. After ten days' confinement, she left the hospital with her baby and returned to her home, at 15,025 118th Avenue, Ozone Park, Queens.

Two years later, on June 20, 1930, Madge Clark called at the Federation of Protestant Welfare Agencies, at 122 East 22d Street, in Manhattan, to ask if it could arrange to look after her son for a couple of weeks. She said she was on sick leave from her job as a waitress in a Childs restaurant and needed rest to recover her health. The social worker who interviewed her found that she had been leaving her son alone or in the care of neighbors much of the time and gave her the option of placing him in a foster home or a day nursery until she got to feeling better. The mother said she would think it over and return the next morning. She did not return.

The records reveal little about Madge Clark—a fact that was in time to cause her son considerable distress. It is known that she was born in Liverpool, England, in 1902, the daughter of Michael and Margaret McConnell Brown. She had four brothers—Philip, Charles, Arthur, and John. Her mother died in England. Her father came to the United States in 1912 or thereabouts with his five children and settled in the suburbs of Jersey City. Madge went through the second year of high school and then took lessons in singing and dancing, in the hope of a career in vaudeville. In 1919, when she was seventeen, she married William Clark, in North Bergen, New Jersey, and on February 19, 1921, a son, whom they named William Clark, Jr., was born to them. In 1926, she left her husband and child and moved to New York City, where she resumed a friendship, she once told a social worker, "with a man I had been engaged to before I was married." Her husband divorced her and married again, but the records do not show whether she ever married the man to whom she said she had once been engaged and who probably fathered her second child. She successfully resisted all efforts the social agencies made to get her to tell his name. For the six months following her visit to the Federation of Protestant Welfare Agencies, there is no record of how she and her son were getting along, but they were very likely having a hard time, for the depression was shaping up.

On December 16, 1930, an agent from the Society for the Prevention of Cruelty to Children knocked on the door of Madge Clark's furnished room, on the upper East Side of Manhattan. The SPCC had received a telephone call about "a woman and child living in a heatless furnished room." The agent took them to Children's Court, on East 22d Street, and filed a complaint charging Madge Clark with neglect of the child. The presiding justice ordered an investigation by the Department of Welfare and, pending its outcome, gave the SPCC permission to lodge the boy in its child shelter, then at 2 East 105th Street. Madge Clark spent Christmas and New Year's without her son and in a state of apprehension about what was going to happen to him. On January 3, 1931, she again appeared in Children's Court. The presiding justice, who had before him a report from the Department of Welfare stating that "the mother was financially unable to give the child proper care," handed down his decision: Society would raise the boy, not his mother. The child was taken by the Department of Welfare and placed in the children's ward at Bellevue, a clearing house for children awaiting foster homes. At this point, Madge Clark drops out of sight, apparently forever.

Madge Brown Clark's son entered the children's ward as Robert Brown, the name he was known by in the voluminous records that were to pile up about him in the years to come. Robert Brown was two years, six months, and twenty-one days old when society took over his rearing. He was still learning to talk and in the last stages of having to be helped with his food. He stayed a little more than a month in the children's ward while the Department of Welfare sought to place him in the care of some Catholic agency, his mother having indicated she was of that faith. On February 6, 1931, the New York Foundling Hospital, a Catholic institution at 68th Street and Lexington Avenue, accepted him, and put him in a wing of the hospital assigned to children destined for foster homes or adoption. (The authorities at the Foundling Hospital have naturally been distressed over the way this particular charge of theirs has turned out. "Thousands of our children have been integrated into the community," Sister Catherine, who directs the institution's child-placement activities, said not long ago. "They are leading normal lives and, we feel, often work out better than children reared by their own parents. The case of Robert Brown is the exception. In his case, we failed.") At the end of three weeks, a home was found for Robert with a family named Korowski, who lived in a six-room house in Jamaica. (The names given here of the families who helped bring up the boy are not their real ones.) Mr. and Mrs. Korowski already had three children of their own and two boarding children

from the hospital. They were not well off, and the twenty-five dollars a month they received for each boarding child was a welcome addition to their income.

Brown has only a dim recollection of living with the Korowskis. "I remember that it was a big family with a lot of kids and the old man was out of work a lot," he has since said. "Plenty of nights, us kids sat down to dinner to nothing but a bowl of turnips. That's why I never been able to stand turnips my whole life. Those Korowskis were all right, but they just didn't have it—money, I mean. It was depression times and the going was rough. I remember they used to call me their little black-haired devil, because I was always in some mischief. I liked them—I used to go back to visit them after I left there. Mrs. Korowski and her old man used to laugh and say, 'Well, well, our little black-haired devil has come back.' "

A Visitor from the Foundling Hospital, who called periodically to check on Robert's adjustment to his foster home, apparently considered the food at the Korowskis' satisfactory. On May 5, 1932, for example, she made a call at dinnertime and noted that the meal consisted of "lamb, spinach, cake, bread, butter, and milk." She also noted that Mrs. Korowski called Robert "Bobby."

During the first three years Robert stayed with the Korowskis, the observations of the Visitor were about what could be expected in the case of any normal child. Shortly before his sixth birthday, however, at the end of his first year in school, the first disturbing note appears in his record. The Visitor wrote on June 6, 1934, that "Robert took pennies from teacher's desk." This report agrees with what Robert recollects of his first stealing. "As far back as I can remember, I was thinking it kind of funny that I didn't have a real mother and father, like other kids," he says. "My name was different than Korowski and—well, I just knew things were different with me than other kids. One day I was out in the playground and a kid said to me, 'How come your name is Brown? Why isn't it Korowski?' I started to tell him that the Korowskis weren't my real parents, but before I could finish, he said, 'Oh, a dirty orphan!' I hadn't been getting along too well with kids, and I figured that it was because I was an orphan—didn't have no mother and father. I noticed that kids who had real mothers and fathers had it better. They had money and things and could give parties. I couldn't, so I figured the next-best thing was to do things for kids and I'd get in good with them. I started swiping pennies the teacher collected from the kids for the milk. Then, at the store, I'd buy candy for the kids, and sodas. Maybe I was trying to be a big shot."

The Visitor called at Robert's school on June 11 to discuss the matter of the pennies with his teacher. It was an unsatisfactory interview. The teacher, obviously antagonistic to Robert, told the Visitor about the boy in such a loud voice that her pupils could overhear everything she said. She complained that Robert pinched other children and was forever putting his head down on his desk instead of sitting up straight, like her other pupils. She admitted that he was clever and learned his lessons easily—too easily. The teacher then publicly questioned Robert's classmates about him. She called to a little girl, "Mary, what does Robert do?" Mary replied, "He doesn't stay in his seat." Then she called to another pupil, "John, what does Robert do?" John replied, "He steals pennies." Afterward, the Visitor wrote in her report, "Robert was becoming more and more uncomfortable. He flushed and seemed almost on the point of crying. When the Visitor looked at him, he smiled."

During his seventh year, the record shows, Robert generally misbehaved both at school and at home. Mrs. Korowski made it clear to the Visitor that she no longer approved of the boy, and on May 15, 1935, the Visitor noted that "Mrs. Korowski criticized Robert in the Visitor's presence. She had been repeatedly asked not to." The following month, another teacher wrote the Foundling Hospital that owing to Robert's "peculiar behavior" she felt it would be a good idea if she could talk with someone from the institution, so that "we might help him." When the Visitor called at the school, the teacher was not encouraging. She said, the Visitor reported, that Robert seemed "unstable and greatly handicapped. He falls off his chair in class, falls into his locker, has a silly grin on his face."

The Foundling Hospital decided that a change in schools might help Robert, and that fall he was sent to St. Monica's Parochial School, operated by the Sisters of Charity, in Jamaica. There the stealing of pennies continued. Again he was caught, and again his teacher rebuked him in front of the other children. She also complained to his foster mother. Mrs. Korowski, in

turn, complained to the Visitor, who noted that "boarding mother talks about transfer in front of him."

On February 7, 1936, Robert was taken to the Foundling Hospital for a psychiatric examination. His intelligence quotient was found to be 109, or slightly above average. "He admitted mild trouble," the psychiatrist wrote. "Chatted incessantly. He did no guessing on the tests, had good attention but seemed restless. His verbal response is good and his nonverbal or written response average. Social orientation and comprehension excellent." The Foundling Hospital decided that there was nothing fundamentally wrong with Robert but that a transfer to another foster home might bring about an improvement.

Robert remained in his second foster home only long enough to learn to call his new foster mother "Mother." Then he came down with diphtheria and was taken to Queensboro Hospital. He recovered after two and a half weeks. By that time, another child had taken his place at the second foster home, so he was sent to a third one. His next father and mother were Mr. and Mrs. Dolson, and they lived in a six-room house in Baldwin, Long Island. The husband was a municipal clerk in New York. Robert is described in the Visitor's record at this time as follows: "He is a nice-looking boy. He is a nicely mannered, friendly, talkative child. He is 47½ inches tall and weighs 50 pounds." The record says nothing of Robert's arrival at the Dolsons', in the spring of 1936, but it made a particularly strong impression on the boy, who was then in his eighth year. He remembers that a few minutes after he and the Visitor entered the house, he noticed a toy pistol lying on the floor. It belonged to the Dolsons' ten-year-old son. While the Visitor and Mr. and Mrs. Dolson discussed arrangements, Robert eyed the pistol. He felt nervous and embarrassed in his new setting, and very conscious of being the object of the adults' attention. For something to do, he walked over and picked up the pistol. As he rose, he heard a loud burst of laughter from Mr. Dolson. "I can see that this one's never going to be any good," Mr. Dolson said, slapping his thigh. "Went straight for the gun." Brown considers it one of the low points of his life. He says that he felt Mr. Dolson was right and that he instantly blamed himself because he wasn't any good. He had by then definitely decided, he adds, that it was because he didn't have a mother that he wasn't any good.

There were times when Robert appeared to be doing well at the Dolsons', as in April, 1936, when the Visitor reported, "He is a regular boy; his mind is on Dick Tracy, marbles, and guns." But she also noted his growing dislike of Mrs. Dolson. In May, she wrote, "Robert is disobedient and spiteful. Mrs. Dolson sent him upstairs as a punishment and he took a scissors, cut the bedspread, a table scarf, and a plant." In August, the Visitor wrote, "Robert is a very destructive child and seems to want to be cutting something or destroying his toys or some article that the boarding mother is particularly fond of."

Presently, Robert began asking Mrs. Dolson whether he had a mother and, if so, where she was. Mrs. Dolson said she didn't know and suggested that he ask the Visitor, but the Visitor could give him no very satisfactory answer, either. As Brown remembers it, he was concerned primarily about his mother and gave little thought to his father. Years later, Dr. Frederic Wertham, a psychiatrist who has devoted much study to the psychology of murderers, examined Brown, by then a murderer, and concluded that the young man's longing for his mother was the dominating force in his life, even driving him to irrational and criminal behavior.

Another episode at the Dolsons' remains fixed in Brown's memory. He described it long afterward in a letter to a social worker who became interested in his case:

"I am going to give you one incident that happened when I was eight years old. At that time I was attending St. Christopher's School [a parochial school in Baldwin]. The school is at least two miles from where I was living. Before leaving in the morning I was given two sandwiches of dubious content. It was usually prunes or lettuce. I also received a nickel, for carfare *to* school. I always had to walk home after school. Once after school I decided to take what I thought was a short cut, to get home. After about four hours of walking I found myself crying somewhere in Hempstead. An elderly woman saw me crying and asked what was wrong. I told her I was lost. She took me in her house and called the police. The police came and took me home. When I reached home, the policeman explained what happened to Mr. and Mrs. Dolson, and when he left, Mr. Dolson slapped me in the face and sent me to bed without supper."

The Visitor reported that Robert was inarticulate about the things that disturbed him. Mrs. Dolson's reports to the Visitor, on the other hand, were distressingly articulate. "He is an irresponsible, heedless boy," she said on one occasion. "He does everything he can to hurt my feelings. The other day he shot off a cap pistol in a girl's face. Robert is jealous of my son, and I have to be careful to give the same to both." Despite this friction, there were periods when Robert seemed happy. In the summer, for instance, he enjoyed camping out with his foster brother in vacant lots around Baldwin.

School went smoothly for Robert during his first couple of years with the Dolsons, but in the fall of 1938, when he was ten, he began to have trouble again. His teacher reported that he was shoving children on the stairs and stealing money from them. Brown thinks that his trouble at school stemmed, just as it had before, from his not having parents like the other children. Some boys in the playground gathered around him one afternoon and asked the old question—"How come your name ain't Dolson?" Again he tried to explain, and again, he says, he was taunted with "Dirty orphan!"

During the Christmas holidays, it was decided by the Foundling Hospital and the teachers at St. Christopher's that Robert should change schools once more. In January, he entered the Shubert Public School, in Baldwin, and in February the Visitor wrote that he "seems quite excited over his new school and is extremely happy there. His clothes are neater and he is studying harder." But when summer came around, things were again not quite right. "Robert seems to grow more nervous as he gets older," the Visitor wrote. "He had a D average in school."

Robert began stealing more frequently in the summer of 1939. Mrs. Dolson told the Visitor in August that he had rifled the drawers in a neighbor's house. And that fall, after he returned to the Shubert Public School, the principal reported that he stole candy. In the hope that a sense of responsibility would cure him of his stealing, the school authorities put Robert in charge of collecting the milk money from his classmates. The following spring, the Visitor wrote that this device had apparently proved effective.

Brown remembers his twelfth birthday— June 13, 1940—vividly. "That morning, I got up feeling good," he recalls. "I went downstairs and said to Mrs. Dolson, 'Today's my birthday.' 'So what?' she says. I felt pretty bad." This version of the birthday is only at slight variance with the version set down by the Visitor, who called that day with a present for Robert. A neighbor of the Dolsons', a Mrs. Berndorff, told her, "Robert came into my house and burst into tears. He said he had reminded his foster mother that this was his birthday and she had not even wished him a happy birthday." Mrs. Berndorff gave her daughter, who was Robert's age, some money, and she took Robert to the corner drugstore and bought ice cream for him and several other children.

In the summer of 1940, the Visitor seems to have detected a certain hostility on Mrs. Dolson's part toward Robert. On August 19, for example, the Visitor wrote, "Robert was taken to the movies by a pal's mother. Mrs. Dolson refused to let Robert go to the World's Fair with some other children. The neighbor felt sorry for Robert and took him to the movies."

Many boys who have as bleak a childhood as Robert Brown grow up to be law-abiding adults. Robert Brown grew up to be an armed robber. In the course of one robbery, he shot and killed the victim. If he had not been so rejected by adults during his childhood, if he had not been shifted from one foster home to another during what must have been his formative years, he might have developed greater capacity to identify with other people as well as stronger commitment to moral norms. Emotional deprivation in childhood often results in abnormal development, although not inevitably. Neuroses and psychoses in adults as well as criminality have been traced to socialization failure in childhood.[5] A rare type of socialization failure, the psychopath, demonstrates how weird a completely unsocialized adult can be.[6]

A psychopath is not "mentally ill" in the ordinary meaning of the term. The psychopath does not have hallucinations or delusions; he is not plagued by guilt feelings; he is not unhappy. The one thing the matter with him is that he has no sense of right or wrong. On superficial acquaintance, this may not seem such a serious defect. Lacking inhibitions, the psychopath is charming, gay, cheerful. He is also a chronic liar, extremely persuasive because he has no respect for truth. He feels no embarrassment when caught in a lie. With a bland smile, he invents a new tale to suit his immediate convenience. He can talk his way into almost any job because he is a supersalesman. But he gets bored easily; hence he rarely stays long in a job. He is fabulously successful with women, perhaps because of his devil-may-care attitude, perhaps because they foolishly expect to reform him. Since he is incapable of identifying with anyone, he cannot love. He exploits women as long as they put up with his monumental irresponsibility and believe his solemn promises to change. He marries often, frequently without troubling to divorce the previous victim of his charm. Since he does not worry about consequences, including consequences to himself, he drinks heavily, philanders relentlessly, and generally does what he pleases. His crimes, like his other behavior, can be understood as impulses of the moment. He forges a check or sells Brooklyn Bridge because he happens to be short of cash; he sets fire to a house for kicks; he provokes a fight to relieve boredom.[7] In short, the psychopath is a public menace because he behaves exactly as an infant behaves—except that he talks and dresses like other adults. Harrison Gough, a psychologist, summed up the subject neatly when he remarked that the psychopath is deficient in role-playing ability.[8]

What causes psychopathy? At one time psychiatrists believed that some constitutional deficiency was responsible. Nowadays psychiatrists emphasize parent-child interaction—although they do not rule out the possibility of constitutional predispositions. Both extremes,

---

[5] Not all criminality is the result of socialization failure. In heterogeneous industrial societies, criminality is sometimes a consequence of institutional malintegration, as Chapters 9 and 10 demonstrate.
[6] Hervey M. Cleckley, *The Mask of Sanity*, St. Louis: Mosby, 1941.

[7] I owe much to Professor A. H. Maslow's unpublished lectures on the psychopath.
[8] Harrison G. Gough, "A Sociological Theory of Psychopathy," *American Journal of Sociology*, Vol. 53, March 1948, pp. 359–366.

rejection and overindulgence, increase the probability of psychopathy.

FAMILY LIFE AND CHILD SOCIALIZATION IN INDUSTRIAL SOCIETIES

In preindustrial societies, the family has important functions in addition to the socialization of children. In industrial societies, the family has lost many economic, political, religious, recreational, and welfare functions.[9] Specialized institutions have assumed them. No longer the dominant institution of society, the family is now one of many institutions, but it is still a major agency of child socialization. Teachers, peers, and neighbors also contribute to the socialization of the child; the family, of course, gets the child first. However, child socialization presents different problems in the small, conjugal families of the United States, Sweden, Great Britain, or even Japan than in the extended families of preliterate societies. Families in industrial societies pass through a life cycle of establishment, development, and dissolution not characteristic of preliterate societies. From the point of view of the individual, *two* families exist rather than one: the family into which he is born, consisting of him, his father, mother, sisters, and brothers, and the family he creates by marriage, consisting of him, his wife, and their dependent children.

In industrial society, the individual leaves the household of his *family of orientation* and sometimes immediately, sometimes after an interval of living by himself or with strangers, establishes a new household for his *family of procreation*. The emphasis on the conjugal relationship in family organization in industrial societies (instead of on the parent-child relationship) guarantees the eventual destruction of every household. Very likely, this is unavoidable; an extended kinship unit would not be mobile enough for an industrial economy. Nevertheless, socialization is less uniform in a conjugal family system than in one with con-

tinuity from one generation to the next. If something goes wrong with a conjugal family, it goes very wrong. Consider, for example, the consequences of the death of a parent. In industrial societies, life expectancy is high; consequently orphanhood is a diminishing problem. But even in low-mortality industrial societies, *some* parents die prematurely. When this happens, no one is readily available to take over—as there would be in a household consisting of an extended family and containing more than two adults. Orphanhood is rarer in industrial societies, but when it comes, it creates more serious socialization problems for children than in preindustrial societies. Similarly, *divorce* has more pernicious consequences for children in industrial societies than it has in societies where socialization is the responsibility of the extended family.

The Varied Consequences of Divorce in Different Types of Societies

Reprinted by permission. From Kingsley Davis, "Children of Divorced Parents," *Law and Contemporary Problems*, Vol. 11, Summer 1944, pp. 700–720.

Theoretically the problem of the post-divorce child is universal—not only because divorce itself in one form or another is universal, but more profoundly because the child of divorce constitutes a potentially anomalous element in social organization. In most societies this potentiality is not allowed to express itself; instead, social institutions exist which take care of the child without undue turmoil. The peoples of Western civilization, on the other hand, have developed a peculiar institutional system that makes the problem very acute and hard to solve in practice. To understand why this is true one must compare the position of the child after divorce in different societies.

Since it dissolves the immediate family (now generally believed to be always and everywhere a part of society), the act of divorce usually offends the sense of order and fitness in social affairs. Hence it is nearly always tolerated in fact but never approved in principle. When children are

[9] William F. Ogburn, "The Family and Its Functions," in *Recent Social Trends in the United States*, New York: McGraw-Hill, 1933, Chap. 13.

INITIAL SOCIALIZATION   267

involved the antagonism to divorce is greater, because dissolution of the marriage runs counter to the main function of the immediate family— namely, the bearing and rearing of children. Having formed a union which is socially defined, which involves mutual rights and obligations, and which clearly has as its main function the rearing of children, the parents separate and thus deprive the child of its socially prescribed milieu. If he remains with one parent he lacks the other—a real loss, because each parent plays a necessary and complementary role in the child's life. If the parent with whom he stays remarries, the child falls into a stepchild situation. If he is shifted back and forth between the parents, he must adjust to two different domestic milieus, possibly two different stepchild situations, and must therefore run the risk of discontinuity in his emotional and intellectual development.

This description seems extremely obvious, but it appears so only because it describes the situation *in our culture*. To millions of people living in non-Western societies the description would appear ludicrous—not because it fails altogether to fit their social systems, but because it fits them only in an abstract or analytic sense. Although the immediate family is a universal group, it is not instinctive; rather it is a cultural phenomenon, and as such its specific form, and above all its connections with the rest of society, vary tremendously from one social system to another. It happens that in countless societies the immediate family is so interwoven with other institutional groups that, in case of divorce, the children do not constitute a social problem. The break-up of the immediate family is the same as in our society, and the anomaly of the child's position is potentially the same, but actually the parents' relation to other persons—often to clansmen and joint householders—is such that the child continues largely under their care.

The success of non-Western societies in solving the problem of the post-divorce child is explained by their wider use of kinship groups other than the immediate family. With them the immediate family is not the sole, nor even the most important kinship unit. Instead the clan, the extended family, and the joint household serve as important parts of social organization and perform functions which with us are left either to non-kinship groups or to the immediate family. Let us take as an example the Ibo society of Southern

Nigeria, whose divorce customs have been ably reported.

The first thing to note is the nature of Ibo marriage. It is not an agreement between the two prospective mates, but rather a contract between the parents and more fundamentally the clans of the mates. Without the prior consent and agreement of the two parental families no marriage could take place. Secondly, the prospective groom or his family must pay a bride-price to the girl's relatives, without which the union would have no legal standing. Thirdly, in spite of the marriage, the husband and wife remain socially and religiously members of their respective clans. The wife joins her husband's family physically but not spiritually. She must participate in the economic activities of his household, and above all she must bear children for his clan. But her underlying allegiance remains with her own family, and she may at any time return to it. The bride-price is the compensation that her parents, having gone to the expense of rearing her, receive for the loss of her services. It is not the price of her person, as such, for she continues to belong to her clan, but the price of her services. In return she has obligations toward her husband and his family. He also has obligations toward her, and unless these are properly observed her services may be withdrawn. She does not share her husband's possessions, inherit any of them after his death, or hold any claim to the children borne by her. Her husband has the right to contract as many marriages as he or his family can afford, and since a man's prestige depends on his wealth, and his wealth is most effectively displayed by the number of wives, he will try to secure as many as possible.

Being a private contract between the two families, a marriage may be revoked at will by either side. If he is willing to forget the bride-price the husband may send his wife back for any cause whatsoever. On the other hand, the wife may not be able to leave her husband even for just cause if her family refuses to refund the bride-price. Only if she has good prospects of remarrying, which means that another man stands ready to pay her family the bride-price (which then is returned to the original husband), may she leave of her own free will.

One of the most frequent causes of the dismissal of Ibo wives is barrenness. If several years elapse without a child being born, the wife may be sent home and the bride-price recovered. If, on the other hand, the wife has fulfilled her duty by bearing at least two children, including one son, it is extremely difficult for the husband to return her to her parents and receive back the bride-price. The charge of barrenness often elicits the counter-charge of impotence. If the wife fails to conceive for some years after marriage, she or her family and possibly her husband may make arrangements for extra-marital relations. A child born under such circumstances is of course the property of the husband and bolsters the position of the wife.

Obviously in Ibo society there can be no question of the custody of the children when a marriage is dissolved. They belong to the husband's family. It was largely for them that the marriage was contracted and the bride-price paid in the first place. The question may be raised as to how they can be taken care of without their mother, but the truth is that the mother's care is not necessary. Since the household usually includes some of the husband's female relatives, perhaps other wives, there is little difficulty about rearing the children.

The case of the Ibo has been chosen because its handling of divorce is, in its major outlines, typical of that in many primitive societies. The marital relation is dominated by lineal kinsmen, and the custody and rearing of the children do not depend on the continuance of the immediate family. The fact that the Ibo are patrilineal in their clan organization means that the child is viewed primarily as a member of the father's clan.[10] This is sometimes thought to be the most difficult case for post-divorce children in kinship societies, because of the young child's physical dependence on its mother. Actually in some patrilineal societies the children do remain with the mother while they are infants and are returned to the father at a later date.

[10] A patrilineal society is one in which descent is traced through *males,* the way names are inherited in Western countries. A matrilineal society is one in which descent is traced through *females;* that is, a woman, all of her children, and the children of her daughters (but not of her sons) belong to the same family. American society is neither matrilineal nor patrilineal; the child is related equally closely to his mother's and to his father's families. A patrilineal society is usually patrilocal; that is, the newly married couple lives in the household of the groom's family. This is logical because the offspring of the union belongs to the groom's family, not to the bride's. On the other hand, matrilineal societies are usually matrilocal. J.T.

In matrilineal and matrilocal societies the problem is easier. There, after divorce, it is the father who must leave; the child belongs to its mother's clan and hence remains in the mother's household. No conflict arises between the biological attachment of young children to the mother and their sociological attachment to the father. This is one reason why divorce is usually easier in such societies. The following description of the situation among the Khasis is typical:

"In the event of a divorce the mother is always allowed the custody of the children. Divorces . . . are of common occurrence, the result being that children in many cases are ignorant of the names even of their fathers. For the mother, on the other hand, the children cherish a very strong affection, all their sympathies and emotions binding them closely to their mother's kin. . . . The great drawback attaching to divorce in ordinary communities, i.e. the effect it has on the lives of the children of the marriage, does not apply to the Khasis, for with them the children always live with their mother and their mother's family, which latter would be bound to maintain them."

In societies where the emphasis on extended kin is bilateral rather than unilateral, or in which residence and descent are at variance, or in which other special conditions obtain, almost any conceivable rule may prevail with reference to the custody of children after divorce. Sometimes the children are divided equally, sometimes the boys are given to the father and the girls to the mother, sometimes the mother gets the younger, the father the older children. Generally, however, there is no major problem of adjustment, because, whoever gets him, the child is likely to live in intimate and stable relationship with other relatives, both male and female, who will perform the functions of the missing parent.

Although there are exceptions and occasional lapses, the general rule among primitive peoples may be summed up in a quotation from an article on Sumatran cultures:

"[In Indonesia] among strictly patrilineal peoples, such as the Batak and the natives of Nias, all the children [of divorced parents] remain with the father. . . . Among sibless people the children are divided between the parents at divorce, and among matrilineal peoples they naturally remain with the mother."

Not only primitive but civilized societies may utilize kinship as an important principle of social organization. This was the case in China before the process of Westernization set in. The immediate family was subordinate in nearly every respect to the extended family. The mates were selected and the marriage arranged by the parents, and the couple usually lived with the parents of the husband. The young bride was subordinate to the older females in her husband's extended household, and the husband was subordinate to his grandfather, father, or older brother. The household was frequently quite large, so that the children were surrounded by adults other than their mother and father—notably by uncles, aunts, and grandparents. The husband could divorce his wife for numerous causes, of which one was barrenness and another disregard of his parents. The wife's right of divorce was virtually nil.

Divorce in China did not imply family disorganization in our sense of the word. Since the dominant kinship unit was the extended patrilineal kin, the dissolution of a particular marriage had little significance, for it took more than this to break up the entire kindred or even a particular household. Furthermore, concubinage and polygyny made divorce less disruptive, because if one consort were divorced the others could maintain the immediate family. In any case the child necessarily remained in the father's household, where he continued to find the milieu much as it had been before. If divorce seldom occurred in Chinese society it was not because the dissolution of wedlock was considered "bad for the child," but because marital harmony did not depend primarily upon personal likes and dislikes.

In a kinship society, whether primitive or civilized, the immediate family is hardly an independent unit. It is the extended family which exercises the main influence, which has the privilege of choosing the mate, determining the residence, controlling the property, watching the morals, and in general managing the affairs of the young couple. The married pair either live with or near their relatives, and the children consequently grow up with the latter. Therefore if one parent is lost through death or divorce the child's domestic environment is not seriously disturbed. He tends to remain in the same household, among the same intimate relatives, feeling just as secure and loved as ever. Also, what might be called the principle of kinship substitution usually operates—the principle that if one kinsman is lost, another is available to take his place.

Such a principle is necessary if kinship is to form the basis of social organization, and it is embodied widely in the so-called classificatory type of kinship terminology, which calls different relatives by the same term (e.g. father and father's brother) because they may be functionally equivalent or capable of substitution. The principle means that the child is seldom left without some relative to function as a parent for him. Being familiar with this mechanism, he accepts it as a part of life. Also, since usually it is sociological rather than biological paternity that counts, the "stepchild" situation does not arise. Actually, so far as daily behavior is concerned, the child may have drawn little distinction between his parents and the other adults in the household anyway. It is therefore easy for him to make the adjustment when a parent is lost. Things remain for him pretty much as they were before.

One of the outstanding peculiarities of Western civilization, in contrast to the cultures discussed above, is the degree to which kinship has lost its social importance. At first sight this might suggest that divorce itself would have lost its importance, but such is not the case. The decline of kinship has affected the extended, not the immediate, family. The latter has lost some of its erstwhile functions in our mobile, urban, industrial society, but because it is virtually the sole remaining kinship unit it has acquired some of the functions formerly performed by other kinship relations. Its burden has therefore become heavy —perhaps too heavy for its inherently frail structure; and divorce, which dissolves the immediate family, has become a much greater problem, because it represents a threat to the family organization that remains.

With the principle of kinship substitution and the custom of the great household abandoned, the child of a deceased or divorced parent has as a rule nowhere to turn except to the other parent. He does not retain the balanced family life that a child in a kinship society is likely to have. He is therefore a "problem" in a much more pressing sense.

Having become the sole important kinship unit, the small family exhibits an unusual emotional concentration within itself. Its members, living apart from other kinsmen and surrounded by temporary acquaintances or strangers, can rely only upon themselves to share the feelings peculiar to blood relationship. The resulting intensity is sometimes extremely great, if not stifling. The loss of nonaffectional functions has further increased the importance of the family's emotional bonds at the same time that it has reduced the mutual cooperation in outside matters which would ordinarily support these bonds. Marriages, instead of being arranged by the elders on the basis of objective standards, are formed on the basis of romantic love and maintained on the strength of mutual likes and dislikes. The custom of having only one, two, or three children, plus the isolation of the parents from any other children than their own, increases the uniqueness and hence the emotionality of the parent-child relation. Consequently any marital discord not only affects the mates acutely but also involves the children. Husband and wife, as a compensation for marital unhappiness, unconsciously seek consolation, revenge, release, prestige, security, or what not in the children. The offspring in turn are victims of divided loyalty, emotional insecurity, and parental interference. This is why many experts believe that chronic discord is worse for the child than divorce; but the emotional intensity of the immediate family in modern society complicates divorce itself. It not only makes divorce more probable (because if things go wrong they go very wrong), but it also makes much harder the emotional readjustments of parents and children after divorce.

Not only do *death, divorce,* or *separation* of parents interfere with child socialization in industrial societies. *Any* kind of parental failing has serious emotional consequences for children: alcoholism, mental illness, unemployability, rejection, neglect. In preindustrial societies, where children spread their dependence over a larger number of kin, the imperfections or misfortunes of parents are not translated as directly into difficulties for children.

When homes break up in industrial societies, as some inevitably do, even financial arrangements for children are precarious. Studies have shown that fathers absent from the home because of divorce, separation, or desertion, are generally unable, unwilling, or both to contribute to the support of their children.[11] An even smaller proportion of the fathers of *illegitimate* children make financial contribu-

tions.[12] These conclusions hold despite the efforts of law-enforcement agencies to *force* absent fathers to support their children—including the imprisonment of substantial numbers of them for desertion and nonsupport.

The Financial Problems of the Fatherless American Family

Reprinted by permission. From Saul Kaplan, *Support from Absent Fathers of Children Receiving ADC,* 1955, Public Assistance Report No. 41, Washington: Government Printing Office, 1960, pp. 1–2.

Why do many broken families have little prospect of obtaining sufficient regular support from absent fathers? Many divorced fathers remarry and establish new family obligations that reduce their ability to support their first family. From January 1950 to April 1953 the number of divorced men remarrying was almost half (48.6 per cent) the number obtaining divorces, and more than half the remarriages occurred in less than 3 years from the time of the divorce. *In addition, absent fathers often completely sever their relations with the family left behind and leave no trace of their whereabouts.*[13] Finally, even when the fathers do not remarry or disappear, their income is often too low to enable them to support themselves in an independent establishment and, at the same time, support their children. The median income of separated men in 1950 was $1750 and that of divorced men was $2242—41 per cent and 24 per cent less, respectively, than the median income of married men living with their wives ($2959). More than half of all separated and divorced men but fewer than a third of all married men living with their wives had an income of less than $2000 in 1949. Almost

---

[11]   A study was made of support by absent fathers to children receiving Aid to Dependent Children assistance in the summer of 1955. Only 18 per cent of fathers currently or previously married to the mothers of the children contributed *anything* to their support. See Saul Kaplan, *Support from Absent Fathers of Children Receiving ADC,* 1955, Public Assistance Report No. 41, Washington: Government Printing Office, 1960, p. 17.

[12]   In the same study reported on in footnote 11, it was found that only 10 per cent of the fathers of *illegitimate* children on A.D.C. contributed *anything* to their support. *Ibid.,* p. 35.

[13]   Italics added by J.T.

a third of all separated and divorced men, more-over, live in rooms with no cooking facilities and have to pay more than a normal amount for their food because they must often eat in restaurants.

With little or no support from the fathers of their children, necessity—not choice—forces many mothers of broken families into the labor market. In 1955 more than half (52.9 per cent) of widowed, divorced, and separated mothers but fewer than a fourth (24.0 per cent) of other mothers were in the labor force. The younger the children, the more difficult it is for the mother to seek outside employment. Sixty-three per cent of the widowed, divorced, and separated mothers of children aged 6–17 were in the labor force, but only 40 per cent of those with children under age six were employed or seeking employment. Thus, while the labor-force rate of mothers in fatherless families is much higher than that for other mothers, almost half of all the mothers in fatherless families and 60 per cent of those with children under age six are not in the labor market.

Even when they do work, the mothers in broken families usually earn fairly little because of low wage rates, part-time employment, or a combination of these factors. Almost a fourth of all female heads of families had no personal income in 1954, and for the other three-fourths the median income ($1489) was almost 60 per cent smaller than that ($3626) of male heads of families. In 1949, fully 87.5 per cent of all separated women and 70 per cent of all divorced women received an annual income of less than $2000.

Faced with these financial problems, some mothers give up the hope of maintaining a home for their children. Some children are sent to live with other relatives, some to foster homes, some to institutions for dependent and neglected children.[14] Some mothers surrender their children for adoption.[15] (This is espe-

[14] On November 30, 1958, more than 54,000 children were in institutions for dependent and neglected children in 45 states. See Helen R. Jeter, *Children Who Receive Services from Public Child Welfare Agencies*, Children's Bureau Publication No. 387, Washington: Government Printing Office, 1960, p. 12.
[15] About 100,000 adoptions were authorized by American courts in 1960. See U.S. Bureau of the Census, *Statistical Abstract of the United States, 1962*, Washington: Government Printing Office, 1962, p. 301.

cially common with newborn illegitimate children.) Some mothers struggle to maintain a home for their children despite the necessity of playing a double role: breadwinner and homemaker. Under urban industrial conditions, however, the mother who works full-time has difficulty arranging for the proper supervision of her young children. Table 35 shows the variety of child-care arrangements made in 1958 by American working mothers in broken homes.

Very little is known about the *quality* of these child-care arrangements—although 91,-000 children under 12 take care of themselves while their mothers are at work, and this is unsatisfactory supervision by any standard. Even this need not be deliberate neglect. Mothers who do not have relatives or neighbors to put in charge of their children may have no alternative but to leave them unsupervised. The cost of group care or paid baby-sitters is usually beyond their resources. A generation ago the federal government recognized the seriousness of this problem and undertook to subsidize child care. The philosophy of the Aid to Dependent Children program is written into the

TABLE 35
Child-Care Arrangements Made by Full-Time Working Mothers in Broken Homes, United States, 1958

Type of Child-Care Arrangement	Children under 12	
	Number	Per Cent
Supervised by father	11,000	1.2
Supervised by relative under 18	123,000	13.9
Supervised by relative over 18	389,000	43.8
Supervised by neighbor	73,000	8.2
Supervised by other nonrelative	90,000	10.1
Group care	54,000	6.1
Self-care	91,000	10.3
Other arrangements	57,000	6.4
All arrangements	888,000	100.0

Source: Henry C. Lajewski, *Child-Care Arrangements of Full-Time Working Mothers*, Children's Bureau Publication No. 378, Washington: Government Printing Office, 1959, p. 21.

originating legislation: "No child shall be deprived of care in his own home because of poverty alone." [16] By 1960 more than two million American children received benefits each year under the Aid to Dependent Children program; more than a billion dollars were disbursed.[17] Some critics of this program are appalled at the large number of recipients and the high cost to the taxpayer; they fear that A.D.C. benefits are being given to persons who do not need them. However, Table 36 shows that the bulk of children receiving A.D.C. benefits come

TABLE 36
The Status of the Fathers of Children Assisted by the Aid to Dependent Children Program, October–December 1958

| Status of Fathers | Children Assisted by A.D.C. | |
	Number	Per Cent
Dead	219,970	10.3
Incapacitated	558,443	26.1
Absent	1,319,165	61.6
Divorced or legally separated	276,979	12.9
Separated without court decree	187,174	8.7
Deserted	397,094	18.5
Not married to mother	335,830	15.7
Imprisoned	101,618	4.7
Absent for other reason	20,470	1.0
Other status *a*	44,818	2.1
Total	2,142,396	100.0

Source: Bureau of Public Assistance, *Illegitimacy and Its Impact on the Aid to Dependent Children Program*, Washington: Government Printing Office, 1960, p. 81.

a Includes father in home as caretaker because of death, incapacity, or absence of the *mother.*

16 For a good discussion of the philosophy and the practicalities of government support of child welfare in the United States, see Eveline M. Burns, "The Government's Role in Child and Family Welfare," in Eli Ginzberg, Ed., *The Nation's Children*, Vol. 3, New York: Columbia University Press for the Golden Anniversary White House Conference on Children and Youth, 1960, pp. 148–179.
17 *Health, Education, and Welfare Trends*, 1961, Washington: Government Printing Office, 1961, pp. 81–82.

from fatherless homes or from homes where the father is unable to provide support because of a physical disability.

Given the system of isolated conjugal families in industrial societies and given the occurrence among them of broken homes (because of divorce, separation, desertion, or illegitimacy), the A.D.C. program may be the most economical way of dealing with society's responsibility for child socialization. Perhaps it may be too economical. The average monthly benefit was only $30 in 1960.[18] For nearly half of the A.D.C. families, total income from all sources (including earnings of family members) did not attain the modest monthly requirements under state assistance standards.[19] Even if the A.D.C. benefits were *doubled*, the cost of A.D.C. would be a fraction of the cost of placing the children in schools for dependent and neglected children.

Those who wish to punish promiscuous women by denying A.D.C. benefits for illegitimate children underestimate the difficulties of making alternate child-care arrangements. The foster-home experiences of Robert Brown, while not necessarily typical, point up a real problem: there is a chronic shortage of foster homes, even marginally satisfactory ones. If the sole criterion is a suitable home for the child, studies have shown that mothers whose sexual behavior shocks the community may nevertheless care for their *children* conscientiously.[20]

Broken families overlap the larger universe of *problem* families, that is, families unable to function adequately by community standards without help from voluntary or governmental agencies.[21] The size of the problem-family universe is difficult to estimate because it is not clear how many health, educational, delin-

18 *Ibid.*, p. 83.
19 "The average amount needed by all families was $143; the shortage for families with unmet needs was $39 per month." Bureau of Public Assistance, *Illegitimacy and Its Impact on the Aid to Dependent Children Program*, Washington: Government Printing Office, 1960, p. 45.
20 *Ibid.*, pp. 49–50, 54–57.
21 An unpublished report of Dr. Sol Chaneles to the Youth Development Program of The Ford Foundation, 1961, defines problem families in this way.

quency, psychological, and economic difficulties turn up in the *same* families—although the popularity of the term, "multiproblem family," suggests a tendency for a sea of simultaneous troubles to flood the same family.[22] Perhaps a quarter of American families have one or more problems necessitating outside help. If so, a *majority* of American families are self-reliant, and in these families a majority of American children are socialized. The self-reliant family is not, however, a static family. Unlike the extended families of preindustrial societies, the normal conjugal family in an industrial society develops through various stages and ultimately disappears when the last parent dies. The following article, based on decennial censuses and reports of the Current Population Survey, traces the life cycle of the normal conjugal family in the United States.

The Life Cycle of the American Conjugal Family

Reprinted by permission. From Paul C. Glick, "The Life Cycle of the Family," *Marriage and Family Living*, Vol. 17, February 1955, pp. 3–9.

MARRIAGE. The average young man in the United States in 1950 entered marriage for the first time at about the age of 23 years and his wife at about the age of 20. (See Table 37 and

[22] Ludwig Geismar and Beverly Ayres, *Measuring Family Functioning*, St. Paul, Minn.: Family Centered Project, 1960.

Figure 10.) Both the groom and the bride in 1950 were more than a year younger, on the average, than the corresponding young persons who were entering their first marriage a decade earlier. This decline stands in contrast with the fact that during the entire 50-year period from 1890 to 1940, the average (median) age at first marriage for grooms had declined only about two years and that for brides only about one-half year, according to the best estimates available.

Earlier marriages have become more common during recent years when married women have found it easier to gain employment outside the home. More and more women now work for a period before marriage, continue their employment after marriage until they start the child-bearing period, then in a few years return to work outside the home. Women who are in the labor force have received more education, on the average, than those not in the labor force. In the marriage boom of the last decade, greater gains in the proportion married in the United States were made by the more-educated than by the less-educated sections of the population.

An interesting sidelight on the changing age at marriage is an apparent decline in the gap between the median ages of husbands and wives at first marriage. The average husband of recent years is his wife's senior by about three years, whereas his grandfather was likely to have been senior by about four years.

To simplify the treatment of our subject, we have limited our discussion to first marriages. It is recognized, of course, that many of these marriages become broken within a relatively short time; in such cases, most of the marriage partners

TABLE 37
Median Age of Husband and Wife at Selected Stages of the Life Cycle of the Family, for the United States: 1950, 1940, and 1890

Stage of the Life Cycle of the Family	Median Age of Husband			Median Age of Wife		
	1950	1940	1890	1950	1940	1890
A. First marriage	22.8	24.3	26.1	20.1	21.5	22.0
B. Birth of last child	28.8	29.9	36.0	26.1	27.1	31.9
C. Marriage of last child	50.3	52.8	59.4	47.6	50.0	55.3
D. Death of one spouse [a]	64.1	63.6	57.4	61.4	60.9	53.3
E. Death of other spouse [b]	71.6	69.7	66.4	77.2	73.5	67.7

[a] Husband and wife survive jointly from marriage to specified age.
[b] Husband (wife) survives separately from marriage to specified age.

are at ages when remarriage rates are relatively high. In 1948, about 13 per cent of the married women living with their husbands had remarried after the dissolution of an earlier marriage; in 1910, the corresponding proportion was probably about seven or eight per cent. Among persons who married since the end of World War II, about one fifth were entering a second or subsequent marriage.

CHILDBEARING. The average mother who was having her first child in 1950 was 22.5 years old, according to vital statistics data on order of birth by single years of age of mother. The difference between the median age at first marriage based on census data and the median age at birth of first child based on vital statistics data, however, provides an unsatisfactory measure of the average interval between marriage and the birth of the first child. Similar data are used here to approximate the average interval between marriage and the birth of the last child only because the relative error is much less in this case. More precise measurement of child-spacing intervals is now being undertaken by the Bureau of the Census

in cooperation with the National Office of Vital Statistics, on the basis of data from the 1950 Census of Population and from the Current Population Survey.

For women who had married and had reached the end of their reproductive period (45 to 49 years old) by 1952, the average number of children born per woman was about 2.35. By making use of this fact in conjunction with 1950 statistics on order of birth, it is estimated that approximately half of the women have borne their last child by the time they are 26 years old. Thus, the median length of time between marriage and the birth of the last child is probably close to six years.

Because families have declined so sharply in size, the usual span of the childbearing years has become only about half as long as it was two generations ago. The average mother whose family reached completion in 1890 had borne 5.4 children, with an estimated interval of ten years between marriage and the birth of the last child. She had not given birth to her last child until she was about 32 years old. For 1940, the last of three (3.0) children was born when the mother was about 27 years old.

Women who had never borne a child constituted only about eight per cent of all women who had married and completed their period of fertility by 1890. This percentage approximately doubled by 1940 (15 per cent); it continued to rise by 1952 to 19 per cent for women 45 to 49 years old but there was evidence that it would fall sharply for younger women.

During the next decade or two the average number of children per completed family is likely to rise moderately and the proportion of women who remain childless throughout their reproductive years is certain to decline. Changes in patterns of marriage and childbearing which have developed since about the beginning of World War II will apparently have the effect of reversing, at least temporarily, the 150-year decline in the average size of completed family.

CHILDREN LEAVING HOME. From the time the last child is born until the first child leaves home, the size of family usually remains stable. Changes in family living during this period are those related to the growth and maturation of the children and the changing economic status of the parents.

If we make some allowance for mortality

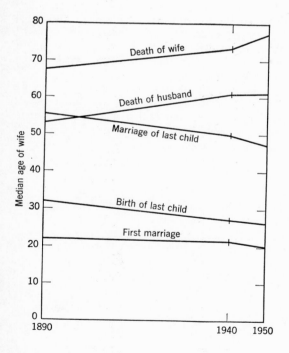

FIGURE 10. Stages of the life cycle of the family in the United States: 1890, 1940, and 1950.

among the children, and if we assume that the children will marry and leave home at the same age that their parents married, we find that the average woman who married in 1950 will be about 48 years of age when her last child leaves home. By comparison, the average woman of her grandmother's day was about 55, if she lived that long, when her last child got married.

DISSOLUTION OF THE FAMILY. The combined effects of earlier marriages, smaller families, and longer average length of life have produced a remarkable change in the length of time that married couples live together after their children have set up homes of their own. Under conditions existing in 1950, a couple could expect to have about 41 years of married life before either the husband or the wife died; during their last 14 years together, the couple would ordinarily have no unmarried children remaining with them. Thus, the couple would have half as many years of married life with no young children at home as they would have with children at home.

By contrast, conditions existing in 1890 assured only about 31 years of joint survival for the husband and wife; in fact, the chances were 50-50 that one spouse or the other would die at least two years before their youngest child married.

Because men are usually older than their wives at marriage and have higher mortality rates, age for age, wives generally outlive their husbands. The wife can expect to live much longer after her husband's death if she is the survivor than the husband can expect to live after his wife's death if he is the survivor. In this final stage of the family life cycle, the length of time that the remaining marriage partner survives has not changed greatly in the last two generations, but the expected ages during which the lone survivor is in this phase have been advanced several years.

CHANGES IN COMPOSITION AND ECONOMIC CHARACTERISTICS

As the family proceeds through its life cycle, it expands in size with the addition of each child and eventually contracts as the children marry and depart from their parental home. Many variations in this pattern exist, of course. Some families have no children; in others, one or more children remain at home longer than usual, often after marriage; and in still other cases, one or more of the parents or parents-in-law spend their later years with their children. Adjustments in living accommodations are commonly made in order to meet the needs of the family and changes in the economic activity of the family members generally occur as conditions make such changes feasible and advantageous.

These dynamic aspects of family living are traced in this section by studying changes in characteristics of married couples as the age of the husband advances. (See Table 38 and Figure 11.)

FAMILY COMPOSITION. On the basis of data for a recent year (1952), about 45 per cent of the married couples of all ages combined have no sons or daughters under 18 years of age in their homes. About four tenths of the husbands below the age of 25 years have no dependent children, but only 21 per cent of those between 25 and 44 have none in the home. Above the age of 45, the proportion of husbands without young children of their own at home rises sharply and continuously until, among those above the age of 65, nearly all have none living with them.

The number of children in homes with children rises until it reaches two or three, on the average, by the time the husband is 35 to 44 years old, then declines. Thus, the average family group, comprising the husband, wife, and young children, grows from two persons to four or five and then diminishes gradually to the original two parents.

There are seldom any additional relatives living with the couple while the husband is under 40 years of age. From that time until old age approaches, however, there are likely to be one or more adult relatives (usually grown children of their own) in about one half of the homes and one or more other young relatives (usually grandchildren) in about one home out of ten. When a young married couple lives with the husband's or wife's parents, the chances are nearly two out of three that the couple will stay with the wife's parents. This arrangement is most common perhaps largely because the wife is likely to spend more time in the home than her husband, and because close daily contacts between a mother and her daughter are less likely to create tensions than similar contacts between a mother-in-law and her daughter-in-law.

RESIDENTIAL LOCATION. About four fifths of the persons who marry change residences at the time of marriage or within the ensuing year. Thereafter, the mobility rate decreases sharply as the number of years married increases. By the time couples have been married 10 to 15 years, only about 20 per cent move to another home in the course of a year's time. By this time, most of the changes of residence required to provide room and a measure of privacy for the various family members have been made. Moreover, the difficulty of moving all of the belongings of the family when it is at its maximum size probably serves as a deterrent to residential changes during this stage of family life. The continued decline, rather than an increase, in mobility during the later years of life perhaps suggests, among other things, that families do not ordinarily move into smaller quarters after their children have left home. Data from the 1950 Census of Housing also suggest that the shifts to smaller homes are relatively few in number during this period of life and that most of them take place after the husband reaches 65 years of age.

LABOR FORCE PARTICIPATION. Half of the young men have begun employment by the time they are about 18 years of age, that is, five years before the median age at marriage. Between the ages of 25 and 60, about 85 per cent or more of the men are in the labor force, and close to half of them remain in the labor force until they reach the age of 70.

Although it is characteristic of husbands to be in the labor force from marriage until the age of retirement, at no time does the proportion of wives in the labor force exceed one half. In 1953,

one fourth of all women living with their husbands were in the labor force, that is, had a job (or were seeking work) other than their own home housework. In 1940, the corresponding pro-

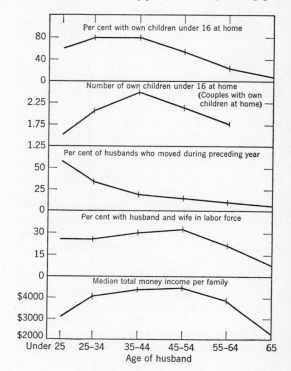

FIGURE 11. Characteristics of married couples by age of husband, for the United States: 1952.

TABLE 38

Characteristics of Married Couples by Age of Husband, for the United States: 1952

Age of Husband	Per Cent of Couples With No Own Children Under 18 at Home	Own Children Under 18 at Home Per Couple With Children	Per Cent of Husbands Who Moved During the Preceding Year	Per Cent of Couples With Husband and Wife in Labor Force [a]	Median Total Money Income Per Family [b]
All ages	44.8	2.15	20.2	24.5	$3,890
Under 25 years	42.4	1.51	55.8	24.9	$3,069
25 to 34 years	20.9	2.08	32.9	24.9	$4,030
35 to 44 years	20.9	2.46	18.2	29.5	$4,339
45 to 54 years	49.4	2.08	⎰ 10.3	30.9	$4,355
55 to 64 years	79.6	1.71	⎱	20.5	$3,805
65 years and over	96.2	[c]	6.6	6.5	$2,276

[a]   Based on 1953 data.
[b]   Income in 1952, for families surveyed in 1953.
[c]   Fewer than 100 cases in sample.

portion was only 15 per cent. This striking change has taken place despite the fact that the average number of children that married women under 35 years of age have borne has increased by about 20 per cent.

During the first year after marriage about 40 per cent of the wives have jobs away from home. During the second or third year many drop out of economic activity to have children and the proportion of working wives falls to about 30 per cent. For the period when women have children of preschool age (under 6 years old), only about 15 per cent are labor force participants. After all of the children have reached school age, nearly one third of the wives are in the labor force. Aside from the first couple of years of marriage, this is the period when the wife is most likely to be supplementing the husband's earnings by working outside the home; it is probably also the period when women are most likely to contribute volunteer service to their communities.

Among older couples, whose children have married and left home, it seems probable that fewer wives feel the necessity to remain in the labor force. Furthermore, as the situation exists at present, the average wife who has reached her upper fifties probably lacks the necessary skills, experience, and other qualifications for remunerative employment. Since many more of the younger wives now than formerly have had work experience, it seems reasonable to expect that a larger proportion of those who advance to later middle age in future years will be qualified to contribute to the family income by engaging in work away from home.

In 1952, one third of the families had two earners—usually the husband and the wife. In one tenth of the families, there were three or more earners, usually including the wife and/or young adult children. . . .

For families that are newly formed, there are many demands for household goods to equip the home and, in some cases, to start a business. Furthermore, within a short time the wife is likely to be preoccupied with child rearing and unable to help her husband make a living. During this period, while the husband's work experience is still limited, the family income is relatively low. Within about ten years, however, the family income generally has increased about one third. Between the ages of 35 and 54, when the wife may have returned to the labor force and some

of the older children who live with their parents may be working, the family income is at its peak, about 40 per cent above the level for newly formed families. After the family head has passed age 65, the family has only about half the income it had at its peak.

Partly as a consequence of declining income in old age and partly as a means of being better cared for at that time, the proportion of married couples who live in the homes of others increases somewhat from a low point of less than three per cent in their late 50's but amounts to only about five per cent for couples above the age of 65 years. Some older couples invite a married son or daughter to move in with them for similar reasons.

As the foregoing discussion makes clear, the American family is not only a child-rearing institution. The average couple has also as many years of married life without young children in the home as with them. The concern of this chapter is, however, with child socialization and therefore with the implications of the family cycle for the socialization of children rather than for companionate marriage or the personality adjustment of the aged. Earlier in this chapter attention was called to the major liability of the small, conjugal family as a child-rearing institution, namely, its vulnerability to personal crisis. It lacks the resilience to cope with serious illness, death, parental incompatibility, and other catastrophes. On the other hand, the conjugal family system has its advantages. Not only is it compatible with the population mobility of industrial societies, which extended families are not; it is also more receptive to expert advice on child rearing than are patrilineal or matrilineal families.[23] The phenomenal sales in the United States of Dr. Benjamin Spock's book on baby and child care are no accident. They reflect the uncertainty of today's parents with a newborn infant and without the guidance of an older, more experienced woman *in the household*. Such parents buy Dr. Spock's book and others like it because they cannot draw so easily on an in-

[23] See footnote 10 for a definition of "patrilineal" and "matrilineal."

formal tradition of child care—as can parents in societies where children are socialized in households where other children have recently passed through the same developmental stage. The uncertainty of parents in industrial societies makes them more receptive to advice from pediatricians, child psychologists, and other transmitters of the latest research. Insofar as it can be assumed that folk traditions of child care are not perfect, this receptivity to change makes improved socialization techniques possible. Whether the changes in socialization practices in the United States in the past couple of generations have been *improvements* is not certain; there is no doubt, however, that *changes* have occurred.[24] If and when a scientific basis for child socialization is established, the introduction of changes in child-rearing practices will not be so difficult.

CONCLUSION

Faced with a barbarian invasion of egocentric infants, every society responds by setting up an informal teaching program, usually run by the family, in which the child learns to behave in accordance with the society's standards for human beings. "Socialization" is the name for this process of learning to play roles, first in one's family and then in other groups. It consists not only of external conformity to social rules but also of learning to like doing what one would be compelled to do anyway, that is, of the development of a certain kind of self-conception. In all societies the individual joins the human community in the same way: by identifying with previously socialized members of the society and by incorporation of *their* values.

Since socialization is a type of learning, failures are inevitable. No educational program is 100 per cent successful. Most forms of mental illness result from the emotional scars of childhood socialization. A bizarre form of socialization failure is the psychopathic personality, whose appearance is adult but whose morality is that of the egocentric infant.

Because industrial societies assign responsibility for child socialization to the conjugal family, they are especially vulnerable to socialization failure. When things go wrong in a conjugal family, they go *very* wrong. The conjugal family system lacks the resilience to absorb the personal catastrophes which past experience would suggest are inevitable. On the other hand, the conjugal family system has a built-in receptivity to change, and this opens the door to improvements in child-rearing techniques as scientific knowledge of socialization grows.

SOME SIGNIFICANT LITERATURE ON INITIAL SOCIALIZATION

Albert Bandura and Richard H. Walters, *Adolescent Aggression: A Study of the Influence of Child-Training Practices and Family Interrelations*, New York: Ronald, 1959. In order to investigate the effect of child-rearing practices on the development of explosively aggressive adolescents, the authors selected for study from the caseload of a probation department 26 adolescent boys

---

[24] Daniel R. Miller and Guy E. Swanson, *The Changing American Parent*, New York: Wiley, 1958; John Sirjamaki, *The American Family in the Twentieth Century*, Cambridge, Mass.: Harvard University Press, 1953; Orville Brim, Jr., *Education for Child Rearing*, New York: Russell Sage Foundation, 1959; Urie Bronfenbrenner, "Socialization and Social Class Through Time and Space," in Maccoby, Newcomb, and Hartley, Eds., *Readings in Social Psychology*, 3rd ed., New York: Holt, 1958, pp. 400–425.

with histories of assaultive behavior. These boys were not members of ethnic minorities; they came from intact homes located in neighborhoods at least average in socioeconomic status. Hence, several factors that might confuse the relationship between child-training practices and aggressive behavior were eliminated in advance. Another group of 26 boys who did not manifest explosive aggressiveness were also interviewed as a comparison group. The parents of the aggressive boys differed from parents of boys in the control group in the following ways: they were less warm toward their sons, more disapproving of dependent behavior, less consistent in their demands, and less likely to make any demands at all. They relied more on physical coercion than on reasoning in attempting to enforce the demands they made. The aggressive boys developed less identification with their fathers, felt more hostile toward them, spent less time with them, and avoided seeking their help. Outside of the home the aggressive boys expressed more direct hostility toward teachers and peers and felt relief rather than guilt following aggressive episodes. This summary is based on a review by Edward C. Devereux, Jr., *American Sociological Review*, Vol. 25, June 1960, pp. 438–439.

Orville G. Brim, Jr., "Family Structure and Sex-Role Learning by Children," *Sociometry*, Vol. 21, March 1958, pp. 1–16. Psychologists have long believed that a girl learns appropriate feminine traits by identifying with her mother and a boy with his father. Sexual pathologies, such as homosexuality, have been traced to obstacles to appropriate identifications. This article explores a neglected source of sex-role education: brothers and sisters. Dr. Brim reanalyzes data on 384 native-white children from *two-child* unbroken families. At the time the original data were collected (in Chicago) the children were five or six years old. Dr. Brim found (1) that children with siblings of the *opposite* sex tended to assimilate more traits of the opposite sex than did children with siblings of the *same* sex and (2) that this effect was especially pronounced if the child was younger than his sibling of the opposite sex. Since siblings closer in age are assumed to interact with one another more extensively, it was hypothesized that the effect of siblings of the opposite sex would be stronger the closer in age were the siblings. The data did not confirm this hypothesis.

Paul C. Glick, *American Families*, New York: Wiley, 1957. A wealth of data on family organization and living arrangements exist in the census reports of modern countries. This monograph, one of a series commissioned by the Social Science Research Council, undertakes to exploit data on American families drawn largely from the 1950 census of population. It covers such topics as: (1) family living arrangements, (2) the life cycle of the family, (3) changes in family composition during the life cycle, (4) first marriages and remarriages, and (5) separation, divorce, and widowhood. As background for understanding American child socialization, a researcher may wish to know such things as the percentage of American families living with relatives or in rooming houses rather than in their own households or the percentage of families without two parents in the home. He has a good chance of finding answers in this monograph. This summary is based on a review by Sheldon Stryker, *American Sociological Review*, Vol. 22, October 1957, pp. 605–606.

Norman Goodman, Stephen A. Richardson, Sanford M. Dornbusch, and Albert H. Hastorf, "Variant Reactions to Physical Disabilities," *American Sociological Review*, Vol. 28, June 1963, pp. 429–435. Research has shown that American children and adults respond more favorably to drawings of a child without handicaps than to drawings of a child with crutches, with a missing left hand, or with a facial disfiguration. And, curiously enough, they respond even more negatively to a drawing of an obese child than to drawings of crippled or disfigured children. The research reported in this paper takes the rank order of reactions to disabilities as the result of normal—albeit subtle—socialization, and goes on to predict that certain categories of children will react differently. Mentally retarded and psychiatrically disturbed children will rank the drawings differently because their intellectual and emotional problems interfere with learning in general and especially with learning values which are implicit rather than explicit. Children from particular ethnic traditions will rank the drawings differently because they have learned special subcultural values at variance with the point of view of the larger society. The research undertaken by the authors confirmed their predictions.

Talcott Parsons, "The Superego and the Theory of Social Systems," *Psychiatry*, Vol. 15, February 1952, pp. 15–25. Along with other insights, this theoretical article suggests an explanation of the child's development from being a pragmatist yielding to superior power to becoming a moral being. Professor Parsons points out that mother-child interaction implicitly teaches the child expressive concepts describing the relationship between his mother's acts and her underlying feelings. This symbolic learning makes possible emotional communication between them. Only after the child has learned the expressive concepts of his culture, concepts already known to his mother and embodied in her responses to him, can he learn to love his mother or to care about her love for him.

Morris Rosenberg, "Parental Interest and Children's Self-conceptions," *Sociometry*, Vol. 26, March 1963, pp. 35–49. Through a questionnaire survey of 1684 juniors and seniors in ten high schools in New York State, the relationship between level of parental interest in their children and children's self-esteem is examined. Three indices of parental interest are used: (1) the parents' knowledge of the child's friends when he was 10 or 11 years of age, (2) the parents' response to his report card when he was in the fifth or sixth grades, and (3) the degree of current participation of the child in mealtime conversation. Dr. Rosenberg reports that children whose parents can be described as disinterested in them (by any of the three criteria) score lower on a test of self-esteem, on the average, than children whose parents are interested in them—lower in fact than children of parents whose interest is mainly punitive. "Very likely such lack of interest in the child goes along with lack of love, a failure to treat the child with respect, a failure to give him encouragement, a tendency to consider the child something of a nuisance and to treat him with irritation, impatience and anger. . . . The feeling that one is important to a significant other is probably essential to the development of a feeling of self-worth."

David M. Schneider and George C. Homans, "Kinship Terminology and the American Kinship System," *American Anthropologist*, Vol. 57, December 1955, pp. 1194–1208. In order to evaluate the consequences of American kinship terminology, the authors asked 209 students and colleagues to describe in detail the exact terms used in their families in referring to relatives. Searching interviews were conducted to find out the reasons for variations from ordinary kinship usage— for example, why some uncles were addressed by their first names and others as Uncle _____. One variation was particularly interesting from the point of view of socialization: the reciprocal use of first names between children and parents. Since this terminology suggests social equality, the authors were not surprised to be told that parents in these situations had greater difficulty asserting their generational authority. "Parents always have the problem of dealing with children who, at certain ages, insist that, 'If you can do it, why can't I?' But where first names are used reciprocally, we find that this problem is especially acute and especially difficult to handle."

Anselm Strauss and Karl Schuessler, "Socialization, Logical Reasoning, and Concept Development in the Child," *American Sociological Review*, Vol. 16, August 1951, pp. 514–523. A series of test items were administered to young children involving coin recognition, comparative value of different coins, and making change. The researchers concluded that because young children were inferior to adults in logical reasoning, they did not have the concepts necessary for learning adult motives and roles. Only when they have mastered these concepts, passing from simple to more complex symbols, can socialization proceed to levels expected by adult society.

Jackson Toby, "The Differential Impact of Family Disorganization," *American Sociological Review*, Vol. 22, October 1957, pp. 505–512. The family not only transmits socially acceptable values to the young child; it also tries to prevent him from being influenced by socially unacceptable values. By means of an examination of American delinquency data, this article explores the differential consequences to girls and boys, to younger and older children, of ineffective parental guidance. Since girls and preadolescents tend to be better supervised by the average urban industrial family than adolescent boys, a defective family situation makes a greater difference to girls and preadolescents than it does to adolescent boys.

Clark E. Vincent, "Unmarried Fathers and the Mores: 'Sexual Exploiter' As an Ex Post Facto Label," *American Sociological Review*, Vol. 25, February 1960, pp. 40–46. In view of the difficulties in providing for the socialization of illegitimate children in industrial societies, unmarried motherhood is relevant to the topic of child socialization. In 1954 Dr. Vincent studied 201 out-of-wedlock births to white women in Alameda County, California, where the identity of the father was known. He reported that the fathers did not conform to the popular stereotype of the exploiting male. By and large, the fathers resembled the mothers in age and education; he concluded that any exploitation present in the relationship when illicit sexual relations were occurring was likely to be reciprocal. This suggests that unmarried parenthood is not explainable in terms of naiveté of inexperienced girls and also that the social obstacles to the marriage of the father and the mother of the child are fewer than were supposed. For a more detailed discussion of the characteristics of the unmarried mothers, including the factors associated with their decision to keep their babies or surrender them for adoption, see Clark E. Vincent, *Unmarried Mothers*, New York: Free Press of Glencoe, 1961.

CHAPTER 9

Nonconformity and Its Control

The more heterogeneous the culture and the more swiftly its norms change, the less consensus there is about right and wrong. In the United States, for instance, moral values differ in upper and lower classes, among Negroes and whites, and in various regions, occupations, religions, and ethnic groups. To speak of a collective conscience for American society as a whole implies resolution or compromising of the moral sentiments of many individuals as they interact with one another. In one sense, that is what the criminal law is: a compromise, a moving equilibrium. But it is not the same compromise that would be arrived at by a random sample of the American population.

THE DIFFERENCE BETWEEN NONCONFORMITY AND IMMORALITY

The legislators and judges who make and interpret the law are, by and large, well-educated, high-status persons. No matter how hard they try to be merely spokesmen of collective sentiments, they cannot help reading the parochial morality of their milieu into their conception of the public conscience. Thus, the administration of the criminal law is not simply the enforcement of morality—except perhaps

for middle-aged, middle-class, male, white Protestants. For members of other groups, the intentional commission of a crime is not necessarily synonymous with defiance of the collective conscience. Everyone perceives the collective conscience from the vantage point of his own place in the social structure. Drunken driving, nonsupport of spouse and children, stealing from large corporations, and cheating on income-tax returns are not universally condemned in American society. When the offender has done nothing wrong in terms of the moral standards of his reference groups, it may be more appropriate to speak of "culture conflict" than of deviant behavior.[1]

That is to say, *illegality and immorality are not synonymous.* Violations of the traffic laws and public drunkenness are far more common than murder, rape, and burglary. Yet traffic violations and drunkenness, even when they result in injuries to persons or in property damage, do not arouse the same moral indignation as the traditional offenses. Neither do white-collar crimes: offenses committed by business and professional people against laws regulating their activities—for example, patent infringe-

[1] Thorsten Sellin, *Culture Conflict and Crime*, New York: Social Science Research Council, 1938.

ment. The term "folk crime" has been coined to tag these violations of law which are tolerated by the general public. H. Laurence Ross has developed an interesting explanation of folk crimes; he believes that the lack of indignation is only temporary and that morality will eventually catch up with the laws required by our complex industrial society.

Folk Crimes: Illegalities Not Considered Immoral

Reprinted by permission. From H. Laurence Ross, "Traffic Law Violation: A Folk Crime," *Social Problems*, Vol. 8, No. 3, Winter 1960–1961, pp. 231–241.

It may be useful to think of both white-collar crime and traffic law violations as sub-species of folk crime. This category is proposed in order to group together violations of laws that are introduced to regulate the novel kinds of behavior that an increasingly advanced technology and an increasing division of labor generate. It should be noted, as Aubert states in connection with white-collar crime, that "the laws . . . are usually not in obvious or apparent harmony with the mores. They are largely an outcome of the increased complexity of modern industrial society, a complexity which requires legal control of activities with long-range and often very indirectly damaging effects."

The characteristics of folk crime are present in Sutherland's description of white-collar crime. However, in proposing the more general category of folk crime, these characteristics are emphasized to the exclusion of Sutherland's focus on the occupational context of the act and the white-collar status of the criminal.

The following propositions are speculatively offered concerning folk crime:

(a) Major increments to the complexity of a society, of which the automobile is a technological example, create a need for regulation where none was previously necessary.

(b) Legislation to regulate the conditions brought about by increasing complexity reclassifies certain prevalent non-criminal behavior as crime.

(c) Especially where the harmful effect of the proscribed behavior is indirect or improbable in most instances, the novel legislation may not be related to previously existing norms.

(d) Criminal behavior in folk crime is rooted, not necessarily in lower-class culture, but in the culture of groups most affected by the social or technological changes that the legislation attempts to control. White-collar crime is the special case of folk crime resulting from legislation regulating business and finance. The automobile, with its impact on all social classes, generates more pervasive forms of folk crime.

(e) In particular instances, large numbers of people, including those of high status, will be involved in law violations related to major social changes.

(f) The lack of congruence between the new laws and established mores, the generally higher social status of the violators, and the possibly large size of the group of violators among the total population, will tend to be associated with preferential treatment of folk criminals in the public image and in the judicial process.

Examples of other law violations with the characteristics of folk crime can be found in the literature. Among them is "chiseling" in unemployment compensation. According to Smigel, chiseling shares with white-collar crime (and traffic law violation) the following characteristics: the participant is not a professional criminal, he is not stigmatized as criminal, he may lack criminal intent, and he is treated differently from "ordinary" criminals. Smigel notes that the chiseler differs from the white-collar criminal in that his action need not be committed in the course of his occupation, and he may be found in any social class.

Another example is participation in the wartime black market. Although Clinard claims this is white-collar crime, he presents statistics showing that 65 per cent of the people imprisoned for these violations had less than a high-school education, thus indicating that high social status need not be involved. Furthermore, it is obvious that at least the consumers engaging in black market transactions did not necessarily commit these crimes in the course of their occupations.

In sum, the category of folk crime is proposed as a convenient way of thinking about traffic law violations, white-collar crime, chiseling, black market dealings, and many other illegal actions that have in common a source in social complexity. As opposed to "ordinary criminals," folk criminals are relatively numerous, unstigmatized, and differentially treated in the legal process. While they tend to be from higher social classes than the typical stigmatized criminal, they need not be predominantly white-collar, and the proscribed acts need not be committed in the course of business.

Let us ignore folk crimes. Let us ignore also nonconformity arising from psychopathology. The individual who suffers from such a defect of reason as to not know what he is doing does not intentionally defy accepted moral standards; an essential ingredient of crime—both from the legal and the common-sense point of view—is lacking. If we ignore subculturally legitimated crime and the offenses of mentally irresponsible persons, what is left to account for? There remains the problem of violations of the law by people who are not mentally ill and who have been brought up to believe that theft, assault, and other acts prohibited by the criminal law are *wrong*. Such persons engage in deviant behavior because training is never perfect. Since human beings do not have the social rules imbedded in their biological make-up, as ants and bees do, the individual must *learn* the group pattern. On any subsequent occasion when he experiences envy, hatred, fear, or other strong emotions, he faces a choice between his own inclinations, which may happen to be illegal, and his desire to obey the rules of his society. This is a chronic problem. It is not only professional criminals who are tempted to defy or evade the collective conscience. The collective conscience formulates universal prohibitions. Yet circumstances occur in the lives of *most* people when they wish to drive an automobile at 80 miles an hour, beat up an enemy, or take something without paying for it. The fact that the rules have to be *learned* makes crime possible; the fact that situations of extraordinary temptation arise makes crime inevitable. It is a commonplace of criminology that quite ordinary people embezzle large sums of money from their employers or kill close relatives in the course of a quarrel.[2]

THE PUZZLE OF CONFORMITY

The problem is not why crime and other forms of deviance exist. The real problem is conformity. Yet conformity is so commonplace that explanations for criminality are thought to be necessary. Does the long arm of organized society explain conformity? Are not police forces a major deterrent to crime? The potential thief may refrain from stealing because he is afraid he will be caught and punished. The classic demonstration of the validity of this argument was provided by the Nazis during the Second World War; they deported all of Denmark's police force and crime increased greatly.[3] This demonstration notwithstanding, laymen exaggerate the deterrent value of the police. In industrial societies, a thief has at least an even chance of not getting caught. For example, in 1961 only about 30 per cent of the auto thefts and burglaries reported to the police in American cities were cleared by the arrest of suspects.[4] Furthermore, the percentage of auto thefts solved was greater in cities of less than 10,000 population than in large cities. (See Table 39.) The police did better in solving crimes against the person: murder, rape, aggravated assault.[5] Apparently the conditions of life in industrial societies— the mobility, the anonymity, the ready marketability of valuables—are not conducive to catching thieves. Since urbanization and industrialization are increasing in the contemporary world, stealing will become *less* risky in

[2] Donald R. Cressey, *Other People's Money: A Study in the Social Psychology of Embezzlement*, Glencoe, Ill.: Free Press, 1953; Marvin E. Wolfgang, *Patterns in Criminal Homicide*, Philadelphia: University of Pennsylvania Press, 1958.
[3] Jörgen Trolle, *Syv Måneder uten politi* (Seven Months without Police), Copenhagen, 1945, quoted in Nils Christie, "Scandinavian Criminology," *Sociological Inquiry*, Vol. 31, Winter 1961, p. 101.
[4] United States Department of Justice, *Uniform Crime Reports—1961*, Washington: Government Printing Office, 1962, pp. 83–84.
[5] *Ibid.*

the decades ahead—barring an unanticipated break-through in police science. In short, the police are necessarily inefficient under contemporary conditions. If the police were the only reason that the temptation to steal did not eventuate in thefts, industrial societies would need a policeman for every ten citizens and special police to watch the police.

Criminologists are prone to stress another factor to explain why the temptation to steal only infrequently results in thefts or attempted thefts. It takes skill to steal successfully. Trying to learn shoplifting or safe cracking through trial-and-error methods is likely to result in swift apprehension. In point of fact, few youngsters steal without previous contact with more sophisticated delinquents.[6] They serve an informal apprenticeship, learning what things are worth stealing and how to dispose of them,

what techniques to use to gain entrance unobtrusively to stores, factories, and private homes, and how to answer the questions of detectives to avoid self-incrimination. This training is not available for the asking. Nor do motion pictures or television programs provide sufficiently detailed instruction. Neighborhoods differ greatly in the opportunities they present for training in deviant activities.[7] High delinquency neighborhoods, for example, are not only neighborhoods where theft and violence are likely to occur; they are also neighborhoods where a growing boy has a better chance than in other neighborhoods to become friendly with persons who will teach him how to steal or to look for "kicks" in gang fighting or drug use.

This ecological perspective highlights the point that crime is not mere negativism; crime usually requires a repertoire of skills that have

[6] Several articles in the summer 1960 issue of *Social Problems* were devoted to theory and research on differential association.

[7] Richard A. Cloward and Lloyd E. Ohlin, *Delinquency and Opportunity: A Theory of Delinquent Gangs*, Glencoe, Ill.: Free Press, 1960, Chaps. 6 and 7.

TABLE 39
Differential Crime and Arrest Rates in American Cities, 1961

	Type of Crime	Size of City					
		Over 250,000	100,000–250,000	50,000–100,000	25,000–50,000	10,000–25,000	Under 10,000
Major crimes Known to Police (rate per 100,000 population)	Murder	7	5	4	3	3	2
	Forcible rape	18	7	5	5	4	4
	Robbery	153	56	39	24	16	13
	Aggravated assault	169	85	63	42	34	29
	Burglary	786	679	536	468	368	305
	Larceny—$50 and over	505	372	360	313	216	159
	Auto theft	417	277	210	165	113	80
Crimes Cleared by Arrest (per hundred crimes reported to police)	Murder	93	94	92	96	90	89
	Forcible rape	72	70	72	77	80	84
	Robbery	43	39	37	40	46	47
	Aggravated assault	78	75	78	86	86	91
	Burglary	31	29	26	29	31	35
	Larceny—$50 and over	23	19	18	21	20	24
	Auto theft	24	30	28	32	40	48
Full time police employees per 100,000 population		258	169	158	146	141	144

Source: Adapted from *Uniform Crime Reports—1961*, Washington: Government Printing Office, 1962, pp. 81–84 and 108–109.

to be learned in a social context. When this has been said, however, the original riddle is still unsolved. The infrequency of deviance cannot be accounted for by lack of opportunity to learn illegitimate skills. Even in high-delinquency neighborhoods, a considerable proportion of youngsters do not engage in delinquency. And persons who happen to live in communities where deviant activities are infrequent are mobile enough in industrial societies to find models for deviant roles in other communities. The *raggare* gangs of Stockholm are a case in point. They recruit youngsters from all over the city. This is necessary because of a deliberate policy (by officials charged with allocating scarce housing) to distribute multiproblem families as widely as possible instead of concentrating them in certain neighborhoods as occurs in the United States and Great Britain.[8] Perhaps the tremendous emphasis on automobiles on the part of *raggare* youth is an adaptation to the difficulties of getting into contact with other deviantly oriented adolescents under Swedish conditions.

It is not easy to explain conformity in terms of the situation external to the individual. True, some people conform because they are afraid of being caught and punished, and others conform because they have not located models to show them how to carry out their deviant impulses. However, neither of these factors, singly or in conjunction with one another, seems adequate to explain widespread resistance to ever-present temptations. Perhaps a better explanation of conformity lies in the *internal* resources for resisting illicit motives, namely, guilt and shame.

GUILT: THE INTERNALIZED POLICEMAN

To the extent that the individual has incorporated within his own personality the "do's" and "don'ts" of the collective conscience, society has mobilized his self-respect

[8] Unpublished report submitted by Jackson Toby to the Youth Development Program of The Ford Foundation dealing with European delinquency as of the summer of 1960.

on the side of conformity. He feels that stealing and murder are *wrong*, not merely acts which might arouse the police force. Suppose, for example, a woman shopper sees a bracelet in a jewelry store which she would like to own but cannot afford; she thinks she could put it in her pocketbook without anyone seeing her. But the norms within her psyche prevent her from taking advantage of this opportunity. She knows that she could not respect herself if she thought of herself as a "thief."

A tremendous amount of conforming behavior can be understood as part of the individual's attempt to maintain his self-conception intact. If the conscience of every member of society were precisely the same, guilt feelings would always work in favor of conformity. In fact, however, the agents of socialization (parents, friends, neighbors, teachers) stress different norms and apply them with varying degrees of pressure. The result is that within the same society (1) notions of right and wrong differ from personality to personality, and (2) even though there may be consensus that certain behavior is wrong, individuals differ in the extent to which they can engage in such behavior without guilt reactions incompatible with their self-conceptions. Some people have such strict consciences that they suffer remorse over deviations which most members of the society would consider trifling. On the other hand, psychiatrists occasionally encounter individuals who have hardly been touched by the socialization process. They are egocentric and amoral (like the infant); they respond to their impulses, oblivious of social rules. Apparently, anything they may wish to do is compatible with their self-conceptions. Chapter 8 discussed psychopaths as an instance of defective socialization.

Psychopaths get into trouble frequently and spend much time in prisons and mental hospitals.[9] However, the perpetrator of a crime is not necessarily a psychopath. A professional burglar might well consider rape to be *wrong*

[9] For an excellent discussion of this strange disorder, see Hervey M. Cleckley, *The Mask of Sanity*, St. Louis: Mosby, 1941.

and might therefore be incapable of such behavior. The concept of crime, geared as it is to the predictability of state sanctions, obscures the motivational distinction between acts compatible with the offender's self-image and acts which are not. Offenders do not challenge the rules on principle. They find laws an obstacle to getting what they want, and, if the particular offense is not too guilt provoking, they take a chance that they will not be caught. Crime is an abstraction; robberies, assaults, auto theft, embezzlements, arsons, forgeries, and so forth, are the concrete realities. Thus, a man with a long criminal record may be psychologically incapable of engaging in 90 per cent of the offenses defined by the criminal code. His conscience is operative, and it prevents most antisocial behavior.

Guilt reactions are exceedingly complex. Even when deviant behavior is entered upon without overt guilt, closer study usually reveals that strong motivation to engage in prohibited behavior overcomes a norm in the psyche. Sometimes the victory of the deviant impulse is temporary, and subsequently remorse overwhelms the offender. Psychiatrists claim that some offenders are so effective at self-condemnation that they unconsciously seek out punishment in order to expiate their guilt feelings. A guilt-ridden offender may confess his crime—and sometimes others he did not commit. One well-publicized and ghastly Los Angeles murder gave rise to 38 "confessions" to the police over a ten-year period. The Black Dahlia mystery is still unsolved.

Those who denounce themselves to the police for other people's crimes are probably psychotic. Offenders who are not psychotic have guilt problems too—as the following techniques for chloroforming the conscience suggest: (1) Liquor is frequently an accompaniment of crime—as well as of lesser forms of misbehavior. This is partly because consciences can be put out of commission by alcohol. (2) Much crime is executed in groups—from burglary to lynching. Social support stills the self-condemnations which the individual might feel if he committed the crime by himself.

(3) Convicted offenders offer elaborate justifications for their crimes. Sykes and Matza systematically questioned juvenile delinquents in a state training school about these justifications. They were persuaded by their research that rationalizations that neutralized guilt were part of the explanation of juvenile delinquency. Here are the specific rationalizations they identified.

How Boys Commit Crimes without Feeling Like Criminals

Reprinted by permission. From Gresham M. Sykes and David Matza, "Techniques of Neutralization: A Theory of Delinquency," *American Sociological Review*, Vol. 22, December 1957, pp. 664–670.

THE DENIAL OF RESPONSIBILITY

Insofar as the delinquent can define himself as lacking responsibility for his deviant actions, the disapproval of self or others is sharply reduced in effectiveness as a restraining influence. As Justice Holmes has said, even a dog distinguishes between being stumbled over and being kicked, and modern society is no less careful to draw a line between injuries that are unintentional, i.e., where responsibility is lacking, and those that are intentional. As a technique of neutralization, however, the denial of responsibility extends much further than the claim that deviant acts are an "accident" or some similar negation of personal accountability. It may also be asserted that delinquent acts are due to forces outside of the individual and beyond his control such as unloving parents, bad companions, or a slum neighborhood. In effect, the delinquent approaches a "billiard ball" conception of himself in which he sees himself as helplessly propelled into new situations. From a psychodynamic viewpoint, this orientation toward one's own actions may represent a profound alienation from self, but it is important to stress the fact that interpretations of responsibility are cultural constructs and not merely idiosyncratic beliefs. The similarity between this mode of justifying illegal behavior assumed by the delinquent and the implications of a "sociological" frame of reference or a "humane" jurisprudence is readily apparent. It is not the validity of this orientation that concerns us here, but its function of deflecting blame attached to violations of social norms and its relative independence of a particular personality structure. By learning to view himself as more acted upon than acting, the delinquent prepares the way for deviance from the dominant normative system without the necessity of a frontal assault on the norms themselves.

THE DENIAL OF INJURY

A second major technique of neutralization centers on the injury or harm involved in the delinquent act. The criminal law has long made a distinction between crimes which are *mala in se* and *mala prohibita*—that is between acts that are wrong in themselves and acts that are illegal but not immoral—and the delinquent can make the same kind of distinction in evaluating the wrongfulness of his behavior. For the delinquent, however, wrongfulness may turn on the question of whether or not anyone has clearly been hurt by his deviance, and this matter is open to a variety of interpretations. Vandalism, for example, may be defined by the delinquent simply as "mischief"—after all, it may be claimed, the persons whose property has been destroyed can well afford it. Similarly, auto theft may be viewed as "borrowing," and gang fighting may be seen as a private quarrel, an agreed upon duel between two willing parties, and thus of no concern to the community at large. We are not suggesting that this technique of neutralization, labelled the denial of injury, involves an explicit dialectic. Rather, we are arguing that the delinquent frequently, and in a hazy fashion, feels that his behavior does not really cause any great harm despite the fact that it runs counter to law. Just as the link between the individual and his acts may be broken by the denial of responsibility, so may the link between acts and their consequences be broken by the denial of injury. Since society sometimes agrees with the delinquent, e.g., in matters such as truancy, "pranks," and so on, it merely reaffirms the idea that the delinquent's neutralization of social controls by means of qualifying the norms is an extension of common practice rather than a gesture of complete opposition.

THE DENIAL OF THE VICTIM

Even if the delinquent accepts the responsibility for his deviant actions and is willing to admit that his deviant actions involve an injury or hurt, the moral indignation of self and others may be neutralized by an insistence that the injury is not wrong in light of the circumstances. The injury, it may be claimed, is not really an injury; rather, it is a form of rightful retaliation or punishment. By a subtle alchemy the delinquent moves himself into the position of an avenger and the victim is transformed into a wrong-doer. Assaults on homosexuals or suspected homosexuals, attacks on members of minority groups who are said to have gotten "out of place," vandalism as revenge on an unfair teacher or school official, thefts from a "crooked" store owner—all may be hurts inflicted on a transgressor, in the eyes of the delinquent. As Orwell has pointed out, the type of criminal admired by the general public has probably changed over the course of years and Raffles no longer serves as a hero; but Robin Hood, and his latter day derivatives such as the tough detective seeking justice outside the law, still capture the popular imagination, and the delinquent may view his acts as part of a similar role.

To deny the existence of the victim, then, by transforming him into a person deserving injury is an extreme form of a phenomenon we have mentioned before, namely, the delinquent's recognition of appropriate and inappropriate targets for his delinquent acts. In addition, however, the existence of the victim may be denied for the delinquent, in a somewhat different sense, by the circumstances of the delinquent act itself. Insofar as the victim is physically absent, unknown, or a vague abstraction (as is often the case in delinquent acts committed against property), the awareness of the victim's existence is weakened. Internalized norms and anticipations of the reactions of others must somehow be activated, if they are to serve as guides for behavior; and it is possible that a diminished awareness of the victim plays an important part in determining whether or not this process is set in motion.

THE CONDEMNATION OF THE CONDEMNERS

A fourth technique of neutralization would appear to involve a condemnation of the condemners or, as McCorkle and Korn have phrased it, a rejection of the rejectors. The delinquent shifts the focus of attention from his own deviant acts to the motives and behavior of those who disapprove of his violations. His condemners, he may claim, are hypocrites, deviants in disguise, or impelled by personal spite. This orientation toward the conforming world may be of particular importance when it hardens into a bitter cynicism directed against those assigned the task of enforcing or expressing the norms of the dominant society. Police, it may be said, are corrupt, stupid, and brutal. Teachers always show favoritism and parents always "take it out" on their children. By a slight extension, the rewards of conformity—such as material success—become a matter of pull or luck, thus decreasing still further the stature of those who stand on the side of the law-abiding. The validity of this jaundiced viewpoint is not so important as its function in turning back or deflecting the negative sanctions attached to violations of the norms. The delinquent, in effect, has changed the subject of the conversation in the dialogue between his own deviant impulses and the reactions of others; and by attacking others, the wrongfulness of his own behavior is more easily repressed or lost to view.

THE APPEAL TO HIGHER LOYALTIES

Fifth, and last, internal and external social controls may be neutralized by sacrificing the demands of the larger society for the demands of the smaller social groups to which the delinquent belongs such as the sibling pair, the gang, or the friendship clique. It is important to note that the delinquent does not necessarily repudiate the imperatives of the dominant normative system, despite his failure to follow them. Rather, the delinquent may see himself as caught up in a dilemma that must be resolved, unfortunately, at the cost of violating the law. One aspect of this situation has been studied by Stouffer and Toby in their research on the conflict between particularistic and universalistic demands, between the claims of friendship and general social obligations, and their results suggest that "it is possible to classify people according to a predisposition to select one or the other horn of a dilemma in role conflict." For our purposes, however, the most important point is that deviation from certain norms may occur not because the norms are rejected but because other norms, held to be more pressing or involving a higher loyalty, are accorded precedence. Indeed, it is the fact that both sets of norms are believed in that gives meaning to our concepts of dilemma and role conflict.

The conflict between the claims of friendship and the claims of law, or a similar dilemma, has of course long been recognized by the social scientist (and the novelist) as a common human problem. If the juvenile delinquent frequently resolves his dilemma by insisting that he must "always help a buddy" or "never squeal on a friend," even when it throws him into serious difficulties with the dominant social order, his choice remains familiar to the supposedly law-abiding. The delinquent is unusual, perhaps, in the extent to which he is able to see the fact that he acts in behalf of the smaller social groups to which he belongs as a justification for violations of society's norms, but it is a matter of degree rather than of kind.

"I didn't mean it." "I didn't really hurt anybody." "They had it coming to them." "Everybody's picking on me." "I didn't do it for myself." These slogans or their variants, we hypothesize, prepare the juvenile for delinquent acts. These "definitions of the situation" represent tangential or glancing blows at the dominant normative system rather than the creation of an opposing ideology; and they are extensions of patterns of thought prevalent in society rather than something created *de novo*.

Resort to these rationalizations—as well as use of alcohol and group-encouraged delinquency—indicates that guilt reactions must be dealt with even when they are not sufficient to *prevent* deviant behavior.

SHAME: SENSITIVITY TO SOCIAL SANCTIONS

Socialization is an effective defense against nonconformity to the extent that deviant impulses arouse in advance sufficient guilt to prevent their overt expression. But guilt is not the only internal control. Reinforcing whatever guilt feelings the individual may have are the pressures exerted upon him by others. In addition to his feeling that certain actions are *wrong* is the individual's awareness that they may arouse disapproval in his family, among his peers, in his school, or in his place of employment. To the extent that he anticipates general disapproval and wishes to avoid it, shame reinforces guilt in the control of nonconformity.

In contemporary society, however, the large variety of subgroups and subcultures makes shame as problematic as guilt. Take the family, for example. If all parents disapproved emphatically of stealing and brawling, children sensitive to their parents' reactions—girls and preadolescents especially—would be less likely to steal and to fight.[10] But family units differ not only in cohesiveness, that is, in the extent to which children are sensitive to parental disapproval, but also in the *strength* of parental disapproval of delinquency. Thus, in one family a boy who brings home a stolen item will be forced to return it to its owner with apologies; in another he will be lectured but allowed to keep it; in some families there will be no questions asked; and in a few he may gain approval for his contribution to the family's possessions.[11] It is too much to expect that millions of family units in a complex and highly differentiated society will react to violations of law in precisely the same way.

To complicate the problem of shame further, relatives by no means exhaust the circle of significant others. Even in the preadolescent years, peers are important to youngsters. By adolescence, however, approval and disapproval from peers is of greater concern to many youngsters than the reactions of their parents.[12] There are, of course, youth groups with conventional values: church groups, 4-H clubs, YMCA groups, and such. But adolescent peer groups in industrial societies are more likely than families to condone nonconformity because their members are struggling to emancipate themselves from family *controls*, and in the process they may also repudiate *values* espoused by their parents.[13] Thus, it is possible to find delinquent and quasidelinquent groups

in suburban communities where parental disapproval of such activities is unequivocal.[14] Such groups derive support from adolescent rebelliousness against parental authority.

Even the normal adolescent in industrial societies exists in a family limbo. He is becoming detached from the family in which he was born and socialized, and he has not yet established a family unit of his own. His peers fill the void and give him roots, but they are an inherently unstable group. Its members grow older, and, unless younger adolescents are admitted to membership, the structure of the group disappears. Groups which enjoy adult sponsorship or support—boys' clubs, settlement house youth groups, Scouts, church youth clubs—do not disintegrate in this way. They recruit younger adolescents to take the place of the older adolescents who lose interest. Hence these adult-sponsored youth groups are permanent in the sense that, although the membership is constantly changing, the basic structure remains intact. On the other hand, the youth groups that develop spontaneously on street corners are much less likely to be age-graded and therefore to preserve their identity beyond the particular cohort of adolescents currently in them. Millions of these spontaneous groups come into being, exist for several years as vehicles for expressing the interests and the solidarity of a particular group of adolescents, and then disintegrate. This flux is conducive to nonconformity because such autonomous groups are structurally isolated from adults whose responsibilities in the larger society are likely to make them sympathetic interpreters of conventional values.[15]

Some peer groups are actively organized to promote delinquent activities: "bopping" (fighting) gangs, drug-using cliques, car

10 Jackson Toby, "The Differential Impact of Family Disorganization," *American Sociological Review*, Vol. 22, October 1957, pp. 505–512.
11 The same point can be made about the expression of aggression. See Albert Bandura and Richard H. Walters, *Adolescent Aggression: A Study of the Influence of Child-Training Practices and Family Interrelations*, New York: McGraw-Hill, 1959.
12 Talcott Parsons, "Age and Sex in the Social Structure of the United States," *American Sociological Review*, Vol. 7, October 1942, pp. 604–616.

13 Herbert A. Bloch and Arthur Niederhoffer, *The Gang: A Study in Adolescent Behavior*, New York: Philosophical Library, 1958.
14 Seymour Freedgood, "Life in Bloomfield Hills," *Fortune*, July 1961, pp. 234–236.
15 Sophia M. Robison, "Autonomous Groups: An Unsolved Problem in Group Loyalties and Conflicts," *Journal of Educational Sociology*, Vol. 20, October 1946, pp. 154–162.

thieves.[16] But much adolescent nonconformity is tolerated rather than required by peers. In the *raggare* clubs of Stockholm (the Road Devils, the Car Angels, the Car Comets, and the Teddy Boys) it is prestigeful to have an American car in which to cruise around the city looking for girls. A boy who stole a squirrel tail to hang on the aerial of his car would probably not be disapproved of by his friends. And he would be able to signal to boys in other cars, by raising or lowering the squirrel tail, indicating how he was making out in his quest.

In short, peer groups vary considerably in their response to delinquent behavior. Among those that *require* stealing or fighting, shame operates in favor of delinquency instead of against it. The more common situation, however, is a peer group that will *tolerate* stealing, drunkenness, or assaultive behavior, often because these are ways of expressing daring or toughness—but not the only ways.

THE DIFFERENTIAL STAKE IN CONFORMITY

The deterrent value of shame depends on the sensitivity of the individual to disapproval from other people. But just as it cannot be assumed that everyone in a person's milieu will approve or disapprove of the same acts, neither can it be assumed that disapproval is equally threatening, no matter who expresses it. The individual is far more sensitive to pressures emanating from small face-to-face groups in which he interacts extensively than to pressures from larger, more inclusive groups like the neighborhood or "society." [17] Disapproval from people one cares about is more threatening than disapproval from strangers. Nevertheless, human beings do feel shame in relationship to strangers they have never seen before or expect to see again. Even in contemporary cities where neighbors are a blurred streak of constantly changing faces, people ask themselves, "What will the neighbors think?" But, of course, the sting of neighbor disapproval is greatly reduced if population mobility and density creates an anonymous atmosphere—as in a rooming-house district. Another factor reducing the effectiveness of neighborhood controls in industrial societies is the extent to which the individual's reference groups are physically separated from the area in which he lives. That is to say, one's home may be the place where one sleeps and little else. One's place of work, one's school, or one's friends may be separated from one's home by a 15-minute (or more) drive in an automobile.

The sting of social disapproval is greater the more approval the individual previously enjoyed. This truism has tremendous implications for the understanding of shame. Shame costs the high-status individual more than the person already disesteemed by his community. The captain of the high-school football team or the president of the Student Council has more to lose by being caught cheating on a test than a below-average student taking the general course and intending to quit school as soon as he reaches 16. More generally, anything that affects the individual's prestige—his occupational prospects or achievements, the social position of his family, the color of his skin, his athletic exploits, even a neighborhood reputation as a "good fellow"—provides a stake in conformity.[18] Part of the reason why unskilled workers and Negroes are disproportionately represented in the criminal statistics is that convictions for crime are less degrading for them than for middle-class white Protestants. One cannot lose what one does not have. Jail is not so threatening to those at the bottom of the social hierarchy; incarceration is easier to bear when it is not also disgrace.

Shame has greater deterrent value—even in the anonymous urban community—for those held in high esteem by respectable members

16   Cloward and Ohlin, *op. cit.*
17   Edward A. Shils, "The Study of the Primary Group," in Daniel Lerner and Harold D. Lasswell, Eds., *The Policy Sciences*, Stanford, Calif.: Stanford University Press, 1951, pp. 44–69.

18   Jackson Toby, "Social Disorganization and Stake in Conformity: Complementary Factors in the Predatory Behavior of Young Hoodlums," *Journal of Criminal Law, Criminology, and Police Science*, Vol. 48, May–June 1957, pp. 12–17.

of society than for those regarded as of no particular consequence. This statistical prediction rests on the principle that the individual's self-respect is in dynamic equilibrium with the deference he is accorded by others.[19] Individual personalities vary in the extent to which they can tolerate adverse judgments from others without unfavorable modifications of their self-conceptions; but the over-all correlation between reputation and self-respect is quite high.[20]

Although high-status people have a greater stake in conformity than low-status people, they also have greater resources for resisting definitions of themselves as nonconformists. Thus, criminologists have shown that white-collar crimes are less likely than blue-collar crimes to result in conviction in a criminal court.[21] Indeed, the criminal violations of business and professional people, such as fraudulent advertising, income-tax evasion, or collusive bidding on government contracts, are not usually regarded with the same repugnance by the general public as burglary or assault. And even when the offense charged is one like shoplifting, which clearly violates community norms, high-status people have a better chance than low-status people to escape condemnation. Their protests of innocence, put forward by skillful lawyers, are more readily believed than the monosyllabic denials of the shabby and uncouth. When they plead "kleptomania" and offer to submit to psychiatric treatment, their superior financial resources are regarded as evidence that they are ill and not antisocial.[22]

[19] Hans L. Zetterberg, "Compliant Actions," *Acta Sociologica*, Vol. 2, 1957, pp. 179–201.
[20] It might be argued from this that guilt and shame are really different aspects of the same phenomenon. The error in this line of reasoning lies in its neglect of the time dimension. At a particular moment, an individual's self-conception may permit him to feel no guilt despite intense disapproval from the people around him. But the norms incorporated in his personality took root in the context of interaction with persons who expressed approval and disapproval—and whose point of view he adopted.
[21] Edwin H. Sutherland, *White Collar Crime*, New York: Holt, Rinehart and Winston, 1949.
[22] Donald R. Cressey, "The Differential Association Theory and Compulsive Crimes," *Journal of Criminal*

SOCIAL DISORGANIZATION: THE BREAKDOWN OF CONTROLS

Crime exists in every community because situations arise where the temptation to violate a rule is more powerful than the deterrent capacity of the individual's guilt feelings and his fear of social disapproval. In some communities, however, the crime rate is unusually high. The term "social disorganization" has been applied to such communities by sociologists on the asumption that high *rates* of deviant behavior are best accounted for in terms of peculiarities of the social structure. The term "social disorganization" calls attention to two basic characteristics of industrial societies: their heterogeneity and fluidity. As compared with preindustrial societies, industrial societies are, because of their heterogeneity and fluidity, far less successful in using guilt and shame to control deviance. Slum neighborhoods manifest this failure to a greater degree than middle-class neighborhoods, as the following analysis shows.

The Slum Neighborhood: A Context for the Weakening of Traditional Controls over the Adolescent Boy

Reprinted by permission. From Henry D. McKay, "Basic Considerations in Delinquency Prevention," testimony at *Hearings before the Subcommittee to Investigate Juvenile Delinquency of the Committee on the Judiciary*, United States Senate, May 28 and 29, 1959, pp. 164–173.

While perfect conformity probably never is achieved, stable societies are bothered little with violative behavior. In contrast, when the rate of change is high, as in the modern American city, delinquency and other nonconforming behavior appear in such volume as to be highly destructive.

The relationship between social change and the disruption of community institutions is easy to follow. Institutions through which the child is socialized and through which the values of the

Law, Criminology and Police Science, Vol. 45, May–June 1954, pp. 35–38.

group are transmitted lag behind technological developments in periods of rapid change.

As a result, these institutions do not function effectively in meeting the needs of the people and fail to furnish the framework within which social life is ordinarily organized and integrated. In addition, during periods of rapid change new problems arise for which there are no institutional solutions. The cumulative effect of this imbalance is seen both in the fact that socialization of children is imperfect and in the weakening of ordinary type of control.

Change takes place as a result of the operation of natural processes. Inventions which improve production, transportation, and communication are basic, and the results of such developments are seen in urbanization, industrialization, the division of labor, and mobility. Special causative factors in the modern era are immigration, migration, or other movements of population which bring people into new situations, or even the movement of families from address to address, which, along with more basic change, tends to destroy the integration and cohesion of communities.

One of the consequences of change is the breakdown of communication between adults and children which arises out of the fact that they live in such different worlds. When the behavior of children is incomprehensible to adults and when adults are not able to make what they do or think comprehensible to children, conflict and stresses are created within the family.

In this situation adults, frightened by conduct which they do not understand, often attempt to explain the delinquency of children in terms of movies, radio, television, comic books, jazz music, and many other such characteristics of modern social life, or, on the other hand, by looking backward and charging that the misbehavior of youth is due to lack of respect for parents, or to the absence of the harsh punishments which characterized earlier eras. While there is no evidence to support these particularistic explanations, it is easy to see how they develop.

Not all age groups or areas are influenced to the same degree by change. There seems to be good reason to believe that in urban centers the adolescent male is influenced more by social alterations than is any other age group. Deprived of a chance to be important in the family by shift from family to wage economy, and by compulsory education, and without any approved way of establishing his importance in the larger community, the adolescent male is without any significant role or without any device to prove that he is a man. The restlessness arising from this role deficiency coupled with the weakening of traditional controls sets the stage for the delinquency problem as it is observed in the modern city. . . .

If . . . disruption associated with change is associated with high rates of delinquents, the degree of disruption should be high in the inner-city areas. Even cursory examination of the process reveals that this is true. The proposition presented here is that as a result of this disruption in the inner-city most of the basic social institutions are so weak, inadequate, and inconsistent that they do not furnish an adequate framework for the control of the conduct of children. This is especially true of the institutions with which the adolescent male might ordinarily be expected to be identified.

Some special elements enter the situation to create the particular type of social structure found in inner-city areas. The first is that the cultural institutions and practices brought to these areas by the successive groups which have occupied them have never been fully adapted to the forms of urban life found in the American city. The European immigrant came largely from backgrounds which were stable and well integrated. But many of the institutions which they brought did not fit the situation in the new world, or if they served the adults well they were often unacceptable to the children.

When one considers the more recent immigrants to the city the problem is even more serious. These groups have the same disabilities as the immigrants in that they represent largely rural backgrounds without much experience in city life but they have others as well. In many instances they lack the stabilizing influence of long-established and well-integrated cultural institutions which European immigrants had as part of their backgrounds, and some of the migrants have had the additional disadvantage of limited freedom and lack of opportunity to participate in some of the basic activities of social life.

Another element in the situation in the inner-city areas where most of the immigrants must make their adaptation to city life is the fact that there are kinds of problems with which they are totally unfamiliar but which must be dealt with in the American city. Foremost among these are problems of employment and participation in the political process, but others almost equally disturbing are those arising out of the fact that adolescent males are not part of the labor force, that child rearing presents new kinds of hazards, or that luxury items can be secured with a small downpayment.

Thus life in the inner-city area lacks integration either because the institutions are weak, or because there are no institutions through which the new problems can be dealt with. Of course, the situation is not the same in all of the inner-city areas. Areas in which there has been some stability have tended to become more integrated because old institutions have been readapted to new problems and have thus brought some order into the community. In others where there has not been time for such an integrative development, persons are largely free from institutional ties and at liberty to operate with relatively little control.

In extreme form this absence of stabilizing influence is seen among the adolescent males who do not only have the freedom which comes from weak institutional structure, but tend also to be detached from whatever basic institutions there are. For this group, ties with family and church tend to be weak and only the school represents the thread which ties them to respectability.

When the boy finishes school, or leaves school because he cannot get along there, this last thread is broken. Ties with church and family are often reestablished when the boy reaches maturity and marries. Then family responsibility tends to bring him back into the economic order and into other conventional activities. But during this period between leaving school and the assumption of adult roles, young men in the inner-city areas of Chicago today are free in a sense seldom known in social life.

These boys without institutional ties tend, in the inner-city areas, to become identified with one another in groupings often called gangs, but for the purpose of this report designated as corner groups. These groups are functional for their members; that is, they take the place of and perform many of the functions performed by conventional institutions in other areas. Sometimes these groups have names or other symbols of identification, and within them the members

have status, win approbation, and achieve a sense of belonging.

These corner groups and the social-athletic clubs into which some of them develop, may be regarded as natural institutions which came into existence to meet the needs of the detached adolescent males. They would represent positive contributions to the stability of the community were it not for the fact that oftentimes they are organized in opposition to middle-class values and conventionality. It is for this reason that it can be said that corner groups represent the center of the organized attack on conventional values such as life and property.

The corner group is not alone in this activity. In the absence of control through conventional institutions, many other forms of illegal, quasi-illegal, or marginal activities become organized as part of the social life of these inner-city areas. Often these activities are known as the rackets, or collectively as the activities of the syndicate. For the task at hand this development is highly significant. It means that children growing up in these areas have intimate and personal knowledge of two moral worlds, each of which offers a livelihood and a path for upward mobility. To the child, each seems to have its advantages and disadvantages, and each recruits some members. This conflict of values is one of the striking characteristics of inner-city areas.

Although less evident, some indigenous conventional institutional forms are probably being germinated and tried out in the inner-city areas. If mobility is high, these activities will probably die out; but if there is some stability, some of them may develop in the direction of basic institutions. Also, there is a tendency for groups to take over institutions from other groups. But none of these developments have been adequate to meet the human needs of the population in the inner-city areas, and quite serious attempts have been made by many groups from outside the area to meet these problems through the development of agencies. The place of these agencies in the community needs to be analyzed.

As community structure has been described here, well-integrated communities need few if any agencies because most of the problems of life are dealt with within the framework of traditional institutions. When communities are disrupted, however, there is need for agencies to meet the problems created by this disruption, and the presence of agencies indicates that such a disruption has taken place.

Most of the organizations or agencies created from outside the inner-city areas to help deal with inner-city area problems may be described as non-indigenous both because they were not developed by the local people to meet local needs, and because the control traditionally has been held by people from outside the area. No doubt many of the persons who created these agencies hoped and intended that they would become indigenous, but the course of development has not been in that direction.

The efforts of people from outside to help deal with the problem in the inner-city areas are seen most clearly in the development of private service agencies such as settlement houses or boys' clubs. Over the years a great variety of useful services have been performed by these agencies for newcomers and their children. More recently there has been a tendency for services such as aid to dependent children, old-age assistance, and the teaching of household arts, formerly furnished by private agencies, to be taken over and administered as functions of government. But private agencies still have some functions and just recently new waves of migration have made it possible to furnish many services for which there has been little demand for several decades.

Services are ends in themselves and need no further justification. Sometimes, however, efforts have been made to justify services in terms of delinquency prevention. In fact, the question is begged through the use of the term "character building institutions," without it having been established either logically or in fact that character building takes place faster in one situation than another. Access to a place to play, a place to learn, and a place to participate should be part of the heritage of every child, but such access does not guarantee that the child will not be an offender.

Three reasons for the limited influence of the inner-city area service agencies on the problem of delinquency deserve detailed discussion:

1. Even though they may give useful services, nonindigenous service agencies do not seem to influence greatly the moral life of the areas where they are located. Seldom do they control, or even reach the centers of political, economic, or religious power and without such power or access to it they cannot be very influential.

2. Conventional agencies have not been very successful in reaching delinquent groups. This has been made explicit in recent years through the use of such terms as "unreached," or "hard to reach." Even if the value differences between delinquents and agencies could be dealt with, the fact remains that no one knows the type of program required to reduce delinquent behavior.

3. More or less explicitly each agency must choose its clientele. If an agency favors conforming boys it may be performing a very fine service, but delinquent boys will stay away. If, on the other hand, an agency tried to encourage the participation of delinquents the conforming boys may stay away, or be kept away by their parents. Because of the tendency of the delinquent boy to be destructive and difficult to control, this question of clientele tends, quite naturally, to be decided in favor of the conformist.

In recent years somewhat more direct attacks on the problem of delinquency called the hard-to-reach, or detached-worker programs have been put into operation in Chicago and other large cities, either by governmental or private agencies from outside the area. In this program the worker seeks out the corner groups and tries to redirect the group activities along conventional lines. The program has not been startlingly successful, but it has focused attention on the fact that the delinquent group must be reached before it can be changed. That, in itself, is progress.

Also, mostly nonindigenous are such facilities as relief, health services, mental hygiene clinics, et cetera. These are basic services and their desirability is not even to be argued. Many families and individuals need services of a great variety, and adequate services will help some children out of trouble. But it can hardly be argued that rates of delinquents vary inversely with either the type or the extent of services available.

Partly indigenous and partly nonindigenous are such institutions as the police department, public parks, and playgrounds, and schools. These institutions perform functions prescribed by law and they can operate without local support. There is reason to believe, however, that the level of performance can be raised through local participation and through improvement of communication between those who are performing the service and those who are being served. During the past few months top officials in the school, park, and police systems have expressed publicly their interest in trying to get support from local communities to improve the effectiveness of their operations.

Finally, two other types of programs, namely, community councils and community committees, should be mentioned along with the other efforts to help deal with the problems of the inner-city areas. In both of these organizations the impetus comes originally from the outside, but in operation one is partly indigenous and the other wholly indigenous. Although often confused, the difference between these two types of organizations is sharp and clear. Community councils are usually made up of representatives of agencies and organizations in the area. Their purposes include the formulation of goals and coordination of efforts. In contrast, community committees represent organizations of local residents created to help deal with local problems. These groups represent new sources of power and personnel for welfare work.

Why should there be this ecological concentration of social disorganization? (See Figure 12.) One reason social disorganization is concentrated in slum neighborhoods is that the unsuccessful members of urban communities cannot pay the rentals in more desirable neighborhoods. Different types of slums exist, however, and they collect different assortments of the casualties of a competitive society:

1. Rooming-house districts are characterized by extreme anonymity. The weakness of interpersonal relations constitutes a serious obstacle to the effective mobilization of shame against potential offenders. On the other hand, rooming-house districts cater to unattached adults, often elderly adults. As a result of these demographic factors, mental illness, alcoholism, and suicide are more typical problems in rooming-house districts than delinquency.[23]

2. Decaying tenement districts are *family* slums

and are sometimes ethnically homogeneous (Italian, Negro, Puerto Rican). Autonomous peer groups are likely to transmit delinquent values. Unless parental controls are unusually strong, *normal* socialization into "street-corner society" makes for delinquency. But parental controls are likely to be *weak* in urban slums because of the concentration in such neighborhoods of families with serious health and welfare problems. Adolescent gangs fill the vacuum.[24]

3. Public-housing projects for low-income families in the United States frequently combine the anonymity of the rooming-house district with the child socialization and control inadequacies of the family slum. The reason is that public housing is usually preceded by complete demolition of existing structures and the dispersal of site residents. Tenants are then recruited on the basis of financial need. They start as strangers to one another, and they are likely to remain so, for the existence of income limits and the high turnover rate give an air of impermanency to project living. These powerful delinquency-producing tendencies are partially offset by the age structure of the child population: many preadolescents and few adolescents, at least in the early years of their existence.[25]

There have been few attempts to measure neighborhood disorganization as well as to discuss it in theoretical terms. All the more noteworthy, therefore, is the following comparison between adult attitudes toward juvenile misbehavior in two neighborhoods of low socioeconomic status.

23 Harvey W. Zorbaugh, "The Dweller in Furnished Rooms: An Urban Type," in Ernest W. Burgess, Ed., *The Urban Community*, Chicago: University of Chicago Press, 1929, pp. 98–105.
24 Frederick M. Thrasher, *The Gang*, Chicago: University of Chicago Press, 1927; Clifford R. Shaw and Henry D. McKay, *Juvenile Delinquency and Urban Areas*, Chicago: University of Chicago Press, 1942.
25 Harrison F. Salisbury, "Problem Youngsters Spring from Housing Jungles," New York *Times*, March 28, 1958.

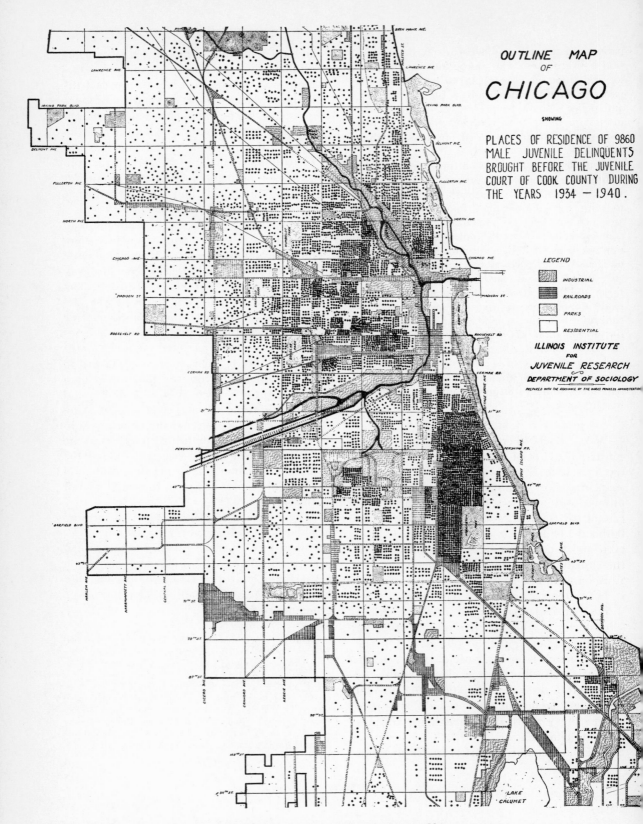

FIGURE 12. Distribution of male juvenile delinquents, Chicago, 1934–1940.

Adult Reactions to Juvenile Misbehavior

Reprinted by permission. From Eleanor E. Maccoby, Joseph P. Johnson, and Russell M. Church, "Community Integration and the Social Control of Juvenile Delinquency," *Journal of Social Issues*, Vol. 14, No. 3, 1958, pp. 38–51.

The important role that community integration and social control are assumed to play in the prevention of delinquency is highlighted by Shaw, in his discussion of the differences in delinquency rates in various parts of Chicago. In the famous Chicago studies, done more than 25 years ago, it was found that delinquency was highest in the center of the city, areas marked by physical deterioration and declining population. Shaw offered the following hypothesis:

"Under the pressure of the disintegrative forces which act when business and industry invade a community, the community thus invaded ceases to function effectively as a means of social control. Traditional norms and standards of the conventional community weaken and disappear. Resistance on the part of the community to delinquent and criminal behavior is low, and such behavior is tolerated and may even become accepted and approved.

"Moreover, many of the people who come into the deteriorating section are European immigrants or southern Negroes. All of them come from cultural and social backgrounds which differ widely from the situations in the city. In the conflict of the old with the new the former cultural and social controls in these groups tend to break down. This, together with the fact that there are few constructive community forces at work to re-establish a conventional order, makes for continued social disorganization." [26]

If community disintegration is indeed a factor producing juvenile delinquency, how precisely are the effects produced? In an attempt to devise an empirical study of the effects of community integration, we reasoned that something like the following process might occur: a child who, for a variety of reasons, has an interest in deviating, tries out one or two deviant acts in a tentative way, to see what the reaction of the community will be.

[26] Clifford R. Shaw and collaborators, *Delinquency Areas*, Chicago: University of Chicago Press, 1929, pp. 204–205.

If he lives in a disorganized community (where the rate of moving in and out will be high and where neighbors are not closely bound by social, religious, or kinship ties) there will be relatively little chance that he will be seen by someone who knows him or knows his parents, so long as the act is committed outside the walls of his own dwelling. The people who do see him may be deviants themselves, and may not consider the behavior especially reprehensible. But even if they do disapprove, they may nevertheless choose not to interfere, being reluctant to mention the incident directly to the child or his parents since they do not know them, and being afraid to attract the attention of the police to themselves by reporting the act to the authorities.

Our basic hypothesis is then, that in disorganized neighborhoods individual adults will feel less responsibility for guiding other people's children into the paths of "good" behavior, and will ignore deviant acts when they see them being committed, unless they themselves are directly involved. Under these circumstances, the children who are making their first tentative explorations into delinquency will find that they have a good chance of escaping any painful consequences of their antisocial activities, and will be emboldened by this knowledge, with the result that delinquency will increase in the disorganized neighborhoods.

To test whether this hypothetical picture represents what actually occurs, we compared two areas of Cambridge, Mass. The areas were chosen to be as similar as possible with respect to socioeconomic status of residents, but still highly different in delinquency rates. We set out to test the following specific hypotheses:

1. The high delinquency area will be less "integrated" than the low, in the sense that people living in the "high" area will be less homogeneous with respect to ethnic and religious background, will be more transient, will be less well acquainted with their neighbors, and have fewer perceived common interests with them.

2. In the high delinquency area, values about pre-delinquent acts will be more "permissive" than in the low delinquency area. That is, there will be a tendency for residents to believe that youthful acts such as fighting, drunkenness, minor shoplifting, and minor vandalism are not especially reprehensible, are "natural" and sometimes to be condoned. Attitudes toward

such behavior in the low delinquency area, on the other hand, should be relatively severe.

3. In the high delinquency area, private citizens will be less likely to take remedial action when they see other people's children engaging in some kind of delinquent or pre-delinquent activity.

We interviewed a sample of adults in each of our two neighborhoods, and our questions covered (a) the respondent's attitudes toward several categories of juvenile misbehavior, (b) the degree of the respondent's integration in his community, and (c) reports of incidents of juvenile delinquent or pre-delinquent behavior in the neighborhood. We asked each respondent to tell us exactly what action (if any) had been taken by people who observed or knew about the incident.

Before we report our findings, let us describe our criteria for choosing the two neighborhoods, and our methods of obtaining the information we required.

THE TWO NEIGHBORHOODS

It is well known, of course, that delinquency rates are higher in neighborhoods where the residents have low socio-economic status. We were not interested in studying this factor, however, and wanted to hold it constant. We therefore selected two census tracts from the city of Cambridge, one with a high delinquency rate and one with a low rate, with socio-economic factors constant as nearly as possible. We were not able to achieve as close a match on all factors as would have been desirable. Table 40 shows how the two areas compared with respect to delinquency and with respect to socio-economic factors. It will be seen that the areas were well matched on education, fairly well matched on occupation, with a difference of over five hundred dollars in median income. The differences in delinquency rates were quite dramatic.[27]

We were unable to find areas which were closer than these two in socio-economic level and which still differed significantly in delinquency rates. It is impossible to tell, of course, whether

the differences which exist between the two areas in socio-economic status are sufficient to produce the differences in delinquency rate. All that we can say is that considering the whole socio-economic range in Cambridge, these neighborhoods are fairly similar on such items as rent, occupation, education, and even income, while they differ by a considerably greater part of the range in delinquency rates.

THE SURVEY METHOD

Having selected our two areas, we chose dwelling units from these areas by probability sampling methods (area sampling) and within households, selected for interview 50 per cent of the adults in the selected households.[28] We defined as adults all individuals who were married plus all unmarried people of 21 or over. Since our interview concerned a "sensitive" topic, and respondents were asked to tell us about certain incidents of delinquent behavior in the neighborhood which may not have come to the attention of the police, we took great pains to try to convince the respondents that we had no connection with any official agency. Even so, there were a number of families who clearly did not want to confide in us; we encountered more suspicion in the high delinquency area, where we suspect that some of our potential respondents believed we had come in connection with some delinquent act of their own children. Altogether 11 per cent of the people approached for interview refused to be interviewed. An additional 16 per cent could not be reached, because they could not be found at home after several call-backs, because of illness, etc. We did not include in the sample anyone who had lived at his present address less than six months, because we felt such people would not be in a good position to give us accounts of neighborhood incidents. In the high delinquency area we interviewed 129 people, in the low delinquency area 107. Our sample contained a somewhat higher proportion of women than census figures would lead us to expect in a complete probability sample.

The interview took between 25 minutes and an hour, and consisted of a standard list of open-

---

27 It will be noted that in the high-delinquency area a higher proportion of the cases which are reported to the police are brought into juvenile court. This may mean either that the offenses committed by juveniles in this area are more serious, or that families in the low-delinquency area are able somehow to keep their children's cases out of court after they have come to the attention of the police.

28 Residents of each household were listed by the interviewers in predetermined order. Each household listing sheet was marked to indicate whether it was the first and third, or the second and fourth, occupants listed who were to be interviewed.

ended questions plus a list of probes that were to be used whenever the respondent mentioned a specific incident of juvenile delinquency occurring in the neighborhood. At the end of the interview, the interviewer filled out an "incident report sheet" recording the age and sex of the children involved in the incident, the relationship of the witness to the deviating children, and the nature of the control action (if any) taken by the respondent or other individuals in the neighborhood. The kinds of delinquency inquired about in the interview were: major and minor thefts, truancy, vandalism, street fighting, drunkenness, and the use of insulting, abusive language.

RESULTS

COMMUNITY INTEGRATION. Our high delinquency area was clearly less integrated in terms of the criteria of integration we employed. First of all, the low delinquency area was highly homogeneous with respect to religion: 93 per cent were Catholic, as contrasted with 53 per cent in the high delinquency area. Furthermore, those who were Catholics were more frequent church-goers in the low delinquency areas than in the high. Thirty-five per cent of the Catholics in the high delinquency area said they attended church less than once a week, while in area "low" only 15 per cent report this. Area "low" was also more homogeneous ethnically: Here our sample shows a fairly high concentration (32 per cent) of people of Canadian origin, quite a few of these being French Canadian, with virtually no Negroes, or people of Eastern European origin. In contrast, our sample from the high delinquency area had 18 per cent Negroes, and 16 per cent East Europeans, with only 9 per cent Canadians.

We expected that the high delinquency area would contain more people who were "transient" —who had lived in the community only a short

TABLE 40

Demographic Characteristics of a High Delinquency and a Low Delinquency Area

	High Delinquency Area	Low Delinquency Area
Juvenile Delinquency		
Average annual rate per 1000 children in 7–16 age group from 1948 through 1950, based on number of cases brought before the juvenile court.	15.2	4.9
Cases handled by Crime Prevention Bureau		
Average annual incidence per 1000 in the 7–16 age group from 1950 through 1952, based on number of cases reported to the Cambridge police dept. .	34.0	22.1
Truancy		
Rate per 1000 in 7–16 age group for five-month period Sept. 1952–Jan. 1953, public and parochial elementary and high schools, as reported by the City Attendance Supervisors.	34.1	4.1
Education		
Per cent adults without high school diplomas 1950 census, computed for those over 25 years of age.	76.1	71.2
Occupation		
Per cent employed males in occupation group, 1950 census:		
Professional, managerial, clerical, and sales	26.5%	27.3%
Craftsmen, foremen	17.9	25.8
Operatives, service workers, laborers.	55.6	46.9
Median Income (1950 Census)	$2630.00	$3176.00
Mean Rent (1950 Census)	$25.72	$30.48
Population (1950 Census)	3976	3818
Per cent of population between 7–16 yrs.	14.8	14.2

time. We found a slight tendency for this to be true, but both areas were highly stable. Sixty per cent of the respondents in the high delinquency area and 71 per cent in the low area had lived in their present neighborhood for ten years or more.

Despite the fact that most of the people in the high delinquency area had lived in their neighborhoods a substantial length of time, they were less integrated in their communities. As Table 41 shows, they knew fewer of their neighbors by name, did not know many people intimately enough to borrow something, less often felt they had common interests with their neighbors, and more often disliked the neighborhood.

These differences between the areas in attitudes toward the neighborhood and relations with neighbors are still found, even if one considers only the people who have lived in the neighborhood ten years or more. Therefore, the differences in "integration" of individual citizens into their communities cannot be attributed primarily to differences in length of residence. We might point out parenthetically that the lower level of integration in our high delinquency area need not reflect a progressively deteriorating situation. This particular low level of social interaction might remain stable for many years.

We do, then, find evidence for the first of our hypotheses. In the high delinquency area, residents do not know each other as well as in the low delinquency area, and do not feel as much a part of the community. Does this mean that they withdraw from playing any role in the informal control of children's deviant actions in their community? Before we examine the answer to this

question, let us take up one other factor that might lead the residents of a high delinquency area to avoid controlling delinquent or pre-delinquent actions; perhaps they do not take such actions as seriously as do the residents of a low delinquency area. Do the two areas differ in their values about certain actions that the larger society defines as "delinquent"?

ATTITUDES TOWARD DEVIANT BEHAVIOR. Measuring attitudes toward deviant behavior is a difficult matter. One clearly cannot ask "Do you think excessive drinking is a good or bad thing? How about theft? Assault?" In our first formulations of questions in this area, we found we were getting universally righteous answers, in which everybody reported (at least to our primarily middleclass interviewers!) being "against sin." In pretesting question wording, we found that the only way we could differentiate among respondents in this area was to ask, not whether certain actions were "right" or "wrong," but *how serious* actions were. That is, while all respondents might agree that stealing a candy bar from the dime store was "wrong," some expressed the view that it was not a very serious matter—that it was the sort of thing all children might be expected to do at some time or another, and that they would outgrow it if no issue were made of it; others regarded such actions as the first step toward more serious criminal actions, and felt that drastic disciplinary action was called for. We inquired about seven different kinds of pre-delinquent behavior. Two of our questions are presented below to illustrate the way we approached these issues:

"Every neighborhood has a certain amount of

TABLE 41
Area Differences in Measures of Integration

	High Delinquency Area	Low Delinquency Area
Per Cent Who:		
Report liking the neighborhood	64%	85%
Know more than ten of their neighbors by name	52%	63%
Know more than five neighbors well enough to borrow something ("Like a hammer or a cup of sugar")	28%	50%
Feel they have "pretty much the same interests and ideas" as the other people in the neighborhood	33%	59%
Number of cases:	129	107

fighting between groups of children. Some people think it's very important to stop these fights, other people think the youngsters are just learning to stand up for themselves and should be left alone. How do you feel?"

"Sometimes we hear of children damaging the property of people who live in the neighborhood—for instance, bending over car aerials or letting the air out of tires or ripping up fences. If children do this sort of thing, do you think it's anything to worry about, or are they just letting off steam?"

Table 42 shows the proportion of respondents in each area who thought each of the seven kinds of act was "serious," who qualified their answers, or who thought the actions were "not serious." The striking thing about the table is the similarity of the attitudes in the two areas. In both areas, drinking is considered the most serious juvenile offence, fighting the least. People in the low delinquency area took a slightly more serious view of minor thefts from stores, damage to public property, and drinking than did their high-delinquency-area counterparts; but this trend was counterbalanced by a tendency for the high-delinquency-area respondents to take a more serious view of abusive remarks and fighting.

Our findings, then, are not consistent with the point of view that the adults in a high delinquency area take a tolerant or indifferent attitude toward delinquent and pre-delinquent activities on the part of children. We see no evidence that "delinquent values" about the "wrongness" or "seriousness" of these actions prevail in the high delinquency area. This issue will be discussed further below.

INFORMAL SOCIAL CONTROL. We have seen that while the two areas did not differ in their views about how serious various kinds of delinquent behavior are (at least if their verbal reports to our interviewers may be trusted), the high delinquency area was less integrated, and we reasoned that this lack of integration might result in individual residents being unwilling to take action if they observed their neighbors' children engaged in some sort of deviant behavior. We asked our respondents hypothetical questions about whether they *would* step in and try to do something about it if they observed abusive language, property damage, fighting, or drunkenness. Table 43 shows that the respondents in the low delinquency area report themselves somewhat more ready to "do something about it," significantly so in the case of fighting and drinking.

TABLE 42
Area Differences in Attitude Toward Types of Pre-delinquent Acts [a]

		Serious	Depends	Not Serious	No Answer	
Abusive remarks	High delinquency area	57	30	12	01	100%
	Low delinquency area	47	33	12	08	100%
Minor thefts from stores	High delinquency area	36	50	12	02	100%
	Low delinquency area	49	46	05	01	100%
Damage to public property	High delinquency area	57	26	10	06	100%
	Low delinquency area	64	22	08	07	100%
Damage to private property	High delinquency area	40	32	22	07	100%
	Low delinquency area	41	36	15	08	100%
Fighting	High delinquency area	28	48	23	02	100%
	Low delinquency area	22	50	27	02	100%
Drinking	High delinquency area	79	17	03	01	100%
	Low delinquency area	87	08	01	04	100%
Truancy	High delinquency area	42	42	12	04	100%
	Low delinquency area	41	42	11	06	100%

[a] The percentages in this table are based upon 129 cases in the high delinquency area, 107 in the low. In none of the seven instances are the two neighborhoods significantly different in the proportion reporting a "serious" attitude.

The actual controlling behavior in real incidents reported by the respondents showed some area differences in the same direction, although the differences are not large. To study the kinds of action that had been taken in actual incidents of neighborhood delinquency, we first recorded all the incidents from the "incident report sheets" in which action by the respondents was both "possible and necessary," and in which the respondent's own children were not involved. If someone else had already taken remedial action about the incident, we did not regard it as necessary for the respondent to do so, even if the respondent observed the incident. And if the respondent knew about the incident but had not actually seen it and/or did not know the identity of the culprits, we did not regard it as possible for the respondent to act. On the other hand, if the respondent heard about the incident without actually witnessing it, and *did* know the identity of the delinquent children, we included the incident in our list of incidents in which some controlling action by the respondent would have been possible. For example, an incident of vandalism in a parochial school was reported, in which a gang of boys had entered the school by breaking windows, and had thrown ink on the floors and slashed furniture. The police had been unable to learn the identity of the vandals. One of our respondents knew who the boys were, having learned the details through her own sons, who were ostensibly not involved. She could have told either the police or church authorities, but had not done so. This incident would be included in the list of incidents in which action by our respondent was both "necessary and possible."

In all, 206 such incidents were reported by the respondents in our high delinquency area, and 130 were reported by the respondents in our low delinquency area. Of course, some respondents reported no such incidents, while others reported several.

Having listed the incidents in which control by the respondent would have been possible, and in which no one else had already taken remedial action, we wished to determine the number of these incidents in which the respondent actually had taken action. Before doing this, however, we divided the incidents according to whether the respondent had or had not been the *victim* of the delinquent act. Our hypothesis about greater social control in the low delinquency area applies especially to acts of delinquency in which the observer is *not* the victim. That is, in both areas, we might expect that when the respondent himself has been stolen from or had his property damaged, he will be motivated to catch and punish the offenders. But we have hypothesized that in well-integrated neighborhoods, individual citizens will act to stop deviant juvenile behavior even if they themselves are not involved.

Table 44 shows that, as expected, when the respondent is himself the victim of an anti-social act on the part of a juvenile offender, he is very likely indeed to take action, and this is true in both the high and low delinquency areas. The kinds of action taken included calling the police, reproving the child directly, or getting in touch with the child's parents. When the respondent is not the victim, there is a somewhat greater tendency for an observer to take action in the low delinquency area than in the high. In 60 per cent of the non-victim incidents reported from the "low" area in which the respondent was in a position to take action, he did so; in the high delinquency area, the comparable figure is 40 per cent. It is difficult to evaluate the statistical significance of the differences between these last two figures, since they are based upon the number of *incidents* reported, rather than upon the number of respondents reporting them. The fact is that, out of the 68 respondents in the high delinquency area who reported at least one incident in which they could have taken action but were not the victim, 30 took no action and 38 took action in at least one of the incidents he reported.

TABLE 43

Area Differences in Percentages Who "Would Do Something about It" in Hypothetical Instances of Delinquency

Child's Hypothetical Act	High Delinquency Area	Low Delinquency Area
Open rudeness, insulting language	26%	31%
Property damage	32%	42%
Fighting	12%	25%
Drinking	8%	21%
Number of cases	129	107

In the low delinquency area, out of the 41 people reporting at least one non-victim incident, 16 took no action and 25 took action in at least one instance. These proportions are quite similar (and not statistically different). The difference between the two areas appears to lie in the fact that in the high delinquency area, each respondent reports more non-victim incidents, and his tendency toward controlling action is not proportional to the number of incidents he reports. That is, the more incidents a respondent reports, the lower the proportion of them he will have attempted to control. And 44 of the respondents in the high delinquency area had *ignored* at least one non-victim incident in which they could have taken action; only 21 respondents in the low delinquency area did this.

One explanation of this fact is that in the high delinquency area, more of the delinquent acts are committed by *gangs* of children (rather than by individual offenders), and the deviant children are older, on the average. Naturally, when an observer sees a delinquent act being committed by a group of five or six boys in their middle or late "teens," the observer will hesitate to interfere because of the physical danger to himself. Several of our respondents told us of people who had been beaten up when they attempted to stop gangs of boys who were engaged in delinquent activity. But the greater frequency of older offenders in the high delinquency area does not fully account for the lower proportion of controlling actions on the part of residents who are not directly involved. Even when the deviant

child is young enough so that it would not be dangerous to try to control him, his deviant action is somewhat less likely to meet with a controlling action in the high-delinquency area (see Table 45).

In both areas, many of our respondents expressed reluctance to interfere in the control of other people's children. We asked: "We're interested in how you feel about whether it's all right to correct somebody else's child. When somebody else's child gets into mischief, and you see it, do you think it's up to you to say anything, or do you think it's better to stay out of it?" One third of the respondents in each area said that they thought it was all right for them to do something, but the majority expressed strong doubts about the propriety of interference, and many said categorically that a child's misbehavior is his parents' responsibility and others ought not to interfere. One respondent expressed this reaction as follows:

"We generally keep out of other people's business with their kids. They just don't want us to do anything about them. Definitely—even if I knew them—I'd just go on and not pay any attention. People wouldn't like it—they'd say what does he know about my kids! We get along fine with everybody and I wouldn't want it to change by sticking my nose somewhere where it's not wanted."

It is interesting that while we found no area differences in respondents' *own* opinions about whether it was all right to interfere with other people's children, we did find some differences when we asked whether *other people in the neigh-*

TABLE 44

Area Differences in the Number of Incidents in Which the Respondent Took Controlling Action

	Number of Incidents Reported	Respondent Took Action	R. Did Not Take Action	Per Cent of Incidents in Which R. Acted	Number of Respondents Reporting at Least One Incident
Respondent the victim:					
High delinquency area	86	72	14	84%	62
Low delinquency area	78	69	9	88%	47
Respondent not the victim: (but control possible)					
High delinquency area	120	48	72	40%	68
Low delinquency area	52	31	21	60%	41

borhood felt it was all right. In the high delinquency area, people more often said that their neighbors believed one ought to mind one's own business (22 per cent said this, as contrasted with 9 per cent in the low delinquency area).

There are a number of reasons, then, why an individual might choose not to interfere. One is the desire to maintain harmonious relations with neighbors. Perhaps one reason why respondents in the high delinquency area ignored more of the incidents they saw is that they did not want to get the reputation of being interfering busybodies; so they therefore took action only in the most serious cases or in the cases where they had hope of being effective. Another concern, mentioned primarily by respondents in the high delinquency area, is that of avoiding retaliation from either the deviant child or his parents. We were told of instances in which an individual had tried to go to the parents of a child who had committed a delinquent act, and had been met with abusive language or even physical violence from the parent. Finally, in our high delinquency area, eight respondents said they had decided not to speak to a delinquent child or his parents because they

already knew that the family would be unresponsive to pressure—that the parents themselves were alcoholic or criminal or indifferent to the activities of their children.

SUMMARY AND DISCUSSION

We compared two areas of Cambridge which were similar in socio-economic status, one having a high rate of juvenile delinquency and the other a low rate. We interviewed a sample of residents in these two communities concerning "community integration," attitudes toward delinquent behavior, and the social control of such behavior. We took 129 interviews in the high delinquency area, 107 in the low, and reached 73 per cent of the people initially designated for interview in a probability sample. Our major findings were:

1. The high delinqency area was less "integrated" than the low. That is, residents of the "high" area, as compared with residents of the low delinquency area, did not like their neighborhood as well, did not know their neighbors as well, and did not so often feel that they shared interests and points of view with their neighbors. This was true despite the fact that both areas had fairly stable residence patterns. The low delinquency area was also somewhat more homogeneous with respect to the religious and ethnic backgrounds of the residents.

2. The areas did not differ in their attitudes toward the "seriousness" of different kinds of deviant juvenile behavior.

3. Residents of the low delimency area, when they saw a child engaged in deviant behavior in which the observer was not directly involved, were somewhat more likely than residents of the "high" area to take some action— either interfering directly with the child's activities, or informing the police or the child's parents. Area differences in this respect were not great, however, and an attitude of reluctance to interfere prevailed in both areas.

Some of our initial speculations about the processes of social control are supported, and some are not. We found, as expected, that people in the high delinquency area do tend to ignore children's pre-delinquent and delinquent actions somewhat more often, and this provides an atmosphere in which delinquency can grow more easily.

We originally thought that one of the reasons residents in a high delinquency area might be slow to take controlling action when they ob-

TABLE 45

Differences in the Willingness of Bystanders to Control the Deviance of Children in High and Low Delinquency Areas (Including only incidents in which the respondent was not the victim)

	No. of Incidents (Action Necessary and Possible)	Action Taken by R.	No Action Taken by R.
Child under 13 yrs. old [a]			
High delinquency area	51	29	22
Low delinquency area	29	20	9
Child 13 or over			
High delinquency area	62	16	46
Low delinquency area	23	11	12

[a] When several children were involved in delinquent activity together, the median age of the group was taken as the age for this tabulation. The number of incidents included is less than the number reported in Table 44, since for some incidents the respondent did not report the age of the child or children involved.

served incidents of delinquent behavior was that they hold delinquent values themselves, and feel that actions of delinquent children are actually quite acceptable. We did not find this to be the case; residents of the high delinquent area were just as quick as the residents of the "low" area to tell us that minor vandalism and small thefts from stores, etc. were serious and should be dealt with severely. How shall we interpret this finding? One possibility is that the respondents did not reveal their real conscious attitudes to our interviewers. We do not know; we can only point out that while a number of respondents *did* express indulgent attitudes about juvenile misbehavior, in response to our particular question-wording, these respondents were found equally often in the two areas, so that the attitudes they expressed do not appear to be differentially related to a high delinquency rate.

Assuming for the moment that most of our respondents told us the truth about their conscious attitudes, how are we to explain the fact that the residents of a high-delinquency area appear to share the values of the larger society about the "wrongness" and "seriousness" of such activities as stealing, damaging property, juvenile drunkenness, etc.? We may be dealing here with the ticklish problem of different "levels" of attitudes—perhaps these people are ambivalent, and while they consciously hold pro-social attitudes, they simultaneously have strong anti-social impulses, so that when they see a child deviating they may consciously disapprove but at the same time experience enough vicarious pleasure in the child's anti-social actions that they do not take steps to stop the child. Or perhaps, while sharing the general values about specific criminal activities, they may hold *other* values which interfere. For example, a strong belief in the value of individual autonomy, or the importance of immediate impulse gratification, might run counter to the effective implementation of anti-criminal values.

Another possible explanation is that the "delinquent values" which have been assumed to prevail in high-delinquency areas actually characterize, not the entire delinquent neighborhood, but only the actual families in which the delinquent children are found. We encountered some evidence that when a family of children got the reputation of being "bad," the neighborhood would withdraw from the family and isolate them. Other children would be forbidden to play with the deviant children, and the parents of the neighborhood, who might have made previous efforts to deal with the parents of the delinquent children, would give up such efforts and leave the family alone. Thus the pro-social values of the larger neighborhood might cease to affect delinquent children.

Within the families themselves in which delinquent children grow up, do "delinquent values" prevail? We have little evidence on this point, but would like to argue against an uncritical assumption that they do. There may, of course, be a few cases in which, for instance, a father is a skilled pickpocket or safe-cracker, and trains his son in these skills while the mother smiles proudly to see her boy growing up "just like daddy." It is equally possible however (and, we suspect, much more common) that the parents in delinquent families do not want to see their children become criminals. Granted that the reasons why the children do in fact become criminals may lie in parent-child interaction; nonetheless, they may be centered in other processes than the direct transmission of values. The literature is full of suggestions as to what these processes may be—e.g., the parents may be too inconsistent, too rejecting, or too brutal in their punishment to transmit values effectively. In our own study, we interviewed a woman one of whose children was already in a reformatory, and whose younger children were notorious in the neighborhood for stealing and property damage. This woman strongly expressed values about the "wrongness" and "seriousness" of juvenile thievery and vandalism. Yet we learned from her neighbors, whom we also interviewed, that she was helping her children to conceal stolen goods. Neighbors also said that the children were forcing their mother to abet their activities in this way by threatening to tell their father about the male visitors she occasionally entertained during his absence. It appears, then, that the lack of maternal control over these particular delinquent children stemmed, not from their mother's failure to adopt the values of the larger society about the "wrongness" of theft and vandalism, but from the special circumstances which gave these children freedom to reject their mother's efforts to inculcate these pro-social values.

Our study suggests that a neighborhood pattern of social isolation of families may be an important factor in delinquency. We see no evidence that this social pattern is either the cause or the result of lack of homogeneity of values *about delinquent activities as such.* But the lack of social integration appears to have certain direct effects in a lowered level of social control of delinquent and pre-delinquent activities.

Nonconformity occurs despite the socialization process, despite *informal* sanctions, and despite the anticipation of *formal* sanctions such as arrest and imprisonment—although it must be pointed out that mechanisms for social control prevent nonconformity most of the time. When nonconformity *does* occur, it forces conformists to reevaluate the normative situation. For example, a student who studies hard and gets a lower grade on a quiz than students who cheat may become cynical about the principle of honest effort on examinations. One socially significant consequence of punishing nonconformists is that punishment may reduce the potentially disruptive effect of their nonconformity.

Why Punishment of Nonconformists Promotes the Morale of Conformists

Reprinted by permission. From Jackson Toby, "Is Punishment Necessary?" *Journal of Criminal Law, Criminology, and Police Science.*[29]

Durkheim considered punishment indispensable as a means of containing the demoralizing consequences of the crimes that could not be prevented. Punishment was not for Durkheim mere vindictiveness. Without punishment Durkheim anticipated the demoralization of "upright people" by defiance of the collective conscience. He believed that unpunished deviance tended to demoralize the conformist and therefore he talked about punishment as a means of repairing "the wounds made upon collective sentiments." [30] Durkheim was not entirely clear; he expressed his ideas in metaphorical language. Nonetheless, we can identify the hypothesis that the punishment

[29] To be published late in 1964.
[30] Émile Durkheim, *The Division of Labor in Society*, Glencoe, Ill.: Free Press, 1947, p. 108.

of offenders promotes the solidarity of conformists.

Durkheim anticipated psychoanalytic thinking as the following reformulation of his argument shows: One who resists the temptation to do what the group prohibits would like to feel that these self-imposed abnegations have some meaning. When he sees others defy rules without untoward consequences, he needs some reassurance that his sacrifices were made in a good cause. If "the good die young and the wicked flourish as the green bay tree," the moral scruples which enable conformists to restrain their own deviant inclinations lack social validation. The social significance of punishing offenders is that deviance is thereby defined as unsuccessful in the eyes of conformists. Thus, conformists are satisfied that the inhibition or repression of their own deviant impulses is worthwhile. The law-abiding person who unconsciously resents restraining his desire to steal and murder has an opportunity, by identifying with the police and the courts, to affect the precarious balance within his own personality between internal controls and the temptation to deviate. A bizarre example of this psychological mechanism is the man who seeks out homosexuals and beats them up mercilessly. Such pathological hostility toward homosexuals is due to the sadist's anxiety over his own sex-role identification. By "punishing" the homosexual, he denies the latent homosexuality in his own psyche. No doubt, some of the persons involved in the administration of punishment are sadistically motivated. But Durkheim hypothesized that the psychic equilibrium of the *ordinary* member of the group may be threatened by violation of norms; Durkheim was not concerned about psychopathological punitiveness.

Whatever the practical difficulties, Durkheim's hypothesis is, in principle, testable. It should be possible to estimate the demoralizing impact of nonconformity on conformists. Clearly, though, this is no simple matter. The extent of demoralization resulting from the failure to punish may vary with type of crime. The unpunished traffic violator may cause more demoralization than the unpunished exhibitionist—depending on whether outwardly conforming members of society are more tempted to exceed the speed limit than to expose themselves. The extent of demoralization may also vary with position in the social structure occupied by the conformist.

Thus, Ranulf suggested that the middle class was especially vulnerable:

". . . the disinterested tendency to inflict punishment is a distinctive characteristic of the lower middle class, that is, of a social class living under conditions which force its members to an extraordinarily high degree of self-restraint and subject them to much frustration of natural desires. If a psychological interpretation is to be put on this correlation of facts, it can hardly be to any other effect than that moral indignation is a kind of resentment caused by the repression of instincts." [31]

Once the facts on the rate and the incidence of moral indignation are known, it will become possible to determine whether something must be done to the offender in order to prevent the demoralization of conformists. Suppose that research revealed that a very large proportion of conformists reacted with moral indignation to *most* violations of the criminal laws. Does this imply that punishment is a functional necessity? Durkheim apparently thought so, but he might have been less dogmatic in his approach to punishment had he specified the functional problem more clearly: making the nonconformist unattractive as a model for imitation. If the violator of norms can be regarded as unenviable through some other process than by inflicting suffering upon him, then punishment is not required by the exigencies of social control.

Punishment can be discussed on three distinct levels: (*a*) in terms of the motivations of the societal agents administering it, (*b*) in terms of the definition of the situation on the part of the person being punished, and (*c*) in terms of its impact on conformists. At this point let us consider the third level, the impact on conformists. Note that punishment of offenders sustains the morale of conformists only under certain conditions. The first has already been discussed, namely, that conformists unconsciously wish to violate the rules themselves. The second is that conformists implicitly assume that the nonconformity is a result of *deliberate defiance* of society's norms. For some conformists, this second condition is not met. Under the guidance of psychiatric thinking, some conformists assume that violation of norms is the result of illness rather than wicked-

ness.[32] For such conformists, punishment of the offender does not contribute to their morale. Since they assume that the nonconformity is an involuntary symptom of a disordered personality, the offender is automatically unenviable because illness is (by definition) undesirable. Of course, one does not really know the relative proportions of the conforming members of society who make the "wicked" or the "sick" assumption about the motivation of the offender, but this can be discovered by investigation.

In Western industrial societies, there is an increasing tendency to call contemporary methods of dealing with offenders "treatment" rather than "punishment." Perhaps this means that increasing proportions of the population are willing to accept the "sick" theory of nonconformity. Note, however, that the emphasis on "treatment" may be more a matter of symbolism than of substance. Although the definition of the situation as treatment rather than punishment tends to be humanizing—both to the offender and to the persons who must deal with him—there are still kind guards and cruel nurses. Furthermore, it would be an error to suppose that punishment is invariably experienced as painful by the criminal, whereas treatment is always experienced as pleasant by the psychopathological offender. Some gang delinquents consider a reformatory sentence an opportunity to renew old acquaintances and to learn new delinquent skills; they resist fiercely the degrading suggestion that they need the services of what they call the "nut doctor." Some mental patients are terrified by shock treatment and embarrassed by group therapy.

What then is the significance of the increasing emphasis on "treatment"? Why call an institution for the criminally insane a "hospital" although it bears a closer resemblance to a prison than to a hospital for the physically ill? Perhaps the increased emphasis on treatment in penological thinking and practice reflects the existence of a large group of conformists who are undecided as between the "wicked" and the "sick" theories of nonconformity. When they observe that the offender is placed in "treatment," their provisional diagnosis of illness is confirmed. Therefore they

[31] Svend Ranulf, *Moral Indignation and Middle-Class Psychology*, Copenhagen: Levin and Munksgaard, 1938, p. 198.

[32] Talcott Parsons has repeatedly suggested the analogy between illness and criminality. See also Vilhelm Aubert and Sheldon L. Messinger, "The Criminal and the Sick," *Inquiry*, Vol. 1, No. 3, 1958, pp. 137–160; and Barbara Wootton, *Social Science and Social Pathology*, New York: Macmillan, 1959, pp. 203–267.

do not feel that he has "gotten away with it." Note that "treatment" has the capacity to make the offender unenviable to conformists whether or not it is effective in rehabilitating him and whether or not he experiences it as pleasant. Those old-fashioned conformists who are not persuaded by official diagnoses of illness will not be satisfied by "treatment"; they will prefer to see an attempt made to visit physical suffering or mental anguish on the offender. For them, punishment is necessary to prevent demoralization.

CONCLUSION

The socialization process generates enough guilt and shame to prevent nonconformity most of the time—even in highly differentiated industrial societies. However, guilt and shame are not completely successful in preventing nonconformity because child socialization is not uniform in millions of families and peer groups. Heterogeneity works against the universal rules laid down in the criminal code. In addition, status differentiation means that there is inequality with respect to the stake in conforming behavior. Adolescents and others whose interpersonal ties with conventional

adults are weak are insensitive to disapproval of their antisocial activities. So are the residents of slum neighborhoods. Being at the bottom of the hierarchy of prestige and other rewards, they are used to lack of approval. What they do not have cannot be taken away. In short, the diversity and the differentiation of an industrial society guarantee that some people some of the time will defy the institutionalized rules.

Formal agencies of social control—the police, the courts, the prisons—attempt to deal with those whom guilt and shame does not deter. In one sense, these formal agencies are fighting a losing battle. It is not possible under contemporary urban conditions for the police to arrest and the courts to convict more than a fraction of the persons who violate the rules. From the point of view of preventing the breakdown of the rules and the demoralization of conformists, however, formal agencies are useful. In punishing the luckless deviants who are caught, formal agencies of control help to define deviance as dangerous as well as immoral. Thus, conformists are reinforced in their self-imposed tendencies to conform.

SOME SIGNIFICANT LITERATURE ON NONCONFORMITY AND ITS CONTROL

Joseph Bensman and Israel Gerver, "Crime and Punishment in the Factory: The Function of Deviancy in Maintaining the Social System," *American Sociological Review*, Vol. 28, August 1963, pp. 588–598. In a large aircraft factory working on United States Air Force contracts, use of a tap to align bolts in recessed nuts is so serious a violation of work rules that a worker possessing a tap, even though he is not caught using it, can be summarily fired. Nevertheless, mass violation of the rule occurs because without using taps this factory cannot attain a high enough level of productivity. The authors therefore regard the use of taps, not as deviant behavior, but as "a permanent unofficial aspect of the organization." What is considered a crime in this factory is not using a tap, which is necessary under some circumstances, but failing to observe the rituals of concealment in its use or of penitence when reprimanded for using one. Informal controls are brought to bear on workers who violate the rules regulating tapping, thus tending to limit the use of the tap to what are considered "necessary" situations. This article

deals with a crime defined by a private organization rather than by the state, but it throws light on an important problem: the redefinition of legitimacy by persons other than the law makers. Tapping is thus a second cousin of traffic violations, public drunkenness, and other folk crimes.

Kettil Bruun, *Drinking Behavior in Small Groups: An Experimental Study*, Stockholm: Almqvist and Wiksell, 1959. Under the auspices of the Finnish Foundation for Alcohol Studies, 15 four-person groups were assembled for six-hour drinking sessions in order to investigate the effects of group drinking. The monograph reports changes in group cohesion and stability as well as changes in the proportions of positive and negative responses to individual members, but these changes were not directly proportional to the amount of alcohol consumed. Apparently personal and cultural attitudes toward acceptance of drinking and of drunken aggression are also involved. See review by Ozzie G. Simmons, *American Sociological Review*, Vol. 25, June

1960, pp. 436–437. For a comparative approach to drinking behavior in industrial societies, see Kettil Bruun and Ragnar Hauge, *Drinking Habits among Northern Youth: A Cross-national Study of Male Teenage Drinking in the Northern Capitals*, Helsinki: Finnish Foundation for Alcohol Studies, 1963.

John A. Clausen, "Drug Addiction," in Robert K. Merton and Robert A. Nisbet, Eds., *Contemporary Social Problems: An Introduction to the Study of Deviant Behavior and Social Disorganization*, New York: Harcourt, Brace & World, 1961, pp. 181–221. The social characteristics of the approximately 50,000 known American drug addicts supports Dr. Clausen's observation that addiction is ". . . primarily a symptom of a deeper pathology that derives from our failure to integrate into the social fabric the more deprived migrants to our metropolitan centers, especially those disadvantaged by minority-group status." "Nearly 60 per cent are Negro, 7 per cent are Puerto Rican, 5 per cent Mexican-American and only 27 per cent native white." Most American drug addicts contract the habit and continue to live in the slum neighborhoods of large cities: New York, Chicago, Los Angeles, Washington, D.C., Detroit, St. Louis, and Dallas.

Albert K. Cohen, "The Study of Social Disorganization and Deviant Behavior," in Robert K. Merton, Leonard Broom, and Leonard S. Cottrell, Jr., Eds., *Sociology Today: Problems and Prospects*, New York: Basic Books, 1959, pp. 461–484. The prospective deviant has several courses in a situation in which conformity is unsatisfactory, yet nonconformity will result in sanctions from persons with whom he interacts. "One [course] is for our hypothetical subject to continue to conform, despite continued frustration, because conformity is the only alternative that is morally and symbolically validated by his reference groups. . . . A second [course] is for him to break with the reference groups and acknowledge other reference groups, whose norms legitimize deviant solutions and attribute favorable role symbolism to them. . . . A third [course] is for the individual to 'go it alone,' violating the institutionalized expectations without the legitimation and validation that come from consensus." Professor Cohen calls attention in this theoretical article to the deviant act as a "cumulative and collective product." By this he means that the deviant act should be examined as the outcome of a social process consisting of: (1) the motivations for nonconformity on the part of its ultimate author, (2) his exploratory moves in the direction of deviance, and (3) the responses of persons in his milieu to these tendencies.

Kingsley Davis, "Prostitution," in Merton and Nisbet, *op. cit.*, pp. 262–288. Professor Davis distinguishes five related, although separable, issues in the understanding of prostitution as a universal phenomenon: (1) the causes of the *existence* of prostitution, (2) the causes

of *different forms* of prostitution, (3) the causes of *differing* rates of prostitution from one society to another, (4) the factors inducing some women to enter the "profession," and (5) the factors inducing some men to patronize prostitutes. As part of his discussion of reasons for the existence of prostitution, Professor Davis compares it with the black market in a controlled economy. When the demand for sexual thrills cannot be satisfied within the framework of marriage or other socially approved practices, some women are tempted to violate the norms by establishing a black market in sex. This is extremely difficult to control in an anonymous commercial society.

Jack P. Gibbs, "Suicide," in Merton and Nisbet, Eds., *op. cit.*, pp. 222–261. Suicide is a form of deviance for which the perpetrator cannot be punished—at least in this world. This makes for difficulties in the control of suicide and thus explains its existence: when individuals get into situations that they define as intolerable, suicide provides escape. Sociologists are particularly interested in explaining variations in the resort to suicide from one society to another and from one social category to another within the same society. For example, why is Denmark's suicide rate three times Norway's? Why does the urban suicide rate exceed the rural rate in virtually all countries? Why does the suicide rate of males exceed the rate for females? Why does the suicide rate of old people exceed the rate for young adults in most industrial countries? Why are divorced persons more prone to suicide than married persons? As contrasted with these sociological interests, psychologists and psychiatrists are more interested in the related question of explaining why one individual in a given society or social category rather than another takes his life. For this purpose, they may interview persons who attempt unsuccessfully to commit suicide.

Solomon Kobrin, "The Chicago Area Project—A 25-Year Assessment," *Annals of the American Academy of Political and Social Science*, Vol. 322, March 1959, pp. 19–25. Assuming as it does that adolescent delinquency in the large city is principally the result of a breakdown in *spontaneous* social controls, the Chicago Area Project attempts to *organize* adult controls over adolescents in high-delinquency neighborhoods. To accomplish this objective, the Project seeks to induce indigenous residents of these neighborhoods to work together on youth problems as the local community perceives them. Through the use of street workers hired by neighborhood committees, the committees reduce somewhat the isolation of the male adolescent peer group from adult controls. (The Area Project apparently invented the technique of sending young adults to work with adolescent gangs on street corners.) The committees also interpret the impersonal operation of police departments, courts, probation and parole systems, and schools to many youngsters so as to make bureaucratic decisions and procedures more acceptable. The Area Project does not claim to have effected permanent reduction of delinquency rates—even in neighborhoods where years of effort have been made—because the social forces working to isolate adolescents from adult controls in the large city have so far proven stronger than the manufactured controls of the committees.

Talcott Parsons, "Youth in the Context of American Society," *Daedalus*, Vol. 91, Winter 1962, pp. 97–123. One of the features of industrial societies and particularly of American society is the increasing differentiation of institutions. Thus, longer schooling means sharper segregation of youngsters from adult society, and this makes for autonomous youth cultures. Furthermore, the differentiation of institutions gives youngsters more choices. ". . . [T]ypes of interest, motivation, and evaluation that were embedded in a less differentiated complex come to be separated out, to become more autonomous and more visible . . ." As an example of increased choices, Professor Parsons points to greater freedom for the expression of erotic interests, not only in the private life of the individual but also on the stage, in movies and television, and in books and magazines. Sex is less confined to the family context. Parsons suggests that new patterns should be expected as a result of increased differentiation and are not necessarily signs of breakdown. Unfortunately, whether they constitute a new, fairly stable way of organizing social life or are temporary maladjustments can be assessed only after the passage of time.

Albert J. Reiss, Jr., and Albert Lewis Rhodes, "The Distribution of Juvenile Delinquency in the Social Class Structure," *American Sociological Review*, Vol. 26, October 1961, pp. 720–732. The theory of relative deprivation suggests that lower-class boys in middle-class neighborhoods feel more disadvantaged and resentful than lower-class boys in lower-class neighborhoods. A deduction from this theory holds that lower-class boys in middle-class neighborhoods have very high delinquency rates. A study of 9238 white boys, 12 years old or older and attending school in the Nashville metropolitan area, provides an opportunity to test this application of the theory of relative deprivation. The authors report that sons of fathers in laboring or service occupations have a much higher delinquency rate in predominantly lower-class neighborhoods than have boys of the same background who live in predominantly middle-class neighborhoods. Apparently the delinquency tradition of a neighborhood is an even more important factor in antisocial behavior than the psychic strains leading to feelings of inadequacy or resentment.

Lyle W. Shannon, "Types and Patterns of Delinquency Referral in a Middle-Sized City," *British Journal of Criminology*, Vol. 4, July 1963, pp. 24–36. Although juvenile and criminal court cases show a definite concentration in the lower socioeconomic neighborhoods of large cities, some criminologists suspect that the police are more lenient to middle-class suspects, thus exaggerating the socioeconomic differences in crime and delinquency rates. In the course of analyzing police contacts with juvenile suspects in Madison, Wisconsin, from 1950 to 1955, Professor Shannon throws light on this issue. The rate of police contacts with juveniles in the Central zone (low socioeconomic status) is about three times the rate in the East zone (highest socioeconomic status). Although the Madison police are less likely to make an official referral of a juvenile contact in the East zone, this is almost entirely because of the less serious offenses in those neighborhoods. ". . . [J]uveniles engaging in comparable types of delinquent behavior receive pretty much the same treatment from Madison police." Nondiscriminatory handling of referrals is characteristic of *first* contacts with the police as well as of subsequent contacts. Unless it is assumed that the police discriminate in their contacts but not in their referrals, which is rather unlikely, this study is evidence of class differences in actual delinquent behavior, not merely in recorded delinquency.

CHAPTER 10

Illegitimate Roles

Most crimes are *not* committed by professional criminals. In proceedings in traffic courts, magistrate courts, or even county criminal courts, most of the defendants think of themselves as law-abiding citizens who have somehow gotten into "trouble." To put it another way, almost everyone has committed a crime at some time or other. Thus, a criminology professor reported that his students had engaged in much the same offenses as were committed by youngsters adjudicated "delinquent" by the courts.[1] And a questionnaire survey revealed a remarkably high percentage of felonies confessed by outwardly respectable adults.[2] If nearly everyone has committed one or more crimes—in the sense of an occasional lapse from an essentially law-abiding style of life—it does not make much sense to define "the criminal" as anyone who has committed a crime. By that definition, we are all criminals.

THE CRIMINAL: AN EXAMPLE OF AN ILLEGITIMATE ROLE

A more restrictive criterion of the criminal is necessary to distinguish the persistently antisocial individual from the rest of us. Many sociologists believe that the criterion should be a social psychological one: whether the individual thinks of himself as a criminal and whether he is so regarded by others.[3] A criminal is a person who plays a certain kind of role: who interacts with other persistent offenders, who looks to them for approval, and who is indifferent to the reactions of conventional persons. By this definition, criminals are rare—even in industrial societies with high crime rates. But they are more dangerous than their numbers might indicate because they are unresponsive to the internal controls (guilt and shame) that influence the noncriminal. They can be deflected from further crime only by fear of arrest and punishment.

As an illustration of this principle, consider the situation of an adolescent boy who wants

[1] Austin L. Porterfield, "Delinquency and Its Outcome in Court and College," *American Journal of Sociology*, Vol. 49, November 1943, pp. 199–208.
[2] James S. Wallerstein and Clement J. Wyle, "Our Law-Abiding Lawbreakers," *Probation*, Vol. 25, March-April 1947, pp. 107–112.
[3] Ernest W. Burgess, testimony in *Hearings before the Committee on Low-Income Family of the Joint Committee on the Economic Report*, 81st Congress, December 1949, Washington: Government Printing Office, 1950, pp. 375–400.

to impress his girlfriend by taking her out in an expensive convertible. He tries to borrow such a car but fails. He feels desperate. This girl is important to him, and he believes that a car is essential to a successful date. So, although he never stole a car before, he "borrows" the red convertible parked half a block from his house with the keys in it. After his big date, he returns the car to the spot from which he had taken it. Since he does not think of himself as a "car thief"—only as a boy whom circumstances compelled to "borrow" a car—he may well ignore future opportunities to steal cars. On the other hand, a boy who has been caught by the police in a stolen car and branded a "car thief" by arrest and trial begins to think of himself not merely as a boy who "borrows" cars for joy rides but as a "car thief." As a car thief, he begins to *look* for opportunities to steal cars, and he may see them in circumstances the first boy would miss. He becomes proud of his skill at stealing cars. He learns from more sophisticated car thieves how to break into a locked car and how to start cars without keys. One 17-year-old car thief specialized in stealing Lincolns. He had stolen 80 Lincolns before he was sent to a reformatory. He would not demean himself by stealing smaller, less expensive cars even though he was aware that he was more likely to arouse suspicion in a Lincoln. "When the police see a young kid driving a $6000 Lincoln, they get suspicious. They stop you and ask to see the registration. That's how I got caught." Whereas the dedicated car thief is on the alert wherever he goes for chances to practice his craft, the occasional offender must rationalize the crime in order to make it acceptable to an essentially conventional self-conception.[4] Granted that human powers of rationalization are great. Nevertheless, the necessity of rationalizing imposes a limitation that does not exist for the criminal. Nothing in the self-conception of the self-defined car thief deters him from stealing cars; on the contrary, his self-conception provides

encouragement for the further development of a delinquent career.

THE DEVELOPMENT OF A DEVIANT SELF-CONCEPTION

A criminal self-conception is the outcome of social processing. Nearly all contemporary criminologists believe that criminals are made rather than born. Criminal self-conceptions develop in much the same way as noncriminal self-conceptions: in the course of the individual's interactions with other people. Consider the outraged attitude of the judge when the boy who had stolen 80 Lincolns was brought before him. He did more than sentence the boy to jail. He helped to define the boy to himself as well as to the community as a person who ought to be imprisoned. Jail is not merely incarceration. For those who use the legitimate community as a reference group, imprisonment is also disgrace. For those who have shifted their allegiance to antisocial groups, however, imprisonment is not disgrace. It may even bring honor—as in some adolescent gangs where it is a mark of delinquent sophistication. For professional criminals, imprisonment is simply one of the hazards of their occupation.

Criminologists do not understand precisely how this change in allegiance takes place, but they believe that the sanctions mobilized by law-enforcement agencies drive a wedge between the offender and law-abiding groups.[5] Perhaps because of the tradition that an individual is innocent until proven guilty, the offender does not usually think of himself as a criminal until the law so labels him. When he is arrested, tried, convicted, and jailed, the resulting stigma simultaneously reduces his status in law-abiding groups and changes his conception of the kind of a person he is. Moreover, it is quite likely that he will find—in correctional institutions or in the free community—persons very much like himself. He and his new friends mutually reinforce one another's delinquent tendencies by turning the values of the law-abiding community upside-down. The boy who stole 80 cars is given credit by fellow reforma-

---

[4] John Bartlow Martin, *My Life in Crime: The Autobiography of a Professional Criminal*, New York: Harper, 1952.

[5] Burgess, *op. cit.*

tory inmates for his enterprise. But he is patronized for his lack of sophistication. He abandoned the cars after using all the gas in the tanks. Didn't he realize that he could make money by stripping the cars of radios, heaters, hub caps, and tires? If he had had "connections," he would have known how to sell the entire car to "fences" who make a specialty of transforming stolen cars and reselling them. His new friends make him feel welcome, but they prove to him that he has much to learn. Thus, he reaches a point where the condemnations of the legitimate community are irrelevant to his self-respect. In the face of the rejecting definition of his behavior by the legitimate community, he gravitates toward other outcasts; he needs *their* approval.

Is it accident then that determines who becomes a criminal (in the role sense) and who does not? Do those who are caught and stigmatized become criminals? This does not seem to be a sufficient explanation. Very likely circumstances may predispose some persons toward illegitimate roles.[6] Personality disturbances may incapacitate the individual for legitimate roles and, if they do not also incapacitate him for criminal roles, may explain why some offenders transfer allegiance so readily from the legitimate community. Social and cultural factors can also pose obstacles to the playing of legitimate roles. Consider the developmental history of the typical reformatory inmate. He came from a low-income family—possibly of minority origin (Negro, Puerto Rican, Mexican). His parents exercised ineffectual control over him, not necessarily because of indifference but because they were preoccupied with their own problems: chronic warfare in the household; desertion by the father; serious illness of the mother; alcoholism; too many children for an unskilled father to support or a harried mother to supervise. When he started school, no one at home made schoolwork seem meaningful to him, so he had little incentive

to try to learn. Within a few years, he was retarded in such basic skills as reading and arithmetic. The more successful students considered him "dumb" and said so; the teachers showed that they thought so too by shunting him into programs for "slow" learners. Being a failure at school increased his disinterest, and he began to truant and to rebel against the authority of the teachers. He quit school "to go to work" as soon as he could legally do so.

He floundered in the labor market, shifting from one blind-alley job to another—with intervals of unemployment between. Employers were reluctant to hire him because of his failure to complete high school, the competition of older, more experienced workers, and the stipulations of the child labor laws. But he was not a desirable worker on other grounds: he had a poor job attendance record; he transferred to supervisors the hostile attitude he had toward teachers; he quit jobs suddenly, usually without notice. In short, he found employment no more interesting than school had been —and no more rewarding in terms of recognition. As a result, he withdrew from the labor market whenever he had the money to do so; he did not regard a job as his normal activity; a job was a chore he assumed when pressed for money. Psychologically uninvolved in school or job, he hung out on the street corner with other unsuccessful youngsters. He became known as a hoodlum. When family and neighbors added their condemnations to those of teachers and employers, all bridges to respectability were burned.

This composite history of a reformatory inmate reveals a boy who was defeated in two of the major arenas of urban industrial life: school and work. Rejected by respectable people, he looked instead to a clique of street-corner loafers for approval. Cultural, social, and (possibly) personality disabilities can incapacitate an individual for legitimate roles and thus make more likely his attraction to illegitimate roles. Bear this interpretation in mind in reading the following account of a delinquent gang in New York City.

6 Michael Argyle, "A New Approach to the Classification of Delinquents with Implications for Treatment," Monograph No. 2, California State Board of Corrections, July 1961, pp. 15–26.

The Fancied Inability to Play a Legitimate Role: The Case of Adolescent Gangs

Reprinted by permission. From Murray Schumach, "The Teen-Age Gang—Who and Why," New York *Times Magazine*, Sept. 2, 1956, pp. 7, 66, 68.

Although no one of the New York City gangs can be considered "typical," most of them have a great deal in common. Membership is almost entirely from the neighborhood. This, more than prejudice, explains the racial character of so many gangs. Dictatorship and strict discipline mark the organization. Force is its guiding social principle. It recruits members by offering "rep"—prestige— and by intimidation. Almost always, each gang is part of a loose federation for warfare that may range from sneak raids with fists to massed attacks —"rumbles"—with guns. Headquarters may be a street corner, lot, park, playground, candy store, cafeteria, hallway or cellar. Most members do not attend school or hold regular jobs. Generally, these youths do not use dope.

In most other respects, however, the gangs vary widely. Some gangs are recruited from slums, others from middle-class environments. Some have members largely from broken homes, others from apparently stable families. Some are children of immigrants, or are themselves immigrants. Others were born to native Americans. Some adorn themselves in flashy blazers, sneakers and Levis and let their hair grow long. Others dress without affectation. Some have auxiliary girl gangs, others repudiate such an idea.

Recently I spent a few days with a gang of juvenile delinquents—they call themselves a "crew" or "clique"—to try to learn its organization and composition; how it lives in peace and war; the forces that bring and hold the gang together; the values and mores that comprise its rather primitive code; the gang members' attitudes toward one another, the community, the police, social workers and adults in general.

The members of this gang—we shall call them the Devils—are almost entirely of Irish and Italian stock, with just a few of Jewish and German origins. Their parents were born in this country, mostly in the same Park Circle section of Brooklyn where they now live. Their environment is middle class, with a family income ranging from $3,000 to $6,000. They live mainly in one- or two-family homes along clean, tree-lined streets. For the most part they are nice-looking boys, who dress like most adolescents, in sport shirts, slacks and shoes. In rainy or cool weather they wear unmarked zipper jackets.

"If you're man enough," explained a Devil, "you don't need a name on your jacket."

The Devils claim a membership of 175. This is probably greatly exaggerated. I met about twenty-five, and their hard-core membership probably does not exceed fifty. They are supreme over a territory—they call it "turf"—of nearly a square mile. Most of them have left school, though their average age is about fifteen and a half, ranging from 13 to 18. (Boys can leave school at 16. Those who are younger usually have truancy records so long they indicate chronic absenteeism.) Very few have regular jobs. Their organization is topped by a Leader, a War Counsellor and two Main Guys.

Tension hangs over the gang members, even now when they are virtually unchallenged and at peace with all except one of eight bordering gangs. When they gather at night at their headquarters outside a playground they are wary of every car that rolls by the bench around which they cluster. The car could contain invaders or detectives. With careful military sagacity they maintain outpost groups in other parts of their realm. Important members of the gang carry a list of telephone numbers for emergency mobilization.

"A clique could get in," conceded a Devil, "but they'd never get out. We'd cut them off before they knew what happened."

The police take no chances. One night a radio car passed slowly by the group at least once an hour for three hours. The last time—it was nearly midnight—the car stopped. One of the Devils whispered:

"Watch this. They're gonna bust us (disperse us). They're gonna pad us down (search us)."

The police studied them slowly and drove off without interfering.

The next night, however, when some twenty of them were being noisy about 9 o'clock along a brightly lighted street, the police ordered their dispersal, then fragmentized the smaller groups. This was done without force. The youths obeyed, reluctantly. One of them muttered, "Some cops need a beating." But another youth had said, the preceding day, "Most cliques are breaking up. The cops are too hot."

The threatening atmosphere that envelops the Devils is accentuated by the incessant tendency to "rank" or "sound" one another. This is a combination of threat and insult in loud, foul language, whereby the members are constantly measuring one another. Their sudden bursts of sparring sometimes seem close to violence. Their derisive laughter, their swaggering, boisterous manner and eternal suspicion are reminders that the Devils are more than just hearty adolescents. So, too, is their warfare.

Their favorite tactic in gang fights, they say, is "pulling a Jap," or sneak raid. A group of Devils will drive at night into enemy territory and park a few blocks from the hangout of the enemy. When the rival gang breaks up, the Devils will follow by car one or two who have broken away from the main body. When these "strays" are beyond help, the group of Devils will beat them up and drive off. Such an attack lasts only a few minutes. The raids continue until the enemy surrenders—"turns it off."

Then there is the military maneuver known as "a fair one." On the surface it seems honorable. Each of the hostile gangs sends forth its champion, accompanied by five cohorts. The figure of six has become accepted because that many fit comfortably in a car. In a "fair one," the champions fight without weapons, but everything goes —kicking, stomping, kneeing. In theory, there is no interference. Actually, the Devils admit their five "seconds" always attack the rival quintet.

The Devils say they have access to guns, but prefer to fight without weapons. They contend they were forced to acquire guns when they learned a rival gang had them. But they avoid the "rumble," or massed gang fight. They say only stupid gangs fight this way; it is the surest way to get picked up by the police.

The fights stem from numerous causes. But these can be boiled down to two—invasion or insult. The Devils assert they always check rumors of boundary violation or of their crew being demeaned by others. They seek out witnesses, question them and then send out emissaries to the other crew for confirmation.

"We talk before we hit," says a Devil. "If we find out it's true, we hit."

I never saw the Devils violate the law. But sixteen of their members or alumni are in jail on charges that include extortion, grand larceny, and violation of the Sullivan Law. Most of those I met said they had been arrested—mostly, they declared, for unlawful assembly. They hinted at serious crimes but, for obvious reasons, refused to discuss them. They admitted they had committed wanton destruction of property in public or private buildings. Some of them, for instance, talked of having destroyed toilet fixtures at a recreation hall. They "used to" extort money from youngsters at school, some admitted, and "when we were kids" used to attack youngsters without gang affiliation "just for the kicks." They admit having carried guns in fights.

Like most organizations created for military operations, the Devils seem to spend a great deal of their time idly hanging around. Usually, they wake up about noon and reach the playground benches between 1 and 2 o'clock. Three or four afternoons a week they go to a nearby movie.

"You go to pick up girls," explained a Devil. "If there's no girls you watch the movie. If there's girls you make out with them—and watch the movie." The term "make out," in this case, usually means vigorous necking.

Occasionally, they will go swimming. Almost invariably they choose an area near Mill Basin not frequented by the public. They say they avoid such places as Coney Island.

"We don't like to go where there's a lot of people," a Devil said. "Anytime we go to a place like Coney Island we get into trouble. A guy gives you a funny look. You say: 'What the —— you lookin' at?' You can't let guys get away with that stuff. Next thing you know there's trouble."

Not long ago, the Devils agreed to accompany social workers on an outing to a Long Island beach. Soon after they arrived, there were objections from another bather about their loud, foul language. They told him to move. When he tried to silence the Devil who had made this suggestion, a few other Devils jumped him. A state trooper ended the picnic a short time later by ordering the Devils back on the bus and home.

Most evenings they loiter at the playground or wander in groups through the neighborhood. Sometimes, on hot nights, they dive from trees in Prospect Park into the lake. Thursday nights they meet at the playground to learn if any enemies have besmirched their rep or violated their turf. At this meeting they also consider whether any of their own members have to be "straightened out," punished. The transgression could be failure to attend meetings without good reason or consorting with an enemy group. Punishment could range from warning to beating. On this night they also plan their campaign for the dance the following night in Prospect Park. There they go in strength because it is alien territory and because they think it might be fruitful for girl-hunting.

Saturday nights they may go to parties, to a Coney Island rock-and-roll session or just drape themselves around the bench and sip a few cans of beer while they argue loudly.

They rise much earlier than usual on Sundays, for the 10 A.M. mass. Afterward, they watch a softball game in the playground, played by alumni of the Devils. They lunch at home—almost all their meals are at home—and return to the bench. In the evening, except for those with dates, they gather at the benches or patrol the turf.

Beneath all their apparently reckless hostility and confusion, the Devils have a strict code—one that seems not too far advanced from the cave. They do not, they insist, attack neutrals, either adolescent or adult. They grant the right of passage to all gangs except the one with which they are currently at war. They believe they have the right to beat up any member of this warring gang found in their territory. They respect, they say, pacts with rivals. They are respectful of their parents and particularly of their mothers—known as "moo" in their jargon. A slighting remark about one's mother must be avenged. The mother-insult is a reliable device for provoking an enemy or making him admit he is a "punk."

One reason they try to avoid trouble near home stems from the wish to keep their gang activities a secret from their mothers. When arrested for unlawful assembly—gathering for a fight—they may tell their mothers they were preparing to defend themselves or that they were arrested unjustly. One boy hangs out with a faction of the gang that meets a few blocks away from the playground because he lives near the playground and doesn't want his mother to see him there. Generally the parents admit their sons are "wild," but hope they will outgrow this phase.

The gang code applies to girls as well as mothers. The Devils brag that "our girls are clean." They literally shout it through the streets, while the girls giggle on near-by benches. By this boast they mean they desist from immoral acts with girls in their neighborhood. These are girls, they say, they will marry some day. However, they crow just as loudly about their lack of restraint with girls outside the neighborhood.

Most important, the code calls for loyalty of gang members to one another. "We stick together," says a Devil. "Everything we do we stick together. We got it made right. The clique is good. When we're men, the guys will still be friends and our wives, too."

At times, carried away by the fervor of their code, they see themselves as protectors of a homeland that, without their resistance and courage, would be overrun by enemy gangs.

That the community does not judge them by this code is irksome to the Devils. They think it unfair that several candy stores and cafeterias will not admit them because they sometimes endanger property by their "fooling around." For the legal arm of the community, the police, they express hatred. To them a policeman is a bully, for sale to "anybody with scratch." Nor do they think much more flatteringly of social workers. The social worker, they say, "makes himself a hero." They make an exception of the Youth Board worker now assigned to them.

At times, in self-appraisal they are capable of withering honesty. In bragging that none of their members takes dope, one of the Devils said sadly, not boastfully, "We're bad enough without dope." The others nodded silently.

The primordial pattern of the Devils emerges clearly in the ritual for admission. The aspirant, having been questioned carefully at earlier interviews, presents himself before the group in the playground on a prearranged night. There he is beaten by any Devils present. He has the right to fight back. If he makes no complaint he is admitted. But if he cries or begs mercy, he is called "punk" and barred from membership. Members are proud of having "caught my beating."

The Devils were not always this sort of organization. The group was formed fifteen years ago as a football team. The game was often marked by fist fights. During World War II, athletics became less important to the Devils and gang fighting increased in importance. Clashes with other gangs led to brushes with the police, and an anti-social group developed.

Many Devils say they joined the gang because they grew up in this neighborhood and wanted to be with their friends—for excitement; for protection against other gangs; for "rep." To them the gang seems a normal transition process before they grow up, leave the gang, get jobs, marry and settle down in the neighborhood, honorably retired from "gang busting."

Adult workers, surveying the whole field of juvenile delinquency, come up with somewhat different explanations of the gang. In the gang, they say, boys find the recognition and status they do not receive elsewhere. They are not good at school, they rarely distinguish themselves in athletics. Only in the gang can they gain "rep." This sense of comparative adequacy in the gang makes them increasingly dependent upon it, increasingly fearful of being deserted by the gang or thrown out of the group. This leads to the irony that these boys who rebel so strongly against the normal discipline of society impose upon themselves the sterner disciplines of the gang.

Researchers in the field also discern other factors in the formation of gangs. First, they point out, it is normal for teen-agers to join groups in the difficult period when they are making the transition from adolescent dependence on the family into adult independence of the family. The vast majority of teen-age groups fit the community pattern and usually contribute a great deal.

In the case of anti-social groups, the members feel cultural deprivation as well as strong personal difficulties. They are convinced they have no future and that society will not give them what they deserve. If, in support of this conclusion, they can find considerable evidence of discrimination—as in the case of Negroes and Puerto Ricans—their leanings toward delinquency are that much stronger. Such youths may think they have no choice but to live for the pleasures of the moment. Delinquents, with little sense of obligation toward society, have little compunction about violating the rules of society.

According to this interpretation of adolescent gangs, many of the members feel, rightly or wrongly, that "they have no future." The gang offers "pleasures of the moment" instead of the future that more fortunate youngsters look forward to. Presumably, the Devils would have trouble recruiting new members if all the boys in the neighborhood stayed in high school until graduation and were confident about getting a good job, or going to college, afterwards. This explanation of the attractions of an illegitimate role assumes that it is adopted in lieu of a legitimate role perceived as unavailable. In order to test this explanation further, let us examine a quite different illegitimate role: that of the stutterer. To be a stutterer is undesirable. A stutterer may receive more sympathy than a delinquent gang member, but neither role is an approved one. From one point of view, the role of stutterer is even more disadvantageous. At least the delinquent has the support of the other members of his gang; the stutterer is characteristically surrounded by fluent speakers. Can the development of stuttering be explained as another instance of the social psychology of defeat? Are stutterers people who encountered obstacles in their childhood which made normal speech seem unattainable? Wendell Johnson, a world-renowned authority on stuttering, states the case for this explanation in the following article.

The Fancied Inability to Play a Legitimate Role: The Case of Stutterers

Reprinted by permission. From Wendell Johnson, "For the Stutterer, a Sympathetic Ear," New York *Times Magazine*, Feb. 13, 1955, p. 42.

The 4-year-old is breathless with excitement as he reports a drama he has just observed.

"And then the dog, the dog," he says, "the dog chased the k-k-kitten right up that, that tree, the one, one by the corner. And J-Jack, Jack was so mad. He hollered and hollered at that old dog. Boy!"

Mother and dad listen to the incident with interest. It's nothing new for an old dog to chase a kitten but they enjoy hearing their young man tell about it. The little fellow is lucky. In some homes his first flow of enthusiasm might have been dammed with a "Stop and start over" or "Take a deep breath" or even "Stop that stuttering." In others, though the parents keep their remarks to themselves, they may show their tension at all these repetitions and start wondering if their youngster is going to be a stutterer. Recent research indicates that stuttering gets its start in just this way—not in the child's mouth but in the parent's ear.

This problem of stuttering, or stammering, affects approximately seven out of every 1,000 persons in the United States—roughly 300,000 youngsters and 700,000 grown-ups, a total of 1,000,000 of all ages. Stutterers make up one of our largest handicapped groups.

Although the problem is as old as civilization—it is, indeed, probably a part of the price we pay for civilization—there was little scientific knowledge of stuttering before 1925. Since that date, however, a great deal of research has been carried out—at the University of Iowa and elsewhere—and while much remains to be done, the substantial research dividends to date are heartening.

University of Iowa studies have involved nearly 1,000 mothers and fathers and 500 children. Half the children were regarded by their parents as stutterers, and for study purposes each of these was compared with a non-stuttering "control" child of like age, sex and socio-economic family status.

It turned out that the original diagnoses of stuttering had been made by persons—usually the supposed stutterer's mother—who lacked essential information regarding normal speech development and the conditions affecting it. In general what was taken for stuttering was the normally hesitant and repetitive speech of early childhood.

A study of approximately 200 normal children, aged 2 to 5, has revealed that the average child repeats a sound or a word or a phrase forty-five times every 1,000 running words. Most parents either disregard or do not notice these repetitions. A few parents worry about them.

While most of the parents studied said they had "done nothing" about these repetitions and "tried not to let the child know" they had been noticed, it was quite clear that through facial expressions, vocal inflections, bodily tensions and other means they had unknowingly conveyed their concern and disapproval to the children. Some, of course, had quite openly and insistently tried to get their youngsters to "stop all that stumbling."

The general consequence appeared, in the usual case, to be a gradual loss of confidence on the part of the child. As a result he spoke somewhat more hesitantly and appeared, as time went on, first to build up a positive fear of speaking in certain situations and then to speak with more and more tension. All the while the parents became more concerned and expressed their anxiety more and more clearly. Thus, without meaning to, they bothered the youngster all the more in his attempts to talk clearly. Generally speaking, that is how stuttering begins—as the child tries not to do something his parents find unacceptable. Full-blown stuttering turns out to be simply what the so-called stutterer does in his effort not to stutter again.

Previous theories on the cause of stuttering were not so simple. Some early research appeared to indicate that stuttering children were physically unstable or emotionally disturbed. One of the most popular theories among speech specialists a generation ago was that stuttering resulted from forcing left-handed youngsters to use the right hand. Recent studies have failed to support these theories, however.

The children who become stutterers, we have found, are like other children physically and psychologically. Moreover, neither the children nor their parents appear to qualify as "neurotics."

It was observed, though, that the parents who felt that their children did not speak smoothly enough tended in general to be overly conscientious. They were somewhat perfectionistic, impatient for their children to meet adult standards. Although their children had developed normally, the parents rated them as relatively slow in development.

These mothers and fathers also tended to rate themselves and each other less favorably than the objective facts merited. By and large, they were striving to rise in social and economic status, and on the average, they seemed to need to have their children "show up well" a bit more than did the control group parents.

If the children evaluated by such parents as stutterers differ in any important respects from other youngsters, the main difference is that they tend to be a little more dependent on their parents and, for this reason, a bit more sensitive to parental disapproval and uneasiness. The comparison, however, is to be expressed in a gray language, not in terms of black and white. The most important fact is that these children are quite within the normal range.

So it turns out that "the patient" is not really

the child but the parent. What is most important is not the way the child speaks but the way his parents listen to his speech and the way they feel about it and influence the child to feel about it, and the way they feel about him—and about themselves. The parents need information about normal speech development and the conditions that foster and retard it.

Another way of stating the foregoing explanation of joining a delinquent gang and of becoming a stutterer is this: People want to conform. They prefer legitimate roles. However, when legitimate roles are unattainable or are thought to be unattainable, people consciously seek an illegitimate role (gang membership) or unconsciously accept a definition of self which makes an illegitimate role commitment unavoidable (stuttering).

THE QUASI-INSTITUTIONALIZATION OF DEVIANT ROLES

This explanation of the attraction of illegitimate roles is inadequate because it considers only the difficulties of attaining *legitimate* roles. What about the ease or difficulty of attaining *illegitimate* roles? Consider that some deviant roles are quasi-institutionalized in complex industrial societies. They are not fully supported; nor is recruitment for them as free as for legitimate roles. But they enjoy *covert* support and protection from *overtly* conforming members of the community. Thus, some illegitimate roles can offer rewards to potential recruits equal to or greater than the rewards of legitimate roles. Take the role of bookie as an example. In a slum neighborhood where there is considerable betting on horse races, a bookie may be an object of envy to the youth of the community. Unlike most of the men in this low-income community, the bookie wears new and expensive clothes, drives a flashy car, and always has money in his pocket. He is by no means an outcast. Not only do the people of the neighborhood place bets with him; not only are ambitious youngsters eager to work for him as "runners"; he is also on familiar

terms with most of the police; he pays them off on a regular basis. A boy may find a bookie more attractive a role model than his own father, a day laborer. After all, the money that the bookie earns from his activities is indistinguishable from the money earned in conventional occupations. When he goes each year to the Cadillac agency to turn in his old car and get a new one, he is deferred to as a valuable customer. No one questions the source of his income. In industrial societies, the market place is differentiated from other institutional contexts. Money is money, no matter where it comes from.

The quasi-institutionalization of the bookie role has significant consequences. Gambling—only part of which is illegal bookmaking—is one of America's largest industries. According to J. Edgar Hoover, Director of the Federal Bureau of Investigation, the gross "take" from gambling in the United States is more than ten billion dollars a year. The complex operations which bookmaking alone requires, the bureaucratic organization of these operations, and the public and governmental tolerance which is a prerequisite for such large-scale activities is explained in the following article.

How Bookies Run Their Businesses: Racket in a Goldfish Bowl

Reprinted by permission. From Fred J. Cook, "Racket in a Goldfish Bowl," *The Nation*, Vol. 191, Oct. 22, 1960, pp. 265–272.

Bookmaking, the most remunerative of the underworld's multi-billion-dollar gambling rackets, has the advantage of a certain degree of secrecy; yet, actually, despite the protestations of police that it is so hard to ferret out, it runs virtually in a goldfish bowl.

The paradox is implicit in the very nature of the business. A bookie handles most of his transactions by telephone, with a minimum of personal contact, and the telephone is of course a private and secretive device. If a bookie's needs could be limited simply to answering a phone and taking bets, he would probably have the world's most cop-proof racket; but unfortunately for him, to operate his business, he needs certain vital services. And these services are a giveaway to his activity.

The pressing needs of a bookie are three: He must get "the line"; he must be able to "lay off" the dangerously heavy play; he must get fast results from the race track.

Getting "the line" means that the bookie must have constant access to an expert and recognized handicapper who can keep him up to the minute on just what the points and odds are on a baseball game, a basketball game or the weekend's college and professional football competition.

In America today there is just one "line" that is recognized nationally as *the* line. In popular parlance, it is known as "the Minneapolis line," and if you take a look at the sports page of your favorite newspaper during any given week this fall, you are almost certain to find recorded there "the Minneapolis line" on the point spread on Notre Dame and Princeton and Harvard. This is an inestimable journalistic service, disclosing the findings of the nation's betting "bible" to alumni engaging in friendly bets—and to patrons of the bookies.

The "Minneapolis line" is the product of a firm known as Athletic Publications Inc., run by Leo Hirshfield, a short, gray-haired man in his sixties. Hirshfield maintains a four-room suite in a large Minneapolis office building. In one room are several desks and a battery of telephones. At each desk and phone sits a man, before him a list containing the printed code numbers representing Hirshfield clients who may be calling for the latest odds. A staff of eighteen persons mans the telephones, runs the office and sets the point spread and the odds on sporting events all over the nation.

Each Monday, Hirshfield mails out to his "clients" a schedule of the week's coming events. In the football season he distributes 25,000 to 30,000 lists each week. Since most customers need more than one copy, this probably means that he has 8,000 to 10,000 "clients" during this peak period of the year. During the remainder of the week, the "clients" call by telephone to get what Hirshfield calls his "early line," his "midweek line," and his "late line." The "client" calling for information always identifies himself by his code number—never by name. For instance, "102" may call from Cincinnati. The Hirshfield

employee answering the phone makes a check by the symbol "102" showing service rendered; then he reads off the odds as fast as tongue can clack the numbers. The man at the other end of the phone would be hopelessly lost if he did not have the printed Hirshfield list on which to jot down the odds in the exact order that they are given.

The printed schedules, so essential to the service, cost Hirshfield subscribers 20 cents each; the phone updating of "the line" costs from $15 to $30 a week, depending on the amount of advice a "client" seeks. . . .

The second of the three musts in a bookie's life involves money in even more fantastic proportions. This is the loot of the "layoff." Inextricably mixed up with the "layoff" is a not-inconsiderable item known in the trade as "vigorish." This is the bookie's guaranteed edge. On horse racing, for example, the "payout" is determined by the odds quoted on the pari-mutuel machines at the tracks. But, as the Massachusetts commission pointed out, the tracks always take a percentage "off the top" to pay taxes to the state and the costs of running the racing plants. In Massachusetts, this "takeout" averages 15½ per cent before the pari-mutuel odds are figured. In illegal betting this 15½ per cent goes to the bookie, who has no race track to maintain, no pari-mutuel tax to pay, nothing to worry about—except, of course, "protection."

This same item of "vigorish" dips its grasping hand into every type of betting. Take a look, for example, at what happens on a heavyweight championship prize fight—an event that, despite the general opprobrium in which the sport is held, does lure heavy betting. In last summer's return battle between Ingemar Johansson and Floyd Patterson, the early odds were "6-5, pick 'em." This means that, if you liked Patterson, you had to wager $6 on the chance of winning $5; similarly, if you liked Johansson, you had to put up $6 to win $5. A bookie having the same amount of money bet on each fighter was rolling in clover. Obviously, only one man could win, and it was a matter of complete indifference to the bookie who it was. For, with neatly balanced books, he would pay out only $11 of each $12 he took in—a clear $1 margin of profit on every twelve.

Clearly, with "vigorish" going so vigorously for him, the only time disaster can overtake a bookie, aside from the unlikely hazards of the law, comes if he allows himself to be overloaded on one betting proposition—one horse, one fighter, one football team. This elemental fact of book-making life has led to the development of the "layoff." This means simply that, if one bookie is overloaded on a horse, he hunts another bookie, not faced with the same problem, with whom he can bet some of the play on the dangerous nag. This is known as "spreading the play," and bookies have a mutual understanding to help each other out in this manner, each balancing his books and letting "vigorish" pour in a green cascade.

Simple "layoff" problems can be handled on a neighborhood or regional basis; but on major events, with heavy play, this is obviously impossible. Huge money, sometimes millions of dollars, may ride on a single event. This means that the "layoff" operation must be bankrolled heavily; it means, almost inevitably, that there has to be a national clearing house, to which small and medium bookies all over the nation can appeal in their need. Throughout the decade of the 1940s and into the early 1950s, the czar of the nation's "layoff" industry was Frank Erickson, the master New York bookie who ran his head-quarters and accounting house just acorss the Hudson River in Bergen County, N.J. There Erickson handled "layoff" play from all of the forty-eight states. When the McCarran Committee, the predecessor of the Kefauver Committee, caught up with Erickson in early 1950, the law finally stepped in, Erickson went to jail, and the scene of activity shifted. But the system remained the same.

That system and the manner in which it still runs today was described in testimony in the New York probe by Joseph P. Manners, of Miami, Fla., a former Assistant U.S. Attorney and special assistant to the head of the Criminal Division of the Justice Department for the thirteen Southern states. Manners headed the active field force under Milton Wessel—the unit that labored all too briefly from September, 1958, to May, 1959, on the national bookmaking problem.

Manners pointed out that the "layoff" begins with the $2 bettor who places his wager with the smallfry handbook operating from the corner newsstand. This $2 bettor likes Black Jack in the third at Hialeah. As the morning passes, it becomes obvious that other bettors in the neighborhood like Black Jack, too, and the first thing the

handbook knows his play is out of whack—he has $20 bet on Black Jack. So he contacts a larger book, one step up the ladder, and wagers $10 of the dangerous Black Jack play with him. Should this larger book find himself overloaded on Black Jack, he in turn tries to "lay off" the dangerous overload with the largest regional book; and if the play tilts the ledgers of the regional book, a large part of the load will be transferred to one of the two national clearing houses that now provide this type of gambling insurance. The smaller of these is located in Biloxi, Miss.; the larger, in Covington, Ky.

Biloxi is a wide-open town. According to Manners, gambling is "the only source of economy it has. . . . You walk down the street and every store has a one-armed bandit [slot machine], contrary to state law. . . ." The "layoff" headquarters is located in what is known as "the 406 Club" at 406 Magnolia Street. The telephone number is Idlewood 2-2633, and this number was extremely popular with upstate New York bookies who kept calling it to "lay off" with someone called "P.J." Manners says the 406 Club is "a typical gambling joint. You walk right in. There are tables. The old-fashioned board. They give you the results, and it's open to the public. The public doesn't want to change it."

In trying to check up on the Biloxi operation, Manners testified, he wrote to the local police and asked for a report on the premises and the phone activity at "the 406 Club." After a considerable lapse of time, this is the reply he got:

"Please pardon my delay in answering your letter. I have been out of office. The above is listed in the name of the 406 Club and this club is owned and operated by local boys whose reputation is, as far as I know, very good. If I can be of further service to you, please let me hear from you."

This bland official endorsement, this high-character reference for the "local boys" who were running an interstate gambling racket that stretched all the way from Biloxi to upstate New York and beyond, is typical of the lethargic forces of modern law. Yet, said Manners, in acid comment on the initiative of Biloxi police, "That phone averages over—I would say 1,500 calls a month going in." The callers, he said, were "federal tax-stamp holders"—in other words, professional bookmakers who have complied with federal law by registering and purchasing a $50 tax stamp.

Important as Biloxi is in the "layoff" operation, it handles only a tithe of the business that flows into the nation's major "layoff" center—the Newport-Covington area of Kentucky. Even in the days of Frank Erickson, Covington had begun to handle a heavy proportion of the play, as the Kefauver Committee found in 1951. Nothing has changed since that memorable exposé except that the rackets in Newport and Covington flourish more rankly and prolifically today than they did then. Indeed, the New York Commission of Investigation this year pinpointed the Newport-Covington area, just a short taxi ride across the Ohio River from Cincinnati, as the "layoff" capital of the country. And it found that some of the same outfits exposed by Kefauver—the Ace Research Service and the New-Cov Bookkeeping Service, to cite just a couple—are still handling big "layoff" money, their location, names and businesses unchanged and unpurified by time. . . .

The New York Commission of Investigation's raids in late 1959 established that upstate New York bookies were funneling their top "layoff" play to both Biloxi and Covington, but principally to Covington. Eliot Lumbard, the commission's counsel, estimated that the Newport-Covington area provides "the basic insurance" for "perhaps 90 per cent of the bookmaking activity in this country." Walsh added that the investigation had shown Covington exercises important controls from the top. For example, he said, he found that Covington "assigns code numbers to upstate New York bookmakers." On one occasion, a New York bookie wanted to get his code number changed, but the Covington headquarters refused to accommodate him "until it could be checked with the boss."

When a bookie in upstate New York has nothing to say about the code number under which he operates, but has to wait for the approval of "the boss" in Covington, Ky., the tight, czaristic control that the underworld exercises over every phase of the bookmaking racket would seem amply demonstrated. This theme was developed in significant detail before the New York commission by Manners, the federal prober. He and his agents had tracked underworld connections by studying thousands of telephone calls crisscrossing the nation and watching the ties

these established between top echelons of the underworld and Covington.

Manners testified that the money not laid off at the tracks—in other words the colossal final take that is insured by "vigorish" and losing bets—

". . . ends up in a top pool, top level of organized crime. This is the amazing feature of organized gambling. That $2 (bet with the corner handbook) finally ends up in part throughout the nation either in Kentucky, in Biloxi or one or two other places in the West. . . . It's strange that after hours, on off days, that the connections between these two spots, Biloxi and Covington, Ky.—the connections are many and frequent between the various gambling casinos' owners that we all know in Las Vegas and Havana. Somehow or other these names come to the same operation. After hours, they come in. Never during the operating day."

Manners said that he could only conclude, since federal investigators are barred from wire tapping and so could not listen in on these conversations, that

"This is the checkup. This is to find out how much have you made today or how much are we doing this week. It's the same few who control everything. The same few are there because of all of us. I feel that gambling is the initial source of moneys. This is their [the underworld's] entire money that they can use for everything. . . ."

No statement could more clearly pose the issue. In Manners' testimony is capsuled a vivid picture of the hidden ties that give the top echelons of the underworld power over literally billions of dollars—and the incalculable prestige and influence that control of such enormous wealth always and inevitably commands.

One instant and graphic demonstration of this influence lies in the fact that there is no secret about all of this. Hirshfield's role in furnishing "the line," the key function of Biloxi and Covington in providing "the layoff"—the first two of bookmaking's essential three services—are truly goldfish-bowl operations. Similarly obvious, as open to observation as the posture of a manikin in Macy's window, is the final step—the supplying of fast results from the tracks.

Lightning speed in flashing the name of the winner of a race is important to a bookie for two reason. First, fast results stimulate "action"; second, if a bookie lags in knowledge, he can become the victim of a neat racket known as "past-posting." One of the axioms of the trade is that the quicker a bettor on the first race finds out how he fared, the quicker he can be lured to bet again. If he has won, he has money to gamble with; if he has lost—for in this the psychology works both ways—he may be tempted to double his bet the next time around in the futile scramble to "get even." Either way, the faster the bookie gets the news from the track, the faster this news gets to the bettor, the greater the volume of the bookie's business is going to be and the greater his take from that ever-mounting "vigorish."

Important as this first motive is, the second is even more so. A bookie cannot afford to be caught asleep, and unfortunately, in his business, there are always a great number of connivers who are trying to do just that. Innumerable gimmicks have been figured out to get the results of races faster than the bookies can get them—and then to get a bet down on a race that has already been run and won before some unsuspecting bookie knows it's over. This tricky practice of "past-posting," is a menace to a hard-working book who has no desire to have the bread taken out of his mouth by a customer with a sure thing. It is vital, then, both from the standpoint of "action" and "past-posting," for bookies around the nation to get results from the track faster than anyone else can get them. This is a need that is most obligingly filled by a father-son combination, Albert and Joseph Tollin, who operate the Delaware Sports Service from offices in a roadhouse-type building at 601 Tathall Street, Wilmington, Del.

Just as Hirshfield provides "the line" from Minneapolis, the Tollins flash "the results" from Wilmington. They serve, by their own admission, some 4,000 to 8,000 bookies all over the United States, in Canada, Cuba and even Europe. They have an especially heavy clientele in the northeastern states, and New York probers identified a full fifty of their raided books as Tollin customers. Like Hirshfield, like the "layoff" operators in Biloxi and Covington, the Tollins have a passion for code names and "client" anonymity. The standard procedure is for customers to contact the Tollins by phone or Western Union and contract for their service. This initial contact establishes a code name like "Joe 13" by which the customer ever after will be known. The Tollins' fees range from $5 to $10 for a report on a single race and up to $50 for a full day's coverage

of the racing program.

Walsh, in the New York hearings, traced the development of the Tollin service. In the days before the Kefauver probe, the furnishing of race results was dominated by the Continental Wire Service, controlled by Al Capone's mob heirs in Chicago. At that time, the Tollins' Delaware Wire Service was a subscriber of Continental. When the Kefauver exposure drove Continental out of business, there was a scramble for the lush proceeds. Several competitors failed, but the Tollins survived. Every bit of information received by both Delaware and New York authorities indicates that this survival was probably aided by underworld muscle. "No one is letting Mr. Tollin carve up this lush melon which was Continental's plush list before," Walsh declared in his testimony before the New York commission. "Syndicate gambling controls this list just as it controls other things in professional gambling."

Walsh and Detective Walter J. Wassmer, of the Delaware Attorney General's Office, described the Tollins' technique. The basic operation involves getting an instantaneous flash on the winner from inside the track. For this, the Tollins rely on what is known as "the pitcher-catcher" system. The "pitcher" is an agent who is stationed inside the track, right on top of the finish line. The "catcher" is spotted outside, with an open telephone line into the Tollin office in Delaware, ready to "catch" and relay the word from the "pitcher."

This word may be flashed visually, if the "pitcher" and "catcher" are stationed so that they have a clear view of each other; if this isn't possible, modern devices like a walkie-talkie arrangement may be used. If the contact is visual, the "pitcher" will wigwag a previously agreed signal to designate the winning horse, or he may merely hold up a card containing the number of the winner. The instant the signal is received, the "catcher" calls the name of the horse into the ear of either Albert or Joseph Tollin, waiting on the other end of the phone line in Wilmington, and the entire Tollin system swings into lightning-fast action.

The Tollin headquarters occupy two floors of the Tathall Street house. On the main floor is the business office; on the second floor, in a box of a room ten feet by twelve, is the result-flashing center. Here are a switchboard and switchboard operator; in the center of the room, a table; and at the table, usually, Albert Tollin and a girl assistant. On the table are three curiously rigged wooden boxes. The boxes are plain wooden crates, about 1½ feet square, padded with foam rubber. They are placed facing Tollin. As race time nears and calls begin coming in, Tollin's girl assistant places just the mouthpieces of telephones in these padded boxes, where they will instantly catch Tollin's shouted announcement of the winner as his voice echoes off the foam-rubber sounding boards.

"About two or three minutes before a race is run, why there is quite a calamity," Detective Wassmer told the New York commission. "The telephones are jumping and jingling. Tollin himself would be holding a telephone in one hand, one in the other. His girl on the other side will be taking the telephone calls. The phones are just jingling."

When all the phone mouthpieces that can be accommodated have been placed in the sounding boxes, the switchboard girl puts a hold key on each of the other incoming calls. She draws the hold keys up in a line, a ruler in her hand, and waits. Tollin, on the open telephone line to his "catcher" outside the race track, gets the winner, shouts the name. Instantly, all the bookie calls dangling in the sound boxes are taken care of; instantly, the switchboard girl relays the winner's name to all those waiting on the first row of hold keys on her switchboard. With one sweep of her ruler, she flips off this line of keys, flips on a new batch. With incredible dispatch, the Tollins' frantic clientele receive their bread-and-butter information.

Telephone and Western Union records clearly establish the tremendous volume of the Tollin business. Walsh estimated that the Tollins' Delaware Sports Service must chalk up a profit of at least $500,000 a year. There is no secret about it. But neither is anything being done about it. As in Minnesota with the Hirshfield operation, the local law in Delaware professes itself helpless. The Tollins, like Hirshfield, are providing a service and are keeping carefully within the bounds of local legality. Their activity, as Walsh pointed out, would perhaps have been impossible had Kefauver been able to secure the passage of a law he recommended to ban the rapid interstate transmission of race results. But a Congress less concerned on the whole about syndicate crime than was its crusading Senator (and one has to

wonder why) turned a deaf ear to Kefauver's plea and let the nation's bookmaking business retain comfortable twilight zones of legality. Taking advantage of every loophole, the books have employed the decade since Kefauver to reap more billions than ever before. No one doubts that the list of Tollin customers, hiding there behind the false face of code numbers, would be the clear giveaway to virtually every major operator in the multi-billion-dollar bookmaking racket of the underworld—but nobody on any level of law enforcement is doing anything to pick up the clues, to follow the trail.

The quasi-institutionalization of deviant roles and the obstacles preventing some people from playing legitimate roles lead to the same consequence: a constant flow of recruits into illegitimate roles. This poses a problem of social control for industrial societies, which is coped with partly by punishing offenders and partly by attempting to induce them to adopt legitimate roles. Unfortunately, it appears that these two social responses work at cross-purposes. However necessary the punishment of deviants may be for sustaining the morale of conformists, most forms of punishment tend to reinforce commitment to the illegitimate role.

PRIMARY GROUP SUPPORT FOR THE DEVIANT ROLE

Why should the imposition of punishment complicate the task of rehabilitating the deviant? Punishment is the purposive imposition of unpleasant experiences like imprisonment on the deviant. But one consequence of imprisonment is to bring the offender into contact with other persons who are being similarly punished. (It is too costly to confine prisoners in strict isolation.) A society of captives is established with its own subculture and its own reward system.[7] In this society within a society, punishment is reinterpreted as injustice, thus

[7] Gresham M. Sykes and David Matza, "Techniques of Neutralization: A Theory of Delinquency," *American Sociological Review*, Vol. 22, December 1957, pp. 664–670.

stifling incipient guilt or shame. The sting of community rejection is neutralized by the acceptance of fellow inmates.[8] In other words, an unintended consequence of group punishment is to create solidarity among offenders, and this primary group support becomes an additional obstacle to the abandonment of the deviant role. Many a reformatory inmate is proud of his criminal record because this record gives him status in the delinquent subculture. He would be ashamed to be a "square" college boy. (He may not have felt this way before incarceration, but he has adopted the values of the "hipsters" whom he admires.) Primary groups have enormous influence over the individual, whether they are legitimate groups like the family or illegitimate groups like the delinquent gang. Of course, some illegitimate roles are stigmatized but not punished in a congregate fashion—for example, the alcoholic. Alcoholics do not ordinarily have the support of a primary group encouraging their continued drinking. From this point of view, the alcoholic is a less difficult problem of rehabilitation than the criminal.

TRAINED INCAPACITY FOR LEGITIMATE ROLES

Primary group support of deviance is not the only obstacle to rehabilitation. Playing an illegitimate role incapacitates the individual to some extent for playing legitimate roles. This principle is equally relevant to the alcoholic and the criminal. The alcoholic eventually becomes unemployable. When this happens, his unemployability adds to his original motivation for drinking and creates a further obstacle to rehabilitation. Similarly, it is an unusual gang delinquent who does well in school or has a steady job. That is to say, inadequacies in playing legitimate roles which preceded the adoption of the illegitimate role become accentuated. Part of the reason for this is that playing one role requires time and energy that is not available for learning and practicing an-

other. But there is another reason, too: the disapproval and suspicion of conformists. For example, it is a rare employer who is enthusiastic about hiring a parolee or an alcoholic.

RELEARNING LEGITIMATE ROLES

In the face of these obstacles to rehabilitation, how can *anyone* be induced to abandon an illegitimate role? One possibility is psychiatric help or other means of making the individual more adequate to cope with social stigma and his other problems. But some incumbents of illegitimate roles do not feel that they have problems. Many delinquent gang members are downright smug; they are not only contemptuous of "nut doctors" but of anyone who uses psychiatric services. Under these circumstances, the most successful force in favor of rehabilitation seems to be the coercive force of primary groups. For instance, an important factor making for the reintegration of delinquent gang members into the legitimate community is that they get interested in conventional girlfriends—and eventually marry them. These girls constantly propagandize against the boys' delinquent associates. "Stop hanging with those bums. They'll only get you into trouble. Stay home with me." Sometimes the marriage breaks up. More often, the gang breaks up as boy after boy gets absorbed in the problems of marriage and children.

Effective though *some* girls may be at inducing *some* boys to abandon the delinquent role, society is not content to rely on the vagaries of romance for delinquency control. Systematic programs exist, and some of these attempt to *contrive* peer groups and to mobilize their coercive force in favor of rehabilitation. The following account describes the Pinehills program conducted in Provo, Utah, with juvenile court probationers.

---

8   Lloyd E. Ohlin and William C. Lawrence, "Social Interaction among Clients as a Treatment Problem," *Social Work*, Vol. 4, April 1959, pp. 3–13.

Primary Group Support to Abandon the Delinquent Role

Reprinted by permission. From Lamar T. Empey and Jerome Rabow, "The Provo Experiment in Delinquency Rehabilitation," *American Sociological Review*, Vol. 26, October 1961, pp. 679–695.

Attempts to involve a boy with the peer group begin the moment he arrives. Instead of meeting with and receiving an orientation lecture from authorities, he receives no formal instructions. He is always full of such questions as, "What do I have to do to get out of this place?" or "How long do I have to stay?", but such questions as these are never answered. They are turned aside with, "I don't know," or "Why don't you find out?" Adults will not orient him in the ways that he has grown to expect, nor will they answer any of his questions. He is forced to turn to his peers. Usually, he knows someone in the program, either personally or by reputation. As he begins to associate with other boys he discovers that important informal norms do exist, the most important of which makes *inconsistency* rather than *consistency* the rule. That which is appropriate for one situation, boy, or group may not be appropriate for another. Each merits a decision as it arises.

Other norms center most heavily about the daily group discussion sessions. These sessions are patterned after the technique of "Guided Group Interaction" which was developed at Fort Knox during World War II and at Highfields. Guided Group Interaction emphasizes the idea that only through a group and its processes can a boy work out his problems. From a peer point of view it has three main goals: (1) to question the utility of a life devoted to delinquency; (2) to suggest alternative ways for behavior; and (3) to provide recognition for a boy's personal reformation and his willingness to reform others.

Guided Group Interaction grants to the peer group a great deal of power, including that of helping to decide when each boy is ready to be released. This involves "retroflexive reformation." If a delinquent is serious in his attempts to reform others he must automatically accept the common purpose of the reformation process, identify himself closely with others engaged in it, and grant prestige to those who succeed in it. In so doing, he becomes a genuine member of the reformation group and in the process may be alienated from his previous pro-delinquent groups. Such is an ideal and long term goal. Before it can be realized for any individual he must become heavily involved with the treatment system. Such involvement does not come easy and the system must include techniques which will impel him to involvement. Efforts to avoid the development of formal structure have already been described as one technique. Group processes constitute a second technique.

Before a group will help a boy "solve his problems" it demands that he review his total delinquent history. This produces anxiety because, while he is still relatively free, it is almost inevitable that he has much more to reveal than is already known by the police or the court. In an effort to avoid such involvement he may try subterfuge. But any reluctance on his part to be honest will not be taken lightly. Norms dictate that no one in the group can be released until everyone is honest and until every boy helps to solve problems. A refusal to come clean shows a lack of trust in the group and slows down the problem-solving process. Therefore, any recalcitrant boy is faced with a real dilemma. He can either choose involvement or relentless attack by his peers. Once a boy does involve himself, however, he learns that some of his fears were unwarranted. What goes on in the group meeting is sacred and is not revealed elsewhere.

A second process for involvement lies in the use of the peer group to perpetuate the norms of the treatment system. One of the most important norms suggests that most boys in the program are candidates for a reformatory. This is shocking because even habitual delinquents do not ordinarily see themselves as serious offenders. Yet, the tradition is clear; most failures at Pinehills are sent to the Utah State Industrial School. Therefore, each boy has a major decision to make: either he makes serious attempts to change or he gets sent away.

The third process of involvement could only occur in a community program. Each boy has the tremendous problem of choosing between the demands of his delinquent peers outside the program and the demands of those within it. The usual reaction is to test the situation by continuing to identify with the former. Efforts to do this, however, and to keep out of serious trouble are usually unsuccessful. The group is a collective board on delinquency; it usually includes a member who knows the individual personally or by reputation; and it can rely on the meeting to discover many things. Thus, the group is able to use actual behavior in the community to judge the extent to which a boy is involved with the program and to judge his readiness for release. The crucial criterion for any treatment program is not what an individual does while in it, but what he does while he is *not* in it.

The fourth process involves a number of important sanctions which the group can impose if a boy refuses to become involved. It can employ familiar techniques such as ostracism or derision or it can deny him the status and recognition which come with change. Furthermore, it can use sanctions arising out of the treatment system. For example, while authorities may impose restrictions on boys in the form of extra work or incarceration in jail, the group is often permitted, and encouraged, to explore reasons for the action and to help decide what future actions should be taken. For example, a boy may be placed in jail over the week-end and told that he will be returned there each week-end thereafter until his group decides to release him. It is not uncommon for the group, after thorough discussion, to return him one or more week-ends despite his protestations. Such an occurrence would be less likely in an ordinary reformatory because of the need for inmates to maintain solidarity against the official system. However, in this setting it is possible because boys are granted the power to make important decisions affecting their entire lives. Rather than having other people do things to them, they are doing things to themselves.

The ultimate sanction possessed by the group is refusal to release a boy from the program. Such a sanction has great power because it is normative to expect that no individual will be tolerated in the program indefinitely. Pinehills is not a place where boys "do time."

When the deviant role receives *encouragement and support* from a primary group, the organization of a countering primary group pressing for *abandonment* of the deviant role is an effective rehabilitative strategy. However, even when the deviant role is *not* supported by a primary group, as with alcoholism, it appears that primary group support can increase the likelihood that the individual will rejoin the legitimate community. The following analysis of Alcoholics Anonymous indicates that the vitality of this organization stems from its ability to make the struggle for sobriety a collective effort.

Primary Group Support in the Overcoming of Alcoholism

Reprinted by permission. From H. Jack Geiger, "Anonymous Struggle for Twenty-five Years," New York *Times Magazine*, June 5, 1960, pp. 26, 74–76.

On the evening of June 10, 1935, a New York stockbroker visited a surgeon in a suburb of Akron, Ohio. Both men were confirmed and "hopeless" drunks. In despair and loneliness, they almost inadvertently made a major medical and social discovery. This month, nearly a quarter of a million people in sixty nations—their lives deeply touched by that event—will mark its twenty-fifth anniversary.

The stockbroker and the surgeon began to realize, that evening, that they could stay sober, and be helped, by helping other alcoholics to stay sober. In the past quarter-century, their realization has been repeated a hundred thousand times over, in strikingly varied settings and involving the whole roster of human types. For from it grew Alcoholics Anonymous, the remarkable fellowship of compulsive drinkers who don't drink.

There is great natural drama in the story of A.A. But now perhaps the drama is less important than the attempt to read its meaning. Beyond the questions—what is A.A., does it work, how often, how well, for whom?—there is an important issue: what has it taught us about alcoholism?

A.A. is not, as some suspect, a herky-jerk parade of stumble-bums shambling up the road from skid row to salvation; it lacks the psalm-singing self-righteousness of the usual crusade. Neither is it a "scientific" or medical organization. Nor is it finally, "the answer" to alcoholism.

But it is—and this is the crucial fact—the top of an iceberg, one of the few visible aspects of a major national health problem. To understand A.A. it is necessary to know something about the underlying structure of alcoholism—the parts of the iceberg that we usually keep below the surface of national awareness and concern.

It is a big iceberg. A recent estimate (and it is probably a serious underestimate) counts more than 4,700,000 alcoholics in the United States —one man in every fifteen over the age of 20, six men for every woman. Only about 8 per cent are on skid row, and only about 750,000 have obvious signs of illness. There are one to two million problem drinkers in industry, hundreds of thousands in the wards of mental hospitals. Five to six million wives, husbands, parents and children are living in the same household with alcoholism and are the victims of its erratic behavior.

The count could be more accurate if researchers had any exact idea of what they were counting.

Alcoholism is not simply synonymous with drinking, heavy drinking or drunkenness, and no one is certain whether it is a symptom, a disease in its own right, or several diseases. Most of the rule-of-thumb definitions (the man who drinks alone, the man who drinks the first thing in the morning, the man who has "lost his will power") are either wrong or inadequate. Most of the scientific classifications (one researcher recently counted thirty-four) are not much better.

One theme, however, keeps recurring. The alcoholic is a man who is either unable to abstain from liquor or unable to stop once he has started; the first drink "pulls a trigger" and his controls disintegrate.

Within this broad definition, some researchers feel, there are at least two distinct types: "addictive" drinkers, driven usually by internal stresses, who seek the biggest, quickest alcoholic jolt they can find, and "habitual excessive symptomatic" drinkers, men in search of a gentle, anxiety-obliterating alcoholic plateau with the longest—not the quickest or most intense—effect. . . .

Alcoholics Anonymous agrees that the alcoholic is forever "one drink away from a drunk" —but there the theorizing stops. In the belief that alcoholism comes in people, not bottles, it takes no stand on prohibition, temperance or liquor laws.

A.A. is a vast network of local organizations, but it has almost no organizational structure. Its growth has been meteoric, but it has never asked anyone to join. Its one goal is sobriety, yet no member ever "takes a pledge." Its tone and

orientation are religious, but its membership includes several thousand agnostics who happily rub shoulders with Protestants, Jews, Catholics and Mormons.

Though it keeps no records, conducts no research and is, if anything, faintly hostile to too much probing ("We're just a bunch of ex-drunks," says one member, "and we don't care how or why it works, so long as it does"), A.A. has been at least indirectly responsible for major strides in the scientific understanding of alcoholism. . . .

What are the methods? The interested visitor can find out, on almost any night in any American city. A typical meeting begins with from thirty to 100 men and women gossiping on rows of wooden chairs in a church meetinghouse or a rented hall. There is a busy traffic to and from a stand with coffee, soft drinks and doughnuts.

In one corner, someone is idly playing a piano. The air is heavy with cigarette smoke, and the talk is loud and cheerful. On the wall are a few signs with messages like "Easy does it" and "First things first." One bears the A.A. motto: "God grant us the serenity to accept the things we cannot change, courage to change the things we can, and wisdom to know the difference."

The visitor who plays guessing games about those present soon discovers he is wasting his time: the seedy-looking young man in the front row is a casual guest who has never been drunk in his life; the white-haired, grandmotherly lady next to him has a record of twenty arrests and six hospitalizations.

Here and there, however, he may be able to spot a newcomer—someone drawn and tense and perhaps tremulous—and he may note that each one is sticking close to a "sponsor," an established A.A. member who is giving him special attention, introducing him to friends, pouring his coffee.

Finally, the chairman calls for order. "My name is Joe and I'm an alcoholic," he begins. He announces that this is the regular weekly "open" meeting of the group (there is a "closed" meeting, for alcoholics only, later in the week). He calls for a moment of silence "to be used as each person sees fit." He announces plans for a dance, a bowling contest, and a party to be sponsored by the local "Alanon"—an auxiliary group in which relatives of A.A. members meet to talk over some of the problems of having an alcoholic in the family.

Then he introduces the first of three speakers from a neighboring A.A. group who have come to "tell their stories." The first speaker begins with the standard line: "My name is _____, and I'm an alcoholic." ("If he can make it anyone can," someone whispers gleefully. "He was the worst wetbrain in history.")

What follows is, perhaps, the last thing the visitor expects: it is at once tragic and uproariously funny, and the hall rocks again and again with laughter.

A steelworker describes his weekly, wobbly odyssey from home to jail to hospital to home again—where his despairing wife, he adds, always covered him with the help-wanted pages from the newspaper while he slept it off.

A business executive recounts his early career as a bootlegger's assistant, hauling home-made gin in a baby carriage until "some drunk stole the wheels." Later, a confirmed alcoholic, his job and family gone, he decided to drink himself to death—only to discover, painfully, that "you don't die that easy."

A suburban housewife wryly displays the sole trophy of her drinking days, a citation as a faithful Cub Scout den mother. "The kids must have had a great time, with me drunk at every meeting," she says, but adds quietly, "except for two of them—my kids."

The laughter that comes is the laughter of recognition. The alcoholic newcomer discovers that the troubles, horrors and tragedies he thought were unique have, in fact, been shared by most of the people in the hall—people who now are not only sober but (to his even greater astonishment) happy.

A number of themes run through the talks. "Easy does it" turns out to be a warning against the grandiose ambitions and unrealistic drives that afflict alcoholics. "First things first" is a reminder of the need for priorities in the long job of rehabilitation.

Another slogan, "Live and let live," is shorthand for the observation that resentment and self-pity push the drinker back toward the bottle. The "24-hour plan" expresses the knowledge that the alcoholic's only hope at present is total abstinence—and that it is easier to quit one day at a time than to face a lifetime without alcohol's solace.

In all the talks there are references to the "Twelve Steps," which are the core of A.A. belief.

Here, the compulsive drinker admits that he has become powerless over alcohol, that his life has become unmanageable. He decides that his fate is in the hands of a "Power greater than" himself, and turns his life over to "the care of God as I understand Him."

He undertakes a searching self-inventory, admits his wrongs, tries to make amends, prays for removal of his shortcomings. Finally—the all-important Twelfth Step—he tries to carry the message of this "spiritual experience" to other alcoholics if and when they seek help.

This is, in essence, what began in Akron in 1935, spread slowly to New York, then to Cleveland and Chicago. In 1938 there were sixty members; by 1940, one man recalls, "there were two's and three's and five's of us in half a dozen cities."

Today, after a period of explosive growth beginning in 1941, there are more than 7,000 groups. Each is autonomous and self-supporting (by voluntary and unrecorded contributions, not dues) and has no permanent chairman or officers.

The individual groups support an over-all "General Service Board"—seven alcoholics, eight nonalcoholics—in New York, and this, together with an annual convention of elected delegates and a national newspaper wryly called "The Grapevine," is all that holds the loose federation together.

A.A. works, its students believe, by overcoming the drinker's biggest barrier—the lack of real, vital emotional contact with any single human or group, the feeling that nobody really understands or cares. In A.A. he finds people essentially like himself, who cannot reject him and whom he finds hard to reject or deceive. The concept of alcoholism as an illness eases his guilt; his identification with a group dilutes it. Gradually, the group itself provides a satisfying alternative to drinking.

How well does it work? A.A. usually claims that of those who really try, 50 per cent sober up at once and stay that way, another 25 per cent remain sober after a few relapses. Unfortunately, the best evidence suggests that these figures are probably wrong. A few careful studies by outside observers report much lower figures, in the 30-to-40 per cent range.

The most important source of error, of course, is the statistical catch in "of those who really try." This means, in effect, counting only those alcoholics who find the program attractive enough to join, and dismissing the failures as persons who don't count.

Clearly, the alcoholics who join A.A. are a self-selected group and may not be representative of all alcoholics. A recent study by Cornell University's Dr. Harrison Trice—one of eight non-alcoholic members of A.A.'s General Service Board—found striking differences in personality and past experience between A.A. members and uncontrolled alcoholics who had come to meetings but failed to join.

But results like these may represent a major step forward, for they suggest that there is no single type of "alcoholic" and no single "cure." The important question then becomes, not "What works?" but "What works best—for whom?"

Twenty-five years ago, when A.A. began, alcoholism made physicians uneasy, frustrated psychiatrists, hardened social workers, wearied judges and jailers, inflamed "wets" and "drys" and, all too frequently, killed the alcoholic.

It still does—but the picture is changing. Tranquilizing drugs can be used to help control alcoholic cravings and ease the pangs of withdrawal—and they give the physician, at last, the knowledge that there is something he can really do for such patients.

Psychiatrists, in recent years, have soft-pedaled their emphasis on alcoholism as a mere symptom of some deeper emotional disorder and focused on the drinking itself. Perhaps more important, they are beginning to abandon the widely held feeling that alcoholism is an incurable personality defect and are trying new, less orthodox therapies.

"The psychiatrist and his techniques have to be less rigid," notes Dr. Morris Chafetz of Massachusetts General Hospital's alcoholism clinic in Boston, "and he has to be a pioneer in his approach to each case. . . .

"The passive, non-directive therapist of alcoholics who follows his usual therapeutic approach usually has no patients to treat after a while."

At this and other clinics, psychiatrists now work in teams with social workers and psychologists. Wherever possible, if the patient has a family, an attempt is made to bring his wife into treatment, too, in individual or group counseling sessions. Almost invariably, such efforts increase the success rate to 30 per cent or better.

In the past decade, finally, a therapy has begun to appear for the skid-row drinkers, the derelicts, the homeless men of the bottle gang who rotate between rented rooms and jail. Observers noted that these men did well while they were jailed—and protected—but always drank when they were tossed out, jobless and unskilled in the simplest tasks of living.

A dozen states now have "half-way houses," small residential units which offer food and shelter, group identification, support from physicians and social workers, and a firm but gentle push toward employment and self-sufficiency. The improvement rate—and these are the "hopeless" men—is better than 30 per cent.

For all these advances, including many in which it has had no direct part, A.A. can claim some real credit—they may, in fact, represent its greatest contribution. Raymond G. McCarthy of Yale's Center for Alcohol Studies, explains:

"The real effect of A.A. extended far beyond its members. A.A. changed the social climate, dramatized alcoholism as an illness, substituted 'alcoholic' for 'drunkard' in public thinking, and demonstrated that something could be done."

. . . A.A.'s 200,000 members are still, statistically, only a drop in the alcoholic bucket. And, as is the case with all other workers in the field of alcoholism, they clearly have a long way yet to go.

But already they have added a strangely social prescription to medicine's stock of remedies. The idea is, after all, very old. "I am my brother's keeper," says one member, "and he is mine, and that's the heart of it."

The method of Alcoholics Anonymous is spreading beyond the problem of alcoholism. Narcotics Anonymous, Youth Anonymous, and Divorcees Anonymous pattern their therapeutic programs after the more famous A.A. Not all illegitimate roles, however, are as amenable to group-facilitated reintegration as alcoholism seems to be. In the case of stuttering, the major therapy is individual; no self-help organization of stutterers has developed. Nevertheless, the social factor cannot be ignored. Just as A.A. tells the alcoholic that he will always be an alcoholic, so the speech therapist tells the stutterer that he will always stutter. This is not the counsel of despair. On the contrary, A.A. has learned from bitter experience with alcoholics that the hope of a miraculous cure turns the slightest slip into a disaster. Similarly, speech therapists have learned that the way to *reduce* stuttering is to enable the stutterer to stutter without feeling that he is a failure. Therefore, he is not promised a cure. Quite the contrary: part of the early therapy is to practice *increased* stuttering, perhaps in a group situation. The paradoxical fact is that the more the stutterer *wants* to stutter, the less able he is to do so. When he reaches the point where he can accept his stuttering without anxiety, he stutters very little. What has this to do with group support? Just this: the stutterer is anxious about his nonfluency because he listens to his own speech from the viewpoint of a condemning group. What therapy does for him is to transform his conception of the group into a more tolerant one.

CONCLUSION

Nonconforming *acts* violate the social rules, but the problem of societal control is more serious when such acts are not occasional lapses from an essentially conformist style of life but are organized into illegitimate *roles*. A deviant role is not mere nonconformity. It is nonconformity supported by the individual's self-conception and by the attitudes or behavior of others. Thus, the usual internal controls of shame and guilt do not operate.

Why should nonconformity sometimes eventuate in illegitimate roles and sometimes not? For two reasons: (1) Some individuals develop feelings of inadequacy during socialization which impair their capacity to play one or more legitimate roles. (2) Illegitimate roles enjoy overt or covert support from outwardly conforming members of society; they are quasi-institutionalized. These two circumstances mutually reinforce one another in industrial societies. Individuals who feel, rightly or wrongly, that they cannot play legitimate roles are attracted to illegitimate roles when they perceive that the disapproval of these roles is far from unanimous.

How can the incumbents of illegitimate roles be induced to abandon them? One possible strategy is to destroy the social support which the illegitimate role enjoys. The difficulties that this strategy must face are great. Gambling, for example, is deeply rooted in American society. Whether it is possible to reorganize American social structure sufficiently so that bookies have no place in it is an intriguing question. Another strategy is to give the present incumbents of *illegitimate* roles hope that they can succeed in playing *legitimate* roles. Peer-group support, natural or contrived, helps to give the individual the self-confidence to attempt this transformation. Even with peer-group support, however, reintegration into legitimate society is difficult. It is impeded not only by the objective disabilities of the individual for playing legitimate roles and by his lack of self-confidence. It is also impeded by the understandably suspicious—and sometimes hostile—attitudes of conventional society.

SOME SIGNIFICANT LITERATURE ON ILLEGITIMATE ROLES

Howard S. Becker, *Outsiders: Studies in the Sociology of Deviance*, New York: Free Press of Glencoe, 1963, Chaps. 3 and 4. Professor Becker reports the insight he gained from interviews with marihuana users, namely, that deviant behavior often produces deviant motivation instead of the more plausible sequence of deviant motivation followed by deviant behavior. When the marihuana user first tries smoking marihuana, he does not enjoy the experience; he must learn how to obtain certain effects and how to enjoy them. He must also come to redefine popular stereotypes of the conse-quences of marihuana use as uninformed and replace ". . . those conceptions with the 'inside' view he has acquired through his experience with the drug in the company of other users."

Richard A. Cloward and Lloyd E. Ohlin, *Delinquency and Opportunity: A Theory of Delinquent Gangs*, Glencoe, Ill.: Free Press, 1960. The underlying maladjustment of recruits to criminal, fighting, or drug-using gangs is an inability to find legitimate means to realize their aspirations for money and the things money will buy. They are resentful because the equalitarian ideology of American society seems to promise them a fair share of the good things of life, and they realize that ethnic and class barriers will prevent them from attaining these goals. The feeling of unjust deprivation underlies alienation, "a process of withdrawal of attributions of legitimacy from established social norms." When youngsters become disenchanted with legitimate society, they seek support from others who are similarly alienated, and they evolve a collective solution to their common problem. Not only do they join in delinquent *acts,* they also develop in concert "a supporting structure of beliefs and values that provide advance justification for deviant conduct." If these groups of alienated adolescent boys live in a slum community containing opportunities to learn and practice criminal skills under the guidance of older thieves, their gang crystallizes around stealing. If they live in a disorganized neighborhood where neither legitimate nor illegitimate opportunities for financial gain are plentiful, their gang crystallizes around "bopping" (fighting for neighborhood hegemony). If the criminal or fighting opportunities disappear—or were never available in the first place—the focus of gang activity becomes drug use or heavy drinking. In short, the type of delinquent gang that forms depends on the availability of legitimate and illegitimate opportunities in the neighborhood. Society can prevent the formation of delinquent gangs only if it can provide sufficient *legitimate* opportunities to choke off the stream of alienated youth who seek gang membership as a solution to the strain of unjust deprivation.

Erving Goffman, "On the Characteristics of Total Institutions," in Donald R. Cressey, Ed., *The Prison: Studies in Institutional Organization and Change,* New York: Holt, Rinehart, and Winston, 1961, pp. 15–106. Although institutional differentiation is characteristic of urban industrial societies—people usually work, play, and sleep in different places—some organizations existing within modern societies concentrate these activities in common locations: prisons, homes for the aged, mental hospitals, military bases, and monasteries. Professor Goffman calls such organizations "total institutions" and describes the systematic invasion of privacy that becomes possible when all spheres of the individual's life are subject to the same authority. In the course of his discussion, he comments perceptively on the mortification of newcomers, the personal reorganization that occurs within the privilege system of the total institution, staff-inmate relations, the inmate culture, and the individual's loss of, or failure to acquire, some of the habits currently in use in the larger society.

Maxwell Jones, *The Therapeutic Community: A New Treatment Method in Psychiatry,* New York: Basic Books, 1953. In April 1947 an Industrial Neurosis Unit opened at Belmont Hospital in England to deal with unemployable neurotics. Dr. Jones and his colleagues assumed that traditional mental hospitals generated a cultural climate which interfered with therapy; hence, they attempted to create a therapeutically favorable culture by breaking down the usual cleavages between staff and patients. They established small discussion groups that included doctors and nurses as well as patients and abolished one-to-one contacts of doctors and patients in offices. These daily discussion groups talked about current events, the psychiatric problems of the patients that incapacitated them for a normal job, and patient behavior in the hospital. Patients stayed in the hospital no more than six months and, on discharge, obtained jobs with the help of a rehabilitation officer trained in job placement. (There was substantially full employment in Great Britain at the time, and this made the placement task easier.) Of the 103 patients whose job performance was followed for six months, 44 per cent made a satisfactory work adjustment. This result sounds impressive in view of the chronic nature of the presenting problems—even in the absence of a comparison group of untreated unemployables. This summary is based on a review by H. Warren Dunham, *American Sociological Review,* Vol. 19, June 1954, pp. 359–360.

Albert J. Reiss, Jr., "The Social Integration of Queers and Peers," *Social Problems,* Vol. 9, Fall 1961, pp. 102–120. In the course of his study of delinquency in Nashville, Professor Reiss gathered sex histories from 187 white boys between 12 and 17. He reports that substantial numbers of lower-class delinquents earn money by participating in homosexual acts with passive homosexual adults. Peer norms condone such activity as long as it is engaged in unemotionally as a form of money raising and not undertaken for pleasure. The boys do not consider themselves either prostitutes or homosexuals, and they give up this "racket" when they grow older and get legitimate jobs. If the adult homosexual violates the expectation of the boys as to acceptable limits of the relationship, he may be beaten up and robbed. All of the information in this article about the integration of "two types of deviators into an institutionalized form of prostitution" comes from the boy prostitutes. For a direct study of the homosexual way of life in a large city, see Maurice Leznoff and William A. Westley, "The Homosexual Community," *Social Problems,* Vol. 4, April 1956, pp. 257–263.

Harold Sampson, Sheldon Messinger, Robert D. Towne, et al. "The Mental Hospital and Marital Family Ties," *Social Problems,* Vol. 9, Fall 1961, pp. 141–155. A strategic consideration for those who operate mental hospitals is ". . . to help preserve and reinforce those ties which link the deviant to the world beyond the walls." This article reports factors conducive to the maintenance of such ties among white, married women whose schizophrenic breakdown occurred in the course of prolonged marital conflict: "First, hospitalization tended to *interrupt* the divisive processes at work in the marital family, narrowing opportunities for conflict and delaying permanent withdrawal by or exclusion of an errant member." Second, hospitalization helped to define the bizarre behavior of the wife as involuntary and thus helped to prepare for the gradual resumption of marital relationships. Finally, absence often made the hearts of both husband and wife grow fonder, partly because each learned the disadvantages of life without the other, partly because the requirements that the hospital placed on the responsible party (the husband) tied him more closely to his wife.

James F. Short, Jr., Ray A. Tennyson, and Kenneth I. Howard, "Behavior Dimensions of Gang Delinquency," *American Sociological Review*, Vol. 28, June 1963, pp. 411–428. The activities, both delinquent and nondelinquent, of 598 members of 16 Chicago gangs were check rated by detached workers who had been in contact with them for at least six months. Sixty-nine activities were rated including basketball, skating, arson, carrying concealed weapons, rape, and attempted suicide. The gangs ranged in size from 16 to 68 members; 11 gangs were Negro and five white. Statistical analysis of the ratings show considerable overlap of delinquent behavior among all the gangs rather than stealing in one type of gang, violence in another, and alcohol or drug use in a third. The authors suggest that an undifferentiated "parent delinquent subculture" may exist out of which more specialized delinquent groups emerge.

Rita Volkman and Donald R. Cressey, "Differential Association and the Rehabilitation of Drug Addicts," *American Journal of Sociology*, Vol. 69, September 1963, pp. 129–142. Synanon is a self-help organization of former drug addicts with a culture that is strongly opposed to drug use. The authors analyze the five rehabilitative principles implicitly embodied in the Synanon program to account for its success with confirmed heroin addicts: (1) Admissions to the program are restricted to addicts who demonstrate by personal sacrifices a willingness to accept the guidance of the group. (2) Indoctrination makes clear that the central purpose of Synanon is not recreation or vocational therapy but keeping addicts away from drugs. (3) Partly as a result of members living and working together voluntarily, the group achieves great cohesiveness and *esprit de corps*. (4) Synanon House "has an explicit program for distributing status symbols to members in return for staying off the drug and, later, for actually displaying antidrug attitudes." Further-

more, status in the outside community is also gained as the individual develops a deeper commitment to the organization. (5) The group sessions (synanons) at which each member of the group is encouraged to evaluate the progress of his fellows provides members an opportunity to be "moral policemen." The identification with the legitimate community implicit in the role of critical evaluator helps members to change.

Stanton Wheeler, "Socialization in Correctional Communities," *American Sociological Review*, Vol. 26, October 1961, pp. 697–712. Criminologists have been interested for a long time in an unintended consequence of imprisonment: deepening the commitment of inmates to criminal values. ("Prisonization" is the term Donald Clemmer coined to identify the process of assimilating the innate culture.) It has been assumed that the longer an inmate remains in prison, the more "prisonized" he becomes. The research reported in this article—based on data from a reformatory in the state of Washington—shows that it is not only how long the inmate stays in prison but also how long he *expects* to stay in prison that affects his choice between inmate and conventional values. ". . . [I]nmates who recently have been in the broader community and inmates who are soon to return to that community are more frequently oriented in terms of conventional values. Inmates conform least to conventional standards during the middle phase of their institutional career." One implication of this research is that shorter sentences would redirect the interests of inmates in prisons and reformatories toward legitimate society.

Lewis Yablonsky, *The Violent Gang*, New York: Macmillan, 1962. Professor Yablonsky presents a detailed case study of a fighting gang in New York City (including excerpts from tape-recorded interviews) which fails to fit the conception of the fighting gang as a tightly integrated group of a hundred boys or more. He argues that most fighting gangs are loose aggregates of youths around a handful of dedicated warriors. On occasion the phantom membership can be mobilized, but a gang fight bears more resemblance to a riot than to the disciplined maneuvers of a modern army. Yablonsky has been criticized strongly by sociological reviewers for failing to link his research to theories of collective behavior, which seek to explain riots, lynchings, and other forms of spontaneous crowd phenomena. See the review by Solomon Kobrin, *American Sociological Review*, Vol. 28, April 1963, pp. 316–317, and the article by Harold W. Pfautz, "Near-group Theory and Collective Behavior: A Critical Reformulation," *Social Problems*, Vol. 9, Fall 1961, pp. 167–174.

CHAPTER 11

Continuing Socialization

Sociologists assume that socialization continues throughout life. As long as the individual lives, he joins new groups and assumes new roles in groups to which he already belongs. These changes require him to learn new ways of relating to other people. The conception of *continuing socialization* is a shorthand way of referring to that necessity.

COMPARISONS BETWEEN INITIAL AND LATER SOCIALIZATION

Sociologists call attention to the similarity between early and later socialization by including them both within the single concept of "socialization." But infant socialization and adult socialization are not *identical* learning experiences. Infant socialization is the first contact with society. In a sense, all later socialization experiences are an anticlimax. Initial socialization is unique in two respects: (1) The infant does not understand language, and therefore he cannot (initially) communicate with the socializing agent. (2) The infant is not (initially) concerned about his mother's reactions to him; he is not even aware that she is reacting.

Subsequent socialization contrasts with infant socialization in both respects. The learn-

ing of language in early childhood means that later socialization experiences will involve symbolic communication between the socializing agent and the individual undergoing socialization. Second, the relationship between mother and child is transferred to all human beings—to some extent. The child's experience with his mother has made it impossible for him to adopt as an adult the devil-may-care attitude of the infant toward other people. In the course of worrying about *her* reactions, the child learned to care about the reactions of practically everybody. Of course, we do not care *as much* about the reactions of strangers as about the reactions of emotionally important people like parents. But early socialization has made us "other-directed," as David Riesman termed it; socialized persons cannot help being sensitive even to the reactions of strangers. Before his mother got to work on him, the infant was no more sensitive to people than to trees or stones.[1]

The sociological literature contains endless demonstrations of the sensitivity of socialized adults to responses from others. Morale studies in military organizations show that *esprit de corps* is primarily a function of a soldier's friend-

[1] David Riesman et al., *The Lonely Crowd*, New Haven, Conn.: Yale University Press, 1950.

334

ship with and loyalty to his "buddies." [2] Studies of voting behavior show that relatives and friends are a more powerful influence than the mass media.[3] Studies of fund raising show that *personal* appeals are more successful than written solicitations or radio and television appeals.[4] The following excerpt from an article about survey research illustrates continuing sensitivity to interpersonal influence.

An Illustration of Sensitivity to Social Pressure

Reprinted by permission. From Rensis Likert, "The Sample Interview as a Tool of Research and Policy Formation," in Daniel Lerner and Harold Lasswell, *The Policy Sciences*, Stanford, Calif.: Stanford University Press, 1951, pp. 239–246.

In 1943 immediately after the Second War Bond Drive, a national sample of about eighteen hundred persons was interviewed to learn why people did or did not buy bonds during the drive and what should be done to increase the effectiveness of the Third War Bond Drive. When respondents were asked why they bought war bonds, most of them gave a patriotic reason in answer, as, for example, that the government needed the money to buy war equipment. Other answers given often were that bonds were a good investment or that money was being set aside for education, retirement, or post-war purchases. Only a small proportion answered that they bought bonds because they were asked to buy or because of social pressure.

In designing the study of the Second War Bond Drive, however, it was felt that personal solicitation might be an important variable affecting bond buying. Consequently, at one point in the interview each respondent was specifically

2 Edward A. Shils and Morris Janowitz, "Cohesion and Disintegration in the Wehrmacht in World War II," *Public Opinion Quarterly*, Vol. 12, Summer 1948, pp. 280–315.
3 Paul F. Lazarsfeld, Bernard Berelson, and Hazel Gaudet, *The People's Choice*, New York: Duell, Sloane & Pearce, 1944; Elihu Katz and Paul F. Lazarsfeld, *Personal Influence*, Glencoe, Ill.: Free Press, 1955.
4 Aileen D. Ross, "The Social Control of Philanthropy," *American Journal of Sociology*, Vol. 48, March 1953, pp. 451–460.

asked whether during the drive he had been asked personally to buy war bonds. At another point in the interview the respondent was asked whether he had bought more bonds than usual during the drive period and how many more.

Of all gainfully employed people 25 percent reported that they had been asked personally to buy war bonds. When these people were grouped together, it was found that 47 percent of them bought more bonds during the Second War Bond Drive than they had been buying. Among the three-fourths of gainfully employed persons who had not been asked to buy, however, only 12 percent bought more bonds than usual.

This relationship between bond buying and solicitation held for every income group, every occupational group, and every geographical region. No matter how the data were grouped, it was found that among those who were asked personally to buy there were about 35 percent more buyers than among those who were not approached in person. Of all the different factors influencing bond-buying behavior, personal solicitation appeared to be one of the most important.

The results from the study of the Second War Bond Drive on the effectiveness of solicitation were called to the attention of T. R. Gamble, Director of the War Finance Division, with the strong recommendation that a major effort be made to increase the amount of personal solicitation in the Third War Bond Drive. The War Finance Division made this an important objective. They presented the research results in regional meetings and published a report making the findings available to state, county, and local war bond committees. In the survey following the Third War Bond Drive, it was found that personal solicitation in the third drive had been doubled: Fifty percent of all gainfully employed persons were solicited. It was expected that the net effectiveness of solicitation would decrease somewhat as a larger proportion of the population was solicited. Actually that did not occur: 59 percent of those who were personally solicited bought more bonds than usual. Among those who were not personally asked to buy, only 17 percent bought additional bonds.

The real test of the effectiveness of solicitation, however, was the relation that was found between the amount of solicitation and the number of bonds sold. The doubling of personal solicitation in the third drive over the second resulted in almost doubling the amount of Series E bonds that were sold. In the second drive one and one-half billion dollars of Series E bonds were sold; two and one-half billion dollars were sold in the third. Throughout all the bond drives, there was a close relationship between the amount of solicitation and the total amount of bonds sold to individuals.

Other indications that the relation between solicitation and buying was not spurious were also found. When the organization and activities of counties and smaller geographical units were examined, a marked relationship was found between the amount of personal solicitation and the success of the unit in selling bonds.

The Treasury Department had feared that soliciting people more than once in a particular drive would result in decreased buying because of resentment upon the part of those who were asked more than once to buy. Before studies were started, the Department had changed the structure of the bond-selling organization in order to minimize the likelihood of multiple solicitation. Actually, the research findings showed that when people were asked once to buy, about 60 percent bought; when asked twice, about 70 percent bought; when asked three or more times, about 80 percent bought. Moreover, no evidence was found of resentment over being asked more than once to buy.

As might be expected from theory, solicitation was more effective at the place of work than at home. Of those who were asked at work to buy, about 65 percent bought additional bonds. Of those who were asked at home to buy, 55 percent bought. These figures varied slightly from drive to drive, but the relation was always the same.

It was also found that men were more effective as solicitors than women. More of the persons asked by men bought additional bonds than of those asked by women, the difference being about 15 percent.

Solicitors asking people to buy could give various reasons. Some of the reasons given were that the government needed the money, that the bonds were a good investment, and that it was better to save then and buy after the war when commodities would be available again. However, the most effective reasons involved references to local quotas, as for example, "Bill, the quota in our shop is so much—how about it?"

Child socialization is different from later socialization partly because it is a *first* experience, and first experiences can never be repeated. The first date, the first job, and the first year away at college are in this sense unique. But in addition the first socialization experience occurs early in the life cycle and is therefore entangled with the mysterious discontinuity between *non*being and being. Later discontinuities are never that radical—although the anthropologist, Ruth Benedict, pointed out that postchildhood socialization experiences present varying learning problems for the individual depending on whether later roles are similar to or different from the early roles played in the family.[5] Thus, Professor Benedict hypothesized that *the greater the number of familiar elements in the new role as compared with earlier roles, the easier it is to learn the new role.* This certainly seems plausible. The son of a farmer has a good chance to gain gradual experience in the role of farmer. Youths in urban areas—where the world of work is more likely to be separated from the place of residence—find occupational roles more disconnected from their childhood roles. In short, there is a possibility of later socialization building on earlier socialization, although this possibility is realized to varying degrees in the actual learning of adolescent and adult roles.

Professor Benedict perceived an additional problem. Early socialization can be misleading from the point of view of later socialization. Far from contributing to the learning of adolescent or adult roles, childhood socialization can constitute an obstacle. This is not a fanciful possibility. Some parents attempt to control childhood sexuality by communicating to children that sex is a nasty, dirty thing. Effective though this may be at preventing premature interest in sex, such attitudes must be *unlearned* before these children marry. In this instance childhood socialization creates what Thorstein Veblen called "trained incapacity." Or, as Ruth Benedict put it, *the less unlearn-*

---

[5] Ruth Benedict, "Continuities and Discontinuities in Cultural Conditioning," *Psychiatry*, Vol. 1, May 1939, pp. 161–167.

ing of elements in previous roles that the new role requires, the easier it is to learn the new role.

In an industrial society socialization experiences subsequent to early childhood are legion. As a sample of later socialization experiences, consider some of the roles that American youngsters learn as they pass from childhood to adulthood. The criteria suggested by Ruth Benedict help evaluate the difficulties of postchildhood socialization at various stages of the life cycle.

SOCIALIZATION INTO THE PEER GROUP

The American family is an island of emotional intimacy in a sea of strangers. In this respect the American family is similar to the British family, the Swedish family, and the Russian family—and different from the family in preindustrial societies. Because the American family is typically a conjugal unit, the child may have brothers and sisters in his household but not usually first or second cousins.[6] This limits considerably his possible experiences with agemates. An older brother or sister, even one who is only a year or two older, is at a different stage of development. An older sibling tends to have an advantage in every game, a younger sibling a disadvantage. In order to learn how to compete on *equal* terms, most children must go *outside* the family and locate agemates in the neighborhood. Given the relative anonymity of urban neighborhoods, this is not easy for less venturesome children. Not only must the child "make friends" with strangers, that is, initiate interaction without the help of an established relationship; he must also relate to these new friends in quite different ways from the patterns established with his mother and father.

In dealing with doting parents, a child learns techniques by which powerless persons get what they want from powerful persons: pleading, appealing for sympathy, cajoling. When he goes out into the neighborhood to interact with peers, his skills at crying, throwing himself on the ground and making a fuss, or smiling winsomely may be useless. He is no longer dealing with benevolent despots. He must therefore *unlearn* the techniques of manipulation which proved successful within the family circle. He must learn to fight for his rights, to bluff, to negotiate. (Presumably an "only" child is at a disadvantage in learning to relate to peers as compared with a child having siblings of about the same age.) Some children never learn how to interact with agemates. They need not necessarily have unhappy childhoods. The world of books or fantasy may provide compensations. Or they may become precociously skillful at interacting with adults, a talent which yields higher dividends as the years go by. But there is evidence that children who do not develop viable peer relationships are more prone to mental illness.[7]

In all societies, children are taught to interact with peers. In American society, however, peer socialization presents special difficulties: (1) In the United States, as in other industrial societies, the isolation of the conjugal family and the anonymity of the urban community accentuate the qualitative differences between relationships *inside* and *outside* the family. (2) In the United States more than in other industrial societies of the contemporary world, ideological pressure for "adjusting" to peers is well nigh inescapable. A youngster who lives in a world of books or dreams is forced by the expectations of his parents and of other adults in the community to come to terms with his peers—sometimes at the cost of his individuality. Riesman argues persuasively that Americans are excessively preoccupied with peer group adjustment.[8] In France, on the other hand, the ideological pressure is quite different; children are expected to orient themselves to

6 Paul C. Glick, *American Families*, New York: Wiley, 1957.

7 Stuart D. Loomis and Arnold Green, "The Pattern of Mental Conflict in a Typical State University," *Journal of Abnormal and Social Psychology*, Vol. 42, July 1947, pp. 342–355; Nicholas J. Demerath, "Adolescent Status Demands and the Student Experiences of Twenty Schizophrenics," *American Sociological Review*, Vol. 8, October 1943, pp. 513–518.

8 Riesman, *op. cit.*

parents rather than to peers.[9] (3) In the United States, geographic and social mobility produces kaleidoscopic instability of interpersonal relations. Adjustment to peers is not settled at any particular age. Equalitarian interaction is a problem for youngsters for two decades after the walking-and-talking stage.

SOCIALIZATION AT SCHOOL

When the American child starts school, he enters a world fundamentally different both from his family milieu and from his peer group. It is his first experience with explicit, long-term goals—in this case the transmission of neatly packaged units of "education." Even though kindergarten provides a transition, cushioning somewhat the shock that is to come, the child has good reason to resist socialization into the student role. The discipline of school is imposed on him by adults. It is not the schoolboy who decides that 9 o'clock is a good time to arrive and 3 o'clock a good time to go home. Nor is his interest in shouting, jumping, or pinching his neighbor given much consideration. Is it any wonder that the early grades are filled with chatterers and squirmers, controlled by the eternal vigilance of their teachers? For an interesting experience, walk through a school, visiting first the lower grades and then the higher grades and observing the gradual decrease of fidgeting and the increasing concentration.

The student role is a difficult one to learn because school represents a curtailment of the freedom of the child for the sake of goals he only dimly understands. Another difficulty is that the student role requires a relationship between adults and children quite different from the one learned in the family. The teacher's reaction to her student is qualitatively different from the mother's reaction to her child. The teacher does not love her students; there are too many of them. The size of classes and the necessity of communicating prescribed lessons militate against diffuse personal relationships between teacher and students. Instead of giving students love, the teacher gives them approval (or disapproval), which is a far more contingent reaction. The teacher's reaction to a child depends preponderantly on what he *does:* on how fast he learns, on how often he throws spitballs, on how readily he raises his hand to volunteer an answer to her questions.[10] At home, on the other hand, his mother's response to him is preponderantly based on the fact that he is *hers*. His beauty, intelligence, and even his naughtiness are secondary considerations. This is not to say that the student role is the child's first experience with contingent reactions. On the contrary, as Chapter 8 tried to show, the contingency of maternal responses is crucial to internalization. But there is a difference between contingency that is a small part of a basically uncontingent relationship and a relationship that is predicated on contingency. The student role is of the second type. So are other roles of industrial societies, notably occupational roles. But the student role comes earlier in the life cycle. This is part of the explanation for the incidence of problems in the first few grades.

LEARNING TO BE INDEPENDENT: THE ADOLESCENT ROLE

The small conjugal family system characteristic of industrial societies tends to make children highly dependent on their parents. Other sources of emotional support are not readily available. Nonetheless, the expectation is that the family into which one is born will disintegrate. Children cannot remain dependent throughout life. They must leave the nest. The expectations surrounding occupational choice and the establishment of a family of one's own (family of procreation) create pressures to be more independent. During adolescence these two forces meet head-on: the structurally fostered *dependence* of an isolated family system

[9] Jesse Pitts, "The Family and Peer Groups," in Norman W. Bell and Ezra F. Vogel, *A Modern Introduction to the Family*, Glencoe, Ill.: Free Press, 1960, pp. 266–286.

[10] Talcott Parsons, "The School Class as a Social System: Some of Its Functions in American Society," *Harvard Educational Review*, Vol. 29, Fall 1959, pp. 297–318.

and the *independence* required by a dynamic society. The turmoil of adolescence in industrial societies is largely due to the collision of these incompatible forces. Adolescents are rebellious not only because parents sometimes try to keep them children too long but also because they must struggle against their own inclinations to remain protected and dependent. In the following autobiographical anecdotes, college students report on adolescent conflicts with their parents and reveal their own ambivalence.

The Struggle for Greater Independence within the Family

Unpublished papers submitted by Rutgers undergraduates as a class assignment in the introductory sociology course.

CASE 1

One of the earliest and most notable clashes of expectations between me and my parents occurred when I was about 15 years old. The matter was precipitated by the wedding of an uncle. It was the type of an affair at which I was supposed to be present, but the thought of being there filled me with dread.

Why did I fear? At this particular age, my awkwardness was appalling. I was painfully aware of this but had never taken any steps toward self-improvement. I predicted my actions at the wedding reception weeks before it took place; I could not and would not dance. Not only that; but I would sit alone, shunning conversation with other people.

I believed my parents understood my shortcomings and consequently would not place me in a position in which those faults would be brought to public attention. My ultimate desire at this assemblage was to enter unseen, sit alone and unnoticed, and leave quietly.

At the reception my parents started prodding me to dance with this girl and that girl, which brought about a slow mounting of anger and some hasty "Leave me alone!"'s from me. The hushed exchange of words continued until suddenly there erupted a verbal argument that reached the ears of everyone. Distinctly mortified at my own behavior, I left the reception.

CASE 2

Mother and father had been separated for a long time and I lived with mother on a farm. Both of us were lonely in this environment. I had few friends and was closely attached to mother, who had practically built her entire life around me. Although not a disciplinarian, mother dominated the scene and I was obedient, having considerable respect for her. Then, when I was 13, we moved into town, and the situation was immediately changed for me. No longer did I desire to remain devoted to mother but rather to the numerous newly found friends that I had acquired. Of course, mother was not prepared for my "breaking away." She never consciously attempted to keep me to herself, for she knew that what was happening was natural. But, nevertheless, I remained to her the little boy, ever so helpless, submissive, and devoted. Meanwhile, I began considering myself a young man—at least as wise as his mother and certainly more up-to-date. I was only dependent on her for room, board, clothing, and a little spending money—just the material things. No longer was she my companion or my boss; in fact I could tell her a thing or two.

Now when she gave me a command, even in the gentlest tones, I flew into a rage. Furthermore, mere advice or the use of words which I associated with domination would bring violent resentment on my part. The fact that good intentions were behind all her behavior towards me meant little, for I was reacting solely against being dominated by mother. On the occasion of the first scenes we had, mother was indignant at my arrogance. How dare her child retaliate! The rebellion must be punished by a good whack across the face, so she thought. But how dare mother hit her son, a man! I increased the violence of my attack, and mother, shocked, recoiled in fear. Then she would cry hard and tell me how mean I was. Immediately I felt ashamed; my poor helpless mother was now drenched in tears. I had to justify my actions, somehow to demonstrate to mother and perhaps to myself that I wasn't a bad boy. "Well you deserved it," I blurted out, "I'm not to be dominated; I'm a man. This was the only way I could make you realize, mother dear." She continued to weep; I became frantic and occasionally broke into tears myself. It was best to leave the scene. Mother treated me coldly for a few days; she was hurt and thought me undeserving of her affection. I tried to make it up to her by being extra good, but not so as to permit her to feel that I was backing down on my demands. Soon the relationship was restored to normal only to be followed by future scenes.

CASE 3

When I was being discharged from the Army last year, I had already planned to attend Rutgers—it was all set. As usual, I didn't consult my parents because they left decisions like that entirely up to me.

But the situation had changed at home. My older brother and sister had recently been married, and my younger brother had just joined the Navy. Unknown to me, my mother was heavily counting on me to reenter Brooklyn College so she would have at least one of her children at home.

When I announced I was going to Rutgers, 35 miles away, I could see she was disappointed. "Do you always want to be away from home?" I remember her bitterly asking me. "First, it was California, then the Army, and now New Jersey." (I had been away to California for a year.)

It took a lot of explaining of the many advantages Rutgers held for me over Brooklyn College, coupled with the faithful promise that I would be home every weekend, before my mother reluctantly gave approval.

At first all seemed to go well. My mother still wanted me home all the time but she seemed satisfied that I was coming home each weekend. When I would come home my mom treated me like a king. She would cook my favorite dishes, wash all my clothes and, in general, dote on me in every way. For the first time I realized my mother got a big kick out of doing things for her kids and now that I was the only one around, lavish attention was heaped upon me.

And then, two things happened to further the split that was growing between myself and my home. I got a job working nights, and I met Marie.

The only time I was able to see Marie, who lives near the University, was during the weekend, and I began staying away from home, sometimes two and three weekends in a row. I didn't realize the effect this was having on my mother until a Saturday afternoon not long ago.

I had arrived home, opened the door and had just laid my laundry on the floor. I saw my mom and grabbed her in an affectionate greeting.

She shoved me away, saying, "That's all you come home for, for me to wash your clothes and for you to sleep and eat for two days!" She was crying. "Don't you love your home and mother any more?" she blurted out as she pushed past me.

What could I say? Of course, I loved my mother but how could I explain the way I felt —how could I reconcile my love for Marie and for my parents and home?

"I'm a grown-up man now," I told my mother. "I've got to make decisions and go my own way. I can't be your little son forever." I talked on it this way for a long time but, in the end, it was to no avail. My mother was convinced that she had forever lost my love and that I no longer needed her. I could see she was terribly hurt.

The 15-year-old boy who had a violent argument with his parents at his uncle's wedding was not merely reacting to nagging. He was also responding to his expectations for himself, namely, that he ought to have been able to dance. In this instance, parents were eager to see their child developing toward adulthood, but the child was not ready to move forward. In the second anecdote, the mother was not fully prepared to see her son grow up. Here the boy faced a double problem: his own inadequacy feelings and his mother's emotional need for his continued dependency.

The theme of the possessive mother is a familiar one; it has inspired plays, novels, short stories, and magazine articles.[11] As clinical descriptions, these accounts are often excellent. As *explanations* of Momism, they leave much to be desired. Consider the relationship between the possessiveness of mothers and their role in society. In industrial societies, women typically live 20 to 30 years after their children are fully grown. Furthermore, they often outlive their husbands, who are usually older to

[11] See, for example, Sidney C. Howard, *The Silver Cord*, in *The Theatre Guild Anthology*, New York: Random House, 1936; Philip Wylie, *Generation of Vipers*, New York: Farrar and Rinehart, 1942.

begin with and who also have a higher mortality rate at every age (for reasons that are not well understood).[12] This results in a situation in which the developing maturity of children may precipitate a crisis for their mothers. Threatened with loss of her child-rearing function, anticipating long years of uselessness, a mother may consciously or unconsciously fight against retirement from active supervision of her children. She has a vested interest in the parental role—unless she has an occupation to return to. Since the moment when the son is able to fend for himself is a matter of judgment, his mother may consider herself crucial to his physical survival long after he no longer needs her guidance and protection. By the time the son is 45, it seems clear that he will not starve to death even if deprived of "Mom's home cooking." But when he is 19 or 20, there is more room for argument, and some mothers are tempted to shade the doubts in favor of their own indispensability.

SOCIALIZATION INTO THE DATING SUBCULTURE

The peer group in preadolescent years is overwhelmingly a single-sex group. As a result, most boys and girls enter adolescence with little experience with the opposite sex. They find that some of the skills which have made for success among peers in preadolescent years are less important now or even irrelevant. Thus, a boy who excels in street fighting may be less attractive to girls than a boy who can dance and is a "smooth" conversationalist. Gradually, boys and girls learn what is expected of them on dates, but the process of learning the "dating" aspect of the adolescent role can be painful— or funny, depending on one's perspective on the miscommunications characteristic of the first date.

[12] Bureau of the Census, *Statistical Abstract of the United States: 1960*, Washington: Government Printing Office, 1960, p. 59.

The First Date

Unpublished papers submitted by Rutgers undergraduates as a class assignment in the introductory sociology course.

CASE 1

I remember walking to Jane's house that night —my first date. I was excited. Jane was so pretty; all the guys said so. Yes, tonight I was to be suave and charming, I would sweep Jane off her feet and, of course, she would fall madly in love with me.

But I felt a lump well in my throat as I neared her house. I felt sort of frightened at the thought of being with a girl all evening, just her and me. All my life had been with boys like myself, playing baseball and football together and talking the same vulgar and sometimes lewd sort of language. "What did *girls* talk mostly about?" I asked myself.

These meditations were abruptly halted as I found myself ringing the doorbell of Jane's house.

A bumbling "hello" later to Jane's parents and a promise to return her before midnight, and Jane and I left for our "big night." My original plan was to attend the neighborhood theater and then, afterwards, go for a coke and hamburger.

It wasn't long before I realized that Jane knew nothing of my favorite topic—sports. And when she asked me if I knew what the "top 10" records were, I realized I knew nothing of her main interest either. This was the first time Jane and I were really alone. Always it had been with a group of mutual friends. Now I felt like a fool when I began talking of something she either didn't know anything about or else was completely disinterested in. When I began talking of something else, she neither encouraged nor discouraged me, most of the time not responding at all.

After a while I was convinced I was saying the wrong thing. This petite girl certainly was quite different from my usual associates.

About two blocks and five minutes of silence later, we arrived at the theater. I thought some of the mounting tension would ease once we were inside, but it only heightened somewhat as I wasn't quite sure just what was the proper thing for me to do. Should I hold her hand—would that be the proper thing? How would I suggest going for a hamburger later?

On the way home (she demurred at my suggestion of a coke) I again tried to strike up a conversation and wasn't very successful. The walk home seemed so long—I thought it would never end. I began to think of how to say "good-night" to her. Should I try to kiss her or should I just hold her hand? Maybe I should ask her for a kiss. But I couldn't bear it if I tried and was rejected by her—my ego wouldn't stand it.

When we reached her door I told her what a nice time I had with her (what a liar) and she thanked me for a "wonderful evening" (another liar).

We looked at each other for a moment and then, in an impulse borne of desperation and desire, I clumsily threw my arms around Jane and attempted to kiss her.

She recoiled from me as if I were a monster, blurting out, "I don't think it's nice to kiss on the first date."

CASE 2

Recently, I had a blind date with a girl recommended to me by a friend. When I called her, I said we would probably go to the movies. I thought she knew how to dress for the occasion so I did not mention it. I called for her, and to my surprise she was wearing an off-the-shoulder cocktail dress. I did not want to press the movie issue, but saw in an instant she either did not want to go to the movies or did not know how to dress. When I noticed the quarter of an inch of powder packed on from her head to her chest, I assumed it was the latter. We said "goodnight" to her parents, and she beat me to every door, including the car door. Ordinarily I would have opened it, but evidently she did not think it was necessary. I suggested that we go to a nightclub to dance, and she agreed. I was hoping then that none of my friends would see me "sporting" this girl, although they could probably smell her, with the amount of perfume she wore. I offered her a cigarette trying to be as polite as possible. What a mistake! I saw in a few moments that she probably had never smoked before. All she had to do was tell me that she didn't smoke. But no! She smoked until she became dizzy and then told me she was not used to that brand of cigarettes. We finally arrived at the nightclub and ordered a few drinks. I noticed that she gulped down liquor like

it was fruit juice. I didn't mind her drinking, but she drank as if liquor were going out of style. I suggested that she stop drinking so fast, but that only made her increase her pace. Soon, she became very pale and loud. I decided it was time to take her home. We had just reached the car when she regurgitated all over the front seat. I was heartsick! Thoroughly disgusted, I did not say a word the entire trip home. When we arrived at her home, I offered to help her to the front door. She bluntly refused to move and said it was too early to go to bed. After much persuasion, I finally got her to the doorstep. She then asked me to kiss her goodbye. I was dumbfounded! I took two steps backward, patted her on the shoulder, and walked away. Needless to say, I never called her again.

CASE 3

My first date was about six years ago with the girl to whom I am now engaged.

The church I belonged to had chartered a bus to go to an amusement park and all members and their friends were invited to go. Since all the young people of the church were going in couples, I asked the minister's daughter, Alice, if she would go with me.

Alice's acceptance of my request was the first example of how our expectations for one another coincided. A few weeks before this event, we had been attracted to each other when we first met in church. From that time on we exchanged love notes and ogles. When it was announced that a trip to an amusement park was to take place, Alice was my choice as a date, and she naturally expected me to ask her—unless I had only been leading her on with my flirting.

On the day of the big affair, a peculiar thing happened when I called for Alice at her home. As she and I were about to leave for the bus, her father handed her a couple of dollars, saying she might need it. Although my experience in dating had been limited up to this time, I knew enough to realize that the guy footed the bill. Undoubtedly, Alice wasn't sure I knew this, so she wanted to be prepared to save me any financial embarrassment.

By the time the bus brought us to the park, we got fairly well acquainted, and I convinced her I was in a position to pay the expenses. (Since it was a church group, tickets were only half-price anyway.)

As we walked around the park, it seemed anything I wanted to do was agreeable to her. If I motioned to hold hands, she put her hand in mine; when I put my arm around her, she didn't resist. In fact, if I didn't take the initiative, she sometimes would. She would either take my hand or walk so close beside me that the only thing I could do with my arm was to put it around her, since I couldn't swing it.

The fifth time through the Tunnel of Love, Alice proved once more that she liked me as I did her. When we were half way through—in the darkest spot—she took hold of the guide rail and stopped the boat, thereby allowing us a few minutes more to smooch. The same thought had occurred to me but Alice acted first.

The entire day went along smoothly. On the return bus trip we sang with the rest of the group and also found time to display affection for each other. After spending so much time in the Tunnel of Love, that goodnight kiss on her front porch —though nice—wasn't completely novel.

MUTUAL SOCIALIZATION IN MARRIAGE

Relating to the opposite sex in dating shades off into courtship—varying degrees of "going steady" with expectations of a permanent relationship. Marriage is not more intimate dating, however, and therefore successful socialization into the dating subculture may have little carryover into marriage.[13] A great deal of additional socialization is necessary to make a successful marriage between a young man and a young woman who have dated one another steadily and consider themselves in love. The responsibilities of the marital role are far removed from the pleasure-seeking dalliance of dating. It is easier to be charming and witty when dancing to nightclub music than while changing a dirty diaper or washing dishes. Even physical appearance changes. A fiancee is more chic than a wife because she has more time to primp. Husbands who expect their wives to look the way they did before marriage are unrealistic. Elaborately manicured nails and an

[13] Jackson Toby, "The Case Against Romance," in Harry C. Bredemeier and Jackson Toby, *Social Problems in America*, New York: Wiley 1960, pp. 461–468.

impeccable coiffure may be obtained at a cost the husband will not like: a dirty house and inedible dinners.

A second reason why additional socialization is necessary is that marriage forces the boy and the girl to look at one another in the context of family and friends. During courtship days they were essentially alone with one another. In industrial societies and especially in the United States, there is no legal or social requirement that the respective families know the future spouse—much less give their consent to the marriage. Romantic songs glamorize this absence of social context: "A sleepy lagoon, a tropical moon, and two on an island. . . ." But a *married* couple is no longer "two on an island." Each spouse has friends and relatives, and these emerge as important factors in the success or failure of many marriages. The following case of marital incompatibility was drawn from the files of a marriage counseling agency in Los Angeles, the American Institute of Family Relations. It is a dramatic illustration of a Chinese notion, namely, that a girl should be more concerned about getting along with her mother-in-law than with her husband.

Unsuccessful Mutual Socialization

Reprinted by permission. From Dorothy Cameron Disney, "Can This Marriage Be Saved?", *Ladies Home Journal*, Vol. 73, March 1956, pp. 73, 199–205.

Ava tells her side:
"When my husband walks into our house he automatically turns on the hi-fi," said twenty-seven-year-old Ava. She was slightly built, had snapping blue eyes and a square, firm jaw. "Chad is a music lover, but he doesn't love music that much. His real object is to keep from hearing me talk. Chad takes no interest in my activities or my feelings and he keeps his own feelings and activities a secret from me.

"Chad is now at liberty to play the hi-fi every evening as loud and as long as he likes. I won't be around any more trying to talk through Haydn and Bach. From now on he is also free to visit his mother and listen while she harps on her imaginary ailments and her unsatisfactory, unsympathetic daughter-in-law. Chad's mother is the worst hypochondriac on record. And Chad, unfortunately for him and for me, is credulous and tenderhearted.

"The children and I are living in my mother's apartment—we've been there since Saturday—and the arrangement suits me fine. Billy and Bobby and I intend to stay put until I can rent a place for us, locate an efficient full-time maid, make connections with a hospital and get back into nursing again. Thank heavens, I'm an R.N. and have a profession and the wit to support my two boys. Chad is welcome to take over the house I've always hated and that both of our savings paid for. He is more than welcome to the exclusive enjoyment of his mother's company.

"Until I married, I thought I could get along with everybody. When I got acquainted with Lady—I call Chad's mother 'Lady' at her specific request, and so does he—I found out different, and that's for sure. I'm a down-to-earth, literal sort of person; when I speak I deal in facts. Lady prefers fiction and drama. . . ."

Ava sighed.

"When I married Chad, I didn't dream he was tangled in apron strings. On the night his ex-girl friend Helen introduced us—we met on New Year's Eve and married on Valentine's Day —I had just broken my engagement to one of those big, grown-up boys with oceans of charm and no strength of character. I was good and fed up with the type of male who expects some woman to lead him by the hand through the storms of life. I wanted to marry a real man, a strong man. Chad was so sweet and so generous —if anything, he is too generous—I couldn't help falling in love with him. In those days, before he became so ingrown and self-centered, he was extraordinarily thoughtful and kind.

"He lived miles from the hospital where I was on duty, but during our courtship we saw each other every night except one. On the evenings I had charge of the floor I could spend only a few minutes with him, but Chad wasn't discouraged by that fact. The only night he missed the long drive was the night before our wedding, and that time he sent flowers. I easily persuaded myself he was strong and dependable and adult.

"I soon learned he wasn't adult at all. On our honeymoon Chad had a tonsillectomy he'd been needing a long while. The hotel doctor happened to be a friend of mine and gave us a courtesy rate. Chad wasn't hospitalized and inside twenty-four hours he felt dandy. Nevertheless, he yearned for his mother. It was all I could do to prevent him from inviting my mother-in-law to join us in the bridal suite.

"When we got back from our trip, Lady had already selected and virtually spoken for the 'bargain' house we now own. I suppose our house might be considered a fair investment, but we live in a moribund community. Everybody else's children are in high school and most of the other wives are twenty years my senior.

"After we settled in the house—I was too dumb to object to the purchase—I quickly discovered how maddeningly childish Chad can be. For one thing, he expected me to shoulder the responsibility for getting him up and off to work in the mornings. Chad is a talented sleeper—I doubt an earthquake would budge him. I didn't mind waking him—once. He demanded to be called six or eight times, at five-minute intervals. If I got impatient and jerked off his blankets or if he took exception to the tone of my voice, he would roll over and stick to the bed for another hour or so. Sometimes he didn't even go back to sleep, just lay there and sulked. Naturally, he was late to work but never did he blame himself. He blamed me.

"Chad's tardiness and the juvenile side of his temperament have seriously hampered his career. He is an expert on air conditioning, but his employment record is as spotty as a shooting-gallery target. Whenever a boss has complained of him—regardless of whether the complaint was justified—Chad's favorite tactic has been to resign from his job. Chad cannot tolerate criticism, constructive or not, and seemingly he is incapable of defending his point of view in a mature discussion. Nearly every time he's met opposition in his business he has pouted and sulked for a few days, hugged his wounded feelings to himself and then quit. Chad interprets his flitting from job to job as a sign of his masculinity and independence. To me it is a sign of weakness. I cannot imagine why he behaves so foolishly.

"Since Chad earns considerably less than he should, it is obvious we should stick to a careful budget. We are up to our eyebrows in debt and installment payments. Holidays and anniversaries register big with Chad. He showers the boys and me with gifts he can't afford. He is equally munificent with his mother on her birthdays. Periodically he goes on spending sprees and buys unnecessary luxuries for himself. A motion-picture camera, a new tool, a new record album. The movie camera enthralled him—for six weeks. He then presented it to the twelve-year-old son of our postman. . . .

"Chad doesn't know how to communicate with me or with anybody else. Even Lady complains he is remote and erratic and almost impossible to get at. My attempts to make contact drive him to the radio, or else he retires to his workshop and locks himself in. He ducks my most trivial questions. If I ask whether he intends to work late or leave his office early, I receive a blank stare. If I ask whether we can accept an invitation to a party, he just grunts. Often he scarcely appears to be aware that I exist. . . .

"Chad is devoted to our sons, but he gets into wrangles with them like another child. They do something irritating and he scowls and stalks off to nurse his offended dignity in private. I hate to bring up my boys without a father, but I'd hate them to grow up and be like Chad. . . ."

Chad tells his side:

"I've been pushed around all my life, usually by some woman," said thirty-year-old Chad. A big man with nervous hands, his words poured forth so fast that he stammered. "All my life I've wanted peace—and I found it only once. That was just after I got out of the Army. In the Army I was really pushed around—by professionals. Rules, regulations, regimentation. Do this, do that, and do it on the double! When the Army finally sprung me into private life, I decided I was really going to have a private life. I wasn't going home to my mother and her rules and regulations. I built myself a small house in a growing community in the desert. I got up when I pleased, I went to bed when I pleased. If I wanted to, I stayed up all night listening to my record collection, watched the stars fade and the sun come up. That was the life! I did air-conditioning installation for local builders. I didn't have too many jobs, but I earned almost as much as I earn now in the city.

"Then I met Ava. She is still the only person in the world with whom I've ever felt really companionable and easy and close. I will never forget our first evening. I had come into the city to attend a New Year's party. Ava was wearing a black dress with a lacy-doily dingus at the top

and a long, full skirt. She put me in mind of a smiling, sparkly-eyed doll.

"I am socially diffident and a poor dancer, but in a few minutes she had me out on the floor and we were laughing together. I knew at once she was the girl for me.

"During our courtship she was sweet and companionable and so helpful to me. Every night in the week she would phone and I would drive all the way in from the desert to see her. She was kept busy at the hospital, but to me Ava's minutes were worth any other girl's hours. In those days my comfort and my wishes rated high with her, and even in small things. If the evening was cool, Ava fetched me a cup of hot coffee from the nurses' kitchen; if the evening was warm, there was a pitcher of lemonade waiting.

"I was sure that she would be the kind of wife who would cheer for and support my ideas. And I was positive I would not lose my independence in marriage. Ava told me she shared my love for the desert too and, daydreaming, I pictured the two of us living our lives in my little house— listening to music and looking at the stars.

"Before we had been married a week I discovered that Ava was as bossy as my mother or my sister. She had been determined all along that I would take a job in the city, and I did. I came back to my mother, my sister, my family, a job, and the old neighborhood. Ava now thinks it was solely my mother's idea that we buy our present house; actually she joined forces with my mother in urging me to buy it. She wanted to get me in town.

"I've never heard of another man whose bride maneuvered him into having a tonsillectomy on his honeymoon. She said she was being practical; it would save money. Well, perhaps it did. But it spoiled the trip. And Ava made trouble for me by not notifying my mother of the operation. When my mother finally got the news she was so upset she had a heart attack. When my mother gets sick—and I think it's my fault—my nerves go haywire. I get a thick choked feeling, I can't seem to breathe and then I get a blinding headache. . . .

"I had some rugged combat in the Army—I fought at both Tarawa and Okinawa—and it may sound ridiculous, but I'd rather face combat than a quarreling, arguing woman. The fact is I've always been afraid of having angry females nag and pick at me. Actually, the first thing I can recall from childhood is sitting with my sister in a stalled automobile, while my dad tried to change a tire and my mother denounced him for having the puncture. My sister—Ruth is two years older and probably was six or seven at the time—was also scolding away at him. I spoke up for my dad and both Ruth and my mother hopped on me. I can still remember my panic. I tried to jump out of the car and get away, but I was caught and got a spanking.

"My sister and my mother, like my wife and her mother, like all women of my acquaintance, are quick on the trigger. Quick-acting, quick-thinking, machine-gun talkers. My wife, my mother, my sister, my mother-in-law can talk rings around me. I take after my dad, I'm slow. Not only was I slow as a boy; I was sickly. Or so Lady says. I had severe whooping cough in the fourth grade—the grade they taught phonetics in my school—and I was kept at home for a year. I never did catch up with my reading. My memory of my boyhood Saturdays is of other kids outside playing and my mother standing over me with a book insisting I read from it, when I didn't know how to read.

"My mother always managed to get me to obey her. My sister would rebel. I just couldn't. The times Ruth would skip out on the dishes I was likely to wash and dry the dishes and run the vacuum cleaner to boot. My mother would make me feel sorry for her, or . . . something.

"Perhaps I tried extra hard to satisfy my mother because I early realized what a disappointment I was to her and my dad. When I was in the seventh grade my parents went to a P.T.A. meeting and my teacher told them I wasn't college material. Both were badly cut up, though dad attempted to hide it. Years later tests I took in the Army indicated that my I.Q. was high and in music and math I scored exceptionally well. . . .

"It is now impossible for me to keep the peace between my wife and my mother or to find any personal peace. Much as I dislike to have Ava bring up our sons by herself—I'm afraid she will boss them around the way I was bossed around— I see little hope of saving my marriage. Ava makes me feel stupid and like a failure. I don't want my boys looking at me with her critical, disappointed eyes. I came to this interview only because I was told Ava needed my help. It seems improbable

Ava either needs or will accept help from me. Long ago she stopped listening to any of my ideas or accepting any of my advice. She knows all the answers herself."

The marriage counselor says:

"Ava didn't know all the answers by any means. On the contrary, she was as badly mixed up and, in some respects, was as emotionally juvenile as Chad. Ava lamented her lack of understanding of her husband without perceiving her serious lack of self-understanding. Her hardships as a small, fatherless girl had left Ava with a healthy distaste for divorce. She loved her sons, knew Chad was devoted to them. Nevertheless, she had such a hazy perspective of her ultimate objectives in life that she seemed to be working almost deliberately to break up her home. She had committed her mind and emotions so thoroughly to the feud with her mother-in-law—by preference she would have discussed her squabbles with Lady in endless detail—that she had lost sight of almost everything else. She put far more time and energy into dreaming up plots against Chad's mother than she put into thinking about Chad or their deteriorating marriage. It just plain didn't occur to Ava that her own attitudes and actions, her character, might be a factor—an important factor—in the deterioration.

"When Chad took refuge from his dissatisfactions in childish fits of the sulks a wiser, more patient wife would have endeavored to overlook the sulking unless she understood and could change his mood. Frustrated by Chad's obstinate silences and her inability 'to get anything out of him,' Ava retaliated with scenes. The scenes didn't help her to 'get at' her husband. Indeed, she succeeded in driving him deeper into himself and farther away from her. Both she and Chad needed to learn how to sense and respond to the other fellow's feelings instead of blindly reacting to the other's exasperating behavior.

"If Chad stubbornly refused to disclose the hour he would leave his office, it was futile for Ava to pay him off with anger and tears and thereby prolong the unpleasantness. Later on, in our conferences, it developed that Chad's seemingly mysterious reticence on the subject of his working hours wasn't mysterious at all. If he told Ava he was leaving early she immediately took charge of his leisure and loaded him with errands to be performed on the way home; if she learned he was working late, she arranged that his additional earnings should come under her direct control.

"Any observant acquaintance could have told Ava that she was bossy and domineering, but she wouldn't have believed it. A psychological test taken here at the Institute indicated that in a random crowd of a hundred people, including both men and women, Ava would rank at the top in extreme aggressiveness. The result of this test startled and disturbed her—like most young women of the present generation, Ava admires gentle, feminine qualities—but it convinced her as no words could have done. She and I then talked over her past history and she viewed it with a little insight. . . .

"Chad's major difficulties with his marriage, his career, the world and himself, of course, dated back to his boyhood and his relationship with his tyrannical mother. A child can react to the over-domination of a parent with either rebellion or submissiveness. Less lucky than his sister who rebelled, Chad started off handicapped by the belief that he was a disappointing son. It was easy for Chad's mother to make him feel guilty when he didn't obey her. If you have the power to make another person feel guilty, it is a psychological truth that you can get that person to do almost anything.

"In his boyhood Chad obeyed, but acquired the habit of dealing with the sometimes intolerable pressures his mother applied by disappearing from the house or by withdrawing into long spells of sullen silence. He learned how to hold his tongue and suppress his natural resentment at the injustice that was his lot. In this way, without realizing it, Chad as a young boy learned how to be a 'lone wolf' and gradually lost the knack of making contact with others. He didn't enjoy his role. His wild bursts of generosity clearly indicated how intense was his longing to share in and reflect the feelings of others, make their feelings a part of his own life experience.

"In his manhood Chad was consistently repeating behavior patterns established long ago in childish skirmishes with his mother. Treated unfairly or criticized in business, he repressed his feelings, sulked and then withdrew from the situation exactly as he had done at the age of five when he felt abused by his mother. His feelings and reactions when he heard a harsh note in Ava's voice duplicated his boyish reaction to the harsh, commanding voice of his mother. His fear aroused by quarreling, arguing women, his sensation of extreme helplessness, was an echo of old clashes with a mother and sister teamed against him."

With the help of a marriage counselor, this particular marriage was saved. It could well have ended in a divorce court. The grievances which Chad and Ava had against one another were not so important in themselves. He said she was bossy. She objected to his childishness: his dependence on his mother, his extravagance, his inability to hold a job. The real significance of these grievances was that they prevented Chad and Ava from developing a mutually acceptable way of life. Another man might have accepted Ava's bossiness as a fact of life—like snow in the winter—and learned to live with it. Another woman might have accepted the task of waking Chad each morning as part of the housework. Chad and Ava needed help because they could not agree on the basis for their relationship. Each had a conception of what their marriage should be, and these conceptions were incompatible.

Marriage involves socialization because the man and the woman must learn new roles in order to live harmoniously with one another. Marriage involves *mutual* socialization because unlike most other socialization experiences, marriage is not a situation in which an individual becomes incorporated into an established structure, that is, a situation in which he feels from the start that *he* is in the minority and it is up to *him* to make the adjustments. Each marriage is a new social system, and in industrial societies each partner thinks he should have an equal voice in the definition of the rules of that system. Consequently, the roles of "husband" and "wife" must be *mutually* defined and accepted in order for the marriage to work.

SOCIALIZATION INTO THE WORLD OF WORK

Among adult males in industrial societies, playing an occupational role is a near universal expectation for the able-bodied. Exceptions are made in some European countries for the aristocracy: for the descendants of the feudal nobility. The United States, however, lacks a feudal past. As a result, even the rich are expected to have an occupation. The playboy may be envied, but he is not respected. The emotional investment in "work" in industrial societies can be assessed by considering the impact of unemployment. Far from being regarded as an opportunity to relax and enjoy life, unemployment is treated as a disaster.[14] This is only partly because employment is the economic basis for the family. In Great Britain, where National Assistance is readily available, unemployment is no less feared than in less welfare-minded societies.[15] The enormous numbers of employed persons in industrial countries and of persons frantically seeking employment are evidence of the success of occupational socialization. Besides these huge totals, the professional criminals, the gamblers, the pimps, and the loafers sink into statistical insignificance.

Absenteeism and high rates of job turnover are regarded as pathological in industrial societies. Consider, however, that there is no timeclock-punching instinct to help men get up early, gulp their breakfasts, pack into crowded buses or subways, and do their day's work. Still, as the rush-hour traffic jams prove, the delights of lounging in bed are foregone by the vast majority; absenteeism is remarkably rare. This may be so because the occupational role is such an important part of the total status of an adult male that most men are prepared to make considerable sacrifices to further their "careers." A plumber is not simply a person who fixes leaky faucets; he *is* a plumber. Even when he is sunning himself on the beach during his summer vacation, the people who know him think of him as a plumber. Furthermore, plumbers are not evaluated as favorably as lawyers.[16] Thus, the choice of an occupation is not simply a search for work that is personally congenial. For status-conscious youngsters —and all youngsters are status-conscious to some degree—occupational choice also involves the selection of a level of community prestige.[17]

Competition is keen for the more desirable occupational roles. Considerable amounts of time, energy, and training are required by way of preparation for them. Not only is this true of the professions: engineering, law, medicine, teaching. It is increasingly characteristic of business, especially in the United States. Most business executives today do not work their way up from blue-collar jobs. They go to college and often to graduate schools of business.[18] The lengthening educational preparation for business and professional careers has implications for occupational socialization. It means that learning an élite occupation necessarily involves a discontinuity. A college student cannot get a part-time executive position to find out how he likes business or an apprenticeship to a pediatrician to find out whether medicine is for him. Occupational reality sometimes has a shocking impact on the conceptions of the role developed in the course of educational preparation. The aeronautical engineer who entered the field because, as a boy, he was fascinated by model airplanes, may not be happy with his work—although he may *grow* to like it as a result of further socialization. Job satis-

14   E. Wight Bakke, *The Unemployed Worker*, New Haven, Conn.: Yale University Press, 1940; Mirra Komarovsky, *The Unemployed Man and His Family*, New York: Dryden, 1940.
15   Barbara Wootton, *Social Science and Social Pathology*, New York: Macmillan, 1959, pp. 41–44.

16   Cecil C. North and Paul K. Hatt, "Jobs and Occupations: A Popular Evaluation," *Opinion News*, September 1947, pp. 3–13. Reprinted in Wilson and Kolb, *Sociological Analysis*, New York: Harcourt, Brace, 1949, pp. 464–473.
17   Theodore Caplow, *The Sociology of Work*, Minneapolis: University of Minnesota Press, 1954, Chap. 9, "Vocational Choice," pp. 214–229; Eli Ginzberg et al., *Occupational Choice*, New York: Columbia University Press, 1951.
18   Seymour M. Lipset and Reinhard Bendix, *Social Mobility in Industrial Society*, Berkeley and Los Angeles: University of California Press, 1960, Chap. 4.

faction, like marital happiness, may be due as much to successful socialization as to judicious selection.

The effects of occupational socialization are most obvious when the job has low status in the community, as the following reading shows.

The Development of an Occupational Self-image: The Case of a Low-Status Job

Reprinted by permission. From Richard L. Simpson and Ida Harper Simpson, "The Psychiatric Attendant: Development of an Occupational Self-Image in a Low-Status Occupation," *American Sociological Review*, Vol. 24, June 1959, pp. 389–392.

Members of occupational groups often develop occupational self-images: sets of beliefs, attitudes, and evaluations regarding their work. By stressing certain highly valued aspects of the work —the skill it requires, its social utility, the perquisites it affords—an occupational self-image can provide work motivation and work satisfaction. The person in a high-status occupation is aided in maintaining a flattering self-image by the social prestige of his occupation. Occupations such as those of the physician and the business executive are widely known to require skill and to carry high income and pleasant working conditions. Low-ranking occupations, however, do not command favorable society-wide evaluations; the public evaluates many jobs as unappealing or, oftentimes, distasteful.

How then do people in low-status occupations maintain favorable self-images? A number of plausible answers may be suggested. One is that they do *not* maintain favorable self-images, but are dissatisfied with their work and would leave it if they could. Another is that they are dissatisfied with their work but project their aspirations onto their children. Still another is that they reject or fail to internalize the value of occupational success, perhaps seeking personal fulfillment in activities off the job. Probably all of these patterns are to be found; yet it also seems likely that many low-status workers are satisfied with their jobs and have favorable occupational self-images. In this paper we try to show one way in which work satisfaction among low-status occupational groups can come about.

Our hypothesis is that people in low-status occupations may seize upon some aspect of their work which is highly valued, either throughout the society or in the work subculture, and build a self-image around it. We present data showing the basis on which workers in a low-status occupation—psychiatric attendants—may maintain a favorable occupational self-image. Attendants tend to minimize the less glamorous features of their work and focus upon the most highly valued element in the hospital's subculture: care of the patient.

SOURCE OF DATA

The findings grew out of a study of psychiatric nursing practices in North Carolina hospitals. Attendants were interviewed about their reasons for choice of the job, their duties, and their attitudes toward work. Interviews were conducted with 81 men and 63 women, selected randomly to include 15 percent of the attendants in each of five hospitals: a state mental hospital for whites, a state mental hospital for Negroes, a Veterans' Administration mental hospital for both races, a private mental hospital for whites, and a psychiatric in-patient clinic for whites in a general hospital affiliated with a medical school. The findings presented below hold for all five hospitals: there are no differences between hospitals significant at the .05 level on a chi-square test.

CHOICE OF THE JOB AND WORK SATISFACTION

Each attendant was asked, in open-ended questions, why he had chosen the job, and why he had remained in the job of attendant. The answers to each question were classified as either intrinsic (pertaining to the work itself) or extrinsic (pertaining to the externals of the job). Answers which incorporated more than one reason were coded according to the first reason given. *Intrinsic reasons* included such explanations as interest in understanding mental illness through contact with patients, humanitarian interest in patients' welfare, satisfaction of working with people rather than things, and affection or sympathy for patients. *Extrinsic reasons* included such explanations as better salary than for former job, not qualified for anything else, spouse or relatives worked in the hospital, convenient transportation from home to hospital, and friendship with co-workers.

As Table 46 indicates, the majority of attendants (82.6 per cent) gave extrinsic reasons for taking their jobs but less than half (46.5 per cent) of the entire group offered the same type of reason for remaining. Thus there is a marked over-all shift in the kind of reason emphasized: from extrinsic to intrinsic. More particularly, about half of those who took their jobs for extrinsic reasons changed their outlook and said that they remained for intrinsic reasons. Among the 17.4 per cent who took their jobs for intrinsic reasons, less than one-third (4.9 per cent) changed to extrinsic reasons for remaining. Despite the fact that this small group shifted in a contrary direction, a general trend toward the intrinsic rather than the extrinsic as reasons for remaining in the job seems to be clear. A chi-square test shows the over-all shift in pattern of the responses, from reasons for taking the job to reasons for staying in the job, to be statistically significant at the .001 level for men and women considered separately and for both sexes combined.

The intrinsic reasons for remaining in their jobs, offered by 53.5 per cent of the attendants, focus on their personal relationships with patients. Except for one individual whose purpose was to gain intellectual understanding of mental illness, the reasons given by these attendants appear to reflect an occupational self-image of the kind hypothesized: one which places heavy emphasis on the importance of the attendant in patient care. Their reasons for taking the job are mainly extrinsic, suggesting that no such self-image existed before they began work. These findings suggest that many attendants acquired a favorable self-image not from the society at large as people in high status occupations often do, but from the subculture of the hospital.

The quotations below illustrate the kinds of reasons the attendants gave for taking and keeping their jobs.

EXTRINSIC REASONS FOR TAKING THE JOB OF ATTENDANT:

Negro male attendant at the Negro state hospital: "I got to where I couldn't conduct the farm as I wanted to, because of my health and high blood pressure. Some of my friends had always worked here, and they pointed me here."

White male attendant at the white state hospital: "I wanted to quit farming; it's all work and no money and you're old before your time. My brother worked here and he told me about it. I had no notion what it was like when I started, but I liked it so I have stayed on."

Negro female attendant at the Negro state hospital: "The lady I worked for as a maid wanted me to find a better job. I didn't know of another job I could do. If I had, I would have chosen it instead."

White male attendant at the veterans' hospital: "The pay looked all right and I wasn't trained for much else, so I thought I'd give it a try."

INTRINSIC REASONS FOR REMAINING IN THE JOB OF ATTENDANT:

White female attendant at the private hospital: "Somebody has to help these people get well, and I feel it's our mission to do that."

TABLE 46

Reasons for Taking and Remaining in the Job of Psychiatric Attendant

Reasons	Men (N = 81)	Women (N = 63)	All Attendants (N = 144)
Took job for extrinsic reason, remained for extrinsic reason	46.9%	34.9%	41.6%
Took job for extrinsic reason, remained for intrinsic reason	38.3	44.5	41.0
Took job for intrinsic reason, remained for intrinsic reason	12.3	12.7	12.5
Took job for intrinsic reason, remained for extrinsic reason	2.5	7.9	4.9
Total	100.0	100.0	100.0

For men, $\chi^2 = 25.48$, d.f. $= 1$, $p < .001$; for women, $\chi^2 = 16.03$, d.f. $= 1$, $p < .001$; for all attendants, $\chi^2 = 40.96$, d.f. $= 1$, $p < .001$.

White male attendant at the veterans' hospital: ". . . I ask myself how I would want my mother or my wife or my kids treated if they got mentally sick, and that's how I try to treat these people here. It could happen to anybody."

Negro male attendant at the Negro state hospital: ". . . They get to feeling so bad they'll just brood all day long unless somebody shows an interest in them. We try to talk to them and cheer them up when they are like that."

White female attendant at the white state hospital: "I have a real interest in the psychiatric nursing (sic) we do. The patients see us more than they see anyone else, and how we act with them is very important to their welfare."

ATTENDANTS' PERCEPTIONS OF THEIR DUTIES

A further indication of the attendants' self-image is the way in which they perceive their duties. They were asked, in open-ended questions, to name the *most important* and *most time-consuming* aspects of their work. The activities mentioned as most important differ somewhat from the activities cited as most time-consuming. Chi-square tests show the patterns of responses to the two questions to differ significantly at the .001 level, for men and women separately and for both

sexes combined. The attendants' answers tend to stress activities directly connected with patient care as most important, although housekeeping tasks such as cleaning floors and making beds may be more time-consuming. Table 47 shows these findings. When the attendants were asked to name the most important duties, 73.8 percent of the 141 who responded mentioned care of patients or interaction with them as most important; only 7.8 per cent referred to housekeeping and miscellaneous tasks. But when they were asked to name the most time-consuming duties, 52 per cent of the 144 indicated housekeeping and miscellaneous tasks while only 34.8 per cent cited care of patients or interaction with them.

DISCUSSION

The data support the hypothesis that people in a low-status occupation can develop or maintain a favorable occupational self-image by focusing upon some highly valued aspect of the work situation. In the case of psychiatric attendants, emphasis is placed on care of the patient.

Professional training, such as that which doctors and nurses receive, not only provides technical competence but usually leads to an occupational self-image. The psychiatric attendant, however, has not undergone such extensive train-

TABLE 47
Activities Mentioned as Most Important and Most Time-Consuming by Psychiatric Attendants

Type of Activity (In order of most patient-centered to least patient-centered)	Percentage of Attendants Mentioning Activity as Most Important			Percentage of Attendants Mentioning Activity as Most Time-Consuming		
	Men ($N = 79$)	Women ($N = 62$)	All Attendants ($N = 141$)	Men ($N = 81$)	Women ($N = 63$)	All Attendants ($N = 144$)
Interaction with patients	25.3%	32.3%	28.4%	6.2%	3.2%	4.9%
Physical care of patients	40.5	51.6	45.4	33.3	25.4	29.9
Supervision and observation of patients' behavior	24.1	11.3	18.4	12.4	14.3	13.2
Housekeeping and miscellaneous	10.1	4.8	7.8	48.1	57.1	52.0
Total	100.0	100.0	100.0	100.0	100.0	100.0

Chi-squares computed from contingency tables including data on most important and most time-consuming activities: for men, $\chi^2 = 32.64$, d.f. $= 3$, $p. < .001$; for women, $\chi^2 = 48.22$, d.f. $= 3$, $p < .001$; for all attendants, $\chi^2 = 76.00$, d.f. $= 3$, $p. < .001$.

ing. Therefore when attendants develop favorable occupational self-images, they are apt to be based on the workers' direct role in the primary function of the hospital, patient care. Cleaning floors and supplying linen closets have only an ancillary relation to patient care—understandably, most attendants do not regard these duties as their most important tasks although they are time-consuming.

This is not to imply that all attendants are entirely happy in their work. In our sample, 46.5 per cent of the attendants gave extrinsic reasons for staying in their jobs, and some of those who gave intrinsic reasons may have felt ambivalent about their work. It seems, however, that a self-image based on patient care brings a measure of job-satisfaction to many attendants. Further research would be needed to determine the factors associated with intrinsic or extrinsic reasons for remaining on the job.

The self-image developed among psychiatric attendants serves the same functions as the ideologies of other occupations. It furnishes ego-enhancement and motivation. It appears likely that other low-status groups may develop self-images similarly, each grasping at whatever symbols of skill or social utility the situation affords.

Socialization to failure is a difficult lesson. It is learned not only at work, where prospective sales do not materialize and promotions are given to others, but also in the family, at school, and among peers. Professor Erving Goffman has pointed out that the humiliation which failure in a role involves poses problems of social control as well as of individual adjustment.[19]

". . . [A] person who can no longer sustain one of his social roles and is about to be removed from it . . . is a person who is losing one of his social lives and is about to die one of the deaths that are possible for him. This leads one to consider the ways in which we can go or be sent to our death in each of our social capacities, the ways, in other words, of handling the passage from the role we had to a state of having it no longer. One might con-

sider the social processes of firing and laying-off; of resigning and being asked to resign; of farewell and departure; of deportation, excommunication, and going to jail; of defeat at games, contests, and wars; of being dropped from a circle of friends or an intimate social relationship; of corporate dissolution; of retirement in old age; and lastly, of the deaths that heirs are interested in."

The commitment that an occupational role requires in industrial societies makes failure especially threatening to the individual's self-conception. Nevertheless, we learn how to fail occupationally—and be reasonably good sports about it. (David Riesman talks about the "nerve of failure.") Retirement from an occupational role is often experienced as failure, partly because retirement is usually abrupt. One week an aging personnel man is so preoccupied with decisions that he feels there are not enough hours in the day, and the next he has more leisure time than he can handle. An even more important reason why retirement is experienced as akin to failure is that one's sense of identity tends to be bound up with one's occupational role; retirement, over and above the problem of hobbies and killing time, may create a feeling of uselessness.

SOCIALIZATION INTO A NEW COMMUNITY

Socialization proceeds throughout the life cycle, much of it following the same sequence for everybody. Some adult socialization is experienced only by a segment of the population—for example, military service.[20] And some socialization is experienced at different stages of the life cycle by various members of the population—for example, moving from one community to another. Although change of residence always involves socialization, the ease of the transition depends partly on the *meaning* of the move to the mover, and this varies with

[19] Erving Goffman, "On Cooling the Mark Out," *Psychiatry*, Vol. 15, November 1952, pp. 462–463.

[20] For a discussion of socialization into military service, see Samuel A. Stouffer et al., *The American Soldier*, 2 vols., Princeton, N.J.: Princeton University Press, 1949, especially Vol. 1, Chaps. 3–5, and Vol. 2, Chap. 5.

the *reason* for the move. An elderly couple may sell a large house in the suburbs after the children have left home and rent a small apartment in the central city; a 30-year-old unmarried engineer may give up his furnished apartment because he is moving to another city to take a better job; a nine-year-old boy may change schools and peer groups because his parents have bought a larger house to accommodate a new addition to the family. In terms of Ruth Benedict's first proposition, some moves involve fewer discontinuities than others because the mover's role in the new community is much the same as his role in the old.

Between 1955 and 1960 about *half* of the American population changed its place of residence.[21] A third of these movers remained within the same county, but the other two-thirds moved to a different county, some to a different state. As in most industrial societies, the American people move frequently and for a variety of reasons, but usually to escape disadvantageous economic situations or to take advantage of occupational opportunities. They also move to further educational goals, to enjoy a more favorable climate, and sometimes out of sheer restlessness. By the standards of peasant societies, where families who have lived in a community for only two hundred years may not be fully accepted, Americans are incredibly rootless. We are a society of transients.[22]

American society works. The transients are absorbed into the communities into which they move, partly because the communities of origin are not so different from the communities of destination, partly because most Americans have adjusted themselves to the changes that moves involve. As one of the editors of *Fortune* observed, men in the middle echelons of the corporate hierarchy *expect* to be transferred from place to place.[23] Varied experiences further their careers. They are as ready to move across the country as are the players in a game of musical chairs to give up their seats when the music starts. Particularly for better-educated, higher-income families and individuals, a move is an adventure, not a disorganizing experience. For some Americans, however, migrations means uprooting themselves: abandoning a secure way of life in exchange for bewildering problems. This is particularly true of poorly educated, unskilled rural people who move to large cities.

The Indian Relocation Program: A Case Study of Rural-Urban Migrants

Reprinted by permission. From La Verne Madigan, "The American Indian Relocation Program," New York: Association on American Indian Affairs, December 1956.

On the reservations of the Southwest and the Plains the Indian people, like people everywhere, are busy leading humdrum daily lives and, also like people everywhere, they are not planning to do any big good or bad thing which will change these lives drastically. If they are in Oklahoma, they are living on inadequate and rapidly shrinking allotments where the reservations used to be. The business of survival fills their days, and they are not humming with discussion of whether Relocation is a brave new way to survive or a way to destroy themselves as Indians. Their tribal governments have discussions like that sometimes and send resolutions to Washington, but Relocation is not the only thing the tribal councils discuss. They discuss the need for more agricultural and industrial opportunity in Oklahoma; per capita payments and oil leases at Fort Berthold in North Dakota; and, always, the loss of Indian land at the big Oglala Sioux reservation in South Dakota. Everywhere they discuss the need for more factories like the Bulova Watch Company's at Turtle Mountain and the new baby furniture plant at Navajo. But those are the remote things that local governments—tribal councils or boards of aldermen—discuss everywhere. The man who may ultimately decide to try Relocation with his family arrives at a private decision which is not made on the basis of whether the

21 Bureau of the Census, *Statistical Abstract of the United States: 1962*, Washington: Government Printing Office, 1962, p. 39.
22 Theodore Caplow, "Transiency as a Cultural Pattern," *American Sociological Review*, Vol. 5, December 1940, pp. 731–739.
23 See pp. 188–189.

Relocation Program is one more form of the protean pressure to end the separate existence of Indians in the United States. . . .

There will be food for tonight, none for tomorrow, and no refrigerator to keep it in if there were. The family will have used up the last of the man's unemployment compensation, and tomorrow he will pay a useless visit to the office of the State Employment Service, located on the reservation perhaps, to seek work as a day laborer to tide him over until the time comes for him to go off again with a road gang for the Santa Fe, or with a group of trained fire-fighters to a burning forest somewhere in the West. When he goes on these jobs he will leave his family behind him for a month or three months or maybe longer. Perhaps instead he will take his wife and all the children off to harvest beets or potatoes in Colorado, Idaho or Nebraska. If he does that, he will be sorry to take the children out of school. He would like his children to be educated, for educated Indians get good jobs with the Indian Service or the tribal councils, at trading posts or in the missions.

If educated Indians do not get these jobs at home, they disappear with their knowledge and aspirations into the world beyond the reservations. It is hard for them to cut loose from their people, and their culture that has no counterpart outside, but education has unfitted them for the feast-and-starve existence of the seasonal laborer. It has unfitted them for the menial, unsteady jobs earmarked for Indians in the white communities on the edge of the reservations—Farmington and Gallup in New Mexico, Globe in Arizona, Rapid City in South Dakota—and for being half-humorously regarded as part of the Indian shanty-town fermenting in the swamp or used-car-dump on the outskirts of the city. Work on the reservation, among and for their people, would make them happy. There is big talk in the Indian Bureau about bringing industry and enterprise to Indian areas, but the man who waits may end up an alcoholic. There is nothing else to become. The educated Indians go off to the cities, therefore, and the Indian communities lose the leaders they will need for the industrial development about which the Indian Bureau is saying so much.

Uneducated Indians live the same experience on a humbler level. They do not go off to the cities on the spur of ambition to succeed in some particular kind of endeavor or even to live in a home-magazine house. They know that men with one to eight years of schooling work for wages, not self-fulfillment. They do not, generally, have the self-confidence or train-fare to start out without assistance or encouragement from anyone. They walk into the Indian Bureau office some morning and say, "What is this Relocation?"

Reservation Indians know about the existence of the Relocation Program from speeches made at tribal council meetings; from little mimeographed folders on the counter at the trader's store, inviting anyone who is interested in year-round employment in a distant city to visit the Bureau office; from letters written home by others who went to the cities under the Program. In 1952 and 1953 they used to learn about it from Relocation Officers who went out on the reservation to recruit as for the Army. Such recruiting is still done in Oklahoma, where the Program is well regarded by Indians, and where Relocation is seen as opportunity. Relocation Officers in other areas do not usually do this now, partly because Indians are seeking relocation on their own initiative, and partly because public criticism of the quota-system used in the Program convinced the Bureau that the American people will tolerate the Program only to the extent that it is voluntary.

Posters in the reservation Relocation Office advertise the attractions of the Relocation cities. Snapshots mounted on pasteboard show the Chicago waterfront, Indians building airplanes in Los Angeles, their wives standing by television sets and electric refrigerators. Two, to be seen in most offices, show Indian-owned ranch houses with front-yard flower gardens. This display material has been denounced as untruthful representation of the conditions under which relocated Indians live in the cities. . . .

The man has seen the posters. Now the Relocation Officer tells him, not as overpoweringly as in 1952 and 1953 before the Program had been taken to task for overselling itself, about the financing and services available to him under it. The Relocation Officer shows the man job and wage reports from the Relocation cities, tells him that the city Relocation Office will help him with money for up to four weeks and with guidance for six months to a year, and assures him that by then he will be his white neighbor's peer in know-how and able to dispense with paternalistic care. Then, the man is sent home to discuss what he has been told with his wife and other relatives whose welfare may be involved.

Finally, in theory, and in practice where the staff is as large as it should be, the Relocation Officer visits the man's family to make clear the problems of adjustment to urban life, to explain to the wife that the success of the Relocation will depend upon her, since, at first, she will sit lonely indoors while her husband works and her children are away at school. If after this interview the family still wants to try Relocation, papers begin to be processed and sent to the chosen city Relocation Office: family histories, employment forms, health certificates. . . .

Service up to this point has, perhaps, been as personal as any the man has ever received. Reservation Relocation Officers sometimes drive 160 miles round-trip for a single visit to a family and make three such visits before the final one whose purpose is to transport the family to the railroad station. They sometimes hustle young relocating couples to priests or ministers in order that "Indian marriages" may be regularized before departure. They pack bags, buy alarm clocks for men who have never had to get to work at 7 in the morning, and buy disposable diapers for use on the way. Some reservation Relocation Officers do not do all these things; most of them do.

The kindly service continues for a little while after the Indian family reaches the city. The man when he arrives at the railroad station has in his pocket an instruction sheet. It tells him to check his baggage, where it may be picked up later by a Relocation Office employee; and advises him, this once, to take a taxi to the Relocation Office. He has been told that he may turn to representatives of the Travelers Aid Society if some unforeseen confusion arises at the station, and he could not be told a better thing.

The Travelers Aid Society, which gives relocated Indians emergency assistance under a national agreement with the Bureau of Indian Affairs, says nothing inflammatory or public about the troubles which beset Indians newly arrived in a city, but it helps them in quick, quiet ways. In cooperation with the Bureau, it guides and counsels Indians who are dazed upon arrival, and it makes emergency loans to the city Relocation Office when an Indian reaches town before his subsistence check has been processed. The Society refers to appropriate local agencies Indians who are not new arrivals in the city but have remained as confused as if they were. And, since freedom of movement is the principle on which the Society stands, it has been known to make arrangements, in justifiable instances, for Indians to go home again. It serves equally Indians who have come to the city under the Program and Indians who have come on their own, uninduced and untempted. . . .

The man and his family present themselves at the Relocation Office. . . . A receptionist, usually Indian, is expecting them. The man is wearing his best pants, a pair of new blue jeans, cowboy boots and, possibly, a ten-gallon hat. His wife is wearing a cotton housedress, wrinkled from the long train ride. Two of her little children will be put in the office play-pen, one will cling to her knees, and she may be nursing the youngest—unless she does that later on the street. She will remain quiet while a Relocation Officer confers with her husband. The Relocation Officer, a woman in most cases where there is guidance work to be done, tells the man how to use the checking account in which his subsistence money will be deposited, and how to operate a dial telephone. She gives him a map of the city and tells him how to use it, although he is tired now and will probably forget what she said. She looks over her check-list of things to be remembered, and asks him whether he owns an alarm clock, promises to see that one is bought if he does not, and slips in a word of advice about getting to work on time. She tells him to rest with his family for the remainder of the day, and to return to the office tomorrow in order that the Relocation Officer in charge of employment may refer him to a job. Then she takes the family to a cheap apartment house or hotel which is used to quarter large families until the man is working and permanent housing can be found near his place of employment. She drives the family to this temporary residence, advises them to eat in a cheap, clean, nearby restaurant, and then goes on to pay a home visit to a couple who arrived the day before.

HOUSING

The temporary housing in which the family and all newcomers will be placed . . . will have been chosen as the newcomers' first stopping place because it is near the Relocation Office which the man will have to visit frequently for the next week; because it is cheap enough not to exhaust the family's subsistence allowance too quickly;

and because it has space for Indian families which seldom number less than four and occasionally number as high as thirteen. The rooms will be shabbily but not wretchedly furnished. In one city there will be cooking facilities in the temporary quarters. In another, the quarters will be in a hotel which has seen better days but does not yet qualify for the skid-row category; here there will be no stove, but there will be pay television. Single men and women are more easily and better housed in Y.M. and Y.W.C.A. residences, and all-male or all-female boarding houses. The temporary housing is used only until the man is employed.

The second quarters into which the family move, today, will be passable according to working-class, inadequate according to middle-class standards. . . .

Currently the Chicago Relocation Office is finding housing for Indians in those erstwhile luxury neighborhoods, familiar in all large industrial or commercial cities: neighborhoods where the streets are wide and tree-lined, the building fronts still elegant, the interiors shabby and in dismal contrast. The shabbiness is the peculiar shabbiness of old hall carpets which were once deeply piled, threadbare over-stuffed divans which were once opulent, a plastic shower curtain hanging at a window which once had a velours drape, an extra bed standing in the living room. That would be a furnished apartment.

The Relocation Offices in all cities are now, with the new $250 furniture allowance, trying to move families as quickly as possible into cheaper, roomier unfurnished flats. The furniture will still be second-hand, purchased from Goodwill Industries or the Salvation Army, but it will be refinished simple furniture, not decaying rococo. . . .

EMPLOYMENT

The day after a man's arrival, or the same afternoon if he is not too tired, and his family feels safe in its temporary quarters, he goes to the Relocation Office for referral to a job. He is interviewed by an employment specialist who discusses his aptitudes and desires. In many cases, the man has had only a few years of schooling, has worked solely as an agricultural stoop-laborer, and the city's lure for him was the possibility of year-round rather than soul-satisfying work. If he had—and a few Indians do have—a developed

skill and a well-defined ambition, opportunity could readily be found for him. It is not difficult, in any event, to place him at the prevailing wage in a given industry, since city Relocation Offices are situated where employment is diversified and plentiful. The problem is that the prevailing wage in the industry may be inadequate for the support of his family. That is not to say that it would be inadequate for the support of a non-Indian family, which would not include five or six school and pre-school children and accept as both agreeable and inevitable the possibility that another child would be born each year. . . .

The city Relocation Offices are usually able to place a man after from one to three referrals; and they themselves cannot be held accountable for the lack of education, urban work experience and emotional serenity which may cause him to fail at this first job, and the third, and, if his troubles are unusually bad, [at] all he ever attempts. The man's ability to adapt himself to and improve his skill in urban employment cannot be predicted before he tries. Whether he should be discouraged from trying at all because he may fail, or whether all Indians should be encouraged to remain in their reservation areas for the years it will take to produce a skilled generation is a question. . . .

While a man is seeking employment, the Relocation staff is performing various services for his family. One member helps hunt the permanent housing referred to above. Another . . . visits the home at least three times to take the mother out to buy clothes with the family's clothing allowance, to help her select used furniture for the $250 permitted for that, to enroll her at the prenatal clinic, to see that the children are registered in school, to learn whether the family is in any kind of trouble it has kept to itself. On these visits Relocation Officers have been known to wash a man's shirt and give a long-braided woman a hair-cut.

Since the limit on home-visiting must be set somewhere, unless the staff is to be indefinitely extended, mail communications are used on some occasions to serve the same purpose. The files of the Chicago office, examined in privacy and at random, revealed that mimeographed notices were broadcast to relocated families telling the date of school opening and warning that all school-age children must be enrolled, and announcing the availability of Salk shots. . . .

Whether the Indian Relocation Program is succeeding is not clear. Unlike the larger migration of rural Negroes into urban areas, however, the Indian migration is sponsored and supported by the federal government. Organized efforts are made to facilitate the socialization of Indians at their urban destinations. This represents a break with American traditions. In the years from 1890 to 1914, when millions of European peasants crowded into the large cities of the East, the federal government did not take responsibility for their socialization—or for the welfare problems resulting from their initial maladjustment. And currently the federal government has no program to facilitate the exodus of Negroes from the rural South and their integration into cities. The unintended consequence of this *laissez faire* policy is that Negro, Puerto Rican, and Spanish-American migrants from rural areas, as well as Appalachian Mountain whites, flounder for months and sometimes years as they try to cope with the urban environment. Private health and welfare agencies and municipal services eventually offer assistance, but it is difficult to undo the demoralizing effects of initial experiences. The rising cost of health and welfare services in large American cities may tempt the federal government to extend the concept of planned relocation to rural communities not served by the specialized Indian Relocation Program. When that happens, one of the major types of adult socialization in industrial societies, socialization of migrants, will receive explicit recognition.

CONCLUSION

Socialization continues throughout life as the individual learns new roles in new groups. Early socialization may facilitate later socialization, as happens when there are familiar elements in the new role. But sometimes early socialization interferes with later socialization, as happens when the new role requires the *unlearning* of elements in previous roles. In any case, socialization can never be regarded as finished. Learning of new roles continues until death.

In industrial societies some socialization experiences outside of the family are predictably difficult. Socialization into the neighborhood peer group involves learning equalitarian relationships. Socialization at school involves learning to participate in an impersonal organization. Socialization into the world of work involves a discontinuity between the educational and the occupational systems. Socialization in marriage involves the joint development of a new social system. It is perhaps premature to attempt to assess the relative difficulty of these various transitions. The problem of the strains involved in continuous socialization is where the cooperative research of psychologists and sociologists can add significantly to knowledge of human development.

SOME SIGNIFICANT LITERATURE ON CONTINUING SOCIALIZATION

Elaine Cumming and William E. Henry, *Growing Old: The Process of Disengagement*, New York: Basic Books, 1961. The authors of this research monograph, having interviewed a large sample of old people in metropolitan Kansas City, address the question, "What are healthy, economically secure old people like?" Aging is conceived of as disengagement, defined as "an inevitable process in which many of the relationships between a person and other members of society are severed and those remaining are altered in quality." This summary is based on a review by Gordon F. Streib, *American Sociological Review*, Vol. 27, August 1962, pp. 561–562.

S. N. Eisenstadt, *The Absorption of Immigrants: A Comparative Study Based Mainly on the Jewish Community in Palestine and the State of Israel*, Glencoe, Ill.: Free Press, 1955. During the nineteenth century the United States was called a "melting pot" because it absorbed a heavy influx of immigrants, largely of European origin. In the twentieth century the State of Israel has faced a proportionately heavier influx of immigrants from Europe, Africa, and the Middle East. Professor Eisenstadt describes and analyzes the emergence of a pluralistic society in Israel which cushions the adult socialization process for immigrant groups and enables them to maintain some degree of separate identity. This summary is based on a review by Arthur Jordan Field, *American Sociological Review*, Vol. 20, August 1955, pp. 487–488.

Nelson N. Foote and Leonard S. Cottrell, Jr., *Identity and Interpersonal Competence: A New Direction in Family Research*, Chicago: University of Chicago Press, 1955. Family research has emphasized concepts like compatibility and adjustment, which do not recognize the interactive character of the marital relationship. Marital success depends less on similar traits in the husband and wife than on mutual participation in the creation of new goals. The authors suggest *interpersonal competence* as a concept that is sufficiently dynamic to handle the complexities of marital socialization. Interpersonal competence is not a unidimensional concept; some of its components—like intelligence—may be innate; others—like judgment—are susceptible to training. The type of training that seems most promising to the authors is empathic identification with other persons possessing interpersonal competence. This summary is based on a review by Thomas Ktsanes, *American Sociological Review*, Vol. 21, August 1956, pp. 510–511.

Renee C. Fox, *Experiment Perilous: Physicians and Patients Facing the Unknown*, Glencoe, Ill.: Free Press, 1959. Professor Fox reports on her participant-observer study of a 15-bed metabolic research ward in a large city hospital. The patients had a variety of chronic and, in some cases, fatal illnesses. Their futures were at best uncertain. Their physicians attempted to treat their illnesses with new drugs, but the prospects of successful treatment were slim. In describing the way patients and doctors handled the stresses of their situations, Professor Fox provides examples of socialization to failure. This summary is based on a review by H. Warren Dunham, *American Sociological Review*, Vol. 25, February 1960, pp. 133–134.

Robert L. Hall and Ben Willerman, "The Educational Influence of Dormitory Roommates," *Sociometry*, Vol. 26, September 1963, pp. 294–318. The effect of college roommates on each other was studied under two conditions: (1) where roommates mutually chose one another and (2) where roommates were assigned to one another on the basis of their high school percentile ranks. (Research indicates that a student's percentile rank in his high school graduating class is the best single predictor of his academic performance in college.) The major hypothesis tested by the *experimental* assignments was that students living with high-ability roommates would get better grades than students living with low-ability roommates; no appreciable tendency for this to happen was observed. However, "roommates were more alike than chance expectancy in attendance at plays and in belonging to student organizations—and this was true for both experimentally assigned and mutually selected roommates. The mutual roommates were also alike in time spent studying . . . and academic achievement. The similarities that occur only between *mutual* roommates are presumably the result of their methods of selecting a roommate, rather than of mutual influence."

Robert K. Merton, George G. Reader, and Patricia Kendall, Eds., *The Student-Physician: Introductory Studies in the Sociology of Medical Education*, Cambridge, Mass.: Harvard University Press, 1957. In urban industrial societies *occupational* socialization is of major importance both to the individual and to the community. This study of medical students thus serves as an illustration of the lengthy process of occupational socialization entailed by some careers. Eight separate reports are included by various members of the research team. One thread running through the reports is the changes in values of medical students as they progress in their training. For example, students farther along in school are more likely to report that they think of themselves as doctors in contacts with patients than students less far along; they are also more capable of bearing the uncertainties inherent in medical treatment. Another thread is Professor Merton's concept of anticipatory socialization: the adoption of the values of a group to which one does not yet belong but which one wishes to join. Medical students are not yet physicians, but their tendency to think of themselves as physicians helps them to learn the role. For a discussion of the sociology of occupations—of which occupational socialization is but one aspect—see Everett Cherrington Hughes, "The Study of Occupations," in Robert K. Merton, Leonard Broom, and Leonard S. Cottrell, Jr., Eds., *Sociology Today: Problems and Prospects*, New York: Basic Books, 1959, pp. 442–458.

C. Wright Mills, Clarence Senior, and Rose Kohn Goldsen, *The Puerto Rican Journey*, New York: Harper, 1950. In 1948 the Bureau of Applied Social Research at Columbia University undertook a survey of Puerto Ricans living in New York City. The characteristics of 5000 Puerto Rican immigrants were studied in an attempt to understand why they had been dissatisfied with Puerto Rico and attracted to New York. The migrants were likely to come from *urban* areas in Puerto Rico and to be otherwise better equipped to compete in a metropolis than the islanders they left behind. Nevertheless, their average educational level of six years, their lack of occupational skills, and their language handicap constituted obstacles to successful adjustment. One-third of the migrants were colored, and this added to their difficulties. For a moving account of the socialization of *nineteenth century* immigrants, based on their own and other contemporary accounts, see Oscar Handlin, *The Uprooted: The Epic Story of the Great Migrations That Made the American People*, Boston: Little, Brown, 1951.

Theodore M. Newcomb, *The Acquaintance Process*, New York: Holt, Rinehart, and Winston, 1961. Professor Newcomb and his research associates at the University of Michigan set up a special residential house for undergraduates in order to observe the process by which newly arrived college students chose their friends. He found that students tended to gravitate toward those students having similar attitudes toward dormitory and university policies, religion, sex, politics, and race. This finding supports the old adage, "Birds of a feather flock together," and contradicts the other adage, "Opposites attract." In each of two successive years, 17 students were selected for the experiment. The findings of the first year were thus confirmed in a repetition of the study. This summary is based on a review by Ithiel De Sola Pool, *American Sociological Review*, Vol. 26, December 1961, pp. 939–940.

Henry W. Riecken, *The Volunteer Work Camp: A Psychological Evaluation*, Cambridge, Mass.: Addison-Wesley, 1952. This study is an example of evaluative research: research aimed at finding out the *actual* impact of an action program as opposed to its *intended* impact. The action program studied was the summer work camps of the American Friends Service Committee. The college students who volunteered for community service during their summer vacations filled out questionnaires three times: (1) before working in the camps in 1948, (2) at the end of camp, and (3) ten months after the closing of the camps. Thus, it was possible to distinguish superficial short-run changes in the participants from more lasting changes. Long-run changes were reported in the direction of less authoritarian, less ethnocentric, and more democratic attitudes. Short-run changes in a pacifist direction were noted immediately following the closing of the camps, but there was a reversion toward nonpacifist attitudes after ten months. Bear in mind, in considering the implications of summer camps for adult socialization, that the participants were self-selected to begin with and were therefore sympathetic to the "liberal" objectives of the program. This summary is based on a review by R. A. Schermerhorn, *American Sociological Review*, Vol. 18, August 1953, pp. 468–469.

Robin M. Williams, Jr., *The Reduction of Intergroup Tensions: A Survey of Research on Problems of Ethnic, Racial, and Religious Group Relations*, New York: Social Science Research Council, 1947. An important type of adult socialization is the reduction of antisocial or divisive attitudes. For instance, many governmental and private agencies attempt to change criminal or prejudiced attitudes. This monograph surveys the research undertaken in conjunction with programs that deal with the latter problem. Generally speaking, modest accomplishments have resulted from the considerable efforts to promote "group understanding." Prejudice results from initial socialization in childhood, which, once developed, is difficult to modify. Although educational institutions often try to promote racial, cultural, and religious tolerance, "the mere giving of objective general information in print or by lecture about a group which is the object of hostility has only a slight effect, or no effect, in reducing hostility—at least in the short run." Programs with greater possibilities for success depend on building solidarities that transcend racial or other cleavages, or on working with groups whose members mutually support one another's increased tolerance. For a recent discussion of the lack of relationship between level of formal education and tolerance, see Charles H. Stember, *Education and Attitude Change: The Effect of Schooling on Prejudice against Minority Groups*, New York: Institute of Human Relations Press, 1961.

PART IV

The Maintenance of Stability
in Urban Industrial Societies

CHAPTER 12

Formal Education

All societies must cope with the task of transmitting their cultural traditions to the new generation. In preliterate societies, this task is handled informally by the family and the community. In industrial societies, the family starts the education of the young, but at an early age a specialized organization, the school, assumes the main responsibility. Modern societies were compelled to create *formal* educational institutions because the universal problem of cultural transmission is more difficult under urban industrial conditions. The tremendous size of the culture base means that no one has detailed knowledge of the entire culture. Members of the society share a common culture in a composite sense: Each person has a general idea of the contents of the culture and also has detailed knowledge of small portions of it. The cultural mosaic is further differentiated (1) by ethnic, regional, and class subcultures and (2) by a rapid rate of cultural change. Under these difficult conditions the school attempts to provide a guaranteed minimum of useful knowledge for everybody as well as specialized education for particular subgroups.

THE EMERGENCE OF MASS PRIMARY AND SECONDARY EDUCATION

Suppose there were no schools, and parents educated their children in accordance with their own notions of what a child ought to know. Would a child who depended on the version of the cultural tradition transmitted by his parents learn enough basic ideas and skills to function in a complicated society? All industrial countries have implicitly assumed a negative answer to this question. They have established systems of mass education at the primary school level to teach basic literacy, arithmetic, and some common knowledge and beliefs. Table 48 documents the extent to which the education of children from five to 14 is *mass* education in the developed countries.

The ability to read and write is hardly a luxury in urban industrial societies. An illiterate gets lost more often than persons who can read street signs and house numbers. He does not understand notices posted on a bulletin board at his place of employment. He probably is not able to get a driver's license. He has trouble making employment applications, signing contracts, and paying bills. Not knowing how to read labels, he has difficulty shopping in the

supermarket. He has difficulty in finding a job.[1]
The emphasis in primary schools on basic literacy is plainly dictated by necessity.

Arithmetic is also a necessity in urban industrial communities. In a society in which nearly everyone at some stage of his life (1) sells his services in the labor market and (2) consumes the goods and services it produces, monetary transactions are inescapable. A person who cannot add and subtract is at a serious disadvantage in such transactions. Arithmetic is also required in other activities, although not

as obviously as in exchange. A carpenter must know how to add and subtract fractions, or his measurements will not be correct. Inventory control requires endless counting. Personal budgeting requires arithmetic, and so does a checking account.

The importance of reading, writing, and arithmetic skills in an industrial society can also be appreciated by a comparative perspective. In the following article, Dr. Hilda Hertz Golden demonstrates (1) that literacy is correlated with economic development and (2) that *mass education* is a necessary condition for economic development.

TABLE 48
School Attendance in Contemporary Nations in Various Recent Years

Country	Base Year	Per Cent of Age Group Enrolled in School			
		5–14 Years	15–19 Years	20–24 Years	5–24 Years
United States	1958	89.9	66.2	12.0	69.9
Canada	1958	87.3	45.9	9.3	63.0
Sweden	1960	82.6	32.3	11.0	54.0
Switzerland	1956	78.6	22.9	3.4	48.7
Luxembourg	1957	76.3	25.2	5.4	44.0
Belgium	1957	95.4	31.5	5.5	60.2
United Kingdom	1957	98.8	17.6	3.9	59.6
France	1958	90.1	30.8	3.8	58.6
Denmark	1957	76.4	18.5	5.6	48.9
Norway	1957	77.3	35.7	9.5	55.2
Germany, F.R.	1958	80.2	17.6	4.6	42.3
Netherlands	1958	85.5	32.8	4.7	57.4
Iceland	1957	73.2	57.9	6.8	56.7
Austria	1957	84.8	13.1	3.7	46.5
Ireland	1957	92.6	19.6	4.2	59.3
Italy	1957	78.8	15.7	3.9	42.5
Yugoslavia	1956	66.3	16.9	4.1	37.8
Spain	1958–59	74.9	13.3	3.3	39.6
Greece	1956–57	74.5	16.9	3.3	40.8
Portugal	1957–58	56.2	8.8	3.1	32.6
Turkey	1959–60	44.7	3.3	1.1	25.1
Soviet Union	1958	71.5	48.6	8.2	49.1

Source: Ingvar Svennilson (in association with Friedrich Edding and Lional Elvin), *Targets for Education in Europe in 1970*, Paris: Organization for Economic Cooperation and Development, January 1962, pp. 107–108.

[1] Eli Ginzberg and Douglas W. Bray, *The Uneducated*, New York: Columbia University Press, 1953.

Literacy: A Prerequisite for the Urban Industrial Way of Life

Reprinted by permission. From Hilda Hertz Golden, "Literacy and Social Change in Underdeveloped Countries," *Rural Sociology*, Vol. 20, February 1955, pp. 1–7.

Literacy affords an excellent index of the level of socio-economic development of a country, for behind the degree of literacy lies the whole institutional structure of a society. Thus, one indication of the differential spread of industrialism through the world is the sharp contrast in literacy between urban-industrial and peasant-agricultural nations. One way of identifying the world's underdeveloped countries is by singling out the highly illiterate countries—those, let us say, with more than half of their adult population illiterate.

But literacy is more than an index: Literacy skills function significantly in the economic advance of underdeveloped areas. Though not essential to traditional agriculture and its related crafts, literacy is required for urban-industrial occupations. Hence, literate and educated manpower constitutes a necessary asset in the transition from peasant agriculturalism to urban industrialism. . . .

DEFINITION AND MEASUREMENT

Educators have long debated the question of where, on the continuum of educational achievement, to draw the line dividing literacy from illiteracy; they are still far from a unanimous answer. Fortunately, almost any point would do for present purposes, since all that is needed is an accurate *indicator* of educational achievement, not a final definition of literacy. The dividing line used here is the one drawn by most governments, particularly governments of underdeveloped countries, for purposes of census enumeration—the ability to read and write one's name. On this basis literacy rates can be readily calculated, and these rates correlate highly with other indices of educational achievement.

The data have been taken mostly from national censuses. Because definitions differ slightly from country to country, census data occasionally have had to be adjusted to conform to one definition and to refer to one date—1950. To achieve world coverage, however, other educational statistics have been converted into estimates of literacy rates whenever census data were lacking. Even though the estimates may be quite rough and the census data not strictly comparable, the information is sufficiently accurate to place all countries, except borderline cases, within broad categories and to provide a basis for exploring the problem in a world-wide context.

THE RELATION OF LITERACY AND INDUSTRIALIZATION

If those countries in which 50 per cent or more of the gainfully occupied males are engaged in agriculture are regarded as underdeveloped, we find, as expected, that the underdeveloped countries are highly illiterate, with the striking exception of those in Europe (Table 49). But even the latter are far more illiterate than the industrial nations. Despite exceptions, then, Table 49 demonstrates the close association between the levels of educational achievement and of industrialization.

The application of correlation analysis to the data provides both a measure of the degree of correspondence of the variables and a regression equation through which deviant cases can be isolated. Literacy and industrialization in 1950 correlate closely: the coefficient of correlation is .87 when industrialization is measured by the proportion of gainfully occupied males in nonagricultural pursuits, and .84 when measured by per-capita income. The closeness of these relationships is further substantiated by historical data for individual countries. In England and Wales, for example, the growth of literacy has been closely associated with that of industrialism, as is con-

firmed here by a coefficient of correlation of .98.

Establishing the close interrelation of the diffusion of literacy and industrialization invites speculation on why it should exist: Literacy is not essential in the training for or the practice of traditional agriculture and its related handicraft occupations. These occupations can be learned through apprenticeship, by watching an experienced person, by attempting to imitate him by trial and error. The knowledge required for such work can be stored in a person's memory; the principles can be transmitted verbally as part of the apprenticeship process. Since neither business documents nor accounts need be kept, and since the work requires no blueprints, reading and writing are not essential to everyday life.

When most parents follow these traditional occupations, they feel no strong incentive to send their children to school or to arrange somehow

TABLE 49
Illiteracy in Developed and Underdeveloped Countries, 1950 [a]

Geographical Division	Percentage of illiterates in the Population Aged 10 and Over		
	All Countries	Developed Countries	Underdeveloped Countries
World	47	6	70
North America [c]	2	2	[b]
Europe	8	3	20
Oceania	11	1	88
U.S.S.R. [d]	11	11	[b]
South America	42	17	51
Middle America [e]	48	20	52
Asia	70	2	75
Africa	88	55	91

[a] Developed countries are those with less than 50 per cent of their economically active males in agricultural pursuits, including hunting, fishing, and forestry; underdeveloped countries are those with 50 per cent or more of their economically active males in these pursuits.

[b] No country in this category.

[c] U.S.A., Canada, and Alaska.

[d] The U.S.S.R. is a borderline case but has been classed here among the developed countries, since today its agricultural labor force is probably slightly below 50 per cent.

[e] The Central American republics and the islands of the Caribbean.

that the children acquire literacy skills; they view with indifferent skepticism the practical benefits to be derived from literacy and education. They are easily discouraged by lack of funds, by long distances from school, by their need for their children's labor. Therefore, unless local governments or outside agents push a program of formal education with unusual vigor or attempt with great persistence to diffuse literacy skills, their prospects of success are slight.

Besides the agriculturalist's apathy toward formal education and his poverty, lack of government funds is an additional obstacle to the diffusion of literacy, since governments of underdeveloped countries cannot provide adequate educational facilities even when they want to. Many impoverished governments, for example, exempt rural children from school attendance because providing school facilities for them is too costly.

In peasant-agricultural countries, literacy begins to diffuse beyond a few traditional occupations (such as the scribe's) and beyond the confines of a literate élite when the society is starting to change in its occupational structure. Since urban-industrial occupations require reading and writing for their acquisition and practice, literacy appears as a skill that leads the individual out of traditional agriculturalism. Education begins to be regarded as a passport from the hard and primitive life of the subsistence farmer to the haven of nonagricultural employment. When parents are no longer employed in traditional agriculture but instead have become unskilled industrial laborers, occupational training of children requires time and skills beyond the power of parents to provide. Parents thus acquire incentives to send their children to school; they acquire some notion of the usefulness of primary education and are less likely to demand their children's services at an early age. They may view education as a channel of mobility from unskilled to skilled occupations, from agriculture to industry. Furthermore, with increasing industrialization governments become more able to provide educational facilities and to enforce school attendance. In brief, the growth and diffusion of literacy in underdeveloped countries is closely tied to the growth and diffusion of an urban-industrial civilization.

LITERACY AS A FACTOR IN SOCIAL CHANGE

Although all underdeveloped countries show a glaring lack of trained manpower, some are far more deficient in this respect than are others at the same stage. The skills of a population are, within limits, subject to manipulation, and a few peasant-agricultural countries have diverted an unusually large share of their means toward the diffusion of literacy, others only a small share. As a result, educational progress when compared with industrial advance may be retarded or advanced. Singling out the deviant countries by using the regression equations mentioned earlier serves a twofold purpose: An analysis of the deviant countries may indicate the factors that account for the differential support of education, and it may also suggest the role of educational achievement in future economic development.

Among the underdeveloped nations, the following are noteworthy for their deviation:

More Literate than Industrial:

Bulgaria	Panama
Colombia	Philippines
Costa Rica	Poland
Ecuador	Rumania
Finland	Thailand

Less Literate than Industrial:

Egypt	Libya
India	Malaya
Indonesia	Nepal
Iran	Union of South
Iraq	Africa

The information available about these countries suggests that two kinds of factors largely account for the retardation or advance of educational *vis-à-vis* industrial development. The first set of factors are those determining the relative claim that a nation's goals, such as mass literacy or the support of religion or an army, have upon a nation's wealth; second, there are those determining the cost of achieving widespread literacy and education, such as linguistic diversity or the esoteric nature of the literary language.

In a few countries the literate and educated class has been particularly narrow in its interests and pursuits; its learning has been oriented away from the everyday life of the community and toward traditionalism, abstruse religious scholarship, and magic. Conversely, in a few nations the literate élite has conceived of education as a means to increased national strength or national independence; the intelligentsia have taken an interest in scientific and technological knowledge, and their scholarship has received the stimulus of daily necessity and economic need. In Bulgaria prior to independence, for example, wealthy persons conceived it their duty to open and to maintain schools despite the opposition of the Turkish state; the élite of the Arab areas of the Ottoman Empire showed no such interest.

One result of a great emphasis on traditionalism by a small literate class in a generally illiterate population is the tendency of the written language to diverge from the spoken vernacular. This process may go so far that the written language becomes meaningless to the masses. If the educated class extols the virtues of the "classical" language instead of working toward reducing the vernacular to writing and toward simplifying the script, there is no chance for widespread diffusion of literacy.

In addition, the great diversity of languages and scripts in some of the world's underdeveloped nations compounds the cost of achieving widespread literacy. Africa south of the Sahara is "a vast mosaic of vernacular languages, spoken by groups ranging in size from a few hundreds to several millions of persons," and this is one of the major difficulties encountered in the diffusion of literacy. Furthermore, the controversy over the medium of instruction, so endemic to the efforts to diffuse literacy and education, is an ample tribute to the magnitude of the problem of linguistic diversity.

In brief, the diffusion of literacy and education in a country beyond the comparable point of economic development, or the retardation behind that point, derives from the factors just mentioned—and perhaps others. Next comes the question of the significance of such retardation or advance for future economic development.

The modernization of peasant-agricultural countries is usually conceived of as a moving equilibrium in which no one element can be for very long out of line with the others, because they are functionally interdependent. On this basis we would expect that countries in which educational retardation is considerable and has lasted for some time would now be making relatively greater headway educationally than economically. Conversely, countries in which the advance is considerable and has lasted for some time should now be making relatively greater progress economically than educationally. Despite the paucity of informa-

tion, it can be shown that this is true for many countries.

Since about 1900, India has exhibited faster educational than economic progress. It has slowly narrowed the gap created by the more rapid economic development of the nineteenth century, although in 1951 the difference had not yet disappeared (Table 50). Again, in nineteenth-century Egypt, economic development, though spasmodic, took place faster than educational change. During the first three decades of this century, both industrial and educational advances were slight.

TABLE 50
Actual and Expected
Illiteracy in Selected Countries

Country and Year	Percentage of Illiterates in the Population Aged 10 and Over		Difference (Actual Percentage Minus Expected)
	Actual	Expected [a]	
India: [b]			
1911	93	64	29
1921	92	65	27
1931	91	64	27
1941	85	67	18
1951	80	61	19
Egypt:			
1907	93	67	26
1917	91	62	29
1927	86	56	30
1937	85	61	24
1947	[c]75	51	24
U.S.S.R.:			
1926	49	80	−31
1939	19	39	−20
Brazil:			
1940	57	61	− 4
1950	52	52	0
U.S.A.:			
1870	20	37	−17
1910	7	5	2

[a] By means of the regression equation, the expected percentages were calculated from the percentages of economically active males engaged in agricultural pursuits in each country (see text).

[b] Data on India's agricultural labor force have been taken from Kingsley Davis, "Social and Demographic Aspects of Economic Development in India," to be published soon as part of a symposium sponsored by the Social Science Research Council.

[c] Estimate.

Since about 1930, educational progress has been faster than economic development, despite the fact that during the period of World War II economic change was rapid. Egypt seems to have entered the phase in which for some time educational advance will remain faster than economic development. The examples of Egypt and India suggest that in countries like them educational progress is likely to accelerate.

Among the underdeveloped countries that are more literate than industrial, there are none for which we have as adequate information as we have for India and Egypt. Nevertheless, the scanty information that is available corroborates the contention. For example, Brazil, which in 1950 had a level of literacy commensurate with its level of industrialization, achieved this condition after a decade of considerably more rapid economic than educational progress. Similarly, Puerto Rico's rapid economic expansion began when educational advance had caught up with economic development. Today, Puerto Rico is more literate than industrial—its actual illiteracy rate is 24 per cent, whereas the expected rate is 32 per cent—and it is also making rapid economic progress. Unfortunately, there is little information available on the Balkan countries; but what there is suggests that they are repeating the pattern characteristic of the U.S.S.R. between 1926 and 1939 and of the U.S.A. between 1870 and 1910 (Table 50).

The differential rates of economic advance for the educationally retarded and the educationally advanced countries point to the importance of the dissemination of literacy and education in the transformation of peasant-agricultural nations into urban-industrial nations. In the "bootstrap" operation in which all underdeveloped countries are engaged, training the population for urban-industrial occupations is crucial to the achievement of higher levels of industrialization. Clearly the countries that today are ahead educationally will find it easier to achieve this goal than those that are behind. The latter countries will find their lack of literate and trained manpower a major obstacle to rapid industrialization. Paradoxically, they will need to spend a great share of their wealth, even though they have almost none, for the long-neglected goal of mass education before they can aspire to become modern industrial states.

As important as is basic literacy, the need for it does not alone explain mass formal education in industrial societies. If reading, writing, and arithmetic were sufficient, mass education would not have reached the secondary school level—and in the United States, the college level. Table 51 shows the increasing proportion of 17-year-old Americans who graduate from high school in the twentieth as compared with the nineteenth century. Mass secondary education began in the United States and is spreading to Western European countries. Table 48 showed that more than 30 per cent of youngsters 15 to 19 are enrolled in school in seven European countries. Secondary education was originally thought of as preparation for humanistic education in the universities, but the philosophy of secondary education has changed.[2] With advancing industrialization, an increasing proportion of jobs require technical skill or the mastery of a body of accumu-

TABLE 51

Graduates from Public and Private Secondary Schools in the United States, 1870–1956

School Year Ending	Secondary School Graduates	
	Number	Per Cent of 17-Year-Olds in Population
1870	16,000	2.0
1880	23,634	2.5
1890	43,731	3.5
1900	94,883	6.4
1910	156,429	8.8
1920	311,266	16.8
1930	666,904	29.0
1940	1,221,475	50.8
1950	1,199,700	59.0
1956	1,414,800	62.3

Source: Bureau of the Census, *Historical Statistics of the United States, Colonial Times to 1957*, Washington: Government Printing Office, 1960, p. 207.

2 A. D. C. Peterson, *A Hundred Years of Education*, rev. ed., New York: Collier, 1962, pp. 145–177.

lated knowledge.[3] The responsibility for preparation for these jobs was gradually assumed by secondary and advanced education. Thus, secondary education in the technological society helps prepare youngsters to assume adult occupational roles. This preparatory function means that education must "keep up" with a *changing* culture base. As the anthropologist Margaret Mead maintains in the following article, a changing culture base requires a dynamic approach to education. Under these conditions education can never be completed.

Educational Obsolescence in a Changing Culture

Reprinted by permission. From Margaret Mead, "Thinking Ahead: Why Is Education Obsolete?," *Harvard Business Review*, Vol. 36, November–December 1958, pp. 23–30.

When we look realistically at the world in which we are living today and become aware of what the actual problems of learning are, our conception of education changes radically. Although the educational system remains basically unchanged, we are no longer dealing primarily with the *vertical* transmission of the tried and true by the old, mature, and experienced teacher to the young, immature, and inexperienced pupil. This was the system of education developed in a stable, slowly changing culture. In a world of rapid change, vertical transmission of knowledge alone no longer serves the purposes of education.

What is needed and what we are already moving toward is the inclusion of another whole dimension of learning: the *lateral* transmission, to every sentient member of society, of what has just been discovered, invented, created, manufactured, or marketed. This need for lateral transmission exists no less in the physics or genetics laboratory than it does on the assembly line with its working force of experienced and raw workmen. The man who teaches another individual the new mathematics or the use of a newly invented tool is not sharing knowledge he acquired years ago. He learned what was new yesterday, and his pupil must learn it today.

[3] Burton R. Clark, *Educating the Expert Society*, San Francisco: Chandler, 1962, pp. 45–58.

The whole teaching-and-learning continuum, which once was tied in an orderly and productive way to the passing of generations and the growth of the child into a man—this whole process has exploded in our faces. Yet even as we try to catch hold of and patch up the pieces, we fail to recognize what has happened. . . .

Likewise, extraordinarily little attention is paid to the fact that two great new educational agencies—the armed services and industry—have entered the field, and there is little awareness of the ways in which operations in these institutions are altering traditional education. Recruitment programs of the armed services now include explicit statements of their role as educational institutions. For instance:

"The United States Armed Forces Institute . . . has enabled thousands upon thousands of young men to finish their high school education and begin college-level studies. A second Army program enables young men to attend courses at many civilian schools and colleges in off-duty hours. . . . [A third program teaches soldiers— on their bases] such subjects as typing, stenography, foreign languages, literature, and many more."

But most important, the pattern itself is hardly questioned. For we *think* we know what education is and what a good education ought to be; and however deficient we may be as a people, as taxpayers, or as educators, we may be actualizing our ideals. An occasional iconoclast can ask wistfully: "Wouldn't it be fine if we could scrap our whole school system and start anew?" But he gets no hearing because everyone knows that what he is saying is nonsense. Wishful dreams about starting all anew are obviously impractical, but this does not mean that someone should not ask these crucial questions:

• Is our present historic idea of education suitable for people in the mid-twentieth century, who have a life expectancy of 70 years, and who live in a world of automation and global communication, ready to begin space exploration and aware of the possibility that we can bring about the suicide of the entire human species?

• As all these present and pressing concerns of the human race are new, is it not possible that a system of education may be out of date which was designed for small societies that were connected by horse-drawn coaches and sailing ships, and where any war could threaten only small sections of the human species at any one time?

• Is it not possible that the problem of the educational system's obsolescence goes beyond such issues as methods of teaching reading or physics, or the most desirable age for leaving school, or the payment of teachers, or the length of summer holidays, or the number of years best devoted to college, or even the comparative advantages of working while going to high school or college?

• Is not the break between past and present —and so the whole problem of outdating in our educational system—related to a change in the rate of change? For change has become so rapid that adjustment cannot be left to the next generation; adults must—not once, but continually —take in, adjust to, use, and make innovations in a steady stream of discovery and new conditions.

• Our educational system, besides being the oldest system of universal free primary education in the world, bears the marks of its long history. But is it not possible to think that an educational system that was designed to teach what was known to little children and to a selected few young men (after which they could be regarded as "educated") may not fit a world in which the most important factors in everyone's life are those things that are not yet, but soon will be, known?

• Is it not equally possible that our present definition of a pupil or a student is out of date when we define the learner as a child (or at best an immature person) who is entitled to those things to which a child is entitled—moral protection and a meager subsistence in a dependency position—and who is denied those things which are denied to a child—moral autonomy, sex and parenthood, alcoholic beverages, and exposure to hazards?

In the picture which we have of the student, we have muddled together *both* a conception of the young child who is unable to fend for himself or to protect himself against moral and physical hazards, and who is entitled to be fed and sheltered *and* our own historical conception of the scholar's role as one in which some few men could claim lifelong support provided they themselves accepted an economic dependency that was demeaning to other men and a type of life in which they were subject to supervision (and, until recently in Christian history, gave up sex and parenthood).

This composite picture is one into which we can fit the scholarly monk, the Cambridge don who was not permitted to marry, and the student who lives in college and whose degree depends on his sleeping there (a touchingly infantile method of attaining a degree). All of these match our conception of the learner as a dependent who is subject to the supervision appropriate to a child and who must pay for his learning by abnegating some of the rewards of maturity.

Yet the combined ideas of the child and the monk do not complete our picture of the student; we have added still other things to it. With the industrial revolution there came new possibilities of exploiting human labor. Work, which through long ages had often been disliked by members of the upper classes and had been delegated to women, slaves, or serfs, became something different—more hazardous, more menacing. In this situation children were the most easily identifiable victims, and their fate was dramatized as a conflict between their right to an education and their subjection to dangerous and ruthless exploitation in the mines, in the factories, in dives, and in the street trades. The common school, born at a period in the United States when we were particularly concerned with extending the rights of the common man, was sponsored and fought for by labor groups. In this way the common school became doubly identified as the means of making all children literate and as the official enemy of child labor. A vote to raise the school-leaving age was a vote against child labor, and, like sin or cancer, child labor became something no one could be in favor of, officially.

So, as inevitably happens when different institutions in a culture become intertwined, raising the school-leaving age came to stand for several things: it was, on the one hand, a way of increasing the privileges of every child born in the United States and, on the other hand, a way of protecting children against the hazards of work to their health and morals.

That our picture of harmful labor is itself very complex can be seen even from a cursory examination of federal and state child labor laws. Looking at these we find that work outdoors is better than work indoors, that work in small cities is better than work in large cities, that work in summer and during vacations is less harmful than work in winter or during school terms, that work done for parents does not count as work, and that there is one form of work in which all the rules can be broken about age, hours, places, hazards from the weather, weight of objects dealt with, being on the streets, going to strange places, and so forth,—which, characteristically and in the best spirit of Horatio Alger, is delivering news-papers. . . .

So, when we think about education and try to identify the student, we have in our minds—whether or not we are aware of it—an exceedingly complex picture, the elements of which are com-pounded and confused in their historic connec-tions. Yet we must identify what they are if we are to remodel our educational system so that it is devoted to the kind of teaching and learning that is appropriate to the United States today. For this purpose a look at education in other societies will be helpful:

• Education which is limited to small chil-dren is appropriate in a very primitive society like that of the Eskimo. The nine-year-old Eskimo child has learned, from father or from mother, the basic skills of a spoken language, the handling of tools and equipment, knowledge of the weather, relevant personal relations, and religious taboos. He must wait until he is physically mature before he can marry; as he grows older he will gain pro-ficiency in hunting, in religious practices, in his knowledge of time, the seasons, and the land-scape; and he may come to exercise leadership. But his education, in the sense of learning what-ever adults could teach him directly, was over long before.

• In other societies that are more complex, education may not be completed before adoles-cence, when some young people may elect, or may be chosen, to learn more complicated skills and may memorize the classics, master complex weaving skills, or become skilled craftsmen or leaders of ritual activities.

After the invention of writing and the de-velopment of mathematics and medicine, these did not become part of the whole tradition which had to be imparted to everyone. Like techniques of gold working or a knowledge of magical charms, they were taught by a few to a few in a long continuum of teaching-and-learning, in which the teacher responded as much to the pupil as the pupil did to the demands of the teacher, and both attempted not so much to add to the sum

total of knowledge as to increase the skill of its manipulation. Under these circumstances, new knowledge was added so gradually that the slow web of transmission of ancient skills was not torn.

Parallel to these developments was the special education given by specially chosen tutors and teachers to the children of the aristocracy; such an education was designed to ground the pupils well in many arts and graces and in a scholarship which they would not practice but would wear as an adornment or use for wise government.

• In a country governed by a conqueror or in a country to which large numbers of immigrants come, there are special problems of education as the government becomes responsible for people who speak a different language and have different customs. For, in these situations, the function—or at least one function—of the educational sys-tem is not the transmission to the next generation of something that all adults or that specialized groups of adults know, but rather the transmission of something the parents' generation does *not* know to children whom the authorities wish to have educated.

So, looking at our educational system today, we can see that in various ways it combines these different functions:

• The protection of the child against ex-ploitation and the protection of society against precocity and inexperience.

• The maintenance of learners in a state of moral and economic dependency.

• Giving to all children the special, wider education once reserved for the children of priv-ileged groups, in an attempt to form the citizen of a democracy as once the son of a noble house was formed.

• The teaching of complex and specialized skills which, under our complex system of division of labor, is too difficult and time-consuming for each set of parents to master or to hand on to their own children.

• The transmission of something which the parents' generation does *not* know (in the case of immigrants with varied cultural and linguistic backgrounds) to children whom the authorities or the parents wish to have educated.

To these multiple functions of an educational system, which, in a slowly changing society, were variously performed, we have added slowly and reluctantly a quite new function: *education for rapid and self-conscious adaptation to a changing world*. Yet we hardly recognize how new this function of our educational system is. It is implicit in the demands of educators that schools develop flexibility, open-mindedness, and creativity; but such demands might equally well have been made 200 years ago, well before the rhythm of change had radically altered.

That we have as yet failed to recognize the new character of change is apparent in a thousand ways. Despite the fact that a subject taught to college freshmen may have altered basically by the time the same students are seniors, it is still said that colleges are able to give students "a good education"—finished, wrapped up, and sealed with a degree. . . .

Thus we avoid facing the most vivid truth of the new age: *no one will live all his life in the world into which he was born, and no one will die in the world in which he worked in his maturity.*

For those who work on the growing edge of science, technology, or the arts, contemporary life changes at even shorter intervals. Often, only a few months may elapse before something which previously was easily taken for granted must be unlearned or transformed to fit the new state of knowledge or practice.

In this world, no one can "complete an education." The students we need are not just children who are learning to walk and talk and to read and write plus older students, conceived of as minors, who are either "going on" with or "going back" to specialized education. Rather, we need children *and* adolescents *and* young *and* mature *and* "senior" adults, each of whom is learning at the appropriate pace and with all the special advantages and disadvantages of experience peculiar to his own age. . . .

In this world the age of the teacher is no longer necessarily relevant. For instance, children teach grandparents how to manage TV, young expediters come into the factory along with the new equipment, and young men invent automatic programing for computers over which their seniors struggle because they, too, need it for their research.

This, then, is what we call the *lateral transmission* of knowledge. It is not an outpouring of knowledge from the "wise old teacher" into the minds of young pupils, as in vertical transmission. Rather, it is a sharing of knowledge by the informed with the uninformed, whatever their ages. The primary prerequisite is the desire to know. . . .

. . . [A]s long as we continue to think that free and, when necessary, subsidized education is appropriate *only* when it is *preliminary* to work (though, exceptionally, it may be continued after some inevitable "interruption"), just so long the guardians of character, of political literacy, and of our store of talent that comes from all classes and in many cases shows itself only very slowly will argue for—and will get—longer and longer years of compulsory education and longer and longer years of free education.

Under these circumstances, the meaning of education and the purpose of schools—especially for young people between the ages of 14 and 20 —will only become more confused. On the one hand, the education that is absolutely necessary for those who, at an early age, are ready to go on to become scientists, statesmen, philosophers, and poets will be hamstrung by the presence of those others who, at the same age, do not want schooling; and on the other hand, the lives and characters of the temporary nonlearners will be ruined, and they will be incapacitated as potential later learners.

What we need to do, instead, is to separate primary and secondary education—in an entirely new way:

By *primary education* we would mean the stage of education in which all children are taught what they need to know in order to be fully human in the world in which they are growing up —including the basic skills of reading and writing and a basic knowledge of numbers, money, geography, transportation and communication, the law, and the nations of the world.

By *secondary education* we would mean an education that is based on primary education and that can be obtained *in any amount* and *at any period* during the individual's whole lifetime.

Secondary education, in this sense, is already well developed. The proliferation of educational upgrading programs in industry, of extension courses offered by universities, and of adult education under a variety of sponsorships shows that education in the technological society tends to continue throughout the life cycle. Adult education goes by different names in different countries; in Japan it is called "social education." [4] But all industrial societies attempt to cope with a rapidly changing technology, which prevents children from learning in school all they must know on the job. Adult education does not, however, solve the problems of how much and what kind of education to give the young. More secondary education, in the old-fashioned sense of high school or vocational school, may be desirable to prepare contemporary children for the changing occupational requirements of industrial societies.

The Changing Educational Requirements of Industrial Societies

Reprinted by permission. From Seymour L. Wolfbein, "Education and Employment," in Eli Ginzberg, Ed., *The Nation's Children*, Vol. 2, New York: Columbia University Press for the White House Conference on Children and Youth, 1960, pp. 138–157.

A recent New York *Times* advertisement by a long established multibranch company calls for applications from persons with experience in:

Transistorized circuitry
Inertial guidance—missiles
Gyrodynamics-supersonic aircraft
Shielding design-atomic power
Ferret reconnaissance
Human factors science
Micro-miniaturization
Data telemetry

This "help wanted ad" contains occupations which were hardly even known just a few years ago. Dealing as they do with some of the frontiers of current work in the physical sciences they are representative of the great forces of change in the world of work. How many persons are there in the United States today who carefully chose, prepared for, and entered these occupations?

This brief listing of occupations is also symptomatic of a basic and overridingly important shift

[4] Ronald S. Anderson, *Japan: Three Epochs of Modern Education*, Bulletin No. 11, United States Office of Education, Washington: Government Printing Office, 1959, pp. 187–204.

in the very industrial and occupational structure of the United States—a shift which took place slowly but almost inexorably throughout this century, reached an historic turning point during the '50s and will continue to be a major force to be reckoned with during the '60s.

In a recent month during 1959, persons who work for a wage or salary (but including farmers as well as farm hands) were distributed as follows among the major industries of the United States:

(in millions)

Manufacturing	16.1	Transportation and	
Construction	2.8	public utilities	3.9
Mining	.7	Trade	11.2
Agriculture	6.4	Finance, insurance	2.4
		Service	6.6
		Government	8.2
	26.0		32.3

On the left we have the workers who produce "goods": all of the items literally manufactured —autos, steel, rubber, apparel, furniture, chemicals, etc.; everything built—the millions of homes every year, bridges, highways, factories, office buildings, etc.; everything mined from the ground —coal, lead, zinc, gold, uranium, etc.; all the food, feed and fiber produced by the agricultural sector of the American economy.

On the right we have the workers who produce "services"—who buy and sell, finance and service, teach, work for the government as firemen, policemen, economists or clerks, etc., etc. They now outnumber the "goods" producers by 6 millions. Had we, in addition to the wage and salary workers, included persons earning their livelihood by owning their own business off the farm, the difference would have been even much greater in favor of the service sector, since most self-employed persons are in such sectors as trade.

Throughout this century, workers in the service producing industries have been gaining on those producing goods; they overtook them in the early part of the '50s, have moved steadily ahead since then, and there is nothing in the offing which will change this trend as we move into the '60s.

Inevitably, this kind of change in industrial structure has brought a corresponding change in the occupations we follow as workers. Here again is a brief recapitulation of past, present, and expected future developments:

	1910	1959	1970
		(in percent)	
All workers	100	100	100
White-collar	22	42	45
Professional and technical	5	11	13
Proprietary and managerial	7	11	11
Clerical and sales	10	20	21
Blue-collar	37	37	36
Skilled	12	13	13
Semiskilled	14	18	18
Unskilled	11	6	5
Service	10	12	13
Farm	31	9	6

In a real way this brief table reflects some of the major social and economic changes of the twentieth century in this country:

1. The almost complete turn-around from a rural to urban economy: in 1910 almost one out of every three workers was on the farm; today the ratio is below one in ten and still going down.

2. The emergence to a majority position of the white-collar group in the late 1950s: in 1910, more than one in three employed persons was a blue-collar worker and only about one in five a white-collar worker; now the white-collar worker outnumbers his blue-collar counterpart and is scheduled to increase his numerical and proportionate advantage during the '60s.

3. The great growth in the professional and clerical and sales groups, which have doubled their standings in the occupational hierarchy over the past fifty odd years.

4. The stable (but key) position of the skilled craftsman.

5. And the enormous decline in unskilled jobs in the United States.

As can be seen from the summary figures, these occupational trends are expected to continue into the '60s, highlighted particularly by the persistent growth in the white-collar jobs. This growth, it may be added, is expected to affect the goods-producing as well as the service-producing sectors of the economy, as indeed it already has.

For example: In 1948 there were among manufacturing (factory) employees a little short of 13 million production workers and about 2.5 million nonproduction workers. The former represent workers in and around the factory production line; the latter include largely the clerical, managerial, and professional personnel in the offices of factory plants. Ten years later (1958) production

workers had fallen by a million under the impact of the business downturn of that year; nonproduction workers had increased by 1.25 million over the same period of time.

These expected trends should not be taken to denigrate the continued importance of at least one major group among the blue-collar workers—the skilled craftsmen, for whom the demand is expected to be substantial in the decade to come. The situation in this field, in fact, illustrates one of the points we are coming to in the following section—the role of training.

For example: The U.S. Bureau of Apprenticeship reports that the number of new building trades craftsmen emerging from apprenticeship training programs between 1950 and 1958 was less than the number of journeymen lost to the trade because of death and retirement.

All in all, then, the '60s are expected to witness a significant increase in the skill level of the labor force across the occupational structure. . . .

As we already have indicated, education and training represent the major catalyst for bringing together and meshing the occupational demands of the future with the resources available to meet them. . . .

The impact of the labor market upon education in the '60s will be highlighted by higher educational and training prerequisites for employment. The almost perfect match between level of educational attainment and the growth areas of the occupational structure can be seen from the following brief summary of the amount of schooling by members of different occupational groupings.

Thus, it is the occupations which require higher educational attainment that represent the

Occupation	Average Years of School Completed
White-Collar	
Professional and technical	16+
Clerical	12.5
Proprietary and managerial	12.4
Sales	12.4
Blue-Collar	
Skilled	10.5
Semiskilled	9.5
Unskilled	8.5
Service	9.6
Farmers	8.6
Farm Workers	8.2

growth areas of the future. And, even in these occupations the educational requirements continue to rise. Witness the increasing time required for an engineering degree; the recent increase from four to five years for a baccalaureate in pharmacy and architecture; the increasing demand for teachers with master's degrees, the rising demand for secretaries and clerical personnel with some post high-school work, etc.

At the same time, there is every indication that young people in ever-increasing numbers and proportions will be going after the increased education and training which our changing job structure will apparently call for. Back in 1940, only 26 percent of the population fifteen years of age and over were high-school graduates; the Census Bureau projects a figure of 45 percent for 1970. Similarly, only 3.8 million in our population twenty years of age and over were college graduates in 1940; the Census projects a tripling of that figure for 1970.

The education-occupation-employment links which we have emphasized so much in this discussion have and will prove themselves out in the acid test of the labor market. One of the more persevering labor force trends in this country is the inverse relationship between educational attainment and occupational status on the one hand and the rate of unemployment on the other. Here was the situation in the spring of 1959; the numbers may change with alterations in the business cycle, but the relationships among the different occupational groups stay on:

Occupational Level	Rate of Unemployment (in percent)
Unskilled	11.8
Semiskilled	7.5
Skilled	5.4
Sales	4.1
Clerical	3.3
Proprietors, managerial	1.4
Professional and technical	1.3

The occupational role structure has been changing rapidly in industrial countries. As the foregoing article shows, the American economy has upgraded its manpower requirements over the past half century in the direction of professional, technical, managerial, clerical, and sales occupations. These demand greater formal education than most blue-collar occupa-

tions. Whether in response to financial incentives or to independent factors, educational levels have been rising. The proportion of American 17-year-olds graduating from high school has grown astoundingly. But *educational upgrading has not kept pace with occupational upgrading* in the United States. Too many youngsters for the economy to absorb drop out of school to seek unskilled laboring jobs. Recall the 1959 unemployment statistics: 11.8 per cent unemployment among unskilled workers as compared to 3.3 per cent among clerical workers. Youngsters who leave school as soon as they can legally do so enter an overcrowded labor market where the pay is low and the work menial.

THE FAILURE OF EDUCATIONAL SUPPLY TO KEEP UP WITH OCCUPATIONAL DEMAND

The technical and scientific manpower needs of an industrial society are not satisfied automatically. The school system attempts to teach youngsters the skills and attitudes appropriate for the places in the occupational system which they want to occupy. Or, to put it the other way around, those youngsters who learn at school the intellectual content and the associated values of white-collar jobs tend to get such jobs. Those youngsters who rebel against the authority of teachers, fail to learn verbal skills, or for some other reasons drop out before graduating from high school are relegated to laboring occupations.[5] Thus, educational success selects youngsters for various occupational levels.

One possible explanation for this failure of educational supply to keep up with occupational demand is that a sizable minority of the population lacks the intellectual ability to absorb the level of education required in a technological society. Compatible with this explanation is the fact that the United States has moved furthest toward mass secondary educa-

[5] Talcott Parsons, "The Social Class as a Social System: Some of Its Functions in American Society," *Harvard Educational Review*, Vol. 29, Fall 1959, pp. 297–318.

tion of any country, and American educators are disproportionately preoccupied with the problem of "slow learners." [6] Lack of intellectual ability is certainly an important factor in learning failure. Dropouts tend to have lower IQs than students who continue in school, although students of average and superior ability also drop out of school.[7] Similarly, better high school students are more likely to attend college, but some get to college who are not good students, and some who terminate their formal education in the twelfth grade have enough ability to succeed in college.[8]

Limitations on innate ability are not the whole story. *Social* as well as intellectual factors affect school achievement. Schools in certain neighborhoods have traditions of high educational achievement; youngsters attending them take school work more seriously than others in schools with a different socioculture clientele. Why should this be so? For two reasons:

1. Children from higher socioeconomic levels do better in school than children from lower socioeconomic levels,[9] and some schools contain higher proportions of these middle-class and upper-class youngsters.

2. Children from schools with a high concentration of well-motivated students have a stronger commitment to academic achievement than would be predicted from knowledge of their IQs or parental backgrounds.[10]

[6] Gordon Liddle and Dale Long, "Experimental Room for Slow Learners," *Elementary School Journal*, Vol. 59, December 1958, pp. 143–149.
[7] New York State Division for Youth, *The School Dropout Problem in Major Cities of New York State: Rochester, Part II*, unpublished research report, April 1963, p. 45.
[8] Bureau of the Census, "Educational Status, College Plans, and Occupational Status of Farm and Nonfarm Youths: October, 1959," Series P-27, No. 30, Washington: Government Printing Office, August 1961; Bureau of the Census, "Factors Related to College Attendance of Farm and Nonfarm High School Graduates: 1960," Series P-27, No. 32, Washington: Government Printing Office, June 1962.
[9] See pages 375–382.
[10] Alan B. Wilson, "Residential Segregation of Social Classes and Aspirations of High School Boys," *American Sociological Review*, Vol. 24, December 1959, pp. 836–845.

The whole is greater than the sum of its parts; the climate of the school depends not only on the characteristics of the students attending it but also on the mutual reinforcement of their values. The former president of Harvard University, James B. Conant, was struck by the contrasting atmospheres of slum schools and suburban schools.[11] In the slum schools, dropping out was normal at the age when the law no longer compelled attendance *regardless of intellectual potentialities;* In the suburban schools, college attendance was expected *regardless of abilities or interests.*

Although there are individual exceptions to the correlation between the socioeconomic status of parents and the school performance of their children, parental status is statistically a good predictor because better-educated parents tend (1) to occupy superior socioeconomic statuses and (2) to communicate their educational values effectively to their children. The following article attempts to probe the mechanisms whereby socioeconomic differences in the parental generation are translated into differential school achievement on the part of the children.

Some Causes and Consequences of Differential Educational Achievement

Reprinted by permission. From Jackson Toby, "Orientation to Education as a Factor in the School Maladjustment of Lower-Class Children," *Social Forces*, Vol. 35, March 1957, pp. 259–266.

Even taking an extremely crude index of school achievement, that of grade placement, *for every age level* the average grade of middle-class urban children is higher than that of lower-class children. (See Tables 52, 53, and 54.) These differences can be observed at 7 and 8 years of age as well as at 17. Apparently whatever produces the difference starts operating to differentiate lower-class from middle-class children from the early grades. Another way of looking at class selec-

[11] James B. Conant, *Slums and Suburbs: A Commentary on Schools in Metropolitan Areas*, New York: McGraw-Hill, 1961.

tivity of the educational process is to observe the proportion of lower-class boys in high school a generation ago (Tables 55 and 56) or in college today.

Why are middle-class children more successful in their studies? Why do lower-class children drop out at younger ages and complete fewer grades? One hypothesis is that school teachers are middle-class in their values, if not in their origins, and penalize those students who do *not* exhibit the middle-class traits of cleanliness, punctuality, and neatness or who *do* exhibit the lower-class traits of uninhibited sexuality and aggression. Some social scientists believe that lower-class children, even though they may have the intellectual potentialities for high levels of academic achievement, lose interest in school or never become interested because they resent the personal

TABLE 52

Median Years of School Completed by Native White Boys by Monthly Rental Value of Home and by Age in Cities of 250,000 Inhabitants or More, 1940

	Monthly Rental Value of Home						
Age	Under $10	$10–$14	$15–$19	$20–$29	$30–$49	$50–$74	$75 and Over
7 years	1.3	1.5	1.6	1.7	1.7	1.7	1.7
8 years	2.1	2.4	2.4	2.5	2.6	2.6	2.7
9 years	2.8	3.2	3.3	3.4	3.5	3.7	3.7
10 years	3.6	4.0	4.2	4.4	4.5	4.6	4.7
11 years	4.4	4.9	5.1	5.3	5.5	5.6	5.6
12 years	5.4	5.7	6.0	6.2	6.5	6.6	6.7
13 years	6.0	6.7	7.1	7.2	7.5	7.7	7.8
14 years	7.2	7.8	7.9	8.2	8.5	8.7	8.8
15 years	8.3	8.5	8.8	9.2	9.4	9.6	9.8
16 years	8.6	9.3	9.6	9.8	10.3	10.5	10.6
17 years	9.4	9.9	10.2	10.7	10.7	11.3	11.5

Source: Bureau of the Census, *Sixteenth Census of the United States* (1940), Monograph on Population Education: *Educational Attainment of Children by Rental Value of Home*, Washington: Government Printing Office, 1945, p. 3.

TABLE 53

Distribution of Retarded and Nonretarded Pupils according to Occupational Status of Father (Sims' Scale) in the New York City Public Schools, 1931–1932

Father's Occupational Status	Total	Slow Progress	Normal Progress	Rapid Progress
Total	100.0	100.0	100.0	100.0
Professional	3.7	1.3	4.4	6.2
Clerical	19.8	11.2	19.4	31.9
Artisan	24.0	22.0	25.5	24.8
Skilled laborer	36.9	43.8	35.1	29.8
Unskilled laborer	15.6	21.7	15.6	7.3

TABLE 54

Percentage Distribution of Pupils according to Father's Occupational Status and Pupils' Progress Status, 1931–1932

Father's Occupational Status		Pupil's Progress Status		
	Total	Slow	Normal	Rapid
Professional	100.0	13.2	39.7	47.1
Clerical	100.0	21.3	32.7	46.0
Artisan	100.0	34.6	35.6	29.8
Skilled laborer	100.0	45.0	31.9	23.1
Unskilled laborer	100.0	53.0	33.6	13.4

Source for Tables 53 and 54: Eugene A. Nifenecker, *Statistical Reference Data Relating to Problems of Over-ageness, Educational Retardation, Non-Promotion, 1900–1934* New York: Board of Education, 1937, p. 233.

TABLE 55

High School Attendance of the Children of Fathers Following Various Occupations, Seattle, St. Louis, Bridgeport, and Mount Vernon, 1919–1921

Parental Occupation	Number in High School for Every 1,000 Men 45 Years of Age or Over
Proprietors	341
Professional service	360
Managerial service	400
Commercial service	245
Building trades	145
Machine trades	169
Printing trades	220
Miscellaneous trades	103
Transportation service	157
Public service	173
Personal service	50
Miners, lumber workers, and fishermen	58
Common labor	17

rejection of their teachers. Such rejection is, they say, motivated by the teachers' mistaken notion that lower-class children are deliberately defying them. Davis and Havighurst show that children are the prisoners of their experience and that lower-class children behave the way they do, not because of any initial desire to defy school authorities, but rather because of their lower-class childhood training.[12]

According to this hypothesis, teacher rejection makes the lower-class boy resentful and rebellious. His attitude is, "If you don't like me, I won't cooperate." Unfortunately for him, however, school achievement is related to later occupational advancement. Failure to cooperate with the teacher cuts off the lower-class boy from a business or professional career. Professor August Hollingshead describes what happens to lower-class boys from a small town in Illinois who withdraw from school to escape the psychic punishment meted out by the teachers and upper-class children.

"The withdrawees' job skills are limited to what they have learned from contact with parents, relatives, friends, and through observations and personal experience, largely within the community; no withdrawee have any technical training for any type of job; furthermore, few have plans to acquire it in the future. . . . The boys have some acquaintance with working on farms, washing cars, loading and unloading grain, repairing cars, driving trucks, doing janitor work, clerking in stores, and odd jobs, but their lack of training, job skills, and experience combined with their youth and family backgrounds severely limit their job opportunities. These factors, along with need, force them to take whatever jobs they can find. . . . Menial tasks, long hours, low pay, and little consideration from the employer produces discontent and frustration, which motivate the young worker to seek another job, only to realize after a few days or weeks that the new job is like the old one. This desire for a more congenial job, better pay, shorter hours, and a better employer gives rise to a drift from job to job." [13]

"The association between education, job levels, and prestige in the social structure is so high that the person with more education moves into the high-ranking job and the person with little education into the low-ranking job. Furthermore, and this is the crucial fact from the viewpoint of the person's relation to the social structure, each tends to remain in the job channel in which he starts as a young worker. This is especially true if he has less than a high school education; then he starts as an unskilled menial and has few opportunities in later years to change to skilled labor, business, or the professions. Therefore, his chances to be promoted up through the several levels of the job channel in which he functions are severely limited. As the years pass, his position in the economic system becomes fixed, and another generation has become stable in the class structure." [14]

In other words, some sociologists point out that the American public school teacher is suspicious of lower-class children and unwilling to

TABLE 56
Percentage of Students in Each of Two High School Years from Each of the Occupational Groups, 1919–1921

Parental Occupation	Freshman Class	Senior Class
Proprietors	17.7	22.9
Professional service	7.7	12.5
Managerial service	15.4	19.1
Commercial service	8.6	11.1
Clerical service	5.9	5.9
Agricultural service	2.3	2.3
Artisan-proprietors	4.4	3.5
Building trades	8.8	5.3
Machine trades	8.3	4.6
Printing trades	1.0	0.8
Miscellaneous trades	4.8	2.3
Transportation service	6.2	3.6
Public service	1.7	1.1
Personal service	1.4	0.9
Miners, lumber workers, and fishermen	0.5	0.3
Common labor	1.8	0.6
Unknown	3.5	3.2

Source for Tables 55 and 56: George S. Counts, *The Selective Character of American Secondary Education*, Chicago: University of Chicago Press, 1922, pp. 33, 37.

[12] Allison Davis and Robert J. Havighurst, *Father of the Man*, Boston: Houghton Mifflin, 1947.

[13] August B. Hollingshead, *Elmtown's Youth*, New York: Wiley, 1949, p. 369.
[14] *Ibid.*, p. 388.

give them a chance. If they withdraw from school to escape the pressures, they must surrender their chance to realize the American dream: social mobility.

Another hypothesis attributes the inferior performance of lower-class children at school *directly* to the economic disabilities of their families. John is a poor student because he lacks the nourishing food for sustained effort or because he is compelled to work after school instead of doing his homework; or he is a truant because he is ashamed to appear at school in ragged clothes or torn shoes. Like the rejecting teacher hypothesis, the economic disability hypothesis treats the child as essentially passive. According to both, he is victimized by a situation over which he has no control, in the one case by teachers who reject him, in the other by an economic system which does not allow him the opportunities to realize his ambitions.

But it is not at all clear that the average lower-class child has academic aspirations which are thwarted by his teachers or his economic circumstances. Studies of withdrawees from high school show that the majority leave school with no regrets; some volunteer the information that they hate school and are delighted to get through with it. These data suggest that some lower-class children view the school as a burden, not an opportunity. Perhaps it is not only teacher prejudice and his parents' poverty that handicap the lower-class child at school. *He* brings certain attitudes and experiences to the school situation just as his teacher does.

"Whereas the middle-class child learns a socially adaptive fear of receiving poor grades in school, of being aggressive toward the teacher, of fighting, of cursing, and of having early sex relations, the slum child learns to fear quite different social acts. His gang teaches him to fear being taken in by the teacher, of being a softie with her. To study homework seriously is literally a disgrace. Instead of boasting of good marks in school, one conceals them, if he ever receives any. The lower-class individual fears not to be thought a street-fighter; it is a suspicious and dangerous social trait. He fears not to curse. If he cannot claim early sex relations his virility is seriously questioned." [15]

[15] Allison Davis, *Social Class Influences on Learning*, Cambridge, Mass.: Harvard University Press, 1949, p. 30.

Of course, not all lower-class children have a hostile orientation to the school. As a matter of fact, the dramatic contrast between the educational attainments of drafted enlisted men in the two World Wars show that the public schools are being used more and more; and some of this increase undoubtedly represents lower-class youths who eagerly take advantage of educational opportunities. Still, many lower-class children do *not* utilize the educational path to social advancement. Apparently, one reason for this is a chronic dissatisfaction with school which begins early in their academic careers. Why should middle-class children "take to" school so much better?

To begin with, it should not be taken for granted that any child, whatever his socio-economic origin, will find school a pleasant experience from the very first grade. On the contrary, there is reason to believe that starting school is an unpleasant shock. The average child cannot help but perceive school as an invasion of his freedom, an obligation imposed on him by adults. Forced to come at set times, to restrain his conversation so that the teacher may instruct the class as a group, he may not see any relationship between what she asks him to learn and what he might be interested in doing. And in terms of maximizing his pleasure at the time, he is quite right. Except for kindergarten and ultra-progressive schools, the curriculum is a discipline imposed on the pupil rather than an extension and development of his own interests. This is not to condemn the school system. But it does point up the problematic nature of school adjustment.

Middle-class parents make it quite clear that school is nothing to be trifled with. They have probably graduated at least from high school, and their child is aware that they *expect* him to do the same or better. If he has difficulty with his studies, they are eager (and competent) to help him. And not only do his *parents* expect him to apply himself to his studies, so do his *friends* and *their* parents. He is caught in a neighborhood pattern of academic achievement in much the same way some lower-class boys are caught in a neighborhood pattern of truancy and delinquency. This concern with education is insurance against the child's fall in social status. Middle-class parents convey to their children subtly or explicitly that they must make good in school if they want to go on being middle-class. This may be phrased in terms of preparation for a "suitable" occupation (an alternative to a stigmatized occupation such as manual labor), in terms of a correlation between a "comfortable" standard of living and educational level, or in terms of the honorific value of education for its own sake.

Middle-class parents constantly reinforce the authority and prestige of the teacher, encouraging the child to respect her and compete for her approval. The teacher makes a good parent-surrogate for him because his parents accept her in this role.[16] They urge him to value the gold stars she gives out and the privilege of being her monitor. But although the middle-class child's initial motivation to cooperate with the teacher may spring from his parents, motivation functionally autonomous of parental pressure usually develops to supplement it. Part of this new motivation may be the intrinsic interest of the subject matter, or at least some of it, once he has gotten well along in his course. *Learning* to read may be a disagreeable chore; but the time soon comes when interesting stories are made accessible by the development of reading skill. An even more important source of motivation favorable to school is the recognition he gets in the form of high marks. He learns that scholastic competition is somewhat analogous to the social and economic competition in which his parents participate. The object of scholastic competition is to win the approving attention of the teacher, to skip grades, and to remain always in the "bright" classes. (In grade school the "bright" and the "dull" classes take approximately the same work, but pupils and teachers have no difficulty in separating the high prestige groups. In high school, "commercial," "trade," and "general" courses have different curricula from the high prestige "college" course. Again, there is consensus among the students as well as the teachers that the non-college courses are for those who are not "college material.")

Of course it is not competition alone that gives the middle-class child an emotional investment in continued scholastic effort; it is the *position* he achieves in that competition. Apparently his preschool training prepares *him* much better for scholastic competition than his lower-class classmate.[17] His parents mingle with lawyers, accountants, businessmen, and others who in their day-to-day activities manipulate symbols. In the course of conversation these people use a sizeable vocabulary including many abstractions of high order. He unconsciously absorbs these concepts in an effort to understand his parents and their friends. He is stimulated in this endeavor by the rewards he receives from his parents when he shows verbal precociousness. These rewards are not necessarily material or conscious. The attention he receives as a result of a remark insightful beyond his years, the pride his mother shows in repeating a bright response of his to her friends, these are rewards enough. This home background is valuable preparation for successful competition in school. For, after all, school subjects are designed to prepare for exactly the occupational level to which his parents are already oriented. Hence he soon *achieves* in school a higher than average status. (See Tables 52, 53, and 54.) To maintain this status intact (or improve it) becomes the incentive for further effort, which involves him deeper and deeper in the reward and punishment system of the school. Thus, *his success cumulates and generates the conditions for further success.*

A similar conclusion was reached after a study of the success and failure of children in certain nonacademic activities. Dr. Anderson concluded that success and practice mutually reinforce one another, producing remarkable differentiations in performance.

". . . [A] child is furnished from early life with the opportunity to hammer nails. In the course of the next ten or fifteen years, the child has 100,000 opportunities to hammer nails, whereas a second child in the same period of time has only ten or fifteen opportunities to hammer nails. At the age of twenty, we may be

---

[16] Professor Green maintains that the middle-class boy is more closely supervised by his mother than the lower-class boy and that this "personality absorption" creates a dependence on adult authority much greater than that of the less well-supervised lower-class boy. If this theory were accepted, we would thus find additional reason for the relative tractability and cooperativeness of the middle-class boy in school. Arnold W. Green, "The Middle Class Male Child and Neurosis," *American Sociological Review*, Vol. 11, February 1946, pp. 31–41.

[17] Millie C. Almy, *Children's Experiences prior to First Grade and Success in Beginning Reading*, New York: Teachers College, Columbia University, Contributions to Education, No. 954, 1949; Doris M. Lee, *The Importance of Reading for Achieving in Grades Four, Five, and Six*, New York: Teachers College, Columbia University, Contributions to Education, No. 556, 1933.

tremendously impressed with the ease and accuracy with which the first child hammers nails and likewise with the awkwardness and incapacity of the second child. We speak of the first child as an expert and the second child as a boob with respect to the nail hitting situation, and we may naively ascribe the ability of the first child to an inherited ability because its appearance is so inexplicable in comparison with the lack of ability of the second child." [18]

"The most significant fact which comes out of these observations is the fact that if we take a particular child and record his relationship to the group, we find that in ninety-five percent of the situations with which he is presented in the play situation, he is the dominating or leading individual, whereas another child under the same conditions is found to be in the leading position only five percent of the time.

". . . the social reactions of these particular children . . . may be the product of hereditary factors, environmental factors, more rapid rate of development, or a large number of factors combined. The important fact for our discussion is that within a constant period one child is getting approximately twenty times as much specific practice in meeting social situations in a certain way as is a second child. Life is something like a game of billiards in which the better player gets more opportunity for practice and the poorer player less." [19]

For the average middle-class child, the effective forces in his life situation form a united front to urge upon him a favorable orientation to school. Of course, this may not be sufficient to produce good school adjustment. He may not have the native intelligence to perform up to the norm. Or he may have idiosyncratic experiences that alienate him from scholastic competition. But, apparently, for the *average* middle-class child, this favorable orientation, combined with the intellectual abilities cultivated in his social milieu, results in satisfactory performance in the school situation.

The other side of the coin is the failure of some lower-class children to develop the kind of orientation which will enable them to overcome

the initial frustration of school discipline. To begin with, the parents of the lower-class child may not support the school as do middle-class parents. His parents probably do not have much education themselves, and, if not, they cannot very well make meaningful to him subjects that they do not themselves understand. Neither are they able to help him surmount academic stumbling blocks. Even more important, they lack the incentive to encourage him in and praise him for school accomplishment at that critical early period when he finds school new and strange and distasteful. Almost the same reasoning can be applied to the inculcation of a cooperative attitude toward school in the child as has been applied to an acceptant attitude toward toilet training. If the parents convey to the child their eagerness to have him adjust to irksome school discipline, he will probably accept it to please them and retain their love just as he learned to urinate and defecate at appropriate times and places. But toilet training and school adjustment training differ in an important particular. Parents *must* toilet train the child because permitting him to soil himself at will is a constant and immediate nuisance.

The consequences of a child's disinterest in school may also be unpleasant, both for him and for his parents, but it is not immediate. In the short run, allowing him to neglect school may be the least troublesome course for his parents to take. If they are neutral or antagonistic toward school, a result (1) of the esoteric nature of the curriculum from the point of view of skills cultivated and appreciated in the lower-class milieu and (2) of their failure to see the relevance of education to occupational advancement into a higher socio-economic class, they do not *have* to give the kind of support to the school given by middle-class parents. There is no reason to assume that the value of education is self-evident. For those lower-class people who have lost hope in social mobility, the school is a symbol of a competition in which they do not believe they can succeed. If they themselves have given up, will they necessarily encourage their children to try to strive harder?

Moreover, coming as he does from a social stratum where verbal skills are not highly developed, the lower-class child finds school more difficult than does his middle-class contemporary. His father, a carpenter or a factory worker, ma-

18 John E. Anderson, "The Genesis of Social Reactions in the Young Child," in E. S. Dummer, Ed., *The Unconscious: A Symposium*, New York: Knopf, 1928, pp. 83–84.
19 *Ibid.*, pp. 81–82.

nipulates concrete objects rather than symbols in his occupational role. In so far as he learns from his father, he is more likely to learn how to "fix things" than the importance of a large vocabulary. This learning does not help him with his school work, for school tends to give a competitive advantage to those with verbal facility.

This disadvantage with respect to verbal skills may account for the poorer showing of lower-class children on standard intelligence tests.[20]

". . . [T]he cultural bias of the standard tests of intelligence consists in their having fixed upon only those types of mental behavior in which the higher and middle socio-economic groups are superior. In those particular areas of behavior, the tests might conceivably be adequate measures of mental differences among individual children within the more privileged socio-economic groups. But they do not measure the comparative over-all mental behavior of the higher and lower socio-economic groups, because they do not use problems which are equally familiar and motivating to all such groups." [21]

In other words, middle-class children have an advantage because they are more familiar with the sort of problems that occur on the tests. This does not necessarily mean that the intelligence tests are invalid. It depends upon what the investigator thinks he is measuring. If he believes he is getting at "innate" ability, abstracted from cultural milieu and idiosyncratic learning, he is naive. An intelligence test is a valid measure of the native intellectual ability of an individual only under special circumstances, one of these being that the respondent's experience is similar to that of the group on which the test was standardized. Thus, a Navaho boy who scores 80 on the Stanford-Binet (Revised Form) may be unusually intelligent. Until a test is designed to tap the experiences of Navahos, there exists no reference point about which to assess superiority and inferiority.

However, it is not only the *content* of the intelligence test that gives middle-class urban children a better chance at high scores. It is the *structure* of the test situation. Even if we could find items equally familiar or unfamiliar to everyone taking the test, differential interest in solving

abstract problems would work against the lower-class student.

". . . [F]inding completely unfamiliar problems is not a possible choice, because such problems (namely, those involving some relationship between esoteric geometrical figures) do not arouse as great interest or as strong a desire to achieve a solution among low socio-economic groups as among high groups. The reason is clear: such an unrealistic problem can arouse the child's desire to achieve a solution only if the child has been trained to evaluate highly any and all success in tests. No matter how unreal and purposeless the problem may seem, the average child in a high socio-economic group will work hard to solve it, if his parents, his teacher, or other school officers expect him to try hard. The average slum child, however, will usually react negatively to any school test, and especially to a test whose problems have no relation to his experience." [22]

However justified the criticisms of the intelligence test as an instrument measuring native intellectual ability, it is highly predictive of academic accomplishment. A student with a high I.Q. score does better in his studies, on the average, than one with a low I.Q. score. Hence the discrepancy between the scores of lower-class students and of middle-class students is an index of the former's disadvantage in the school situation.

One possible response of the lower-class child to his disadvantages in the school situation is to increase his efforts. But his initial orientation drives him in the opposite direction. He is more likely to respond to competitive failure by going on strike psychologically, neglecting his homework, paying no attention in class, annoying the teacher. Uninterested in the curriculum, he learns as little as he can. Instead of a situation where the student and the teacher work toward a common goal, the development of the student's understanding of certain ranges of problems, he and his teacher are oriented antagonistically to one another. The teacher tries to stuff into his head as much of the curriculum as possible; he tries to absorb as little as is consistent with his own safety, in terms of sanctions mobilized by the school and his parents.

But school subjects are cumulative. Within a few years he is retarded in basic skills, such as reading, absolutely necessary for successful performance in the higher grades. Whether he is

[20] Walter S. Neff, "Socio-economic Status and Intelligence: A Critical Survey," *Psychological Bulletin*, Vol. 35, December 1938, pp. 727–757.
[21] Allison Davis, *op. cit.*, p. 48.

[22] *Ibid.*, pp. 68–69.

promoted along with his age-mates, "left back," or shunted into "slow" programs makes relatively little difference at this point. For whatever is done, he finds himself at the bottom of the school status hierarchy. He is considered "dumb" by the more successful students and by the teachers. This makes school still more uninteresting, if not unpleasant, and he neglects his work further. Eventually he realizes he can never catch up.

Without realizing what he was doing, he had cut himself off from the channels of social mobility. In those crucial early grades where the basis for school adjustment was being laid, he had not yet known that he wanted more out of life than his parents. Or, if he knew, he did not realize that school achievement and high occupational status are related. And he was not lucky enough to have parents who realized it for him and urged him on until he was old enough to identify with the school through choice. There is a certain irreversibility about school maladjustment. The student can hardly decide at 18 that he wants to become a lawyer if he is five years retarded in school. It is no longer possible for him to "catch up" and use school as a means to realize his ambitions. Sometimes lower-class men will rue their failure to take advantage of the opportunities presented by the school. James T. Farrell captures the flavor of this regret in the following passage from one of his novels:

"Walking on, seeing the lights of Randolph Street before him, he wondered if they were college football players [referring to the young men walking in front of him]. That was what Studs Lonigan might have been. Even if he did admit it, he had been a damn good quarterback. If he only hadn't been such a chump, bumming from school to hang around with skunky Weary Reilley and Paulie Haggerty until he was so far behind at high school that it was no use going. It wouldn't have been so hard to have studied and done enough homework to get by, and then he could have set the high school gridiron afire, gone to Notre Dame and made himself a Notre Dame immortal, maybe, alongside of George Gipp, the Four Horsemen, Christie Flannagan and Carideo. How many times in a guy's life couldn't he kick his can around the block for having played chump." [23]

If, on the other hand, the social milieu of the lower-class boy supported the school and encouraged him to bend every effort to keep up with his work, he would finish high school whether he enjoyed it or not—the way middle-class boys do. At graduation he might decide that he would like to become a plumber. That is, he might not crave middle-class status enough to suffer the discipline of continued education. But if he were not content with a lower-class status, if he wanted above all things to "be somebody," the educational route to high status would still be open. He would still have a *choice*; he would not be forced to accept a menial occupational role whether he liked it or not. As it is, the crucial decision is made before he is old enough to have a voice in it; it is made by his parents, his neighbors, and his friends.

To sum up, the middle-class child has the following advantages in school compared with the lower-class child: (1) his parents are probably better educated and are therefore more capable of helping him with his school work if this should be necessary; (2) his parents are more eager to make his school work seem meaningful to him by indicating, implicitly or explicitly, the occupational applications of long division or history; (3) the verbal skills which he acquires as part of child training on the middle-class status level prepare him for the type of training that goes on in school and give him an initial (and cumulating) advantage over the lower-class child in the classroom learning situation; and (4) the coordinated pressure of parents, friends, and neighbors reinforce his motivation for scholastic success and increase the probability of good school adjustment.

If the foregoing analysis is valid, an important reason for the failure of educational supply to keep pace with occupational demand is the anti-intellectual biases of poorly educated blue-collar parents. These biases are transmitted in subtle ways; an English sociologist has evidence that the structure of the language spoken in working-class homes reduces the possibilities for certain kinds of learning.[24] And the more limited the contact of "culturally de-

23   James T. Farrell, *Judgment Day*, New York: Vanguard Press, 1935, p. 24.

24   Basil Bernstein, "Social Structure, Language and Learning," *Educational Research*, Vol. 3, June 1961, pp. 163–176.

prived" children with persons having higher educational horizons, the more likely they will accept the values of their own families.[25] This is one important significance of racially segregated education. Since Negroes are much more likely than whites to be immersed in the culture of poverty (discussed in Chapter 6), Negro children who attend school only with members of their own race have less contact with the liberating educational values of the larger society. Negro business and professional parents, who usually do not share the culture of poverty, understand that segregated education means that their children will be exposed to a predominantly anti-intellectual milieu in school, and they are bitter about it.[26]

Another reason for the failure of educational supply to keep up with occupational demand is that a system of formal education, which is differentiated from the larger society, develops its own cultural tradition, and this tradition may resist change. One component of the cultural tradition of the school is contributed by teachers. Through the concepts and values absorbed in the course of professional training, through reading professional journals, and through continuing contact with their colleagues, teachers contribute professional values to the culture of the school. Professional values are not necessarily concerned with the ultimate occupational placement of students; this depends on the central concerns of the leading educational philosophers and the ideologies of the centers of teacher training. Thus, American educators have been as much concerned about the *social* adjustment of students (*life adjustment*) as about occupational preparation.[27] They have aspired to promoting wholesome family living, less juvenile delinquency, and better citizenship. To the extent that these aspirations are unrealistic, teachers

may confuse students as to what can be accomplished through continued education.

A second component of the cultural tradition of the school is contributed by who controls the school. In most European countries, schools are agencies of the central government. In the United States, schools are controlled through locally elected (or appointed) boards of education.[28] Different as are these methods of channeling societal support to the school, both involve budgetary dilemmas. Inadequate school budgets can prevent teachers from dealing effectively with the educational difficulties that arise. Mass education implies fairly large numbers of students being taught by a single teacher. Indeed, with the advent of educational television and other audiovisual aids, increasing numbers of students can be taught by one teacher. Considering the variety of interests and abilities within the class, a uniform method of instruction is inherently inappropriate for some students. Professional educators have attempted to grapple with this problem by urging community support for small classes, thus making possible greater individualization of instruction. But the community does not always accept the definition of the problem offered by professionals, especially in the United States where educators are a weak professional group. This is partly because so many teachers are women, partly because many of them have been trained in teachers' colleges rather than in prestigious universities, and partly because local control over education encourages laymen to set educational goals.

The third component of the culture of the school is contributed by the students themselves. In the United States, college preparatory students, future dropouts, and youngsters whose formal educations will end with high school graduation interact within the comprehensive high school. This creates a different type of student subculture from Great Britain where a two-track system exists; "grammar"

25 Frank Riessman, *The Culturally Deprived Child,* New York: Harper, 1962.

26 Marya Mannes, "School Trouble in Harlem," *The Reporter,* Vol. 20, Feb. 5, 1959, pp. 13–19.

27 Martin Mayer, *The Schools,* New York: Harper, 1961, Chaps. 2 and 3. Myron Lieberman, *Education as a Profession,* Englewood Cliffs, N.J.: Prentice-Hall, 1956.

28 Neal Gross, Ward S. Mason, and Alexander W. McEachern, *Explorations in Role Analysis: Studies of the School Superintendency Role,* New York: Wiley, 1958.

schools contain the academic youngsters and "secondary modern" schools contain vocationally oriented youngsters, largely of working-class origins. The student subculture in the American high school must cover a wider range of student background and interest than in European school systems where the two-track system is common. This necessity helps to explain why studies of American secondary schools show that student subcultures often promote athletic and social success more ardently than academic success.[29] The following article, written a generation ago, attempts to place the American student subculture in the context of other components of the culture of the school.

The Independent Culture of the High School

Reprinted by permission. From Willard Waller, *The Sociology of Teaching*, New York: Wiley, 1932, pp. 104, 106–110, 112–115, 119.

Certain cultural conflicts are at the center of the life of the school. These conflicts are of two sorts. The first and most obvious is that which arises from the peculiar function of the school in the process of cultural diffusion. A conflict arises between teachers and students because teachers represent the culture of the wider group and students are impregnated with the culture of the local community. Where the differences concern matters of religion or of fundamental morality, the struggle which then ensues may become quite sharp and may seriously affect the relation of the school to the community. A second and more universal conflict between students and teachers arises from the fact that teachers are adult and students are not, so that teachers are the bearers of the culture of the society of adults, and try to impose that culture upon students, whereas students represent the indigenous culture of the group of children. . . .

Age is not the only factor that separates people who nominally drink of the same cultural stream from actual community of culture. Mental

[29] James S. Coleman, "The Adolescent Subculture and Academic Achievement," *American Journal of Sociology*, Vol. 65, January 1960, pp. 337–347.

ability, education, subtle differences of interests and of personality may likewise sort people into cultural pigeonholes. So completely is the individual immersed in the culture of his own age and social level that he often has difficulty in realizing that any other kind of culture exists. He is separated by invisible walls from those about him who follow different gods. Persons living in different segments of our culture, as determined by age and life situation, may find difficulty in communicating with each other or in understanding each other at all. The old cannot understand the young, the prudent cannot understand the heedless, the married can have little sympathy for the unmarried, parents can never commune with nonparents; each person in the world is surrounded by many with whom he must communicate by smoke signals and by only a few with whom he can converse. But the greatest chasm is that which separates young persons and old.

The journey from the world of the boy to the world of the man is rarely smooth and continuous. But it has fewer sharp corners to turn if the members of the adult world are able to project themselves back into the psychic world of childhood. The adult who can live in the childish world with sufficient intensity to understand children from within can help them intelligently to develop those complex and unstable syntheses upon which the adult adjustment depends. Teachers have tried to make the transition easier by presenting to children a finely graded and continuously evolving culture, organized into ever more complex configurations. (They have succeeded very well in grading and sorting academic subject matter.) So have arisen those teacher-initiated and teacher-managed "activities," ceremonials, traditions, etc. So were produced, in fact, most of the things which we shall treat in discussing the culture of the school. The purpose of all these things is to soften the conflict of cultures between old and young.

Though an enlightened pedagogy may ameliorate the conflict of adults and children, it can never remove it altogether. In the most humane school some tension appears between teacher and students, resulting, apparently, from the rôle which the situation imposes upon the teacher in relation to his students. There are two items of the teacher's duty which make it especially likely that he will have to bring some pressure to bear upon students: he must see to it that there is no retrogression from the complexity of the social world worked out for students of a certain age level, and he must strive gradually to increase that complexity as the child grows in age and approximates adult understanding and experience. Activities may reduce conflict, but not destroy it.

Children have something which can be regarded as a culture of their own. Its most important loci are the unsupervised play group and the school. The unsupervised group presents this culture in a much purer form than does the school, for the childish culture of the school is partly produced by adults, is sifted and selected by adults, and is always subject to a certain amount of control by teachers. The culture of the school is a curious mélange of the work of young artisans making culture for themselves and old artisans making culture for the young; it is also mingled with such bits of the greater culture as children have been able to appropriate. In turning to more concrete materials, we may note certain aspects of tradition in the school. It will illustrate well this mingling of cultures if we divide the tradition which clusters about the school into three classes: tradition which comes entirely, or almost entirely, from the outside; tradition which is in part from outside the school and in part indigenous; and tradition which is almost entirely indigenous. It is roughly true that tradition of the first class exists in the community at large, that of the second class among teachers, and that of the third class among students.

Tradition of the first class, that which for the particular school comes altogether from the outside, is a manifestation of a culture complex diffused throughout the whole of West European culture. The historic school has of course had a part in the formation of this complex, but any particular school is largely the creation of it. Tradition of this sort governs the very existence of schools, for, without such a culture complex, schools would not exist at all. This traditional culture complex governs also the general nature of the life in the schools. It determines that the old shall teach the young, and not that the young shall ever teach the old, which would be at least equally justifiable in a world that changes so rapidly that an education twenty years old is out of date. Tradition governs what is taught and it holds a firm control upon the manner in which it is taught. . . . It is this same sort of tradition also which largely determines how students and

teachers shall think of each other.

The best example of a mingled tradition in part absorbed from the general culture of the group and in part produced in the particular institution is the tradition of teachers. In so far as this tradition of teachers is derived from outside a particular school, it is drawn by teachers from the general culture, and from association with members of the teaching profession everywhere. In so far as it is a purely local product, it is produced by the teachers in the institution and is passed on from one teacher to another. We may mention some cardinal points of the teacher tradition as it is usually encountered, making due allowance for local variations. There is a teacher morality, and this morality regulates minutely the teacher's relations with his students and with other teachers; it affects his relations with other teachers especially where the standing of those teachers with students might be affected. There is a character ideal of the teacher; nearly every group which lives long in one stereotyped relation with other groups produces its character ideal, and this ideal for teachers is clearly observable. When teachers say of a colleague, "He's a school teacher," they mean that he conforms to this local character ideal. (It usually implies that the individual puts academic above other considerations, is conscientious in his duties, and exacting in the demands he makes upon himself and others.) There is a taboo on seeking popularity among students, and this taboo operates with dreadful force if it is thought that popularity seeking is complicated by disloyalty to the teacher group. There is a traditional attitude toward students; this attitude requires that a certain distance be kept between teachers and students. The desire to be fair is very likely not the strongest motive that teachers have for keeping students at a distance, but it is certainly one of the consequences of the policy, and it has in its own right the compelling value of an article of faith. None may violate the code of equality with impunity. Teachers have likewise a certain traditional attitude toward each other. The most obvious manifestation of this traditional attitude is the ceremoniousness of teachers toward each other and toward the administration of the school. It seems clear that this is the ceremoniousness of a fighting group which does not care to endanger its prestige with underlings by allowing any informality to arise within itself. Another interesting observation that has often been made about particular groups of teachers is that they discriminate markedly between veterans and new men. . . .

The indigenous tradition of the school is found in its purest form among students. This tradition, when it has been originated on the spot, is passed on, largely by word of mouth, from one student to another. Some of the indigenous tradition has been originated by the faculty, and then imposed upon the students; once it has been accepted by students, however, it may be passed on by student groups. Some of the traditional observances which students follow are not home-grown; there is a great literature of school life, and students occasionally appear who are obviously playing the parts of story-book heroes. Besides, there exists in the culture of any community a set of traditional attitudes toward school and school life, varying from one social class to another, and from family to family; these attitudes influence profoundly the attitudes which students have toward school life. Nevertheless the tradition of students is very largely indigenous within the particular school. Although this sort of tradition varies much in detail from one school to another, we may mention certain characteristics of the fundamental patterns.

Like teacher morality, student morality is the morality of a fighting group, but differences appear in that the student group is subordinate, and its morality is relevant to that situation. Social distance between student and teacher seems as definitely a part of the student code as of the teacher code. The student must not like the teacher too much, for that is naïveté. There is the well-known school-boy code, the rule that students must never give information to teachers which may lead to the punishment of another student. Certain folkways grow up in every group of school children, as the folkway of riding to grade school on a bicycle or of not riding to high school on a bicycle, and these folkways have a great influence over the behavior of all members of the group. These groups of children are arranged in stair-steps. Membership in the older group implies repudiation of the folkways of the younger group. No one more foolish than the high-school boy on a bicycle, or the college boy wearing a high-school letter! Interlocking groups look forward only, each group aping its elders and despising its juniors. In modern schools, there is a whole complex of traditions pertaining to activities; it seems that all activities are meritorious, that they are in some way connected with the dignity and honor of the school, that some activities are more meritorious than others.

Sometimes a whole social system is carried in the tradition of students, and such social systems are very resistant to change. The fagging system, or a system of any sort of hazing, may persist for decades against the best efforts of highly efficient teachers and administrators to change them. A collegiate institution comes to mind which has conducted such a struggle for upwards of a hundred years. We are led to believe that hazing, at least, having its roots in the desire of those already in the group to dominate new members (and having its parallel on the faculty), would be destined to have some place in the culture which the young work out for themselves even if it had no sanction in tradition. In other words, the manner in which the young experience the universe recreates a hazing problem in every generation of students. . . .

These culture patterns of activities are partly artificial and faculty-determined, and partly spontaneous. In so far as they have been evolved by the faculty, they have been intended as means of control, as outlets for adolescent energies or substitutes for tabooed activities. They represent also the faculty's attempt to make school life interesting and to extend the influence of the school. Any activity, however, which is to affect the life of students at all deeply, any activity, then, which aspires to a greater influence than is exerted by the Latin Club or the Cercle Français, must have a spontaneous basis, and must appeal to students by presenting to them behavior patterns of considerable intrinsic interest. Each activity usually has some sort of faculty connection, and the status of the faculty adviser is thought to rise or fall with the prosperity or unprosperity of the activity which he promotes. Activities, then, increase in importance and gain recognition from the faculty through the efforts of interested faculty members, as well as through their own intrinsic appeal to students. . . .

Of all activities athletics is the chief and the most satisfactory. It is the most flourishing and the most revered culture pattern. It has been elaborated in more detail than any other culture pattern. Competitive athletics has many forms. At the head of the list stands football, still regarded as the most diagnostic test of the athletic prowess of any school. Then come basketball, baseball, track, lightweight football, lightweight basketball, girls' basketball, girls' track, etc. Each of these activities has importance because the particular school and its rivals are immersed in a culture stream of which competitive athletics is an important part. Each school has its traditional rivals, and a greater psychic weighting is attached to the games with traditional rivals than to those with other schools. Schools are arranged in a hierarchy, and may therefore win moral victories while actually suffering defeats. Pennsylvania wins, but Swarthmore triumphs.

Games, the most interesting phase of competitive athletics, are complex and elaborate cultural patterns. Other culture patterns reside in them. Some form of game is to be found in most cultures. The history of games is one of the most fascinating chapters of anthropology of the historical sort. Enthusiasts of the modern games played with balls claim for them a most ancient origin. (Basketball is an exception.) The game acquires a clearly defined pattern, and this is passed on with little variation. (Even minor changes in the rules usually meet with determined opposition.) Skill is relevant to the culture pattern of the game; if the form of the game is changed, skill vanishes. It is interesting, too, that a "form" which is partly cultural comes to reside in every feature of competitive athletics. The most flexible and skillful performance, with irrelevant motions most completely eliminated, represents "form" in a particular performance. Lack of form usually limits the perfectability of a performance sufficiently to keep the athlete out of competition. Thus there is "form" for batting a baseball, for a drop-kick, for putting the shot. It is possible that an athlete, by long practice, might develop this form through trial and error and the gradual removal of imperfections in his performance. But it is more likely that the athlete gets this form through cultural diffusion. Form itself may represent the accumulated improvements in technique of many generations of athletes. Form, produced by the internal mechanisms making for the perfection of responses, has thus a cultural character as well.

Competition between schools in athletics comes to a focus in games. The game is in fact disguised war. There is a continual tendency for the game to revert to actual war. "Now go out and fight," says the coach. "Fight," says the school orator. "Fight," scream the spectators. Everyone treats the game as a fight and thinks of it as a fight except perhaps the referee. It is small wonder that the political order worked out for this conflict situation, the political order consisting of the rules and the referee to back them, is maintained with such difficulty and only by penalties which impose the direst disabilities upon the offenders. There is, it is true, a whole code of sportsmanship which arises from this conflict situation, a code which internalizes the rules and makes for the principle of fair play. This code of sportsmanship is a central part of the athletic tradition, and as such an important aspect of the cultural life of the school.

The code of sportsmanship becomes a very important ethical principle, one almost says the very source and spring of all ethics, for youngsters and for those adults who hold to the conflict theory of human life. There are men who insist that they learned the most important lessons of life upon the football field. They learned to struggle there and to hold on, and they learned to respect the rights of others and to play according to the rules. It may be surmised that men who have such a conception of life do not live in a very complex world. It is difficult to generalize about the effect of athletics upon the personalities of those participating. One might guess that it is in general favorable, and that its favorable effects are in the line of a growing into such rôles as those mentioned above. Part of the technique, indeed, of schools and teachers who handle difficult cases consists in getting those persons interested in some form of athletics. This constitutes a wholesome interest, opens the way to a normal growth of personality, and inhibits abnormal interests and undesirable channels of growth.

There arise some problems of the relations of professionals and amateurs in school athletics, and these have their effect upon the culture patterns of the game and sportsmanship. All coaches are professionals, and live by the prowess of their teams. All players are forced to be amateurs. It often happens that the preachments concerning the sporting code which drop so frequently from the lips of the coaches are more than neutralized in practice by the pressure which these men put upon their players to win games. A more serious indictment of a social system which allows the livelihood of a man and his family to depend upon the athletic achievements of boys is that the coach is so pressed that he uses his human material recklessly. He trains his "men" (aged sixteen) a bit too hard, or he uses his star athletes in too many events, or he schedules too many hard games; all this he does from a blameless desire to gain a better position or a rise in salary for himself, but he often fails to consider the possible effects upon the physical well-being of the rising generation. . . .

Unquestionably, activities contribute much to make the schools livable and are more effective than any other feature of the school in the molding of personality. But we should not allow these facts to blind us to the truth that they often tend to interfere with other important features of school life. Every activity has its faculty sponsor, who in addition to his teaching is charged with the promotion of that particular activity. His prestige among the faculty and students, and often his salary as well, are largely determined by the success of that activity; it is no wonder, then, that activities accumulate and make increasing demands upon the school time and the attention of students. It would, of course, be perfectly possible to educate through activities alone, and the present writer would be the last to argue against such a system if one could be devised, but we must not forget that education through activities as at present organized is at best scattering and sporadic, and needs systematic supplementation through the basic training in facts and skills which it is the formal purpose of the schools to give.

Why should student values fail to support academic effort? Do students not realize that their futures depend on their academic records? Why do they allow athletics or other extracurricular activities to distract them from the task of realizing their intellectual potentialities? Talcott Parsons offers an intriguing hypothesis to account for student ignorance of or indifference to the school's effect on their futures: too much is at stake for many youngsters to admit it.[30] Seeming indifference to academic achievement can be a cloak to conceal deep

anxieties. High school students, for instance, may be uncertain as to whether they are performing well enough to get into college, and they may pursue popularity as a more attainable goal. Intellectually able children of poorly educated parents may be tempted by the opportunities offered by higher education, yet be reluctant to turn their backs on parental and neighborhood values. Athletic interests might serve to compromise this inner conflict. Similarly, James Coleman argues that academic achievement is *individual* and that the superior performance of one student necessarily involves the relative failure of others.[31] Thus, academic achievement is too threatening to be given unlimited scope. Athletic achievement, on the other hand, occurs within the framework of interschool competition; hence, athletic triumphs contribute to the morale of the entire school—including the nonathletes. These explanations of anti-intellectualism in secondary schools gain additional force from studies of students who fail at college.[32] A surprisingly large number of college casualties are students who have the intellectual capacity to do college work but who are "unmotivated." Perhaps they unconsciously rebel against parental pressure. Sometimes the stakes can be *too* high.

A NEW FUNCTION FOR HIGHER EDUCATION IN THE TECHNOLOGICAL SOCIETY

Industrial societies did not invent the university; it was medieval Europe's contribution. But the function of universities in medieval Britain or France was vastly different from their function in contemporary societies.[33] The medieval university was concerned with theologi-

[30]   Talcott Parsons, "The Social Class as a Social System: Some of Its Functions in American Society," *Harvard Educational Review*, Vol. 29, Fall 1959, p. 312.

[31]   James S. Coleman, "Academic Achievement and the Structure of Competition," *ibid.*, pp. 330–351.
[32]   John Summerskill, "Dropouts from College," in Nevitt Sanford, Ed., *The American College*, New York: Wiley, 1962, pp. 627–657.
[33]   A. H. Halsey, "The Changing Functions of Universities in Advanced Industrial Societies," *Harvard Educational Review*, Vol. 30, Spring 1960, pp. 119–127; Joseph Ben-David and Awraham Zloczower, "Universities and Academic Systems in Modern Societies," *European Journal of Sociology*, Vol. 3, Spring 1962, pp. 45–84.

cal and humanistic knowledge, not with science and technology. The secularization of learning proceeded slowly; even in the United States, a majority of the early graduates of Harvard and Yale became clergymen.[34] When universities gained a measure of independence of religious institutions, they did not immediately become a dynamic force in their societies. Until the nineteenth century, universities catered to the aristocracy. Their aim was to produce gentlemen and to train a tiny fraction of the population in law, medicine, and theology. This meant familiarity with the languages, the literature, and the ideas that gentlemen were expected to know. It meant extracurricular education also: an accent from Oxford or a dueling scar from Heidelberg. Grades were not important because the young men who attended a university had a place waiting for them in the top rank of their society; it was their birthright. The "gentleman C" dates from an era in the history of higher education when *who* one was overshadowed *what* one learned.

The scientific revolution gave the universities a new function. Because developments in physics, chemistry, biology, and mathematics are intimately related to economic and technological change, industrial societies needed *the systematic production of new knowledge.* When established universities were not prepared to satisfy this demand, new universities, institutes, and research centers were created. While Oxford and Cambridge wavered between being cloistered finishing schools for the élite and the means whereby new knowledge was transmitted to the administrative, professional, and research personnel required in an advanced society, the universities of London, Manchester, Birmingham, Leeds, and Liverpool came into being. Oxford and Cambridge seemed unwilling at first to recognize the legitimacy of illuminating a scientific and technological age.

[34] Richard Hofstadter and C. De Witt Hardy, *The Development and Scope of Higher Education in the United States*, New York: Columbia University Press, 1952, pp. 6–9.

The Reluctance of Eighteenth-Century Oxford and Cambridge to Illuminate Tomorrow

Reprinted by permission. From Sir Eric Ashby, *Technology and the Academics: An Essay on Universities and the Scientific Revolution*, New York: Macmillan, 1958, pp. 6–13.

In the accomplishment of the scientific revolution British scientists played a notable and distinguished part. But British universities (except fortuitously and incidentally) played no part whatever. They had allowed the revolution to pass over their heads and still, a century later, they were providing no lead in scientific thought. They reflected yesterday: they did not illuminate tomorrow. This isolationism on the part of the universities cannot be attributed to any one cause; indeed, the causes differed from one university to another. . . .

Oxford was weighed down by every imaginable device for inertia. Dissenters, who were the greatest enthusiasts for science and technology, were not admitted to the University. Power lay with the colleges, which were obliged by their statutes to elect fellows on all sorts of criteria other than that of intellectual distinction. The teaching staff was comprised of celibates in holy orders, members of the Church of England, committed to a curriculum drawn up in the time of Charles I. Such natural science as was taught was Aristotelian, dogmatic and desiccated. These circumstances alone would have been enough to prevent Oxford from adapting itself to the new scientific age. But there was a further circumstance which, had it not been for the University's wonderful powers of adaptation in the 1850's, might have threatened the very viability of Oxford as a university. This was the almost complete atrophy, in the eighteenth and early nineteenth centuries, of half the University's function.

On paper the pattern of Oxford was consistent with its generic status as a mediaeval university. It had a dual function: as a group of colleges where young men could study the trivium and quadrivium as a preliminary to their professional training; and as a group of professional schools providing advanced study in theology, medicine, and law. The first function was discharged by college tutors. Among these tutors there was scarcely any differentiation of teaching duties: each tutor was responsible for teaching his group of students all the subjects for the degree of B.A.: ancient history, Latin and Greek, poetry, philosophy and logic, mathematics. They were in fact schoolmasters. That this course of liberal studies was intended for boys was evident from some of the statutes still in force at Oxford in 1800, for example, a statute directing corporal chastisement for those who neglect their lessons.

It was an integral part of the pattern of the University that this preliminary liberal education should be followed by advanced study in a professional school; and it is clearly for this reason that Oxford had, in addition to college tutors, public university professors and lecturers in the faculties of theology, law, and medicine. Public teachers in science subjects were attached to the Faculty of Medicine. Thus chairs in medicine, natural philosophy, botany, and geometry had existed since the seventeenth century and (as a gesture toward the advocates of reform) chairs of chemistry and experimental philosophy were added in the early nineteenth century. But this second function of the University, though nominally recognised, was actually ignored. Even as late as 1852 the Regius Professor of Medicine reported that he had discontinued his lectures. He formerly had 10 students a year and the numbers had dwindled to 4. The Professor of Geometry gave tuition in his house to about 3 students a year. The Professor of Botany was obliged to give 12 lectures a year, but there were often no students to attend. The newly created chair of chemistry attracted only 12 students a year, even though the length of the course had been halved. There was actually a reduction in the numbers attending science lectures between the 1820's and the 1840's. This can be attributed partly to Oxford's preoccupation in the Tractarian movement and partly to the increasing competition for University honours, which could not be secured through scientific studies. The position in legal studies was similar. In brief, two of the professional schools in Oxford had atrophied, and science teaching (with the singular exception of lectures in mineralogy) was at a very low ebb. Lawyers went to London and medical men to Edinburgh or Leyden or to one of the hospital schools in London.

It needs no imagination to realize how for-midable these barriers were to the introduction of science into Oxford. Most of the students who went there were candidates for the priesthood of the Church of England or were drawn from the upper classes, destined to preside over their country estates or to enter public life through politics. Those who aspired to academic life had to get fellowships, and in so far as election to fellowships depended upon intellectual qualifications, they were qualifications in the classics, not in science, not even in logic. Accordingly, eighteenth-century Oxford had become a self-perpetuating machinery for safeguarding the interests of college fellows; most of its teaching was concentrated upon what even a fourteenth-century university would have regarded as only the prerequisites of a university education.

In Cambridge the barriers to the introduction of science were less formidable, but it could not be said, even as late as 1852, that scientific work had taken root there. However, Cambridge had produced Newton and was proud of the fact; and even before the opening of the nineteenth century mathematics and mechanics were essential ingredients for a degree. The mathematics of those days had a strong Greek flavour. Consider, for example, this problem set in an examination at St. John's College in 1794:

"A countryman, being employed by a poulterer to drive a flock of geese and turkeys to London, in order to distinguish his own from any he might meet on the road, pulled 3 feathers out of the tails of the turkeys and 1 out of those of the geese, and upon counting them found that the number of turkey feathers exceeded twice those of the geese by 15. Having bought 10 geese and sold 15 turkeys by the way, he was surprised to find as he drove them into the poulterer's yard, that the number of geese exceeded the number of turkeys in the proportion of 7:3. Required the number of each."

When, in 1822, a classical tripos was introduced at Cambridge, aspirants to the tripos still had first to obtain honours in the mathematical tripos. In justice to Cambridge it should not be forgotten that the judges, statesmen, and bishops of that day who graduated in classics were more familiar with such concepts as mass, velocity, and inertia than most modern classicists are.

The lectures on applied chemistry by W. Farish (who succeeded to the chair of chemistry in 1793) were well attended, although they did not "count" toward a degree or toward the elections to college fellowships. Furthermore, Cambridge, although it excluded dissenters from its degrees as rigorously as Oxford did, was not so prejudiced toward their thinking; and Cambridge was not so helplessly bound by the authoritarian teaching of the Anglican Church. Perhaps that is why it was able to abandon the Aristotelian tradition in science teaching, while Oxford still retained it.

Nevertheless, even a century after the death of Newton, it could not for one moment be said that Cambridge was alight with the flame of science. The overwhelming majority of students who read seriously read for holy orders. Even the mathematics and mechanics courses, suffering from a sort of Newtonian scholasticism, were not taking account of advances in knowledge since Newton's day. When a Royal Commission examined the affairs of Cambridge during 1850–52 they heard from the Professor of Chemistry (the Rev. J. Cumming, who was appointed in 1815):

"A course of about 28 lectures was given annually by the present Professor . . . until the year 1831. From that time thirty lectures were given in the Lent and twenty in the Easter Term. This was continued until 1845, but the attendance in the Easter Term was so small, consisting of only four or five medical students, that the original plan was resumed of giving lectures only in one Term. . . . There is no residence, museum, library, collection, or apparatus attached to the Professorship . . . and there are no funds for this purpose. There are no opportunities afforded to students for instruction in the actual manipulation of instruments. . . . Hitherto the study of Chemistry has not only been neglected but discouraged in the University, as diverting the attention of pupils from what have been considered their proper academical studies. . . ."

To sum up: Oxford at the turn of the century was offering young men of 18 a course of study intended under the Laudian Code for boys. The more advanced studies in the professional faculties, which the Laudian Code assumed would follow the liberal education in the arts, had atrophied. Cambridge, though more sensitive to the age than Oxford, could not by any stretch of imagination be said to have responded to the scientific revolution. England's two ancient universities were—in Matthew Arnold's words— "places where the youth of the upper class prolong to a very great age, and under some very admirable influences, their school education . . . they are in fact still schools."

The purpose of this analysis is not to pass judgment on early Victorian Oxford and Cambridge, still less to pass judgment on the merits of a classical versus a scientific education. It is simply to establish the fact that scientific thought, which by 1800 was already consolidated in the foundations of modern physics and chemistry (those of biology were still to be laid by Darwin), and which had caught the imagination of the general public (even of artisans, who crowded to Anderson's 'anti-toga' lectures in Glasgow), had scarcely influenced the universities of England. The scientific revolution had occurred not through, but in spite of, the English universities.

The English universities did not embrace science and technology as enthusiastically as did the American universities, but by the middle of the *nineteenth* century, Oxford and Cambridge had both humanistic and scientific commitments. By the middle of the *twentieth* century, Sir Charles Snow created an intellectual stir by writing about "the two cultures" in English universities and the chasm between them.[35] Many English, French, and German universities are prisoners of their medieval past. They give less emphasis than American or Soviet universities to applied science and to organized research because they are dominated by scholars who underestimate the relevance of science or who have exclusively humanistic interests.[36] As a result, European business executives and engineers are less likely to have university degrees than their American or Soviet counterparts.[37] The Soviet Union has gone farther than any other industrial society in rejecting humanism and establishing a scientific-technological ideal for higher education.[38] This

35   Charles P. Snow, *The Two Cultures and the Scientific Revolution*, Cambridge, England: Cambridge University Press, 1959.
36   Ben-David and Zloczower, *op. cit.*, p. 82.
37   Seymour Martin Lipset and Reinhard Bendix, *Social Mobility in Industrial Society*, Berkeley: University of California Press, 1959, pp. 40–42.
38   Nicholas DeWitt, "Soviet Science Education and the School Reform," *School and Society*, Vol. 88, Summer 1960, pp. 297–300.

vocational emphasis in Soviet education stems from a belief on the part of Soviet leaders that industrial managers and government officials need such training. In Western Europe and in the United States, a liberal arts education is more acceptable as preparation for executive roles and government service.

Before assuming that the Soviet Union is correct in its rejection of liberal education, recall that for two thousand years Chinese emperors selected ministers, generals, and government officials from candidates who had passed examinations *in Confucian literature*.[39] It was assumed that cultivated minds could apply their wisdom to a wide range of problems. Recall further that Julius Caesar and other military geniuses of the Ancient World did not attend military academies. Possibly industrial societies have evolved to the point where native talent and humanistic education are not enough and therefore specialized training is crucial. Certainly, technical education is necessary for *some* industrial occupations—chemical engineering, for example. Certainly, too, the *belief* that a technical or scientific education is essential for factory managers can result in their being selected on the basis of training in engineering. But this is an illustration of the self-fulfilling prophecy and not proof that such training improves performance in the role. Urban industrial societies need more scientists and technicians than previous generations dreamed of producing, but whether they require a monolithic emphasis remains an open question.

Vocational training is not really a new function of higher education. Universities have long been responsible for training physicians, lawyers, and the clergy. What is new is the *number* of university students who regard higher education as vocational preparation—not only in the traditional professions, the pure sciences, or technical specialties like aeronautical engineering, but also in applied fields like business administration and elementary education. Some

critics of the heavy emphasis on vocational applications of higher education have pointed out that such emphasis may delude students into thinking they are being prepared for high-level occupations when they are not.[40] In a changing culture, general education may be better vocational preparation than elaborate specialization. One implication of Margaret Mead's point that education must continue throughout life is that premature specialization does not produce an individual who can make all the readjustments demanded by life.

In the United States, where college and university enrollments reached 38 per cent of the 18-to-21-year-old population in 1961, the emphasis on applied subjects is great.[41] American educational institutions can be classified in terms of their postures toward vocational preparation. The small, selective liberal-arts colleges teach the arts and sciences for their educational value and assume that a well-educated man is not disadvantaged in the labor market. (A study of the careers of a large number of graduates from a variety of American colleges provides empirical support for this assumption; graduates of Ivy League colleges earned more than graduates of other colleges—even with the economic background of the family controlled.[42]) Community junior colleges try to be "practical"; they teach an array of service and vocational courses. The large state universities are committed both to liberal and to vocational education, usually in different divisions, but with much overlapping. Generally speaking, students from working-class backgrounds are more likely than students from middle-class families to perceive higher education as vocational education, to choose applied curricula and courses, and to attend municipal

39   H. H. Gerth and C. Wright Mills, *From Max Weber: Essays in Sociology*, New York: Oxford University Press, 1946, pp. 416–444.

40   See the bibliographical reference to William H. Whyte, Jr., at the end of this chapter.
41   This paragraph leans heavily on data and interpretation of Martin Trow, "The Democratization of Higher Education in America," *European Journal of Sociology*, Vol. 3, Fall 1962, pp. 231–262.
42   Patricia Salter West, "Social Mobility among College Graduates," in Reinhard Bendix and Seymour Martin Lipset, Eds., *Class, Status and Power*, Glencoe, Ill.: Free Press, 1953, p. 476.

commuting colleges or state universities where this type of education is available. Thus, the increasing rate of college and university attendance—an average increase of 1 per cent per year in the United States since the end of the Second World War—means that American higher education is increasingly serving vocationally oriented students.

CONCLUSION

In an urban industrial society, the cultural tradition is so vast and is being augmented so rapidly that informal methods of transmitting ideas and skills to the younger generation are insufficient to the task. Formal educational institutions have been established in the industrial societies to guarantee that all children know how to read, write, and do simple computations. Mass elementary education has not been enough to equip children for adult roles, however, and therefore educational levels are still rising. Moreover, adult education under a wide variety of sponsorships—industry, the armed services, voluntary associations—attempts to compensate for the continuing obsolescence of childhood education. A system of formal education develops traditions of its own, which sometimes interfere with learning and, therefore, with producing sufficient numbers

of highly educated youngsters to fill managerial, technical, and professional roles. An anti-intellectual class culture is such an interference. So are student cultures in certain schools.

The occupational structure of an industrial society requires, as industrialization advances, increasing proportions of better-educated white-collar workers and less unskilled labor. But an industrial society does not require high levels of education for all workers. Hence, the school system attempts to guarantee that all children possess a minimum of useful knowledge and skills; above this minimal level, the population is increasingly differentiated in accordance with additional educational accomplishment. Differential educational achievement is the major mechanism for allocating youngsters to various status levels in industrial societies. Education has been related to social status in preindustrial societies also, but the educational horse followed the status cart. Preindustrial educational differentiation was either humanistic or dogmatic; special education was defined as suitable for the élite—the gentry in feudal China or preindustrial England. Industrial education, on the other hand, tends to be pragmatic, technical, vocational; it *generates* social status instead of being a *result* of it.

SOME SIGNIFICANT LITERATURE ON FORMAL EDUCATION

David P. Ausubel, *Maori Youth*, Wellington, New Zealand: Victoria University of Wellington Publications in Psychology, No. 14, 1961. Although New Zealand makes great efforts to achieve racial equality, interviews with 50 white and 50 Maori secondary school boys in two communities, one rural and the other urban, show that Maori youths are educationally disadvantaged in both. They have as high vocational and educational aspirations as white youngsters, but they are less likely to implement their ambitions through successful school performance, partly because of white prejudice and partly because the Maori culture does not prepare them adequately to internalize an achievement pattern. Apparently, different as New Zealand is from the United States in many ways, the educational difficulties of racial minorities are similar in the two countries. This summary is based on a review

by Richard Robbins, *American Sociological Review*, Vol. 27, February 1962, pp. 106–107.

George Baron and Asher Tropp, "Teachers in England and America," in A. H. Halsey, Jean Floud, and C. Arnold Anderson, *Education, Economy, and Society: A Reader in the Sociology of Education*, New York: Free Press of Glencoe, 1961, pp. 545–557. In England the teaching profession has a greater voice than in the United States both in setting educational goals and in their application. The main reason for this difference is that the British system of *national* control over education minimizes parental influence over their children's education; whereas the American system of *local* control enables nonprofessionals in the community to interpret the educational task to the teacher. Another factor reinforcing the authority of teachers in

England vis-à-vis parents is that British teachers are more likely than American teachers to be better educated than the parents of their students. ". . . [I]n England, where education for the larger part of the population ceases at the age of fifteen, the teacher will have had more education than all except a minority of parents." For these reasons teaching in England is more often regarded by the teacher as a lifetime career than in the United States. A 1957 study of 7150 beginning American teachers showed that relatively few of them planned to remain in teaching. The women intended to leave teaching for homemaking responsibilities, and the men aspired to becoming educational administrators. See Ward S. Mason, Robert J. Dressel, and Robert K. Bain, "Sex Role and Career Orientations of Beginning Teachers," *Harvard Educational Review*, Vol. 29, Fall 1959, pp. 370–383.

Basil Bernstein, "Social Structure, Language and Learning," *Educational Research*, Vol. 3, June 1961, pp. 163–176. The linguistic usages typical of the lower class in England form a relatively condensed language supplemented by gestures and implicit meanings. Such language is adequate ". . . for expressing and receiving concrete, global, descriptive relationships organized within a relatively low level of conceptualization." It is adequate, however, only in a community ". . . in which complex verbal procedures are made irrelevant by the system of nonverbal, closely shared identifications which serve as a backdrop to the speech." Formal education requires a shift of emphasis from nonverbal to verbal signals and, concomitantly, greater conceptual resources for expressing applications of the general case to the specific instance. Thus, Dr. Bernstein explains why the lower-class subculture incapacitates many English children from succeeding in school. See also his article, "Some Sociological Determinants of Perception," *British Journal of Sociology*, Vol. 9, June 1958, pp. 159–174.

Orville G. Brim, Jr., *Sociology and the Field of Education*, New York: Russell Sage Foundation, 1958. "Education has the inescapable problem of somehow integrating the various aims of its two major bodies of personnel, the educators and the students." Thus begins this survey of sociological research in the field of education. After examining the *goals* that have been assigned to educational institutions, Dr. Brim considers research on the *allocation of societal resources* to educational systems, including differential allocation depending on the clientele served. In these areas research is scarce, and Dr. Brim points out gaps that need filling. When he comes to discuss the *allocation of personnel*, which includes selection and promotion both of teachers and students, research is more plentiful. The *role prescriptions* for teachers include expectations governing community behavior, classroom interaction with students, and professional associations. All of these have been studied. The *role prescriptions* for students include classroom behavior and community participation —although neither of these aspects of the student role has been investigated systematically. On the other hand, the third aspect of the student role, relationships with fellow students, has received much attention. Dr. Brim concludes with a consideration of the consequences of different types and quantities of education on the student.

James S. Coleman, "The Adolescent Subculture and Academic Achievement," *American Journal of Sociology*, Vol. 65, January 1960, pp. 337–347. The student status systems in ten Midwest high schools were examined, five schools in small towns, one in a working-class suburb, one in a wealthy suburb, and three in cities of various sizes. In answer to the question, "How would you most like to be remembered in school: as an athletic star, a brilliant student, or most popular?" a majority of boys in all the schools were more interested in being remembered as athletic or popular than as a brilliant student. Professor Coleman explains the emphasis on athletic values as partly due to the fact that an outstanding athlete represents his school and not himself alone when he plays on a varsity team. "The outstanding student, in contrast, has little or no way to bring glory to his school. His victories are always personal, often at the expense of his classmates, who are forced to work harder to keep up with him." Professor Coleman suggests that establishing academic games and tournaments between schools might enable the brilliant student to contribute to the prestige of his school and would tend to increase his prestige within the school.

Neal Gross, *Who Runs Our Schools?*, New York: Wiley, 1958. Lengthy interviews with 105 superintendents of school and 508 school-board members in Massachusetts show the professional and lay pressures on school superintendents in the United States. Cross-pressures are analyzed from the point of view of the school superintendent, from the point of view of the school-board member, and, finally, from the point of view of the researcher. This summary is based on a review by Robert J. Havighurst, *American Sociological Review*, Vol. 24, August 1959, p. 605. See also Neal Gross, Ward S. Mason, and Alexander W. McEachern, *Explorations in Role Analysis: Studies of the School Superintendency Role*, New York: Wiley, 1958.

David Riesman, "The Influence of Student Culture and Faculty Values in the American College," *Year Book of Education*, 1959, Yonkers-on-Hudson, N.Y.: World, 1959, Chap. 2. Professor Riesman reviews a number of researches directly or indirectly concerned with the influence of student subcultures on the values of college students. He concedes that student subcultures may work at cross-purposes with faculty values, especially at large universities. School spirit ". . . is all too easily achieved at those big American state universities of the second and third rank where student solidarity, enshrined in fraternities and sororities, confronts a faculty culture so comparatively feeble and unprotected that nothing the latter would do could readily influence the former; students at such colleges, when asked to read a book they think beyond them, or which is not a free text, will turn in blank pages on the exam." On the other hand, notes Professor Riesman, public-opinion polls make clear that the values of the college educated differ from the values of the rest of the population. Unless it is assumed that these differences can be entirely attributed to self-selection among youngsters who go to college, student cultures do not prevent the faculty from wielding some influence. For an examination of the student subculture in medical schools, see Everett C. Hughes, Howard S. Becker, and Blanche Geer, "Student Culture and Academic Effort," in Nevitt Sanford, Ed., *The American College: A Psychological and Social Interpretation of the Higher Learning*, New York: Wiley, 1962, pp. 515–530.

Robert Singleton and Paul Bullock, "Some Problems in Minority-Group Education in the Los Angeles Public Schools," *Journal of Negro Education*, Vol. 32, Spring 1963, pp. 137–145. During the 1959–1960 and 1960–1961 academic years four Los Angeles high schools enrolled predominantly Negro students, and two high schools enrolled mainly Mexican-American youngsters. In each of those years, the proportion of enrollees who left these six schools without indicating an intention of entering another school was more than 20 per cent of the total enrollment. In Los Angeles high schools as a whole, however, the dropout rate was 10.5 per cent in 1959–1960 and 11.1 per cent in 1960–1961. Thus, Negro and Mexican-American high school students attended school in a milieu where dropping out rather than graduating was a prevalent expectation. Students expecting to quit school probably lack motivation to do homework conscientiously or attend regularly. In such a situation discipline problems are chronic. A negativistic student subculture is also characteristic of secondary modern schools in Great Britain, not because the students are predominantly from ethnic minorities but simply because most of them leave school to go to work at the age of 15. See John Webb, "The Sociology of a School," *British Journal of Sociology*, Vol. 13, September 1962, pp. 264–272. For a study showing that the sociocultural climate in a secondary school influences the grades and the aspirations of youngsters beyond what could be expected from knowledge of *individual* student characteristics, see Alan B. Wilson, "Residential Segregation of Social Classes and Aspirations of High School Boys," *American Sociological Review*, Vol. 24, December 1959, pp. 836–845.

B. F. Skinner, "Teaching Machines," *Science*, Vol. 128, October 1958, pp. 969–977. Professor Skinner argues that education must become more efficient in order to cope with the problems of mass education, and he suggests that the development of teaching machines is an important step in this direction. Teaching machines are not mere presentational aids (like closed-circuit television). The most important part of a teaching machine is its instructional program: a cunningly designed series of questions presented in such a way that the student must learn the correct answer to one question before he is permitted to go on to the next. What are the advantages of teaching machines? (1) They make possible individualized instruction; the slow student and the bright student each learns at his own pace—something impossible in large classes. Thus, teaching machines can cope with a common reason for educational failure: differences in learning speeds. (2) Teaching machines encourage the student to take an active part in the instructional process. The student must respond to the program correctly in order to advance to the next question; hence, he cannot remain a passive recipient of information as he could if he lolled in front of a television set or sat inertly in a large lecture hall. (3) Teaching machines reinforce the student's correct response immediately—unlike the ordinary test situation where the student must wait several days to find out whether his answers are correct. This immediate feedback facilitates retention. Professor Skinner argues that a teaching machine is an approximation to an individual tutor. "Like a good tutor the machine presents just that material for which the student is ready. It asks him to take only that step which he is at the moment best equipped and most likely to take. Like a skillful tutor the machine helps the student to come up with the right answer. It does this in part through the orderly construction of the program and in part with techniques of hinting, prompting, suggesting. . . ." In short, the teaching machine is, according to Professor Skinner, the least painful way to communicate most kinds of information to large numbers of students. See also Lawrence M. Stolurow, *Teaching by Machine*, Cooperative Research Monograph No. 6, Office of Education, Washington: Government Printing Office, 1961.

William H. Whyte, Jr., "The Training of Organization Man," in *The Organization Man*, Garden City, N.Y.: Doubleday, 1957, pp. 69–152. Whyte argues in this section of his book that American colleges are trying too hard to prepare youngsters to take their places in a technological society. He deplores the growth of enrollments in vocationally oriented curricula like business administration not only because he believes that a liberal-arts education is intellectually "liberating" but also because he does not agree that future business men need ". . . more and more . . . training in the minutiae of organization skills . . ." To be sure, he notes (with obvious sadness) (1) that corporate recruiting procedures penalize the liberal-arts major as against the vocationally "trained" under-graduate and (2) that the growing vocational emphasis of the colleges is helping to reduce the discontinuity between education and work. "For the senior who is headed for the corporation [to join its training pro-gram] . . . the locale shifts; the training continues, for at the same time that the colleges have been changing their curriculum to suit the corporation, the corporation has responded by setting up its own cam-puses and classrooms."

CHAPTER 13

Political Institutions:
Achieving a Precarious Consensus

From one point of view, the political process determines who gets what, when, and where.[1] This conception emphasizes the differential advantages resulting from concrete decisions: the awarding of a contract to produce military equipment, the location of a school, the imposition of tariffs, the passing of a new law regulating minimum wages. Such a conception of political institutions is valid; many of the activities of government are concerned, directly or indirectly, with the relative advantages of various segments of the population. The graduated income tax is clearly redistributive: income is taken from wealthier citizens and, through governmental expenditures, allocated to poorer ones. More subtly perhaps, so are the decisions of agencies like the Interstate Commerce Commission, the Reconstruction Finance Corporation, and the Food and Drug Administration.[2] Still, redistribution is only one aspect of the political process. A more fundamental problem is the achievement of consensus.[3] How can acceptable decisions be arrived at? To what ends should the resources of the society be applied? Although the choice between war and peace has redistributive implications, most people would agree that the substantive importance of these alternatives overshadows the redistributive implications.

The larger and more differentiated the society, the harder it becomes to resolve differences in point of view as well as conflicts of interest. Consensus and solidarity are not achieved automatically. As early as the seventeenth century, the British social philosopher Thomas Hobbes recognized the precariousness of social order.[4] He imagined what social existence would be like in the absence of government and concluded that it would be "a war of all against all"—that is, chaos. Life for the individual would be "solitary, poor, nasty, brutish, and short." Since Hobbes did not want

1 Harold D. Lasswell, *Politics: Who Gets What, When, How*, New York: McGraw-Hill, 1936.
2 Blair Bolles, *How to Get Rich in Washington: Rich Man's Division of the Welfare State*, New York: Norton, 1952.
3 Seymour Martin Lipset, "Political Sociology," in

Merton, Broom, and Cottrell, Eds., *Sociology Today: Problems and Prospects*, New York: Basic Books, 1959, pp. 81–114; Talcott Parsons, " 'Voting' and the Equilibrium of the American Political System," in Burdick and Brodbeck, Eds., *American Voting Behavior*, Glencoe, Ill.: Free Press, 1959, pp. 80–120.
4 Thomas Hobbes, *Leviathan; or the Matter, Forme and Power of a Commonwealth, Ecclesiasticall and Civill*, Cambridge, England: Cambridge University Press, 1904; Talcott Parsons, *The Structure of Social Action*, New York: McGraw-Hill, 1937, pp. 89–94.

to live such an unpleasant and insecure existence, he argued for strong government, which
in his time meant monarchy.

THE PROBLEM OF DECISION
MAKING IN INDUSTRIAL SOCIETIES

In contemporary industrial societies, consensus is at least as problematic as it was
in Hobbes' lifetime. Whenever alternatives
confront a community, regardless of whether
they are economic, educational, religious, or
military, disagreement over them is a possibility. Hence, there is a political dimension to
every issue that can potentially divide or disrupt a society. Whether individuals should be
allowed to select their own pattern of religious
behavior is a political question. So is the extent to which people are permitted to buy,
sell, and produce goods. Americans do not ordinarily think of these as political questions because they were settled long ago. The American solution was to place the authority (and
the coercive force) of government behind individual freedom in both religious and economic behavior. The Soviet solutions to these
political questions are obviously different.

The political institutions of a society are
mechanisms for reevaluating previous decisions
in the light of recent experience and for making
decisions about newly presented alternatives.
At one time, parents could decide whether to
send their children to school and for how long.
Today, all of the industrial countries have compulsory school-attendance laws, and the number of years of compulsory attendance continues to rise. Compulsion is implicit in every
governmental decision because a decision cannot be effective unless opponents are compelled
to accept it. Sometimes people have to be
physically removed from homes condemned
under the right of eminent domain for a new
highway or school. Usually, though, governmental decisions are complied with, half because they are felt to be legitimate, half because of an awarenes that resistance is useless.

Industrial societies are too complicated to
permit everybody to participate in every decision. Part of the political process consists of
the selection of persons authorized to make decisions on behalf of the society: legislators,
judges, administrators. Even in totalitarian political systems, where government officials are
less dependent on popular support, decision
makers need acceptance of their *authority* as
well as fear of their *power*. Authority, a pivotal
concept in political sociology, refers to a recognition of the decision's legitimacy by those
subject to the decision.[5]

No matter what level of the political process
is examined, local, national, or international,
decision makers constitute a tiny fraction of
the total population. Furthermore, they are
obviously not a random sample of their society. For example, Max Weber, the German
sociologist, called attention to the *charismatic*
quality of some leaders.[6] ("Charisma" is rare;
it is the personal magnetism enabling a politician to command loyalty from followers—
apart from the authority of his office or his
power to confer rewards.) In addition to
charismatic qualities, which are difficult to define precisely, persons who wield political power
differ from the larger population in more
tangible ways: by age, sex, profession, education, and so forth. One of the intriguing problems for empirical research is the effect of
characteristics of the decision makers on the decision-making process. In the following article,
Peter Rossi surveys the literature on decision
making *in the local community*.

[5] Robert M. MacIver, *The Web of Government*,
New York: Macmillan, 1947, p. 83; Chester I. Barnard,
The Functions of the Executive, Cambridge, Mass.:
Harvard University Press, 1938, p. 163.
[6] Max Weber, *The Theory of Social and Economic
Organization*, New York: Oxford University Press,
1947.

Research on Decision Making in American Local Communities

Reprinted by permission. From Peter H. Rossi, "Community Decision Making," *Administrative Science Quarterly*, Vol. 1, March 1957, pp. 415–443.[7]

A community decision is a choice among several modes of action which is made by an authoritative person or group within the community institutions and of which the goals are the change or maintenance of community-wide institutions or facilities.

We shall not be concerned whether the motives of the actors involved are personal profit, power, or the general welfare of the community. If a decision undertaken by an authoritative group

[7] The following references from Professor Rossi's bibliography are mentioned in the course of his article: Bernard Berelson, Paul F. Lazarsfeld, and William N. McPhee, *Voting*, Chicago, 1954; W. W. Charters, Jr., "Social Class Analysis and the Control of Education," *Harvard Educational Review*, Vol. 23, Fall 1953; George S. Counts, *The Social Composition of Boards of Education*, New York, 1927; Oliver Garceau, *The Public Library in the Political Process*, New York, 1949; August B. Hollingshead, *Elmtown's Youth*, New York, 1949; Floyd A. Hunter, *Community Power Structure*, Chapel Hill, N.C., 1953; Elihu Katz and Paul F. Lazarsfeld, *Personal Influence*, Glencoe, Ill., 1955; Robert K. Lamb, "Suggestions for a Study of Your Home Town," *Human Organization*, Vol. 11, Summer 1952; Paul F. Lazarsfeld, Bernard Berelson, and Hazel Gaudet, *The People's Choice*, New York, 1949; Seymour Lipset, Paul F. Lazarsfeld, Allen Barton, and Juan Lenz, "The Social Psychology of Voting," in Gardner Lindzey, *Handbook of Social Psychology*, Vol. II, Cambridge, Mass., 1954; Robert S. Lynd, *Middletown in Transition*, New York, 1937; Donald R. Matthews, *The Social Background of Political Decision Makers*, New York, 1954; Robert K. Merton, "Patterns of Interpersonal Influence," in Paul F. Lazarsfeld and Frank Stanton, *Communications Research: 1948–49*, New York, 1949; Martin Meyerson and Edward C. Banfield, *Politics, Planning and the Public Interest*, Glencoe, Ill., 1955; C. Wright Mills and Melville Ullmer, "Small Business and Civic Welfare," *Report of the Smaller War Plants Corp.*, U.S. Senate Document No. 135, Washington, D.C., 1946; Peter H. Rossi, J. Leiper Freeman, and James M. Shipton, "Politics and Education in Massachusetts," manuscript in preparation; John T. Salter, *Boss Rule*, New York, 1935; Samuel A. Stouffer, *Communism, Conformity and Civil Liberties*, New York, 1955; W. Lloyd Warner and Paul S. Lunt, *The Social Life of a Modern Community*, New Haven, 1941.

or person involves actions directed toward change or nonchange within the community as such, this is a community decision.

Note that this definition contains two specifications. To qualify as a community decision, a choice must be made by an authoritative person or group, that is, one which either by law or by custom has the legitimate and recognized right to make the decision in question. The second specification indicates that the decision must involve community-wide institutions such as local government, locally oriented private associations, and so on.

What sorts of decisions does this concept exclude? It excludes, first, the myriad decisions whose goals are not community oriented, for example, the market decisions of business organizations, migration decisions of individuals, and so on. Second, decisions made by "outside" agencies or persons, for example, the state and national governments, are not covered. Finally, it excludes decisions made by persons who are not in authoritative positions.

The range of decisions included is considerable. On the broadest level, the citizen casting his vote in a local election is an authoritative decision maker in his role as voter. A mayor acting in the capacity of his office makes community decisions of a wide variety. So do the members of the board of directors of community organizations such as the community chest.

Implicit in our concept of community decisions is the idea of "community issues," which may be defined as choices as to policy open to the authoritative decision makers. Thus the issue before the voters in a local election are choices among slates of candidates, approval or disapproval of referenda, and so forth. The issues before a city council may involve decisions within each of a wide variety of sets of alternatives, ranging from budget allocation for the whole municipality to the repair of a sidewalk in front of a particular citizen's house. Note that the issue defines the relevant decision maker according to the rules laid down by law and customs.

Issues, of course, involve more persons and groups than just the decision makers to which they are ultimately referred. Other members and groups within the community express preferences to each other and to the decision makers, attempt to persuade or even coerce decision makers, and so on. Each issue thus has its partisans, a category which may include—depending on the issue involved—almost the entire community or just one or two individuals. A *partisan* is some one person or group who is concerned to see that one or another alternative is chosen by a decision maker.

The definitions offered are not as precise as might be desired. It is not always easy to locate the decision maker for a given issue, although this may be less of a problem *post factum*. Nor is it always clear whether an issue involves the community and its status or noncommunity matters. Our definitions are designed to make rough distinctions, and their utility can be judged in the discussion which follows.

Our objective is to review and evaluate research on community decisions. How are such decisions made? How are issues settled? What factors have been found to be crucial in affecting the outcomes of issues? What general statements may be made about the decision-making process? What are the research designs employed and the problems which they seem best suited to study? . . .

One basic approach to the study of decision making has been concerned with the characteristics of *decision makers*, attempting to relate the social and personal differences among decision makers to the kinds of decisions made. The research techniques employed have ranged from the analysis of detailed quasi-clinical case histories through the statistical analysis of official biographical notes.

A second approach has given central attention to the *partisans* of issues, seeking to find in their actions vis-a-vis the decision makers the "ultimate" determinants of the outcome of decisions. Studies which focus on "pressure groups," or propaganda, or which search for the "power structure" belong to this class of research designs.

A third approach employs *decisions* as its reference point, seeking to understand the choices of decision makers as the outcome of relatively complex processes. Studies of decision making in contrived groups within laboratory settings fall into this category as well as analyses of retrospective accounts of the decision-making process obtained from interviews with the decision makers.

The remainder of this section will be devoted to taking up each approach in turn, presenting a few examples of each, abstracting the major substantive findings, and evaluating each approach.

THE DECISION-MAKER APPROACH

In outline form, the typical design of research in this category is constructed along the following lines. Decision makers, usually of a particular type, for example, precinct captains, school board members, voters, and so on, are located, and certain of their characteristics are noted and compared with some sort of reference population. The technique furnishing the essential characteristics of the decision makers may range from extensive life histories, as in the case of John T. Salter's study of Philadelphia "bosses," to published official biographical notes, as in the case of Donald R. Matthews' study of national and state legislators. The characteristics studied may range from the relatively simple ones of age, occupation, and education to the more complex attitudinal data such as are supplied in detailed interviews.

From a consideration of the ways in which the decision makers differ from the general population or from some other norm, inferences are made concerning the types of decisions which they are thereby disposed to make. Thus from the finding that the age of city councilmen is higher than that of the voters, the conclusion might be drawn that city councils tend to be conservative and resistant to change. Several brief examples follow:

• An early study by George S. Counts showed that school-board members throughout the nation are primarily recruited from among the business and professional occupations. Hence the essentially conservative and business-oriented character of the public schools.

• As a part of a study of adolescent behavior in a small midwest community, August B. Hollingshead made a detailed study of the social-class membership of the community's school board and top school officials. Finding that school-board members and school officials were recruited entirely from among the upper strata of the community, he concluded that the character of the school system stemmed at least in part from this pattern of recruitment.

• W. Lloyd Warner's now-classic study of "Yankee City" contains data showing that the higher the office held in the local government, the higher the social class of the officeholder. The "class character" of the local political system is inferred from this pattern of officeholding.

• In a very recent study of attitudes toward political nonconformists, Samuel A. Stouffer found that "community leaders" (mayors, heads of library boards, and so on) were more tolerant toward nonconformists than the general population of their communities. He suggests that those responsible for important decisions concerning civil liberties on the local level are more tolerant in their actions than would be the average citizen.

• Oliver Garceau's study of the compositions of library boards in a sample of American communities indicated that there was little relationship to be discerned between the composition of these boards and the excellence of the library's services. The members of library boards tended to be concentrated in the higher social and economic strata of their communities.

• Practically every modern study of voting behavior has relied heavily on the analysis of the way in which classes and regional groups display different electoral choices. . . .

The most strongly established finding of these studies of decision makers concerns their differential recruitment. Whether we are concerned with the electorate or with elected or appointed officials, as a group decision makers tend to be drawn disproportionately from the higher age categories, classes, and ethnic groups of higher status. Furthermore, the higher the authority level of the decision maker, the more marked are the differences between decision makers and ordinary citizens. In other words, the upper, as compared with the lower, status groups are somewhat more likely to hold public or semipublic offices.

Most of the studies cited above go beyond the fact of differential recruitment, however, to make inferences concerning how decision making is affected by this pattern. This approach has been most successful when applied to mass voting behavior as a decision-making process, where, for most national and local elections, clear divisions may be discerned in the electorate along class, ethnic, and regional lines.

When applied to decision makers on higher levels, the inferences drawn from the differential recruitment pattern are somewhat shaky. For example, to demonstrate that a school board composed of business and professional men is bound to show a "class bias," it is necessary first to demonstrate that the classes in the community hold different opinions on the issues confronting a school board. Is there, for example, a class posi-tion on education policy? Or on the alternative solutions to a community's traffic problems?

In other words, it is open to question whether for many issues there are clear and consistent differences among class groups, ethnic groups, age levels, and so on, which could manifest themselves in different decisions dependent on what kind of decision maker holds office. The substitution of sets of decision makers of radically different background need not necessarily result in groups holding radically different positions on many issues.

Secondly, there is an assumption of a close association between an individual's background and personal characteristics and the behavior which he will manifest in office. While it is true that *in the general population* class position correlates with opinion on a variety of issues . . . , these correlations are low enough to ensure a rather large number of deviants from the majority opinion on every class level. *It is precisely to these deviants on the upper occupational levels that the popular support of the lower strata of the community may be attracted*. Among elected decision makers, at least, social background may be a very poor predictor of decisions made, particularly on class-related issues. In other, nonelected positions, for example, membership on library boards, the community chest, and so on, some decision makers may owe their appointments to the fact that they represent deviant views among the upper strata.

Thirdly, to look to social background and personal characteristics as the major explanation of a man's behavior in a decision-maker role is to deny that a given individual may act differently when placed in different roles. It is noteworthy that this approach has been most successful when applied to the decision-making role of voter, which is the least demanding of all such roles under discussion. The higher-level decision-maker roles with which we are mainly concerned here are ordinarily rather well defined in both law and custom, by virtue of the concern with which the community has regarded them. Each role involves its incumbents in a set of structured relationships to other roles and is accompanied by formally and informally defined criteria for its proper performance. Thus a local bank executive on a local school board is pressured to come to grips with the organizational problems of his school system in a way that he would never do as just a private citizen. His actions on the school board are at least in part determined by the demands of his role as school-board member. Especially when the role is professionalized—as in the case of school officials, public health officials, social workers, and so forth—and incumbents are specially trained to fill their positions, role expectations will probably be particularly important determinants of decisions. A school superintendent trained in a teachers' college will have been exposed to a very self-conscious view of educational policy and of the way a superintendent should behave in his role.

Finally, the decision maker does not operate entirely within a social vacuum. On many issues, particularly those which intimately affect the interests of significant persons or groups, he is bombarded with communications from partisans of one or another policy alternative. Attempts are made to persuade, influence, or coerce him to support particular policies. He is supplied with information, presented with arguments, offered rewards extending from the intangibles of social acceptance to the hard reality of money, and threatened with reprisals either to himself or to his organization. Undoubtedly the actions of partisans play some part, over and above predisposition and role, in the outcome of many issues. . . .

THE "PARTISAN APPROACH": STUDIES OF POWER AND INFLUENCE

So dramatic have been the documented instances in which partisans have managed to affect the outcome of issues that we can hardly overlook their actions as an important set of determinants of community decisions. The dramatic quality of these incidents stems in large part from their semilegitimate status in the light of our democratic values. On the one hand, we recognize the right of citizens to advocate and defend their individual interests as against the individual interests of others. On the other hand, we demand that the decision maker should be above partisan views and should act in line with the interests of the community, without, however, specifying how one might identify in any particular issue what they may be. *Hence when we examine the outcome of an issue, it is easier to see which individual interests have been served than to judge whether the community interests as such have been upheld.*

The effects of partisan activity have been studied on many levels of decision making. Recent research on voting has documented the existence of informal opinion leaders, persons of more than ordinary concern with politics, who affect the behavior of those voters with whom they may be in personal contact. On higher levels of decision making, the concept of power has been used to describe how persons and organizations controlling significant amounts of wealth or solidarity employ their resources to affect the outcome of issues. Power and influence are both relational terms, concepts employed to describe relationships between persons and/or groups. When we say that a man is influential or powerful, we mean that his behavior has significance for some other persons. In the case of power, we imply a relationship in which individual A affects the behavior of individual B because B wishes to avoid the sanctions which A would employ if B did not comply with his wishes. In the case of influence, B's behavior is affected in the absence of sanctions. Thus although the process in each case by which A affects B is different, the general form of the relationship is the same, and hence researches on power and influence tend to follow the same basic designs. Indeed, so close is the relationship between power and influence that it is difficult empirically to distinguish between the two.

Roughly, there are three basic research designs which have been employed in the study of power and influence. First, we have studies of the potentials for power and influence, inventories of persons and organizations in a community who are in positions to influence or apply power to decision makers. Second, we have studies of power or influence reputations, researches on what community members consider the influence or power structures to be. Finally, there are researches on actual influence or power, studies of particular issues in which influence or power have played a part in the determination of the outcome.

POWER AND INFLUENCE AS POTENTIAL. Since social relationships are notoriously difficult to study directly, some researchers have centered their attention on producing inventories of those positions in the community which have the necessary attributes for the wielding of influence or power. In the case of power, these studies document who within a community controls significant amounts of economic resources. By virtue of their control over economic organizations—banks, industrial and commercial enterprises, public utilities, and so forth—such persons are in a position to wield sanctions of an economic sort over decision makers. In the case of influence studies, inventories are obtained of "leaders," persons at the heads of various private associations or occupying important public offices. By virtue of their position, leaders can influence the opinions of their followers on a variety of issues. A few examples of these researches follow:

• In his study of Middletown, Robert Lynd devotes a chapter to the X family showing how this family group either owns or controls a large number of enterprises and has representation in most of the other significant enterprises in the community.

• Advising students how they may undertake surveys of communities, Robert K. Lamb stresses the procedure of obtaining a list of the banking and industrial officials, newspaper editors, owners of large blocks of real estate, and so forth. Such lists may be used to outline the power structure of the community.

• The community leaders studied by Samuel A. Stouffer in his research on attitudes toward political nonconformity were chosen in part because their positions made them the likely leaders of public opinion in their communities.

• C. Wright Mills and Melville Ullmer, in a study of single- and diversified-industry cities, identify the real leaders of their communities as the industrial and mercantile elite within each community. . . .

Implicit in this approach is the assumption that the potential for power or influence undoubtedly will be employed. Business leaders, in fact, exercise their power to affect the decisions made by formal authorities. Furthermore, the potential for power is often regarded as equally effective regardless of the point at which it is applied—whether within the community chest or within the city council—and results in decisions which are different from those which would occur in the absence of such power. Similarly, the potential for influence is often regarded as equally effective regardless of the topic involved—whether political opinions, attitudes toward mental disease, and so forth—and when employed, it results in a different distribution of opinion among the public than would have occurred in its absence. . . .

STUDIES OF POWER OR INFLUENCE REPUTATION: THE PERCEIVED POWER OR INFLUENCE STRUCTURE. With the development of sociometric techniques, it was almost inevitable that these devices be applied to the study of both power and influence in the local community. These techniques allow the researcher literally to chart the interrelationships within a group of people. Obviously, except for communities of very small size, some modification of sociometry was necessary before this technique could be used in the study either of power or of influence. In the case of power-reputation studies, informants are asked whom they perceive to be powerful within the community. Persons receiving a large number of "votes" from informants are identified as constituting the power structure. Similarly, in the case of "influence-reputation" studies, informants are asked to designate whose opinion would influence them on a variety of topics. Several examples of research along these lines follow:

• Floyd Hunter, in his study of the power structure of "Regional City," asked a sample of community-organization leaders to designate who were the "top" as "civic, governmental, business and status" leaders in the community. The persons receiving the highest number of "votes" were designated as comprising the power structure of the community.

• Robert K. Merton asked a sample of "Rovere" citizens to designate to whom they would look for advice on a variety of topics, e.g., on educational problems, political matters, health problems, and so forth. Persons receiving more than a minimum number of designations were termed influentials. Their characteristics were studied in direct interviews.

• My associates and I, in a study of "Bay City," a small Massachusetts industrial city, asked members of the community's elite to choose the most important persons on a prepared list of some twenty-five names culled from among industrial, political, religious, and civic leaders. Interviews were obtained from members of this group, and an analysis was made of the factors which led them to be highly chosen by their fellows.

• Elihu Katz and Paul F. Lazarsfeld report on a study of women who were asked to designate persons whom they "could trust to let them know what was really going on." Designated persons were then interviewed in order to identify their characteristics as compared with the persons who designated them.

• In a study of the public administrators in "Bay City," J. Leiper Freeman obtained ratings from each public official of the importance for their operations of other officials and various groups in the city, e.g., the city council, mayor, chamber of commerce, and so forth. Persons designated as important for an official were considered potential sources of influence upon him.

Note that the power or influence structure is defined in terms of the "reputations" accorded to individuals by a set of judges. While the "reputations" involved are probably deserved in the sense that these are persons who are likely to exercise power or influence, it is still open to question whether, on a variety, let alone a majority, of issues outcomes of issues are heavily affected by their actions.

For example, in the case of Hunter's study, the range of issues with which the power structure concerns itself is delimited by example. The instances cited in which members of the power "structure" undertook to provide the leadership for community projects covered considerable ground. The implication is left that there are few areas of community life in which the power structure does not take a hand. Yet the total set of issues is unspecified, and hence the impact of the power structure on the life of the community is hard to assess.

Similarly, Merton's study of influentials is also on a general plane. Influentials are persons who are regarded as potential sources of trusted advice by members of the community; we do not know how frequently, in fact, they are employed as sources. That this is a relevant issue to raise is demonstrated in Katz and Lazarsfeld, where it is shown that *the persons who actually influenced specific opinion changes are likely to be very different from persons designated as potential sources of influence.*

The same question may be raised about the power reputation studies. It seems likely that they specify one of the important ways in which the outcomes of issues are settled, but we are not confident that this represents either the *typical* way for every decision or for every decision-maker role.

What have these studies established? First, it is clear that some individuals by virtue of their economic strength can and, on occasion, do exercise more than ordinary influence over decision makers. Secondly, this control is especially effective over some rather than other decision makers. Civic associations dependent on voluntary finan-

cial contributions seem particularly vulnerable. Thirdly, informal opinion leaders exist on all levels of the community and on occasion affect the opinions of the mass of citizens. It can be shown, furthermore, that these opinion leaders do not entirely overlap with the official public and organizational leaders of the community. . . .

Granted that power is wielded and influence exists, as we must concede from the number of examples which these researches have collected, the question still remains as to the *proportion* of all decisions affected in this way. The method of collecting examples probably emphasizes the efficacy of the power or influence structure, as compared, for example, with some of the researches cited below which focus on decisions rather than partisans. It seems obvious, furthermore, that for any urban community of any size, the number of decision makers and the decisions made is so great that complete monitoring by the power structure is impossible, especially since the persons involved are usually engaged in other enterprises as well. . . .

STUDIES OF DECISIONS: THE PROCESS APPROACH

. . . The blame for the neglect of decisions as a major research focus must be placed to a large degree on the nature of the phenomenon itself. Most of the issues in which we are most interested ordinarily entail a settlement process in which complicated chains of choices are made by a large number of decisions makers. A description of the events involved, for example, in the approval of a municipal budget by a city council would result in a large document, while more complicated issues would demand even more complicated descriptions.

Nor would our task be more manageable if we concentrated on the choices made by a decision maker rather than on issues. The work of a mayor or city councilman involves a large number of choices of a great variety. Few of the decisions would be comparable in content, and those which were would be likely to be relatively trivial, e.g., a councilman's votes on public-works maintenance orders.

For these reasons the study of decisions has ordinarily been carried out either within the controlled environment of the laboratory or, in the field, on decisions which are relatively simple and hence comparable. Only a few studies have attempted to follow a particular issue from start to settlement. . . .

Outside of the laboratory the study of decisions has been most successful when confined to mass observations of simple issues, as in mass voting behavior. Observations are made of large numbers of decision makers, each of whom has to make much the same choice among a small number of alternatives. A small group of researchers have attempted to follow the career of more complicated issues, observing the decisions made with respect to them by a large number of decision makers acting in different capacities.

Typically, the researcher isolates a population which has either made a decision of a particular kind or will shortly be faced with the necessity for doing so. The decision makers are interviewed concerning their past decisions or they are questioned periodically as they come to a choice on an issue which faces them.

Vote decisions are particularly suited to this approach. The issues before each voter and the form of the decision are identical. Two of the most valuable accounts of vote behavior (Paul Lazarsfeld, Bernard Berelson, and Hazel Gaudet and Berelson, Lazarsfeld, and William N. McPhee) studied the decisions made by samples of voters interviewed repeatedly during the presidential campaigns of 1940 and 1948. Voters who came to their choices or shifted their preferences during the period of the interviewing were asked to tell how they came to their decisions. . . .

Katz and Lazarsfeld report a study of changes in marketing habits, fashions, and political opinions. A sample of women were interviewed concerning the reasons for their shifts of preference and opinion, with particular emphasis on the roles of the mass media and interpersonal contacts.

Studies of more complicated issues have been relatively rare:

Perhaps the most elaborate study of the career of an issue is the description of how sites were selected in Chicago during 1949 and 1950 for new public housing. Martin Meyerson and Edward C. Banfield (the former Planning Director of the Chicago Housing Authority during the period under study) have provided a fascinating account of the way in which sites were finally selected after much pulling and hauling among the housing authority, the city council, the mayor, local neighborhood groups, and so on. Basic data for the study came from documents of the various groups involved and interviews with participants.

A number of the cases collected by the Inter-University Case Program bear on community decisions. Presented as descriptive accounts, the cases follow through controversies from their beginnings to their final settlements.

In our own study an attempt was made to account for the outcome of two local issues: the selection of a superintendent of schools by a local school board and the approval of a municipal budget by a city council. School-board members and councilmen were intensively interviewed concerning their relationships to each other, their contacts with persons outside the decision-making groups, and their reasons for their particular positions on the issues. . . .

CONCERNING DECISION MAKERS

It seems likely that the most important source of variation among decision makers lies in their roles rather than in the personal qualities which they bring to their offices. The more of the decision maker's total interests and activities are invested in the role itself, the more likely are role expectations to determine his decision-making behavior. Thus, at the one extreme, we would expect that the role of voter, being poorly defined and undemanding, would have little effect on the voter's choices; while at the other extreme, the professional social worker in charge of a community organization would be acting according to a well-defined conception of the best way he might fill the demands of his office.

At the higher level of decision making, roles vary widely in three respects, each of which seems likely to affect the vulnerability of the decision maker's role both to the demands of the would-be power wielder and to those of his organization. First, the higher the prestige of the office, the more the decision maker will be able to act independently. In this connection, we may note that Supreme Court Justice achieved the highest prestige rating of all the occupations studied by the National Opinion Research Center. Secondly, decision-maker roles in organizations which have an independent financial base are less vulnerable than those in organizations dependent on support controlled by other persons or organizations, thus the vulnerability of the civic associations dependent on voluntary contributions and the relatively greater independence of public officials whose organizations are supported by taxing powers. Finally, decision makers may derive independence from their basis of tenure: tenured officials might be expected to be more independent than elected officials, who in turn may be more independent than those who are removable at will.

As a result of his survey, Professor Rossi tentatively concluded that the requirements of the *role* have more weight in the decision-making process than the personal qualities of the decision maker or the pressures brought to bear on him by outsiders. This conclusion rests on American studies and should be checked against comparative data from other industrial societies. Furthermore, only decision making in *local* communities was considered. Nevertheless, it is an encouraging finding. If Professor Rossi is right, decision makers are neither so parochial nor so vulnerable to pressure as the more pessimistic political analysts think. They are capable of representing the entire community, of adopting what Walter Lippmann called "the public philosophy." [8]

Professor Rossi suggested at various points in his article that his conclusions were less relevant to voting behavior than to other community decisions. Yet in democratic societies *voting* is the mechanism for selecting key government officials. If voting decisions are more parochial and vulnerable to pressure than other community decisions, what implications are there for the organization of the political process in democratic societies?

DESPOTIC AND DEMOCRATIC SOCIETIES

The most conspicuous difference between democratic and despotic societies is that voting affects the personnel in decision-making roles more in the former than in the latter. Insofar as elections are genuine contests between rival groups of potential leaders, the incumbents have only a precarious grasp on decision-making roles. A two-party system, prescribed

[8] Walter Lippmann, *Essays in the Public Philosophy,* Boston: Little, Brown, 1955.

intervals between elections, rules limiting the number of terms in office, and certain conditions of equilibrium among the groups and organizations within the society help keep elections vehicles for the transfer of power instead of mere rituals. In the following article, Gerard DeGré demonstrates the subtle connection in a free society between the autonomy of non-governmental groups and the actual power of political authorities.

The Sociological Basis of Freedom

Reprinted by permission. From Gerard DeGré, "Freedom and Social Structure," *American Sociological Review*, Vol. 11, October 1946, pp. 529–536.

Man, as a political animal, lives his life in groups, and the concrete freedoms which he enjoys derive their sustenance and vitality from the backing of his group *vis à vis* other groups. The romantic, highly individualized conception of freedom, so popular in the literature of the nineteenth century, and useful as it may be in motivating individual thought and action, fails, nevertheless, to provide a realistic theory of freedom which can do justice to the sociological and historical roots of social action. Romanticism provides an ideal of freedom rather than an explanation or analysis. In its emphasis on the ideal of personal autonomy, Romanticism brushes aside the problem of the situational determination of freedom. . . .

A sociological theory of freedom, therefore, must take as its starting point the *socius,* that is, the individual as a member of a group, class, or social type, rather than the abstract individual-as-such that forms the nucleus of Romanticism.

Studies in the field of the sociology of knowledge have demonstrated that the idea of freedom is itself conditioned by the group membership of the individual. For the conservative, freedom usually means the freedom to exercise his prerogatives and to conduct his affairs with a minimum of interference from the state or other organized groups. Although at first glance this conception might not seem to run contrary to our general definition of freedom, in practice it tends to violate social freedom to the degree to which it refuses to recognize the claims of other groups to free action. In other words, it recognizes freedom only *for its own class,* and endeavors to keep other social strata subordinated to its will.

The revolutionist, on the other hand, defines freedom primarily in terms of freedom from the restrictions and prerogatives of a strongly intrenched dominant class, and, in its revolutionary fervor, calls for the destruction of that class. This is as true of the ascendant bourgeoisie in its struggle against the feudal aristocracy as it is of the revolutionary proletariat of our day.

A little reflection makes it clear that both of these groups are operating with a *particularistic* conception of freedom, for they both define freedom in terms of their own class interest. The unreconstructed conservative and the reactionary admit freedom as a good only for their own group, and wish to deny it to others just as soon as they feel that their class interests are threatened. The revolutionist, in reaction to this situation, wishes to deny the very basis of freedom to the dominant group, that is, their continued existence.

A *pluralistic* or *total* definition of freedom must take into account the interests and aspirations of all societal groupings: economic, political and cultural. . . .

If the degree of freedom is dependent upon the relative absence of external constraint, it will be correlated also with those societal conditions which tend to limit the power of social groups in relationship to one another. . . .

Within a specific socio-historical situation, the existing system of power relationships will determine the degree of freedom which is present. The system of power relationships itself is the resultant of the relative power of the component groups of a society. The social freedom of any individual, in turn, is largely dependent upon the relative freedom of the group of which he is a member.

Inasmuch as the freedom of the individual is rooted in the social situation of his group, and derives efficacy and stability through the backing of his group in the social field of action, the problem of inter-group relations is definitive in determining the conditions of freedom.

What types of social intergroup structures are to be analyzed? The strictly political classifications are misleading, for they refer primarily to forms of government rather than types of society. The Aristotelian classification into monarchy, aristocracy and democracy is not of much help, for specific freedoms have flourished under all three forms. Economic classifications, as well, are often irrelevant, for commercial, industrial and agricultural communities exhibit varying degrees of freedom. A socio-economic classification is perhaps more to the point, but even the categories: feudal, bourgeois-capitalist, proletarian-socialist, fascist, etc., fail when viewed in historical perspective, for all of these types may take a totalitarian form whenever one of the constituent social groups achieves a relative monopoly of control and power. This does not mean that political or economic forms are irrelevant to freedom, for certain historical correlations can be demonstrated to exist, but only that the social basis of freedom is broader than its economic or political base.

Our classification of societal types must therefore be *sociological,* rather than economic or political. A sociological classification of inter-group structures has its basis, as has been indicated, in the group structure as such. This means that the typology is to be constructed on the most general level of analysis, i.e., on the basis of the inter-group relations within the total system of social relationships.

Emile Durkheim in his *Division of Labor in Society* has suggested one such classification which we may take as our starting point. He divides societies into those based on *mechanical* solidarity and those based on *organic* solidarity. According to his system, mechanical social structures are those which are characterized by such features as homogeneity, little or no division of labor, a minimum degree of individuality and a maximum degree of social constraint. These conditions exist primarily in primitive societies where differentiation of groups, individuals and social functions is at a minimum. Since practically no differentiation is present, there is little diversification of group interests, values or attitudes. Such societies, to use a biological analogy, may be said to be *amorphous.*

A later differentiation, which occurs when institutions began to crystallize out of the division of society according to a more clear cut differentiation of the religious from the secular, the economic from the recreational, etc., is the *segmental* society. The division here, however, is still primarily *institutional* rather than *associational.* There is as yet little differentiation into functional groups, the division is rather on the basis of different collective interests of the community.

As individuals begin to specialize according to institutional interests, and start to perform more specialized economic functions, definite groups with specific group interests begin to emerge. The greater the degree of specialization which is reached, the larger becomes the amount of interdependence of the specialized segments, and the more diverse become the interests and attitudes of the component groups. In this way the *organic* society emerges, characterized by a high degree of group differentiation, multiplication of interests, specialization of function, increasing interdependence and wide *heterogeneity*. Because of the diversification of interests and values which is concomitant with this increasing heterogeneity, the amount of collective constraint decreases, since the unanimity of attitudes which prevailed in amorphous societies is no longer present, and the divergent social groups must learn to accommodate themselves to one another.

According to Durkheim, this transition from primitive amorphous societies through segmental to organic social structures is an evolutionary process intimately correlated with the division of labor and an increasing specialization of function. This development has as its consequence the multiplication of societal groups as well as the increasing individualization of their members. Inasmuch as freedom is closely correlated with group structure, Durkheim's theory of group differentiation as a general historical process provides a preliminary orientation to our problem of constructing a typology of social structures.

We have seen that the multiplication of groups caused by the division of labor in an organic society has as its consequence an increasing need for accommodation between the divergent social groups. As long as no specific group obtains a monopoly of power, the various groups can protect the interests of their constituent individuals. On the other hand, as soon as one particular group begins to achieve a relative monopoly of power, the concrete freedoms of the members of other groups begin to decline proportionately. This is true, apparently, no matter which group obtains a dominant position to the extent that it no longer needs to take into account the interests and values of other groups.

During some periods of history it has been the priesthood that has achieved an almost complete monopoly of politico-hierocratic power; Egypt, Medieval Christendom, Zwingli's Geneva,

Cotton Mather's New England. At other times, the land-owning aristocracy arrogated to itself an almost complete control over the machinery of the state. In its turn, the ascendant bourgeoisie has been able to control the Legislatures to the virtual exclusion of other social classes. Proletarian governments have rooted out the vestiges of any opposition, not only from other class alignments, but from within their own "classless" stratum as well. In Fascist societies it has been the government party machine and bureaucracy itself which has achieved the greatest monopoly of force and control the world has ever seen.

In most of these cases political dominance has been achieved through a disproportionate degree of economic control of certain groups as compared to the other groups within a society. The source of the initial advantage may have been due originally to conquest, e.g., early feudalism. Sometimes it has been the result of greater technical competence as in the case of Rome. Perhaps in most cases it has been due to the fact that certain groups were strategically situated historically to take full advantage of a changing economic situation, and the lack of enterprise, interest or imagination of other more firmly intrenched strata; e.g., the bankers and merchants of Renaissance Florence *vis à vis* the old Florentine aristocracy.

Although it would be difficult to overestimate the importance of economic control in determining the structure of power relationships, this should not blind us to the relevance of ideological and political factors as well. The fact that certain political doctrines may be considered extremely useful by particular groups in furthering their own ends does not mean necessarily that the parties expressing these doctrines are the "tools" of these groups. The political party, rather, may be their accomplices and eventually their masters. A case to the point is Nazi Germany where the National Socialist party eventually achieved dominance over the economic interests which originally backed them in their ascent to power. At other times, ecclesiastical, military, ideological or charismatic groups have attained strategic positions in the distribution of power relationships which enabled them to dominate politically the historical situation in spite of a relatively secondary economic position.

Inasmuch as the amount of power of any specific group is restricted by the social pressure which other groups can bring against it, it follows that a hyper-individualized or atomized society is in greater danger of falling under the dominance of the first organized group that comes along than is a society where various units of possible resistance already exist. A society split into too large a number of tiny conflicting groups, as well, will find it difficult to organize a significant opposition in case of need. On the other hand, when one or two groups have obtained control of the social structure, the resulting oligarchy is in a position to dominate the majority for its own purposes. The optimum condition for freedom, therefore, lies somewhere midway between totalitarianism at one extreme and atomized individualism at the other.

In order to visualize the relationship between freedom and social structure just described, a graphic device may prove useful. The optimum condition for freedom may be represented by the high point of a bell-shaped curve; the decline of the probability of freedom in the directions of both atomism and totalitarianism is indicated by the declining slopes to the left and right of the medial distribution. (Figure 13.)

In this statistical analogy the horizontal ordinate represents a continuum from a completely disorganized social structure (atomism) to the absolutely regimented society (totalitarianism). The intervening steps represent degrees of group organization and concentration. The vertical ordinate represents the varying degrees of probability that free institutions will be present in relationship to the underlying social inter-group structure.

Thus the minimal degree of group integration (extreme individualism) is correlated with a low degree of freedom and would be illustrative of Hobbes' "war of all against all." This provides the first type of our projected classification, and may be designated as *atomistic*. Historical types tending to fall within this area of the curve are anarchy, frontier democracy, and the magic-ridden, cut-throat competitive economy of Dobu.

The minoral degree of societal integration is characterized by the shattering of society into a multitude of small competing groups, resulting in a relatively low degree of social stability which in turn can pave the way for dictatorship and the monolithic state. It is characterized by a multiplication of small groups: many autonomous economic organizations, a large number of competing sects, a multi-party system where no one party can achieve a parliamentary majority or significant minority, and a society lacking a basic consensus concerning its ends, institutions or organization. In the world-political sphere we have the example of the Holy Roman Empire and the Italian City States which were at the mercy of unified national powers. Societal types are more difficult to find, although in certain respects the French political scene during the thirties approximated this condition. To designate a *multipartite* system an alternative botanical term suggests itself: *multifid*, cloven into many segments.

The high, medial segment of the curve represents the optimum condition for the development and maintenance of freedom. It is the *pluralist* society characterized by the presence of large, well integrated groups representing significant divisions of interests and values. The various groups are limited in their power by the fact that the interests of other groups must be taken into account. The power of the state is limited by the power of organized public opinion and large special interest groups; the pressure exercised by business interests is counterbalanced by the forces of organized labor; both management and labor must take into account the interests of an integrated consumers' movement and other public agencies; no one religious group possesses a monopoly of spiritual values, and the various religious groups learn to accommodate themselves to one another; religious thought is denied absolute sovereignty over ideas by the presence of independent secular thought maintained by a free press, free univer-

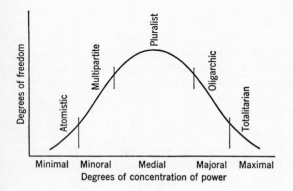

FIGURE 13. Variations of freedom in relation to systems of power relationships.

sities, free literary movements, learned societies and organized scientific research. In the sphere of production, a pluralist society might allow for the operation of more than one form of economic organization: not only corporations and single entrepreneurships, but worker owned cooperatives and state organized collectives as well. Probably no community has ever achieved the optimum degree of pluralist organization, but the United States of America, Great Britain and Sweden may be considered as illustrative of societies tending to approximate the conditions of a pluralist society. The problem of the citizenry of these states is to extend the equilibrating democratic forces which tend to secure the pluralistic conditions of freedom, while combating the twin dangers of monolithic totalitarianism and atomistic individualism. In this connection it must be stressed that a consensus must exist amongst the various groups concerning the relative desirability and validity of the underlying institutional structure. This consensus exists to the degree to which the groups are convinced that they can realize their aims within the framework of the society as a going order. Without this basic agreement, the pluralist society degenerates into a conflict society of warring strata, classes, organizations and pressure groups.

The ancient term, *oligarchy*, may be retained to designate the declining slope of our hypothetical curve. The chief index is the increasing concentration of power into the hands of specific vested interests; irrespective of whether these interests are aristocratic, bourgeois, military, proletarian, ecclesiastic or bureaucratic. It is inevitable, perhaps, that this tendency will manifest itself at critical historical junctures and revolutionary periods. The role of the moderate (if he keeps his head) during these periods is to provide a critical oasis during the transition, while adapting himself realistically to the logic of events and the pattern of history. This means that the role of the moderate is a progressive rather than a reactionary one; but that, at the same time, he cannot share the fanaticism of the extreme left any more than he can that of the extreme right, and still be the carrier of general human and cultural values: the dignity of man, individual responsibility, judicial impartiality, the preference of persuasion to force; in a word, all of the *values* which make him prefer freedom to domination. In normal times, the moderate or pluralist will tend to support those social strata which have not as yet achieved relative equality of status within the society.

Located at the bottom of our declining slope is the *totalitarian* society. It is totalitarian precisely because it has systematically destroyed all independent groups and autonomous opinion. It resembles the atomistic society in that the individual again operates without the backing of any group of his own. It differs from the atomistic society, however, in the fact that this time the atomized individual faces the full power of an omnipotent Leviathan state. Because of this it might be preferable to label the process as "massification" rather than "atomization." For while "atomization" takes place more or less spontaneously, "massification" is the product of the deliberate policy of the totalitarian state to destroy all possible social groups which could some day challenge its authority.

The purpose of constructing the hypothetical curve was to provide a frame of reference within which the relationship of freedom and social structure might be shown as a continuum. The curve, obviously, does not represent an experimentally derived frequency distribution. It might be described as an "ideal-typical" curve, arbitrarily divided into five segments, each segment representing a formal "pure type" of social structure. On the basis of this ideal typical distribution it is then possible to define societal types more precisely, and to locate roughly on the curve historically given social structures. The curve serves as a reminder, as well, that freedom is a matter of degree, rather than an "all-or-none" affair, and that it is correlated with the structure of group relationships present in society.

As Professor DeGré points out, freedom requires a delicate balance among the groups making up a complex society. If an organized group of official decision makers (a "party") is so powerful compared with potential competitors that its voice in the decision-making process cannot be effectively challenged, freedom cannot exist. The despotism may be benevolent, but meaningful elections cannot take place. An implication of Professor DeGré's conception of pluralism is the *legitimacy of opposition* to current authorities. Thus, in democratic countries, parties not in power are permitted (and even encouraged) to criticize the incumbents of political office and to solicit support to "throw the rascals out" at the next election. The British have a phrase that epitomizes the legitimacy of dissent from the policies of current decision makers. The party out of power is known as Her Majesty's *Loyal* Opposition. Note the word "loyal." If a party in power manages to define opposition parties, or the policies of opposition parties, as illegitimate, disloyal, and, ultimately, illegal, elections become empty ceremonials, and democracy is dead.[9] This is the situation today in the Soviet Union, Spain, Portugal, Yugoslavia, Egypt, Communist China, Nationalist China (Formosa), and several South American countries.

Although democratic countries have solved the problem of succession, totalitarian societies cannot ensure an orderly transfer of power because they do not permit meaningful elections. The death of a dictator like Khrushchev or Franco creates a more serious crisis than the death of a president or prime minister in a democratic society. This is a weakness of despotic societies. If elections are not available for changing the decision makers, the dissatisfactions that build up can only be expressed in a struggle for power, culminating perhaps in revolution. In democratic countries, elections are safety valves that prevent pressures of dissatisfactions from building up to a revolutionary explosion. From the antidemocratic viewpoint, free elections may be regarded as institutionalized chaos.

Legitimacy of opposition implies that the government does not dominate all groups within the society. Churches, universities, labor unions, business firms, youth organizations, and other voluntary associations have genuine independence. Normal though this may be in democracies, and even in conservative oligarchies like Portugal and Saudi Arabia, it is intolerable in totalitarian societies because independent groups might become the nucleus

for opposition to the regime. Thus, in the Soviet Union, not only is the *economy* controlled by the state; so are universities, labor unions, youth organizations, professional associations, and so forth. One reason totalitarian leaders get into conflict with organized religion—a struggle with the Catholic Church proved the downfall of Perón in Argentina—is that the churches are notoriously reluctant to surrender their independence to secular authorities. Yet totalitarian leaders cannot help but be jealous of independent associations; independence means potential opposition, and opposition is, by definition, subversive in the totalitarian society.

Totalitarian leaders seek to dominate all groups within the society as insurance against loss of power. They go further, however. They demand *ideological* conformity to the regime as well as obedient *actions*. For instance, in the Soviet Union, there is a Communist Party "line" on political and economic issues—and also on art, music, literature, history, genetics, architecture, pedagogy. Those who do not express the "correct" ideas, or do not shift ground rapidly enough when the "line" changes, are looked upon with suspicion. Why should Soviet leaders care about artistic, musical, or literary ideas? Because it is difficult to deny intellectual freedom on political and economic issues and permit it on other topics. Totalitarian leaders fear that people free to think independent thoughts may start thinking about new leaders. Freedom, like peace, is indivisible.

The lack of freedom of association and of intellectual freedom in a totalitarian society does not necessarily produce political stability. True, organized opposition is difficult. But covert disaffection is more likely than in democratic societies because so little of life is permitted to be nonpolitical. Whereas American painters, writers, scientists, musicians, ministers, physicians, and architects can ignore politics, comparable professionals in the Soviet Union cannot. The Communist Party "line" in their field forces them to take stands, to pass endless loyalty tests, to risk punishment for intellectual "unreliability." These restrictions on profes-

9 Morton Grodzins, *The Loyal and the Disloyal: Social Boundaries of Patriotism and Treason,* Chicago: University of Chicago Press, 1956.

sional freedom undoubtedly alienate some Soviet citizens who, in a democratic society, would not care who governs the country. Bear in mind that only a minority of Soviet citizens are enrolled in the Communist Party or its subdivisions. Consensus is difficult to attain in complex societies, totalitarian or democratic, but it may be easier in democracies.

Classical democratic theorists exaggerated the importance of rational and knowledgeable voters because they implicitly assumed that majority rule could not be based on anything less. Recent research dealing with voting decisions has demonstrated widespread voter apathy as well as powerful tendencies to vote in response to the influence of friends, family, and political predisposition rather than in response to arguments presented during the campaign. This being so, a feeble-minded deaf-mute running on the Democratic or Republican ticket would have a good chance of polling 40 per cent of the votes cast in most American communities. How then can the viability of the American political system be explained? The authors of one of the best empirical studies of voting behavior address this issue in the concluding pages of their study.

The Sociological Basis for Democracy

Reprinted by permission. From Bernard R. Berelson, Paul F. Lazarsfeld, and William N. McPhee, *Voting: A Study of Opinion Formation in a Presidential Campaign*, Chicago: University of Chicago Press, 1954, pp. 306–321.

Perhaps the main impact of realistic research on contemporary politics has been to temper some of the requirements set by our traditional normative theory for the typical citizen. "Out of all this literature of political observation and analysis, which is relatively new," says Max Beloff, "there has come to exist a picture in our minds of the political scene which differs very considerably from that familiar to us from the classical texts of democratic politics."

Experienced observers have long known, of course, that the individual voter was not all that

the theory of democracy requires of him. As Bryce put it:

"How little solidity and substance there is in the political or social beliefs of nineteen persons out of every twenty. These beliefs, when examined, mostly resolve themselves into two or three prejudices and aversions, two or three prepossessions for a particular party or section of a party, two or three phrases or catch-words suggesting or embodying arguments which the man who repeats them has not analyzed."

While our data do not support such an extreme statement, they do reveal that certain requirements commonly assumed for the successful operation of democracy are not met by the behavior of the "average" citizen. The requirements, and our conclusions concerning them, are quickly reviewed.

INTEREST, DISCUSSION, MOTIVATION. The democratic citizen is expected to be interested and to participate in political affairs. His interest and participation can take such various forms as reading and listening to campaign materials, working for the candidate or the party, arguing politics, donating money, and voting. In Elmira the majority of the people vote, but in general they do not give evidence of sustained interest. Many vote without real involvement in the election, and even the party workers are not typically motivated by ideological concerns or plain civic duty.

If there is one characteristic for a democratic system (besides the ballot itself) that is theoretically required, it is the capacity for and the practice of discussion. "It is as true of the large as of the small society," says Lindsay, "that its health depends on the mutual understanding which discussion makes possible; and that discussion is the only possible instrument of its democratic government." How much participation in political discussion there is in the community, what it is, and among whom—these questions have been given answers in an earlier chapter. In this instance there was little true discussion between the candidates, little in the newspaper commentary, little between the voters and the official party representatives, some within the electorate. On the grass-roots level there was more talk than debate, and, at least inferentially, the talk had important effects upon voting, in reinforcing or activating the partisans if not in converting the opposition.

An assumption underlying the theory of democracy is that the citizenry has a strong motivation for participation in political life. But it is a curious quality of voting behavior that for large numbers of people motivation is weak if not almost absent. It is assumed that this motivation would gain its strength from the citizen's perception of the difference that alternative decisions made to him. Now when a person buys something or makes other decisions of daily life, there are direct and immediate consequences for him. But for the bulk of the American people the voting decision is not followed by any direct, immediate, visible personal consequences. Most voters, organized or unorganized, are not in a position to foresee the distant and indirect consequences for themselves, let alone the society. The ballot is cast, and for most people that is the end of it. If their side is defeated, "it doesn't really matter."

KNOWLEDGE. The democratic citizen is expected to be well informed about political affairs. He is supposed to know what the issues are, what their history is, what the relevant facts are, what alternatives are proposed, what the party stands for, what the likely consequences are. By such standards the voter falls short. Even when he has the motivation, he finds it difficult to make decisions on the basis of full information when the subject is relatively simple and proximate; how can he do so when it is complex and remote? The citizen is not highly informed on details of the campaign, nor does he avoid a certain misperception of the political situation when it is to his psychological advantage to do so. The electorate's perception of what goes on in the campaign is colored by emotional feeling toward one or the other issue, candidate, party, or social group.

PRINCIPLE. The democratic citizen is supposed to cast his vote on the basis of principle— not fortuitously or frivolously or impulsively or habitually, but with reference to standards not only of his own interest but of the common good as well. Here, again, if this requirement is pushed at all strongly, it becomes an impossible demand on the democratic electorate.

Many voters vote not for principle in the usual sense but "for" a group to which they are attached—their group. The Catholic vote or the hereditary vote is explainable less as principle than as a traditional social allegiance. The ordinary voter, bewildered by the complexity of modern political problems, unable to determine clearly what the consequences are of alternative lines of action, remote from the arena, and incapable of bringing information to bear on principle, votes the way trusted people around him are voting. A British scholar, Max Beloff, takes as the "chief lesson to be derived" from such studies:

"Election campaigns and the programmes of the different parties have little to do with the ultimate result which is predetermined by influences acting upon groups of voters over a longer period. . . . This view has now become a working hypothesis with which all future thinking on this matter will have to concern itself. But if this is admitted, then obviously the picture of the voter as a person exercising conscious choice between alternative persons and alternative programmes tends to disappear."

On the issues of the campaign there is a considerable amount of "don't know"—sometimes reflecting genuine indecision, more often meaning "don't care." Among those with opinions the partisans *agree* on most issues, criteria, expectations, and rules of the game. The supporters of the different sides disagree on only a few issues. Nor, for that matter, do the candidates themselves always join the issue sharply and clearly. The partisans do not agree overwhelmingly with their own party's position, or, rather, only the small minority of highly partisan do; the rest take a rather moderate position on the political considerations involved in an election.

RATIONALITY. The democratic citizen is expected to exercise rational judgment in coming to his voting decision. He is expected to have arrived at his principles by reason and to have considered rationally the implications and alleged consequences of the alternative proposals of the contending parties. Political theorists and commentators have always exclaimed over the seeming contrast here between requirement and fulfillment. Even as sensible and hard-minded an observer as Schumpeter was extreme in his view:

"Even if there were no political groups trying to influence him, the typical citizen would in political matters tend to yield to extra-rational or irrational prejudice and impulse. The weakness of the rational processes he applies to politics and the absence of effective logical control over the results he arrives at would in themselves suffice to account for that. Moreover, simply because he is not 'all there,' he will relax his usual moral standards as well and occasionally give in to dark urges which the conditions of private life help him to repress."

Here the problem is first to see just what is meant by rationality. The term, as a recent writer noted, "has enjoyed a long history which has bequeathed to it a legacy of ambiguity and confusion. . . . Any man may be excused when he is puzzled by the question how he ought to use the word and particularly how he ought to use it in relation to human conduct and politics." Several meanings can be differentiated.

It is not for us to certify a meaning. But even without a single meaning—with only the aura of the term—we can make some observations on the basis of our material. In any rigorous or narrow sense the voters are not highly rational; that is, most of them do not ratiocinate on the matter, e.g., to the extent that they do on the purchase of a car or a home. Nor do voters act rationally whose "principles" are held so tenaciously as to blind them to information and persuasion. Nor do they attach efficient means to explicit ends.

The fact that some people change their minds during a political campaign shows the existence of that open-mindedness usually considered a component of rationality. But among whom? Primarily among those who can "afford" a change of mind, in the sense that they have ties or attractions on both sides—the cross-pressured voters in the middle where rationality is supposed to take over from the extremes of partisan feeling. But it would hardly be proper to designate the unstable, uninterested, uncaring middle as the sole or the major possessor of rationality among the electorate. As Beloff points out: "It is likely that the marginal voter is someone who is so inadequately identified with one major set of interests or another and so remote, therefore, from the group-thinking out of which political attitudes arise, that his voting record is an illustration, not of superior wisdom, but of greater frivolity."

The upshot of this is that the usual analogy between the voting "decision" and the more or less carefully calculated decisions of consumers or businessmen or courts, incidentally, may be quite incorrect. For many voters political preferences may better be considered analogous to cultural tastes—in music, literature, recreational activities, dress, ethics, speech, social behavior. Consider the parallels between political preferences and general cultural tastes. Both have their origin in ethnic, sectional, class, and family traditions.

Both exhibit stability and resistance to change for individuals but flexibility and adjustment over generations for the society as a whole. Both seem to be matters of sentiment and disposition rather than "reasoned preferences." While both are responsive to changed conditions and unusual stimuli, they are relatively invulnerable to direct argumentation and vulnerable to indirect social influences. Both are characterized more by faith than by conviction and by wishful expectation rather than careful prediction of consequences. The preference for one party rather than another must be highly similar to the preference for one kind of literature or music rather than another, and the choice of the same political party every four years may be parallel to the choice of the same old standards of conduct in new social situations. In short, it appears that a sense of fitness is a more striking feature of political preference than reason and calculation.

If the democratic system depended solely on the qualifications of the individual voter, then it seems remarkable that democracies have survived through the centuries. After examining the detailed data on how individuals misperceive political reality or respond to irrelevant social influences, one wonders how a democracy ever solves its political problems. But when one considers the data in a broader perspective—how huge segments of the society adapt to political conditions affecting them or how the political system adjusts itself to changing conditions over long periods of time—he cannot fail to be impressed with the total result. Where the rational citizen seems to abdicate, nevertheless angels seem to tread.

The eminent judge, Learned Hand, in a delightful essay on "Democracy: Its Presumptions and Reality," comes to essentially this conclusion.

"I do not know how it is with you, but for myself I generally give up at the outset. The simplest problems which come up from day to day seem to me quite unanswerable as soon as I try to get below the surface. . . . My vote is one of the most unimportant acts of my life; if I were to acquaint myself with the matters on which it ought really to depend, if I were to try to get a judgment on which I was willing to risk affairs of even the smallest moment, I should be doing nothing else, and that seems a fatuous conclusion to a fatuous undertaking."

Yet he recognizes the paradox—somehow the system not only works on the most difficult and complex questions but often works with distinction. "For, abuse it as you will, it gives a bloodless measure of social forces—bloodless, have you thought of that?—a means of continuity, a principle of stability, a relief from the paralyzing terror of revolution."

Justice Hand concludes that we have "outgrown" the conditions assumed in traditional democratic theory and that "the theory has ceased to work." And yet, the system that has grown out of classic democratic theory, and, in this country, out of quite different and even elementary social conditions, does continue to work—perhaps even more vigorously and effectively than ever.

That is the paradox. *Individual voters* today seem unable to satisfy the requirements for a democratic system of government outlined by political theorists. But the *system of democracy* does meet certain requirements for a going political organization. The individual members may not meet all the standards, but the whole nevertheless survives and grows. This suggests that where the classic theory is defective is in its concentration on the *individual citizen*. What are undervalued are certain collective properties that reside in the electorate as a whole and in the political and social system in which it functions.

The political philosophy we have inherited, then, has given more consideration to the virtues of the typical citizen of the democracy than to the working of the *system* as a whole. Moreover, when it dealt with the system, it mainly considered the single constitutive institutions of the system, not those general features necessary if the institutions are to work as required. For example, the rule of law, representative government, periodic elections, the party system, and the several freedoms of discussion, press, association, and assembly have all been examined by political philosophers seeking to clarify and to justify the idea of political democracy. But liberal democracy is more than a political system in which individual voters and political institutions operate. For political democracy to survive, other features are required: the intensity of conflict must be limited, the rate of change must be restrained, stability in the social and economic structure must be maintained, a pluralistic social organization must exist, and a basic consensus must bind together the contending parties.

Such features of the system of political democracy belong neither to the constitutive institutions nor to the individual voter. It might be said that they form the atmosphere or the environment in which both operate. In any case, such features have not been carefully considered by political philosophers, and it is on these broader properties of the democratic political system that more reflection and study by political theory is called for. In the most tentative fashion let us explore the values of the political system, as they involve the electorate, in the light of the foregoing considerations.

REQUIREMENTS FOR THE SYSTEM

Underlying the paradox is an assumption that the population is homogeneous socially and should be homogeneous politically: that everybody is about the same in relevant social characteristics; that, if something is a political virtue (like interest in the election), then everyone should have it; that there is such a thing as "the" typical citizen on whom uniform requirements can be imposed. The tendency of classic democratic literature to work with an image of "the" voter was never justified. For, as we will attempt to illustrate here, some of the most important requirements that democratic values impose on a system require a voting population that is not homogeneous but heterogeneous in its political qualities.

The need for heterogeneity arises from the contradictory functions we expect our voting system to serve. We expect the political system to adjust itself and our affairs to changing conditions; yet we demand too that it display a high degree of stability. We expect the contending interests and parties to pursue their ends vigorously and the voters to care; yet, after the election is over, we expect reconciliation. We expect the voting outcome to serve what is best for the community; yet we do not want disinterested voting unattached to the purposes and interests of different segments of that community. We want voters to express their own free and self-determined choices; yet, for the good of the community, we would like voters to avail themselves of the best information and guidance available from the groups and leaders around them. We expect a high degree of rationality to prevail in the decision; but were all irrationality and mythology absent, and all ends pursued by the most coldly rational selection of political means, it is doubtful if the system would hold together.

In short, our electoral system calls for apparently incompatible properties—which, although they cannot all reside in each individual voter, can (and do) reside in a heterogeneous electorate. What seems to be required of the electorate as a whole is a *distribution* of qualities along important dimensions. We need some people who are active in a certain respect, others in the middle, and still others passive. The contradictory things we want from the total require that the parts be different. This can be illustrated by taking up a number of important dimensions by which an electorate might be characterized.

INVOLVEMENT AND INDIFFERENCE. How could a mass democracy work if all the people were deeply involved in politics? Lack of interest by some people is not without its benefits, too. True, the highly interested voters vote more, and know more about the campaign, and read and listen more, and participate more; however, they are also less open to persuasion and less likely to change. Extreme interest goes with extreme partisanship and might culminate in rigid fanaticism that could destroy democratic processes if generalized throughout the community. Low affect toward the election—not caring much—underlies the resolution of many political problems; votes can be resolved into a two-party split instead of fragmented into many parties (the splinter parties of the left, for example, splinter because their advocates are *too* interested in politics). Low interest provides maneuvering room for political shifts necessary for a complex society in a period of rapid change. Compromise might be based upon sophisticated awareness of costs and returns —perhaps impossible to demand of a mass society—but it is more often induced by indifference. Some people are and should be highly interested in politics, but not everyone is or needs to be. Only the doctrinaire would deprecate the moderate indifference that facilitates compromise.

Hence, an important balance between action motivated by strong sentiments and action with little passion behind it is obtained by heterogeneity within the electorate. Balance of this sort is, in practice, met by a distribution of voters rather than by a homogeneous collection of "ideal" citizens.

STABILITY AND FLEXIBILITY. A similar dimension along which an electorate might be characterized is stability-flexibility. The need for change and adaptation is clear, and the need for stability

ought equally to be (especially from observation of current democratic practice in, say, certain Latin American countries).

How is political stability achieved? There are a number of social sources of political stability: the training of the younger generation before it is old enough to care much about the matter, the natural selection that surrounds the individual voter with families and friends who reinforce his own inclinations, the tendency to adjust in favor of the majority of the group, the self-perpetuating tendency of political traditions among ethnic and class and regional strata where like-minded people find themselves socially together. Political stability is based upon social stability. Family traditions, personal associations, status-related organizational memberships, ethnic affiliations, socioeconomic strata—such ties for the individual do not change rapidly or sharply, and since his vote is so importantly a product of them, neither does it. In effect, a large part of the study of voting deals not with why votes change but rather with why they do not.

In addition, the varying conditions facing the country, the varying political appeals made to the electorate, and the varying dispositions of the voters activated by these stimuli—these, combined with the long-lasting nature of the political loyalties they instil, produce an important cohesion within the system. For example, the tendencies operating in 1948 electoral decisions not only were built up in the New Deal and Fair Deal era but also dated back to parental and grandparental loyalties, to religious and ethnic cleavages of a past era, and to moribund sectional and community conflicts. Thus, in a very real sense any particular election is a composite of various elections and various political and social events. People vote for a President on a given November day, but their choice is made not simply on the basis of what has happened in the preceding months or even four years; in 1948 some people were in effect voting on the internationalism issue of 1940, others on the depression issues of 1932, and some, indeed, on the slavery issues of 1860.

The vote is thus a kind of "moving average" of reactions to the political past. Voters carry over to each new election remnants of issues raised in previous elections—and so there is always an overlapping of old and new decisions that give a cohesion in time to the political system. Hence the composite decision "smooths out" political change. The people vote *in* the same election, but not all of them vote *on* it.

What of flexibility? Curiously, the voters least admirable when measured against individual requirements contribute most when measured against the aggregate requirement for flexibility. For those who change political preferences most readily are those who are least interested, who are subject to conflicting social pressures, who have inconsistent beliefs and erratic voting histories. Without them—if the decision were left only to the deeply concerned, well-integrated, consistently-principled ideal citizens—the political system might easily prove too rigid to adapt to changing domestic and international conditions.

In fact, it may be that the very people who are most sensitive to changing social conditions are those most susceptible to political change. For, in either case, the people exposed to membership in overlapping strata, those whose former life-patterns are being broken up, those who are moving about socially or physically, those who are forming new families and new friendships—it is they who are open to adjustments of attitudes and tastes. They may be the least partisan and the least interested voters, but they perform a valuable function for the entire system. Here again is an instance in which an individual "inadequacy" provides a positive service for the society: The campaign can be a reaffirming force for the settled majority and a creative force for the unsettled minority. There is stability on both sides and flexibility in the middle.

PROGRESS AND CONSERVATION. Closely related to the question of stability is the question of past versus future orientation of the system. In America a progressive outlook is highly valued, but, at the same time, so is a conservative one. Here a balance between the two is easily found in the party system and in the distribution of voters themselves from extreme conservatives to extreme liberals. But a balance between the two is also achieved by a distribution of political dispositions through time. There are periods of great political agitation (i.e., campaigns) alternating with periods of political dormancy. Paradoxically, the former—the campaign period—is likely to be an instrument of conservatism, often even of historical regression.

Many contemporary campaigns (not, however, 1952) must be stabilizing forces that ac-

tivated past tendencies in individuals and reasserted past patterns of group voting. In 1948, for example, the middle-class Protestants reaffirmed their traditional Republican position, the working-class Protestants reverted toward their position of the 1930's and the working-class Catholics toward their position not only of the 1930's but of a generation or more earlier. In this sense the campaign was a retreat away from new issues back toward old positions.

Political campaigns tend to make people more consistent both socially and psychologically; they vote more with their social groups and agree more with their own prior ideas on the issues. But new ideas and new alignments are in their infancy manifested by inconsistency psychologically and heterogeneity socially; they are almost by definition deviant and minority points of view. To the extent that they are inhibited by pressure or simply by knowledge of what is the proper (i.e., majority) point of view in a particular group, then the campaign period is not a time to look for the growth of important new trends.

This "regressive tendency" may appear as a reaction to intense propaganda during decisive times. The term "regressive" need not imply a reversion to less-developed, less-adaptive behavior; in fact, one might argue that the revival of a Democratic vote among workers was functional for their interests. What it refers to is simply the reactivation of prior dispositions—dispositions in politics that date back years and decades, often to a prior political era.

Its counterpart, of course, is what we believe to be an important potential for progress during the periods of relaxed tension and low-pressure political and social stimuli that are especially characteristic of America between political campaigns. The very tendency for Americans to neglect their political system most of the time—to be "campaign citizens" in the sense that many are "Sunday churchgoers"—is not without its values. Change may come best from relaxation.

Again, then, a balance (between preservation of the past and receptivity to the future) seems to be required of a democratic electorate. The heterogeneous electorate in itself provides a balance between liberalism and conservatism; and so does the sequence of political events from periods of drifting change to abrupt rallies back to the loyalties of earlier years.

CONSENSUS AND CLEAVAGE. We have talked

much in the text, and perhaps implied more, about consensus and cleavage. Although there were certain clusters of political opinion in Elmira, at the same time there were a number of opinions that did not break along class or party lines. American opinion on public issues is much too complex to be designated by such simple, single-minded labels as *the* housewife opinion or *the* young people's opinion or even *the* workers' opinion. If one uses as a base the central Republican-Democratic cleavage, then one finds numerous "contradictions" within individuals, within strata and groups, and within party supporters themselves. There are many issues presented, cafeteria-style, for the voter to choose from, and there are overlaps in opinion in every direction.

Similarly there are required *social* consensus and cleavage—in effect, pluralism—in politics. Such pluralism makes for enough consensus to hold the system together and enough cleavage to make it move. Too much consensus would be deadening and restrictive of liberty; too much cleavage would be destructive of the society as a whole.

Consider the pictures of the hypothetical relationships between political preference (e.g., party support) and a social characteristic as presented in this chart:

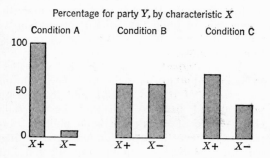

Percentage for party Y, by characteristic X

In Condition A there is virtual identity between the characteristic and political preference; all the people of type X+ vote one way, and all the people of X— vote the other way. In Condition B the opposite is the case, and there is no relationship between vote and the characteristic; both parties are supported equally by people of the two types. In Condition C there is neither a complete relationship nor a complete absence; more X+'s than X—'s are partisans of a given side, but there are some members of each type in each political camp.

Now a democratic society in which Condition A was intensified would probably be in danger of its existence. The issues of politics would cut so deeply, be so keenly felt, and, especially, be so fully reinforced by other social identifications of the electorate as to threaten the basic consensus itself. This might be called "total politics"—a conception of politics, incidentally, advanced by such leading theorists of National Socialism and communism as Carl Schmitt and Lenin. This involves the mutual reinforcement of political differences and other social distinctions meaningful to the citizen. The multiplication of Condition B, on the other hand, would suggest a community in which politics was of no "real" importance to the community, in which it was not associated with special interests. Condition C is a combination of Conditions A and B —that is, a situation in which special interests are of some but not of overriding importance. It portrays neither the extremist or fanatical community like A nor the "pure" or utopian community like B.

There is nothing in Elmira that represents Condition A; the closest approximation would be the relationship between vote and religion or minority ethnic status, and even here there are group overlaps in vote amounting to from a quarter to a third of the members. The nearest approximation to Condition B is the relationship between vote and sex, which is another way of saying that there is little relevance of this characteristic to political matters, at least so far as party preference is concerned. The relationships between vote and socioeconomic status or vote and occupation are examples of Condition C.

The social and political correlations we find in places like Elmira (that are not a priori meaningless) are of the C type to a greater or less extent. What this means is that there is a good deal of cross-group and cross-party identification and affiliation within the community. The political lines are drawn in meaningful ways but are not identical with the lines of social groupings. The same social heterogeneity that produces self-interest also produces a cross-cutting and harmonious community interest.

Thus again a requirement we might place on an electoral system—balance between total political war between segments of the society and total political indifference to group interests of that society—translates into varied requirements for different individuals. With respect to group or bloc voting, as with other aspects of political behavior, it is perhaps not unfortunate that "some do and some do not."

INDIVIDUALISM AND COLLECTIVISM. Lord Bryce pointed out the difficulties in a theory of democracy that assumes that each citizen must himself be capable of voting intelligently:

"Orthodox democratic theory assumes that every citizen has, or ought to have, thought out for himself certain opinions, i.e., ought to have a definite view, defensible by argument, of what the country needs, of what principles ought to be applied in governing it, of the man to whose hands the government ought to be entrusted. There are persons who talk, though certainly very few who act, as if they believed this theory, which may be compared to the theory of some ultra-Protestants that every good Christian has or ought to have . . . worked out for himself from the Bible a system of theology."

In the first place, however, the information available to the individual voter is not limited to that directly possessed by him. True, the individual casts his own personal ballot. But, as we have tried to indicate throughout this volume, that is perhaps the most individualized action he takes in an election. His vote is formed in the midst of his fellows in a sort of group decision— if, indeed, it may be called a decision at all—and the total information and knowledge possessed in the group's present and past generations can be made available for the group's choice. Here is where opinion-leading relationships, for example, play an active role.

Second, and probably more important, the individual voter may not have a great deal of detailed information, but he usually has picked up the crucial *general* information as part of his social learning itself. He may not know the parties' positions on the tariff, or who is for reciprocal trade treaties, or what are the differences on Asiatic policy, or how the parties split on civil rights, or how many security risks were exposed by whom. But he cannot live in an American community without knowing broadly where the parties stand. He has learned that the Republicans are more conservative and the Democrats more liberal—and he can locate his own sentiments and cast his vote accordingly. After all, he must vote for one or the other party, and, if he knows the big thing about the parties, he does

not need to know all the little things. The basic role a party plays as an institution in American life is more important to his voting than a particular stand on a particular issue.

It would be unthinkable to try to maintain our present economic style of life without a complex system of delegating to others what we are not competent to do ourselves, without accepting and giving training to each other about what each is expected to do, without accepting our dependence on others in many spheres and taking responsibility for their dependence on us in some spheres. And, like it or not, to maintain our present political style of life, we may have to accept much the same interdependence with others in collective behavior. We have learned slowly in economic life that it is useful not to have everyone a butcher or a baker, any more than it is useful to have no one skilled in such activities. The same kind of division of labor—as repugnant as it may be in some respects to our individualistic tradition—is serving us well today in mass politics. There is an implicit division of political labor within the electorate.

Note the implications of this line of reasoning: the strength of a democratic political system lies not so much in the *individual voter* as in the balance it achieves in the *society*. The stability of the system as a whole could not be predicted from examining the characteristics of the average voter because stability depends on competition among various pressure groups for voter support. Even when the majority of voters are ignorant of the issues or apathetic toward them, the democratic process may be working well. Apathy in a democracy means that some people are satisfied enough with the status quo to ignore the opportunity to make changes presented by the ballot box. The importance of an election is not how many people vote but how many *could* vote if they were motivated to. As long as that potentiality exists, current decision makers must tremble during an election campaign even though they are aware that most people pay little attention to campaign oratory and that half of the eligible voters may not bother to vote. Table 57 shows the proportion of eligible voters who cast bal-

TABLE 57

Percentage of Eligible Voters Voting in Presidential and Congressional Elections, 1920–1960

Presidential Elections		Congressional Elections	
Election Years	Per Cent of Eligible Voters Voting for Presidential Electors	Per Cent of Eligible Voters Voting for U. S. Representatives	Election Years
1920	44.2	32.4	1922
1924	44.3	30.1	1926
1928	52.3	34.1	1930
1932	52.9	41.8	1934
1936	57.5	44.5	1938
1940	59.7	32.7	1942
1944	56.3	37.6	1946
1948	51.5	41.6	1950
1952	62.0	42.2	1954
1956	60.1	43.4	1958
1960	63.8		

Source: U. S. Bureau of the Census, *Statistical Abstract of the United States: 1962*, Washington: Government Printing Office, 1962, p. 373.

lots in presidential and congressional contests from 1920 to 1960.

Given widespread apathy and ignorance, many voters cast their ballots for reasons that might have horrified Thomas Jefferson. In particular, political machines in large cities appeal to voters on a personal basis or as reciprocation for past favors. The following article shows how votes are controlled in a Negro slum community in Nashville, Tennessee.

How a Political Machine Controls Votes: A Case Study

Reprinted by permission. From David Halberstam, " 'Good Jelly's' Last Stand," *The Reporter*, Vol. 24, Jan. 19, 1961, pp. 40–41.

The other day the [Nashville] police raided a Negro barbecue and beer joint and arrested nine people. The raid and the arrests came as something of a shock to the owner. "I don't know why they're bothering me," said Henry ("Good Jelly") Jones, restaurateur, bootlegger, and politician, "It ain't election time." But bother him they did, and because Good Jelly (or just "Jelly" to his friends) is something of a local celebrity these days, there was a sizable press section on hand for his trial.

The reporters were not disappointed. Good Jelly's wife, when asked whether a gallon jug was the same jug found during the raid, answered, "I don't know. Jugs don't have no names." Later the white prosecuting attorney asked her why she found it so easy to answer defense questions and so hard to understand his. "Mr. City Attorney," said Robert Lilliard, her Negro attorney, "she's a little confused by all your high-class words. You just talk like we talk down at Good Jelly's and we'll be all right." "High-class words," snorted the city attorney. "What's so high-class about the words 'white corn'?"

The case came out as everyone knew it would: the charges against Good Jelly and his friends were dismissed. For if Good Jelly has a striking ability to get into trouble, he has an even more remarkable ability to get out of it. Fifteen times he has been called before the bar of justice in recent years, fourteen times he has been set free. The explanation of this enviable batting average lies deep in the structure of Southern politics, the Negro's role in it, and the specific power structure of Nashville. Henry Jones, with his golfer's cap, big flashing smile, and long police record, is a power. He is among the last of the ward heelers. Very simply, he controls the votes of a large number of unbelievably poor people, and for a minimum of service, protection, and financial reward, he delivers these same votes without the slightest concern for ideology.

In Nashville, he is the Negro whom many Negroes like least to think about; he is the Negro whom many whites like most to think about. In his own blunt word, he is a "nigger"; what is worse, that is all he wants to be. Respectable Negro society shuns him, yet to some of the Negro poor he is perhaps the only truly big man in their lives.

Good Jelly first became interested in politics at an early age. Because he was an uneducated Negro there were distinct limitations to the ambitions he might reasonably entertain and yet many people who govern his city and who dedicate schools and other buildings in the highest of ideals are perfectly willing to deal with him. "Call him a backdoor Negro," said one white leader; "they won't have their picture taken with him, and they won't pose with him, even at Negro functions. But they know how to get hold of him." When a white man once complained about Jelly's police record and about his bootlegging and the fact that he has many friends among politicians, a Negro answered: "That's the way you people really want him."

It is hardly surprising, then, that the complexities of playing the system at both ends have produced two Jellies. They are separate but equal Jellies. There is a Jelly for whites and a Jelly for Negroes. The whites' Jelly is an ingratiating Uncle Tom, laughing, smiling, hiding from any slightly serious question or threat behind the big smile and a joke (in which old Jelly is always the butt). The Negroes' Jelly is something different. He is kind: he has clothed many of his people, housed more, and fed them all. If he calls one and gives him the key to the big black Cadillac and says it's time to move the Caddy, the man is honored by the assignment; if he calls eight of them together and says that the newspaper wants their picture and that he, Jelly, approves of the idea, then a picture of eight smiling faces is taken; if he tells them to vote this way or that, they vote this way or that.

"I carry a lot of weight around here," Jelly admits. " 'Bout half the people in this precinct I control. Two hundred, three hundred people. They're my people."

"I DON'T TURN THEM DOWN"

Good Jelly is a dark, stocky man of about fifty, whose use of minstrel-show techniques in front of whites is a legitimate heritage. As a young man he left his Nashville home and joined the cast of the Mandy Green from New Orleans Minstrel Show (the poor man's version of the famous Silas Green show). For Mandy Green he traveled the South as what he calls "one of those black-face comedians, and I was pretty good." Then he returned to Nashville, where he became associated with the then ruling Negro ward heeler, "Pie" Hardison. "I was Pie's chauffeur. He thought I was a pretty good fellow, and I was a good driver and a good talker, and so he got me into politics. One time Pie said I ought to be in there pitching for the mayor, and I said: 'If you want the mayor, then I'm pitching one hundred per cent,' and so I got him the votes."

Pie Hardison is gone now and his heir does his pitching from a small hut off a dark alley deep in the Negro slums. In a small half-masonry, half-wooden café, he cooks, bootlegs, and politicks. There is one small sign over the door—it is upside down—and it says "BEST." Jelly says this is not the name of the café, that the name is "Jones Barbecue." It is a small café and there are no menus, only signs on the walls. At one end of the café white beans cost twenty-five cents, at the other they cost twenty-one cents. There, with regular violations of local whiskey laws ("We have some whiskey but we don't have no beer—we have to send out for the beer"), he operates his machine: the restaurant is essential to his success as a politician.

For Good Jelly's machine has been described by one reporter as "the lame, the sick, the poor, and a few of the penniless." Good Jelly himself says: "Down in this part folks don't have but a little money and so they come over here when they have a little and we feed them, and they come over here when they don't have any money and we still feed them. I don't turn them down. I always feed them and I get them a place to sleep, most times right here, and get them to a hospital, and even a job sometimes. They get what I got, these folks, and they don't forget."

If the voters don't forget, neither does Good Jelly. He keeps a thorough file on each of his debtors: name, favors granted, address—or frequently the address of someone who will know where to find the debtor. Before election day Good Jelly will make sure all his friends are registered; he will also send out cards reminding them of their civic responsibility. Come election day and Good Jelly takes out his big Cadillac and herds his people to the polls. He likes to start early; it gives him more time later in the day for rounding up slackers. "I'll tell you why Good Jelly has got so many friends," said Robert Lilliard, the Negro attorney who is also a city councilman. "A lot of these politicians just like him: you can really count on Jelly. If he's for you, why you can check his precinct the next day and his votes will be there. If you treated him right."

Good Jelly himself says that he asks little for his interest in politics. "I'm for any man that's a good man," he is fond of saying. How does he tell who's a good man? "I read about this man, see, and I can tell if he's for me. I want to know all the issues."

Is that all? What issues? "A lot of these men, they want to be politicians and so they come and see Jelly and I see how friendly they are, and they're pretty friendly. They're good men. We talk about these issues. All of these issues." He repeated emphatically: "I'm for any man that's a good man."

Other interpretations of Good Jelly's political motivations have been offered from time to time. "I'd say he gets an average of about $300 for an election," one white politician told me. "It depends. On a close local election with a lot at stake I expect he's gotten $500 or more. Maybe a thousand."

"How much money did you get for the sheriff's race?" I asked him point-blank.

"Money? Money? I wouldn't do none of that," he said. "The man, he come down here and he was a good man and he said how he wanted to do right . . ."

It is not without a touch of regret that many white politicians, worried by the new power of the sit-in leaders and the young Negro ministers, foresee the demise of Good Jelly and his kind. "You make the deal with Jelly," one politician said, "and that's it. You don't have to worry about him coming downtown with a bunch of his damn people and sitting down at some nice restaurant, or calling the damn newspapers and announcing he's going to picket some company for

better jobs. Jelly's all right. Take care of him on the drunk and disorderly and that kind of thing, and that's it."

"He comes through?" I asked.

"We take care of him and he takes care of us," the man answered. . . .

Jelly's lack of concern about civil rights galls many young Negroes in Nashville. "If John Kasper were running against Thurgood Marshall and it was a local race and the right people went to see Jelly for Kasper, that's all it would take," said one Negro bitterly. Jelly himself has said: "My folks, they're not the integration type. They're not interested in all that. All they want is a little food." Attorney Robert Lilliard has explained Jelly's continuing popularity in just about the same terms: "Those folks, they aren't going to eat at Woolworth's or Grant's or anything like that. But they got to eat. Jelly's the only thing those people have, and he looks mighty good to them."

But even Lilliard concedes that sooner or later other political leaders will supplant Good Jelly Jones and his kind among the Negroes. "You take this city, growing all the time, and the city limits going out, and the Negro making a little more money all the time—a thing like Jelly got, it's getting to be less and less important all the time. Five, ten years from now there probably won't be any Good Jelly. Pretty soon both sides [will be] too busy worrying about this middle-class vote to pay for Jelly. That's where the next battle will be."

The significance of precinct leaders like Good Jelly Jones is that they involve people in the political process who are too apathetic to participate on their own initiative. Good Jelly's friends do not vote in response to television debates or to paid political advertisements in the newspaper. They vote the way Good Jelly tells them to vote because that is how they reciprocate his kindnesses. Whether Good Jelly's constituency is a burden to the democratic process in Nashville is not clear. Perhaps a political machine offers the best chance for poorly educated minorities to have a voice in the community. However, with the breakup of ethnic ghettoes and the educational upgrading of the population, political machines are declining in importance. American democracy survived the first three decades of the twentieth century during which political machines controlled cities like New York, Chicago, Philadelphia, Jersey City, Memphis, and Boston, and were a factor on state and national levels. It will certainly survive Good Jelly Jones.

Mass communications pose a more serious threat to democracy than political machines. In totalitarian countries, government control of press, radio, and television gives the party in power an opportunity to repeat its propaganda messages without fear of contradiction. Monopoly of the instruments of mass communication enables a totalitarian regime to put across "the big lie." Even when the regime is not perpetrating an outright lie, its ability to determine what information to allow the citizenry to receive, and in what context, may enable it to engineer consensus instead of allowing consensus to develop naturally. In democratic countries, the mass media are not monopolized by the state, but neither does a free market in ideas exist. People wealthy enough to own a newspaper have a better chance than less affluent citizens to influence public opinion. In the United States, for instance, the Republican Party usually has greater support in the editorial columns of newspapers and magazines than the Democratic Party.[10] This does not, however, give an insuperable advantage to Republican candidates.

Are the mass media, then, irrelevant to the political process in a democracy? They are not irrelevant, but their influence is indirect. Their initial impact is on the opinion leaders of the community.[11] Due to the personal influence of these leaders on politically apathetic segments of the population, ideas about issues and candidates percolate through the electorate. Therefore, even though the mass media *are* influential, no one should expect votes to be exactly

proportional to the linage of political propaganda. Professional politicians have a saying that reflects the uncertainty of efforts at mass persuasion: "Half of the money spent on campaigns is wasted. But which half?"

Mass communication has aroused *fears* about mass manipulation of voters. Research has shown that these fears have been based on a wrong assumption: that all citizens are oriented to the political messages of mass media. Only a minority is interested in campaign literature and devotes the time and effort necessary to understand the issues involved. Mass communication has also aroused *hopes* for a more enlightened electorate. Nineteenth-century liberals thought that the rise in the educational level in democratic countries was bound to make a better world. H. G. Wells spoke for his generation when he remarked, "Human history becomes more and more a race between education and catastrophe." These hopes for an enlightened electorate have also proved illusory. Universal education resulted in mass literacy, but mass literacy has not produced greater reason and good will in politics. Teaching people to read does not guarantee that they will prefer to read speeches rather than comic books. Educational television has proved far less popular than cowboy dramas.

THE PROBLEM OF THE RATIONAL ENFORCEMENT OF LEGITIMATE DECISIONS

Complex societies face two problems in carrying out political decisions. One is the efficient coordination of the efforts of persons required to administer decisions in a large society. (This is the task of bureaucracy and will be considered in Chapter 15.) The other is the problem of applying decisions *uniformly* throughout the society and in conformity with popular notions of *justice*. This is the responsibility of the legal system.

Take the matter of dealing with burglars. Americans clearly do not want thieves breaking into homes and stores. So policemen patrol the streets to deter the potential thief and to ap-

10 Frank Luther Mott, "Newspapers in Presidential Campaigns," *Public Opinion Quarterly*, Vol. 8, Fall 1944, pp. 348–367.
11 Robert K. Merton, *Social Theory and Social Structure*, rev. ed., Glencoe, Ill.: Free Press, 1957, pp. 387–420.

prehend persons who actually "break and enter." But what happens when a policeman discovers an 18-year-old boy trying to open the safe in the back office of a supermarket? Does he whip out his gun and execute the young burglar on the spot? Or does he talk to him like a Dutch uncle and send him home? Neither, if he follows American legal procedures. He arrests the suspect and takes him to police headquarters. The accused is held in a lockup until he can be formally charged with "breaking and entering" in a hearing before a magistrate. The accused has a right to have a lawyer represent him in this hearing and to advise him whether to plead "guilty" or "not guilty." If he pleads "not guilty," he is entitled to release on bail until the time of trial—on the assumption that his guilt has not yet been established. If he pleads "guilty," he is also entitled to release on bail until he is sentenced by a judge having jurisdiction over his case. When and if he comes before a judge for sentencing, the judge ordinarily has discretion as to whether to imprison the convicted offender or to place him on probation—and, if to imprison him, for how long. But the judge does not have limitless discretion; he cannot sentence a person to the electric chair for "breaking and entering." The range of possible penalties for this offense have been established by the legislature of the state in which the prohibited act took place.

Why this time-consuming fuss? The boy was caught committing a crime. The process of punishing a burglar is anchored with rules of procedure because the alternative is to allow the community reaction to burglary to be capricious. Recall that urban industrial populations are heterogeneous. The range of values among policemen and judges is sufficiently great that their spontaneous reactions to a suspected offender may not coincide with the collective conscience. A legal system limits official discretion and thereby tends to produce uniformity of treatment.

Laws must still be administered by human beings with parochial biases; hence, the ideal of equal treatment under the law is never fully achieved. For example, the sentencing practices of judges in criminal courts show wide variation within the same jurisdiction.[12] And those punished relatively severely for crimes that are leniently handled in other cases feel unfairly treated. But existing resentment of "injustice" is mild compared with the explosive indignation that would result if the legal system did not limit variations in police and court practices.

Law helps to justify the naked force behind political decisions in other ways besides guaranteeing some uniformity in the processing of individual cases. The American Constitution forbids *ex post facto* laws because the American conception of fairness requires the state to specify in advance what acts will be punished and how severely. This means that if someone thinks up a type of crime that existing laws do not forbid, he cannot be punished for it—even though it outrages his society. Of course, legislatures constantly add to the criminal code so as to keep brief the periods during which crime pays.

The American Constitution also protects substantive rights: freedom of speech and assembly, security in one's home against unreasonable searches by law-enforcement personnel, the right to petition public officials. Sometimes these rights of citizens are regarded by officials as obstacles to carrying out their jobs. Police often have well-founded suspicions about the identity of an armed robber or a murderer. They believe that they could get a confession from the suspect, complete with corroborative evidence (like a gun), if only the law permitted them to use "third degree" methods. The law does not permit the police to torture suspects, no matter how convincing the suspicions, and therefore the courts are required to protect the citizenry *against their own officials*. The seeming inefficiency of legal procedures and the opportunities which they offer for the guilty to escape punishment have an important by-product: they transform *might* into *right*.

---

[12] F. J. Gaudet, G. S. Harris, and C. W. St. John, "Individual Differences in the Sentencing Tendencies of Judges," *Journal of Criminal Law and Criminology*, Vol. 23, January–February 1933, pp. 811–818.

The following article by Talcott Parsons analyzes the complex relationship between law and government.

Law, Lawyers, and Social Control

Reprinted by permission. Adapted from Talcott Parsons, "Law and Social Control," in William M. Evan, *Law and Sociology*, New York: Free Press of Glencoe, 1962, pp. 56–72.

A legal system serves to mitigate potential elements of conflict and to oil the machinery of social intercourse. Only by adherence to rules can systems of social interaction function. The rules formulated in the system should not subject the individuals under their jurisdiction to incompatible expectations or obligations—or, more realistically, not too often or too drastically. Since individuals act in many roles, they will be subject to various sets of rules. But all the rules must somehow build up to a single, relatively consistent system.

FUNCTIONAL PROBLEMS OF A LEGAL SYSTEM

There are difficulties involved in institutionalizing a viable legal system in a large-scale, highly differentiated society.

SANCTIONS. Law depends on political organization because laws may require enforcement. If physical force were altogether excluded, the ultimate coercive sanction would be expulsion, as in excommunication from a church. In some cases, however, expulsion will not be a sufficiently severe sanction to prevent undesirable action from taking place. And if it is not sufficient, resort must be had to force. Force is the ultimate negative sanction.

Thus, if rules are taken sufficiently seriously, resort will sometimes be necessary to physical sanctions to prevent deviance. On the other hand, the use of force is a potential source of disruption of order in social relationships. For this reason, in all societies, the state has a monopoly of the more serious uses of physical force. If, then, it becomes necessary to use or threaten physical force as a sanction for the enforcement of legal norms, the legal system must have an adequate connection with the state in order to use governmental agencies as the administrators of physical sanctions.

JURISDICTION. The problem of jurisdiction is closely linked with that of sanctions. One of the reasons that the jurisdiction of political bodies is geographically defined is that physical force can be applied only if the individual to whom it is directed can be reached at a given time. Hence a legal system that relies on sanctions of physical force must also be linked to a geographic jurisdiction.

When a rule has been defined as a rule, it must be impartially applied to all persons or other social units that fall within the criteria that define the application of the rule. It is only within geographic areas that enforcement of defined rules can effectively be carried out. Therefore, enforcement agencies in a legal system are generally organs of the state.

Enforcement agencies are, however, not the *central* organs of the state. They do not make policy but rather are put at the service of the many different interests that are regulated by legal norms. What enforcement agencies may do, and to a considerable degree how they may do it, is defined and supervised by the courts. Where enforcement agencies gain virtual independence of the courts, as in totalitarian societies, the legal system is subordinated to political considerations.

In a democratic society, the judiciary is expected to enjoy considerable independence of the central political authority. Unless holding office for specified terms, judges enjoy tenure; they are not removable except for cause; and it is considered improper for political authority to put pressure on them to influence their specific decisions. Furthermore, though not a constitutional requirement in the United States, judges are generally lawyers. The judicial function is centered in a special type of social organization: the court. This organization applies laws to specific cases. This is done, of course, through the bringing of cases to the court for adjudication, in the course of which not only are the rights and obligations of individual petitioners settled but the rules themselves are given authoritative interpretations.

INTERPRETATION AND LEGITIMATION. The lawyer tends to take justice for granted. Neither the attorney nor the judge decides whether the existence of a given rule is morally or politically justified. Its interpretation and application *to particular cases* is the lawyer's concern. Nevertheless, the legal system must always rest on faith in its legitimacy. This may take forms analogous to the legal process itself, such as the issue of proper procedures in the enactment of legislation by duly authorized bodies. But in back of proper procedure and due authorization of law-making bodies lie deeper questions of ultimate values. Does justice result from the political decisions applied by the courts?

Anglo-American law relies heavily on the accumulation of precedents resulting from judicial decisions. But the problem of maintaining the internal consistency of the precedent system is formidable. Furthermore, current judicial decisions must be oriented to the authority of basic constitutional documents, which necessitates continual reinterpretation of them.

The interpretive problems faced by the legal profession may be compared with interpretive problems faced by other professions. First, there is an analogy with the professions concerned with the application of scientific knowledge, such as engineering and medicine. In these cases, the available knowledge is far from adequate to cover practical needs. Nevertheless, established scientific knowledge exists, and the relevant professional groups are recognized as competent to interpret such established knowledge. The second type is different, involving a fountainhead of authority beyond which there is no appeal. The Roman Catholic Church is the most conspicuous large-scale example, though the Soviet Communist Party is in certain respects similar. "Correct doctrine" is assumed not to be dependent on any human will, but to be infallibly specific, with a clearly authorized human agency for its implementation.

As compared with both of these, secular law is less subject to authoritative interpretation. The Constitution is less clear-cut than the canons of the Church, and the Supreme Court is less "canonical" than is the papacy. The legal profession, then, has to maintain difficult balances in a tradition that is in itself exceedingly complex, that is applied to changing conditions, subject to severe pressures from interest groups, authoritatively based only on very general and partly ambiguous documents, and subject to change within considerable limits by the unpredictable "will of the people."

THE ROLE OF LAWYERS IN A LEGAL SYSTEM

The practicing attorney is an officer of the court. As such, he bears a certain public responsi-

bility. But at the same time, he is a private adviser to his client, depending on the client for his remuneration and enjoying a privileged relation to the client. This relation between lawyer and client parallels that between physician and patient, its confidential character being one of the principal clues to this parallel. It is focused, however, on situations of actual or potential social conflict and the adjudication and smoothing over of these conflicts.

The legal profession shares certain characteristics with the other professions. Its members are trained in and integrated with a distinctive part of our cultural tradition, having a fiduciary responsibility for its maintenance, development, and implementation. They are expected to provide a "service" to the public without regard to immediate self-interest. The lawyer has a position of independent responsibility, so that he is neither a servant of the client, though he represents his interest, nor of *any* other group—even a group embodying public authority.

The member of a profession stands *between* two major aspects of our social structure; in the case of the law, between public authority and its norms and the private individual or group whose conduct or intentions may or may not be in accord with the law. In the case of the physician, it is between the worlds of sickness and of health; he himself is defined as not sick, but he participates more intimately with the sick than any other category of well person. In the case of the teacher, it is between the world of childhood— or, on advanced levels, of relative "untrainedness"—and the status of being fully trained.

The professions may be regarded as agencies of social control. Some professions—for example, teaching—help to socialize the young, to inculcate in them the expectations of full membership in the society; others, like the medical profession, bring members of the society *back* into accord with normal expectations when they have deviated (resocialization). The legal profession contributes to both these processes. The private attorney forestalls deviance by advising the client in ways that will "cool him off." Second, the lawyer, like the physician, helps his client to "face reality," to confine his claim to what he has a real chance of making "stand up" in court or in direct negotiation, and to realize that the other fellow may have a case, too. The element of delay in bringing things to a head, though carried too far because of crowding of court calendars, may help the lawyer bring about this realization. On the other hand, a person under strain should have some opportunity for expressing his tensions in an institutionally legitimate way. This the lawyer does, too. In order to be psychologically capable of "getting things off his chest," a person must be assured that negative sanctions will be suspended. This implies a protected situation like the confidential character of the lawyer's relation to his client. The client can talk freely to an understanding and knowledgeable ear without fear of immediate repercussions. What is relayed beyond this confidential relationship is selected through the screen of the lawyer's judgment.

In situations of strain, there must be also some assurance of "support" or "acceptance" within broader limits than would otherwise be the case. The physician tends to be tolerant of human beings; he does not judge them morally, but tries to help them as best he can. Certain features of legal practice also fits this pattern. Although the attorney is not supposed to attempt to "get off" a person he knows to be guilty of a crime, there is the presumption that the client is entitled to a "fair trial" not only in the formal sense, but a hearing from his attorney as well as assistance within the bounds of professional ethics.

While the lawyer tends to be both permissive and supportive in his relation with his clients, there is another side to the picture. He is schooled in the tradition of the law. As a member of a great profession, he accepts responsibility for its integrity. He must not only give clients what they want—that is, to teach them what they can expect to "get away with"—but also to inform them what the law expects them to do. Here, the lawyer stands as a kind of buffer between the illegitimate desires of his clients and the social interest. He "represents" the law rather than the client.

From the combination of the interpretive function and that of legitimation, we may begin to understand some of the reasons for the emphasis in the law on procedural matters. As Max Weber put it, "the rationality of law is formal rather than substantive." One of the basic conceptions in the Anglo-Saxon legal systems, that of "due process of law" is concerned with what to laymen are legal technicalities rather than with substantive justice or injustice. "Due process of law" is satisfied as long as correct formal procedure has been observed. If pressure becomes strong

with reference to either the question of enforcement or the question of legitimation, the integrity of procedural traditions and rules is in danger. People who are vexed about questions of substantive justice and injustice are not strong respectors of complicated legal procedure. Similarly, if disobedience to law is sufficiently scandalous, citizens may demand direct action that by-passes the rules of procedure. Law flourishes in a society in which the most fundamental questions of social values are not currently under agitation. Where there is sufficiently acute value conflict, law is likely to go by the board. It flourishes also in a society in which the enforcement problem is not too acute because of strong *informal* forces reinforcing conformity with the legally institutionalized tradition. Modern England illustrates this possibility.

Law has special importance in a pluralistic society where there are many different kinds of interests that must be balanced against each other. In the totalitarian type of society, which is in a great hurry to settle some fundamental general social conflict or policy, law tends to lack independent authority. Both individually and collectively, law imposes restraints on precipitate and violent action. Recall the words with which the recipients of law degrees are greeted by the President of Harvard University at every Commencement. He says, "You are now qualified to help administer those wise restraints which make men free."

CONCLUSION

In every society conflicts must be resolved and decisions made. In less differentiated societies, this political function can be handled informally. Leadership exists but not necessarily government. Industrial societies are sufficiently large and differentiated that formal political institutions are inevitable. The differences between democratic and despotic government hinge on the method of *selecting current decision makers, the extent to which opposition to them is legitimate, and the degree of independence of the legal system from them or their administrative subordinates.*

On a more philosophical level, the difference between democracy and despotism hinges on different conceptions of human nature and of social life. Despotic political philosophies tend to make either or both of two extreme assumptions:

1. that *consensus* is so difficult to achieve that freedom must be sacrificed to order. (The roots of this assumption can be traced to the "war of all against all" argument of Thomas Hobbes.)

2. that *justice* is so easy to achieve that political authority can be entrusted to a wise man or to a benevolent party. (The confidence of Marxists that a one-party dictatorship will result in greater social justice than capitalist democracy rests on the assumption that despotism can be permanently benevolent.)

Democratic political philosophies tend to steer a middle course between pessimism about the possibilities of consensus and optimism about the possibilities of justice. The Protestant theologian, Reinhold Niebuhr, put it very well when he said, "Man's capacity for justice makes democracy possible; but man's inclination to injustice makes democracy necessary." [13] That is, belief in the viability of democracy rests on faith that man is a moral animal and not a jungle cat. Being moral, human beings have the capacity to transcend their own partial perspectives and partisan interests—at least sometimes. Hence, democratic decision making approximates a moral consensus and not a triumph of the most powerful interest group. On any given issue, interest groups contend with each other for a favorable decision, but no group is dominant, so that all interest groups must ultimately appeal to the disinterested and somewhat apathetic majority. Belief in democracy rests on hope that the verdict of this majority will be just.

On the other hand, this hope that the democratic process will result in a just consensus has not blinded democratic theorists to potentialities for injustice. The framers of the American Constitution were careful to build checks and balances into the system because they were afraid of the tyranny of a temporary majority. For the same reason, influential leaders in the 13 colonies opposed ratification of the Constitution until a Bill of Rights was tacked on (the first ten amendments). When Professor Niebuhr says ". . . man's inclination to injustice makes democracy necessary," he is echoing the pessimism of the Founding Fathers about political authority generally, and he is asserting that *self*-government is the best protection against tendencies to injustice. He suggests that it is an inconsistency of totalitarian political philosophies to place so little faith in the citizen and so much in the rulers. "If men are inclined to deal unjustly with their fellows, the possession of power aggravates this inclination. That is why irresponsible and uncontrolled power is the greatest source of injustice." [14] That, argues Niebuhr, is why democracy is *necessary*.

[13] Reinhold Niebuhr, *The Children of Light and the Children of Darkness: A Vindication of Democracy and a Critique of Its Traditional Defence*, New York: Scribner's, 1950, p. xi.
[14] *Ibid.*

SOME SIGNIFICANT LITERATURE ON POLITICAL INSTITUTIONS

Daniel Bell, *The End of Ideology: On the Exhaustion of Political Ideas in the Fifties*, rev. ed., New York: Collier Books, 1961. Ideologies that once gave intellectuals a sense of political direction have lost the power to arouse passion. "Few serious minds believe any longer that one can set down 'blueprints' and through 'social engineering' bring about a new utopia of social harmony. . . . Few 'classic' liberals insist that the State should play no role in the economy, and few serious conservatives, at least in England and on the Continent, believe that the Welfare State is 'the road to serfdom.' In the Western world, therefore, there is today rough consensus among intellectuals on political issues: the acceptance of a Welfare State; the desirability of decentralized power; a system of mixed economy and of political pluralism." Professor Bell hopes that a new age has dawned in which political goals will be chosen more rationally rather than on the basis of "apocalyptic fervor." For an explanation of the decline in ideology in terms of the extension of voting rights to previously disenfranchised segments of the population, see Reinhard Bendix, "The Lower Classes and the 'Democratic Revolution,'" *Industrial Relations*, Vol. 1, October 1961, pp. 91–116.

Reinhard Bendix, "Social Stratification and the Political Community," *European Journal of Sociology*, Vol. 1, No. 2, 1960, pp. 3–32. Professor Bendix traces the emergence of national states in medieval Europe in an effort to understand the relationship between two aspects of social life: (1) individual economic concerns and group solidarities and (2) centralized, depersonalized decision-making institutions. He concludes that urban industrial societies produce an irreversible differentiation ". . . between the forces making for social solidarity independently of government and the forces accounting for the continuous exercise of central authority in the national political community." The resulting loss of governmental functions on the part of secondary groups means that they possess less cohesion than in a politically undifferentiated society. "Whereas solidarity has been based on the individual's participation in a 'law community' or on his membership in a privileged status group possessing certain governmental prerogatives, it must arise now from the social and economic stratification of society aided by the equality of all adult citizens before the law and in the electoral process." Solidarity is thus problematic in contemporary societies.

William A. Faunce, "Size of Locals and Union Democracy," *American Journal of Sociology*, Vol. 68, November 1962, pp. 291–298. At the 1959 convention of the United Automobile Workers, 1815 delegates representing 753 U.A.W. locals filled out questionnaires dealing with participation in union affairs. After the convention, 108 delegates from locals in Lansing and Flint, Michigan, were interviewed at length not only about their participation in the national convention but also about politics in the U.A.W. locals. Delegates from *small* locals were less likely than delegates from *large* locals to take an active part in convention proceedings and to express concern about representing rank-and-file views at the national level. Although delegates from small locals reported a higher proportion of members voting in local elections than delegates from large locals, they also reported fewer contested elections and less well-developed opposition parties. Professor Faunce concludes that large locals appear to contribute more than small locals to democratic processes in unions both on the national and on the local levels. For other studies of the conditions favoring democratic processes in trade unions, see Seymour Martin Lipset, Martin A. Trow, and James S. Coleman, *Union Democracy: The Internal Politics of the International Typographical Union*, Glencoe, Ill.: Free Press, 1956; and Seymour Martin Lipset, "The Law and Trade Union Democracy," *Virginia Law Review*, Vol. 47, January 1961, pp. 1–50. These studies are interesting partly because

the political process on the governmental level is paralleled in the private governments of voluntary associations. They are important also because political sociologists seek to understand the limits of compatibility between a democratic central government and undemocratic organizations within the same society.

Morton Grodzins, *The Loyal and the Disloyal: Social Boundaries of Patriotism and Treason*, Chicago: University of Chicago Press, 1956. Democratic and totalitarian nations have different methods of sustaining loyalty. In a democracy, loyalty is a by-product of satisfaction achieved within the family, the economic system, the church, and other non-national solidarities that the nation is implicitly assumed to symbolize. ". . . The democratic system of limited government presupposes that national loyalty will be a limited loyalty." In a totalitarian society, all identifications that the ruling party might not be able to control are regarded as signs of disloyalty. "Every effort is made to blast the individual from his non-national identifications. Then he is offered the single identification with the state." Professor Grodzins illustrates these contrasting conceptions of loyalty by citing the more than six thousand American citizens of Japanese descent who, during the Second World War, formally declared that they were not loyal to the United States. The government program of evacuation and relocation of West Coast Japanese had so disturbed their primary group relations as to make the United States a negative symbol instead of the positive symbol it had been before. Therefore, when they were registered and forced to reply to a question, "Will you swear unqualified allegiance to the United States of America . . . and forswear any form of allegiance to the Japanese emperor?" six thousand out of the 37 thousand Japanese-American citizens in relocation centers said, "No." Grodzins implies that this loyalty test implicitly assumed a totalitarian rather than a democratic concept of loyalty. This summary is based on a review by S. Frank Miyamoto, *American Sociological Review*, Vol. 21, October 1956, p. 657.

Joseph R. Gusfield, "Mass Society and Extremist Politics," *American Sociological Review*, Vol. 27, February 1962, pp. 19–30. Some sociologists maintain (1) that traditional solidarities—family, class, neighborhood, ethnic group—have little significance in societies characterized by mass communications, bureaucratized relationships in large-scale organizations, and equalitarian ideologies and (2) that the resulting rootlessness of degrouped individuals creates opportunities for demagogues and extremist political parties. Professor Gusfield criticizes this theory on both theoretical and empirical grounds: (1) The mass society theorists emphasize only the disruptive consequences of urban industrial culture. Homogeneous experiences with mass media and with formal education may *increase* consensus and integration—particularly on the national level. (2) The chief source of political extremism seems to be the population elements most isolated from the institutions and the values of mass society as, for example, in the desegregation crisis. "Opposition to a national culture of race relations is found most intensively among those most localistic, least educated, least urban, least exposed to mass media, and least integrated into the national economy." For an exposition of the views Gusfield is criticizing, see William Kornhauser, *The Politics of Mass Society*, Glencoe, Ill.: Free Press, 1959; and Philip Selznick, *The Organizational Weapon: A Study of Bolshevik Strategy and Tactics*, New York: McGraw-Hill, 1952.

Morris Janowitz and Dwaine Marvick, *Competitive Pressure and Democratic Consent*, Ann Arbor: Bureau of Government, Institute of Public Administration, University of Michigan, 1956. Professors Janowitz and Marvick assess American voting behavior in the 1952 presidential election in terms of a theory of "democratic consent." Five criteria are suggested in terms of which the election can be evaluated: (1) competition among rival candidates is sufficiently intense to generate widespread citizen participation; (2) the citizenry is concerned about the outcome but is willing to accept the verdict of the electoral process; (3) the campaign stimulates effective deliberation on the candidates and the issues; (4) no party or candidate monopolizes the mass media; (5) mass-media influences and personal influences of friends and relatives are independent. Although the authors identify segments of the electorate which did not participate in 1952 in a process of democratic consent (Negroes and lower-class persons), they conclude that in general the 1952 election fulfilled their criteria. This summary is based on a review by Duncan MacRae, Jr., *American Sociological Review*, Vol. 22, April 1957, p. 238.

Seymour Martin Lipset, "Party Systems and the Representation of Social Groups," *European Journal of Sociology*, Vol. 1, No. 1, 1960, pp. 3–38. Even when social and economic conditions are conducive to a stable democratic system, formal political institutions may contribute to stability or to instability. Professor Lipset demonstrates by means of comparative analysis of stable and unstable democracies that a two-party system is more conducive to stability than a multiparty system except when the society is polarized by class, race, or religion. If under these circumstances ". . . the political lines follow those of social cleavage, a two-party system may intensify internal conflict rather than help integrate the society." But how is a two-party system developed? Professor Lipset shows that proportional representation favors the development of a multiparty system whereas an electoral system wherein the candidate wins who receives a plurality of the votes tends to be a two-party system. The reason for this tendency in a plurality system is that voters are reluctant to "waste" their votes on a weak party. Lipset explicitly credits political scientists with this insight and chides sociologists for assuming that underlying social cleavages must result in multiparty instability.

Seymour Martin Lipset, *Political Man: The Social Bases of Politics*, Garden City, N.Y.: Doubleday, 1960. A major concern running through the various essays included in the book is the conditions conducive to stable democracy. Professor Lipset considers, for example, whether high voter turnout is desirable. On the one hand, a low voting rate usually means that the socially and economically disadvantaged groups are under-represented in government. On the other hand, an extremely high turnout is usually a symptom of political crisis and the decline of consensus. He concludes that it is the *sudden* introduction of previously apathetic nonvoters into politics that is dangerous for democracy. "To the extent that the lower strata have been brought into [the] electoral process *gradually* (through increased organization, an upgrading of the educational system, and a growth in their understanding of the relevance of government action to their interests), increased participation is undoubtedly a good thing for democracy." In another section of his book Professor Lipset considers the relationship between economic development and democracy by comparing more democratic and less democratic countries by indices of wealth, industrialization, education, and urbanization. He concludes from the statistical correlations that stable democracy is difficult to attain before a minimum level of economic development is reached.

Paul W. Massing, *Rehearsal for Destruction: A Study of Political Anti-Semitism in Imperial Germany*, New York: Harper, 1949. Professor Massing traces the anti-Semitism of the Nazi regime in Germany to its ideological roots in German culture. He shows how anti-Semitism was used as a political weapon by Bismarck's enemies and how it served as the rallying cry of extremist groups after Bismarck's fall from power. Massing suggests that racial anti-Semitism was strongest among the urban lower middle class. "The most virulent anti-Semitism was spread by teachers, students, white-collar workers, petty officials, the free professions. . . . In contrast, conservative Junkers, peasants, and other rural inhabitants had no special love for Jews but their dislike was circumscribed." This summary is based on a review by Bart Landheer, *American Sociological Review*, Vol. 15, April 1950, p. 319. Although anti-Semitism was an important part of the Nazi program, the strongest support for the Nazis in the 1932 elections, the year before Hitler took power, came from *rural* voters. See Lipset, *Political Man, op. cit.*, p. 144. Professor Lipset reviews the evidence showing that in the years of economic crisis, 1930–1933, the Nazis picked up crucial support from relatively uneducated and previously unpolitical segments of the German population. Nonetheless, Lipset believes, as Massing does, that the *sustained* support that carried the Nazi movement to an eventual mass following came from the middle class.

C. Wright Mills, *The Power Élite*, New York: Oxford University Press, 1957. This polemical work was far better received by the general public than by professional sociologists. As Leonard Reissman put it in his review in the *American Sociological Review*, C. Wright Mills ". . . moves from the fact to the observation with ease and without warning." Professor Mills' central thesis is that a small unified group mans the political, economic, and military "command posts" of American society and has increased its relative power over the past generation. In a long review article, Talcott Parsons criticizes this thesis for the following reasons: (1) Mills had a limited and somewhat paranoid conception of power; he perceived only the distributive aspect of it. If he recognized that power was the capacity to mobilize societal resources for the realization of common goals, he might be less worried that differences in power existed among members of American society. (2) Given the nature of an industrial society and of the United States as a particularly rich and influential industrial society, the

differentiation of a distinct leadership group in business and government should occasion no surprise. Leadership is a specialized function in all social systems. When the increase in scale goes far enough, leadership roles become more clearly defined. (3) Even though the recruitment of top business and governmental leadership is informal, this does *not* mean that executive competence is irrelevant to the selection process. Mills' suspicion that the power élite arbitrarily selected personally congenial, socially acceptable successors is unproven. (4) Mills' conception of "the power élite" tacitly assumed that those who wield power were necessarily élite, or conversely, that those without power could not be part of the élite. Sociologists who think of the élite in prestige terms would maintain that prestige need not necessarily be accompanied by power. (5) Government officials have greater independence of the business community than Mills believed. Mills asserted—and perhaps he was right—that big business tycoons had more power than judges, civil servants, college professors, and lawyers. He then went on to assume that these groups had no power at all, that only business men "count." This evaluation is based on a review article by Talcott Parsons, "The Distribution of Power in American Society," *World Politics*, Vol. 10, October 1957, pp. 123–133.

CHAPTER 14

Religion

In every society, human beings seek reassurance that life has meaning. Experience produces evidence that life is ". . . a tale told by an idiot, full of sound and fury, signifying nothing." Examples of such evidence are (1) the inevitability of physical death; (2) the unpredictability and uncontrollability of events in whose outcomes people have deep emotional investments; and (3) the failure of moral determinism.

Death is a threat to the meaning of life because human beings develop in the course of socialization the capacity to treat themselves as objects. Once self-awareness develops, the individual loves himself or hates himself, is proud of himself or ashamed of himself; his emotional investment in himself is too great for him to be indifferent to the possibility of oblivion. His intellectual awareness that the organism must perish creates a chronic feeling of anxiety. We are born; we suffer; and we die. To what purpose? [1] Poets have expressed in

vivid language the universal suspicion that death reduces life to an absurdity. For example, T. S. Eliot ends "The Wasteland" with the line, "This is the way the world ends, not with a bang but a whimper." And Shelley expressed the futility of power and glory in the following well-known poem:

I met a traveler from an antique land
Who said: Two vast and trunkless legs of stone
Stand in the desert. Near them, on the sand,
Half sunk, a shattered visage lies, whose frown
And wrinkled lip, and sneer of cold command,
Tell that its sculptor well those passions read
Which yet survive, stamped on those lifeless
    things,
The hand that mocked them, and the heart
    that fed:
And on the pedestal these words appear:
"My name is Ozymandias, King of Kings:
Look on my works, ye Mighty and despair!"
Nothing beside remains. Round the decay
Of that colossal wreck, boundless and bare
The lone and level sands stretch far away.

[1] This chapter leans heavily on Talcott Parsons' analysis of the motivation for religious belief and behavior as set forth in "Religious Perspectives of College Teaching in Sociology and Social Psychology," pamphlet, New Haven, Conn.: Edward W. Hazen Foundation, pp. 9–21. But parallel analyses exist in the theological literature. See, for example, Paul Tillich, *The Courage to Be*, New Haven, Conn.: Yale University Press, 1952; and Reinhold Niebuhr, *The Nature and Destiny of Man: A Christian Interpretation*, New York, Scribner's, 1949.

Curiously enough, the anxiety about life's significance aroused by the certainty of death does not guarantee a preference for life over death. The French sociologist Émile Durkheim demonstrated in his classic study that a feeling of purposelessness increases the probability of suicide; the best insurance against self-destruction is the belief that life has meaning.[2] On the other hand, the act of self-destruction can fulfill life's meaning instead of negating it, as, for example, the Kamikaze pilots during the Second World War who dived their planes laden with explosives into American battleships; they believed that self-destruction, under these circumstances, would win them eternal glory.

A second threat to the meaning of life is the uncertainty of human efforts and plans. As the poet Robert Burns put it:

But, Mousie, thou art no thy lane,
In proving foresight may be vain;
The best laid schemes o' mice an' men
    Gang aft agley,
An' lea'e us nought but grief an' pain
    For promised joy.

In preliterate societies, the exposure of agriculture to unpredictable and uncontrollable weather illustrates the limitation of human planning. Hard work makes a good crop more likely, but hard work cannot guarantee it. The anthropologist Bronislaw Malinowski suggested that the greater the uncertainty of human effort, the more likely would supernatural means be sought to increase the *feeling* of control.[3] He cited the difference between lagoon fishing and open-sea fishing in the Trobriand Islands. Lagoon fishing is safe and sure, and no rituals are associated with it; open-sea fishing is dangerous, the yields are uncertain, and rituals abound. In contemporary industrial societies, science and technology have provided greater control over crops and even weather. But the

future continues to be unpredictable. The threat of war and economic crises—as well as personal problems of health and unemployment—remind us that the investment of hope and effort is a gamble.

A third threat to the meaning of life is the partial failure of moral determinism in all societies.[4] As the Bible put it, "The good die young while the wicked flourish as the green bay tree." The biblical statement exaggerates the actual state of affairs. Every society makes an effort to balance the moral economy: to reward the virtuous and punish the wicked. But all societies fail to some extent because social control is never complete. In every society, good people can be found who fare badly and corrupt people can be found who seem to be enjoying life immensely. This partial failure of moral determinism suggests that social life is little better than a jungle. If those who abide by ethical principles are pushed aside by those who have no principles, might makes right, and life has no meaning.

ULTIMATE VALUES AND THE PROBLEM OF SOCIAL ORDER

Unless human beings are somehow reassured that life has meaning, demoralization ensues. Émile Durkheim introduced the term *"anomie"* into sociology to describe a demoralized society—without goals or norms. Several centuries earlier, Thomas Hobbes tried to imagine life in a demoralized society ("a state of nature"); he emphasized the insecurity which would result from "a war of all against all." Neither Durkheim nor Hobbes could accurately describe a demoralized society because reorganization occurs before demoralization becomes unbearable; thus, *anomie* is the hypothetical result of a process that is never carried to its conclusion.

What prevents demoralization from be-

2 Émile Durkheim, *Suicide*, Glencoe, Ill.: Free Press, 1951.
3 Bronislaw Malinowski, "Magic, Science and Religion," in Joseph Needham, Ed., *Science, Religion and Reality*, New York: Macmillan, 1925, pp. 31–32.

4 The phrase "moral determinism" is used by Kingsley Davis in *Human Society*, New York: Macmillan, 1948, pp. 530–531, in the course of a penetrating chapter on religious institutions. In lectures and writings, Talcott Parsons has repeatedly pointed out the discrepancies between conformity to moral standards and secular rewards.

coming total? The efforts of the society to affirm its ultimate values. On the most concrete level, these efforts underlie child socialization. Suppose a five-year-old raises his metal shovel menacingly over the head of a playmate. The child's mother happens to be near enough to avert the disaster. "You must not do that!" she cries. "Why not?" he might ask as she pulls the shovel out of his hands. "Because I do not want you to," is a polite way of saying, "Shut up and do what you are told." It settles the issue in power terms rather than by asserting the existence of ultimate values. However, the mother can justify her determination to prevent bloodshed by citing religious tradition and thereby obtaining transcendental justification for her peaceful policy. "Because God is up there watching, and He does not want you to beat up anyone with a shovel." Perhaps the mother could have gotten the child to accept a more mundane justification this time, but, sooner or later, ultimate questions call for ultimate answers. If the child keeps asking, "Why?" as children have been known to do, his mother has either to resort to naked force or to justify secular rules in moral terms. On those occasions when the question "Why?" is a challenge to the arrangements that make possible the peaceful coexistence of people in a society, religion can step into the breach. Voltaire is reported to have said, "If God doesn't exist, we must invent him."

Children are not the only ones to ask difficult questions. When a loved one is killed in an automobile collision and his relatives exclaim, "Why did it happen to *him?*" they are not satisfied with a detailed explanation of the technology of the accident. A reasonably satisfactory answer is possible for bereaved relatives with faith in the goodness of God and the inscrutability of His ways. They may be consoled for their loss by the thought that the victim is going to his reward in a better world.

The efforts of a society to affirm its ultimate values are evident not only in the crises of socialization and death but also in day-to-day applications of social norms. Religion supports the social order on this level, too. Some

70 years before the birth of Jesus, Rabbi Hillel provided a classic statement of such support in reply to a challenge that he sum up all of the rules of conduct in the Torah and the Talmud while standing on one foot. He said, "Do *not* do to others what you would *not* want others to do to you." At first hearing, this may sound like a mere ethical maxim. But the occasion for its enunciation makes the transcendental reference clear. Hillel was saying that God forbade men to commit aggressions against one another. He claimed only to be summarizing the religious law of the Hebrew people. However, the abstractness of the formulation makes it sociologically classic; it can apply equally well to cannibal as to Hebrew society. In short, every society prohibits aggressive behavior *within* the group, and religious beliefs sanctify these prohibitions. The variation arises from *what* is considered aggression and *who* is included within the group. Wife beating is grounds for divorce in American society; among some peasant groups in Eastern Europe, a woman whose husband did not slap her occasionally would have reason to fear he had lost interest.

Every society must prohibit behavior which is divisive. But social solidarity does not result from the absence of rape, murder, and theft. True, solidarity could not exist if these harms were freely perpetrated, but lack of them or any overt aggression is not solidarity. Solidarity is the feeling of mutual obligation among members of a group. A family in which each member "minds his own business" has no solidarity even though no arguments or fist fights take place; it has the atmosphere of a rooming house. Family solidarity requires that parents be actively concerned about the welfare of their children and that children consider the feelings of their parents. Religion promotes social solidarity by prescribing positive obligations as well as by prohibiting aggression. The classic statement of religious support of group solidarity is that of Jesus: "Do unto others as you would have others do unto you." The phraseology is reminiscent of Hillel, but the elimination of the double negative effects a shift in emphasis.

To put the difference crudely, Hillel was forbidding "bad" acts, Jesus was prescribing "good" ones.

Note that the Golden Rule, because it requires *universal* solidarity, depends on guilt rather than shame to motivate conformity. Violations of the commandment "Honor thy father and thy mother" are easy to detect. If one does not treat one's parents according to the customs of the community, the parents are likely to be resentful, and one may become a subject for neighborhood gossip. On the other hand, the failure to manifest universal love is difficult to measure. Therefore, the universalistic norms of religions that prescribe human brotherhood depend on conscience rather than on social pressure. Since urban industrial societies are too fluid for informal group pressure to achieve solidarity, a universalistic religion is more necessary in contemporary than in nonliterate societies.

Even in a nonliterate society, religion helps to underwrite the minimum cohesiveness without which the community could not function. But a conception of the brotherhood of man is not required to achieve this minimum because parochial rules suffice in a society where interpersonal relations depend on kinship ties. Among the Australian Murngin, for instance, a tribesman lives with relatives, hunts with relatives, and is cared for when sick by relatives. Parochial rules are sufficient to ensure solidarity. If a Murngin fulfills his obligations to his sisters and brothers as well as to his other kinsmen, he has been loyal to everybody. Everyone in the tribe is a relative. Isolated though the Murngin are, awkward situations arise when visitors approach the camp site. On these occasions, long conferences become necessary during which the genealogy of the stranger is traced in exhaustive detail. If the visitor is a relative of a member of the tribe, even a sixth cousin, he can stay as long as he likes. During his visit he is treated as warmly as the member of the tribe whose relative he is. If no relationship is discovered, the Murngin do not know what to do with him. Who is to feed him? In whose hut will he sleep? With whom will he hunt?

Not encumbered by universalistic rules, the Murngin may spear the stranger to death out of sheer embarrassment.[5]

Modern society is, of course, a long way from the particularistic unity of the Murngin. For all practical purposes, industrial man lives in a society of strangers. If Americans refused to deal with anyone but kinsmen, American society could not function. A typical city family depends on strangers for food (grocers, butchers, restaurateurs), on strangers for clothing (haberdashers), on strangers for entertainment (movie ushers)—as well as for employment, medical care, police and fire protection, garbage disposal, and water supply. And the more urban, impersonal, and anonymous the community, the greater is the need for mutual cooperation among strangers. In such cases, universalistic values contribute to a solidarity which is at best precarious. Fortunately, the major religions support universalistic values.

THE IMPACT OF SUPERNATURAL COMMITMENTS

Since no one can prove scientifically that life is worth living, an act of faith is necessary to affirm the meaningfulness of life. When this act of faith is anchored to a belief in a supernatural world shared by a group of persons, the concept of "religion" can be invoked. Distinguishing religion from ideology or philosophy is not easy, especially when one wishes to define religion so as to include the religions of nonliterate peoples as well as religions like Buddhism and Confucianism which lack the Western idea of a personal God. Talcott Parsons feels that any religion must contain the following features: [6]

1. *Beliefs* concerning sacred entities which are "set apart" from the workaday world and on which the meaning of life depends, e.g., God.
2. *Symbols* for expressing the emotional states

---

[5] Talcott Parsons uses this illustration to contrast the universalism of urban industrial societies with the particularism of the folk society.

[6] Parsons, *op. cit.*, pp. 7–8.

appropriate to this supernatural sphere, e.g., the cross for Christians.

3. Prescribed *activities* for a believer although they are not supposed to help him realize secular goals, e.g., attendance at church services.

4. A conception of a *moral community,* a universe of persons who subscribe to the beliefs and participate in the activities and thereby constitute a solidary group. (In nonliterate societies, the boundaries of the tribe and of the religious community coincide; in contemporary societies, many religious communities exist side-by-side depending on the number of separate denominations.)

5. A faith that the sacred entities in the supernatural world have prescribed certain *rules of conduct* and moral values for believers, e.g., the Ten Commandments.

Within organized religions that include these features, the individual receives help in dealing with the crises of existence, and the group is protected from the demoralization of its members. Bronislaw Malinowski analyzes the contribution of organized religion to the individual and the community in nonliterate societies faced with death's challenge to the meaning of life.

Crisis Religion in Preliterate Societies

Reprinted by permission. From Bronislaw Malinowski, "Magic, Science and Religion," in Joseph Needham, Ed., *Science, Religion and Reality,* New York: Macmillan, 1925, pp. 57–62.

Let us start with the religious act par excellence, the ceremonial of death. Here the call to religion arises out of an individual crisis, the death which threatens man or woman. Never does an individual need the comfort of belief and ritual so much as in the sacrament of the viaticum, in the last comforts given to him at the final stage of his life's journey—acts which are well-nigh universal in all primitive religions. These acts are directed against the overwhelming fear, against the corroding doubt, from which the savage is no more free than the civilized man. These acts confirm his hope that there is a hereafter, that it is not worse than present life; indeed, better. All

the ritual expresses that belief, that emotional attitude which the dying man requires, which is the greatest comfort he can have in his supreme conflict. And this affirmation has behind it weight of numbers and the pomp of solemn ritual. For in all savage societies, death, as we have seen, compels the whole community to forgather, to attend to the dying, and to carry out the duties towards him. These duties do not, of course, develop any emotional sympathy with the dying —this would lead merely to a disintegrating panic. On the contrary, the line of ritual conduct opposes and contradicts some of the strongest emotions to which the dying man might become a prey. The whole conduct of the group, in fact, expresses the hope of salvation and immortality; that is, it expresses only one among the conflicting emotions of the individual.

After death, though the main actor has made his exit, the tragedy is not at an end. There are the bereaved ones, and these, savage or civilized, suffer alike, and are thrown into a dangerous mental chaos. We have given an analysis of this already, and found that, torn between fear and piety, reverence and horror, love and disgust, they are in a state of mind which might lead to mental disintegration. Out of this, religion lifts the individual by what could be called spiritual co-operation in the sacred mortuary rites. We have seen that in these rites there is expressed the dogma of continuity after death, as well as the moral attitude towards the departed. The corpse, and with it the person of the dead one, is a potential object of horror as well as of tender love. Religion confirms the second part of this double attitude by making the dead body into an object of sacred duties. The bond of union between the recently dead and the survivors is maintained, a fact of immense importance for the continuity of culture and for the safe keeping of tradition. In all this we see that the whole community carries out the biddings of religious tradition, but that these are again enacted for the benefit of a few individuals only, the bereaved ones, that they arise from a personal conflict and are a solution of this conflict. It must also be remembered that what the survivor goes through on such an occasion prepares him for his own death. The belief in immortality, which he has lived through and practiced in the case of his mother or father, makes him realize more clearly his own future life.

In all this we have to make a clear distinction between the belief and the ethics of the ritual on the one hand and on the other the means of enforcing them, the technique by which the individual is made to receive his religious comfort. The saving belief in spiritual continuity after death is already contained in the individual mind; it is not created by society. The sum total of innate tendencies, known usually as "the instinct of self-preservation," is at the root of this belief. The faith in immortality is, as we have seen, closely connected with the difficulty of facing one's own annihilation or that of a near and beloved person. This tendency makes the idea of the final disappearance of human personality odious, intolerable, socially destructive. Yet this idea and the fear of it always lurk in individual experience, and religion can remove it only by its negation in ritual.

Whether this is achieved by a Providence directly guiding human history, or by a process of natural selection in which a culture which evolves a belief and a ritual of immortality will survive and spread—this is a problem of theology or metaphysics. The anthropologist has done enough when he has shown the value of a certain phenomenon for social integrity and for the continuity of culture. In any case we see that what religion does in this matter is to select one out of the two alternatives suggested to man by his instinctive endowment.

This selection once made, however, society is indispensable for its enactment. The bereaved member of the group, himself overwhelmed by sorrow and fear, is incapable of relying on his own forces. He would be unable by his single effort to apply the dogma to his own case. Here the group steps in. The other members, untouched by the calamity, not torn mentally by the metaphysical dilemma, can respond to the crisis along the lines dictated by the religious order. Thus they bring consolation to the stricken one and lead him through the comforting experiences of religious ceremony. It is always easy to bear the misfortunes—of others, and the whole group, in which the majority are untouched by the pangs of fear and horror, can thus help the afflicted minority. Going through the religious ceremonies, the bereaved emerges changed by the revelation of immortality, communion with the beloved, the order of the next world. Religion commands in acts of cult, the group executes the command.

But, as we have seen, the comfort of ritual is not artificial, not manufactured for the occasion. It is but the result of the two conflicting tendencies which exist in man's innate emotional reaction to death: the religious attitude consists merely in the selection and ritual affirmation of one of these alternatives—the hope in a future life. And here the public concourse gives the emphasis, the powerful testimony to the belief. Public pomp and ceremony take effect through the contagiousness of faith, through the dignity of unanimous consent, the impressiveness of collective behavior. A multitude enacting as one an earnest and dignified ceremony invariably carries away even the disinterested observer, still more the affected participant.

But the distinction between social collaboration as the only technique necessary for the enactment of a belief on the one hand, and the creation of the belief or self-revelation of society on the other, must be emphatically pointed out. The community proclaims a number of definite truths and gives moral comfort to its members, but it does not give them the vague and empty assertion of its own divinity.

In another type of religious ritual, in the ceremonies of initiation, we found that the ritual establishes the existence of some power or personality from which tribal law is derived, and which is responsible for the moral rules imparted to the novice. To make the belief impressive, strong, and grandiose, there is the pomp of the ceremony and the hardships of preparation and ordeal. An unforgettable experience, unique in the life of the individual, is created, and by this he learns the doctrines of tribal tradition and the rules of its morality. The whole tribe is mobilized and all its authority set in motion to bear witness to the power and reality of the things revealed.

Here again, as at the death, we have to do with a crisis in the individual life, and a mental conflict associated with it. At puberty, the youth has to test his physical power, to cope with his sexual maturity, to take up his place in the tribe. This brings him promises, prerogatives, and temptations, and at the same time imposes burdens upon him. The right solution of the conflict lies in his compliance with tradition, in his submission to the sexual morality of his tribe and to the burdens of manhood, and that is accomplished in the ceremonies of initiation.

The public character of these ceremonies

avails both to establish the greatness of the ultimate lawgiver and to achieve homogeneity and uniformity in the teaching of morals. Thus they become a form of condensed education of a religious character. As in all schooling, the principles imparted are merely selected, fixed, emphasized out of what there is in the individual endowment. Here again publicity is a matter of technique, while the contents of what is taught are not invented by society but exist in the individual.

In other cults again, such as harvest festivals, totemic gatherings, first-fruit offerings and ceremonial display of food, we find religion sacralizing abundance and security and establishing the attitude of reverence towards the beneficent forces without. Here again the publicity of the cult is necessary as the only technique suitable for the establishment of the value of food, accumulation and abundance. The display to all, the admiration of all, the rivalry between any two producers, are the means by which value is created. For every value, religious and economic, must possess universal currency. But here again we find only the selection and emphasis of one of the two possible individual reactions. Accumulated food can either be squandered or preserved. It can either be an incentive to immediate heedless consumption and light-hearted carelessness about the future, or else it can stimulate man to devising means of hoarding the treasure and of using it for culturally higher purposes. Religion sets its stamp on the culturally valuable attitude and enforces it by public enactment.

The public character of such feasts subserves another sociologically important function. The members of every group which forms a cultural unit must come in contact with each other from time to time, but besides its beneficent possibility of strengthening social ties, such contact is also fraught with the danger of friction. The danger is greater when people meet in times of stress, dearth, and hunger, when their appetite is unsatisfied and their sexual desires ready to flare up. A festive tribal gathering at times of plenty, when everyone is in a mood of harmony with nature and consequently with each other, takes on, therefore, the character of a meeting in a moral atmosphere. I mean an atmosphere of general harmony and benevolence. The occurrence of occasional licence at such gatherings and the relaxation of the rules of sex and of certain strictures of etiquette are probably due to the same course.

All motives for quarrel and disagreement must be eliminated or else a big tribal gathering could not peacefully come to an end. The moral value of harmony and good will is thus shown to be higher than the mere negative taboos which curb the principal human instincts. There is no virtue higher than charity, and in primitive religions as well as in higher it covers a multitude of sins; nay, it outweighs them.

It is, perhaps, unnecessary to go in detail over all the other types of religious acts. Totemism, the religion of the clan, which affirms the common descent from or affinity with the totemic animal, and claims the clan's collective power to control its supply and impresses upon all the clan members a joint totemic taboo and a reverential attitude towards the totemic species, must obviously culminate in public ceremonies and have a distinctly social character. Ancestor cult, the aim of which is to unite into one band of worshippers the family, the sib or the tribe, must bring them together in public ceremonies by its very nature, or else it would fail to fulfill its function. Tutelary spirits of local groups, tribes, or cities; departmental gods; professional or local divinities must one and all—by their very definition —be worshipped by village, tribe, town, profession, or body politic.

In cults which stand on the borderline between magic and religion, such as the Intichuma ceremonies, public garden rites, ceremonies of fishing and hunting, the necessity of performance in public is obvious, for these ceremonies, clearly distinguishable from any practical activities which they inaugurate or accompany, are yet their counterpart. To the co-operation in practical enterprise there corresponds the ceremony in common. Only by uniting the group of workers in an act of worship do they fulfill their cultural function.

In fact, instead of going concretely into all the types of religious ceremony, we might have established our thesis by an abstract argument: since religion centers round vital acts, and since all these command public interest of joint co-operative groups, every religious ceremony must be public and carried out by groups. All crises of life, all important enterprises, arouse the public interest of primitive communities, and they have all their ceremonies, magical or religious. The same social body of men which unites for the enterprise or is brought together by the critical event performs also the ceremonial act.

FUNCTIONAL EQUIVALENTS OF RELIGION IN THE SCIENTIFIC AGE

Despite the greater life expectancy in urban industrial societies over nonliterate societies, death remains a challenge to the meaning of life, and funerals in contemporary societies perform much the same functions as in nonliterate communities. Science has not saved us from corrosive fears. But science has made it more difficult for industrial man to obtain the reassurance offered by the traditional religions. When astronomers can calculate the number of light-years separating the earth from various stars and rocket experts plan to send men to the moon, people find it harder to believe in a supernatural world. The *natural* universe seems so immense that supernatural phenomena are crowded out. In previous generations, children thought that heaven lay above the clouds. Where do they imagine heaven to be in the space age?

The religious problems of human beings are inescapable. Insofar as traditional faith is shaken, secular commitments must be substituted. For example, a deep identification with spouse and children enables the individual to ignore the inevitability of his own death. For such a person, his death does not necessarily imply extinction of the self; he is linked to life through loved ones who survive him. On the other hand, the individual who makes such commitments runs the risk that disasters will befall the persons with whom he is identified. As Francis Bacon put it, a wife and children are "hostages to fortune." The fire in a Boston nightclub in which more than 100 persons lost their lives showed how shattering premature death can be on the bereaved.[7] Dr. Erich Lindemann, the psychiatrist who tried to get the survivors to accept their loss, found "morbid identification" with the victims a serious obstacle. That is, some survivors were so emotionally entangled with persons lost in the fire that they

[7] Erich Lindemann, "Symptomatology and Management of Acute Grief," *American Journal of Psychiatry*, Vol. 101, September 1944, pp. 141–148.

regarded life without them as meaningless. They developed psychosomatic symptoms, including ulcerated colitis, as well as emotional disturbances. Dr. Lindemann was able to treat some "morbid grievers" successfully, especially those who were oriented to traditional religion and were responsive to the condolences offered by ministers, priests, or rabbis.

Other kinds of secular commitments provide a functional equivalent for religious faith. Some scientists have a quasireligious devotion to the pursuit of truth, some artists to the creation of beautiful paintings. Nationalistic fervor is another secular religion. In its milder version, commitment to one's country is commendable patriotism. In its fanatical version, nationalism can inflame mobs against foreigners in Cairo, Caracas, or Calcutta—and explain arrogant political speeches in Moscow and Washington. Nationalism enables the individual to identify with something that existed before he was born and will presumably last forever: his country. For the nationalist, this identification adds meaning to life. In the following article, a British and an American sociologist jointly explore the effect of the coronation of Queen Elizabeth on the solidarity of the British community.

A *Secular Ritual in an Industrial Society*

Reprinted by permission. From Edward A. Shils and Michael Young, "The Meaning of the Coronation," *Sociological Review*, Vol. 1, December 1953, pp. 63–81.

The heart has its reasons which the mind does not suspect. In a survey of street parties in East London nothing was more remarkable than the complete inability of people to say why they thought important the occasion they were honoring with such elaborate ritual, and the newspapers naturally took for granted the behavior on which this essay is a comment. What is perhaps more strange is that on the monarchy, at a Coronation or any other time, political science and philosophy too are silent. About this most august institution there is no serious discussion at all.

Some political scientists, as if sure that the

end of so many nineteenth century reformers has been achieved, tend to speak as if Britain is now an odd kind of republic,[8] which happens to have as its chief functionary a Queen instead of a President. It seems that even the most eminent scholars lose their sureness of touch when they enter the presence of Royalty. Sir Ivor Jennings has nothing to say in his volume on *Parliament*,[9] and in his *Cabinet Government*,[10] pausing only to note that the Sovereign still possesses considerable influence on legislation and that the King is also an important part of the "social structure," he gives nearly all his space on this subject to an historical treatment of the Victorian period. The late Professor Harold Laski was more discerning, even though his preferences belong to the more rationalistic phase of recent intellectual history. "Eulogy of its habits," he says, speaking of the monarchy, "has reached a level of intensity more comparable with the religious ecstasy of the seventeenth century, when men could still believe in the divine right of kings, than of the scientific temper of the twentieth, which has seen three great imperial houses broken, and the King of Spain transformed into a homeless wanderer."[11] For the rest, while lightly attributing this change in attitude to the imperial propaganda conducted since Victoria was proclaimed Empress of India, he too devotes himself to constitutional history, with special reference to the tangled events of 1911 and 1931. Recent British political philosophy is as applicable to a republic as it is to a monarchy, whose place in a modern society is a subject most studiously avoided.[12]

[8] The virtual disappearance of republican sentiment is obvious. John Gollan (*Communist Review*, June 1953) and Emrys Hughes, M.P., are indeed unorthodox. The current Labour attitude was expressed by Mr. Attlee in the House of Commons on 9 July, 1952. Speaking against sweeping economies in Royal expenditure, he said "It is a great mistake to make government too dull. That, I think, was the fault of the German Republic after the First World War. They were very drab and dull, the trouble was that they let the devil get all the best tunes." See also Sir Stafford Cripps (*Hansard*, 17 December 1947).
[9] "Of the King we need say nothing. His part in the process of legislation has become little more than formal." *Parliament*, Cambridge, 1939, p. 3.
[10] *Cabinet Government*, Cambridge, 1947.
[11] *Parliamentary Government in England*, Allen & Unwin, London, 1938, p. 389.
[12] Sir Ernest Barker scarcely refers to Monarchy in his *Reflections on Government* (Oxford, 1942) and passes over it entirely in his brief "Reflections on Eng-

Kingsley Martin is almost the only modern political writer to concern himself [13] with the theme to which Walter Bagehot gave such prominence when he set out in 1867 to trace "how the actions of a retired widow and an unemployed youth become of such importance." [14] Bagehot firmly recognized that the role of the Crown was not so much constitutional as "psychological." He supported the monarchy for the precise reason that republicans opposed it: because it enabled the educated ten thousand to go on governing as before. By commanding their unbounded loyalty, it tamed the uncouth "labourers of Somersetshire" who, in their simplicity, needed a person to symbolize the State. In this way "the English Monarchy strengthens our government with the strength of religion. . . . It gives now a vast strength to the entire constitution, by enlisting on its behalf the credulous obedience of enormous masses." [15] Mr. Martin in our day, does not, of course, share Bagehot's outlook. But up to a point he puts the same stress on the psychological functions which the Sovereign performs so well because of the sacredness with which he is invested. Once this assertion is made even he falls back, for in the greater part of the book, on the amusing story of the relations of the Sovereign with Lord Melbourne, Lord Beaconsfield, Mr. Gladstone, and the glittering host whose lives are the constitutional history of the realm.

The careful avoidance of the monarchy's role in British life appears to the authors of this essay, to be the consequence of an "intellectualist" bias. It is avoided because the monarchy has its roots in man's beliefs and sentiments about what he regards as sacred. The decline in the intensity of religious belief, especially in the educated classes, has produced an aversion towards all the sentiments and practices associated with religion. They do not acknowledge the somewhat alarming existence of these sentiments within themselves and refuse to admit that these are at work in others. They are acknowledged only when they are dero-

lish Political Theory" (*Political Studies*, I, 1, Oxford, 1953, pp. 6–12.)
[13] *The Magic of Monarchy*, Nelson, London, 1937. The article by J. G. Weightman, "Loyal Thoughts of an Ex-Republican," and other articles in the June 1953 issue of *The Twentieth Century* must also rank as shining exceptions.
[14] *The English Constitution*, Oxford, 1936, p. 30.
[15] *Op. cit.*, pp. 35, 39.

gated as "irrational" [16]—a charge which is both true and misleading, because it serves to dismiss them from further consideration.

The frequency with which the Coronation was spoken of by ordinary people as an "inspiration," [17] and as a "rededication" of the nation, only underscores the egregiousness of the omission. This essay, using the Coronation as a point of departure, seeks to advance, in some slight measure, the analysis of a neglected subject.

In all societies, most of the adult members possess some moral standards and beliefs about which there is agreement. There is an ordering and assessment of actions and qualities according to a definite, though usually unspoken, conception of virtue. The general acceptance of this scale of values, even though vague and inarticulate, constitutes the general moral consensus of society. Only philosophical intellectuals and prophets demand that conduct be guided by explicit moral standards. In the normal way, the general moral standards are manifested only in concrete judgments, and are seldom abstractly formulated. Persons who conduct themselves in accordance with rigorous and abstract schemes of moral value, who derive and justify every action by referring it to a general principle, impress most others as intolerable doctrinaires. To the doctrinaires, of course, the ordinary man is even more shocking; they would shake the *homme moyen sensuel* from his spiritual slothfulness and elevate him to a higher plane on which he would act knowingly only in the service of the highest good. To the doctrinaire, to the ideological intellectual, the ordinary sociable man is a poor thing—narrow, unprincipled, unmoral. The ordinary man, is, of course, by no means as poor a thing as his educated detractors pretend. He too is a moral being, and even when he evades standards and dishonours obligations, he almost always concedes their validity. The revivalist reassertion of moral stand-

ards in highly individualistic frontier groups, or among detribalized primitive societies in the process of yielding before the pressure of a modern economy, are instances of the respect vice pays to virtue. The recourse to the priestly confessor and the psychoanalyst testify to the power of moral standards even in situations where they are powerless to prevent actual wrongdoing.

We do not claim that men always act in conformity with their sense of values, nor do we claim that the measure of agreement in any society, even the most consensual, is anywhere near complete. Just as no society can exist without moral consensus, without fairly far-reaching agreement on fundamental standards and beliefs, so is every society bound to be the scene of conflict. Not only is there a clash of interests, but moral and intellectual beliefs too are in collision. Yet intertwined with all these conflicts are agreements strong enough to keep society generally peaceful and coherent.

What are these moral values which restrain men's egotism and which enable society to hold itself together? A few can be listed illustratively: generosity, charity, loyalty, justice in the distribution of opportunities and rewards, reasonable respect for authority, the dignity of the individual and his right to freedom. Most people take these values so much for granted that argument about them seems neither necessary nor possible. Their very commonplaceness may seem to place them at the very opposite pole from the sacred. Yet these values are part of the substance of the sacred, and values like them have sacred attributes in every society.

Life in a community is not only necessary to man for the *genetic* development of his human qualities. Society is necessary to man as an object of his higher evaluations and attachments, and without it man's human qualities could not find expression.[18] The *polis* or community is not just a group of concrete and particular persons; it is, more fundamentally, a group of persons acquiring their significance by their embodiment of values which transcend them and by their conformity with standards and rules from which they derive their dignity. The sacredness of society is at bottom the sacredness of its moral rules, which itself derives from the presumed relationship between these rules in their deepest significance and the

---

16 See, for instance, Percy Black, *The Mystique of Modern Monarchy*, Watts, London, 1953.
17 Not only in Britain and the Commonwealth. Sebastian Haffner speaks of the way in which the Coronation has "taken hold of the public consciousness of America, France and Germany. . . . There is, instead, an absorbed participation which almost, momentarily, removes the barriers of statehood—as if these foreign countries were celebrating, with mourning or rejoicing, great events in their own ruling Houses, or as if the British Monarchy had become a common possession of the Western world at large." *The Twentieth Century*, June 1953, p. 418.

18 *The Politics of Aristotle*, trans. by Sir Ernest Barker, Oxford, 1946, p. 2.

forces and agents which men regard as having the power to influence their destiny for better or for worse.

Man, as a moral creature with the capacity to discriminate among degrees of rightness and wrongness, feels not only safe but also terribly unsafe in the presence of the abstract symbols of these moral rules. *This is one reason why there is a recurrent need in men to reaffirm the rightness of the moral rules by which they live or feel they ought to live.* The reaffirmation of the moral rules of society serves to quell their own hostility towards these rules and also reinstates them in the appropriate relations with the greater values and powers behind the moral rules.

The need to reaffirm the moral rules comes then, not only from their sacred character, which require that they and their sources be respected in the most serious manner, but also from the struggle against morality being continuously enacted in the human mind. Dr. Ernest Jones, in a perceptive essay,[19] has pointed to the fundamental ambivalence in the attitude to authority —first towards the parents, then towards the wider authorities of State and Church, and finally towards the rules which emanate from these authorities. This ambivalence can be overcome in a number of ways of which reaction-formation and displacement are the most prominent. In order to curb an impulse to contravene a moral law, men will sometimes put all their energy into the fulfillment of the contrary impulse. Connection with the symbols of morality or proximity to them helps in this exertion and reinforces the strength which the individual can muster from his own resources to keep the moral law uppermost. It re-establishes the preponderance of positive devotion to the moral rules to enter into contact with them in their purest form. Contact with them in their most sacred form—as principles, or when symbolized in ritual activities, or when preached in moving sermons or speeches —renews their potency and makes the individual feel that he is in "good relations" with the sacred, as well as safe from his own sacrilegious tendencies.

If this argument be accepted, it is barely necessary to state the interpretation of the Coronation which follows from it: that the Coronation was the ceremonial occasion for the affirmation of the moral values by which the society lives. It was an act of national communion. In this we are merely restating the interpretation, in a particular context, of a more general view (which can apply to Christmas, Independence Day, Thanksgiving Day, May Day, or any other great communal ritual) expressed by a great sociologist. "There can be no society," said Durkheim, "which does not feel the need of upholding and reaffirming at regular intervals the collective sentiments and the collective ideas which make its unity and its personality. Now this moral remaking cannot be achieved except by the means of reunions, assemblies and meetings where the individuals, being closely united to one another, reaffirm in common their common sentiments; hence come ceremonies which do not differ from regular religious ceremonies, either in their object, the results which they produce, or the processes employed to attain these results. What essential difference is there between an assembly of Christians celebrating the principal dates of the life of Christ, or of Jews remembering the exodus from Egypt or the promulgation of the decalogue, and a reunion of citizens commemorating the promulgation of a new moral or legal system or some great event in the national life?" [20]

The Coronation is exactly this kind of ceremonial in which the society reaffirms the moral values which constitute it as a society and renews its devotion to those values by an act of communion.

In the following pages, this interpretation of the Coronation will be illustrated by a brief analysis of the Service itself and of some aspects of public participation in it.

The Coronation Service itself is a series of ritual affirmations of the moral values necessary to a well-governed and good society. The key to the Coronation Service is the Queen's promise to abide by the moral standards of society. The whole service reiterates their supremacy above the personality of the Sovereign. In her assurance that she will observe the canons of mercy, charity, justice and protective affection, she acknowledges and submits to their power. When she does this, she symbolically proclaims her community with

[19] Ernest Jones, "The Psychology of Constitutional Monarchy" in *Essays in Applied Psychoanalysis*, Vol. I, Hogarth, London, 1951.

[20] *Elementary Forms of Religious Life*, Allen & Unwin, London, 1915, p. 427. Cf. also Radcliffe-Brown, A. R., *The Andaman Islanders*, Cambridge, 1922, Ch. V.

her subjects who, in the ritual—and in the wider audience outside the Abbey—commit themselves to obedience within the society constituted by the moral rules which she has agreed to uphold.

This intricate series of affirmations is performed in the elaborate pattern which makes up the Coronation ceremony.

THE RECOGNITION

When the Archbishop presents the Queen to the four sides of the "theatre," he is asking the assembly to reaffirm their allegiance to her not so much as an individual as the incumbent of an office of authority charged with moral responsibility and for which she has the preliminary qualifications of a *blood-tie*. The "People" who signify their willingness to "do homage and service" were once the actual members and representatives of the Estates whose participation was necessary for the security of the realm. Now, those within the Abbey, although many of great power stand among them, are no longer its exclusive possessors. The "homage and service" of the entire society is far more important than it was in earlier Coronations and their offering is no more than a dramatic concentration of the devotion which millions now feel.

THE OATH

The Queen is asked whether she will solemnly promise and swear to govern the people of the United Kingdom and the Dominions and other possessions and territories in accordance with their respective laws and customs. When she does so, she clearly acknowledges that the moral standards embodied in the laws and customs are superior to her own personal will. The Queen agrees to respect justice and mercy in her judgments, and to do her utmost to maintain the laws of God and the true profession of the Gospel. In doing this, she acknowledges once more the superiority of the transcendent moral standards and their divine source, and therewith the sacred character of the moral standards of British society.

Apart from the momentary appearance of the Moderator of the General Assembly of the Church of Scotland, the Church of England administers the entire ceremony (though the Duke of Norfolk—a Roman Catholic—organised it), and yet there is no indication that this was regarded as anomaly in a country where only a small proportion of the population actively adheres to that church. Britain is generally a Christian country, it is certainly a religious country, in the broad sense, and in the Coronation Service the Church of England served the vague religiosity of the mass of the British people without raising issues of ecclesiastical jurisdiction or formal representation. As with so much else in the Coronation Service, behind the archaic façade was a vital sense of permanent contemporaneity.

PRESENTING THE HOLY BIBLE

When the Moderator presents the Bible to the Queen, the Archbishop says that this act is performed in order to keep Her Majesty "ever mindful of the Law." The Bible is a sacred object which contains in writing the fundamental moral teachings of the Christian society. Since this Bible is to go with her always, her moral consciousness is to be kept alive by means of continuous contact with the Book in which God's will is revealed. As the Moderator says, "Here is Wisdom; This is the royal Law; [21] These are the lively Oracles of God." The Bible which is handed to the Queen is not simply a closed and final promulgation of moral doctrine. It is the "lively Oracles of God," in which moral inspiration and stimulus for the mastery of constantly emerging new events are to be found. The Bible is the vessel of God's intention, a source of continuous inspiration in the moral regulation of society.

THE ANOINTING

When the Queen is divested of her regalia, she is presented as a frail creature who has now to be brought into contact with the divine, and thus transformed into a Queen, who will be something more and greater than the human being who has received the previous instruction. When the Queen sits in the saintly King Edward's Chair she is anointed by the Archbishop with consecrated oil which sanctifies her in her regal office. When he makes the cross on both her hands, her breast and the crown of her head, he places her in the tradition of the Kings of Israel and of all the rulers of England. He anoints her saying "And as Solomon was anointed king by Zadok the priest and Nathan the prophet, so be thou anointed, blessed, and consecrated Queen over the Peoples." It is not merely an analogy; it is

21 It is the law which is to govern Royalty, and only in this way does it refer to the law made by Royalty for the government of society.

a symbolization of reality, in conformity with sacred precedent. She shows her submission before the Archbishop as God's agent, kneeling before him while he implores God to bless her.

PRESENTING THE SWORD AND THE ORB

The Queen is then told that she will be given power to enforce the moral law of justice and to protect and encourage those whose lives are in accordance with the law. She is commanded to confirm what is in good order, and to restore to order what has fallen away from it. The sword is an instrument of destruction. It is as dangerous as the sacred foundations of the moral rules themselves and its terrible power, for evil, as well as good, must never be forgotten by the Queen. To stress this dual potentiality of authority, it is, throughout the rest of the ceremony, carried naked before her by the peer who redeemed it. In this way, the terrible responsibilities and powers of royal authority are communicated to the Queen and the people. The people are thus made aware of the protection which a good authority can offer them when they themselves adhere to the moral law, and of the wrathful punishment which will follow their deviation. She is next invested with the bracelets of sincerity and wisdom and is dressed in the Robe Royal, which enfolds her in righteousness. With these dramatic actions, she is transformed from a young woman into a vessel of the virtues which must flow through her into her society. Thus transformed, she is reminded of the wide sphere of her power, and of the responsibilities for its moral and pious use, by the Orb which she takes in her hand and places on the altar which is the repository of the most sacred objects. In doing this, she resanctifies her own authority. She is told to execute justice but never to forget mercy.

THE BENEDICTION

The communal kernel of the Coronation becomes visible again in the Benediction when the duties of the subjects are given special prominence by the Archbishop. In his blessing, he says: "The Lord give you faithful Parliaments and quiet Realms; sure defence against all enemies; fruitful lands and a prosperous industry; wise counsellors and upright magistrates; leaders of integrity in learning and labour; a devout, learned, and useful clergy; honest, peaceable, and dutiful citizens." The circle of obligation is completed:

the Queen to God's rule, and to her subjects in the light of God's rule, and then, her subjects to her by the same standard.

The Coronation Service and the Procession which followed were shared and celebrated by nearly all the people of Britain. In these events of 2nd June the Queen and her people were, through radio, television and press and in festivities throughout the land, brought into a great nation-wide communion. Not only the principals and the spectators inside the Abbey, but the people outside also, participated in the sacred rite. There is no doubt about the depth of the popular enthusiasm. Only about its causes is there disagreement. Some claim that it is the product of commercially interested publicity, others that it is the child of the popular press, others simply dismiss it as hysteria or "irrationality." There are those who claim (with rather more justice) that the involvement in the Coronation was no more than an expression of an ever-present British love of processions, uniforms, parades and pageants. Still others see the whole affair as a national "binge," or an opportunity for millions of people to seize the occasion for a good time. The youth and charm of the Queen and the attractiveness of her husband and children are also cited to explain the absorption of the populace.

Which of these explanations is correct? All of them, it seems to us, are at best partial answers. They all overlook the element of communion with the sacred, in which the commitment to values is reaffirmed and fortified. As we said earlier, the rationalistic bias of educated persons in the present century, particularly those of radical or liberal political disposition, is liable to produce abhorrence towards manifestations of popular devotion to any institution which cannot recommend itself to secular utilitarianism.

The collision between the latter viewpoint and the devoted gravity of the popular attitude was revealed most strikingly in the uproar which followed the publication of Mr. David Low's cartoon in the *Manchester Guardian* on 3rd June. This cartoon showed a Blimp-like figure, "the morning after," a paper crown awry on his head, the remains of the tinsel and crepe paper of a gay party littered about him, a television receiver in the corner and over it all a grim reminder that £100,000,000 had been spent on the spree. It was in the radical "debunking" tradition. It called forth a storm of denunciation. Moral sentiments had been affronted by Mr. Low's frivolity at a time when they were at a high pitch of seriousness.[22] The first flood of letters expressed indignation that a cynical reference to monetary costs should intrude upon a state of exhilaration, of "inspiration," of "uplift," upon "a unique and inspiring experience" of "heartfelt national rejoicing," upon a "spirit of service and dedication and the inspiring unity of all the people who rejoiced together (and who rededicated themselves) on this wonderful occasion." The second stage of the correspondence was no less significant. Although the anti-Low letters continued, the outburst of sentiment affirming the sacred character of the national participation in the Coronation made the more sceptical uncomfortable. Some of those who sprang to Low's defence found the expression of such intensely serious moral indignation "frightening."

The solemn sense that something touching the roots of British society was involved found expression in many other ways as well. An experienced observer of the London crowd said that the atmosphere on 1st June was like that of Armistice Day 1918 and of VE and VJ Days 1945: there was an air of gravity accompanied by a profound release from anxiety. The extraordinary stillness and tranquillity of the people on the route all through the early morning of 2nd June was noted by many who moved among them. Churches received many persons who came to pray or to meditate in the quiet, and in at least one famous London church—All Hallows Barking—communion services were held every hour.

Just as the Coronation Service in the Abbey was a religious ceremony in the conventional sense, so then the popular participation in the

service throughout the country had many of the properties of the enactment of a religious ritual. For one thing, it was not just an extraordinary spectacle, which people were interested in as individuals in search of enjoyment. The Coronation was throughout a collective, not an individual experience.

W. Robertson Smith in his great work, *Lectures on the Religion of the Semites*,[23] points out that acts of communion (of which the Coronation can be regarded as an example) are never experienced by individuals alone: they are always communal occasions. They are acts of communion between the deity or other symbols of the highest values of the community, and persons who come together to be in communion with one another through their common contact with the sacred. The fact that the experience is communal means that one of the values, the virtue of social unity or solidarity, is acknowledged and strengthened in the very act of communion.

The greatly increased sensitivity of individuals to their social ties, the greater absorption of the individual into his group and therewith into the larger community through his group found expression not only on the procession route but in the absent people as well, notably through their families. The family, despite the ravages of urban life and despite those who allege that it is in dissolution, remains one of the most sinewy of institutions. The family tie is regarded as sacred, even by those who would, or do, shirk the diffuse obligations it imposes. The Coronation, like any other great occasion which in some manner touches the sense of the sacred, brings vitality into family relationships. The Coronation, much like Christmas, was a time for drawing closer the bonds of the family, for re-asserting its solidarity and for re-emphasizing the values of the family—generosity, loyalty, love—which are *at the same time* the fundamental values necessary for the well being of the larger society. When listening to the radio, looking at the television, walking the streets to look at the decorations, the unit was the family, and neither mother nor father were far away when their children sat down for cakes and ice-cream at one of the thousands of street and village parties held that week. Prominent in the crowds were parents holding small children on their shoulders and carrying even

22 Durkheim, to whose understanding of the function of great communal rituals we have already referred, designated the side of life which includes action on behalf of or in accordance with the sacred moral values as "la vie serieuse." Durkheim might have been referring to the "Low crisis" when he wrote: "What social danger is there in touching a tabooed object, an impure animal or man, in letting the sacred fire die down, in eating certain meats, in failure to make the traditional sacrifice over the graves of parents, in not exactly pronouncing the ritual formula, in not celebrating certain holidays, etc.? We know, however, what a large place in the repressive law of many peoples ritual regimentation, etiquette, ceremonial, and religious practices play." . . . "An act is criminal when it offends strong and defined states of the collective conscience." *The Division of Labor in Society*, Macmillan, New York, 1933, pp. 72, 80.

23 *Lectures on the Religion of the Semites*, Black, London, 1927.

smaller ones in cradles. In all towns over the country, prams were pushed great distances to bring into contact with the symbols of the great event infants who could see or appreciate little. It was as if people recognized that the most elementary unit for entry into communion with the sacred was the family, not the individual.

The solidarity of the family is often heightened at the cost of solidarity in the wider community. Not so at the Coronation. On this occasion one family was knit together with another in one great national family through identification with the monarchy. A general warmth and congeniality permeated relations even with strangers. It was the same type of atmosphere, except that it was more pronounced, that one notices at Christmas time when, in busy streets and crowded trains, people are much more warmhearted, sympathetic and kindly than they are on more ordinary occasions. Affection generated by the great event overflowed from the family to outsiders, and back again into the family. One correspondent of the *Manchester Guardian*, reporting the Coronation procession, observed: "The Colonial contingents sweep by. The crowd loves them. The crowd now loves everybody." Antagonism emerged only against people who did not seem to be joining in the great event or treating with proper respect the important social values—by failing, for example, to decorate their buildings with proper splendour. A minor example of the increase in communal unity was the police report that, contrary to their expectations, the pickpockets, usually an inevitable concomitant of any large crowd, were entirely inactive during Coronation Day.

An occurrence in a new housing estate on the outskirts of London provides another instance. There the organizer of a street party had for many months been engaged in a feud with a neighbour so violent that they had at one time summoned each other to the local court. The origin of the feud—a minor quarrel about trespassing by children—was forgotten, and there were continuous outbursts of aggression which reached a climax in May when the neighbour poured hot water over the fence on to some flowers which had just been planted. The neighbour's children were not enrolled for the Coronation party until near the day itself. Then the neighbour came to the organizer and asked in a very humble way whether her own children might be included. They were

accepted, and the two who had not exchanged friendly words for so long began to greet each other in the streets as they passed. On the day itself, the organizer, out of her generosity for everyone, went so far as to ask the neighbour to come in and watch her television set. When the neighbour had been in the house for half an hour she asked whether her husband, who was waiting alone next door, could join them. He came in, and when the Service was over, the long standing feud was finally ended over a cup of tea.

Something like this kind of spirit had been manifested before—during the Blitz, the Fuel Crisis of 1947, the London smog of 1952, even during the Watson-Bailey stand in the Lord's Test or Lock's final overs at the Oval—and to some extent the broad reasons were probably the same. There was a vital common subject for people to talk about; whatever the individual's speciality, the same thought was uppermost in his mind as in everyone else's, and that made it easier to overcome the customary barriers. But not less important than the common subject is the common sentiment of the sacredness of communal life and institutions. In a great national communion like the Coronation, people became more aware of their dependence upon each other, and they sensed some connection between this and their relationship to the Queen. Thereby they became more sensitive to the values which bound them all together. Once there is a common vital object of attention, and a common sentiment about it, the feelings apt for the occasion spread by a kind of contagion. Kindness, met with on every side, reinforces itself, and a feeling of diffuse benevolence and sympathy spreads; under these circumstances the individual loses his egoistic boundaries and feels himself fused with his community.

The need to render gifts and sacrifices, so central in religious ceremonies, was also apparent in various forms. Many persons sent gifts directly to the Queen, and the vast scale of individual and collective gifts to persons known and unknown has been the occasion of much comment. Very many municipalities arranged "treats for old folks," local authorities gave gifts to school children and gift-giving within and between families was very widespread. The joint viewing of the Coronation Service and Procession on the television called forth many presentations. The universal decorations attest not merely to the sense of festivity but also to the disposition to offer valuable objects on such an occasion of entry into contact with the sacred values of society. Low's cartoon in the *Manchester Guardian* certainly portrayed one aspect of the truth when he saw the whole thing as "one gigantic binge." But it was not just a "good time" or an "opportunity for a good time," as some persons grudgingly said in justification for giving themselves up to the Coronation. There was an orgy, in a certain sense, but it was not just one of self-indulgence. Students of comparative religion have shown that an orgy following an act of communion with the sacred is far from uncommon. It aids the release of tension and reduces the anxiety which intense and immediate contact with the sacred engenders. Moreover, what appears to be simply an orgy of self-indulgence is often one of indulgence with goods which have been consecrated or which have some sacred, communally significant properties.

Surcease from drabness and routine, from the commonplaceness and triviality of daily preoccupation, is certainly one reason for the exaltation. There is surely wisdom in the remark of a philosophical Northern villager: "What people like is the sheer excess of it. We lead niggling enough lives these days. Something a bit lavish for a change is good for the soul." [24] But he did not go far enough. The British love of processions, of uniforms, and ceremonial is not just simple-minded gullibility—it is the love of proximity to greatness and power, to the charismatic person or institution which partakes of the sacred. The crowds who turned out to see the Queen, who waited in the rain in quiet happiness to see the Queen and her soldiers, were waiting to enter into contact with the mighty powers who are symbolically and to some extent, really responsible for the care and protection of their basic values and who on this day had been confirmed in these responsibilities. The crowds who clamoured for the Queen outside Buckingham Palace or who lined the streets on the days following Coronation Day when she made her tours of London were not just idle curiosity-seekers. They were, it is probably true, looking for a thrill but it was the thrill of contact with something great, with something which is connected with the sacred, in the way that authority which is charged with obligations to provide for and to protect

[24] *Manchester Guardian*, 3 June 1953.

the community in its fundamental constitution is always rooted in the sacred.

Let us now assume that this interpretation of the Coronation is at least plausible and perhaps correct. Why then, should it have taken place in this way in Great Britain at this time? Not all coronations, British or foreign, have drawn such deep sentiments of devoted participation. Whereas a century ago republicanism had numerous proponents in England, it is now a narrow and eccentric sect. Although the stability of the British monarchy became well established in the course of the nineteenth century, persons who have lived through or studied the four coronations of the present century seem to agree that the Coronation of Elizabeth II stirred greater depths in the people than any of its predecessors.

Over the past century, British society, despite distinctions of nationality and social status, has achieved a degree of moral unity equalled by no other large national state. The assimilation of the working class into the moral consensus of British society, though certainly far from complete, has gone further in Great Britain than anywhere else, and its transformation from one of the most unruly and violent into one of the most orderly and law-abiding is one of the great collective achievements of modern times. Whatever its origins, the past century has certainly witnessed a decline in the hostility of the British working and middle classes towards the symbols of the society as a whole and towards the authorities vested with those symbols and the rules they promulgate and administer.

It is true that the discredit into which the British "ruling class" fell as a result of the First World War, the General Strike and the Great Depression, diminished this moral unity. But consensus on fundamental values remained. The Second World War greatly contributed to the strengthening of attachment to society. The care which officers, junior and senior, took to avoid the waste of life, the provision for families at home, the steadiness of the emergence of victory, made for widespread solidarity and for absence of rancour even across gaps in that solidarity. The subsequent General Election was soberly fought. Following that, the Labour Government, by its concern for the under-privileged, by its success in avoiding the alienation of the middle and upper classes, and by the embodiment of certain prized British virtues in its leaders, brought this moral unity of British society to a remarkably high level. Moreover, many British intellectuals who in the 1920's and 1930's had been as alienated and cantankerous as any, returned to the national fold during the War.[25] Full employment and Government patronage on a large scale, as well as a growing repugnance for the Soviet Union and a now exacerbated but hitherto dormant national pride or conceit also played their part in this development. The central fact is that Britain came into the Coronation period with a degree of moral consensus such as few large societies have ever manifested.

The combination of constitutional monarchy and political democracy has itself played a part in the creation and maintenance of moral consensus, and it is this part which we shall now briefly consider. The late John Rickman and Ernest Jones have argued that the deep ambivalence towards authority and towards moral rules has promoted the widespread acceptance of the monarchy in Britain and in other countries where constitutional monarchy has become firmly established. Whereas the lands where personal or absolute monarchy prevailed were beset by revolution, countries of constitutional monarchy became politically stable and orderly, with a vigorously democratic political life. Hostility against authority was, it is said, displaced from royalty onto the leaders of the opposition party and even onto the leaders of the government party. Constitutional monarchies and their societies were fortified by drawing to themselves the loyalties and devotion of their members while avoiding the hostility which is always, in varying measure, engendered by submission to morality. When protected from the full blast of destructiveness by its very *powerlessness*, royalty is able to bask in the sunshine of an affection unadulterated by its opposite. The institution of the constitutional monarchy is supported by one of the mechanisms by which the mind defends itself from conflict, namely, by the segregation of mutually antagonistic sentiments, previously directed towards a single object, onto discrete and separate objects.[26]

It might therefore be said that the vigour of British political life is actually rendered possible by the existence of the constitutional monarchy. But the aggressiveness which is channelled into the political arena is in its turn ameliorated and checked by the sentiments of moral unity which the Crown helps to create. Here it is not only the symbolism of the Crown but also the painstaking probity of Kings George V and VI in dealing with the Labour Party, both when it was in opposition and when it formed the Government, which have helped to weld the Labour Party and its following firmly into the moral framework of the national life.

An effective segregation of love and hatred, when the love is directed towards a genuinely love-worthy object, reduces the intensity of the hatred as well. Just as the existence of a constitutional monarchy softens the acerbity in the relations between political parties, so it also lessens the antagonism of the governed towards the reigning government. Governments are well known to benefit whenever the virtues of Royalty are displayed.[27] It appears that the popularity of the Conservative Administration was at least temporarily increased by the Coronation, and at the time much newspaper speculation centred on the question whether Mr. Churchill would use the advantage to win a large majority for his Party at a General Election.

Thus we can see that the image of the monarch as the symbolic custodian of the awful powers and beneficent moral standards is one weighty element in moral consensus. But the monarch is not only symbol. Personal qualities are also significant. Hence it is appropriate at this point to refer to the role of the Royal Family in attaching the population to the monarchy. Walter Bagehot said: "A family on the throne is an interesting idea also. It brings down the pride of sovereignty to the level of petty life." [28] More and more has this become true since then. Where once to mention the family of the King, like Charles II or George IV, would have provoked laughter, it is now common form to talk about the Royal Family. The monarchy is idealised not so much for the virtue of the individual sovereign as for the virtue which he expresses in his family life.

---

[25] Cf. Arthur Koestler's penetrating article on Richard Hillary in *The Yogi and the Commissar*, Cape, London, 1945, pp. 46–67.
[26] Anna Freud, *The Ego and the Mechanisms of Defence*, Hogarth, London, 1937.

[27] The Secretary of the Labour Party once told one of the authors of this essay that he had always been confident that Labour would win the hotly contested Gravesend by-election in 1947 because the then Princess Elizabeth had been married a short time before.
[28] *Op. cit.*, p. 34.

Devotion to the Royal Family thus does mean in a very direct way devotion to one's own family, because the values embodied in each are the same. When allowance is also made for the force of displacement, if it is accepted that a person venerates the Sovereign partly because he is associated, in the seat of the emotions, with the wondrous parents of phantasy, and if it is accepted that there is also a sort of re-displacement at work, whereby the real parents and wives and children are thought of more highly because they receive some of the backwash of emotion from their Royal counterparts,[29] it is easy to see that the emotional change is a reciprocal one, and all the more powerful for that. Some aspects of this relationship become clear in the Christmas broadcast in which the Sovereign year after year talks about the Royal Family, the millions of British families, and the nation as a whole, as though they are one.[30] On sacred occasions, the whole society is felt to be one large family, and even the nations of the Commonwealth, represented at the Coronation by their prime ministers, queens, and ambassadors, are conceived of as a "family of nations."

In other ways the monarchy plays on more ordinary occasions the same kind of role as it does at a Coronation—only in a far less spectacular way. Thus British society combines free institutional pluralism with an underlying moral consensus. The universities, the municipalities, the professional bodies, the trades unions, the business corporations—all seek to enforce and protect their internal standards and to fend off external encroachment. Yet they coexist and cooperate in a remarkable atmosphere of mutual respect and relative freedom from acrimony. There are many reasons for this (which we hope to treat more elaborately and with adequate documentation in subsequent publications). In the present context we wish only to stress the unifying function of the monarchy and the orders of society which derive their legitimacy from connection with it. Every corporate body which has some connection with the sacred properties, the *charisma*, of the Crown thereby has infused into it a reminder of the moral obligations which extend beyond its own corporate boundaries. It is tied, so to speak, to the central value system of the society as a whole through its relationship with Royalty. Quite apart from the Armed Forces, with their multiplicity of royal connection, by fleet, regiment and squadron, a thousand institutions of all kinds are also recognized by the presence of a member of the Royal Family as Patron, President, or Visitor. Royalty presides over such diverse organizations as the Royal Society and the Royal Institute of British Architects, the Royal Academy and the Royal College of Veterinary Surgeons, the British Medical Association and the Institution of Civil Engineers, the Marylebone Cricket Club and the Lawn Tennis Association, the Red Cross and the National Playing Fields Association, St. Mary's Hospital and the Royal Yacht Squadron, the Royal Forestry Society and the University of London.[31] There are the Royal Charters, the patronage of charities, the inaugural ceremonies of hospitals and ships, gardens and factories. The monarchy is the one pervasive institution, standing above all others, which plays a part in a vital way comparable to the function of the medieval Church as seen by Professor Tawney—the function of integrating diverse elements into a whole by protecting and defining their autonomy.[32]

Even where the monarchy does not assume

---

[29] One of the authors, during an interview in a London slum district, asked a mother the age of her small son. "Just the same age as Prince Charles," she replied, looking at him with a smile of pride and love.

[30] We have mentioned above the significance of the reconciliation between the intellectuals and the monarchy as part of the general re-acceptance of society by the intellectuals. With respect to the family, the change is equally impressive. Who among the figures of the high intelligentsia would now accept the critical views on the family of Shaw, Wells, Havelock Ellis, Edward Carpenter, D. H. Lawrence or the Bertrand Russell of the 1920's? Who among well known British intellectuals today would be sympathetic with H. G. Wells' pronouncement?: "The family can remain only as a biological fact. Its economic and educational autonomy are inevitably doomed. The modern state is bound to be the ultimate guardian of all children, and it must assist, replace or subordinate the parents as supporter, guardian and educator; it must release all human beings from the obligation of mutual proprietorship and it must refuse absolutely to recognize or enforce any kind of sexual ownership." *Experiment in Auto-Biography*, Vol. II, Gollancz and Cresset Press, London, 1934, p. 481.

[31] The Queen is Visitor to all the Universities in England, Wales and Ulster except Oxford, Cambridge and Durham; and even in Scotland one University, Edinburgh, has the Duke as Chancellor. In the Dominions the Queen's representative often plays the same part— at McGill, for instance, the Governor General is Visitor and at Melbourne the Governor of Victoria.

[32] "Religion . . . the keystone which holds together the social edifice . . ." *Religion and the Rise of Capitalism*, John Murray, London, 1926, p. 279.

ceremonial offices of the type just referred to, the function of holding together the plurality of institutions is performed in some measure by the peerage and the system of honours. In all institutions and professions, all forms of individual achievement and merit are recognized and blessed by this system. The outstanding actors and poets, doctors and scientists, leaders of trade unions and trade associations, scholars and sportsmen, musicians and managers, the brave, the brilliant and the industrious, all receive confirmation of their conformity with the highest standards of society by an honour awarded by the Sovereign. The Sovereign acts as agent of the value system, and the moral values of the society are reinforced in the individuals honoured.

To sum up: A society is held together by its internal agreement about the sacredness of certain fundamental moral standards. In an inchoate, dimly perceived, and seldom explicit manner, the central authority of an orderly society, whether it be secular or ecclesiastical, is acknowledged to be the avenue of communication with the realm of the sacred values. Within its society, popular constitutional monarchy enjoys almost universal recognition in this capacity, and it is therefore enabled to heighten the moral and civic sensibility of the society and to permeate it with symbols of those values to which the sensitivity responds. Intermittent rituals bring the society or varying sectors of it repeatedly into contact with this vessel of the sacred values. The Coronation provided at one time and for practically the entire society such an intensive contact with the sacred that we believe we are justified in interpreting it as we have done in this essay, as a great act of national communion.

THE DIFFERENTIATION OF RELIGIOUS ORGANIZATIONS

Religion in an urban industrial society is certainly different from religion in a nonliterate community. So are the family and the economy. This difference does not imply that secular commitments will displace supernatural religion completely. However, the relationship between religious behavior and other activities is looser in industrial societies than in less differentiated societies. Whereas in a nonliterate community a religious dimension permeates every aspect of life from agriculture to warfare, in an industrial society religion tends to be segregated from economic, political, educational, and other secular activities and embodied in a special-purpose organization, the church. Furthermore, the local church is usually affiliated with a larger organization having national and sometimes international interests.

Religious organizations, despite otherworldly values, must come to terms with the principles governing large-scale organizations; for instance, the Roman Catholic Church cannot avoid bureaucracy. Furthermore, an organized religion, like other special-purpose organizations, must compete for societal resources and support. In American society, this means going into the market and buying land for a church, paying a contractor to put up a structure, and hiring a minister to lead the congregation. Thus, religious organizations cannot be indifferent to money because money is a means for realizing religious as well as secular goals. The dilemma of religion in industrial societies is that organizational requirements have a logic of their own and may necessitate compromises with traditional values. Some evangelical sects condemn drinking, smoking, dancing, and gambling despite the likelihood that this ascetic attitude will alienate potential support. Instead of having full-time, salaried ministers, who attended divinity school in order to achieve professional status, they may rely on unpaid, part-time "ministers" with meager religious education and much enthusiasm. On the other hand, established denominations are more likely to sponsor dances for young people and bingo for their elders, and to counsel long-winded ministers that "no souls are saved after 15 minutes." The compromise which a particular denomination strikes between traditional values and the necessities of gaining support from a secular society helps explain the differences in the values of adherents of various religious groups.

Sociologists have long been interested in empirical studies showing the social consequences of differentiated religious organizations with a variety of value commitments. For instance, Robert Merton showed that the Puritan contribution to English scientific development in the seventeenth and eighteenth centuries was disproportionately great. Professor Merton's explanation of the disproportion is that the Puritan value complex demanded ". . . the systematic, rational, and empirical study of Nature for the glorification of God in His works and for the control of the corrupt world." [33] Merton, like Max Weber before him, showed that Karl Marx was mistaken in his belief that organized religion necessarily supported the status quo. Weber's studies in the sociology of religion are classics.[34] He demonstrated through comparative analysis of Europe, China, India, and ancient Judea that the Protestant attitude toward economic activities made Western Europe more receptive to capitalism than otherwise comparable societies. Weber did not maintain that the growth of Protestantism in Western Europe *caused* capitalism to develop, but he showed that certain religious values were a necessary ingredient. He showed further that early entrepreneurs in Western Europe and the United States were likely to be members of certain Protestant sects. A recent study in the Weber tradition sought to discover whether membership in Protestant denominations continues to differentiate the population in a mature industrial society. Do economically successful Americans come disproportionately from certain denominations?

[33] Robert K. Merton, "Puritanism, Pietism and Science," in *Social Theory and Social Structure*, rev. ed., Glencoe, Ill.: Free Press, 1957, pp. 574–606.
[34] Max Weber, *The Protestant Ethic and the Spirit of Capitalism*, New York: Scribner's, 1930; Max Weber, *The Religion of China: Confucianism and Taoism*, Glencoe, Ill.: Free Press, 1951; Max Weber, *Ancient Judaism*, Glencoe, Ill.: Free Press, 1952; Max Weber, *The Religion of India: The Sociology of Hinduism and Buddhism*, Glencoe, Ill.: Free Press, 1958.

Relationship between Denominational Preference and Secular Success

Reprinted by permission. From Albert J. Mayer and Harry Sharp, "Religious Preference and Worldly Success," *American Sociological Review*, Vol. 27, April 1962, pp. 218–227.

An inquiry into the meaning of religion to different denomination groups and the strength of religious expression, valuable as this would be, is beyond the scope of the present paper. Rather, we are here accepting only the denominational label with which an individual associates himself, and investigating the hypothesis that differing religious preferences are associated with varying degrees of worldly success.

This hypothesis is founded on the assumption of a basic distinction in the life orientations which are held by Catholics as compared with Protestants. The powerfully reinforced and traditional Roman Catholic Church tends to orient its members toward the hereafter; successful performance in the market place and the acquisition of the symbols of economic achievement are of relatively little importance as an indication of the Catholic's status after death. On the other hand, adherents of Protestantism are assumed to be highly concerned with worldly success and the attainment of material possession, status, and the prestige that is associated with upward social mobility. These things often are viewed as indications that salvation is assured, or at least is more probable.

To the degree that religious orientations toward life are reflected in behavior, this theory would lead us to expect Protestants to excel Catholics in the race for worldly success. Protestantism in contemporary America, however, is hardly a homogeneous religious faith. We expect variations among the major Protestant denominations both with respect to adherence to the Protestant ethic and to economic achievement. Thus, this research does not group all Protestants under a common rubric, but considers the major denominations separately.

Members of the Jewish faith and adherents of the Eastern Orthodox Church do not fit into the theory as summarized above. According to Sombart, the Jews played a prominent supportive role in the rise of capitalism.[35] On this basis, we would hypothesize that the Jewish group should bear a greater resemblance to Protestants rather than to Catholics, were all religious groups measured by a scale of economic achievement. The comparative standing on an achievement scale of the adherents of Eastern Orthodoxy was not predicted at the start of the research.

Religion does not exist as an independent attribute of the individual, but is closely bound to important cultural variables such as urbanism, ethnicity, nativity, and experience in a specific community. Thus, in an investigation of the type proposed here, the question must be answered: Is it the religion itself, operating through a network of values stemming from one's religious faith, that produces varying degrees of economic success? Or are other factors, correlated with but not "caused by" a given religious preference, instrumental in the degree of success achieved by a given religious group?

THE DATA

The data employed in this research were collected by the University of Michigan's Detroit Area Study. Each year since 1952 the Detroit Area Study has conducted a survey of the metropolitan Detroit community. The present discussion focuses on data obtained from 1954 through 1959. The objectives of these surveys required a sample of the adult population of greater Detroit that would be representative, within known confidence limits, of all non-institutionalized adults in the community.

For this research, strict probability samples were constructed which allowed the assignment of specific addresses at which interviews were to be obtained. No substitutions of any kind were permitted. Certain information was obtained about every adult who lived in the sampled dwelling units. Although the specific topics covered by each annual survey varied, demographic and socio-economic data were collected in a uniform manner. In this paper, the six surveys taken between 1954 and 1959 were combined and analyzed as though they constituted a single operation. By doing so, we are able to work with a maximum N of over 9,000 adults.

Adults in the sample were classified by reli-

gious preference on the basis of their answers to these questions:

"Do you have a religious preference?"

(If Yes) "Are you Protestant, Catholic, Jewish, or something else?"

(If Protestant) "What specific denomination is that?"

For purposes of analysis, the total sample was grouped into twelve denominational categories: Catholic, Jewish, Eastern Orthodox, Episcopalian, Lutheran, Calvinist,[36] Methodist, Baptist, Small Neo-Fundamentalist Protestant Sects,[37] Non-Denominational Protestant, Semi-Christian Churches,[38] and No Religious Preference.

ANALYSIS PROCEDURE

From one perspective, life in a modern community may be viewed as a hotly contested foot race in which families vie with one another in the hope of material reward. The rewards are rather well defined in western society; they include such achievements as economic success, collection of worldly assets, and the status to be derived from the attainment of these culturally approved goals.

Through the use of a number of indices, all of which repeatedly have been shown to be highly interconnected, we have measured the relative success of the major religious denominations in this race. At the same time, we have attempted to account for the fact that not all denominations are equally favored with background factors that are helpful in the winning of economic success in a metropolitan community.

Each of the variables measured by the indices used here can be categorized as *achieved* or *ascribed*, following the conceptualization developed by Linton.[39] The relative position of a given religious group on an *achieved* variable index may be regarded as the result of the efforts of the individuals comprising that group. Correspondingly, the position of a given group on the *ascribed* vari-

---

[35] Werner Sombart, *The Jews and Modern Capitalism*, London: Unwin, 1913.

[36] Included in this classification are Presbyterians, Congregationalists, Evangelical and Reformed, and Dutch Reformed.

[37] Jehovah's Witnesses, United Missionary, Pentecostal Churches.

[38] This category includes such groups as the Latter Day Saints, the Christian Scientists, and the Spiritualists. The classification, of course, represents more of a residual grouping than a meaningful distinction.

[39] Ralph Linton, *The Study of Man*, New York: Appleton-Century, 1936, Chap. 8.

able index is here regarded as an "accident of birth"; ascribed status is given to the individual when he is born or while he is still a dependent minor.

Continuing with the analogy to a foot race, a system of "handicapping" has been devised which at least partially removes the effect of ascribed factors on worldly success. The handicapping consists of weighting the ascribed variables in such a way that no group has an unfair advantage at the start of the contest. Thus, the relationship of religion to achievement can be more clearly seen.

ASCRIBED FACTORS

Ascribed background factors were analyzed through the use of three continua: rural-urban background, foreign-native background, and extent of experience in metropolitan Detroit. Each major religious group in the Detroit area was ranked with respect to these factors. In this ranking, one polar extreme would be a religious group all of whose members had no rural experience, were born in this country of fathers who were also native-born, and had spent their entire adult lives in greater Detroit. The advantages for this hypothetical group are maximal since its members would have had the greatest opportunity to acquire property, education, and maximum familiarity with the cultural setting in which they now live. The opposite extreme would consist of a group all of whose members had a rural background, are of foreign birth, and have had a relatively short residence in greater Detroit. For this hypothetical denomination, familiarity with the ways and customs of a modern metropolis, and hence opportunities for success, would be at a minimum; their ascribed advantage would therefore be minimal.

Each of these ascribed background factors was further redefined. Rural-urban experience was measured in three ways: (1) percentage of each group having no farm experience (the higher the proportion without farm experience, the greater the presumed familiarity with an urban way of life); (2) percentage of each group born in cities of 50,000 or more persons; and (3) percentage of each group born outside the rural South. An additional handicap was given for rural southern United States birth under the assumption that cultural differences between the North and the South constitute a substantial disadvantage for those residents of metropolitan Detroit who were born in the southern United States.

Three indices, each with a somewhat different connotation, were used in measuring the effect of foreign background: (1) percentage of each group whose fathers were born in the United States; (2) percentage of each group whose fathers were of Northwestern European derivation (this measure attempts to "correct" for ethnically based differences in social status by assigning a higher handicap to persons of non-Northwest European stock); and (3) percentage of the members of each group who themselves are native-born Americans or were born in Canada.

It was also assumed that adults who have spent all or a major share of their lives in greater Detroit have an economic advantage over more recent arrivals in the community. Two indices were built for this ascribed factor: (1) the proportion of a given group's adherents who are native Detroiters; and (2) the percentage of each group's members who came to the Detroit area before the age of fifteen. Together, these indices measure specific experience in this particular cultural environment.

Table 58 presents the data for the ascribed factors. White and Negro Detroiters are considered separately in this table; given the social significance of race in American society, it would be completely unrealistic to do otherwise.

Although the figures in Table 58 reveal some striking relationships, full comprehension of these data is difficult without further summarizing. Therefore, in Table 59 each index of the three ascribed factors was analyzed in terms of quartiles. Of the twelve religious preferences in the white population, the three ranking highest on each ascribed characteristic were given the weight of four, the next three highest were given the weight of three, and so forth. The four religious categories in the Negro population were handled in a comparable manner on the relevant variables, with the obvious exception that only one preference was in each quartile of the index.

For whites, the foreign and rural background categories each consisted of three indices. The third factor (Specific Detroit Background) consisted of two indices. Specific Detroit Background was given a weight equivalent to each of the first two factors by increasing it 50 per cent. As a result, each of the three ascribed variables had a possible maximum weight of twelve (4 × 3, or

6 × 2). The grand total maximum weight for the ascribed factors in the white population would therefore be 12 × 3, or thirty-six.

For Negro Detroiters, quartile rankings on Specific Detroit Background were also increased by 50 per cent. Since foreign background was not a variable for Negroes, the grand total weight for this population group was 12 × 2, or twenty-four.

In the white population, Lutherans (with a value of 28.8) are in the most advantageous position with respect to the ascribed factors, followed by a cluster of three groups: Jews (27.0), Episcopalians (26.7), and Calvinists (26.5). Detroiters of the Eastern Orthodox faith possess the least advantage (12.3) with the members of the small sects (16.0) and the Baptists (18.0) also at a comparative disadvantage.

The rankings on the ascribed variables are generally in accord with preconception. Detroit area Lutherans, Jews, Episcopalians, and Calvin-

ists are highly urban, and, as a group, have a very large proportion of native-born Detroiters. The Jewish advantage is tempered, however, by the greater proportion of foreign-born among Jews as compared to other religious preferences. The Eastern Orthodox are economically handicapped, not only because a majority of these persons are foreign-born, but also because of their limited urban background before coming to Detroit and the comparatively late age at which they arrived in this community. The Baptists, although largely of native birth, are among the lowest of the religious groups in urban background and specific Detroit experience.

Among Negro Detroiters, the Baptist faith is by far the most common denomination. Negro Baptists also are in the least advantageous position with respect to the possession of those ascribed characteristics which, we have assumed, lead most readily to economic achievement. Negro Catho-

TABLE 58

Ascribed Factors, by Religious Group and Race

| | Ascribed Factors | | | | | | | | |
| | Rural Background | | | Foreign Background | | | Specific Detroit Background | | |
Religious Group and Race	% with No Farm Background	% Born in Cities of 50,000+	% Not Born in Rural South	% with Native Born Fathers	% with Fathers of N-W European Stock	% Born in U.S. or Canada	% Born in Detroit Area	% in Detroit before Age 15	Number of Cases [a]
White									
Catholic	77	54	99	36	46	81	45	68	3,307
Episcopalian	84	44	100	46	95	82	32	42	289
Lutheran	74	53	99	52	84	90	42	55	778
Calvinist	75	46	98	59	90	90	33	46	723
Methodist	64	34	92	69	92	95	24	36	750
Baptist	44	24	72	80	96	97	17	29	727
Small sects	49	26	85	68	87	93	21	33	232
No denomination	60	35	70	68	91	92	12	42	194
Semi-Christian	64	50	92	63	89	96	26	39	96
Jewish	90	63	100	4	10	70	42	58	234
Eastern Orthodox	61	33	99	3	8	42	19	33	169
No preference	74	44	94	49	64	85	39	54	239
Negro									
Catholic	76	50	89	..	..	..	23	41	75
Methodist	62	39	73	..	..	..	12	26	316
Baptist	43	23	68	..	..	..	7	20	938
Other	60	36	72	..	..	..	18	32	164

[a] The N's given here are applicable to all following tables.

lics (a minority within a minority, to be sure) are a comparatively urban group and therefore rank at the top of each of the indices of ascribed factors.

In following the above procedure, we obviously have assumed that one unit of urban experience, one unit of specific Detroit experience, and one unit of foreign birth can be considered as equivalent. This assumption was necessary as a result of summing these different measures to produce a unique index value. Given the present level of knowledge, the degree to which this assumption is in error cannot be evaluated. We offer this procedure as an admittedly rough approximation to "reality," and hope that further research in this area will result in progressively more accurate refinements.

ACHIEVED FACTORS

Five indices were used in measuring the social and economic achievements of the major religious groups in greater Detroit: (1) relative ranking on family income, given as the percentage of each group earning $2,000 or more *above* the median Detroit area family income for a given year; (2) percentage of self-employed in each group; (3) percentage of the members of each group who are in high status white-collar occupations (professionals, managers, proprietors, or officials); (4) median school year completed; and (5) percentage of persons of each religious preference who are members of three or more formal social groups.[40]

TABLE 59

Quartile Ranking and Total Weights of Ascribed Factors, by Religious Group and Race

| | Quartile Ranking on Ascribed Factors | | | | | | | | |
| | Rural Background | | | Foreign Background | | | Specific Detroit Background [a] | | |
Religious Group and Race	% with No Farm Background	% Born in Cities of 50,000+	% Not Born in Rural South	% with Native-Born Fathers	% with Fathers of N-W European Stock	% Born in U.S. or Canada	% Born in Detroit Area	% in Detroit before Age 15	Grand Total All Ascribed Factors
White									
Catholic	4	4	3.3	1	1	1	6	6	26.3
Episcopalian	4	2.5	4	4	2	2	4.5	3.8	26.7
Lutheran	3	4	3.3	2	2	2.5	6	6	28.8
Calvinist	3	3	3	3	3	2.5	4.5	4.5	26.5
Methodist	2	2	2	4	4	4	3	3	24.0
Baptist	1	1	1	4	4	4	1.5	1.5	18.0
Small sects	1	1	1	2	3.5	3	3	1.5	16.0
No denomination	1	2	1	3	3.5	3	1.5	3.7	18.7
Semi-Christian	2	3	2	3	3	4	3	3	23.0
Jewish	4	4	4	1	1	1	6	6	27.0
Eastern Orthodox	2	1	3.3	1	1	1	1.5	1.5	12.3
No preference	3	2.5	2	2	2	2	4.5	4.5	22.5
Negro									
Catholic	4	4	4	..	..	..	6	6	24.0
Methodist	3	3	3	..	..	..	3	3	15.0
Baptist	1	1	1	..	..	..	1.5	1.5	6.0
Other	2	2	2	..	..	..	4.5	4.5	15.0

[a] Quartile weights for Specific Detroit Background inflated by 50 per cent to equalize weights between background factors.

[40] The relationship of formal group membership to economic success has been repeatedly demonstrated. For example, see Morris Axelrod, "Urban Structure and Social Participation," *American Sociological Review*, Vol. 21, February 1956, pp. 13–18.

These five indices, then, attempt to measure worldly success. They are shown in Table 60.

The quartile grouping described above for the ascribed factors was applied in a comparable manner to the achieved factors. For both whites and Negroes, the total maximum weight that any religious group might have on the achieved factors would be twenty (4×5). The results of these operations may be seen in Table 61.

With respect to the white population, Jews (with a rating of 20.0) show the greatest achievement as we have measured it. They are followed by Episcopalians (17.7), Calvinists (16.7) and the Semi-Christian group (16.0). The other end of the scale represents low achievement. Here are found Baptists (5.0), and Catholics and small Protestant sects (both with a rating of 8.0).

Among Negroes, the greatest achievement is shown by adults who are categorized as "Other" in Table 61. They score 17.5 on our measure. Negro Methodists rank second on achievement (13.5), and are followed closely by Negro Catho-

lics (12.0). Negro Baptists are a rather distant fourth with a rating of 7.0.

In general, the achievement rankings shown here are consistent with the findings of previous research, both on a national basis and for individual communities. Episcopalians, Calvinists, and Unitarians are usually ranked high on economic status. Also, Jews generally are a relatively high economic status group in metropolitan centers other than New York City. Moreover, the very low status of Baptists and small Protestant sects is not surprising, although the relatively low ranking of Detroit area Catholics is not consistently reported by other studies.

RELATIONSHIP OF ASCRIBED TO ACHIEVED FACTORS

To evaluate the contribution of ascribed background factors to variations in socio-economic status, the ascription handicap was subtracted from a *weighted* achievement rating for each religious group. Weighting of the achievement meas-

TABLE 60
Achieved Factors, by Religious Group and Race

Religious Group and Race	Achieved Factors				
	% $2,000 and Above Median Income	% Self-employed	% in High Status Occupations	Median School Year Completed	% in Three or More Formal Groups
White					
Catholic	27	7	19	10.0	14
Episcopalian	35	9	42	12.5	42
Lutheran	30	6	28	12.2	17
Calvinist	35	11	37	12.5	21
Methodist	32	8	27	12.3	23
Baptist	21	6	15	9.8	8
Small sects	16	11	17	9.5	9
No denomination	29	11	26	12.0	17
Semi-Christian	24	15	39	12.4	19
Jewish	42	41	62	12.5	45
Eastern Orthodox	35	15	13	9.3	8
No preference	23	9	28	10.0	7
Negro					
Catholic	6	4	7	10.0	8
Methodist	7	5	6	9.8	12
Baptist	8	3	3	9.1	7
Other	12	10	15	9.8	10

ure was necessary to convert this variable to the same scale as the ascribed rating. The total achievement rating for each white denomination was weighted by nine-fifths; for Negro religious groups, the weight was six-fifths. It should be noted that this process in no way changes the relative weights, but simply facilitates comparison between achieved and ascribed factors. The results of this procedure are shown in Table 62.

Returning once more to the analogy of a foot race, we are now in a position to judge the results of this contest. To review, in investigating the relationships between religious preference and worldly success in metropolitan Detroit, we endeavored to place all denominations on an "equal footing" with respect to those background factors which are conducive to high economic achievement in an urban environment. Actual achievement was then measured against the potential for this performance. The final ranking of the religious groups, taking the starting handicaps into consideration, is as follows:

White: Jewish
       Eastern Orthodox
       Semi-Christian
       Episcopalian
       Calvinist
       Protestant, no denomination
       Methodist
       Small sects
       No preference, Lutheran (tie)
       Baptist
       Catholic
Negro: Other than the below
       Baptist
       Methodist
       Catholic

For many religious groups, the handicapping produced a final ranking which was comparable to that based on achievement alone. However, several interesting exceptions may be seen. The most significant change in rank occurred in the Eastern Orthodox group which, when its handicap was applied, jumped high on the scale. The Baptists also rose one notch on the scale, thereby

TABLE 61

Quartile Ranking and Total Weights of Achieved Factors, by Religious Group and Race

Religious Group and Race	Quartile Ranking on Achieved Factors					
	% $2,000 and above Median Income	% Self-employed	% in High Status Occupations	Median School Year Completed	% in Three or More Formal Groups	Grand Total All Achieved Factors
White						
Catholic	2	1	1	2	2	8.0
Episcopalian	3.7	2	4	4	4	17.7
Lutheran	3	1	3	3	2.5	12.5
Calvinist	3.7	3	3	4	3	16.7
Methodist	3	2	2	3	4	14.0
Baptist	1	1	1	1	1	5.0
Small sects	1	3	1	1	2	8.0
No denomination	2	3	2	2	2.5	11.5
Semi-Christian	2	4	4	3	3	16.0
Jewish	4	4	4	4	4	20.0
Eastern Orthodox	3.7	4	2	1	1	11.7
No preference	1	2	3	2	1	9.0
Negro						
Catholic	1	2	3	4	2	12.0
Methodist	2	3	2	2.5	4	13.5
Baptist	3	1	1	1	1	7.0
Other	4	4	4	2.5	3	17.5

surpassing Catholics among both whites and Negroes.

A striking picture emerges from these data. Members of the Jewish, Greek Orthodox, and Semi-Christian faiths appear to have made the greatest achievements, given the system followed here. Behind these three groups are the several major Protestant denominations, with Baptists ranking below those white Detroiters who have no religious preference. For both whites and Negroes, the Catholics have had the least economic success as measured by our index.

Although these indices are crude and the resultant quantification somewhat specious, the major findings are not easily dismissed. We believe that no amount of statistical manipulation, even if more precise or elegant than that employed here, would appreciably change the broad outline of these rankings. To summarize our findings as

TABLE 62

Total Inflated Weights of Achieved Factors Less Total Weights of Ascribed Factors, by Religious Group and Race

| Religious Group and Race | Total of Factors | | |
	Achieved Factors [a]	Ascribed Factors	Achieved Less Ascribed
White			
Catholic	14.4	26.3	−11.9
Episcopalian	31.9	26.7	+ 5.2
Lutheran	22.5	28.8	− 6.3
Calvinist	30.0	26.5	+ 3.5
Methodist	25.2	24.0	+ 1.2
Baptist	9.0	18.0	− 9.0
Small sects	14.4	16.0	− 1.6
No denomination	20.7	18.7	+ 2.0
Semi-Christian	28.8	23.0	+ 5.8
Jewish	36.0	27.0	+ 9.0
Eastern Orthodox	21.0	12.3	+ 8.7
No preference	16.2	22.5	− 6.3
Negro			
Catholic	14.4	24.0	− 9.6
Methodist	16.2	15.0	+ 1.2
Baptist	8.4	6.0	+ 2.4
Other	21.0	15.0	+ 6.0

[a] Totals inflated by 1.8 for whites and by 1.2 for Negroes to equalize weights between ascribed and achieved factors.

they apply to white residents of greater Detroit: (1) Jews, followed closely by Episcopalians and Calvinists, have achieved the greatest worldly success. In the middle range are the remaining Protestant groups, with Baptists falling toward the end of the economic scale. Catholics have achieved the least. (2) If an ascription "handicap" is considered, the Eastern Orthodox group, closely followed by adherents of the Semi-Christian faiths, join the Jewish group at the top of the scale. An additional conclusion is that Catholicism is related to economic achievement among Negroes much as it is among whites.

INTERPRETATION

Previous research, in general, has failed to reach agreement as to the nature of the relationship between religious preference and economic achievement. Several investigations have discovered a comparative absence of Catholics among the economic and social élite of America. Low Catholic achievement motivation has also been pointed out. On the other hand, a number of researchers have found little evidence for the proposition that the Protestant ethic hypothesis is descriptive of the relationship between religious preference and worldly success in contemporary urban society.

The results of the present study may be interpreted as supporting the Weberian approach in part, while presenting some important modifications. Religious preferences appear to have meaningful consequences for economic success, quite apart from other background factors associated with religion. It would seem, therefore, that religion continues to play an essential role in controlling, limiting, and guiding economic behavior. As Weber proposed, most Protestant denominations far exceed the Catholics in economic standing. The various Protestant denominations are ranked in a general order which further supports the Weberian thesis. As Sombart proposed, moreover, the Jews seem to be the most successful and worldly oriented. Thus, where it has been hypothesized that a general ordering would appear, it has appeared.

Not all religious preferences, however, fall into a neat, predictable rank order. This finding leads to a further interpretation in which religion per se is of lesser importance in guiding economic achievement in contemporary society than are other cultural factors associated with the religion.

As part of their cultural heritage, members of particular religious groups may have certain occupational roles. The Eastern Orthodox in Detroit, for example, are primarily Syrians, Lebanese, and Greeks—traditionally traders, shopkeepers, merchants, and entrepreneurs. Granting that originally their religion strengthened, abetted, and possibly even forced them into these pursuits, their total cultural environment presently is consistent with entry into these occupations.

Much the same case can be made for Jews. Although three or four generations ago the Jewish religious link to worldly success was probably direct, the contemporary teachings of this religion may not be nearly as crucial as are other cultural characteristics which foster success and achievement patterns. Thus, the presence of intervening variables may alter the original linkage between religion and worldly success.

Religious values seem to affect sexual as well as economic behavior. Studies have demonstrated that Catholics have larger families, on the average, than Protestants even when economic factors are equated.[41] This is understandable in view of the Catholic doctrine that mechanical techniques of contraception are equivalent to infanticide. Nevertheless, the obedience of Catholics to official Church values is noteworthy considering that this involves *private* behavior where social control is difficult. The relationships found between religious affiliations and social behavior suggest that being a member of one denomination instead of another makes a real difference in the operative values of one's life.[42] Religion is not simply a matter of nomenclature. In America, as Will Herberg points out, Protestantism, Catholicism, and Judaism have accommodated to secular values to a considerable (and perhaps a comparable) extent.[43] But this does not mean that traditional religious values have evaporated. What happened in the United States is that many religious denominations struck parallel compromises with secular society; this prevented a sharp cleavage between anticlerical and clerical communities, as occurred in some European countries.[44]

SOME CONSEQUENCES OF THE DIFFERENTIATION OF RELIGIOUS ORGANIZATIONS

The problems of organized religion are different in the United States from what they are in some other industrial societies. In the United States, nearly everyone claims a religious affiliation; an outspoken atheist could probably not be elected to public office. But ignorant friends may be more dangerous to religion than prejudiced enemies. In a society where everyone is "for" religion, communicating the content of particular religions to the young is difficult. And this problem is complicated by denominational pluralism: by the tacit agreement among religious factions of one another's legitimacy. Given such religious diversity, tolerance may be the only workable arrangement, but, as G. K. Chesterton remarked, tolerance is the easy virtue of people who do not believe in anything.

The Dilemma of Religious Education in a Pluralistic Society

Reprinted by permission. From William Lee Miller, "The Fight over America's Fourth 'R'," *The Reporter*, Vol. 14, March 22, 1956, pp. 20–26.

The current religious revival is full of patriotism, and nowhere more urgently than in the effort to teach the "fourth R"—religion—in the public schools.

"These troubled times," declared the New York Board of Regents in 1954, ". . . call for the teaching of 'Piety and Virtue' in the schools, and of that dependence upon Almighty God so clearly recognized in the Declaration of Inde-

41 William Peterson, *Population*, New York: Macmillan, 1961, pp. 222–226.

42 Evon Z. Vogt and Thomas F. O'Dea, "A Comparative Study of the Role of Values in Social Action in Two Southwestern Communities," *American Sociological Review*, Vol. 18, December 1953, pp. 645–654.

43 Will Herberg, *Protestant, Catholic, Jew*, Garden City, N.Y.: Doubleday, 1955.

44 Talcott Parsons, "Some Comments on the Pattern of Religious Organization in the United States," in *Structure and Process in Modern Societies*, Glencoe, Ill.: Free Press, 1960, pp. 295–321.

pendence, the Constitution of the United States, the Constitution of the State of New York, and in the pronouncements of the great leaders of our country." Just where the Federal Constitution so clearly recognizes dependence on Almighty God the Regents did not say, but in these troubled times that may not be the kind of question one should ask.

The Florida State Superintendent of Public Instruction, Thomas D. Bailey, last fall proposed a statewide plan to give religious training in the public schools, arguing that it is "impossible to teach democracy in a Godless atmosphere." At about the same time, in the godly atmosphere of Jersey City, former Mayor John V. Kenny proposed that lessons in Protestantism, Judaism, and Roman Catholicism be given to the appropriate children in the city's public schools. He said such a move would help to fight juvenile delinquency.

Back in 1951, W. Kingsland Macy, then one of the thirteen members of the New York Board of Regents, which has supervision over the public schools in the state, had a similar idea: He urged that successful completion of a course in religion be made a prerequisite for graduation. The reception given General MacArthur on his return showed that the nation wanted godliness, Mr. Macy said, and educators should "shift their emphasis from erudition to the teaching of true values . . ."

THE "GUIDING STATEMENT"

The most significant expression of this desire for piety and virtue in the schools is the development of a form of literature known as the "guiding statement" for teachers. The one for the Los Angeles schools, with a genial Southern Californian syncretism, starts off with versions of the Golden Rule from seven different religions, including Taoism, Sikhism, and Hinduism. The San Diego statement lists "the existence of God" as the basic assumption underlying "loyalty to American Ideals." A statement called "the Basic Structure for the Study of the Fundamental Principles of Civic Ethics," proposed in 1954 for special classes at the junior-high-school level in the Indianapolis public schools, even provides an interfaith, all-American public-school definition of God.

These attempts are the most recent phase of the long, perplexing struggle over religion, morality, and public education. Heretofore, the main focus of controversy has been the intricate problem of "released time" (letting pupils be taught religion by their own religious groups on school time).

The "released time" debate concerned the way schools might cooperate in the churches' teaching of their own children; the present debate concerns the way religion and morality might be taught in civics and history classes—and maybe even in home economics and girls' gym—of the public school itself. The biggest furor on the issue has been in New York City and State.

THE GREAT ELECTRICIAN

Last June, after a series of very devotional recommendations by the State Board of Regents, the New York City superintendents issued their proposed "guiding statement." This document explained how and why teachers should inculcate the ubiquitous "moral and spiritual values." That much was all right. But along with unexceptionable affirmations about the worth of the individual were others: ". . . the public schools must reinforce the program of the home and church in strengthening belief in God," and ". . . identify God as the ultimate source of natural and moral law." These caused an uproar.

The statement went on to suggest how teachers in the various disciplines could get these points across to students, and it found opportunities all over the place. In science and mathematics, for example, ". . . consideration of the vastness and the splendor of the heavens, the marvels of the human body and mind, the beauty of nature, the mystery of photosynthesis, the mathematical structure of the universe, . . . cannot do other than lead to humbleness before God's handiwork. . . ." In industrial arts, "the composition of metals, the grain and the beauty of woods, the ways of electricity and the characteristic properties of the materials used, invariably give rise to speculation about the planning and the orderliness of the natural world and the marvelous working of a Supreme Power."

The response of the "three faiths" to this guiding statement must have come as something of a jolt to those who want a common American religious front. The Roman Catholic Archdiocese promptly supported the statement: the Protestant Council of the City of New York, representing a constituency that ranged from strong supporters to strong opponents, debated awhile and finally made some comments that were partly appreciative but mostly critical: the New York Board of Rabbis solidly opposed it, issued a negative analysis of it, and organized concerted preaching against it in the city's temples and synagogues.

In New York City the number of Catholics and Jews is so large (fifty-two and twenty-five per cent of the population, respectively) that the nature of the major religious groups is made inescapably apparent. It is possible to see very clearly that each of the "three faiths" is really a quite different phenomenon from the others. They are not, as tolerance literature sometimes suggests, just three indiscriminable outlets selling three slightly different brands of the one basic product, religion. They differ, to continue this unfortunate metaphor, not only in brand names but also in marketing and packaging, and even in the contents of the packages.

Many Christians, accustomed to a more or less doctrinal religion and to a more or less dominant status in society, had a hard time understanding the Jewish opposition to the New York guiding statement—particularly because the opposition was unanimous. Orthodox, Conservative, and Reform Jews stood side by side, and rabbis of quite widely differing positions in other matters joined together, five hundred strong, to preach against the statement throughout the city. "And they say *we* are monolithic!" remarked a bemused Catholic priest.

The universal and doctrinal character of Christianity, especially Catholicism, bumped squarely against the communal and ritualistic character of Judaism. A Catholic, with his commitment to a fully worked-out, intellectually formulated truth for all men, may try to get as much of that truth as possible taught wherever he can —as for example to every child in the schools: "Because we are convinced that moral and spiritual values have their ultimate source in God and are meaningless without God," said the Archdiocesan statement, "we are anxious to see God given due recognition in our public schools." But for a Jew, the formulations of theology do not have the same authority, and religious words are not so easily separated from the context of the ritual and history of the group. The Jew's faith centers instead in a whole fabric of historic observances of a particular law by a particular community. "We deny," said the rabbis, "that a non-Jewish teacher, however deeply devoted he may be to his own faith, can conscientiously and properly teach Jewish children the fundamentals of their faith . . ."

The New York controversy made plain another important fact, overlooked in much interfaithism: There is a big difference between being in the majority and in the minority. It is easier to settle for a religious stew if the meat of one's own faith determines the dominant flavor. In the nineteenth century, when Roman Catholics were a small minority, they led the fight against religion in the public schools because they knew it would have a Protestant taste to it. Their situation has changed. But the Jewish community has an ancient awareness of the situation of a religious minority from long years of experience with Christian majorities and their "truth." It knows that public religion tends to include more what Christians think Jews believe than what Jews do in fact believe. In this period when religion is surrounded with a rosy glow of popularity, the Jew may enter the reminder that for a child in the minority, religion can be a very uncomfortable business.

Plenty of others joined in opposition to the New York City guiding statement: the Society for Ethical Culture, some Unitarian ministers, the United Parents Association, the New York Civil Liberties Union, Americans for Democratic Action, and the Teachers Guild. The New York Board of Education was to have adopted the superintendents' guiding statement last fall, but it has not done so. As of this writing, the statement is still being reworked in an attempt to meet the various objections. The Board of Education may never adopt it.

CORNERSTONES, FOUNDING FATHERS

This New York effort has been marked throughout by a devoutly celebrational tone. The various resolutions and statements are full of exalted phrases about Lincoln's "sublime thought," the "unequaled clarity" of the Declaration of Independence, and the "solemn words" of the Constitution. The first sentence of the first pronouncement on the subject by the Board of Regents, in 1951, reads: "Belief in and dependence on Almighty God was the very cornerstone upon which our Founding Fathers builded." The New York City superintendents quote a version of this same thought in their guiding statement. The Board of Regents themselves were so taken with it that last March they issued a new document, quoting it again and expatiating on it by citing reverently some brief, familiar, and often peripheral references to God and Values from the Supreme Court, the Constitution of New York State, President Eisenhower, and the dollar bill. They also found quotations from the Declaration of Independence (". . . endowed by their Creator . . ."), Washington ("The event is in the hand of God"), Lincoln (". . . with firmness in the right as God gives us to see the right . . ."), Woodrow Wilson ("God helping me . . ."), Benjamin Franklin (". . . God governs in the affairs of men . . ."), and Thomas Jefferson ("I have sworn upon the altar of God . . .").

The phrase the Regents picked to describe this new education, "Piety and Virtue," with its staid, upright, classically Roman overtones, reflects the traditional and nostalgic flavor of the whole effort. America is seeking eagerly for a "faith" to match the Communists'; the nation is trying to find, all at once and in a hurry, religion, morality, and a heritage. (The word "heritage" ranks almost with "crusade" as a symbol of our period.) Just as millions of Americans are reading eagerly about the American past, so they are also gathering in large numbers about the churches and talking everywhere about morality. The trouble with this otherwise praiseworthy development is that it tends to take short cuts, avoiding the hard paths by which that national enrichment it rightly seeks could be achieved.

Then there are those almost forgotten folks, the nonbelievers, the semibelievers, and the unaffiliated believers. But in the guiding statement one finds this passage: ". . . as a rule the American teacher is religious in character, in action, and in belief. He belongs to a church or synagogue. . . ." As a statement of fact this may be true, but one can almost hear a voice muttering, "He'd better, or else. . . ."

THIN SOUP

The New York effort represents quite clearly all three salient assumptions of the current national religion: that there is an essential common core of "religion" in America, that morality depends upon it, and that Americanism depends upon it. Each of the three needs to be challenged, on religious as well as nonreligious grounds.

The liberal Catholic magazine *Commonweal* said it doubted whether a "religion of the least common denominator" could fill the religious vacuum in the schools; the New York Civil Liberties Union predicted that the result would be a "vague theism"; the New York Board of Rabbis said, ". . . some teachers are bound to become missionaries for their own religious convictions. . . . Other teachers will, no doubt, become advocates of a watered, meaningless 'public school religion,' glossing over differences among religious groups which stem from vitally important convictions. . . . [making] little more than a collection of platitudes and truisms."

A supporter of "common American beliefs" might say that thin soup is better than none, but that's one of the chief mistakes: to think any "religion" whatever is good. If what one seeks is depth, then teaching shallowness won't help.

The public school cannot possibly rise any higher in teaching of religion than the general opinion of the community: Its religious platitudes would become an official ideology. Teachers, untrained in religion, would be called upon to teach or "recognize" it; political agencies, chosen on nonreligious grounds, would formulate the core religion. Of the results of that process we already have a sample in the Regents' literature, and it's not encouraging.

The problems of reducing a deep and determinant faith to a public-school religion are acute with all denominations, and particularly with the Roman Catholics. On the basis of their understanding that some basic truths are available to the natural reason of every man, unaided by revelation, they may suggest that some of these —God and the natural law, for example—be taught in the general schools. But in a non-Catholic American environment, with all its pressures toward what a Catholic would call "indifferentism," the teaching of those "common beliefs" soon would certainly imply to many students a shoulder-shrugging conclusion that one religion that contained these basic beliefs was quite as good as another. These common beliefs, taught to everybody in the schools, would tend to become the important ones, and the particular doctrinal or institutional forms in which they were embodied would become, by implication, secondary. When the teaching moved ever so slightly toward that conclusion, the Roman Catholics would be the first and most emphatic to withdraw support of the program. . . .

"A MISTY MIDDLE RANGE"

A chief reason for the effort to have basic American religion taught is its allegedly essential relation to morality. "The American people," said the first sentence of the New York superintendents' guiding statement, "are, characteristically, a religious people who derive their accepted moral and spiritual values from religion." Americans are very much concerned with the morality of their children, and many insist that moral principles necessarily depend upon religion. But other Americans, with equal vigor, say, "No. Morality can and should be taught independently of religion." That's the heart of the fight.

In America it is common to equate religion and morality: Religion is "doing good"; "It was a Christian thing to do." The result is a kind of misty middle range, where ideals and doctrines, religion and morality, blend into something called "spiritual and moral values." This is a confusion. They are really two separate though intimately related questions, in the public schools as elsewhere. One has to do with the teaching of religion; the other has to do with moral training. They aren't the same. True, the attempt at moral training may often involve religion; for example, a counselor must of course appeal to what is there in an individual student, which sometimes would include his religious faith. But that is not the same as having the whole society, through its public schools, formally commit itself to the claim that morality must be linked to religion.

The fact that there are good men who are not religious—and, unfortunately, vice-versa—is plain for all to see, and it is fully taken care of in the believer's understanding of the broad and mysterious purposes of God. To pretend otherwise, to make religion and morality rigidly related, denies the higher and subtler doctrines of faith. It also tends to add to the unpleasant tendency to justify religion on the basis of services rendered, a pervasive and dubious theme in the "religious revival."

THE WONDER PILL

The Regents' 1951 statement said that Americans' belief in God is "the best security against the dangers of these difficult days." "We believe," they said of their moral and spiritual program, "that such is the best way of insuring that this government and our way of life shall not perish from the earth." Just as the appeal to the individual in popular religion now tends to say that it will do useful things—give success, happiness, peace of mind, peace of soul, peace with God—so the appeal to the nation is that religion will solve oppressing problems: answer juvenile delinquency, give security against Communism, create a moral fiber for the nation. Religion is recommended because, like Chesterfields, it satisfies. It is promoted for its helpfulness in meeting pre-existing needs and desires; a possibility that it might transform, criticize, or negate those desires is not included. . . .

Even a much more sophisticated position may make too close a link of religion to morality and Americanism. The Christian educator, arguing against "secularism" in the public schools, says that without the belief in God and the soul our human values will eventually disappear. But even those who find some force in the argument may want to question its defensive and apologetic form: It starts off on the wrong foot, arguing from morality to religion rather than from religion to morality. It tends to start with values taken for granted and then to argue that religion is their necessary support. Sometimes it seems to say to a reluctant world, "If you want your lovely civilization and your nice morality you have to take our tired old religion, too. Christianity and Judaism are the pill society must take to get the sugar coating of moral virtues and national strength."

The place for believers to begin is not with results but with faith and truth. Otherwise, the truth is tailored to fit function, and out of religious faith only that part is selected which surely does serve the particular purposes it has been presented to fulfill. . . .

THE LIMITS OF SECULARISM

Opponents of the New York guiding statement, oddly enough, sometimes speak in words that, to a reader of the Regents' and superintendents' literature, have a familiar ring: "We must never forget," said a rabbi in Brooklyn, "that the separation of church and state is the very foundation stone upon which the superstructure of our American democracy has been builded." There is that foundation stone again, and with it, elsewhere, the Constitution, the Supreme Court, and the Founding Fathers. Only this time they are invoked not for their Godliness but for their insistence upon a separation of church and state.

When a freshman religion class writes about the various denominations and religious groups in America, the student who writes about the Baptists explains that the Baptist heritage of Roger Williams and religious freedom is America's own; the Presbyterian says that the American form of government, representative and tripartite, is molded on the Presbyterian, and that the Constitution is full of a Calvinist and Presbyterian sense of the need to check and balance human sinfulness; the Congregationalists find the American pattern set by the Puritans and the Congregational New England town meeting; the Catholic writes that the founding documents are based upon the Catholic doctrine of natural law, which, for example, Jefferson got from the Catholic Bellarmine; the Unitarian, having read a book by A. Powell Davies, explains that the deist-Unitarian heritage, shared by Tom Paine, Jefferson, Lincoln, and almost everybody important, is America's true religion; and so it goes. There is a cornerstone in every corner.

Much writing about America's religious heritage is less an attempt to understand the past than to shape the present by a selective appeal to the past. The position many opponents of the guiding statement want to promote is that religion is strictly a matter for home and church, to be left out of the school, where it may create "divisive intergroup tension," be unfair to the unbeliever, and harm the role of the school as a "builder of American democracy."

To each side of the debate its own propositions seem perfectly self-evident, and the answer relatively easy. The proponents say, "Well, for heaven's sake, we simply want God and the moral law recognized in the schools. Who could object to that?"

The opponents, with equal ingenuousness, say, "We just want religion left in church where it belongs, and not put in school where it is divisive and out of place—a perfectly obvious American position." But the intensity of feeling on both sides shows that the struggle is real, and that, speaking of "spiritual and moral values," both sides have some important ones they are guarding. No simple, purist answer to the problem will suffice.

Arguments in the debate tend to cut both ways. For example, there may be a conflict of authority, baffling to the child, between a nonreligious parent and a Bible-quoting teacher who finds God in the grain of wood. But there also may be the same between a devout parent who tells her child that religion undergirds all of life and a teacher whose consideration of life is antiseptically free of any religious understanding.

Much Christian polemic, full of that theologian's cuss word "secularism," overstates its case. The overwhelming majority of Christians in America, no doubt, do not believe what some spokesmen seem to say, that "secularism" is a bad thing. Most Americans, religious or not, want secular politics, without any churchly parties; they want secular public schools, not committed to any doctrine or under any religious control. But the religious man stops there; he does not want secular men and secular children.

The adamant opponents of every "breach" in the "wall" between church and state sometimes do not realize the position of the adherent of a doctrinal religion. His faith is not just a private, incidental, and peripheral matter of taste, a quaint hangover, adding a bit of color to our pluralistic democracy, like the costumes of national backgrounds worn on U.N. Day. Rather, his faith is a total world view, and the fact that his child spends five days every week being taught important matters in a determinedly secular atmosphere raises problems.

The opponents of the guiding statement tend to be devotees of aggressively "democratic" philosophies, full of praise for the "public" control of the schools. But it is from the public, after all—the very democratic public—that the current pressure for religion in the schools is mainly coming. . . .

THE JOB IS TEACHING

The question has, as one might guess, been talked about by experts. Formidable groups of them have been meeting under the aegis of the American Council on Education and, after the habit of experts, making studies. They incline toward this position: You can't and shouldn't teach as true any common core of American religious beliefs; at the same time, you can't and shouldn't eject all mention of religion from the schools. Instead, they suggest "the factual study of religion."

One of the facts about religion is that it is a field in which people do not stop with, or agree upon, the facts about religion. They go on to make personal commitments one way or another. That raises the most emotional and touchy problems. It isn't easy to deal with religion, even "objectively," for young and impressionable minds in the mixed and nonreligious school. There are high schools, we are told, that felt they had to drop teaching about the Reformation from the history course because pressures were so great.

Practically, local schools deal with, or avoid dealing with, religion in a large variety of ways: What happens in Little Rock will be different from what happens in Jersey City. Those differences, reflecting the different composition of communities, will and maybe even should continue. But surely every school ideally ought to be able to do its own job—to teach. The one subject of religion, despite its peculiar difficulties, shouldn't be taboo. Teachers of history should bring in the influence of religion wherever it is appropriate to the teaching of history; social-studies classes should be able to tell about religious institutions as well as about banks and factories. The American Council studies show that in some places classes can develop as a project the study of the different faiths with what all admit are very good results.

Perhaps the teacher, who is the one who really has to work with the problem, should not be pressured either into or out of dealing with religion. Many teachers will continue to stay miles away from the subject of religion, fearful of angry calls from parents. But it ought to be possible for teachers who are competent to do it to approach religion in a way appropriate to the general school: not to teach for commitment but for knowledge and understanding. Information, yes. Proselytizing, no.

That isn't the same as "putting God in the schools." The public school didn't bring "secularism" to America, and it won't and can't bring "religion." These are the consequences of more profound events. The question about the whole religious "revival" nowadays is how much of it will be exhausted in the shallow surface of popular religiosity—and how much of it may run deeper. The place that question will be settled is not in the public schools but, for the most part, in the churches.

It is in the churches that a definite religious content *can* be taught, with authority and commitment. Such religion as may legitimately come into the school will come, as "secularism" does, not by the fiat of a board of education but in the underlying assumptions of some devoted teachers.

Any true influence of religion on the school—and on the society, for that matter—must take such long ways around. . . .

Writers often say the public schools are the "battleground of democracy," or something like that. Usually, frightened by the implications of the statement, they propose some massive attack to win, and thus end, the battle. Some wrongly make religion a dogmatic set of propositions instead of a faith; others wrongly make democracy an anti-dogmatic dogma instead of a political process; both may try to force their positions onto the children in school. But in a nation of many faiths the public schools will also remain mixed.

The real ways faith and democracy are learned are hard and long, in their very nature not to be forced. And one thing is sure about "moral and spiritual values," whatever they are: They have to be paid for.

If such payment is made and such long ways taken, committed religion and noncommittal democracy need not clash. Profound religion, like democracy, wants no compulsion, for a voluntary decision is of its essence. It doesn't go well in mixtures and stews, for its specific affirmations are crucial to it. It can't be talked about at every drop of an eraser—nothing would more surely drive kids away from religion than to have it rammed at them in every course from math to basketball. And it can't be won too easily. Young people are often not too hard to persuade but too easy; they take positions and choose up sides before they know what they are talking about. A good teacher in the public schools may do religion a service by holding back the headlong rush to take positions and set beliefs, indicating that there is vastly more to the subject of religion than can possibly be dealt with in the public school. Maybe that's what those parents who are eager for a heritage also need to learn.

Professor Miller was arguing deductively in the foregoing article. That is, he hypothesized that the kind of religion which could be taught in a pluralistic society would not satisfy anybody. It would have to be least-common-denominator religion. Several years after Professor Miller wrote his article, a journalist reported in the New York *Times* the experience of one high school with a nonsectarian ritual.

A *Case Study of Least-Common-Denominator Religion*

Reprinted by permission. From Maxwell Nurnberg, "Of Thee I Sing—Maybe," New York *Times Magazine*, Nov. 26, 1961, p. 86.

As not every schoolboy knows, the fourth stanza of "America," as originally written by Samuel Francis Smith, goes as follows:

Our fathers' God to thee
Author of liberty,
To thee I sing;
Long may our land be bright
With freedom's holy light;
Protect us by thy might,
Great God, our King!

If our schoolboy lives anywhere in the city of New York, however, he ought to know these words, because every day—from the moment he enters the lower grades until the day he graduates—he is required by law to sing stanza four. On Nov. 30, 1951, the State Board of Regents adopted a "Statement of Moral and Spiritual Training in the Schools" recommending that "at the commencement of every school day the Pledge of Allegiance to the Flag be joined with an Act of Reverence to God." And on Jan. 15, 1953, the Board of Education of the City of New York resolved that "at the commencement of each school day the Pledge of Allegiance to the Flag be followed by the singing in unison of the fourth stanza of 'America' "—selected for its reverent quality. . . .

In view of the great emphasis given stanza four, one might assume that by the time our schoolboy gets to high school, he would know the words—if not backward, at least forward. One New York City high school principal who had his doubts decided to test this assumption and had pupils in half a dozen assorted English classes write down their versions of the fourth stanza—as recollected in tranquillity.

Some were able to reproduce a reasonable facsimile—with the expected variations in punctuation and spelling. Several didn't know the words at all and merely wrote: "I don't no the words," or "I don't now the words." (The second seems to give promise of future commitment.)

The others? The variations of and deviations from the original—the improvements—were legion.

The first line ("Our fathers' God to thee") appeared in such various guises as:

Our father art to thee
Our father's gone to thee
Our father's guard to thee
Our father's scout to thee
Our fathers guide to thee

The second and third lines were comparatively free of mutilation with only "Offer, thy liberty," and "All thou of liberty," "To thee we see" and "To thee we sign" appearing as variants.

Line four ("Long may our land be bright") offered some interesting opportunities:

Law made our land be bright
Lord make our land be bright
Lord made our land be bright
Lord maid our land be bright

There was still some restraint shown in their treatment of line five:

With freedom's holly light
With freedom's holey light
With freedom hold thy night
With freedom's whole delight
With freedom all delight

With line six the floodgates opened wide:

Protect us by thy mite
Protect us by the night
Protect us from thy might
Protect us spy die might
Protect us spy they might
Protect us spy thy might

Line seven closed on a minor note with:

Gray God our King
Grant God our King
Pray God our key
God save the Queen

A few of the girls and boys confusing stanza one with stanza four came up with:

Land of the pilgrim's bride
Land of the pilgrim sprite
Land where the pilgrims pried

One or two, thinking that a line or two from "America the Beautiful" would somehow add something, gave us the lovely line:

God shed His grease on thee

So—to recapitulate—here, with only some punctuation added, are the "best" lines of stanza four in a composite reconstruction worthy of a Pogo or a James Joyce (sing along with me):

Our father's gone to thee,
Offer thy liberty,
To thee we sign.
Lord made our land be bright
With freedom's whole delight;
Protect us—spy they might—
God save the Queen!

CONCLUSION

During the nineteenth century and the early years of the twentieth, readers of Darwin, Freud, Marx, Pareto, and Spencer tended to consider traditional religion an anachronism and an obstacle to scientific progress. The Civil War hero and former Attorney General of Illinois, Colonel Robert G. Ingersoll, denounced the Judeo-Christian tradition as superstitious nonsense during successful lecture tours of the United States. "Everybody talks about the Bible," said Colonel Ingersoll, the son of a Congregational minister, "and nobody reads it; that is the reason it is so generally believed. I am probably the only man in the United States who has read the Bible through this year. I have wasted that time. . . ." [45] When Marx said that religion was the opiate of the people, many of the thinking men of his era agreed that religion was unnecessary in a scientifically advanced society.

Contemporary sociology cannot evaluate the truth or falsity of particular religions. Non-empirical ideas are, by definition, beyond the scope of an empirical discipline. However, most sociologists believe that scientific knowledge is insufficient to give meaning to human exist-ence. Life raises ultimate questions, and science provides partial and provisional answers. On the other hand, traditional religion interprets the human situation in ways that protect the believer against the threat of meaninglessness. For this reason, sociologists anticipate that religious institutions will persist—even in industrial societies in which the development of science has shaken faith in the miraculous aspect of traditional religion.

Karl Marx assumed that religion was hostile to change. Study of the relationship between Protestantism and the development of a market economy demonstrates that religion is not necessarily conservative.[46] When sociologists talk of religious support of the social order, they refer to the basic values inculcated during the socialization process. Considerable variation in economic and political arrangements can occur within the same value framework.

Secular equivalents of religion exist in contemporary society: commitments to family, country, art, and science. These secular commitments are a substitute for traditional religion in an age of skepticism about the supernatural world. They are capable of helping the individual transcend his own existence and perceive a pattern of meaning greater than himself. But secular equivalents of religion, since they are anchored to human beings or to human institutions, are vulnerable to the vicissitudes of human life, as Dr. Lindemann showed in his study of morbid grievers. Supernatural religion has, *for the believer*, greater possibilities for reassurance.

The differentiation of religious organizations in industrial societies poses additional problems for supernatural religion. To begin with, the religious organization must strike some kind of compromise with secular values. Its supporters are necessarily persons who interact mainly in secular contexts, and its facilities depend on secular resources. Second, the multiplicity of religious organizations in large, heterogeneous societies limits the support any one of them can receive from the state and from other secu-

[45] Robert Green Ingersoll, *Colonel Robert G. Ingersoll's 44 Complete Lectures*, New York: Donohue, 1924, p. 10.

[46] Weber, *The Protestant Ethic and the Spirit of Capitalism, op. cit.*

lar institutions. A necessary condition for religious freedom and religious tolerance is that no religious organization may have a predominant advantage over others. In the United States, this condition is formalized in the constitutional principle of separation of church and state. But even in England and Sweden, countries with established churches, education is firmly under secular control, a good indication of the limitations on state support. Under these conditions, each denomination must struggle to win *voluntary* support and enthusiasm; this is an additional reason for compromising with secular values.

SOME SIGNIFICANT LITERATURE ON THE SOCIOLOGY OF RELIGION

James S. Coleman, "Social Cleavage and Religious Conflict," *Journal of Social Issues*, Vol. 12, No. 3, 1956, pp. 44–56. ". . . The potential for social conflict exists by the very way in which people identify themselves with groups, forming lines of consensus and cleavage in society. . . ." The potential for conflict among adherents of different religions is greatest when these religious differences are reinforced by other distinctions: ethnic background, education, geographic location, social class. On the other hand, a religious difference is less likely to generate conflict when people divided by religious affiliation are united by other solidarities. Professor Coleman refers to "the cross-pressured man . . . whose attachments lead him in both directions at once. . . ." This conception of cross-pressures reducing the motivation for decisive action originated in studies of voting behavior. Coleman believes that recent changes in American society have increased the extent of cross-pressures that dampen and dissipate religious conflict. ". . . Catholics have diffused upwards in the economic structure, and outward geographically to the suburbs; Jews similarly are less concentrated in particular economic roles and geographic locations than before; Protestants who grew up in one sect in a community are dispersed and recongregated in communities where sects must combine to survive. In sum, economic and geographic mobility is imposing new conditions of association and group identification on persons of different religious groups." For a discussion of the religious organizations of urban industrial societies as sources of malintegration and conflict, see Allan W. Eister, "Religious Institutions in Complex Societies: Difficulties in the Theoretic Specification of Function," *American Sociological Review*, Vol. 22, August 1957, pp. 387–391.

Joseph H. Fichter, S. J., *Dynamics of a City Church: Southern Parish*, Vol. 1, Chicago: University of Chicago Press, 1951. Father Fichter, a Ph.D. in sociology from Harvard University as well as a priest, describes in this book St. Mary's parish, a Catholic congregation located in a city within the American Bible Belt. The study is largely descriptive: the numbers attending mass, going to confession, taking communion, giving donations, and the like. Professor Forrest E. LaViolette reported in his review, *American Sociological Review*, Vol. 17, April 1952, p. 255, that the remaining volumes of Father Fichter's study might not be published. High officials in the Catholic Church feel that confidences of the Church were violated in the study. Be that as it may, the remainder of Father Fichter's study has not yet appeared. He did publish a collection of essays on various aspects of Catholic parish life: *Social Relations in the Urban Parish*, Chicago: University of Chicago Press, 1954.

Charles Y. Glock and Benjamin B. Ringer, "Church Policy and the Attitudes of Ministers and Parishioners on Social Issues," *American Sociological Review*, Vol. 21, April 1956, pp. 148–156. In 1951–1952, questionnaires were filled out by a sample of American ministers and laymen of the Protestant Episcopal Church, the latter being randomly selected from the parishes of the ministers included in the study. The questionnaires gathered attitude data on nine public issues ranging from the acceptability of war as an instrument of international policy to permissiveness toward intermarriage with Roman Catholics. Since the Episcopal Church passed resolutions on public questions at its triennial denomination meetings, it was possible to compare the attitudes of ministers and laymen with the official position of the Church. "Ministers' attitudes clearly tend to reflect church policy. Where the church has elected to compromise on an issue, the minister also has compromised with the view of his parishioners. However, where the church has taken a partisan point of view, the minister generally identifies with this view despite the opposition of a substantial segment of his parishioners."

Benton Johnson, "On Church and Sect," *American Sociological Review*, Vol. 28, August 1963, pp. 539–549. The usefulness of a typology of religious organizations explains the popularity of Ernst Troeltsch's distinction between *church* and *sect*. Troeltsch defines the sect as a small, voluntary fellowship of converts constituting a community apart from the world around it; he defined the church as a more conservative religious community ". . . that seeks to dominate all elements within society, to teach and guide them, and to dispense saving grace to them by means of sacraments administered by ecclesiastical office holders." Unlike the sect, the church regularly includes the infant offspring of members. Professor Johnson analyzes the Troeltsch definitions, which were derived from a study of Christian Europe prior to 1800, and concludes that they have limited relevance to the contemporary world. He suggests the following unidimensional criterion for distinguishing between church and sect: "A sect is a religious group that rejects the social environment in which it exists." A church accepts the secular milieu. Professor Johnson recognizes that his criterion defines a continuum rather than a polarity, and he tests its utility by applying it to the American religious scene. He points out that Methodists, Presbyterians, Congregationalists, and Episcopalians are close to the church end of the continuum; Reform and Conservative Jews are intermediate as are Mormons, Seventh Day Adventists, Orthodox Presbyterian, and Christian Reformed; Roman Catholics and Orthodox Jews are the most sectarian of American religious organizations. Notwithstanding these distinctions, Professor Johnson contrasts the American religious situation with that in other parts of the world. "The most striking fact about the American religious situation is that the vast majority of religious bodies seems to accept the dominant value system."

Gerhard E. Lenski, "Social Correlates of Religious Interest," *American Sociological Review*, Vol. 18, October 1953, pp. 533–544. Individual interest in religion in urban industrial societies varies from fanatical zeal at one extreme to utter indifference at the other. This Indianapolis study of 860 native-white married couples of Protestant background explores possible explanations of the variation in religious interest in this population. Based on intensive interviews conducted with husbands and wives separately in 1941, the findings are as follows: (1) Women are more interested in religion than men. (2) Couples with children are more interested in religion than couples without children. (3) Middle-income families express more interest in religion than either upper-income or lower-income families. (4) The greater the educational attainment, the less is the interest in religion. (5) Greater interest in religion is expressed by persons who have suffered large income *losses* since marriage, and the least interest is expressed by those with the largest income *gains*. (6) Husbands and wives from different denominations are less interested in religion than couples from the same denominational background. Despite these relationships, Professor Lenski feels that the relationships between social factors and religious interest are not strong enough for sociologists to make more than tentative generalizations about underlying causal factors. For a study by the same author of the *effects* of religious

interest rather than its causes, see *The Religious Factor: A Sociological Study of Religion's Impact on Politics, Economics and Family Life*, Garden City, N.Y.: Doubleday, 1961.

Dennison Nash and Peter Berger, "The Child, the Family and the 'Religious Revival' in Suburbia," *Journal for the Scientific Study of Religion*, Vol. 2, Fall 1962, pp. 85–93. The authors interviewed a sample of adults who recently joined one of three churches of the Congregational-Christian denomination in a rapidly growing suburb of Hartford, Connecticut. "For most of these people the decision to join was prompted by the prospect or presence of children in the family." In general, joining was *not* preceded by a conversion experience of the sort described by William James in *The Varieties of Religious Experience*, nor was it motivated by crises in their personal lives. Joining appears to have been a rational decision connected with the religious education and moral guidance of their children.

Thomas F. O'Dea, *The Mormons*, Chicago: University of Chicago Press, 1957. In the first five chapters Professor O'Dea traces the rise and expansion of the Mormon Church. He then turns to a consideration of Mormon theology, the organizational structure of the Mormon Church, the social ethnic of the church, and, finally, the sources of strain and conflict within the church and between Mormons and other Protestants. The continued vitality of Mormonism is puzzling in view of characteristics that might be expected to reduce its appeal in a scientifically oriented democracy where women approximate equality of status with men. Mormonism is a fundamentalist religion with an authoritarian priesthood that excludes women. One implication of this study is that religious beliefs and values have consequences for the secular behavior of communicants. This summary is based on a review by Kimball Young, *American Sociological Review*, Vol. 23, February 1958, pp. 103–104. For a study showing the relevance of Zoroastrian values for the economic behavior of present-day Zoroastrians in India, see Robert R. Kennedy, Jr., "The Protestant Ethic and the Parsis," *American Journal of Sociology*, Vol. 68, July 1962, pp. 11–20.

Talcott Parsons, "The Pattern of Religious Organization in the United States," *Daedalus*, Vol. 87, Summer 1958, pp. 65–85. Some sociologists as well as some theologians have discounted the religious element in the current "religious revival" in the United States. One interpretation stresses the security needs of rootless people in a mass society. According to this interpretation, the increase in church membership can be explained in terms of sociability and status seeking. Professor Parsons feels that this explanation is incomplete and argues that the increased religiosity is genuine. Strains are produced by rapid economic growth in a society where the individual is expected to sub-ordinate his personal needs to an objective task (such as his occupational role) to which he is supposed to devote his full energies. Heightened concern with reli-gion, with mental health, with family life, and with other personal matters should be expected to accom-pany the processes of socialization into different adult roles. Parsons believes that the major contribution of religion in urban industrial societies is the regulation of the commitment of the individual to the values of his society and through these values to his roles in it. In short, Professor Parsons interprets the American religious revival as genuine because he believes that coexistence is possible between religious and secular elements in urban industrial societies. Beyond the secu-larization of education and politics that has already occurred, he does not anticipate a further erosion of traditional religion.

Sylvia L. Thrupp, Ed., *Millennial Dreams in Action*, Supplement II to *Comparative Studies in Society and History*, The Hague: Mouton, 1962. The conference out of which this book grew aimed at drawing together the conclusions of anthropologists and sociologists on religious movements ". . . animated by the idea of a perfect age or a perfect land." One of the contributors, Norman Cohn, defines as *millenarian* any religious movement including a fantasy of salvation that is to be:

"(*a*) collective, in the sense that it is to be enjoyed by the faithful as a group;

(*b*) terrestrial, in the sense that it is to be realized on this earth and not in some otherworldly heaven;

(*c*) imminent, in the sense that it is to come both soon and suddenly;

(*d*) total, in the sense that it is utterly to transform life on earth, so that the new dispensation will be no mere improvement on the present but per-fection itself;

(*e*) accomplished by agencies which are consciously regarded as supernatural."

By this standard, a contemporary secular religion, Com-munism, cannot be called millenarian, yet Communism resembles millenarian cults in the hopes and the dis-illusionments it inspires. See Gabriel A. Almond, *The Appeals of Communism*, Princeton, N.J.: Princeton University Press, 1954.

W. Lloyd Warner, *The Living and the Dead: A Study of the Symbolic Life of Americans*, New Haven, Conn.: Yale University Press, 1959. Professor Warner brings his anthropological background to bear on the cere-monial and symbolic activities of a modern community (Newburyport, Massachusetts) in this, the sixth and concluding volume of the Yankee City series. He starts with a living symbol: the career of a mayor and politi-cal boss who is a hero to some and a villain and clown to others. Warner moves on to a discussion of the ritualization of the past: Memorial Day, Lincoln as a patriotic symbol, Catholic and Protestant symbolism, and the place of the cemetery in the community. The question has been raised about this volume, as about the other five Yankee City books, of the generality of the conclusions. Is the symbolic life of a small Ameri-can city typical of the large metropolis? This summary is based on a review by Orrin E. Klapp, *American So-ciological Review*, Vol. 25, October 1960, p. 757.

CHAPTER 15

Bureaucratic Organizations

Organized interaction in industrial societies is characterized by elaborate division of labor. In a university, for example, the activities of teachers and students are facilitated by an army of specialists: accountants, switchboard operators, secretaries, librarians, maintenance men, housemothers, policemen, postal clerks, editors, physicians, architects, scheduling officers, cooks, receptionists, and dozens more. Specialization by task promotes efficiency because specialists are usually faster and more skillful than generalists. However, this differentiation of an interactive system into highly specific roles poses a difficult problem of coordination. Who or what will see to it that the many activities mesh?

Informal communication integrates a small social system like a family, but it is not reliable enough to ensure the continued operation of General Motors, Rutgers University, the Federal Bureau of Prisons, the Roman Catholic Church, or the Ford Foundation. Therefore, all large organizations tend to formalize the coordination of activities. Sociologists use the term "bureaucracy" to refer to the way large-scale administrative tasks tend to be organized.[1] For the sociologist, "bureaucracy" is not

[1] Peter M. Blau, *Bureaucracy in Modern Society,* New York: Random House, 1956, p. 14.

an evil word. Once political mechanisms have resulted in policy decisions, bureaucracy is an efficient way to carry them out on a large scale.

THE CHARACTERISTICS OF BUREAUCRATIC ORGANIZATIONS

One of the most obvious—and most irritating—characteristics of bureaucracy is formality. Positions in the organization are precisely defined; often detailed job descriptions are available. In practice, this means that an outsider has to know with *whom* to get in touch in the organization to get action. If a high school graduate wishes to apply for admission to college, he may wander around the campus for some time before he locates the Admissions Office and finds someone who will discuss his situation. He may think that the Dean of the College, the Dean of Students, and the Chairman of the Department in which he would like to major are giving him a "runaround." They do not mean to. Being aware that the admissions function is the responsibility of specialists better qualified than they to answer the applicant's questions, they know that it would waste their time (and that of the applicant) to interfere.

Bureaucracies manifest formality in other ways besides allocating definite functions to definite positions. Bureaucracies promulgate highly specific procedural rules and do not allow idiosyncratic variations—even when justice or efficiency would seemingly be better served by stretching them. Thus, when a psychology professor needs to purchase a tape recorder for recording interviews with experimental subjects, he must submit a requisition, probably in triplicate, to the Purchasing Department of the University; the Purchasing Department follows its usual procedure of inviting several suppliers to submit competitive sale prices. Six weeks later, the tape recorder may arrive. Certainly, this is not the fastest way to supply a researcher with a tape recorder. But centralized purchasing may be the most economical method for the University to make thousands of purchases every year. The individual has to fuss and fume while he conforms to a seemingly arbitrary procedure in order to enable this centralized system to work.

Formal rules make the operation of a bureaucracy predictable. For instance, at one college a student must have an over-all average of no higher than 3.2 in order to graduate. (The grades of this college are reminiscent of golf scores: that is, the lower the numerical grade, the higher the achievement it represents.) Is there something so sacred about 3.2 that a student with a cumulative average of 3.25 should be denied his diploma? The particular average used to qualify for graduation is not crucial, but it *is* crucial to have a cutoff point. The 3.2 requirement is sufficiently clear that students, faculty, and the clerical personnel in the various offices concerned with academic bookkeeping know precisely *who is entitled to graduate and who is not*. Without the rule, there would be endless wrangling between students and parents, on the one hand, and college personnel, on the other. The outcomes of these controversies would not be uniform. Persuasive or persistent students might graduate with a 3.4 average. Timid students or students unfortunate enough to talk to grouchy administrators might *fail* to graduate despite a 3.1 average. However arbitrary they may seem, formal rules make organizational behavior predict-

able. Furthermore, they guarantee that everyone will be treated uniformly.

The codification of bureaucratic rules in bulky manuals may seem unnecessary. But formal organizations must look to the future. In the long run, we are all dead. Hence the organization must take measures to maintain efficiency despite loss of personnel through death, illness, marriage, military service, firing, and promotion. A file clerk who uses her own system—say, one who files material under the second letter of the main topic rather than the first—thereby makes herself indispensable; nothing can be found in the files unless she locates it personally. But she violates the bureaucratic ideal of continuity. A bureaucracy assumes not merely that everyone is replaceable, but also that everyone's task can be routinized and codified in standard operating procedures, thus permitting a replacement to take over on short notice.

Just as bureaucratic formalism is criticized, so is bureaucratic impersonality. The *coldness* of bureaucracies is contrasted with the friendliness of a small group. Yet impersonality is the best insurance against either favoritism or discrimination. The prison administrator knows that the guard who is friendly with the inmates he supervises is bound to be *more* friendly with some than with others. Where will this lead? To a letter smuggled *out* without going through normal prison censorship? To a gun smuggled *in* to be used in an escape attempt? Prison administrators do not want friendly guards because they are aware, from bitter experience, that friendship corrupts the integrity of a guard more often than money.[2] This does not imply that prison administrators want unfriendly or cruel guards; they want guards who apply the rules *fairly*, and this means *impersonally*. Prison administrators prefer impersonal guards for another reason; emotional involvement in inmate problems may sap the energies of guards and reduce their efficiency.

[2] Lloyd W. McCorkle and Richard R. Korn, "Resocialization within Walls," *Annals of the American Academy of Political and Social Science*, Vol. 293, May 1954, pp. 88–98.

Bureaucracies are not only formalistic and impersonal; they are also hierarchical. This characteristic results from the fact that the number of persons an individual can direct is limited. Hence, large numbers of subordinates have to be coordinated through a smaller number of supervisors who are themselves supervised. The hierarchy in a bureaucratic organization is graphically represented in the table of organization, which a large organization may distribute to its members (Figure 14). The table of organization shows who reports to whom at each echelon—not, of course, the names of individuals but rather in terms of roles (offices). Policy is supposed to be made at the top of the hierarchy. In practice, however, decisions have to be made at every level in the organization; the *responsibility* for decision making remains with the top bureaucrats, but they cannot know in detail about all the policy problems of the organization. If something goes wrong, however, the top bureaucrats cannot claim ignorance of what is occurring five echelons down. They are supposed to know. This pressure to make rational decisions on the basis of what is at best partial knowledge is one of the strains of the executive role.

THE BUREAUCRATIZATION OF THE ECONOMY

Large-scale organization characterizes all phases of life in industrial societies, but is best exemplified in the government agency and in the business corporation. When the business corporation was invented several hundred years ago in response to the problems of British trade, no one anticipated that it would transform economic behavior. The building and operation of sailing vessels was costly, and the investment was risky. In order to encourage this form of enterprise, the Crown chartered trading corporations and endowed them with certain attractive characteristics, the most important of which was that owners were not liable for debts of the corporation.[3] The most they could lose was their investment. Some of these cor-

porations became rich and famous like the East India Company. On the other hand, Adam Smith wrote in his *Wealth of Nations* (published in 1776) that corporations could never be a major force in the economy; no man pays as much attention to his employer's affairs as to his own, and therefore the corporation is necessarily inefficient.[4]

Karl Marx also underestimated the corporation. When he predicted the division of capitalist society into a tiny group of owner-managers ("exploiters") and a vast majority of propertyless employees ("proletarians"), he did not count on the enormous growth of corporate size and power. When a company gets to be the size of General Motors—it had more than *half a million* employees in 1961—large numbers of managerial, technical, and professional employees fit neither the capitalist nor the proletarian stereotype. In the following article, Reinhard Bendix discusses the bureaucratization of business management in Western industrial countries. Professor Bendix is interested not only in the growing proportions of workers in administrative and technical categories, but also in the qualitative changes in business careers since capitalism has grown more bureaucratic.

Bureaucratic Management of Business Firms

Reprinted by permission. From Reinhard Bendix, *Work and Authority in Industry: Ideologies of Management in the Course of Industrialization*, New York: Wiley, 1956, pp. 211–216, 226–236.

The most useful, single index of the internal bureaucratization of economic enterprises is the proportion of salaried employees in the occupational structure of a country. With industrialization the proportion of independent individual proprietors declines and that of economically dependent employees increases. Among dependent employees the proportion of salaried workers increases more rapidly than that of manual workers

3 Scott Buchanan, "The Corporation and the Republic," New York: Fund for the Republic, 1958.

4 Adolph A. Berle, Jr., "Economic Power and the Free Society," New York: Fund for the Republic, 1957, p. 4.

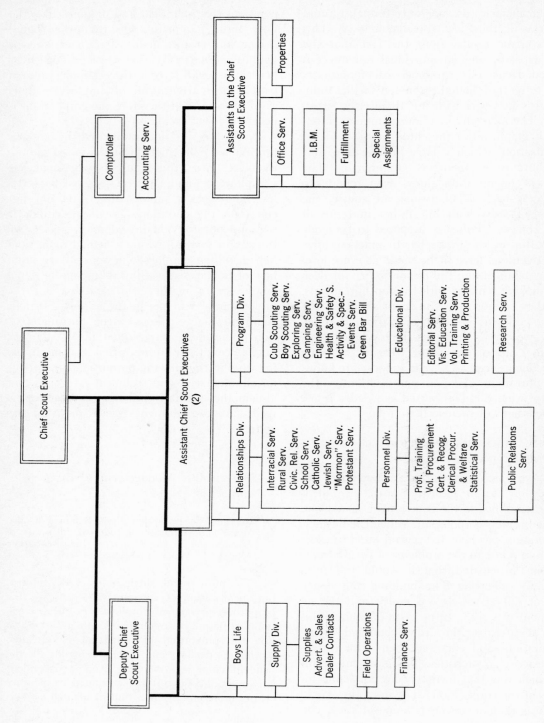

FIGURE 14. Organizational chart of the National Office of the Boy Scouts of America, 1960.

wherever the number of large-scale economic enterprises increases rapidly. In the United States, for instance, the total gainfully occupied population increased by 49 per cent from 1910 to 1940. During this period individual proprietors increased by 17 per cent, manual workers by 49 per cent, and salaried employees by 127 per cent. These illustrative figures point to significant changes in the occupational structure, which are relatively recent. The bureaucratization of economic enterprises, however, began with the Industrial Revolution.

At one time individual entrepreneurs performed a large variety of routine administrative tasks in addition to their "distinct economic function of undertaking new things," which Schumpeter has singled out for special emphasis. Seen historically, bureaucratization may be interpreted as the increasing subdivision of the functions which the owner-managers of the early enterprises had performed personally in the course of their daily routine. These functions may be divided into labor management, technical staff work, administrative management, and mercantile functions of purchasing, sales, and finance. As the work involved became more extensive and complex with the development of economic enterprises, it came to be delegated to subordinates both with regard to routine work and with regard to selected aspects of the entrepreneurial function proper. During the initial period of growth, the most important subordinates were likely to be relatives of the founder or persons who had earned his confidence and who frequently married into his family. The administrative and managerial work of early entrepreneurs, the importance of family ties, and the rather gradual increase of salaried employees in the early period (compared with the increase of workers) are reflected in [Table 63].

This increase in the number of salaried employees was coterminous with changes in the organization of economic enterprises. These changes can be understood most clearly by contrasting the system of subcontracting with the position of the foreman in modern industry. Subcontracting typically involved a contract between a merchant enterpriser and one or several subcontractors, in which the latter obliged themselves to deliver a given quantity of goods at a stipulated quality and price. The organization of labor and sometimes also of production was left to the subcon-

tractors. Today, subcontracting in this sense has disappeared completely from industries which require heavy capital investments, the concentration of operations in single plants and highly technical as well as long-run planning of production. Most of the functions which the subcontractors performed have been assigned to separate departments, and the immediate foreman of the workers has retained only the function of direct supervision. . . .

This transformation in the management of labor has made the foreman of today into an executive agent of various departments which specialize in one or another of the separate functions of contract negotiation, personnel recruitment, training, and so on. Increasingly, it has become a matter of discretion whether or not these departments consult the foreman. The following summary, based on a study of one hundred American companies which were sampled for the purpose of analyzing the *best* practices in American industry, illustrates this point clearly.

Hiring. In two-thirds of the companies replying, the personnel department interviews and selects new employees, while the foreman has final say; but in one-third the foreman has no voice in hiring.

Discharge. Foremen have some say in discharge, but only in one-tenth of all cases can they discharge without any consultation.

Pay Increases and Promotion. These must almost always be approved by other authorities.

TABLE 63
Number of Salaried Employees and Workers in a Swedish Firm, 1845–1873

Year	Plant Managers and Draftsmen	Bookkeeper and Correspondent	Total Salaried	Total Number of Workers
1845	2	1	3 *a*	30
1855	4	3	7 *b*	210
1865	6	6	12	288
1873	9	6	15	435

a All members of the family.
b Includes four members of the family.
Source: Fritz Croner, *Die Angestellten in der Modernen Gesellschaft*, Frankfurt: Humboldt, 1954, p. 103.

Discipline. In only one-tenth of all cases do foremen have complete charge of discipline.

Grievances. Discussion with the foreman is generally the first step in the grievance procedure, but the extent to which he settles grievances is not clear. A small sample in the automotive-aircraft industries shows that this may range from 45 per cent to 80 per cent.

Policy-making. Only 20 per cent of the companies replying held policy-meetings with foremen.

These findings illustrate the process of internal bureaucratization in the most advanced industries with regard to the management of labor. That process consists in the subdivision of this (as of other) entrepreneurial functions with the result that each phase, such as recruitment, pay administration, etc., becomes the task of a separate administrative staff consisting of technical and administrative specialists as well as of a number of salaried employees performing routine work. . . .

Sources for Table 64:

United States: Recomputed from Seymour Melman, "The Rise of Administrative Overhead in the Manufacturing Industries of the United States, 1899–1947," *Oxford Economic Papers*, Vol. III, 1951, p. 66.

France: Ministère du Travail et de la Prévoyance Sociale, *Résultats du Recensement Général de la Population 1906*, Vol. I, 2nd section, p. 187, Table IV (for 1901 and 1906); *ibid.*, 1927, Vol. XLVII, pp. 11, 13 (for 1921). Sous-secretariat d'état et d'Economie Nationale, Bureau de la Statistique Générale, *Recensement Général de la Population*, Vol. I, 3rd section, 1931, p. 95 (data for 1926), p. 94 (data for 1931); Institut National de la Statistique et des Etudes Economiques, Statistique Générale de la France, *Annuaire Statistique*, Vol. LVI, 1946, pp. 17, 19 (for 1936).

Great Britain: Seymour Melman, *Dynamics of Industrial Productivity*, Chap. 11, Table 1, unpublished manuscript, by permission of the author.

Germany: Statistik des Deutschen Reichs, Berlin, Vol. 466, 1937, Table 7, p. 194.

Sweden: Croner, *op. cit.*, pp. 120–121.

Great care has been taken to make the figures for each country internally consistent and to make them as comparable as possible for all five countries. Success in this respect, however, can only be proximate, and it is best to think of comparisons among several countries in terms of orders of magnitude and over all trends.

TABLE 64

Number of Administrative and Production Employees in Industry for Selected Countries and Selected Years

Year	(A) Administrative Employees [a]	(P) Production Employees	A/P
I. United States			
1899	348,000	4,496,000	7.7%
1909	750,000	6,256,000	12.0
1923	1,280,000	8,187,000	15.6
1929	1,496,000	8,361,000	17.9
1937	1,518,000	8,553,000	17.7
1947	2,578,000	11,916,000	21.6
II. France			
1901	425,000	3,609,000	11.8
1906	392,000	3,772,000	10.4
1921	671,000	4,650,000	14.7
1926	699,000	5,458,000	12.8
1931	762,000	5,496,000	13.9
1936	635,000	4,355,000	14.6
III. Great Britain			
1907	408,000	4,755,000	8.6
1924	627,000	4,708,000	13.0
1930	589,000	4,286,000	13.7
1935	676,000	4,482,000	15.0
1948	1,126,000	5,651,000	20.0
IV. Germany [b]			
1895	266,000	5,530,000	4.8
1907	606,000	7,922,000	7.6
1925	1,122,000	9,463,000	11.9
1933	802,000	5,718,000	14.0
V. Sweden			
1915	25,000	374,000	6.6
1920	37,000	417,000	8.9
1925	34,000	392,000	8.7
1930	45,000	455,000	9.9
1935	54,000	471,000	11.5
1940	76,000	555,000	13.7
1945	111,000	639,000	17.3
1950	140,000	663,000	21.0

[a] The figures for administrative employees *exclude* owners and top executives.

[b] The German and French series were not extended beyond the 1930's because the more recent figures cannot be put on a basis comparable with the earlier figures. Taken independently, however, the more recent data also show an increasing bureaucratization.

The proportion of administrative employees varies over time as well as between enterprises of different types and sizes today. These variations have been paralleled by changes in the task and the careers of "business leaders," which in turn reflect changes in the management of economic enterprises. It will be useful to examine the internal bureaucratization of contemporary enterprises before turning to a study of the changing career patterns of entrepreneurs and managers.

The increasing size of industrial enterprises entails certain administrative problems which in each case require for their solution the addition of salaried personnel.[5] Dale points out that in the smallest enterprise the major problem involves the division of work among the owner-manager, perhaps some member of his family, and a few employees. As the enterprise increases in size, it becomes necessary for the owner-manager to delegate to subordinates responsibility for many functions, which he has performed personally in the past. Subsequently, it becomes necessary to delegate further managerial functions, and the problem arises how to do this without overburdening the chief executive officer of the company (span of control). With further increases in size this problem is solved in part by making one or several staff assistants available to the executive so that his energies can be concentrated on the essential tasks of his position. In still larger enterprises, it may become necessary to hire staff specialists, who will be charged with responsibility for developing plans in several departments of the enterprise. A further increase in size is likely to bring to the fore the problem of decision-making, since the complexity of the enterprise makes it impossible for any one person to have sufficient information for intelligent decision-making; hence, the different management functions become coordinated through group decision-making. And finally it becomes necessary to increase the degree to which responsibility is delegated to subordinates by decentralizing the operations of the enterprise so that each of its branches can be operated efficiently.

This list of managerial devices is a useful guide to an understanding of bureaucratization. According to Dale, these devices are employed as an enterprise passes through different stages

of growth to solve the problems of organization that arise as a result of this growth. Of course, these problems of organization continue to demand attention even after the "stage" at which they had to be dealt with initially. Both the addition of administrative staff and changes in the functions of management are concomitants of the managerial devices which Dale has listed. I turn now to a consideration of the career patterns among the business elite as another index of internal bureaucratization.

Since the beginning of the nineteenth century the organization of industry has been transformed. In order to analyze the effect of bureaucratization on the career patterns of the business and industrial elite, it has been necessary to devise a typology of careers that would facilitate such an analysis. The career types of business and industrial leaders may be designated by the terms: heirs, entrepreneurs, and bureaucrats. The career pattern of heirs is most easily characterized. Their outstanding trait is that they have inherited considerable wealth and, hence, have come to control a firm either through direct legacy or through purchase. Neither entrepreneurs nor bureaucrats are "heirs" in this sense, although this does not preclude their having received assistance from their families at the start of their careers. But if entrepreneurs and bureaucrats are clearly distinguished from heirs, the distinction between entrepreneurs and bureaucrats is not equally simple. Entrepreneurs start firms of their own at some point in their careers; bureaucrats do not. At the climax of their careers entrepreneurs are substantial owners of a firm, while bureaucrats are typically salaried executives. Entrepreneurs sometimes spend a part of their careers as salaried employees; bureaucrats do so invariably and for a major portion of their careers. These are important distinctions, but in some cases they are distinctions of degree. Thus, the careers of bureaucrats tend to show a succession of salaried jobs, which lead to an executive position; but then the man may buy into an old firm or may be hired as an executive and become a part-owner. Entrepreneurs, on the other hand, may hold several salaried jobs before they assume a proprietary position. In such cases it is a matter of judgment how the careers are to be classified; in this instance, that judgment depends upon the length of time the individual has held a salaried position.

Table 65 shows the major results of our study.

---

5   Ernest Dale, *Planning and Developing the Company Organization Structure*, Research Report No. 20, New York: American Management Association, 1952.

It presents the classification of a little over 1,000 biographies of prominent businessmen and industrialists by career type. It shows clearly that the proportion of entrepreneurs has sharply declined in the course of American industrialization at the same time that the proportion of "industrial bureaucrats" has increased.

Table 65 shows that the proportion of heirs in the business elite of each generation has gradually increased. This increase of heirs may indicate a proportionate increase in the success with which prominent families of industrialists have managed to facilitate the careers of their descendants. It is difficult to regard this result with confidence until it is confirmed by an independent check. But on the face of it, the study seems to indicate that in spite of the increasing capital requirements of giant firms, there were enough investment opportunities in smaller firms, where a wealthy individual could still acquire a substantial interest. And it should be remembered that the *National Cyclopedia of American Biography* contains profiles of all business leaders judged prominent enough by rather general criteria.

It should be obvious that this differentiation of career patterns is based on over-all judgments of each career. The differences between career patterns are not likely to be evident with the same clarity in any single index that may be devised. For one thing, entrepreneurs, bureaucrats, and heirs alike have participated in the on-going changes of American society; hence, there are no significant differences between them in some respects, while in others the differences may be small. Thus, detailed compilations show that all three types of businessmen and industrialists have predominantly come from families which already occupied a privileged economic position. Likewise, all three types have participated more than the average in the rising educational level of the general population.

One important difference in educational attainment is to be noted. Of the prominent businessmen born between 1831 and 1875 who became entrepreneurs and bureaucrats about two-thirds attained at most a high-school education, while about one-third went to college or beyond. (The heirs divide evenly in this respect.) Yet, for those businessmen born between 1876 and 1920 the educational picture changes: two-thirds or more of the bureaucrats and the heirs attended college, while the educational attainment of the entrepreneurs remained the same.

One can infer from these data that the higher level of educational attainment which both the bureaucrats and the heirs show in the second period was the result of very different conditions. For men who depend in part upon education for success in their careers, higher education is a means to career advancement; but for the heirs who are secure in their career chances, higher educational attainment simply reflects their high status and the increasing importance of education in the population generally. It is significant in this respect that the decline of entrepreneurs is reflected in their failure to increase their educa-

TABLE 65

Percentage Distribution of the American Business Elite, by Career Type and by Date of Birth [a]

Career-Type	1771–1800 (N = 121)	1801–1830 (N = 75)	1831–1860 (N = 332)	1861–1890 (N = 344)	1891–1920 (N = 131)
Entrepreneurs	76	68	56	36	18
Bureaucrats	5	16	21	29	48
Heirs	19	16	23	35	34
Total	100	100	100	100	100
Not classifiable	1 (1%)	12 (14%)	21 (6%)	34 (9%)	11 (7%)
Total subjects	122	87	353	378	142

[a] Subjects have been classified by the time-period into which their year of birth fell.

Sources: *National Cyclopedia of American Biography; Dictionary of American Biography; Current Biography.*

tional "preparedness." For the increasing educational requirements of modern industry are likely to militate against individuals without educational background. Although this factor is probably a secondary one, it shows clearly that the anti-educational bias of the self-made man has taken its toll.

Another bias of the self-made man is the belief that the young man must start to work early in his life if he wants to get ahead. By tabulating our three career types in terms of the age at the time of the first job, we find that the entrepreneurs were most reluctant to part with this tradition. While the proportion of bureaucrats and heirs who had been born between 1831 and 1875 and who started work before they were twenty years old had already dropped to less than one-third (26 per cent and 30 per cent, respectively), the corresponding proportion of entrepreneurs was still 45 per cent. Of the subjects born after 1876, however, over three-quarters in each career type started work at age twenty-one or over, a finding which suggests that by the last decade of the nineteenth century the age at the start of the work career no longer distinguished between career types.

The bureaucrats among business leaders seem to have participated more than heirs and entrepreneurs in another secular change. The first job

an individual takes may not be a good predictor of his subsequent career, especially in the case of future business leaders whose careers are by definition mobile and unpredictable; but the first job is an index of the prevailing outlook on economic activities, for it has been part of the "ideological equalitarianism" in American society to esteem an eminent man if in his youth he also did lowly jobs like everyone else. It seems that his rise to fame is more praiseworthy if he began his career in a humble position. And it might be added that the strength of this value is not notably diminished by the fact that many of those who started so humbly did not really have to do so, inasmuch as their families were quite well off. It is, therefore, of interest that business and industrial leaders seem to be on the way toward abandoning this tradition, while it seems to have remained strongest among the heirs. Of course, this distinction between the high or the low status of a first job is quite crude, and the interpretation of these figures is inevitably speculative. Yet a comparison between the two periods shows a clear trend in the same direction for each type of career: an increasing proportion of business leaders begin their work careers in a job of relatively high status. To be sure, a majority still start their careers in the traditional manner. And

TABLE 66

Percentage of American Business Leaders Attaining Different Levels of Education, by Career Type and Date of Birth

Period and Educational Attainment	Entrepreneurs	Bureaucrats	Heirs
1831–1875	(N = 234)	(N = 115)	(N = 143)
High school or less	66	62	50
College or more	34	38	50
	100	100	100
1876–1920	(N = 117)	(N = 145)	(N = 165)
High school or less	62	35	28
College or more	38	65	72
	100	100	100

Source: Same as Table 65.

TABLE 67

Percentage Distribution of First Jobs of the American Business Elite, by Status Level and Date of Birth

Period and Status Level of First Job	Entrepreneurs	Bureaucrats	Heirs
1831–1875	(N = 219)	(N = 110)	(N = 125)
High status [a]	31	24	33
Low status [b]	69	76	67
	100	100	100
1876–1920	(N = 51)	(N = 103)	(N = 79)
High status	43	43	39
Low status	57	57	61
	100	100	100

[a] Includes first jobs as proprietors, firm members, executives, government officials, and professionals.
[b] Includes first jobs as white-collar workers, salesmen, and manual laborers.

Source: Same as Table 65.

it is improbable that this practice will be abandoned, since it is an important experience for the future executive to have worked in the lower rungs of the enterprise hierarchy (quite apart from the symbolic meaning attached to the idea of "working from the ground up"). But it may well become even less common than it is in the modern generation of business leaders to start their careers in this manner, since few of them really need to take first jobs of low status and since there are many training substitutes for the experience itself. The men we have classified as "bureaucrats" have so far gone most rapidly in the direction of beginning their careers in positions involving considerable skill and responsibility. If their precedent presages a more general development in the future, then we may see a further impairment of the "rags to riches" myth. As we shall see later, there are signs already that the myth itself is superseded gradually by alternative beliefs, even in the United States, where that myth has swayed the popular imagination more than in any other country.

The bureaucratization of economic enterprises is reflected in the career patterns of business leaders in still another way. As we have seen, bureaucratization involves a detailed subdivision of administrative organization in the enterprise, and such subdivision involves by definition a considerable increase in the number of jobs between the top and the bottom of the administrative hierarchy. This increase means two things: a larger number of ranks and an increase in the number of positions at each rank. These facts should have a decisive influence upon the careers of industrialists. The entrepreneurs, whose careers frequently develop with the enterprise they have helped to initiate, need not spend their time in moving up an administrative hierarchy, and they may, therefore, achieve success at a relatively early age. The industrial bureaucrat, on the other hand, is characterized by a career which involves his gradual advancement from job to job within an administrative hierarchy. Hence, he can be expected to achieve economic success relatively late. For the heirs it is not possible to hypothesize a typical "age of first success."

It would follow from these findings that the careers of entrepreneurs and bureaucrats especially should also show significant differences with reference to the number of positions which each has held during the whole course of his career. In part, this is simply a correlative of age. If entrepreneurs achieve their economic success early, they cannot have held as many positions as the industrial bureaucrats who achieve their success relatively late. The two variables, however, are not synonymous. "First success" at an early age is theoretically quite compatible with a large number of positions held throughout a career, unless it is characteristic for the man who achieves success early to have subsequently a relatively stable career in which he changes his jobs rather infrequently. Of course, the converse is not true, since the man who achieves success relatively late is likely to have held a rather large number of positions. While the figures bear out these considerations, it is of interest that the career pattern of entrepreneurs shows the effects of bureaucratization, even though entrepreneurs tend to hold fewer positions during their work history than do bureaucrats. Of the entrepreneurs born between 1771 and 1830 (N = 143), 28 per cent held five positions or more throughout their careers, a percentage which rose to 44 per cent for the period 1831–1875 and fell slightly to 39 per

TABLE 68

Percentage Distribution of Entrepreneurs, Bureaucrats, and Heirs, by Age at the Time of "First Success" and by Date of Birth

Period and Age at Time of "First Success" [a]	Entrepreneurs	Bureaucrats	Heirs
1831–1875	(N = 137)	(N = 107)	(N = 143)
30 years or under	72	25	56
31 years or over	28	75	44
	100	100	100
1876–1920	(N = 59)	(N = 108)	(N = 84)
30 years or under	76	24	48
31 years or over	24	76	52
	100	100	100

[a] We have classified our subjects by the age at which they achieved their "first success," since no other dividing point within the careers of different men is equally comparable.

Source: Same as Table 65.

cent for the period 1876–1920. But if an increasing proportion of entrepreneurs held a relatively large number of jobs, a majority of them (72, 56, and 61 per cent, respectively) has continued to hold four positions or less. By way of contrast it should be mentioned that the proportion of bureaucrats who held five or more positions during their careers increased from 62 per cent (1831–1875) to 82 per cent (1876–1920).

Similar contrasts between career patterns are obtained, if they are compared with regard to two other criteria: transfers between firms and between industries. As can be expected, the heirs

TABLE 69

Percentage Distribution of Interfirm and Interindustry Transfers of Entrepreneurs and Bureaucrats, by Frequency of Transfer and by Date of Birth

Period and Number of Interfirm and Interindustry Transfers [a]	Entrepreneurs	Bureaucrats	Per Cent Difference between Career Types
1831–1875			
Interfirm transfers	(N = 277)	(N = 99)	
2 or less	66	51 ⎫	
3 or more	34	49 ⎬	±15
	100	100	
Interindustry transfers	(N = 277)	(N = 120)	
1 or none	63	75 ⎫	
2 or more	37	25 ⎬	±12
	100	100	
1876–1920			
Interfirm transfers	(N = 59)	(N = 110)	
2 or less	68	55 ⎫	
3 or more	32	45 ⎬	±13
	100	100	
Interindustry transfers	(N = 60)	(N = 108)	
1 or none	58	71 ⎫	
2 or more	42	29 ⎬	±13
	100	100	

[a] Transfers between firms occur more readily than between industries. Hence, a different measure of mobility had to be used for the two types of transfers.

Source: Same as Table 65.

among the business elite showed the least mobility: about 90 per cent of them made two or less transfers between firms and one or no transfer between industries, in each of the periods. Entrepreneurs as well as bureaucrats show more mobility than that. There is no significant change in the mobility pattern of entrepreneurs between these two periods, except possibly a slight increase in the number of interindustry transfers in the recent past. Likewise, there is no significant change over time in the mobility pattern of the bureaucrats, but there is a rather striking difference between them: entrepreneurs show more mobility between industries, while bureaucrats show more mobility between firms. The difference reflects the major characteristics of each type. As Schumpeter has emphasized, the entrepreneur is characterized primarily by his innovating function in the economy. Consequently, he shows a tendency to work in several industries, presumably prompted by the demands of his innovating activity. The bureaucrat, on the other hand, has a primary interest in regular advancement up the administrative hierarchy, and detailed knowledge of the problems of one industry will facilitate his career. This experience can be gained in many firms, and indeed his chances for promotion increase the more he is "in demand" by other firms. Hence, bureaucrats show a greater mobility between firms compared with their entrepreneurial colleagues, but a lesser mobility between industries.

Karl Marx had in mind entrepreneurs and heirs, not bureaucrats, when he talked about bourgeois exploiters. If he had anticipated the development of bureaucratic management, he might have recognized that "ownership of the means of production" was less important than *control*. Bureaucrats tend to control the means of production in all industrial societies. Communist as well as free-enterprise societies give high pay and considerable autonomy to professional managers.[6] For those American executives who are not sizable stockholders in the

6 James Burnham, *The Managerial Revolution*, New York: John Day, 1941; Alex Inkeles, "Social Stratification and Mobility in the Soviet Union, 1940–1950," *American Sociological Review*, Vol. 15, August 1950, pp. 465–479.

company, ownership is almost as remote as it is for the factory manager in the Soviet Union. A Soviet citizen who strode airily into a Leningrad factory and explained that he was one of the owners would be ejected as quickly as a United States Steel stockholder who arrived unannounced to inspect one of "his" plants. Karl Marx underestimated the revolutionary implications of large-scale organizations in the economy.

The bureaucratization of business management and the separation of *ownership* from *control* mutually reinforce one another in giant corporations. The stockholders own the corporation, but they are usually too numerous to take an active part in the management of its affairs. They are entitled to profits, which they receive in the form of dividend checks. They are entitled also to vote in proportion to their stock holdings for or against the incumbent board of directors. But ordinarily, stockholders have little choice but to mail in their proxies to the hands that feed them, and the incumbent board is overwhelmingly reelected. Occasionally, a large stockholder tries to wrest control from the existing management in a costly proxy fight. The late financier Robert Young took control of the New York Central Railroad in this way. Such contests are so rare that they generate enormous excitement. As A. A. Berle, Jr., put it, "In practice, institutional corporations are guided by tiny self-perpetuating oligarchies. These in turn are drawn from and judged by the group opinion of a small fragment of America—its business and financial community." [7]

Peter F. Drucker has argued that the emergence of "the employee society" requires a new conception of economic behavior in industrial societies. "The divorce of the worker from product and means of production is essential and absolute. It has nothing to do with legal control or political institutions. The worker by himself cannot produce. He must have access to that highly complex organization of men, machines, and tools we call a plant." [8] This sounds faintly like the Marxian idea of the propertyless proletarian, but Professor Drucker (1) applies it to top management as well as to wage workers and (2) uses it to demonstrate that remuneration within the large corporation has little to do with *market* criteria. Consider the General Dynamics Corporation, which had in 1961 $2,062,378,000 in sales, $816,357,000 in assets, 106,000 employees—and a *loss* for the year of $143,203,000! [9] No doubt, this staggering loss pleased neither top management nor stockholders, but it could not be attributed to the way individual employees of the company did their jobs. The loss was generated by the bureaucracy that organized the corporate effort and as such was not susceptible to breakdown—except for purposes of recrimination. Employee remuneration was, for the most part, independent of these bookkeeping matters. A man's salary was determined by the nature of his work and the evaluation of his performance by personnel people.

Losses are unusual for large corporations, except in time of depression, because their operations are so diversified that the profits of one division ordinarily cancel the losses of another. According to *Fortune*, only 24 of the 500 largest industrial corporations in the United States reported losses for 1961. But whether the corporation suffers a loss or makes a profit, approximately the same remuneration is paid to employees because, as Drucker argues, *there is no determinate way to relate the market success or failure of the corporation as a whole to individual contributions*. Top management in a large corporation cannot use the market yardstick to evaluate lower-echelon employees, and therefore remuneration of employees becomes a bureaucratic decision. One's salary and one's chances for promotion depends on convincing superiors in the administrative hierarchy of one's worth. This is one of the reasons

[7]   Adolph A. Berle, Jr., *The Twentieth Century Capitalist Revolution*, New York: Harcourt, Brace, 1954, p. 180.

[8]   Peter F. Drucker, *The New Society*, New York: Harper, 1959, p. 5.
[9]   *Fortune*, Vol. 66, July 1962, pp. 172–173.

for wasteful empire building in big organizations. What better testimony to one's value than a large staff?

Drucker's argument assumes not only that a corporation is large but also that it is eternal. Is a corporation really eternal? How long could General Dynamics go on losing more than 100 million dollars per year? If a giant corporation ignores market considerations, will it not go bankrupt? Giant corporations can lose money for a long time and continue to operate. Consistent losses are more likely to produce mergers than bankruptcies. And even if a bankruptcy occurs, as has happened with several railroads, the enterprise continues to operate, sometimes with the same management and usually with the same employees. One would not have known, for example, from riding one of its trains on the day after the public announcement, that the New York, New Haven, and Hartford Railroad had gone into bankruptcy. But giant corporations rarely lose money consistently. On the contrary, most large corporations pay handsome dividends to stockholders and also save enough capital to finance new investment. Sixty-four per cent of the $150,000,000,000 spent by industrial concerns for plant and equipment between 1946 and 1953 came from internal sources (profits not distributed to stockholders as well as depreciation and depletion reserves).[10] In short, large corporations tend to grow larger, to become, as the lawyers put it, "a trust for perpetual accumulation." [11] This growth trend allows corporate management a comfortable margin of safety for new ventures. For example, there is little risk for the Great Atlantic and Pacific Tea Company in opening a supermarket. With profits of $57,464,000 in 1961, A & P management can afford to operate some stores at a loss.[12] The growth trend also allows corporate

management considerable freedom of action in distributing wages, salaries, and dividends among the employees and owners of the company.

The business corporation has become prominent in the economies of Western countries partly because it is a convenient way of pooling venture capital and partly because it fits the organizational requirements of industrial societies. Many economic activities are most efficiently performed by highly differentiated organizations with long time perspectives, and self-perpetuating corporate bureaucracies meet this specification. Large-scale business organizations tend to generate large-scale organizations in other parts of society; the economist John Kenneth Galbraith calls this tendency "the principle of countervailing power." [13] Thus, many governmental agencies—the Interstate Commerce Commission, the Securities and Exchange Commission, the Food and Drug Administration, the Federal Power Commission—came into being to regulate corporations so large and powerful as to require specialized measures. Similarly, the existence of corporations employing tens of thousands of workers stimulated the growth of bureaucratic unions capable of bargaining with employers on more nearly equal terms.

Bureaucratic Unions: A Response to Bureaucratic Management

Reprinted by permission. From Seymour Martin Lipset, "The Political Process in Trade Unions: A Theoretical Statement," in Galenson and Lipset, Eds., *Labor and Trade Unionism: An Interdisciplinary Reader*, New York: Wiley, 1960, pp. 216–241.

Management bureaucracies usually demand "responsible union leadership" as their price for recognizing the union's position. "Quickie" or wildcat strikes over grievances, jurisdictional or factional fights, militant demands by a member-

10 Berle, *The Twentieth Century Capitalist Revolution*, *op. cit.*, pp. 37–38.
11 Berle, "Economic Power and the Free Society," *op. cit.*, p. 6.
12 *Fortune*, Vol. 66, August 1962, p. 120; John William Andrews, "U.S. vs. A&P: Battle of Titans," *Harper's Magazine*, Vol. 201, September 1950, pp. 64–73.

13 John Kenneth Galbraith, *American Capitalism: The Concept of Countervailing Power*, Boston: Houghton Mifflin, 1952.

ship in excess of those agreed upon by the union officials, and all other kinds of actions outside the control of the union officers upset the routine of production or profit making, and management demands their elimination. This insistent cry for union "responsibility" often leads to undemocratic unionism since it sometimes becomes a demand that unions coerce their members.

There is a basic conflict between democratic unionism and "responsible" unionism, which many conservatives and business leaders do not recognize, at least in their public pronouncements. The dictatorial mechanisms found in many unions are an adaptation to management's insistence that its yielding on union security issues must be followed by union responsibility.

At least one major industrial union has openly acknowledged this problem. In *The Dynamics of Industrial Democracy*, Clinton Golden and Harold Ruttenberg, then officials of the United Steelworkers, pointed out that this union has consciously developed a number of mechanisms, partly educational and ideological and partly formal control devices, to prevent variations in local practices. They describe a case in which a militant and loyal local union officer was expelled from the union because he refused to recognize that he could not set local policies which violated national agreements. The problem of the local leader under a national bureaucracy was well put by this expelled leader: "Being a good union man is agitating—that's what I always knew as a union man—and I got fired for agitating. . . . The company has had it in for me since 1933. I'm a thorn in the flesh to it. Now the union sides with the company and I am out."

Adaptations to the need to adjust to bureaucratic industry which preserve union organizational stability also serve the interests of the leaders of trade unions by reducing the hazards to their permanent tenure of office. By increasing the power of the administration over local units, the officials reduce the sources of organized opposition. The United Automobile Workers has given its international executive board the right to suspend the officials of local unions for violating international policies. This modification in the union's constitution was defended as necessary for contract negotiations, but it also enabled the international officials to eliminate potential rivals. In both their conciliatory tone—as when they call for intraunion discipline and responsi-

bility—and in their militant tone—as when they call for union solidarity in a dispute with management—union leaders strengthen their own hands and justify their monopolization of internal power in the course of articulating organizational needs and purposes.

Unions that are small or that do not deal with large centralized industries may permit local units a great deal of autonomy. The International Typographical Union, for example, permits its locals considerable freedom in negotiations. It is operating, however, in an industry which does not have large national companies and which is, in part, non-competitive from one section of the country to another. But even this union limits its locals' freedom to strike or to make concessions to management on issues involving union security, or jurisdiction over various mechanical processes. The ITU, like many other unions, is faced with the problem that a prolonged series of strikes in different parts of the country could bankrupt the union's strike funds.

A somewhat different situation giving rise to increased bureaucratization is found in industries that are highly competitive. Here the pressure for bureaucratization may come from the union; large unions are often unable to stabilize their own position unless the industry becomes less competitive, and therefore more predictable, in character. Unions such as the garment unions have developed highly centralized structures so as to be able to force employers to develop similar collective bargaining practices. In some cases, the unions have been able to force bureaucratic structures on employers by forcing them to join industrial associations and set up codes of business practice. In such industries, unions are as constrained to prevent their local units from violating standard policy as are unions operating within highly bureaucratized industries.

The participation of government boards in collective bargaining may also increase trade union bureaucracy. Local unions yield powers they once possessed to their international, as the locus of decision shifts from a local to a national governmental level. This phenomenon is an illustration of the functional interrelationship between patterns of social organization. The reaction to increased bureaucracy in one institutional area, in this case, the government, increases the need for bureaucratization of other institutions like trade unions, which interact with it.

As control over decisions shifts away from the local levels, there is a decrease in membership participation, and interest in local affairs. Similarly, disagreements over policy are increasingly limited to conflicts over national policies, knowledge about which is limited to members of the bureaucracy itself. Thus conflicts occur more and more as administrative fights at international headquarters and less and less as political struggles between groups in the locals. The implications of this shift were once graphically expressed to a friend of mine by a steelworker who said, explaining his lack of interest in the local union: "We don't have a union any more, we have a contract. The economists and statisticians negotiate contracts—all we can do is vote 'yes' or 'no' to them."

Increased bureaucratization within the union does, of course, help protect the rights of the workers as well as reinforces the position of leadership. Insofar as unions operate to protect their members from management arbitrariness and caprice in hiring and promotion, they emphasize rational and impersonal norms and standards such as seniority and "equal pay for equal work." These standards, systematized, standardized, and administered, are a bulwark of the worker's security and freedom.

Bureaucracy as an organizational pattern which effectively meets so many and varied needs —of the organization, of leadership, of the members—has deep roots in the trade union movement. It may be stated as a general proposition, however, that the greater the bureaucratization of an organization, the less the potential for membership influence over policy.

COMMUNICATIONS WITHIN UNIONS

One major source of administrative power, which is exclusively available to the incumbent bureaucratic hierarchy, is control over the formal means of communication within the organization. The right of free speech of individual members means little as an effective check on administrative power if the union leaders have control over all public statements made by members of the administrative or field staff, the union newspaper, and the expense account which enables officials to travel around the country to see and talk to local members and leaders. The monopolization of the channels of communication is one of the basic conditions for shaping attitudes and behav-

ior by propaganda. This condition is indigenous to the structure of totalitarian states; it is also characteristic of the one-party structure of most labor unions.

This particular form of control has a number of consequences for the power structure of a union. The only viewpoints about union matters that are widely available to the membership under such conditions are those of the administration. Official policy is justified, opposing proposals or programs discredited if mentioned at all, and the only information concerning union affairs that reaches the general membership is that which officialdom wishes them to hear. Secondly, this control obstructs the crystallization and organization of opposition. Even if the membership is not thoroughly convinced of the correctness and efficiency of administration policies and there is widespread discontent, organizing active opposition presupposes a means of "getting together," of communicating. The reduction of "collective ignorance" is impossible without widespread contact and information.

To be sure, no administration group can exercise a total control over the flow of communications within its organization. And different organizations vary in the degree to which the administration "party" approaches a monopoly. Any attempt to analyze the factors which differentiate democratic from non-democratic organizations must consider the determinants of such variations. A few are suggested here:

Communications reaching the membership from sources outside of the organization may weaken administrative control. For example, political parties, in the United States at least, do not control the newspapers which their members read. Such newspapers, by criticizing acts of party leaders, can help create the basis for factional opposition. In the labor and Socialist parties of Europe, the party usually owns or controls the newspapers which support it, and this facilitates continued domination by party leaders.

The internal structure or political processes in trade unions are not usually exposed in the press. There have, however, been a number of cases in which outside media have attempted to reach trade union members. In New York, the Yiddish press, especially the *Forward*, a Socialist paper, played a major role in the life of the garment unions for a long period. This paper, which was widely read by immigrant Jewish garment workers, criticized union policies and often acted as the organ of groups within the union. As might be expected, the union leadership resented the independence of the *Forward*. In many unions today, the press of the Catholic Church reaches Catholic workers with propaganda about internal union issues, and it has played an important role in factional situations. Radical political groups have played a similar role in furnishing union members with information and propaganda about their union.

Certain occupational groups have supported newspapers or magazines that are devoted to news of the trade but independent of union control. This has been true in the entertainment and printing fields, whose unions have significantly more internal democracy than have most trade unions.

In small union locals, interpersonal or oratorical communication may be effective in reaching the members, and control of the organizational machinery is not an important communications asset. In larger one-party organizations, however, the effective monopolization of communications will vary inversely with the extent to which communications media stemming from extraorganizational sources are directed to the members of the organizations. Such independent organs can be based on an ethnic community or religious group which overlaps with an occupation, on political groups that are concerned with the internal policies of trade unions, and, in a few special cases, on interest in occupational affairs.

THE MONOPOLY ON POLITICAL SKILLS

In most unions, one of the principal factors that perpetuates incumbent power is the administration's almost complete monopoly of the chances for learning political skills. One of the few roles open to a manual worker in which he can learn such skills is that of union leader. In the political life of the nation as a whole, leaders are recruited mainly from occupations which themselves require political skills—largely those of organization and communication. The legal profession, of course, is the one that best trains its members for these activities; but many business executive positions run law a close second, since the successful executive must be able to make speeches, secure assent, mediate conflict, and so forth. Anyone who has been concerned with public relations work must learn these skills,

and so must the leaders of mass organizations, such as trade unions, farm groups, and professional societies. In large measure, the existence in the society at large of many and diverse "political" leadership roles means that almost every group can find politically trained people to present and organize support for its viewpoints.

The average worker has little opportunity or need to learn political skills. He is rarely, if ever, called upon to make a speech before a large group, to put his thoughts down in writing, or to organize a group's activities. The officers' monopoly of political skills within the union may therefore be suggested as one of the major factors which prevents the effective organization of opposition sentiment in labor organizations, and which enables an incumbent administration to use its superior communicative skills to subdue or divert discontent.

The one-party union organization may offer office-seeking union members the opportunity to learn organizational skills through formal educational programs or through participation in unpaid voluntary positions. Such aspiring members, however, are usually subjected to a barrage of administration views on economics, politics, and union organization. Mobility within the union structure requires that the aspirant take over the norms and orientations dominant in the organization, that is, those held by the leaders. It is also likely that active members, the potential leaders, will be receptive to the viewpoint—broad or narrow—of the administration and develop a loyalty to it as the source of a more interesting and rewarding pattern of life activity than they have formerly experienced. In this sense a union organization provides ambitious workers who are confined to their occupation opportunities that few other agencies in society do.

Aside from education or indoctrination, the aspiring leader has literally one place to go if he is to go anywhere—into the administration. Unless some opposition group exists, his political activity has to be within the bounds set by the incumbents. Union officers, who are often faced with a paucity of skilled prospective subordinate officials and the lack of any means to train them, are usually willing and even anxious to recruit capable union activists into the administrative structure.

The major advantage accruing to union officers from their possession of the skills of politics may be lessened, however, and even eliminated if the members of their union have other extraorganizational sources of developing these skills. For example, actors must learn to deliver speeches effectively, and observers of the membership meetings of Actors' Equity report that there is a high degree of membership participation in discussion, as well as a long history of internal factional politics.

But most workers who belong to unions do not gain these abilities through their jobs, and research studies indicate that they do not usually belong to formal organizations outside of the union. There are, however, at least two organizations that have contributed to the training of workers in political skills—churches and radical political parties. In the United States and Great Britain many workers belong to churches whose membership is predominantly working class and whose lay leaders or ministers are themselves workers. Various observers of the British labor movement have pointed to the fact that a great many of the early leaders of British trade unions and labor political groups were men who first served as officers or Sunday School teachers in the Methodist or other non-conformist churches. In the United States, many of the early leaders of the United Automobile Workers, which had a large membership from the South, were men who had been active in Southern sects. Today, the Catholic Church, through the Association of Catholic Trade Unionists and Catholic Labor Schools, seeks to train Catholic workers in the skills of oratory, parliamentary procedure, organization, and administration. In situations in which Catholics as a group wish to fight the incumbent leadership, Catholics trained in these church groups often form the active core of opposition groups.

On the other side, left-wing political parties like the Communists and Socialists have contributed a large number of the labor leaders of America. Workers who join such parties are trained, formally or informally, in the skills of organization and communication and become potential union leaders. During the late thirties, John L. Lewis, though a political conservative, was forced to hire many Socialists and Communists as CIO organizers because these parties were the only reservoirs of organizing talent and skill that were friendly to the labor movement. One of the things that has enabled Communists to

gain support from non-Communists within the labor movement is the fact that in many unions Communists, although they are a small minority, are the only persons not in the union administration who know how to organize an effective opposition.

THE SOCIAL STATUS OF UNION LEADERS

It has been noted frequently that labor union officials become set apart from the rank and file in both their styles of life and their perspectives and modes of thought. This cleavage is most clearly visible in the upper rungs of union administrative hierarchies, where the income differential between union officials and working members is sizable, and where the more or less permanent tenure of most national officials makes their higher income more secure and more regular than many workers can ordinarily expect. This higher, more secure income, together with the different range of experience that is involved in being a union official—desk work, travel, association with business, government, and other union leaders—provides the basis and the substance for styles of life markedly different from that of the men in the shop. At the local level there is generally not a large difference between the official's income and the worker's pay, but the local officer still has an advantage in the security of his income, the greater chances he has to rise within the union structure, and (by no means least important) the fact that the union job gets him out of the shop into a much pleasanter, more varied, and more rewarding type of work.

The special interests and kinds of activity union officials experience, both on and off the job, create bonds of sentiment, and a common orientation and perspective, which, while sharpening the cleavage between officials and the rank and file, serve as important cohesive elements within the leadership group. The members of a union officialdom, who share far more in common with each other than they do with the rank and file, develop a self-consciousness regarding their common interests which finds expression in their use of the organization machinery for the defense of their individual tenures and group retention of power.

If a trade union structure is further viewed as part of the total system of social stratification, other factors that contribute to the tendency toward oligarchy and undemocratic behavior on the part of labor officials become clear. Status—the honor and deference accorded individuals by certain others—has no meaning except as it locates an individual, group, or stratum relative to others in the same frame of reference. Psychiatrists and social psychologists have indicated the tremendous importance to an individual of the position accorded him by those from whom he claims a given status. In American society, an individual's status is most closely related to his occupation, but it is also influenced in some contexts by such attributes as kinship, power, length of residence, and other factors. A look at the status of the working members of a union compared to that of their officers may suggest how these relative positions affect the degree and nature of the two groups' participation in union affairs.

In general, the officers of local and international unions do not appear to be accorded status by virtue of their association with their particular trade or industry, but rather in regard to the quite different roles they play in their occupation of "trade union official." That this status is very much higher, in the eyes of both the general public and their own rank and file, than the status of almost all working class occupations, can hardly be doubted. A study of the relative job prestige of different occupations (as ranked by a national cross section of the population) indicated that an "official of an international union" ranks about the same as "proprietors, managers, and officials." The following comment by the authors of an evaluation of the United Auto Workers, Irving Howe and B. J. Widick, illustrates the strong evidence that workers themselves generally accord higher status to their officers than to their fellow workers.

"The status of the union official can be very high; . . . he is usually highly respected by the workers for his presumed superior knowledge and greater articulateness; he earns a larger and more steady income than they do; he does not have to submit to factory discipline and can keep comparatively flexible hours; and he enjoys what is for most Americans a very great privilege and mark of social authority: he can wear 'white collar' clothes rather than work clothes."

Each of the grounds on which this deference is accorded—knowledge, skills, income, job control, head instead of hand work—tends to separate the official from the ranks in terms of style of life, perspectives, and so forth. Taken together they support a status differential which tends to *justify* the leader's monopolization of union functions and important activities which his position in the union hierarchy only makes *possible*. He not only wields his power and makes his decisions by virtue of his office, but, equally important, the high status accorded him by the members serves to make his authority legitimate in a familiar self-reinforcing pattern of power and status: union office carries with it power, develops skills, supports a middle-class style of life, and is in fact a middle-class occupation. All of these factors, together with the position itself, are accorded relatively high status by the rank and file—a status which makes the entire role and the actions of its incumbent legitimate.

There is a basic strain between the democratic values of the trade union movement and this system of status placement. With few significant exceptions, every trade union official has moved up in the hierarchy through his own achievements. The occupation is one of the few high-status ones in which status is secured almost completely by achievement rather than ascription. Most high-status positions necessarily carry with them some security of tenure once a given position is reached. Democracy, however, implies permanent insecurity for those in governing positions —the more truly democratic the governing system, the greater the insecurity. Turnover in office is inherent in the democratic value that demands equal access by all members of the system to positions of power. Thus, every incumbent of a high-status position of power within a democratic system must, of necessity, anticipate a loss of position if democratic values are accepted.

It is not in harmony with what is known of the psychological needs of individuals to expect persons in such positions to accept this insecurity with equanimity. Once high status is achieved, there is usually a pressing need to retain and protect it. This is particularly true if the discrepancy between the status and the position that one is apt to be relegated to upon losing it is very great. In other words, if the social distance between the trade union leader's position as an official and as an ordinary member is great, his need to retain the former will be correspondingly greater.

It is quite true that this insecurity is faced by holders of public office in any democratic society, but there are important differences. Politicians in the larger society are more than likely to be drawn from what Weber so perceptively termed the "dispensable" occupations like those of law and journalism. These occupations are dispensable in the sense that the practitioner is able to leave them for extended periods and enter politics without any loss of skill during his period of absence (perhaps the opposite is true in the case of the lawyer!) and return to the practice of his profession without too great a financial loss or dislocation. Actually, former public officials, whether lawyers or not, are usually able to capitalize on the skills and informal relations they have established while in office. A defeated politician is often in a better financial and status position after leaving office than while he was a public official. And, significantly for the democratic process, he may continue to play the role of political leader outside of office and be of use to his party in opposition.

The trade union leader, on the other hand, if he is one of the relatively few who are defeated after serving in high union office, cannot find a position which will enable him to both maintain his high-status position and continue to take part in the union's political system. This may explain why so many union leaders who lose office for one reason or another do not return to the shops but leave the occupation entirely, or secure an appointive office in some other union hierarchy. The absence of an experienced trained cadre of leaders in the ranks, which defeated office holders could provide, makes very much more difficult, if not impossible, the maintenance of an active opposition which could present alternative sets of leaders and policies at union elections. When all the men of experience in union affairs are either in the administration or out of the union, there is no nucleus of skills, ideas, and reputations around which an opposition can crystalize. The history of the United Automobile Workers is a good example: three former presidents and the former international secretary-treasurer, as well as a number of past vice-presidents and other high officials, have left the union for jobs in private industry or other unions.

The alternative to leaving the union for a defeated leader is a return to the assembly line or the mine pit. It is impossible to imagine John L. Lewis digging coal after defeat by the Miners' convention. Return to the shop, even by local leaders, in addition to making for a sharp reduction in their style of life, is often regarded as humiliation and failure, both by the defeated leader and by his fellow workers.

The strenuous efforts on the part of many trade union leaders to eliminate democracy (the possibility of defeat) from their unions, are, for them, necessary adaptive mechanisms. The insecurity of leadership status (endemic in democracy), the pressures on leaders to retain their high-status achievement, their control over the organizational structure, the differential skills that leaders possess vis-à-vis other union members are all strong factors in the creation of dictatorial oligarchies.

The relation of a leader's status to his efforts to minimize democracy in a union are quite direct. The hold of a union machine on officials does not lie simply in the fact that lower- and middle-level leaders retain their jobs at the pleasure of the top administrative leaders. It is primarily the attractiveness and status of these positions compared with work in the shops that gives the union office holders their huge stake in their positions and, depending on their rank, makes them dictatorial (if they hold high rank) or subservient to their union superiors (if they hold a low or intermediate position).

The effect of high but insecure achieved status becomes clear if we examine the consequences for the union structure of an occupation which gives status to the worker equivalent or superior to that of union official. Under these conditions, union machines cannot be as strong and cohesive, or demand and receive complete devotion and obedience from subordinate officials. The lack of a clear and significant differential of privilege (and style of life) between the officers and the rank and file will mean that the elected leader is not under as great a strain to eliminate democratic procedures and the possibility of turnover.

Actors' Equity and the American Newspaper Guild are trade unions whose members may aspire to higher income and status than their officials. Far from suffering from entrenched oligarchies, these two unions have had difficulty recruiting members to serve as full-time officials. Their solution has been to create a number of unpaid policy-making positions, so that members may continue their occupational careers while serving as union officials. In Actors' Equity, few members of the Executive Council ever run for re-election. In the guild, many of the officers come from the lower-status non-journalist occupations which the union has organized. Recently, the highest full-time official of the guild, who previously had not been a journalist, resigned to become editor of a labor newspaper. This action conforms to the value system of the craft, which ranks the occupation of journalist higher than that of union officer. Another union with a history of continuous opposition to administrations and frequent turnover in officialdom is the International Typographical Union. The members of this union are among the best paid, highest-status groups of American workers, a situation that may help account for the fact that in the ITU defeated union leaders return to the printshop after losing office. Interviews with members and leaders of this union suggest that they have a strong attachment to their craft, and also look upon it as an important high-status job. . . .

THE PROBLEM OF SUCCESSION. In any organization which does not have a democratic system for replacing leaders or in which there is no formally prescribed system of promotion or selection, the problem of succession often precipitates a crisis. The death of the leader of a one-party structure necessarily upsets the power equilibrium. The more the power structure was organized around personal allegiance to the "leader" the more likely it is that his death or retirement will result in major internal conflict.

In large measure, the passing of a dictatorial union leader creates or re-creates the situation that exists in a union which has been formed from a merger of existing autonomous groups. With the elimination of the person at the top of the pyramid, the leaders immediately below him may each claim equal rights of succession. As in the earlier case, the union may be faced with the problem of creating a power hierarchy out of equals. Each of the claimants has reputation, and skill in union politics, and the resources of control of a segment of the organization.

A recent situation which illustrates this pattern occurred in the United Steelworkers. Philip Murray became seriously ill during 1950 and was not expected to live. During his long stay in the hospital, several members of the International Executive Board began preparing for the struggle to succeed him. The apparent monolithic character of the union broke down. Murray, upon recovering, learned of this struggle and, according to reports, attempted to rearrange the internal power hierarchy so as to prevent a succession conflict. It is clear that Murray died before he was able to complete his internal rearrangements. No open conflict developed immediately as David McDonald, the secretary-treasurer, stepped into the presidency before his opponents could successfully organize against him. However, a number of top Steelworker leaders resented McDonald's succession, and close observers of the union predicted that open factional conflict would develop, a prediction that has been borne out.

There is an interesting similarity between the succession problem of the Steelworkers and that which developed in the Soviet Union in 1923–1924 around the illness and subsequent death of Lenin. Like Murray, Lenin took ill, and several members of the Central Committee began immediately to struggle over succession. Lenin was aware of this and attempted to eliminate Stalin as a candidate, but, as history has recorded, failed. Lenin's death brought about a bitter internal fight for succession in which at least five members of the Central Committee attempted to succeed to his mantle.

Within the trade union movement, there have been situations in which the death of a strong dictatorial leader did not result in a succession crisis. The death of Sidney Hillman, the president of the Amalgamated Clothing Workers, for example, was not followed by any open internal cleavage. This seeming exception to the succession crisis, however, was not due to a lack of conflict among Hillman's lieutenants. Two major groupings exist within the union, led by Hyman Blumberg and Frank Rosenblum. Each is very powerful in his own right, with power based largely in different regions of the country. Blumberg's power rests in the East, Rosenblum's in the Midwest and other sections of the country. Instead of an open conflict developing over control of the entire union, the previous secretary-treasurer, Jacob Potofsky, was made president, even though he has little backing of his own. It is significant that in this union, in which a strong leader did not succeed a powerful president, the old leader, Hillman, has been deified. The union constantly erects monuments of various kinds to him, and his name is used to give legitimacy to all present actions. Here the existence of regional blocs may lead to a permanent division of power, as has occurred at times in the history of nations. Such distribution of power contains within it the seeds of a secession movement.

Max Weber, in dealing with the succession problem in one specific context, has pointed out that the death of a charismatic leader (one to whom his followers impute extraordinary personal qualities) may cause his staff and followers, whose power does not rest on any traditional or legitimate basis, to experience tremendous insecurity about the consequences of succession. He considered that one solution is the bureaucratization of the structure, but his formulation of the problem does not clearly indicate the manner in which succession would bring about increased bureaucratization. More recent investigators have extended his analysis, pointing out that resistance to the authority of a new leader by the remaining staff of the old one leads him to institute allegiance to rationalized rules, that is, to increased bureaucratization. We might hypothesize on the basis of this analysis that when a trade union leader with charismatic attributes is succeeded without conflict, as in the case of Hillman, the union will become more bureaucratic, thus reducing rather than increasing the potentialities for democracy. There is evidence to suggest that such has been the case in the Amalgamated Clothing Workers. However, there is as yet little definitive evidence to substantiate this hypothesis.

There appear to be trade unions in which the process of bureaucratization has reduced the problem of succession to one of moving up a recognized ladder. It is possible to raise, if not answer on the basis of existing evidence, a number of questions which relate aspects of organizational structure to the process of leadership succession. Under what conditions will succession crises occur so as to give the membership some voice in the choice of a new leader? Under what conditions do the leaders of a union hierarchy feel constrained to keep the struggle within the hierarchy itself? When does a succession crisis open the door for new and independent groups to contest for union leadership? Under what conditions does the process become one of moving up within the hierarchy?

The succession crisis actually may give students of union organizations the opportunity to test many of the hypotheses in this chapter. The conditions which determine variations in patterns of succession should be the same ones that have been suggested here as determining variations in union political structure. A study of a large number of cases of succession should enable us not only to shed more light on the process of succession itself but may be the best way to test hypotheses bearing on the factors making for different degrees of leadership control and oligarchy. . . .

CONCLUSIONS

The analysis developed in this [article] obviously implies some pessimistic conclusions about the long-term chances for democracy in trade unions. To recapitulate the major points:

1. The structure of large-scale organization inherently requires the development of bureaucratic patterns of behavior. The conditions making for the institutionalization of bureaucracy and those making for democratic turnover in office are largely incompatible; and the degree of incompatibility varies with the degree of bureaucratization imposed by the need to come to stable terms with other bureaucratized institutions in the union's environment.

2. The structure of large-scale organization gives an incumbent administration very great power and advantage over the rank and file, or even over an organized opposition. This advantage takes such forms as control over financial resources and internal communications, a large permanently organized political machine, a claim to legitimacy, and a monopoly of political skills.

3. The ease with which an oligarchy can control a large organization varies with the degree to which the members are involved in the organization. The more important membership is considered, and the more participation in it there is, the more difficult it will be for an oligarchy to enforce policies and actions that conflict with the values or needs of the members. The concept of business unionism, which assumes that a union performs only the one major function for its members of securing the best possible contracts, helps prevent internal politics and conflict and encourages only limited participation on the part of the members. Any conception of trade union functions that increases the involvement of the members in the organization increases the potentialities for democratic conflict.

4. The inherent instability of democracy in trade unions is revealed by the implications of a trade union as a status-placing mechanism.

a. A functional requirement of the leadership role is that it be assigned higher status, that is, be a higher achievement than the follower role.

b. A dominant value of achievement is that upward mobility is a cultural goal.

c. One key attribute of a democratic political structure is the possibility for the circulation or rotation of leadership. This means that oligarchy can be avoided only if a mechanism exists by which leaders can be retired from office.

d. In society at large, political leaders may leave office and assume positions of equivalent or higher status. In the trade union movement, the defeated leader moves from a high-status to a low-status position if he remains within the union.

e. The institutionalization of movement from high to low status, which is what democracy in trade unions would mean for the leaders, would be a major deviation from the dominant value of achievement.

f. Fulfillment of these contradictory norms would result in anomie for the leaders and is a psychologically impossible situation.

The obvious conclusions of this analysis are that the functional requirements for democracy cannot be met most of the time in most unions. For example, the conflict between democratic and achievement norms means that democracy can exist as a stable system in unions only where the status differentiation between leaders and followers is very small. This may help account for the fact that democracy is found mostly in high-status unions and in local unions. Instead of suggesting that power corrupts in all situations, this analysis suggests that such "corruption" is a consequence of specific social structures, where conformity to one norm necessarily involves violation of another norm.

Nevertheless, the general proposition still holds that trade unions, like many other internally oligarchic organizations, help sustain political democracy in the larger body politic. As the American political scientist Franz Neumann, among others, has made clear, many internally dictatorial associations operate to protect the interests of their members by checking the encroachments of other groups. Even the most dictatorial union is a better protector of workers' economic interests, and of political democracy within the larger society, than no union, provided that the union is not a tool of either the state or the employer. In large measure, the chance that the collectivist society which is developing in most countries will be democratic rests in the possibility that trade unions, although supporters of Socialist objectives, will maintain their independence of the state. The behavior of the trade unions in the British Commonwealth and the Scandinavian countries furnishes real evidence that such a pattern is possible.

It is also necessary to remember that even the most dictatorial trade union leaders must be somewhat responsive to the economic needs of their members. A union oligarchy that does not defend the economic interests of the rank and file may find its membership disappearing, as John L. Lewis found in the twenties. Lewis, then a trade union as well as a political conservative, almost lost the United Mine Workers. Only after adopting the militant tactics for which he is now famous was he able to rebuild the union. A trade union that is not an economic defense organization has no function and will not long remain on the scene. But the fact that most unions do represent their members' interests must not be confused with the problem of internal democracy, for as Howe and Widick have pointed out:

"There is one decisive proof of democracy in a union (or any other institution): oppositionists have the right to organize freely into 'parties,' to set up factional machines, to circulate publicity and to propagandize among the members. . . . The presence of an opposition . . . is the best way of insuring that a union's democratic structure will be preserved. . . . To defend the right of factions to exist is not at all to applaud this or that faction. But this is the overhead (well worth paying!) of democracy: groups one considers detrimental to the union's interest will be formed. The alternative is dictatorship."

In the foregoing article, Professor Lipset raises the question of the compatibility of bureaucratic authority with democracy in large trade unions. He reaches a pessimistic conclusion on the basis of two assumptions: (1) that the structure of a large-scale organization gives an incumbent administration great power over the rank and file; and (2) that the status degradation usually involved in loss of office motivates union leaders to use this power to prevent effective opposition. Lipset is probably right about the decision-making structure in most unions but not necessarily about the protection of minority rights. Especially when union membership is essential to employment, as in some skilled trades or when there are union-shop agreements with employers, expulsion from the union means loss of livelihood. Under these circumstances, public opinion is intolerant of an autocratic union in which dissident elements are intimidated or expelled. When the McClellan Committee Hearings of 1957 and 1958 revealed gangster control of some unions, public opinion was aroused to the need for governmental protection of the right of union members to oppose the bureaucracy. Congress enacted the Labor-Management Reporting and Disclosure Act of 1959 which gave the Secretary of Labor and the Federal courts authority to guarantee some democratic procedures in unions.[14] At about the same time (1957), the United Auto Workers established *voluntarily* a system of appeal from decisions of the executive board of the UAW to a board of eminent outsiders.[15] Although the United Auto Workers pays the cost of operating the Public Review Board, six of the 29 initial cases carried to the Board were decided against the leadership of the UAW. Neither existing laws nor voluntary programs have transformed American trade unions into models of democratic decision making, but they place limits on undemocratic procedures.

Large corporations have also established machinery to guarantee procedural rights to workers—although not a voice in decision making. Sometimes this machinery is established to forestall government intervention, sometimes as a direct result of collective bargaining with unions, sometimes as a by-product of bureaucratization. The following article suggests how democratic values seep into the large corporation through the establishment of personnel administration as a specialized staff function.

14 Walter E. Oberer, "Union Democracy and the Rule of Law," in *Democracy and Public Review: An Analysis of the UAW Public Review Board*, Santa Barbara, Calif.: Center for the Study of Democratic Institutions, 1960, p. 50.
15 *Ibid.*, pp. 7–32.

Corporate Bureaucracies and the Institutionalization of Employee Rights

Reprinted by permission. From Howard M. Vollmer and Patrick J. McGillivray, "Personnel Offices and the Institutionalization of Employee Rights," *Pacific Sociological Review*, Vol. 3, Spring 1960, pp. 29–34.

Growth in the size and organizational complexity of modern American industrial enterprises has given rise to special concern in some quarters about the position of individual employees within these enterprises. Where an increasingly bureaucratized supervisor-worker relationship has come to replace the more personalized employment relationship characteristic of smaller firms, the question may be raised: What happens to the individual? Does he tend to become more and more anonymous and depersonalized—simply an economic commodity to be bought and sold in an impersonal labor market? Or are there any forces which tend to enhance human dignity and status among employees in larger firms?

There are indications that such forces do exist. They typically originate both in the external environment and in the internal conditions that are characteristic of modern large scale enterprises. Perhaps the most obvious and most dramatic of the forces that have contributed to increasing managerial recognition of employee claims to job security and protection from arbitrary treatment have been the interrelated processes of unionization, collective bargaining, and grievance arbitration.

But these processes reflect external pressures; there are also other forces that have their origin and nurture in the dynamic development of bureaucratic enterprise itself. This paper will discuss one such force—the way in which "staff" personnel agencies and specialists within these agencies act to support the institutionalization of concepts of employee "rights."

More specifically, it shall be indicated that the "privileges" that firms have granted employees ostensibly for the purposes of increasing morale and loyalty to the organization have now become more or less irrevocable commitments on the part of these enterprises. They have become "institutionalized" as part of the established pattern of mutual expectations of management officials and employees alike. They cannot be abandoned without changing significantly the character of the enterprises concerned. The structural support for this development is embodied in the activities of personnel specialists.

The evidence offered here in support of this thesis must be considered as illustrative, rather than conclusive, at this stage of research. This evidence is based in part upon exploratory interviews with forty-four personnel executives in leading enterprises in a large metropolitan area. The interviews were conducted during the course of a survey in 1958 under the auspices of the Institute of Industrial Relations of the University of California, Berkeley.

To understand what has occurred within industrial enterprises, it is useful first to review briefly the formal position of personnel departments as "staff" agencies in business enterprises.

PERSONNEL OFFICES: STAFF OR LINE?

Personnel administration as a specialized staff function has arisen, in part, out of the functional necessities of large-scale bureaucratic enterprises and partly as a result of certain historical circumstances.

As industrial enterprises have increased in size and complexity, they have become characterized by what Max Weber described as the characteristics of bureaucracy in its "ideal type." Among these characteristics is functional specialization and impersonality in the relationship of top management to employees at the lowest levels of the organizational hierarchy. Impersonality in the employment relationship has necessitated specialized personnel agencies which are charged with the function of establishing uniform personnel practices to integrate employees into an impersonalized organizational context. Specialization of the personnel function has proceeded along the same lines as specialization of other functions in the enterprise; e.g., finance, public relations, purchasing, transportation, etc.

Among the historical conditions that particularly contributed to the establishment of staff personnel and industrial relations departments in American industrial enterprises are: the concern with efficient utilization of manpower arising out of the scientific management movement and developments in World War I; labor legislation in the 1920's and 1930's that imposed special conditions of employment and employee treatment upon affected organizations; the growth of the trade union movement and resultant management concern with the "divided loyalty" of employees; and the human relations movement, emphasizing employee counseling procedures and attention to the "human" element in production.

Personnel offices may operate under a number of different titles. Among these titles are "labor relations office," "industrial relations office," "employment office," "manpower management office," and "employee relations office." A distinction frequently is made between "personnel" functions, as those concerned with intra-firm problems of personnel administration, and "labor relations" functions, as those concerned with union-management relations. Only intra-firm problems of personnel administration are considered in this paper.

A study by Dale Yoder in 1954 reported that at least 70 per cent of firms surveyed reported the following functions for their "employment relations" departments: (1) administration of the staff division; (2) planning of personnel policy, programs, and organization; (3) job analysis, recruitment, and selection; (4) training of personnel; (5) promotion, transfer, and release; (6) labor relations; (7) employee benefits and services; (8) medical and safety functions; (9) wage and salary administration; (10) personnel records and reports; and (11) personnel research.

Regardless of what functions personnel offices perform, their formal position within the managerial structure is usually conceived of by management as a *staff* position. Nevertheless, in actual practice it may be maintained that personnel departments in many cases exercise line functions; that is, *direct* control over personnel management affairs within the firm, in spite of their formal position as staff agencies.

This control over personnel matters is manifested in the written personnel policies of some firms. In the Jones and Laughlin Steel Company, for example, the Director of Personnel Relations is responsible for continuous review of the personnel relations activities in the various operations of the corporation and for compliance with corporation-wide objectives, policies, and programs in this regard. Similarly, a personnel executive in a large railroad transportation company told the authors:

"We have an enlightened management as far as labor relations is concerned. Our president has pointed out repeatedly that anything that affects labor relations must be approved by the personnel department. He has also said that in doubtful matters the personnel department will determine whether the particular matter affects labor relations or not."

In a mineral processing company, the director of industrial relations stated:

"In some firms labor relations departments have very little authority—the authority in personnel matters is vested in the line management. But here we do have considerable authority over line operations on labor relations and personnel matters."

Frequently, the formal authority of personnel departments is most strongly developed in matters which have to do with discipline and discharge, and grievance actions arising therefrom. A Bureau of National Affairs study reported that most companies provide some type of procedure for the review of disciplinary and discharge actions before such actions become effective. It was found that in approximately one-third of all companies surveyed this review is made by the personnel or industrial relations department. In another third of the companies the review is conducted by the personnel department plus one or more line management executives. In the remaining firms the review procedure is commonly handled entirely by line supervision—for example, by the department head or the plant manager.

An example of a management initiated policy which includes review procedures by the personnel department is the following excerpt regarding "relief from duty in departments" from a non-unionized department store:

"It is our desire that all separations be conducted in a manner which will satisfy the employee that we have attempted to extend him every consideration and that we are willing to reopen his case on the basis of any facts presented by him which may not have been given adequate consideration.

"Immediate supervisors of employees may request the Relief from Duty within their department of any employee considered unsatisfactory with the concurrence of the Department Heads, but under no circumstances may terminate any employee from the Store's employ.

"Department Heads shall consult the Employment Department on all questions pertaining to the Relief from Duty of any employee considered unsatisfactory, prior to the discussion of the matter with such employee.

"Department Heads shall, when requesting the Relief from Duty of any employees, justify such requests by submitting to the Employment Department written reports covering the record of warnings.

"The Employment Department shall, whenever possible, recommend the transfer of employees Relieved from Duty, provided the Merit Rating of the employee is satisfactory. In the consideration of all cases of Reliefs from Duty, the Employment Department shall consult with the Merit Rating Department, Training Department, and others interested in order to determine that all pertinent facts have been considered. . . ."

This mixture of staff and line functions in the operation of personnel offices may be more evident than in the case of other "staff" specialties. The primary function of line management in productive enterprises is to produce certain products. Financial, public relations, purchasing, transportation, legal, and other staff functions are clearly ancillary to the primary line management objective of achieving production goals. On the other hand, as management officials themselves are likely to point out, production goals cannot be achieved except through the cooperative efforts of the employees involved. Thus, it is not surprising that personnel management often becomes a "line" function.

In this discussion, however, we are not interested merely in the confusion of staff-line distinctions which characterize modern personnel management; we are also interested in changes in certain value orientations which arise out of this dilemma within the organization of industrial enterprises.

EMERGENT VALUES IN PERSONNEL POLICIES

The managerial rationale behind the establishment of personnel offices in most firms has given prominent emphasis to the promotion of employee morale, harmony, and loyalty to the goals of the organization. The Carborundum Company, for example, includes the following statement among its personnel policies in regard to the functions of its personnel department:

"To maintain high morale, enthusiasm, and loyalty to the interests of the company. To promote good understanding and cooperation among the company's personnel. To create a sense of belonging, so that all employees are working toward a common goal."

This orientation is expressed also in the personnel policies of the Lukens Steel Company, S. C. Johnson and Son, and others.

In such policies, high value is placed upon cooperative effort. The means proposed to achieve this objective is manipulation of employee attitudes toward the firm. Involved here is the assumption that it is within the ability of personnel specialists, using the technical skills of their trade, to select and motivate employees toward a high degree of harmonious cooperation and productive effort.

The philosophy of manipulation has had its eloquent exponents in the literature of management. Mr. L. A. Appley wrote at the time of his presidency of the American Management Association:

". . . competitive survival depends upon the capacity of management to increase the individual productivity of workers. . . . *The emergence of a new management era is the transferring of emphasis from technology to humanics*. It is the application of the same time, skill, effort, logic, understanding, knowledge, and competency to human resources which management applied so successfully in the past to physical resources."

Similarly, a writer in *Personnel Journal* expressed explicitly the manipulative orientation in his discussion of "supervision by suggestion":

"The effective supervisor today is a specialist in dealing with human relations. Understanding the forces that motivate people to cooperate is a powerful tool. It allows for the manipulation of human behavior to the mutual satisfaction of both the supervisor and those supervised.

"The successful supervisor is frequently distinguished by his ability to make it appear that his wishes originated with the other person. The employee who usually displays a negative attitude is studied very carefully to find some way in which an idea he expresses, or something he says, can be interpreted to mean what the supervisor would like to have it mean. The supervisor then tries to get the employee to express the desired thought himself. When the worker can be made to feel that he himself originated the idea, he is committed to it in advance and rejection of the supervisor's instruction is circumvented. At the same time the worker is made to feel personally adequate and even influential."

This manipulative orientation, however, is also reacting upon the character of industrial enterprises through the actions of the very agencies which were established with the explicit objectives of specializing in manipulation—personnel departments. Personnel specialists have operated in many firms to promote an attitude of adaptation to the presumed rights and interests of individual employees. The emergent concept of employee rights in personnel philosophy has perhaps been expressed most aptly by James Worthy of Sears, Roebuck and Company:

"These ideals are usually expressed in terms of 'rights'—the very word 'rights' implying their essentially moral and ethical nature . . . we may summarize some of the more significant of these rights as follows:

1. The right of every man to be treated as an individual and respected as a person;
2. The right of every man to a voice in his own affairs, which includes his right to contribute to the best of his ability to the solution of common problems;
3. The right of every man to develop and make use of his highest capacities;
4. The right of every man to fairness and justice in all his relationships with his superiors."

Mutual recognition of employee rights concepts, which is promoted by the activities of personnel specialists, may be rationalized and expressed verbally in different ways. For example, a personnel executive in a chemical firm stated what he believed to be a relationship between employee rights concepts and "the American way of life":

"Because of the type of country we live in, where the individual is more important than any company, a man carries this idea about his rights into his work—this idea of his 'dignity.' Employees are particularly concerned with their rights to job security, fair treatment, and being respected by management and their fellow workers."

A personnel executive in a food processing and packing firm mentioned the relevance of employee rights concepts to the implicit meaning of the employment relationship to the parties concerned:

"There are actual rights and there are implied rights. Actual rights are overtly expressed in company policies and practices. Implied rights are implicit in the expectations of the mutual parties to a relationship—like the employment relationship. Usually, when employees talk about their rights, they are not referring to contract provisions. Employees use the term in a broader sense. For example, if an employee feels his supervisor has treated him ill, he speaks of his rights as an individual with human dignity. For an instance of this, an employee who is publicly reprimanded in front of other employees is likely to feel that his rights as a human being with dignity have been violated by the supervisor."

INSTITUTIONALIZED RECOGNITION OF EMPLOYEE RIGHTS

The value orientations expressed in the previous comments of personnel specialists, however, tend to be merely ideological statements, rather than expressions of actual policy, if they lack institutionalized support. There seem to be three general sources of institutionalized support for the continued recognition of employee rights and their expanded acceptance in the future: (1) further formalization of the "line" authority of personnel offices in personnel management matters; (2) professionalization of personnel specialists; and (3) establishment of formal personnel policies that specify safeguards for employee rights.

Melville Dalton has pointed out that staff-line conflict is to be expected in industrial enterprises as a result of the differing personal backgrounds and organizational functions of staff and line managerial personnel. The additional point may be made that everyday conflicts between personnel specialists and line managerial officers are especially likely to occur because of confusion between "line" and "staff" responsibilities.

Arguments about proper personnel management practices are especially likely to occur in regard to disciplinary actions. Such disagreements were often indicated in the authors' survey of personnel executives. The personnel executives interviewed frequently reported that they see it as their responsibility to "sell" line management on what personnel specialists believe to be the proper procedures in disciplinary practices. Where their selling techniques are unsuccessful, they see it as their duty to take their cases to higher management for policy decisions. A personnel executive in the regional division of a large steel corporation reported:

"There are times when we believe line management at the plant level is wrong. Then they

say, 'God damn you, you're selling us down the river.' Then we must sell them on the right way to handle discipline. We may even have to go to the company president if we have a firm disagreement with plant managers." (Steel manufacturing)

A personnel director in a shipyard stated:

"I have as many arguments with the back office (line management) as I do with union leaders. Yesterday I had a fight with one of our managers to get him to give an employee adequate notice before discharging him." (Marine construction and repair)

A personnel executive in a petroleum company reported:

"I'm employed by the company, but my responsibility is to the employee as well as to the company. Sometimes I have to fight for an employee with management. I have to ward off the impulsive actions of division heads. Believe me, one has to have the courage of his convictions to do this." (Petroleum products)

Insofar as personnel specialists "win" their arguments on personnel matters of these types, particularly in regard to disciplinary procedures, they act to limit the arbitrary powers of line management officials over employees. They promote a new orientation within the firm directed toward the acceptance of what has come to be considered the legitimate "rights" of employees.

Also, to the degree to which personnel specialists become professionalized and identified with status considerations with regard to their occupational associates in local communities and even nationally, they become more committed to standards of practice and codes of ethics which emphasize fair treatment and "due process" principles in dealing with employees. Several of the national professional personnel societies, such as the personnel section of the American Management Association and the Society for Personnel Administration, have been concerned with the establishment and general recognition of ethical codes that emphasize employee rights concepts. Where such codes are accepted, the activities of personnel specialists within firms become less attributable to the individual ideas of individual personnel specialists and more referable to commonly accepted standards of personnel practice.

What is perhaps the most significant and potent mechanism for the institutionalized recognition of employee rights concepts has been the development of formalized personnel policies within industrial enterprises. In the Yoder study referred to earlier, it was indicated that "employment relations divisions" participate in the planning of policy programs and organization in eighty-six per cent of the firms surveyed. The formal policies which result from this planning activity not only may give personnel specialists considerable authority in "line" personnel management functions, but also may specify in considerable detail the safeguards established to protect employee rights, particularly in disciplinary actions.

The Bureau of National Affairs has reported that about three-fourths of business firms have such written disciplinary regulations in the form of "plant rules." Many companies in the remaining fourth operate under rules that are well known to employees, even though they are not in written form. The outlook for the future was summarized by a personnel executive in a paper products company in the following terms:

"In the future I see a continuing trend toward specifying and tightening disciplinary policies. Employees like to have a tight-run ship. They like to know that their supervisor will take the same action each day. They like to have rules and to have a part in creating them. They expect their discipline to be fair."

Formal disciplinary regulations not only have become more likely to specify causes for discipline but also more likely to define the severity of disciplinary action permitted in specified circumstances. Many plant rules have specific penalties attached to the violation of certain regulations. A high proportion of these simply state, "The following offenses may result in immediate dismissal."

In other cases, however, plant rules may list certain types of actions for which an employee ordinarily is not subject to discharge in a first offense. For example, the rules of an electronics firm studied by the authors state:

"For offenses against safety, plant working, and employee conduct rules, other than those specifically mentioned under Section B below, an employee shall not be discharged without first having been notified that repetition of the offense will be cause for dismissal. The record of this notification shall be incorporated in the personnel record at the time it is given. . . ."

In a shipyard, the disciplinary regulations make the following distinctions:

"Any employee committing any of the following violations shall be subject to discharge: (thirteen types of offenses are listed). . . .

"For any of the following offenses an employee will be given a pink (reprimand) slip: (six types of offenses are listed). . . .

"Any employee issued a second pink slip will be given five days off. . . .

"Any employee issued a third pink slip for any of the above violations shall be discharged."

In the procedure for disciplinary action of a small parts manufacturing company, offenses are classified into three types with correspondingly greater severity of discipline: "minor offenses," "major offenses," and "intolerable offenses." In the same company the following instructions, written by the personnel director, are given to supervisors regarding discharge policy:

"Not every rule violation justifies dismissal. But there is a point at which discharge becomes proper by reason of either a single serious infraction or an accumulation of minor infractions. The following 'yardstick' is suggested to determine whether this point has been reached:

1. Has the employee seriously or irreparably damaged the employer's trust and confidence in him? The importance of this test depends on the type of work done by the employee.

2. Does it seem likely that the employee will correct his deficiencies within a reasonable period of time if he is not fired?

3. What effect would retaining the employee have on the discipline and morale of other employees?

4. What about the individual himself? Does he have a long period of good service and, therefore, deserve special consideration? How would a discharge affect his job prospects elsewhere?

5. Finally, does discharge seem fair, all things considered? In other words, does the punishment fit the crime, taking into account any mitigating circumstances that might be present?"

The existence of such gradated penalties for different types of offenses and a discharge policy such as that just cited both tend to restrain management from arbitrary disciplinary action.

The Bureau of National Affairs study reported that among larger firms which have written plant rules about fifty per cent spell out the penalties for breaking each rule. According to this study, penalties for chronic absenteeism most frequently take the form of one or two warnings, then suspension, and then discharge—although in many firms suspension is not used and employees are discharged after one or two warnings. Insubordination is the basis of immediate discharge in about one-third of larger companies, although about the same proportion of companies report they do not discharge an employee until after one

warning about insubordination. The penalty for fighting is immediate discharge in about half of the companies studied, whereas other companies treat a first offense with a warning or suspension. As these disciplinary procedures are formalized, they become part of the pattern of legitimate expectations for both employers and employees. They establish standards of fair treatment that have become institutionalized.

TABLE 70

Paid Civilian Employment in the Federal Government, by Agency, January 31, 1962

Agency	Number of Employees	Agency	Number of Employees
Executive Office of the President:		Federal Home Loan Bank Board	1,144
White House Office	441	Federal Mediation and Conciliation	
Bureau of the Budget	455	Service	355
Executive Mansion and Grounds	72	Federal Power Commission	898
National Security Council	43	Federal Trade Commission	1,000
Office of Civil and Defense Mobilization	476	Foreign Claims Settlement Commission	62
All Other	72	General Services Administration	30,682
Executive Departments:		Housing and Home Finance Agency	12,401
Agriculture	91,279	Information Agency	11,005
Commerce	28,487	Interstate Commerce Commission	2,398
Department of Defense:		National Aeronautics and Space Administration	19,654
Office of the Secretary	13,874	ministration	19,654
Department of the Army	387,737	National Capital Housing Authority	420
Department of the Navy	351,507	National Labor Relations Board	1,841
Department of the Air Force	306,862	National Mediation Board	139
Health, Education, and Welfare	73,347	National Science Foundation	786
Interior	54,020	Panama Canal Company	11,853
Justice	30,899	Railroad Retirement Board	2,116
Labor	8,083	Renegotiation Board	202
Post Office	580,433	St. Lawrence Seaway Development Corporation	
State	38,999	poration	154
Treasury	80,763	Securities and Exchange Commission	1,210
Independent Agencies:		Selective Service System	6,804
American Battle Monuments Commission		Small Business Administration	2,922
mission	413	Smithsonian Institution	1,471
Atomic Energy Commission	6,783	Soldiers' Home	1,032
Board of Governors, Federal Reserve		Tariff Commission	269
System	603	Tax Court of the United States	149
Canal Zone Government	2,655	Tennessee Valley Authority	18,429
Civil Aeronautics Board	787	Veterans Administration	176,716
Civil Service Commission	3,823	Virgin Islands Corporation	585
Commission on Civil Rights	56	All other	591
Export-Import Bank	257	All agencies	2,445,598
Farm Credit Administration	235		
Federal Aviation Agency	43,295		
Federal Communications Commission	1,360		
Federal Deposit Insurance Corporation	1,274		

Source: U. S. Bureau of the Census, *Statistical Abstract of the United States: 1962*, Washington: Government Printing Office, 1962, pp. 405–406.

BUREAUCRATIC TENDENCIES IN POLITICAL, EDUCATIONAL, PHILANTHROPIC, AND WELFARE ACTIVITIES

Large-scale organization characterizes all of the institutions of industrial societies, not only the economy. Government bureaucracy is, however, the most conspicuous form of large-scale organization. In 1962, the budget of the federal government was nearly 90 billion dollars, and the number of civilian employees about two and a half million.[16] Table 70 shows the distribution of civilian workers among federal agencies. Note that the majority of federal workers are either in the Department of Defense or in the Post Office Department. Despite fears about the development of a "welfare state," the Department of Health, Education, and Welfare had only about 73,000 employees in 1962, less than the Treasury Department and far less than the half million persons employed by General Motors. State and local governments are more deeply involved in health, education, and welfare activities; about 60 per cent of the expenditures for these activities is borne by state and local governments.[17] Actually, the number of federal employees working in the health, education, and welfare fields is less than the large federal expenditures in these fields might suggest because much federal participation is financial rather than direct operation of programs. In 1960, the various social-insurance activities of the federal government (old-age, survivors, and disability insurance, unemployment compensation, etc.) disbursed $22,640,000,000 to beneficiaries.[18] And, as Table 71 shows, federal grants-in-aid to state and local governments—more than three billion dollars in 1960—help these governments operate their own health, education, and wel-

fare programs. Thus, more of the money than of the bureaucracy in the health, education, and welfare fields is federal.

TABLE 71
Federal Grants-in-Aid to State and Local Governments for Health, Education, and Welfare, 1960

Type of Service Supported	Amount of Federal Grants (in Millions of Dollars)
Health	
General health	16.0
Disease control	11.5
Mental health	4.9
Hospital construction	145.4
Water pollution control	43.2
Maternal and child health	17.4
Crippled children	17.1
Education	
Vocational education	39.1
Colleges of agriculture and mechanical arts	5.1
National Defense Education Act	68.5
Contributions to local school systems serving federal personnel	237.3
Library services	7.0
American Printing Home for the Blind	.4
Cooperative agricultural extension work	59.9
State marine schools	.5
Welfare	
Old-age assistance	1,170.5
Aid to dependent children	668.8
Aid to the blind	49.3
Aid to the permanently disabled	170.3
H.E.W. grants for child welfare	12.9
Public housing	127.4
State and territorial homes for disabled veterans	6.2
Agricultural commodity donation to schools and institutions	149.0
School milk program	80.6
School lunch program	151.3
Vocational rehabilitation	48.6

Source: Department of Health, Education and Welfare, *Health, Education, and Welfare Trends: 1961*, Washington, Government Printing Office, 1961, pp. 98–102.

[16] Bureau of the Census, *Statistical Abstract of the United States: 1962*, Washington: Government Printing Office, 1962, pp. 381, 405.
[17] Department of Health, Education, and Welfare, *Health, Education, and Welfare Trends: 1961*, Washington: Government Printing Office, 1961, p. 95.
[18] Bureau of the Census, *Statistical Abstract of the United States: 1962*, Washington: Government Printing Office, 1962, p. 278.

Private philanthropy is not usually thought of in terms of bureaucracy. Yet there are 129 American foundations with assets of at least ten million dollars; and in 1960 these foundations made grants totaling nearly $350,000,-000.[19] The largest foundation, the Ford Foundation, made grants in 1963 of nearly $250 million dollars.[20] To allocate such sums of money wisely and efficiently requires task specialization, formal procedures, and impersonality. The Ford Foundation has, in addition to its board of trustees and its president, Henry T. Heald, several vice-presidents who direct a New York headquarters staff of about 100 specialists in fields the Foundation is interested in helping and a supporting staff of several hundred secretarial and clerical workers. These full-time staff members are assisted by part-time expert consultants engaged as the need arises.

About 20,000 letters arrive at the New York headquarters of the Ford Foundation each year asking for financial support for projects or causes. Often they are addressed to "The Ford Foundation"—with no direction to a particular person within the organization. Sometimes they are addressed to "The President." In either case, they are opened by the Central Secretariat, the unit of the administrative staff of the Foundation concerned with correspondence. A member of the Central Secretariat reads each letter, attaches to it a form that includes a summary of its contents, a control number, and a target date for a reply, and routes it to the appropriate office within the Foundation. Usually, a reply is promptly made by the office to which the inquiry was directed by the Central Secretariat, and a carbon copy of the reply is sent to the Secretariat. If a reply is not made within a reasonable time after the target date, the Central Secretariat follows up with a reminder so that the letter cannot remain buried beneath a pile of papers on someone's desk or otherwise ignored. This procedure ensures (1) that letters are answered and

(2) that the person answering a letter is the individual most appropriate to deal with it.

Any one of the following programs of the Foundation might have a grant inquiry referred to it: Education, Humanities and the Arts, Science and Engineering, International Training and Research, Public Affairs, Economic Development and Administration, International Affairs, Population, or Overseas Development. If a grant request does not fit the categories of established programs, the Secretariat refers the letter to the program most closely related to the subject of the inquiry. That program sends a reply to the writer explaining that the Foundation does not maintain a grant program covering his field of interest. Of course, many letters come addressed to particular people in particular programs. These letters are also processed by the Central Secretariat—unless the writer takes the precaution of marking his communication "personal."

If a proposal fits an established program interest and if the staff member handling it thinks tentatively that it is worthy of support, a searching investigation begins. The qualifications of the applicant are explored. This may mean dozens of long-distance telephone calls, extensive correspondence, and travel to the part of the world in which the project would be located. A routine inquiry will be made about the tax-exempt status of the potential grantee since the Ford Foundation makes grants only to such organizations. In a short time, many letters and other items of information will have accumulated concerning this possible grant. If the proposal survives the initial screening by the professional staff, the further review by officers of the Foundation, and, in certain cases, a final review by the Board of Trustees, the applicant is notified by telephone that a *grant letter* will shortly be issued by the Secretary of the Foundation. This formal notification will contain all the terms and conditions of the grant—including the amount of the grant and the procedures for obtaining funds from the Treasurer's Office. At this point, all of the pieces of paper concerning the project (in-

---

[19] *Ibid.*, p. 307.
[20] Ford Foundation, *Annual Report*, New York: 1963.

cluding a carbon copy of the grant letter) will be placed in a chronological file, and this file will be stored in the Records Center adjacent to the Central Secretariat. Even if a grant is not made, all of the correspondence would be filed in the Records Center. This means that every Foundation staff member has ready access to the correspondence of every other program. It also means that staff members must send down to the Records Center when they wish to consult previous correspondence.

The foregoing account of the internal procedures for grant processing in the Ford Foundation could be duplicated for Rutgers University, the Roman Catholic Church, or the Red Cross. Bureaucracy is not confined to economic or political organizations. It arises wherever a large number of operations must be carried out in a uniform manner. An especially interesting case of bureaucratization lies in the field of social casework. Casework involves a highly personal relationship between a client with a problem and a professional helper (social worker). Yet, as the following selection shows, even the activities of this helping profession tend to become bureaucratized in contemporary society.

The Bureaucratization of Welfare Administration

Reprinted by permission. From Harold L. Wilensky and Charles N. LeBeaux, *Industrial Society and Social Welfare*, New York: Russell Sage Foundation, 1958, pp. 233–246.

Suppose an individual wants help on a personal problem from a family counseling agency. Except in case of emergency, he cannot apply for and expect immediate service. He must first talk with a receptionist, who will give him an appointment with a caseworker for a more or less distant date.[21] Already, in a minor way, service has been controlled: by a receptionist, working under agency rules, and by the use of a waiting period, possibly "therapeutic." [22]

21 Even getting this far may be difficult and discouraging. A receptionist who acts like a clerk can be disturbing to someone seeking help on a delicate, personal problem.

When the appointed time comes the client will meet with the caseworker not in his home but in an agency office, furnished with a desk behind which the worker sits. The "intake" interview will last, typically, about an hour. If his case is acceptable he will "continue in treatment" on some regular weekly basis, not because life's problems turn in a weekly cycle, but because the agency as a complex social structure finds it necessary to regularize activities if it is to function at all. Thus far, agency rules and professional codes of conduct have shaped the client's experience in obvious ways.

Beyond the worker are a supervisor and perhaps a case consultant with whom the worker will share case information and responsibility for diagnostic and treatment decisions. They help to decide what will be done with the client. Above them still is the agency director. All of them, from receptionist to director, make decisions about the casework service—either general policies and rules or specific case decisions. Codes, agency and professional, written and unwritten, formal and informal, govern *their* interaction, too, and thereby what is done for the client.

The caseworker, however, will not help him in just any way he needs and she (the worker) is able. Rather, the agency has certain "functions." If the client's needs lie outside the declared limits of these, he will be "referred" to another agency. He may be passed on through several before he receives service. He may find none to fit his need, or give up the search. Or he may receive service simultaneously from several agencies, each dealing with an aspect of his problem. He is faced, probably unwittingly, with the fact that agencies are themselves specialized, dividing the total welfare function in a web of interdependence whose complexity has fateful consequences for service.

Decisions affecting daily practice in and among agencies, matters of "small policy," will be made by all their personnel. Where "big policy" is concerned, however—large expenditures, major shifts in service—authority resides at a higher level. For the voluntary agency there is almost always a "lay board," legally responsible

22 Some agencies have maintained, with professional backing, that a waiting period may have therapeutic value in motivating a client to accept help when it is finally given. Research at one counseling agency, however, indicates that a two-month waiting period resulted in more resistance, greater lack of emotional control, and more likelihood of dropping out of treatment.

and the final arbiter of which clients will receive what services. But if the agency is "Chest"-supported, even the board's authority is circumscribed, for there remains a "budget committee," typically including "hardheaded businessmen," to decide the amount of money the agency may have. In the public agency such decisions will be made, within the confines of existing legislation, by local or state "welfare commissions," and by public officials running up to federal Cabinet level. And most of these board members, commissioners, and officials come by these positions so crucial for welfare as a result of their power and status in the larger society. Their interests, and the stereotypes and opinions they hold about social welfare and social work, powerfully affect the nature of services available to the client.

This brief picture of social agency operation reveals an organization marked by specialization of function among workers, who are arranged in a hierarchy. Their relations are, to a degree, formalized, their activities routinized. The agency is, in short, a *bureaucracy*, a form of organization typical of the complex industrial society. The agency is, further, one of a host specialized by program purpose, skill emphasis, clientele, location, and auspices. . . .

Bureaucracy (or, simply, formal organization) exists in degree—the degree to which certain distinguishing characteristics are present and emphasized. Many people would list these characteristics as red tape, buck passing, inaction, inflexibility. These, however, are but the "pathologies" of bureaucracy—they derive from a number of more basic features of organization. The purpose of this section is to discuss essential characteristics of bureaucracy, the implications of these characteristics for social service, and the conditions which promote their development in the social agency.

DISTINGUISHING CHARACTERISTICS. To say bureaucracy is to say *specialization*; and to say specialization is to say *hierarchy*. Most social agencies have, broadly speaking, two main levels of authority and status (representing also the major functional division)—the clerical-technical staff, typists to accountants, and the professional staff, each subdivided in standard ways. Within the professional staff the major ranks of worker, supervisor, and executive are found. From one to six or seven caseworkers (or groupworkers) may be directed by one supervisor who, if his supervisory

load is light, may also carry a caseload. In a large agency there may be a case supervisor, supervisor of supervisors. We see here the standard pyramid of the "line" organization. The essence is authority; the right to command by virtue of position passes successively from many hands to fewer to an integrating peak. Any organization of appreciable size and complexity, comprising people of different but interrelated skills, inescapably is driven to such a system in order to achieve a framework within which goals can be set and efforts can be mustered and coordinated with maximal efficiency. Internal agency hierarchy is most fully worked out when the agency is public, or, if private, participates in joint fund-raising. Then central authorities create finely graded classifications or civil service schemes, running from the lowest filing clerk to the topmost brass.

The hierarchy is also a congealed model of the career pattern. It provides a set of steps through which the individual may advance, a promotional horizon for the motivation of those lower down. The caseworker aims to become supervisor, the supervisor to become an executive. Social agency structure thus accords with the need in industrial society for a highly motivated workforce. Not all achieve their goals, of course, but there is some evidence that the hierarchical organization of social work allows a comparatively large opportunity for advancement above the basic caseworker and groupworker jobs. Among all welfare workers in 1950, 37 per cent were above client-contact jobs; among members of professional social work associations some 60 per cent hold the higher positions (though not all of these are supervisors and directors—some are teachers, public relations specialists, and the like). An ironic commentary on the extraordinary speed with which social groupworkers become supervisors came from an experienced social worker observing operations in a modern settlement house: "Heaven forbid that a groupworker should lead a group!"

Although the supervision pattern may be required by bureaucratic organization in the agency, the ways in which authority is exercised, the styles of leadership, are quite as much an outgrowth of unique elements in social work professional culture. In an extensive literature devoted to developing effective supervisory technique, and in courses in supervision in schools of social work, leadership is more often conceived in terms of education than of command, as a channel for obtaining collaboration among workers on difficult problems than as a method of case review by higher authority. Supervision is also a key element in the training of caseworkers, who spend about half their two years of graduate training in an agency under a selected teacher-supervisor. Since sensitivity to the motivational and emotional states of the client—perhaps the prime objective of social work training—must be preceded by self-awareness, the student is himself subjected to a near-psychotherapeutic experience. He is persistently called to account for his own behavior, not in cognitive but in emotional terms—not "Why do you think this way?" but "Why do you feel this way?" . . .

First, then, we have specialists, and to coordinate and motivate their efforts we have hierarchy. A second feature of bureaucracy—and agency—is an emphasis on rules, on doing things "by the book." This appears as *routinization of activity* on the one hand, and on the other as *formalization of relationships* between functionaries and clients, and to a lesser extent among functionaries themselves. Compare the handout at the door of the monastery in fourteenth century Europe, or at the relief agency in nineteenth century America, or at a Salvation Army slum mission today, with the two-inch thick "Manual of Regulations" guiding the administration of contemporary public assistance. Or contrast the informal mixing and exchange of "culture" between University "settlers" and slum dwellers envisaged by the founders of the Settlement House movement with the elaborately planned program of activities offered by settlement houses today, even though they are among the least formal of our modern leisure-time agencies. . . .

Within any good-sized agency rules and some formality will be found. They function to smooth communication and command between the hierarchical ranks, to regulate relations between occupational specialists working side-by-side, and to realize the objectives of a planned program. Without stable, comfortable, certified ways of talking and writing to one another, people of different rank or different function do not easily maintain harmony. Without prescribed goals and rules that fit the goals, specialized efforts tend to be random and to cancel one another.

Because a bureaucracy coordinates interdependent specialists, each person must be proficient in his task, and must not presume to intrude upon anyone else's. Thus, further features of the social agency are *assignment of roles on the basis of technical qualifications*, and clear and official *areas of jurisdiction* for the several roles. In the non-bureaucratic organization—an early-day social agency or a contemporary agency not yet caught up in the swing toward professionalism and formal organization—little attention is paid to technical qualifications for role performance. In rural areas teachers without formal certificates of training are still hired, judges without law degrees are elected, and juvenile court probation officers and Children's Aid Society workers need only "be of good character." To qualify for employment in a modern, high-standard agency, in contrast, the worker must possess a MSW degree at least, and often also a "specialization" in psychiatric, family, or child welfare work. The supervisor not only must have such training, but in addition must give evidence of years of experience, and of interest in "professional improvement" by attendance at postgraduate institutes and the like.

In the nonbureaucratic organization, areas of jurisdiction will be hazy—anyone may do anything, within limits, even if he is unskilled at it. In the family, father may cook dinner and diaper the baby; mother may drive the car and mow the lawn. In the early-day social agency, anyone might pitch in to help investigate a rush of relief applicants. But in the modern agency, the case worker will not take over a dictaphone in the stenographic pool even if she is able; the stenographer would not dream of conducting a treatment interview; and, although alternation of roles occurs, the worker who is not "on intake" will not casually wander in and do an intake interview.

EFFECTS ON SERVICE. Bureaucracy, especially as it becomes joined with professional culture, plainly has many implications for agency operation and social service. The essential characteristics of formal organization—specialization and hierarchy, emphasis on rules, technical qualifications for functionaries operating in clearcut areas of jurisdiction—are not designed to interfere with the giving and getting of service. Quite the opposite. From the viewpoints of both client and worker, however, they often appear as obstacles and impediments.

The rules and red tape that swathe the agency within, for instance, also reach out to mold the client. He has a role to play too; he must behave like a "case" if he is to use the service. He must fall into certain categories by need or other attribute—a dependent child, over 65, a marital problem, "motivated for treatment." There are applications to complete or sign, appointments to be kept. He must be willing to cooperate, to bare his life's secrets in relevant areas, to bring spouse or children to the office, to file charges in court, to be "cleared" through a Social Service Exchange.

Within the agency, specialists in a hierarchy find effective communication an increasingly severe problem. There is much truth in the observation that ours is the "paper age" (soon, perhaps, to become the "magnetic tape age"), that we are a nation of paper shufflers and file-keepers. Small, informal groups can maintain identity, continuity, and tradition through word of mouth. Families need few records, and those, such as income tax returns, are required by the outside bureaucratic society. But anyone who has worked in either small or large agencies or in business firms knows that paper-work is central to all operations; in the largest organizations, whole divisions simply maintain records. Several necessities of organizational life prompt the piles of paper. First, these organizations have a long time-perspective. They undertake long-range tasks, and therefore need to perceive long-range changes and to make continuing evaluations of organizational efforts and results, unclouded by personal or memory bias. Second, in so far as they assign positions on the basis of technical ability, they must keep records for periodic review of individual performance. Third, agencies are accountable to some board or legislative body or other authority; so they keep records to justify themselves should they come under attack or scrutiny. Most important, continuity of function dictates that records be kept, for people die, retire, quit, fail, are promoted. The next occupant of the position, the next worker on the case must get oriented. Some of this is done informally. But contacts and information are of such complexity and scope that even the memory of an "old office Joe" with a reputation for knowing everything cannot be trusted. To the extent that their time perspective is long, that accountability to officials is required, and continuity of specialized roles must be maintained, even small organizations will devote much effort to the record department.

The well-run social casework agency is a champion record-keeper. The Hill and Ormsby cost study in the Family Service of Philadelphia (primarily a casework agency) arrived at the following distribution of a $100 expenditure for casework services: [23]

Interviewing costs	$42.49
Case recording	32.15
Supervisory conferences	13.17
Case consultations	5.77
Miscellaneous	6.42
Total	$100.00

Thirty-two per cent of all expenditures related to providing casework services were for recording. Moreover, if we focus not simply on recording but on the total process of *maintaining communication* within a bureaucratic structure, then supervisory conferences and case consultations may be added to case recording, resulting in a total of 51 per cent of all expenditures for this purpose. These bulk so large along with other necessary costs that only 42 per cent is spent for direct contact with clients. The expense of maintaining communication appears to be very great. But where there is a long-range program with outside accountability, a complex division of labor, and frequent changes of staff, communication within an organization becomes necessarily a matter of prime importance—we do not know, really, whether or not a cost distribution such as the above is optimal for a family agency.

Because of the time that must be spent in maintaining communication, and the general intricacy of its inner workings, bureaucracy affects the speed with which service is given. The writers know of an instance in a small city where a midday radioed public appeal for bedding for a burned-out family brought fifty mattresses, flung upon their doorstep, by evening. Agencies oppose public appeals of this sort, but that is the way informal welfare operates. The formal agency, in contrast, has its own built-in tempo and reaction time. Although not typical, the time schedule of one large high-standard family agency in early 1955 was substantially as follows. When a prospective client first made contact with the agency, unless a well-defined emergency existed, he was asked to call back some two or three weeks later to arrange an appointment. When he called back,

[23] John G. Hill and Ralph Ormsby, "The Philadelphia Cost Study," *Social Work Journal*, Vol. 34, October 1953, p. 168.

he was given an appointment three or four weeks later for an intake interview. At the completion of this, if he needed further consultation, he was scheduled for a second appointment some three to six months later. From then on he was seen every week or fortnight on regular schedule. This situation is perhaps extreme and may have been due largely to lack of personnel to meet the demand. But the impress of bureaucracy is plain; no informal organization can ever operate with such deliberation in the face of a request for help.

Bureaucracy tends to minimize urgency, which may be counted a disadvantage. But the gains associated with it are clear: reliability, continuity, fairness. Although he may wait as long as six months for service, the client will receive dependable attention. The agency will not forget him, as the public will forget its mattress-buried family after a few days. Those same files whose maintenance eats up 32 cents of the agency dollar assure him definite attention at the appointed time. Other agency procedures also assure continuity of service—not just this burned-out family but others to come will get predictable help. Finally, while bureaucratic procedures may seem impersonal to the client—he cannot have his favorite worker, or perhaps even the one to whom he unburdened at intake—by the same token he is assured of equality of treatment. Class background, the worker's feelings, "pull," personal charm or lack of it, make little difference to the agency; in informal welfare they are often the very basis on which aid is given.

The model for the foregoing discussion has been the "ideal type" bureaucracy. Along with its gains—efficiency, reliability, precision, fairness—come what many students have called its pathologies: timidity, delay, officiousness, red tape, exaggeration of routine, limited adaptability. The agency as a means, a mechanism—the *agency*—for carrying out welfare policy becomes an end in itself. Between the altruist with his desire to help and the client with his need lies the machine, with its own "needs." These needs can result in an emphasis on technique and method, on organizational routines and records, rather than on people and service.

FACTORS AFFECTING DEGREE OF BUREAUCRACY. Much of what goes on in social agencies fits this model of bureaucracy. And much does not. Several factors affect the degree to which bureaucratic gains and pathologies will be present in an organization. Among the most important are size, proportion of personnel which is professionally oriented, and degree of public control.

First, consider size: the bigger, the more bureaucratic. Even in large organizations, however, a network of informal, personal relations among workers infiltrates the bureaucratic skeleton, infusing it with qualities quite unbureaucratic. In the social agency lines of communication may bypass the supervisor; a client will be seen out of turn or transferred to a worker he knows; hours set for "dictation" will be disregarded—all with the knowledge and tacit approval of everyone in the agency. This so-called "informal organization," which arises in part as a reaction against the pathologies of bureaucracy, is often essential to the survival of the agency and the accomplishment of its goals. It sometimes has a powerful effect in reshaping the goals of an organization.

In the small agency informal colleague relations and a deemphasis of hierarchy and rules are still more common, and the model of bureaucracy a still poorer fit. But even in the small agency many fundamental elements of bureaucracy—assignment of roles on the basis of technical qualification, division of responsibility, record-keeping—must still exist, with effects heightened by the professional culture of social work. It seems clear, also, that the day of the small agency is nearly past. Many such agencies exist, but mergers —both by geography to cover metropolitan areas and by program purposes to cover related functions—are now frequent. Finally, there are a limited number of ways to organize work—and if the schools and churches we attend, the stores we patronize, the voluntary associations and political parties we belong to, the government agencies we encounter, and the defense establishment we support all accustom us to elements of bureaucracy, we become predisposed to adopt this organizational form in new areas for different problems, appropriate or not. The atmosphere and pattern of bureaucracy tend to be copied in small agencies even when size and degree of specialization do not require them.

A second major factor affecting degree of bureaucracy in the agency is *the proportion of personnel that is strongly committed to a profession.* A professional orientation among functionaries works both ways—toward accentuating and toward reducing bureaucratic tendencies—but on balance the reduction effect may be stronger.

Considering that both professionalism and bureaucracy are responses to complex specialization in modern society, it is not surprising that they play into each other at many points. The impersonality of relations governed by rules that the formal organization requires finds its counterpart in the professional emphasis on formality of client-worker relations. Insistence that recruitment and promotion of workers be on the basis of technical qualifications is common to both; and both strive toward clarity in the definition and jurisdiction of roles. We have also suggested that some unique stresses in social work culture may further accentuate bureaucratic tendencies, for example, the emphasis on supervision and records, and a possible tendency to carry rules for worker-client relations over to colleague relations.

On the other hand, to be professional is to behave in many ways counter to the bureaucratic pattern. The service code of the professional requires him to give foremost attention to the needs of the client, with several unbureaucratic results: he may disregard or short-circuit formal rules and regulations in order to meet client needs; he will be concerned about red-tape impediments to efficient operation, and will be ready to make adjustments; he will strive to maintain or improve existing standards of work; he will often seek to evaluate service on the basis of results achieved rather than by techniques used. Professionalism gives one not only the incentive but also the strength to avoid excesses of bureaucratic proceduralism—for membership in a cohesive group with its own standards, and with roots outside any given agency, frees the functionary from the fears and insecurity which would lead him to take refuge in fixed rules. "A professional orientation neutralizes feelings of dependency. . . ." [24] Where professionalism is strong, Blau finds, the feeling of freedom is also strong, and the proliferation of rules less necessary.

A third factor affecting bureaucracy is *auspices*. Among the various types of auspices, the public versus private alternative is most crucial on the American scene. The public agency is larger on average than the private agency, and less often professionally staffed. Thus, the factors discussed above, size and method of staffing, enter again. Not only has the public agency a bigger local operating office, it is also more often

tied in with extensive state and federal hierarchies of control. People in the ADC program, for instance, or in unemployment insurance, work in local, state, regional, and federal offices; a mass of regulations issues at all levels; and there may be a dozen supervisory layers stacked above the local-bureau visitor and employment-office interviewer. Such towering organizational pyramids require an emphasis on the basic characteristics of bureaucracy and invite the exaggerations which we have called "pathologies" of bureaucracy.

Two other conditions of public agency life tend further to accentuate bureaucracy: public welfare programs are framed in law, and the agency operates in a "goldfish bowl." The basic law setting up a program is usually brief; administration of the program requires an endless flow of regulations which comprise the ever-changing "Manual." Operation in the glare of publicity may create an atmosphere of insecurity which, as Blau shows, tends to foster rigidity and proceduralism. It is no accident that Weber found his model of the bureaucrat in the public official.

CONCLUSION

Bureaucracy is *not* the antithesis of democracy. Democracy is a procedure for achieving consensus through free competition among opposing interest groups. Democracy is contrived to be somewhat unstable because it is predicated on the assumption that current decision makers are temporary. Bureaucracy, on the other hand, is a structure for carrying out decisions with maximum efficiency; it is predicated on the assumption that a best way exists, irrespective of who administers it, to realize current objectives. Peter Blau put the contrast well: "When people set themselves the task of determining the social objectives that represent the interests of most of them, the crucial problem is to provide an opportunity for all conflicting viewpoints to be heard. In contrast, when the task is the achievement of given social objectives, the essential problem to be solved is to discover the efficient, not the popular, means for doing so." [25] In short, bureaucracy is compatible with democracy.

[24] Peter M. Blau, *The Dynamics of Bureaucracy*, Chicago: University of Chicago Press, 1956, p. 188.

[25] Blau, *Bureaucracy in Modern Society, op. cit.*, p. 107.

But bureaucracy is also compatible with tyranny. The political indifference of bureaucratic procedures explains why administrative structures in the Soviet Union and in the United States are so similar. In both societies, large-scale organizations exist characterized by task specialization, formal rules of procedure, and impersonality, and members of both societies complain about bureaucratic "red tape."

SOME SIGNIFICANT LITERATURE ON BUREAUCRATIC ORGANIZATIONS

Morroe Berger, *Bureaucracy and Society in Modern Egypt: A Study of the Higher Civil Service*, Princeton, N.J.: Princeton University Press, 1957. In 1954, 249 higher civil servants in the Egyptian ministries of Agriculture, Education, Finance and Economy, and Municipal and Rural Affairs responded to questions asked them in Arabic by trained interviewers. Professor Berger analyzed their replies in order to discover ". . . the social origins of higher civil servants [in Egypt] today; the reasons for the attraction this career has for so many of the educated elite; the changing socioeconomic status of the higher civil servants; their loyalties and the extent of their professionalization; and their attitudes toward such norms of bureaucratic behavior as impartiality, impersonality, subordination to one's superior, and the exercise of the permitted degree of initiative." In particular, Berger was interested in finding out how the public bureaucracy in Cairo differed from that of most Western countries. ". . . The study of bureaucracy in a non-Western setting points to the limitation of current bureaucratic theory, developed mainly in the West." This summary is based on a review by George L. Harris, *American Sociological Review*, Vol. 23, April 1958, pp. 223–224.

Peter M. Blau, *The Dynamics of Bureaucracy: A Study of Interpersonal Relations in Two Government Agencies*, Chicago: University of Chicago Press, 1955. Professor Blau studied the behavior of lower officialdom in a state employment agency to test the hypothesis that informal interactions need not constitute idiosyncratic deviations from bureaucratic regulations but may instead be work-facilitating innovations. He found that change in patterns of informal activities followed the introduction of statistical performance records. He concluded that bureaucracy did not inevitably resist change; it did so only under specific conditions. For example, workers whose statuses are insecure tend to resist change, but job tenure arrangements, professionalization, established work groups, and the absence of basic conflict between work group and management reduce this insecurity and thereby the opposition to change. This summary is based on a review by Sheldon L. Messinger, *American Sociological Review*, Vol. 21, February 1956, pp. 102–103.

William M. Evan and Morris Zelditch, Jr., "A Laboratory Experiment on Bureaucratic Authority," *American Sociological Review*, Vol. 26, December 1961, pp. 883–893. The subjects of this experiment did not realize they were anything but part-time coders in a nonprofit research organization. One group of subjects were supervised by a coding supervisor whose technical knowledge seemed superior to theirs, one group by a supervisor whose knowledge seemed about equal to theirs, and one group by an apparently incompetent supervisor. Although all of the subjects acknowledged the legitimacy of commands given them by the supervisors, the *grounds* for defining legitimacy of authority tended to be different. Subjects with equal-knowledge or inferior-knowledge supervisors justified authority in terms of *office*. Subjects with superior-knowledge supervisors justified authority in terms of *technical competence*. Thus, Professors Evan and Zelditch experimentally separated the effects of rational and legal authority. Ideally, the holder of legal authority in an organization also possesses the appropriate knowledge.

Robert H. Guest, "Managerial Succession in Complex Organizations," *American Journal of Sociology*, Vol. 68, July 1962, pp. 47–54. This paper compares two studies of the succession of a new leader at the top of a bureaucratic hierarchy. In one case, Alvin Gouldner's study of a small gypsum plant, the new manager felt under pressure from his superiors in the central office of the corporation to institute more bureaucratic routines and to use disciplinary measures to make the organization more efficient. He instituted what Gouldner called "punishment-centered" discipline, and the result was an increase in internal organizational tensions. In the other case, Guest's own study of succession in one of six identical plants of a large corporation, the new manager felt free to use a more democratic technique of wielding authority; he permitted the initiation of interaction from lower levels in the hierarchy, and he established group meetings at all levels of the organization to cope with problems. Quantitative indices showed that this democratic leader made a significant improvement in the productive efficiency of the plant. ". . . [T]here emerges from both studies encouraging evidence suggesting that it is possible for democratic processes to function in an otherwise authoritarian bureaucratic social system." For a more detailed description of the studies compared in this paper, see Alvin W. Gouldner, *Patterns of Industrial Bureaucracy*, Glencoe,

Ill.: Free Press, 1954; and Robert H. Guest, *Organizational Change: The Effect of Successful Leadership*, Homewood, Ill.: Irwin-Dorsey, 1962.

Morris Janowitz, *The Professional Soldier: A Social and Political Portrait*, Glencoe, Ill.: Free Press, 1960. Professor Janowitz traces the changes among American professional soldiers over the past half century: the changing social backgrounds, skill distribution, and career patterns. Concomitantly, the basis of discipline in the military establishment has shifted from domination by arbitrary command toward authority maintained by persuasion, manipulation, and concern with morale. Janowitz used historical, documentary, and biographical sources in analyzing a historical sample of 760 generals and admirals covering the years 1910, 1920, 1935, and 1950. He also obtained questionnaire data from contemporary members of his sample, and he interviewed 113 Army, Navy, and Air Force officers on duty at the three Service headquarters. One of his most interesting conclusions is that the careers of the most distinguished military leaders deviate from the pattern of advancement by seniority usual in the military establishment. This summary is based on a review by Hans Speier, *American Sociological Review*, Vol. 25, December 1960, pp. 970–971.

James G. March and Herbert A. Simon, *Organizations*, New York: Wiley, 1958. A search of the literature on organizations yielded three models of organizational behavior, each accounting for some features of formal organizations: (1) One model assumes ". . . that organization members, and particularly employees, are primarily *passive instruments*, capable of performing work and accepting directions, but not initiating action or exerting influence in any significant way." (2) Another model assumes that members ". . . have to be motivated or induced to participate in the system of organizational behavior; that there is incomplete parallelism between their personal goals and organizational goals; and that actual or potential goal conflicts make power phenomena, attitudes, and morale centrally important in the explanation of organizational behavior." (3) A third model conceives of the participant as a decision maker and consequently assumes ". . . that perception and thought processes are central to the explanation of behavior in organizations." This summary is based on a review by Philip Selznick, *American Sociological Review*, Vol. 24, December 1959, pp. 911–912.

Charles Perrow, "The Analysis of Goals in Complex Organizations," *American Sociological Review*, Vol. 26, December 1961, pp. 854–866. The relative emphasis upon one or another of four organizational tasks depends on the nature of the work the organization does and the stage of development within the organization. The operative goals of an organization, as opposed to its verbalized goals, depend upon its relative emphasis on one or another of the following organizational tasks:

(1) securing facilities for conducting and expanding organizational production, (2) obtaining legitimacy and acceptance for the organization from the community, (3) recruiting persons with necessary skills, and (4) coordinating the activities of members of the organization and relating these activities to nonmembers and to outside organizations.

Arthur L. Stinchcombe, "Institutions of Privacy in the Determination of Police Administrative Practice," *American Journal of Sociology*, Vol. 69, September 1963, pp. 150–160. Police bureaucracies started little more than a century ago when Sir Robert Peel organized the London Metropolitan Police (thenceforth called "bobbies" after Sir Robert). Professor Stinchcombe shows that the character of police administrative practices is influenced by the tasks assigned to the police by increasingly urbanized societies. For example, rural police depend much more on complaints from people who are injured by a crime or who observe it than do urban police who rely heavily on patrol of public places. This difference in administrative practice is a consequence of the greater intensity of use of public places in big cities and the greater feasibility of police surveillance of public places. Stinchcombe goes on to suggest (1) that different types of crimes have varying probabilities of being committed in public places where they are vulnerable to police intervention and (2) that persons occupying different positions within an urban industrial society have varying opportunities to escape police observation by entering private places. (By definition, the police cannot penetrate private places except under special circumstances—for instance, if they have a search warrant.) Stinchcombe hypothesizes that some of the difference between the arrest rates of lower-class and middle-class persons may be the result of differential observability of their behavior by the police.

James D. Thompson, "Organizations and Output Transactions," *American Journal of Sociology*, Vol. 28, November 1962, pp. 309–324. "Classic bureaucratic theory is preoccupied with behavioral relations ordered by a single, unified authority structure from which the client is excluded. . . ." In point of fact, though, purposive organizations distribute the organization's ultimate product, service, or impact to nonmembers through persons who occupy what Professor Thompson calls *output roles*, as, for example, salesmen, caseworkers, checkout clerks in supermarkets. He develops a typology of output transactions and analyzes for each one the interactive possibilities between nonmembers and persons in the output roles. Four types of output transactions are generated (1) by the degree of control by the organization over the behavior of the member in the output role and (2) by the degree to which the nonmember finds interaction with the organization optional. Maximum organizational control over the member in the output role occurs when ". . . the member is equipped with a single, complete program —a standard procedure which supposedly does not vary, regardless of the behavior of the nonmember." An example of minimum nonmember discretion about interacting with the organization is the prisoner who must deal with his guard.

Stanley H. Udy, Jr., "Administrative Rationality, Social Setting, and Organizational Development," *American Journal of Sociology*, Vol. 68, November 1962, pp. 299–308. Members of bureaucratic organizations are supposed to behave rationally. (Social behavior is rational "in so far as it is purposefully directed toward explicit empirical objectives and planned in accordance with the best available scientific knowledge.") On the basis of a study of formal organizations engaged in the production of material goods in 34 nonindustrial so-

cieties, Professor Udy suggests that administrative rationality involves a cumulative emphasis on the following characteristics: (1) central management, (2) compensatory rewards for participation, (3) the concurrent performance of three or more qualitatively different operations by different members ("specialization"), (4) continuous job assignment by management of particular people to particular roles, (5) rewards contingent on the amount and quality of the work done ("performance emphasis"), (6) explicit definition of the terms of participation by mutual agreement ("segmental participation"), and (7) limited organizational objectives. By a cumulative emphasis, Udy means that organizations with characteristic (4) will tend to possess characteristics (1), (2), and (3) and that organizations with characteristic (7) will tend to possess all of the other rational characteristics.

PART V

Individual Mobility and Social Change in Urban Industrial Societies

CHAPTER 16

Changes of Status
and Their Interpretation

In all societies, children start life on the social level occupied by their parents. In many societies, they remain on that level throughout their lives. The term "caste" refers to the lack of appreciable mobility from generation to generation in societies like India or Ceylon.[1]

In industrial societies, the child initially shares the status of his family, but by late adolescence he moves into social limbo. His social evaluation becomes unclear because his own activities in school or in the labor market foreshadow his future status about as well as the social standing of his parents. By adulthood, the impact of parental status has receded further. Family origins affect social status *indirectly* by influencing opportunities for educational and occupational achievement, but this is a far cry from the *direct* inheritance of status which occurs in aristocratic societies, as when a title passes from father to son. Inheritance of status in industrial societies occurs mainly because high-status parents help and low-status parents hinder their children in preparing educationally for white-collar employment.

This generalization is, of course, a statisti-

cal one. Some working-class youngsters go to college, presumably with the help and encouragement of their families, and some youngsters from economically advantaged backgrounds do not. Table 72 presents data from a survey of

TABLE 72
1960 *High School Graduates Enrolled in College, by the Occupations of the Household Heads in 1959*

Occupations of the Household Heads in Families of 1960 High School Graduates	1960 Graduates Who Attended College in 1960		Total Number of 1960 High School Graduates
	Number	Per Cent	
White-collar workers	363,000	62.7	579,000
Manual or service workers	220,000	29.3	752,000
Farm workers	40,500	27.0	150,000
Unemployed or not in labor force	33,000	33.3	99,000
Total	656,500	41.6	1,580,000

Source: Bureau of the Census, "Factors Related to College Attendance of Farm and Non-farm High School Graduates: 1960," Series P-27, No. 32, Washington: Government Printing Office, June 1962, p. 16.

[1] Bryce F. Ryan, *Caste in Modern Ceylon: The Sinhalese System in Transition*, New Brunswick, N.J.: Rutgers University Press, 1953.

a national sample of American households; these data show a greater rate of college attendance for the children of parents in the higher occupational strata. Nevertheless, about three-tenths of working-class high school graduates went to college in 1960, and the absolute number of youngsters from white-collar backgrounds going to college (363,000) was only a little more than the number of youngsters from all other backgrounds (293,500).

THE HIGH RATE OF SOCIAL MOBILITY IN INDUSTRIAL SOCIETIES

The concept of "social mobility" spreads like an umbrella, covering several distinct departures from the rigidity of a caste system. One is *vertical mobility*: upward and downward changes of status. Another is the sidewise movement from one social system to another within the same society. Rural-urban population flow exemplifies this *horizontal mobility*, but geographic relocation is not a necessary condition for it. When an office worker takes another typing job with a different employer, the job change is also a horizontal movement. Sometimes geographic mobility is accompanied by vertical mobility. However, vertical mobility is clearest when the community setting is unchanged. When *different* social systems are involved, as, for example, when a person moves from one community to another, precise evaluation of vertical movement is difficult.

Even if a discussion of social mobility were confined to vertical movement, problems of specification would remain. Vertical mobility can be defined (1) in terms of comparisons between members of one generation and the next —*inter*generational mobility—or (2) in terms of comparisons between different stages in the life of members of the *same* generation—*intra*generational mobility. This may seem like splitting hairs. After all, the infant starts life on the same status level as his parents. What difference does it make whether the status he finally achieves is compared with the status he started with or with the status of his parents? It would not make much difference if status changes during a lifetime were progres-

sively up or progressively down. What causes difficulty is that some individuals enjoy their highest status in middle age; others enjoy it in youth, and others in old age. To ignore the ups and downs occurring within the lifetime of an individual tends to exaggerate the immobility of the society. Thus, a study of labor mobility in the East Bay section of metropolitan San Francisco demonstrated that a large proportion of the family heads whose work histories were surveyed had "worked in different communities, in different occupations, and in many different jobs." [2] Indeed, the greater the *intra*generational mobility, the more complicated is the task of measuring *inter*generational mobility. Consider a study of the comparative statuses of fathers and sons. The results are affected by the stage of the life cycle at which the comparisons are made. Gunnar Boalt faced this difficulty in his comparison of the occupations of 24-year-old Stockholm men in 1949 with the occupations of their fathers in 1936.[3] The fathers of 11-year-old boys were doubtless more than 24 years old. Sons at an early stage of their careers were compared with their fathers at a later stage, thus minimizing the extent of *upward* mobility and exaggerating the incidence of *downward* mobility.

When sociologists speak of vertical mobility, they sometimes mean *gross* mobility: the proportion of persons in a society who have been *either* upwardly or downwardly mobile. At other times, however, they mean *net* mobility: the *difference* between the amounts of upward and downward changes in status. A society could have no net mobility at all and still have a high rate of gross mobility, the upward moves of some members being balanced by the downward moves of others. In point of fact, industrial societies are characterized by appreciable net upward mobility. This is due partly to the changing occupational

[2] Seymour Martin Lipset and Reinhard Bendix, *Social Mobility in Industrial Society*, Berkeley: University of California Press, 1960, p. 180.
[3] Gunnar Boalt, "Social Mobility in Stockholm: A Pilot Investigation," in *Transactions of the Second World Congress of Sociology*, Vol. 2, London: International Sociological Association, 1954, pp. 67–73.

structure, which permits an increasing proportion of the population to enjoy middle-status levels, and partly to the tendency for white-collar families to have a lower birth rate than blue-collar families, thus creating more room at middle- and top-status levels.[4] Net mobility could be the main component of gross mobility, but it apparently is not. Joseph A. Kahl has estimated that net mobility accounted for only about 40 per cent of the gross mobility in the United States between 1920 and 1950.[5]

Theoretical considerations do not enable sociologists to predict a definite level of gross mobility in industrial societies. Although *net* mobility is related to occupational changes tied to processes of industrialization and urbanization, *gross* mobility also reflects a society's mechanisms for social ascent and descent. Presumably, societies differing in values will also differ in readiness to accept radical redistributions of status from generation to generation. All the more interesting, therefore, are the conclusions of a comparative study of gross mobility in six industrial countries which suggest that gross mobility rates are about the same in all industrial countries.

Comparative Data on Social Mobility

Reprinted by permission. From Seymour Martin Lipset and Hans L. Zetterberg, Chap. 2, in Lipset and Bendix, *Social Mobility in Industrial Society*, Berkeley: University of California Press, 1960, pp. 11–17, 19–21, 24–26, 42–43, 57–60.

Widespread social mobility has been a concomitant of industrialization and a basic characteristic of modern industrial society. In every industrial country, a large proportion of the population have had to find occupations considerably different from those of their parents. During the nineteenth century, the proportion of the labor

[4] Elbridge Sibley, "Some Demographic Clues to Stratification," *American Sociological Review*, Vol. 7, June 1942, pp. 322–330.
[5] Joseph A. Kahl, *The American Class Structure*, New York: Rinehart, 1957, pp. 251–262. Lipset and Bendix, *op. cit.*, pp. 86–88, refer approvingly to Kahl's technique for partitioning total mobility into gross and net mobility.

force in urban occupations increased rapidly, while the proportion in agriculture decreased.

In the twentieth century the West has been characterized by a rapid growth of trade and of service industries, as well as of bureaucracy in industry and government; more people have become employed in white-collar work, and the comparative size of the rural population has declined even more rapidly than before. These changes in the distribution of occupations from generation to generation mean that no industrial society can be viewed as closed or static.

This apparently simple statement runs counter to widely held impressions concerning the different social structures of American and Western European societies. According to these impressions, America has an "open society" with considerable social mobility, but the countries of Western Europe (specifically England, France, Italy, Germany, the Low Countries, and the Scandinavian nations) have societies that are "closed," in the sense that the children of workers are forced to remain in the social position of their parents. This judgment reflects earlier European beliefs. In the age of the French Revolution, America appeared to be a land free from traditional institutions and historical legacies: the country of the future, Hegel called it, where each man was master of his fate just as American democracy itself was the product of human reason. This notion has been reiterated in many analyses, all contrasting American and European societies. . . .

The questions implicit in these alternative interpretations can be answered today with somewhat more assurance than was possible even two decades ago because of recent research in social mobility. In this [article] we attempt to summarize the findings available for a number of countries. Since our object is to assemble a large amount of empirical evidence, it will be useful to state at the outset that *the overall pattern of social mobility appears to be much the same in the industrial societies of various Western countries.* This is startling—even if we discount the mistaken efforts to explain differences in political institutions by reference to different degrees of social mobility in the United States and in Western Europe. Further, although it is clear that social mobility is related in many ways to the economic expansion of industrial societies, it is at least doubtful that the rates of mobility and of expansion are correlated. Since a number of the countries for which we have data have had different rates of economic expansion but show comparable rates of social mobility, our tentative interpretation is that the social mobility of societies becomes relatively high once their industrialization, and hence their economic expansion, reaches a certain level.

OCCUPATIONAL MOBILITY

Before World War II, studies of social mobility were usually limited to investigations of the social origins of different occupational groups, employees of single factories, or inhabitants of single communities. Since World War II there have been at least fifteen different national surveys in eleven countries which have secured from representative samples of the population information that relates the occupations of the respondents to the occupations of their fathers. In addition, there have been a number of studies conducted in different cities of various countries. Taken together, these investigations permit the comparison of current variations in occupational mobility, as well as some estimate of differences during the past half century.

To make such comparisons and estimates is difficult. Few of the studies were made with the intention of facilitating the comparison of findings in different countries. Many of them employ systems of classifying occupations which cannot be compared with each other and the questions concerning the occupations of respondents and fathers are seldom similar. In order to use the results for a comparative analysis, we have reduced the occupational categories for most countries to the closest approximation of manual, nonmanual, and farm occupations. In presenting these materials, we make the assumption that a move from manual to nonmanual employment constitutes upward mobility among *males*. This assumption may be defended on the following grounds:

1. Most male nonmanual occupations have more prestige than most manual occupations, even skilled ones.
2. Among males, white-collar positions generally lead to higher incomes than manual employment.
3. Nonmanual positions, in general, require more education than manual positions.
4. Holders of nonmanual positions, even low-paid white-collar jobs, are more likely than manual

workers to think of themselves as members of the middle class and to act out middle-class roles in their consumption patterns.
5. Low-level nonmanual workers are more likely to have political attitudes which resemble those of the upper middle class than those of the manual working class.

It is true, of course, that many white-collar positions are lower in income and prestige than the higher levels of skilled manual work; however, most of these poorly paid white-collar positions are held by women, and male white-collar workers are often able to secure higher-level supervisory posts. Consequently, we believe that using the break between manual and nonmanual occupations as an indicator of low and high occupational status is justified whenever a dichotomous division of males in urban occupation is used. It is important to remember, however, that like all single-item indicators of complex phenomena this one will necessarily result in some errors; that is, some nonmanual positions which have lower status than some manual occupations will be classified in the high group though they should be in the low.

POSTWAR NATIONAL SAMPLES

Figure 15 presents the inter-generational shifts between manual and nonmanual occupations for adult males in six countries. The data indicate that a large minority of the sons of the industrial labor force achieve nonmanual positions. In France this group comprises 35 per cent of the sons, in Germany 26 to 30 per cent, in Switzerland 44 per cent, in Sweden 29 per cent, in Japan 33 per cent, and in the United States 31 to 35 per cent. A smaller minority in each country declines from nonmanual to manual positions, the percentages ranging from a low of 13 per cent to a high of 38 per cent. . . .

The lack of comparable classifications in nationwide surveys of social mobility makes it difficult to conclude this summary with more than general impressions. Moreover, we must bear in mind that we deal here exclusively with a single index to complex and quite diverse societies, so that inferences can carry us only part of the way and should be made with caution. Yet, the value of a comparative approach to social mobility becomes apparent when we set side by side for each country the figures which are most clearly indicative of upward, downward, and total mobility across the line between the middle and the working class (Table 73). . . .

The figures in the first column give the proportion of all sons of manual workers who now occupy middle-class positions. In the second column the figures indicate the proportion of all sons of middle-class fathers who are now in manual occupations. In order to get some index of the total mobility in society, the figures in the third column were computed: out of all the sons of fathers in urban occupations who are themselves in urban occupations, those who were mobile in either direction were added together, and this figure was expressed as a percentage of the total.

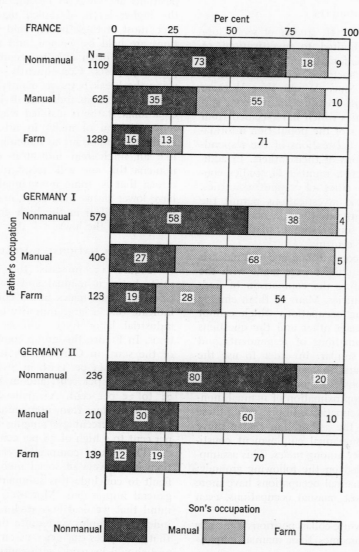

FIGURE 15. Mobility between manual and nonmanual occupations and between agriculture and nonagriculture. Details do not always add to 100 per cent because of rounding. Source: France: M. Bresard, "Mobilité sociale et dimension de la famille," *Population*, Vol. 5, 1950, pp. 553–566. Germany: (I) From data supplied by Dr. Erich Reigratski, Cologne, Germany, from his study *Soziale Verflechtungen in der Bundesrepublik*, Tubingen: Mohr-Siebeck, 1956; (II) From data supplied by Institut für Demoskopie, Allensbach, Germany.

For example, of those persons in the nonfarm population of the United States who were sons of fathers in nonfarm occupations, 30 per cent had either fallen into a manual position from their fathers' nonmanual position, or had risen from their fathers' working-class occupation into a middle-class one. Though this is, to be sure, a very crude index, it should give a rough indication of the fluidity of the urban occupational structure. It expresses the proportion of the native urban population which has, in one way or another, "changed class."

The first impression one gains from Table 73 is that all the countries studied are characterized by a high degree of mobility. From one generation to another, a quarter to a third of the nonfarm population moves from working class to middle class or vice versa. Second, there is among

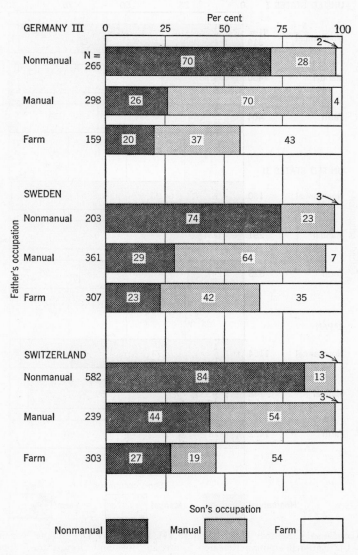

FIGURE 15 (continued). Source: Germany: (III) From data supplied by DIVO, Frankfurt A. M. Sweden: From data collected by H. L. Zetterberg, partly reported in "Sveriges fem rangrullor," Vecko-Journalen, Vol. 48, 1957, p. 40. Switzerland: Recalculated from information supplied by Professor Roger Girod.

the first six countries a high degree of similarity in this total mobility rate. The total range is between 23 and 31 per cent, and five of the six countries (United States, Germany, Sweden, Japan, France) range between 27 and 31 per cent. Such narrow differences lead quickly to one interpretation: total mobility rates in these countries are practically the same. . . . The previous discussion should not be interpreted to mean that occupational mobility is the sole or even the primary basis for assessing the availability of opportunities in an industrial society. An individual may rise occupationally and economically and yet find himself excluded from those social groups

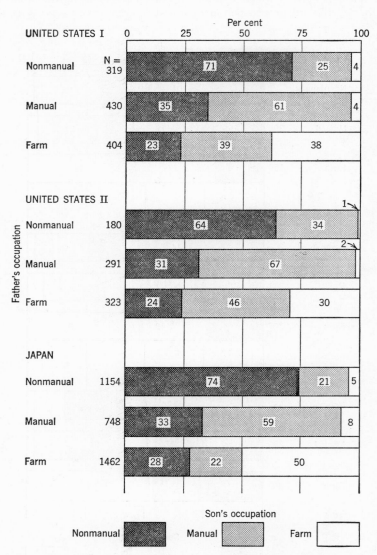

FIGURE 15 (continued). Source: United States: (I) Derived by Dr. Natalie Rogoff from data published by the National Opinion Research Center in "Jobs and Occupations," *Opinion News*, September 1, 1947, pp. 3–33; (II) From data supplied by the Survey Research Center of the University of Michigan from their study of the 1952 presidential election. Japan: Research Committee on Stratification and Social Mobility of the Japanese Sociological Association, *Social Stratification and Mobility*, Tokyo: 1956, mimeographed, p. 13.

to which, he feels, his economic position entitles him to belong; this exclusion may have an adverse effect on his later career, though this need not be true. The degree of emphasis on "aristocratic" values and privileges, that is, on the inheritance of position, may therefore be reflected in the extent to which men claiming high status because of their family's position will accept as social equals those who have but recently climbed the economic ladder. Few studies bear directly on this problem, but the most nearly relevant data deal with intermarriage across class lines by contrasting the occupations at marriage of husbands and wives, the occupations of the fathers of the bride and groom, and the husbands' occupations with those of their fathers-in-law.

The most detailed European study comparing the class status of husbands and wives is based on all marriages in the state of Bavaria in 1927; comparable American material is from one of the earliest, but in many ways best, of American studies, based on Philadelphia marriage licenses for the years 1913 to 1916. These studies clearly suggest that barriers to marriage across the

TABLE 73
Comparative Indices of Upward and Downward Mobility (Percentages)

	Nonfarm Populations		
Country	Upward Mobility (Nonmanual Sons of Manual Fathers)	Downward Mobility (Manual Sons of Nonmanual Fathers)	Total Vertical Mobility (Nonfarm Population Mobile across the Line between Working and Middle Class)
United States [a]	33	26	30
Germany [b]	29	32	31
Sweden	31	24	29
Japan	36	22	27
France	39	20	27
Switzerland	45	13	23

[a] Average of three studies: two cited in Figure 15, and the third computed from data in R. Centers, "Occupational Mobility of Urban Occupational Strata, *American Sociological Review*, Vol. 13, 1948, p. 203.
[b] Average of three studies cited in Figure 15.
Source: See Figure 15.

manual-nonmanual class line are equally strong (or weak, depending on one's interpretation) in Germany and America. . . .

MOBILITY TRENDS AND SOCIAL STRUCTURE

Several different processes inherent in all modern social structures have a direct effect on the rate of social mobility, and help account for the similarities in rates in different countries: (1) changes in the number of available vacancies; (2) different rates of fertility; (3) changes in the rank accorded to occupations; (4) changes in the number of inheritable status-positions; and (5) changes in the legal restrictions pertaining to potential opportunities.

By examining the relationship between these features of the social structure and the trends of mobility in different countries, we may be able to account for the similarities and differences among these trends.

1. The number of vacancies in a given stratum is not always, or even usually, constant. For example, in every industrialized or industrializing country, the increase in the proportion of professional, official, managerial, and white-collar positions and the decline in the proportion of unskilled-labor jobs creates a surge of mobility, which is upward—provided these positions retain their relative standing and income. More and more people are needed to manage industry, to distribute goods, to provide personal services, and to run the ever-growing state bureaucracy. A comparison of the ratio of administrative (white-collar) to production (manual) workers in manufacturing industries over the last half-century in the United States, the United Kingdom, and Sweden shows that the correspondence in trends is very great. Thus, in the United States in 1899 there were 8 administrative employees per 100 production workers, in 1947 there were 22 administrative employees per 100 production workers, and in 1957 there were 30 administrative employees per 100 production workers. The corresponding rise in Britain between 1907 and 1948 is from 9 to 20 administrative employees per 100 production workers, and in Sweden the number rose from 7 to 21 between 1915 and 1950. In none of these countries did the proportion of those self-employed in urban occupations decline.

2. An important determinant of upward mobility is the difference in rates of fertility. In all industrialized countries for which we have data,

fertility tends to vary inversely with income. Although changes in the economic structure are increasing the proportion of persons engaged in high-level occupations, the families of men who are now in such occupations are not contributing their proportionate share of the population. Consequently, even if every son of a high-status father were to retain that status, there would still be room for others to rise.

A similar consideration also applies to the process of urbanization. In all industrialized countries the urban centers continue to grow, requiring migrants to fill new positions or to replace urbanites, who characteristically fail to reproduce themselves. Although the urban birth rate is below reproduction level, the proportion of the population living in large cities (100,000 and over) grew in England from 26 per cent in 1871 to 38 per cent in 1951; in Germany from 5 per cent in 1870 to 27 per cent in 1950; in France, from 9 per cent in 1870 to 17 per cent in 1946; and in the United States from 11 per cent in 1870 to 30 per cent in 1950. And . . . the process of migration into urban areas permits a large proportion of the sons of workers who grow up in metropolitan centers to fill the newly created or demographically vacated middle-class positions, while the manual jobs left open are filled by migrants from small towns or rural areas.

3. In our rapidly changing world some positions lose, some gain, prestige. Thus, a person can be mobile in the eyes of society without changing his job. Admittedly, most of these losses or gains are barely noticeable within one generation. For example, a rating of twenty-five occupations made in 1925 was compared with a rating made in 1947, and a correlation of .97 was obtained, indicating practically no change. However, another study of the same period has indicated that government positions in the United States have enhanced their prestige since the 'twenties. Moreover, the addition of new occupations may sometimes inadvertently alter the prestige of certain ranks; for example, the emergence of the occupation of airplane pilot during the last generation served to deglamorize such occupations as ship captain and locomotive engineer. And significant changes in a given profession such as were effected in those of physicist, mathematician, and others by the atomic research programs during World War II, are also likely to better—or to lower—its prestige. However, we do not have studies with which to test such guesses.

4. In modern social structures there is a relative decline in the number of inheritable positions. Many middle-class fathers in salaried positions have little to give their children except a good education and motivation to obtain a high-status position. If for any reason, such as the early death of the father or family instability, a middle-class child does not complete his higher education, he is obviously in a poorer position, in terms of prospective employment, than the son of a manual worker who completes college. Clearly, some of the children of the middle class are so handicapped, others simply do not have the ability to complete college or to get along in a bureaucratic hierarchy, and many of these fall into a status below that of their fathers. Whatever the reason, persons of middle-class origin who fall in status leave room for others of lower-class background to rise.

The importance of this factor is emphasized by the sharp increase in the educational level among the working classes. No nation approaches the United States in terms of the number of university students who come from the working class. Even sons of working-class Negroes in the United States are more likely to go to college than sons of European workers. The effect of the difference in university attendance among workers on the two continents, of course, is reduced by the fact that higher education is a more certain way of achieving a privileged position in Europe than in the United States.

5. Many earlier legal restrictions upon the right of a person to create a new and higher occupational status for himself have been removed. The abolition of the guild system is the classic example of this. All the countries we have discussed . . . have legal guarantees of the freedom of occupational choice. A peculiar consequence of such guarantees is the phenomenon of "increased upward mobility" during depressions. In these periods many manual workers are fired and cannot find jobs in their normal occupations. To survive, many of them become small entrepreneurs and, thus, according to the conventional classification, move upward on the social ladder.

Gross mobility rates may be about the same in industrial countries. Yet within any society opportunities for mobility may be very different for particular groups. For example, while the Negro population of the United States amounts to 10 per cent of the total population, the bulk of Negroes cannot easily obtain white-collar work. Minorities sharing the culture of poverty are immobile not because of legal restrictions but because of traditional prejudice and discrimination. In an average mobility rate for the United States as a whole, the immobility of these minorities can pull down the high mobility rate of white Americans. Even if sons of working-class Negroes in the United States are more likely to go to college than sons of European workers, they cannot be mobile, in accordance with the criterion of mobility used in the foregoing article, without obtaining white-collar jobs. Hence, the crucial question is whether a college education gives them better opportunities for white-collar employment than sons of European workers have without higher education.

Ethnic minorities may find it somewhat more difficult to use educational achievement as a means of occupational mobility. Nevertheless, in all industrial societies formal education tends to allocate people to occupational levels. In contemporary Japan, for example, educational attainment is important enough in personnel recruitment so that educational attainment and occupational status correlate extremely well in the large factory.[6] Whether this necessarily means intergenerational mobility depends on the correlation between *parental status* and the *education* of offspring.

Data from the Boalt study of social mobility in Stockholm permit an examination of this possibility.[7] Table 74 shows a strong relationship between the occupational status of fathers

and the educational attainment of sons. More than half of the sons of high-status fathers (173 out of 282) graduated from college.[8] Sons of fathers of medium or low occupational statuses were much less likely to have gone this far in school. On the other hand, *some* of the sons of fathers of medium or low occupational statuses also attained this educational level, and the majority of them (138 out of 208) had high occupational status at the time of the study. In short, higher education may be the normal expectation on middle- and upper-class levels, but higher education is also a socioeconomic escalator for intellectually able youngsters from working-class backgrounds. If Stockholm is typical of contemporary large cities, formal education is a genuine channel of social

---

[6] James C. Abegglen, *The Japanese Factory: Aspects of Its Social Organization*, Glencoe, Ill.: Free Press, 1958, p. 28.

[7] Boalt, *loc. cit.*

[8] The labels in Table 74 attempt to translate levels of the Swedish educational system into their closest American equivalent. Thus, "college graduate" is the closest approximation of passing the student examination, which is required for university attendance in the Scandinavian countries. "Some college" refers to attendance at the *gymnasium* but without passing the student examination.

TABLE 74

Education of Sons Related to the Occupational Status of Their Fathers in 1936 and Their Own Occupational Status in 1949, Stockholm

Occupational Status of Sons	Education of Sons				
	College Graduate	Some College	Secondary School Graduate	Some Secondary School	Primary School Only
(of fathers of high occupational status)					
High	135	1	...	...	...
Medium	38	52	15	31	6
Low	...	...	...	2	2
(of fathers of medium occupational status)					
High	115	...	...	...	...
Medium	49	65	96	99	143
Low	...	2	7	24	116
(of fathers of low occupational status)					
High	23	...	...	...	...
Medium	21	11	101	61	404
Low	...	2	21	37	515
(of fathers of all occupational statuses)					
All statuses	381	133	240	254	1186

Source: Gunnar Boalt, "Social Mobility in Stockholm: A Pilot Investigation," in *Transactions of the Second World Congress of Sociology*, Vol. 2, London: International Sociological Association, 1954, p. 68.

mobility in industrial societies—and probably an increasingly important one. Bureaucratized economies can deal more rationally with qualifications like education than they can with personal factors like family connections. Besides, the size of urban societies creates staggering problems of social sifting; educational criteria offer a simple approach to screening.

Are the systems of formal education in contemporary societies sufficiently alike to account for the similarities in mobility rates? A recent study has shown that university students are less likely to come from working-class backgrounds in Germany, France, The Netherlands, Switzerland, and Austria than in Great Britain or the United States.[9] That is, industrial societies differ in the extent to which they approach equality of educational opportunity. They probably differ also in the extent to which educational achievement and occupational achievement are correlated. All the more puzzling, therefore, is the observed similarity in mobility rates reported in the previous reading. If such similarities persist in comparative studies conducted under the same auspices and using the same methods, this would suggest that industrial societies dip into lower strata to the same extent for persons of ability. Very likely, educational systems serve to provide opportunities for social ascent to such persons in all the industrial societies, although not to *all* young persons of talent. But educational achievement need not guarantee high occupational status. In the United States, for example, one out of five 24-year-olds in 1960 completed one year of college or more.[10] It is unlikely that all of these persons will achieve high occupational status, partly because there are not sufficient opportunities, partly because the American educational system is not as selective of talent as some of the European systems.

[9] David V. Glass and René Koenig, *Soziale Schichtung und Soziale Mobilität*, Cologne: Westdeutcher Verlag, 1961, reviewed by Kurt B. Mayer in *American Sociological Review*, Vol. 28, August 1963, pp. 638–639.
[10] Bureau of the Census, *United States Census of Population: 1960, United States Summary, Detailed Characteristics*, Washington: Government Printing Office, 1963, p. 398.

High rates of gross mobility involve social *descent* as well as social *ascent*. Systems of formal education in all industrial societies alert parents to the prospect of downward mobility for their children; school failure conveys the same meaning in the suburbs of Tokyo, Paris, London, and New York: the likelihood of a *fall* in social status.

IDEOLOGICAL INTERPRETATION OF OBJECTIVE OPPORTUNITIES

The objective situation never speaks for itself; it must always be interpreted by participants. Let us apply this sociological axiom to social mobility. Even if mobility rates of industrial societies are comparable, they may be interpreted as "high" or "low," "good" or "bad," depending on the cultural values of a particular tradition. Professors Lipset and Bendix argue that the American belief in "opportunity" can be better understood in terms of the equalitarian ideas of a new country than in terms of greater objective opportunities for social mobility on this side of the Atlantic Ocean.

Ideological Equalitarianism in America

Reprinted by permission. From Seymour Martin Lipset and Reinhard Bendix, "Ideological Equalitarianism and Social Mobility in the United States," *Transactions of the Second World Congress of Sociology*, Vol. 2, London: International Sociological Association, 1954, pp. 34–54.

We can only speculate when we assess the absence of a feudal past in America. Clearly it has not meant the absence of status distinctions, which have frequently been every bit as invidious on this side of the Atlantic as on the other. But it has led, among other factors, to an ideological equalitarianism, which is not any the less important because it has been contradicted throughout and on every side by the existence of status differences. No act is perhaps as symbolic of this persuasion as Thomas Jefferson's order to have a round table replace the rectangular one at the White House, because this would relieve him of the necessity to stipulate the order of precedence at official receptions. The implication of this act was not to deny the existing differences in rank and authority; it was rather a testimony to the belief that these were the accidental, not the essential, attributes of man. Among men of equal worth, it is not good form to insist on the accidental distinctions which divide them.

Such ideological equalitarianism has played, and continues to play, an important rôle in facilitating social mobility in the United States. It enables the person of humble birth to regard mobility as an attainable goal, for himself or for his children. It facilitates his acceptance as an equal, if he succeeds in rising socially and economically. It mitigates the emotional distance between persons of different social rank. And it fosters in any existing elite the persuasion (however mistaken this may be in fact) that its eminence is the result of individual effort, and hence temporary. The point worth emphasising is not that these beliefs are often contradicted by the experience of those who hold them and that distinctions of status exist in fact. What calls for analysis is the persistence of this equalitarian ideology in the face of facts which contradict it. We would suggest that the absence of hereditary aristocracy has aided in this respect. Americans have rarely been exposed to persons whose conduct implies their own inherited and God-given superiority as well as the demand that others demonstrate their recognition of this fact by deferential behaviour.

The American ideological emphasis on equality provides a lens through which American mobility is viewed. Insofar as it is possible, this mobility is interpreted as evidence of an open society. This optimistic interpretation of mobility in America perhaps explains why Horatio Alger found 50 million readers for his 135 novels—despite devastating criticism of his literary talents.[11] On the other hand, European traditions of élitism fostered disbelief in the reality of mobility on their side of the Atlantic Ocean. European observers were more prone to notice *immobility* because they were ideologically prepared to see it.

If ideological considerations exaggerate the actual differences in mobility rates between Europe and America, they also exaggerate the differences between mobility in nineteenth-century America and mobility in the contemporary United States. What schoolboy has not learned to associate the frontier with opportunity and the closing of the frontier with increasing social rigidity? Yet careful studies have not succeeded in demonstrating a tendency for mobility to decrease since 1900.[12] Even though opportunities have not decreased, it is what people *believe* to be true about mobility rather than the actual distribution of opportunities to rise or fall in status which produces satisfaction or discontent. We come back again to the principle of relative deprivation mentioned in Chapter 4.

AMBITION AND DEVIANCE IN AMERICAN CITIES

For several reasons, vertical mobility tends to be greater in large cities than in small towns or rural areas.[13] Large cities are characterized by far more elaborate division of labor than small towns. This means that youngsters are presented with more potential choices as to the roles they will play. Second, the anonymity of the metropolis allows the youngster who is unwilling to accept the same status as his parents more chance to avoid community pressures favoring status inheritance. Third, the concentration of high-quality educational institutions in large cities gives ambitious youngsters a better chance to utilize educational channels of mobility than they would have in smaller communities. Finally, the demographic characteristics of cities make for *net* upward mobility; the *growth* of cities creates new occupational opportunities—including high-level positions. And apart from the effect of growth, the larger the city, the greater is the proportion of the labor force in white-collar jobs.

Whether these additional opportunities for

11   R. Richard Wohl, "The 'Rags to Riches Story': An Episode of Secular Idealism," in Bendix and Lipset, Eds., *Class, Status and Power: A Reader in Social Stratification*, Glencoe, Ill.: Free Press, 1953, pp. 388–395.

12   Lipset and Bendix, *Social Mobility in Industrial Society, op. cit.*, p. 90.
13   *Ibid.*, pp. 203–226, is the source of the data on which this paragraph is based.

vertical mobility make city dwellers more ambitious depends, as Professors Lipset and Bendix point out, on the ideology of the society. A society may discount small moves upward or downward and consider only meteoric careers as examples of mobility.[14] If, however, situations in which the son of a machinist becomes a mechanical engineer or the son of a salesman becomes an electrician are discounted, the citizen may recognize fewer possibilities for mobility than the sociologist. In the United States, one result of the tradition of celebrating meteoric careers and paying less attention to the more prosaic, step-by-step mobility is a counter-ideology of disbelief in the possibilities of social ascent.

Disbelief in the existence of occupational opportunities is especially pronounced in slum neighborhoods. The culture of poverty generates apathy and resentment rather than ambition. Dissatisfaction leads to ambition only when it is coupled with hope. When dissatisfaction occurs in conjunction with disbelief in legitimate opportunities, it promotes a willingness to utilize illegitimate opportunities. The slum boy sees the urban industrial economy from a peculiar perspective. He and his family have a low standard of living. Many of the people he observes in films and reads about in newspapers live more comfortably, and he would like to move up to their level. He has little chance to see the educational achievements and the occupational responsibilities that make a luxurious standard of living possible. The mass media do not, it is true, portray the idle rich to the exclusion of business and professional men, but élite occupational roles are represented vaguely and romantically. The middle-class child can "fill in" the details from observations in his milieu; he knows what a lawyer or a business executive does at work and the preparations such careers entail. But a boy with few sources of information about high-status people may think that their only talent is a talent for spending money. Besides, illegitimate opportunities may seem accessible; legitimate opportunities may not.[15]

Social psychological research is capable of specifying how an objectively disadvantaged youngster perceives the alternative between legitimate and illegitimate opportunities *subjectively*. For example, Richard Stephenson studied the occupation aspirations and expectations of 1000 ninth-grade students in New Jersey high schools.[16] He demonstrated that the occupational aspirations of ninth graders were uniformly high even though their concrete educational and job goals were correlated with their fathers' occupational status. They dream, but they know the difference between dream and reality. And Arthur Stinchcombe, in a study of a California high school, found that youngsters who could not perceive bright educational futures for themselves were likely to feel resentful and to act rebellious.[17] Unfortunately, neither of these studies was specifically concerned with economically deprived adolescents. Other studies have provided insights into the subjective reactions of slum youth. Nevertheless, many gaps remain in our knowledge of the assessment of legitimate and illegitimate opportunities. Any attempt at analysis is necessarily speculative.

Is the slum boy likely to believe that the way to a higher standard of living than his parents enjoy is through starting a business of his own? A careful study of the work histories of 935 wage earners in Oakland, California, showed that self-employment was one of the few positions of higher status attainable by manual workers.[18] Although the number of self-employed businessmen at any given time is small, a considerable number of manual workers have tried at some time in their lives to

---

14   *Ibid.*, p. 117.

15   Richard A. Cloward, "Illegitimate Means, Anomie and Deviant Behavior," *American Sociological Review*, Vol. 24, April 1959, pp. 164–176.
16   Richard M. Stephenson, "Mobility Orientation and Stratification of 1,000 Ninth Graders," *American Sociological Review*, Vol. 22, April 1957, pp. 204–212.
17   Arthur Stinchcombe, "Social Sources of Rebellion in a High School," unpublished Ph.D. dissertation, University of California at Berkeley, 1960.
18   Lipset and Bendix, *Social Mobility in Industrial Society, op. cit.*, pp. 156–181.

become self-employed. Most of them do not succeed because they are swimming against the tide. The trend in industrial societies is toward more bureaucratic organization of economic activity, greater capital investment per enterprise, and high mortality rates for new businesses.[19] But many try, and some thrive. Whether a slum youngster thinks about owning a gas station or a bar, or about starting some other small business probably depends on whether people he has known have ventured into self-employment. If he is a Negro, the chances of his knowing someone with this kind of experience are small because so few American Negroes are self-employed businessmen; the maldistribution is self-perpetuating.

The slum boy not optimistic about starting a business of his own will not aspire to a managerial position in a large corporation either. This is feasible only for a youngster who plans to complete high school and then go on to college or engineering school. Working one's way up is no longer common.

"Today fewer men rise from the bottom to the top places in industry and business than did a generation ago . . . more and more top jobs are being filled by men coming from the technical and engineering schools or from the universities. The route up for them is no longer through a hierarchy of increasing skill to management and ownership as it was two generations ago. The prudent mobile man today must prepare himself by education . . ."[20]

A middle-class personnel officer mans the gate of the large corporation and lets pass only those working-class youngsters who have demonstrated their potentialities by educational achievement. For the slum boy who lacks scholastic aptitude, becoming a business executive may be as difficult as becoming a physician or a lawyer.

For low-status youngsters with special talents, careers in professional sports or entertainment offer possibilities for high prestige and income. For instance, for three-quarters of a century boxing has reflected the aspirations of disadvantaged minority groups in American cities. Fifty years ago, the leading boxers were Irish, German, and English; 30 years ago, they were Italian and Jewish; today they are Negro.[21] Boxing shares with careers in acting, singing, football, and baseball an emphasis upon performance rather than upon formal educational qualifications. But boxing differs from most careers in professional sports or in the entertainment field because the physical dangers are greater. Weinberg and Arond report that a majority of boxers sustain brain injuries which leave them mildly or severely "punch-drunk." The risks of a boxing career, its necessary brevity, and the handful of boxers who earn substantial money serve to discourage middle-class competition. This explains why professional boxers are recruited disproportionately from the minority currently on the socio-economic floor—and why managers believe that a "hungry" boxer is better motivated.

Working-class boys are not disadvantaged in competing for baseball careers, either. Although preadolescent boys dream of becoming baseball players (in the United States and Japan), middle-class parents smile benignly and refuse to regard baseball as a potential career. How can one plan on doing something that depends in part on muscular maturation? Since it is easier to predict that a 12-year-old boy has the aptitude for law school than the muscular coordination and the timing of a Joe DiMaggio, middle-class parents prefer to regard sports as recreation and school as vocational preparation. Professional football and tennis are more likely to recruit from the ranks of college players, thus restricting opportunities for nonacademic youngsters; but even in these sports, circumstances and talent sometimes catapult an unlikely person to fame and fortune.

[19] Kurt B. Mayer, "Business Enterprise: Traditional Symbol of Opportunity," *British Journal of Sociology*, Vol. 4, June 1953, pp. 160–180.

[20] W. Lloyd Warner, Marcia Meeker, and Kenneth Eells, *Social Class in America*, Chicago: Science Research Associates, 1949, p. 24.

[21] S. Kirson Weinberg and Henry Arond, "The Occupational Culture of the Boxer," *American Journal of Sociology*, Vol. 57, March 1952, pp. 460–469.

A Rags-to-Riches Story

Reprinted by permission. From Marshall Smith, "From a Waif to a Winner, the Clown of the Courts," *Life*, Vol. 50, Jan. 13, 1961, pp. 95–102.

The entrance is always the same. When the loudspeaker announces "The Two-Fisted Killer from Ecuador," he rises on short, crooked legs and sucks in air through nostrils that flare extravagantly down to the corners of his mouth. Absent-mindedly he hands his wallet to the person standing next to him. Instead of striding to the center of the court in the clean-cut, dignified fashion that has endured since Bill Tilden's day, he lowers his shaggy black head, aims himself and charges. One arm has a death grip on six tennis rackets. The other, flailing as if to supply additional propulsion, beats the air in a mad circle. His feet execute a series of maneuvers that outrage the principles of locomotion. With every pigeon-toed stride his right foot threatens to collide with his left, and he seems certain to disintegrate in a horrible tangle of arms, legs and rackets. But, with a monstrous sigh, he comes abruptly to rest, determined in spite of his preposterous appearance to play professional tennis. Pancho Segura is on-stage.

A TWO-FISTED CLOWN

It is evident to every spectator that this figure is not a two-fisted killer but a clown. And yet from the moment he swings his racket with his unorthodox, two-handed baseball grip, every spectator is brought under the spell of the most accomplished underdog in the history of professional sport. Pancho Segura's eagerness makes up for his deficiencies in style and stature. Scuttling around the court on his crooked legs, he staves off disaster after disaster. He gives himself frenzied pep talks, crying out, "*Vamos, Pancho! Vamos!*" He slaps his leg and grimaces. When he connects for a winner, he breaks into a tricky little jog and throws out his chest Mussolini-style. When he manages to fool his opponent with a lob or drop shot, he taps his forehead significantly. On questionable calls that go against him he appeals dramatically to heaven, holding up thumb and forefinger half an inch apart to emphasize the injustice. It is all a fine and funny show—but when the match is over, it is often the clown who is taking the winner's bows, giggling and wagging his head as he calls for more applause.

Surely the victory is a mistake: the funny man has stepped out of character and slain the dragon. No one seems to remember that Pancho Segura has twice been professional champion of the U.S., for the curse of his life has been to perform heroic deeds and be rewarded with laughter. As he toddles off the court after his triumph, he is struck by a distressing thought: to whom did he entrust his wallet?

It is the same question he asks himself every time he finishes a match, and he always gets the same answer. He scans the faces of his fellow players, searching hopefully for a clue. The old game of making a goat of Pancho is under way. Before it ends there will be heated accusations, and Pancho will be told that he is out of his idiotic mind. Eventually he will get his wallet back—but not before he has been reduced to begging for his supper.

At the venerable age of 39 Pancho Segura is permanently cast as the "animal act." He started professional tennis that way 13 years ago, going on in the preliminary match for appropriately animal wages. He has played the role in every country on earth visited by Jack Kramer's pro tennis tour. He is too enthusiastic to be downcast, too humble to be demanding, too grateful to complain. "If it wasn't for tennis," he says, "I'd be checking coconut trees in Ecuador."

Pancho spent the first 19 years of his life in Ecuador, most of it being called *Pata de Loro*, or parrot-foot. His legs were deformed by premature birth, rickets, double hernia and malaria. He lived in a sugar-cane house on the outskirts of Guayaquil with only the earth for a floor, and every time his mother contemplated his emaciated body and twisted legs she reached for her rosary.

In Guayaquil, where only the rich and healthy play tennis, these drawbacks were more than enough to keep anybody off the courts. In addition to his physical handicaps, he was a *cholo*, with the mixed blood of one Spaniard and many Incas in his veins. In class-conscious Ecuador it was unthinkable for a half-crippled urchin of mixed blood to be accepted in the tennis circle. The only thing in Pancho's favor was his godfather, Juan José Medina, one of the wealthiest men in Ecuador and a director of Guayaquil's only tennis club.

Pancho's father worked for Juan José and later became caretaker at the tennis club. When Juan José suggested that tennis might help his puny godchild, Pancho took to the courts after hours with a balsawood tennis paddle made by his mother. He also earned a little money as a ball boy, scrabbling around the court like a crab. The constant, day-after-day exercise strengthened his scrawny legs, even though it could never straighten them. To build himself up, he also took long swims in the filthy Guayas River.

At 11 he got his first real racket, a beaten-up Top Flight discarded by a visiting Brazilian player. Because it was too heavy for him to swing with one hand, he used two. When his godfather gave him permission to use the club's rowing machine, Pancho jumped at the opportunity and rowed hundreds of theoretical miles, building up his arms, legs and chest. He soon became strong enough to swing the racket with one hand, but he had become so proficient with his *dos manos* grip that he kept on swinging that way. By the time he was 15, Pancho was the best tennis player in Ecuador.

In 1938 he got a bitter lesson in what happens to a *cholo* who tries to rise above his station. That year, when it was suggested that he play for the club in the big annual match against Quito, the capital, all hell broke loose. The members were aghast at the idea of having a *cholo* on the club team. They said he was a professional. After all, he had taken up to 10 sucres (60¢) to play matches with members. The complaints were overridden by the club president, who threatened to resign unless Pancho played.

On the train ride up to Quito the caretaker's son was snubbed by his teammates. He was made to sit off to one side by himself. When the train stopped overnight, the others went off to the hotel for steaks while he bought green bananas from a sidewalk vendor. But Pancho won all three of his matches, enabling Guayaquil to defeat Quito. On the ride home he was allowed to sit with his teammates.

That same year he was entered by Ecuador in the Bolivarian Olympics at Bogotá and once again felt the sting of abuse. Other countries, led by Peru, tried to bar him from competing on the grounds that he was a pro. But when Ecuador threatened to boycott the games, Pancho was allowed to play. Once again he won, but with insults from other contestants ringing in his ears.

On his return from Bogotá, however, he was hailed by 20,000 hero-worshiping Ecuadorians. His name appeared on bus lines, barbershops and haberdasheries. The street on which he lived became Pancho Segura Calle, and his picture appeared on a 50-centavos postage stamp. The lowly *cholo* was too bewildered by it all to do anything but grin, and when his fame evaporated like morning mist two years later, he still had the contagious grin which is now his trademark.

In the field of sports, Pancho Segura, Joe Louis, and Babe Ruth are exceptions: one-in-a-million possibilities that came true. In the entertainment world, Louis Armstrong and Harry Belafonte are similar rarities. Unless slum-dwelling youngsters are incurably optimistic, as some no doubt are, they realize the small likelihood of legitimate success without higher education. This realization makes *illegitimate* opportunities more attractive. A slum boy may think of the money he would have by robbing a bank, a lower-class girl of the pretty clothes she could wear if she made herself sexually available to men with money. Parents may caution about avoiding "trouble." But what do parents know? The slum youngster hears that gamblers are not strictly legitimate, but he observes that they suffer less for their sins than honest laborers for their virtues. He may disregard parental advice because he does not wish to forego the good things of life as his parents have done. On the other hand, his parents may be oriented to short-cut methods of making money also. To be sure, the numbers racket and other forms of gambling flourish in slum neighborhoods.[22] The poor "waste" money on long-shots because they believe that the gulf between what they have and what they would like to have can be bridged only by luck. They gamble even though they are aware of the odds against winning.[23] Armed robbery, like gam-

22 Edward C. Devereux, "Gambling and the Social Structure," unpublished Ph.D. dissertation, Harvard University, 1950, Part V.
23 In an experiment directed by Professor Frederick Mosteller of the gambling behavior of Harvard undergraduates (middle class) and National Guardsmen (lower class), Mosteller provided all visitors to his ex-

bling, is a way of getting money by techniques that repudiate the exchange principle embodied in the economic institutions of industrial societies.

Lower-class youngsters, then, who are not able to utilize the educational escalator, may seek illegitimate means to avoid entrapment at the bottom of the socioeconomic heap. The values of the particular subculture in which they are socialized affects the choice between legitimate and illegitimate courses, as a comparison between second-generation Jewish and Italian children shows.

Ethnic Factors in the Choice between Legitimate and Illegitimate Opportunities

Reprinted by permission. From Jackson Toby, "Hoodlum or Business Man: An American Dilemma," in Marshall Sklare, Ed., *The Jews*, Glencoe, Ill.: Free Press, 1958, pp. 542–550.

Jews and Italians came to the United States in large numbers at about the same time—the turn of the century—and both settled in urban areas.[24] There was, however, a very different attitude toward intellectual accomplishment in the two cultures. Jews from Eastern Europe regarded religious study as the most important activity for an adult male. The rabbi enjoyed great prestige because he was a scholar, a teacher, a logician. He advised the community on the application of the Written and Oral Law. Life in America gave a secular emphasis to the Jewish reverence for learning. Material success is a more important motive than salvation for American youngsters,

Jewish as well as Christian, and secular education is better training for business and professional careers than Talmudic exegesis. Nevertheless, intellectual achievement continued to be valued by Jews—and to have measurable effects. Second-generation Jewish students did homework diligently, got high grades, went to college in disproportionate numbers, and scored high on intelligence tests.[25]

Immigrants from Southern Italy, on the other hand, tended to regard formal education either as a frill or as a source of dangerous ideas from which the minds of the young should be protected.[26] They remembered Sicily, where a child who attended school regularly was a rarity. There, youngsters were needed to help on the farm. Furthermore, hard-working peasants could not understand why their children should learn classical Italian (which they would not speak at home) or geography (when they would not travel in their lifetime more than a few miles from their birthplace). Sicilian parents suspected that education was an attempt on the part of Roman officials to subvert the authority of the family. In the United States, many South Italian immigrants maintained the same attitudes. They resented compulsory school-attendance laws and prodded their children to go to work and become economic assets as soon as possible. They encouraged neglect of schoolwork and even truancy. They did not realize that education has more importance in an urban-industrial society than in a semi-feudal one. With supportive motivation from home lacking, many second-generation Italian boys did not make the effort of Jewish contemporaries. Their teachers tried to stuff the curriculum into their heads in vain. Their lack of interest was reflected not only in low marks, retardation, truancy, and early school leaving; it even resulted in poor scores on intelligence tests.[27] They accepted their parents'

perimental gambling casino with precise odds before taking bets. Nevertheless, the National Guardsmen bet more heavily than the college students. See James Olds, "Gambling and the Value of Money," *Lab Bulletin*, Vol. 2, October 1949, Laboratory of Social Relations, Harvard University, pp. 1–5.
24 Bureau of the Census, *Immigrants and Their Children*, 1920, Washington: Government Printing Office, 1927, p. 62. An official comparison of the rural-urban distribution of Jews and Italians is not possible with United States data. In Canada, however, 96.45 per cent of the Jewish population was urban in 1931 as compared with 81.55 per cent of the Italian population. Dominion of Canada, Bureau of Statistics, *Rural and Urban Composition of the Canadian Population*, Ottawa: 1938, p 81.

25 For documentation, see Jackson Toby, "Educational Maladjustment as a Predisposing Factor in Criminal Careers," unpublished Ph.D. dissertation, Harvard, 1950, Chap. 7, "The Orientation of the School Contributed by the Jewish Cultural Tradition," pp. 178–207.
26 Leonard Covello, "The Social Background of the Italo-American School Child: A Study of the Southern Italian Family Mores and Their Effect on the School Situation in Italy and America," unpublished Ph.D. dissertation, New York University, School of Education, 1944.
27 Nathaniel D. M. Hirsch, "A Study of Natio-Racial Mental Difference," *Genetic Psychology Monographs*,

conception of the school as worthless and thereby lost their best opportunity for social ascent.

Some of these youngsters did not reconcile themselves to remaining on the bottom of the heap; they rebelled. Second-generation Italian boys became delinquent in disproportionately large numbers. In New York City, 39 per cent of the white delinquents of foreign-born parents in 1930 were of Italian origin, although less than 22 per cent of the white families with foreign-born heads were of that ethnic group.[28] In Chicago, second-generation Italian boys in the years of 1927–33 had an appearance rate in the Cook County Juvenile Court twice as high as white boys generally.[29] Among older and more serious offenders, too, a disproportionate representation of Italian-Americans occurred. In 1933, second-generation Italian men were committed to state prisons and reformatories proportionately more frequently than the average second-generation American.[30]

Second-generation Jewish youths had less reason to become hoodlums. Whether they lived in slums or not, they usually perceived a constructive alternative to continued lower-class status. Their parents kept legitimate channels of social ascent open for them by inculcating the traditional attitude of respect for education and by transmitting the business know-how gleaned from hundreds of years of urban life in Europe. Why should they have rebelled against success in the marketplace as a criterion of status? Their chances in the marketplace were excellent. As a matter of history, although Jewish immigrants took menial jobs and lived in overcrowded ghettos during the first two decades of the twentieth century, their children became overwhelmingly middle class. The shift from unskilled and skilled trades worked at by one generation, to clerical, managerial, and professional occupations in the next, probably was not duplicated by any other immigrant group.[31] Jewish parents did not consider them-

selves engaged in crime prevention, but consequences do not have to be foreseen to be real.

Did second-generation Jewish youths avoid delinquency, as these considerations suggest? Data on the offense rates of Jews are difficult to come by.[32] Official agencies in the United States rarely identify offenders by religious affiliation and do not consider Jews to be a nationality.[33] Some statistics on Jewish offenders exist, however, and, fortunately, they refer to periods shortly after large-scale Jewish migration to the United States —so that they are, in effect, second-generation rates. In New York City, for example, Jewish

Vol. 1, 1926, pp. 239–406; Covello, *op. cit.*; Sophia M. Robison, *Can Delinquency Be Measured?*, New York: Columbia University Press, 1936, "Truants," pp. 127–155.

[28] Robison, *op. cit.*, p. 182.

[29] Clifford R. Shaw and Henry D. McKay, *Juvenile Delinquency and Urban Areas*, Chicago: University of Chicago Press, 1942, p. 154.

[30] Donald R. Taft, "Nationality and Crime," *American Sociological Review*, Vol. 1, December 1936, pp. 724–736.

[31] Nathan Goldberg, *Occupational Patterns of American Jews*, New York: Jewish Teachers' Seminary and People's University, 1947.

[32] Not only is it difficult to identify Jewish offenders, but in the United States it is also no small problem to count the Jewish population at large. The Bureau of the Census does not collect information on the religious affiliation of individuals. As a result, the number of Jews in the United States is something of a mystery. Estimates are available, especially in large cities where the bulk of American Jewry lives, but no one knows how accurate these are. Even in New York, Boston, and Chicago, detailed data on age composition and nativity do not exist. Since an accurate count of the base population is necessary in order to compute a crime rate, Jewish crime statistics in the United States must be considered approximations even in instances in which the Jewish offenders have been validly identified.

[33] Insofar as Jews are identified in population surveys, e.g., the Canadian Census, it is because they call themselves Jewish or are considered Jewish by others. Thus, their solidarity with other "Jews" is measured rather than their commitment to Jewish values. From the point of view of preventing crime, however, whether the individual has internalized the intellectual achievement values of the Jewish cultural tradition is more relevant to his developing a stake in conformity than the fact that he calls himself "Jewish." In the United States and Canada, where ethnic groups are in process of assimilation, the values of the ethnic tradition may be sloughed off by an individual before he disaffiliates from his group. This is particularly true of Jews because prejudice may enforce a solidarity upon them that is unjustified by usual ethnic traditions. In short, there is reason to believe that a statistical effort to document the crime-preventing effect of the Jewish cultural tradition cannot fully succeed; statistics about Jewish offenders and about the Jewish population at large employ an operational definition of "Jewishness" geared to solidarities rather than to cultural commitment.

The author's survey of the case histories of a sample of Jewish juvenile delinquents tended to confirm this line of reasoning. These youngsters were, in their attitudes toward school and their occupational aspirations, much like juvenile delinquents from other backgrounds. That is, they did not have the orientations which one would expect of youngsters immersed in the Jewish cultural tradition.

youngsters constituted in 1930 about a quarter of the white delinquents—although the Jewish population at large was estimated to be about a third of the total white population of the city.[34] To be sure, only nine-tenths of the Jewish delinquents in 1930 were the offspring of foreign-born parents, but it is unlikely that a recalculation of the Jewish delinquency rate for youngsters whose parents were born abroad would have made an appreciable difference.[35] Out of 394,080 prisoners sent to the prisons and reformatories of the 48 states from 1920 to 1929, 6846 (1.74 per cent) were Jews.[36] (The Jewish population of the country was estimated then to be 3.43 per cent of the total.) Crude though these data are, they show that the probability of becoming a hoodlum was not the same for second-generation Jews and second-generation Italians.

The foregoing analysis can explain why Italian delinquents are more common than Jewish delinquents in American cities, but it does not throw much light on illegitimate opportunities for success. Delinquents typically commit petty, crudely executed thefts. They force open the back door of a grocery store and rifle the cash register; they drive off a car and "strip" it of radio, heater, and tires; they break into a darkened house and look for valuables; they beat up a drunk on the street and take his wallet. A professional con-man or safe-cracker would be ashamed to "pull jobs" so lacking in craftsmanship. Similarly, the businessmen of crime, who operate lucrative rackets, have political friends to intercede with police and prosecutors, and hire top-notch lawyers, bear slight resemblance to these young hoodlums who gain little from crime but incarceration.

Yet there is a connection. Although some juvenile delinquents remain the unskilled workers of crime, enjoying a trifling income and spending most of their lives in custody, a few

graduate into the ranks of organized crime, as Al Capone did. In the annals of illegitimate opportunity, Al Capone was a Horatio Alger story, a Brooklyn boy who made good in Chicago.[37] Organized crime has to staff openings in its ranks without the benefit of formal educational preparation. Important racketeers do not write books explaining their recruiting methods, but they probably look for promising youngsters among alumni of reformatories and prisons. Organized crime, because its operations are conspicuous, must also have collaborators in politics and law enforcement. Thus, the slum boy who joins the local political club, working first as a precinct captain, then as a ward leader, may develop a close relationship with local gambling interests. This relationship may be even closer if the racketeers and the politicians are members of the same disadvantaged ethnic group striving to move up the ladder. Daniel Bell of Columbia University lays great emphasis on the parallel strivings of racketeers and politicians in his analysis of the relationship between politics and crime in American cities.

Urban Rackets in America: An Alternative Channel of Social Ascent

Reprinted by permission. From Daniel Bell, "Crime as an American Way of Life," *Antioch Review*, Vol. 13, Summer 1953, pp. 131–156.

. . . [T]he urban rackets—the illicit activity organized for continuing profit rather than individual illegal acts—is one of the queer ladders of social mobility in American life. Indeed, it is not too much to say that the whole question of organized crime in America cannot be understood unless one appreciates (1) the distinctive role of organized gambling as a function of a mass consumption economy; (2) the specific role of various immigrant groups as they one after another became involved in marginal business and crime; and (3) the relation of crime to the changing character of the urban political machines.

As a society changes, so does, in lagging fashion, its type of crime. As American society be-

34   Robison, *op. cit.*, p. 72; pp. 222–226.
35   Julius B. Maller, "The Maladjusted Jewish Child," *Jewish Social Service Quarterly*, Vol. 10, December 1933, p. 160.
36   H. S. Linfield, "Jewish Inmates of the State Prisons of the United States," *American Jewish Year Book*, Vol. 33, Philadelphia: Jewish Publication Society of America, 1931.

37   Frank Tannenbaum, *Crime and the Community*, New York: Columbia University Press, 1938.

came more "organized," as the American business-man became more "civilized" and less "buccaneer-ing," so did the American racketeer. And just as there were important changes in the structure of business enterprise, so the "institutionalized" criminal enterprise was transformed too.

In the America of the last fifty years the main drift of society has been toward the rationaliza-tion of industry, the domestication of the crude self-made captain of industry into the respectable man of manners, and the emergence of a mass-consumption economy. The most significant trans-formation in the field of "institutionalized" crime was the increasing relative importance of gambling as against other kinds of illegal activity. And, as a multi-billion-dollar business, gambling under-went a transition parallel to the changes in Amer-ican enterprise as a whole. This parallel was ex-emplified in many ways: in gambling's industrial organization (e.g., the growth of a complex tech-nology such as the national racing wire service and the minimization of risks by such techniques as lay-off betting); in its respectability, as was evidenced in the opening of smart and popular gambling casinos in resort towns and in "satel-lite" adjuncts to metropolitan areas; in its func-tional role in a mass-consumption economy (for sheer volume of money changing hands, nothing has ever surpassed this feverish activity of fifty million American adults); in the social acceptance of the gamblers in the important status world of sport and entertainment, i.e., "café society."

In seeking to "legitimize" itself, gambling had quite often actually become a force against older and more vicious forms of illegal activity. In 1946, for example, when a Chicago mobster, Pat Manno, went down to Dallas, Texas, to take over gambling in the area for the Accardo-Guzik combine, he reassured the sheriff as to his intent as follows: "Something I'm against, that's dope peddlers, pickpockets, hired killers. That's one thing I can't stomach, and that's one thing the fellows up there—the group won't stand for, things like that. They discourage it, they even go to headquarters and ask them why they don't do something about it."

Jimmy Cannon once reported that when the gambling raids started in Chicago, the "combine" protested that, in upsetting existing stable rela-tions, the police were only opening the way for ambitious young punks and hoodlums to start trouble. Nor is there today, as there was twenty or even forty years ago, prostitution of major organized scope in the United States. Aside from the fact that manners and morals have changed, prostitution *as an industry* doesn't pay as well as gambling. Besides, its existence threatened the tacit moral acceptance and quasi-respectability that gamblers and gambling have secured in the American way of life. It was, as any operator in the field might tell you, "bad for business."

The criminal world of the last decade, its tone set by the captains of the gambling industry, is in startling contrast to the state of affairs in the two decades before. If a Kefauver report had been written then, the main "names" would have been Lepke and Gurrah, Dutch Schultz, Jack "Legs" Diamond, Lucky Luciano, and, reach-ing back a little further, Arnold Rothstein, the czar of the underworld. These men (with the exception of Luciano, who was involved in nar-cotics and prostitution) were in the main indus-trial racketeers. Rothstein, it is true, had a larger function: he was, as Frank Costello became later, the financier of the underworld—the pioneer big businessman of crime, who, understanding the logic of co-ordination, sought to *organize* crime as a source of regular income. His main interest in this direction was in industrial racketeering, and his entry was through labor disputes. At one time, employers in the garment trades hired Legs Dia-mond and his sluggers to break strikes, and the Communists, then in control of the cloakmakers union, hired one Little Orgie to protect the pickets and beat up the scabs; only later did both sides learn that Legs Diamond and Little Orgie were working for the same man, Rothstein. . . .

But in the last decade and a half, industrial racketeering has not offered much in the way of opportunity. *Like American capitalism itself, crime shifted its emphasis from production to consumption.* The focus of crime became the di-rect exploitation of the citizen as consumer, largely through gambling. And while the protection of these huge revenues was inextricably linked to politics, the relation between gambling and "the mobs" became more complicated.

Although it never showed up in the gross na-tional product, gambling in the last decade was one of the largest industries in the United States. The Kefauver Committee estimated it as a twenty-billion-dollar business. This figure has been picked up and widely quoted, but in truth no one knows what the gambling "turnover" and "take" actually is, nor how much is bet legally (pari-mutuel, etc.) and how much illegally. In fact, the figure cited by the committee was arbitrary and arrived at quite sloppily. As one staff member said: "We had no real idea of the money spent. . . . The California crime commission said twelve billion. Virgil Peterson of Chicago estimated thirty billion. We picked twenty billion as a balance between the two."

If comprehensive data are not available, we do know, from specific instances, the magnitude of many of the operations. Some indications can be seen from these items culled at random:

—James Carroll and the M & G syndicate did a 20-million-dollar annual business in St. Louis. This was one of the two large books in the city.

—The S & G syndicate in Miami did a 26-million-dollar volume yearly; the total for all books in the Florida resort reached 40 millions.

—Slot machines were present in 69,786 establishments in 1951 (each paid $100 for a license to the Bureau of Internal Revenue); the usual average is three machines to a license, which would add up to 210,000 slot machines in operation in the United States. In legalized areas, where the betting is higher and more regular, the average gross "take" per machine is $50 a week.

—The largest policy wheel (i.e. "numbers") in Chicago's "Black Belt" reported taxable net profits for the four-year period from 1946 through 1949, after sizable deductions for "overhead," of $3,656,968. One of the large "white" wheels reported in 1947 a gross income of $2,317,000 and a net profit of $205,000. One CIO official estimated that perhaps 15 per cent of his union's lower echelon officials are involved in the numbers racket (a steward, free to roam a plant, is in a perfect situation for organizing bets).

If one considers the amount of betting on sports alone—an estimated six billion on baseball, a billion on football pools, another billion on basketball, six billion on horse racing—then Elmo Roper's judgment that "only the food, steel, auto, chemical, and machine-tool industries have a greater volume of business" does not seem too far-fetched.

While gambling has long flourished in the United States, the influx of the big mobsters into the industry—and its expansion—started in the '30's when repeal of Prohibition forced them to look about for new avenues of enterprise. Gambling, which had begun to flower under the nour-

ishment of rising incomes, was the most lucrative field in sight. To a large extent the shift from bootlegging to gambling was a mere transfer of business operations. In the East, Frank Costello went into slot machines and the operation of a number of ritzy gambling casinos. He also became the "banker" for the Erickson "book," which "laid off" bets for other bookies. Joe Adonis, similarly, opened up a number of casinos, principally in New Jersey. Across the country, many other mobsters went into bookmaking. As other rackets diminished, and gambling, particularly horse-race betting, flourished in the '40's, a struggle erupted over the control of racing information.

Horse-race betting requires a peculiar industrial organization. The essential component is time. A bookie can operate only if he can get information on odds up to the very last minute before the race, so that he can "hedge" or "lay off" bets. With racing going on simultaneously on many tracks throughout the country, this information has to be obtained speedily and accurately. Thus, the racing wire is the nerve ganglion of race betting.

The racing-wire news service got started in the '20's through the genius of the late Moe Annenberg, who had made a fearful reputation for himself as Hearst's circulation manager in the rough-and-tumble Chicago newspaper wars. Annenberg conceived the idea of a telegraphic news service which would gather information from tracks and shoot it immediately to scratch sheets, horse parlors, and bookie joints. In some instances, track owners gave Annenberg the rights to send news from tracks; more often, the news was simply "stolen" by crews operating inside or near the tracks. So efficient did this news distribution system become, that in 1942, when a plane knocked out a vital telegraph circuit which served an Air Force field as well as the gamblers, the Continental Press managed to get its racing wire service for gamblers resumed in fifteen minutes, while it took the Fourth Army, which was responsible for the defense of the entire West Coast, something like three hours. . . .

While Americans made gambling illegal, they did not in their hearts think of it as wicked—even the churches benefited from the bingo and lottery crazes. So they gambled—and gamblers flourished. Against this open canvas, the indignant tones of Senator Wiley and the shocked righteousness of Senator Tobey during the Kefauver investigation rang oddly. Yet it was probably this very tone of surprise that gave the activity of the Kefauver Committee its piquant quality. Here were some Senators who seemingly did not know the facts of life, as most Americans did. Here, in the person of Senator Tobey, was the old New England Puritan conscience poking around in industrial America, in a world it had made but never seen. Here was old-fashioned moral indignation, at a time when cynicism was rampant in public life.

Commendable as such moralistic fervor was, it did not make for intelligent discrimination of fact. Throughout the Kefauver hearings, for example, there ran the presumption that all gamblers were invariably gangsters. This was true of Chicago's Accardo-Guzik combine, which in the past had its fingers in many kinds of rackets. It was not nearly so true of many of the large gamblers in America, most of whom had the feeling that they were satisfying a basic American urge for sport and looked upon their calling with no greater sense of guilt than did many bootleggers. After all, Sherman Billingsley did start out as a speakeasy proprietor, as did the Kreindlers of the "21" Club; and today the Stork Club and the former Jack and Charlie's are the most fashionable night and dining spots in America (one prominent patron of the Stork Club: J. Edgar Hoover). . . .

Most intriguing of all were the opinions of James J. Carroll, the St. Louis "betting commissioner," who for years had been widely quoted on the sports pages of the country as setting odds on the Kentucky Derby winter book and the baseball pennant races. Senator Wiley, speaking like the prosecutor in Camus's novel, *The Stranger*, became the voice of official morality:

SENATOR WILEY: Have you any children?

MR. CARROLL: Yes, I have a boy.

SENATOR WILEY: How old is he?

MR. CARROLL: Thirty-three.

SENATOR WILEY: Does he gamble?

MR. CARROLL: No.

SENATOR WILEY: Would you like to see him grow up and become a gambler, either professional or amateur?

MR. CARROLL: No . . .

SENATOR WILEY: All right. Is your son interested in your business?

MR. CARROLL: No, he is a manufacturer.

SENATOR WILEY: Why do you not get him into the business?

MR. CARROLL: Well, psychologically a great many people are unsuited for gambling. . . .

Carroll, who admitted to having been in the betting business since 1899, was the sophisticated —but not immoral!—counterpoint to moralist Wiley. Here was a man without the stigmata of the underworld or underground; he was worldly, cynical of official rhetoric, jaundiced about people's motives, he was—an "againster" who believed that "all gambling legislation originates or stems from some group or some individual seeking special interests for himself or his cause."

Asked why people gamble, Carroll distilled his experiences of fifty years with a remark that deserves a place in American social history: "I really don't know how to answer the question," he said. "I think gambling is a biological necessity for certain types. I think it is the quality that gives substance to their daydreams."

In a sense, the entire Kefauver materials, unintentionally, seem to document that remark. For what the Committee revealed time and time again was a picture of gambling as a basic institution in American life, flourishing openly and accepted widely. In many of the small towns, the gambling joint is as open as a liquor establishment. The town of Havana, in Mason County, Illinois, felt miffed when Governor Adlai Stevenson intervened against local gambling. In 1950, the town had raised $15,000 of its $50,000 budget by making friendly raids on the gambling houses every month and having the owners pay fines. "With the gambling fines cut off," grumbled Mayor Clarence Chester, "the next year is going to be tough."

Apart from the gamblers, there were the mobsters. But what Senator Kefauver and company failed to understand was that the mobsters, like the gamblers, and like the entire gangdom generally, were seeking to become quasi-respectable and establish a place for themselves in American life. For the mobsters, by and large, had immigrant roots, and crime, as the pattern showed, was a route of social ascent and place in American life.

The mobsters were able, where they wished, to "muscle in" on the gambling business because the established gamblers were wholly vulnerable, not being able to call on the law for protection. The Senators, however, refusing to make any distinction between a gambler and a gangster, found it convenient to talk loosely of a nationwide conspiracy of "illegal" elements. Senator Kefauver asserted that a "nationwide crime syndicate does exist in the United States, despite the protestations of a strangely assorted company of criminals, self-serving politicians, plain blind fools, and others who may be honestly misguided, that there is no such combine." The Senate Committee report states the matter more dogmatically: "There is a nationwide crime syndicate known as the Mafia. . . . Its leaders are usually found in control of the most lucrative rackets in their cities. There are indications of a centralized direction and control of these rackets. . . . The Mafia is the cement that helps to bind the Costello-Adonis-Lansky syndicate of New York and the Accardo-Guzik-Fischetti syndicate of Chicago. . . . These groups have kept in touch with Luciano since his deportation from the country."

Unfortunately for a good story—and the existence of the Mafia would be a whale of a story—neither the Senate Crime Committee in its testimony, nor Kefauver in his book, presented any real evidence that the Mafia exists as a functioning organization. One finds police officials asserting before the Kefauver committee their *belief* in the Mafia; the Narcotics Bureau *thinks* that a worldwide dope ring allegedly run by Luciano is part of the Mafia; but the only other "evidence" presented—aside from the incredulous responses both of Senator Kefauver and Rudolph Halley when nearly all the Italian gangsters asserted that they didn't know about the Mafia—is that certain crimes bear "the earmarks of the Mafia." . . .

There is, as well, in the American temper, a feeling that "somewhere," "somebody" is pulling all the complicated strings to which this jumbled world dances. In politics the labor image is "Wall Street," or "Big Business"; while the business stereotype was the "New Dealers." In the field of crime, the side-of-the-mouth low-down was "Costello."

The salient reason, perhaps, why the Kefauver Committee was taken in by its own myth of an omnipotent Mafia and a despotic Costello was its failure to assimilate and understand three of the more relevant sociological facts about institutionalized crime in its relation to the political life of large urban communities in America, namely: (1) the rise of the American Italian community, as part of the inevitable process of ethnic succession, to positions of importance in politics, a process

that has been occurring independently but almost simultaneously in most cities with large Italian constituencies—New York, Chicago, Kansas City, Los Angeles; (2) the fact that there are individual Italians who play prominent, often leading roles today in gambling and in the mobs; and (3) the fact that Italian gamblers and mobsters often possessed "status" within the Italian community itself and a "pull" in city politics. These three items are indeed related—but not so as to form a "plot."

The Italian community has achieved wealth and political influence much later and in a harder way than previous immigrant groups. Early Jewish wealth, that of the German Jews of the late nineteenth century, was made largely in banking and merchandising. To that extent, the dominant group in the Jewish community was outside of, and independent of, the urban political machines. Later Jewish wealth, among the East European immigrants, was built in the garment trades, though with some involvement with the Jewish gangster, who was typically an industrial racketeer (Arnold Rothstein, Lepke and Gurrah, etc.) Among Jewish lawyers, a small minority, such as the "Tammany lawyer" (like the protagonist of Sam Ornitz's *Haunch, Paunch* and *Jowl*) rose through politics and occasionally touched the fringes of crime. Most of the Jewish lawyers, by and large the communal leaders, climbed rapidly, however, in the opportunities that established and legitimate Jewish wealth provided. Irish immigrant wealth in the northern urban centers, concentrated largely in construction, trucking and the waterfront, has, to a substantial extent, been wealth accumulated in and through political alliance, e.g. favoritism in city contracts. Control of the politics of the city thus has been crucial for the continuance of Irish political wealth. This alliance of Irish immigrant wealth and politics has been reciprocal; many noted Irish political figures lent their names as important windowdressing for business corporations (Al Smith, for example, who helped form the U.S. Trucking Corporation, whose executive head for many years was William J. McCormack, the alleged "Mr. Big" of the New York waterfront) while Irish businessmen have lent their wealth to further the careers of Irish politicians. Irish mobsters have rarely achieved status in the Irish community, but have served as integral arms of the politicians, as strong-arm men on election day.

The Italians found the more obvious big city

paths from rags to riches pre-empted. In part this was due to the character of the early Italian immigration. Most of them were unskilled and from rural stock. Jacob Riis could remark in the '90's, "the Italian comes in at the bottom and stays there." These dispossessed agricultural laborers found jobs as ditch-diggers, on the railroads as section hands, along the docks, in the service occupations, as shoemakers, barbers, garment workers, and stayed there. Many were fleeced by the "padrone" system, a few achieved wealth from truck farming, wine growing, and marketing produce; but this "marginal wealth" was not the source of coherent and stable political power.

Significantly, although the number of Italians in the U.S. is about a third as high as the number of Irish, and of the 30,000,000 Catholic communicants in the United States, about half are of Irish descent and a sixth of Italian, there is not one Italian bishop among the hundred Catholic bishops in this country, or one Italian archbishop among the 21 archbishops. The Irish have a virtual monopoly. This is a factor related to the politics of the American church; but the condition also is possible because there is not significant or sufficient wealth among Italian Americans to force some parity.

The children of the immigrants, the second and third generation, became wise in the ways of the urban slums. Excluded from the political ladder—in the early '30's there were almost no Italians on the city payroll in top jobs, nor in books of the period can one find discussion of Italian political leaders—finding few open routes to wealth, some turned to illicit ways. In the children's court statistics of the 1930's, the largest group of delinquents were the Italians; nor were there any Italian communal or social agencies to cope with these problems. Yet it was, oddly enough, the quondam racketeer, seeking to become respectable, who provided one of the major supports for the drive to win a political voice for Italians in the power structure of the urban political machines.

This rise of the Italian political bloc was connected, at least in the major northern urban centers, to another important development which tended to make the traditional relation between the politician and the protected or tolerated illicit operator more close than it had been in the past. This is the fact that the urban political machines had to evolve new forms of fund-raising since the

big business contributions, which once went heavily into municipal politics, now—with the shift in the locus of power—go largely into national affairs. (The ensuing corruption in national politics, as recent Congressional investigations show, is no petty matter; the scruples of businessmen do not seem much superior to those of the gamblers.) One way urban political machines raised their money resembled that of the large corporations which are no longer dependent on Wall Street: by self-financing—that is, by "taxing" the large number of municipal employees who bargain collectively with City Hall for their wage increases. So the firemen's union contributed money to O'Dwyer's campaign.

A second method was taxing the gamblers. The classic example, as *Life* reported, was Jersey City, where a top lieutenant of the Hague machine spent his full time screening applicants for unofficial bookmaking licenses. If found acceptable, the applicant was given a "location," usually the house or store of a loyal precinct worker, who kicked into the machine treasury a high proportion of the large rent exacted. The one thousand bookies and their one thousand landlords in Jersey City formed the hard core of the political machine that sweated and bled to get out the votes for Hague.

A third source for the financing of these machines was the new, and often illegally earned, Italian wealth. This is well illustrated by the career of Costello and his emergence as a political power in New York. Here the ruling motive has been the search for an entrée—for oneself and one's ethnic group—into the ruling circles of the big city.

Frank Costello made his money originally in bootlegging. After repeal, his big break came when Huey Long, desperate for ready cash to fight the old-line political machines, invited Costello to install slot machines in Louisiana. Costello did, and he flourished. Together with Dandy Phil Kastel, he also opened the Beverly Club, an elegant gambling establishment just outside New Orleans, at which have appeared some of the top entertainers in America. Subsequently, Costello invested his money in New York real estate (including 79 Wall Street, which he later sold), the Copacabana night club, and a leading brand of Scotch whiskey.

Costello's political opportunity came when a money-hungry Tammany, starved by lack of patronage from Roosevelt and La Guardia, turned to him for financial support. The Italian community in New York has for years nursed a grievance against the Irish and, to a lesser extent, the Jewish political groups for monopolizing political power. They complained about the lack of judicial jobs, the small number—usually one—of Italian Congressmen, the lack of representation on the state tickets. But the Italians lacked the means to make their ambitions a reality. Although they formed a large voting bloc, there was rarely sufficient wealth to finance political clubs. Italian immigrants, largely poor peasants from Southern Italy and Sicily, lacked the mercantile experience of the Jews, and the political experience gained in the seventy-five-year history of Irish immigration.

During the Prohibition years, the Italian racketeers had made certain political contacts in order to gain protection. Costello, always the compromiser and fixer rather than the muscle-man, was the first to establish relations with Jimmy Hines, the powerful leader of the West Side in Tammany Hall. But his rival, Lucky Luciano, suspicious of the Irish, and seeking more direct power, backed and elected Al Marinelli for district leader on the Lower West Side. Marinelli in 1932 was the only Italian leader inside Tammany Hall. Later, he was joined by Dr. Paul Sarubbi, a partner of Johnny Torrio in a large, legitimate liquor concern. Certainly, Costello and Luciano represented no "unified" move by the Italians as a whole for power; within the Italian community there are as many divisions as in any other group. What is significant is that different Italians, for different reasons, and in various fashions, were achieving influence for the first time. Marinelli became county clerk of New York and a leading power in Tammany. In 1937, after being blasted by Tom Dewey, then running for district attorney, as a "political ally of thieves . . . and big-shot racketeers," Marinelli was removed from office by Governor Lehman. The subsequent conviction by Dewey of Luciano and Hines, and the election of La Guardia, left most of the Tammany clubs financially weak and foundering. This was the moment Costello made his move. In a few years, by judicious financing, he controlled a block of "Italian" leaders in the Hall—as well as some Irish on the upper West Side, and some Jewish leaders on the East Side—and was able to influence the selection of a number of Italian judges.

The most notable incident, revealed by a wire tap on Costello's phone, was the "Thank you, Francisco" call in 1943 by Supreme Court nominee Thomas Aurelio, who gave Costello full credit for his nomination.

It was not only Tammany that was eager to accept campaign contributions from newly rich Italians, even though some of these *nouveaux riches* had "arrived" through bootlegging and gambling. Fiorello La Guardia, the wiliest mind that Melting Pot politics has ever produced, understood in the early '30's where much of his covert support came from. (So, too, did Vito Marcantonio, an apt pupil of the master: Marcantonio has consistently made deals with the Italian leaders of Tammany Hall—in 1943 he supported Aurelio, and refused to repudiate him even when the Democratic Party formally did.) Joe Adonis, who had built a political following during the late '20's, when he ran a popular speakeasy, aided La Guardia financially to a considerable extent in 1933. "The Democrats haven't recognized the Italians," Adonis told a friend. "There is no reason for the Italians to support anybody but La Guardia; the Jews have played ball with the Democrats and haven't gotten much out of it. They know it now. They will vote for La Guardia. So will the Italians."

Adonis played his cards shrewdly. He supported La Guardia, but also a number of Democrats for local and judicial posts, and became a power in the Brooklyn area. His restaurant was frequented by Kenny Sutherland, the Coney Island Democratic leader; Irwin Steingut, the Democratic minority leader in Albany; Anthony DiGiovanni, later a Councilman; William O'Dwyer, and Jim Moran. But, in 1937, Adonis made the mistake of supporting Royal Copeland against La Guardia, and the irate Fiorello finally drove Adonis out of New York.

La Guardia later turned his ire against Costello, too. Yet Costello survived and reached the peak of his influence in 1942, when he was instrumental in electing Michael Kennedy leader of Tammany Hall. Despite the Aurelio fiasco, which first brought Costello into notoriety, he still had sufficient power in the Hall to swing votes for Hugo Rogers as Tammany leader in 1945, and had a tight grip on some districts as late as 1948. In those years many a Tammany leader came hat in hand to Costello's apartment, or sought him out on the golf links, to obtain the nomination for a judicial post.

During this period, other Italian political leaders were also coming to the fore. Generoso Pope, whose Colonial Sand and Stone Company began to prosper through political contacts, became an important political figure, especially when his purchase of the two largest Italian-language dailies (later merged into one), and of a radio station, gave him almost a monopoly of channels to Italian-speaking opinion of the city. Through Generoso Pope, and through Costello, the Italians became a major political force in New York.

That the urban machines, largely Democratic, have financed their heavy campaign costs in this fashion rather than having to turn to the "moneyed interests," explains in some part why these machines were able, in part, to support the New and Fair Deals without suffering the pressures they might have been subjected to had their source of money supply been the business groups. Although he has never publicly revealed his political convictions, it is likely that Frank Costello was a fervent admirer of Franklin D. Roosevelt and his efforts to aid the common man. The basic measures of the New Deal, which most Americans today agree were necessary for the public good, would not have been possible without the support of the "corrupt" big-city machines.

There is little question that men of Italian origin appeared in most of the leading roles in the high drama of gambling and mobs, just as twenty years ago the children of East European Jews were the most prominent figures in organized crime, and before that individuals of Irish descent were similarly prominent. To some extent statistical accident and the tendency of newspapers to emphasize the few sensational figures gives a greater illusion about the domination of illicit activities by a single ethnic group than all the facts warrant. In many cities, particularly in the South and on the West Coast, the mob and gambling fraternity consisted of many other groups, and often, predominantly, native white Protestants. Yet it is clear that in the major northern urban centers there was a distinct ethnic sequence in the modes of obtaining illicit wealth, and that uniquely in the case of the recent Italian elements, the former bootleggers and gamblers provided considerable leverage for the growth of political influence as well. A substantial number of Italian judges sitting on the bench in New York today are indebted in one fashion or another to Cos-

tello; so too are many Italian district leaders—as well as some Jewish and Irish politicians. And the motive in establishing Italian political prestige in New York was generous rather than scheming for personal advantage. For Costello it was largely a case of ethnic pride. As in earlier American eras, organized illegality became a stepladder of social ascent.

To the world at large, the news and pictures of Frank Sinatra, for example, mingling with former Italian mobsters could come somewhat as a shock. Yet to Sinatra, and to many Italians, these were men who had grown up in their neighborhoods, and who were, in some instances, bywords in the community for their helpfulness and their charities. The early Italian gangsters were hoodlums—rough, unlettered, and young (Al Capone was only twenty-nine at the height of his power). Those who survived learned to adapt. By now they are men of middle age or older. They learned to dress conservatively. Their homes are in respectable suburbs. They sent their children to good schools and had sought to avoid publicity. Costello even went to a psychiatrist in his efforts to overcome a painful feeling of inferiority in the world of manners.

As happens with all "new" money in American society, the rough and ready contractors, the construction people, trucking entrepreneurs, as well as racketeers, polished up their manners and sought recognition and respectability in their own ethnic as well as in the general community. The "shanty" Irish became the "lace curtain" Irish, and then moved out for wider recognition. Sometimes acceptance came first in established "American" society, and this was a certificate for later recognition by the ethnic community, a process well illustrated by the belated acceptance in established Negro society of such figures as Sugar Ray Robinson and Joe Louis, as well as leading popular entertainers.

Yet, after all, the foundation of many a distinguished older American fortune was laid by sharp practices and morally reprehensible methods. The pioneers of American capitalism were not graduated from Harvard's School of Business Administration. The early settlers and founding fathers, as well as those who "won the west" and built up cattle, mining and other fortunes, often did so by shady speculations and a not inconsiderable amount of violence. They ignored, circumvented or stretched the law when it stood in the way of America's destiny, and their own—or, were themselves the law when it served their purposes. This has not prevented them and their descendants from feeling proper moral outrage when under the changed circumstances of the crowded urban environment later comers pursued equally ruthless tactics.

Ironically, the social development which made possible the rise to political influence sounds, too, the knell of the Italian gangster. For it is the growing number of Italians with professional training and legitimate business success that both prompts and permits the Italian group to wield increasing political influence; and increasingly it is the professionals and businessmen who provide models for Italian youth today, models that hardly existed twenty years ago. Ironically, the headlines and exposés of "crime" of the Italian "gangsters" came years after the fact. Many of the top "crime" figures long ago had forsworn violence, and even their income, in large part, was derived from legitimate investments (real estate in the case of Costello, motor haulage and auto dealer franchises in the case of Adonis) or from such quasi-legitimate but socially respectable sources as gambling casinos. Hence society's "retribution" in the jail sentences for Costello and Adonis was little more than a trumped-up morality that disguised a social hypocrisy. . . .

With the rationalization and absorption of some illicit activities into the structure of the economy, the passing of an older generation that had established a hegemony over crime, the general rise of minority groups to social position, and the break-up of the urban boss system, the pattern of crime we have discussed is passing as well. Crime, of course, remains as long as passion and the desire for gain remain. But big, organized city crime, as we have known it for the past seventy-five years, was based on more than these universal motives. It was based on certain characteristics of the American economy, American ethnic groups, and American politics. The changes in all these areas means that it too, in the form we have known it, is at an end.

CONCLUSION

Despite difficulties in measuring social mobility with precision, many studies of mobility have been made in industrial countries. They show (1) that all industrial societies are characterized by high rates of social mobility and (2) that all industrial societies have approximately the *same* mobility rates. This latter finding is especially surprising in view of the variety of histories and values. Perhaps more precise methods of comparing mobility rates will reveal differences in mobility patterns which we do not now appreciate. If it turns out, however, that industrial societies from varying cultural backgrounds have the same mobility rates, this would suggest that industrialization and urbanization are making developed countries more similar to one another than might be inferred from superficial differences in language and customs.

A high rate of social mobility does not imply either a harmonious or a disharmonious society. If, however, a high rate of mobility is regarded by the members of a society as a sign of strength and flexibility, its consequences will be less disruptive than if mobility is considered an indication of societal disintegration. Interestingly enough, both the United States and the Soviet Union are proud of high rates of social mobility. To a lesser extent, so are the countries of Western Europe. In India, on the other hand, the high mobility rates resulting from industrialization can be achieved only by breaking down the caste organization of Indian society and the isolation of Indian villages; hence, mobility is regarded as a mixed blessing. Nevertheless, the leaders of India are pushing industrial development as fast as an impoverished economy and an overpopulated country can go.

Educational upgrading can be regarded as a crude index of the commitment of a society to high rates of mobility. Even for the sociologically unsophisticated, it is apparent that the system of formal education is the main mechanism of social mobility in contemporary societies. Of course, there are other reasons for the worldwide effort to upgrade education besides acceptance of high mobility rates. It has been argued that some underdeveloped countries put more resources into education than is necessary for their level of economic development and that therefore educational upgrading can be a form of conspicuous consumption. Education can also be valued for its own sake without concern for pragmatic consequences. The likelihood is, however, that the tremendous expansion of educational facilities throughout the world would not have taken place without an acceptance of its logical consequences: increased utilization of education as a mechanism of social designation.

High rates of mobility tend to generate a belief in an open society. However, mobility may be defined in terms of meteoric careers; hence, it is possible for a society to have high rates of step-by-step mobility without ideological recognition of it. Some research has shown that mobile individuals have a greater tendency than the immobile to break down psychologically (possibly because mobility disconnects the mover from some of his primary groups) and to be politically apathetic (possibly because the mover must choose between the values of the group he has left and the values of the group he has joined).[38] A special case of immobility are those members of the society trapped at the bottom of the socioeconomic pile. Slum-dwelling minorities are less likely to believe that they can move up—except by a stroke of luck. Among minorities immersed in the culture of poverty, the principle of relative deprivation helps to explain a counter-ideology of disbelief in mobility. Skeptical about legitimate opportunities, minority group members may become demoralized, may use deviant means of social ascent, or may support social change to increase equality of opportunity.[39]

SOME SIGNIFICANT LITERATURE ON CHANGES OF STATUS AND THEIR INTERPRETATION

Otis Dudley Duncan and Robert W. Hodge, "Education and Occupational Mobility: A Regression Analysis," *American Journal of Sociology*, Vol. 68, May 1963, pp. 629–644. Data collected for a six-city survey of labor mobility in 1951 are reanalyzed to throw light on social mobility. The Chicago cases, consisting of 1105 male workers ranging from 25 to 64 years of age at the time of the original survey, are examined on four bases: (1) the number of years of school completed by the respondent, (2) the longest job held during 1950, (3) the job held in January 1940, and (4) his father's longest job. The analysis shows that fathers' occupational statuses were only weakly related to the occupational statuses of their sons. Educational attainment of the respondents was a more important factor in occupational status. In fact, part of the relationship between the occupational levels of fathers and sons is explainable through an intervening tie between the occupational statuses of fathers and the educational opportunities of sons. The authors are cautious in interpreting one of their most interesting findings: that the relationship between educational attainment and occupational status was stronger in 1950 than in 1940. If this finding is not due to peculiarities in their data or to artifacts of their data processing, it means that formal education is becoming *more important* as a mechanism of social placement.

G. Franklin Edwards, *The Negro Professional Class*, Glencoe, Ill.: Free Press, 1959. A sample from the rosters of Negro physicians, dentists, and lawyers in Washington, D.C., and the entire Washington population of Negro college teachers in the arts and sciences were interviewed in a study of the origins and the mobility of male professionals. If this group is typical of Negro professionals in other cities, the Negro professional is drawn largely from the middle class. The fathers of the men interviewed averaged 11.3 years of schooling and were mainly in white-collar occupations. This summary is based on a review by Leonard Broom, *American Sociological Review*, Vol. 25, October 1960, p. 759.

Daniel Kubat, "Social Mobility in Czechoslovakia," *American Sociological Review*, Vol. 28, April 1963, pp. 203–212. When the Communists came into power in Czechoslovakia in 1948, their ideological and administrative policies tended to restrict opportunities for mobility: (1) The Communist Party denied the existence of class differences and ridiculed the acquisition of a car and other symbols of success. (2) Income differences between manual and nonmanual occupations narrowed, thus reducing the incentive to leave manual occupations. (3) Since small business careers no longer existed, the main channel of mobility for children of

38 For a summary of these studies, see Lipset and Bendix, *Social Mobility in Industrial Society, op. cit.*, pp. 64–72.
39 Robert K. Merton, "Social Structure and Anomie," and "Continuities in the Theory of Social Structure and Anomie," in *Social Theory and Social Structure*, Glencoe, Ill.: Free Press, 1957, pp. 131–194.

manual workers became higher education. In addition to the financial and cultural obstacles similar to those experienced by children of workers in other industrial societies, higher education became unpalatable to workers' children in Czechoslovakia because it required verbalization of an ideological commitment to the regime. "We would thus hazard a conclusion—however tenuous because of the inaccessibility of many data—that the command economy of totalitarian societies discourages processes of social mobility once the rank order of the social structure has been set."

Julius Roth and Robert F. Peck, "Social Class and Social Mobility Factors Related to Marital Adjustment," *American Sociological Review*, Vol. 16, August 1951, pp. 478–487. Professors Roth and Peck examined the marital adjustments of a sample of couples in order to discover how cross-class marriages compared with marriages in which the partners came from the same social level. They found that cross-class marriages were less likely to produce marital satisfaction and that the likelihood of success *decreased* with the initial social distance between the partners. Cross-class marriages in which the wife came from a higher social level than her husband had more failures than cross-class marriages in which the husband came from a higher social level than his wife.

Melvin Seeman, "Social Mobility and Administrative Behavior," *American Sociological Review*, Vol. 23, December 1958, pp. 633–642. Professor Seeman calls attention to the possibility that occupational advancement is not necessarily due to a desire for upward mobility; sometimes it is the unintended consequence of intrinsic interest in one's work. He constructed a Mobility-Achievement scale to identify those whose social strivings take precedence over more intrinsic interests in health, family, community, and the like. Forty-four school executives filled out a questionnaire containing the scale and a job history, thus enabling Professor Seeman to place them in one of four categories: "(1) the mobile status-seeker, (2) the unsuccessful status-seeker, (3) the mobile non-striver, and (4) the stable non-striver. The crucial point is that this typology, derived exclusively from the executive's standpoint, is related to the behavioral descriptions of him provided by the staff members and school board members." It helps to predict administrative behavior.

Ralph H. Turner, "Sponsored and Contest Mobility and the School System," *American Sociological Review*, Vol. 25, December 1960, pp. 855–867. Industrial societies with the same *rate* of upward social mobility may nevertheless be characterized by different modes of recruitment into the élite. Specifically, Professor Turner contrasts British "sponsored mobility" with American "contest mobility." *Sponsored mobility* "involves controlled selection in which the élite or their agents choose recruits early and carefully induct them

into élite status." Thus, the British educational system selects from the population of 11-year-old students those who will attend "grammar schools" and receive the education appropriate for those in high-status occupations. In *contest mobility* "élite status is the prize in an open contest, with every effort made to keep lagging contestants in the race until the climax." The American education system (and specifically the comprehensive high school) avoids sharp social separation between superior and inferior students and enables youngsters to transfer into the college preparatory curriculum at a fairly late stage of their education. Professor Turner relates the absence of revolutionary movements in the United States to the American emphasis on contest mobility. Hope for future success is kept alive much longer than in a system of sponsored mobility. Individual rebellion is still possible (the beatnik or the criminal), but organized opposition to the system is less likely. The delinquent's complaint is less that the system is unjust than that he has not gotten what he wanted out of it.

Y. C. Wang, "Western Impact and Social Mobility in China," *American Sociological Review*, Vol. 25, December 1960, pp. 843–855. Until the end of the nineteenth century, civil-service examinations offered broad opportunities to rural youth. "Education was relatively inexpensive, and once a scholar passed the examination at the provincial or national level, he joined the privileged group and assumed a leadership role in society." However, in 1902 the Chinese government established a modern educational system based on Japanese and Western models, and in 1905 civil-service examinations were abolished. Study abroad and a diploma from American or European universities became the most efficient route to fame and power. Prestigious education had become expensive; ". . . the opportunity to receive a higher education was virtually limited to men from official, professional, and mercantile families. . . . The only way a peasant could rise into officialdom was within a channel of violence—banditry or soldiery." Professor Wang believes that the lack of mobility opportunities for rural youth and the resulting preponderance of urban-born officials in the central government helped create political instability in twentieth-century China. "The needs of the rural masses were neglected. . . ."

W. Lloyd Warner and James C. Abegglen, *Occupational Mobility in American Business and Industry, 1928–1952*, Minneapolis: University of Minnesota Press, 1955. This study compares the social origins of top American business leaders in 1928 with top American business leaders in 1952. Professors Warner and Abegglen conclude that the likelihood of men from laboring and lower white-collar backgrounds entering the élite *increased* between 1928 and 1952. Occupational mobility is facilitated by the impersonal, rational selection procedures of large corporations and the increasing importance of higher education as a prerequisite for business executives. This summary is based on a review by Natalie Rogoff, *American Sociological Review*, Vol. 21, June 1956, pp. 384–385. Dr. Rogoff's own study of comparative occupational mobility a generation apart is based on the analysis of marriage-license applications in Marion County, Ohio, in 1910 and 1940. She concludes that occupational mobility for the population as a whole, not just the business élite, was about the same in 1910 and 1940. See Natalie Rogoff, *Recent Trends in Occupational Mobility*, Glencoe, Ill.: Free Press, 1953.

Harold I. Wilensky and Hugh Edwards, "The Skidder: Ideological Adjustments of Downwardly Mobile Workers," *American Sociological Review*, Vol. 24, April 1959, pp. 215–231. In 1951 the Survey Research Center of the University of Michigan obtained questionnaire responses on occupational history from 495 male manual workers of urban backgrounds in two plants of a manufacturing company in a midwestern city. Of these, 20 per cent were *worklife skidders*: workers who entered the factory from a previous white-collar occupation; and 19 per cent were *intergenerational skidders*: blue-collar sons of white-collar fathers. Both types of skidders were more likely than nonskidders to reject identification with the working class, to believe in ability rather than seniority as a proper basis for promotion, to aspire to middle-class positions, to anticipate leaving

the factory soon, to say they would accept the job of foreman if it were offered to them, and to expect middle-class positions for their children. Apparently early socialization was a more important influence than subsequent or anticipatory socialization. "The ideological conservatism of skidders can be explained almost entirely by the presence of . . . *older* worklife skidders and . . . *young* intergenerational skidders." [Emphasis added.]

Charles V. Willie, "Age Status and Residential Stratification," *American Sociological Review*, Vol. 25, April 1960, pp. 260–264. Dr. Willie rated the socioeconomic level of 59 census tracts in Syracuse, New York, in 1940 and 55 census tracts in 1950. He then correlated the socioeconomic level of a census tract with the proportions of the tract's population in various age brackets. He discovered a tendency in 1940 for a preponderance of people from 18 to 29 to be associated with *low* socioeconomic status and a preponderance of people from 35 to 54 to be associated with *high* socioeconomic status. In 1950 the same general pattern was found, but the ages shifted somewhat; the ages from 20 to 34 were associated with low socioeconomic status and 40 to 59 with high socioeconomic status. Dr. Willie infers that young adults, on leaving their families of orientation, live first in a neighborhood of lower socioeconomic status than their parents. Then, as they progress in age and status, they move into more expensive neighborhoods suitable for child rearing.

CHAPTER 17

Sociocultural Change:
An American Example

In contemporary industrial societies, technological development and the growth in scientific knowledge are so much a part of everyday life that they serve in the public mind as the prototype of change. This is unfortunate because technological and scientific development has a cumulative character different from all other kinds of cultural and social change. On the reasonable assumptions that knowledge is superior to ignorance and that greater resources for carrying out objectives, whatever they are, are more desirable than fewer resources, the cumulative nature of technological and scientific development generates "progress" (in the sense of improvement over the past). There is no inherent reason why other types of sociocultural change constitute analogous improvements.

During optimistic periods of world history, such as the late nineteenth century, intellectuals argued that evolutionary progress was not limited to science and technology but was the principal behind all sociocultural change.[1] One hundred years ago, intelligent people believed that the future was getting brighter in every way, that poverty and war were on the verge of elimination, and that human beings would

soon reach new plateaus of happiness and morality. Twentieth-century experience cast doubt on the validity of the idea of *general* progress. The First World War, the Second World War, and the period of international tension following the Second World War demonstrated that peace is no easier to attain today than it was a thousand years ago. The brutalities perpetrated by the Nazi regime in Germany—including concentration camps and gas chambers where millions of men, women, and children were put to death because they belonged to supposedly inferior "races"—showed that industrial development was not necessarily accompanied by moral development. German atrocities were more disillusioning for believers in "progress" than the rape of nuns in the Congo or ritual murders in Haiti because Germany was an advanced industrial society with impressive cultural achievements behind it: the poetry of Goethe and Schiller, the music of Beethoven. Yet this society invented a technique for manufacturing soap out of the fatty tissues of corpses removed from gas chambers and used this technique on a large scale. In the face of such lapses into barbarism, contemporary intellectuals are reluctant to assume that change necessarily means improvement.[2] To be

[1] J. B. Bury, *The Idea of Progress*, New York: Macmillan, 1932.

[2] See, for example, the writings of Reinhold Niebuhr.

sure, change sometimes is improvement; the abolition of slavery was so regarded. In contemporary society, the reduction of racial segregation is generally considered progress.

With the assumption of automatic progress abandoned, it becomes more difficult to explain why some changes occur and others do not. Why, for example, was the automobile permitted to transform American life whereas the Mormon practice of polygamy was short-lived, even in Utah?[3] The automobile is not a self-evident blessing. Nearly 40,000 Americans are killed every year in highway accidents, and hundreds of thousands are injured.[4] Between the cost of vehicles and the cost of the highways that carry them, automotive transportation is almost as expensive as litter bearers.[5] Furthermore, the speed and convenience of automobile transportation is declining as traffic jams and parking problems grow.[6] On the other hand, the Mormon attempt to reestablish the polygamous households described in the Hebrew Bible could be justified by the American tradition of religious freedom. The Mormons did not insist that every man have several wives. They merely wished to *permit* a man to have more than one wife if he could induce more than one woman to marry him. If the triumph of the automobile and the repression of polygamy cannot be explained as instances of "progress," then some other explanations are necessary.

FACTORS CONDUCIVE TO CULTURAL AND SOCIAL CHANGE

Social change refers to altered patterns of interaction in a society or social system. *Cul-*

---

[3] Kimball Young, *Isn't One Wife Enough?*, New York: Holt, 1954.
[4] Department of Health, Education, and Welfare, *Vital Statistics of the United States*, annual report; National Safety Council, *Accident Facts*, annual report.
[5] For a thoughtful discussion of the traffic problems of large cities, see Scott Greer, "Traffic, Transportation, and Problems of the Metropolis," in Merton and Nisbet, Eds., *Contemporary Social Problems*, New York: Harcourt, Brace and World, 1961, pp. 605–650.
[6] Francis Bello, "The City and the Car," in The Editors of Fortune, *The Exploding Metropolis*, Garden City, N.Y.: Doubleday Anchor, 1958, pp. 32–61.

tural change refers to any change in the stock of ideas of the society: an advance in scientific knowledge, a new religion, a new political ideology, a change in fashion, an addition to the poetry, music, or literature of the society, or a new technique for adapting to the environment. Technological and scientific change is only one type of cultural change, but it is the most prominent type of change in industrial societies. Technological innovations and scientific discoveries are frequent; they produce modifications in economic organization and social life; and their cumulative character makes them appear so automatic as to obscure the human element behind them. Nevertheless, it is reasonable to ask *why* technological and scientific progress should proceed so rapidly.

THE SIZE OF THE CULTURE BASE. One reason for the quasiautomatic character of technological and scientific progress is the sheer size of the culture base. Knowledge breeds new knowledge, not because books write themselves, but because the larger the stock of ideas the more are the possibilities for combining them in a novel way. As Sir Isaac Newton put it, "If I have accomplished anything, it is because I stood on the shoulders of giants." Newton was being modest about his own contributions, but he stated a principle applicable to any scientist, engineer, or inventor. The capacity of one generation to make innovations depends on what preceding generations have transmitted to them. What could Albert Einstein have accomplished if he had been born in a preliterate society—for example, the Murngin?

In a sense, all the industrial societies share a common stock of inventions and discoveries. Transportation and communication are so well developed that the cultural traits of one country are readily available for diffusion to another. In previous centuries, societies were more isolated culturally, and diffusion of traits was more selective. Still, as anthropologist Ralph Linton shows in the following passage, cultural borrowing has been going on for a long time.

Diffusion of Culture Traits

Reprinted by permission. From Ralph Linton, *The Study of Man*, New York: Appleton Century, 1936, pp. 326–327.

Our solid American citizen awakens in a bed built on a pattern which originated in the Near East but which was modified in Northern Europe before it was transmitted to America. He throws back covers made from cotton, domesticated in India, or linen, domesticated in the Near East, or wool from sheep, also domesticated in the Near East, or silk, the use of which was discovered in China. All of these materials have been spun and woven by processes invented in the Near East. He slips into his moccasins, invented by the Indians of the Eastern woodlands, and goes to the bathroom, whose fixtures are a mixture of European and American inventions, both of recent date. He takes off his pajamas, a garment invented in India, and washes with soap invented by the ancient Gauls. He then shaves, a masochistic rite which seems to have been derived from either Sumer or ancient Egypt.

Returning to the bedroom, he removes his clothes from a chair of southern European type and proceeds to dress. He puts on garments whose form originally derived from the skin clothing of the nomads of the Asiatic steppes, puts on shoes made from skins tanned by a process invented in ancient Egypt and cut to a pattern derived from the classical civilizations of the Mediterranean, and ties around his neck a strip of bright-colored cloth which is a vestigial survival of the shoulder shawls worn by the seventeenth-century Croatians. Before going out for breakfast he glances through the window, made of glass invented in Egypt, and if it is raining puts on overshoes made of rubber discovered by the Central American Indians and takes an umbrella, invented in southeastern Asia. Upon his head he puts a hat made of felt, a material invented in the Asiatic steppes.

On his way to breakfast he stops to buy a paper, paying for it with coins, an ancient Lydian invention. At the restaurant a whole new series of borrowed elements confronts him. His plate is made of a form of pottery invented in China. His knife is of steel, an alloy first made in south-ern India, his fork a medieval Italian invention, and his spoon a derivative of a Roman original. He begins breakfast with an orange, from the eastern Mediterranean, a cantaloupe from Persia, or perhaps a piece of African watermelon. With this he has coffee, an Abyssinian plant, with cream and sugar. Both the domestication of cows and the idea of milking them originated in the Near East, while sugar was first made in India. After his fruit and first coffee he goes on to waf-fles, cakes made by a Scandinavian technique from wheat domesticated in Asia Minor. Over these he pours maple syrup, invented by the Indians of the Eastern woodlands. As a side dish he may have the egg of a species of bird domesticated in Indo-China, or thin strips of the flesh of an animal domesticated in Eastern Asia which have been salted and smoked by a process developed in northern Europe.

When our friend has finished eating he settles back to smoke, an American Indian habit, consuming a plant domesticated in Brazil in either a pipe, derived from the Indians of Virginia, or a cigarette, derived from Mexico. If he is hardy enough he may even attempt a cigar, transmitted to us from the Antilles by way of Spain. While smoking he reads the news of the day, imprinted in characters invented by the ancient Semites upon a material invented in China by a process invented in Germany. As he absorbs the accounts of foreign troubles he will, if he is a good conservative citizen, thank a Hebrew deity in an Indo-European language that he is 100 percent American.

Despite the effectiveness of diffusion of new traits among contemporary industrial countries, there exist isolated backwaters which have smaller cultural bases than, say, urban communities. Until recently, the Ozark Mountain region of the United States was such a backwater; but radio, television, and good highways are making available to the Ozark region the larger culture base of the outside world.[7] If we are prepared to make exceptions of isolated communities, the concept of a world culture base,

[7]   Walter O. Cralle, "Social Change and Isolation in the Ozark Mountain Region of Missouri," *American Journal of Sociology*, Vol. 41, January 1936, pp. 435–446.

enormous in size and oblivious to national boundaries, seems valid.

THE PREFERENCE FOR RATIONALITY OVER TRA-DITION. Rural populations characteristically resist change, even in otherwise advanced countries like France. In the United States, however, farmers are receptive to new techniques for raising productivity. Some of the credit for this receptivity to change must be given to the Cooperative Extension Service of the Department of Agriculture which disseminates to farmers the latest research findings of 80 agricultural experiment stations. The 15,000 extension agents of the Service do not wait passively for farmers to come seeking knowledge; they reach out aggressively to farmers with all their resources: written materials, oral advice, on-farm demonstrations.[8] Still, the system of county extension agents depends ultimately on certain values of the American cultural tradition—specifically on a readiness to abandon traditional methods of doing something provided it can be demonstrated that newer methods are more efficient. Without this acceptance of a rational approach to problem solving, scientific evidence alone would not persuade farmers to adopt new practices. For example, suppose a county extension agent recommended contour plowing to a tradition-minded farmer who was losing valuable top-soil through the run-off of rainwater. The farmer's attitude would be essentially this: "Maybe straight furrows do increase soil erosion. And maybe soil erosion will eventually decrease the yield per acre. But I'm trying to farm this land exactly the way my grandfather did, and he didn't think a farmer was worth a damn if he couldn't plow a straight furrow." This argument is unbeatable —as long as the farmer is willing to pay in inefficiency for adherence to tradition. In the United States, relatively few farmers, except for

the adherents of fundamentalist sects like the Amish, are willing to pay this price.[9] *Rationality* is positively valued.

Societies differ in their adherence to tradition. The United States tends to look ahead rather than behind. Societies with a long (and, to them, glorious) history are more concerned with maintaining continuity with the past. In Paris, for example, no structural changes are permitted in old and crumbling buildings lest the charm of the city be destroyed. Obviously, the greater the preference for tradition, the harder it is to make cultural changes.

THE INSTITUTIONALIZATION OF INVENTIVE-NESS. The Constitution of the United States gives Congress the power "to promote the progress of science and useful arts, by securing for limited times to authors and inventors the exclusive right to their respective writings and discoveries." Table 75 shows the growth of inventions (patents) in the United States from 1790 to 1890, a period of rapid industrialization. The patent system was designed to encourage invention by holding out hope of considerable financial reward to the technological innovator. Thomas A. Edison became a rich man as a result of his development of the electric light, the phonograph, and other useful

TABLE 75

Patents Issued for Inventions by the United States Patent Office, 1790–1890

Year	Number of Inventions Patented
1790	3
1800	41
1810	223
1820	155
1830	544
1840	458
1850	883
1860	4,357
1870	12,137
1880	12,903
1890	25,313

Source: Bureau of the Census, *Historical Statistics of the United States: Colonial Times to 1957*, Washington: Government Printing Office, 1960, pp. 607–608.

8   U.S. Department of Agriculture, "Farming in the United States," Agricultural Information Bulletin No. 246, Washington: Government Printing Office, 1961.
9   Charles S. Rice and Roland C. Steinmetz, *The Amish Year*, New Brunswick, N.J.: Rutgers University Press, 1956; John A. Hostetler, *Amish Society*, Baltimore: Johns Hopkins Press, 1963.

gadgets. The patent system also legitimizes the role of the inventor. During the eighteenth and nineteenth centuries, the inventor was mainly an amateur; very few persons were full-time inventors. The twentieth century has witnessed the bureaucratization of invention. Private industry, government agencies, and universities have established laboratories with full-time jobs for technological and scientific innovators.[10] One result was that corporations started patenting more inventions than private individuals in 1932, and the trend to corporate and governmental patents has continued.[11]

However dedicated the scientist may be, he is also filling a role that demands innovation as part of its requirements. Perhaps he would rather listen to television, play with his children, or go on a picnic instead of working in his laboratory or writing articles for scholarly journals. He knows, however, that his chances for promotion and perhaps his job itself depends on his "productivity"—on the impact of his research on the existing state of knowledge. Even without this pressure, he might wish to do research out of disinterested curiosity and to publish the results for the benefit of humanity. But bureaucratization means that scientific and technological discoveries do not depend on curiosity and humanitarianism alone. Once a man has become a scientist, he cannot escape the pressure to do research. Granted that he had curiosity and creativity to begin with, or he would not have chosen a scientific career. Once in the role, he had better mobilize all his curiosity and creativity in a search for innovations. Contrast this situation with that of a preliterate inventor, who, if he builds a better canoe than his neighbor, may be suspected of witchcraft. In preliterate societies, the balance of rewards and punishments operates to stifle

creativity; in contemporary societies, patent systems, laboratory organizations, and professional specialization encourage the maximum expression of creativity.

Although the institutionalization of inventiveness is most obvious in the technological and scientific fields, the differentiation of specialized roles also favors change in other fields. For example, the prospect of professional recognition encourages the social worker to discover more efficient ways of alleviating human distress, the surgeon to reduce postoperative mortality, and the teacher to communicate his subject matter more efficiently. Even when innovations arouse the opposition of the general public, the professional has an incentive to make them to impress his reference group, his colleagues. The existence of specialized roles dedicated to innovation means that self-interest is mobilized in behalf of cultural change.

THE MARKET MECHANISM. The freedom to sell goods and services in the open market is likewise conducive to technological innovations. Henry Ford did not need authorization from federal, state, or local governments in order to manufacture and sell his early cars. Nor did he have to win the approval of a majority of the American people. A minority interest has representation in the market place, and eventually it may win over the majority. At first, only the farsighted and the eccentric bought cars. Eventually the automobile became crucial to the American way of life, and Henry Ford became a billionaire.

In retrospect, the triumph of the automobile was inevitable. When "horseless carriages" first appeared on the dirt roads of America, however, the children who ran after them shouting derisively, "Get a horse!" were the hard-headed realists of the day. Vested interests opposed the car: blacksmiths, livery stable keepers, horse breeders, and carriage makers. Moreover, everyone accustomed to horse transport could be expected to resist learning how to drive a "horseless carriage." But what could the partisans of the horse do to prevent the new "fad" from spreading? They could refrain from buying automobiles themselves, and they

10   Simon Marcson, *The Scientist in American Industry: Some Organizational Determinants of Manpower Utilization*, New York: Harper, 1960; for a parallel development in the social sciences, see Paul F. Lazarsfeld, "The Sociology of Empirical Social Research," *American Sociological Review*, Vol. 27, December 1962, pp. 757–767.
11   Bureau of the Census, *Historical Statistics of the United States: Colonial Times to 1957*, Washington: Government Printing Office, 1960, p. 607.

could fight against government expenditures for paving roads. But they could not pass laws forbidding the manufacture and sale of automobiles; such laws were incompatible with the private-enterprise system and would have seemed like sinking the ship to drown the rats. In short, the economic and political system facilitated the change from horse to automotive transport. Not only were the promoters more interested in selling cars than the general public was in clinging to an old habit. Vested interests could also be whittled away gradually as support for the automobile grew.[12] In the Soviet Union, on the other hand, the introduction of the automobile required a political decision.

Private enterprise promotes technological innovations only when they are made in the form of products or services that consumers wish to buy. Not all technological innovations, even in the automotive field, are attractive to consumers. For example, American car manufacturers are reluctant to incorporate safety features in automobiles because experience has convinced them that the car market is more responsive to horsepower, chromium strips, and sleek lines than it is to interior design capable of reducing injuries to passengers in the event of accidents.[13] Thus, when the Ford Motor Company introduced new safety features during the first half of 1956, Ford car sales fell markedly compared with Chevrolets. Where the market works *against* a technological innovation, as appears to be the case in the field of automotive safety, political decisions (laws and administrative regulations) are necessary to force change on an apathetic public.

THE SOCIAL FACTORS

Technological and scientific development is an important factor in social change in industrial societies. This observation is at the heart of William Ogburn's theory of *cultural lag*, which holds that patterns of interaction change *in response to* maladjustments brought on by technological progress.[14] For instance, the automobile not only made outlying suburban areas more accessible.[15] The automobile has also influenced the ways Americans commute to work, shop in shopping centers, travel during vacations (stopping in motels), attend drive-in movies, and carry on courtships. Even in industrial societies, however, not all social change can be adequately accounted for by cultural lag. Certainly recent changes in race relations in the United States have been the result of many forces: the declining manpower requirements of Southern agriculture, the embarrassing discrepancy between equalitarian ideals and segregated reality, new knowledge of racial characteristics and human relations, organized protests against racial discrimination, and planned efforts by the federal government to speed up desegregation. To conclude this long look at contemporary society, let us now turn to a major, current sociocultural change—what many have called America's Negro Revolution.

THE CHANGING PLACE OF NEGROES IN AMERICAN SOCIETY

When Eli Whitney invented the cotton gin in 1794, the demand for cheap labor in the cotton fields spurred the slave trade, which had been declining, and thousands of Negroes were brought from Africa to serve white plantation owners.[16] The ignorance and degradation of Negro slaves is one historical thread; another is the Western tradition of the brotherhood of man.

The history of the belief in human dignity

12 Talcott Parsons discusses the role of vested interests in social change in Chapter 11 of *The Social System*, Glencoe, Ill.: Free Press, 1951.
13 Daniel P. Moynihan, "Epidemic on the Highways," *The Reporter*, Vol. 20, April 30, 1959, pp. 16–23; Ralph Nader, "The *Safe* Car You Can't Buy," *The Nation*, Vol. 188, April 11, 1959, pp. 310–313.

14 William F. Ogburn, *Social Change*, New York: Huebsch, 1922; William F. Ogburn, *The Social Effects of Aviation*, Boston: Houghton Mifflin, 1946.
15 In 1920, 63.7 per cent of the population in United States standard metropolitan areas lived in central cities, but each decennial census thereafter showed declining percentages in central cities and increasing percentages in suburban areas. See Amos H. Hawley, *The Changing Shape of Metropolitan America: Deconcentration Since 1920*, Glencoe, Ill.: Free Press, 1956.
16 Gunnar Myrdal, *An American Dilemma: The Negro Problem and Modern Democracy*, New York: Harper, 1944, pp. 86, 118.

is a long one.[17] Greek philosophers speculated about the essential rights of human beings more than 2000 years ago. These speculations were not taken sufficiently seriously to challenge the institution of slavery in Greece or Rome, perhaps because slavery provided the margin of leisure and comfort upon which civilization then depended. Nevertheless, even the Roman emperor, Marcus Aurelius, was intrigued by the idea that all human beings have intrinsic dignity, and many thinkers in less prominent positions were stimulated by this noble but impractical notion. Christianity gave the ideal new vitality. The early Christians expected the Second Coming of the Messiah imminently; hence, they were not concerned with the contribution of slavery to the maintenance of civilization. They took over the Platonic doctrine of the freedom of the human soul and applied it to everyone, slaves included. But the world did not end; and a dominant Christianity accepted for many centuries human degradation in this life if not in the next.

In the eighteenth century, the belief in human dignity won new and eloquent adherents. The French Declaration of the Rights of Man and the American Declaration of Independence expressed the same humanitarianism. Yet slavery continued. Jefferson, who wrote in the Declaration of Independence "that all men are created equal; that they are endowed by their Creator with certain unalienable rights; that among these are life, liberty, and the pursuit of happiness . . . ," himself owned slaves. But the Founding Fathers had a bad conscience. The American Constitution never used the word "slave" although it provided that only "three fifths of all other persons" would be counted in determining a State's delegation in the House of Representatives and that "the migration or importation of such persons as any of the States now existing shall think proper to admit, shall not be prohibited by the Congress prior to the year 1808. . . ." Congress passed a law outlawing the slave trade as

soon as the Constitution permitted it to do so (1808), but this prohibition was not effectively enforced. About half a million slaves were smuggled into the United States between 1808 and 1860.[18]

Pushed by the Methodist movement, Great Britain abolished the slave trade in 1808 and purchased and freed all slaves in British Dominions in 1833. Pushed by religious and by secular abolitionists, the United States fought the Civil War over slavery. After the South had been defeated, the thirteenth amendment to the Constitution was adopted. "Neither slavery nor involuntary servitude, except as a punishment for crime whereof the party shall have been duly convicted, shall exist within the United States, or any place subject to their jurisdiction." The thirteenth amendment could not, of course, erase decades of social, educational, and economic disadvantages. A great change had occurred in the *legal* status of Negroes. But this did not mean that Negroes were in a position to compete with whites on equal terms. Even if there were no prejudice against them, Negroes would have had great difficulty breaking out of the underprivileged status which was their legacy from slavery. Discriminatory treatment reinforced their existing socioeconomic disadvantages and served to perpetuate them. Still, as the Swedish economist and sociologist Gunnar Myrdal pointed out, white Americans are torn between equalitarian ideals and discriminatory practices.[19] Most whites cannot deny equality of opportunity to Negroes with a clear conscience. Writing in October 1942, Myrdal predicted that white Americans, pressed to choose between their ideals and their prejudices, would prefer to change their behavior: ". . . not since Reconstruction has there been more reason to anticipate fundamental changes in American race relations, changes which will involve a development toward the American ideals." [20]

---

[17] Alfred North Whitehead, *Adventures of Ideas*, New York: Macmillan, 1933, Chap. 2, "The Human Soul."

[18] Myrdal, *op. cit.*, p. 119.
[19] *Ibid.* The dilemma referred to in the title of the book is this problem of squaring discrimination with American ideals.
[20] *Ibid.*, p. xix.

Events of the past 20 years have justified Myrdal's optimism. American Negroes have markedly improved their educational, economic, and social status. The ideological dilemma, upon which Myrdal laid so much stress, is only one among several factors responsible for the change. Another factor is the migration of hundreds of thousands of Negroes from the rural South to cities of New York, New Jersey, Pennsylvania, Ohio, Michigan, Illinois, Missouri, and California.[21] This migration, a consequence of the shrinking manpower requirements of Southern agriculture, was accelerated by industrial expansion during the Second World War and the postwar years in Northern cities. The massive redistribution of the Negro population—from one-party states in the South to big industrial states in the North—gave Negro voters "potentially irresistible political power." [22] Table 76 illustrates this point with data from the presidential election of 1960. The margin by which John F. Kennedy won the

[21] Samuel A. Stouffer, *Social Research to Test Ideas,* New York: Free Press of Glencoe, 1962, p. 232.

[22] *Ibid.*

TABLE 76

1960 *Votes for the Democratic and the Republican Candidates, by States, and Negro Population, by States*

| State | Number of Votes in the Electoral College in 1960 | Votes Cast in 1960 (to nearest thousand) | | Negro Population in 1960 |
		For John F. Kennedy (Democrat)	For Richard M. Nixon (Republican)	
New York	45	3,830,000	3,446,000	1,417,511
California	32	3,224,000	3,260,000	883,861
Pennsylvania	32	2,556,000	2,440,000	852,750
Illinois	27	2,378,000	2,369,000	1,037,470
Ohio	25	1,944,000	2,218,000	786,097
Texas	24	1,168,000	1,122,000	1,187,125
Michigan	20	1,687,000	1,620,000	717,581
Massachusetts	16	1,487,000	977,000	111,842
New Jersey	16	1,385,000	1,363,000	514,875
North Carolina	14	713,000	655,000	1,116,021
Indiana	13	952,000	1,175,000	269,275
Missouri	13	972,000	962,000	390,853
Georgia	12	459,000	274,000	1,122,596
Virginia	12	362,000	405,000	816,258
Wisconsin	12	831,000	895,000	74,546
Alabama	11	324,000	238,000	980,271
Minnesota	11	780,000	758,000	22,263
Tennessee	11	481,000	557,000	586,876
Florida	10	749,000	795,000	880,186
Iowa	10	551,000	722,000	25,354
Kentucky	10	522,000	603,000	215,949
Louisiana	10	407,000	231,000	1,039,207
Maryland	9	566,000	490,000	518,410
Washington	9	599,000	629,000	48,738
Kansas	8	363,000	561,000	91,445
Mississippi	8	108,000	74,000	915,743
Oklahoma	8	370,000	533,000	153,084
South Carolina	8	198,000	189,000	829,291
West Virginia	8	442,000	396,000	89,378
Arkansas	8	215,000	185,000	388,787

TABLE 76 (continued)

State	Number of Votes in the Electoral College in 1960	Votes Cast in 1960 (to nearest thousand)		Negro Poulation in 1960
		For John F. Kennedy (Democrat)	For Richard M. Nixon (Republican)	
Connecticut	8	657,000	566,000	107,449
Colorado	6	331,000	402,000	39,992
Nebraska	6	233,000	381,000	29,262
Oregon	6	367,000	408,000	48,738
Maine	5	181,000	241,000	3,318
Arizona	4	177,000	221,000	43,403
Idaho	4	139,000	162,000	1,502
Montana	4	135,000	142,000	1,467
New Hampshire	4	138,000	158,000	1,903
New Mexico	4	156,000	154,000	17,063
North Dakota	4	124,000	154,000	777
Rhode Island	4	258,000	148,000	18,332
South Dakota	4	128,000	178,000	1,114
Utah	4	169,000	205,000	4,148
Alaska	3	30,000	31,000	6,771
Delaware	3	100,000	96,000	60,688
Hawaii	3	92,000 [a]	92,000	4,943
Nevada	3	55,000	52,000	13,484
Vermont	3	69,000	98,000	519
Wyoming	3	67,000	77,000	2,183
Total	561	34,227,000	34,108,000	18,871,831

[a] Democrats carried Hawaii by a small margin.

Source: Bureau of the Census, *Statistical Abstract of the United States: 1962*, Washington: Government Printing Office, 1962, pp. 30, 363–364.

crucial industrial states was much smaller than the Negro electorate of those states. Postelection surveys have in fact shown that a substantial majority of Negro voters preferred Mr. Kennedy to Mr. Nixon and that these votes provided the margin of victory.[23] Certainly the political leverage of American Negroes has improved as a result of population redistribution. On the other hand, Negro support might not help a candidate if the bulk of white voters were ideologically committed to white supremacy. Under such circumstances, a call for greater opportunities for Negroes would lose a candidate more *white* votes than it would gain him *Negro* votes.

Another factor in the changed status of the Negro in the United States is educational up-

23 Stanley Kelley, "The 1960 Presidential Election," in Ivan Hinderaker, Ed., *American Government Annual, 1961–62*, New York: Holt, Rinehart, and Winston, 1961, p. 74.

grading. As Table 77 shows, the past generation has witnessed nearly a threefold increase in the proportion of *nonwhite* youngsters who have completed at least four years of high school. The increase in the proportion of *white* youngsters who have completed at least four years of high school has been more modest. Even today, white youngsters as a group complete more years of school than colored youngsters, but the gap narrowed between 1940 and 1960. The improvement in Negro education has been qualitative as well as quantitative. As Negroes moved out of the rural South and into Northern cities, they automatically obtained access to better educational facilities for their children. Ever since the First World War, psychologists have been aware of the fact that Northern Negroes test higher, on the average, than Southern Negroes on standard intelligence tests, but at first it was thought that more intelligent Negroes were more likely to migrate. Then Otto Klineberg of Columbia University conducted a series of studies which demonstrated that "selective migration" could not explain the intellectual superiority of Northern Negroes; better educational opportunities made the difference.

TABLE 77
White and Colored Americans Age 14–24 with Four Years of High School Education or More, 1940–1960

In Census Year	Whites 14–24 Years		Nonwhites 14–24 Years	
	Total	Per Cent with 4 Years High School or More	Total	Per Cent with 4 Years High School or More
1940	23,428,642	30.4	2,898,446	9.3
1950	21,367,060	36.8	2,852,860	15.7
1960	23,461,963	37.4	3,215,044	22.6

N.B.: For the sake of comparability with 1940 data, Hawaii and Alaska are not included in this table.
Source: Bureau of the Census, *United States Census of Population: 1960, United States Summary, Detailed Characteristics*, Washington: Government Printing Office, 1963, pp. 420–421.

TABLE 78
Northern and Southern Negroes, Army Results

Test Scores	Southern Negroes (N = 14,994)	Northern Negroes (N = 8,165)
D—	55.7%	19.6%
D	26.4	27.6
C—	9.8	22.1
C	6.2	21.4
C+	1.4	6.7
B	0.4	2.3
A	0.1	0.6

TABLE 79
Southern Whites and Northern Negroes, by States, Army Results

Whites		Negroes	
State	Median Score	State	Median Score
Mississippi	41.25	Pennsylvania	42.00
Kentucky	41.50	New York	45.02
Arkansas	41.55	Illinois	47.35
Georgia	42.12	Ohio	49.50

Why Northern Negroes Have Higher IQ's than Southern Negroes

Reprinted by permission. From Otto Klineberg, *Negro Intelligence and Selective Migration*, New York: Columbia University Press, 1935, pp. 1–2, 24–26, 30, 37–38, 56–58.

Since the days of the Army intelligence-testing program a very large amount of material dealing with the question of Negro intelligence has been collected. The summaries of the results by Garth, Pintner, Witty and Lehman and others make it quite clear that Negroes rank below Whites in almost all studies made with intelligence tests. An analysis of these results soon shows, however, that the amount of difference between the two groups varies very considerably from one part of the country to another. More specifically, northern Negroes do very much better in the tests than Negroes in the South, and approximate much more closely the records made by the Whites with whom they are compared.

This difference between northern and southern Negroes was first clearly demonstrated in the results obtained during the War [World War I]. One comparison between 14,994 southern, and 8,165 northern Negroes gave the percentage distribution of letter grades [shown in Table 78].

Although the northern Negroes still rank below the northern Whites, they are clearly superior to the larger group of Negroes from the South. It is well known that the Negroes in certain of the northern states actually exceeded the median scores obtained by White recruits from a number of the southern states, as shown in Table 79.

Very few of the studies made since the War have been directly concerned with the comparison of scores made by Negroes in different parts of the country. It is interesting, however, to list separately the studies made in the North and in the South to see whether the difference found by the Army testers in the case of recruits also holds for the more recent studies of Negro children. . . .

This part of the study attempts to discover whether the admittedly superior northern environment has any effect in raising the intelligence-test scores of southern-born Negro children. The method used was to compare the scores obtained by different groups of New York Negro children, all born in the South, but differing in the number of years which they had lived in New York City. If the environment has an effect, there should be a rise in intelligence at least roughly proportionate to length of residence in New York. If there is no environmental effect, and if the superiority of the New York City Negroes is entirely due to selective migration, length of residence ought to make little or no difference.

This technique has already been used by the writer in connection with a study of differences in speed of motor activity, as measured by the rate of movement during the solution of various performance tests. It was shown that Negro boys who had lived longer in New York reacted more quickly than those who had come more recently from the South. A somewhat similar method was used also by Peterson and Lanier in connection with intelligence tests; they divided their New York City group into "Northern born" and "born elsewhere" (that is, in the South and in the West Indies), and found a superiority in the former group. This superiority was not entirely reliable statistically, but it was slightly more than three times its probable error, which, considering the relatively small number of cases, seems reasonably significant.

The present investigation includes nine distinct studies made under the direction of the writer by candidates for the degree of Master of Arts in the Department of Psychology in Columbia University. Together they represent the findings on 3,081 subjects, consisting of ten and twelve-year-old Negro boys and girls in the Harlem schools; three of the studies were made with the National Intelligence Test, scale A, form I; three with the Stanford-Binet; one with the Otis Self-administering Examination, Intermediate Form; one with the Minnesota Paper Form Boards; and one with an abbreviated Pintner-Paterson Performance Scale. The results of these studies will be presented separately, and also combined, wherever possible, so as to give a more general and at the same time more reliable picture of the environmental effect.

The three studies with the National Intelligence Test, scale A, form I, were made upon 1,697 twelve-year-old boys and girls in the Harlem schools in 1931 and 1932. In all three studies the subjects at the time of testing had passed their twelfth, and had not yet reached their thirteenth birthdays. The attempt was made in each

case to secure every Negro boy or girl within this age range at the various schools at which the studies were made, and it is not likely that many were omitted. The scores were so combined as to make possible a comparison between a northern born control group and the southern born children who had been in New York one year, two years and so on up to eleven years. In every case note was taken of the average school grade of these various groups, so that degree of retardation or acceleration in school might also be used as a rough measure of present intellectual level. As might be expected, the intelligence-test scores and the school grades show a high degree of correspondence. . . .

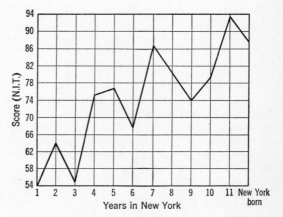

FIGURE 16. National-intelligence-test scores and length of residence in New York, 12-year-old boys (Lapidus).

The study by Marks throws some light on an important problem which arises in connection with this whole investigation. If the subjects who have been in New York six years are superior to those who have been there only two, it is probable, as we have suggested, that length of residence in a superior environment definitely affects the test score. There is, however, another possibility. It may be that the quality of the more recent migrants is inferior to that of the earlier arrivals. The superiority of the six-year over the two-year group may be due, not to environmental influences, but to the fact that each year the northward migrants are inferior to those who preceded them. It is not very probable that such a difference would appear in successive years; one year or even two or three would hardly suffice to alter the conditions of migration sufficiently, although when migrants are compared after, let us say, a ten-year interval, such a difference in selective factors might possibly show an effect.

This problem arose in connection with the Army results as reported by Brigham. He pointed out that those European immigrants who had been in America longer scored higher in the Army tests than the more recent arrivals. His conclusion was that the migrants who came earliest were intellectually superior to those who followed. It may also be that those who have been longer in this country have had more time to learn the language and to acquire the information essential to high scores on the Army Alpha. (It should be added that Brigham no longer subscribes to the general position of his earlier writings.)

In the present investigation an attempt was made to throw light on this problem by having two studies made under exactly the same conditions, with similar subjects and the same test, but one year apart. The studies by Lapidus and Marks fulfilled these conditions; they were both on twelve-year-old boys with the National Intelligence Test, the study by Lapidus in 1931 and the one by Marks in 1932.

If the findings by Lapidus are due to a progressive deterioration in the quality of the migrants rather than to an environmental effect, the results obtained by Marks in 1932 should be consistently *below* those obtained by Lapidus in 1931. A specific example will make this reasoning clearer. The twelve-year-old boys in the 1931 study who have been in New York four years, for example,

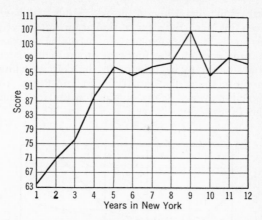

FIGURE 17. National-intelligence-test scores and length of residence in New York, 12-year-old girls (Yates).

TABLE 80
National-Intelligence-Test Score and Length of Residence (Marks)

Residence Years	1 and 2 Years	3 and 4 Years	5 and 6 Years	7 and 8 Years
Number of cases	36	40	38	34
Average score	87.53	78.70	81.18	85.82
Standard deviation	29.9	37.5	28.4	31.5
Reliability of average	5.0	5.9	4.6	5.4

Residence Years	9 Years and Over	Northern Born	Total Southern Group
Number of cases	63	350	211
Average score	96.19	90.78	87.02
Standard deviation	32.3	35.1	32.9
Reliability of average	4.1	1.9	2.3

TABLE 81
Comparison of 1931 and 1932 Averages

Group	1931 Average	1932 Average	Difference	Sigma Difference	Difference / Sigma Difference
1 and 2 years	64.21	89.71	25.50	6.5	3.92
3 and 4 years	66.86	79.06	12.20	7.8	1.56
5 and 6 years	72.32	81.86	9.54	7.0	1.36
7 and 8 years	83.58	85.06	1.48	7.6	.19
9 years and over	84.64	97.15	12.51	6.2	2.02
Northern residence	86.93	90.23	3.30	2.5	1.32

arrived in 1927; those in the 1932 study who have been in New York for a similar period arrived in 1928. If the migrants are becoming inferior as time goes on, the four-year group in the later study ought to be inferior to the corresponding group in the earlier one. Table 81 and Figure 18 show the average scores obtained in the 1931 and the 1932 studies. . . .

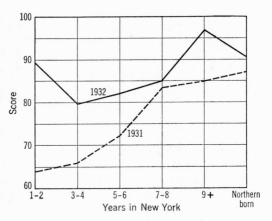

FIGURE 18. Comparison of results obtained in 1931 and 1932 (Lapidus and Marks).

To anyone with any acquaintance with the Negro school system in the South, it will hardly come as a surprise that a period of residence in the superior New York school environment should improve the intelligence of Negro children. This is not the occasion for a discussion of the intricate relationship between schooling and intelligence as measured by the intelligence test; in the ordinary linguistic tests (of the type of the Binet or the National Intelligence Test) the success in many of the tasks to be performed depends so clearly upon the type of training received in school that it is not surprising that better schooling should mean a higher intelligence quotient. The opinion expressed in the earlier days of the testing movement in America, that the tests measure native endowment altogether apart from the influence of training and background, is now held by few if any of the psychologists who have concerned themselves with tests. The question is no longer whether training has an effect, but rather how great that effect can be.

Better schooling is of course not the only environmental factor which influences the test scores, but it is probably the most important one.

The other factors—superior economic status, better opportunities for "extra-curricular" activities, greater motivation resulting from a better chance of success—also play their part, although it is a part which cannot very easily be evaluated. The difference in the school systems in the North and the South is, however, clear and definite, and the influence of the change upon the southern Negro child, especially when that change occurs early in life, can hardly be overestimated.

Woofter comments as follows on the southern schools:

"The South is not only poorer than the North, but also less disposed to distribute such funds as are available according to the school population. The Negro schools are a secondary consideration. In comparison with schools for White children they have fewer seats in proportion to the school population, more pupils per teacher, more double sessions, fewer teachers, poorer salaries, fewer and smaller playgrounds, and less adequate provision for the health and comfort of pupils and teachers."

The per-capita expenditure for the education of White and Negro children in the South shows an illuminating contrast. The report of the Phelps-Stokes fund for 1910–1920 states that

". . . the per capita in the Southern states was found to be $10.32 for each White child, and $2.89 for each Colored child. The per capita figures for the different states vary widely. In the border states where the proportion of Negroes is relatively small, the per capita for Negroes is higher than in the other states. The most striking differences, however, are in the county expenditures. State school funds are apportioned to each county on the basis of population without regard to race. The county officers then divide these funds according to their interpretation of the needs of the White and Colored pupils."

The report gives a table of expenditures in southern counties, arranged according to the proportion of Negroes in each county.

Charles S. Johnson also points out the wide disparity in per-capita expenditures for White and Negro children in the southern states. For example, South Carolina spends $4.48 per Negro child, and $45.45 per White child; the figures for Alabama are $5.45 and $37.63; for Georgia, $7.44 and $35.24; for Louisiana, $8.02 and $46.67; for Mississippi, $9.34 and $42.17; for Virginia, $14.86 and $54.21. In Tennessee the proportion is considerably more equitable, $20.15 to $33.47. In the border states, Kentucky and West Virginia, the per-capita expenditures for the two groups are about the same.

Embree in *Brown America* comments:

"Studies of eight Southern states show average expenditures of $44.31 per capita for Whites and only $12.50 for Negroes. . . . The inadequacy of these provisions for either race is seen when one compares them with the average expenditure throughout the United States as a whole, which is $87.22 per school child."

In the light of these figures the educational handicap under which the average southern Negro child suffers hardly requires further comment. It may be noted in this connection that Clark Foreman, who administered achievement tests to colored children in a number of rural counties in Georgia and Alabama, found a close correspondence between the standing of the various counties in these tests and the per-capita expenditure for the education of Negro children.

The marked discrepancy between educational facilities in the North and in the South throws considerable light on the question of school retardation among Negro children. A large number of the children who are retarded in the northern schools have come from the South and have suffered certain educational handicaps which they have not yet been able to overcome. The data on school retardation presented elsewhere in this study show that northern born children are only very slightly over age, and that the degree of retardation is very much greater among the newcomers from the South. Similar results are reported by Johnson for the Negro school population of Detroit. In the Detroit schools Negro children born in Michigan show only 4.76 percent retardation, while those born in the South are very much more retarded, in proportions closely approximating the condition of the school

system in their home states; for example, children from Virginia show 20 percent retardation, and those from Mississippi, 25 percent. Another important factor in retardation is delay in entering school, rather than slow progress. Woofter points out that a great many of the colored children are "merely pedagogically retarded, not mentally deficient, and these tend to progress faster and to catch up with their normal grade."

The picture is a clear one. The southern states are relatively poor, have much less money to expend on elementary and secondary education, and divide that money in such a way that Negro children obtain far less than their proportionate share of educational opportunities. This discrepancy is more marked in some states than in others, and more marked also in rural than in urban districts, but in general it is certainly fair to assume that those Negro children who have received part of their education in the South are placed at a definite disadvantage in competition with others. Those who have come North at an early age, and have had all or nearly all their schooling in the North, have been very nearly able to overcome the handicap; those who have come North in recent years still suffer from it very definitely.

Professor Klineberg's studies of Negro intelligence are not only illustrative of well-designed research. They also demonstrate how advances in social-science knowledge can contribute to social change. As evidence accumulated relating poor Negro performance on intelligence tests to insufficient and inadequate schooling, the belief in inherent Negro inferiority grew less tenable, and race prejudice became less respectable, especially among better-educated segments of the white population. The Supreme Court decision on May 17, 1954, outlawing racial segregation in public schools, is a further illustration of the effect of social-science research on white decision makers.[24] In holding that "separate educational facilities are inherently unequal," the Court considered

TABLE 82
Per Capita Expenditure on Education

County Groups	White	Negro
Under 10 percent Negro	$7.96	$7.23
10–25 percent Negro	9.55	5.55
25–50 percent Negro	11.11	3.19
50–75 percent Negro	12.53	1.77
75 percent and over Negro	22.22	1.78

[24] For a survey of Supreme Court decisions dealing with race relations, see Rayford W. Logan, "The United States Supreme Court and the Segregation Issue," *Annals of the American Academy of Political and Social Science*, Vol. 304, March 1956, pp. 10–16.

explicitly the *psychological* consequences of segregated education, not merely the usual superiority of white schools in physical facilities and budget. The 1954 Supreme Court decision will help equalize Negro and white education further. The gradual elimination of segregation will improve the quality as well as increase the quantity of Negro education. Probably though, the decision is too recent to explain the upgrading shown in Table 77 (on page 551). This upgrading is more likely a consequence of the redistribution of Negro population and of the rising aspirations of Negro parents for their children.

Although factors in social change have to be discussed one at a time, the joint effect of all of them together may be considerably greater than the additive effect of each separate one. (Statisticians call this phenomenon "interaction" and can measure it precisely with analysis of variance techniques.) Thus, the changed status of Negroes in American society is not due to any factor, however important, acting alone: to ideological dilemmas, to social-science research, to the redistribution of Negro population, to rising Negro demands, or to governmental sponsorship of integration. All of these factors exist in a dynamic equilibrium; a change in one makes a change in another easier to achieve.[25] Take government sponsored change, for example. The 1954 Supreme Court decision rested on ideological and social scientific as well as Constitutional foundations. But it also depended on the existence of a Negro protest movement one arm of which (the National Association for the Advancement of Colored People) paid the legal expenses enabling four test cases to be appealed to the Supreme Court. Another arm of that protest movement sponsors sit-ins, freedom rides, and other nonviolent challenges to segregation. The following article recounts the development of nonviolent techniques for challenging segregation in the United States. What it does not recount, although the discussion implicitly suggests the point, is the dependence of the Negro protest

[25] See Myrdal, *op. cit.*, pp. 1065–1070, for a discussion of vicious circles and benevolent circles.

movement on the rising level of Negro education.

How the Sit-in Movement Started

Reprinted by permission. From Carleton Mabee, "Evolution of Non-violence," *The Nation*, Vol. 193, Aug. 12, 1961, pp. 78–81.

The non-violent movement for desegregation was born during World War II. The war created tensions which were sometimes transferred—often unconsciously—to hatred of minorities. At the same time, the Negroes' awareness of their second-class citizenship was heightened by the contrast between Jim Crow and the professed American war aim of opposition to the Nazi race theory. There was uneasiness in war plants, where white and colored often worked side by side for the first time.

In this situation, pacifists, once they had lost their effort to prevent United States entry into the war, decided to emphasize the development of non-violent techniques to improve race relations. As they proceeded, they consciously learned from Gandhi, whose non-violent movement for the independence of India was then reaching its climax.

As early as April, 1942, the pacifist Fellowship of Reconciliation's Youth Secretary, Bayard Rustin, a young Negro of compelling charm, was trying one-man sit-ins. He believed that American Negroes were peculiarly fitted to experiment with non-violent action, he said, because they not only had a history of enduring suffering without bitterness, but also a rich religious heritage of which non-violence was a part.

When Rustin went into a restaurant in a small Midwestern town, the manager refused to serve him, because, she explained, if she did, "everybody would walk out." Rustin proposed that they try an experiment: he would sit at a table with a hamburger in front of him, and they both would watch for ten minutes to see if anyone walked out because he was there. If anyone did, Rustin would also walk out. After some hesitation, the manager agreed to try the experiment. Rustin waited the ten minutes without anyone's walking out, and then the manager served him a hot hamburger. Thereafter the restaurant continued to serve Negroes.

Rustin found other opportunities to refuse to cooperate with segregation. On a bus near Nashville, he sat up front with whites, was dragged out of the bus and kicked, but did not retaliate. Attending a Quaker conference at Cape May, N.J., he appeared with white friends one afternoon at a "whites only" section of a beach. When guards asked him to go elsewhere, he expressed concern for the difficult position of the guards. He explained that it was against his principles to acquiesce in segregation and therefore he could not willingly leave, but suggested various humorous ways by which they could remove him. The guards were so taken aback that they left him alone; during the rest of the conference, Rustin and his friends continued to use the beach. When he arrived late one rainy night by train in Baltimore, Rustin found that the taxi drivers at the station refused to pick him up because of his color. He walked into the middle of the narrow taxi driveway alongside the station, and stood there, blocking all taxi traffic for ninety minutes, until he got a taxi.

During 1942 Rustin described his one-man sit-ins, ride-ins, swim-ins and stand-ins to many audiences, and thus prepared the way for the organized non-violent movement.

In February, 1942, James Farmer, the young Race Relations Secretary of the Fellowship of Reconciliation, proposed to the Fellowship that it attempt to create an organization, composed of both pacifists and non-pacifists, committed to non-violent action against racial discrimination. It was hoped that, after a period of five to ten years of education and experiment, the organization would be ready to use on a large scale "relentless non-cooperation, economic boycott, [and] civil disobedience." In April, 1942, the Fellowship's National Council decided to endorse such a campaign, and authorized Farmer to work on it. The decision was soon to bear fruit.

Meanwhile, among the several Fellowship of Reconciliation "cell" groups in Chicago, one, composed largely of University of Chicago students, was devoted to race relations. One evening two members of this group—Farmer, who is colored, and James Robinson, white—went into Jack Spratt's, a restaurant in their neighborhood. They were served reluctantly. Later, a larger interracial party from the same "cell" also went into the restaurant. They were also served reluctantly; and after they had eaten, their waiter refused to give them a bill. They left money in payment, but the waiter followed them into the street to throw the money after them.

By this time the group working on Jack Spratt's had grown to include several non-students and non-pacifists. The enlarged group deliberately planned a non-violent demonstration, patterned on a combination of Gandhian methods and the methods of the 1936–7 "sit-down strikes" in auto factories (the sitters first called their demonstrations "sit-down strikes"), in an attempt to change the restaurant's policy.

One day in May, 1942, the group sent an all-white party into Jack Spratt's, and it was served; then a mixed party went in, and was seated; finally, an all-Negro party entered. The hostess told the all-Negro group it would not be seated except in the basement, but the group refused to leave. The hostess called the police who, upon finding only a quiet group of people waiting to be served, refused to arrest anyone. Patrons in the restaurant who were not part of the sit-in became curious about it and stayed on, occupying seats, thus in effect helping the cause. After two hours in which business in the restaurant was almost at a standstill, the management decided to change its policy, and the hostess personally served the waiting Negroes.

Deciding that they had found a technique that worked, the sitters led in forming, in June, 1942, the Chicago Committee on Racial Equality to experiment further with non-violent direct action. The following year the committee, with the help of the Fellowship of Reconciliation, led in creating a national federation of groups devoted to non-violent, direct action, called the Congress of Racial Equality (CORE) which chose Farmer as its chairman. The major vehicle of the non-violent movement of the 1940s had been created.

During most of the decade, CORE remained a loose federation of local groups, without a paid national staff. Its leaders were generally young, and among them were both colored and white. Aside from Farmer (a graduate of the School of Religion of Howard University, who later became Program Director of the NAACP, but who this year returned to CORE as National Director), the leaders included George Houser, an ordained Methodist minister who later became Executive Secretary of the American Committee on Africa; and Bayard Rustin, who recently has been active in working with the Rev. Martin Luther King, Jr., and the War Resisters League.

In its early years, CORE's leaders—national and local—were generally pacifists, but this was not true of the rank and file. Some CORE leaders had been conscientious objectors during World War II. Officially, CORE was neutral on pacifism, but much of its non-violent emphasis was nourished by the pacifists in its membership.

At first, CORE's national office was in a church in Chicago; from 1944 it shared offices with the Fellowship of Reconciliation in Cleveland; and from 1946 it shared the Fellowship's national office in New York. CORE's unpaid Executive Director, for most of the decade, was George Houser, whose paid occupation was that of a staff member of the Fellowship. There was some friction within CORE over whether the identification of CORE with the pacifist Fellowship scared non-pacifists away.

CORE was an interracial, urban movement, centered in the North, with only a few member groups south of the Mason-Dixon Line at any time during the 1940s, and these all in the upper South—in Baltimore, Washington, St. Louis and Bartlesville, Oklahoma (where, under pressure from "patriotic" societies, the leader of the CORE group was eventually forced from the library post which she had held for thirty-five years). The number of local groups affiliated with CORE was ten in 1945, thirteen in 1947, fifteen in 1949 and twenty in 1950; and there was usually a number of cooperating non-affiliated groups. Most of the affiliates tended to be unstable, flourishing briefly, dying down, then re-forming. They were likely to be small, with perhaps fifteen to a hundred members, an exception being the affiliate in Columbus —the Vanguard League—which had 2,000 to 3,000 members.

Not all of the activities of CORE and CORE-related groups were carried out along strictly non-violent, direct-action lines. Some activities followed conventional patterns, and in these CORE was often able to work with other organizations. CORE encouraged letter-writing campaigns to government officials or owners of businesses; petitions (as in Washington, D.C., to protest segregation in the public parks); and publicity by press releases. (In Denver, after a Negro was refused a room at a YMCA on Christmas Day with the explanation that there was no room available, a CORE press release drew a parallel with what happened, a long time ago, at another inn at Christmas time.)

Some activities were less conventional, and in these it was harder to find cooperating organizations. When the "Freedom Train" was circulating the country to exhibit copies of the Constitution and the Declaration of Independence, CORE groups picketed it with signs saying, "There is no freedom till all are free."

CORE groups conducted opinion surveys to find out if department store patrons objected to being served by Negro sales clerks (in Cleveland, where department stores employed only white sales clerks, 68 per cent of patrons were willing to be served by Negroes); listed restaurants, outside of Negro sections, which had no racial bars (in Washington, sitters could recall when there were only four such restaurants; by 1950, there were still only seventeen they could list); printed cards for CORE friends to leave on the tables of desegregated restaurants expressing appreciation of their policy; solicited business for newly desegregated enterprises; bought stock in companies which practiced segregation—like the Greyhound bus company—and then appeared at stockholders' meetings to protest company policy; distributed leaflets at Pennsylvania Station in New York and the interstate bus terminal in Washington, informing passengers that in interstate travel, despite custom, the Supreme Court had ruled in the *Morgan* case in 1946 that segregation was unconstitutional; and promoted a song that urged interstate travelers to sit where they liked:

"And if the driver-man says 'Move,'
And if the driver-man says 'Move,'
And if the driver-man says 'Move,'
Speak up polite,
But sit there tight,
You're in the right,
You don't have to ride Jim Crow."

But it was in the more clearly non-violent, direct-action projects that the CORE and CORE-related groups found their real métier. They adapted Gandhian methods imaginatively to the American scene, developing the techniques which sitters and freedom riders have made well known in the last few years.

Sitters in the 1940s, as now, found eating places their most convenient target. As early as 1944, the CORE group in Washington, D.C., decided that dime-store lunch counters were excellent places to hold "sit-down strikes"—and for some of the same reasons that present-day sitters also find them so: "Because there is a good deal of Negro trade in these stores," they explained and "also because colored people are served at the present time standing up at the [lunch] counter." But they did not at that time discover that the dime stores were also a good choice because sympathy boycotts might spread against chain dime stores all over the nation; that idea would not catch hold while the non-violent movement remained small.

In the 1940s, CORE groups also held sit-ins at fancy restaurants, like the "plush and hush" restaurant in Los Angeles where a hundred persons at a time "sat-in." Sit-ins were held in a Negro-owned restaurant in Washington which discriminated against whites; at drug-store lunch counters and in department-store restaurants.

In addition to eating places, there were also sit-ins in churches, as in Frankfort, Kentucky, and Bartlesville; in theatres, as in Yellow Springs, Ohio, and Baltimore; in swimming pools, as in Palisades Park, N.J., and Cleveland; in roller-skating rinks, as in Chicago; and in the religious services of prisons, as by the conscientious-objector inmates of the federal prison in Ashland, Kentucky.

Other planned forms of non-violent, direct action included stand-ins to buy tickets at discriminatory theatres, as in Washington, D.C., or at discriminatory swimming pools, as in Los Angeles, or to buy food at discriminatory cafeterias, as in Detroit; the picketing of segregated YMCAs, as in New York, and offices which promoted restrictive covenants for real estate, as in Chicago; small-scale boycotts, as of a tavern in Yellow Springs (it lost 60 per cent of its business), or metropolitan-wide boycotts protesting discrimination against Negro employment, as of Carnation milk in San Francisco and Los Angeles, and of Wonder bread in Chicago (both these actions were successful in changing company policy); testing for hotel discrimination in Boston; hunger or work strikes against segregated dining in prisons, as by conscientious-objector inmates of the federal prisons at Lewisburg, Pennsylvania, and Danbury, Connecticut; sitting desegregated on buses and trains, as on a long "Journey of Reconciliation" through Virginia, North Carolina, Kentucky and Tennessee in 1947, for which Rustin and three others were sentenced to thirty days in a North Carolina road gang on the charge of disobeying state segregation laws. (Among the riders on this trip was Jim Peck, one of CORE's recent "Freedom Riders," who was severely beaten in Alabama last May.) CORE tested the interracial use of parks which by custom had become segregated, as in Chicago; and set up new enterprises, such as unsegregated barber shops in Oberlin, Ohio, and State College, Pennsylvania, interracial cooperative houses in Chicago and Detroit, and an interracial cooperative store in Detroit.

All this activity by CORE and its friends naturally stimulated opposition. According to the demonstrators' reports, if they were served food at all, they sometimes were served ants in their pie, sour cream for their coffee, or garbage in their sandwiches; sometimes they were charged higher prices; sometimes employees tried to break the "polluted" dishes from which they had eaten. Occasionally, when demonstrators arrived, managers would close their businesses; or, especially if their businesses were swimming pools or roller-skating rinks, would pretend they were running a private club. Sometimes employees or onlookers kicked demonstrators, pushed them out of line in front of theatre ticket windows, shoved them against glass windows in swimming pools till the windows broke, hounded them with ammonia fumes, had them arrested, beat them, played fire hoses on them—or, as the demonstrators went limp, dragged them away.

The members and friends of CORE were likely to differ about its primary function. According to some, this was simply to stop discrimination against Negroes by non-violent means. When such was the purpose, sitters sometimes occupied all seats in a restaurant or encouraged boycotts to force a change in policy. But according to others, forcing a change in policy was not justified: the function of CORE was rather to stop discrimination by *changing the attitudes* of the persons responsible for it. As Chaplain Howard Thurman of Howard University put it, the purpose of non-violent direct action was "to tear men free from the alignment to the evil way, to free them so that they may be given an immediate sense of acute insecurity and out of the depths of their insecurity to be forced to see their kinship with the weak and insecure." When such was the purpose, sitters were likely to occupy only some of the seats in a restaurant, with the object of appealing to the conscience of customers and managers. In practice, however, as Houser admitted, CORE activities sometimes brought desegregation without changing managers' attitudes.

There was continuous study of CORE methods. The executive committee admitted in 1945 that CORE suffered from "immature leadership," and pointed out that the lack of a paid national staff reflected inadequate organization. Houser stated that many who participated in direct-action projects simply didn't have time to carry through with all the patient steps required for effectiveness. After the Executive Secretary had led an unsuccessful direct-action project to desegregate a roller-skating rink in Cleveland, during which patrons had bullied the CORE group, Houser decided that "a really tough racial situation cannot be handled by the tactics which we have used to date."

CORE leaders also frankly faced the problem posed by the participation in CORE activities of certain "undesirables"—including neurotics, leftists who were using the movement for their own not necessarily non-violent ends, and those insufficiently disciplined to resist opportunity to retaliate with violence.

There was a barrage of criticism of CORE even from those who were foursquare for desegregation. Leftists blamed it for concentrating on racial injustice without recognizing that discrimination was merely part of an unjust social order. Activists said that CORE groups spent too much time investigating and negotiating, and too little in direct action. Purists complained that CORE sometimes succumbed to public prejudice by not permitting mixed colored-white couples to appear publicly on its behalf. Strategists condemned CORE for not doing much in the South, where the need was greatest.

Professor Douglas Steere of Haverford College, a leading Quaker pacifist, answering a Fellowship of Reconciliation request that he sponsor a CORE project, wrote as follows:

"I have watched the CORE groups function in a number of cities, and there have been a number of these that I should certainly not be prepared to sponsor, for they were simply 'expressing themselves' and gaining experience at the expense of those they worked on, and the ultimate result did not really advance the cause, in my way of thinking. Other CORE groups, however, who went about the process of thoroughly acquainting the persons they meant to seek to influence with what they were about, and at every point continuing this education, have seemed to me extremely useful instruments in the present situation. . . . There is still a strong element of the John Woolman approach to the slaveholders in my way of seeing the solution to these problems, and unless that is wedded to the direct-action techniques, and unless those who undertake them are exceptionally well-disciplined and mature, I do not see this kind of program resulting in one which the Fellowship can helpfully sponsor. On the other hand, I realize the necessity of some action which will give us opportunities to see whether the Gandhi technique can function in the West."

Nevertheless, CORE-sponsored action was often successful, and strong claims were made on CORE's behalf. Educator John Dewey wrote that the direct-action method "is education in action through solving life problems, and its value can hardly be overestimated." Labor leader A. Philip Randolph declared that CORE's adaptation of Gandhi's methods "has resulted in a novel and successful technique for removing discriminatory practices." Unitarian minister Homer Jack, of the Chicago Council against Racial and Religious Discrimination, said of a CORE summer project in Chicago: "A small interracial group of young people fought on more fronts and got more accomplished than most of the professional high-salaried race relations experts in Chicago."

The current non-violent movement bears many marks of its origins in the movement of the 1940s. Today, as twenty years ago, the motivation of many of the participants has a religious basis; now, as then, there is an attempt to slough off extreme leftist or neurotic hangers-on; now, as then, the techniques are much the same: sit-ins, stand-ins, picketing, boycotts and "freedom rides." There are, however, significant ways in which the two movements differ. In the earlier movement, most of the participants were young adults; now most are students. In the 1940s, the major action took place in the North, in a generally friendly climate, with the law often in its favor; today, though there is supporting action in the North, the major projects are undertaken in the South, in a generally hostile climate and more often than not in defiance of state and local law. In the earlier movement, the action was strongly interracial; now it is more nearly dominated by Negroes. The earlier movement was on a small scale, featuring action by fairly cohesive, more or less disciplined groups, chiefly under the sponsorship of a national organization, CORE, with support from the Fellowship of Reconciliation; today it has become a mass movement, with action often spontaneous, beyond the control of any one organization. In the 1940s, the movement lacked general support by either whites or colored, or even by pacifists; today it has the support of many of the major forces of the nation, thus bearing witness to a striking reversal of public opinion.

This "striking reversal of public opinion" must be understood in the context of several interrelated factors including the *nonviolent* approach adopted by Negro leaders. Nonviolence is a palatable form of protest to middle-class Christians. The Reverend Martin Luther King, Jr., one of the main figures in the sit-in movement, gives credit to the Indian leader, Gandhi, for demonstrating the effectiveness of nonviolent resistance. Gandhi in turn was convinced of the value of nonviolent resistance from reading Henry David Thoreau's essay on "Civil Disobedience." [26] Thus, the sit-in movement carries on an American tradition—started in 1848 when Thoreau refused to pay taxes and went to jail to protest what he regarded as an unjust war against Mexico. Needless to say, nonviolent resistance is resistance, although a type of resistance suited to a minority group lacking access to major sources of power.[27] Nonviolence enables American Negroes to protest their status without breaking with the Christian tradition which taboos hatred. As one sociologist put it, Dr. King "has aided Negroes to redefine as moral and acceptable what otherwise would be defined as immoral and unacceptable." [28] Because it emphasizes its Christian roots, this militant Christianity is more acceptable to *white* Christians than other forms of militancy. It is also more acceptable to the Negro community where ministers along with lawyers, labor leaders, teachers, businessmen,

[26] Louis Fischer, *The Life of Mahatma Gandhi*, New York: Harper, 1950.
[27] James W. Vander Zanden, "The Non-violent Resistance Movement against Segregation," *American Journal of Sociology*, Vol. 68, March 1963, pp. 544–550.
[28] *Ibid.*, p. 547.

and physicians constitute the unpaid, real leadership.

Negro Leadership

Reprinted by permission. From Daniel C. Thompson, *The Negro Leadership Class*, Englewood Cliffs, N.J.: Prentice-Hall, 1963, pp. 34–39, 52–54.

With few exceptions, Negro leadership in New Orleans is an avocation. Those who perform leadership functions in the area of race relations usually do so in addition to their full-time occupational pursuits.

By and large, the Negro leadership class is composed of successful representatives of the following occupational groups: The Protestant ministry, law, labor, business, the intelligentsia (teachers), professional leaders, and medicine.

THE PROTESTANT MINISTRY

Negro ministers constitute the largest segment of the leadership class. A relatively large percentage of them, with the backing of their congregations, have been able to contribute to local and national "uplift" efforts.

There may be several reasons why Negro ministers have become widely recognized symbols of the Negroes' struggle for equal citizenship status. Some of the most tenable explanations are:

1. The Negro Protestant Church was the first, and in some respects it remains the only, major social institution in which a significant number of Negroes with varying talents and academic preparation have found opportunities for self-expression, the development of self-respect and racial pride, professional employment, and leadership training.

2. The Negro church is the "parent" of most other organizations and agencies in the Negro community. In some instances the apparentization is widely recognized, as is the case with insurance companies that developed from burial-aid societies. Also, most Negro institutions of higher education still claim affiliation with the various religious bodies that founded them. There is also a kind of indirect apparentization whereby benevolent orders and certain Negro "uplift" organizations are nurtured by Protestant Churches as an extension of their

missionary functions. Important in this connection are lodges and racial-improvement associations, which look to the church for their legitimization or a major portion of their social and financial support.

Finally, the Protestant ministry is a more or less easily accessible profession. Standards for admission are sufficiently flexible on the whole so that Negro ministers are recruited from every academic, economic, and social segment of the community. This means that those with leadership ambitions will find some denomination or particular church that will be willing to accept them in apprenticeship positions which will provide them opportunities to develop and refine their leadership talents.

Ministers, like all other leaders in the Negro community, may be classified as *intraracial* or *interracial*. The activities of the intraracial leaders tend to center around two major approaches.

THE OTHER-WORLDLY. As might be expected, the vast majority of ministers are primarily interested in their pastoral role. The peculiar characteristic of the other-worldly is their lack of interest in mundane affairs. They have little apparent interest in or even feeling of responsibility for the general citizenship status of their own parishioners, to say nothing about that of the Negro masses. Their sermons are essentially biblical, dealing only tangentially with social issues. The most obvious goal of their church services is to create an atmosphere of "enjoyment." Little time is spent in attempts to motivate members to assume the social responsibilities generally considered to be incumbent upon responsible citizens. Thus, one such minister made it clear that he regarded the church solely as a "place of worship," and that "the church is no place to encourage people to register and vote or to discuss controversial issues."

Some few ministers in this category do, however, contribute indirectly to racial uplift, in the sense that their church programs provide opportunities for the development of talents, such as in music, public speaking, and leadership.

THE DENOMINATION-CENTERED. A second large segment of intraracial leaders is composed of ministers who are imprisoned in their own denominational worlds. Some of these ministers are so interested in their personal advancement within the denominational hierarchy that they are often mistaken for genuine community leaders. That is, in order to insure their own promotion they express real or feigned interest in a wide number of social issues. We find that these various social issues are almost always championed in meetings with members representing cross sections of their own particular denominations. It would appear that their avowed concern with social issues seldom extends beyond a more or less nominal, or verbal, or at best financial, support of the limited social programs adopted by their national church bodies.

Yet, again, these intraracial leaders often contribute to racial uplift. Members of their congregations get some limited opportunity, at least, to become acquainted with a few vital social issues. Some even get opportunities to develop leadership potentials, as chairman of various boards or committees for which certain social problems are of major concern.

One other contribution denomination-centered leaders often make to the advancement of Negroes in American society is their effort to provide church scholarships for a small number of young persons who have manifested leadership ability. In this way, some give tangible sanction to the value of education, which is the most estimable avenue of social mobility for Negroes in American society.

Of primary concern to this study of the Negro leadership class are the *interracial* leaders among Protestant ministers. There are two major functional groups constituting this category.

THE VIRTUOSO. There is a small number of ordained Protestant ministers who are not primarily engaged in pastoring. They are employed in such secular fields as business, teaching, and labor unions. Very often they are college graduates, and some hold graduate and professional degrees as well. Generally, they are uncommonly conscious of and sensitive to racial segregation, discrimination, and injustice. They are avowed critics of white supremacy in all forms and champions of civil rights.

Some are highly skilled orators and lecturers and are in great demand to deliver keynote speeches and formal addresses and to conduct forums. In these roles, they appear regularly as spokesmen for the Negro's cause before various types of audiences. In this way a few become leaders who are well known and respected by a cross section of the community.

Though they rarely become official representatives of organizations with mass following, practically all of the ministers in this category do hold membership in several organizations whose main purpose it is to improve the lot of Negroes in some area of community life. They often serve on the boards of these organizations, in which capacity they become important in determining what issues the Negro leadership class will champion, and what techniques and strategies will be employed.

THE COMMUNITY-CENTERED. In New Orleans, as in most other cities, there are a few prominent Negro ministers who can always be found in the vanguard of the Negro's march toward full participation in community affairs. These ministers are generally well trained, articulate, and courageous. Their churches are made available for mass meetings, forums, and other types of programs designed to acquaint the Negro masses with major social issues affecting them.

These pastors are often heads of secular organizations the major purpose of which is to accomplish social goals sought by Negro people. Some have become outstanding in voter-registration drives and fund-raising for civic organizations, and as organizers of protest movements. Occasionally some have campaigned vigorously for political candidates, and have themselves run for public office.

When Negroes get opportunities to have representation on interracial committees and boards, their representatives are often chosen from among the community-centered pastors. In this capacity these pastors are able to represent the Negro community as common participants with white leaders in the solution of such problems as health and welfare. Some serve as advisors to white groups where certain problems directly affecting Negroes are concerned.

Community-centered Negro pastors have traditionally received recognition from white men of power. White authorities usually respect the influence they have with their Negro followers. Occasionally they are appointed, officially or unofficially, to serve as liaison persons between them and intraracial Negro leaders. In that role they are privileged to negotiate with white authorities for some recognition or right sought by special-interest groups in the Negro community.

As we shall have occasion to point out again and again in the following pages, community-centered pastors continue to make valuable contributions to the Negro's struggle to achieve equal rights in all aspects of the total society. One of the most outstanding of the community-centered ministers in our sample defined the role of the minister as that of "giving responsible leadership." He contended that ministers

". . . cannot ignore violence toward any man, nor injustice toward any people, nor at any time; especially can we least afford it in a free and democratic society whose basic guarantees are toward the enhancement of life and of the person. Therefore, we are dedicated to the winning of freedom."

LAW

It may be said that Negro lawyers in New Orleans are young. Almost all of them graduated from law schools and entered practice during the past ten years. Thus, only a few of the twenty Negro lawyers may be classified as top leaders. Yet all of them, because of their professional positions, do perform significant leadership functions. These functions may be summarized under four general categories. Lawyers who may be classified in the first two categories we designate as intraracial leaders, and those who can best be placed in the last two categories we designate as interracial leaders.

THE LEGAL ADVISORS. Negro attorneys falling within this classification feel that their primary role in the achievement of first-class citizenship for Negroes can best be fulfilled by providing legal advice and counsel to organizations and groups in the community the goals of which include racial uplift. They frequently lend direction and guidance to groups in the formulation of such by-laws and constitutions as are necessary for these organizations to qualify for charters, while at the same time being flexible enough to achieve civil rights goals. They also perform a necessary advisory function when uplift organizations set about to devise programs of legal redress. As we shall see, during the period when powerful legislative forces were attempting to outlaw or seriously handicap certain Negro organizations (particularly the NAACP), Negro lawyers were constant advisors to ad interim organizations designed to carry on their several programs. These lawyers are readily available to advise Negro organizations on what they may or may not legally do in the area of civil rights.

THE JOINERS. A number of the Negro lawyers may be classified as joiners. That is, they join and participate in groups for several reasons. One is that this is a means whereby they become known to potential clients. Another is that they get an opportunity to develop certain leadership potentials that they would not otherwise develop by participating in the activities of various social and uplift groups. . . . They have no opportunity to exercise leadership in interracial legal associations, or in the many all-white civic organizations in which white attorneys may develop their leadership ability.

Whatever may be the personal reasons why some lawyers are inveterate joiners, one thing is definite: these lawyers are drawn into the membership of some groups because a type of leadership vacuum exists in what would otherwise be effective community organizations. The younger lawyers, therefore, become an active part of these groups, because their training and personalities naturally equip them for the kind of leadership some of these organizations need to be effective.

Some Negro attorneys, then, are affiliated with several intraracial social and uplift organizations. Generally, they immediately become members of the board of directors or are elected to some official position from which they might aspire to become interracial leaders.

Perhaps the most significant contribution this type of lawyer makes to racial uplift is that of educating the Negro masses about the legal techniques and strategies that may be employed in getting things done within the framework of law and government.

THE POLITICAL PARTICIPANTS. Some of the New Orleans Negro lawyers have been involved in one way or another with politics. A few of them are heads of political organizations, and become interracial leaders through their contacts with white "men of power" in the broader New Orleans community. They have been instrumental in helping to elect white candidates to office.

Perhaps, however, their most significant leadership role is that of running for public office themselves. As will be discussed in a later chapter, Negro political candidates have made several significant contributions in the field of race relations. Among the most important are the following:

1. Through running for public office Negro attorneys have been able to get a considerable number of Negroes registered to vote.

2. Dissemination of political knowledge to the Negro community has been another of their contributions. This has been one of the most successful means by which knowledge about the whole political process and the responsibility of citizenship has been presented to the Negro masses.

3. Negro lawyers who have run for public office have, in a sense, become symbols of Negro achievement. They have done much to establish the fact that there are Negroes who are willing and qualified to fill responsible public positions. Further, they have provided stimulating competition for white political candidates, who have frequently adopted important planks of the Negro candidate's platform. These lawyers have often succeeded in forcing white political candidates to take some definite stand on important racial issues which may otherwise have been ignored.

THE CIVIL RIGHTERS. The major leadership responsibility of this group is, perhaps, in the realm of constitutional law. That is, because of specialized legal knowledge, some have been most effective in protecting the civil rights of Negroes through litigation. The outstanding Negro lawyer in the city summarized his leadership role in this way: The legal process is "slow but sure." He is convinced that the Constitution of the United States and federal laws, as they now exist, provide ample opportunities for Negroes to achieve first-class citizenship. Therefore, he considers the education and encouragement of Negroes in the pursuit of their rights within the framework of our existing legal system as his primary community leadership role.

A few of the lawyers in this category have become widely recognized interracial leaders. Their skill in handling federal cases is highly respected by the legal profession and by the courts. The dean of Negro lawyers in New Orleans, who is the legal representative of the NAACP in the state, has an enviable record of successes before the federal judiciary, because of which he is the official and unofficial spokesman on the civil rights of Negroes. He is frequently called upon to speak before Negro audiences when technical points of civil rights are under consideration. In addition, white groups and individuals seek his opinion on race relations issues. He is, consequently, one of the most respected interpreters of the philosophy of race relations as it may be applied to the Negroes' goal of equal citizenship.

It must be kept in mind that at certain points these leadership categories may overlap. Therefore, a number of Negro attorneys may participate to some extent in all areas outlined above, but heuristically it may be assumed that their major or primary activity is in one category. . . .

PROFESSIONAL LEADERS

Another significant element of the Negro leadership class in New Orleans is composed of a small group of top officials of Negro uplift organizations, particularly the NAACP and the Urban League, journalists, public relations officers, and radio news commentators. These share at least one basic responsibility with the intelligentsia. They are expected to impart information. However, unlike teachers, to whom education or enlightenment is the chief end in itself, professional leaders impart knowledge in order to achieve some concrete, specific social goal. As we shall see, these goals are clearly enunciated in the policy statements of the organizations they represent.

The Negro radio news commentators, though adhering tacitly to virtually the same set of racial uplift principles as do the others, cannot, of course, pursue these ends with as much directness and vigor. They are more restricted in their expression because all of the radio stations are owned and managed by white businessmen, whose interest in the Negro community is primarily financial.

One of the main things that sets this group apart from intellectuals is this: *Leadership is their main job.* All the others who perform leadership functions must do so in addition to their full-time occupational commitments.

These professional leaders render four important, even indispensable, community services: fact-finding, protest, the creation of solidarity, and the formation of public opinion.

FACT-FINDING. A central service of professional leaders is that of gathering facts. The Urban League, for example, has a long record in connection with vital community surveys. In New Orleans, as in other cities with Urban League chapters, this organization has gathered facts concerning welfare which often form the basis for intelligent social amelioration.

The NAACP, too, has always maintained a research staff. Though the New Orleans Chapter does not have its own research staff, it does base its program upon facts gathered by the national organization and share in the gathering of facts for the national organization. The NAACP research staff has been able to uncover pertinent facts concerning the many civil rights cases it has handled. Perhaps the best testimony regarding the competence of this staff is the phenomenal proportion of cases NAACP lawyers have won in federal courts.

Since the local white newspapers report only a minimum of facts concerning the Negro's place in community life, and since very little space is given to issues of vital importance to the segregated Negro community, the Negro masses must turn to the local Negro paper for information and guidance in community affairs. The fact is, the local white daily newspapers are obviously dedicated to the defense of the biracial status quo. Over the years, therefore, Negro publications in New Orleans, especially the *Louisiana Weekly*, have done a gigantic job of collecting and interpreting information on vital issues affecting Negroes and the Negro community. There is some feeling among Negro leaders, however, that this information reaches very few white men of power.

Radio news commentators are in some respects similar to journalists. They, too, gather facts of concern to Negro people that otherwise would be ignored. Yet they have made a distinct additional contribution in the realm of education by bringing before the radio public outstanding Negro talent and leaders, and scholarly discussions of issues of interest to Negroes.

PROTEST. One of the characteristic roles of professional leaders is that of protest. Both the Negro community and the white power structure expect protest from professional leaders. When they do not protest the inequities Negroes experience, Negro intraracial leaders accuse them of being indifferent or Uncle Toms, and some white authorities interpret their silence as meaning that Negroes are satisfied with segregation and discrimination.

At this point a generalization is in order: *White authorities do not effect positive changes in the status of Negroes in any area of community life until professional Negro leaders have voiced long, loud, concerted protest.*

SOLIDARITY. A third function performed by professional leaders is the creation of solidarity and unity in the Negro community. This has been occasioned by times of crisis. This need for unity was succinctly voiced by the executive secretary of the New Orleans Urban League. He said, "We are experiencing a social revolution. In this revolution all segments of the Negro community must participate. There must be protest meetings, sit-ins, mass demonstrations, letter-writing, and negotiation." He, and several other Negro leaders, are convinced that only through unity can the Negro community achieve first-class citizenship. On another level, the president of the Coordinating Council of Greater New Orleans urged unity among community leaders. He said, "We, as community leaders, must achieve organization and unity among ourselves in order that we might attain a common goal—dignity and freedom."

Not only do professional leaders call for abstract unity, but from time to time they make concrete proposals about how actual unity might be achieved. Thus, they appeal to all segments in the Negro community to unite behind definite programs, such as registering voters, reducing juvenile delinquency, and supporting Negro institutions. These leaders use several techniques in attempts to bring about unity among Negroes. They not only appeal to race pride, but they make deliberate efforts to create it. Those working in communications do an especially noteworthy job in this connection. They emphasize Negro achievements in all fields, and when there are Negro "firsts" in certain jobs or positions they dramatize their success stories. Another technique used by professional leaders to create unity is to point out that all Negroes, regardless of social status, are subject to the same racial indignities. They document the fact that "segregation and discrimination are common to us all."

PUBLIC OPINION. Professional leaders are among the main creators of a public opinion favorable to advancements in civil rights. This is done mostly through informal education. The leaders frequently make speeches, write editorials, publish reports, and conduct hearings of one kind or another in order to get pertinent information across to the public. A relentless campaign also is carried on "for the minds of men," as one leader stated it.

One of the major points reiterated by professional leaders is that segregation and discrimination, as practiced in American society, especially in the South, do "irreparable damage to the United States's internal strength and international prestige." This thesis is illustrated by examples

from various facets of American life—business, politics or government, housing, education, and religion. As a matter of fact, some Negro leaders strongly believe, as voiced by one, that "if white Americans could ever be brought to see and understand the high cost of prejudice and racial discrimination, they would gladly join forces with Negroes and abolish them. Because of ignorance they have turned the struggle for democracy over to Negroes."

Professional leaders are frequently accepted as spokesmen for the Negro people. Their statements and interpretations regarding the status of Negroes and, in a broader sense, race relations, are given national (often international) prominence. Thus, in some measure, they have participated in the creation of a national and international public opinion that is increasingly unfavorable to racial segregation.

Like all leaderships, Negro leadership is ultimately validated by its constituency. Mass support among Negroes for nonviolent protests against segregation has cost leaders who continued to advocate unacceptable "compromise" tactics their leadership. In Tallahassee, Florida, for example, a bus boycott was the issue on which the old, established leaders were supplanted by militantly nonviolent leaders.[29] Boycotts, sit-ins, and freedom rides are far more dramatic than the accommodating, behind-the-scenes tactics of previous leaders. Widespread as is Negro support for nonviolent protest, it is far from unanimous. Less well-educated segments of the Negro community confuse nonviolence with acquiescence. G. Franklin Edwards of Howard University demonstrated this communications gap in an experiment sponsored by the Youth Development Program of the Ford Foundation. Professor Edwards conducted a seminar in race relations with five Howard University students who had participated in sit-ins (four Negro students and one white) and five inmates of the federal reformatory at Lawton, Virginia (four Negro inmates

[29] Lewis M. Killian and Charles U. Smith, "Negro Protest Leaders in a Southern Community," *Social Forces*, Vol. 38, March 1960, pp. 253–257.

and one white). The reformatory inmates understood what the students were trying to accomplish and respected them for it. What they could not understand was their nonviolent methods: letting their enemies slug them without defending themselves. This same communications gap exists in the larger Negro community between the well-educated leaders of organizations like the National Association for the Advancement of Colored People and the bitter, impatient members of the Black Muslims.

The N.A.A.C.P. versus the Black Muslims: The Task of Justifying Gradualism to American Negroes

Reprinted by permission. From Gertrude Samuels, "Two Ways: Black Muslim and N.A.A.C.P." New York *Times Magazine*, May 6, 1963, pp. 26–27, 86–88.

Throughout the American Negro community —nearly 20,000,000 people, or one-tenth of the nation—there is a growing bitterness over the slow pace of progress on civil rights. On all sides the frustrations have been deepening since the historic Supreme Court decision of 1954, banning segregation in schools. Today, nine years after that decision, less than 10 per cent of Negro students are in nonsegregated schools in the South. Opportunities for Negroes generally remain bound by the shackles of race. As Dr. C. Eric Lincoln, who teaches sociology at Clark College in Atlanta, writes: "Every intelligent Negro experiences a feeling of quarantine when he ponders his future and the avenues of creative existence open to him."

On these beliefs—that equality must come, and that it must come more quickly—the Negro community is united. But it is deeply split over how it should proceed: whether it should continue to move democratically though more militantly; or whether it should alienate itself completely from American white society.

This schism shows up in the diametrically opposed approaches of two main groups: the National Association for the Advancement of Colored People—N.A.A.C.P.—for fifty years the best known group identified with Negro aspirations,

and considered moderate; and the radical Black Muslims, who oppose integration and for months have been increasingly active in their challenge to the N.A.A.C.P.

THE BLACK MUSLIMS

This is a religion of protest and rebellion, which preaches black union against the white man. It rejects Christianity. It preaches that the black man is "divine" and that all whites are "devils." An Islamic sect, it believes that it alone has the answer for the Negro masses who are groping for social dignity and for social action. Its avowed goal is to separate from America, to set up its own state with its own flag.

The Muslims reject integration as vehemently as do Mississippi's Gov. Ross Barnett and Senator Eastland. They contemptuously reject the Negro moderates who are fighting for integration as "Toms" and "white man's niggers." They appeal deliberately to the Negroes at the bottom of the social totem pole—the lower working class, the poor and the illiterate. They identify with Moslems overseas, and obey the rules that forbid smoking, gambling, drinking and the eating of pork. They are secretive about their membership, estimated at 100,000.

Their doctrine of black supremacy is offering a minority people, confined in racial ghettos, the escape of fantasy—a "nation" of their own—to counteract the reality of their despair. This is what the Muslims recognize and exploit.

The movement began back in 1930, when a peddler—who may have been an Arab and who was known by various names but chiefly as W. D. Fard, Professor Ford and "The Prophet"—appeared in Detroit and shocked his listeners with denunciations of Christianity. He taught slum Negroes that their enemy was the white man. He set up a temple of Islam, and appointed Elijah Muhammad (born Elijah Poole in Georgia) as his "Messenger." Then, in the way of prophets, he "disappeared." Under Muhammad, who lives in a mansion in Chicago's South Side, the sect thrived.

Temples now abound in various cities. Muslim real-estate holdings and commercial enterprises have grown. Many members were recruited in prisons. The most flamboyant of these and Muhammad's chief lieutenant is the New York leader Malcolm X.

Minister Malcolm X is today both personal

magnet and political threat, a fascinating study in human contradictions.

In Temple 7 Restaurant in Harlem, one of the many Muslim holdings, you meet Malcolm X under a large framed portrait of "The Honorable Elijah Muhammad, Messenger of Allah." No-smoking signs abound in the well-appointed restaurant where white-jacketed waiters serve well-dressed diners. A mural of the Sphinx fills one wall. Even the juke box seems toned down. It is like a stage set.

For three and a half hours, Malcolm X virtually mesmerizes the listener with his ingratiating manners, an endless flow of ideas, Biblical quotations, boyish smiles and bland insults. He is tall (6 feet 3 inches), a light-brown, 37-year-old, ruggedly handsome man with coldly appraising eyes behind horn-rimmed glasses. With pauses for phone calls or to sip water (he was on a monthly three-day fast), he roams widely over religious, economic, cultural and racial subjects on which he has educated himself.

He never got beyond a formal eighth-grade education. He attributes "all that I am and all that I know" to his teacher, Mr. Muhammad. When he pronounces the name, it is with the same awe that Catholics refer to St. Peter, or Jews to Moses.

He was born Malcolm Little in Omaha, Neb., one of 11 children and the son of a Baptist minister. He tells you he was 6 years old when the Ku Klux Klan burned his home to the ground; later his father was found killed. These terrible memories have never left him. The family broke up and Malcolm went to a boys' institution. Eventually, he moved East and into the underworld. Known as "Big Red," he went to prison for larceny in Massachusetts on an 8-to-10-year sentence, and served seven years. In prison he began to absorb the Muslim religion and to correspond with Muhammad. He likes to say that "Christianity took me to prison and Islam brought me out."

"This Elijah," he tells you, "is teaching us that just as Moses solved the problem of the Jews by taking them to a land of their own, this Moses, our Elijah, will lead us to a land of our own."

"Where?" (Some reports have identified the site as three Southern States.)

Malcolm X flashes his smile. "Moses never told the Jews where it was to be. It was part of the Mosaic strategy politically just to lead them out

toward the 'promised land.'

"The reason that Muslims don't want integration with the white man," Malcolm X continues, "is because we see what's coming to the white man, what's in store for him. It's a sinking ship.

"We're not anti-white. We're anti-oppression, and the oppressor is white. That's why I say there is a guilt complex among the whites.

"The N.A.A.C.P. is not a Negro organization, so Roy Wilkins [N.A.A.C.P. executive director] is not a Negro leader. As long as Arthur Spingarn is the president, it's a Jewish organization. And it's the same with the Urban League, CORE, the N.A.A.C.P. Legal Defense Fund—all those are white organizations.

"When Negroes in those organizations open their mouths to speak words of praise, it's always for white people—the good liberals, the good Jews, the good white folks. When they say anything good about Mr. Muhammad, it's always with reservations to let people know that 'I'm not a Muslim.' These are statements by scared men."

Asked whether he feels his racism is comparable to Hitler's he replies, blandly: "Uncle Sam was practicing racism and white supremacy before Hitler was born. Hitler learned from Uncle Sam. Kennedy exploited the Negro to get in office and since then he bucked everyone on this earth—U.S. Steel, Khrushchev, Castro, everybody—but he won't buck the Southern segregationists. Tokenism—minimum integration—is a political trick."

But is not race irrelevant? Shouldn't man be judged as a human being, not on his color?

"It's too late to undo the chain reaction of events that has been set in motion by the white supremacists. There is some Muslim in a whole lot of Negroes. The only movement with mass appeal today is the Muslim movement. Why? Because Negroes are fed up. The most dangerous thing that confronts whites today is the white man's attempt to minimize the intense dissatisfaction among Negroes."

Malcolm X likes to say that he has no political ambitions, yet like other Muslim ministers, he is constantly recruiting—on speaking tours, at outdoor rallies, on college campuses, in pool halls, prisons and drugstores—inviting Negro Christians to attend lectures at the mosque.

So strong is Malcolm X's drawing power in Harlem today that Congressman Adam Clayton

Powell, a Baptist preacher, has begun to link himself to the Muslims.

The other week, at a huge, outdoor rally in Harlem Square, the Congressman declared:

"I tell you again and again, we are not going to get anything more in this life except that which we *fight* for and *fight* for with all our power. Unless we can seize completely the administration of our national Negro organizations, then we must say there is no hope there for us. This may sound like black nationalism. If it is, then what is wrong with it?"

Powell added that he did not agree with "some things" that Malcolm X preached, but he said Malcolm X was his "friend." In wrathful tones that won loud approval, he attacked on racist grounds such nonviolent, interracial groups as N.A.A.C.P. (of which he happens to be a life member), the Urban League, CORE, and the Rev. Martin Luther King's Southern Christian Leadership Conference. They had, he said, white people in leadership positions.

Malcolm X rose at the same meeting to declare: "We won't get our problems solved depending on the white man." Both speakers obliquely singled out for attack those leaders with Jewish names.

The leading Negro press has been scathing in reaction to the attacks on the N.A.A.C.P. But in Harlem, the Muslims and Powell have been given a curious boost by the writings of James Hicks, executive editor of *The Amsterdam News,* a Harlem Negro weekly. Hicks has been trying to paint N.A.A.C.P. leaders and Negroes high in government as in league with "the enemy," calling them "stupid." (His paper, paradoxically, has been advertising that its "great" columnists are the very men he is criticizing—Roy Wilkins and Dr. King.)

During the newspaper strike, when reaction was necessarily mute, the paper charged that "Jews control New York's top jobs." Recently, Hicks wrote that he was "fed up" with leaders who criticized Malcolm X for "fighting the wrong war in the wrong place at the wrong time."

"Who is the enemy?" asked Mr. Hicks.

THE N.A.A.C.P.

The enemy, answers N.A.A.C.P., is race hatred—whether it comes from men with white skins or black skins.

The N.A.A.C.P. rejects segregation or, as the Muslims call it, "separation." It is biracial. It was founded fifty years ago by liberal whites and Negroes. N.A.A.C.P. fights in three nonviolent ways —legal, legislative and educational—to help Negroes break out of their ghettos. It is trying to teach all people that race is irrelevant, that man must be judged as man.

In contrast with the Muslims, N.A.A.C.P. seeks to bring about complete integration in all phases of American life. It wants equal justice under law, the right to vote (Muslims discourage voting), personal security against mob and police violence, and nondiscriminatory treatment in housing and all public facilities. It is the largest civil rights organization in the nation with some 400,000 paying members and probably millions of supporters, Negro and white.

For traditional reasons, all presidents of N.A.A.C.P. have been white. The board of directors, which sets policy, numbers 60, of whom 11 are whites. The board has included such public figures as Mrs. Eleanor Roosevelt, Ralph Bunche, Gov. Herbert Lehman, Rabbi Stephen S. Wise, Walter Reuther. Arthur Spingarn, 85-year-old Jewish lawyer, who heads N.A.A.C.P., was for nearly a quarter-century the association's entire "legal department," serving on a no-fee basis.

Today the N.A.A.C.P. Legal Defense Fund, a separate, nonprofit group, works for civil rights through legal actions. Its nine lawyers (six of whom are Negro) have 121 cases pending in the Southern states. Of these, 66 are school segregation cases; six involve admission of physicians to hospital staffs and patients to treatment facilities; the remainder are sit-in and Freedom Rider cases.

N.A.A.C.P. is also encouraging the economic boycott—what it calls "selective buying." Negro purchasing power is estimated at $15 billion a year; N.A.A.C.P. reports that planned boycotts of certain merchants and retail stores in Jackson, Miss.; Savannah, Ga.; Macon, Ga., and St. Petersburg, Fla., are "effective" and that the idea is spreading.

The chief legal counsel until recently was Thurgood Marshall, a Negro who is now a Federal judge. When asked to comment on the appointment of Jack Greenberg, his successor as director-counsel (now under attack by the Muslims and Congressman Powell), Judge Marshall said: "As those who are fighting discrimination, we cannot afford to practice it."

Urbanity is the word for Roy Wilkins,

N.A.A.C.P.'s graying executive director, who looks younger than his 62 years. The son of a Methodist minister, tall, lean, known as a cool strategist, Wilkins worked his way through the University of Minnesota (as a redcap and a railroad dining-car waiter). He was managing editor of The Call, a Negro weekly in Kansas City, Mo., until he joined the association some thirty years ago. At N.A.A.C.P. headquarters in mid-Manhattan the other day, Wilkins discussed Powell and spoke with contempt of the Muslims and their hate philosophy.

"What is Adam Powell doing in Congress," asked Wilkins, "if he doesn't believe in integration? Logically, if he's given up on the system, or doesn't support what most Negroes want—integration—he ought to resign.

"I don't think that there's any doubt that Negroes are frustrated, bitter and impatient, but I don't see that as identical with the Muslim objectives. This Muslim group is a cult. The first point of departure is its anti-Christianity which gives them the cult aspect and is attention-getting. But Christianity has been for the American Negro part and parcel of his development and his life. So when he is asked to get rid of it and to adopt Islam and Allah, well, it is bound to get attention.

"And, let's face it," he went on coolly, "the white community brought it on themselves. The whites are responsible for the seeds of this cult being even an inch high—their rebuffs to the Negro, their rejection of his worthiness no matter how worthy.

"The supreme push to this defeatist Muslim philosophy was given by the tolerated defiance of the Supreme Court decision. Negro citizens had a right to believe that once the Supreme Court in 1954 had affirmed that segregation was unconstitutional, things would change. But instead of progress, there has been token integration—driplets of compliance. Of course, the Muslims capitalize on all this.

"But for all his frustrations, the Negro is still an American. This is his country. He's sore about a lot of things. But most Negroes—the vast majority—have decided to fight it out, fight for what is their due. The Negro is convinced that he can do something about it. If he didn't believe it, you wouldn't have the steady membership in N.A.A.C.P., the personal following of Martin Luther King, the kneel-ins at the churches, the sit-ins at the lunch-counters, and the demonstrations."

What is the meaning of the present schism for the Negro community and for America?

Many people believe that the influence of the Muslims is growing. They seem to have plenty of money. Their code, emphasizing race pride and individual decorum, is helping to shatter the Negro stereotype of shiftlessness and lawlessness and has undeniable appeal. As one non-Muslim Negro put it: "No one can calculate the psychological and emotional impact throughout the nation." Though their political power is latent, it is a threat. The immediate danger is that, through them, a growing number of colored people are beginning to experience a real sense of alienation from American society.

Partly in reaction to the rise of the Muslims but mostly because of its own impatience with the slow progress on civil rights, the N.A.A.C.P. and other moderate groups are being forced into more militant positions. The militancy, especially of the young Negro American, has been dramatized in recent days by the various "freedom walks" and the hundreds of arrests of young Negroes in Birmingham, Ala., in the demonstrations against segregation. Some believe that the very existence of the Muslims points to a failure of the N.A.A.C.P. to reach the grass roots where the cult is having success.

As Roy Wilkins moves about the South, he encounters redcaps, porters and bellhops who keep abreast of events, reading the papers and watching TV. They are apt to ask him: "How're things going? You think those folks are going to act right down there in Washington?"

"I think so," Wilkins replies, "if you keep up the pressure."

"We're going to do it," they answer, "but sometimes—" and they shake their heads—"I don't know . . . I don't know. Adam flies off the handle—but he gets white folks *told*."

The warnings are clear. The Muslims exist and their influence will remain potent so long as they are able to give the Negro masses something that articulates their pent-up frustrations.

Dr. Kenneth B. Clark, professor of psychology at City College, chief of HARYOU (the federally supported Harlem Youth Opportunities Unlimited) and himself a target of the Muslims, puts it this way:

"The danger of the Muslim movement is that

it exploits chaos. It is really the other side of the White Citizen Councils of the South. It can put terror into people and intimidate the responsible elements. The anti-Semitism is part of the demagoguery. The Muslims have again demonstrated the ease with which masses of human beings can be aroused by hatred. There is no reason to believe that Negroes are any more immune to this type of hate appeal than are whites."

X THE UNKNOWN

Asked about his family name, Minister Malcolm X says that he long ago took the surname X: "The last white man to own my foreparents was Little, and it would be an insult to call me by that name."

He told the writer to call him Malcolm X, or Mr. Malcolm X, or Mr. X.

"The X means that I don't know who I am," he said. "No one knows who these Negroes are— their identity was destroyed during slavery. All of the Muslims take X—the unknown. Sixty-seven brothers in our mosque alone have the name James X with the number of their sequence— James X-11, James X-12, etc. We have done this deliberately.

"I feel more intelligent saying my name is X," he added, icily, "than I would saying my name was Little—or Bunche or Powell or King. They don't know that they don't know what their name is."

The Black Muslim movement capitalizes on the inability of established protest organizations like the N.A.A.C.P. and the Urban League to improve the position of the Negro *rapidly*. It offers no real alternative to gradualism. But it does make available to uneducated or naive Negroes a channel for the expression of resentment. In opposing cooperation with white liberals, the Black Muslims express hopelessness about the white conscience. Unlike Gunnar Myrdal, who perceived the American Creed as an immense asset in the struggle for racial equality, Malcolm X considers white liberals hypocrites and Negroes who cooperate with them "suckers." The Black Muslim movement feeds on the impatience of Negroes, especially the young and the uneducated, with

the *pace* of desegregation. For those not able or willing to take the long view, Malcolm X has a case. Southern school desegregation, integrated housing, and equality of occupational opportunity seem far away. But social change can speed up suddenly, especially when it is government promoted. Take the history of the desegregation of the American Armed Forces.

Military Desegregation: An Example of Government-Promoted Change

Reprinted by permission. From James C. Evans and David A. Lane, Jr., "Integration in the Armed Services," *Annals of the American Academy of Political and Social Science*, Vol. 304, March 1956, pp. 10–16.

The feature article, "The U. S. Negro, 1953: A decade of progress . . . ," in the May 11, 1953, issue of *Time* asserted, "The biggest single blow against segregation in the U. S. has been struck by the armed forces." Similarly, the *New York Times* of February 14, 1954, called the Armed Forces racial integration "one of the biggest stories of the twentieth century. *Per se* it warrants no lesser description." Elsewhere the observation has been made that one of the most significant aspects of the achievements of our forces in the Korean conflict was the validation, in the field and under fire, of the racial integration program through which co-operation and cohesion were at last substituted for conflict and confusion.

As late as 1941 a War Department spokesman, addressing Negro newspaper representatives at a conference on the problem of racial segregation, held in the Munitions Building in Washington on December 8, stated the position that had governed policy since 1914 and that was to continue at least through 1944 and probably longer:

"The Army did not create the problem. . . . Military order, fiat or dicta will not change these viewpoints [in support of racial segregation]. The Army . . . cannot be made the means of engendering conflict among the mass of the people because of a stand with respect to Negroes which is not compatible with the position attained by the Negro in civilian life. This principle must necessarily govern the Army not only with [respect to] this subject of contention but with respect to [any] other dogma, be it religious, political or economic. The Army is not a sociological laboratory; to be effective it must be organized and trained according to principles which will insure success. . . ." [30]

Nevertheless, the years between 1941 and 1953 saw a change in the racial policies and practices of the armed services that was so nearly a transformation that it evoked statements of genuine surprise and sometimes enthusiasm from those concerned with advances in human relations. Increasingly, as the press carried summaries of such advances, it gave priority to the continuing success of the integration program in the Army, Navy, Air Force, and Marine Corps. One recent summary said:

"Historians agreed that the three most momentous events of the Golden Decade [1945–55] were: (1) The Supreme Court decision banning segregation in the schools; (2) the abolition of segregation in the Armed Forces; and (3) the decisions invalidating subterfuges that kept Negroes from voting in the South." [31]

Earlier a United States Senator characterized Armed Forces integration as "the first truly effective step that has been made in implementing the Emancipation Proclamation." [32]

The military establishment, in effect, executed an "about face," discarded the markers so long and supposedly so firmly established, and set out in a new direction. In so doing, with the primary objective of improving military efficiency and strengthening national defense, it took cognizance of the pressures engendered by the nation's urge toward justice and equity for all citizens in uniform, by the world-wide deployment of our forces, and by the United States position of leadership in a world in which attitudes and practices with respect to race and color were becoming more and more significant.

It is the purpose of this account to trace the outlines of this development, pointing out both its accomplishments and its limitations, as a basis of analysis and possibly of application.

HISTORICAL BACKGROUNDS

There is clear evidence that Negroes served widely, without being segregated, in the nation's early fighting forces. They served in the French and Indian Wars, and when Washington took "command of the Continental Army, Negroes were already in the ranks of the revolutionary militias which constituted that Army." [33] It is difficult to determine the total number of Negroes in the Revolutionary Army, for many of the state rolls carry no designation of race. They served, however, principally in the ranks, along with other patriots, and the separate Negro company did not appear until near the end of the conflict.

Moreover, "the Revolutionary Navy had a larger proportion of Negroes than the Army. . . . Negro pilots, because of their intimate knowledge of coastal waters, were in demand. . . ." [34] Another record reads:

"In 1816 I was surgeon of the *Java* under Commodore [sic] Perry. The white and Negro seamen messed together. About one in six or eight were Negroes. . . . There seems to have been an entire absence of prejudice against the blacks as shipmates among the crew. . . ." [35]

Despite the patriotic service of Negroes in all the wars from the founding of the Republic, the separate Negro unit, with all its inherent limitations, almost always with white officers, was destined to become the established pattern for decades. Moreover, the Negro citizen had to fight to maintain his right to a place in the fighting forces. Following the Civil War, the 24th and 25th Infantry and 9th and 10th Cavalry Regiments were maintained as Regular Army units pursuant to a statute of 1866 which provided that "the enlisted men of two regiments of Infantry [and] . . . the enlisted men of two regiments of Cavalry shall be colored men." The authorization of these four units, which later achieved distinguished records, served to prevent total exclusion of Negroes from the regular forces. The record of the separate units fittingly drew to a close with the 24th Infantry Regiment achieving, at Yechon, the first decisive American victory of the Korean conflict.

At the beginning of World War II Negro officers in the Regular Army numbered three line officers and three chaplains. There were possibly five hundred Negro Reserve and National Guard

---

30   Official release to the press.
31   *Ebony*, November 1955, p. 135.
32   Senator Hubert H. Humphrey, jacket endorsement for Lee Nichols, *Breakthrough on the Color Front*, New York: Random House, 1954.
33   Army Service Forces Manual M-5, *Leadership and the Negro Soldier*, October 1944, p. 74.
34   *Ibid.*, p. 79.
35   Dennis D. Nelson, *The Integration of the Negro into the U.S. Navy*, New York: Farrar, Straus, and Young, 1951, p. 4.

officers, but few were in the grade of major or higher.

Procedures for overcoming this shortage in the face of officer requirements for the expanding forces were, to some degree, a forerunner of the program of integration that was to follow a decade later. In World War I a separate officer candidate school for Negroes had been established. In World War II, however, both white and Negro personnel, upon qualifying, were trained in the same officer candidate schools. In 1942 Judge William H. Hastie, then the Civilian Aide to the Secretary of War, wrote in *The Annals:* [36]

". . . Negro officer candidates are attending classes and participating in field exercises with other outstanding young Americans of every race and religion from every part of the country. These soldiers have been and are a living demonstration that ability and leadership are not racial characteristics. It is to be remembered that many of their classmates have never had an opportunity to work with or even to observe Negroes equipped by training and experience to compete with them on a basis of equality."

During World War II also there were limited efforts at various times to improve the internal co-ordination of Army effort by lessening the impact upon Negro troops of regulations and practices enforcing racial segregation. Among them was the issuance by the Army, in 1944, of Army Service Forces Manual M-5, *Leadership and the Negro Soldier*, designed "to provide the main substance for a course of ten periods of instruction in schools for officers." Although not presuming to anticipate change in the established pattern of segregation, this document was in many respects a forthright statement of advanced principles that foreshadowed change.

POSTWAR PRINCIPLES AND POLICIES

Following World War II a step of great significance was taken when the Gillem Board submitted, in November 1945, the report of its study, "The Utilization of Negro Manpower in the Postwar Army." Based on experiences of the war, this report led to the announcement in 1946 of a policy which assured the Negro citizen of a continuing place in the Army; established a numerical ratio based on that in the civilian population; abolished the "all-Negro" division; authorized the

grouping of Negro units and white units of smaller size into composite organizations; and for the first time took the position that, in the event of another major war, all personnel assignments should be made without regard to race. Perhaps of even greater significance, this study, in the light of the subsequent necessity for large military forces deployed world-wide, led to a revealing and a re-evaluation of all policy positions concerning the utilization of Negro manpower during both peace and war.

Subsequent attention, increasingly affirmative, led to the establishment, by Executive Order 9981, dated July 26, 1948, of the Fahy Committee, which was charged with the responsibility of examining all existing Armed Forces regulations and practices, with a view of putting into effect an announced national policy of "equality of treatment and opportunity for all persons in the armed services without regard to race, color, religion or national origin."

This committee inquired into the position, long held by military planning staffs, "that (1) Negroes do not have the education and skills to perform efficiently in the more technical military occupations, and (2) Negroes must be utilized, with few exceptions, in segregated units." It "believed the assumption that equality of treatment and opportunity would impair efficiency, was of doubtful validity" and after extended study and hearings it "found, in fact, that inequality had contributed to inefficiency." The committee was "convinced that a policy of equality of treatment and opportunity . . . [would] strengthen the nation." [37]

The report of this committee, made in 1950 and entitled *Freedom to Serve*, provided the philosophy and the working basis for the program of racial integration, with no restrictions as to racial quotas, that has advanced with significant success in the Army, Navy, Air Force, and Marine Corps.

IMPLEMENTING POLICY

There follow now brief accounts of action taken and results effected as the services have moved to implement policy directives on racial integration.

[36] Vol. 223, September 1942, p. 59.

[37] President's Committee on Equality of Treatment and Opportunity in the Armed Services, *Freedom to Serve*, Washington: Government Printing Office, 1950, pp. 11, 67.

INTEGRATED UNITS. As an item of general impact, June 30, 1954, was eventually agreed upon as the time limit for the dissolution of all-Negro units in the Forces. The program proceeded even ahead of schedule, so that on that date answers to the often-asked question about the number of Negro units remaining had come to be a matter of definition. There are no longer any all-Negro units in any of the services proper, though some exceptions are found in civilian components, principally a number of school and college Reserve Officers' Training Corps units. Integrated activities include organization, assignment, training, billeting, mess, supervised recreation, and all other unit operations.

REMOVAL OF RACIAL QUOTAS. Contrary to some predictions, removal of racial quotas and other restrictions has not resulted in any disturbing imbalance of the ratio of Negro personnel to white personnel. In a positive direction, the abolition of racial quotas for service school selection and subsequent training and assignment has more than doubled the number of Negro officers and enlisted personnel attending such schools. Significant evidence is given, moreover, by the table indicating percentages of Negro personnel in the total personnel of the various services, in 1949 and 1954. The tabulation is of more than usual value because the current position in the Department of Defense toward eliminating all racial statistics will make future compilation of such comparative data practically impossible.[38]

ASSIGNMENT ACCORDING TO MERIT. Racial integration in the Armed Forces has given Negro personnel the opportunity to demonstrate skill and ability without limitations imposed by race. Furthermore it has released all personnel from numerous useless limitations centering around race. While the program has perhaps been under way for too short a time to bring about complete equity, Negroes are in responsible and important staff and field assignments on a fully integrated basis. Moreover, no unusual difficulties such as had been anticipated in some quarters have arisen out of the assumption of the command function by Negro officers and noncommissioned officers. In the Air Force one Negro officer is on active duty in the grade of brigadier general. In both the Army and the Air Force the promotion of more Negroes to that grade in the not-too-distant future is indicated. Advancement of qualified Negroes throughout the hierarchy increasingly becomes routine.

NAVY RECRUIT TRAINING. In the Navy the concentration of Negro personnel in the stewards branch has been traditional. A significant step toward change was taken when the Department of the Navy announced on March 1, 1954, that separate recruitment of stewards was being abolished. The effect of this change in policy was to give all seaman recruits an equal opportunity to qualify for service in any of the Navy's specialty groups at the end of recruit training. The racial concentration in the stewards branch was not immediately dissolved under the new program, but Negro recruits are now assured of the same opportunity as that of all other recruits to seek their branch of service on the basis of recruit orientation, testing, and training.

THE MARINE CORPS. A tradition of 167 years was broken when the United States Marine Corps accepted Negroes in 1942. The total inclusion approached twenty thousand before the end of World War II. After baptism of fire on Saipan, the Commandant of the Marine Corps announced, "The Negro Marines are no longer on trial. They are Marines, period." [39]

Service records of individuals and of units facilitated another departure from tradition in implementing the integration policy. This, when promulgated, proceeded without incident on the same timetable as the other services.

AIR FORCE TECHNICAL TRAINING. The Air Force accumulated considerable experience in in-

Percentage of Negroes in the Personnel of the Armed Forces, by Services, July 1, 1949, and July 1, 1954

	July 1, 1949	July 1, 1954
Army officers	1.8	2.97
Army enlisted men	12.4	13.7
Navy officers	0.0	0.1
Navy enlisted men	4.7	3.6
Air Force officers	0.6	1.1
Air Force enlisted men	5.1	8.6
Marine Corps officers	0.0	0.1
Marine Corps enlisted men	2.1	6.5

[38] *Integration in the Armed Services: Progress Report*, prepared by the office of James C. Evans, Civilian Assistant, Office of Assistant Secretary of Defense, Washington, January 1955, p. 4.

[39] Jean Byers, "A Study of the Negro in Military Service," unpublished, 1947, p. 253.

tegration as a result of a policy decision made in connection with Air Force training contracts with schools in states with racial segregation laws. The policy statement read:

"The Air Force will let contracts for technical training in civilian schools in accordance with the effectiveness of the service that the school can render to the Air Force. When airmen are to be sent to schools in States having statutes requiring segregation, Negro airmen will be given the option of not going if they choose. In that event, the Negro airman will be sent to a school which can accept both white and Negro airmen."

SCHOOLS FOR DEPENDENTS. Without any formal directive, in a number of states several schools for dependents, located on government property, had been operating for some time, without incident, on a racially integrated basis. As the question of integration in public schools received widespread attention, it was determined as a matter of policy that with the beginning of the 1953 fall term all such schools operated by the military on military posts and stations would be organized and conducted on an integrated basis. This policy was carried out on schedule.

Policy concerning schools located on military installations but operated by local educational agencies was announced on January 12, 1954, when the Secretary of Defense directed "that the operation of all school facilities located on military installations shall be conducted without segregation on the basis of race or color," regardless of other considerations. He stipulated that this policy would be put into effect "as soon as practicable, and under no circumstances later than September 1, 1955." It will be noted that the United States Supreme Court decision against segregation in public schools followed four months after the announcement of the Secretary of Defense.

Desegregation of the Armed Forces might have been postponed, but it could not have been prevented entirely. American Negroes were sufficiently educated to be aware that segregation violated equalitarian ideals and sufficiently powerful politically not to be ignored. Furthermore, most white Americans were ideologically prepared to make concessions. When President Truman signed the executive order of July 26, 1948, leading to sweeping changes, this was official sponsorship of a reform which had to come. Once desegregation of the Armed Services was carried out, segregation in civilian life became less practicable. It seemed anomalous that soldiers and sailors stationed in southern bases were integrated on the base and segregated while off duty. With schools on military installations desegregated, a precedent for integrated civilian schools existed. Thus, the pace of desegregation is likely to increase as one change prepares the ground for another. This means that the Black Muslim movement is bound to lose out in the end. For a time, however, it may grow because the pace of desegregation, even though increasing, will fall short of rising Negro expectations. Responsible white and Negro leaders are concerned about this possibility. The larger the number of extremists, white or colored, fishing in the troubled waters of American race relations, the greater is the chance of race riots. Desegregation is inevitable. Whether it will be peaceful desegregation or turbulent desegregation depends on the struggle for leadership within the Negro community. Whether responsible Negro leaders will continue to lead depends, in part, on their ability to demonstrate to their constituencies that responsibility pays off in progress toward racial equality.

CONCLUSION

Early sociologists were impressed with the cumulative character of technological and scientific development and with the impact of technological change on social life. They tended to assume that evolutionary improvements would automatically occur in family organization, intergroup relations, and social ethics. Contemporary sociologists, like contemporary historians and philosophers, are less confident that social change is synonymous with social progress. They are sensitive to a wider range of factors capable of changing patterns of interaction than were the nineteenth-century evolutionists.

The theory of cultural lag, though not explicitly evolutionary, also placed too little emphasis on the noncumulative factors in change. While a large cultural base makes technological innovations easier to *devise*, the *acceptance* of innovations depends on social values and institutions. The more rationally oriented the society, the more acceptable will be technological innovations; and when the innovator occupies a differentiated role in the context of which innovation is rewarded, the likelihood is increased that inventiveness will result in inventions.

Once technological innovations are made, social values and institutions do not cease being important. Technological and scientific development does not produce social change automatically. Other factors must be considered. The ideals and ideas of a society provide a basis for evaluating current patterns of interaction. Demographic and educational processes disturb the balance of power supporting the status quo. Social movements organize the proponents of change so as to influence the general public or specific decision makers. Political authorities support changes opposed to a greater or lesser degree by vested interests within the society. In short, technological and scientific development is an important factor in social change in industrial societies, perhaps the most important single factor, but it is by no means the only one.

"We must base our hopes, not on a progress that is to be achieved for us by the inexorable movement of historical law, but on ourselves and our children and our children's children, who will make the world better or worse according to the goodwill, the courage, and the skill with which they face the tasks of the present and the future. In place of the belief in a progress guaranteed by the order of nature we need to put a faith in our collective power to make the good prevail, if we try hard enough —but not otherwise." [40]

[40] G. D. H. Cole, "The Idea of Progress," *British Journal of Sociology*, Vol. 4, September 1953, pp. 282–283.

SOME SIGNIFICANT CONTRIBUTIONS TO THE STUDY OF SOCIOCULTURAL CHANGE

H. M. Blalock, Jr., "Urbanization and Discrimination in the South," *Social Problems*, Vol. 7, Fall 1959 pp. 146–152. In 150 counties selected at random from a universe of all Southern counties reporting at least 250 nonwhite households in the 1950 census, the following data were obtained for whites and nonwhites: (1) percentages of homeowners, (2) percentages of dwelling units not overcrowded, (3) percentages of families having incomes of $1500 or more, and (4) percentages of males 25 and over who completed more than six years of schooling. Professor Blalock uses the difference between the white and the nonwhite percentages for each of these four indices as a measure of discrimination. Although both whites and nonwhites enjoyed higher living standards in the more urbanized counties, the *differences* between whites and nonwhites were equally great in urban and rural counties. Bear in mind that the survey is limited to *Southern* counties. In a study of school desegregation in Kentucky and Missouri, it was found that the more prosperous and urbanized counties of these border states were much more likely to desegregate than the poorer rural counties. See Thomas F. Pettigrew, "Demographic Correlates of Border-State Desegregation," *American Sociological Review*, Vol. 22, December 1957, pp. 683–689.

G. D. H. Cole, "The Idea of Progress," *British Journal of Sociology*, Vol. 4, September 1953, pp. 266–285. Professor Cole takes his point of departure from a book by the distinguished social theorist, Morris Ginsberg, *The Idea of Progress: A Revaluation*. The notion of social progress was originally linked to a belief in a benevolent deity who was the force behind it. When skepticism arose about the existence of God, confidence in progress could continue only under special assumptions. For example, Karl Marx and his followers assumed that the class struggle was the force that would impel mankind "toward a classless society in which social co-operation would find its complete expression, and a return would be made . . . to the Communism that was supposed to have prevailed in primitive societies." A second course was to develop an optimistic conception of human nature, such as that of Condorcet, who equated moral failure with ignorance. Condorcet assumed that the advance of knowledge was an impetus to higher moral achievement, and therefore he insisted on the importance of universal education. A third possibility was to assume that social institutions were generating moral advance even though individual weaknesses remained unchanged. Although Professor Cole criticizes all three of these assumptions, he shares some of the sociological optimism of the third view. He points out that social life requires ". . . rules of behavior, assignment of things to be done, and means of deciding disputed points." This results in laws and means of enforcing them, and these tend to generate a demand for fairness (justice). Professor Cole refers to T. H. Marshall's book, *Citizenship and Social Class*, for a concept of developmental stages of increasing justice in Western civilization: stage 1, the right to equality before the law and the concomitant abolition of slavery; stage 2, the extension of political rights, particularly the right to vote for political leaders; stage 3, the claim to economic rights and social security.

Raymond Firth, *Social Change in Tikopia: Re-study of a Polynesian Community after a Generation*, New York: Macmillan, 1959. Professor Firth first studied this 1300-person society in 1929; his book, *We the Tikopia*, was a report of this early field work. In 1952, Firth returned to the tiny island of Tikopia and carefully noted the changes in the way of life since his first visit. For example, Christians had been a deviant minority in 1929; in 1952 they constituted a majority of the population. Firth interviewed informants to learn when and how changes occurred between 1929 and 1952; he also studied official and other records. Observing that kinship ties have begun to weaken, he expects that basic structural change is in the offing. This summary is based on a review by Felix M. Keesing, *American Sociological Review*, Vol. 25, August 1960, pp. 604–605.

Elihu Katz, Martin L. Levin, and Herbert Hamilton, "Traditions of Research on the Diffusion of Innovation," *American Sociological Review*, Vol. 28, April 1963, pp. 237–252. The authors of this article compare approaches to the study of diffusion of innovation in cultural anthropology, rural sociology, education, public health, marketing, and other fields. Although the basic idea of diffusion as a source of change is the same, different aspects of the process have been emphasized in different traditions. Combining these approaches gives a more adequate conceptualization of diffusion and a better basis for further research. "Viewed sociologically, the process of diffusion may be characterized as the (1) *acceptance*, (2) over *time*, (3) of some specific *item*—an idea or practice, (4) by individuals, groups, or other *adopting units*, linked (5) to specific *channels* of communication, (6) to a *social structure*, and (7) to a given system of values, or *culture*."

C. Eric Lincoln, *The Black Muslims in America*, Boston: Beacon Press, 1961. This book contains a scholarly account of the origin and growth of the Black Muslim movement and its relationship to non-Muslim Negroes. "Information on the movement's recruitment practices is presented, particularly those revolving around its proficiency in stealing ministers and religious 'bigwigs' from Baptist and other Negro congregations." This quota-

tion is from a review by Nathan Hare, *American Sociological Review*, Vol. 27, June 1962, p. 423.

Margaret Mead, *New Lives for Old: Cultural Transformation—Manus, 1928–1953*, New York: Morrow, 1956. In 1928 Margaret Mead studied the Manus, a New Guinea tribe only casually exposed to Western technology, religion, and law. *Growing Up in New Guinea*, published in 1930, was her report of the Manus culture. During the Second World War, the Australian administration of New Guinea was interrupted, first by Japanese invasion and occupation and then by the use of Manus Island by American troops as a staging area. The American reliance on machine technology and American equalitarianism impressed the 14,000 Manus who had led essentially a Stone Age existence. Led by middle-aged men who had observed Western ways as youths employed by plantation owners and the police, the Manus changed their society radically. This summary is based on a review by Leonard Mason, *American Sociological Review*, Vol. 22, February 1957, pp. 125–126.

Gunnar Myrdal, *An American Dilemma: The Negro Problem and Modern Democracy*, New York: Harper, 1944. In the summer of 1937 the president of the Carnegie Corporation of New York, Frederick P. Keppel, invited Professor Myrdal of the University of Stockholm to take charge of "a comprehensive study of the Negro in the United States, to be undertaken in a wholly objective and dispassionate way as a social phenomenon." This 1500-page book is the end-product of that research project. At least one hundred social scientists worked on Myrdal's staff, producing dozens of research memoranda and several books, which Myrdal integrated in his monumental assessment of the changing place of Negroes in American society. The unpublished memoranda were deposited in the Schomburg Collection of the New York Public Library for scientific reference. One of the important books to be published out of material gathered for the Myrdal study was E. Franklin Frazier's analysis of ". . . the emergence of the Negro as a minority group and his gradual integration into American life." See Frazier, *The Negro in the United States*, New York: Macmillan, 1949.

Wilson Record, *The Negro and the Communist Party*, Chapel Hill: University of North Carolina Press, 1951. This book is concerned with the unsuccessful efforts of the American Communist Party to woo the Negro since the First World War. One reason for the failure was the ignorance of American Communists of the Negro community, which was reflected in inept tactics. Professor Record estimates that Negro Communists never numbered more than 8000 at any one time. This summary is based on a review by Maurice R. Davie, *American Sociological Review*, Vol. 16, October 1951, pp. 740–741.

Louis Ruchames, *Race, Jobs and Politics: The Story of FEPC*, New York: Columbia University Press, 1953. The main emphasis in this book is the history of origins and achievements of the President's Committee on Fair Employment Practice—created in 1941 by Executive Order 8802 of President Franklin D. Roosevelt. This Order prohibited discrimination in defense employment and in government agencies; the Committee was established to secure compliance with the Order. For material on the Negro protest movement that preceded the issuance of the Order, see Herbert Garfinkel, *When Negroes March: The March on Washington Movement in the Organizational Politics for FEPC*, Glencoe, Ill.: Free Press, 1959. Although a march on Washington to demand racial equality was proposed by Negro labor leader A. Philip Randolph in January 1941, it was abandoned during the Second World War at the request of President Roosevelt. Not until the summer of 1963 was it actually held.

Neil J. Smelser, *Social Change in the Industrial Revolution: An Application of Theory to the British Cotton Industry, 1770–1840,* Chicago: University of Chicago Press, 1959. Professor Smelser suggests a seven-stage model to describe social change resulting from the increasing differentiation of a complex society: (1) dissatisfaction, (2) unconstructive disturbances, (3) efforts to cope with dissatisfaction without structural change, (4) social encouragement of new approaches, (5) efforts to specify innovation, (6) implementation of the change, and (7) routinization. He applies his model to the history of the British cotton industry and specifically to the readjustments in English family life when British factories successively introduced major innovations. Even though cotton spinners enjoyed a higher standard of living than other workers, the necessity of working long hours away from home tended to disrupt the family; the reduction of the working day to ten hours helped to reintegrate the family because it enabled common activities to develop outside of the home. This summary is based on a review by Leland H. Jenks, *American Sociological Review*, Vol. 25, October 1960, pp. 764–765.

FIGURES

579

TABLES

NAME INDEX

Contributors' names are shown in CAPITALS.

SUBJECT INDEX

Defined words are shown in CAPITALS.

Abilities, 375
Abolitionists, 548
Abstinence, 329
Accounting practices, 22
Accra, 146
ACHIEVED ROLE, 164
Achievement, academic, 381, 388
  socioeconomic, 455–456
Actors' Equity, 487, 489
Administrative behavior, 540
Administrative rationality, 510
Administrative tasks, 471
Adolescence, 59–61, 292–293
Adolescent aggression, 278
Adolescent rebelliousness, 289
  dependent aspect, 338
  independent aspect, 339
ADOLESCENT ROLE, 338–341
Adoption, 271
Adult education, 371
Advertising, 66, 69
Agemates, 337; see also Peers
Aggression, 308, 434
  as a lower-class trait, 376
Aggressiveness, 347
Aging, 357
Agribusiness, 143
Agriculture, Department of, Exten-
  sion Service as overcoming re-
  sistance to change, 545
Aid to Dependent Children, 270,
  271, 272
Air Force, 574
Akron, 327, 329
Alcoholics Anonymous, 327
Alcoholism, 325, 327, 328
Alienation, 104, 332
Amalgamated Clothing Workers,
  490, 491
Ambivalence, 339
"America," 466
American Bowling Congress, 124
American Committee on Africa,
  557
American Communist Party, 577
American Council on Education,
  464
American Farm Bureau Federation,
  192
American Friends Service Commit-
  tee, 359
American Institute of Family Re-
  lations, 343
American Management Associa-
  tion, 496, 497
American Newspaper Guild, 489
Americans for Democratic Action,
  461

American Sociological Association, x
Amish, 545
Amsterdam News, 569
Anglo-Saxon culture, 238
Ankara, 154, 157, 162, 163
Anna, an isolated child, 250
ANOMIE, 433
Anomie, 11, 469, 492
Anonymity, 166, 173, 283, 295,
  323, 337, 523
Anti-intellectualism, 388
Anti-Semitism, 430
Antwerp, 138
Apaches, 60
Apprentices, 87
Arab areas, 366
Archbishops, 535
Archery, 125
Aristocracy, 94, 348, 407
Aristotelian tradition, 391
Arithmetic, 363
Armistice Day, 445
Artifacts, cultural, 66
ASCRIBED ROLE, 164
Ascription, 11, 164, 453–455
Aspirations, 115
  educational, 210
Assembly lines, 102, 110
Association of Catholic Trade
  Unionists, 487
Athens, 138
Athletics, school, 386–388
Atlanta, 211, 567
Atomized society, 409; see also
  Anomie, Social disorganization
Atrocities, 542
Attitude change, 359
AUTHORITY, 398
Authority, 398, 508
  teacher, 34
Automation, 16, 111, 127
Automobile industry, 115
  workers, 110
Automobiles, 546, 547
Autonomy in work, 109

Baby boom, 182
Babylon, 137
Balgat, 154–163
Baltimore, 193, 195, 557, 558, 559
Banditry, 540
Bangkok, 172
Bankruptcy, 483
Barbarian invasion, 250; see also
  Socialization
Bartlesville, 558, 559
Baseball, 128

Batak, 268
Bay City, 403
Beacon Hill, 150
Belching, 58
Belmont Hospital, 332
Berbers, 158
Bereavement, 436–437
Bibliographies, *ix*
Big Business, 20
Bill of Rights, 428
Biloxi, 321, 322
Birmingham, Ala., 211, 570
Birth-control clinics, 209
Birth rate, 129, 130, 175, 182, 183
Black belt, 196, 199
"Black ghetto," 211
Black Muslims, 567–571
Black supremacy, 567
Blight, 150, 172
Boards, civic, 401
Boating, 123, 124
Bogotá, 527
Bookies, 319, 532, 535
Bookmaking, 319–324
Book reviews, *ix*
Bootleggers, 533
Boredom, 127
Boston, 56, 144, 150, 200, 211, 559
Boycott, 569
  of Carnation milk, 559
  of Wonder bread, 559
Boys' clubs, 294
Braceros, 191
Bride, age of, 273
Bride-price, 267
Broken homes, 41, 210
Bronx, 151, 152
Brooklyn, 151, 152
Brutalities, 542
Buck passing, 503
Buddhism, 238, 435
Buenos Aires, 148, 149
Building trades, 373
Bureaucracy, 450, 471–510
  in Egypt, 508
  pathologies of, 506–507
Bureaucratization, of invention, 546
  of unions, see Unions
Bureau of Applied Social Research,
  177, 358
Bureau of Indian Affairs, 355
Bureau of National Affairs, 498
Business leaders, 540
BUSINESS UNIONISM, 491
Busybodies, 304

Café society, 531
Caliente, 16

589